Lecture Notes in Computer Science 3804

George Bebis Richard Boyle
Darko Koracin Bahram Parvin (Eds.)

Advances in Visual Computing

First International Symposium, ISVC 2005
Lake Tahoe, NV, USA, December 5-7, 2005
Proceedings

Volume Editors

George Bebis
University of Nevada, Computer Vision Laboratory
Department of Computer Science and Engineering
Reno, USA
E-mail: bebis@cse.unr.edu

Richard Boyle
NASA Ames, BioVis Technology Center
Moffett Field, CA, USA
E-mail: Richard.Boyle@nasa.gov

Darko Koracin
Desert Research Institute, Atmospheric Sciences
Reno, NV, USA
E-mail: darko@dri.edu

Bahram Parvin
Lawrence Berkeley National Laboratory, Imaging and Informatics
Berkeley, CA, USA
E-mail: B_Parvin@lbl.gov

Library of Congress Control Number: 2005936803

CR Subject Classification (1998): I.4, I.5, I.2.10, I.3.5, I.2.6, F.2.2

ISSN 0302-9743
ISBN-10 3-540-30750-8 Springer Berlin Heidelberg New York
ISBN-13 978-3-540-30750-1 Springer Berlin Heidelberg New York

Springer is a part of Springer Science+Business Media

springeronline.com

Printed in Germany

Typesetting: Camera-ready by author, data conversion by Scientific Publishing Services, Chennai, India
Printed on acid-free paper SPIN: 11595755 06/3142 5 4 3 2 1 0

Preface

It is with great pleasure that I welcome you to Lake Tahoe for the 2005 *International Symposium on Visual Computing* (ISVC). ISVC provides a common umbrella for the four main areas of visual computing: vision, graphics, visualization, and virtual reality. The goal of ISVC is to provide a common forum for researchers, scientists, engineers, and practitioners throughout the world to present their latest research findings, ideas, developments, and applications in the broader area of visual computing.

The program consists of six oral sessions, two poster sessions, seven special tracks, four keynote presentations, and one invited presentation. The response to the call for papers for the general ISVC 2005 sessions was very good. We received over 110 submissions from which we accepted 33 papers for oral presentation and 26 papers for poster presentation. Special track papers were solicited separately through the organizing and program committees of each track. A total of 32 papers were accepted for inclusion in the special tracks.

All papers were reviewed with an emphasis on their potential to contribute to the state of the art in the field. Selection criteria included accuracy and originality of ideas, clarity and significance of results, and presentation quality. The review process was quite rigorous, involving two or three independent double-blind reviews followed by a one-week discussion period. During the discussion period we tried to correct anomalies and errors that might have existed in the initial reviews. Despite our efforts, we recognize that some papers worthy of inclusion may not have been included in the program. We offer our sincere apologies to authors whose contributions might have been overlooked.

I wish to thank everybody who submitted their work to ISVC 2005 for review. It was because of their contributions that we succeeded in having a technical program of high scientific quality. In particular, I would like to thank the ISVC 2005 area chairs, the organizing institutions (i.e., UNR, DRI, LBNL, and NASA Ames, the industrial sponsors (i.e., Intel, DigitalPersona, and Equinox), the International Program Committee, the special track organizers and their Program Committees, the keynote speakers, the reviewers, and especially the authors that contributed their work to the symposium.

I sincerely hope that ISVC 2005 will offer opportunities for professional growth. I wish you a pleasant time in Lake Tahoe.

September 2005 George Bebis

Organization

ISVC 2005 General Chair

George Bebis, University of Nevada, Reno, USA

ISVC 2005 Area Chairs

Computer Vision:
George Bebis, University of Nevada, Reno, USA
Bahram Parvin, Lawrence Berkeley National Laboratory, USA

Computer Graphics:
Lijun Yin, Binghamton University, USA
Ramesh Raskar, MERL, USA

Virtual Reality:
Richard Boyle, NASA Ames Research Center, USA
Reinhold Behringer, Rockwell Scientific, USA

Visualization:
Darko Koracin, Desert Research Institute, USA
Paolo Cignoni, ISTI - CNR, Italy

Publicity/Website:
Ali Erol, University of Nevada, Reno, USA

Local Arrangements:
Kostas Veropoulos, University of Nevada, Reno, USA

Publications:
Junxian Wang, University of Nevada, Reno, USA

ISVC 2005 International Program Committee

Ara Nefian, Intel, USA
Babak Hamidzadeh, The Library of Congress, USA
Christa Sommerer, ATR, Japan
Kenneth Wong, University of Hong Kong, Hong Kong, China
Anthony Maeder, CSIRO ICT Centre, Australia
Alexei Sourin, Nanyang Technological University, Singapore

Mircea Nicolescu, University of Nevada, Reno, USA
J.K. Aggarwal, University of Texas, Austin, USA
Ioannis Pavlidis, University of Houston, USA
Godfried Toussaint, McGill University, Canada
Marc Pollefeys, University of North Carolina, USA
Mohan Trivedi, University of California, San Diego, USA
Anders Heyden, Malmo University, Sweden
Emanuele Trucco, Heriot-Watt University, UK
Riad Hammoud, Delphi Corp., USA
Reinhard Klette, Auckland University, New Zealand
Nadia Magnenat-Thalmann, University of Geneva, Switzerland
Swarup Medasani, HRL, USA
Xiangjian He, University of Technology, Australia
Shaogang Gong, University of London, UK
Salil Prabhakar, DigitalPersona, USA
Gian Luca Foresti, University of Udine, Italy
Andrea Selinger, The College of New Jersey, USA
Matthew Turk, University of California, Santa Barbara, USA
Alexander Belyaev, Max-Planck-Institut für Informatik, Germany
Carlo Regazzoni, University of Genoa, Italy
Tieniu Tan, Chinese Academy of Sciences, China
Stefanos Kollias, National Technical University of Athens, Greece
Bogdan Georgescu, Siemens, USA
James Davis, Ohio State University, USA
Davide Maltoni, University of Bologna, Italy
Karen Sutherland, Augsburg College, USA
Alessandro Verri, University of Genoa, Italy
Jos Roerdink, University of Groningen, The Netherlands
Eam Khwang Teoh, Nanyang Technological University, Singapore
Kenneth Tobin, Oak Ridge National Laboratory, USA
Mark Allmen, Perceptek, USA
Joaquim Jorge, University of Lisbon, Portugal
Paolo Remagnino, Kingston University London, UK
Michael Strintzis, Aristotle University of Thessaloniki, Greece
Yunhong Wang, Chinese Academy of Sciences, China
Ismail Haritaoglu, IBM Almaden, USA
Philippe Palanque, University of Paul Sabatier, France
Nikos Paragios, Ecole Nationale des Ponts et Chaussées, France
Vladimir Brajovic, CMU, USA
Nikolaos Bourbakis, ITRI Wright State University, USA
Gopi Meenakshisundaram, University of California-Irvine, USA
Manuel Oliveira, Univ. Fed. do Rio Grande do Sul, Brazil
Xander Twombly, NASA Ames Research Center, USA
Chandrika Kamath, Lawrence Livermore National Lab, USA
Antonis Argyros, ICS-FORTH, Greece

Hanspeter Bieri, University of Bern, Switzerland
Alexei Skourikhine, Los Alamos National Lab, USA
Mark Billinghurst, University of Canterbury, New Zealand
Sabine Coquillart, INRIA, France
Rahul Singh, San Francisco State University, USA
Vana Kalogeraki, University of California, Riverside, USA
Nello Cristianini, University of California, Davis, USA
George Papadourakis, TEI Heraklion, Greece
Zehang Sun, eTreppid Technologies, USA

ISVC 2005 Special Tracks

Computer Vision Methods for Ambient Intelligence

Organizers:

Paolo Remagnino, DIRC, Kingston University, UK
Gian Luca Foresti, DIMI, Università di Udine, Italy
Ndedi D. Monekosso, DIRC, Kingston University, UK
Sergio Velastin, DIRC, Kingston University, UK

Program Committee:

Jan-Olof Eklund, KTH, Sweden
Yoshinori Kuno, Saitama University, Japan
Matt Brand, MERL, USA
Giulio Sandini, Università di Genova, Italy
Hani Hagras, Essex University, UK
Rita Cucchiara, Università di Modena, Italy
James Ferryman, Reading University, UK
Mohan Trivedi, UC San Diego, USA
Dimitrios Makris, Kingston University, UK
James Orwell, Kingston University, UK

Intelligent Vehicles and Autonomous Navigation

Organizers:

Fatih Porikli, MERL, USA
Ara Nefian, Intel, USA
Swarup Medasani, HRL Laboratories, USA
Riad Hammoud, Delphi Electronics and Safety, USA

Program Committee:

George Bebis, Univ. of Nevada, USA
Thorsten Graf, Volkswagen AG, Germany
Kikuo Fujimura, Honda Research, USA
Riad Hammoud, Delphi E&S, USA
Narayan Srinivasa, HRL Laboratories, USA

Swarup Medasani, HRL Laboratories, USA
Mohan Trivedi, Univ. of California, San Diego, USA
Alexander Zelinsky, Seeing Machines, USA
David Schwartz, Delphi
Ying Zhu, Siemens
Fatih Porikli, MERL

Pattern Analysis and Recognition Applications in Biometrics

Organizers:
Nello Cristianini, University of California, Davis, USA
Salil Prabhakar, DigitalPersona, USA
Kostas Veropoulos, University of Nevada, Reno USA

Visual Surveillance in Challenging Environments

Organizers:
Wei-Yun Yau, Institute for Infocomm Research, Singapore
How-Lung Eng, Institute for Infocomm Research, Singapore
Anastasios N. Venetsanopoulos, University of Toronto, Canada
Monique Thonnat, INRIA Sophia Antipolis, France
Tieniu Tan, CAS Institute of Automation, China

Program Committee:
Tele Tan, Curtin University of Technology, Australia
Weimin Huang, Institute for Infocomm Research, Singapore
Liyanage C De Silva, Massey University, New Zealand
Kap-Luk Chan, Nanyang Technological University, Singapore
Chin-Seng Chua, Nanyang Technological University, Singapore
Yap-Peng Tan, Nanyang Technological University, Singapore

Virtual Reality and Medicine

Organizers:
Fabio Ganovelli, VCG ISTI-CNR, Italy
Cesar Mendoza, Universidad Politécnica de Madrid, Spain
Min-Hyung Choi, University of Colorado at Denver, USA
John Dingliana, Image Synthesis Group, Trinity College, Dublin

Mediated Reality

Organizers:
Reinhold Behringer, Rockwell Scientific, USA
Steve Feiner, Columbia University, USA
Steve Mann, University of Toronto, USA
Jose Molineros, Rockwell Scietific, USA
Mohammed Yeasin, University of Memphis, USA

Visualization Techniques Applied to Geophysical Sciences Research

Organizers:

Darko Koracin, Desert Research Institute, USA
Robert Rabin, NOAA/National Severe Storms Laboratory, USA
Joseph Scire, Earth Tech, USA
William Sherman, Desert Research Institute, USA

Additional Reviewers

Sebastien Bougleux
Ananda Chowdhury
Renan Coudray
Ajay Daptardar
Jerome Darbon
Pablo Diaz-Gutierrez
Guoliang Fan Fan
Luiz Gonzaga da Silveira Jr
Haiying Guan
Fred Harris
Shinji Hayashi
Zhiyu He
Elsayed Hemayed
Altab Hossain
Bo Hu
Mao Lin Huang
Runzhen Huang
Kohei Inoue
Luca Iocchi
George Kamberov
Hang-Bong Kang
Kyungnam Kim
Julien Lamy
Minh Tuan Le
Woobeom Lee
Jongseok Lim
Nathan Lovell
Ruijiang Luo
Yunqian Ma
Aamir Saeed Malik
Aparecido Nilceu Marana
Isabelle Marchal
Yoshitaka Masutani
Satoru Morita
Ken'ichi Morooka
Masayuki Mukunoki
Jeffrey Mulligan
Congdu Nguyen
Jun-Taek Oh
Jonghyun Park
Nicolas Passat
Peeta Basa Pati
Stefano Piva
Andrea Salgian
Raul San Jose Estepar
Frutuoso Gomes Mendes da Silva
Gaetano Somma
Chung-Yen Su
Qingchuan Tao
Olaf J Thiele
David Thirde
Thanos Vasilakos
Inteck Whoang
Xinwei Xue
Chunrong Yuan
Yossi Zana

Sponsoring Institutions

UNR - Computer Vision Laboratory

DRI - Atmospheric Sciences

LBNL - Imaging Group

NASA Ames - BioVis Lab

Table of Contents

An NPR Technique for Pointillistic and Mosaic Images with Impressionist Color Arrangement

Linlin Jing, Kohei Inoue, and Kiichi Urahama

Kyushu University, Fukuoka-shi, 815-8540 Japan
{k-inoue, urahama}@design.kyushu-u.ac.jp

Abstract. A simple non-photorealistic rendering (NPR) technique is presented for creating pointillistic and mosaic images with color arrangement resembling the impressionist paintings. An input image is partitioned into rectangular tiles which are grouped into blocks. The color of tiles is changed to ones maximally far apart from each other while their local average approximates the color of the input image. The resultant mosaic image with the tile size of only one pixel is used for creating pointillistic images like to ones by George Seurat. Their blending with the original image produces a mosaic image resembling that by Chuck Close. Some modifications are also incorporated into the color transformation to improve the reproducibility of mosaic images blended with a collection of tiny images.

1 Introduction

In this paper, we focus on the color arrangement in non-photorealistic rendering (NPR) techniques especially for pointillistic and mosaic images. Most NPR techniques are devoted to generation of stroke textures, while their colors are naively copied from the input photograph only with small random perturbation. This is also the case with photo-mosaics[1, 2, 3] and more elaborated artificial mosaic images[4]. Little attention has been attracted to isoluminant properties in NPR color modulation techniques[5, 6]. No systematic procedure has been reported for color modulation in NPR methods for pointillistic and mosaic images.

On the other hand, it has been well-known to artists that color configuration is artificially altered from natural views to impressive ones where nearly isoluminant but largely different hue colors are painted adjacently, for instance the famous dull color of the sun in the "Impression Sunrise" in Fig.1(a) by Claude Monet, the pointillistic painting "Le Grande Parade" in Fig.1(b) by George Seurat, many mosaic images by Chuck Close as shown in Fig.1(c), and so on. In these images, we show only the green channel for monochromatic printing. This paper with color images can be seen in our homepage: http://www.design.kyushu-u.ac.jp/~urahama/. We can observe nearly isoluminant color configuration in those color images by converting them to gray-scale ones.

Recently Luong et al.[7] have presented an approach for making mosaic images where adjacent tiles are almost isoluminant. Although the images created

G. Bebis et al. (Eds.): ISVC 2005, LNCS 3804, pp. 1–8, 2005.

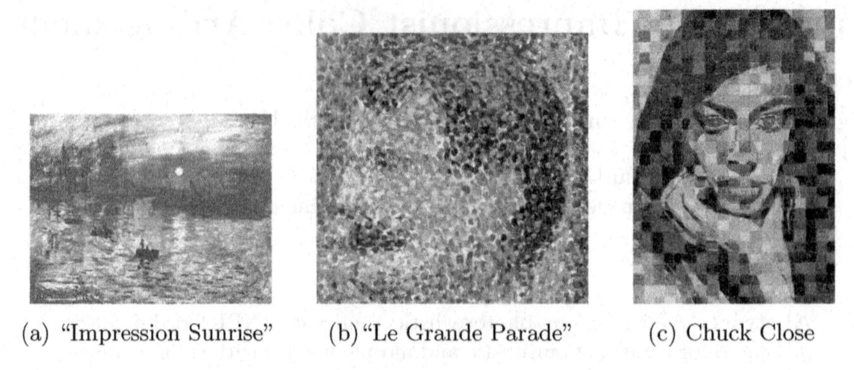

(a) "Impression Sunrise" (b) "Le Grande Parade" (c) Chuck Close

Fig. 1. Paintings with impressionist color arrangement

with their method is interesting, their procedure is complex and includes numerical solution processes. In this paper, we present a simple technique for making mosaic images where the hue of colors of neighbor tiles is maximally different while they are isoluminant and approximate locally the original color of the input image in average. We also apply this technique to generation of pointillistic images like the one by George Seurat. Images created by our method satisfy the following three requirements:

(1) Adjacent colors are isoluminant.
(2) Adjacent colors are maximally far apart from each other in the 3-dimensional color space.
(3) Local averages of colors are equal to those of the input image.

2 Color Arrangement of Blocks

In the method proposed in this paper, we partition an image into equally-sized rectangular tiles and several tiles are grouped into blocks as shown in Fig.2(a). The tiles are rectangular boxes of several (possibly one) pixels and blocks are sections composed of several tiles. We arrange the colors of tiles in a way that the average color of tiles in blocks coincides with those in the input image. For simplicity, we adopt 2×2 grouping, i.e. $2 \times 2 = 4$ tiles constitute one block.

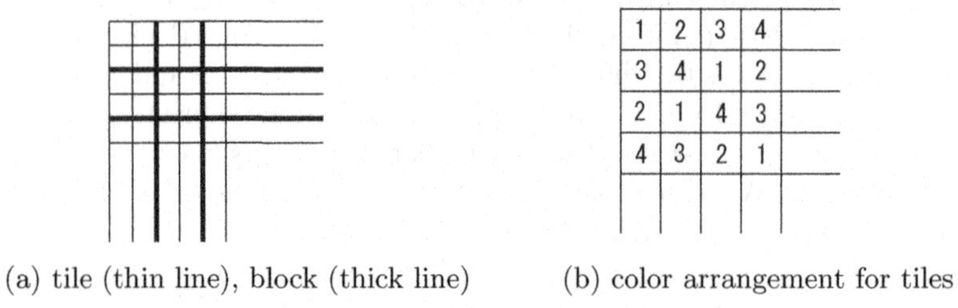

(a) tile (thin line), block (thick line) (b) color arrangement for tiles

Fig. 2. Image partition

Let the average color in a block be $\bar{\boldsymbol{C}}= (\bar{R}, \bar{G}, \bar{B})$ from which we calculate four colors $\boldsymbol{C_1}= (R_1, G_1, B_1)$, $\boldsymbol{C_2}= (R_2, G_2, B_2)$, $\boldsymbol{C_3}= (R_3, G_3, B_3)$, $\boldsymbol{C_4}= (R_4, G_4, B_4)$ as folloows:

The average luminance in this block is $\bar{Y} = \alpha\bar{R} + \beta\bar{G} + \gamma\bar{B}$ (we adopt the Y in the YIQ color hence $\alpha = 0.299, \beta = 0.587, \gamma = 0.114$). We draw two mutually orthogonal lines on the isoluminant plane $\alpha R + \beta G + \gamma B = \bar{Y}$ and pick up four points on these lines equidistant from the center color $\bar{\boldsymbol{C}}$. One example of such four points are $\boldsymbol{C_1}=\bar{\boldsymbol{C}}+\mathrm{t}\boldsymbol{u}$, $\boldsymbol{C_2}=\bar{\boldsymbol{C}}-\mathrm{t}\boldsymbol{u}$, $\boldsymbol{C_3}=\bar{\boldsymbol{C}}+\mathrm{t}\boldsymbol{v}$, $\boldsymbol{C_4}=\bar{\boldsymbol{C}}-\mathrm{t}\boldsymbol{v}$ with mutually orthogonal unit vectors $\boldsymbol{u}=(\delta, \delta, -\epsilon)$ and $\boldsymbol{v}=(\lambda, -\mu, \nu)$ where $\delta = 1/\eta, \epsilon = (\alpha + \beta)/\gamma\eta, \lambda = [\beta(\alpha+\beta)+\gamma^2]/\gamma(\beta-\alpha)\xi, \mu = [\alpha(\alpha+\beta)+\gamma^2]/\gamma(\beta-\alpha)\xi, \nu = 1/\xi$,

$$\eta = \sqrt{2 + (\frac{\alpha+\beta}{\gamma})^2}, \quad \xi = \sqrt{1 + \frac{[\beta(\alpha+\beta)+\gamma^2]^2}{\gamma^2(\beta-\alpha)^2} + \frac{[\alpha(\alpha+\beta)+\gamma^2]^2}{\gamma^2(\beta-\alpha)^2}} \tag{1}$$

These four colors are isoluminant and $(\boldsymbol{C_1} + \boldsymbol{C_2} + \boldsymbol{C_3} + \boldsymbol{C_4})/4 = \bar{\boldsymbol{C}}$ for arbitrary $t(> 0)$. We set the value of t as large as possible for these four colors staying within the color cube $[0, 255]^3$. Such value of t is given by the minimum among

$$\begin{array}{l} (255-\bar{R})/\delta,\ (255-\bar{G})/\delta,\ \bar{B}/\epsilon,\ \bar{R}/\delta,\ \bar{G}/\delta,\ (255-\bar{B})/\epsilon, \\ (255-\bar{R})/\lambda,\ \bar{G}/\mu,\ (255-\bar{B})/\nu,\ \bar{R}/\lambda,\ (255-\bar{G})/\mu,\ \bar{B}/\nu \end{array} \tag{2}$$

The above procedure is summarized as:

(1) We compute the average color $\bar{\boldsymbol{C}}$ of each block.
(2) We compute twelve values in eq.(2) and denote their minimum t_m.
(3) We compute $\boldsymbol{C_1}=\bar{\boldsymbol{C}}+t_m\boldsymbol{u}$, $\boldsymbol{C_2}=\bar{\boldsymbol{C}}-t_m\boldsymbol{u}$, $\boldsymbol{C_3}=\bar{\boldsymbol{C}}+t_m\boldsymbol{v}$, $\boldsymbol{C_4}=\bar{\boldsymbol{C}}-t_m\boldsymbol{v}$ and paint them to four tiles as illustrated in Fig.2(b) where only the numbers are written.

All rows and columns in Fig.2(b) contain 1, 2, 3 and 4 once in order to avoid perception of artificial horizontal or vertical stripes in output mosaic images.

We perform this color processing at every block independently and paint obtained colors in the arrangement shown in Fig.2(b) for every section of 2×2 blocks. This color processing transforms the input image into a color mosaic image.

3 Application to Pointillistic Images

A mosaic image obtained with the above procedure from the famous image "lena" is shown in Fig.3(a) where the tiles are composed of only one pixel. Though we cannot see each tile in this print-size, colors vary drastically as is zoomed up in Fig.3(b) (these images are also the green channel for monochromatic printing).

Fig.3 is, however, close to a dither image because the tile size is only one pixel. Hence its NPR effect is subtle, but as is shown in the following, it is useful as a basic image for creating pointillistic pictures.

(a) tile image

(b) partial zoom-up

Fig. 3. Color tile image of "lena"

(a) disk dots

(b) ellipsoidal dots

Fig. 4. Pointillistic image of "lena"

We transform Fig.3(a) into a pointillistic image in the following way. We adopt disk dots and set their radius arbitrarily. We paste colored dots according to the Poisson disk sampling, i.e. we sample pixels randomly and adopt them as centers if no pixel has been adopted yet within their disk. After this random search, we paste dots with colors of adopted center pixels. A result is shown in Fig.4(a) where the radius of the dots is five pixels. In Fig.4(a), the color of nearby dots is very different but they are isoluminant hence the color arrangement in Fig.4(a) is resemblant to that in Fig.1(b). Fig.4(b) is a similar result with ellipsoidal dots instead of circular ones. The orientation of ellipsoids is aligned to the gradient of the luminance of pixels. The fidelity of Fig.4(b) to the original image "lena" is superior than Fig.4(a), i.e. errors in gray-scaled images from the gray-scaled original "lena" is smaller in Fig.4(b) than that in Fig.4(a).

4 Mosaic Images

We described above the color transformation technique which produces a color tile image where each tile is painted with one color. We next blend other small images with these color tiles after this color transformation. Such blending produces an interesting NPR mosaic image.

4.1 Color Transformation

We divide an input image into tiles of $m \times m$ pixels and group $2 \times 2 = 4$ tiles into one block. We average the colors in the block and compute four colors $\boldsymbol{C_1}, \boldsymbol{C_2}, \boldsymbol{C_3}, \boldsymbol{C_4}$ and arrange them as in Fig.2(b). A mosaic image with color tiles made from a photograph in Fig.5(a) is shown in Fig.5(b). Blending the input image in Fig.5(a) with the mosaic image with $m = 36$ is shown in Fig.5(c) which seems like Fig.1(b).

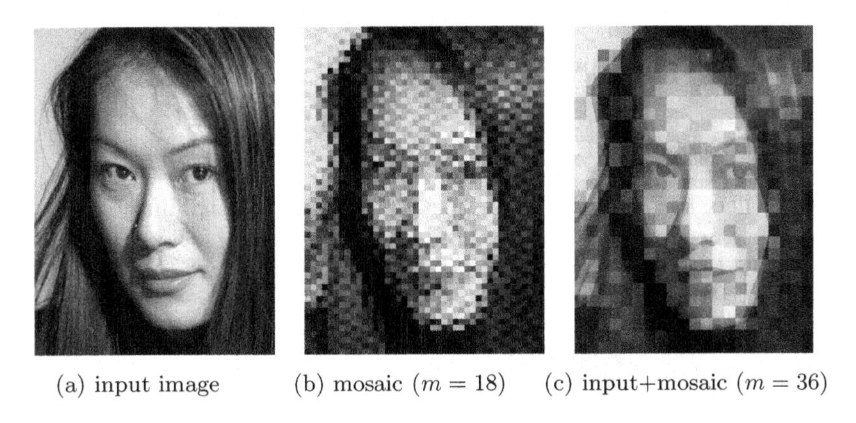

(a) input image (b) mosaic ($m = 18$) (c) input+mosaic ($m = 36$)

Fig. 5. Input image, its mosaic and their blending

4.2 Blending with Small Images

We next prepare four small images with the size $m \times m$ and blend them with four color tiles. Let us consider the first tile denoted by "1" at the upper-leftmost in Fig.2(b). Its color is $\boldsymbol{C_1} = (R_1, G_1, B_1)$. Let the color of the (i, j) pixel in a small image be (r_{ij}, g_{ij}, b_{ij}) and their average be $(\bar{r}, \bar{g}, \bar{b})$. From them, we compute

$$r'_{ij} = r_{ij}\bar{R}/\bar{r}, \quad g'_{ij} = g_{ij}\bar{G}/\bar{g}, \quad b'_{ij} = b_{ij}\bar{B}/\bar{b} \tag{3}$$

and we paint the color $R'_{ij} = (R_1 + r'_{ij})/2$, $G'_{ij} = (G_1 + g'_{ij})/2$, $B'_{ij} = (B_1 + b'_{ij})/2$ to the (i, j) pixel of the first tile in the output image. Other tiles are similarly processed. Thus blended tiles are still isoluminant in each block and their average is preserved at $\bar{\boldsymbol{C}}$.

The image shown in Fig. 6(a) is the result of blending the image in Fig.5(b) with four small images of insects. Fig.6(b) is a zoomed portion in Fig.6(a).

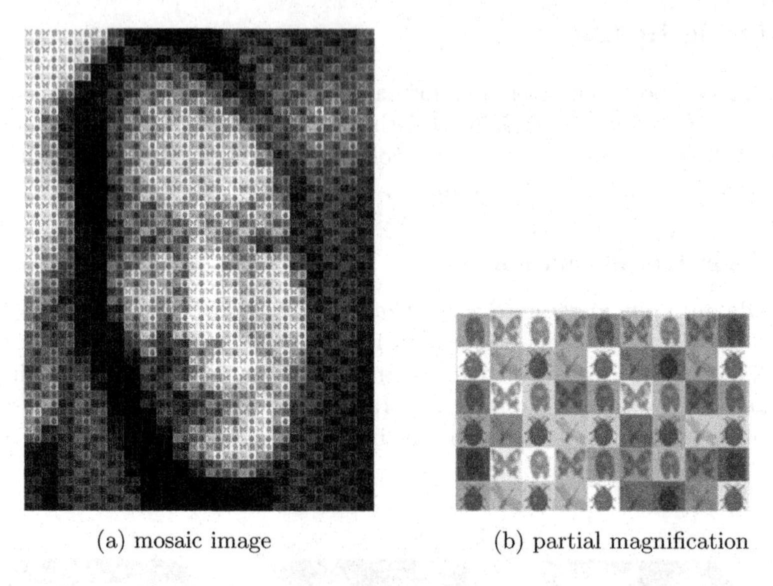

(a) mosaic image (b) partial magnification

Fig. 6. Mosaic image blended with tiny pictures

4.3 Improvement of Reproducibility

The NPR effect in Fig.6(a) is interesting, however the original image in Fig.5(a) is blurred in Fig.6(a). This blur is caused from two factors: blocky partitioning in mosaics and color transformation. Smoothing by blocky division is unavoidable

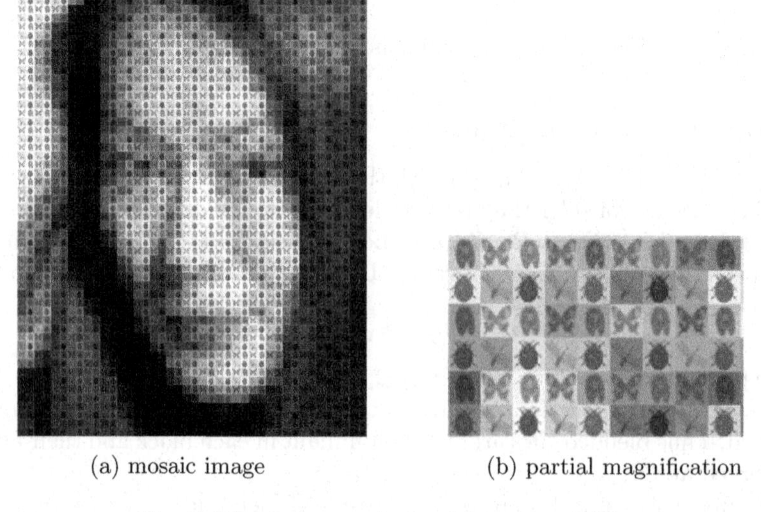

(a) mosaic image (b) partial magnification

Fig. 7. Mosaic image obtained by using eq.(4)

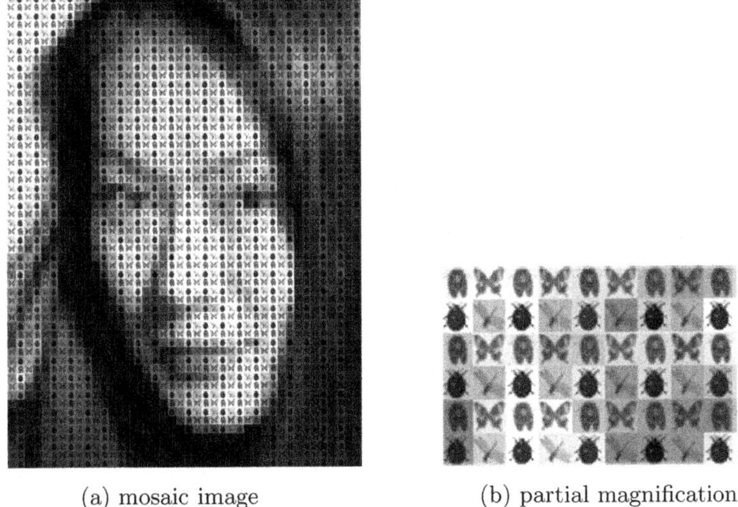

(a) mosaic image

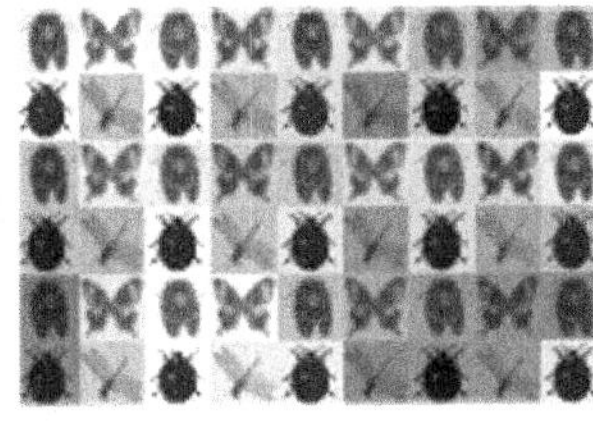

(b) partial magnification

Fig. 8. Mosaic image with higher fidelity

but we can improve the color transformation scheme for raising the reproducibility by converting eq.(3) into

$$r'_{ij} = r_{ij}\bar{R}_1/\bar{r}, \quad g'_{ij} = g_{ij}\bar{G}_1/\bar{g}, \quad b'_{ij} = b_{ij}\bar{B}_1/\bar{b} \tag{4}$$

where $(\bar{R}_1, \bar{G}_1, \bar{B}_1)$ is the average color of the tile "1h in the input image. This conversion breaks the isoluminantness of four tiles while their average color is still preserved at $\bar{\boldsymbol{C}}$. Since the color of the tiles are adjusted to the input image through eq.(4), its reproducibility is expected to be raised. The result of this modification is shown in Fig.7(a) and its partial zooming is shown in Fig.7(b). Errors in smoothed images from Fig.5(a) is smaller in Fig.7(a) than that of Fig.6(a). However as is seen in Fig.7(b), the local color variation is more flat in Fig.7 than Fig.6 where the tiles are more colorful.

4.4 Improvement of Luminance Fidelity

Though the reproducibility of Fig.7 is improved from Fig.6, the contrast in both images is decreased from the original image. Hence we further modify the color transformation scheme to improve the luminance reproducibility. The colors of four tiles $\boldsymbol{C_1}, \boldsymbol{C_2}, \boldsymbol{C_3}, \boldsymbol{C_4}$ before blending with tiny images are identical in both of the above subsections 4.2 (Fig.6) and 4.3 (Fig.7) and their luminance is equal to that of $\bar{\boldsymbol{C}}$. The difference between Fig.6 and Fig.7 is caused by the difference in the color of the pasted tiny images, i.e. eq.(3) versus eq.(4). We proceed further and break the isoluminantness of $\boldsymbol{C_1}, \boldsymbol{C_2}, \boldsymbol{C_3}, \boldsymbol{C_4}$, to improve the luminance fidelity.

In section 2, we set $\boldsymbol{C_1}=\bar{\boldsymbol{C}}+\mathrm{t}\boldsymbol{u}$, $\boldsymbol{C_2}= \bar{\boldsymbol{C}}-\mathrm{t}\boldsymbol{u}$, $\boldsymbol{C_3}=\bar{\boldsymbol{C}}+\mathrm{t}\boldsymbol{v}$, $\boldsymbol{C_4}=\bar{\boldsymbol{C}}-\mathrm{t}\boldsymbol{v}$, i.e. these four colors depart from $\bar{\boldsymbol{C}}$ equidistantly on the isoluminant plane. In this section, we set $\boldsymbol{C_1}=\bar{\boldsymbol{C}}_1+t\boldsymbol{u}$, $\boldsymbol{C_2}=\bar{\boldsymbol{C}}_2-t\boldsymbol{u}$, $\boldsymbol{C_3}=\bar{\boldsymbol{C}}_3+t\boldsymbol{v}$, $\boldsymbol{C_4}=\bar{\boldsymbol{C}}_4-t\boldsymbol{v}$ where $\bar{\boldsymbol{C}}_i$ is the average color in the tile i. In this case, the four colors depart from the average of each tile on each isoluminant plane separately. Their stopping rule is the same as in section 2, i.e. t is stopped when any one of R,G,B of $\boldsymbol{C_1}, \boldsymbol{C_2}, \boldsymbol{C_3}, \boldsymbol{C_4}$ reaches the surface of the color cube. Additionally the blending is extended to the weighted one $R'_{ij} = (w_1 R_1 + w_2 r'_{ij})/(w_1 + w_2)$. Though this modification breaks the isoluminantness of four tiles as is the same as section 4.3, their average color is still preserved at $\bar{\boldsymbol{C}}$. A result of this improved method with $w_1 = 1, w_2 = 5$ is shown in Fig.8(a) which is partially magnified in Fig.8(b). Fig.8(a) is closer to Fig.5(a) than Fig.7(a) and its contrast is also regained. However the colorfulness of tiles deteriorates further from Fig.7, much inferior than Fig.6.

In summary, we recommend the scheme in section 4.2 if the colorfulness of tiles is desired, while the scheme in this section is recommended if the reproducibility of the input image is crucial. The scheme in section 4.3 is moderate between them.

5 Conclusion

We have presented a simple NPR scheme for generating a novel type of mosaic images where small images are blended after color transformation of tiles resemblant to the impressionist color arrangement. The increase in the number of colors of tiles, the combination of various forms of tiles and the application of the present method to video mosaics[8] are under study.

References

1. Silvers, R. and Hawley, M.: Photomosaics. Henry Holt and Co., Inc. (1997)
2. Finkelstein, A. and Range M.: Image mosaics. EP/RIDT (1998) 11-22
3. Di Blasi, G. and Petralia, M.: Fast photomosaic. WACG (2005)
4. Kim, J. and Pellacini, F.: Jigsaw image mosaics. SIGGRAPH (2002) 657-664
5. Ostromoukhov, V. and Hersch, R.: Multi-color and artistic dithering. SIGGRAPH (1999) 425-432
6. Gooch, A., Gooch, B., Shirley, P. and Cohen, E.: A non-photorealistic lighting model for automatic technical illustration. SIGGRAPH (1998) 447-452
7. Luong, T.-Q., Seth, A., Klein, A. and Lawrence J.: Isoluminant color picking for non-photorealistic rendering. Graphics Interface (2005)
8. Klein, A. W., Grant, T., Finkelstein, A. and Cohen, M. F.: Video mosaics. NPAR (2002) 21-28

Active View Optimization for Viewing Objects in Motion

Matt Berger[1], Lijun Yin[1], and Jason Moore[2]

[1] Department of Computer Science, SUNY Binghamton
[2] Air Force Research Lab, Rome, NY

Abstract. This paper introduces a novel method to automatically generate camera animation for scenes with objects in motion. A means of bounding the scene is first discussed, in order to provide a restricted surface for the camera to move along. Methods for generating static views of a scene are then developed, based on prior literature in the field of optimal camera views. Methods for producing smooth animations for camera paths are developed. This is broken up into two constraints; the minimum distance constraint and the minimum angle constraint. Finally, a camera path is produced based on the two prior constraints. This framework is then applied to the problem of facial tracking and visualizing a large scene.

1 Introduction

Automatic view optimization is a very useful tool in the visualization of 3D scenes. With standard 2D or 3D input devices it is very difficult to navigate to an optimal view effectively. During the course of manual camera navigation the user has to know a priori where all the important objects already are in order to place the camera effectively. This problem is confounded when they are obscured or out of sight, making automatic view optimization essential. While the problem of automatic camera placement in static scenes has been researched for many years, there are many instances in which a scene consists of objects in motion. Once objects are in motion, naively choosing the optimal view using the aforementioned research can result in large changes to the camera's location and orientation. This can lead to being disoriented and create visualizations with little value. These types of dynamic scenes pose a more difficult problem for maintaining an optimal view. It is often crucial to be able to visualize the relationship between multiple mobile objects. For instance, in car accident recreation the entire problem consists of understanding and being able to portray the dynamic relationship of the vehicle's locations. The object of this paper is to create a framework for solving this type of problem. The first portion of the algorithm describes a method of bounding the scene, in order to restrict possible camera positions to a defined surface. Metrics are then developed to help define what is considered an optimal static view. There are three different metrics being considered; the object normals metric, the frustum volume metric, and the object occlusion metric. The novel portion of the algorithm is automatically generating a non-disorienting smooth animation through the optimal static views over the entirety of the scene. Based on the surface definition and the static view metric solver,

G. Bebis et al. (Eds.): ISVC 2005, LNCS 3804, pp. 9 – 16, 2005.

candidate camera positions are generated on the surface to represent where optimal static views are considered. Two constraint solvers, the minimum distance constraint and the minimum angle constraint, determine the most appropriate camera path to follow. These constraints are aimed at minimizing the amount of disorientation that may occur when a camera is moving around the scene, in addition to maintaining optimal dynamic views at all times over the scene.

2 Related Work

The related work in the field of automatic camera manipulation can be divided between producing optimal views and producing optimal camera animations [4, 5]. The main issue with producing optimal views is in the definition of optimal. There is no universal standard of an optimal view: it is rather subjective. Regardless, there is an extensive amount of literature providing a variety of different constraints as to what is considered an optimal static view. In contrast, there is very little work done on producing optimal camera animations. Regarding ***camera animation for static scenes***, Salomon et al. [1] proposed an algorithm for clustering areas of interest together in order to visualize large information spaces. The clustered areas of interests are based on a few constraints including distance parameters between data. The clustered data points then form graphs under Delaunay triangulation. Various graph algorithms are then applied to map out a specific camera path to follow. Once the path is found, the paper uses a partial constraint solver to define metrics that represent how exactly to orient, not locate, the camera at each point. A major problem inherit with the clustering is the absence of measuring how well the view may be at each area of interest. Thus, even though the partial constraint solver will be used to find the best orientation, the view may still be insufficient due to poor camera placement. Dennis et al [2] proposed a method of navigating complex environments via path planning. The environment is restricted to a surface for an avatar to walk upon. The entire surface that the avatar can walk on is then heavily random sampled. A global roadmap is computed using the idea of reachable and unreachable nodes, via distance heuristics. The global roadmap produces all paths for which the camera can navigate around. Although optimal views are disregarded for this algorithm, the paper proposes a novel method of efficiently navigating an environment. The graph construction method, as described in section 5, was influenced by this work. For ***camera animation for dynamic scenes***, there has been very little research in this area. Stoev et al [3] provided a means of visualizing time-dependent historical data. The paper, much like [1], makes use of a partial constraint solver to find the best static optimal view for portions of the scene. Regarding camera motion, the paper proposes to bind active data into a bounding box. The camera views this dynamically changing bounding box over time. The algorithm fails to mention the specifics of the time interval used. For large time intervals, the algorithm will likely produce poor static views, as the active data will change too much. However, for small time intervals, the animation of the camera will likely be very rough and disorienting. This is caused by the fact that the bounding box to view will always be changing, and there is no mention of smoothing out the camera path.

3 Bounding the Scene

The 3D scene must first be bounded for potential camera placement at any given time. The scene is bounded by first determining the minimum and maximum values of all objects, in order to produce a bounding box, similar to [3]. The distance between the center of the box and any corner of the box is then taken to be the radius of a bounding sphere, whose center is the center of the box. This bounding sphere represents all locations where the camera can be placed.

4 Optimal Static View Metrics

Optimal static view metrics are developed in order to measure the quality of a view at a particular time. Three metrics are defined: the normals metric, the camera frustum metric, and the object occlusion metric. Each metric is quantified in the range of [0, 1] where each metric is of equal significance to the overall effectiveness of the camera view metric. The metrics can have different weights however, depending on what the user wants to see.

(1) Normals Metric: The normals metric *N* is designed to obtain how much detail an object has for a given view. The metric is calculated for a particular camera position and orientation and a particular object. For each polygonal patch on the object, the angle between the camera view and the normal of the patch is calculated. There is an inverse relationship between the angle and the metric, an angle of 0 results in the value 1 for the metric. Intuitively, the higher the metric is, the more of the surface of the model will be shown. The following calculations are done to normalize the *N* to be in the range of [0, 1], where the number of normals a model has is weighted, making all models of equal significance:

$$N = \frac{1}{numObjects} \sum_{j} \left(\sum_{i} \left(1 - \frac{ang(\vec{x}_j, \vec{n}_i)}{\pi/2}\right) / totalNormals_j \right) \tag{1}$$

j refers to all objects in the scene and *i* refers to all polygonal patches on a model. *x* is the vector formed from the camera location to an object *j* and *n* is the polygonal patch's normal. *ang* is the minimum angle between vectors x and n. This metric generally produces good results for scenes where models have a wide distribution of normals. For scenes where models all have very similar normals, the optimal view will be considered the view facing straight down on these normals, giving very poor depth perception of the environment. As a more concrete example, flat terrain would likely result in this metric to provide an optimal view that looks straight down on the terrain, with poor depth perception regarding all other models in view.

(2) Camera Frustum Volume Metric: The camera frustum volume metric is designed to measure how much information is contained within the camera's view for a camera position and orientation. It measures how close all objects are to the camera. The computation done to quantify this is the ratio between the total volume of the objects in the scene and the total volume of the camera frustum. Bounding box intersection tests must be done to account for objects overlapping in computing the total volume for objects. This metric has a strong inverse relationship on the complexity of the scene. For a scene with few objects that have a large distribution in their location over time, this metric will give poor results. This is partially due to the spherical surface that bounds the environment regarding where the camera can be positioned. Since the camera can not zoom in and out, the camera has the potential to always be far away from the main concentration of the scene.

(3) Object Occlusion Metric: The object occlusion metric is designed to quantify the amount of objects that are seen from a particular camera position and orientation. The greater the metric ϑ, the less objects are occluding other objects. In order to efficiently quantify this metric, an algorithm approximating angular obstructions between objects is used. The metric is quantified by: $\vartheta = \frac{1}{totalOcc} \sum_k \sum_j \sum_i r(i,j,k)/6$

$$\text{Where } r(i,j,k) = \begin{cases} \frac{ang(\overrightarrow{cenLook_k}, \vec{v}_{ki})}{ang(\overrightarrow{cenLook_k}, \vec{v}_{ji})} & if\ \frac{ang(\overrightarrow{cenLook_k}, \vec{v}_{ki})}{ang(\overrightarrow{cenLook_k}, \vec{v}_{ji})} < 1 \\ 1 & otherwise \end{cases} \tag{2}$$

i refers to the center of one of the six sides of the bounding box, i goes from 1 to 6. j is all objects excluding k, k is the object being tested. The vector as denoted by $\vec{v}_{ki}$ is the vector formed from the camera position to the center of the ith side of the kth bounding box. The vector as denoted by $cenLook_k$ is the vector formed from the camera position to the center of the kth object. The vector as denoted by $\vec{v}_{ji}$ is the vector formed from the camera position to the center of the ith side of the jth bounding box. *totalOcc* is a constant defined as the number of objects squared minus the number of objects. For a given object k, this algorithm first determines the angle between vectors $cenLook_k$ and $\vec{v}_{ki}$. That angle is then divided by the angle between vectors $cenLook_k$ and $\vec{v}_{ji}$. If this ratio exceeds 1, then the value is clamped to 1. This metric is testing object occlusion where 0 implies complete occlusion and 1 is not occluded. Therefore, values greater than 1 are clamped as to not over bias excessively non-occluded objects. That summed angle relationship is then divided by 6 in order to normalize the value between 0 and 1. If the summation is 0 then there is complete occlusion of object j with object k. Despite the fact that this is an approximation to test object-to-object occlusion, it produces very accurate results. It is able to disregard how large objects are and their depth from the camera, focusing on their relationships to one another. Occasionally the metric fails however, as a result of the bounding box inaccurately representing the true shape of an object.

5 Smooth Camera Path Generation

Now that the optimal static view metrics have been defined, the next step is to generate the camera path. The camera path will be represented in terms of five degrees of freedom, a look at / look from pairing. The lost degree of freedom is the roll of the camera. Furthermore, the path will be represented by key-frames; that is, for a given time step, a camera look at / look from pair will be plotted, and interpolation will occur between the key-frames to give the path. The main goal is to generate a camera path that results in as little disorientation as possible and providing the optimal static view. Setting up the camera look at points is fairly trivial. For each time step, the current bounding box of all objects in the scene is obtained and the center of the bounding box is taken as the look at point. The camera look at key-frames will linearly interpolate between time steps. Obtaining the optimal camera look from positions is not so trivial. This is accomplished through first representing the spherical surface in terms of a graph, and then applying the two smooth camera path constraints to this graph: the minimum distance constraint and the minimum angle constraint.

5.1 Graph Representation

For each time step, the graph is constructed via random sampling of the spherical surface. Only a certain percentage of camera positions are accepted; these will be referred to as candidate camera positions (CCPs). The CCPs are assumed to be camera look from points where an optimal static view of the scene is obtained. For all random sampled points, the metric process described in section 4 is applied. A predefined percentage of these points are kept as being the candidate camera positions. Refer to figure 1 for an illustration of the sampling. The edges of the graph are formed by connecting all nodes between each time step. Note that this gives a set of bipartite graphs between each time interval, which is helpful in computing the constraint solvers.

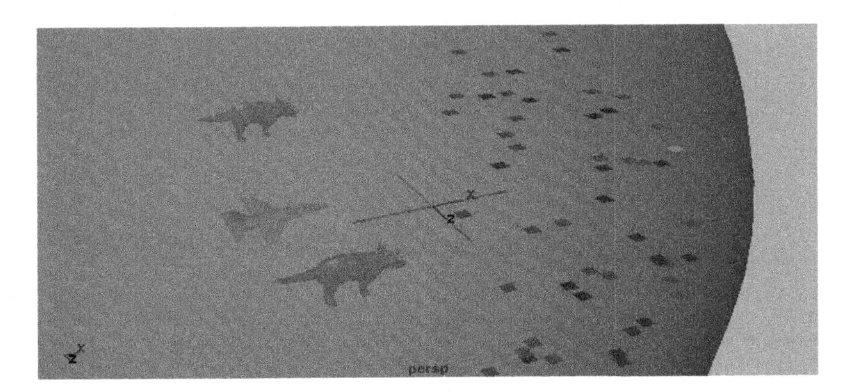

Fig. 1. This image represents the bounded scene with the darker squares representing CCPs at time step n and the lighter squares representing CCPs at time step n+1

Note that at this point three critical heuristics must be accurately defined: the time step, the total number of random sampling to do at each time step, and the percentage of points to keep at each time step. The time step dictates how much time in between CCPs. The greater the time step is the more the optimal view will suffer, but the smaller the time step is the more difficult it will be to find the optimal path. As the number of random sampling per time step increases, the performance and execution time of the algorithm will increase. When the percentage of CCPs taken at each time step is large, it will be easier to find the optimal camera path at the cost of the views being semi-optimal. Thus much caution must be taken in choosing these heuristics.

5.2 Minimum Distance Constraint

The minimum distance constraint is based on the idea to minimize the amount of "jumpiness" the camera path may encounter. This jumpiness is caused by the lack of uniformity between the distances of all the candidate camera position pairs. It is possible that for time step n, the distance to the next CCP is very large. It is also possible that the distance to the next CCP is very small. Therefore, the minimum distance constraint solver determines the smallest distance paths that exist from all CCPs at time 0, to all other CCPs at the end time. It is assumed that the minimum distance it takes to get from time 0 to the end time will result in as little "jumpiness" between time steps as possible. The algorithm developed for the minimum distance constraint solver is a variation of Dijkstra's algorithm. The algorithm is applied separately to every candidate camera position at time 0, resulting in the shortest-distance path to all CCPs at the end time. First, all distances to the first time step n are initialized, such that we can assume that this is the shortest distance to each of these CCPs. At the next time step, the CCP with the shortest distance is added to the current path. The reason this holds true is due to the property of the entire graph being a set of separate bipartite graphs. Therefore, there is no way for a CCP at time step n+1 to have any other edges coming into it, other than edges formed by CCPs at time step n. As in Dijkstra's algorithm, this method of adding CCPs to paths is incremental, and can be repeated for all time steps. Refer to Figure 2(a) for an illustration of this algorithm.

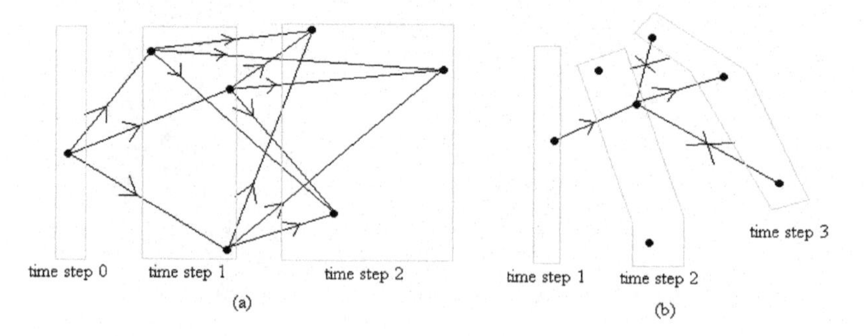

Fig. 2. The two constraint solvers. (a) the minimum distance constraint solver will compare all CCPs at each time step, and choose the one resulting in minimum distance; (b) the minimum angle constraint solver will find the straightest path.

5.3 Minimum Angle Constraint

The minimum angle constraint is based on the idea to minimize the amount of "jerkiness" the camera path may encounter. This "jerkiness" refers to the following example: at time step n to time n+1, a smooth camera animation will always be observed. However, going from time step n+1 to n+2, if the direction taken to get to n+2 significantly differs from n to n+1, the camera motion will experience a sharp tug. The minimum angle constraint solver finds the path that will result in as little angle variation between time steps as possible. The algorithm for the minimum angle constraint solver is very similar to the algorithm for the minimum distance constraint solver. The obvious difference is that it compares angles between vectors instead of distances. Furthermore, it must keep track of the previous vector for each time step, for comparison purposes. Otherwise, the algorithm strictly follows the minimum distance algorithm. Refer to Figure 2(b) for an illustration of this algorithm.

5.4 Path Matching Algorithm

The last phase of the algorithm is to narrow down the specific path to choose. The two sets of paths are based on the results of the minimum distance constraint solver and the minimum angle constraint solver. For each CCP at time 0, the constraint solvers are used to produce two separate sets of paths to each CCP at the end time. These sets are compared as to ensure that the chosen path will share as many nodes as possible with the two constraint solvers. The number of shared points in these sets is summed and the path with the most shared points is chosen as the best path. This path represents the best possible animation, for which the "jumpiness" and "jerkiness" described above will be minimized and additionally maintains near optimal views throughout. This process is repeated, finding the matched path that contains the shortest distance, ultimately reducing the "jumpiness" even further.

6 Experiments and Evaluation

This framework was applied and modified to perform two separate applications. The first application dealt with providing automatic camera animation for 3D scenes with multiple object movement. The second application dealt with automatic facial tracking, for faces that can move around in any manner.

6.1 Visualizing Large 3D Scenes

In visualizing scenarios with multiple 3D objects moving around, the bounding sphere of the scene is constant: it is the sphere encompassing all bounding boxes of all objects over all times. This will provide smoother camera position interpolations, as opposed to a constantly-changing bounding sphere. All other aspects of the framework remain unchanged. The algorithm is very effective for scenes with uniform object motion. That is, the objects are all moving in a general direction. This makes it easier for the algorithm to find a smooth path. Another advantage of the algorithm is its consistency in finding a single optimal path. For instance, when the algorithm is applied to the same scene multiple times, the camera paths produced tend to converge into a single path.

6.2 Automatic Facial Tracking

In automatically tracking facial movement, the only input given is the vertex information of the face over time (no translation/rotation factors). For this application the bounding sphere of the scene is dynamically changing. The optimal static view metrics described in section 4 are also modified. In this application, it is assumed that the user sets up the optimal view of the face to begin with, and that this will be considered optimal throughout the tracking. Therefore, the object occlusion and bounding volume metrics are not effective in this situation. The normals metric is modified as follows: the angles between the normals of the face and the initial view vector are considered to be the optimal angles. For any given time step, the view vector produced compares the angles with the face with these angles, measuring view quality. The minimum angle constraint is not used in this application since it is assumed that the face will be moving in any manner. The modified algorithm tracks the face rather well, as shown in the supplemental video. The minimum distance constraint bounds the camera to better view the face over interpolations. Unfortunately the removed degree of freedom described above results in the camera not being able to view the head roll in any manner.

7 Conclusions and Future Work

This paper presents a unique approach for automatically calculating an optimal camera animation between optimal static views. The algorithm presented takes into consideration how smooth the produced animation is instead of solely focusing on optimal views. The future work will be to use a damping function or control points to guide the path for reducing disorientation, and use a different means of random sampling for solving the face-roll problem. We will also apply the algorithm to visualizing a car chase scenario. Regardless of the particular application, this framework can adjust and adapt to the scene and provide sufficient camera animation.

References

[1] Salomon, B., Garber, M., Lin, M., et al. 2003. Interactive Navigation in Complex Environments Using Path Planning. *Symposium on Interactive 3D Graphics, p*41-52.

[2] Dennis, M., and Healey, C. 2002. Assisted Navigation for Large Information Spaces. *Proceedings of the Conference on Visualization '02,* 419-426.

[3] Stoev, S., and Strasser, W. 2002. A Case Study on Automatic Camera Placement and Motion for Visualizing Historical Data. *IEEE Visualization, p*545-548.

[4] Singh, K., and Balakrishnan, R. 2004. Visualizing 3D Scenes using Non-Linear Projections and Data Mining of Previous Camera Movements. *3rd International Conference on Computer Graphics, Visualization and Interaction in Africa,* 41-48.

[5] Otaduy, M. , and Lin, M.. 2001. User-Centric Viewpoint Computation for Haptic Exploration and Manipulation. *IEEE Visualization '01,* p311-318.

Adding Hand Motion to the Motion Capture Based Character Animation

Ge Jin and James Hahn

Computer Science Department, George Washington University, Washington DC 20052
{jinge, hahn}@gwu.edu

Abstract. Most character motion capture data does not contain secondary motions like detailed hand motion, therefore the resultant animation looks unnatural due to the stiffness of hand motion. In this paper, we analyzed the pose space distance from the character's motion capture data and used stepwise searching algorithm to find the key poses for hand motion synthesis. We adaptively changed the contrast of the local distance map to capture the small motions. If an appropriate hand motion data available, temporal alignment with speed matching and spatial warping of motion data can produce realistic hand motion. If there is no motion capture data available, key frame with cubic or gaussian based interpolation can be used to generate in between frames.

1 Introduction

Motion capture based character animation has become major trend in the computer animation and computer game industry. The skeleton driven mesh deformation is an efficient approach for real-time applications like computer games and virtual reality. Although the motion capture technology can capture realistic human character motions, there has been less effort to simultaneously capture the secondary motions, like hand motion. There are some difficulties to capture gross body motion and intricate hand motion simultaneously. For the vision based motion capture device, the simultaneous capturing of hand motion is restricted due to the occlusion and capturing volume. Further more, most of currently available motion capture data does not contain the detailed hand motion. If we use motion data with no detailed hand motion, the skeleton driven character animation will look unnatural due to the stiffness of hand motion. Current researches in motion capture based character animation concentrate on utilizing existing motion capture data to synthesize new motion. Secondary motions, like hand motion is often neglected in motion synthesis research. Animation of human hand motion has been studied separately in regard to the full body animation. Early works in human hand animation focused on grasping and gesture motion using inverse kinematics and hand motion constraint. Recent works in hand animation concentrated on ASL (American Sign Language) animation, music driven hand animation and realistic hand deformation. Data glove and Cyber glove can be used to capture the hand motion in real time. However, by our knowledge, there has been no work reported for adding hand motion detail to the full body motion capture based character animation.

Local arm motion is closely related with the hand motion. This type of motion includes basketball dribble, catching and throwing motion but not limited to. We have

G. Bebis et al. (Eds.): ISVC 2005, LNCS 3804, pp. 17 – 24, 2005.

analyzed the pose space distance map and found out that the local extreme points in the pose space distance map are the important transition point for the hand motion synthesis. Some of the hand motions are not closely related with the arm motion, like counting with fingers. If we use the global pose space distance map, these small features will be neglected. In order to capture these small changes in the motion capture data, we give more weight to the hand tip difference and increase the contrast of the local region in the pose space distance map. Using adaptively changed pose space distance map, we can detect the local extreme point for small hand motions.

If the hand motion and character animation is closely matched, for example, throwing and catching hand motion to the same throwing and catching character motion, temporal alignment with speed matching is used to seamlessly combine hand and character motion. With similar but not exactly same hand motion, like throwing and catching hand motion to the basketball batting motion, we have used spatial warping of hand motion data to approximate the basketball batting motion. If there is no hand motion capture data available, we defined some key frames and used hermite curve based and gaussian based interpolation to generate in between hand poses.

2 Related Works

Motion synthesis from existing motion capture data has been studied for many years. Early works in motion editing includes motion warping, motion retargeting, motion interpolation, and motion signal processing. Motion warping [1] can make small changes to the end effect of existing motion clip. Motion interpolation [2] method uses pre-existing motion samples to generate new motion clip with linear interpolation. Motion retargeting with space-time constraint [3] [4] has been proposed to map a character's motion to different character while maintaining important constraint. Motion signal processing approach [5] [6] can be used to modify locomotion like exaggerating the motion or changing the step size. Noise based [7] method used procedurally defined motions to simulate nervousness. Recent approaches try to find the closet transition point among various motion clips to synthesize natural long sequence of new motion. Motion graph [8] is used to organize the motion clip into graph structure and automatically generate a transition between the graph nodes.

Introducing secondary motion (like hand motion) to the motion captured character animation has not been reported. But this work is closely related with motion transition and key pose selection work. A seamless transition point is detected using distance between point clouds driven by the skeleton [9]. Another approach uses the translation and weighted average of joint rotation vectors to detect the transition point. [4] An affinity matrix composed of joint position, joint angle, joint velocity and joint angular velocity is used to detect the global key poses for illustrating an animation with a few key poses [10].

In motion transition, the minimum distance between two poses is good candidate point for motion transition. In our case, we are interested in the maximum distance between two poses, which will be potential hand motion transition point. Our key pose detection method for hand motion synthesis is closely related with key pose illustration work [10]. However, for our purpose, only the local arm motion will be considered for the key pose selection. Another difference is the key pose illustration work [10] pays more attention to the global extreme poses, while for hand animation we only need to consider the locally continuous and related transition positions. By adaptively changing the weight of local area of pose space distance map, we can detect subtle motions that could have been neglected by global pose space distance map.

Early works in hand motion animation has discovered a commonly used joint angle dependency $\theta_{DIP}=2/3\theta_{PIP}$ [11]. More detailed hand constraint is reported in [12]. They defined the lower and higher bound of finger joint angles and discovered that the transition from one hand pose to another pose is a linear transformation. We have used the joint angle dependency $\theta_{DIP}=2/3\theta_{PIP}$ to capture the hand motion using electro magnetic trackers. Procedural algorithm and neural net approach have been introduced to synthesize the hand motion of playing musical instrument [13] [14]. Realistic hand skin deformation methods have been reported using bone and muscle structure [15] and pose space deformation [16].

3 Skeleton Structure and Vertex Weight Calculation

We manually choose the feature points on the 3D surface mesh to generate human skeleton structure for limbs, torso and hand. We select the major joint position on the front and backside of 3D mesh model. The skeleton structure can be generated using median position of front and backside feature points. The vertex to skeleton weight is automatically calculated using angular median of skeleton vectors. For every vertex, we choose the shortest and second shortest distance skeleton as weight calculation candidate. The dot product of the angular median vector and vertex to skeleton joint vector is used to calculate the weight for each skeleton. Each mesh vertex has two weights ($w1,w2$) for two nearest skeletons. The constraint is: $0 \le w1 \le 1$, $0 \le w2 \le 1$, and $w1 + w2 = 1$. Random color is assigned to each skeleton to show the controlling vertexes. For the vertexes that affected by two skeletons ($w1>0$, $w2>0$), the vertex color was alpha-blended to show the region controlled by two skeletons.

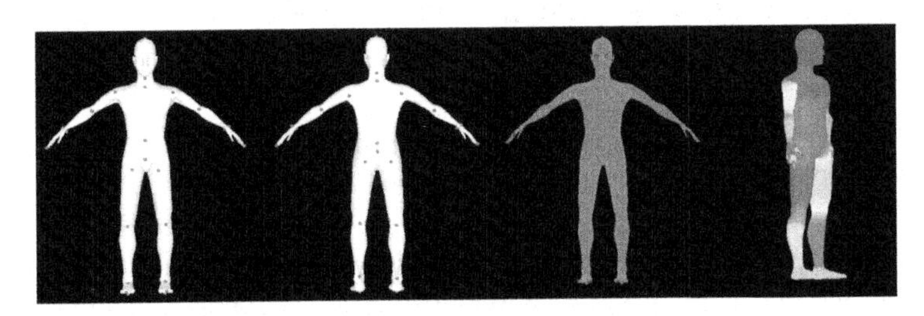

Fig. 1. The first two images show the feature point selection on front and backside of 3D model, the third image shows the skeleton structure from these surface points, the last image shows the result of vertex to skeleton weight calculation

4 Key Pose Selection from Character Motion Capture Data

We are interested in the key poses that are closely related to the hand motion. For this purpose, we only consider local arm motion for key pose selection. We choose the shoulder, elbow, wrist and hand tip position to calculate pose space distance map. Since the global translation and pelvis rotation will affect the joint location, we modified the motion data so that the global translation and pelvis rotation remain unchanged. We used the corresponding joint distance between two frames in motion sequence to generate a pose space distance map. P_t^i, P_t^j is the 3D position of certain joint in ith and jth animation frame. w_t is the weight for each different joint. A distance map pixel value $D_{i,j}$ is calculated using equation (1).

$$D_{i,j} = \sum_{t \in \text{joint}} w_t dist(P_t^j - P_t^i) : dist\ is\ \text{euclidian distance} \tag{1}$$

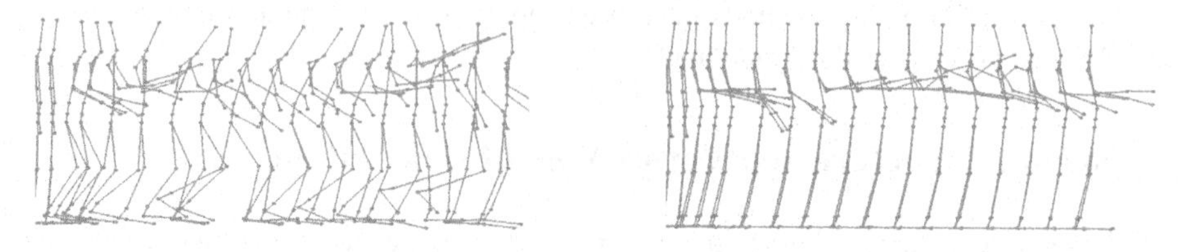

Fig. 2. The sequence of basketball dribble animation and the standing and counting animation

We have computed pose space distance map of right arm for dynamic motion such as basketball dribble and static arm motion like standing and counting (Figure 2). Initially, we give the same weight to the different joints (shoulder, elbow, wrist and tip).

Fig. 3. Left image pair is pose space distance map of basketball and counting motion and right image pair is stepwise searching for key poses from them

For the highly dynamic motions, the resultant pose space distance map shows the clear cue of the maximum distance between two arbitrary frames (Figure 3). For the static arm motion, the distance map could not provide clear cue of counting motion with fingers, only the big movement is indicated (Figure 3).

In order to catch the small motions related with hand tip movement, we give more weight to the hand tip distance and increased the intensity contrast with certain areas: where the mean distance value is less than certain threshold. By doing so we can discover the small motion details like tiny hand tip movement (Figure 4). For the real static frames, increasing the contrast will not provide more cues of motion (Figure 4). Using adaptively weighted and contrast increased pose space distance map, we can detect the key poses from both high dynamic and static arm movement.

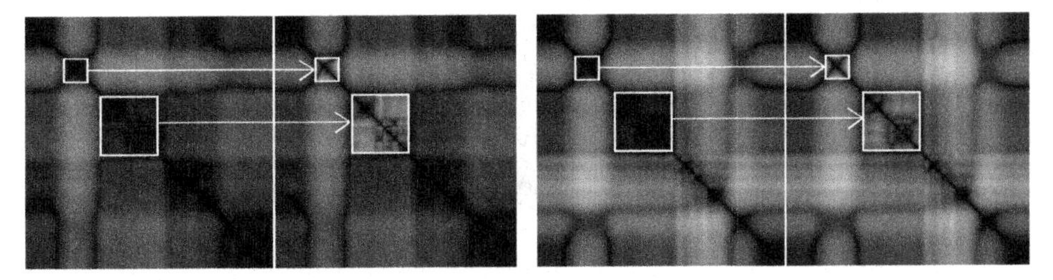

Fig. 4. The pose space distance map of counting motion and contrast increased maps

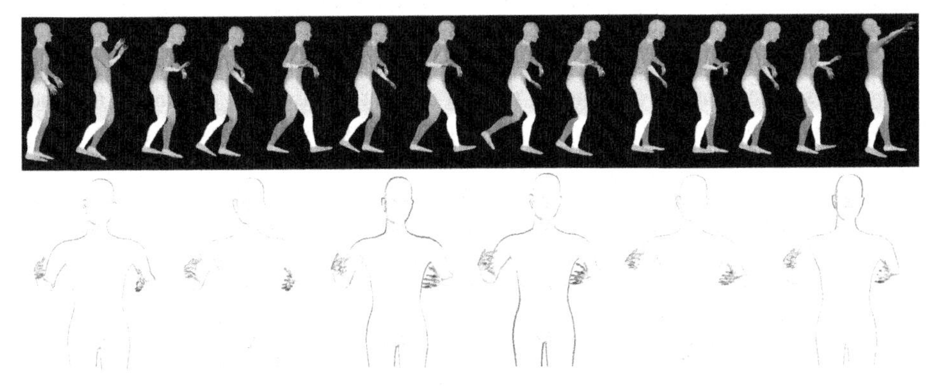

Fig. 5. Automatically calculated key poses from basketball batting motion (upper) and difference of two consecutive key poses in standing and counting motion (lower)

Searching for the key poses from pose space distance map works as follows: we started from the first frame and search for the first local maximum distance with first frame, we searched for local area around this extreme point to find if there is higher local maximum value in this area. The local maximum point $D_{ij}(i<j)$ indicates the frame i and j have maximum distance in pose space. We jump over to the next frame j, and repeat the search with same method. The figure 3 shows the stepwise searching algorithm from basketball batting motion and local contrast increased standing and counting motion. The result of key pose selection is shown in figure 5.

5 Hand Motion Synthesis

In order to add realistic hand motion to the full body motion capture data, we need the hand motion that matches with the character motion. We started from the simple case:

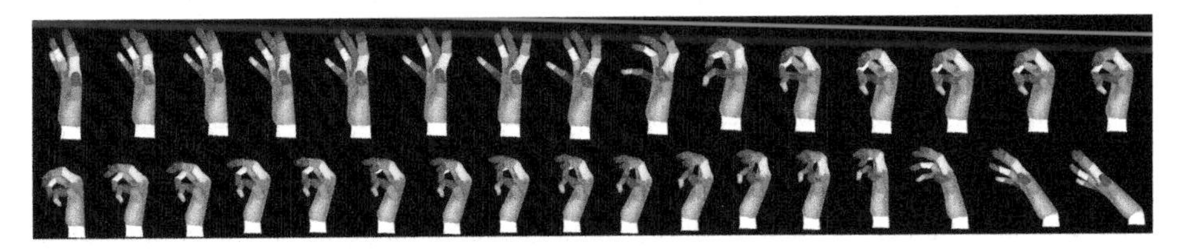

Fig. 6. Capture of catching (upper image) and throwing (lower image) motion

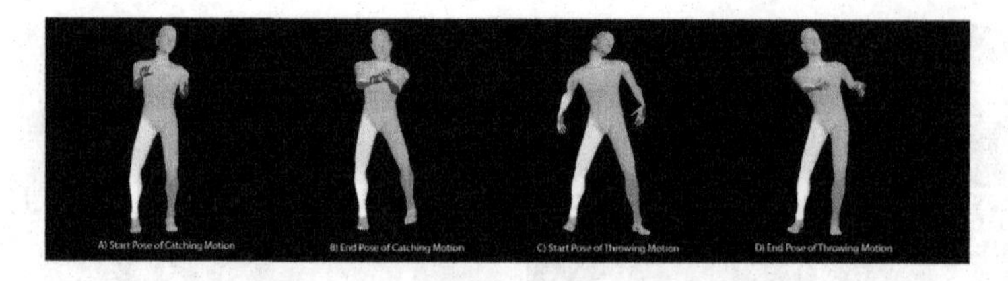

Fig. 7. Extracted motion cycle from the catching and throwing motion

adding catching and throwing hand motion to the catching and throwing motion of character animation. The captured hand motion is illustrated in figure 6.

The extracted key poses (Figure 7) from pose space distance map indicate the motion cycle such as starting and ending pose of catching motion. If we simply add the hand motion cycle to these key poses, the animation will look strange due to the speed mismatch. The motion capture data contains the frame rate information, and we can use this information to calculate the speed of these motion cycles. Another constraint is that: the end pose of hand motion and end pose of arm swing motion should be matched. By matching the end poses and the speed, we can align hand motion capture data to the character animation in temporal domain.

If there is no exact hand motion that matches the character animation, we can use the similar hand motion with spatial warping to synthesize new hand motion. We can use the catching and throwing hand motion to synthesize basketball-batting motion. The main difference in basketball-batting and throw-catch motion is the flexion degree of fingers. We warped the flexion degree of throwing and catching hand motion to approximate the basketball batting motion.

If there is no similar hand motion that can be used with the character animation, key frame interpolation between several predefined hand poses will generate smooth hand motion. For a finger bending motion, the angular velocity at start and end pose is smaller than the velocity at the middle of bending motion. We have experimented with linear, hermite curve and gaussian based interpolation. In hermite curve based interpolation, the interpolation parameter $t(0 \leq t \leq 1)$ is not a constant time interval. Suppose X is time axis and Y is the finger angle axis, the interpolation between two hand pose can be expressed as: $X(t) = f(t)$, $Y(t) = g(t)$ ($f(t)$, $g(t)$: cubic function). We solved general cubic function for $f(t) = x$(certain time), and used the resultant t to get the interpolation value $g(t)$. A gaussian function with appropriate standard deviation will generate good interpolation curve. Both the hermite curve based and gaussian based interpolation generate good result.

6 Results and Discussions

The figure 8 is the animation result of our approach. The resulting hand motion is smoothly integrated into the original human character animation. However, one limitation in our approach is: the predefined hand motion should be close enough to the real hand motion in human character motion capture data. Some of the character animation does not show clear cue of hand motion, or the rough hand motion is missed due to the occlusion in motion capture device. In this case, it is hard to apply our method. Inverse Kinematics based approach is a good candidate when the end constraint of hand tip is already known. But in most case, motion capture data does not contain this kind of constraint. Inverse Kinematics or the Neural Network based optimization for hand motion synthesis usually takes long time to calculate. For our approach the calculation of pose space distance map is done during the preprocessing stage, and the merging of hand animation to the motion capture data can be done in real time.

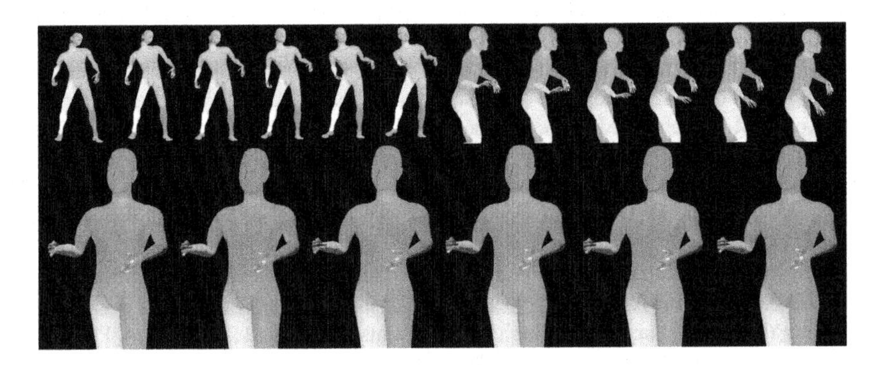

Fig. 8. Catching motion with hand animation, Basketball batting motion using spatial warping, Counting motion with key frames and gaussian based interpolation kernel

7 Conclusions

We have proposed a stepwise searching algorithm to capture key poses from local pose space distance map. The pose space distance map can be locally adjusted to capture subtle motions. Temporal alignment with speed matching and spatial warping was used to add hand motion capture data to the character motion capture data. If there is no hand motion data available, we can use key frame based interpolation with hermite curve or gaussian kernel to generate in between frames. The future research will be focused on more practical and general method: like dubbing a movie, while playing the character animation, simultaneously capture hand motion using data glove. The main challenge will be the seamless synchronization of two motions.

The character motion capture data, which we used in our experiment, are downloaded from http://www.animazoo.com/bvh/. The 3D human character and hand models are downloaded from INRIA Gamma Team Website Collections. (http://ftp-rocq.inria.fr/Eric.Saltel//download/download.php) The hand motion is captured using 3D Articulograph from Carstens Medizinelektronik. (http://www.articulograph.de/)

Acknowledgement

The authors wish to thank anonymous reviewers for their careful comments.

References

1. A. Witkin and Z. Popovic: Motion Warping, Proc. SIGGRAPH (1995) 105-118
2. D. Wiley, J. Hahn: Interpolation Synthesis of Articulated Figure Motion, IEEE CG&A, Vol. 17. No. 6. November/December (1997), 39-45
3. M. Gleicher: Retargetting Motion to New Characters, Proc. SIGGRAPH (1998) 33-42
4. J. Lee and S. Yong Shin: A hierarchical approach to interactive motion editing for human-like figures, Proc. SIGGRAPH (1999) 39-48
5. A. Bruderlin, L.Williams: Motion signal processing. Proc. SIGGRAPH (1995) 97-104.
6. M. Unuma, K. Anjyo, R. Takeuchi: Fourier Principles for Emotion-based Human Figure Animation, Proc.SIGGRAPH (1995) 91-96
7. K. Perlin, L. Velho: Live paint: painting with procedural multiscale textures. Proc. SIGGRAPH (1995) 153-160
8. L. Kovar, M. Gleicher, F. Pighin: Motion Graphs. Proc. SIGGRAPH (2002) 473-482
9. L. Kovar, M. Gleicher: Automated extraction and parameterization of motions in large data sets, Proc. SIGGRAPH (2004) 559-568
10. J. Assa, Y. Caspi, D. Cohen-Or: Action Synopsis: Pose Selection and Illustration, Proc. SIGGRAPH (2005)
11. H. Rijpkema , M. Girard, Computer animation of knowledge-based human grasping, Proc. SIGGRAPH (1991) 339-348
12. J. Lin, Y. Wu, T. Huang: Modeling the Constraints of Human Hand Motion, Proc. of the Workshop on Human Motion (2000) 121-126
13. G. ElKoura, K. Singh: Handrix: animating the human hand, Proc. of ACM SIGGRAPH/Eurographics SCA (2003) 110-119
14. J.Kim, F. Cordier, N. Magnenat-Thalmann: Neural Network-Based Violinist's Hand Animation, Proc. of International Conference on Computer Graphics (2000) 37-41
15. I. Albrecht, J. Haber, H. Seidel: Construction and animation of anatomically based human hand models, Proc. of ACM SIGGRAPH/Eurographics SCA (2003) 26-27
16. T. Kurihara, N. Miyata: Modeling deformable human hands from medical images, Proc. of ACM SIGGRAPH/Eurographics SCA (2004) 355 - 363

Oversimplified Euler Operators for a Non-oriented, Non-manifold B-Rep Data Structure

Frutuoso G.M. Silva and Abel J.P. Gomes

IT - Networks and Multimedia Group,
Department of Computer Science and Engineering,
University of Beira Interior, Portugal
{fsilva, agomes}@di.ubi.pt

Abstract. Traditionally, B-rep geometric kernels possess oriented data structures, i.e. they possess oriented cells (e.g. half-edges, co-edges, face uses, etc.). The use of explicit oriented cells makes these data structures quite verbose and expensive in terms of memory space. Although orientation is important for visualization and engineering analysis purposes, it gives rise to difficult issues at the representation level; for example, keeping inclusion relationships between incident surfaces at a non-manifold vertex. Instead, we propose a non-manifold B-rep data structure whose cells are not oriented. This facilitates the design and implementation of its associated Euler operators, each one of which then reduces itself to a sequence of insertion and removal operations of cells into or from a list. Besides, these Euler operators call a single query operator to retrieve *all* incidence and adjacency information through a minimal number of accesses. As a result, we obtain a *simple*, *responsive*, *concise* and *general* non-oriented, non-manifold B-rep geometric kernel.

1 Introduction

3D data structures can be classified in three main categories: boundary representation (B-rep), celular decomposition (for example, octrees) and CSG trees [1][2][3][4][5]. Traditionally, B-reps have been used as geometric kernels of CAD systems, but they are also used to support the development of virtual reality and animation systems, and more recently multiresolution schemes. Usually, B-reps incorporate oriented data structures, but recently some non-oriented data structures have appeared in the literature (e.g. cell-tuple data structure [6], PSC (Progressive Simplicial Complexes) [7] and DiX data structure [8]). The emergence of non-oriented B-rep data structures enables the development of geometric kernels that are easier to develop and use, which in a way constitutes a return to Baumgart's spirit [3, 9].

The rationale behind oriented boundary representation data structures (Winged-Edge [3], Half-Edge [1], Quad-Edge [10] or Radial Edge [2]) is in part to enable speeding up traversal algorithms for retrieving adjacency and incidence information as fast as possible. However, they need more storage space to cope

G. Bebis et al. (Eds.): ISVC 2005, LNCS 3804, pp. 25–34, 2005.

with oriented cells. In a way, these oriented cells are redundant. For example, in the Radial Edge data structure, each face has two associated loops, one for each face side; hence, three faces incident along an edge require six oriented edges. Lee and Lee [11] proposed a new data structure, called Partial Entity structure, that reduces in half the storage burden of the Radial Edge data structure.

This paper presents a non-oriented, non-manifold B-rep data structure (in short, NNB-rep) and its corresponding Euler operators. The NNB-rep data structure represents only cells, not their oriented counterparts, as described in [12]. Thus, it does not include loops or any oriented entities. In this way, we have reduced the storage size of the NNB-rep data structure to a minimum, though preserving its time efficiency. In fact, as shown later, it is an optimal C_4^9 data structure. On the other hand, Euler operators are ruled by the most general Euler formula for 2-dimensional inhomogeneous, non-manifold geometric objects with complete boundaries in $\mathbb{R}^3$. Despite its generality, the computational complexity (number of steps or operations) of these Euler operators is rather small. Altogether, they form a new geometric kernel that was designed to satisfy four major important requirements, namely: *simplicity*, *responsiveness*, *conciseness*, and *generality*.

This paper is then organized as follows. Section 2 describes the NNB-rep data structure. Section 3 presents its companion query operator, called mask operator, for fast retrieval of adjacency and incidence information. The Euler operators for NNB-rep appears in Section 4. At last, Section 5 draws some conclusions and future work.

2 NNB-Rep Data Structure

The NNB-rep data structure *explicitly* implements a $C_{2n}^{(n+1)^2}$ representation, i.e. it represents $2n$ out of $(n+1)^2$ adjacency and incidence relations between cells of a n-dimensional complex (Fig. 1). In particular, it represents 4 out of 9 relations between cells of a 2-dimensional complex, namely: two basic adjacency relations, $V \prec E$ and $E \prec F$, and their inverse relations or incidence relations, $E \succ V$ and $F \succ E$. These four basic relations can be compound to form those nine adjacency relations introduced by Weiler [13]. According to Ni and Bloor [14], these four basic relations form the best representation in the class C_4^9 in terms of

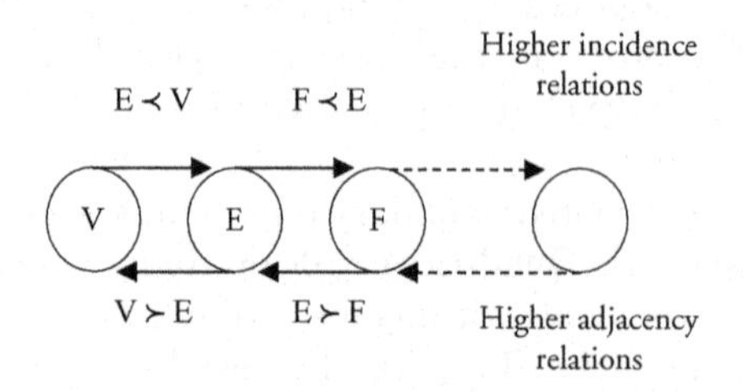

Fig. 1. NNB-rep diagram

information retrieval performance, i.e. it requires a minimal number of direct and indirect accesses to the data structure to retrieve those four explicit topological relations and the remaining five implicit topological relations, respectively. A direct access involves a single call to the query operator, while an indirect access requires two or more calls.

In this paper, we are interested in presenting and constructing 2-dimensional objects in NNB-rep data structure. Each NNB-rep object is defined by means of a triple $M = \{V, E, F\}$, where V is a finite set of vertices, E is a finite set of edges, and F is a finite set of faces. Recall that all NNB-rep objects have complete boundaries. That is, they follow the construction principle that attaching any cell requires that its bounding cells are already in the data structure.

A *vertex* $v \in V$ is represented by a non-ordered k-tuple of its incident edges, i.e. $v = \{e_1, e_2, e_3, ..., e_k\}$, where e_i $(i = 1...k)$ is an incident edge at v; hence, $E \succ V$ relation is embedded in the NNB-rep data structure. For an isolated vertex, its set of edges is empty. The set of edges is also empty in the degenerated case of a single vertex in a face; in this case, a set with a single face must be considered in the representation of v.

An *edge* $e \in E$ is a pair of tuples $e = \{\{v_1, v_2\}, \{f_1, f_2, ..., f_k\}\}$, where the first tuple contains the vertices v_1 and v_2 bounding e, and the second tuple consists of the faces $f_1, f_2, ..., f_k$ incident on e. So, we have $V \prec E$ and $F \succ E$ relations. An isolated ring edge appears as an empty set of vertices and an empty set of faces.

A *face* $f \in F$ is represented by a k-tuple of its bounding (adjacent) edges, i.e. $f = \{e_1, e_2, e_3, ..., e_k\}$, where each e_i $(i = 1...k)$ is an edge bounding f; hence, the $E \prec F$ relation. A self-closed face homeomorphic to a 2-sphere is represented with an empty set of edges. In the degenerated case of a surface homeomorphic to a 2-sphere having a face bounded by a single vertex, we have to consider a singular set with such a vertex in the representation of f.

As described above, the NNB-rep data structure is not an oriented topological data structure viewing that it does not include any oriented cells. Instead, NNB-rep is an orientable data structure. That is, an orientation can be topologically induced over an object as a way of computing a geometric orientation (a normal vector for each face). Inducing an orientation on a face f begins by traversing its frontier either clockwise or counterclockwise. For that, we use a query operator, called mask operator, for retrieving vertices and edges bounding f alternately. This procedure is repeated again and again for all faces using the same order, either clockwise or counterclockwise. After that, the object is said to be consistently oriented.

3 Mask Operator

Let us now pay attention to the incidence scheme of the NNB-rep. It can be described in terms of a set of cell-tuples T=$\{v_i, e_j, f_k\}$, where f_k is a face incident on an edge e_j (symbolically, $f_k \succ e_j$) and e_j is incident at a vertex v_i ($e_j \succ v_i$). Conversely, v_i is adjacent to e_j ($v_i \prec e_j$) and e_j is adjacent to f_k ($e_j \prec f_k$).

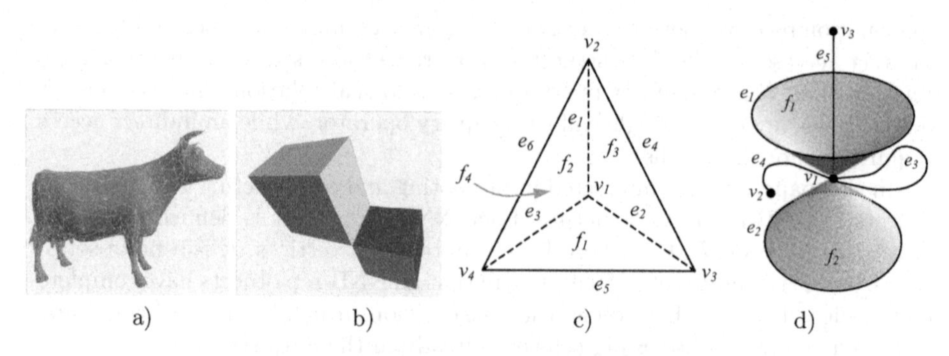

Fig. 2. Manifold and non-manifold objects

This incidence scheme can be considered as a data structure on its own. It is known as the cell-tuple data structure, and is due to Brisson [2]. The NNB-rep data structure has then the same adjacency and incidence descriptive power as the cell-tuple data structure, but it is more concise and less time-consuming in retrieving topological information. This is so because NNB-rep model consists of a set of cells (not a set of cell-tuples), with each cell representing one or two *explicit* topological relations.

Retrieving topological information from the NNB-rep data structure is carried out by means of a single query operator, called mask operator. It is defined by $\blacktriangleright\!\!\triangleleft_d : V \times E \times F \rightarrow C$, being $C = V \cup E \cup F$ the union of the set V of vertices, the set E of edges, and the set F of faces, such that $\blacktriangleright\!\!\triangleleft_d(v_i, e_j, f_k) = \{c_l^d\}$, i.e. a set of d-dimensional cells.

The arguments of $\blacktriangleright\!\!\triangleleft_d$ are cells in the set $V \times E \times F$. These arguments establish adjacency and incidence relations between them. Let x a cell argument of dimension n. If $x = NULL$, there is no restrictions on the cells of dimension n, i.e. all the n-cells are being considered. If $x \neq NULL$, all n-cells are being considered, except x itself. So, the $\blacktriangleright\!\!\triangleleft_d$ operator returns all the d-cells incident on the $(d-1)$-cells and adjacent to the $(d+1)$-cells, after considering the restrictions imposed by non-NULL arguments.

Let us show how the query operator works in conjunction with the NNB-rep data structure. For that, let us consider the manifold object in Fig. 2(c):

1. $\blacktriangleright\!\!\triangleleft_1(v_1,\text{NULL},\text{NULL}) = \{e_1, e_2, e_3\}$ directly returns all edges incident at v_1.
2. $\blacktriangleright\!\!\triangleleft_2(v_1,\text{NULL},\text{NULL}) = \{f_1, f_2, f_3\}$ indirectly returns all faces incident at v_1. This requires an intermediate call to $\blacktriangleright\!\!\triangleleft_1(v_1,\text{NULL},\text{NULL})$ to return all edges e_1, e_2, e_3 incident at v_1. Then, the operator $\blacktriangleright\!\!\triangleleft_2(\text{NULL}, e_i,\text{NULL})$ is called for each edge e_i in order to compute faces incident on e_i and v_1.
3. $\blacktriangleright\!\!\triangleleft_0(\text{NULL}, e_1,\text{NULL}) = \{v_1, v_2\}$ directly returns bounding vertices of e_1.
4. $\blacktriangleright\!\!\triangleleft_2(\text{NULL}, e_1,\text{NULL}) = \{f_2, f_3\}$ directly returns faces incident on e_1.
5. $\blacktriangleright\!\!\triangleleft_0(\text{NULL},\text{NULL}, f_1) = \{v_1, v_3, v_4\}$ indirectly returns all vertices bounding f_1. This requires an intermediate call to $\blacktriangleright\!\!\triangleleft_1(\text{NULL},\text{NULL}, f_1)$ to first determine all edges bounding f_1. Then, the operator $\blacktriangleright\!\!\triangleleft_0(\text{NULL}, e_i,\text{NULL})$ is called for each edge e_i in order to determine vertices bounding e_i and f_1.

6. $\bowtie_1$(NULL,NULL, f_1) $= \{e_2, e_3, e_5\}$ directly returns all edges bounding f_1.
7. $\bowtie_2(v_3, e_1$,NULL) $= \{f_3\}$ directly returns faces incident on e_1 and v_3.
8. $\bowtie_1(v_1, e_2, f_1) = \{e_3\}$ directly returns all edges bounding f_1 and incident at v_1, with the exception of e_2.
9. $\bowtie_0(v_1$,NULL,NULL) $= \{v_2, v_4, v_3\}$ indirectly returns all vertices neighboring v_1. This requires an intermediate call to $\bowtie_1(v_1$,NULL,NULL) to first determine all edges incident at v_1. Then, the operator $\bowtie_0(v_1, e_i$,NULL) is called for each edge e_i in order to determine vertices bounding e_i, with the exception of v_1.

Note that the operator $\bowtie_d$ needs not handle all the data structure constituents to retrieve local topological information. It handles a model locally by using the adjacency and incidence relations stored in the cells of the data structure. Thus, its time performance holds independently of the model size. This is very important for handling large models, in particular in operations at interactive rates.

4 Euler Operators

The Euler operators were introduced in the geometric modeling literature in the 70s. They provide a method for constructing geometric objects that are topologically valid (i.e. closed and orientable) and satisfy some Euler formula. The operators proposed here follow the Euler formula given by

$$v - (e - e_h) + (f - f_h + f_c) = C - C_h + C_c \tag{1}$$

where f, e and v denote the number of faces, edges and vertices; e_h, f_h, C_h stand for the number of holes or handles of an edge, a face, and an object component, respectively; f_c and C_c stand for the number of voids or interior cavities of a face and object components, respectively. This Euler formula is valid for *any* 2-dimensional non-manifold objects with complete boundaries in $\mathbb{R}^3$. It generalizes the formula proposed by Lee and Lee [11] because we have considered two more variables for self-closed edges e_h and self-closed faces f_c which are homeomorphic to 1-spheres and 2-spheres, respectively. The nine variables of the formula (1) form a base of a vector space such that we only need a minimal set of nine Euler operators (and their inverses) to construct any NNB-rep objects in $\mathbb{R}^3$.

In Table 1, we present such a minimal set of Euler operators, whose names are defined according to the Baumgart's convention [9]. These operators causes the addition/subtraction of a cell (that is, vertex, edge or face) but, as shown in the third column of Table 1, the equality of the Euler formula (1) is kept for topological validity. The first three operators change the local and global shape of the object that is being constructed, while the remaining operators only alter the local shape of the object. In fact, a careful glance over the formula (1) shows that its left side denotes the shape of cells (here called local shape) of a geometric object, while its right side represents the global shape, i.e. the shape

Table 1. Minimal set of Euler operators

Name	Description	$(v, e, e_h, f, f_h, f_c, C, C_h, C_c)$
mvC	make vertex and component	(1, 0, 0, 0, 0, 0, 1, 0, 0)
meC_h	make edge and component hole	(0, 1, 0, 0, 0, 0, 0, 1, 0)
mfC_c	make face and component hollow cavity	(0, 0, 0, 1, 0, 0, 0, 0, 1)
$mvke_h$	make vertex, kill edge hole	(1, 0, 1, 0, 0, 0, 0, 0, 0)
mvf_h	make vertex and face hole	(1, 0, 0, 0, 1, 0, 0, 0, 0)
$mvkf_c$	make vertex, kill face hollow cavity	(1, 0, 0, 0, 0, 1, 0, 0, 0)
mve	make vertex and edge	(1, 1, 0, 0, 0, 0, 0, 0, 0)
mvf	make vertex and face	(1, 0, 0, 1, 0, 0, 0, 0, 0)
mee_hff_h	make edge, edge hole, face and face hole	(0, 1, 1, 1, 1, 0, 0, 0, 0)

of a geometric object as a whole. Thus, Euler operators are essentially shape operators, as they change the local and global shape of a geometric object. They use the mask operator to access to adjacency and incidence information to reasoning about connectivity and geometry of objects.

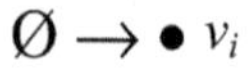

```
mvC (vi, ci) Begin
  vi <- new vertex
  ci <- new empty component
  ci <- add vi
  vi <- assign ci
End.
```

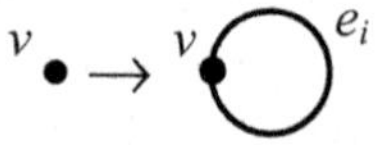

$\emptyset \rightarrow \bullet\, v_i$

```
meCh (v, ei) Begin
  ei <- new empty edge
  v <- add ei
  ei <- assign v
End.
```

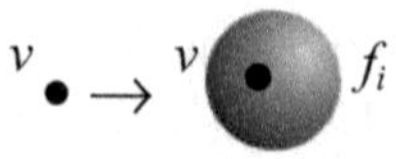

v $\bullet \rightarrow$ v e_i

```
mfCc (v, fi) Begin
  fi <- new empty face
  v <- add fi
  fi <- assign v
End.
```

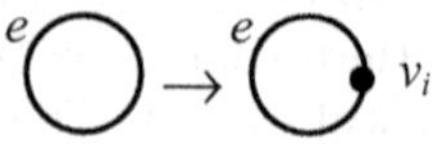

v $\bullet \rightarrow$ v f_i

```
mvkeh (e, vi) Begin
  vi <- new vertex
  vi <- add e
  e <- add vi
End.
```

e $\rightarrow$ e v_i

```
mvfh (f, vi) Begin
  vi <- new vertex
  vi <- add f
  f <- add vi
End.
```

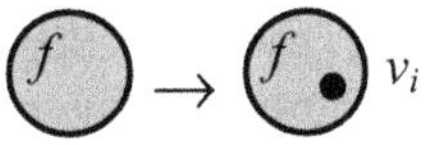

```
mvkfc (f, vi) Begin
  vi <- new vertex
  f <- add vi
  vi <- add f
End.
```

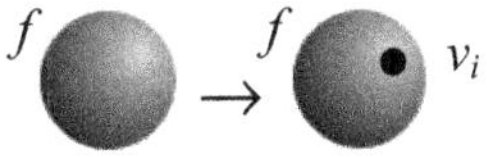

```
mve (e, vi, ei) Begin
  vi <- new vertex
  ei <- new empty edge
  lfaces <- MaskOperator(2, Null, e, Null)
  v_aux <- get vertex v1 from e
  e <- add vi to v1 of edge e
  ei <- add v_aux and vi
  vi <- add e and ei
  v_aux <- remove e
  v_aux <- add ei
  for each f of lfaces
    f <- add ei
End.
```

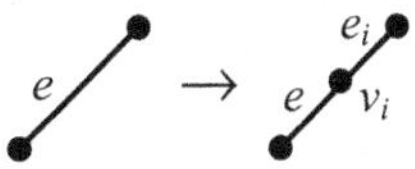

```
mve (v, vi, ei) Begin
  vi <- new vertex
  ei <- new empty edge
  ei <- add v and vi
  vi <- add ei
  v <- add ei
End.
```

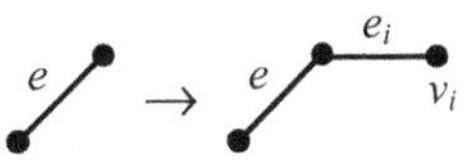

```
mve (v, f, vi, ei) Begin
  vi <- new vertex
  ei <- new empty edge
  ei <- add v and vi
  ei <- add f
  vi <- add ei
  v <- add ei
  f <- add ei
End.
```

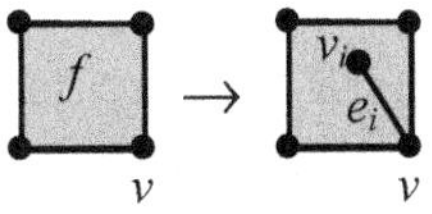

```
mef (v, ei, fi) Begin
  ei <- new empty edge
  fi <- new empty face
  v <- add ei
  ei <- add v and fi
  fi <- add ei
End.
```

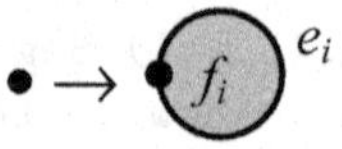

```
mef (e, ei, fi) Begin
  ei <- new empty edge
  fi <- new empty face
  fi <- add ei and e
  ei <- add fi
  e <- add fi
End.
```

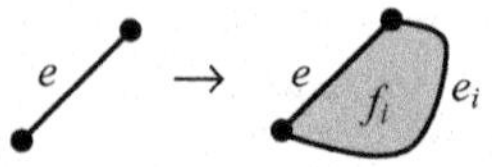

```
mef (v1, v2, f, ei, fi) Begin
  ei <- new empty edge
  fi <- new empty face
  if (v1 != v2) {
    iedges <- MaskOperator(1, v1, Null, f)
    e <- get edge from iedges
    v <- MaskOperator(0, v1, e, Null)
    while (v != v2) {
      f <- remove e
      fi <- add e
      e <- MaskOperator(1, v, e, f)
      v <- MaskOperator(0, v, e, Null) } }
  ei <- add vertices v1 and v2
  fi <- add ei
  f <- add ei
End.
```

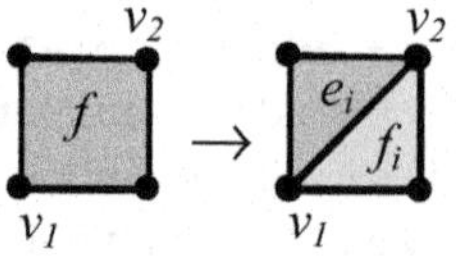

```
meehffh (v, ei, fi) Begin
  ei <- new empty edge
  fi <- new empty face
  ei <- add fi
  fi <- add ei and v
  v <- add fi
End.
```

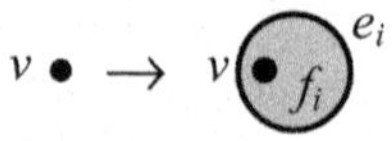

```
meehffh (e, ei, fi) Begin
  ei <- new empty edge
  fi <- new empty face
  ei <- add fi
  e <- add fi
  fi <- add ei and e
End.
```

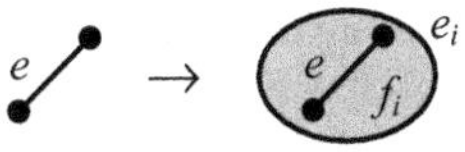

```
meehffh (f, ei, fi) Begin
  ei <- new empty edge
  fi <- new empty face
  ei <- add f and fi
  fi <- add ei
  f <- add ei
End.
```

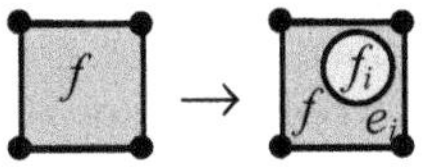

Due to space limitations, we have only presented the nine operators that allow us to build up non-manifold objects. However, their nine inverses would be simple to code likewise. As an example, the object represented in Fig. 2(d) might be construct through the following sequence of Euler operators:

```
mvC(v1, c1)          // vertex v1
mve(v1, v2, e4)      // v2 and e4
meCh(v1, e3)         // e3
mve(v1, v3, e5)      // v3 and e5
meehffh(v1, e1, f1)  // e1 and f1
meehffh(v1, e2, f2)  // e2 and f2
```

5 Conclusions and Future Work

The geometric kernel proposed in this paper is based on the NNB-rep data structure. As shown above, it is an non-oriented, responsive, concise and generic data structure for 2-dimensional inhomogeneous non-manifold geometric objects in $\mathbb{R}^3$. Besides, it is a optimal C_4^9 data structure. Consequently, we have a very efficient query operator to retrieve incidence and adjacency information. The result is a set of oversimplified and efficient Euler operators to model geometric objects.

References

1. Mäntylä, M.: An Introduction to Solid Modeling. Computer Science Press (1988)
2. Weiler, K.: The radial edge structure: a topological representation for non-manifold geometric boundary modelling. Geometric Modelling for CAD applications (1988) 3–36

3. Baumgart, B.G.: Winged-edge polyhedron representation. Technical report, STAN-CS-320, Stanford University (1972)
4. Meagher, D.: Geometric modeling using octree encoding. Computer Graphics and Image Processing **19** (1982) 129–147
5. Requicha, A.: Representation for rigid solids: theory, methods and systems. ACM Computing Surveys **12** (1980) 437–464
6. Brisson, E.: Representing geometric structures in d dimension: topology and order. Discrete & Computational Geometry **9** (1993) 387–426
7. Popovic, J., Hoppe, H.: Progressive simplicial complexes. In: Proceedings of Siggraph, ACM Press (1997) 217–224
8. Gomes, A.J.P.: A concise b-rep data structure for stratified subanalytic objects. In: Proceedings of the 2003 Eurographics/ACM SIGGRAPH Symposium on Geometry Processing, Eurographics Association (2003) 83–93
9. Baumgart, B.G.: A polyhedral representation for computer vision. In: Proceedings of AFIPS Natl. Comput. Conf. Volume 44. (1975) 589–596
10. Guibas, L., Stolfi, J.: Primitives for the manipulation of general subdivisions and the computation of voronoi diagrams. ACM Transactions on Graphics **4** (1985) 74–123
11. Lee, S.H., Lee, K.: Partial entity structure: A fast and compact non-manifold boundary representation based on partial topological entities. In: Proceedings of the Sixth ACM Symposium on Solid Modeling and Applications. (2001) 159–170
12. Silva, F.G.M., Gomes, A.J.P.: AIF - a data structure for polygonal meshes. In: Proceedings of Computational Science and Its Applications (ICCSA'03), Lecture Notes in Computer Science, Vol. 2669, Part III, V. Kumar, M. Gravilova, C. Tan and P. L'Ecuyer (eds.), Springer-Verlag (2003) 478–487
13. Weiler, K.: Edge-based data structure for solid modelling in curved-surface environments. IEEE Computer Graphics & Applications **5** (1985) 21–40
14. Ni, X., Bloor, M.S.: Performance evaluation of boundary data structures. IEEE Computer Graphics and Applications **14** (1994) 66–77

The Number of Gaps in Binary Pictures

Valentin E. Brimkov[1], Angelo Maimone[2], Giorgio Nordo[2],
Reneta P. Barneva[3], and Reinhard Klette[4]

[1] Mathematics Department, SUNY Buffalo State College, Buffalo, NY 14222, USA
brimkove@buffalostate.edu

[2] Dipartimento di Matematica, Università di Messina, 98166 Messina, Italy
{angelo.maimone, giorgio.nordo}@unime.it

[3] Department of Computer Science, SUNY Fredonia, Fredonia, NY 14063, USA
barneva@cs.fredonia.edu

[4] CITR Tamaki, University of Auckland, Building 731, Auckland, New Zealand
r.klette@auckland.ac.nz

Abstract. This paper identifies the total number of gaps of object pixels in a binary picture, which solves an open problem in 2D digital geometry (or combinatorial topology of binary pictures). We obtain a formula for the total number of gaps as a function of the number of object pixels (grid squares), vertices (corners of grid squares), holes, connected components, and 2×2 squares of pixels. It can be used to test a binary picture (or just one region: e.g., a digital curve) for gap-freeness.

Keywords: digital geometry, 2D binary pictures, gaps, gap-freeness.

1 Introduction

This paper identifies the total number of *gaps* of object pixels in a 2D binary picture, which are defined in analogy to the topological concept of *tunnels*. Tunnels in topology are rather counted than identified; the number of tunnels is a topological invariant. In 2D or 3D binary pictures, gaps have been defined based on separability properties, and the total number of gaps is also a property characterizing the "topological" structure of a binary picture. Gaps in 3D binary pictures have also been studied in the context of rendering voxelized scenes [5]. Arising questions are, for example, as follows: is a binary picture gap-free or it has gaps of certain type. This is particularly interesting when dealing with digital curves or surfaces in image analysis and geometric modeling.

With this in mind, our objective was to obtain a formula for the total number of gaps based on basic parameters of a 2D binary picture (such as the number of object pixels, vertices, holes, or connected components). Results of this kind belong to the area of combinatorial topology, which originated with the Descartes-Euler formula $\alpha_2 - \alpha_1 + \alpha_0 = 2$ that (in its first occurrence) combined the number of vertices (α_0), edges (α_1), and facets (α_2) of a convex polyhedron. For results in combinatorial topology in the context of image analysis, see Chapters 4 and 6 in [7].

G. Bebis et al. (Eds.): ISVC 2005, LNCS 3804, pp. 35–42, 2005.

The main result of this paper is the formula $g = v - 2(p + c - h) + b$, where g is the number of gaps, v the number of vertices, p the number of pixels, h the number of holes, c the number of connected components, and b the number of 2-*blocks* (i.e., 2×2 pixels squares) of all object pixels in a binary picture. This equality implies corollaries for the important cases of simple digital curves, simple digital arcs, or for the general case of digital curves.

The next section introduces basic notions and notations. Section 3 presents our main results, including a proof, and we conclude in Section 4.

2 Preliminaries

2.1 Basic Definitions

In this section we recall some basic notions of digital geometry following [7]. The reader is also referred to [1, 2, 8, 11, 15].

A regular orthogonal grid subdivides $\mathbb{R}^2$ into unit squares called *pixels*, that are centered at the points of $\mathbb{Z}^2$. A unit square is a 2-cell (note: "2" as "two-dimensional"), whose frontier contains four 1-cells (edges) and four 0-cells (vertices). Two non-identical pixels are called 0-*adjacent* iff they share a vertex, and 1-*adjacent* iff they share an edge. We identify a binary picture S with its finite set of object pixels (e.g., all those having value 1 in the picture). We use 0-adjacency for object pixels, and 1-adjacency for non-object pixels. It is known that this corresponds to a topology on binary pictures, where 0-adjacency defines closed sets, and 1-adjacency defines open sets [7].

In the following definitions, we have $k = 0$ or $k = 1$. A *k-path* in S is a sequence of pixels from S such that every two consecutive pixels on the path are k-adjacent. Two pixels of a digital object S are *k-connected* (in S) iff there is a k-path in S between them. A subset G of S is *k-connected* iff there is a k-path connecting any two pixels of G. The maximal (by inclusion) k-connected subsets of a binary picture S are called *k-components* of S. Components are nonempty, and distinct k-components are disjoint.

Let M be a subset of a binary picture S. If $S \setminus M$ is not k-connected then the set M is said to be *k-separating* in S. Now let M be a finite set of pixels that is k-separating in $\mathbb{Z}^2$ (note: $k = 0$ or $k = 1$). The infinite 1-component of $\mathbb{Z}^2 \setminus M$ is called the *background component* of M, while the other (finite) 1-components of $S \setminus M$ are called *1-holes* of M (see Fig. 1).

Let a set M of pixels be 1-separating but not 0-separating in a digital object S. Then M is said to have 0-*gaps* (see Fig. 1a, top-left). For a set M of pixels that is not separating in another set of pixels we can identify a gap with a vertex that is incident with two and only two pixels of M, and it is the only common point of these two pixels (see Fig. 1a, top-right). A digital object without any 0-gaps is called *gap-free* (Fig. 1a, bottom).

2.2 Pixel Language

To facilitate the further description, below we present a simple graphical language (similar to Venn diagrams in set theory), which we call the *pixel language*.

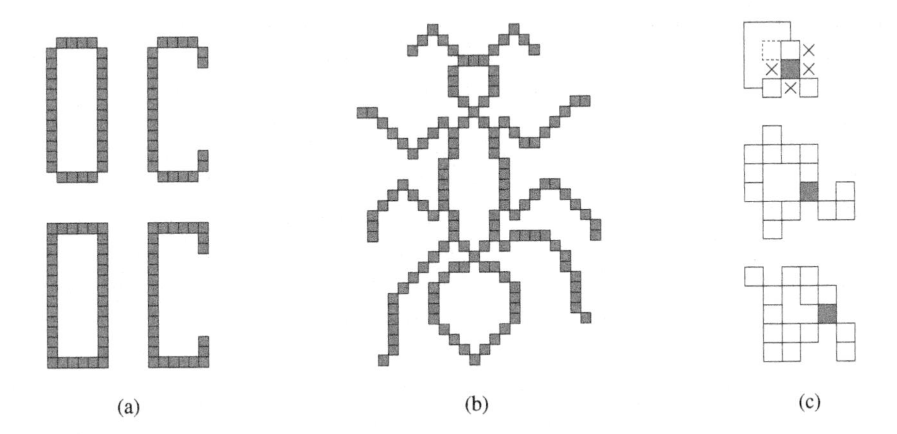

Fig. 1. (a) *Top:* digital curves with 0-gaps. *Bottom:* gap-free digital curves. Both '0's define one 1-hole each. (b) A general digital curve with three 1-holes. (c) Pixel language configuration (*top*) representing two different digital pictures (*middle*, *bottom*).

This language is defined by different *configurations* of pixels, where in each of them there will be a *key pixel*, highlighted in grey, whose neighborhood is studied. For illustrations, see Figures 1c,2,3, and 4. A few rules define the graphical pixel language.

0-adjacent pixels of the key pixel will be drawn with normal continuous lines. Pixels that may or may not exist in a configuration will be drawn with dashed lines. Any subset of such pixels (in particular, no one or all of them) may belong to the configuration or may be missing. Sometimes (i) at least, (ii) at most, or (iii) exactly one (or more) of these pixels will have to exist in a configuration. In order to keep our pixel language simple, we will prefer to add relevant explanations in the text rather than to introduce further special graphical markings. Positions of pixels that are excluded from the configuration will be marked by $\times$.

Additionally to these standard rules, sometimes we also assign labels to pixels for a more detailed analysis of certain possibilities. The existence of a path in a binary picture which connects two pixels in a configuration and does not intersect or "touch" other pixels from it is marked by connecting both pixels with an arc (as in some cases of Figures 3 and 4; see also Fig. 1c).

3 Gap Formulas

3.1 Total Number of Gaps in a Binary Picture

Theorem 1. *Consider a finite set $D \subset \mathbb{Z}^2$, which contains p pixels, v vertices, h 1-holes, c 0-connected components, and b 2-blocks. Let g be the number of 0-gaps of D. Then we have the following:*

$$g = v - 2(p + c - h) + b. \tag{1}$$

Proof. We use induction on the number of pixels. The statement is obviously true for a set consisting of a single pixel. We have $p = 1$, $v = 4$, $c = 1$, and $h = b = g = 0$; those values satisfy formula (1).

Assume that the statement is true for a set composed of p pixels, where $p \geq 1$. We will show that it is then true for any set composed by $p' = p+1$ pixels. Consider such a set D' and remove an arbitrary pixel P from it. Then $D = D' - \{P\}$ is a set of p pixels to which the induction hypothesis applies. Let the number of its vertices, 0-components, 1-holes, 2-blocks, and 0-gaps be v, c, h, b, and g, respectively. Then $g = v - 2(p + c - h) + b$. We will see how adding pixel P to D can influence this last equality. We aim to show that

$$g' = v' - 2(p' + c' - h') + b', \tag{2}$$

where $p' = p+1, v', c', h', b'$, and g' are the counts of pixels, vertices, 0-components, 1-holes, 2-blocks, and 0-gaps of D', respectively. In doing so, we distinguish between 43 essentially different configurations which we group into 10 cases, some of which involve subcases[1]. We analyze all of them with the help of illustrations using our pixel language. For the sake of better readability of the paper, we display the illustrations within Figures 2, 3, and 4, where labels of subfigures match the numeration of the cases considered below. Everywhere, pixel P is in dark grey. We outline the main points of the proof. For full details we have to refer to a forthcoming full length paper.

Remember that throughout we have $p' = p+1$. Upon adding P to D, for the other parameters v', c', h', b', and g' we may have various possibilities. Depending on how the parameters c, h, and b change, we distinguish the 10 basic cases. For the first two we also indicate how v and g change, while for the remaining eight cases this trivial operation is skipped for brevity.

Case 1. *c, h, and b do not change.*

The only possible configurations under these conditions are displayed in Fig. 2. We have $c' = c$, $h' = h$, and $b' = b$.

In Case 1a we have $v' = v+2$ and $g' = g$. In Case 1b, $v' = v+3$ and $g' = g+1$. In Case 1c, $v' = v + 1$ and $g' = g - 1$. In Case 1d, $v' = v$ and $g' = g - 2$.

Case 2. *h and b do not change, while c increases by 1.*

Obviously, adding P to D can increase the number of components of $D' = D \cup \{P\}$ only if P is disjoint from D. Then c will increase by 1, while h, b, as well as g will not change (see Fig. 2 (2)).

We have $v' = v + 4$, $c' = c + 1$, $h' = h$, $b' = b$, and $g' = g$.

Case 3. *h and b do not change, while c decreases by 1, 2, or 3.*

The possible configurations are displayed in Fig. 2. We have $h' = h$ and $b' = b$.

In Case 3a we have $c' = c - 1$, which is possible for the seven configurations displayed in Fig. 2 (3a). In Case 3b we have $c' = c-2$. The possible configurations are given in Fig. 2 (3b). In Case 3c we have $c' = c - 3$ (Fig. 2 (3c)).

[1] Note that any configuration containing dashed pixel(s) and/or path(s), actually represents a number of different configurations, one for each possibility, as all of them feature analogous characterization.

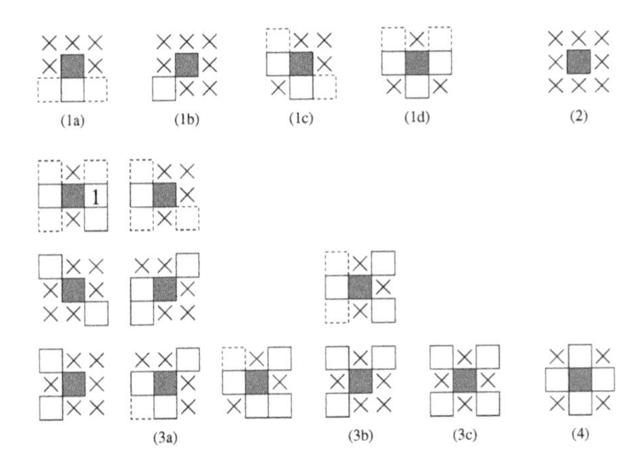

Fig. 2. Illustrations to the proof of Theorem 1. Cases 1, 2, 3, and 4.

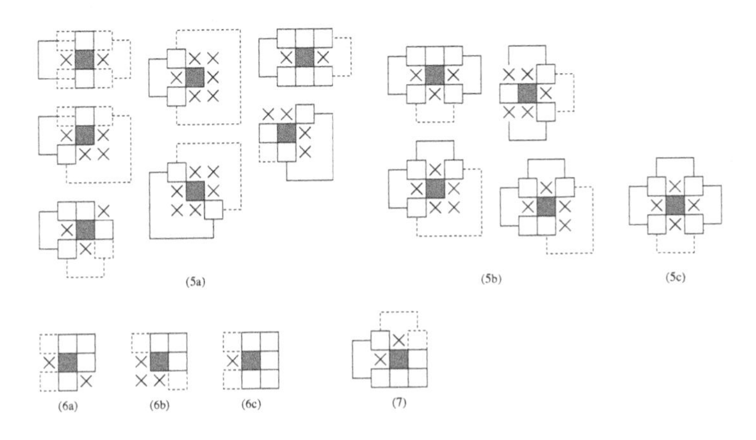

Fig. 3. Illustrations to the proof of Theorem 1. Cases 5, 6, and 7.

Case 4. *b and c do not change, while h decreases by 1.*

The only possible configuration is displayed in Fig. 2 (4). We have $h' = h+1$, $c' = c$, and $b' = b$.

Case 5. *c and b do not change, while h increases by 1, 2, or 3.*

The possible configurations are displayed in Fig. 3. We have $c' = c$ and $b' = b$.

In Case 5a we have $h' = h + 1$, for which there are seven possible configurations displayed in Fig. 3 (5a).

In Case 5b we have $h' = h + 2$, which is possible for the four configurations displayed in Fig. 3 (5b).

In Case 5c we have $h' = h + 3$, which may occur in the configuration in Fig. 3 (5c). Note that if the dashed path is missing, three new 1-holes may appear in a hole-free component, while if the dashed path exists, an existing 1-hole is partitioned into four 1-holes. (In both cases $v' = v$ and $g' = g + 4$.)

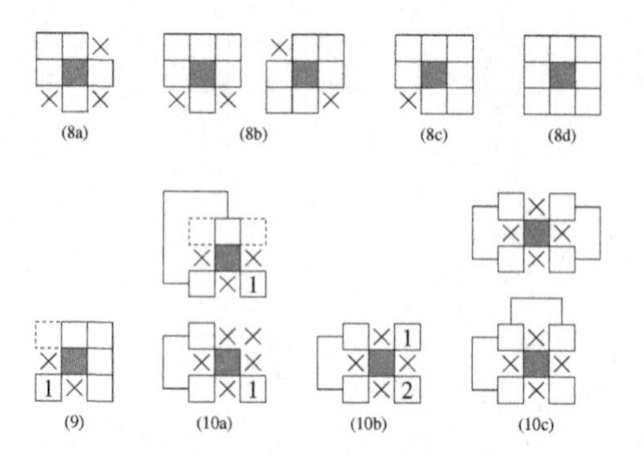

Fig. 4. Illustrations to the proof of Theorem 1. Cases 8, 9, and 10.

Case 6. *c and h do not change, while b increases by 1 or 2.*

In the former case there are two possible configurations displayed in Fig. 3 (6a,b). We have $c' = c$, $h' = h$, and $b' = b + 1$.

In the latter case, we have the configuration displayed in Fig. 3 (6c). We have $c' = c$, $h' = h$, and $b' = b + 2$.

Case 7. *c does not change, while h and b increase by 1.*

The only possible configuration is displayed in Fig. 3 (7). We have $h' = h+1$, $b' = b + 1$, and $c' = c$.

Case 8. *c does not change, h decreases by 1, and b increases by 1,2,3, or 4.*

The possible configurations are displayed in Fig. 4. We have $c' = c$ and $h' = h - 1$.

In Case 8a we have $b' = b + 1$ (Fig. 4 (8a)); in Case 8b we have $b' = b + 2$ (Fig. 4 (8b)); In Case 8c we have $b' = b+3$ (Fig. 4 (8c)); and in Case 8d we have $b' = b + 4$ (Fig. 4 (8d)).

Case 9. *h does not change, while b increases by 1 and c decreases by 1.*

The only possible configuration is displayed in Fig. 4 (9). Note that before adding P to D, the pixel marked by 1 is not connected to the component to which the other pixels of the configuration belong. We have $h' = h$, $b' = b + 1$, and $c' = c - 1$.

Case 10. *b does not change, while h increases by 1 and c decreases by 1 (Case 10a), or h increases by 1 and c decreases by 2 (Case 10b), or h increases by 2 and c decreases by 1 (Case 10c).*

The two possible configurations for Case 10a are displayed in Fig. 4 (10a). Case 10b features the configuration displayed in Fig. 4 (10b), and Case 10c the ones in Fig. 4 (10c).

Note that in all figures differently numbered pixels belong to different components that are not connected to the pixel P.

Having all possible cases determined, simple substitution in (2) for the respective values of h', b', and c', as well as for v' and g' show that this last equality holds in all cases.

It is easy to realize that the considered cases are the only possible (up to certain symmetries). Simple reasoning reveals that adding a pixel to D can neither result in decreasing b, nor in increasing both h and c, nor in increasing both b and c, nor in decreasing h and changing c. This completes the proof of the theorem. □

Corollary 1. *Let M be a gap-free finite set of pixels. Then* $v-2(p+c-h)+b=0$.

3.2 Gaps in Curves

A digital curve admits various equivalent definitions [3]. One of them is the following. A *simple digital k-curve* is a set $\rho = \{c_1, c_2, \ldots, c_l\}$ of pixels that satisfy the following two axioms: (A1) c_i is k-adjacent to c_j iff $i = j \pm 1 (\text{modulo } l)$, and (B1) ρ is one-dimensional with respect to k-adjacency, for $k = 0$ (Fig. 1a, top-left) or $k = 1$ (Fig. 1a, bottom-left). To get acquainted with the classical definition of dimension of a digital object the reader is referred to [10]. For further developments and various results see [3, 7] and the bibliography therein. For example, we have the following:

Fact 1. *Let M be a finite set of pixels which is one-dimensional with respect to adjacency $k \in \{0, 1\}$. Then M does not contain any 2-block.*

Any connected subset of a digital simple k-curve is a *simple digital k-arc* (Fig. 1a, right). More in general, by analogy to the classical definition of a curve in the plane[2], a digital curve can be defined as a set of pixels that is connected and one-dimensional with respect to k-adjacency (see Fig. 1b). Applied to digital curves, Theorem 1 and Fact 1 imply the following:

Corollary 2. *Let M be a general digital curve. Then* $g = v - 2(p + 1 - h)$.
If M is gap-free, then $v = 2(p + 1 - h)$.
If M is a simple digital arc, then $g = v - 2(p + 1)$.
If M is a simple gap-free digital arc, then $v = 2(p + 1)$.
If M is a simple digital curve, then $g = v - 2p$.
If M is a simple gap-free digital curve, then $v = 2p$.

4 Conclusions

In this paper we derived a formula for the total number of gaps in a binary picture, which contributes to combinatorial topology in the context of image analysis, pattern recognition, or geometric modeling. In particular, it can be used to test a binary picture (e.g., a digital curve) for existence of gaps. As already mentioned, the number of gaps characterizes the topological structure of a binary picture. The parameters involved (i.e., g, v, p, c, h and b) are either locally defined (namely, g, v, p, b) or global topological values (h and c). Quantitative interrelationships between local and global properties are of potential value in

[2] A curve in $\mathbb{R}^2$ is a one-dimensional continuum, where *continuum* is any nonempty subset in a given topological space that is compact and topologically connected [9, 14].

property-based image analysis. The identification of gaps is of particular interest when characterizing different ways of defining digital surfaces (2D manifolds) in 3D imaging, e.g., if they exclude the existence of gaps or not (see [4]). In 2D, this corresponds to the question whether a way of defining borders (see [7]) ensures gap-freeness of a digital picture. Work in progress is pursuing extension of the given results to higher dimensions.

Acknowledgements

The authors thank the three anonymous referees for their useful comments.

References

1. Brimkov, V.E., E. Andres, and R.P. Barneva, Object discretizations in higher dimensions, *Pattern Recognition Letters* **23** (2002) 623–636
2. Brimkov, V.E., R.P. Barneva, and Ph. Nehlig, Minimally thin discrete triangulations, In: *Volume Graphics*, A. Kaufman, R. Yagel, M. Chen (Eds.), Chapter 3, Springer Verlag, 2000, pp. 51-70
3. Brimkov, V.E. and R. Klette, Curves, hypersurfaces, and good pairs of adjacency relations, *Lecture Notes in Computer Science* No 3322, Springer Verlag (2004) 270–284
4. Chen, Li, *Discrete Surfaces and Manifolds*, Scientific & Practical Computing, 2004
5. Cohen-Or, D. and A. Kaufman, 3D line voxelization and connectivity control, *IEEE Computer Graphics and Applications* **17** (6) (1997) 80–87
6. Kaufman, A., D. Cohen, and R. Yagel, Volume graphics, *IEEE Computer* **26**(7) (1993) 51–64
7. Klette, R. and A. Rosenfeld, *Digital Geometry - Geometric Methods for Digital Picture Analysis*, Morgan Kaufmann, San Francisco, 2004
8. Kong, T.Y., Digital topology, In: Davis, L.S., editor. *Foundations of Image Understanding*, Kluwer, Boston, Massachusetts, 2001, pp. 33–71
9. Menger, K., *Kurventheorie*, Teubner, Leipzig, Germany, 1932
10. Mylopoulos, J.P. and T. Pavlidis, On the topological properties of quantized spaces. I. The notion of dimension, *J. ACM* **18** (1971.) 239–246
11. Pavlidis, T, *Algorithms for Graphics and Image Processing*, Computer Science Press, Rockville, MD, 1982
12. Rosenfeld, A., Arcs and curves in digital pictures, *Journal of the ACM* **18** (1973) 81–87
13. Rosenfeld, A., Adjacency in digital pictures, *Information and Control* **26** (1974) 24–33
14. Urysohn, P., Über die allgemeinen Cantorischen Kurven, Annual meeting, Deutsche Mathematiker Vereinigung, Marbourg, Germany, 1923
15. Voss, K., *Discrete Images, Objects, and Functions in* $\mathbf{Z}^n$, Springer Verlag, Berlin, 1993

Video Codec for Classical Cartoon Animations with Hardware Accelerated Playback

Daniel Sýkora, Jan Buriánek, and Jiří Žára

Czech Technical University in Prague,
Digital Media Production

Abstract. We introduce a novel approach to video compression which is suitable for traditional outline-based cartoon animations. In this case the dynamic foreground consists of several homogeneous regions and the background is static textural image. For this drawing style we show how to recover hybrid representation where the background is stored as a single bitmap and the foreground as a sequence of vector images. This allows us to preserve compelling visual quality as well as spatial scalability even for low encoding bit-rates. We also introduce an efficient approach to play back compressed animations in real-time on commodity graphics hardware. Practical results confirm that for the same storage requirements our framework provides better visual quality as compared to standard video compression techniques.

1 Introduction

Generations of children and adults enjoy classical cartoon animations and want to see them again and again in the best possible quality. However, the lifetime of traditional archive formats (such as celluloid negative) is strongly limited. Variety of physical degradations may significantly reduce visual quality or completely destroy the original artwork. When one decides to rescue these amazing works, it is necessary to perform *telecine* [1], i.e. to transfer motion picture from film negative into a digital video format. During this process two important factors leverage the final visual quality and the amount of required storage space: resolution and compression technology.

In the movie industry cartoon animations are typically intended for television broadcasting or DVD production, therefore PAL or NTSC resolution is used for digital conversion. Regarding compression the most popular format for broadcasting is *Digital Betacam* tape [2] that can run up to 124 minutes of high-quality video with nearly lossless 2:1 compression. For DVD production MPEG-2 [3] is used with average bit-rates around 3.5 Mbps which is lower quality but still acceptable for most cases. However these commercial standards produce video stream that requires large storage space and is not simply spatially scalable.

In this paper we adopt well known concept of layered compression which has been standardized in MPEG-4 video compression scheme [4]. We show how to detach the dynamic foreground layer and how to reconstruct the static background layer in outline-based cartoon animations. We also introduce a novel space-saving vectorization scheme which allows to preserve high visual quality

G. Bebis et al. (Eds.): ISVC 2005, LNCS 3804, pp. 43–50, 2005.

and resolution independency even for low encoding bit-rates. Finally an efficient decompression scheme is addressed to play back compressed animations in real-time on consumer graphics hardware.

The rest of paper is organized as follows. First we present a brief overview of related work on video compression. Next, we describe our method including implementation details and optimization issues. Finally we present several results on real cartoon animations to confirm the efficiency of proposed solution and conclude with plans for future work.

2 Related Work

For decades video compression was and still is a very active research area (for survey see [5, 6]). However to our best knowledge there has been only one method published [7] which takes into account visual aspects of cartoon animations. In this approach each region is first represented as a 3D volume by sweeping its 2D shape through the time. Then edge-breaker compression scheme is used to encode volume geometry. Decoding is done by intersecting compressed volume with image plane using GPU-based solid clipping technique. Unfortunately this compression is suitable only for regions that change their shape and/or position slightly. Authors also did not address the problem of region shape extraction for more complicated color and gray-scale image sequences.

Standard approaches to video compression such as MPEG-2 assume that strong discontinuities are not frequent in natural image sequences and thus 2D discrete cosine transform (DCT) [8] can by used to efficiently encode small image blocks. However blocking and ringing artifacts may arise when DCT is applied to cartoon images that contain lots of sharp edges. Even promising discrete wavelet transform DWT [9] does not overcome this problem while quantization errors still produce visible ringing artifacts. To suppress such degradations various post-processing techniques have been developed [10, 11]. However they are usually computationally expensive and thus not tractable for real-time applications. Another possibility is to completely avoid coding along strong edges as in segmentation and object-based compression techniques [12, 13]. Here the aim is to divide the input image into a set of homogeneous regions and then compress each of them separately. Unfortunately these methods require usually much higher encoding bit-rates due to over-segmentation.

3 Framework

Shortcomings of previous approaches lead us to develop our novel framework. It consists of five independent phases: unsupervised segmentation, background reconstruction, foreground vectorization, temporal coherency issues and playback. In this section we describe each step in more details.

3.1 Segmentation

First we need to separate the original image into a set of regions. For this task we adopt image segmentation technique first presented in [14] and later refined in [15, 16]. This approach has been designed directly for outline-based cartoons. The main idea is to exploit negative response of Laplacian-of-Gaussian ($\mathbf{L} \circ \mathbf{G}$) to locate outlines. Similarly to [16] we additionally perform interpolation in the $\mathbf{L} \circ \mathbf{G}$ domain to reach fourfold sub-pixel precision [17]. In this case unsupervised σ-fitting [15] helps us to suppress spurious regions that arise inside outlines when extrapolating $\mathbf{L} \circ \mathbf{G}$ response to the higher resolution.

Next we want to detach foreground regions and reconstruct one single image of the whole background layer. To do that we first roughly estimate whether a given region belongs to the background layer using region area size thresholding as in [15]. Then a hierarchical motion estimation [18] helps us to register parts of the background layer using consecutive animation frames. After the registration fragments of background are stitched together and stored as a single image using standard JPEG compression [19]. We also store estimated camera motion vectors. Later this information allows us to extract currently visible portion of the background layer.

In the second phase we refine classification of smaller regions. We accumulate normalized sum of absolute differences between region pixels and corresponding pixels in the reconstructed background. When this sum falls under a specified limit then the region is classified as a background. This approach may fail to classify very small regions while anti-aliased outlines can significantly bias the sum of absolute differences. However such regions are usually homogenous and thus from the visual point of view it does not matter when they remain in the foreground layer.

Finally, it is necessary to assign visually dominant color to each region in the foreground layer. To avoid flickering due to biased mean color estimation we apply mean-shift clustering [20] to obtain static palette of most used colors.

3.2 Vectorization

After the segmentation we need to convert shapes of homogeneous regions into a scalable vector representation. There are various techniques suitable for this task. In our framework we experiment with cubic B-splines [21] and 1D DCT [22]. B-splines are optimal in the sense of rate distortion and DCT representation is more suitable for scalable compression.

In order to combine advantages of both approaches we first apply standard contour tracing algorithm [23] to fit a set of cubic B-splines to the raster representation of the original shape. Then we perform curvature sensitive subdivision using central differencing [24] to obtain adaptive sampling of the original shape that is much more suitable for compression in the frequency domain than uniform sampling (see Figure 1). Moreover in our experiments we found that there is a high correlation between the optimal number of DCT coefficients and the optimal number of control points in the original B-spline representation. We use this feature to estimate the number of DCT coefficients needed to store vector representation without significant loss of precision.

Finally, when DCT coefficients are extracted, we normalize them and quantize uniformly to 16-bit representation. Burrows-Wheeler block transform [25]

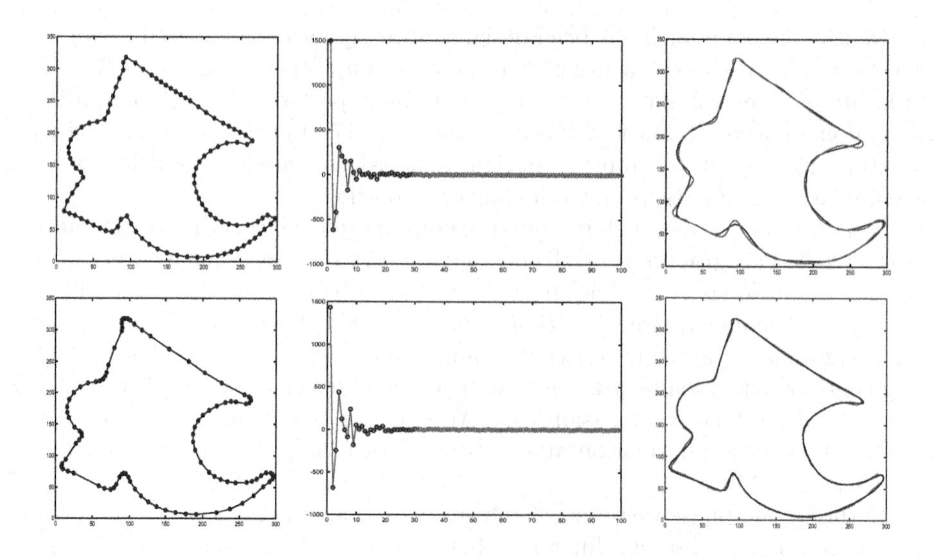

Fig. 1. Compare the efficiency of 1D DCT-based vector compression for uniformly (top) and adaptively (bottom) sampled shape. For the same number of DCT coefficients adaptive sampling produces better approximation.

together with Huffman coding [26] is used to store them into the output stream. In contrast to the original B-spline representation DCT-based compression can save up to 50% of storage space with negligible loss of precision.

3.3 Temporal Coherency

Usually it is not necessary to store foreground layer for each frame since in cartoon animations lots of frames are identical. To alleviate tedious manual inbetweening artists usually decide to significantly reduce frame rate. Typically only every second frame is different. For long animations they also use repetitive sequences of same frames. In our framework we exploit this redundancy by maintaining pool of already stored frames in which we search for duplicities.

The search itself is hierarchical and the similarity is computed only for outline-extracted images. We use phase correlation [27] to align and preselect similar down-sampled thumbnails of past frames. Then we apply bitwise XOR and distance transform [28] to obtain weighted difference bitmap which emphasizes large changes against small global shifts. Finally we sum up weights in this bitmap and if the sum falls under the user-specified threshold we store only the identification number of the corresponding frame. By tuning this threshold we can further lower encoding bit-rate by omitting frames containing insignificant changes.

3.4 Playback

In order to reach compelling visual quality as well as real-time performance during the playback, we implement a simple OpenGL-based player that utilizes GPU to render anti-aliased background and foreground layer for each animation frame. See our web-site[1] where this player is available together with short testing sequence.

During the playback we first activate hardware accelerated full screen anti-aliasing (FSAA) to preserve smooth polygon boundaries. Then the background layer is rendered as a textured rectangle with proper shift and scale according to the estimated camera motion vectors. In front of this background we put the foreground layer. For each region we first apply zero-padding in the frequency domain to increase the resulting number of control points. Then we use IDCT together with proper normalization to obtain coordinates of control points. Thanks to prior adaptive sampling this process yields a good piecewise linear approximation of the region shape that can be directly used for polygon rendering. Extra processing is required only for non-convex polygons that have to be tesselated into convex triangle strips.

Rendering phase itself is time critical since we need to generate all control points and tessellation of non-convex polygons in real-time (typically tens of polygons with hundreds of vertices 25 times per second). To achieve this performance it is necessary to utilize fast FFT-based implementation of the IDCT [29]. For tessellation of non-convex polygons we exploit standard framework gluTess* [30]. However for larger polygons we recommend to use FIST [31].

4 Results

In this section we present several results obtained on real cartoon animations scanned in PAL resolution (720x576) from the original celluloid negative of Czech cartoon *O loupežníku Rumcajsovi*. We encode five different sequences using our codec and using DivX with comparable storage requirements. We set the parameters to reach average encoding bit-rate of 256 kbps. Using AMD Athlon A64 2800+ with ATI Radeon 9700 and 6x FSAA it takes in average 10 seconds to compress and 30 milliseconds to decompress and render one frame. See our website[1] and compare visual quality with accompanied AVI encoded using DivX codec.

In Figure 2 three still images from different sequences are presented. To render them we use the original PAL resolution. However the resolution itself can be much higher (to see this try to maximize rendering window in our player). The limiting factor is bilinear interpolation of the background texture which is fortunately not so disturbing while the background layer usually does not contain sharp edges. In Figure 2 no blocking or ringing artifacts are visible in the output of our codec, only several shape details are omitted. There are also a few examples of small misclassified regions that are not disturbing during the playback while the background layer is almost homogeneous at the same position.

[1] http://www.cgg.cvut.cz/~sykorad

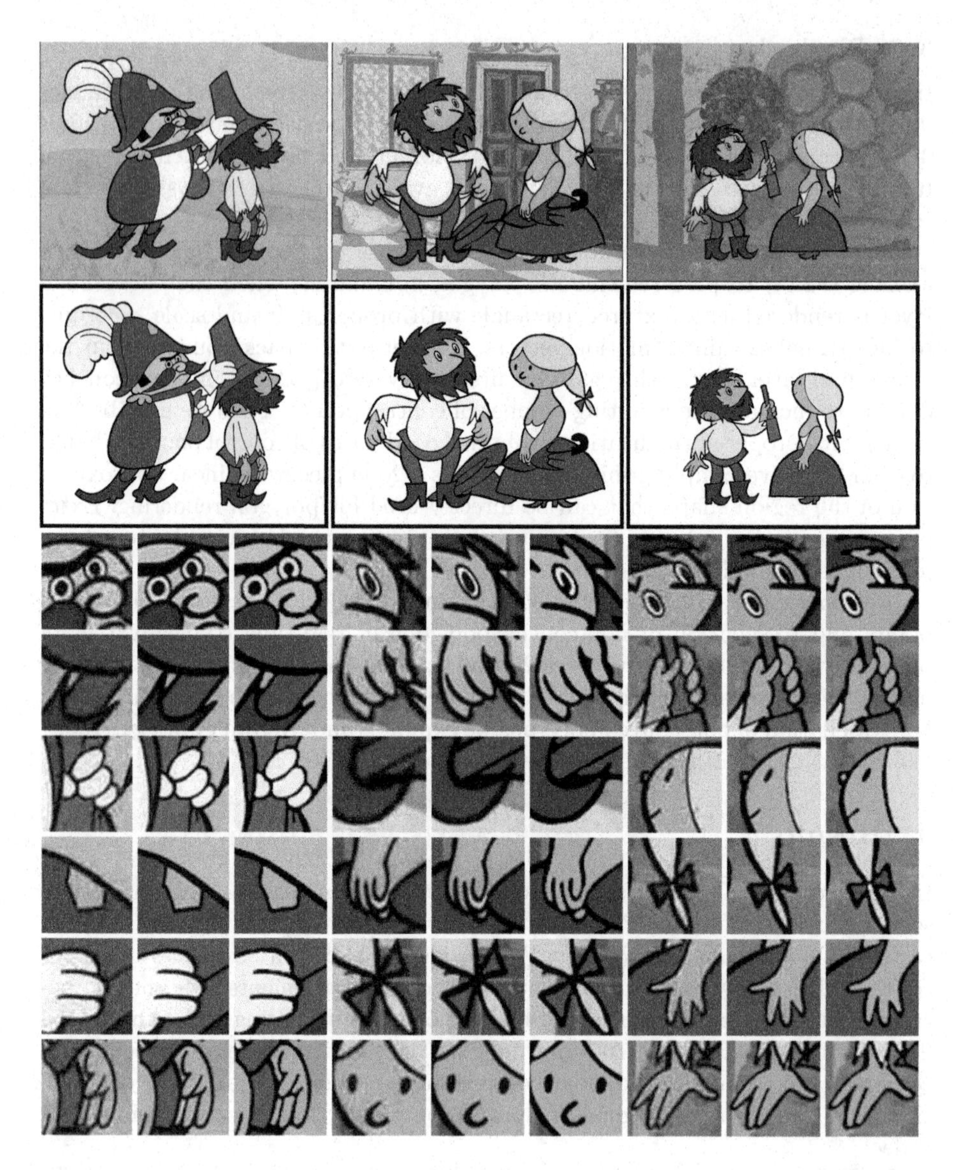

Fig. 2. Still image results – in each column see: the original image (top), vectorization of the foreground layer (middle), and detail views of different compression techniques (bottom). Small nested columns: detail views of `DivX` with comparable storage requirements (left), the original image (middle), and the output of our codec (right). In the vectorization of the foreground layer see misclassified foreground regions (e.g. small region between general's boot and leg). They are not disturbing during the playback while the background layer is homogeneous at the same position (images in this figure are published with permission of © *Vít Komrzí, Universal Production Partners* and *Lubomír Celar, Digital Media Production*).

5 Conclusions and Future Work

A novel video compression scheme for traditional outline-based cartoon animations has been presented. Practical experiments performed on real cartoon animations confirm that for comparable encoding bit-rates our approach achieve better visual quality as compared to standard video compression techniques.

As a future work, we plan to significantly speed up compression phase and further lower encoding bit-rates by estimating warping transformation between corresponding regions. Next we also contemplate to adopt our approach for other drawing styles e.g. cartoon animations that contain only outlines and homogeneous regions. Another issue is an automatic sequence annotation which is desirable for consistent background reconstruction.

Acknowledgements

This work has been supported by the Ministry of Education, Youth and Sports of the Czech Republic under research program No. MSM-6840770014 (Research in the area of information technologies and communications) and under the student research program: FRVŠ-2005-1170.

References

1. Bancroft, D.J.: Advanced and economical telecine technology for global DTV production. In: Proceedings of Broadcast Engineering Conference. (2000)
2. Sykes, P.J.: Digital Betacam: A new approach to broadcast digital recording. In: Proceedings of International Conference on Storage and Recording Systems. (1994) 9–14
3. Wong, A.H., Chen, C.: Comparison of ISO MPEG1 and MPEG2 video-coding standards. In: Proceedings of SPIE Visual Communications and Image Processing. Volume 2094. (1993) 1436–1448
4. Ebrahimi, T., Horne, C.: MPEG-4 natural video coding – An overview. Signal Processing: Image Communication **15** (2000) 365–385
5. Reid, M.M., Millar, R.J., Black, N.D.: Second-generation image coding: An overview. ACM Computing Surveys **29** (1997) 3–29
6. Clarke, R.J.: Image and video compression: A survey. International Journal of Imaging Systems and Technology **10** (1999) 20–32
7. Kwatra, V., Rossignac, J.: Space-time surface simplification and edgebreaker compression for 2D cel animations. International Journal on Shape Modeling **8** (2002) 119–137
8. Ahmed, N., Natarajan, T., Rao, K.R.: Discrete cosine transform. IEEE Transactions on Computers **C** (1974) 90–93
9. Shapiro, J.M.: Embedded image coding using zerotrees of wavelet coefficients. IEEE Transactions on Signal Processing **41** (1993) 3445–3463
10. Yang, Y., Galatsanos, N.P., Katsaggelos, A.K.: Projection-based spatially adaptive reconstruction of block-transform compressed images. IEEE Transactions on Image Processing **4** (1995) 896–908

11. Fan, G., Cham, W.K.: Model-based edge reconstruction for low bit-rate wavelet-compressed images. IEEE Transactions on Circuits and Systems for Video Technology **10** (2000) 120–132
12. Kwon, O., Chellappa, R.: Segmentation-based image compression. Optical Engeneering **7** (1993) 1581–1587
13. van Beek, P.J.L., Tekalp, A.M.: Object-based video coding using forward tracking 2-D mesh layers. In: Proceedings of SPIE Visual Communications and Image Processing. (1997) 699–710
14. Sýkora, D., Buriánek, J., Žára, J.: Segmentation of black and white cartoons. In: Proceedings of Spring Conference on Computer Graphics. (2003) 245–254
15. Sýkora, D., Buriánek, J., Žára, J.: Colorization of black-and-white cartoons. Image and Vision Computing **23** (2005) 767–852
16. Sýkora, D., Buriánek, J., Žára, J.: Sketching cartoons by example. In: Proceedings of Eurographics Workshop on Sketch-Based Interfaces and Modeling. (2005) 27–34
17. Huertas, A., Medioni, G.: Detection of intensity changes with subpixel accuracy using Laplacian-Gaussian masks. IEEE Transactions on Pattern Analysis and Machine Intelligence **8** (1986) 651–664
18. Odobez, J.M., Bouthemy, P.: Robust multiresolution estimation of parametric motion models. Journal of Visual Communication and Image Representation **6** (1995) 348–365
19. Wallace, G.K.: The JPEG still picture compression standard. Communications of the ACM **34** (1991) 30–44
20. Comaniciu, D., Meer, P.: Mean Shift: A robust approach toward feature space analysis. IEEE Transactions on Pattern Analysis and Machine Intelligence **24** (2002) 603–619
21. Spaan, F., Lagendijk, R.L., Biermond, J.: Shape coding using polar coordinates and the discrete cosine transform. In: Proceedings of International Conference on Image Processing. (1997) 516–519
22. Zaletelj, J., Pecci, R., Spaan, F., Hanjalic, A., Lagendijk, R.L.: Rate distortion optimal contour compression using cubic B-splines. In: Proceedings of European Signal Processing Conference. (1998) 1497–1500
23. Weber, M.: AutoTrace: A utility for converting bitmap into vector graphics (2004) `http://autotrace.sourceforge.net`.
24. Clark, J.H.: A fast scan-line algorithm for rendering parametric surfaces. IEEE Transactions on Image Processing **13** (1979) 289–299
25. Burrows, M., Wheeler, D.J.: Block-sorting lossless data compression algorithm. Technical Report 124, SRC, Palo Alto, USA (1994)
26. Salomon, D.: Data compression: The complete reference. Springer Verlag (1998)
27. Kuglin, C.D., Hines, D.C.: The phase correlation image alignment method. In: Proceedings of IEEE International Conference on Cybernetics and Society. (1975) 163–165
28. Borgefors, G.: Distance transformations in digital images. Computer Vision, Graphics, and Image Processing **34** (1986) 344–371
29. Frigo, M., Johnson, S.G.: FFTW: Library for computing the discrete Fourier transform (2005) `http://www.fftw.org`.
30. Woo, M., Davis, T., Sheridan, M.B.: OpenGL Programming Guide: The Official Guide to Learning OpenGL. Addison-Wesley (1999)
31. Held, M.: FIST: Fast industrial-strength triangulation of polygons. Algorithmica **30** (2001) 563–596

Retinal Image Registration for NIH's ETDRS

Thitiporn Chanwimaluang and Guoliang Fan

School of Electrical and Computer Engineering,
Oklahoma State University, Stillwater, OK 74078

Abstract. This paper presents a retinal image registration approach for National Institute of Health (NIH)'s Early Treatment Diabetic Retinopathy Study (ETDRS) standard. The ETDRS imaging protocol specifies seven fields of each retina and presents several major challenges for image registration. The proposed method effectively combines both area-based and feature-based methods in three steps. First, the vascular tree is extracted by using a local entropy thresholding technique. Next, zeroth-order translation is estimated by maximizing mutual information based on the binary image pair (area-based). Specifically, a local entropy-based peak selection and a multi-resolution searching schemes are developed to improve accuracy and efficiency of translation estimation. Third, we use two types of features (feature-based), landmark points and sampling points, for affine/quadratic model estimation. Simulation on 504 pairs of ETDRS retinal images shows the effectiveness of the proposed algorithm.

1 Introduction

A broad range of image registration methods have been proposed for different medical imaging applications including retinal image registration. Typically, retinal image registration techniques are classified as feature-based and area-based methods. Area-based techniques are generally based on pixel intensities and certain optimized objective functions. Feature-based methods are somewhat similar to manual registration. The approach assumes that point correspondences are available in both images, and the registration process is performed by maximizing a similarity measure computed from the correspondences. In [1], the bifurcation points of a vascular tree, also called landmark points, are labeled with surrounding vessel orientations. An angle-based invariant is then computed to give a probability for every two matching points. After that, the Bayesian Hough transform is used to sort the transformations according to their respective likelihoods. In [2], the similarity matrix for all possible correspondences is computed based on the orientations of vascular centerlines, and the transformation is estimated in a hierarchical way, from the zeroth-order model to the first-order model and finally to the second-order model. In [3], the dual-bootstrap iterative closest point (dual-bootstrap ICP) algorithm was introduced. The approach starts from one or more initial, low-order estimates that are only accurate in small image regions called bootstrap regions where the method iteratively refines the transformation estimation, expands the bootstrap region, and tests to see if a higher-order model can be used.

G. Bebis et al. (Eds.): ISVC 2005, LNCS 3804, pp. 51–59, 2005.

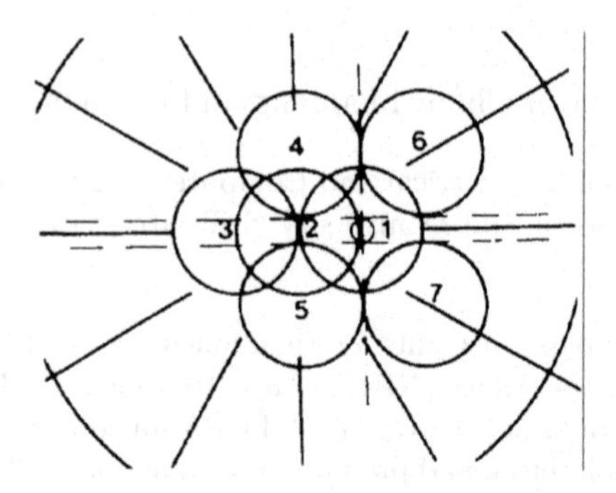

Fig. 1. ETDRS seven-standard fields (right eye)

In this paper, we study retinal image registration in the context of the National Institutes of Health (NIH), Early Treatment Diabetic Retinopathy Study (ETDRS) standard protocol. The ETDRS protocol defines seven 30° fields of each retina with specific field coverage, as shown in Fig. 1. There are two motivations to develop a specific retinal image registration method that can (1) assess image quality in terms of ETDRS field coverage, and (2) support ETDRS-based disease diagnosis. Three challenges exist here. First, small overlaps between adjacent fields, which lead to inadequate landmark points for feature-based methods. Second, the contrast and intensity distributions within an image are not spatially uniform or consistent. This can deteriorate the performance of area-based techniques. Third, high-resolution ETDRS images contain large homogeneous nonvascular/textureless regions which result in difficulties for both feature-based and area-based techniques. In this work, we propose an ETDRS compliant registration algorithm which effectively combines both area-based and feature-based methods and is evaluated based on 504 ETDRS image pairs in the simulation.

2 Preliminaries

2.1 ETDRS Protocol and IQA

The ETDRS protocol standardizes retinal imaging and disease diagnosis, and it also develops an internationally recognized disease severity scale for diabetic retinopathy. As shown in Fig. 1, the overlap of fields 1 and 2 (or fields 1/2) as well as that of fields 2/3 are roughly 50% of the image size. For other field pairs, the overlapping parts are typically less than 25%. It is worth mentioning that the field displacements are not always consistent and depend on patient cooperation and photographer skills. The importance of the ETDRS protocol and the challenges in its practical implementation call for automated software tools for image quality assessment (IQA) that checks the relative positions, i.e., horizontal/vertical displacements, of every image pair according to Fig. 1. By comparing the offset, which is the difference between the ideal vertical/horizontal displacements and actual ones, i.e., T_o, with the diameter of optic disc (DD), an image pair is categorized as good ($T_o < 1/2DD$), fair ($1/2DD \leq T_o \leq 1DD$), or poor ($T_o > 1DD$). Therefore, the IQA of ETDRS field definition boils down to a problem of image registration followed by displacement verification.

2.2 Area-Based Retinal Image Registration

We focus on mutual information (MI) that shows the similarity between one image pair based on the histograms and the joint histogram. The definition of mutual information can be presented in various ways. For the registration purpose, the MI is computed for the overlapping parts of the images. It is, therefore, sensitive to the size of the overlapping parts. The entropy correlation coefficient (ECC) is a normalized measure of MI [4], which is less sensitive to area changes in overlapping regions, as defined in the following:

$$ECC(\mathbf{I}_u, \mathbf{I}_v) = 2 - \frac{2H(\mathbf{I}_u, \mathbf{I}_v)}{H(\mathbf{I}_u) + H(\mathbf{I}_v)}, \tag{1}$$

where $H(\mathbf{I}_u)$ and $H(\mathbf{I}_v)$ represent the global entropy of images $\mathbf{I}_u$ and $\mathbf{I}_v$ respectively, and $H(\mathbf{I}_u, \mathbf{I}_v)$ is the joint entropy between them.

2.3 Feature-Based Retinal Image Registration

Feature-based methods rely on correspondence points in both images. The matching process identifies reliable correspondences by maximizing an objective function related to features. Then the transformation is estimated by minimizing the correspondences' displacement, i.e., the registration error, defined as follows:

$$\hat{\mathbf{M}} = \arg\min_{\mathbf{M}} \text{median}_{\mathbf{p}\in\mathbf{P}} \min_{\mathbf{q}\in\mathbf{Q}} \|\mathbf{p} - T(\mathbf{q}; \mathbf{M})\|^2, \tag{2}$$

where $\mathbf{P}$ and $\mathbf{Q}$ denote the feature point sets from two images. $T(\mathbf{q}; \mathbf{M})$ represents the transformation operation of point $\mathbf{q}$ given model $\mathbf{M}$. As listed in Table 1, the transformation models often used include the translation model, the affine model, and the quadratic model [2,3]. The estimated transformation model, $\hat{\mathbf{M}}$, can be further adjusted by using the Iterative Closest Point algorithm (ICP) to refine correspondences [5]. The ICP is a procedure for iteratively

Table 1. The Transformation Models

Model	Transformations	DoF
Translation	$\begin{pmatrix} p_x \\ p_y \\ 1 \end{pmatrix} = \begin{pmatrix} 1 & 0 & m_2 \\ 0 & 1 & m_8 \\ 0 & 0 & 1 \end{pmatrix} \begin{pmatrix} q_x \\ q_y \\ 1 \end{pmatrix}$	2
Affine	$\begin{pmatrix} p_x \\ p_y \\ 1 \end{pmatrix} = \begin{pmatrix} m_0 & m_1 & m_2 \\ m_6 & m_7 & m_8 \\ 0 & 0 & 1 \end{pmatrix} \begin{pmatrix} q_x \\ q_y \\ 1 \end{pmatrix}$	6
Quadratic	$\begin{pmatrix} p_x \\ p_y \end{pmatrix} = \begin{pmatrix} m_0 & m_1 & m_2 & m_3 & m_4 & m_5 \\ m_6 & m_7 & m_8 & m_9 & m_{10} & m_{11} \end{pmatrix} \begin{pmatrix} q_x & q_y & 1 & q_x^2 & q_y^2 & q_x q_y \end{pmatrix}^T$	12

matching a set of points in two images. Given an initial transformation model, for $\mathbf{p} \in \mathbf{P}$, we need to find the closest point $\mathbf{q} \in \mathbf{Q}$ by following:

$$d(\mathbf{p}, \mathbf{Q}) = \min_{\mathbf{q} \in \mathbf{Q}} \| \mathbf{p} - T(\mathbf{q}; \hat{\mathbf{M}}) \|, \tag{3}$$

where $d(,)$ is a distance metric. Then the transformation model will be re-estimated according to (2) after correspondence refinement, and so on. The iteration will be terminated when $d(,)$ in (3) is stable.

3 Proposed Algorithm

In this work, we propose a hybrid registration approach for ETDRS image, which takes the advantages of both area-based and feature-based methods, and adopts the idea of hierarchical model estimation used in [2, 6], as shown in Fig. 2.

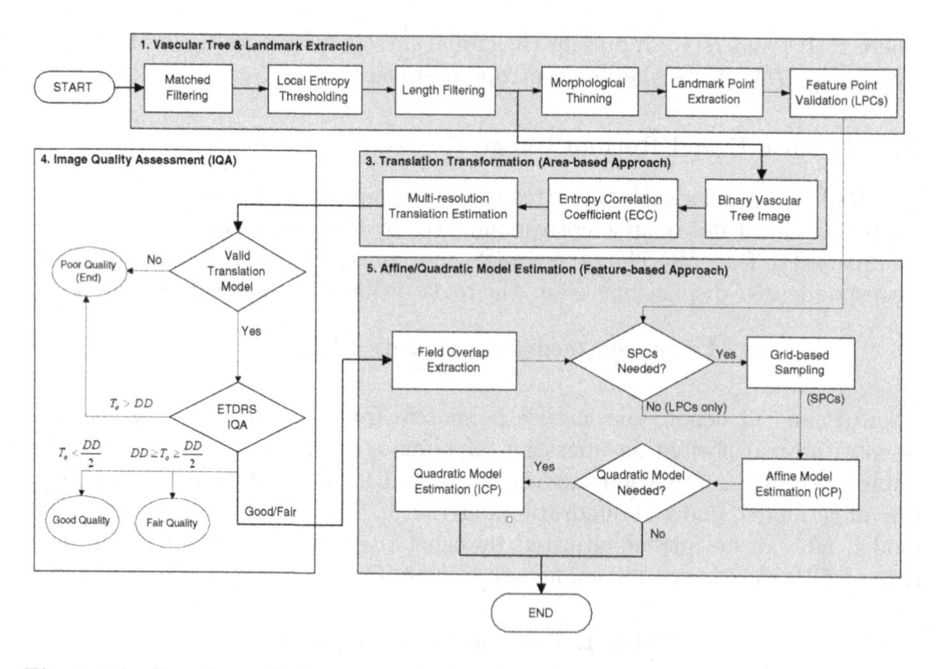

Fig. 2. The flowchart of the proposed algorithm (LPCs: landmark point correspondences and SPCs: sampling point correspondences)

3.1 Vascular Tree Extraction

Vascular tree extraction plays an important role in most retinal registration algorithms since the vascular tree is the most prominent anatomical structure in the retina. Vascular tree segmentation can be very useful for various purposes such as diagnosis and registration. As mentioned in [1], the vascular tree is considered to be the most appropriate representation for retinal image registration due to: 1) it maps the whole retina; 2) it does not move except in very few diseases; 3) it contains enough information for the localization of some anchor points. We develop an efficient method to extract the vascular tree which is composed of four steps. First, a match filter is applied to enhance the prominence of blood vessels [7]. Second, a local entropy-based thresholding scheme is used which takes into account the spatial distribution of gray levels and can well preserve the spatial structures in the binarized image [8]. Subsequently, a length filtering technique is used to remove misclassified pixels or insignificant small segments. The binary vascular tree will be used for area-based translation estimation. Then the morphological thinning is used to obtain the centerline of the vascular tree. Finally, crossover/bifurcation points, which will be used for feature-based registration, are located by a window-based probing process.

3.2 Translation Estimation

The translation estimation here is implemented by an area-based method which is based on a binary vascular tree due to the following three reasons. 1) The vascular tree is the most prominent structure and spans all ETDRS seven fields. 2) The computation of ECC may not be robust when the contrast/intensity distributions are not consistent within each image (invaliding the statistical dependency across images). 3) Geometric distortion in ETDRS image pairs usually are not significant due to negligible rotation and scaling. Given two binary vascular trees images, $\mathbf{I}_u^{'}$, and $\mathbf{I}_v^{'}$, we estimate the translation model between $\mathbf{I}_u$ and $\mathbf{I}_v$ by maximizing the ECC between them, as defined in the following:

$$\hat{\mathbf{M}} = \arg\max_{\mathbf{M}} ECC(\mathbf{I}_u^{'}, T_0(\mathbf{I}_v^{'}; \mathbf{M})), \tag{4}$$

where $T_0(\mathbf{I}_v^{'}; \mathbf{M})$ translates image $\mathbf{I}_v^{'}$ with model $\mathbf{M}$. We also tested XOR which fails to give a distinguishable narrow peak as ECC does. Moreover, in the case of retinal images with moderate geometric distortions, XOR does not provide the noticeable peaks, or it sometimes fails to locate the accurate translation.

It is possible that there are multiple competitive peaks in ECC outputs. Sometimes the highest peak does not necessarily represent the optimal translation due to the geometric distortion and the dissimilarity of binary image pairs. We use the local entropy to evaluate resemblance between two overlapping parts. Let $\mathbf{I}^{(u)}$ and $\mathbf{I}^{(v)}$ represent the overlapping parts from binary vascular tree images $\mathbf{I}_u^{'}$ and $\mathbf{I}_v^{'}$ respectively. The unique optimal translation is obtained by

$$\hat{\mathbf{M}} = \arg\min_{\mathbf{M}\in\Omega} \left| H^{(2)}(\mathbf{I}^{(u)}) - H^{(2)}\left(T_0(\mathbf{I}^{(v)}; \mathbf{M})\right)\right|, \tag{5}$$

where $\Omega = \{\mathbf{M}_1, \ldots, \mathbf{M}_N\}$ is a set of possible translations with significant ECC values, and $H^{(2)}(\mathbf{I})$ is the second-order local entropy of image $\mathbf{I}$ [8].

Moreover, a multi-resolution searching scheme is developed in order to improve the efficiency and accuracy of translation estimation. A binary image is first represented in a pyramid of multiple resolutions from the coarsest scale to the finest scale. Let $\mathbf{I}_u^{'} = \{\mathbf{I}_u^{(0)}, \mathbf{I}_u^{(1)}, \mathbf{I}_u^{(2)}, \ldots, \mathbf{I}_u^{(J)}\}$ and $\mathbf{I}_v^{'} = \{\mathbf{I}_v^{(0)}, \mathbf{I}_v^{(1)}, \mathbf{I}_v^{(2)}, \ldots, \mathbf{I}_v^{(J)}\}$ represent the finest to the coarsest scales of binary images $\mathbf{I}_u^{'} = \mathbf{I}_u^{(0)}$ and $\mathbf{I}_v^{'} = \mathbf{I}_v^{(0)}$, respectively. First, the algorithm finds a binary-ECC peak, an optimal translation, at the coarsest scale, i.e., $\mathbf{I}_u^{(J)}$ and $\mathbf{I}_v^{(J)}$, $\mathbf{M}^{(J)} = \{(r_u^{(J)}, s_u^{(J)}), (r_v^{(J)}, s_v^{(J)})\}$, where $(r_u^{(J)}, s_u^{(J)})$ and $(r_v^{(J)}, s_v^{(J)})$ are two coordinates in two images showing the optimal translation between them. Then $\mathbf{M}^{(J)}$ can specify a constrained searching neighborhood at the finer scale, i.e., $\mathcal{N}(\mathbf{M}^{(J)}) = \{(2r_u^{(J)}+i, 2s_u^{(J)}+j), (2r_v^{(J)}+m, 2s_v^{(J)}+n)|i,j,m,n = -5, ..., 5\}$. where the optimal translation at scale $J-1$ scale can be obtained as follows:

$$\mathbf{M}^{(j-1)} = \arg \max_{\mathcal{N}(\mathbf{M}^{(J)})} ECC(\mathbf{I}_u^{(j-1)}, \mathbf{I}_v^{(j-1)}), \tag{6}$$

where $j = J, J-1, ..., 1$. This procedure starts from the coarsest scale, and it is repeated until the finest scale is reached where an optimal translation, $\mathbf{M}^{(0)}$, is achieved at the pixel-level for two images, i.e., $\mathbf{I}_u^{(0)}$ and $\mathbf{I}_v^{(0)}$.

3.3 Affine/Quadratic Transformations

Usually, feature-based methods are supposed to be more reliable than area-based approaches if sufficient and accurate feature points are available. Specifically, two types of feature points, i.e., landmark points and sampling points, are involved for higher-order model estimation, as illustrated in Fig. 2.

Landmark points are the crossover/bifurcation points of vascular tree. The initial translation model and landmark points are employed as the rudimentary guideline to establish the initial set of *Landmark Point Correspondences* (LPCs), $C^{'}$, which is used to estimate the first-order affine model.

$$C^{'} = \{(\mathbf{p}_i, \mathbf{q}_j)|dist(T(\mathbf{q}_j; \hat{\mathbf{M}}), \mathbf{p}_i) \leq err, \mathbf{p}_i \in \mathbf{P}, \mathbf{q}_j \in \mathbf{Q}\}, \tag{7}$$

where $\mathbf{P}$ and $\mathbf{Q}$ are the sets of N_u and N_v landmark points from $\mathbf{I}_u^{'}$ and $\mathbf{I}_v^{'}$, respectively, $\hat{\mathbf{M}}$ is the initial translation model, $dist(,)$ denotes the Euclidean distance, and err is a threshold (e.g., 30). We create a similarity matrix, $S = \{s_{i,j}|i = 1, ..., N_u; j = 1, ..., N_v\}$, with the purpose of assuring one-to-one matching for every LPC. The similarity between $\mathbf{p}_i$ and $\mathbf{q}_j$, $s_{i,j}$ is defined below:

$$s_{i,j} = \begin{cases} \mathbf{x}_i \cdot \mathbf{y}_j, & (\mathbf{p}_i, \mathbf{q}_j) \in C^{'} \\ 0, & \text{otherwise} \end{cases} \tag{8}$$

where $\mathbf{x}_i$ and $\mathbf{y}_j$ are obtained by placing a 9×9 window centered at $\mathbf{p}_i$ and $\mathbf{q}_j$ on the thinned binary images. One-to-one LPC matchings are achieved by

$$C = \{(\mathbf{p}_i, \mathbf{q}_j)|j = \arg \max_{j \in 1,...,N_v} s_{i,j}, i = 1, ..., N_u\}. \tag{9}$$

After C is obtained, we need to examine the reliability of LPCs. Let σ_x and σ_y be the second central moments of vertical/horiztonal coordinates of LPCs in the overlap of size $H_o \times W_o$. We define $H_o/\sqrt{\sigma_x}$, $W_o/\sqrt{\sigma_y}$ to show how the LPCs spread. If they are large (e.g., > 4.0), LPCs are likely to cluster together in a small area. Then sampling is needed to involve more feature points for image registration. Sampling Point Correspondences (SPCs) are acquired by imposing grid lines on the thinned vascular tree which may facilitate feature-based registration. However, SPCs are usually less trustable compared with LPCs, since they are acquired from the thinned vascular tree which often exhibits strong linearity characteristics and SPCs are likely be linearly dependent if the vascular tree is sparse. Therefore, SPCs are only involved when it is necessary.

Both LPCs and SPCs are the input for the ICP algorithm which is an iterative procedure to refine the model estimation by finding the closest point $\mathbf{q} \in \mathbf{Q}$ for every $\mathbf{p} \in \mathbf{P}$ given transformation $\mathbf{M}$. During the ICP iteration, the LPCs/SPCs with significant error (e.g., 5 pixels) after the transformation are eliminated. The affine model is re-estimated at each iteration, and the iteration is terminated when the model is stable or there is no change to LPCs/SPCs. We will proceed to the quadratic model if the registration error of the affine model is significant and we have at least 6 LPCs. However, in the case of ETDRS, we prefer not to proceed to the second-order when overlapping regions between two images are very limited, since it may not be robust to estimate the transformation of the whole image based only on small overlapping parts.

4 Simulations and Discussions

504 ETDRS image pairs (600×900) were used in the simulation (Table 2).

The error of the translation model is 21.30 which is acceptable for the IQA purpose, since DD is usually near 200 pixels. Out of 504 registered pairs, 39 pairs are rejected by manual validation, and the success rate of translation estimation is 92.3%. Two criteria (energy concentration and peak distinction) are derived from the ECC output to determine the credibility of the translation model. The ETDRS IQA can be performed based on the translation model (Fig. 1). Then the

Table 2. The registration error and overlaps between fields. Totally, there are 84 image pairs for each field pair. (N_1, N_2) : N_1 indicates the number of image pairs are registered. N_2 specifies the number of registered pairs after manual validation.

Field Pairs	Median Registration Errors (pixels)					
(overlap, %)	Translation	LPCs Only		LPCs+SPCs		Proposed
		Affine	Quadratic	Affine	Quadratic	Algorithm
1/2 (53.0%)	$19.2^{(84,82)}$	$3.2^{(78,76)}$	$2.4^{(78,76)}$	$2.9^{(82,78)}$	$2.1^{(82,78)}$	$2.2^{(82,78)}$
1/6 (18.9%)	$27.8^{(84,68)}$	$2.4^{(47,43)}$	$1.4^{(34,32)}$	$2.3^{(69,66)}$	$1.9^{(69,58)}$	$1.9^{(69,66)}$
1/7 (22.5%)	$22.6^{(84,72)}$	$2.6^{(53,49)}$	$1.8^{(32,30)}$	$2.3^{(73,68)}$	$2.1^{(73,61)}$	$2.0^{(73,68)}$
2/3 (44.2%)	$20.8^{(84,78)}$	$3.6^{(68,63)}$	$3.0^{(68,66)}$	$3.4^{(79,74)}$	$2.4^{(79,72)}$	$2.6^{(79,74)}$
2/4 (25.4%)	$19.1^{(84,84)}$	$2.0^{(76,75)}$	$1.1^{(62,59)}$	$2.0^{(84,81)}$	$1.2^{(84,80)}$	$1.8^{(84,81)}$
2/5 (32.2%)	$18.4^{(84,81)}$	$2.4^{(67,66)}$	$2.0^{(62,59)}$	$2.7^{(81,78)}$	$2.0^{(81,74)}$	$2.1^{(81,78)}$
Mean	$21.3^{(504,465)}$	$2.7^{(389,372)}$	$1.92^{(336,322)}$	$2.6^{(468,443)}$	$1.9^{(468,423)}$	$2.0^{(468,445)}$

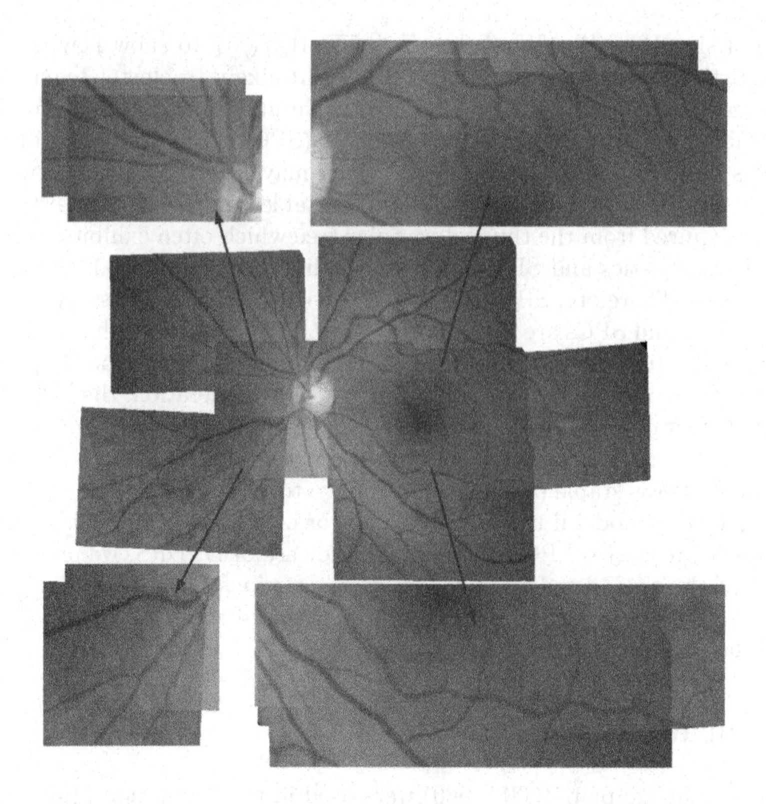

Fig. 3. One registration result. The quadratic model is applied to fields 2/3. The affine model is applied to other field pairs. SPCs are used fields 1/6, 2/3 and 2/4.

accepted 468 pairs proceed to higher order models. The error of the affine model (at least 3 LPCs) is 2.68, and the success rate is 79.5% (372/468). The error of the quadratic model (at least 6 LPCs) is 1.92, and the success rate is 68.8% (322/468). After involving SPCs, all 468 pairs can proceed to affine/quadratic models, among which 443 pairs (94.7%) and 423 pairs (90.4%) are manually validated for the affine and quadratic models, respectively. Moreover, SPCs slightly reduce for the registration error of the affine model. SPCs also improve the accuracy of the quadratic model in fields 1/2 and 2/3 with sufficient LPCs, and SPCs have some negative effect in other field pairs with limited LPCs. Therefore, three if-then conditions are developed to control the algorithm process.

- Condition 1. If $\Psi_3 > 13\%$ (the energy percentage of top three peaks) or $\Phi > 2.0$ (the ratio between top two peaks), the translation model is accepted based on which the IQA is performed, and the registration proceeds to higher-order models. Otherwise, the algorithm terminates.
- Condition 2. For ETDRS images, the affine model is usually sufficient in most field pairs, and the quadratic model is only applied when there are at least 6 LPCs.

- Condition 3. SPCs have to be involved: (1) When the number of LPCs is less than 3; (2) Or if LPCs cluster together in a small area, i.e., $H_o/\sqrt{\sigma_x} > 4.0$ or $W_o/\sqrt{\sigma_y} > 4.0$.

By incorporating above three conditions, we can develop an ETDRS compliant image registration algorithm by combing both area-based and feature-based methods into one flow. The major contribution of this work is to study advantages and limitations of traditional registration methods in the context of ETDRS and to integrate them together to obtain the best registration performance, i.e., the highest success rate (95.1%) and the lowest registration error (2.0 pixel). The proposed method can be used for the ETDRS IQA purpose and to facilitate the implementation of ETDRS protocols in clinical trails.

Acknowledgement

This work was supported by an OHRS award of project number HR03-33 from the Oklahoma Center for the Advancement of Science and Technology (OCAST).

References

1. Zana, F., Klein, J.: A multimodal registration algorithm of eye fundus images using vessels detection and hough transform. IEEE Trans. Biomedical Engineering **18** (1999) 419–428
2. Can, A., Stewart, C.V., Roysam, B., Tanenbaum, H.L.: A feature-based, robust, hierarchical algorithm for registering pairs of images of the curved human retina. IEEE Trans. Pattern Anal. Machine Intell. **24** (2002) 347–364
3. Stewart, C.V., Tsai, C.L., Roysam, B.: The dual-bootstrap iterative closest point algorithm with application to retinal image registration. IEEE Trans. Med. Imag. **22** (2003) 1379–1394
4. Maes, F., Collignon, A., Vandermeulen, D., Marchal, G., Suetens, P.: Multi-modality medical image registration by maximization of mutual information. IEEE Trans. Medical Imaging **16** (1997) 187–198
5. Besl, P.J., McKay, N.D.: A method for registration of 3-d shape. IEEE Trans. Pattern Anal. Machine Intell. **14** (1992) 239–256
6. Sawhney, H.S., Kumar, R.: True multi-image alignment and its application to mosaicing and lens distortion correction. IEEE Trans. Pattern Analysis and Machine Intelligence **21** (1999) 235–243
7. Chaudhuri, S., Chatterjee, S., Katz, N., Nelson, M., Goldbaum, M.: Detection of blood vessels in retinal images using two-dimensional matched filters. IEEE Trans. Medical Imaging **8** (1989) 263–269
8. Pal, N.R., Pal, S.K.: Entropic thresholding. Signal processing **16** (1989) 97–108

Using Multimodal MR Data for Segmentation and Topology Recovery of the Cerebral Superficial Venous Tree

N. Passat[1,2], C. Ronse[1], J. Baruthio[2], J.-P. Armspach[2], M. Bosc[3], and J. Foucher[4]

[1] LSIIT, UMR 7005 CNRS-ULP, Strasbourg 1 University, France
[2] IPB-LNV, UMR 7004 CNRS-ULP, Strasbourg 1 University, France
[3] L2TI, EA 3043, Paris 13 University, France
[4] INSERM U405, France

Abstract. Magnetic resonance angiography (MRA) produces 3D data visualizing vascular structures by detecting the flowing blood signal. While segmentation methods generally detect vessels by only processing MRA, the proposed method uses both MRA and non-angiographic (MRI) images. It is based on the assumption that MRI provides anatomical information useful for vessel detection. This supplementary information can be used to correct the topology of the segmented vessels. Vessels are first segmented from MRA while the cortex is segmented from MRI. An algorithm, based on distance maps and topology preserving thinning, then uses both segmented structures for recovery of the missing parts of the brain superficial venous tree and removal of other vessels. This method has been performed and validated on 9 MRA/MRI data of the brain. The results show that the venous tree is correctly segmented and topologically recovered with a 84% accuracy.

1 Introduction

Magnetic resonance angiography (MRA) proposes non-invasive and non-irradiant techniques providing 3D images of flowing blood. These techniques are frequently used to study the vascular structures of the brain. Indeed, the availability of precise information about brain vascular networks is fundamental for detecting pathologies or to use the vessels as anatomical landmarks.

Despite the development of numerous methods to perform blood vessel segmentation of 3D angiographic data (see [1] for an overview), there is still none that is able to provide completely satisfactory results. In order to improve the segmentation accuracy, methods have been designed to process multimodal angiographic data (DSA and MRA in [2], or DSA and IVUS in [3]), taking advantage of the supplementary information provided by each image. More recently, a new kind of vessel segmentation strategy involving angiographic and non-angiographic data has been developed. This new approach enables to consider a priori knowledge concerning relations between vessels and non-vascular structures, and to use this knowledge for guidance of segmentation algorithms. The

G. Bebis et al. (Eds.): ISVC 2005, LNCS 3804, pp. 60–67, 2005.

first method based on this approach has been proposed in [4] for segmentation of the superior sagittal sinus from cerebral MRA and T1 MRI.

In this paper, a new segmentation method devoted to the cerebral superficial venous tree is proposed. The main purpose of this method is to provide a correct representation of this structure prior to transcranial stimulation procedures. For such procedures, an accurate segmentation of the cerebral superficial venous tree is fundamental, since vessels can be used as landmarks for determining specific cerebral areas. More especially, it is important that the segmented tree presents correct topological properties.

The method described in this paper is based on a preliminary step, providing segmentation of brain vessels. It then uses a priori knowledge about relations between cerebral vessels and the cortex to discriminate superficial venous structures from other vessels and to recover a topologically correct representation of the whole cerebral superficial venous tree. This method is inspired from a strategy based on topological thinning proposed in [5], but is however quite new since it uses multimodal angiographic and non-angiographic data, and high level anatomical knowledge for guidance of the segmentation process.

This paper is organized as follows. In Section 2, related work on topology preserving vessel segmentation is discussed. The main purpose leading to the method proposed in this paper is then detailed, justifying the chosen strategy. The successive steps of the method are described in Section 3. In Section 4, the method is tested and analyzed on a 9 image database. Discussion and further works are presented in Section 5.

2 Related Work and Purpose

Angiographic data acquisition processes such as MRA or computed tomography angiography (CTA) enable to visualize complex 3D vascular structures. Several methods devoted to vessel segmentation from such 3D data have been proposed. Although few of them can deal with topology modifications (some can detect junctions or bifurcations [6], or can generate a graph of the segmented vessels [7]), nearly none of them have been designed to preserve correct structural properties when applied on complex vascular structures.

To the best of our knowledge, there exists only one method, proposed in [5], enabling to segment a whole vascular tree presenting correct topological properties. By assuming that a vascular tree (*i.e.* a structure composed of one connected component with no hole and no cavity) is topologically equivalent to the volume of the whole image, it proposes to apply a thinning algorithm starting from this whole image and iteratively removing simple points. This method has been applied for liver vascular tree segmentation from CTA.

A topologically correct segmentation of the cerebral superficial venous tree[1] can be quite useful for determining specific brain areas for transcranial magnetic

[1] The whole superficial venous structures of the brain can present cycles generated by anastomoses. However, MRA of the top of the head only visualize a part of them really presenting a tree topology.

stimulation. The angiographic data provided for such applications are generally MRA visualizing vascular structures of the top of the head. Unfortunately, the method proposed in [5] presents many limitations making it inapplicable to MRA. First, it assumes that all the vessels located in the image belong to a same vascular tree. However, this is not true for cerebral images where intra and extracranial veins and arteries are organized in a more complex way. Second, the proposed thinning process is guided by the angiographic data intensity, assuming that the whole vascular tree presents a higher signal than the remaining tissues. This is no longer true for MRA where data signal loss can be caused by turbulences of the blood flow.

A correct segmentation of the cerebral superficial venous tree from MRA then requires to be able to discriminate the vessels belonging to this tree from the other ones, and to recover their correct topology despite signal loss in the angiographic data. A possible way to solve this problem can then consist in using a priori anatomical knowledge concerning these vascular structures. It is proposed here to use knowledge about the spatial relation existing between these searched venous structures and the cortex. This approach requires to determine information not only on vascular structures but also on non-vascular ones. To do so, the method described hereafter uses both MRA and MRI data.

3 Method

3.1 Input and Output

The method takes as input two MR data. The first one is a classical MRI of the whole head, denoted by $f_{mri} : I \to \mathbb{Z}$ (with $I \subset \mathbb{Z}^3$). The second one is a MRA of the top of the head, only containing information about the flowing blood, denoted by $f_{mra} : I \to \mathbb{Z}$. Both MRA and MRI have to be correctly registered (if they were not generated during the same image acquisition, a rigid registration is sufficient since both images correspond to the same patient). In the proposed application, the used images are T1 MRI and time-of-flight (TOF) MRA of the top of the head which are already correctly superimposed (Fig. 1). The method provides as output a binary image $V_{seg} \subset I$ of the segmented cerebral superficial venous tree.

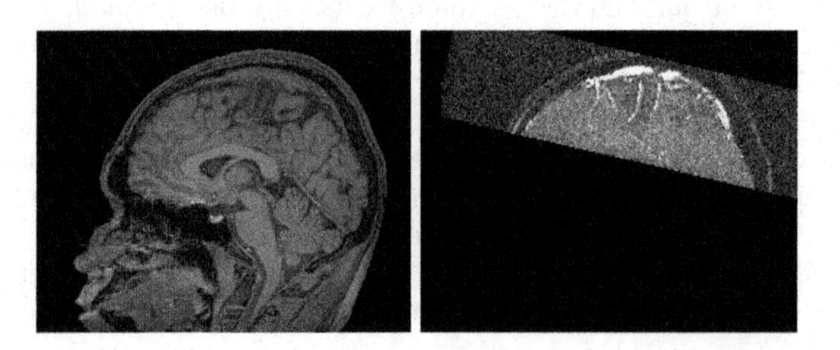

Fig. 1. Sagittal slices of the processed data. Left: T1 MRI of the whole head. Right: TOF MRA of the top of the head.

3.2 Preliminary Step: Vessel and Brain Segmentation

This first step consists in computing preliminary segmentations of the vessels from f_{mra} and of the brain from f_{mri} (middle and left parts of Fig. 2).

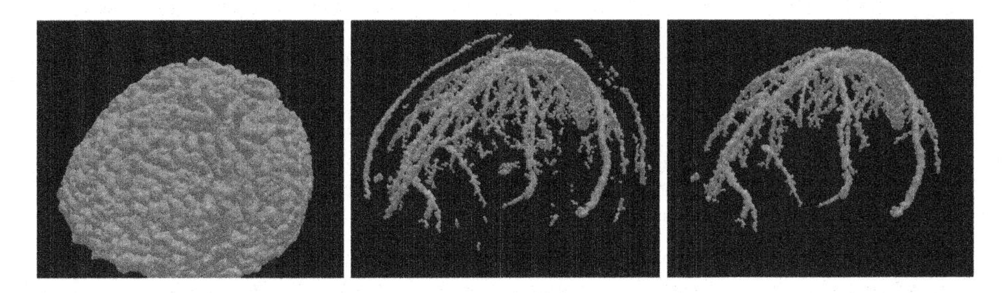

Fig. 2. Left: gray matter (C_{GM}) segmented from f_{mri}. Middle: vessels (V_{ini}) segmented from f_{mra}. Right: segmented vessels belonging to the cerebral superficial venous tree (V_{min}).

All the vessels (*i.e.* the flowing blood) visualized in f_{mra} are segmented using a region-growing method described in [8]. The obtained segmentation is a set $V_{ini} \subset I$, assumed not to contain false positives, composed of several connected components corresponding to deep cerebral vessels, superficial venous vessels and scalp vessels. It has to be noticed that these components do not contain any holes or cavities, since the region-growing segmentation uses topologically simple points.

The brain is segmented from f_{mri}, using an energy minimization method proposed in [9]. This method discriminates the intracranial volume into three categories corresponding to white matter (WM), gray matter (GM) and cerebro-spinal fluid (CSF). The result $(C_{CSF}, C_{GM}, C_{WM}) \subset I^3$ is composed of three sets respectively corresponding to these three kinds of tissues.

3.3 Vascular Tree Reconstruction

Vessel Labeling. Let $V_{seg} \subset I$ be the vascular tree being searched (V_{seg} has to present a tree topology, being composed of one connected component with no hole and no cavity). Correct initialization and termination of the vascular tree reconstruction require to determine two sets $V_{max}, V_{min} \subset I$ such as:

$$V_{min} \subseteq V_{seg} \subseteq V_{max}, \tag{1}$$

with V_{max} having the same topology as V_{seg} and V_{min} containing no hole and no cavity. As already proposed in [5], it is possible to assume that $V_{max} = I$. The determination of V_{min} is now described.

The set V_{min} is assumed to only contain vascular structures which will constitute the basis for the topology recovery procedure. The preliminary segmentation step provides a set V_{ini} containing all the vessels of f_{mra}. However, V_{ini} is composed of connected components corresponding not only to superficial venous vessels but also to scalp and deep cerebral vessels. A vessel labeling procedure is then necessary to determine the vessels belonging to V_{ini}.

Several assumptions can be made about the position of these vessels with respect to the different brain structures. Indeed, deep cerebral structures are located far from the skull (*i.e.* far from the external border of the CSF). Moreover, superficial venous vessels are located close to the cortex (*i.e.* close to the external border of the GM), while scalp vessels are located far from it.

In order to classify the connected components of V_{ini}, two distance maps are computed. The first one (d_{CSF}) indicates the signed distance to the external border of the set C_{CSF} (distances positive inside the brain and negative outside). The second one (d_{GM}) indicates the signed distance to the external border of the set C_{GM} (distances positive outside the brain and negative inside). For each connected component $v_{ini} \subset V_{ini}$, the distance d to the CSF (resp. to the GM) is defined as the minimal value between the CSF (resp. the GM) and any voxel of v_{ini}:

$$d(C_\alpha, v_{ini}) = \min\{d_\alpha(p) \mid p \in v_{ini}\}, \text{(with } \alpha = \text{CSF or GM).} \quad (2)$$

The set V_{min} (right part of Fig. 2) can then be defined by:

$$V_{min} = \bigcup_{d(C_{CSF}, v_{ini})<20 \text{ mm and } d(C_{GM}, v_{ini})<5 \text{ mm}} v_{ini}. \quad (3)$$

The threshold values of this formula have been established for brains presenting a volume of 1200 cm^3. They can then be adapted to the size of any brain by applying a correction coefficient $\sqrt[3]{V/1200}$ where V cm^3 is the current brain volume estimated from C_{GM} and C_{WM}.

Topology Recovery. The topology recovery step consists in determining the vascular tree V_{seg} which has to contain the segmented structures V_{min} and to present correct topological properties. Although V_{min} can contain several connected components, V_{seg} must be composed of only one connected component with no hole and no cavity. This can be done by iteratively removing simple points from V_{max} until obtaining set uniquely composed of voxels belonging to V_{min} or being non-simple. Such a strategy then enables to reconnect the different branches of V_{min}. However, it does not guarantee that these branches will be reconnected according to the anatomical reality. In [5], the CTA image was used as a weight function to indicate which voxels had to be removed first. This strategy was justified by the assumption that the likeliness of a voxel to belong to a vessel was proportional to its gray-level intensity. This assumption is no longer true for MRA data where signal losses are frequent, making such a strategy unusable. It is then necessary to define a new weight map modeling a vessel-likeliness measure for each voxel, then providing a correct priority for their removal from V_{max}.

Still assuming that the vessels of the cerebral superficial venous tree are located at the surface of the cortex, it is proposed to use a weight function f_{weight}

defined as the geodesic distance map providing the distance of each point to the closest connected component of V_{min} inside the mask $I \setminus (C_{GM} \cup C_{WM})$. This weight function $f_{weight} : I \to \overline{\mathbb{Z}}$ is then defined by:

$$f_{weight}(p) = \begin{cases} 0 & \text{if } p \in V_{min} \\ +\infty & \text{if } p \in C_{GM} \cup C_{WM} \\ d_g & \text{otherwise} \end{cases}, \tag{4}$$

where d_g is distance of the shortest path between p and V_{min}, not intersecting $C_{GM} \cup C_{WM}$.

The vascular tree reconstruction can then be summarized as follows.

1. $L = \{F_i\}_{i=\min_I f_{weight}}^{\max_I f_{weight}}$ (L is a set of empty FIFO lists).
2. $V_{cur} = V_{max}$.
3. For all voxel p belonging to the border of V_{cur}, p is put in $F_{f_{weight}(p)}$.
4. While $\exists i \in [\min_I f_{weight}, \max_I f_{weight}]$, $F_i \neq \emptyset$:
   (a) get p from $F_{\max\{i|F_i \neq \emptyset\}}$;
   (b) if p is a simple point of V_{cur} and $p \notin V_{min}$ then $V_{cur} = V_{cur} \setminus \{p\}$ and for all neighbors q of p not already in $F_{f_{weight}(q)}$, add q to $F_{f_{weight}(q)}$.
5. $V_{seg} = V_{cur}$.

4 Experiments and Results

A database of 9 MRI/MRA cases has been used to validate the efficiency of the proposed algorithm. Both TOF MRA and T1 MRI exams (see Fig. 1) were performed on a 2 Tesla whole-body imager (Tomikon S200 Bruker) using a head transmitter and receiver RF coil. The algorithm presented in this paper has been implemented by using the ImLib3D [10] open source C++ library. The obtained results, summarized in Tables 1 and 2, have been validated by an expert. An example of segmented vascular tree is illustrated in Fig. 3.

Table 1. Validations of the labeling step. Mean values of the classification obtained by the method (Results) compared to the real classification of the connected components (c.c.) of V_{ini} (Reference).

Set	Results		Reference		False positives		False negatives	
	voxels	c.c.	voxels	c.c.	voxels	c.c.	voxels	c.c.
V_{min}	11197	15.3	11223	15.8	0 (0%)	0 (0%)	26 (0.2%)	0.5 (3.1%)
$V_{ini} \setminus V_{min}$	2191	21.3	2165	20.8	26 (1.2%)	0.5 (2.4%)	0 (0%)	0 (0%)

Table 2. Validations of the topology recovery step. From left to right: mean number of reconnections, number and ratio of correct and incorrect reconnections.

Reconnections	Correct	Incorrect
14.3	12.1 (84.6%)	2.2 (15.4%)

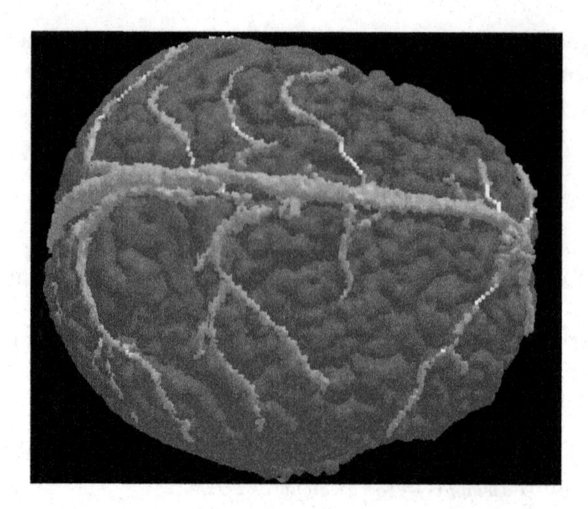

Fig. 3. Cerebral superficial venous tree (V_{seg}) segmented by the proposed method. (brain ($C_{GM} \cup C_{WM}$) in dark gray, initial segmentation (V_{min}) in light gray, topological reconstruction ($V_{seg} \setminus V_{min}$) in white).

One can observe that the results are quite satisfactory for the labeling step. The set V_{min} generated by the method then constitutes a reliable basis for the topology recovery. The results obtained for this topology recovery step are also satisfactory, even if not perfect. Most of the vessels have been correctly reconnected. However, approximately 16% of the reconnections are erroneous. These errors can be classified into two categories. The first ones are composed of false reconnections (*i.e.* reconnections of vessels which should not be connected). These errors occur when the distance between vessels which should be connected is high (generally more than 30 mm). The second ones are composed of reconnections which are topologically correct (*i.e.* reconnections of vessels which should be connected) but which does not exactly correspond to the real vessel trajectory. This analysis seems to prove that the use of geodesic distance between the vessels allows to correctly recover most of the venous tree topology but is not sufficient to deal with the most difficult cases, corresponding to very tortuous vessels and largest signal loss in MRA. A solution could then consist in also considering the signal of vessels, no longer in MRA but in MRI and to fuse it with geodesic distance information to provide a most representative weight map.

5 Conclusion

This paper has presented a novel method using both MRI and MRA for segmentation and topology recovery of the cerebral superficial venous tree. The algorithm uses a priori anatomical knowledge concerning the spatial relations between vessels and brain structures, to discriminate the cerebral venous tree from non-cerebral vessels and to recover the topology of vessel missing parts.

The method has been tested on 9 patients, providing satisfactory results in most cases. The main originality of this work consisted in using both angiographic and non-angiographic images to model anatomical knowledge and integrate information on non-vascular structures in a vessel segmentation process. Further works will consist in improving the reliability of this method by using the MRI signal of vessels as proposed in the previous section. Other methods, taking advantage of multimodality and anatomical a priori knowledge are also being developed for segmentation of the whole cerebral vascular tree.

References

1. Kirbas, C., Quek, F.: A review of vessel extraction techniques and algorithms. ACM Computing Surveys **36** (2004) 81–121
2. Sanderson, A., Parker, D., Henderson, T.: Simultaneous segmentation of MR and X-ray angiograms for visualization of cerebral vascular anatomy. In: International Conference on Volume Image Processing - VIP'93. (1993) 11–14
3. Bloch, I., Pellot, C., Sureda, F., Herment, A.: 3D reconstruction of blood vessels by multi-modality data fusion using fuzzy and Markovian modelling. In: Computer Vision, Virtual Reality and Robotics in Medicine - CVRMed'95. (1995) 392–398
4. Passat, N., Ronse, C., Baruthio, J., Armspach, J.P., Foucher, J.: Using watershed and multimodal data for vessel segmentation: Application to the superior sagittal sinus. In: International Symposium on Mathematical Morphology - ISMM'05. (2005) 419–428
5. Dokládal, P., Lohou, C., Perroton, L., Bertrand, G.: Liver blood vessels extraction by a 3-D topological approach. In: Medical Image Computing and Computer-Assisted Intervention - MICCAI'99. (1999) 98–105
6. Flasque, N., Desvignes, M., Constans, J., Revenu, M.: Acquisition, segmentation and tracking of the cerebral vascular tree on 3D magnetic resonance angiography images. Medical Image Analysis **5** (2001) 173–183
7. Zahlten, C., Jürgens, H., Peitgen, H.O.: Reconstruction of branching blood vessels from CT-data. In: Visualization in Scientific Computing'95, Eurographics Workshop. (1995) 41–52
8. Passat, N., Ronse, C., Baruthio, J., Armspach, J.P., Maillot, C., Jahn, C.: Region-growing segmentation of brain vessels: An atlas-based automatic approach. Journal of Magnetic Resonance Imaging **21** (2005) 715–725
9. Bosc, M., Heitz, F., Armspach, J.P.: Statistical atlas-based sub-voxel segmentation of 3D brain MRI. In: International Conference on Image Processing - ICIP'03. (2003) 1077–1080
10. Bosc, M., Vik, T., Armspach, J.P., Heitz, F.: ImLib3D: An efficient, open source, medical image processing framework in C++. In: Medical Image Computing and Computer-Assisted Intervention - MICCAI'03. (2003) 981–982

Loop Removal from Colon Central Path Through Skeleton Scale-Space Tracking

Julien Lamy[1,2], Christian Ronse[1], and Luc Soler[2]

[1] LSIIT, UMR 7005 CNRS-ULP, Pôle API, boulevard Sébastien Brant, BP 10413, F-67412 Illkirch Cedex, France
ronse@lsiit.u-strasbg.fr
[2] Ircad, 1 place de l'Hôpital, F-67091 Strasbourg Cedex, France
{julien.lamy, luc.soler}@ircad.u-strasbg.fr

Abstract. The central path of the colon is an important tool in computer-assisted diagnosis: it is an aid to navigation during a virtual colonoscopy and allows an easier follow-up of the patient pathologies. However the computation of this central path remains a difficult task: on both MR and CT medical images, the wall of the colon is too thin with respect to the resolution of the acquisition and thus does not appear on images. Hence, when two sections of the colon are in contact, a loop is created in the image, and causes a wrong central path. In this paper, we propose an algorithm to remove those loops, based on the tracking of the colon skeleton in a scale-space. An evaluation of our algorithm on 20 patients showed that every loop was successfully removed, yielding a centered, anatomically and topologically correct central path.

1 Introduction

The central path of the colon is a very useful tool in computer-assisted diagnosis, for virtual colonoscopy, and patient follow-up. Concerning virtual colonoscopy, the convoluted nature of the colon makes the navigation complicated. The central path, used either as a visual guide or in an automated navigation system, solves this problem. Concerning the follow-up of a patient, the central path allows to localize and match the pathologies with precision without having to process the whole volume of the colon.

However, all central path algorithms strongly depend on the segmented, binary volume of the colon, since they have to preserve geometrical and topological features of the colon. This dependency might be problematic in the case of the colon: due to its complicated shape, one segment of the colon might pass very close to another, the walls of both segments being in contact. On current images, both CT and MR, the resolution is not sufficient to distinguish that wall, as it is very thin. This results in a loop in the original image, which has no anatomic counterpart, and which is kept in the central path as it is a topological feature. Small loops often appear near haustrations [1], and larger loops often exist in images of pathological colons. Examples of how these loops appear are presented in Fig 1.

G. Bebis et al. (Eds.): ISVC 2005, LNCS 3804, pp. 68–75, 2005.

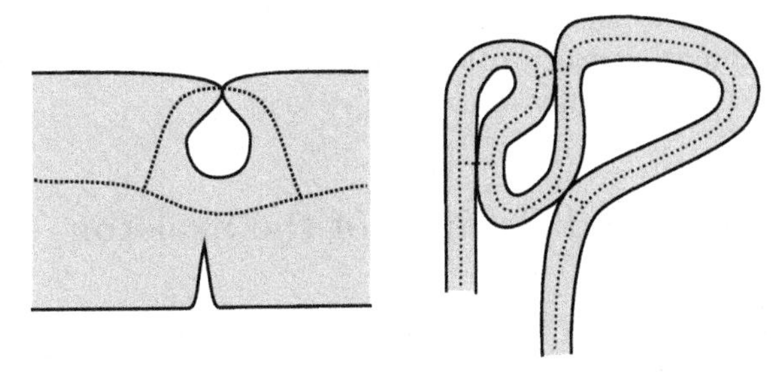

Fig. 1. Loops in the central path of the colon. *Left*: loop around a haustration. *Right*: loops in the whole colon.

As presented by Sadleir and Whelan [2], previous work concerning the computation of the central path of the colon falls into two broad categories: methods based on a distance map, and methods using homotopic thinning. The former compute the distance of every point inside the colon to the colon wall, and then compute the central path from this map, using clusters of points (*e.g.* [3, 4, 5]) or by computing the shortest path between two user-defined markers at the extremities of the colon and then centering the given path using a snake [6, 7].

Methods based on homotopic thinning are less comonly used [1, 2]. These methods involve an "onion peeling" process, where voxels are iteratively removed from the surface of the object, without changing the topology of the object. Homotopic thinning has been considered computationally expensive, as it involves massive neighborhood scans, but such optimizations as binary decision diagrams [8] or the use of lookup tables [2] have solved the problem, with a minor trade-off concerning the memory usage. The central path obtained by homotopic thinning is centered when using Pudney's distance-ordered homotopic thinning [9]. As these algorithms preserve the topology of the original object, all the loops appear in the central path.

The methods based on a distance map will either yield a path that is not centered near the sharp turns of the colon or that is not anatomically correct, taking every shortcut possible. As an erroneous central path cannot be used to obtain a reliable diagnosis, we decided to use the homotopic thinning approach. Indeed, this approach provides a skeleton that contains the correct central path, albeit with loops. Provided an adapted loop removal algorithm, the central path can therefore be extracted from the skeleton.

Concerning the loop removal, to our knowledge, the only methods are those by Zhou and Toga [5], Ge *et al.* [1], and Sadleir and Whelan [2]. The first method is based on the traversal of a directed acyclic graph, which misses some configurations where one loop branches from another. The two last methods only deal with small simple loops mainly caused by haustral folds, neglecting the more "macroscopic" loops mentionned above.

In this paper, we present an algorithm able to remove both kinds of loops. We first explain in section 2 a method to obtain a skeleton without unnecessary branches. Then, we describe our algorithm and show how the tracking of the skeleton through a scale-space allows the removal of loops, whatever their size is. Finally, we evaluate our algorithm on the images from 20 patients and show its reliability, as it successfully remove every loop.

2 Computation and Pruning of the Skeleton

In the following, the colon is assumed to be already segmented, using a classical region growing algorithm [10].In this section, we describe our method to compute a pruned skeleton of the colon, which will be used in the loop removal algorithm. Homotopic thinning is a simple yet powerful framework to obtain the skeleton of a binary object: until stability, voxels are removed from the object if they satisfy two conditions: (a) their removal does not change the topology of the object, and (b) some of the geometrical characteristics of the object are preserved. The first condition (homotopy) is easily tested using the topological numbers of a point p in an object X [11], defined as:

$$\begin{cases} T_6(p, X) = \#CC_6(N_{18}(p) \cap X) \\ T_{26}(p, X) = \#CC_{26}(N_{26}(p) \cap X) \end{cases}, \tag{1}$$

where the 6, 18, and 26 subscripts denote the connectivity of the object, N_n denotes the n-neighborhood, and where $\#CC_n(Y)$ is the number of n-connected components of object Y. Using these numbers, the removal of a point p does not affect the topology of object X iff $T_n(p, X) = 1$ and $T_{\overline{n}}(p, \overline{X}) = 1$, where $\overline{n} = 6$ if $n = 18$ or $n = 26$ and $\overline{n} = 26$ if $n = 6$. Such a point is called *simple.*

The second condition depends on the application. In our case, we want to obtain a one-dimensional skeleton, and thus preserve the voxels at the extremity of a line, defined by having a single neighbor in the foreground, and every other in the background.

This framework is a sequential one, as the parallel removal of simple points might affect the topology of the object [12]. Depending on the order of the removal, the result might not be centered, and thus be useless for the computation of the central path. We use Pudney's distance-ordered homotopic thinning [9] to generate a centered skeleton.

Pruning. A skeleton still contains many branches, and most of them are useless in our application, as we only want the central path. To prune these branches, we perform a second pass of homotopic thinning, where only two simple points are preserved, one at each end of the path. We propose to detect these markers automatically. The first one is the lowest point of the skeleton, and thus is located near the rectum. The second one is the farthest point in the skeleton from the rectum marker, according to the geodesic distance in the skeleton. This second marker is located near the cæcum, at the junction between the small bowel and the colon.

These operations gives us a thin, topologically-correct central path with no side branch, but which might still have loops.

3 Loop Removal

Any loop present in the original image is preserved in the skeleton by the homotopic thinning process. Topologically, the loops are called *tunnels*, defined by the existance of a closed path that cannot be continuously deformed to a single point. Our loop removal algorithm embeds the binary image of the colon in a scale-space in which an increase of the scale parameters closes the tunnels. We compute the skeleton of the object seen at two different scales by homotopic thinning and pruning as described above, and match the branches of the skeleton at the smallest scale to the branches of the skeleton at the largest scale. If no match can be found for a given branch, this means that this branch was part of a loop that disappeared at the largest scale, and that the branch can be discarded.

We will now present the different blocks of the algorithm: the scale-space, a graph representation of the skeleton, and the matching algorithm, working first on the vertices, then on the edges.

3.1 Scale-Space

The scale-space is built using the topological hull algorithm of Aktouf *et al.* [13]. This algorithm closes tunnels and cavities in an object that are smaller than a user-defined size θ. We will note I_θ the topological hull of object I where all tunnels smaller than θ are closed. The object I_0 is the same as object I and the object I_∞ is a superset of I with no tunnel. For any two scales $\theta_1 < \theta_2$, $I_{\theta_1} \subseteq I_{\theta_2}$. The family I_θ, with $\theta \in \mathbb{Z} \cup \infty$, forms a scale space where an increase of the scale parameter θ reduces the number of tunnels in the object I.

3.2 Graph Representation of a Skeleton

Our graph representation of the skeleton is close to the one described by Ge *et al.* [1]. Vertices of the graph are defined by branching voxels, and the paths between those vertices form the edges of the graph. Ge *et al.* defined a branching voxel as a voxel having three or more neighbors, we define it through the topological numbers, where a junction point p is defined by $T_n(p, I) > 2$ and $T_{\overline{n}}(p, \overline{I}) = 1$ [14].

We note the graph of the skeleton G, its vertex set V and its edge set E. Whenever this is possible, for clarity reasons, we assimilate a vertex in the graph to the corresponding voxel in the skeleton, and an edge to the corresponding path.

3.3 Matching of the Vertices

Once the graphs G_{θ_1} and G_{θ_2} of the skeletons S_{θ_1} and S_{θ_2} of the objects I_{θ_1} and I_{θ_2}, where $\theta_1 < \theta_2$, are computed, we will first match every vertex from V_{θ_2} to a vertex in V_{θ_1}. Once this is done, we will back-project every un-matched vertex from V_{θ_1} to V_{θ_2}, thus modifying G_{θ_2} so that its vertex set is similar to V_{θ_1}. This step is presented in Figure 2.

Step 1. For every vertex of V_{θ_2}, we look for the closest vertex in V_{θ_1}, according to the euclidean distance. Let $V_{matched}(V_{\theta_2})$ be the set of vertices matched during this step.

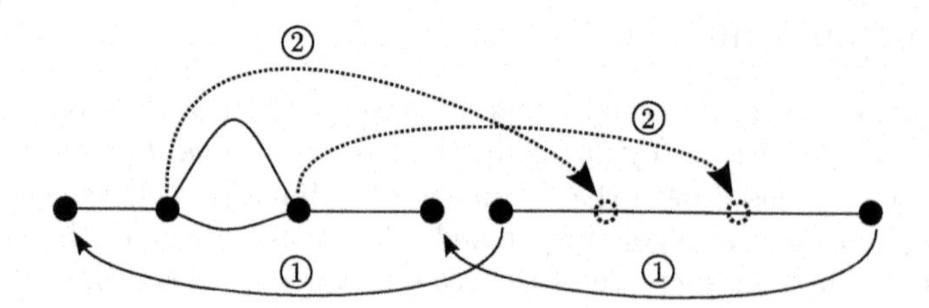

Fig. 2. Steps of the vertex matching. *Left*: G_{θ_1}. *Right*: G_{θ_2}. *Solid lines*: first step, matching of the vertices in G_{θ_2} to the vertices in G_{θ_1}. *Dotted lines and circles*: second step, back-projection of unmatched vertices of G_{θ_1} on G_{θ_2} and edge splitting.

Step 2. For every vertex of $V_{\theta_1} \setminus V_{matched}(V_{\theta_2})$, we look for the voxel of the skeleton S_{θ_2} that is the closest to the label of that vertex. If no vertex in V_{θ_2} has such coordinates, we add one, split the edge of E_{θ_2} on which that voxel was and adjust the labels of the two new edges. This step is made possible as the graphs, corresponding to similar objects, will have almost the same topology.

3.4 Matching of the Edges

The vertices sets V_{θ_1} and V_{θ_2} are now similar, and the vertices of both graphs are matched. For each edge of E_{θ_1}, we then determine if it is still present in E_{θ_2} and, if it is, to which one it corresponds.

For an edge $e \in E_{\theta_2}$, we say that edge $e' \in E_{\theta_1}$ is a possible match for e if the vertices of e' are matched to the vertices of e. For each edge $e \in E_{\theta_2}$, we compute its possible matches in E_{θ_1} and, from this set, compute the best match. According to the number of possible matches – exactly one, more than one, and none – three cases are possible.

Exactly One Possible Match. This is the simplest case: if there is only one possible match for an edge $e \in E_{\theta_2}$, then it is the best match. This is shown in Fig. 3, where the edge w_2, w_3 is matched to the edge v_2, v_3.

More Than One Possible Match. When there is more than one possible match for an edge $e \in E_{\theta_2}$, every candidate is compared to e, and the closest is

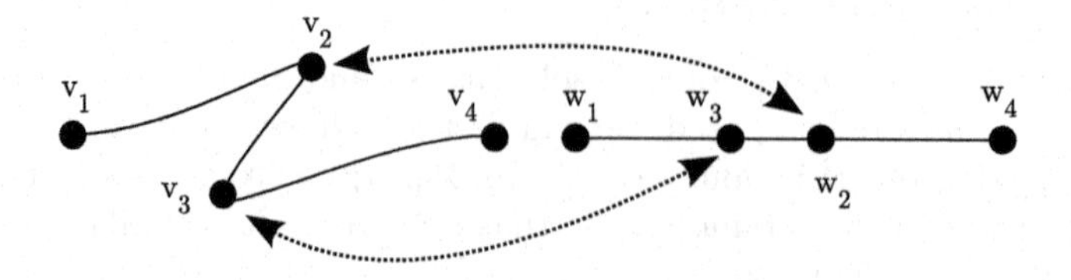

Fig. 3. Matching of edges. *Left*: G_{θ_1}. *Right*: G_{θ_2}. v_i is matched to w_i. The edge (w_2, w_3) is matched to (v_2, v_3). The edge (w_1, w_3) has no possible match in G_{θ_1} as the edge (v_1, v_3) does not exist: (w_1, w_3) is matched to the path (v_1, v_2, v_3).

defined as the best match. This comparison is computed on the voxel sequences labelling the edges, approximated by B-splines [15]. The mean distance between the B-spline γ approximating a candidate and the B-spline γ_{ref} approximating the edge e is defined by

$$D(\gamma, \gamma_{ref}) = \int_{\omega} |\gamma(u) - \gamma_{ref}(u)| \, du \,, \tag{2}$$

where ω is the domain of the B-splines. We approximate this integral by a mean over 100 equally spaced values of the parameter u.

No Possible Match. If the set of possible matches for an edge $e \in E_{\theta_2}$ is empty, two interpretations are possible. First, the edge e was not present in G_{θ_1} and appeared in G_{θ_2}. This is not possible in our case, as the graph becomes simpler when the scale increases. Second, some vertices might have been "swapped" with the diminution of details, as shown in Fig. 3. In that case, we look for a path in G_{θ_1} to match to the edge e. Note that this match is not the best one, but is sufficient in our case, as we only want to determine the existence of a such a match.

The paths in G_{θ_1} that could possibly be matched to an edge $e \in G_{\theta_2}$ are computed using the Dijsktra algorithm [16]. If several such paths exist, the shortest one is kept as the best match for the edge e.

3.5 Deleting Edges

At this point, every edge of G_{θ_2} is matched to an edge or to a path of G_{θ_1}. Any unmatched edge of G_{θ_1} corresponds to an edge going around a tunnel that was closed by the topological hull algorithm: all unmatched edges in G_{θ_1} are deleted, yielding a graph – and hence a central path – with no loop.

4 Experimental Results

We have evaluated our loop removal algorithm on the images from 20 patients. The small scale was set to $\theta_1 = 0$ and the large scale was set to $\theta_2 = +\infty$. We used the 6-connectivity for the foreground, for all topological operations, as the 26-connectivity causes problem for the detection of the junctions [14].

To verify the correctness, both versions of the central path (with and without loops) were superimposed on a semi-transparent mesh of the segmented colon.

Every central path contained loops before the loop removal algorithm. Every path contained small loops, due to haustrations, and 8 contained larger loops. Every loop was removed from the path, and the resulting paths are all anatomically correct. Figure 4 presents the results of our algorithm both for small loops and for a complete colon with large loops.

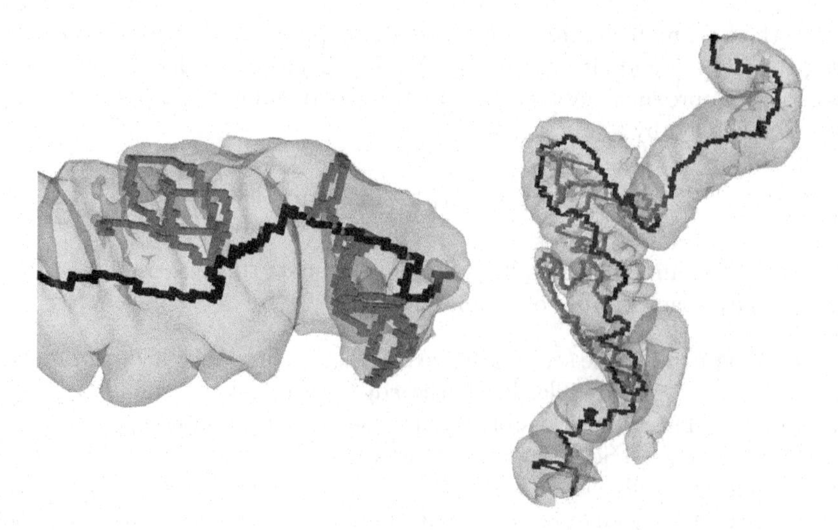

Fig. 4. Results of the loop removal algorithm (details). *Black*: final central path. *Gray*: central path with loops. *Left*: small loops. *Right*: large loops.

5 Conclusion

We have presented a complete algorithm to compute a topologically and anatomically correct central path of the colon. This algorithm includes a new loop removal method based on the scale-space tracking of the skeleton which automatically identifies spurious branches that remain in the skeleton obtained by homotopic thinning. This algorithm was tested on images from twenty patients and loops were successfully removed in every case. On a PC equipped with a 1.4 GHz CPU and 512 MB of RAM, the runtime for one patient is about 10 minutes.

In the future, we will validate this algorithm on a larger set of patients, with the aid of an expert in radiology and/or colonoscopy. We will also investigate the use of a classical gaussian scale-space [17], which should intuitively have the tunnel-closing property we require. This would allow a speedup in the runtime of the algorithm, the bottleneck being currently the thinning process and the computation of the topological hull.

Acknowledgements

We wish to thank the Hpitaux Universitaires de Strasbourg (Strasbourg, France) for providing the medical images upon which this work is based. We also thank Sébastien Lefèvre of the LSIIT for the discussions that led to this work and Stéphane Nicolau of the Ircad for the constructive criticism.

References

1. Ge, Y., Stelts, D.R., Wang, J., Vining, D.J.: Computing the centerline of a colon: a robust and efficient method based on 3D skeletons. Journal of Computer Assisted Tomography **23** (1999) 786–794
2. Sadleir, R.J., Whelan, P.F.: Fast colon centreline calculation using optimized 3D topological thinning. Computerized Medical Imaging and Graphics **29** (2005) 251–258
3. Bitter, I., Kaufman, A.E., Sato, M.: Penalized-distance volumetric skeleton algorithm. IEEE Transactions on Visualization and Computer Graphics **7** (2001) 195–206
4. Chaudhuri, P., Khandekar, R., Sethi, D., Kalra, P.: An efficient central path algorithm for virtual navigation. In: Proceedings of the Computer Graphics International (CGI'04), IEEE (2004) 188–195
5. Zhou, Y., Toga, A.W.: Efficient skeletonization of volumetric objects. IEEE Transactions on Visualization and Computer Graphics **5** (1999) 196–209
6. Cuisenaire, O.: Distance transformations: fast algorithms and applications to medical image processing. PhD thesis, Universit catholique de Louvain (UCL) (1999)
7. Deschamps, T., Cohen, L.D.: Fast extraction of minimal paths in 3D images and applications to virtual endoscopy. Medical Image Analysis **5** (2001) 281–299
8. Robert, L., Malandain, G.: Fast binary image processing using binary decision diagrams. Technical Report 3001, INRIA (1996)
9. Pudney, C.: Distance-ordered homotopic thinning : a skeletonization algorithm for 3D digital images. Computer Vision and Image Understanding **72** (1998) 404–413
10. Wyatt, C.L., Ge, Y., Vining, D.J.: Automatic segmentation of the colon for virtual colonoscopy. Computerized Medical Imaging and Graphics **24** (2000) 1–9
11. Bertrand, G., Malandain, G.: A new characterization of three-dimensional simple points. Pattern Recognition Letters **15** (1994) 169–175
12. Ma, C.M.: On topology preservation in 3D thinning. Computer Vision, Graphics, and Image Processing: Image Understanding **59** (1994) 328–339
13. Aktouf, Z., Bertrand, G., Perroton, L.: A three-dimensional holes closing algorithm. Pattern Recognition Letters **23** (2002) 523–531
14. Malandain, G., Bertrand, G., Ayache, N.: Topological segmentation of discrete surfaces. International Journal of Computer Vision **10** (1993) 183–197
15. Farin, G.: Curves and Surfaces for CAGD: a Practical Guide. 5th edn. Academic Press (2002)
16. Dijkstra, E.W.: A note on two problems in connexion with graphs. Numerische Mathematik **1** (1959) 269–271
17. Lindeberg, T.: Scale-space for discrete signals. IEEE Transactions on Pattern Analysis and Machine Intelligence **12** (1990) 234–254

Multiscale Segmentation of HRCT Images Using Bipolar Incoherent Filtering

Aamir Saeed Malik[1] and Tae-Sun Choi

Gwangju Institute of Science and Technology,
1 Oryong-Dong, Buk-Gu, Gwangju 500712, Korea
aamir@gist.ac.kr, tschoi@gist.ac.kr

Abstract. In this paper, we present a new Multiscale segmentation method based on an optical transfer function implemented in the Frequency domain and with this new segmentation technique, we demonstrate that it is possible to segment the HRCT (High Resolution CT) images into its various components at multiple scales hence separating the information available in the HRCT image. In the literature, several image segmentation techniques have been proposed for the segmentation of the medical images. However, there are few Multiscale segmentation methods that can segment the medical image so that various components within the image could be separated at multiple resolutions or scales. We show that the HRCT image can be segmented such that we get separate images for bones, tissues, lungs and anatomical struc-tures within the lungs.

1 Introduction

There are a variety of lung diseases, for example, pulmonary emphysema, nodules, interstitial lung disease etc. And the objective is to successfully assess these diseases. Experienced observers typically make correct global diagnosis of parenchymal lung diseases in 40% to 70% cases. While on the other hand, High-resolution CT (HRCT) is capable of imaging the lung with excellent spatial resolution. Thin slice CT scans can capture the alterations in the lung anatomy caused by different lung diseases. Hence the advantage of HRCT image is increasingly better anatomic resolution because of very thin image slices. Therefore, the need arises for some type of automated segmentation technique to analyze the HRCT images. In this paper, we present a solution to this problem by proposing a technique for multiscale segmentation based on an optical transfer function implemented in the Frequency domain.

2 Previous Work

Bin Zheng et. al. [1] suggested a fully automated segmentation process that included a series of six simple steps. Jan-Martin Kuhnigk et. al. [2] used anatomy guided 3D watershed transform for lung lobe segmentation. Zhang et. al. [3] proposed an interactive method to extract the oblique fissures using a fuzzy reasoning system followed by

---

[1] Senior Member IEEE.

G. Bebis et al. (Eds.): ISVC 2005, LNCS 3804, pp. 76–83, 2005.

a graph search. They later [4] extended the same system to include 3D shape constraints. Hence, they used fuzzy reasoning system for 3D shape. M.S. Brown et. al. [5] used explicit anatomical knowledge to generate an anatomical model. They showed [8] that 86% of the lung segmentation was correct while 14% required manual corrections while considering 104 data series comprising of 1313 images. S. Hu et. al. [9] used an iterative searching method to compute an optimal threshold value for each CT case and used conditional morphological operations to segment lung regions. Zhang and Valentino [10] suggested using artificial neural networks to classify each pixel in the CT slice into different anatomical structure. The method for image segmentation presented in this paper differs from the methods mentioned above.

3 Method

A new Multiscale segmentation method is proposed to split a range of anatomical structures in a HRCT image. This Multiscale segmentation technique is based on bipolar incoherent image processing [11]. We introduce a transfer function which is used to find the segmented edges by classifying the sharp pixels with maximum intensity.

Transfer function is based on optical image processing. We denote it with O_Ω. To calculate O_Ω, conside the following parameters:

f = focal length of the lenses
k_0 = wave number of light
k_x, k_y = spatial frequencies
p_1 = difference of Gaussian aperture function
p_2 = small pin hole aperture

Using the above parameters, we find the transfer function O_Ω as cross correlation of the two pupils (p_1 and p_2) in the incoherent optical system. The result is bipolar point spread function. O_Ω is a filtering operation that provides the sharpness at pixel points in an image. The filtering operation depends upon two parameters σ_1 and σ_2. These values are adjusted to provide the desired filter shape and it can be adjusted to low pass, band pass and high pass filter operations. Therefore, the operator parameters can easily be adjusted to respond to the high frequency variations in the image intensity. The parameters σ_1 and σ_2 are given by the following equations:

$$\sigma_1 = a_1\,(f/\,k_0)^2$$
$$\sigma_2 = a_2\,(f/\,k_0)^2$$

where a_1 and a_2 are constants, f is the focal length and k_0 is the wave number of light (as mentioned above). Two pupil functions are given as:

$$p_1 = \exp[-a_1(x^2 + y^2)]-\exp[-a_2(x^2 + y^2)]$$
$$p_2 = \delta(x,y)$$

And finally, the transfer function is given by the following equation:

$$O_\Omega\,(k_x, k_y) = \exp[-\sigma_1(k_x^2 + k_y^2)]-\exp[-\sigma_2(k_x^2 + k_y^2)] \quad (1)$$

For our algorithm, first the Fourier transform is applied to the input image so that we can simply multiply our transfer function O_Ω with the input image. To apply the fourier transform, first we find out the spectrum of the intensity image by:

$$S = |S(x, y)|^2 \quad (2)$$

Where S is the spectrum of the intensity image and S(x,y) is the input image. Then we apply fourier tranform to equation (1):

$$S_f = F(S) \quad (3)$$

Where F indicates Fourier Transform, S is the spectrum of the intensity image and S_f is the transformed image in frequency domain. Our transfer function has spatial frequencies denoted as k_x and k_y. Hence our transfer function is O_Ω with spatial frequencies k_x and k_y. So in time domain, the transfer function $h_\Omega(x, y)$ is obtained by taking the inverse Fourier transform of O_Ω and hence it is given as:

$$h_\Omega(x, y) = F^{-1}\ \{O_\Omega(k_x, k_y)\} \quad (4)$$

where F^{-1} is for Inverse Fourier Transform. Now we multiply our transfer function O_Ω with the transformed image S_f (obtained from equation 2). Hence, the complex operation of convolution has been reduced to multiplication. So we get the convolved image by the following equation:

$$I_f = (S_f)(O_\Omega) \quad (5)$$

Where I_f is the convolved image, S_f is the transformed image in frequency domain and O_Ω is the transfer function in frequency domain that has spatial frequencies k_x and k_y. The final computed image I is obtained by taking the inverse Fourier transform of equation (5):

$$I = F^{-1}\ (I_f) \quad (6)$$

Simply, the above mentioned procedure can be explained by the following equation:

$$I = \mathrm{Re}\ [|S(x, y)|^2 * h_\Omega(x, y)\}] \quad (7)$$

where '*' indicates convolution, Re indicates real part, I is the computed image, $|S(x, y)|^2$ is the Spectrum of the Intensity Image and $h_\Omega(x, y)$ is the Transfer Function.

The high frequency component of an image area is determined by processing in the Fourier domain and analyzing the frequency distribution. Fourier transform used to be computationally expensive but with high speed personal computers available today, this computational complexity has decreased exponentially and it is not a matter of concern anymore. The processing in the frequency domain is particularly useful for noise reduction too as the noise frequencies are easily filtered out.

Once the transfer function is applied to the HRCT images, the next step is to select the boundary points for the segmented regions in the HRCT segmented image. So the selection at a point (i,j) is computed in a small window around (i,j) and value at (i,j) is replaced by the sum of computed values of all pixels in that window only after enhancing extracted edges and removing noise, if any. This operation is similar to that used for Sum of Modified Laplacian [6,7]. Window size of 3x3 was used for our experiments. Therefore, the segmented point is given as S_O:

$$S_O\,(i, j) = \sum_{x=i-N}^{i+N}\ \sum_{y=j-N}^{j+N} I\,(x, y) \quad (8)$$

4 Results and Discussion

We tested our algorithm on a variety of images. A database of HRCT lung images of resolution 512x512 pixels was used to test the algorithm. All the images were of DICOM format. All the subsequent results shown in this paper are calculated when the HRCT image is processed using Fast Fourier Transform. We demonstrate the results with one slice only for clarity purposes. The original image slice that is used for demonstrating the results is shown in fig 1 below and we show all the subsequent results with this image slice.

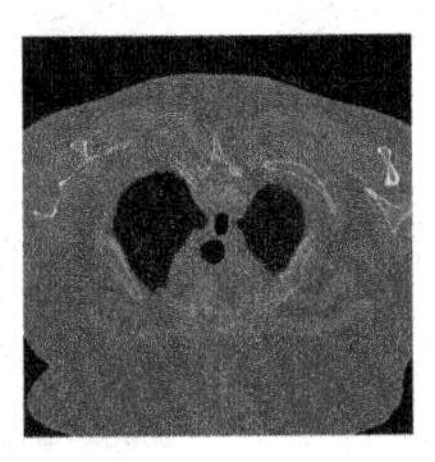

Fig. 1. HRCT Image Slice

Now consider fig 2. HRCT image shown in fig 1 is processed using the Optical Segmentation technique (S_O) given by equation 8. The corresponding filters are also shown in fig 2 with the values of σ_1 and σ_2 that were used for processing the HRCT image. It can be seen from the images in figure 2, the result changes with the variation of the two parameters, i.e., σ_1 and σ_2, of the filter. Consider the images of the filter in figure 2. It is evident that we can design a low pass filter, band pass filter and high pass filter by selecting different values for σ_1 and σ_2. We have organized the images in figure 2 in such a way that we start with low pass filtering and end with high pass filtering. The transition from low pass to band pass and then to high pass is smooth.

The images in row one and row 2 of fig 2 are low pass filtered with no information from medium and high frequencies. As a result, the image does not have sharp edges and it has the blurring effect. As we move towards the images in row 3 of fig 2, some edge information is now accounted for in those images. Hence, the result is less blurring and increased sharpness of pixel values. Another point is quite clear from the images depicted in row 1, i.e., the lungs are quite pronounced in these set of images while the other anatomical structures (bones, structures within the lungs etc) are not obvious. Hence, using the images in row 1, we can easily separate lungs from the rest of the image. Also, there is some tissue information present in the images in row 2. Hence, we can also separate tissues from the HRCT image using low pass filtering.

In fig 2, we can also see the band pass filtered images when the parameter values fall in between σ_1=.09, σ_2=.1 and σ_1=.008, σ_2=.009. So they have medium frequency component present in the images. The bones start to appear in the images while lungs remain present in the image when the parameter values are in between σ_1=.09, σ_2=.1 and σ_1=.06, σ_2=.07. However, the anatomical structures within the lungs are not so prominent in this range. The anatomical structures become prominent when the parameter values fall in between σ_1=.05, σ_2=.06 and σ_1=.008, σ_2=.009. The structure of bones becomes more obvious in between σ_1=.007, σ_2=.008 and σ_1=.001, σ_2=.002.

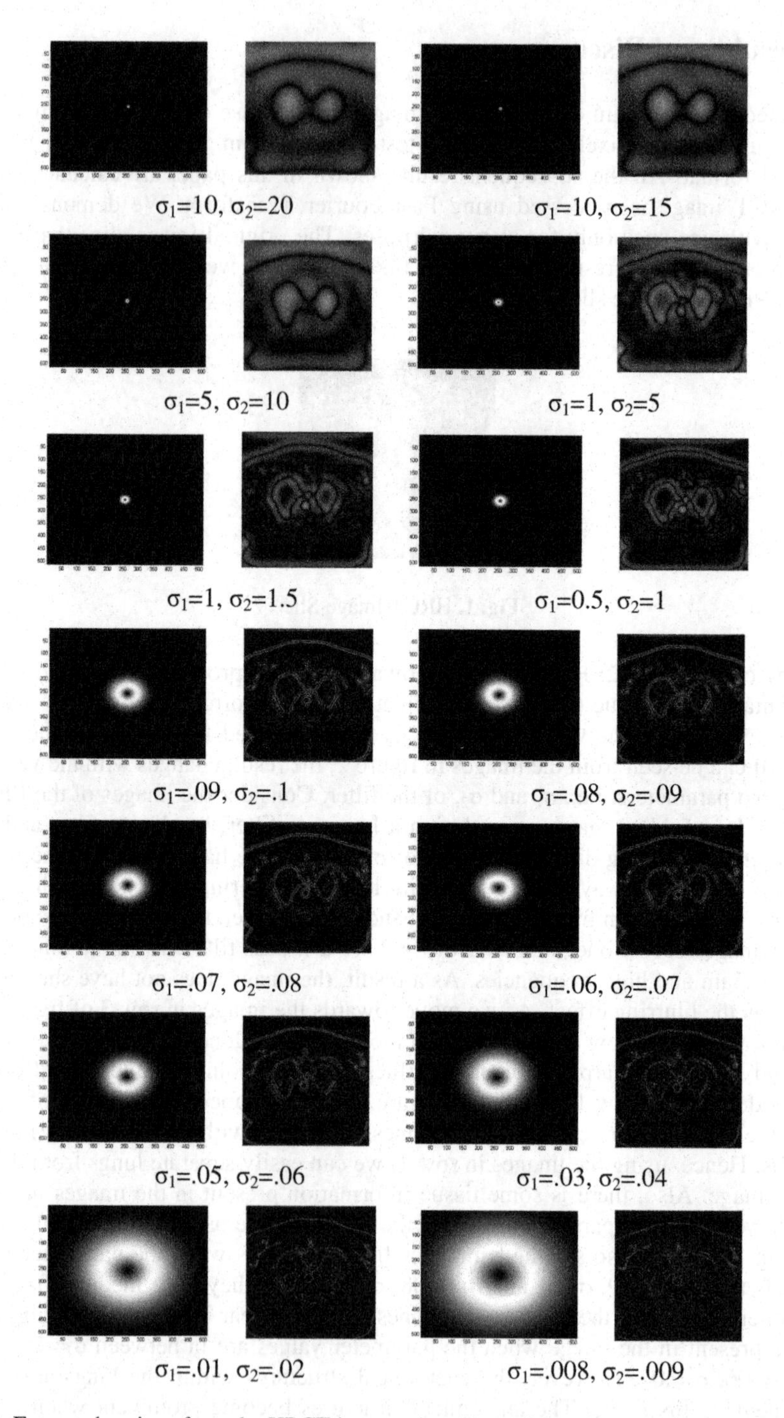

Fig. 2. Extracted regions from the HRCT image when filter with various values of σ_1 and σ_2 is applied

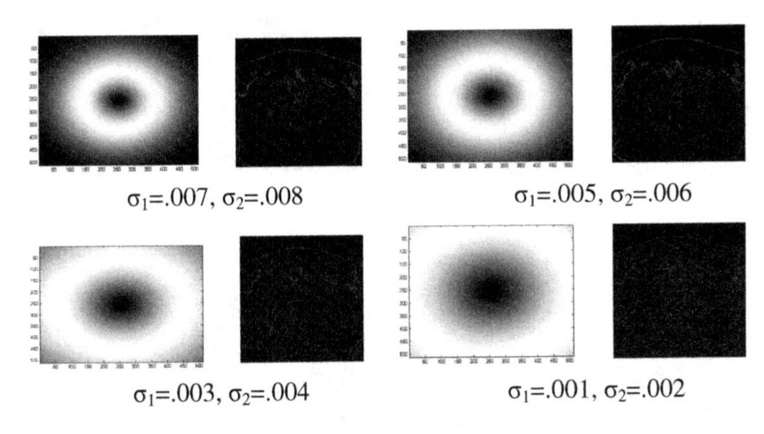

Fig. 2. *(Continued)*

Now consider the filter designed with parameters falling in the range between σ_1=.007,σ_2=.008 and σ_1=.001,σ_2=.002. These images are the result of allowing only the high frequency part of the image to remain within the image while eliminating all other frequency components. Hence, these images are filtered with high pass filter. There is one very interesting point that can be observed from these images, i.e., only the bones structure is visible in these images and we cannot observe lungs, tissues and other anatomical structures within lungs. So we can easily separate the bones from the rest of the anatomical structures present within the image.

Therefore, it is possible to separate the tissues, lungs, bones and the anatomical structures within the lungs from the HRCT images with the usage of precise filter parameter values. Hence, we can perform the multiscale segmentation by using the filter based on optical transfer function to segment the HRCT image at various levels or scales. The white rings in the filter images in fig 2 indicate the region where the frequencies are allowed to pass while the rest of the dark region shows that the frequency components present in that part are blocked.

Similarly, fig 3 shows the different anatomical structures extracted by using a set of filters with different parameter values for σ_1 and σ_2 as compared to those used in fig 2. The difference between these filter values and those used earlier as shown in fig 2 is that these filters cover more frequency components while those used earlier provide narrow rings for filtering. The discussion made earlier for fig 2 is also valid for fig 3.

Now consider fig 4. This is the post processing stage. The result shows the various anatomical structures separated from the HRCT image by further processing. We have simply used thresholding on images shown in fig 2 to separate and then label the anatomical structures. Much better processing techniques can be employed for separating them and labeling each of the anatomical structure after obtaining the results as shown in fig 2 and fig 3. But, description and analysis of such techniques and processing of images using such techniques is beyond the scope of this paper. However, it is part of our on-going research and their results will be presented in the future.

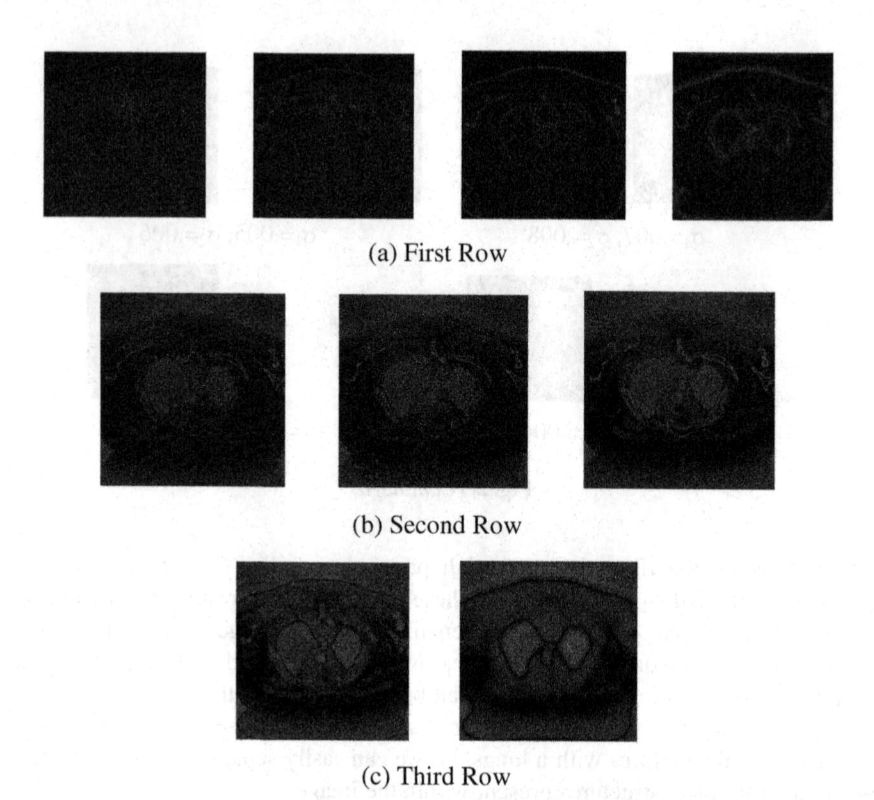

Fig. 3. Extracted regions from the HRCT image when another set of filters with different values of σ_1 and σ_2 is applied

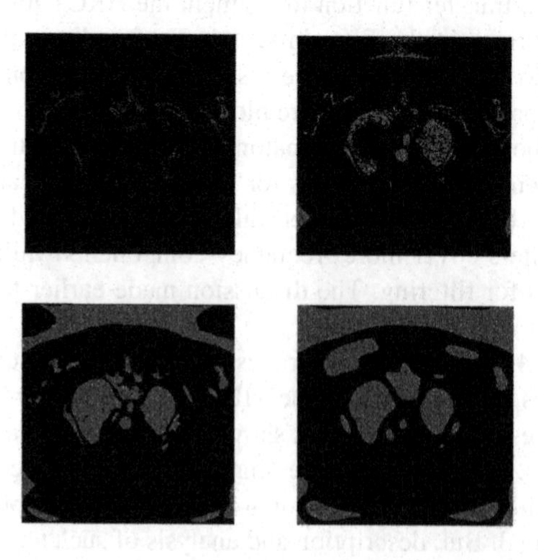

Fig. 4. Using thresholding to separate anatomical structures within HRCT image

5 Conclusions

In this paper, we proposed a new algorithm for multiscale segmentation of High Resolution CT (HRCT) images. The algorithm convolves a filter with the input image. The filter has two very important parameters which can be adjusted to make it a low pass or band pass or high pass filter. We demonstrated that various anatomical structures are segmented with the designed filter. For example, we gave examples of the extraction of tissues, lungs, bones and anatomical structures within the lung using the filter designed by optical transfer function at different resolutions.

References

1. Bin Zheng, Joseph K. Leader, Glenn S. Maitz, Brian E. Chapman, Carl R. Fuhrman, Robert M. Rogers, Frank C. Sciurba, Andrew Perez, Paul Thompson, Walter F. Good, David Gur, "A simple method for automated lung segmentation in X-ray CT images", Medical Imaging, Proc SPIE, 5032: 1455-1463, 2003.
2. Jan-Martin Kuhnigk, Horst K. hahn, Milo Hindennach, Volker Dicken, Stefan Krass, Heinz-Otto Peitgen, "Lung lobe segmentation by anatomy guided 3D watershed transform", Medical Imaging, Proc SPIE, 5032: 1482-1490, 2003.
3. L. Zhang, J.M. Reinhardt, "Detection of lung lobar fissures using fuzzy logic", Physiology and Function from Multidimensional images, Proc SPIE, 3660: 188-199, 1999.
4. L. Zhang, E.A Hoffman, J.M. Reinhardt, "Lung lobe segmentation by graph search with 3D shape constraints", Physiology and Function from Multidimensional images, Proc SPIE, 4321:204-215, 2001.
5. M.S. Brown, M.F. McNitt-Gray, N.J. Mankovich, J.G. GOldin, J. Hiller, L. S. Wilson, D.R. Aberle, "Method for Segmentation chest CT image data using an anatomical model: Preliminary results", IEEE Transactions on Medical Imaging, 16: 828-839, 1997.
6. Shree K. Nayar and Yasuo Nakagawa, "Shape from Focus: An effective Approach for Rough Surfaces", CRA90, pp 218-225, 1990.
7. Shree K. Nayar and Yasuo Nakagawa, "Shape from focus", IEEE Transactions on Pattern Analysis and Machine Intelligence, Vol. 16, No. 8, pp 824-831, August 1994.
8. M.S. Brown, M.F. McNitt-Gray, N.J. Mankovich, J.G. GOldin, J. Hiller, L. S. Wilson, D.R. Aberle, Knowledge based segmentation of thoracic computed tomography images for assessment of split lung function", Medical Physics, 27:592-598, 2000.
9. S. Hu, E.A. Hoffman, J.M. Reinhardt, "Automatic segmentation of accurate quantitation of volumetric X-ray CT images", IEEE Transactions on Medical Imaging, 20: 490-498, 2001.
10. D. Zhang, D.J. Valentino, "Segmentation of anatomical structures in X-ray computed tomography images using artifical neural networks", Proc SPIE 4684:1640-1652, 2001.
11. Ting-Chung Poon, Partha P. Banerjee., "Contemporary optical image processing", 1st ed. New York : Elsevier Science Ltd., 2001

Building Statistical Atlas of White Matter Fiber Tract Based on Vector/Tensor Field Reconstruction in Diffusion Tensor MRI

Yoshitaka Masutani, Shigeki Aoki, Osamu Abe, Mariko Yoshida, Haruyasu Yamada, Harushi Mori, Kenji Ino, and Kuni Ohtomo

Image Computing and Analysis Laboratory, Department of Radiology, The University of Tokyo Hospital, 7-3-1 Hongo, Bunkyo-ku, 113-8655 Tokyo, Japan
{masutani-utrad, saoki-tky, abediag-tky, myoshida-tky, hyamada-tky, hmori-tky, ino-rac, ohtomo-rad}@umin.ac.jp
http://www.ut-radiology.umin.jp/ical

Abstract. The diffusion tensor tractography has drawbacks such as low objectivity by interactive ROI setting and fiber-crossing. For coping with such problems, we are constructing a statistical atlas of white matter fiber tracts, in which probability density maps of tract structures are stored with diffusion tensor parameters on spatially normalized brain data. In building the atlas, our fiber tract modeling method plays a key role, which is based on a novel approach of vector/tensor field reconstruction avoiding fiber-crossings. In this abstract, we describe the modeling method, our statistical atlas, and the preliminary results.

1 Introduction

The diffusion tensor tractography (DTT) based on MR diffusion tensor imaging (DTI) is widely used as a powerful tool for visualizing and analyzing white matter fiber tract [1][2][3]. As is often discussed, however, one of the most important problems in DTT is tracking over fiber crossing. Though many improvement methods have been proposed [4], the problem still remains as a major weakness of DTT. For instance, it become clear when we try to extract a minor structure such as the auditory radiation fibers.

Another important problem of DTT is its low objectivity due to interactive configurations of regions of interest (ROI) for limiting structures for depiction. It is natural that such variation of results is produced because current DTT methods are categorized in the group of interactive segmentation methods [4].

Based on these backgrounds, we are currently constructing a statistical atlas in which probability density maps of fiber tract structures are stored with statistics of tensor parameters on spatially normalized brain data. Such atlas can provide objective information for configuring ROI in DTT. Indeed, our final goal of this study is development of a fully automated DTT method based on the atlas. In building the atlas, our tract modeling method plays a key role, which can cope with every specific structures of fiber tract even if it passes crossing area. It is used both in an interactive way and in a fully automated manner. First, the method is used interactively for building our statistical atlas. Then, once the atlas is constructed, it works in fully automated way for DTT. Fig.1 shows the scheme of our automated DTT.

G. Bebis et al. (Eds.): ISVC 2005, LNCS 3804, pp. 84 – 91, 2005.

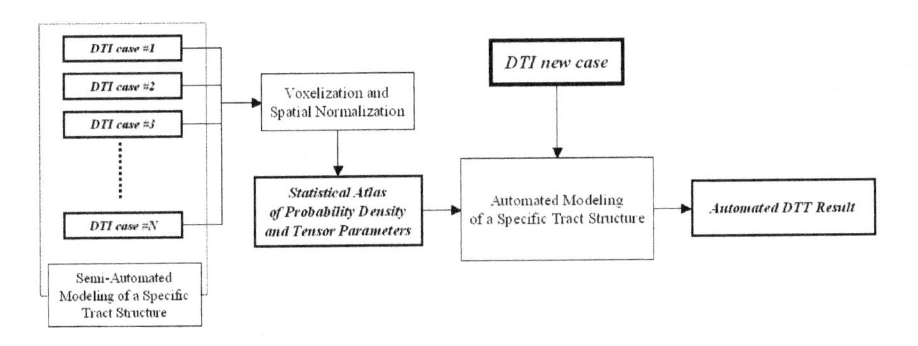

Fig. 1. Schematic Diagram of Our Automated DTT Method

In this abstract, we focus on the following two topics; (1) Development of a new fiber tract modeling method based on vector/tensor field reconstruction, and (2) Building a statistical atlas of specific fiber tract as probability density map and normalized DTI data. Several important works related to ours are found in the literatures as followings.

Regarding normalized DTI, Jones et al. have shown the first normalized DTI data with tensor statistics from 10 data sets [5], and then Park and his colleagues have presented a result with 16 DTI data sets by using registration algorithms of higher degrees of freedom (DOF) [6]. We follow their basic methodology regarding normalized DTI map, except for our dispersion representation by covariance matrix. In addition, we will build probability density maps of specific tract structures for our purpose, which are our original contribution from this study.

An anatomical atlas of specific fiber tract systems was built by Wakana et al. by using single DTI data set [7]. It seems that their atlas is missing several minor structures such as the auditory radiation fiber that is hard to depict with conventional algorithms. Our atlas covers such structures based on our modeling method, and describes further statistical information of spatial probability density and tensor parameters for each specific tract system based on multiple DTI data sets.

Another important concept of statistical analysis of DTT similar to ours was used in the study by Corouge and her colleagues [8], in which statistical analysis of line data as fiber tract model is performed. They presented a successful result of modal modeling of the cortico-spinal tract by eigen analysis of line data sets from multi-subject. In the viewpoint of describing variation of fiber tract shapes, it is effective and is applicable to segmentation or automated modeling of specific fiber tract. One of our purposes includes, however, describing variations of tensor parameters. Therefore, our atlas should be in the form of volume data set.

2 Materials and Methods

2.1 Fiber Tract Modeling Based on Partial Vector/Tensor Field Reconstruction

Our fiber tract modeling method is based on partial reconstruction of vector/tensor field that represent fiber orientation. The reconstruction is performed by using radial basis function (RBF)-based interpolation. The typical modeling process is as follows.

(1) Interactive selection of control voxels by ROI setting except for crossing area, and calculation of diffusion tensor (and its principle vector; $\mathbf{e}_1$)* for the voxels.
(2)* Intra-ROI rectification, and inter-ROI rectification of the $\mathbf{e}_1$ vectors based on analysis of vector field topology.
(3) RBF-based interpolation of vector/tensor field with limited number of control voxels in component-wise manner
(4) Streamline propagation in the field from the location of control voxels. Termination criteria, such as FA etc., are similar to conventional tracking algorithms.

Note that * shows a process used only in the vector field reconstruction version [9]. An example of the results is shown in Fig.2.

The parts of fibers through the corpus callosum (CC) run across vertical tracts such as cortico-spinal tracts (CST). A conventional $\mathbf{e}_1$ tracking started from the CC often merges the vertical tract group and mostly fails to pass through the crossing (Fig.2b). In our approach, by selecting ROI consisting of over 1000 voxels avoiding the crossing part as shown in Fig.2c, fibers through CC and beyond the crossing can be also depicted as shown in Fig.2d. The selected ROI voxels exist not only on the shown slice but also spread on several adjacent slices.

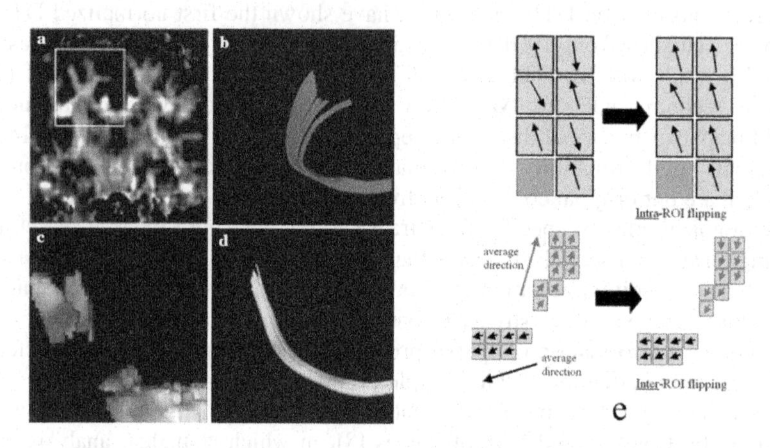

Fig. 2. Modeling based on Partial Vector Field Reconstruction. (a) coronal section of color-coded $\mathbf{e}_1$ image, (b) fiber tracking from the corpus callosum by conventional e_1 tracking, (c) ROI (FA>0.3) used for vector field reconstruction, (d) a modeling result by proposed method (background in b-d is FA image), and (e) vector rectification considering vector field topology in two steps.

One of the most important advantages of this technique is that fiber modeling can be performed smoothly over fiber crossing region by using original tensor information included in the data set without prior knowledge.

The important difference between vector version and tensor version is that, as shown in the step (2) and in Fig.2, part of the control vectors must be rectified (flipped) so that whole vector field is smooth and has no singular point such as attracting focus. This condition is realized by analyzing vector field topology [10, 11] so that the number of singular points is minimized.

2.2 Building Statistical Atlas of Fiber Tracts

2.2.1 Normalized DTI Data of Whole Brain

We construct our original version of normalized DTI data set for our purpose. We currently employ SPM software for registration [12] of multi-subject DTI data sets. We performed registration with single channel of T2WI data sets. For describing statistics of diffusion tensor, we adopted mean tensor and covariance matrix of the sample tensors. Beyond the scalar metric for tensor dispersion, we introduced covariance matrix for computing Mahalanobis distance used as tensor dissimilarity in classifying control tensors for the subsequent tensor field reconstruction.

A feature vector $\mathbf{d}(\mathbf{x})$ derived from a diffusion tensor is defined at a location $\mathbf{x}$. The feature vector has six components corresponding to independent six components of diffusion tensor as;

$$\mathbf{d}(\mathbf{x}) = (D_{xx}(\mathbf{x}), D_{yy}(\mathbf{x}), D_{zz}(\mathbf{x}), D_{xy}(\mathbf{x}), D_{yz}(\mathbf{x}), D_{zx}(\mathbf{x}))^t . \quad (1)$$

The mean vector $\mathbf{m}$ and covariance matrix $\mathbf{S}$ of the diffusion feature vectors calculated from N samples are;

$$\mathbf{m}(\mathbf{x}) = \frac{1}{N}\sum_i^N \mathbf{d}_i(\mathbf{x}) \text{, and} \quad (2)$$

$$\mathbf{S}(\mathbf{x}) = \sum_i^N (\mathbf{d}_i(\mathbf{x}) - \mathbf{m}(\mathbf{x}))(\mathbf{d}_i(\mathbf{x}) - \mathbf{m}(\mathbf{x}))^t . \quad (3)$$

Thus, each voxel has statistical parameters of diffusion tensors in our DTI atlas.

2.2.2 Probability Density Map for Fiber Tract Structures

Probability density map is created for each structure of fiber tract system. The results of interactive modeling by using our method are line node data in the first state. Next, they are converted to a volume data set in which a voxel has non-zero value only if the line data pass through the voxel. The voxel values are graded by the total intersection length of the voxel and lines for anti-aliasing purpose. Then, same transformation as source DTI data for normalization is applied to each probability map. Finally, by averaging the maps of the samples and by proper scaling between 0 and 1, probability density map $P(\mathbf{x})$ for each structure is completed. In addition, the tensor parameters collected in the reconstructed tensor field are also stored.

2.3 Tensor Dissimilarity Definition Based on Mahalanobis Distance

In performing DTT with a new data set based on our automated scheme, it is necessary to classify diffusion tensors in new data set for selecting tensors used for tensor field reconstruction. It is determined based on the Mahalanobis distance (MD) [13], which is superior to other scalar metric such as Euclidean distance because parameter distribution is taken into account in MD. The Mahalanobis distance D^2_M between

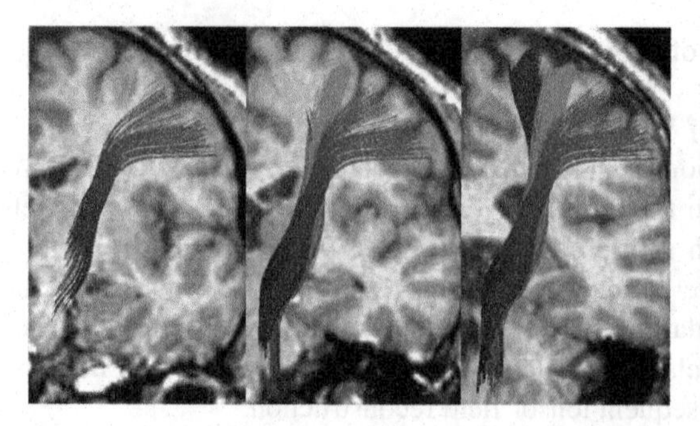

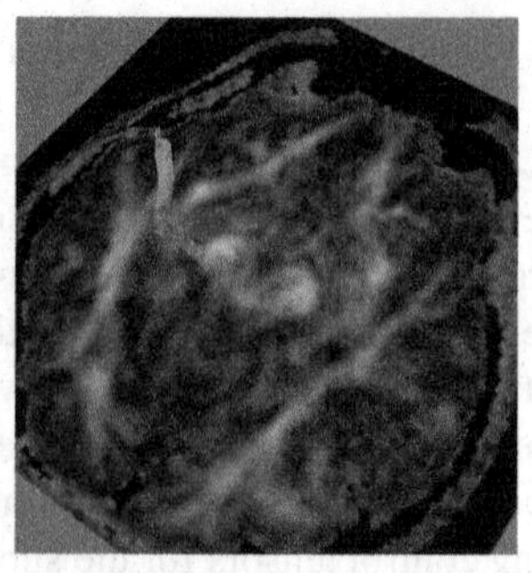

Fig. 3. Examples of Semi-Automated Modeling based on Our Modeling Method. Left: CBT (red), CST from hand motor area (green), and CST from lower limb motor area (blue) are shown with coronal slice images of three different positions (the slice in the left is in the most front position). Right: The auditory radiation fibers with a slice of FA image.

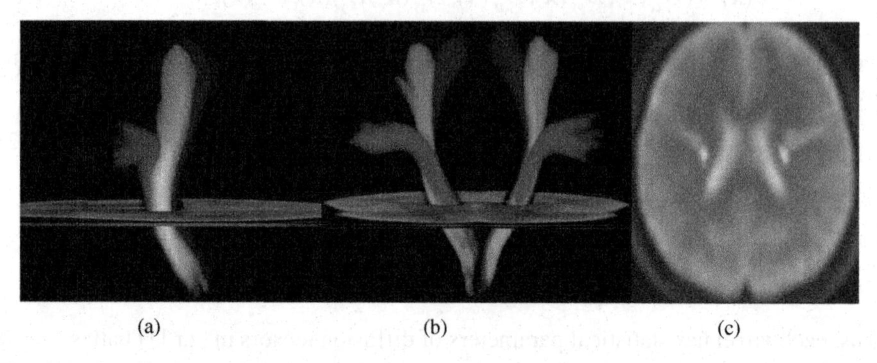

(a) (b) (c)

Fig. 4. Probability Density Map of the CBT and the CST. CBT (red), CST from hand motor area (green), and CST from lower limb motor area (blue) are displayed by volume rendering with a slice of normalized brain in (a) side view and (b) front view. (c) a slice of the probability density map superimposed with the normalized T2WI.

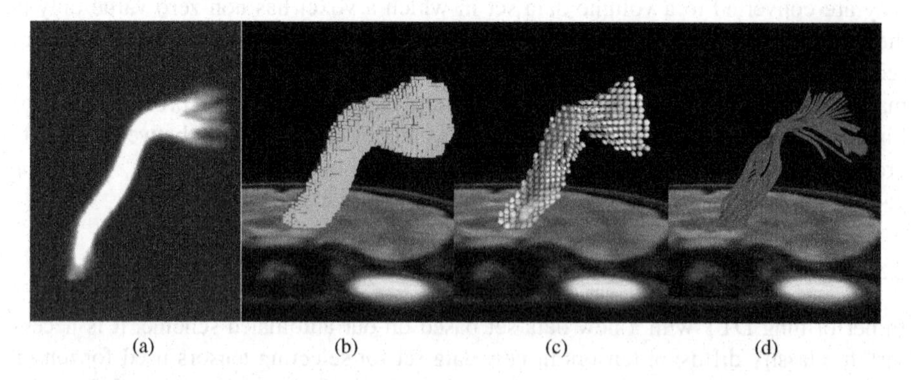

(a) (b) (c) (d)

Fig. 5. DTT based on Probability Density Atlas: example of the left CBT. (a) Probability density map, (b) isosurface of probability density map ($P_{LCBT}(\mathbf{x})>0$), (c) captured diffusion tensors visualized by ellipsoids with anisotropic color coding, and (d) the result of DTT. Except for (a), an axial slice of T2WI at the pons level is superimposed.

sample tensor as feature vector **d** and normalized tensor statistics (**m** and **S**) at the corresponding location is defined as;

$$D_M^2(\mathbf{d},\mathbf{m}) = (\mathbf{d}-\mathbf{m})^t \mathbf{S}^{-1}(\mathbf{d}-\mathbf{m}) \cdot \quad (4)$$

The simplest way to pick up tensors based on our atlas is to select tensors that satisfy $D^2_M(\mathbf{x}) < T_D$, and $P(\mathbf{x}) > 0$. An example is shown in the next section.

3 Results

(1) *Semi-Automated Modeling*
By using clinical data sets, fiber tract modeling was performed for several types of structures. In Fig.3, examples of the corticobulbar tract (CBT), the CST from motor areas and the auditory radiation fibers are shown. The numbers of ROI used for modeling were typically from 3 to 5. Note that the CBT and the auditory radiation fibers are often very hard to depict with the conventional tracking algorithms. The CBT and CST from motor areas that are categorized in the pyramidal tracts are important for neurosurgery. For our neurosurgical purpose [14][15], we have started our atlas construction from the pyramidal tracts.

(2) *Building Atlas by 10 Data Sets*
By using 10 data sets of normal volunteers, we have constructed the first version of our statistical atlas. The DTI data sets are in 256x256 matrix size of axial planes with 30 directions of MPGS, which were virtually optimized by Jones et al. [16]. The left and right CBT and CST from the motor areas were modeled by using our interactive method. The results were spatially normalized onto normalized brain. Fig.4 shows the probability density maps of the CBT and CST visualized by volume rendering.

(3) *Semi-Automated Atlas-based DTT*
Though we did not reach to the fully automated DTT of our final goal, we performed our first atlas-based DTT, by using a new DTI data set that is not included in the atlas. DTT was performed for the left CBT after capturing tensors by probability density $P(\mathbf{x})$ and MD threshold T_D adjusted interactively (Fig.5). The colors of tensors show degree of anisotropy (red is high, and yellow is low). Several undesired trajectories, such as ones reaching to the sensory areas, were manually removed.

4 Discussion

Our modeling method has high flexibility and high DOF based on the vector/tensor field reconstruction. In that sense, however, the method requires the user's neuro-anatomical knowledge at expert level because it can create any shape of tracts by bridging several ROI apart. In our study, all the modeling was done by experienced neuro-radiologists. In addition, the ROI configuration is performed quantitatively by using tensor parameter-based region growing implemented in our software [17]. For more objective ROI configuration, we are currently developing a scheme for detecting fiber crossing interface based on our extended definition of "tensor degeneracy" derived from tensor field topology analysis [18]. The method proposed by Donell et al. [19] may also be helpful.

In building our atlas, registration plays key role because it determines degree of dispersions. It is natural that a registration method with low DOF yields high dispersion. However, too high DOF in registration causes too low dispersion of statistical atlas, which is not useful for control tensor capturing. It is needed a new scheme for determining optimal DOF for building such atlases, which is included in our future work. For achieving our final goal of fully automated DTT, the methods for grouping trajectories such as [20] seem to be necessary as an additional processing for removing undesired trajectories. Though such processes are needed to be automated, our scheme of atlas based DTT seems to be a promising approach for yielding objective and quantitative results of DTT. It is expected that many applications are feasible with our atlas in addition to DTT. Currently, we consider our application for analysis of aging, Alzheimer disease, schizophrenia, and infarction, in which deformation of white matter is rarely observed. In such cases, tensor parameters, mainly diffusion anisotropy, can be significantly changed.

Though the most important work is validation of our DTT, it is not so simple. One solution can be the leave-one-out method for cross-validation between learning samples for the atlas and new data. Currently, the validation study is in progress in parallel with increasing the number of samples.

5 Summary

We have developed a novel fiber tract modeling technique based on vector/tensor field reconstruction, and built a statistical atlas of fiber tracts from 10 DTI data sets.

Acknowledgement

This work was partially supported by the grant-in-aid for scientific research on priority areas; "Intelligent Assistance in Diagnosis of Multi-Dimensional Medical Images" from the ministry of education, culture, sports, science, and technology, Japan.

References

1. Mori S, Crain BJ, et al. : Three-dimensional tracking of axonal projections in the brain by magnetic resonance imaging. Ann Neurol 45:265-269, 1999
2. Conturo TE, Lori NF, Cul TS, et al., Tracking neuronal fiber pathways in the living human brain. Proc. Natl. Acad. Sci. 96:10422-10427, 1999
3. Basser PJ, Pajevic S, Pierpaoli C, et al., In Vivo Fiber Tractography Using DT-MRI Data. Magnetic Resonance in Medicine 44:625-632, 2000
4. Mori S., and van Zijl PCM, Fiber Tracking: Principles and Strategies – A Technical Review, NMR Biomed. Vol.15, 468-480, 2002
5. Jones DK, et al., Spatial Normalization and Averaging of Diffusion Tensor MRI Data Sets, NeuroImage vol.17, pp592–617, 2002
6. Park HJ, et al., Spatial normalization of diffusion tensor MRI using multiple channels, NeuroImage vol.20, pp.1995–2009, 2003

7. Wakana S., et al., Fiber Tract–based Atlas of Human White Matter Anatomy, Radiology vol.230, pp.77-87, 2004
8. Corouge I., et al., A Statistical Shape Model of Individual Fiber Tracts Extracted from Diffusion Tensor MRI, proc. of MICCAI2004, pp.671-679, 2004
9. Masutani Y, Aoki S, et al., RBF-based reconstruction of fiber orientation vector field for white matter fiber tract modeling, proc. of ISMRM'04, 2004
10. Globus A., et al., A tool for visualizing the topology of three-dimensional vector fields, proc. of the 2nd conference on Visualization '91, pp.33-40, 1991
11. Helman JL. and L. Hesselink, Visualization of Vector Field Topology in Fluid Flows, IEEE CG&A, vol.11, no.3, pp. 36-46, 1991.
12. Ashburner J, Friston, KJ, Nonlinear spatial normalization using basis functions. Hum. Brain Mapp. Vol.7, no.4, pp.254–266, 1999
13. Taguchi G and Jugulum R, The Mahalanobis-Taguchi Strategy: A Pattern Technology System, John Wiley & Sons, 2002
14. K. Kamada, A. Morita, Y. Masutani, et al., Combined utilization of tractography-integrated functional neuronavigation and direct fiber stimulation, Journal of Neurosurgery, vol.202, no.4, pp.664-672., 2005
15. K. Maruyama, K Kamada, S. Aoki, et al., Integration of three-dimensional corticospinal tractography in treatment planning of gamma-knife radiosurgery, Journal of Neurosurgery, vol.202, no.4, pp.673-677, 2005
16. Jones DK, Horsfield MA, Simmons A, Optimal strategies for measuring diffusion in anisotropic systems by magnetic resonance imaging, Magnetic Resonance in Medicine 42, pp.515–525, 1999
17. http://www.ut-radiology.umin.jp/people/masutani/dTV.htm
18. Hesselink L., et al., The Topology of Symmetric, Second-Order 3D Tensor Fields, IEEE trans. visualization and CG, vol.3, no.1, pp.1-11, 1997
19. Donnell LO, Grimson WEL, and Westin CF, Interface Detection in Diffusion Tensor MRI, proc. of MICCAI2004, pp360-367, 2004
20. Brun A., Knutsson H., et al., Clustering Fiber Traces Using Normalized Cuts, proc. of MICCAI2004, pp.368-375, 2004

Interactive 3D Heart Chamber Partitioning with a New Marker-Controlled Watershed Algorithm*

Xinwei Xue

School of Computing, University of Utah
xwxue@cs.utah.edu

Abstract. Watershed transform has been widely used in medical image segmentation. One fundamental problem with it is over-segmentation. There are mainly two approaches to deal with this problem: hierarchical segmentation and segmentation with markers. The markers, either automatically extracted or interactively generated, are mostly used in the homotopy modification of morphological gradients prior to the watershed segmentation. Most of the current techniques does not incorporate domain knowledge of the data. In this paper, we propose a two-step marker-controlled watershed segmentation algorithm with simple domain knowledge incorporated: (1) Modified image foresting transform (IFT) algorithm is used to produce the initial segmentation; (2) The marker-controlled watershed region merging process is incorporated with domain knowledge. A min-cut criterion for region merging is proposed. This approach is effectively applied to the interactive 3D heart chamber partitioning.

1 Introduction

Image segmentation is a very important task in medical image analysis, which provide important information for medical diagnosis, surgical procedures, and realtime navigation. Various techniques has been developed for different medical subjects from different imaging modalities. Cardiac imaging has been such a subject, where heart chamber segmentation plays an essential role. Due to clinical demands, left ventricle(LV) segmentation has attracted lots of attention, and a vast literature exists for this subject, as shown in Suri's survey [1].

In our medical application, we are interested in the segmentation of each heart chambers, especially left and right atriums from 3D CT data. The result of the segmentation is used for heart registration and surgical navigation.

There are several categories in segmentation techniques: point based techniques, region based techniques, and contour based techniques [2]. Point based techniques rely heavily on intensity values and is prone to noise. Contour-based segmentation techniques such as active contours or level set methods are iterative processes and computationally intensive. Simple image editing tools requires lots of interaction of user, and is not effective for our application: the left and right sides of the heart are usually connected in a way that is difficult to determine the connection by eyeballing. The fast competitive region growing feature provided by watershed algorithm suggests a promising approach for this task.

* We are thankful to Dr. Chenyang Xu and Dr. Yiyong Sun for helpful discussions.

G. Bebis et al. (Eds.): ISVC 2005, LNCS 3804, pp. 92–99, 2005.

Though fully automatic segmentation is desirable, it is not reliable in reality due to variations in acquired image quality. Here we propose a semi-automatic approach using watershed algorithm controlled by interactively placed markers. Once the markers are in place, our algorithm can automatically segment the heart into four chambers. Due to the effect of the contrast agent, the whole heart can be easily extracted by interactively selecting a intensity threshold. Then the proposed marker-controlled algorithm is applied on the binary heart volume. The main contribution of this paper lies in the following aspects:

1) We incorporate domain knowledge, i.e. the shape property of heart into the algorithm. The anatomy shows that the heart has "neck-like" shape (or concave) in the connections between left and right sides of the heart and between the chambers.

2) A min-cut criterion is proposed for the new marker controlled watershed segmentation. The min-cut concept originally comes from graph-cut algorithms, here we use it as a region merging criterion. Firstly, a modified image foresting transform(IFT) is applied to produce primitive regions; then the regions, treated as a graph, and controlled by markers, are merged by this criterion. The segmentation cuts at the minimum-connection between neighbored regions.

3) Our algorithm has been successfully applied to heart chamber segmentation and is currently being used in imaging product. And it is effective in partitioning binary data where objects has neck-like concave shape.

The rest of the paper is organized as follows: Section 2 describes the related work; Section 3 introduces our approach in detail; In Section 4, we discuss the results. And finally, conclusion is drawn in Section 5.

2 Related Work

The watershed transform, generally defined in terms of SKIZ (skeleton by influence zone) [3] has been widely applied to image segmentation, especially for medical images (e.g. [4]), ever since introduced by Lantuejoul and Beucher [5]. Watershed segmentation can be applied to both gray scale images or binary images. For gray scale images, the watershed transform is applied to the morphological gradient of the images. For binary images, the transform is applied to the inverted distance transform. Basically, the watershed algorithm transforms the image into local minima-based catchment basins and watersheds.

One problem of watershed segmentation is its severe over-segmentation. Two approaches exist to overcome this problem: hierarchical segmentation [6], and segmentation with markers [7, 8, 9]. In the former approach, the height of the watershed (the lowest saddle point separating two neighbored basins), also called dynamics, is used to control the region merging process. In the marker-controlled approach, the markers, either automatically extracted or interactively placed, are used in homotopy modification of the morphological gradient prior to watershed transform, reducing the number of local minima of the image, and thus the number of primitive regions.

The markers are usually applied in the pixel level, which controls the flooding process. An alternative approach is to apply markers in a region level, controlling the merging process of the primitive regions resulted from the initial watershed transform. Haris [10] combined region adjacency graph (RAG) representation of image regions and a nearest neighbor graph in the hierarchical segmentation. Meyer [11] describes a unified framework for watershed segmentation with markers in both pixel and region level, and minimum spanning tree algorithm is used. Markers in the region level, gives flexibility for interactive segmentation.

In terms of implementation, Vincent and Soille's algorithm based on immersion simulation [8] has been widely used in medical image processing. Roerdink and Meijster [12] gives a survey of existing watershed implementation algorithms. Recently, Lotufo and Falcao [13] developed an optimal watershed algorithm based on the Image Foresting Transform(IFT), where the watershed is seen as the solution of the shortest-path forest problem in the graph theory framework. Nguyen et al. [14] reformulates the watershed segmentation as energy minimization problem and boundary smoothness prior is incorporated.

Our algorithm is different from the algorithms available from literature. Firstly, most of the existing watershed algorithms does not incorporate the domain knowledge of the image data. We incorporate simple yet effective domain knowledge; Secondly, we propose a min-cut criterion for region merging, which is different from measures like watershed height or its analogy [15], nearest neighbor, or minimum distance, etc. Thirdly, we apply the marker in region-level with a novel implementation.

3 The Proposed Approach

3.1 The 3D Heart Chamber Segmentation Work Flow

The work flow for the heart chamber segmentation is shown in Figure 1. The input is 3D CT/MR gray-scale volume. The binary whole heart is first extracted from the gray-scale image. Since the heart is solid structure, we can apply a hole-removal algorithm on the binary image. Then the Euclidean distance transform is performed on the holes-filled binary image. Prior to applying watershed transformation, the distance map is filtered (by a median filter, for example) and inverted. The local minima of the inverted distance map is detected. The hole-removal and filtering process helps to reduce the number of minima in the image, which, in turn, reduces the number of primitive regions generated by the watershed algorithm. Finally the IFT watershed algorithm is applied, and our marker-controlled region merging algorithm is performed on the primitive regions. If four markers are placed in the four chambers area, then the final output is a labeled volume with labels ranging from 1-4. We can then extract each chamber by label. As shown in Figure 1, to the right of the dashed vertical line, all the operations are performed internally and need only to perform once, while the marker-controlled region merging part is an interactive process. The user can visually manipulate markers to generate desirable results. If the result is not satisfactory, the user can erase the old markers and place new ones.

The markers can be placed by picking marker points from 2D slice views or from the 3D volume view. For each region of interest, the number of markers

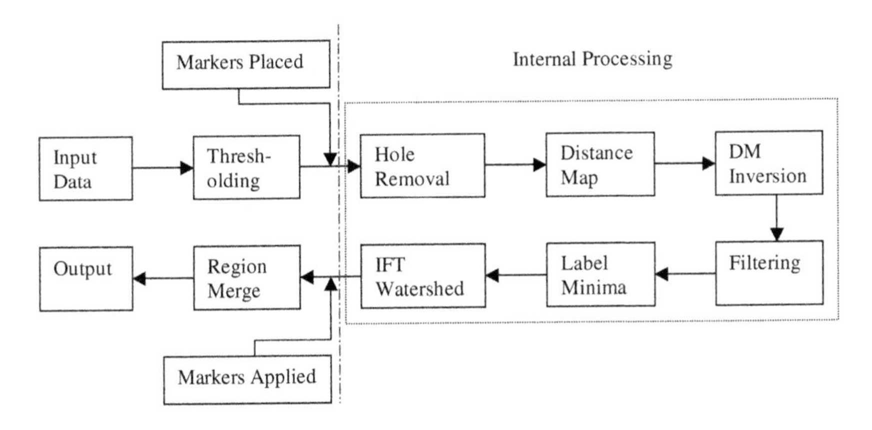

Fig. 1. Heart Chamber Segmentation Work Flow

to be placed are not necessarily limited to one. Instead, a set of markers can be used to represent one heart chamber, but with the same marker label. Thus we can get robust segmentation.

3.2 The Modified IFT Watershed Algorithm

The flooding process in watershed segmentation starts from the original or modified local minima. The IFT algorithm [13] treats the image as a graph, each pixel/voxel as a node. The watershed transform is solved as a shortest-path forest problem. It finds for each node the shortest path connecting it to the nearest root node, which are the marker nodes or local minima nodes. Let $C(u)$ denote the cost along the path from its nearest marker up to node u, $W(u, v)$ (here, $W(u, v) = InvDist(v)$) denote the weight associated with the arc (u, v), $L(p)$ is the input marker image(the minima node of inverted distance transform are initialized to different labels) and also the output of the watershed partitioning. flag(p) indicates whether a node has been processed or not. The modified IFT algorithm works as follows: The queue used in figure 2 is an ordered queue. More detailed information about this algorithm can be found in [13, 16]. We chose IFT watershed algorithm because it is specifically appropriate for segmenting binary images, where the Euclidean distance transform is used. There is great similarity between the Euclidean distance transform and the IFT flooding process.

We made several important modifications to the original IFT algorithm to incorporate our shape prior. First, the markers nodes in the figure are the minima nodes of the inverted distance transform. The cost of marker nodes are initialized to its minima values. Second, we label the watershed pixels while labeling the primitive regions, as shown in the bold font in Figure 2. For each newly labeled pixel, if it has a neighbor labeled as belonging to another region, then it is relabeled as a watershed pixel. To make sure that the watershed is one thin layer of pixels, 6-connected(for 3D) neighborhood is used for labeling primitive

```
1. Initialization
   a) for all nodes p do
        flag(p) = TEMP;
   b) for all non-marker nodes p do
        C(p) = infinity;
   c) for all marker nodes p do
        C(p) = 0; EnQueue(p,0);
2. Propagation
 While QueueNotEmpty() do
   a) v = DeQueueMin();
   b) flag(v) = DONE;
   c) for each p neighbor of v with flag(p) == TEMP do
        if max{C(v), W(v,p)} < C(p)
          C(p) == max{C(v), W(v,p)}; L(p) = L(v);
        IsWS = false;
        for each neighbor q of p and q is not background
           if L(q) != L(p)
              L(q) = WShed; IsWS = true; continue;
       Endfor
       If IsWS == false
          if p is in queue then DeQueue(p);
          EnQueue(p,C(p));
```

Fig. 2. Modified IFT Algorithm

```
For each primitive region Ri
  Ri.mlabel = -1;

For each watershed element Wi in the list
    R1 = Wi.R1;
    R2 = Wi.R2;
    WS = Wi.wslabel;
    If R1.mlabel = = -1 && R2.mlabel = = -1
         Put R1, R2 and WS on to the equivalency table.
    If R1.mlabel != -1 && R2.mlabel = = -1
         Put R1, R2 and WS onto equivalency table
         R2.mlabel = R1.mlabel
         For all region Ri equivalent to R2
            Ri.mlabel = R1.mlabel
            Put Ri on to equivalency table of R1
         End For
    If R1.mlabel = = -1 && R2.mlabel ! = -1
         Put R1, R2 and WS onto equivalency table
         R1.mlabel = R2.mlabel
         For all region Ri equivalent to R1
            Ri.mlabel = R2.mlabel
            Put Ri on to equivalency table of R2
         End For
    If R1.mlabel != -1 && R2.mlabel != -1
         Do nothing
End For
```

Fig. 3. Region Merging with Markers

regions, while 26-connected neighborhood is used for watersheds. This algorithm creates a list of primitive regions and a labeled image.

3.3 The Marker-Controlled Region Merging Algorithm

After applying the IFT watershed algorithm, we get the primitive regions and watersheds. The regions are then merged according the min-cut criterion: the neighbored regions with largest physical connection is merged first, while the merging stops at the regions with minimum connections. Here the watershed size, i.e. the number of pixels in the watershed that separates two neighbored regions, is used as a measure of physical connection of the regions. Our new approach to the marker-controlled region merging algorithm lies in the following three steps:

1) Relabel watersheds.
Relabel watershed pixels according to the two regions it separates. The watershed pixels that separates the same two regions, will be assigned to a unique label. A list of watershed elements is created. Each watershed element records the neighbored region label and watershed size. In the end, a watershed table is produced.

2) Sort the watershed list in the descending order of watershed size.
The watersheds are processed in the descending order of their size. This is where our shape prior knowledge and min-cut criterion are incorporated: the shape of the heart indicates that connections between chambers is narrower than connections between regions residing in the same chamber, thus we can merge regions with larger connections first and safely cut at the regions with minimum connections. Also, it is very important to process the larger regions earlier. This helps

to avoid mistakenly splitting large neighbor regions that belongs to the same chamber. Usually the larger the neighbored regions, the larger the watersheds. Thus, we can be sure that the segmentation will not result in major errors.

3) Marker-controlled region merging and relabeling.
In this step, the markers picked interactively are bound with the primitive regions where they fall on. The corresponding region is assigned a label associated with the marker. If the marker falls on a watershed, one of the neighbored regions is selected and assigned the marker label. A region equivalency table(of regions merged) is maintained during the merging process.

Starting from the watershed element list, the neighbored regions that are separated by the largest watershed size are merged first. There are four cases depending on the fact that whether the two neighbored regions has been relabeled with a marker label, as shown in figure 3. If the two primitive regions were not assigned marker label previously, the watershed and the two regions are placed on the equivalency table. If only one of them has a marker label, the watershed, the other region and its equivalent regions are assigned to the same new marker label. If the two primitive region have different marker labels, they are not placed onto equivalent table, and the watershed is assigned to the marker label of one of the neighbored regions. The merged regions will be updated to the same marker label.

The merging process terminates when each watershed element in the list has been processed. Thus the image is relabeled with the new marker labels. Each region of interest(associated with a marker) can then be selected by specifying a marker label.

4 Results and Analysis

The proposed algorithm has been successfully applied to the 3D heart chamber partitioning task. Several 3D CT/MR heart datasets from different patients have been experimented. The radiologists in a major hospital has done clinical validation and show very positive results. We used a PC with 2.0 Hz CPU with 1GB Memory to measure the performance. The fairly optimized algorithm can segment the 256x256x256 and 512x512x512 volumes in less than 20 seconds and 2 minutes respectively. Felkel et al. [17] discusses optimization methods of the IFT algorithm to further improve performance. Figures from (a) to (h)in figure 4 shows the volume view of original CT, the extracted binary whole heart image, the left side, right side, and the four chambers segmented by our algorithm. Experiments have been conducted to compare the interactive segmentation using our algorithm with the hierarchical watershed segmentation application implemented in ITK (Insight Segmentation & Registration Toolkit) [18], and our approach generates better result. The comparison pictures are not shown here due to limited space. This algorithm can be applied to other images that have similar shape property, and it is especially good for binary image segmentation.

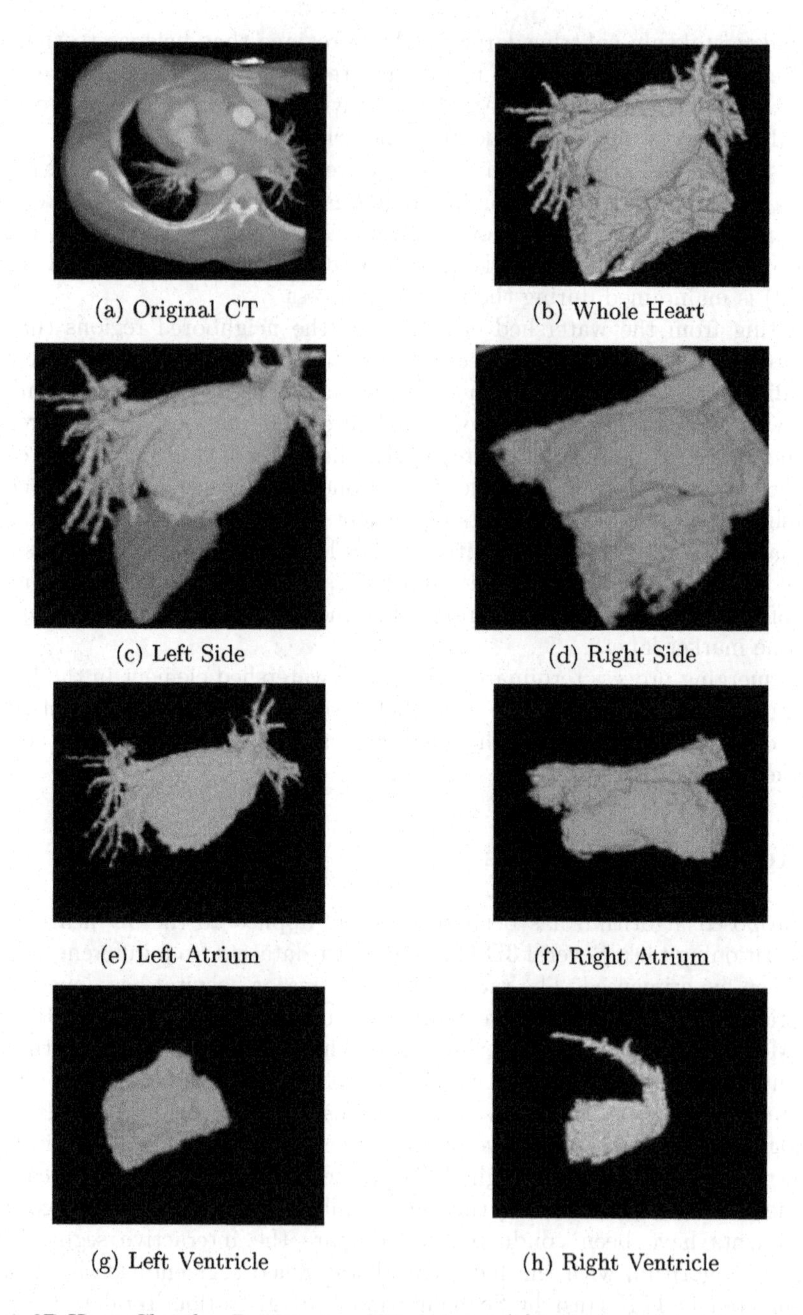

(a) Original CT
(b) Whole Heart
(c) Left Side
(d) Right Side
(e) Left Atrium
(f) Right Atrium
(g) Left Ventricle
(h) Right Ventricle

Fig. 4. 3D Heart Chamber Partitioning. Whole heart (b) is first extracted from original data(a): our algorithm can also be used to segment the whole heart (b) from (a) by placing one set of markers in object, while another set on the background. Then left side (c) and right side (d) are extracted from (b) by placing two sets of markers. The four champers (e)-(h) are segmented by placing four sets of markers on (b).

5 Conclusions

A new approach to the marker-controlled watershed segmentation algorithm incorporated with object shape property and min-cut region merging criterion has been proposed. It is simple, yet very effective. The two-step segmentation algorithm introduced in this paper has been successfully applied to the interactive 3D heart chamber partitioning problem. Extension of this algorithm to solve other partition tasks with similar neck-like shape is readily available.

References

1. Suri, J.: Computer vision, pattern recognition and image processing in left ventricle segmentation: the last 50 years. Pattern Analysis and Applications **3** (2000) 209–42
2. Pham, D., Xu, C., Prince, J.: A survey of current methods in medical image segmentation. Annual Review of Biomedical Engineering **2** (2000) 315–337
3. Soille, P.: Morphological Image Analysis. Springer-Verlag (1999)
4. Riddell, C., Brigger, P., Carson, R., Bacharach, S.: The watershed algorithm: a method to segment noisy pet transmission images. IEEE Transactions on Nuclear Science **46** (1999) 713–719
5. Lantuejoul, C., Beucher, S.: Use of watersheds in contour detection. In: Proc. Int'l Workshop on Image Processing, Real-Time Edge and Motion Detection/Estimation, Rennes, France (1979)
6. Najman, L., Schmitt, M.: Geodesic saliency of watershed contours and hierarchical segmentation. IEEE Transactions on PAMI **18** (1996) 1163–1173
7. Meyer, F., Beucher, S.: Morphological segmentation. Journal of Visual Communication and Image Understanding **1** (1990) 21–46
8. Vincent, L., Soille, P.: Watersheds in digital spaces: an efficient algorithm based on immersion simulations. IEEE Transactions on PAMI **13** (1991) 583–598
9. Rivest, J., Beucher, S.: Marker-controlled segmentation: an application to electrical borehole imaging. Journal of Electronic Imaging **1** (1992) 136–142
10. Haris, K., Efstratiadis, S., Maglaveras, N., Katsaggelos, A.: Hybrid image segmentation using watersheds and fast region merging. IEEE Transaction on Image Processing **7** (1998) 1684–1699
11. Meyer, F.: An overview of morphological segmentation. International Journal of Pattern Recognition and Artificial Intelligence **15** (2001) 1089–1118
12. J.B.T.M., R., Meijster, A.: The watershed transform: definitions, algorithms and parallelization strategies. Fundamenta Informaticae **41** (2001) 187–228
13. Lotufo, R., Falcao, A.: The ordered queue and the optimality of the watershed approaches. In: Math. Morphology and its Applications to Image and Signal Processing. Volume 18. Kluwer (2000) 341–350
14. Nguyen, H., Worring, M., van den Boomgaard, R.: Watersnakes: Energy-driven watershed segmentation. IEEE Trans. on PAMI **25** (2003) 330–342
15. Mangan, A., Whitaker, R.: Partioning 3d surface meshes using watershed segmentation. IEEE Transactions on Visualization and Computer Graphics **5** (1999)
16. Falcao, A., Stolfi, J., Lotufo, R.: The image foresting transform: theory, algorithms, and applications. IEEE Transactions on PAMI **26** (2004) 19–29
17. Felkel, P., Wegenkittl, R., Bruckschwaiger, M.: Implementation and complexity of the watershed-from-markers algorithm computed as a minimal cost forest. In: Proc. Eurographics. (2001)
18. Cates, J.: Itk application:segmentation editor. http://www.itk.org (2003)

Inferring Cause/Effect Relationships in Multi-sensor Ambient Intelligence Systems

S. Piva and C.S. Regazzoni

Department of Biophysical and Electronic Engineering, University of Genoa

Abstract. In this work a learning technique to provide an Ambient Intelligence (smart space) system with the capacity of predicting variation events in its own internal state is presented. The system and the interacting users are modeled through the instantaneous state vectors obtained as output of two trained Self Organizing Map-based classifiers. The information processed by the system is collected by two sensors sets monitoring several internal and external system variables. Starting from the hypothesis that the user actions have a direct influence on internal system state variables (e.g. work load on personal computers computation or storage devices in a University laboratory, in our current test implementation) we developed a statistical voting algorithm for inferring cause/effect relationships in these instantaneous variations. Logical connections are obtained in unsupervised mode with no a priori information and leads to the definition of a knowledge base the system can exploit to predict its own near future internal state variations, given the observation of the lab users.

1 Introduction

Ambient Intelligence (AmI) technology defines a new paradigm in human/machine interaction: it offers the creation of an environment which is responsive to the activities and presence of people. Designing this type of environment needs a new approach: instead of thinking of technology as a resource inside a 'black box', the meaning of Ambient Intelligence is that a distributed network presents facilities to people wherever they are in multiple forms which are offered through old, new and hybrid interfaces [1].

Ambient intelligence should also be "unobtrusive, often invisible: everywhere and yet in our consciousness – nowhere unless we need it. Interaction should be relaxing and enjoyable for the citizen, and not involve a steep learning curve" [2].

The metaphor of Ambient Intelligence tries to picture a vision of the future where all of us will be surrounded by intelligent electronic environments, and this ambience has claims of being sensitive and responsive to our needs. A multitude of sensors and actuators are already embedded in very-small or very large information and communication technologies, and it is only a question of time when better use can be gained from these complex (yet still primitive) technology systems. Yet early experimental results suggest design choices for new computer-enriched environments promising enhanced features (e.g. extending human capacity to remember, or imagine, or redefine spatial positioning, navigation, and adapt to novel situations).

G. Bebis et al. (Eds.): ISVC 2005, LNCS 3804, pp. 100 – 107, 2005.

There are a number of application areas where such systems can be useful. Representative examples could include specific areas (tele-operation, assembly, maintenance and repairing, new working environments, biomedicine and neurosciences, education & training, surveillance, real time interactive gaming and entertainment, archiving, new communication standards, etc) [3]. Creating the needed sense of immersion into the system remains a major challenge [4] and is strictly connected to the development of more and more complex human-machine interfaces where tomorrow only machines will have to learn how to serve users.

Following this technological trend, after this introduction we describe the motivation guiding the study presented in this paper; then in section 3 we describe the implemented system and in section 4 the proposed technique to infer cause/effects relationships. Some results are proposed in section 5, while section 6 draws some conclusions.

2 Motivation

One of the key points of an Ambient Intelligence system is then the extended interaction with users. Complex technologies are becoming more and more friendly and do not force the user to hard trainings to access them. This apparent simplification hides heavy consequences in the designing of such systems and the external interface requires strong efforts to make such complex working logics easy to manage.

In the direction of this user-centered paradigm, we are developing a smart space controlling a University laboratory where the vision system is augmented by two sensors sets to monitor the activity of people entering and using laboratory resources (external sensors) and the internal activity of the devices themselves (internal sensors).

In particular the approach of the present work is the study of the joint evolution of the two state vectors representing user and system. The definition of *events* occurring in the two opposite vectors and the properly filtered collection of these events yield data about delay and likelihood of the expected relationships and provide new and automatically found associations. In other words we define a learning technique in order to allow a smart space to be able to predict -with a reasonable probability- the logical consequence of a user action. This knowledge gives the system an inference capacity to try and foresee its own devices' behavior and the user's requirements and to adapt accordingly.

3 System Description

The base sensory system is represented by two calibrated partially overlapped cameras providing the most important information to interact with the user: his position inside the controlled environment. Visual information however only provides data about the user and is definitely not enough for our purposes of studying human-system behavioral relationships. Then a more complex sensory system is needed to observe also system behavior. Today the implemented system is then composed by two sensors sets, grouped according to their target: the adjectives internal and external do not refer to hardware features but to the nature of the observed quantity. That is to say the former group collects information about system behavior, the latter about the user. As instance this justifies the fact that a mouse activity sensor is an external sensor because it is useful to guarantee the presence of a human user in front of a personal computer.

In the current implementation the interested machines are three: two computers used by the students (*PC1-2*) and a third (*CU*) collecting data and running the central fusion and processing tasks.

The exerted sensors are partly hardware and partly software routines. For the external set we employ: a software simulated badge reader (*BR*); two video cameras with partially overlapped fields of view to cover the room and locate the users (*TLC*); 2 mouse activity sensors (*M*); 2 keyboard sensors (*KEY*). On the internal variables sensing side we use: 2 login controllers (*LOG*); 2 *CPU* computational load sensors (*CPU*); 2 network adapter activity monitors (*LAN*); 2 hard disk usage meter (HD). They collect data at a rate of 1 Hz and send them to the *CU* where they are filtered and put in the two following vectors:

$$\overline{S}_I(t) = [CPU_{1,2}(t), LAN_{1,2}(t), HD_{1,2}(t), LOG_{1,2}(t)] \quad (1)$$

$$\overline{S}_E(t) = [TLC_{1,2}(t), M_{1,2}(t), KEY_{1,2}(t), BR(t)] \quad (2)$$

Then the information are stored and processed to locate significant events as described in the following section.

4 Cause/Effect Relationships

In the central elaboration unit, vectors (1) and (2) are processed to obtain two global system labels (*I(t)* and *E(t)*) defining the instantaneous situation of the two system sides (internal and external). *I/E(t)* labels was obtained thanks to appropriately trained neural network classifiers based on Self Organizing Maps (S.O.M.) [5].

Table 1. *I(t)* labels

I(t) LABEL	MEANING
LOGIN	New access to a PC
LOGOUT	User disconnection
WL1	High load on PC1
WL2	High load on PC2
WF	PC1 and PC2 in low load
WLA	High load on both PCs
NULL	No activity

Training the unsupervised internal map with real-time actual data, 7 significant clusters were identified and labeled with the corresponding *I(t)* listed in Table 1, as well as 7 *E(t)* clusters were found by the external SOM classifier and were labeled as in Table 2 (a portion of the trained and labeled SOM map used for internal state is shown in figure 1 as an example).

Table 2. E(t) labels

E(t) **LABEL**	**MEANING**
EMPTY	Empty lab
ARRIVE	New user entering
EXIT	A user exits the lab
WH1	Users presence near to PC1
WH2	Users presence near to PC2
WHA	Users presence near to both PC1 and PC2
WA	No users detected near to the machines

Considering the classifiers provide the system with these 2 global states once per second, we are interested in evaluating which are the differential relationships connecting state changes occurring on the two maps.

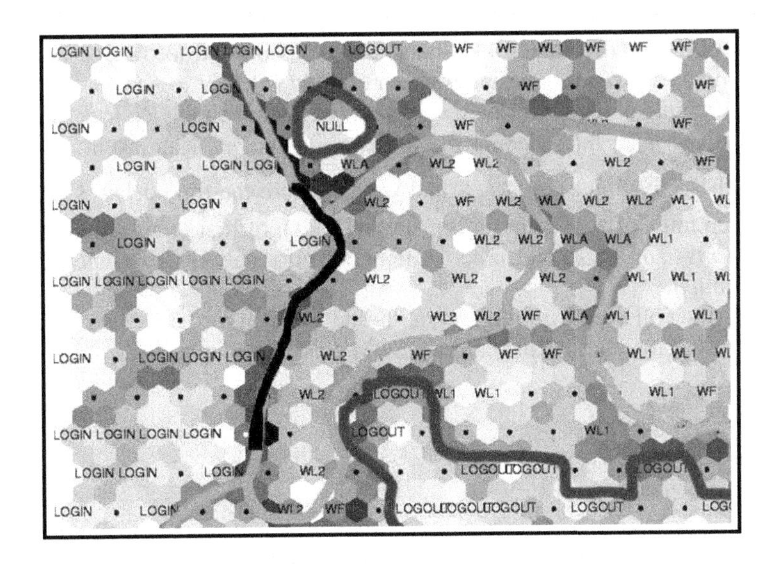

Fig. 1. Portion of the trained and labeled internal SOM map

We define an *event* as the transition between two different clusters on the map, that is to say the changing of the global state label in the internal or external classifier output. Formally we have an event when:

$$I/E(t) - I/E(t - \Delta t) \neq 0 \tag{3}$$

where Δt is the sampling time (1 second in the proposed test application).

The activation is the changing of a global state but an internal global state event is represented by the initial and the final *I(t)* labels.

$$e_I(t) = \{I(t - \Delta t), I(t)\} \tag{4}$$

For instance, writing

$$e_I(t) = \{WL1, WLA\} \tag{5}$$

we mean the global internal state is changing at time *t* from a situation in which PC1 sensors observe a high working load state to the situation of high load on both the computers.

Once the events of interests are defined, we are interested in finding how a user state change has an influence on the variation of the system internal state and how the perception of this change can be used to somehow predict a variation in the smart space state.

With the aim of automatically find these relationships we exploit a properly defined voting algorithm: without any kind of a priori knowledge, a voting algorithm can seize the actual logical connections among a large number of data and noise. The only hypothesis we make is that we look for internal state variations we can consider as consequences of the user activity. Frequently repeating $\{e_E(t), e_I(k\Delta t)\}$ couples with a similar $k\Delta t$ time delay, can be definitely considered actual cause/effect relationships and a time distributed likelihood can be associated to the events couple if the obtained votes exceeds the established threshold (*Th*).

In order to build a more informative data set, we do not simply collect $\{e_E, e_I\}$ couples but we also take into account the most recent internal state event $e_I(t - k_2\Delta t)$ preceding the activation event $e_E(t)$ and we also store the time delay $k_1\Delta t$. In this way we keep track of zero-order information (*labels*), of first order differential information (*events*) and of second order differential information (*variations of internal state variations*).

After having collected a training set in on-line working mode, we process the time-ordered series of the internal and external SOM classifier output:

```
for ∀ e_E(t)
{
   find the time-closest e_I(t - k_2Δt);
   if k_1 < k_win
      vote ∀ {e_I(t - k_2Δt), e_E(t), e_I(t + k_1Δt), k_1Δt}
}
```

with k_{win} heuristic time window extension, set to 30 seconds in our test application.

A graphical representation of the voted quadruplet is shown in figure 2.

After having processed the whole training set, noisy non significant votes are eliminated cutting all the sequences receiving a number of votes below threshold *Th*, set to preserve the 75 % of the assigned votes. What we obtain is a statistical knowledge data base carrying information on logical cause/effect relationships together with the effect likelihood distribution along time axis. If the training set was properly collected, the AmI system can exploit this knowledge to guess its own near-future internal state activity and act proactively: given an $e_E(t)$ observed by the sensors, the time-closest (minimum k_1) $e_I(t-k_1\Delta t)$ stored is recalled and the prediction system returns the next most probable event in the internal state along with its time distribution. An example of the forecast response is shown in Table 3, where only the most likely internal event is indicated.

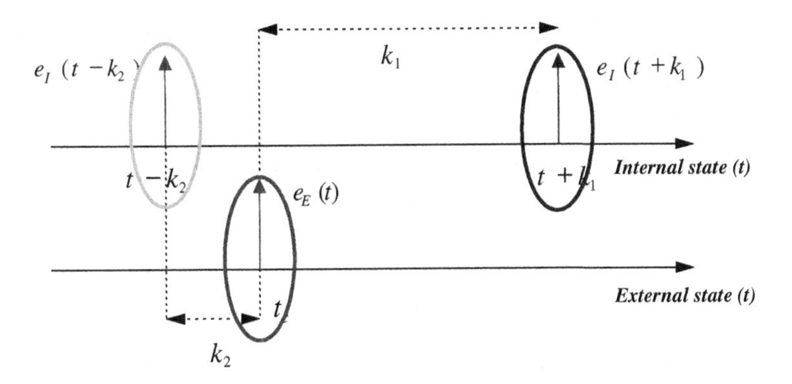

Fig, 2. Graphical depiction of a voted quadruplet with $e_E(t)$ activation event

Table 3. Examples of predicted events with likelihood and time delay

$e_I(t-k_2\Delta t)$	$e_E(t)$	Predicted $e_I(t+k_1\Delta t)$	Likelihood	Delay $k_1\Delta t$
NULL_NULL	EMPTY_ARRIVE	NULL_LOGIN	0.24	17 s
WL1_WF	EXIT_WH1	WL1_WF	0.45	5 s
LOGOUT_WL1	WHA_WH1	WL1_WF	0.50	26 s
WL1_WL1	ARRIVE_WH1	WL1_LOGIN	0.23	13 s
.....	.....	.....	.....	.....

In figure 3 an example of the time distributed likelihood information contained in the obtained knowledge database is presented.

In figure 3 an example of the time distributed likelihood information contained in the obtained knowledge database is presented. The probability of a new NULL_LOGIN event $P\left(e_I(t^+)\,|\,e_I(t-k_1\Delta t),e_E(t)\right)$ is provided as a function of relative time (*t=0* is the external activation event instant).

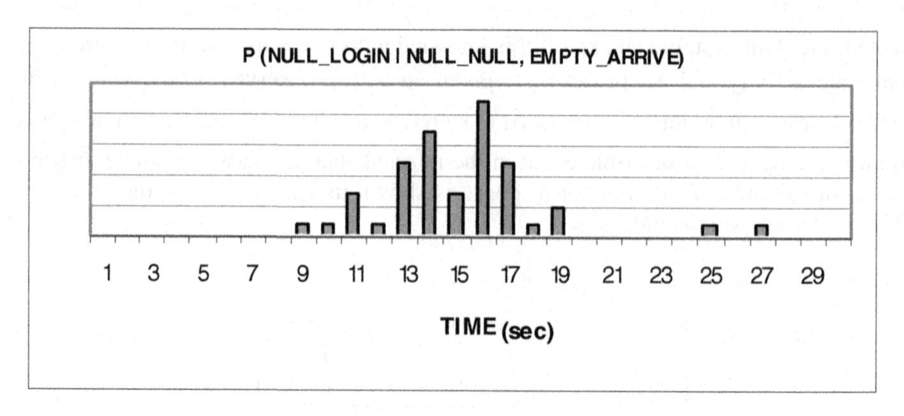

Fig. 3. Example of predicted time distributed NULL_LOGIN internal event likelihood given an activation external event EMPTY_ARRIVE and no previous internal event (NULL_NULL) in the observation window

5 Results

Preliminary tests on a trained predictive system have been conducted to evaluate system performances: the knowledge base was built through an about 180 minutes long training set. 530 $e_E(t)$ events and 1380 $e_I(t)$ events were found by the system with a number of 2484 total votes assigned. Setting the voting filtering threshold to a minimum of 10 votes, approximately the 76% of the votes were saved.

In real-time prediction mode, indicating only the most likely event and its most probable time delay we obtained the encouraging results summarized in Table 4.

Table 4. Real-time prediction test results

NUMBER OF TEST SESSIONS	20
TEST SESSION LENGHT	5 min
CORRECT PREDICTION RATIO	86%
TIME OFFSET MEAN ERROR	3sec

6 Conclusions

In this work a learning technique based on a voting algorithm has been presented in order to train an Ambient Intelligent multi-sensor system and to create a knowledge base keeping track of the cause/effect relationships taking place in a system described in terms of instantaneous internal and external states. These states are obtained through a couple of trained neural network based classifiers. The knowledge provided to the smart space by the voting algorithm, can be used to predict near-future events occurring in the system internal state given the observation of the user activity (mapped in the external state). Preliminary tests show interesting results in the prediction of simple first order differential information but open even more interesting ways to automatic inference of complex consecutive events patterns, based on second order differential information.

Acknowledgements

This work was performed under co-financing of the MIUR within the project FIRB-VICOM.

References

[1] McAra-Mc William, "Foreword" in P. Remagnino, G.L. Foresti T. Ellis eds., Ambient Intelligence, A Novel Paradigm, Springer, USA, ISBN 0-387-22990-6, 2005, pp. xi-xiii.
[2] ISTAG Scenarios for Ambient Intelligence in 2010 [Online]. Available: http://www.cordis.lu/istag.htm
[3] L. Anania "Preface", in Riva, G., Davide, F., Vatalaro, F. e Alcañiz, M., Ambient Intelligence: The Evolution of Technology, Communication and Cognition Towards the Future of Human-Computer Interaction, IOS Press, Amsterdam, ISBN 1-58603-490-1, 2005.
[4] F. Davide, G. Riva, W.A. IJsselsteijn, "Introduction", in F. Davide, G. Riva, W.A. IJsselsteijn, Being There: Concepts, Effects and Measurements of User Presence in Synthetic Environments, The Netherlands, IOS Press, 2003, pp. ix-xiii.
[5] L. Marchesotti, S. Piva and C. Regazzoni "Structured Context Analysis Techniques in Biologically Inspired Ambient Intelligence Systems", IEEE Trans. on Systems, Man and Cybernetics, Part A, Special Issue on Ambient Intelligence, N.1, Vol.35, January 2005, pp. 106-120.

Toward a Unified Probabilistic Framework for Object Recognition and Segmentation

Huei-Ju Chen[1], Kuang-Chih Lee[2],
Erik Murphy-Chutorian[3], and Jochen Triesch[1,4]

[1] Dept. of Cognitive Science, UC San Diego,
9500 Gilman Drive, MC 0515, CA 92093-0515, USA
{hjchen, triesch}@cogsci.ucsd.edu
[2] OJOS Inc.
kclee@ojos-inc.com
http://www.ojos-inc.com/
[3] Dept. of Electrical and Computer Engineering, UC San Diego,
9500 Gilman Drive, MC 0407, CA 92093-0407, USA
erikmc@ucsd.edu
[4] Frankfurt Institute for Advanced Studies, J.W. Goethe University,
Max-von-Laue-Str. 1, D-60438 Frankfurt/Main, Germany

Abstract. This paper presents a novel and effective Bayesian belief network that integrates object segmentation and recognition. The network consists of three latent variables that represent the local features, the recognition hypothesis, and the segmentation hypothesis. The probabilities are the result of approximate inference based on stochastic simulations with Gibbs sampling, and can be calculated for large databases of objects. Experimental results demonstrate that this framework outperforms a feed-forward recognition system that ignores the segmentation problem.

1 Introduction

The recognition of objects in cluttered real-world scenes is a complicated task for computer vision systems. Traditional approaches that first try to segment a scene into its constituent objects and then recognize these objects have had little success, since accurate segmentation is often a subjective measure derived from a priori knowledge of an object. There are two potential approaches to overcoming this problem. The first approach completely ignores the segmentation problem and tries to directly detect or recognize objects in cluttered, unsegmented images. Under this approach, specific views of objects are frequently modeled as constellations of localized features, e.g. [1]. Various formulations of such techniques have achieved excellent performance, and some can also work efficiently with large object databases by sharing features within and between different object models [2, 3]. The second approach tries to simultaneously segment and recognize objects, an idea which seems consistent with our current understanding of visual processing in primate brains [4] but has only recently

G. Bebis et al. (Eds.): ISVC 2005, LNCS 3804, pp. 108–117, 2005.

been considered as a single inference problem [5, 6, 7, 8, 9]. Yu *et al.* used a graph cut framework that combined object patches with spatial configurations and low-level edge groups, to detect and segment people [9]. Leibe *et al.* integrated local cues (e.g. image patches) and global cues (e.g. silhouettes) to detect and segment multiple pedestrians in crowded scenes [7]. Ambiguities between overlapping hypotheses were solved by a serious of evidence aggregation steps: using an implicit shape model [6] to generate hypotheses and initialize segmentation of objects, Chamfer matching to enforce global constrains, and the MDL framework. Tu *et al.* proposed a Bayesian framework that unites segmentation and recognition based on a Data Driven Markov Chain Monte Carlo method [8]. Using two specific detection engines, they successfully segmented and classified faces and text.

This paper proposes a novel probabilistic framework that merges object segmentation and recognition in a Bayesian belief network. Instead of looking for a joint interpretation of the whole image, we first obtain a set of promising candidates using a one-pass model [2, 10] and then evaluate each candidate sequentially using a generative approach. Our model can simultaneously process many objects using the same set of features to represent every object. We test our system on a database of cluttered scenes, and demonstrate robust object recognition and segmentation amid significant occlusions.

2 Problem Formulation

Given an observed image I, our goal is to detect the objects in the scene and segment them from the background. Our system solves this problem by the following steps. First, a set of promising object candidates are selected using a discriminative method proposed by Murphy-Chutorian and Triesch [2], and the identities of these candidates are denoted as $\{V_k, k = 1 \cdots K\}$. K is the number of object candidates. For each candidate, we construct a generative model with the same structure and use it to further evaluate whether this candidate is really present. Denote the constructed set of graphical models as $\{\Omega_k, k = 1 \cdots K; \beta\}$, Ω_k associated with the object of the identity V_k. β is the graphical structure shared by every element of $\{\Omega_k\}$ and will be described in Section 3.

Given Ω_k, we want to decide whether the object of the identity V_k is present as well as to compute its segmentation. We formulate this problem in the context of Bayesian inference. The results are denoted as the object hypothesis H and segmentation S (for simplicity, the subscript k is dropped.). This section introduces all the observed and latent variables in a model Ω_k.

2.1 Observations: I, G_i, and E

Let I be an image with $c \times r$ pixels (we use $c = 640$ and $r = 480$). Let E be a corresponding edge map obtained with the boundary detection algorithm developed by Fowlkes et al. [11].

Let N^I denote the number of detected interest points[1] in I. The properties of these interest points are represented by $\{G_i|i = 1, \cdots, N^I\}$, in which each element, G_i, is a two-tuple vector, $\{\mathbf{g}_i^g, \mathbf{l}_i^g\}$. $\mathbf{l}_i^g$ is the pixel location of the ith interest point, and $\mathbf{g}_i^g$ is a local feature vector at $\mathbf{l}_i^g$, consisting of a 40-dimensional *Gabor-jet*[2] [2]. Two Gabor-jets J_1 and J_2 can be compared by calculating the cosine of the angle between them:

$$\mathtt{Sim}(J_1, J_2) = \frac{J_1^T J_2}{||J_1|| ||J_2||}, \tag{1}$$

where J_1^T denotes the transpose of J_1 and $||\cdot||$ is the Euclidean norm.

2.2 Object Hypothesis H and Segmentation S

Assuming there are N_o types of objects in the database, X^h, is a random variable indicating if the object V_k is present or not. An object hypothesis H can be specified by

$$H \equiv \{X^h, \mathbf{l}^h\}, \tag{2}$$

where X^h and $\mathbf{l}^h$ denote object presence and its location in the test image, respectively. Priors of $X^h, \mathbf{l}^h$ are described as follows. $P(X^h = 1) = P(X^h = 0) = 0.5$. In our system, $\mathbf{l}^h$ is computed in a 2D-Hough transform space which partitions the image space into a set of 32×32 bins [2] and then converted back in $c \times r$ space. We assume that the prior $P(\mathbf{l}^h)$ is uniformly distributed in this $c/32 \times r/32$ 2D-Hough space.

A segmentation S is represented by

$$S \equiv \{m^s, \mathbf{l}^s, c^s, \phi^s\}, \tag{3}$$

$\mathbf{l}^s$ is the position relative to the location of the object hypothesis in the image. m^s is a discrete random variable indexing which of a number of trained contours of the object V_k is present in the scene. Each index value is associated with a set of contour points which are represented as their positions relative to the reference point, $\mathbf{l}^s$. To generate a contour in the training stage, we first manually choose a small set of the contour points. Then we interpolate the rest of the contour points by fitting a B-spline to these points. We repeat this process for N^{V_k} training views of each object, constructing the value space of m^s as a set of indexes of these N^{V_k} contours. Note the superscript, V_k, allows for different objects to have a different number of contour models associated with them. c^s is the scale of the contour and we make $P(c^s)$ uniformly distributed between 0.5 and 1.5 in 21 steps. ϕ^s, the contour score of segmentation, is a continuous random variable with a value domain between 0 and 1. Priors are all uniform distributions: e.g. $P(m^s) = 1/N^{V_k}$, $P(\mathbf{l}^s) = 1/(rc)$, and $P(c^s) = 1/21$.

---

[1] We use the interest operator proposed in [12] with the minimum distance between interest points set to five pixels and the eigenvalue threshold set to 0.03.

[2] Our Gabor jets contain the absolute responses of complex Gabor wavelets at 8 orientations and 5 spatial scales. For details, see [2].

2.3 Shared Features $\{F_i\}$

In order to expedite the process of object recognition and segmentation, we adopt the feature-sharing method proposed by [2] to cluster a large set of Gabor-jets into a shared feature vocabulary. Each cluster center corresponds to a shared feature and is associated with many different objects. In the training stage, N^f shared features are learned along with their relative displacements from the centers of the different objects. In our system, we use a vocabulary with $(N^f = 4000)$ features.

Given an image I, each Gabor-jet extracted at each detected interest point will activate a shared feature. Let F be a collection of these activated features and denote them as

$$F \equiv \{F_i\} \equiv \{f_i^{id}, \mathbf{l}_i^f | i = 1, ..., N^I\}. \quad (4)$$

Each individual feature, F_i, contains the following attributes: f_i^{id} denotes the shared feature identity, and $\mathbf{l}_i^f$ denotes its location. As described in the last paragraph, each shared feature has two attributes: the Gabor jet and the relative displacements from the centers of the objects. We denote these two attributes: $\mathbf{g}_i^f$ as the Gabor-jet of the shared feature of the identity f_i^{id}, and $\delta_{\mathbf{i}}^{\mathbf{f}}$ as the positions relative to the centers of all the object hypotheses that share this feature. Both $\mathbf{g}_i^f$ and $\delta_{\mathbf{i}}^{\mathbf{f}}$ are learned in the training stage. The prior distribution, $P(F_i)$, is the product of $P(f_i^{id})$ and $P(\mathbf{l}_i^f)$. We choose uniform distributions for both, i.e. $P(f_i^{id}) = 1/N^f$ and $P(\mathbf{l}_i^f) = 1/(rc)$.

3 Graphical Representation

The right-most diagram in Figure 1 illustrates the structure of the Bayesian belief network. Given this model, the following three important posterior probability distributions can be decomposed into the following formulations,

$$\begin{aligned} P(F_i|\{G_i\}, H, S, E) &\propto P(F_i|H)P(G_i|F_i), \forall i \\ P(H|\{G_i\}, \{F_i\}, S, E) &\propto P(H)P(S|H)\prod_{i=1}^{N^I} P(F_i|H), \\ P(S|\{G_i\}, H, \{F_i\}, E) &\propto P(S|H)P(E|S), \end{aligned} \quad (5)$$

Each posterior probability in Equation 5 captures the problems of feature activation, object recognition, and segmentation, respectively. The probabilities on the right hand side of Equation 5 can be readily evaluated. The formulation of each likelihood is described in Section 3.1, and the inference process by stochastic simulation is detailed in Section 3.2.

3.1 Likelihood Models

In this section we describe the conditional distributions of the graphical model Ω_k. Let $X_{f_i^{id}}$ be a Bernoulli random variable describing the presence of feature

f_i^{id} in I. Let $\mathbf{d}$ be a location offset of object V_k from feature f_i^{id}. $\mathbf{d}$ is a function of object identity and shared feature identity, and this function is learned during the training stage. $P(F_i|H)$ is formulated as

$$P(F_i|H) \propto \begin{cases} P(X_{f_i^{id}} = 1|X^h) \exp^{-\alpha\|\mathbf{l}^h - \mathbf{l}_i^f - \mathbf{d}\|^2}, \forall i, & \text{if } \|\mathbf{l}^h - \mathbf{l}_i^f - \mathbf{d}\|^2 \leq R \\ \frac{1}{rcN^J} & \text{, otherwise} \end{cases} \tag{6}$$

where $P(X_{f_i^{id}} = 1|X^h)$, the associations between object models and shared features, are learned during training [10]. R is a small constant which allows small variations of positions. R is set to 2 in current implementation.

$P(G_i|F_i)$ represents the likelihood of a shared feature, F_i, activated by the interest point, G_i, and can be denoted as

$$P(G_i|F_i) \propto \exp^{\texttt{Sim}(\mathbf{g}_i^f, \mathbf{g}_i^g)} \delta(\|\mathbf{l}_i^f - \mathbf{l}_i^g\|), \forall i. \tag{7}$$

$P(S|H)$ represents the probability distribution of the segmentation, S, given an object hypothesis, H. $P(S|H)$ can be denoted as

$$P(S|H) \propto P(\phi^s|X^h) \sum_{(x,y)^T \in A} \delta(\|\mathbf{l}^s - (x,y)^T\|), \tag{8}$$

where A is a 2D discrete space $\{-L_a, \cdots, +L_a\}^2$. $L_a = 10$ in current implementation. We assume both $P(\phi^s|X^h = 0)$ and $P(\phi^s|X^h = 1)$ are Gaussian distributions parametrized by (μ_0, σ_0) and (μ_1, σ_1) respectively, which are learned in the training stage. The learning algorithm of these two distributions is explained as follows. Given a training image, we used the same one-pass system [2] to compute a set of image locations that each object is most likely present, i.e. each object is associated with a image location, no matter whether the object is present or not. Then for each object, we used our trained contours to match edges in the image around the neighborhood of the associated location. We also allow some transitions and scale variations during matching. Then we take the average of the edge values at every point of a contour and call this a contour score. This matching is repeated for all training images and for each object. In the end we obtain two distributions of the contour score for each object, one associated with its presence and the other associated with its absence. In this paper, we will show that the associations between contour scores and object presence help to improve recognition.

$P(E|S)$ represents the likelihood of the segmentation, S, given an edge map, E. Let $\texttt{Edge}(E, S)$ compute the sum of edge values of E only at every point location of the contour of identity m^s, at a reference point $\mathbf{l}^s$ and scaled by c^s. Let $\texttt{Length}(m^s)$ be the number of contour points of the contour m^s. $P(E|S)$ can be denoted by

$$P(E|S) \propto \exp^{\frac{1}{\texttt{Length}(m^s)} \texttt{Edge}(E,S)}. \tag{9}$$

3.2 Stochastic Simulation

So far we have presented our belief network. Stochastic simulations are used for approximate inference. The simulation is based on Gibbs sampling, a scheme of Markov Chain Monte Carlo, which is commonly used to approximate the Bayesian inference of a high-dimension probability distribution. Our algorithm consists of two steps. First, we obtain a set of promising object candidates from Murphy-Chutorian and Triesch's system [2]. The number of the candidates, denoted by K, determines the number of Gibbs sampling processes we need to run. We construct K graphical models, $\{\Omega_k\}$, one model for each candidate. Second, we perform Gibbs sampling for each model to determine the presence of each candidate, and also obtain its segmentation if this candidate is determined to be present. The sampling process is as follows. In the beginning of a Gibbs sampling process, we pick an initial sample using the procedure described in Box 1, Step 1 of Gibbs Sampling. Then we draw $T + T_m$ samples sequentially based on the conditional probability distributions described in Equation 5. The first

---

Obtain a set of promising object candidates

We pick a set of K object candidates based on the system proposed by Murphy-Chutorian and Triesch [2]. A candidate is picked if the posterior probability of its presence of is larger than 0.1. For each object candidate, k, we construct a graphical model, Ω_k, to further verify whether this object is present or not in an input image I.

Approximate the joint distribution of each model

Begin

Set a counter $k = 1$.

Set L, the number of the objects found in the input image I, to 0.

(*) In model Ω_k,

Observations: $(I,\ E,\ \{G_i, i = 1 \cdots N^I\})$

I: input image; E: edge map; $\{G_i, i = 1 \cdots N^I\}$: Gabor-jets at interest points

Latent Variables: $(H,\ S,\ \{F_i, i = 1 \cdots N^I\})$

H: object hypothesis; S: segmentation; $\{F_i, i = 1 \cdots N^I\}$: a set of activated shared features

Gibbs sampling

1. Initialization: Set the iteration counter $t = 1$ and set initial values $\theta^0 = (\theta^0_H, \theta^0_S, \theta^0_{F_1}, \cdots, \theta^0_{F_{N^I}})$. $\theta^0_{F_i}$ is set to $\arg\max_{F_i} P(G_i|F_i), \forall i$. We initialize θ^0_S as follows. m^s is initialized by randomly picking an integer between 1 and N^{V_k}. $\mathbf{l}^s$ is set to 0, and c^s is set to 1. ϕ^s is set to 0.2, which is close to the average contour score for the training images. To initialize θ^0_H, we set the value of X^h to 1 and set $\mathbf{l}^h$ to the location of the kth object candidate.
2. Obtain a new value $\theta^t = (\theta^t_F, \theta^t_H, \theta^t_S)$ from θ^{t-1} through successive generations of values
   $\theta^t_{F_i} \sim P(F_i|\theta^{t-1}_H, \theta^{t-1}_S, G, E), \forall i$
   $\theta^t_H \sim P(H|\theta^{t-1}_S, \{\theta^t_{F_i}\}, G, E)$
   $\theta^t_S \sim P(S|\theta^t_H, \{\theta^t_{F_i}\}, G, E)$
3. Change the iteration counter t to $t + 1$. Loop back to Step 2 until $t > T + T_m$. (T=3000 and T_m=1000).

Performing Recognition and Segmentation: Discard the first T samples and compute the expectation value of the state using the next T_m samples. Denote this expectation as θ^*_k. If the component, X^h, of θ^*_k is larger than 0.5, increase L by one and θ^*_k is a new detection. Set $k = k + 1$. Loop back to Step (*) to perform approximate inference for the next model, Ω_k, until $k > K$.

End

Resolving Partial Occlusion (Optional): Please refer to Section 3.3.

Box 1. Summary of the proposed stochastic simulation algorithm

T samples are discarded, and then the rest of T_m samples are used to compute expectation of the state value. Denote this expectation as θ^*. If the component, X^h, of θ^* is larger than 0.5, we determine that this object is present and also obtain its segmentation simultaneously. The algorithm is summarized in Box 1.

3.3 Resolving Partial Occlusion

After all objects have been detected and segmented in the input image, the partial occlusion can be further resolved by checking the edge consistency at the boundaries of all the overlapped areas between each pair of objects. Ideally the contour of a frontal object has stronger edge responses than that of the occluded object does in the overlapped areas. By checking edge consistency we can remove the overlapped areas from the segment of the occluded object and achieve a better segmentation result.

4 Experimental Results

We evaluate our probabilistic framework using the CSCLAB [2] database, which consists of 1000 images of ($N_o = 50$) everyday objects with significant occlusions and 10 different cluttered backgrounds. Among the 1000 images are 500 single object scenes and 500 multiple object scenes. Each multiple-object scene has 3 – 7 objects. Each object model is trained on all single-object scenes and the first 200 multiple-object scenes in which it appears. All the objects are presented in different scales and positions and in slightly different viewing directions. Scale varies over more than an octave.

Figure 1 and Figure 2 display several examples of successful segmentation and recognition in different cluttered scenes. These results demonstrate the capability of our system to deliver precise recognition and segmentation results for complex objects with significant partial occlusions and scale variations. Further, note

Fig. 1. Left: A simple scene with three objects (*Nuts Can, Suisse Mocha Box, and Becks Beer*) on a table. **Middle:** The segmentation and recognition results from our proposed algorithm. **Right:** Graphical representation of the proposed Bayesian belief network. The shaded box nodes denote the evidences. The circles denote the hidden variables. The ellipse denotes the hypernode composed of hidden variables. The big plate around F_i and G_i comprises N^I number of i.i.d. F_i and i.i.d. G_i.

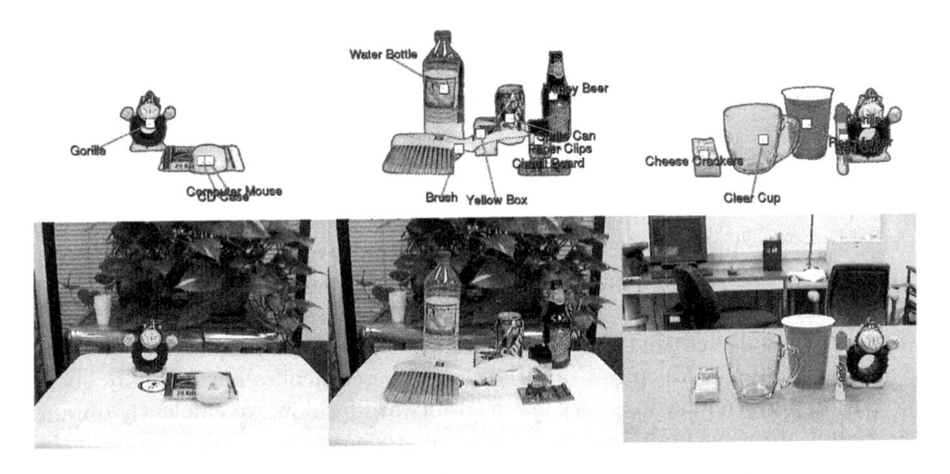

Fig. 2. Recognition and Segmentation results: the red lines depict the contour of each object. The partial occlusion has been resolved correctly for each object.

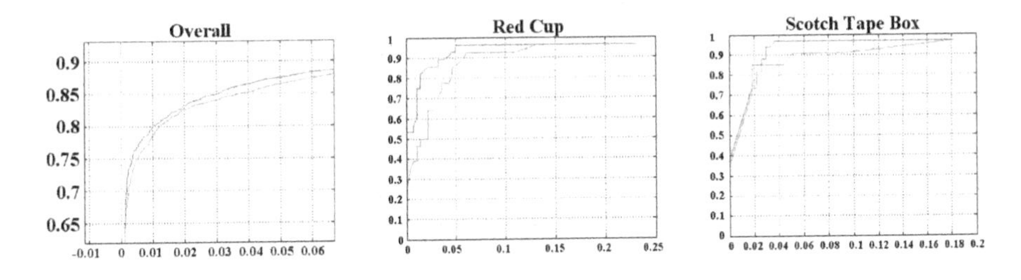

Fig. 3. ROC curves of the integrated system (*pink line*) and the recognition-alone system (*green line*) **Left:** Overall performance **Middle:** Performance comparison with respect to the "Red Cup" object **Right:** Performance comparison with respect to the "Scotch Tape Box" object

that even some of the transparent objects in our database, such as the clear cup and the water bottle, can also be segmented and recognized well under this framework.

The ROC curves in Figure 3 compare the performance of the unified model with the feed-forward recognition system that has no segmentation and does not compute contour scores for recognition. Our unified segmentation and recognition system performs well with a 87.5% true positive rate at a 5% false positive rate on the difficult 50 object detection task. As can be seen, our framework, by integrating segmentation, improves detection rate for any fixed false positive rate. More interesting, the performance improvement is quite significant for some most difficult objects with features like little texture, small sizes, and/or strong occlusions. For example, for the object "Red Cup", the detection rate increases from 39% to 60% at 1% false positive rate, and from 87% to 96% at 5% false positive rate. For the object "Scotch Tape Box", the detection rate increases from 74% to 85% at 2% false positive rate, and from 85% to 96% at 4% false positive rate. The results show that our integrated segmentation and recognition framework achieves performance improvement for the majority of the objects.

5 Conclusion

In this paper we propose a novel probabilistic framework that integrates image segmentation and object recognition based on a Bayesian belief network. Our model consists of three latent nodes: *object hypothesis*, *segmentation*, and *wavelet features*. The joint distribution is approximated by Gibbs sampling. Because the system proposed by Murphy-Chutorian and Triesch achieves reasonably good recognition performance in a very fast feed-forward fashion, we efficiently obtain a good initialization point, which makes the stochastic simulation more likely and quickly to converge to the true distribution. We expect the advantage of this property to be more significant in our future work in which we increase the state space of our model, such as allowing rotations in contour matching, or allowing part of the contour points to move. Segmentation can be also further improved using active contour algorithms such as Snakes [13]. Due to the shared feature vocabulary, our system is scalable to recognizing large numbers of objects. Experimental results demonstrate that our method outperforms a feed-forward version of the system that does not try to segment the objects. Our probabilistic framework can easily incorporate different types of features for both recognition and segmentation, which could further improve performance.

Our current system can be extended to perform full 3-D object recognition and segmentation (in contrast to the single pose version described here) by simply adding more training images of different poses of each object. An important direction for further research is to develop a method for learning the contour models without manual segmentation of training images.

Acknowledgments. Parts of this research were supported by NSF under grant IIS-0208451.

References

1. Lowe, D.G.: Distinctive image features from scale-invariant keypoints. International Journal of Computer Vision **60** (2004) 91–110
2. Murphy-Chutorian, E., Triesch, J.: Shared features for scalable appearance-based object recognition. In: Proc. of IEEE Workshop on Applications of Computer Vision), Breckenridge, Colorado, USA (2005)
3. Torralba, A.B., Murphy, K.P., Freeman, W.T.: Sharing features: Efficient boosting procedures for multiclass object detection. In: Computer Vision and Pattern Recognition. Volume 2. (2004) 762–769
4. Peterson, M.A.: Shape recognition can and does occur before figure-ground organization. Current Directions in Psychological Science **3** (1994) 105–111
5. Leibe, B., Schiele, B.: Interleaved object categorization and segmentation. In: British Machine Vision Conference. (2003)

6. Leibe, B., Leonardis, A., Schiele, B.: Combined object categorization and segmentation with an implicit shape model. In: ECCV'04 Workshop on Statistical Learning in Computer Vision, Prague, Czech Republic (2004) 17–32
7. Leibe, B., Seemann, E., Schiele, B.: Pedestrian detection in crowded scenes. In: Computer Vision and Pattern Recognition. (2005) 878–885
8. Tu, Z., Chen, X., Yuille, A., Zhu, S.C.: Image parsing: Segmentation, detection, and object recognition. In: International Conference on Computer Vision. (2003)
9. Yu, S., Gross, R., J. Shi, a.: Concurrent object segmentation and recognition with graph partitioning. Proceedings of Neural Information Processing Systems (2002)
10. Murphy-Chutorian, E., Aboutalib, S., Triesch, J.: Analysis of a biologically-inspired system for real- time object recognition. Cognitive Science Online (accepted paper) (2005)
11. Martin, D., Fowlkes, C., Malik, J.: Learning to detect natural image boundaries using local brightness, color and texture cues. Pattern Recognition and Machine Intelligence **26** (2004) 530–549
12. Shi, J., Tomasi, C.: Good features to track. Proc. of IEEE Conf. on computer Vision and Pattern Recognition (1994)
13. Kass, M., Witkin, A., Terzopoulos, D.: Snakes: Active contour models. In: International Conference on Computer Vision. (1987) 259–268

Distributed Multi-camera Surveillance for Aircraft Servicing Operations

David Thirde[1], Mark Borg[1], James Ferryman[1],
Josep Aguilera[2], and Martin Kampel[2]

[1] Computational Vision Group, The University of Reading, UK
{D.J.Thirde, M.Borg, J.M.Ferryman}@reading.ac.uk
http://www.cvg.reading.ac.uk/
[2] Pattern Recognition and Image Processing Group,
Vienna University of Technology, Austria
{agu, kampel}@prip.tuwien.ac.at
http://prip.tuwien.ac.at/

Abstract. This paper presents the visual surveillance aspects of a distributed intelligent system that has been developed in the context of aircraft activity monitoring. The overall tracking system comprises three main modules — Motion Detection, Object Tracking and Data Fusion. In this paper we primarily focus on the object tracking and data fusion modules.

1 Introduction

This paper describes work undertaken on the EU project AVITRACK[1]. The main aim of this project is to automate the supervision of commercial aircraft servicing operations on the ground at airports (in bounded areas known as *aprons*). A combination of visual surveillance algorithms are applied in a decentralised multi-camera environment with overlapping fields of view (FOV) [1] to track objects and recognise activities predefined by a set of servicing operations. Each camera agent performs per frame detection and tracking of scene objects, and the output data is transmitted to a central server where data association and fused object tracking is performed. The system must be capable of monitoring a dynamic environment over an extended period of time, and must operate in real-time (defined as 12.5 FPS with resolution 720×576) on colour video streams.

The tracking of moving objects on the apron has previously been performed using a top-down model based approach [2] although such methods are generally computationally expensive. An alternative approach, bottom-up scene tracking, refers to a process that comprises the two sub-processes *motion detection* and *object tracking*; the advantage of bottom-up scene tracking is that it is more generic and computationally efficient compared to the top-down method.

Motion detection methods attempt to locate connected regions of pixels that represent the moving objects within the scene; there are many ways to achieve this including frame to frame differencing, background subtraction and motion

[1] This work is supported by the EU, grant AVITRACK (AST3-CT-3002-502818).

G. Bebis et al. (Eds.): ISVC 2005, LNCS 3804, pp. 118–125, 2005.

analysis (e.g. optical flow) techniques. Background subtraction methods, such as [3], store an estimate of the static scene, which can be accumulated over a period of observation; this background model is subsequently applied to find foreground (i.e. moving) regions that do not match the static scene.

Image plane based object tracking methods take as input the result from the motion detection stage and commonly apply trajectory or appearance analysis to predict, associate and update previously observed objects in the current time step. The tracking algorithms have to deal with motion detection errors and complex object interactions in the congested apron area e.g. merging, occlusion, fragmentation, non-rigid motion, etc. Apron analysis presents further challenges due to the size of the vehicles tracked, therefore prolonged occlusions occur frequently throughout apron operations. The Kanade-Lucas-Tomasi (KLT) feature tracker [4] combines a local feature selection criterion with feature-based matching in adjacent frames; this method has the advantage that objects can be tracked through partial occlusion when only a sub-set of the features are visible. To improve the computational efficiency of the tracker motion segmentation is not performed globally to detect the objects. Instead, the features are used in conjunction with a rule based approach to correspond connected foreground regions; in this way the KLT tracker *simultaneously* solves the problems of data association and tracking without presumption of a global motion for each object.

The data fusion module combines tracking data seen by each of the individual cameras to maximise the useful information content of the observed apron. The main challenge of data fusion for apron monitoring is the tracking of large objects with significant size, existing methods generally assume point sources [1] and therefore extra descriptors are required to improve the association. People entering and exiting vehicles also pose a problem in that the objects are only partially visible therefore they cannot be localised using the ground plane.

In this paper, Section 2 introduces the use of visual surveillance in ambient intelligence systems. Section 3 reviews the per camera motion detection, objects tracking and categorisation. Section 4 describes the data fusion module and Section 5 contains evaluation of the presented methods.

2 Visual Surveillance for Ambient Intelligence

A real-time cognitive ambient intelligence (AmI) system requires the capability to interpret pervasive data arising from real-world events and processes acquired from distributed multimodal sensors. The processing systems local to each sensor require the capability to improve the estimation of the real-world events by sharing information. Finally, this information is shared with the end users, suggesting decisions and communicating through human terms to support them in their tasks. The work presented on the AVITRACK project represents the initial steps in the development of such a system, with intelligent interpretation of the scene via distributed vision based agents. In the longer term it is anticipated that the vision based agents will be able to share information with e.g. GNSS location agents, PTZ camera agents, infra-red camera agents, radar-based agents and RFID tag agents etc. The sharing of information between multimodal sensors provides a more accurate, more complete, representation of the events as they unfold in the scene.

The long term aim of airport surveillance in this context is to provide the end users with the capability to use the information distributed by the AmI system. The cognition of human actions through aural, visual and neural sensors coupled with intelligent processing is a fundamental part of such a system since it is this cognition that allows such a system to detect and understand the behavioural patterns of the human actors within the observed scene. Coupled with this is the requirement that the end user can communicate with the system to facilitate complex activities in the environment; this communication can be achieved either through context aware mobile devices that can adapt to dynamically changing environmental and physiological states or by external sensing and interpretation of the end user actions.

The driving goal of this research is to improve the efficiency, security and safety of airport based operations within the AmI paradigm. From a computer vision point of view this means the requirement of distributed visual surveillance and interpretation of a complex dynamic environment over extended time periods. In this paper we focus on the object tracking and data fusion modules from such a visual surveillance system; more details of the complete system are given in [5].

3 Scene Tracking

A motion detector segments an image into connected regions of foreground pixels, which is then used to track objects of interest across multiple frames. The motion detection algorithm selected for AVITRACK is the colour mean and variance algorithm (a background subtraction method based on the work of [3]). The evaluation process that led to this selection, is described in more detail in [6]. The colour mean and variance algorithm has a background model represented by a pixel-wise Gaussian distribution $N(\mu, \sigma^2)$ over the normalised RGB space, together with a shadow/highlight detection component based on the work of [7].

For per camera scene tracking, the feature-based KLT algorithm is incorporated into a higher-level tracking process to group features into meaningful objects; the individual features are subsequently used to associate objects to observations and to perform motion analysis when tracking objects during complex interactions.

For each object O, a set of sparse features S is maintained, with the number of features determined dynamically from the object's size and a configurable feature density parameter $\boldsymbol{\rho}$. The KLT tracker takes as input the set of observations $\{M_j\}$ identified by the motion detector, where M_j is a connected set of foreground pixels, with the addition of a nearest neighbour spatial filter of clustering radius r_c, i.e., connected components with gaps $\leq r_c$. Given such a set of observations $\{M_j^t\}$ at time t, and the set of tracked objects $\{O_i^{t-1}\}$ at $t-1$, object predictions $\{P_i^t\}$ are generated from the tracked objects. A prediction P_i^t is then associated with one or more observations, through a matching process that uses the individual tracking results of the features S of that object prediction and their spatial and/or motion information, in a rule-based approach.

The spatial rule-based reasoning method is based on the idea that if a feature belongs to object O_i at time $t-1$, then it should remain spatially within the foreground region of O_i at time t. A match function f is defined which returns the number of tracked features of prediction P_i^t that reside in the foreground region of observation M_j^t. The use of motion information in the matching process, is based on the idea that features belonging to an object should follow approximately the same motion (assuming rigid object motion). Affine motion models (solving for $w_t^T F w_{t-N} = 0$ [8]) are fitted to each group of k neighbouring features of P_i. These motion models are then represented as points in a motion parameter space and clustering is performed in this space to find the most significant motion(s) of the object. These motions are subsequently filtered temporally and matched per frame to allow tracking through merging/occlusion and identify splitting events.

On the apron, activity tends to happen in congested areas with several vehicles stationary in the proximity of the aircraft. To differentiate between stationary and moving objects, the motion detection process was extended to include a multi background layer technique. The tracker identifies stopped objects by performing region analysis of connected 'motion' pixels over a time window and by checking the individual motion of features of an object. Stationary objects are integrated into the motion detector's background model as different background layers. The advantage this method has over pixel level analysis (e.g. Collins *et al* [9]), is that for extended time periods (e.g. 30 minutes) pixel level methods tend to result in fragmented layers that do not represent cohesive objects.

To improve reasoning in the data fusion module we introduce a confidence measure that the 2-D measurement represents the whole object. The localisation is generally inaccurate when clipping occurs at the left, bottom or right-hand image borders when objects enter/exit the scene. The confidence measure ψ is estimated in an n pixel border of the scene as $\psi_e = \max(|\text{loc}_e(O_i) - \text{loc}_e(I_t)| / n, 1.0)$ where $e \in \{(\text{left}, x), (\text{bottom}, y), (\text{right}, x)\}$ determines for which edge of the image / object the confidence is measured, O_i is the object and I_t is the current image frame. ψ is in the range $0.0 - 1.0$, a single confidence estimate ψ_{O_i} is computed as a product over the processed bounding box edges for each object.

In the AVITRACK project both top-down and bottom-up approaches have been applied to the problem of object categorisation. The challenges faced in apron monitoring are the quantity (28 categories) and similarity of objects to be classified e.g. the majority of vehicles have similar appearance and size; therefore the simple descriptors used in many visual surveillance algorithms are likely to fail. The top-down approach [10, 2] applies a proven method to fit textured 3D models to the detected objects in the scene; the performance of this module is excellent for many of the vehicle categories with few false matches; the disadvantage of this method is the computational cost which is currently prohibitive. The bottom-up alternative to this approach is similar to the eigenwindow approach of Ohba and Ikeuchi [11]; this method has the advantage that objects can be classified even when partly occluded. The accuracy of the bottom-up method is currently 70% for limited classes of object. A more detailed description of the scene tracking process can be found in [12].

4 Data Fusion

The method applied for data fusion is based on a discrete nearest neighbour Kalman filter approach [1] with a constant velocity model; the main challenge in apron monitoring relates to the matching of tracks to observations; this is not solved by a probabilistic filter, therefore the simpler deterministic filter is sufficient. The (synchronised) cameras are spatially registered using coplanar calibration to define common 'world' co-ordinates. To localise objects in the world co-ordinates we devised a simple heuristic strategy that estimates the ground plane centroid using the camera angle to the ground plane, object category and the measured object size.

The data association step associates existing track predictions with the per camera measurements. In the nearest neighbour filter, the nearest match within a validation gate is determined to be the sole observation for a given camera. For multiple tracks viewed from multiple sensors, the nearest neighbour filter is:

1. For each track, obtain the validated set of measurements per camera.
2. For each track, associate the nearest neighbour per camera.
3. Fuse associated measurements into a single measurement.
4. Kalman filter update of each track state with the fused measurement.
5. Inter-sensor association of remaining measurements to form candidate tracks.

The validated set of measurements are extracted using a validation gate [1]; this is applied to limit the potential matches between existing tracks and observations. In tracking work the gate generally represents the uncertainty in the spatial location of the object; in apron analysis this strategy often fails when large and small objects are interacting – the uncertainty of the measurement is greater for larger objects, hence using spatial proximity alone, larger objects can often be mis-associated with the small tracks. To circumvent this problem we have extended the validation gate to incorporate velocity and category information, allowing greater discrimination when associating tracks and observations.

The observed measurement is a 7-D vector $\mathbf{Z} = [x, y, \dot{x}, \dot{y}, P(p), P(v), P(a)]^T$ where $P(\cdot)$ is the probability estimate that the object is one of three main taxonomic categories (p = Person, v = Vehicle, a = Aircraft). This extended gate allows objects to be validated based on spatial location, motion and category, which improves the accuracy in congested apron regions. The effective volume of the gate is determined by a threshold τ on the normalised innovation squared distance between the predicted track states and the observed measurements:

$$d_k^2(i,j) = \left[\mathbf{H}\widehat{\mathbf{X}}_k^-(i) - \mathbf{Z}_k(j)\right]^T \mathbf{S}_k^{-1} \left[\mathbf{H}\widehat{\mathbf{X}}_k^-(i) - \mathbf{Z}_k(j)\right] \quad (1)$$

where $\mathbf{S}_k = \mathbf{H}\widehat{\mathbf{P}}_k^-(i)\mathbf{H}^T + \mathbf{R}_k(j)$ is the innovation covariance between the track and the measurement; this takes the form:

$$\mathbf{S}_k = \begin{bmatrix} \sigma_x^2 & \sigma_{xy} & 0 & 0 & 0 & 0 & 0 \\ \sigma_{yx} & \sigma_y^2 & 0 & 0 & 0 & 0 & 0 \\ 0 & 0 & \sigma_{\dot{x}}^2 & \sigma_{\dot{x}\dot{y}} & 0 & 0 & 0 \\ 0 & 0 & \sigma_{\dot{y}\dot{x}} & \sigma_{\dot{y}}^2 & 0 & 0 & 0 \\ 0 & 0 & 0 & 0 & \sigma_{P(p)}^2 & 0 & 0 \\ 0 & 0 & 0 & 0 & 0 & \sigma_{P(v)}^2 & 0 \\ 0 & 0 & 0 & 0 & 0 & 0 & \sigma_{P(a)}^2 \end{bmatrix} \tag{2}$$

For the kinematic terms the predicted state uncertainty $\widehat{\mathbf{P}}_k^-$ is taken from the Kalman filter and constant *a priori* estimates are used for the probability terms. Similarly, the measurement noise covariance $\mathbf{R}$ is estimated for the kinematic terms by propagating a nominal image plane uncertainty into the world coordinate system using the method presented in [13]. Measurement noise for the probability terms is determined *a priori*. An appropriate gate threshold can be determined from tables of the chi-square distribution [1].

Matched observations are combined to find the fused estimate of the object; this is achieved using *covariance intersection*. This method estimates the fused uncertainty $\mathbf{R}_{fused}$ for N matched observations as a weighted summation:

$$\mathbf{R}_{fused} = \left(w_1\mathbf{R}_1^{-1} + \ldots + w_N\mathbf{R}_{numcams}^{-1}\right)^{-1} \tag{3}$$

where $w_i = w_i'/\sum_{j=1}^{N} w_j'$ and $w_i' = 1/\psi_i^c$. ψ_i^c is the confidence of the i'th associated observation (made by camera c) estimated using the method in Section 3.

If tracks are not associated using the extended validation gate, the requirements are relaxed such that objects with inaccurate velocity or category measurements can still be associated. Remaining unassociated measurements are fused into new tracks, using a validation gate between observations to constrain the association and fusion steps. Ghosts tracks without supporting observations are terminated after a predetermined period of time. To track objects that cannot be located on the ground plane, we have extended the tracker to perform epipolar data association (based on the method presented in [13]).

5 Experimental Results

The Motion Detection module is evaluated in previous work [6]. The Scene Tracking evaluation assesses the performance on representative test data containing challenging conditions for an objective evaluation. Two test sequences were chosen, Dataset 1 (2400 frames) contains the presence of fog whereas Dataset 2 (1200 frames) was acquired on a sunny day; both sequences contain typical apron scenes with congested areas containing multiple interacting objects.

The tracker detection rate ($TP/(TP+FN)$) and false alarm rate ($FP/(TP+FP)$) metrics defined by Black et al. [14] were used to characterise the overall tracking performance (where TP, FN and FP are the number of true positives,

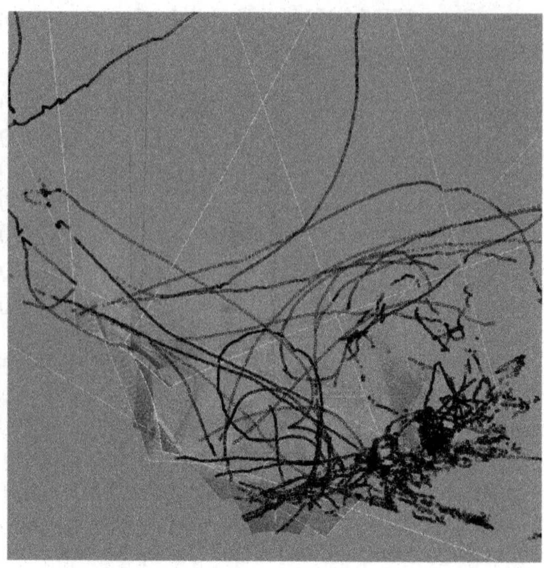

Fig. 1. (Left) Results obtained from the scene tracking module showing (Top) Dataset 1 and (Bottom) Dataset 2. (Right) Result obtained from the data fusion module.

false negatives and false positives respectively). For Dataset 1 3435 true positives, 275 false positives and 536 false negatives were detected by the KLT based tracker. This leads to a tracker detection rate of 0.87 and a false alarm rate of 0.07. For Dataset 2 3021 true positives, 588 false positives and 108 false negatives were detected by the KLT based tracker. This leads to a tracker detection rate of 0.97 and a false alarm rate of 0.16. Representative results of the scene tracking module are presented in Figure 1. It can be seen that strong shadows are tracked as part of the mobile objects such as the tanker from Dataset 1 and the transporter from Dataset 2. In Dataset 1 a person (bottom-right of scene) leaves the ground power unit and in Dataset 2 a container is unloaded from the aircraft; these scenarios leave a ghost track in the previous object position.

The Data Fusion module is qualitatively evaluated for an extended sequence of Dataset 1 (9100 frames). The data fusion performance is shown in Figure 1 where estimated objects on the ground plane are shown; it can be seen that many of the estimated objects are contiguous. The results are encouraging, for many scenarios the extension of the validation gate provides much greater stability, especially when objects are interacting in close proximity. Track identity can be lost when the object motion is not well modelled by the Kalman filter or when tracks are associated with spurious scene tracking measurements.

6 Discussion and Future Work

The results are encouraging for both the Scene Tracking and Data Fusion modules; however, tracking is sensitive to significant dynamic and static object occlusions. Care must be taken to handle errors propagated from earlier modules, which can influence later processing stages (e.g. ghosts). Future work will look into using perspective projection motion models in the Scene Tracking module, speeding up the model based categorisation and using robust descriptors for the bottom-up method. In the Data Fusion module a particle filter based approach will be evaluated to improve performance in the presence of noise.

References

1. Bar-Shalom, Y., Li, X.: Multitarget-Multisensor Tracking: Principles and Techniques. YBS Publishing (1995)
2. Sullivan, G.D.: Visual interpretation of known objects in constrained scenes. In: Phil. Trans. R. Soc. Lon. Volume B, 337. (1992) 361–370
3. Wren, C.R., Azarbayejani, A., Darrell, T., Pentland, A.: Pfinder: Real-time tracking of the human body. In: IEEE Transactions on PAMI. Volume 19 num 7. (1997) 780–785
4. Shi, J., Tomasi, C.: Good features to track. In: Proc. of IEEE Conference on Computer Vision and Pattern Recognition. (1994) 593–600
5. Thirde, D., Borg, M., Valentin, V., Fusier, F., Aguilera, J., Ferryman, J., Brémond, F., Thonnat, M., Kampel, M.: Visual surveillance for aircraft activity monitoring. In: Proc. Joint IEEE Int. Workshop on VS-PETS, Beijing. (2005)
6. Aguilera, J., Wildernauer, H., Kampel, M., Borg, M., Thirde, D., Ferryman, J.: Evaluation of motion segmentation quality for aircraft activity surveillances. In: Proc. Joint IEEE Int. Workshop on VS-PETS, Beijing. (2005)
7. Horprasert, T., Harwood, D., Davis, L.: A statistical approach for real-time robust background subtraction and shadow detection. In: IEEE ICCV'99 FRAME-RATE Workshop. (1999)
8. Xu, G., Zhang, Z.: Epipolar Geometry in Stereo, Motion and Object Recognition: A Unified Approach. Kluwer Academic Publ. (1996)
9. Collins, R., Lipton, A., Kanade, T., Fujiyoshi, H., Duggins, D., Tsin, Y., Tolliver, D., Enomoto, N., Hasegawa, O., Burt, P., Wixson, L.: A system for video surveillance and monitoring. In: Tech. Report CMU-RI-TR-00-12. (2002)
10. Ferryman, J.M., Worrall, A.D., Maybank, S.J.: Learning enhanced 3d models for vehicle tracking. In: Proc. of the British Machine Vision Conference. (1998)
11. Ohba, K., Ikeuchi, K.: Detectability, uniqueness, and reliability of eigen windows for stable verification of partially occluded objects. In: IEEE Transactions on Pattern Analysis and Machine Intelligence. Volume 19 num 9. (1997) 1043–1048
12. Thirde, D., Borg, M., Aguilera, J., Ferryman, J., Baker, K., Kampel, M.: Evaluation of object tracking for aircraft activity surveillance. In: Proc. Joint IEEE Int. Workshop on VS-PETS, Beijing. (2005)
13. Black, J., Ellis, T.: Multi Camera Image Measurement and Correspondence. In: Measurement - Journal of the International Measurement Confederation. Volume 35 num 1. (2002) 61–71
14. Black, J., Ellis, T., Rosin, P.: A Novel Method for Video Tracking Performance Evaluation. In: Joint IEEE Int. Workshop on VS-PETS, Nice, France. (2003) 125–132

Mining Paths of Complex Crowd Scenes

B. Zhan, P. Remagnino, and S.A. Velastin

DIRC, Kingston University, UK
{B.Zhan, P.Remagnino, sergio.velastin}@kingston.ac.uk

Abstract. The Ambient Intelligence (AmI) paradigm requires a robust interpretation of people actions and behaviour and a way for automatically generating persistent spatial-temporal models of recurring events. This paper describes a relatively inexpensive technique that does not require the use of conventional trackers to identify the main paths of highly cluttered scenes, approximating them with spline curves. An AmI system could easily make use of the generated model to identify people who do not follow prefixed paths and warn them. Security, safety, rehabilitation are potential application areas. The model is evaluated against new data of the same scene.

1 Introduction

This paper describes the first steps towards automatic crowd analysis. Machine Vision research has been mainly concerned with accurate measurements of object dynamics and many algorithms have been proposed to track one of more individuals in more or less complex scenes. Not so long ago some researchers started to work on behaviour analysis, mainly concerned with the building of a reusable spatial-temporal model of a scene. Notable work is research carried out to identify patterns in time series of people working in an office, people and vehicles moving in a car park [1][2]. The basic problem with these approaches is that they tend to rely on accurate information extracted by trackers [3], or they make use of coarse information, extracted from video data of individuals or small numbers of people frequenting the analysed environment. What we are interested in are highly cluttered scenes, with many people moving about, with no apparent structure, such as those of large crowds recorded in highly frequented public spaces, such as railway or metro stations. This paper presents an initial study on how to tackle the described scenarios with simple machine vision algorithms that do not require sophisticated image understanding processing algorithms and that can be eventually implemented in hardware. Two examples are shown in Figure 1.

The paper is the first step to bridge two worlds: on the one hand machine vision research that attempts to deliver stochastic models of dynamics while on the other hand mathematical modelling of dynamics, such as fluid or aerodynamics, recently employed to describe the complex and apparent chaotic crowd dynamics [4][5][6][7]. Here we make use of simple image processing techniques to extract foreground data of a dynamic scene. We then build the probability

G. Bebis et al. (Eds.): ISVC 2005, LNCS 3804, pp. 126–133, 2005.

Fig. 1. Two frames of typical video data

distribution function (PDF) of the occurrence of the detected foreground and the motion orientation of the foreground so as to build a local model for it. We then make use of the two PDFs to trace the main paths of people who frequented the scene. These paths are then considered as the modes of paths in the scene and uncertainty around them is used to estimate an error measure to evaluate the performance of the proposed algorithm.

The paper is organised as follows. Section 2 describes the algorithm; Section 3 discusses how paths can be extracted, and spline curves can be employed to interpolate the extracted paths. Section 4 reports on preliminary results of the proposed algorithm tested on a few scenes. Concluding remarks are given in Section 5.

2 Proposed Method

The proposed method can be summarised in the following steps, described in later sections of the paper:

- Occurrence PDF: foreground detection, connected components, accumulator,
- Orientation PDF: correlation matrix, accumulator of block matching,
- Path discovery: previous orientation, probability calculation, path split.
- Path fitting: spline interpolators, path masks.

In step 1 a probability density function for occurrence of foreground is constructed. This entails building the now well known pixel-based multivariate model of image dynamics, use of connected components to remove noise and the populating of an accumulator that, normalised to unit volume, represents a discrete probability density function of the occurrence of the foreground from the single view. Attempts to segment such PDF have been tried before, but in this paper we leave the PDF as is. This is because segmenting continuous paths is not particularly interesting or useful. Also, we split the image into cells which might be interpreted as a fine and unorganised segmentation of the PDF. Finally, we prefer to keep an implicit representation of the PDF. In step 2 a PDF is built on the direction of structure. Structure for us are foreground connected components that move in the scene and whose local motion can be estimated by some similarity measure between consecutive frames. In this first implementation, a conventional block matching technique was implemented to identify the next position of the foreground data. Each cell/block in the image is then associated with a discretised orientation histogram, representing the occurrence of direction over the analysed sequence. In step 3 paths are discovered, by merging the information of both PDFs. In step 4 paths are approximated by spline curves and masks generated to rapidly calculate the foreground blob-path distance and estimate fitting error.

The rationale of the outlined approach is justified by the need to identify main paths of direction in a complex scene, regardless of individual dynamics. Discovering modes of dynamics in a complex scene could be employed to build a coarse natural language narration of the scene and used to identify anomalies, such as people going in an unusual direction.

2.1 Occurrence PDF

It is unrealistic to precompile a background model of a complex real world scene, such as those video recorded by security cameras in public spaces. This is because of sudden or continuous changes in illumination, shadows and noise in the video signals. We have therefore adopted the Gaussian mixture model proposed by Stauffer [8] [9] that builds a dynamic and updatable background scene model on a pixel basis. The use of Stauffers algorithm allows a robust identification of foreground data. This foreground detector assumes background can be built, and therefore that the background stationary part of the scene can be seen over a large number of frames. This might not be the case in more complex scenes, for which a crowd might make invisible the background. In such cases other techniques will need to be employed. The foreground data is further processed to reduce noise. In particular, connected components have been implemented. Connectivity of foreground pixels gives more robustness to the foreground data and assures that only large foreground blobs are accepted for further analysis, while smaller blobs are rejected as likely noise.

For each frame we accumulate foreground features for every pixel, so that after a relatively long video sequence we have the accumulator of the foreground occurrence throughout the whole image. Figure 2 illustrates a typical occurrence PDF. The image can be segmented into cells, to speed the process of estimation of the PDF.

2.2 Orientation PDF

The image plane is segmented into a regular grid of cells ($N \times M$). The dimension of each cell is a multiple of 2 and each cell is square-shaped ($K \times K$). The idea is to speed up the matching process employed as a coarse estimator of motion between frames. Motion is estimated between consecutive frames, using the foreground blocks of the first frame as a reference/template and searching for an optimal

Fig. 2. Typical occurrence PDF

match in the second frame. In the current implementation, block matching is carried out in a 3×3 neighbourhood, around the selected foreground cell. A cell is labelled as foreground if the majority of its pixels are indeed foreground. Matching performance is improved by matching only between foreground cells, ignoring background cells.

A correlation measure [10] is used to calculate the distance between cells. Correlation for an entire cell is then calculated by summing over all the pixels of the cell:

$$D = \sum_{x,y \in C} \frac{1}{1 + \|P - P'\|} \tag{1}$$

where P and P' are respectively the pixel in the reference cell and the pixel in the neighbouring cell. The measurement of the correspondence between two cells uses the normalised cross correlation. This results in a distance falling in the $(0, 1]$ range. The distance is 1 when the two cells are exactly the same and becomes very small when the two cells bear large differences.

Each cell is therefore associated with a histogram representing the eight possible directions of motion. The intention here is to build a local representation of motion, similar to a discrete reinforcement learning technique [11] , where each cell of the table has associated a quality array, indicating the likelihood of transition from the current cell to a neighbouring cell. The final outcome is an orientation PDF, which could be interpreted as the global optical flow of the scene.

3 Path Discovery

The work described in the previous sections provides two PDFs: one for the occurrence and one for the orientation of a scene. To discover the main paths, we need to combine the information and extract those corresponding to higher likelihood/probability. Ideally we would like to identify the paths corresponding to the modes of a probability density function that combines both occurrence and orientation information.

In order to estimate the main paths we make a number of assumptions.

Path origin: we make the assumption that all paths originate from the boundaries of the scene. Consequently path discovery is started from a cell the boundary of the scene and having high occurrence probability. This assumption would not work if the scene had an entrance or exit in the middle of the image, but this can be overcome relatively easily by using user-defined boundaries.

Graceful continuation/Smooth trajectory: We observed that paths have a high probability to maintain their orientation (e.g. people are more likely to go on a straight line, and seldom go backwards.) So we model the expected direction of motion with a *Poisson* distribution, with its maximum in the neighbouring cell along the current direction of motion.

The idea is to spread the likelihood of change in direction unevenly, maintaining the previous orientation as the one at highest probability and forcing the other directions (change in direction) to have a lower likelihood. Table 1 illustrates the probabilities used given the distance from the current orientation.

Table 1. Likelihood as function of orientation distance

d	0	1	2	3	4
P_d	0.6830	0.1335	0.02	0.0045	0.0001

From the start point, we calculate the probability for each neighbouring block using the occurrence pdf (PDF_{occ}), the block matching accumulator represents the orientation probability, that is PDF_{or}, and also the direction likelihood P^d. Furthermore, to avoid repeating calculations from the same block, we mark the visited cells, and set their probability to 0 each time the path discovery process has to deal with them. The probability of each neighbouring cell $i : i \in [0..8]$ to be the next path cell is:

$$P_i = \frac{m_i \cdot PDF_i^{occ} \cdot P_i^d \cdot PDF_i^{or}}{\sum_k m_k \cdot PDF_k^{occ} \cdot P_k^d \cdot PDF_k^{or}} \quad where \quad k \in [0..8], m_i = \begin{cases} 1 \; marked \\ 0 \; unmarked \end{cases}$$

The process will follow the highest probability block and stop at a probability $\epsilon : \epsilon \to 0$. We also devised a way of deciding when to split a trajectory in two or more sub-trajectories. This technique works on a threshold that estimates whether two or more paths are viable given their associated likelihoods. However, we enforce only a single split along a trajectory, so as not to generate too many branches.

Once all paths are identified, a fitting process takes place. This serves two purposes: (i) to have a compact representation of the path, (ii) to have a faster way of estimating the distance between a blob/bounding rectangle, identified by new foreground data, and the spline, and consequently estimating an error. The following figure (Figure 3) illustrates splines approximating the identified paths. The scene of Figure 3 left is highly complex, due to clutter, poor illumination and reflections. Although some of the paths are incorrect, most paths reflect the main dynamics of the scene: people moving from the gates to the exit and viceversa. Future implementations will include a refining process of the paths. Apriori knowledge about the scene might also help, if semi-automatic analysis was enabled.

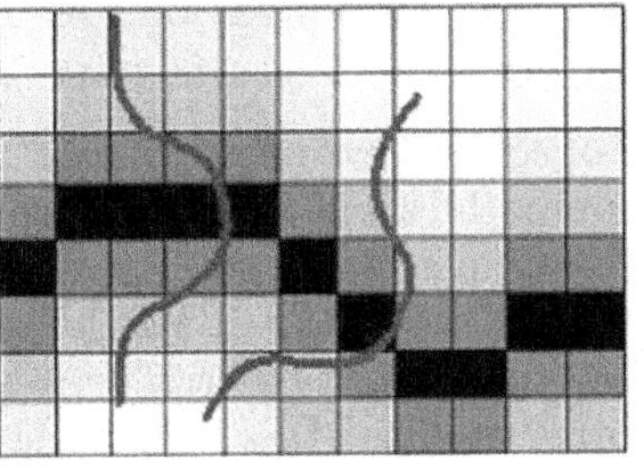

Fig. 3. Left: spline interpolators superimposed on a sequence frame. Right: The stripe.

4 Experimental Results

Paths extracted using the method described in the previous sections correspond to the main modes of trajectories followed by people in the analysed scene. Rather than using the two PDFs (occurrence and orientation) to estimate an error and evaluate the performance of the technique, we provide a simplififed evaluation. We employed the idea of a stripe along the discovered paths using a decay factor (a Gaussian weighting) along the perpedicular to the trajectory.

4.1 Support Masks

The stripe is illustrated pictorially in the Figure 3 right. Suppose the black area represents the discovered path $f = f(x, y, t)$. A Gaussian distribution $G(\mu, \sigma)$ is then centred on the trajectory (μ corresponding to the generic path pixel), and σ being a predetermined standard deviation directly proportional to the size of the blobs estimated by the connected component process.

An approximated estimate of the error between a new sequence of the same scene and the built model can then be calculated by weighting the contribution of a foreground blob, making use of the described weighting scheme. Since error estimation can be performed off-line, when the model already exists, a mask for the entire image can be built before testing.

Masks are built once for all at the end of the path modelling process.

- We build an image look-up table (LUT), where each pixel is assigned a label, identifying the closest path in the scene.
- For each path we build a stripe mask. The mask contains the weights, inversely proportional to the distance between a pixel and the path/spline. To calculate the weights we sampled the curve of the path at equally spaced intervals Δt and used the line segment between samples to calculate the weight.

For each FG blob we detected, we examine it pixel by pixel with the image label LUT, and determine the closest path by taking the most frequent label of its pixels.

4.2 Measuring Goodness of Fit: An Information Theoretic Approach

A number of scenes have been analysed and following the conventional machine learning approach each sequence was split in two halves, to build and test the model. Different percentages of frames to build the model were used, and to test the robustness of the approach. We chose the Kullback-Leibler (KL) dissimilarity measure to estimate the similarity between the PDF_{occ} and PDF_{or} of the model and the corresponding PDFs built using a fixed percentage of test data.

$$\hat{D}_{KL} = (D(PDF^{model}||PDF^{test}) \oplus D(PDF^{test}||PDF^{model})) \qquad (2)$$

where $D_{LK}(p||q) = \sum_t p(t) \log_2 \frac{p(t)}{q(t)}$ and, for PDF_{occ} the sum is over the entire image, and for PDF_{or} is a weighted sum over all the cells. The following table illustrates some preliminary results. Table 2 illustrates results for a scene,

Table 2. Result of goodness of fit

	PDF_{occ}			PDF_{or}		
N_{frames}	$D(p\|\|q)$	$D(q\|\|p)$	$D(p\|\|q) \oplus D(q\|\|p)$	$D(p\|\|q)$	$D(q\|\|p)$	$D(p\|\|q) \oplus D(q\|\|p)$
200	1.38744	6.41181	3.89963	0.992265	3.71003	2.35115
400	1.22145	4.72941	2.97543	0.74336	2.3779	1.56063
600	1.30149	4.22187	2.76168	0.550128	0.870776	0.710452
800	5.32319	1.50177	3.41248	0.960938	0.405281	0.68311
1000	5.43141	1.37666	3.40404	1.61853	0.448835	1.03368
1200	5.83901	1.39313	3.61607	2.20614	0.508669	1.3574
1400	5.87275	1.38677	3.62976	2.48443	0.547993	1.51621

indicating the dissimilarity for PDF_{occ} and PDF_{or} independently. The composit, shown with the symbol $\oplus$, is a type of balanced non-negative dissimilarity measure that, in theory, is zero for $p \equiv q$, and should decrease as the model is refined and better represents the studied scene. These preliminary outcomes illustrate that a decresing trend is present for PDF_{or} but not quite for PDF_{occ}. The number of frames we used is still fairly low. Our next goal will be to use longer sequences, for instance as long as hours.

5 Conclusions and Future Work

In this paper we wanted to prove that a spatial-temporal model of the main modes of dynamics can be captured simply, without the use of a tracker. This is important, as a tracker might not work in very cluttered scenes. Approximating the main paths, means generating a model of normality which can in turn be used to identify anomalies. This is the very first step towards a formalisation of crowd dynamics. We firmly believe that density estimation of dynamics can be built and left in implicit form, the table shows some preliminary results and a possible way of evaluating the goodness of fit of the estimated functions.

References

1. Makris, D., Ellis, T.: Learning semantic scene models from observing activity in visual surveillance. IEEE Transactions on Systems Man and Cybernetics - Part B **35** (2005) 397–408
2. M.Brand: learning concise models of visual activity. Technical Report TR1997-025, MERL (1997)
3. Buzan, D., Sclaroff, S., Kollios, G.: Extraction and clustering of motion trajectories in video. In: Proceedings of the 17th International Conference on Pattern Recognition. Volume 2. (2004) 521–524
4. Still, K.: Crowd Dynamics. PhD thesis, University of Warwick (2000)
5. D.Helbing, L.Buzna, A.Johansson, T.Werner: Self-organised pedestrian crowd dynamics: experiments, simulations and design solutions. Transportation Science **39** (2005) 1–24
6. Helbing, D., Farkas, I., Vicsek, T.: Simulating dynamical features of escape panic. Nature **407** (2000) 487–490
7. Musse, S., Thalmann, D.: Hierarchical model for real time simulation of virtual human crowds. IEEE Transactions on Visualization and Computer Graphics **7** (2001) 152–164
8. C.Stauffer, W.E.L.Grimson: Adaptive background mixture models for real-time tracking. In: IEEE Computer Society Conference on Computer Vision and Pattern Recognition. Volume 2. (1999) 23–25
9. Stauffer, C., Grimson, W.E.L.: Learning patterns of activity using real-time tracking. IEEE Transactions on Pattern Analysis and Machine Intelligence **22** (2000) 747–757
10. M.Sonka, V.Hlavac, R.Boyle: Image Processing: Analysis and Machine Vision. 2nd edn. Thomson Learning Vocational (1998)
11. S.Sutton, A.G.Barto: Reinforcement Learning: an Introduction. MIT Press (1998)

Geometric and Photometric Analysis for Interactively Recognizing Multicolor or Partially Occluded Objects

Md. Altab Hossain, Rahmadi Kurnia, and Yoshinori Kuno

Department of Information and Computer Sciences, Saitama University,
255 Shimo-Okubo, Sakura-ku, Saitama-shi, Saitama 338-8570, Japan
{hossain, kurnia, kuno}@cv.ics.saitama-u.ac.jp

Abstract. An effective human-robot interaction is essential for wide penetration of service robots into the market. Such robots need vision systems to recognize objects. It is, however, difficult to realize vision systems that can work in various conditions. More robust techniques of object recognition and image segmentation are essential. Thus, we have proposed to use the human user's assistance for objects recognition through speech. Our previous system assumes that it can segment images without failure. However, if there are occluded objects and/or objects composed of multicolor parts, segmentation failures cannot be avoided. This paper presents an extended system that can recognize objects in occlusion and/or multicolor cases using geometric and photometric analysis of images. If the robot is not sure about the segmentation results, it asks questions of the user by appropriate expressions depending on the certainty to remove the ambiguity.

1 Introduction

Service robotics is an area in which technological progress leads to rapid development and continuous innovation. One central aim is to enable future service robots to be instructed intuitively by laypersons, such as elderly or handicapped people, rather than needing to be programmed by experts, as is still the case with stationary industry robots utilized in factories. Recently, service robots which interact with humans in welfare domain have attracted much attention of researchers [1][2]. Such robots need user-friendly human-robot interfaces. Multimodal interfaces [3][4] are considered strong candidates. Thus, we have been developing a helper robot that carries out tasks ordered by the user through voice and/or gestures [5][6][7]. In addition to gesture recognition, such robots need to have vision systems that can recognize the objects mentioned in speech. It is, however, difficult to realize vision systems that can work in various conditions. Thus, we have proposed to use the human user's assistance through speech [5][6][7]. When the vision system cannot achieve a task, the robot makes a question to the user so that the natural response by the user can give helpful information for its vision system.

In our previous work, however, we assumed that we could obtain perfect image-segmentation results. Each segmented region in images corresponds to an object in the scene. However, we cannot always expect this one-to-one correspondence in the real world. Segmentation failures are inevitable even by a state-of-the-art method. In

G. Bebis et al. (Eds.): ISVC 2005, LNCS 3804, pp. 134 – 142, 2005.

this paper, we address this problem. Although segmentation fails due to various reasons, we consider two most typical cases here: occlusion and multi-color objects. If a part of an object is occluded by another object, these two objects might be merged into one region in an image. If an object is composed of multiple color parts, each part might be segmented as a separate region. We propose to solve this problem by combining a vision process with geometric and photometric analysis of images and interaction with the user.

There has been a great deal of research on robot systems understanding the scene or their tasks through interaction with the user [8][9][10][11][12]. These conventional systems mainly consider dialog generation at the language level. Moreover, all of them consider relatively simpler scene containing single color objects without occlusion. In this research, however, we concentrate on computer vision issues in generating dialogs for complex scenes where multicolor or occluded objects may exist.

2 Problems of Segmentation

The system first carries out image segmentation. We have proposed a robust approach of feature space method: the mean shift algorithm combined with HSI (Hue, Saturation, and Intensity) color space for color image segmentation [13]. Our previous system [7] can work as long as the segmentation results satisfy one-to-one correspondence, that is, each region in the image corresponds to a different object in the scene. However, we cannot always expect this in complex situations. Two most typical cases that break this assumption are occlusion and multi-color object situations. If an object is composed of multiple color parts, each part might be segmented as a separate region. If a part of an object is occluded by another object, it is not clear that the regions are from the same object or from different objects. Segmentation failure means failure of object recognition, because recognition is carried out based on the segmentation result. In this paper, we solve this problem by using geometric and photometric analysis of the image in the interaction framework.

3 Reflectance Ratio for Photometric Analysis

The reflectance ratio, a photometric invariant, represents a physical property that is invariant to illumination and imaging parameters. Nayar and Bolle [14] presented that reflectance ratio can be computed from the intensity values of nearby pixels to test shape compatibility at the border of adjacent regions. The principle underlying the reflectance ratio is that two nearby points in an image are likely to be nearby points in the scene. Consider two adjacent colored regions r_1 and r_2. If r_1 and r_2 are part of the same piece-wise uniform object and have a different color, then the discontinuity at the border must be due to a change in albedo, and this change must be constant along the border between the two regions. Furthermore, along the border, the two regions must share similar shape and illumination. If r_1 and r_2 belong to different objects, then the shape and illumination do not have to be the same.

If the shape and illumination of two pixels p_1 and p_2 are similar, then the reflectance ratio, defined in Eq. (1), where I_1 and I_2 are the intensity values of pixels p_1 and p_2, reflects the change in albedo between the two pixels [14].

$$R = \left(\frac{I_1 - I_2}{I_1 + I_2} \right) \quad (1)$$

For each border pixel p_{1i} in r_1 that borders on r_2, we find the nearest pixel p_{2i} in r_2. If the regions belong to the same object, the reflectance ratio should be the same for all pixel pairs (p_{1i}, p_{2i}) along the r_1 and r_2 border.

We use this reflectance ratio to determine whether or not geometrically adjacent regions in an image come from a single object. If the adjacent regions come from a single object, the variance of reflectance ratio should be small. Otherwise, large. In addition, we examine the reflectance ratio for isolated regions if their boundaries have discontinuous parts. If the ratio varies much along the line connecting the discontinuous points, multiple objects might form the region due to occlusion.

4 Intensity Profile for Geometric Shape Continuity Analysis

So far, we have discussed the shape compatibility between two adjacent regions using a measure based on the intensity values of border pixels. Now, we concentrate on the compatibility of the shape of adjacent regions by analyzing the intensity values within the two adjacent regions. Actually, if two regions are part of the same object, then the surface form of two regions must have a continuous profile. Thus we should represent the surface profile of two regions and compare them in the matter of compatibility or non-compatibility of their form. The intensity value of pixels within the regions gives a good indication of the form of region surfaces. As a matter of fact, we have allowed all variations of pixel intensity values within the regions by solely using the chromatic components of HSI space to perform the segmentation. These variations (or intensity profiles) represent the shape of regions in the image. In general, the intensity profile of regions in the image form 3D patches and their analysis and modeling which are a challenging task are out of the subject of this work.

Rather than observing the intensity profile in 3D case, we reduce the problem to a simpler domain by analyzing it along the horizontal or vertical line crossing through both regions. In other words, we convert the pixels to a line profile that records the pixel intensity as a function of position. To obtain the line profile for a region pair, we take into account the middle pixel (p_1, p_2) along the border of the adjacent regions r_1 and r_2. We then fit the line profile of the line segments s_1 and s_2 that are passing through this point and crossing both regions using quadratic regression. Fig. 1 shows an example.

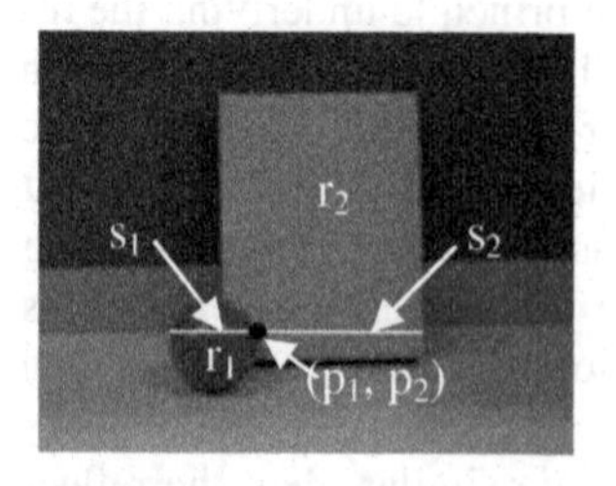

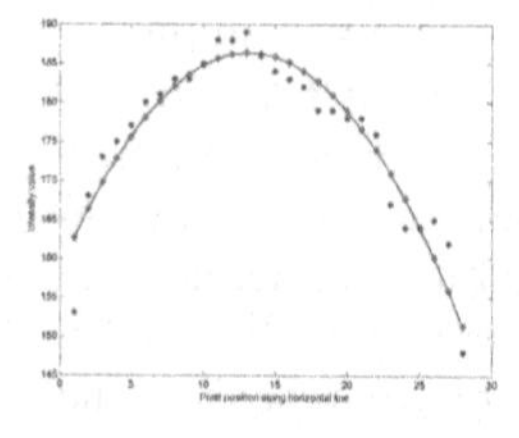
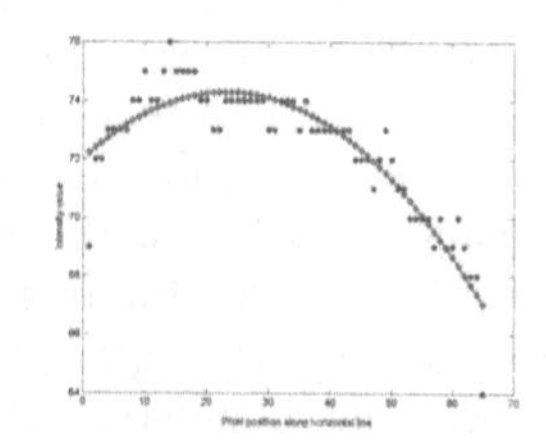

Fig. 1. Original image with the horizontal line in the middle of adjacent regions(*left*), the line profile of line segment s_1(*middle*) and the line profile of line segment s_2 (*right*)

After calculating the parameters and fitting the line profile for each region, we examine the continuity between adjacent regions. One drawback of this test tool could be that it cannot, in general, be used on small regions of an image because it violates basic assumptions necessary for the tool to function properly. However, in this situation, the problem can be solved with the user interaction using the reflectance ratio (Experiment 4).

5 Interactive Object Recognition

The system applies the initial segmentation method described in section 2 to the input image to find uniform color regions in the image. Once the process of color segmentation is completed, the merging process of adjacent regions begins. The system examines one-to-one correspondence between a region and an object. A simple measure for this check is the variance of the reflectance ratio. If r_1 and r_2 are part of the same object, this variance should be small (some small changes must be tolerated due to noise in the image and small-scale texture in the scene). However, if r_1 and r_2 are not parts of the same object, the illumination and shape are not guaranteed to be similar for each pixel pair, violating the specified conditions for the characteristic. Differing shape and illumination should result in a larger variance in the reflectance ratio.

We performed experiments to examine the usefulness of this measure. We measured the variance of reflectance ratio from 80 test images that were taken in different illumination conditions. The images consist of 40 multicolor object cases and 40 occluded object cases. Fig. 2 shows the result. From this experimental result, we classify situations into the following three cases depending on the variance values of the reflectance ratio.

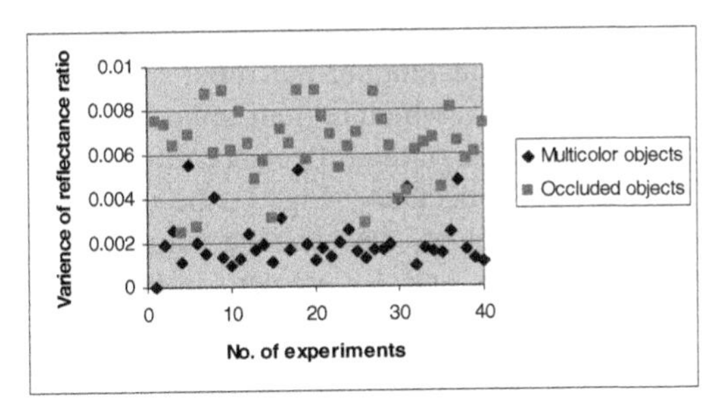

Fig. 2. Distribution of variances of reflectance ratio for multicolor and occluded objects

Case 1: If the value is from 0.0 to 0.0020, we confirm that the regions are from the same objects.

Case 2: If the value is from 0.0021 to 0.0060, we consider the case as the confusion state.

Case 3: If the value is greater than 0.0060, we confirm that the regions are from different objects.

In cases 1 and 3, the system proceeds to the next step without any interaction with the user. In case 1, the system considers that the regions are from the same object, while in case 3, they are from different objects. In case 2, however, the system cannot be sure whether the regions are from the same object or different objects. The system must further investigate the image in such complex situation. We use intensity profile in addition to the reflectance ratio in this case. We use the quadratic regression to the intensity values along horizontal line for a straight line or curve. Then, we check the continuity of the straight line or curve of adjacent regions for their compatibility.

It is helpful for the robot to segment and recognize the target object from the scene if it knows the number of objects in the scene. Thus the robot asks to know the number of objects or to confirm its investigation result regarding the number of objects in the scene. This kind of question is plausible if the number of multicolor or occluded object is not more than six in a cluster by considering user's easiness. However, if the user's response differs from the robot's initial assumptions, it should reinvestigate to adjust the result. Thus, all region pairs that have lower reflectance ratios must undergo for further analysis because the higher values of reflectance ratios specify regions are definitely from different objects. The robot asks questions to the user as a last resort to disambiguate any complexities depending on the scene.

6 Experiments

We performed 80 experiments for various cases in different illumination conditions. Here, we show four typical example cases. They represent four different problems found in our experiments.

6.1 Experiment 1: Robot's Assumption Is Correct

In the scene shown in Fig. 3, there exist three objects: two single color objects and one multicolor object. Two objects are partially occluded by the third object. After applying the initial segmentation technique, the robot obtained four connected regions, R_1, R_2, R_3 and R_4. To confirm which regions are parts of the single or different objects, the robot examines the value of the reflectance ratio of the adjacent regions.

According to the value of the reflectance (Fig. 3), the robot concludes that regions R_1 and R_2 are parts of different objects, because the value of the variance is greater than 0.0060 (case 3). Regions R_1 and R_4 are parts of the same object, because the

Robot: "Are there three objects?" **User:** Yes.

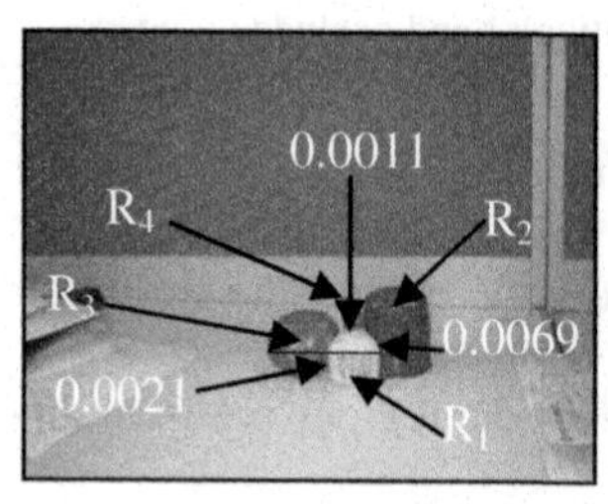

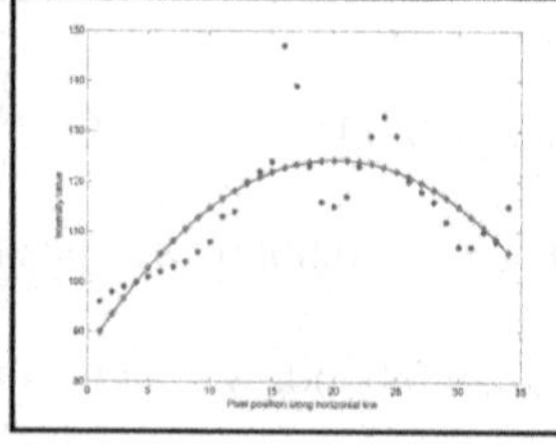
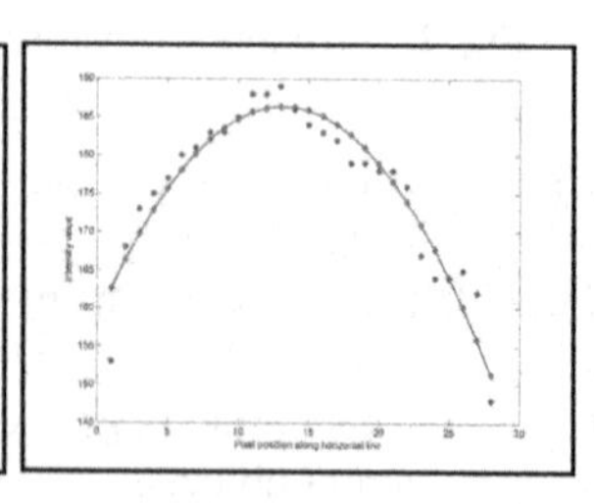

Fig. 3. Image containing single color, multicolor and occluded objects (*left*), Intensity profile of region R_2(*middle*) and R_1 (*right*)

value of the variance is less than 0.0020 (case 1). However, the robot is not certain about the regions R_1 and R_3, because the value of the variance is in the range of case 2. From the value of the reflectance ratio, the robot assumes that these two regions may be parts of a single object. However, after investigating the intensity profile along the horizontal line, it is certain that the regions are parts of different objects. So, the robot asks its user for confirmation.

6.2 Experiment 2: Robot's Assumption Is Wrong

Fig. 4 shows six regions R_1, R_2, R_3, R_4, R_5, R_6. According to the value of the reflectance, the robot concludes that region pairs (R_1, R_6), (R_2, R_6), (R_4, R_6) and (R_4, R_5) are parts of different objects. Regions R_1 and R2 are parts of the same object. However, the robot is not sure about the region pairs (R_2, R_3), and (R_1, R_4). After investigating the intensity profile along the horizontal line for the region pairs (R_2, R_3), and (R_1, R_4), it will be sure that the regions are parts of different objects. So, the robot asks its user for confirmation.

Robot: "Are there five objects?" **User:** No.
Robot: How many object in the scene? **User:** Six.

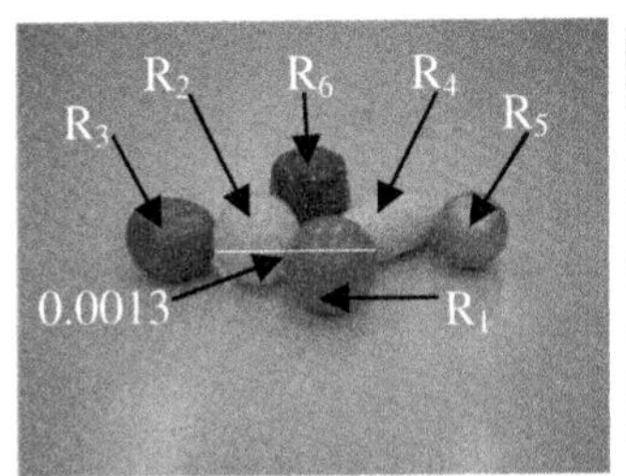

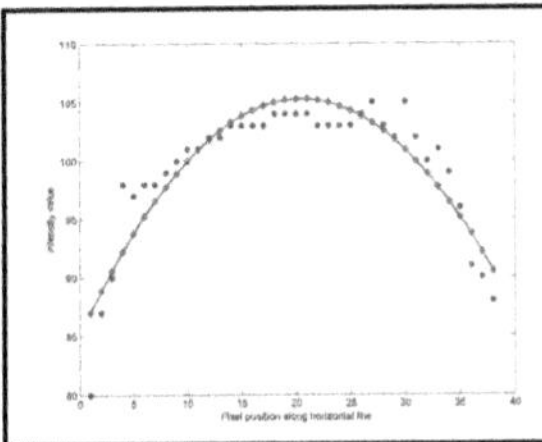
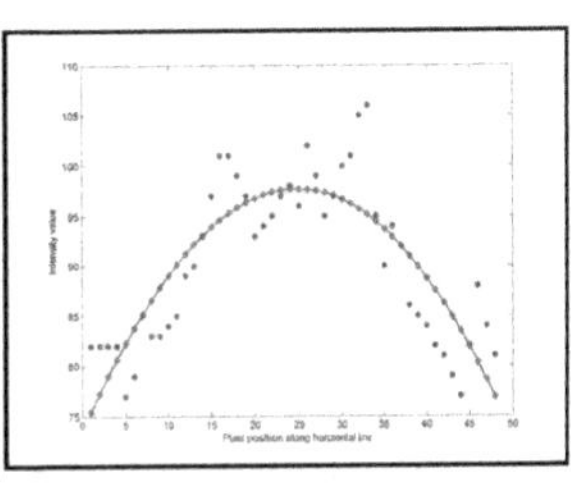

Fig. 4. Image containing single color occluded objects (*left*), Intensity profiles of region R_2 (*middle*) and R_1 (*right*)

As the robot's initial assumption is wrong, it should reinvestigate to adjust the result. Although the test using reflectance ratio has a strong ability to measure the compatibility of region shape, it only specifies which regions are definitely not compatible. Thus, all region pairs that have lower values must undergo for further analysis. In this case, after investigating the intensity profile along the horizontal line for the region pair (R_1, R_2), it will be sure that the regions are parts of different objects.

6.3 Experiment 3: Robot's Assumption About the Total Number Is Correct But Segmentation Is not Correct

In the occluded object case shown in Fig. 5, two regions, yellow and red are found after initial segmentation. Since the variance of the reflectance ratio in the region boundary is 0.0052, the robot needs further image investigation. From the analysis result of the intensity profile, the robot will come up into an assumption that there are two single color objects. To make sure it's assumption, the robot asks:

Robot: Are there two single color objects? **User:** No.

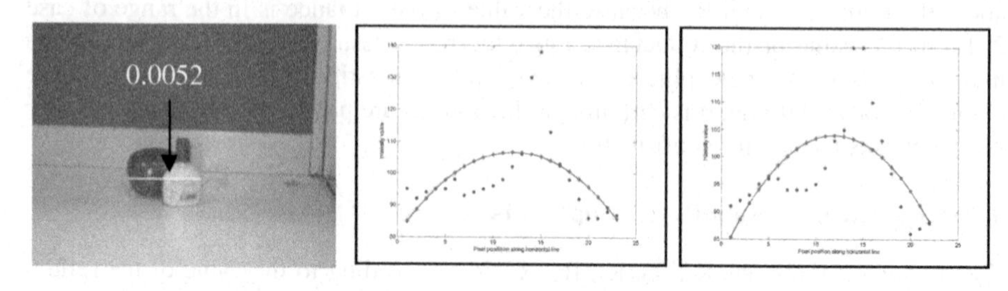

Fig. 5. Occlusion case where parts of two objects are merged into one region with intensity profile

As the robot's initial assumption is wrong, it will ask for the user's assistance by considering all possible combinations. Since the robot generates dialogue based on one-to-one correspondence between regions, it makes the following dialogue to disambiguate the scene.

Robot: How many object in the scene? **User:** Two.
Robot: Choose the combination: **User:**B

A: One yellow and another multicolor.
B: One red and another multicolor.
C: Both multicolors.

Now the robot can identify the target as multicolor one. Still it is difficult for the robot to segment out two objects, red one, and multicolor one containing red and yellow parts. The robot concentrates on the yellow part to pick up the multicolor object.

6.4 Experiment 4: Robot Cannot Conclude

The robot obtained four connected regions (Fig. 6), after applying the initial segmentation technique. To confirm which regions are parts of single or different objects, the robot examines the value of the reflectance ratio of the adjacent regions. According to the value of the reflectance, the robot concludes that both regions pairs (R_1, R_3) and (R_3, R_4) are parts of different objects. Regions R1 and R4 are parts of the same object. However, the robot can not tell the relation between the regions R_1 and R_2. The robot

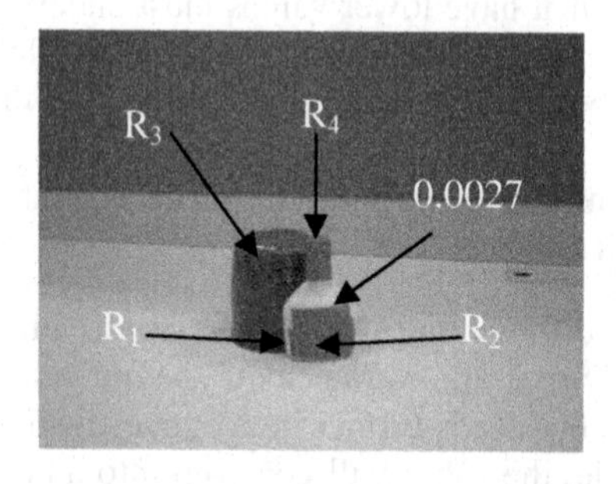

Fig. 6. Image containing single color, multicolor and occluded objects

needs further image investigation. However, the region R_1 is too small for analyzing the intensity profile along the horizontal line of the two regions R_1, R_2. So, this profile is not reliable. The Robot interacts with the user in the following way,

Robot: "Are those regions parts of the same object?" **User:** Yes.

Then, the robot confirms that regions R_1 and R_2 are parts of the same object. Finally, the robot concludes that there are two objects, one single color and another multicolor.

However, in complex cases like the above, the user may not know which part the robot is talking about. The robot should make this clear to the user. The system shows the regions of interest on the display screen to the user in the current implementation. We would like the robot to do this by speech and gesture as humans do. For example, the robot will point at the regions by its finger when they speak. And/or the robot will give more information by speech, such as saying, "I am talking about the objects besides the blue one," in the above case. The user now knows that the robot is talking about the red and yellow objects. These are left for future work.

The proposed method is expected to reduce the user's verbal interaction through the analysis of image properties. We have examined our experimental results for 80 cases composed of several objects from 17 single and multicolor objects from this point. Table 1 shows the result. There were 335 adjacent regions, 81% of which were correctly judged by the method. The robot needed the user's assistance for 19% cases. This result confirms the usefulness of the method in terms of the reduction of user's burden.

However, in some more complicated cases like similar color objects occluded by each other or more than two object regions merge into one region, it is difficult to find out the border for the robot. We are now working on this problem. We are planning to use the robot's arm to disambiguate the scene.

Table 1. Experimental results

Total experiments	Adjacent regions in experiments	Automatic region merging /splitting	User assistance needed for merging / splitting
80	335	81%	19%

7 Conclusion

Interactive systems such as the one proposed here are good in that they can be expected to work under various conditions owing to human assistance. However, if they need too much human assistance, they cannot be used. This paper proposes to use photometric invariance and geometric analysis of images to reduce segmentation failure cases. This can reduce the amount of interaction and make the system more acceptable.

References

1. Ehrenmann, M., Zollner, R., Rogalla, O., Dillmann, R. Programming service tasks in household environments by human demonstration. ROMAN 2002, pp.460-467.
2. Hans, M., Graf, B., Schraft, R.D. Robotics home assistant care-o-bot: past-present-future. ROMAN 2002, pp.380-385.
3. Berry, G. A., Pavlovic, V., Huang, T. S. BattleView: a multimodal HCI research application. Workshop on Perceptual User Interfaces, pp. 67-70, 1998.
4. Raisamo, R. A multimodal user interface for public information kiosks. Workshop on Perceptual User Interfaces, pp. 7-12, 1998.
5. Takahashi, T., Nakanishi, S., Kuno, Y., Shirai, Y. Human-robot interface by verbal and nonverbal communication. IROS 1998, pp.924-929, 1998.
6. Yoshizaki, M., Kuno, Y., Nakamura, A. Mutual assistance between speech and vision for human-robot interface. IROS 2002, pp.1308-1313, 2002.
7. Kurnia, R., Hossain, M. A., Nakamura, A., Kuno, Y. Object recognition through human-robot interaction by speech. ROMAN 2004, pp.619-624, 2004.
8. Takizawa, M., Makihara, Y., Shimada, N., Miura, J., Shirai, Y. A service robot with interactive vision- objects recognition using dialog with user. First International Workshop on Language Understanding and Agents for Real World Interaction, Hokkaido, 2003.
9. Inamura, T., Inaba, M., Inoue, H. Dialogue control for task achievement based on evaluation of situational vagueness and stochastic representation of experiences. International Conference on Intelligent Robots and Systems, Sendai, pp. 2861-2866, 2004.
10. Cremers, A. Object reference in task-oriented keyboard dialogues, multimodal human-computer communication: system, techniques and experiments. Springer, pp. 279-293, 1998.
11. Winograd, T. Understanding natural language. New York: Academic Press, 1972.
12. Roy D., Schiele B., Pentland A. Learning audio-visual associations using mutual information. ICCV, Workshop on Integrating Speech and Image Understanding, Greece, 1999.
13. Hossain, M. A., Kurnia, R., Nakamura, A., Kuno, Y. Color objects segmentation for helper robot. ICECE 2004, pp. 206-209, 2004.
14. Nayar S.K., Bolle R.M. Reflectance based object recognition, Inter. Journal of Computer Vision, vol. 17, no. 3, pp. 219-240, 1996.

A Three-Level Graph Based Interactive Volume Segmentation System

Runzhen Huang and Kwan-Liu Ma

University of California at Davis
rzhuang@ucdavis.edu
klma@ucdavis.edu

Abstract. We present a new *hierarchical graph* representation for volume data as well as its associated operations to enable interactive feature segmentation for high-resolution volume data. Our method constructs a low-resolution graph which represents a coarser resolution of the data. This graph enables the user to interactively sample and edit a feature of interest by drawing strokes on data slices. A subgraph representing the feature is derived with a growing process, and is used to extract the high-resolution version of the feature from the original volume data by performing an automatic mapping and refinement procedure. Our three-level, graph-based approach overcomes partial volume effects that are introduced by downsampling the volume data, and enables interactive segmentation of fine features. We demonstrate the effectiveness of this approach with several challenging 3D segmentation applications.

1 Introduction

Modern 3D imaging techniques such as Computed Tomography (CT) used in Non-destructive Testing (NDT) can generate very high resolution volume data, as large as 2048×2048×1024 voxels, taking over 4GB of storage space. The high resolution of the data provides more accurate information about the subject of study, but also presents great challenges to the associated feature segmentation, modeling and visualization tasks. Most of the conventional segmentation algorithms, such as region growing, are computationally expensive and therefore fail to offer the desired interactivity for large volume data.

In this paper we present an interactive segmentation technique for high-resolution volume data. Interactivity is made possible by using a graph representation of a down-sampled version of the data. The graph becomes *hierarchical* when those nodes belonging to the same feature are fused into a higher-level graph node to represent the feature; meanwhile, these nodes can also be used to construct a lower-level, high-resolution graph from their corresponding high-resolution region in the original data. One problem caused by down-sampling is the *partial volume effects* which introduce fuzzy boundaries due to multiple objects contributing to one boundary voxel. Our hierarchical graph representation and its accompanying operations can effectively address this problem.

An MRI head data set (Figure 3) and two NDT CT data sets (Figure 4 and Figure 5) were used to test our approach. Our test results show that the features of interest in these three data sets can be correctly and efficiently segmented.

G. Bebis et al. (Eds.): ISVC 2005, LNCS 3804, pp. 143–150, 2005.

2 Related Work

Volume segmentation partitions a 3D image into regions in which the voxels share similar characteristics. One popular segmentation approach is graph-based, which represents an image as a graph and employs a graph-partitioning algorithm to find a globally optimal solution for segmentation[1][2]. Our graph representation is different in that it is hierarchical so it can fuse mutiple resolutions of a volume data and enable interactive segmentation of large volume data.

Another related technique called fuzzy segmentation can handle voxels that belong to more than one object. For example, in a partial volume multiple objects may contribute to the value of a voxel. One fuzzy segmentation algorithm is the fuzzy-C means[3]. Another methodology is to model the statistical properties of fuzzy regions and seek the global optimization of a metric, e.g. *Maximum a posteriori*[4]. But all these methods are costly due to global optimization.

Multi-resolution techniques have been studied to handle large data sets. Loke et al.[5] use an octree to smooth and organize multi-resolution data sets. The initial segmentation obtained in low-resolution data is then refined by performing filtering and interpolation along the tree until the highest resolution level is reached. But their approach does not apply connectivity constraints and does not consider partial volume effects, which can lead to inaccurate segmentation results. The octree representation also lacks the flexibility to compactly represent complicated features.

3 Data Representation

To gain interactive rendering and segmentation, a low-resolution version of the data is generated and then partitioned to subvolumes each of which consists of connected voxels that likely belong to the same feature.

3.1 Data Partition

Our data partition is based on a bottom-up merging process which starts from an initial graph in which a node consists of a voxel, an edge connects two adjacent voxels and the edge weight equals the difference of their voxel values. The graph nodes are merged iteratively based on a merge function M:

$$M(a,b) = \frac{N_a + N_b}{N_g}\left(\frac{N_a}{N_a + N_b} e_a + \frac{N_b}{N_a + N_b} e_b\right) + \frac{N_g - N_a - N_b}{N_g} e_g - e_{ab}$$

where a and b are the two graph nodes connected by an edge, N_a and N_b are their voxel number respectively, N_g is the total number of homogeneous voxels in the data set, e_a and e_b are the average edge weight of a and b, respectively; e_g is the average edge weight of all edges connecting homogeneous voxels in the data, and e_{ab} is the edge weight for a and b. N_g and e_g are global variables and calculated from homogeneous voxels which are thresholded by the average gradient magnitude of all non-zero voxels. So the merge function considers both the local and global information of the data set.

A sorted list of the merge function values for all edges is maintained and updated dynamically to decide the merging order. When all edges output non-positive merge function values, the merging process stops and outputs the partitioned subvolumes of the data.

3.2 Graph Representation

The subvolumes are organized as a hierarchical graph to support feature segmentation from high-resolution volume data. Each subvolume becomes a graph node and an edge is created for every pair of adjacent subvolumes. The weight of the edge equals the difference of the average voxel values of the two subvolumes. Each graph node also caches the statistical properties and the boundary voxels of the corresponding subvolume.

A three level graph can be constructed as shown in Figure 1(Left). First, the low-resolution graph consists of the graph nodes generated from the down-sampled data. Second, a group of low-resolution graph nodes that belong to the same feature can be clustered into a feature node which becomes a part of the feature graph. Finally, a low-resolution region represented by a set of low-resolution graph nodes can be used to extract their corresponding high-resolution region from the original high-resolution volume data. A high-resolution graph then is generated from this high-resolution region with the method described above. This graph can help segment the fine feature which is difficult with the low-resolution graph.

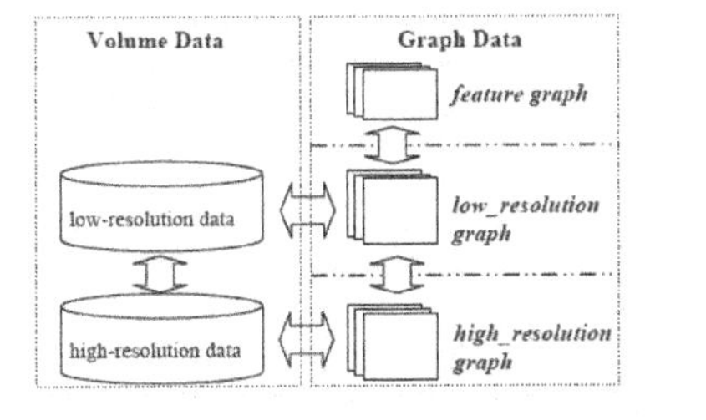

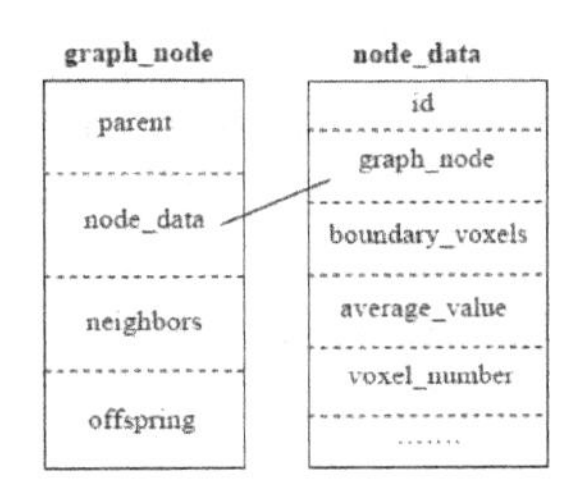

Fig. 1. Left: three levels of detail based on the graph; Right: the data structure of a graph node where *node_data* stores the boundary voxels and the statistical properties of the subvolume and the *graph_node* maintains the pointers

Figure 1(Right) illustrates the data structure of a graph node. Compared to other data structures supporting LOD, such as the octree, the hierarchical graph representation is constructed based on the features of interest. Each graph node associates a likelihood of belonging to one feature, and the hierarchical graph representation is thus feature-centric, which is more flexible and intuitive for feature segmentation.

4 Interactive Feature Segmentation

The user segments a feature by interactively drawing on the slices of the down-sampled data or original data while previewing the images of the segmented volume. An uniformity metric is provided for the user to direct a greedy growing process which starts from the seed nodes selected by the user. This subgraph and the statistical properties of the feature are used to obtain the high-resolution version of the feature from the original volume data through a mapping and refinement procedure. Fine features inside blurry regions in down-sampled data can also be segmented by partitioning the high-resolution graph constructed from its corresponding high-resolution region. Figure 2 displays the user interface.

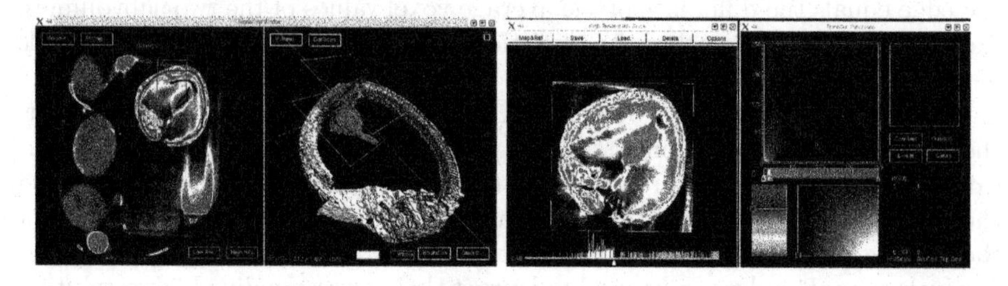

Fig. 2. The system interface while segmenting the watch in the Box data set. (a) Left: sampling and editing the watch by drawing strokes on the low-resolution slice: adding nodes with the red stroke; blocking nodes with the blue stroke; deleting nodes with the cyan stroke; (b) Middle Left: the bounding voxel facets of the high-resolution watch under segmentation; the 3D window defines the region which is used to generate a high-resolution graph, and its intersection area on the slice is also shown in (a); (c) Middle Right: the high resolution slice of the watch; the white boundary lines in (a), (b) and (c) depict the intersection between the slice and the bounding voxel facets for previewing; (d)Right: 2D transfer functions used to volume render the data.

4.1 Uniformity Criterion

An uniformity function U is defined to grow the feature based on the graph, which measures the overlap of two subvolumes' histograms and their edge weight:

$$U(a,b) = \frac{1}{2}[\sum_{i=0}^{n} MIN(\frac{h_a(i)}{N_a}, \frac{h_b(i)}{N_b})] + \frac{1}{2}(1 - \frac{e_{ab}}{e_{max}})$$

where a and b are the two subvolumes in evaluation, h_a and h_b are the corresponding histograms, n is the maximum data voxel value, MIN is a minimum function, N_a and N_b are the voxel number of a and b respectively, e_{ab} is the edge weight for a and b, and e_{max} is the maximum edge weight in the data set.

The uniformity value has a range between zero and one. The larger the value, the more likely the node belongs to one feature. Whenever seed nodes are selected, the uniformity values of their neighboring nodes are calculated.

The middle right window in Figure 2 shows the sorted uniformity values of the neighboring nodes with line markers along the bottom slider. The height of a marker is proportional to the number of voxels in the corresponding node.

4.2 Feature Growing and Editing

An automatic growing method based on the graph has been developed to segment the feature of interest. Whenever a node is merged into the region, the automatic growing step brings the node's neighbors into consideration, and recalculates the uniformity values of all candidate nodes. This procedure is performed iteratively until no more nodes can be merged into the region. The uniformity threshold used in growing is defined by moving the bottom slider shown in Figure 2(c).

The graph representation also supports editing operations including adding, deleting, blocking, merging, and splitting nodes. Since the graph is invisible to the user, the editing operations are applied to the graph according to the user's drawing on the slice with different types of strokes.

Adding and deleting have been discussed in section 3.2. The blocking operation prevents overgrowing by explicitly defining some nodes which are absolutely out of the feature. Merging is similar to the merging in preprocessing to reduce the graph size, or alternatively it uses a feature node to replace all its offspring nodes. Splitting separates one graph node into at least two nodes and is used to modify incorrect merging.

4.3 Fine Feature Segmentation

Fine features cannot be segmented directly with the down-sampled data and its low-resolution graph. Due to their small size, more details from the original data are extracted with a 3D window as in Figure 2(b) and are represented as a high-resolution graph. The high-resolution slice of this region as shown in Figure 2(c) is also provided to facilitate feature segmentation and editing.

4.4 Mapping and Refinement

The mapping procedure maps the boundary voxels of a low-resolution feature to the original volume data, and then refines the fuzzy boundaries to obtain the high-resolution ones. One voxel in the low-resolution data corresponds to a voxel block whose position and size can be calculated with the down-sampling rate.

A refinement method is employed to obtain the accurate boundary of the high-resolution feature. This process uses an inflation algorithm to refine candidate voxels including all mapped boundary blocks and all neighboring blocks obtained by morphologically dilating the mapped boundary blocks[6]. The inflation refinement grows the boundary voxels from the outer-most internal voxels surrounded by the boundary blocks to the outer-most candidate voxel layer. The criterion used in inflation is calculated from the average voxel value v and the standard deviation σ of all internal block voxels.

Segmented features can be displayed with surface rendering and hardware volume rendering. When a segmentation is under way, the bounding facets of segmented voxels are rendered for previewing. Smoother surfaces can be obtained with a method described in [7]. In short, the boundary is low-pass filtered to remove high frequency[8] and then the marching cubes method[9] is applied to extract the feature's surface.

5 Results

We present the test results with three data sets listed in Table 1 which also includes the preprocessing time and memory usage for the low-resolution graphs.

The middle two images in Figure 3 shows the tumor and damaged brain tissue segmented from the MRI head data with our method. The intersection lines of the slice and the bounding voxel facets in Figure 3(Right) reveal the accuracy of the results. Figure 4 shows the NDT Box data and the segmented watch with our approach. The watch contains several materials and has low-contrast to its neighboring objects. Figure 5 shows the segmented components of the flash light. Each component shares fuzzy boundaries with at least one component. Our approach can overcome the partial volume effects and can separate these small components.

In our experiments, the tumor and the damaged tissue were segmented, respectively, in about 30 seconds; the flashlight mechanics took around 1 minute per component; the watch took 6 miniutes because the wristband contains fine parts and consumes more time to operate on the high-resolution graph. Table 2 compares the performance of the feature growing plus the mapping to the per-

Table 1. Tested Data Sets

Data Set	Dimension	Feature	Preprocessing	Low-resolution	Memory
MRI Brain	256x256x256	tumor	5.14 Sec.	64x64x64	11.65MB
CT Box	1024x1024x1024	watch	14.2 Sec.	256x256x128	57.354MB
CT Maglight	512x512x2048	mechanics	51.73 Sec.	128x128x512	111.157MB

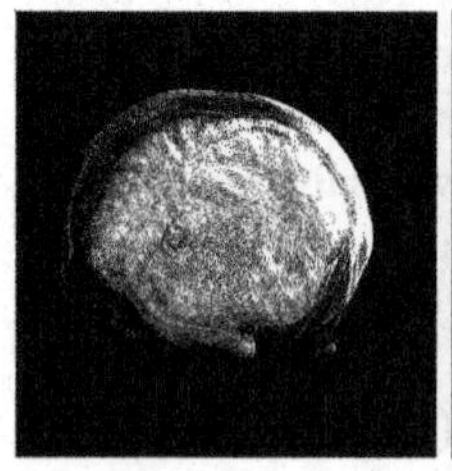
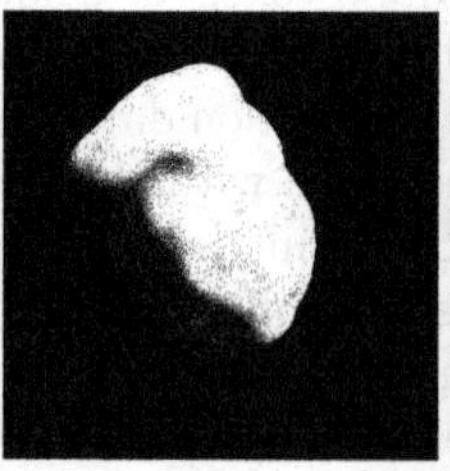
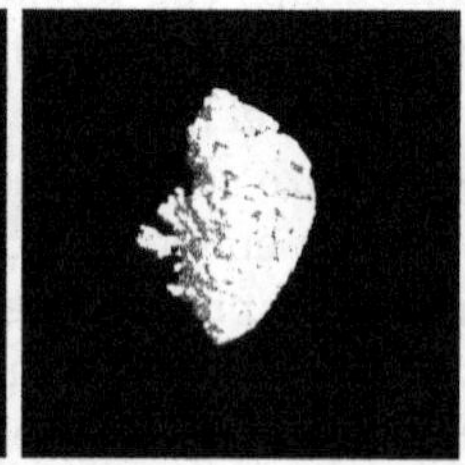
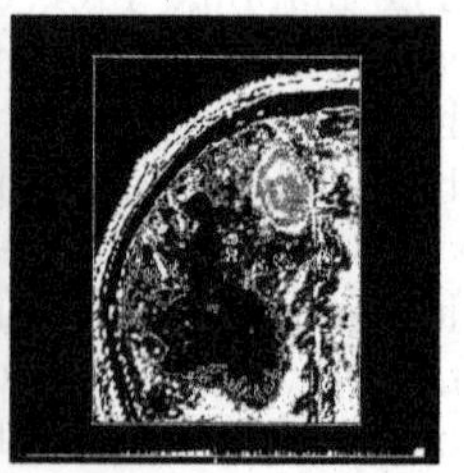

Fig. 3. Left: the head tumor; Middle Left: surface rendering of the segmented tumor; Middle Right: the volume rendering of the segmented damage brain tissue; Right: the high-resolution slice of the segmented damaged tissue shown in the middle right image

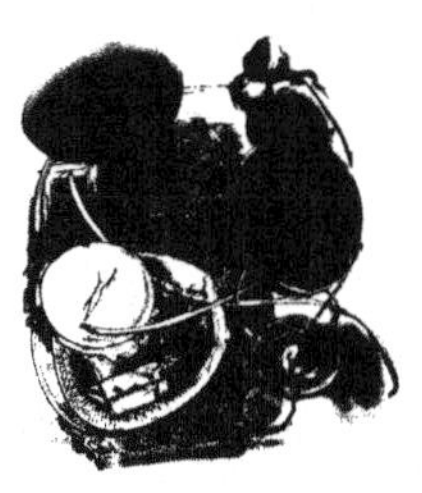 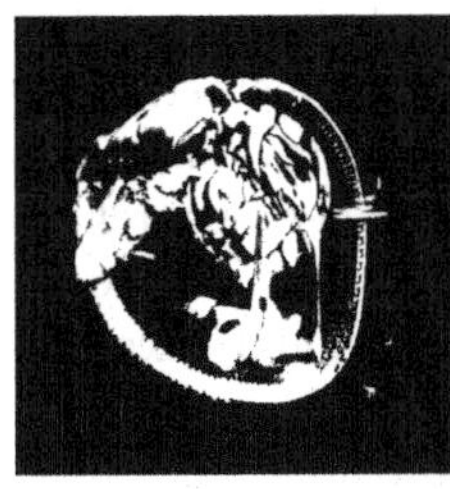 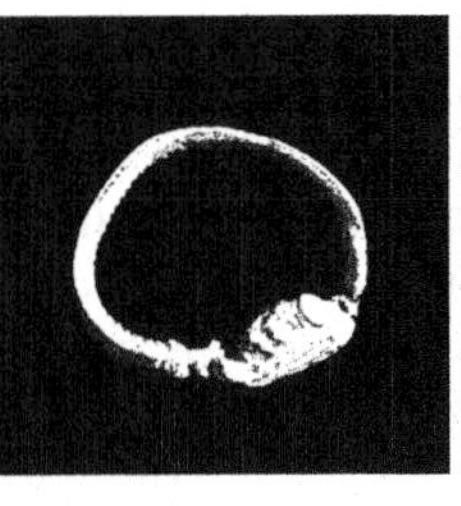 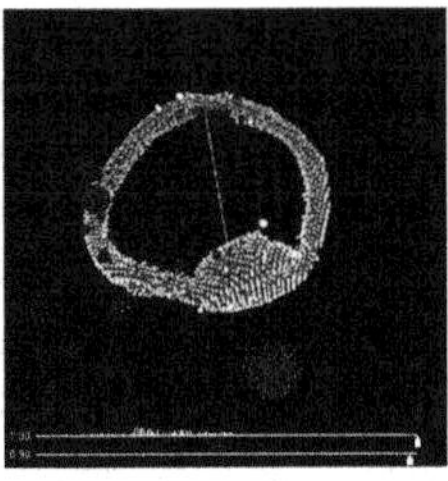

Fig. 4. Left: The Box rendered with hardware-accelerated NPR. Middle Left: Rendering of the watch using a conventional transfer function method; Middle Right: volume rendering of the segmented watch; Right: its internal graph representation: the colors differentiate grown nodes, candidate nodes and blocking nodes. Note that the graph is invisible to the user.

   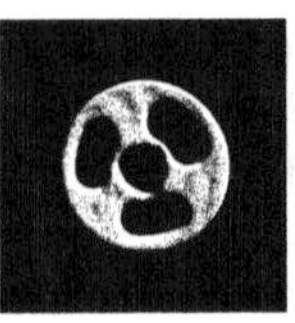  

Fig. 5. Left: the Maglight; Others: five components from the circled part

Table 2. Performance Results

Approach	Region Growing	Graph-based Method	
Feature	time(sec.)	growing	mapping
tumor	0.2327	0.002	0.024
damaged tissue	2.5658	0.03	0.787
watch	4.3712	0.048	1.052

formance of the region growing without criterion selection. The timing numbers show that our method is faster than the region growing, and the feature growing are always sub-seconds therefore the process is interactive.

The graphs can take more than 100MB memory as presented above. However, since low-resolution datasets must fit in video memory and therefore have limited size, the graph size is also limited.

6 Conclusions

The main contribution of our work is that we have developed a new hierarchical graph representation for volume data and a set of associated operations to enable interactive segmentation of high-resolution volume data on a single PC. With such a hierarchical graph-based approach, volume segmentation is conducted through interactively operating on the linked 2D and 3D displays of the data. Hardware acceleration of both the segmentation and rendering steps gives the user immediate visual feedback, making possible more intuitive and editable 3D feature segmentation. The capability to edit segmented features directly allows the user to segment complex 3D features that previous methods fail to do well.

There are two promising directions for further research. First, we will study how to automate the growing process as much as possible so the user can focus on the results rather than the process. Second, we plan to exploit the programmable features of commodity graphics cards to accelerate some of the volume segmentation operations to increase interactivity further.

References

1. Shi, J., Malik, J.: Normalized cuts and image segmentation. IEEE Transactions on Pattern Analysis and Machine Intelligence **22** (2000) 888–905
2. Nyúl, L.G., Falcão, A.X., Udupa, J.K.: Fuzzy-connected 3d image segmentation at interactive speeds. Graphical Models **54** (2002) 259–281
3. Dun, J.C.: A fuzzy relative of the isodata process and its use in detecting compact well-separated cluster. Journal of Cybernetic **3** (1974)
4. Choi, H.S., Haynor, D.R., Ki, Y.M.: Partial volume tissue classification of multichannel magnetic resonance images - a mixel model. IEEE Transactions on Medical Imagin **10** (1991) 395–407
5. Loke, R.E., Lam, R., Buf, J.M.H.d.: Fast segmentation of sparse 3d data by interpolating segmented boundaries in an octree. In: Proc. 11th Portuguese Conf. on Pattern Recogn. (2000) 185–189
6. Lohmann, G.: Volumetric Image Analysis. Wiley & Teubner Press (1998)
7. Huang, R., Ma, K.L.: RGVis: Region growing based techniques for volume visualization. In: Proceedings of the Pacific Graphics 2003 Conference. (2003) 355–363
8. Rosenfeld, A., Kak, A.: Digital Picture Processing, Volume 2. second edn. Academic Press (1982)
9. Lorensen, W.E., Cline, H.E.: Marching cubes: A high resolution 3d surface construction algorithm. Computer Graphics (Proceedings of SIGGRAPH '87) **21** (1987) 163–169

Self-organizing Deformable Model: A New Method for Fitting Mesh Model to Given Object Surface

Ken'ichi Morooka and Hiroshi Nagahashi

Imaging Science and Engineering Laboratory,
Tokyo Institute of Technology,
4259 Nagatsuta-cho, Midori-ku, Yokohama 226-8503, Japan
{morooka, longb}@isl.titech.ac.jp

Abstract. This paper presents a new method for projecting a mesh model of a source object onto a surface of an arbitrary target object. A deformable model, called Self-organizing Deformable Model(SDM), is deformed so that the shape of the model is fitted to the target object. We introduce an idea of combining a competitive learning and an energy minimization into the SDM deformation. Our method is a powerful tool in the areas of computer vision and computer graphics. For example, it enables to map mesh models onto various kinds of target surfaces like other methods for a surface parameterization, which have focused on specified target surface. Also the SDM can reconstruct shapes of target objects like general deformable models.

1 Introduction

Recent developments of measurement devices enable us to deal with 3D object models. In the 3D modeling, users prefer to not only display original models but also generate new models by editing original ones, or create animations from them. However, the direct use of original models is computationally expensive because they are composed of a large number of points on the object surfaces.

One of the solutions for this problem is a surface parameterization which is to find a relationship between an object of complex shape and a primitive object of simple shape. This relationship makes it possible to deal with the models of complex shape efficiently and easily through their corresponding primitives. Moreover, since objects can be represented by a unified form, it is easy to establish a correspondence between multiple models. Therefore, the parameterization method is a powerful tool in the areas of computer vision and computer graphics including 3D object morphing[1], object recognition[2], and texture mapping.

Many techniques for the parameterization have been reported. One of them is to reconstruct object surfaces by using deformable models [2, 3, 4, 5]. Practically, the initial deformable model is a mesh of plane or sphere. The mesh model is deformed by moving its vertices so that it fits to a target object. The other method for the parameterization is to compute a mapping function[6, 7], which enables us to project the object mesh model onto a primitive object surface such

G. Bebis et al. (Eds.): ISVC 2005, LNCS 3804, pp. 151–158, 2005.

as planar or spherical one. There are some types of mapping functions including harmonic mapping and conformal one.

However, most of the traditional methods using a mapping function have been designed only for their specific primitives. Users must choose the mapping function according to the shape of the target object. This mapping technique is desired to be able to map any mesh models onto arbitrary surfaces. On the contrary, the fitting of a deformable model to a target object is formulated as an optimization problem of an energy function that measures the deviation of the model from the surface points of the target. Since the deformation of the model from the points on the target surface uses a lot of points and vertices of the model, it is necessary to find an optimum solution in the large search space which includes many local minima. Accordingly, some initial conditions of the deformable model greatly influence on both the computational cost of the recovery and the accuracy of the obtained model. However, the estimation of the initial model becomes more difficult when the shape of the object is complicated. It is difficult for users to implement the preferable deformation. For example, the inadequate movement may lead to some problems such as the self-intersection of the model. Therefore, the traditional methods using deformable models are required to find an optimal movement of vertices through trial-and-error.

This paper presents a new method for fitting a deformable model to the points of a target object. The deformable model is called Self-organizing Deformable Model(SDM), which can reduce the computational cost while keeping the quality of the obtained model. Our proposed method is composed of two major steps: 1)generate the rough model of the object by deforming the SDM based on a competitive learning, and 2)improve the accuracy of the model by minimizing an energy function. Our SDM can specify a correspondence between an arbitrary point and a vertex of the deformable model, while this specification is a difficult task for traditional methods using deformable models.

2 Self-organizing Deformable Model

2.1 Notations

First, we describe some notations for our SDM. The SDM is a deformable mesh model represented by triangular patches. The deformation of the SDM is made by the combination of a competitive learning and an energy minimization method. The purpose of deforming the SDM is to fit it to a target surface. The target surface is represented by a set of points on the surface, called control points. We can choose arbitrary shapes for both initial shape of the SDM and target surface. As shown in Fig. 1, both of the initial SDM and the target surface can be selected from various kinds of models including sphere, animals and human faces. Here note that the SDM and the target surface must have the same topological type.

Using notations adopted in [8], the SDM $\mathcal{M}$ can be regarded as a two-tuple $\mathcal{M} = (\mathcal{V}, \mathcal{K})$, where $\mathcal{V}$ is a set of 3D positions $\boldsymbol{v}_i$ $(1 \leq i \leq N_v)$ of N_v vertices, and $\mathcal{K}$ is an abstract simplicical complex which contains all adjacency information of $\mathcal{M}$. Moreover, $\mathcal{K}$ includes three types of subsets of simplices: a subset of

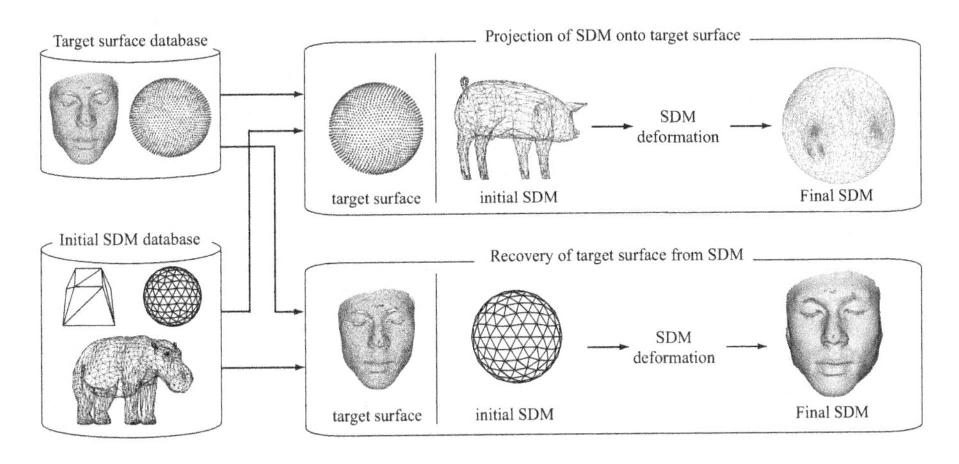

Fig. 1. Concept of our proposed method

vertices $i \in \mathcal{K}_v$, a subset of edges $e = \{i, j\} \in \mathcal{K}_e$, and a subset of faces $f = \{i, j, k\} \in \mathcal{K}_f$. Therefore, $\mathcal{K} = \mathcal{K}_v \cup \mathcal{K}_e \cup \mathcal{K}_f$. Here, our edge representation has a commutative property. For example, the edge e_3 as shown in Fig. 2 is composed of two vertices i_3 and i_4 ($i_3, i_4 \in \mathcal{K}_v$), and is described as $e_3 = \{i_3, i_4\} = \{i_4, i_3\}$. We represent each face of the SDM with a list of its three vertices arranged in counterclockwise direction, i.e., the face f_2 as shown in Fig. 2 is described by $f_2 = \{i_2, i_4, i_3\} = \{i_4, i_3, i_2\} = \{i_3, i_2, i_4\}$.

When two vertices in $\mathcal{K}_v$ are connected only by one edge in $\mathcal{K}_e$, these vertices are topological neighbors of each other. Given two vertices i_1 and i_4 as shown in Fig. 2, a path from i_1 to i_4 is defined as a series of edges. Then, a topological distance $L(i_1, i_4)$ between them is defined as the number of edges of the shortest path from i_1 to i_4. Hence, another topological distance $L(i_4, i_1)$ from i_4 to i_1 is equal to $L(i_1, i_4)$. The shortest path between i_1 and i_4 is illustrated by dashed lines, and the topological distance $L(i_1, i_4)$ $(= L(i_4, i_1))$ is 2.

2.2 Formulation of SDM Deformation

There are two purposes of deforming the SDM: one is to fit the SDM to a target surface $\mathcal{S}$, and the other is to recover $\mathcal{S}$ from the SDM. Considering our SDM notation, the first purpose of the SDM deformation is to project the SDM onto $\mathcal{S}$ by changing the vertex positions in $\mathcal{V}$ while keeping the original topology among vertices represented by $\mathcal{K}$. This projection is called the topology-preserving mapping. Given an initial SDM $\mathcal{M}^b$ and a final SDM $\mathcal{M}^d$, the topology-preserving mapping Φ is formulated as

$$\Phi : \mathcal{M}^b = (\mathcal{V}^b, \mathcal{K}) \longmapsto \mathcal{M}^d = (\mathcal{V}^d, \mathcal{K}) \quad (1)$$

To formulate the second purpose of the SDM deformation, we define an error function for reconstructing the target surface $\mathcal{S}$ from the SDM $\mathcal{M}$. Each control

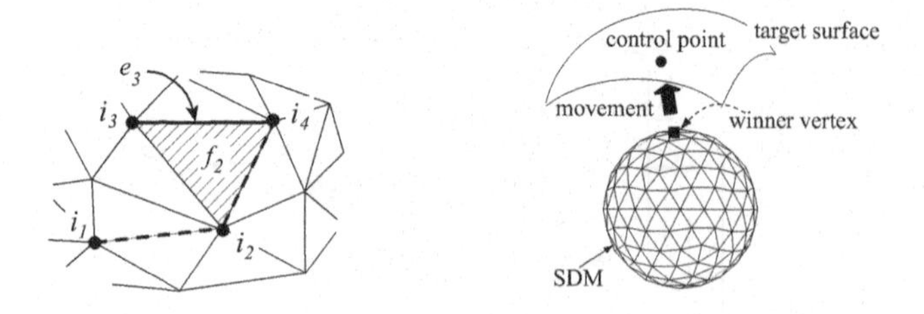

Fig. 2. Example of notations in our SDM **Fig. 3.** SDM Deformation

point $\boldsymbol{p}_u$ on $\mathcal{S}$ is corresponded to its closest vertex among all vertices of $\boldsymbol{\mathcal{M}}$. Let $\boldsymbol{\Omega}_i$ be a set of control points that are made correspondence with a vertex i. Also we denote as $\boldsymbol{\Gamma}_i$ a set of faces $f_m \in \boldsymbol{\mathcal{K}}_f$ which include the vertex i. Then, the error function is defined as a distance $D(\boldsymbol{\mathcal{M}}, \mathcal{S})$ between $\boldsymbol{\mathcal{M}}$ and $\mathcal{S}$:

$$D(\boldsymbol{\mathcal{M}}, \mathcal{S}) = \frac{1}{3}\frac{1}{|\boldsymbol{\Gamma}_i||\boldsymbol{\Omega}_i|}\sum_{i\in\boldsymbol{\mathcal{V}}}\sum_{f_m\in\boldsymbol{\Gamma}_i}\sum_{\boldsymbol{p}_u\in\boldsymbol{\Omega}_i}\{H(\boldsymbol{p}_u, f_m)\}^2, \tag{2}$$

where $|\boldsymbol{\Gamma}_i|$ and $|\boldsymbol{\Omega}_i|$ is the total amounts of elements in $\boldsymbol{\Gamma}_i$ and $\boldsymbol{\Omega}_i$, respectively. A function $H(\boldsymbol{p}_u, f_m)$ returns the Euclidean distance between $\boldsymbol{p}_u$ and f_m.

From eqs.(1) and (2), the deformation of $\boldsymbol{\mathcal{M}}^b$ is formulated by the optimization problem of finding $\boldsymbol{\mathcal{M}}^d$ and $\tilde{\Phi}$ which satisfy the following conditions:

$$\boldsymbol{\mathcal{M}}^d = \tilde{\Phi}(\boldsymbol{\mathcal{M}}^b); \tag{3}$$

$$\tilde{\Phi} = \arg\min_{\Phi} D(\Phi(\boldsymbol{\mathcal{M}}^b), \mathcal{S}). \tag{4}$$

3 SDM Deformation

3.1 Overview

This section explains how to deform a SDM. Generally, the projection function Φ in eq.(1) is nonlinear, and a deformation from $\boldsymbol{\mathcal{M}}^b$ to $\boldsymbol{\mathcal{M}}^d$ is not always unique. Here, as shown in Fig.3, the SDM introduces a framework of Self-Organizing Map (SOM)[9] so that the SDM and control points on a target surface are regarded as a network and input data of the SOM, respectively. Then, vertices of the SDM and their 3D positions correspond to units of the network and positional vectors of units, respectively.

SOM is one of the well-known methods for finding a topology-preserving mapping. By using SOM, we can obtain a network which represents the distribution of given input data. The network consists of units and edges. Each unit has a positional vector which provides a position in the input data space. The algorithm using SOM consists of three steps. The first step is to compute the Euclidean distance between an input data randomly selected and every unit of the network. Next, the unit with the minimum distance is selected as a winner unit of the input data. For the winner unit and its neighbor units, their positions are modified so that these units become closer to the input data. These processes are repeated until all units are not modified. In the algorithm, the network is deformed by moving units in the input data space.

From the geometrical point of view, the model resulting from SOM has the character that the Voronoi region of each vertex of the SDM includes almost the same number of control points. This means that the final SDM $\mathcal{M}^d$ can not always recover the object surface completely because $\mathcal{M}^d$ may not be satisfied with the equation (4). In order to cope with this problem, we further deform the SDM by minimizing an energy function to improve the accuracy of the reconstructed target surface by the SDM. The energy function in our method is based on the error function in eq.(2). When the vertex i is located at the position $\boldsymbol{v}_i$, the value of the energy function E for the vertex i is computed by

$$E(\boldsymbol{v}_i) = \sum_{f_m \in \boldsymbol{\Gamma}_i} \sum_{\boldsymbol{p}_u \in \boldsymbol{\Omega}_i} \{H(\boldsymbol{p}_u, f_m)\}^2. \quad (5)$$

3.2 Algorithm

Our deformation of the SDM is composed of the following steps:

1. Initialize a time parameter t to $t = 0$.
2. From the set of control points on a target surface $\mathcal{S}$, randomly choose a control point $\boldsymbol{p}^{(t)}$ at time t.
3. Determine a winner vertex $k^{(t)} \in \mathcal{K}$ by

$$k^{(t)} = \arg\min_{i \in \mathcal{K}} \; [\boldsymbol{n}_p \cdot (\boldsymbol{p}^{(t)} - \boldsymbol{v}_i)], \quad (6)$$

   where $\boldsymbol{n}_p$ is a normal vector at $\boldsymbol{p}^{(t)}$. The expression $\|\boldsymbol{x}\|$ is the Euclidean norm of a vector $\boldsymbol{x}$.
4. For the winner vertex $k^{(t)}$ and its neighbors, adapt their positions according to the topological distances from $k^{(t)}$:

$$\boldsymbol{v}_i \leftarrow \boldsymbol{v}_i + \epsilon(t)\lambda(i|k^{(t)})(\boldsymbol{p}^{(t)} - \boldsymbol{v}_i). \quad (7)$$

   where $\epsilon(t)$ is a learning rate which determines the extent to which the vertex is adapted towards the point, and is defined by $\epsilon(t) = \epsilon_b(\frac{\epsilon_d}{\epsilon_b})^{t/T_c}$. Here, ϵ_b and ϵ_d are, respectively, an initial value and a final value of ϵ, and these values are set to $\epsilon_b = 3.0$ and $\epsilon_d = 0.1$. T_c is the maximum number of repeating from step 2 to 5.
   The neighborhood function $\lambda(i|k)$ in eq.(7) means an adaptation rate of an arbitrary vertex i for a winner vertex k. It is a decreasing function of the topological distance between two vertices. The value of $\lambda()$ is computed by

$$\lambda(i|k) = \exp[-\frac{1}{2}\{\frac{L(i,k)}{\sigma(t)}\}^2]. \quad (8)$$

   The standard deviation $\sigma(t)$ of the Gaussian is obtained by $\sigma(t) = \sigma_b(\frac{\sigma_d}{\sigma_b})^{t/T_c}$ for a initial value σ_b and a final value σ_d. We empirically set σ_b and σ_d to $\sigma_b = 0.1$ and $\sigma_d = 0.005$, respectively.

5. If all vertices are not moved, or $t \geq T_c$, then go to step 6. Otherwise, $t \leftarrow t+1$ and go to step 2.
6. For each vertex i:
   (a) Choose potential vectors $\tilde{\boldsymbol{v}}_i$ by $\tilde{\boldsymbol{v}}_i = \boldsymbol{v}_i + w(\boldsymbol{p}_{-}\boldsymbol{v}_i)$ for updating the position $\boldsymbol{v}_i$ of the vertex i. Then, $\boldsymbol{p}_u$ included in $\boldsymbol{\Omega}_i$ is a corresponding control point of the vertex i. The parameter w is a variable which gives a rate for moving $\boldsymbol{v}_i$ to $\boldsymbol{p}_u$.
   (b) Find the vector $\boldsymbol{v}_i^*$ satisfying

$$\boldsymbol{v}_i^* = \arg\min_{\tilde{\boldsymbol{v}}_i} E(\tilde{\boldsymbol{v}}_i), \tag{9}$$

   where $E(\boldsymbol{v}_i)$ is the energy function in eq.(5). And update $\boldsymbol{v}_i$ by $\boldsymbol{v}_i \leftarrow \boldsymbol{v}_i^*$.
7. If the SDM $\mathcal{M}$ is satisfied with $D(\mathcal{M}, \mathcal{S}) < \theta_e$, the process is terminated. Otherwise, go to step 6. Here, θ_e is a threshold.

Our algorithm can control the deformation of the SDM by changing the ways how to choose a control point in step 2, and how to determine a winner vertex in step 3. For example, a user can have the constraint that an arbitrary vertex i is always selected as the winner of a special control point $\boldsymbol{p}_u$. Under this constraint, the SDM is deformed so that the vertex i constantly moves toward $\boldsymbol{p}_u$. When choosing probability of control points on a particular region of the target surface is higher than that of other points, the vertices of the SDM tend to move toward the region. Therefore, the way to choose points makes an influence on the density of vertices of the SDM on the target surface.

4 Experimental Results

In order to verify the applicability of our proposed method, we made some experiments of applying the SDM to various kinds of 3D object models. The models "bone", "venus" and "rabbit" downloaded from Cyberware webpage are contained in the models used in our experiment. When a set of range points on a target surface are given, these range points are directly used as control points. On the other hand, when the target surface is represented by some parametric functions, control points are calculated from the functions.

At first, a face model of a male is generated by applying the SDM to the range data of the face as shown in Fig.4(a). The range data is composed of about 85,000 points on the facial surface. The initial shape of the SDM is the tessellated sphere by subdividing each triangular facet of an icosahedron recursively [10]. Fig.4(b) shows the surface resulting from our SDM at level 3, which is obtained by 4 times subdivision. It takes about two minutes to obtain the result on a PC platform with Intel Pentium IV 2.8[GHz]. To improve the accuracy of the model, we increase the number of vertices by performing 1-to-4 subdivision for all patches of the SDM twice, and obtain the SDM at level 5. The newly obtained vertices are moved by repeating steps 6 and 7 in the algorithm of our SDM deformation. The final result is shown in Fig.4(c). Here, an approximation error by the SDM

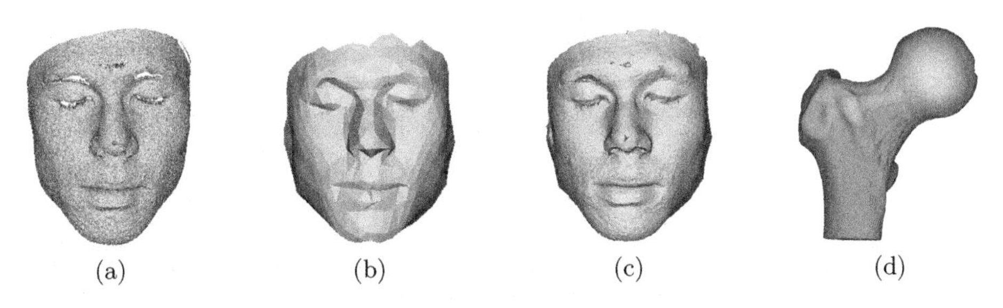

Fig. 4. Recovery of an object shape by SDM: (a)range data of a male face; (b)face model obtained by deforming SDM at level 3; (c)face obtained by deforming SDM at level 5; (d)reconstructed bone model

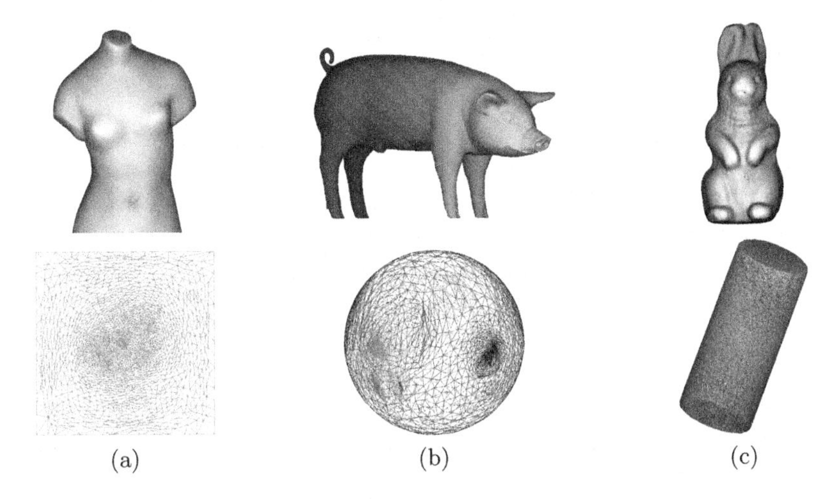

Fig. 5. Projection of object model onto some kinds of surfaces by our SDM. Top row: mesh models of (a)venus, (b)pig and (c)rabbit; bottom row: models mapped onto (a)plane, (b)spherical surface and (c)cylinder.

is defined as the average distance between each patch of the model and points on the face. The errors of two models as shown in Fig.4(b) and (c) are 0.27 and 0.12[mm], respectively. Since these models is obtained by the recursive division of patches, it is easy to generate the multiresolution model of the face. Our SDM is applied to other kinds of models. Fig. 4(d) shows an example of bone reconstructed from a spherical SDM.

The second experiment is to project some mesh models of objects onto simpler surfaces such as plane and sphere. The top row in Fig. 5 shows the initial SDMs. The model of the "venus" is projected onto a plane, where each grid point on the plane is used as a control point. In the projection of both models of a "pig" and a "rabbit", all control points on the target surfaces are calculated from their surface functions. The number of control points used in each projection is ten times larger than that of vertices included in a mesh model to be projected. The bottom row in Fig. 5 displays the projected models. From these results, we can conclude that our method can project mesh models onto some kinds of mapping surfaces in a unified framework.

5 Conclusion

This paper proposed a new method for projecting mesh models onto a given surface by Self-organizing Deformable Model(SDM). The basic idea behind the SDM is the combination of the competitive learning and the energy minimization. Some experimental results show that our SDM is a powerful tool for various fields in computer vision and computer graphics. For example, the SDM enables us to establish the correspondence between two mesh models by mapping them onto a common target surface. One of its applications using this correspondence is a morphing between the models. Now we have developed some applications using the SDM.

Acknowledgment

This research was partially supported by the Ministry of Education, Science, Sports and Culture, Grant-in-Aid for Young Scientists (B), 15700149, 2005, and Scientific Research (B), 17300033, 2005.

References

1. Morooka, K., Sugisawa, K., Nagahashi, H.: 3d morphing between objects with different topologies. In: Proc. IASTED Int. Conf. on CGIM. (2002) 1–7
2. Matsuo, H., Kimura, M., Iwata, A.: Multi-scale and hierarchical description using energy controlled active balloon model. In: Proc. ICPR'98. (1998) 205–209
3. Duan, Y., Qin, H.: A subdivision-based deformable model for surface reconstruction of unknown topology. Graphical Models **66** (2004) 181–202
4. Gibson, S., Mirtich, B.: A survey of deformable modeling in computer graphics. Technical report (1997)
5. Bro-Nielsen, M.: Active nets and cubes. Technical report (1994)
6. Eck, E., DeRose, T., Duchamp, T., Hoppe, H., Lounsbery, M., Stuetzle, W.: Multiresolution analysis of arbitrary meshes. Computer Graphics **29** (1995) 173–182
7. Floater, M., Hormann, K.: Recent advances in surface parameterization. In: Multiresolution in Geometric Modeling 2003. (2003) 259–284
8. Lee, A., Sweldens, W., Schröder, P., Cowsar, L., Dobkin, D.: Maps: Multiresolution adaptive parameterization of surfaces. In: SIGGRAPH 98. (1998) 95–104
9. Kohonen, T., ed.: Self-Organizing Maps. Springer-Verlag, Berlin Heidelberg New York (1996)
10. Horn, B., ed.: Robot Vision. MIT Press, Cambridge (1986)

Image-Based Deformation of Objects in Real Scenes

Han-Vit Chung and In-Kwon Lee

Dept. of Computer Science, Yonsei University
sharpguy@cs.yonsei.ac.kr, iklee@yonsei.ac.kr

Abstract. We present a new method for deforming an object in a static real scene, which interacts with animated synthetic characters. Unlike the existing method - making a new synthetic object to substitute for the interacting object in the real scene, we directly deform the object in image space using an image-warping technique with assistance from a simplified 3D sub-model. The deformed image sequence is processed further using the Expression Ratio Image (ERI) technique to apply the illumination changes generated by the deformation. Using this method, we can maintain the photo-realistic rendering quality of the scene efficiently by preserving the appearance of the object in the real scene as it is.

1 Introduction

Rendering synthetic objects into real scenes is a popular technique used in many applications such as film production and augmented reality [1]. To render an existing object in a real scene (we call this object an "image-object" in this paper) that is being deformed by the interaction with a synthetic character, the image-object should also be modelled and animated as another synthetic object (we call this method "synthetic-copy" in this paper). The simulation of interaction between the character and image-object can be rendered with original textures and lighting conditions extracted from the real scene. Then, a final animation would be created by the careful composition of the real and the synthetic scenes.

When an image-object is complex enough as a part of a complex environment, the object is strongly coupled with other objects in the environment. Separating the object from the original scene is not easy. If the deformations of the object generated by the interactions with a synthetic character are not too large, the animator may want to find another method instead of using synthetic-copy. For example, if an image includes a bed with very complex shapes and textures, and a synthetic ball is thrown on the bedspread, we may try to find a more efficient way rather than modelling and animating the deformations of the bedspread synthetically. In the film making process, the interacting real objects are often deformed with the aid of a virtual object such as a transparent glass stick. Before the final composition of the real scene and synthetic characters, the glass stick in the real scene is erased frame by frame.

In this paper, we suggest a new method for handling the interactions between a synthetic character and an image-object in a static real scene. A simplified 3D

G. Bebis et al. (Eds.): ISVC 2005, LNCS 3804, pp. 159–166, 2005.

sub-model representing the image-object is used in the simulation of the interactions with the synthetic character. The geometric change of the 3D sub-model generated by the simulation is used to deform the original image-object using warping techniques in image space. To reflect the illumination change generated by the deformation, we apply the Expression Ratio Image (ERI) technique to the deformed image. Because we only need the change of silhouette and the ratio of illumination in our process, a simplified white 3D sub-model can be used in the simulation. Using this method, we can maintain the photo-realistic rendering quality of the image-object by preserving the textures and lighting conditions in the original real scene more effectively than the synthetic-copy method.

There are some assumptions and restrictions in our method. First, we consider only a single static real scene as the background image; thus, the position and orientation of the camera are always fixed during the animation. Second, we assume the positions and directions of a camera and lights in the real scene are already known. This is feasible because those parameters can be known when the real scene is newly photographed for the animation. If not, we can use conventional methods (see next section) to estimate the camera and light parameters. Third, we assume the size of the deformation of the image-object is not too large, so any special case such as "cloth folding" does not arise in the simulation.

2 Related Work

Various image-based lighting techniques [2] have been developed for recovering reflectance properties of real surfaces under unknown illumination. Liu et al. [3] proposed a method of capturing the illumination change of one person's expression. They map ERI to any different faces to generate more expressive facial expressions. There have been many research projects for getting camera attributes from several images, but it is still a challenge to extract camera parameters from a single image [4]. Much effort has also gone into the area of deforming an image. According to Gomes et al. [5], the numerous warping methods can be roughly classified into parameter- [6], free-form- [7, 8], and feature-based [9, 10] techniques. There have been a lot of research results of generating animations from 2D pictures or photographs. Image-based rendering methods generate new images having an arbitrary viewpoint, using a lot of 2D input images [11, 12, 13, 14, 15], or by creating 3D graphical models or animations from an image [16, 17, 18].

3 Image-Based Deformation

3.1 3D Sub-model

To deform an image-object according to a given scenario, we need appropriate 3D deformation data. In our method, a 3D sub-model (see Fig. 1) that corresponds to the image-object is used in the simulation of interaction. This model can be constructed using image-based modelling methods [16, 17] combined with a

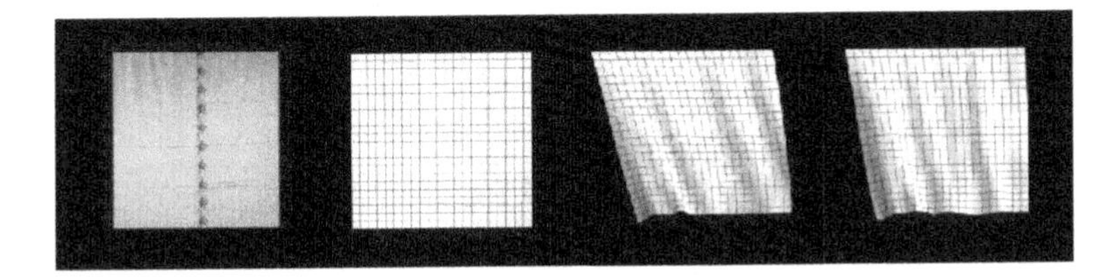

Fig. 1. The top left is an image-object. The rest are the frames in the animation of a 3D sub-model corresponding to the change of geometry and illumination of the image-object.

known camera position. The shapes of 3D sub-models should be similar enough to those of the original image-objects, but some simplifications may be made as follows:

- The back of shapes hidden from the fixed camera view can be omitted.
- The shapes, which are not deformed by the interaction, can be omitted. For example, we can use the sub-model of the bedspread only, excluding other parts of bed in the "ball on the bed" example in Section 1.
- The complex shapes, which do not have any serious effect on the change of silhouette in the 2D view of the model, can be ignored.

The colors and textures of the 3D sub-model do not have to be considered because the sub-model will not be rendered into the final rendered output. We used plain white color for all sub-models in our experimental examples, which is also helpful in measuring the illumination change in the ERI process.

3.2 Geometric Change

The two same 2D grids are generated: G_I and G_M, which cover the image-object and the initial projected view of the 3D sub-model, respectively (see

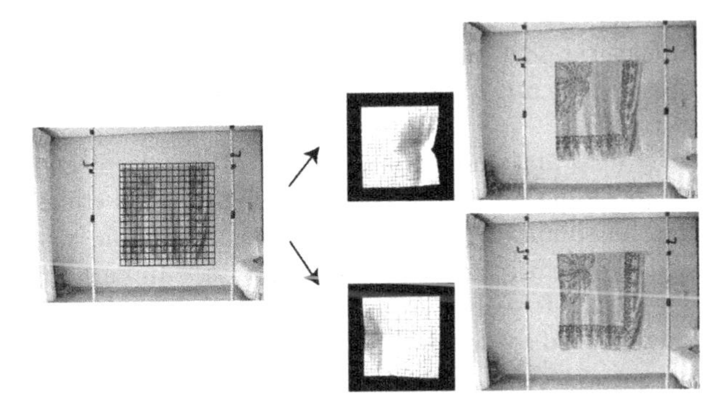

Fig. 2. Geometric Change: The leftmost image shows the 2D grid on the image-object. According to the deformations of 3D sub-model (*middle white models*), the image-object is geometrically deformed (*right*).

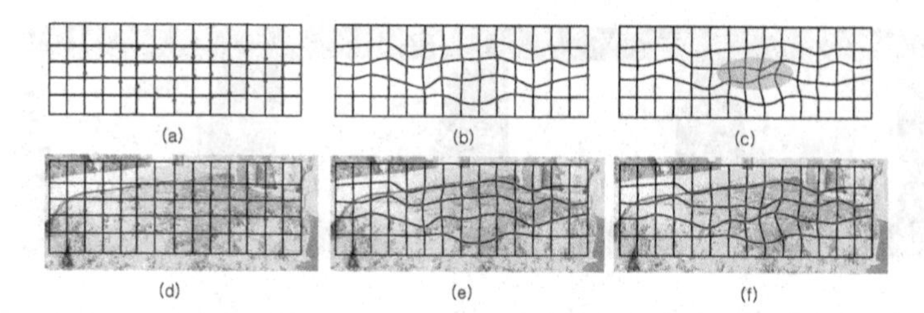

Fig. 3. (a) Grid G_M for a 3D sub-model. (b) Vertices in G_M are aligned to the feature points. (c) Changed grid G_M is in the middle of the simulation. (d) Initial static image. (e) Aligned grid G_I is identical to G_M. (f) Warped image according to the grid change in (c).

Fig. 2 and 3). Some feature points are defined on the deformed surface of the 3D sub-model. Initially, G_M is aligned to the feature points by moving each grid vertex to the projected 2D coordinates of the closest feature point from the grid vertex (see Fig. 3(b)). When the surface is deformed, some feature points are moved, the corresponding grid vertices in G_M can be moved automatically to the changed projected coordinates of the feature points (see Fig. 3(c)). The grid G_I is deformed to be identical to G_M for each frame, and the image-object is warped using a conventional, two-pass warping method [7, 8] using the deformed grid G_I (see Fig. 3(f)).

We need to control the resolution of the set of feature points and grid so that each feature point corresponds exclusively to a single grid vertex. Simultaneously, it is desirable to maintain the resolution of the grid as low as possible, because the unbound grid vertices that do not correspond to any feature point cannot move in the deformation process, which prevents the exact deformation of the image-object. Sometimes the background pixels around the image-objects should be warped together with the pixels that are included in the image objects. Especially, in the "waving cloth" example shown in Fig. 2, the background pixels near the boundary of the cloth object are shown and hidden alternately in the animation. In this case, we make the grid cover a slightly larger region, including some of the boundary pixels as well as the object. Then, the warping process can generate the natural deformation of the background pixels, which prevents annoying clipping and composition of the image-object from the background scene, frame by frame.

We assume the deformation of the object is always local enough that the degenerate cases, including self-intersections among the grid edges, do not arise in the middle of the simulation. Because of this restriction, we cannot treat scenes including large deformations, for example, a flapping flag in a strong wind, using our method. If such a large deformation is needed, we need to use the synthetic-copy method for the image-object.

3.3 Illumination Change

As Fig. 4 shows, the geometric warping alone cannot generate a convincing deformation result. In the first row of the figure, we cannot see the realistic de-

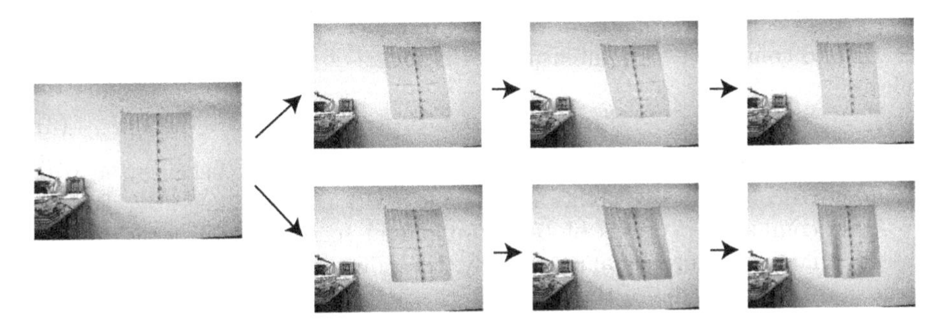

Fig. 4. Applying Illumination Change: The image sequence in the first row shows the geometrically warped images. Applying the change of illumination, gives the result shown in the second row, which looks more expressive and convincing.

formation effects because the resulting image sequence does not show the details such as wrinkles and illumination changes. Using the known light positions, we can construct virtual light sources to illuminate the 3D sub-model in the simulation process. The intensities and other properties of the lights are manually controlled to be as similar as possible to the real scene. Because, we only measure the ratio of illumination change, this rough approximation of light properties is usually acceptable in most cases. The rendered white 3D sub-model shows the illumination changes, which can be applied to the image-object using the ERI technique [3].

Assume there are m light sources illuminating some point $\mathbf{p}$ on a surface. Let $\mathbf{n}$ denote normal vector of the surface at $\mathbf{p}$, and $\mathbf{l}_i$ and I_i, $1 \leq i \leq m$, denote the light direction from $\mathbf{p}$ to the ith light source and the intensity of the light source, respectively. Suppose the surface is diffuse, and let ρ be its reflectance coefficient at $\mathbf{p}$. ERI ($\Re$) is defined as the ratio of light intensity at the same point $\mathbf{p}$ between two arbitrary lightened images:

$$\Re \equiv \frac{I'}{I} = \frac{\rho \sum_{i=1}^{m} I_i \mathbf{n}' \cdot \mathbf{l}'_i}{\rho \sum_{i=1}^{m} I_i \mathbf{n} \cdot \mathbf{l}_i}. \tag{1}$$

From the above equation, we have $I' = \Re I$ for a point $\mathbf{p}$ on the surface.

To apply the illumination change computed by ERI to the image-object at the ith frame, we need the following images:

- $\mathcal{A}_0$: rendered image of the 3D sub-model at the initial frame.
- $\mathcal{A}_i$: rendered image of the deformed 3D sub-model at the ith frame.
- $\mathcal{A}'_0$: warped image generated by warping $\mathcal{A}_0$ to have the same geometry as $\mathcal{A}_i$.
- $\mathcal{B}_i$: the geometrically deformed image-object at the ith frame.

As proven in [3], we can compute the ERI ($\Re$) easily by comparing two pixel values at same position:

$$\Re(u,v) = \frac{\mathcal{A}_i(u,v)}{\mathcal{A}'_0(u,v)}, \tag{2}$$

where (u, v) is the coordinates of the pixel in image space. Then, we can apply the ERI to compute a new intensity of the image-object at the pixel (u, v) as follows:

$$\mathcal{B}_i'(u, v) = \Re(u, v)\mathcal{B}_i(u, v). \quad (3)$$

Note that the algorithm requires a warping from $\mathcal{A}_0$ to $\mathcal{A}_0'$, because the ERI should be calculated at two points at the same position in two images $\mathcal{A}_0'$ and $\mathcal{A}_i$.

After computing a series of background real scene, including the image-objects that are deformed appropriately, the composition of the background scene and the animation of the synthetic characters using conventional composition techniques [19] produces the final animation.

4 Results

In the animation in Fig. 5, a ball is thrown on the laundry to shoo away a fly. The time and position of each collision between the laundry and the ball are predefined in a scenario, which also implies the collision force related to the velocity and mass of the ball. We used a well-known mass-spring model [20] to simulate the deformation of the laundry generated by the collision. We used a 23×23 grid for the geometric warping. The original real scene is an image of 1400×1050 pixels.

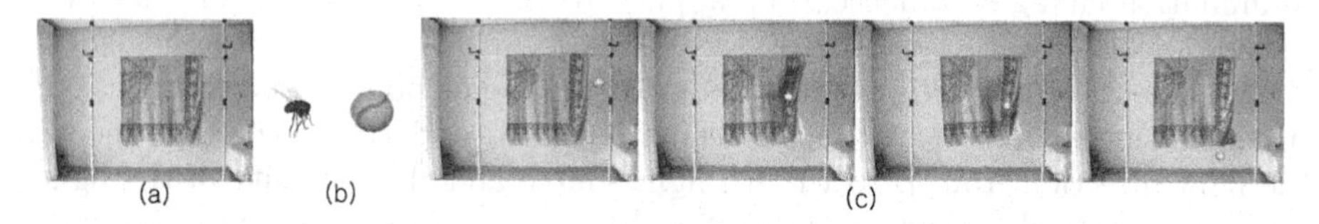

Fig. 5. Example 1: (a) The original, fixed real scene. (b) Two synthetic objects: a fly and a ball. (c) Composition result with proper deformations of the laundry object interacting with the synthetic ball.

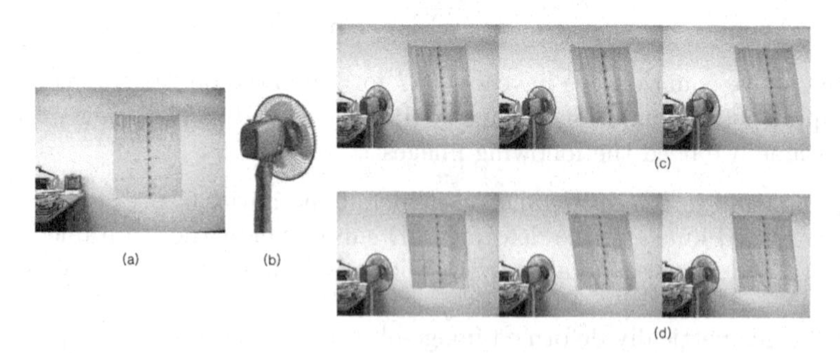

Fig. 6. Example 2: (a) The original fixed real scene. (b) A synthetic electric fan. (c) The animation resulting from using our image-based deformation method. (d) The animation resulting from modelling and animating the synthetic cloth model: the cloth is rendered separately using texture mapping.

Fig. 6 shows an example of a piece of cloth flapping in the wind generated by an electric fan. A 23×23 grid is used for this example. We can observe the differences between the animations generated using image-based deformation (Fig. 6(c)) and the synthetic-copy method (Fig. 6(d)). When both the electric fan and a piece of cloth are synthetic models, the quality of the rendering for the synthetic models depends on the animator's skill and time invested in modelling and animating the characters. Our result looks sufficiently expressive and convincing compared to the result of the traditional method.

5 Conclusions and Future Work

This paper suggests a new method for rendering the deformations of an image-object that is interacting with a synthetic character rendered into a real scene. With the aid of a 3D sub-model, we can deform the image-object directly in image space, using warping and ERI techniques. Some convincing experimental results are shown in this paper.

The most important advantage of this approach is that we can maintain the photo-realistic rendering quality of the image-object because we directly use the original image-object to deform it. Doing so prevents going through the complex process of extracting the exact lighting information from the original real scene.

The image-warping technique exploited for geometric deformation has some limitations. A large amount of deformation cannot be handled with this approach. In that case, it still seems that there is no way to solve the problem without using the synthetic-copy method. Moreover, when the deformed face in the 3D sub-model is nearly parallel to the viewing direction, the face becomes too small to be deformed with the image warping. We need more investigation for these cases.

Applying our method to the real video scene with a dynamically changing viewpoint and direction may be another extension. We are also trying to improve our method to be applied to real-time environments like 3D games. When the interaction happens, the 3D sub-model for the background object is deformed with great rapidity, and other processes such as image warping and ERI should be enough fast to support the real-time speed.

Acknowledgement

This work was supported by grant No. R01-2004-000-10117-0(2004) from the Basic Research Program of the Korea Science & Engineering Foundation.

References

1. Birn J. Digital Lighting & Rendering. New Riders Press, 2000.
2. Debevec P. HDRI and Image-Based Lighting. *SIGGRAPH '2003 Course Notes No.19*, 2003.

3. Liu Z., Shan Y., and Zhang Z. Expresive Expression Mapping with Ratio Image. *Proceedings of SIGGRAPH '2001*, 2001, pp. 271-276.
4. Gabor Blasko. Vision-based Camera Matching Using Markers, *Proceedings of CESCG '2000*, 2000
5. Gomes J., Darsa L., Costa B., and Velho L. Warping and Morphing of Graphical Objects, *SIGGRAPH '95 Course Notes No.3*, 1995
6. Barr A.H. Global and Local Deformations of Solid Primitives. *In Proceedings of SIGGRAPH '84*, 1984, pp. 21-30.
7. Smith A.R. Planar 2-Pass Texture Mapping and Warping, *Proceedings of SIGGRAPH '87*, 1987, pp. 263-271.
8. Smithe D.B., A Two-Pass Mesh Warping Algorithm for Object Transformation and Image Interpolation, *Technical Report 1030*, ILM Computer Graphics Department, Lucas_lm, 1990.
9. Beier T., Neely S. Feature-Based Image Metamorphosis, *Proceedings of SIGGRAPH '92*, 1992, pp. 263-271.
10. Lee S.-Y., Chwa K.-Y., Shin S.-Y., Wolberg G. Image Metamorphosis Using Snakes and Free-Form Deformations, *Proceedings of SIGGRAPH '95*, 1995, pp. 439-448.
11. McMillan L., Bishop G. Plenoptic modeling : An Image-based rendering system, *Proceedings of SIGGRAPH '95*, 1995, pp. 39-46
12. Chen S. E. QuickTime VR - An Image-Based Approach to Virtual Environment Navigation, *ACM SIGGRAPH '95 Conference Proceedings*, 1995, pp. 29-38.
13. Mark W. R., McMillan L., and Bishop G. Post-Rendering 3D Warping, *Proceedings 1997 Symposiums on Interactive 3D Graphics*, 1997, pp. 7-16.
14. Chen S. E., Williams L. View Interpolation for Image Synthesis, *In SIGGRAPH '93 Conference Proceedings*, 1993, pp. 279-288
15. Shade J., Gortler S. J., He L. W., Szeliski R., Layered Depth Images, *Proceedings of SIGGRAPH '98*, 1998, pp. 231-242.
16. Liebowitz D., Criminisi A., and Zisserman A. Creating Architectural Models from Images, *In EuroGraphics '99 Conference Proceedings*, 1999, pp. 39-50.
17. Debevec P., Taylor C., and Malik J. Modeling and Rendering Architecture from Photographs: A Hybrid Geometry- and Image-Based Approach, *Proceedings of SIGGRAPH 96*, 1996, pp. 11-20.
18. Chuang Y., Goldman D., Zheng K., Curless B., Salesin D., Szeliski R. Animating Pictures With Stochastic Motion Textures, *Proceedings of SIGGRAPH 2005*, 2005, pp. 853-860.
19. Wright, S. 2001. Digital Compositing for Film and Video. Focal Press.
20. Witkin A., Baraff D., Blum M., and Monheit G. Physically Based Modeling: Principles and Practice. *SIGGRAPH Course Notes 19*, 1997.

Comparing Sphere-Tree Generators and Hierarchy Updates for Deformable Objects Collision Detection

M. Garcia, S. Bayona, P. Toharia, and C. Mendoza

Universidad Rey Juan Carlos,
c/Tulipan s/n E-28933 Mostoles (Madrid)
{marcos.garcia, sofia.bayona, pablo.toharia, cesar.mendoza}@urjc.es

Abstract. This paper presents a quantitative evaluation of the accuracy of different sphere-tree construction methods when they are used in deformable bodies. The methods evaluated are Grid (an extension of octrees), Hubbard, Adaptive Medial Axis and Spawn. We also present a new approach to update the sphere-tree hierarchy that ensures lower loss of accuracy than in traditional update techniques.

1 Introduction

One of the main concerns in surgery simulation is achieving a realistic framework such that interactions between virtual human tissues are as natural as in the real world. This implies to process, in real-time, the collision and contact responses between deformable virtual objects. Collision detection has always been a bottleneck to obtain real-time simulations and an extensively research topic in computer graphics. Most of the work has been focused on solving the rigid body collision detection problem, but, in the last years, collision detection between deformable objects has become a hot topic of research. Typical algorithms to detect the collision between deformable bodies are based on using bounding volumes and spatial decomposition techniques in a hierarchical manner.

This work addresses the collision detection problem for deformable objects when bounding sphere hierarchies are used. In the last years, the sphere-tree construction process has been significantly improved [1]: the sphere-tree approximations are tighter and the object's surface is better covered by the leaf spheres of the hierarchy. However, when an object deforms, the hierarchies need to be updated at each time-step to keep the accuracy of the collision checking. This update can be very slow and can affect the interactivity of the simulation.

1.1 Contributions and Outline

To the best of our knowledge, there is not a quantitative evaluation, in terms of accuracy, for different sphere-tree hierarchies when they are used in deformable objects. We present a quantitative evaluation of the accuracy of different sphere-tree hierarchies by measuring the *looseness* with which the sphere-tree fits an

G. Bebis et al. (Eds.): ISVC 2005, LNCS 3804, pp. 167–174, 2005.

object in a deformable body. Additionally, we develop different update techniques for the sphere-tree hierarchies that keep the tightness to the object and we compare their accuracy.

The rest of the paper is organized as follows. Section 2 gives an overview of collision detection methods and a brief description of the different sphere-tree hierarchies that we evaluate. Next, in section 3, we identify some aspects of the sphere-tree hierarchies that affect the looseness of the spheres and present our sphere-tree hierarchy update techniques. We also describe how we measure the looseness of the spheres on the object. After that, experiments and comparisons are presented in section 4. Finally, some possible future work and conclusions that can be drawn from our comparisons are described in section 5.

2 Related Work

Refer to [2, 3] for recent surveys in collision detection for deformable objects. Most of the algorithms developed for collision detection use bounding volumes hierarchies such as oriented bounding boxes (OBBs) [4], k-dops [5], including the 6-dop special case: the axis-aligned bounding boxes (AABBs) [6], and sphere trees [1, 7]. According to Van den Bergen [6], AABBs are better option than OBBs for objects undergoing deformations, in terms of memory storage and hierarchy updates. Larsson and Akenine-Möller [8] compared different methods for the hierarchy updating process (i.e. bottom-up and top-down strategies). They proposed an hybrid method that uses both strategies. Mezger et al. [9] speeded up the process by updating only parts of the hierarchy where the vertices have not moved farther than a given distance. Sphere-trees are a key factor in *time-critical collision detection* [10] which has only been applied in rigid body collision detection. Some works compared the performance of different bounding volumes for rigid bodies [1, 4]. Recently, James et al. [11] presented a method to update sphere-tree hierarchies by using reduced deformable structures. For deformable objects there has been some evaluations for axis-aligned and oriented bounding boxes [6, 8], but to our knowledge there is not evaluation of different sphere-trees hierarchies when they are used for deformable bodies.

2.1 Background

A collision detection algorithm, based on sphere hierarchies, checks for collisions between successively tighter approximations of the objects surface. These approximations are composed of a set of spheres that bound, in some manner, primitives of the surface object (e.g. facets, vertices). The better fit of these approximations to the surface object, the more accurate the collision algorithm is. Each level of the hierarchy represents a tighter fit that its parent and the children covering the object's surface are totally wrapped by the parent sphere. We describe some techniques to construct these hierarchies.

The *Grid algorithm* [12] is based on the octree algorithm [13, 14, 15] where the bounding cube of the object is subdivided into 8 sub-cubes (nodes). Each sub-cube can also be subdivided into another set of sub-cubes until a given depth.

These cubes are used to generate the sphere tree. The grid algorithm instead of producing an equal subdivision of the parent node as in the octree, allows more freedom in the sub-division. The idea is to find a grid that produces the fewest number of spheres to approximate the object. Thus, the spheres can be of any dimension. The algorithm can therefore be seen as an optimization problem by considering how well filled (by the object) each sphere is. The optimization technique will aim to increase the area covered by some spheres so others spheres can be discarded.

The *Hubbard's algorithm* [7] generates the sphere-tree from an approximation of the object's medial axis surface. To span the surface, first a set of points are uniformly placed on the object's surface and used to construct a 3D Voronoi diagram. Then, the Voronoi vertices inside the polyhedron are identified to span the surface. Each of these vertices define a sphere, and these spheres tightly approximate the object. Hubbard reduces the number of spheres while preserving as much tightness of the approximation as possible by merging the spheres. The *Adaptive Medial Axis algorithm* [1] is based on Hubbard's algorithm. Hubbard [7] uses a static medial axis approximation while Bradshaw et al. [1] proposed to update the medial axis approximation during the construction of the sphere tree by adding more sample points. Location of these new points is chosen so that the worst sphere is replaced (or merged) with tighter fitting ones.

The *spawn algorithm* [12] distributes the error evenly across the approximation. Each sphere is expanded the same amount until they protrude past the surface a given distance, a stand-off distance. A search algorithm is used to obtain this distance that will yield the desired number of spheres. Additionally, instead of using the object's medial axis for the construction, a local optimization algorithm is used to generate the set of spheres. For each sphere in the set, the optimization algorithm chooses the location that best covers the object, hence keeping small the set of spheres. The algorithm is named spawn as each sphere grows from its predecessor.

3 Updating Hierarchies

The sphere-tree hierarchies, described previously, keep a constant accuracy during collision detection between rigid bodies. However, for deformable objects, where the hierarchies are modified (i.e. the radius and center of the spheres are changed), there is a loss in the accuracy. A standard manner to obtain the new position of a center is by adding to the original center the average displacement vector of the enclosed vertices. James et al. [11] relocated the center by the weighted average displacements of the vertices inside a sphere. The radius is computed by obtaining the distance from the new center to the farthest enclosed vertices. This might excessively increase the radius of the new sphere and largely affect the accuracy of the sphere-tree hierarchy. Additionally, for the latest sphere tree construction methods [1], in certain cases, the spheres do not enclose any vertex. For example, when lots of long, thin triangles are being used. We name these spheres *void spheres*. Next, we propose some approaches that avoid an excessive increment of the radius of the sphere, keeping suitable levels of accuracy, and that take into account the vertices that are not inside the spheres to relocate the sphere.

3.1 Update of the Center

We first correctly link all the spheres to the vertices of the object's surface to avoid the existence of void spheres. For each intersecting facet F_i with a given sphere, s, we obtain the vertices v_j such that $v_j \in F_i$ and associated to s. This can include internal and external vertices with respect to s. Repeated vertices are excluded. Next, let BB be the bounding box of the set of vertices v_j associated to s and c_{BB} the center of BB. Let u be the displacement vector of the bounding box center, i.e. $u = c_{BB_{new}} - c_{BB_{original}}$. Thus, the new position of the center, c, of the sphere is given by:

$$c_{new} = c + u. \tag{1}$$

This process is repeated for all the spheres in the hierarchy.

3.2 Update of the Radius

Let d_j be the distance from the associated vertices $v_j \in s$ to the sphere's center, c, in the undeformed configuration and let $d_{j_{new}}$ the distance of the new positions (i.e. in the deformed object) of v_j to the new center position. Define the distance increment ratio as $\alpha_j = d_{j_{new}}/d_j$. Thus, for a given leaf sphere, the new radius, r_n, is computed as follows:

$$r_n = r \max(\alpha_j) \tag{2}$$

where r is the original radius. This is done hierarchically, so that for upper levels, instead of using the vertices, we use the distance to its children spheres. Let dc_j be the distance between the centers of s and of its associated child sphere s_j, and r_j the original radius of s_j. For non-leaf spheres, d_j is calculated as follows:

$$d_j = dc_j + r_j. \tag{3}$$

Consequently, if $dc_{j_{new}}$ is the distance between the new center of s and the new center of s_j and $r_{j_{new}}$ is the new radius of s_j, then $d_{j_{new}}$ is calculated as follows:

$$d_{j_{new}} = dc_{j_{new}} + r_{j_{new}}. \tag{4}$$

Hence the radius is obtained as in Equation 2.

Alternatively, we can modify the radius using the bounding box, BB, of the elements (vertices or children spheres) associated to the given sphere. Redefine d_j as the distance from the original center of the sphere to the j corner of BB and $d_{j_{new}}$ the distance from the new center of the sphere to the j corner of the new bounding box. Hence we can compute the radius as:

$$r_n = \frac{\max_j(d_{j_{new}})}{\max_j(d_j)} r. \tag{5}$$

For leaf spheres, the bounding box is calculated using its associated vertices and for non-leaf spheres it is computed using its children spheres.

3.3 Proposed Update Approaches

We have proposed two approaches based in how we update the radius and center of each sphere of the hierarchy. Both approaches use our *linking* method to associate spheres to the object's surface and avoid the existence of void spheres.

- Approach 1: The center of the sphere is updated using the traditional approach, i.e. weighting the displacement of the sphere center and the radius is computed using our method in Equation 2.
- Approach 2: The center of the sphere is updated using the displacement of the center of the bounding box of the associated particles or children spheres, Equation 1. Similarly, the radius update is based on the bounding box as in Equation 5.

3.4 Accuracy Measure

We have measured the accuracy of a sphere-tree by measuring the *looseness* of the spheres, that is, a measurement of how much of the sphere protrude outside the object. Hubbard [16] uses Hausdorff distance from each sphere to the object's surface. However, when the object is non-convex, the distance needs to be approximated. We measure the error by considering the volume outside the object but inside the spheres. Both measures are computationally expensive and prohibited for real-time simulations. Next, we explain how we measure the volume between the object and the spheres.

Define a voxel grid, G_j, from the bounding box of the level j of the sphere hierarchy. Let Δ_{ji} be a unit voxel of G_j, $V_{\Delta_{ji}}$ the volume of Δ_{ji} and $c_{\Delta_{ji}}$ the center of the voxel Δ_{ji}. Define Π_j as the union of spheres of a level j in the hierarchy. Assume that the sphere-tree approximations totally cover the object, O. The error, e_{ji}, of the voxel, Δ_{ji}, is calculated as follows:

$$e_{ji} = \begin{cases} V_{\Delta_{ji}} & c_{\Delta_{ji}} \in \Pi_j \ \wedge \ c_{\Delta_{ji}} \notin O \\ 0 & \text{otherwise.} \end{cases} \tag{6}$$

Thus the total error for level j is:

$$e_j = \sum_i e_{ji} \tag{7}$$

The resolution of the error can be increased by subdividing in more voxels the grid G_j. We took the center of the voxel to test for intersections.

4 Results

We have constructed the sphere-tree hierarchies using Bradshaw's toolkit [1] (http://isg.cs.tcd.ie/spheretree/) with a depth of three (four levels including the root) and a branching factor of eight. We have measured the looseness error of different parametric deformations (bending, twisting, stretching), see Figure 1.

Fig. 1. *(Top row)* Deformations: bending, twisting, stretching, and the original position. *(Middle row)* Approach 2 for level 2. *(Bottom row)* Approach 2 for level 3 (leaves).

To evaluate the update approaches, we have used an Adaptive Medial Axis approximation [1] for the object. Figures 2.a,b show how the accuracy of the two deepest levels of the sphere-tree hierarchy, levels two and three (leaves), evolves during a stretch deformation. Observe that the error obtained using the *update approach 1* (i.e. weighting the displacement for the center and obtaining a ratio of the distance from the vertices to the center to update the radius) grows exponentially for a stretching deformation. The accuracy using the *update approach 2* (i.e. radius and center modified based on the bounding boxes of the associated particles or children spheres) is largely better. In both approaches, the center and radius of each sphere of the hierarchy can return to their initial conditions if the object returns to its initial condition as well.

Next, we compare the error of the different sphere-trees hierarchies when they are exposed to deformations, see Figure 2.c,d. Sample zero shows the error of the hierarchy in a rigid body collision detection process and the next samples show the error in intermediate deformed configurations. This accuracy changes during deformations. Note that for the level two of the hierarchy, Hubbard and the Adaptive Medial approximations show better accuracy results. However, surprisingly, for level three (leaves), the grid method resulted slightly better than the others. This indicates that although it is more conservative for rigid body collision detection, it can have better accuracy results for deformable bodies.

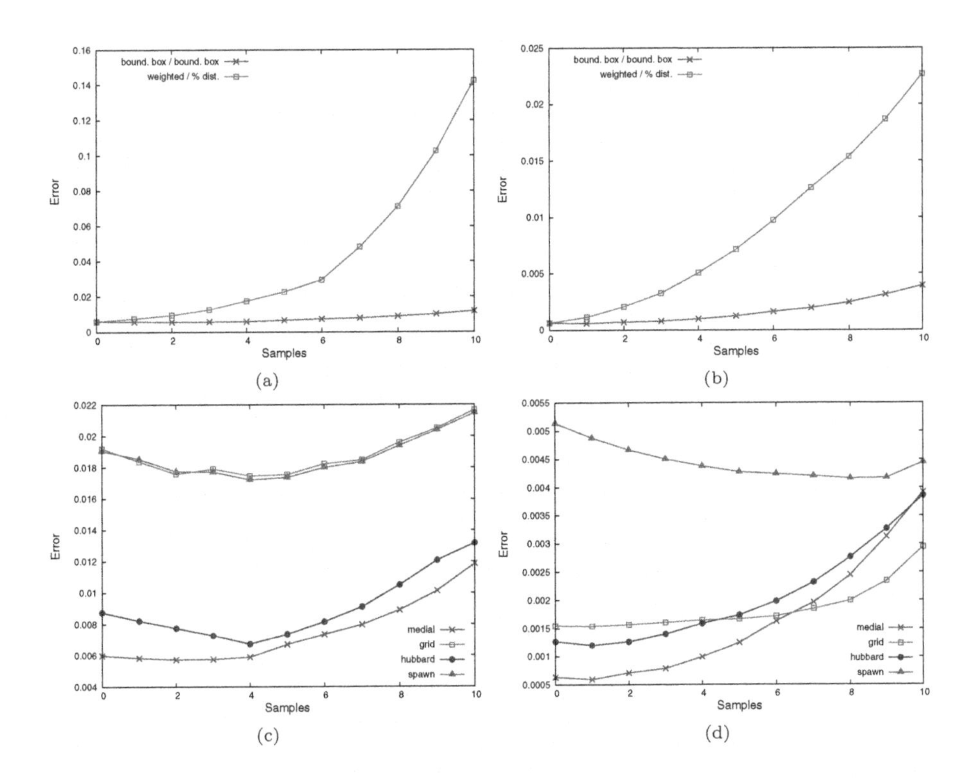

Fig. 2. *Top* Accuracy errors (measured in object dimensions) for the update approaches in level *(a)* two and *(b)* three (leaves). *Bottom* Accuracy errors for sphere-three generators in level *(c)* two and *(d)* three (leaves).

5 Conclusion and Future Work

In this paper we have presented a simple method to measure the accuracy of the sphere-tree hierarchy and we have used it to evaluate our proposed approaches to update the sphere-tree hierarchy (i.e. the center and the radius of each sphere). The approach based on the bounding box presented the best results. In terms of computational cost, it might be similar to updating an AABB, however, the fact that we update sphere-trees is particularly useful for time-critical collision detection or in cases where the contact response is computed using the leaves nodes. Moreover, we have compared the different sphere-tree hierarchies using our best update approach (bounding box based). The Adaptive Medial Axis approximation has turned out to have the best average accuracy for the different levels, however, it was surprising to obtain low error results for a Grid approximation in the leaves level.

Currently, we are investigating the accuracy of the hierarchy update when we combine the approaches, one different for each level of the hierarchy. Additionally, we are also developing a method to measure, in an easy manner, the error in the coverage of spheres on the surface's object when it deforms.

References

1. Bradshaw, G., O'Sullivan, C.: Adaptive medial-axis aproximation for sphere-tree construction. ACM Transactions on Graphics **23** (2004) 1–26
2. Jimenez, P., Thomas, F., Torras, C.: 3d collision detection: A survey. Computer and Graphics **21** (2001) 269–285
3. Teschner, M., Kimmerle, S., Heidelberge, B., Zachmann, G., Raghupathi, L., Fuhrmann, A., Cani, M.P., Faure, F., Magnenat-Thalmann, N., Strasser, W., Volino, P.: Collision detection for deformable objects. In Schilick, C., Purgathofer, W., eds.: Proc. State of the Art Reports, Eurographics '04. (2004) 119–140
4. Gottschalk, S., Lin, M.C., Manocha, D.: Obbtree: a hierarchical structure for rapid interference detection. In: SIGGRAPH '96: Proceedings of the 23rd annual conference on Computer graphics and interactive techniques, ACM Press (1996) 171–180
5. Klosowski, J.T., Held, M., Mitchell, J.S.B., Sowizral, H., Zikan, K.: Efficient collision detection using bounding volume hierarchies of k-dops. IEEE Transactions on Visualization and Computer Graphics **4** (1998) 21–36
6. van den Bergen, G.: Efficient collision detection of complex deformable models using aabb trees. J. Graph. Tools **2** (1997) 1–13
7. Hubbard, P.: Approximating polyhedra with spheres for time-critical collision detection. IEEE Transactions on Visualization and Computer Graphics **15** (1996) 179–210
8. Larsson, T., Akenine-Möller, T.: Collision detection for continuously deforming bodies. In: Eurographics, short presentations. (2001) 325–333
9. Mezger, J., Kimmerle, S., Etzmuss, O.: Hierarchical techniques in collision detection for cloth animation. Journal of WSCG **11** (2003) 322–329
10. Dingliana, J., O'Sullivan, C.: Graceful degradation of collision handling in physically based animation. Computer Graphics Forum **19** (2000) 239–248
11. James, D., Pai, D.: BD-Tree: Output-sensitive collision detection for reduced deformable models. ACM Transactions on Graphics (SIGGRAPH 2004) **23** (2004)
12. Bradshaw, G.: Bounding volume hierarchies for level-of-detail collision handling. In: PhD Thesis, Trinity College Dublin, Ireland (2002) 161
13. Liu, Y., Noborio, J., Arimoto, S.: Hierarchical sphere model and its application for checking an interference between moving robots. In: IEEE International Workshop on Intelligent Robots and Systems, IROS. (1988) 801–806
14. Hubbard, P.: Interactive collision detection. In: IEEE Symposium on Research Frontiers in Virtual Reality. (1993) 24–31
15. Palmer, I., Grimsdale, R.: Collision detection for animation using sphere-trees. Computer Graphics Forum **14** (1995) 105–116
16. Hubbard, P.: Collision detection for interactive graphic applications. IEEE Transactions on Visualization and Computer Graphics **1** (1995) 218–230

Simulating Complex Organ Interactions: Evaluation of a Soft Tissue Discrete Model

Maud Marchal, Emmanuel Promayon, and Jocelyne Troccaz

TIMC-GMCAO Laboratory,
Institut d'Ingénierie de l'Information de Santé,
Faculté de Médecine,
38706 La Tronche Cedex, France

Abstract. Computer assisted procedures play a key role in the improvement of surgical operations. The current techniques in simulation potentially lead to more accuracy, more safety and more predictability in the surgical room. Despite the important number of algorithms proposed for interactively modelling deformable objects such as soft human tissues, very few methods have attempted to simulate complex anatomical configurations. In this paper, we present a new approach for soft tissue modelling whose novelty is to integrate the interactions between a given soft organ and its surrounding organs. The proposed discrete model is compared to finite element method in order to quantify its performance and physical realism. The model is applied to the simulation of the prostate-bladder set.

1 Introduction

The human body is a system of complex interactions between organs and tissues. These interactions are particularly intricate in the case of soft tissues. Actually soft tissues are undergoing deformations depending on their own physical characteristics and contiguous organs motions. Two main directions are taken to model human soft tissues: the biomechanical approach and the computational discrete approach [1].

The biomechanical approach is based on continuum mechanics. The most frequently used framework of this approach is the Finite Element Method (FEM) which offers the advantage of being based on a strong theoretical background. However researchers face two kinds of difficulties when applying this method to computer aided medical simulation: high computational cost and awkward construction and updating of complex anatomical environments where rigid, elastic and active structures are present and interact.

Computational discrete approaches, such as mass-spring networks, offer a simpler alternative to the construction of such complex structures and can be more easily modified to match changing structures in a particular simulation. While they are not computationally demanding, these approaches are difficult to control and assess.

For both methods, there are few examples for the integration of multiple dynamic interactions between soft organs and their environment. This study

G. Bebis et al. (Eds.): ISVC 2005, LNCS 3804, pp. 175–182, 2005.

presents a new soft tissue modelling method based on a discrete approach that allows such interactions to take place. The method named Phymul is a volumetric evolution of a surface model developed by Promayon et al. [2]. It allows to model the objects with interior nodes. In addition, the method can integrate the incompressibility constraint for each component of the environment. It has been validated by comparisons with a finite element method as a "gold standard" of soft tissue modelling.

Our medical aim is to model the prostate and the surrounding organs and to simulate deformations in real time. Prostate cancer is the second leading cause of cancer deaths in men in several countries. The prostate is therefore subject to an increasing number of diagnostic and therapeutic procedures that are evaluated by physicians for potential improvements in care. Modelling the interactions between the prostate and its environment may allow more accurate procedures to be developed and accepted by urologists.

The paper is structured as follows. At first, the model and its operation are described. Then, comparisons with well-proven soft tissue modelling methods are presented. Finally the modelling of the prostate and its environment is introduced.

2 Phymul: A Volumetric Evolution for a Soft Tissue Modelling Method

In this section, a volumetric version of Phymul is presented. Phymul is a discrete model based on computer graphics modelling. The new proposed approach allows to define objects not only with surfacic nodes as in the original Phymul [2] but with interior nodes. The first paragraph presents the geometrical description of models with Phymul. Then, dynamics are described and finally, as soft tissue modelling is one of the major interest in our application, the specific modelling of elastic components is detailled.

2.1 Geometrical Description

Phymul allows building separated objects with their own properties and choosing the interactions between them. The components of our model are all derived from a main basis: a set of nodes describing the geometry of the object to model. Each node has a position, a neighbourhood and different properties depending on what kind of component it belongs to. The nodes can be placed by the user either on the surface or inside the component. A mass is assigned to each node in order to generate forces and dynamics. Moreover the user can choose to model each component with a surfacic description (only nodes on the surface) or with a volumetric description (nodes are present inside the component), depending on their physical properties.

Living structures are governed by three main kinds of components: rigid components to model skeleton, deformable components to model soft tissues and active deformable components to model muscles. The latter inherit deformable components properties. Components with different properties can be

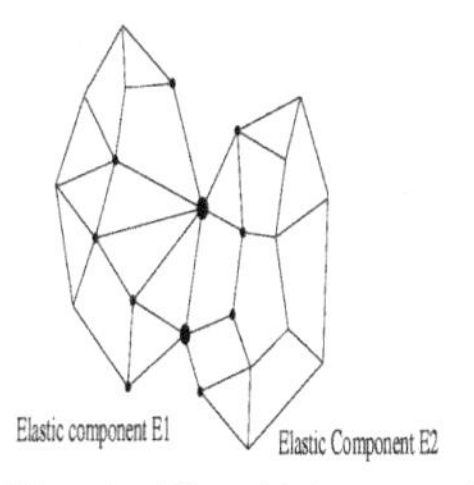

(a) Elastic-Elastic interaction

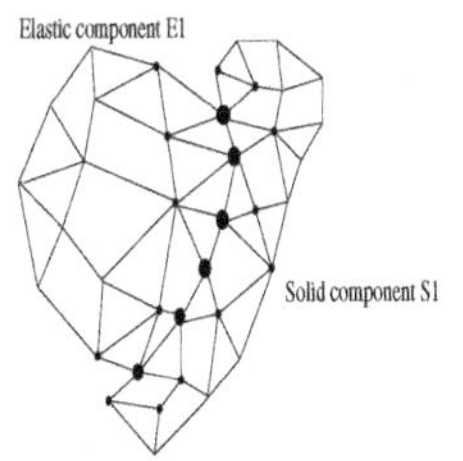

(b) Solid-Elastic interaction

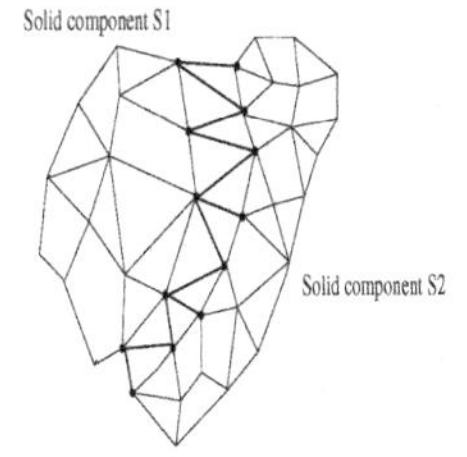

(c) Solid-Solid interaction

Fig. 1. Interaction configurations: (a) Border nodes (bigger black nodes) of elastic components belong to one component but have neighbours in the other elastic component. (b) Border nodes of solid and elastic components are doubled but constrained to be in the same position, whatever the forces applied on them. The forces on elastic component can thus be transmitted to solid component (for example, a link between a bone and a muscle). (c) Solid components are linked together by an elastic component (for example, two bones linked by a ligament).

easily stitched together in Phymul. Figure 1 shows different configurations: interactions between two elastic components or two rigid components and interactions between an elastic and a rigid component.

2.2 Modelling Description

Besides the geometrical description, forces acting on each component and generating displacements and deformations have to be considered. Three kinds of forces can be used in the model: force fields (e.g. gravitation force), locally applied forces (e.g. forces generated by the user) and local shape memory forces to model deformable properties.

In addition to forces, constraints have to be implemented to model complex behaviours and to maintain some conditions such as non-penetrating volume. Phymul can deal with two kinds of constraints:

- local constraints that are applied to a single node, for example to keep a node in a particular region of space
- global constraints that are applied to a set of nodes, for example to enforce an object volume constraint.

The algorithm considers constraints as non-quantified force components: their satisfaction is guaranteed by using a direct projection algorithm based on the gradient vector of the constraint function. Position constraints can be easily defined at each node. For example volume preservation can be satisfied with a simple algorithm whose basis is detailled in [2]. In this method, nodes belonging to the surface are distinguished from nodes located inside the component to model. The algorithm works with all types of polyhedra: the mesh used for the geometrical description does not interfer in the volume computation.

Finally, to solve the system dynamics, at each time t, the forces on each node are summed and the equations of motion are integrated taking into account the local and global constraints. The discrete integration scheme used for the equation of motion is Newton-Cotes scheme.

2.3 Elastic Component

Soft tissue modelling being our aim, let focus on the elastic component of Phymul, and detail how the elasticity property is built and computed. The elastic property is the ability for an object component to come back to its original shape once deformed, independently of the global object position. The elasticity in Phymul is described using an original formulation that has better stability properties than mass-spring networks, as shown by Promayon et al. [2]. To model the elastic property of a node we define a local elasticity memory. The local shape memory force is generated on each node as follows: at each iteration, given the neighbour positions, we compute a shape ideal position: "an attraction node". Its position is ensured to locally minimize the deformation energy. When the node is at the shape nominal position, the local deformation and the shape memory force are both zero.

The difference between a mass-spring network and the local shape memory force is illustrated Fig. 2 with three nodes. Two nodes are fixed and a force is applied on the third node. With mass-spring system, the elasticity force is generated with two springs between the node and its neighbours. With the local shape memory, the elasticity force is represented by a spring between the node and its attraction node. The unique elasticity parameter of a given component is the stiffness of the spring on each node. Like mass-springs, local shape memory is easy to use for topological modifications.

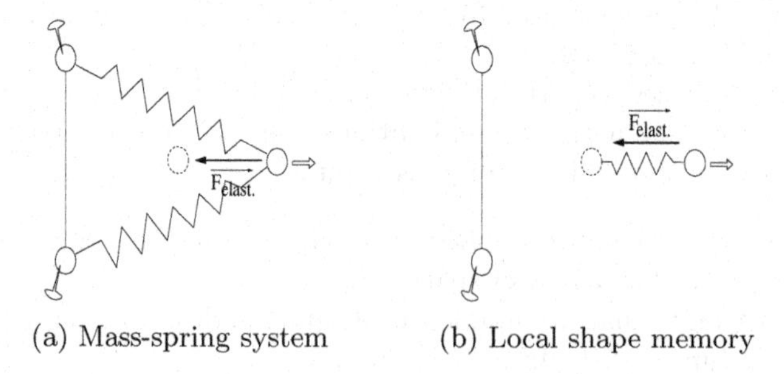

(a) Mass-spring system (b) Local shape memory

Fig. 2. Difference between mass-spring system and local memory shape

To compute the elastic property, a local shape coordinate system is defined on each node in order to find the shape ideal position whatever the object space orientation. Each node position is defined in the local coordinate system relatively to its neighbourhood at rest shape. During simulations, according to the neighbouring nodes position, a target position is computed for each node of an elastic component.

3 Comparisons with the Truth Cube Data and FEM

New approaches of soft tissue modelling can be more easily experimented with phantoms than with complex tissue structures. The validation through these phantom studies are then considered to be applicable to various tissues using their own biomechanical properties.

In 2003 in a project named "Truth cube"[1], Kerdok et al. [3] validated their finite element deformation using the volumetric displacement data of 343 beads embedded in a silicone rubber cube and tracked by Computed Tomography. Material properties and geometry were known and boundary conditions had been carefully controlled while CT images were taken. Using this Truth cube data, we have been able to compare real data with both Phymul and the Finite Element Method.

A finite element model of the "Truth cube" has been built using commercial FE modelling software (ANSYS 8.0 software, Ansys Inc., Cannonsburg, PA). The material properties are isotropic and linear (with a Young Modulus of 14.9 kPa and a Poisson ratio of 0.499). The cube edge dimension is 8 cm and the mesh is made of 8-node solid hexahedral linear elements, as in the model used by Kerdok. Large deformations are employed. For Phymul, the mesh was the same as the FEM mesh. The nodes are linked to form hexahedra. Comparisons have been achieved for three compression levels of 5%, 12.5% and 18.25%. We focus on the distances between measured bead positions and those predicted by the two modelling methods. As measurement, we used the following formula with d the Euclidian distance:

$$\frac{d(realBeads\_position\_afterCompression, simulatedBeads\_position)}{d(realBeads\_position\_init, realBeads\_position\_afterCompression)} \times 100 \quad (1)$$

to obtain a distance between real data and simulated date relative to the real beads displacement. The latest results are in mean:

- for the 5% compression level (mean real displacement: 2.64 mm): 35.6% (Phymul) and 33.8% (Ansys),
- for the 12.5% compression level (mean real displacement: 6.12 mm): 21.5% (Phymul) and 20.2% (Ansys),
- for the 18.25% compression level (mean real displacement: 9.17 mm): 16.9% (Phymul) and 16.8% (Ansys).

FEM produces lower mean errors than our model. Nevertheless, distances are very small compared to global characteristics. More precisely differences between FEM and our model are less than 0.2 mm for 5% compression. Concerning the computational cost, our method presents like other discrete approaches the advantage to be linear in the number of nodes and so enables the building of complex models with as necessary nodes as needed. On a Pentium 4 2.4 GHz, it takes 0.017 ms per node for each iteration. The number of iterations depends

[1] Data are available: `http://www.medicalsim.org/truthcube/`

on the integration scheme. The FEM time results obtained with Ansys cannot be directly compared with Phymul's values, since a single step computational cost cannot be determined. Indeed, simulation time strongly depends on the hypothesis (non-linearity for example).

4 Prostate Modelling in Its Environment

After the validation with simple objects, more complex models containing several objects and better fitting to the prostate shape have been introduced. Modelling the prostate and its environment remains difficult because many factors are influencing prostate motion and deformation. Indeed, measurements of prostate position have demonstrated movements [4] and deformations [5] of the organ mainly due to rectum and bladder filling and recently due to breathing [6] and patient position.

In this paper, our aim is to simulate the influence of an endorectal echographic probe on prostate shape in function of bladder filling. The model presented contains three components: the prostate, the bladder and the rectum. An anatomic view of the prostate and its environment during a biopsy is represented in Fig. 3.

The prostate and the bladder are represented by two deformed spheres. Bladder shape is deformed under gravity and is described with surfacic nodes (like an envelope). Prostate has a volumetric description. The echographic probe inside the rectum is simulated by the applied forces with a cylinder shape. Proportional scales of all organs are respected. Bladder and prostate are stitched together with a limited number of nodes. Top node of the bladder is fixed for each simulation with a different bladder shape (see Fig. 3 b) simulating different bladder repletions. During simulations, a pressure equivalent to real applied forces for biopsy is applied inside the rectum upward to deform the prostate.

After simulations with variations of bladder volume, it appears that the measured deformations correspond to those observed during surgical gestures. The prostate tends to deform more when the bladder is empty (10% of its height) than when the bladder is full (5% of its height). The simulated deformations match to experiment measurements performed during a biopsy or a brachytherapy.

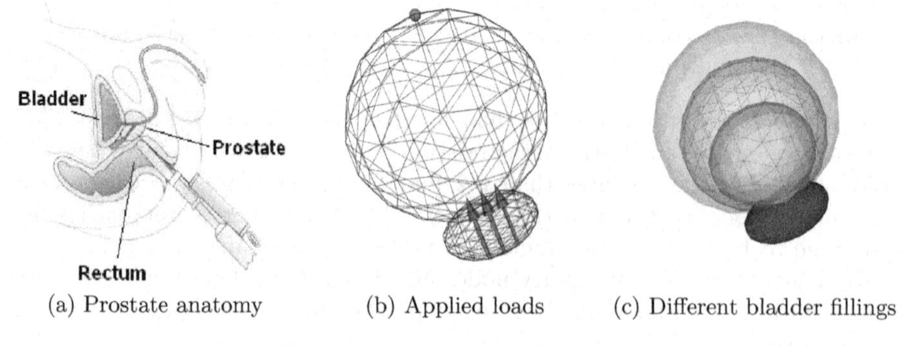

(a) Prostate anatomy (b) Applied loads (c) Different bladder fillings

Fig. 3. Model of the prostate and different bladder fillings

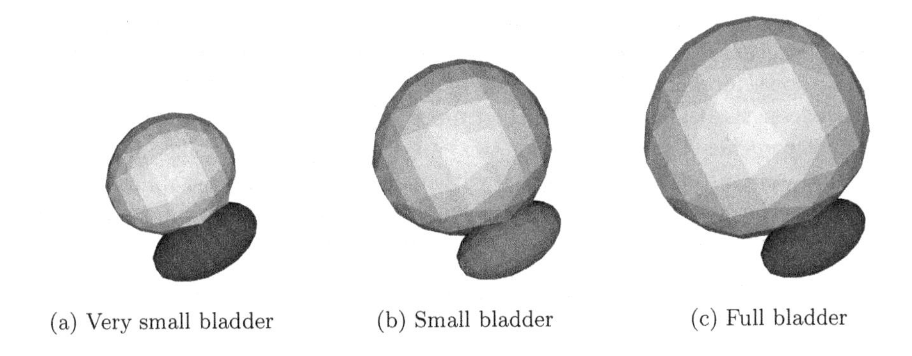

(a) Very small bladder (b) Small bladder (c) Full bladder

Fig. 4. Prostate and bladder in different states

5 Discussion and Conclusion

In this paper, Phymul model and first simulations have been validated with objects of simple geometry. The first validation is a comparison with the Truth cube data and a finite element method. Results show that our method is relatively close to the FEM in terms of accuracy. A second set of experiments concerning the external shape of the cube has also been performed. Results show that our method performs similarly to the FEM in predicting deformations. It is important to note that there are a lot of other measurements to compare modelling methods. The distance choosen in this paper, although emphasis on a particular aspect, seems to us to be more relevant to compare both the discrete model and FEM to real data. The difference, even for FEM, shows us that simplistic modelling of object can induce relatively large difference in deformations, even for simple real object such as Truth cube. In a future work it could be of major interest to classify comparison measurements.

The second validation is directly linked to the prostate application. The model presented here is very simplified but allows to demonstrate how more complex models can be defined with simplicity with our method. We currently extend the work to a more realistic prostate and environment in terms of shape.

The incorporation of physical parameters in the model is a key element of soft tissue modelling. Even if it is possible to measure these parameters in isolated tissue [7], their determination is still very difficult to perform in vivo, especially since these parameters are patient and pathology specific. In addition the complexity of tissue interactions makes it difficult to perform a backward validation process. Prostate properties are reported in few papers [8]. Elastography has opened new possibilities to determine elasticity. Recently, Kemper et al.[9] published elasticity coefficients for the prostate. We have also performed another parallel study concerning the ability to translate FEM parameters (Young modulus for instance) in a local shape memory force. We plan to directly introduce Young modulus into Phymul through a force as a function of deformations. Future work will deal with modelling interactions with needles and ultrasound probe frequently used in biopsy or brachytherapy.

Finally in this paper, a new approach to soft tissue modelling, well-suited to model interactions between organs has been proposed. Our object-oriented based method allows modelling several organs simultaneously. Contacts and interactions between tissues can be described more easily than in FEM for example. Compared to other discrete methods, we can define constraints like incompressibility and express objects properties with more accuracy and stability. By incorporating the interactions with instruments and by modelling more realistic organs, we will also be able to model the prostate behaviour by taking into account not only the organ itself but also its environment.

References

1. Delingette, H.: Towards realistic soft tissue modeling in medical simulation. IEEE Special Issue on Virtual and Augmented Reality in Medicine **86** (1998) 512–523
2. Promayon, E., Baconnier, P., Puech, C.: Physically-based model for simulating the human trunk respiration movements. In: Proceedings of CVRMed II - MRCAS III. (1997) 379–388
3. Kerdok, A., Cotin, S., Ottensmeyer, M., Galea, A., Howe, R., Dawson, S.: Truthcube : Establishing physical standards for real time soft tissue simulation. Medical Image Analysis **7** (2003) 283–291
4. Melian, E., Mageras, G., Fuks, Z., Leibel, S., Niehaus, A., Lorant, H., Zelefsky, M., Baldwin, B., Kutcher, G.: Variation in prostate position quantitation and implications for three-dimensional conformal treatement planning. Int. J. Radiation Oncology Biol. Phys. **38** (1997) 73–81
5. Forman, J., Mesina, C., He, T., Devi, S., Ben-Josef, E., Pelizarri, C., Vijayakumar, C., Chen, G.: Evaluation of changes in the location and shape of the prostate and rectum during a seven week course of conformal radiotherapy. Int. J. Radiation Oncology Biol. Phys. **27** (1993) 222
6. Malone, S., Crook, J., Kendal, W., Szanto, J.: Respiratory-induced prostate motion: quantification and characterization. Int. J. Radiation Oncology Biol. Phys. **48** (2000) 105–109
7. Fung, Y.C.: Mechanical Properties of Living Tissues. 2nd edn. Springer-Verlag (1993)
8. Krouskop, T., Wheeler, T., Kallel, F., Garra, B., Hall, T.: Elastic moduli of breast and prostate tissues under compression. Ultrasound Imaging **20** (1998) 260–278
9. Kemper, J., Sinkus, R., Lorenzen, J., Nolte-Ernsting, C., Stork, A., Adam, G.: Mr elastography of the prostate: initial in-vivo application. Rofo **176** (2004) 1094–1099

Face Verification in Polar Frequency Domain: A Biologically Motivated Approach

Yossi Zana[1], Roberto M. Cesar-Jr[1], Rogerio S. Feris[2], and Matthew Turk[2,*]

[1] Dept. of Computer Science, IME-USP, Brazil
{zana, cesar}@vision.ime.usp.br
[2] University of California, Santa Barbara
{rferis, mturk}@cs.ucsb.edu

Abstract. We present a novel local-based face verification system whose components are analogous to those of biological systems. In the proposed system, after global registration and normalization, three eye regions are converted from the spatial to polar frequency domain by a Fourier-Bessel Transform. The resulting representations are embedded in a dissimilarity space, where each image is represented by its distance to all the other images. In this dissimilarity space a Pseudo-Fisher discriminator is built. ROC and equal error rate verification test results on the FERET database showed that the system performed at least as state-of-the-art methods and better than a system based on polar Fourier features. The local-based system is especially robust to facial expression and age variations, but sensitive to registration errors.

1 Introduction

Face verification and recognition tasks are highly complex task due to the many possible variations of the same subject in different conditions, like facial expressions and age. Most of the current face recognition and verification algorithms are based on feature extraction from a Cartesian perspective, typical to most analog and digital imaging systems. The human visual system (HVS), on the other hand, is known to process visual stimuli by fundamental shapes defined in polar coordinates, and to use logarithmical mapping. In the early stages the visual image is filtered by neurons tuned to specific spatial frequencies and location in a linear manner [1]. In further stages, these neurons output is processed to extract global and more complex shape information, such as faces [2]. Eletrophysiological experiments in monkey's visual cerebral areas showed that the fundamental patterns for global shape analysis are defined in polar and hyperbolic coordinates [3]. Global pooling of orientation information was also showed by psychophysical experiments to be responsible for the detection of angular and radial Glass dot patterns [4]. Thus, it is evident that information regarding the global polar content of images is effectively extracted by and is available to the HVS. Further evidence in favor of a polar representation use by the HVS

* This work was supported by FAPESP (03/07519-0, 99/12765-2) and CNPq (150409/03-3).

G. Bebis et al. (Eds.): ISVC 2005, LNCS 3804, pp. 183–190, 2005.

is the log-polar manner in which the retinal image is mapped onto the visual cortex area [5]. An analogous spatial log-polar mapping was explored for face recognition [6]. One of the disadvantages of this feature extraction method is the rough representation of peripheral regions. The HVS compensates this effect by eye saccades, moving the fovea from one point to the other in the scene. Similar approach was adopted by the face recognition method of [6].

An alternative representation in the polar frequency domain is the 2D Fourier-Bessel transformation (FBT) [7]. This transform found several applications in analyzing patterns in a circular domain [8], but was seldom exploited for image recognition. In [9] we suggested the use of global FB descriptors for face recognition algorithms. The present paper is a major development of this idea. The main contribution of the current work is the presentation and exhaustive evaluation of a face verification system based of local, in contrast to global extraction of FB features. Results show that such a system achieve state-of-the-art performance on large scale databases and significant robustness to expression and age variations. Moreover, we automated the face and eyes detection stage to reduce dependency on ground-truth information availability.

The paper is organized as follows: in the next two sections we describe the FBT and the proposed system. The face database and testing methods are introduced in Section 5. The experimental results are presented in Section 6 and in the last section we discuss the results.

2 Polar Frequency Analysis

The FB series [8] is useful to describe the radial and angular components in images. FBT analysis starts by converting the coordinates of a region of interest from Cartesian (x, y) to polar (r, θ). The $f(r, \theta)$ function is represented by the two-dimensional FB series, defined as

$$f(r,\theta) = \sum_{i=1}^{\infty}\sum_{n=0}^{\infty} A_{n,i} Jn(\alpha_{n,i} r)\cos(n\theta) + \sum_{i=1}^{\infty}\sum_{n=0}^{\infty} Bn, iJn(\alpha_{n,i} r)\sin(n\theta) \quad (1)$$

where J_n is the Bessel function of order n, $f(R, \theta) = 0$ and $0 \leq r \leq R$. $\alpha_{n,i}$ is the ith root of the J_n function, i.e. the zero crossing value satisfying $J_n(\alpha_{n,i}) = 0$ is the radial distance to the edge of the image. The orthogonal coefficients $A_{n,i}$ and $B_{n,i}$ are given by

$$A_{0,i} = \frac{1}{\pi R^2 J_1^2(\alpha_{n,i})} \int_{\theta=0}^{\theta=2\pi} \int_{r=0}^{r=R} f(r,\theta) r J_n(\frac{\alpha n, i}{R} r) dr d\theta \quad (2)$$

if $B_{0,i} = 0$ and $n = 0$;

$$\begin{bmatrix} A_{n,i} \\ B_{n,i} \end{bmatrix} = \frac{2}{\pi R^2 J_{n+1}^2(\alpha_{n,i})} \int_{\theta=0}^{\theta=2\pi} \int_{r=0}^{r=R} f(r,\theta) r J_n(\frac{\alpha_{n,i}}{R} r) \begin{bmatrix} \cos(n\theta) \\ \sin(n\theta) \end{bmatrix} dr d\theta \quad (3)$$

if $n > 0$.

However, polar frequency analysis can be done using other transformations. An alternative method is to represent images by polar Fourier transform descriptors. The polar Fourier transform is a well known mathematical operation where, after converting the image coordinates from Cartesian to polar, as described above, a conventional Fourier transformation is applied. These descriptors are directly related to radial and angular components, but are not identical to the coefficients extracted by the FBT.

3 The Algorithm

The proposed algorithm is based on two sequential steps of feature extractions, and one classifier building. First we extract the FB coefficients from the images. Next, we compute the Cartesian distance between all the FBT-representations and re-define each object by its distance to all other objects. In the last stage we train a pseudo Fisher classifier. We tested this algorithm on the whole image (global) or the combination of three facial regions (local).

3.1 Spatial to Polar Frequency Domain

Images were transformed by a FBT up to the 30th Bessel order and 6th root with angular resolution of 3°, thus obtaining to 372 coefficients. These coefficients correspond to a frequency range of up to 30 and 3 cycles/image of angular and radial frequency, respectively, and were selected based on previous tests on a small-size dataset [9]. We tested FBT descriptors of the whole image, or a combination of the upper right region, upper middle region, and the upper left region (Fig. 1). In order to have a better notion of the information retained by

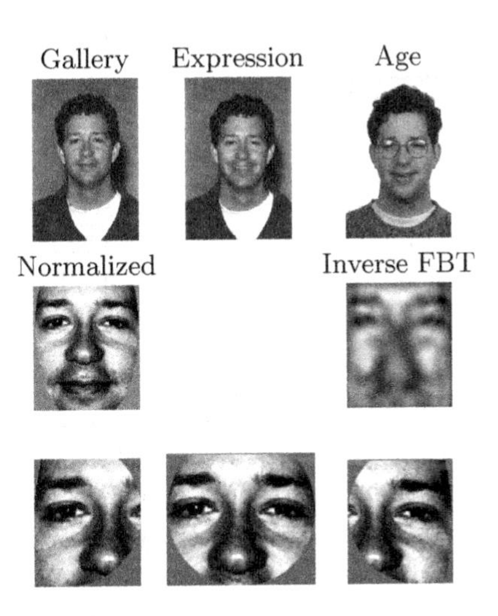

Fig. 1. 1st row: Samples from the datasets. 2nd row: Normalized whole face and the FB inverse transformation. 3rd row: The regions that were used for the local analysis.

the FBT, we used Eq. 1 to reconstruct the image from the FB coefficients. The resulting image has a blurred aspect that reflects the use of only low-frequency radial components. In the rest of this paper, we will refer to the FB transformed images as just images. When using the PFT, the angular sampling was matched and only coefficients related to the same frequency range covered by the FBT were used. Both amplitude and phase information were considered.

3.2 Polar Frequency to Dissimilarity Domain

We built a dissimilarity space $D(\mathbf{t}, \mathbf{t})$ defined as the Euclidean distance between all training FBT images $\mathbf{t}$. In this space, each object is represented by its dissimilarity to all objects. This approach is based on the assumption that the dissimilarities of similar objects to "other ones" is about the same [10]. Among other advantages of this representation space, by fixing the number of features to the number of objects, it avoids a well known phenomenon, where recognition performance is degraded as a consequence of small number of training samples as compared to the number of features.

3.3 Classifier

Test images were classified based on a pseudo Fisher linear discriminant (FLD) using a two-class approach. A FLD is obtained by maximizing the (between subjects variation)/(within subjects variation) ratio. Here we used a minimum-square error classifier implementation [11], which is equivalent to the FLD for two-class problems. In these cases, after shifting the data such that it has zero mean, the FLD can be defined as

$$g(\mathbf{x}) = \left[D(\mathbf{t}, \mathbf{x}) - \frac{1}{2} (\mathbf{m}_1 - \mathbf{m}_2) \right]^T \mathbf{S}^{-1} (\mathbf{m}_1 - \mathbf{m}_2) \tag{4}$$

where $\mathbf{x}$ is a probe image, $\mathbf{S}$ is the pooled covariance matrix, and $\mathbf{m}_i$ stands for the mean of class i. The probe image $\mathbf{x}$ is classified as corresponding to class-1 if $g(\mathbf{x}) \geq 0$ and to class-2 otherwise. However, as the number of objects and dimensions is the same in the dissimilarity space, the sample estimation of the covariance matrix $\mathbf{S}$ becomes singular and the classifier cannot be built. One solution to the problem is to use a pseudo-inverse and augmented vectors [11]. Thus, Eq. 4 is replaced by

$$g(\mathbf{x}) = (D(\mathbf{t}, \mathbf{x}), 1) (D(\mathbf{t}, \mathbf{t}), I)^{(-1)} \tag{5}$$

where $(D(\mathbf{t}, \mathbf{x}), 1)$ is the augmented vector to be classified and $(D(\mathbf{t}, \mathbf{t}), I)$ is the augmented training set. The inverse $(D(\mathbf{t}, \mathbf{t}), I)^{(-1)}$ is the Moore-Penrose Pseudo-inverse which gives the minimum norm solution. The current L-classes problem can be reduced and solved by the two-classes solution described above. The training set was split into L pairs of subsets, each pair consisting of one subset with images from a single subject and a second subset formed from all the other images. A pseudo-FLD was built for each pair of subsets. A probe image was tested on all L discriminant functions, and a "posterior probability" score was generated based on the inverse of the Euclidean distance to each subject.

4 Database, Preprocessing, and Testing Procedures

The main advantages of the FERET database [12] are the large number of individuals and rigid testing protocols that allow precise performance comparisons between different algorithms. We compare our algorithm performance with a "baseline" PCA-based algorithm [13] and with the results of three successful approaches. The PCA algorithm was based of a set of 700 randomly selected images from the gallery subset. The three first components, that are known to encode basically illumination variations, were excluded prior to image projecting. The other approaches are: Gabor wavelets combined with elastic graph matching [14], localized facial features extraction followed by a Linear Discriminant Analysis (LDA) [15], and a Bayesian generalization of the LDA method [16].

In the FERET protocol, a "gallery" set of one frontal view image from 1196 subjects is used to train the algorithm and a different dataset is used as probe. We used the probe sets termed "FB" and "DupI". These datasets contain single images from a different number of subjects (1195 and 722, respectively) with differences of facial expression and age, respectively. The "age" variation subset included several subjects that started or quited wearing glass or grow beards since their "gallery" pictures were takes. Images were normalized using the eyes ground-truth information or coordinates given by an eyes detector algorithm. This face detection stage was implemented using a cascade of classifiers algorithm for the face detection [17] followed by an Active Appearance Model algorithm (AAM) [18] for the detection of the eyes region. Within this region, we used flow field information [19] to determine the eye center. Approximately 1% of the faces were not localized by the AAM algorithm, in which cases the eyes regions coordinates were set to a fix value derived from the mean of the other faces. The final mean error was 3.7 ± 5.2 pixels. Images were translated, rotated, and scaled so that the eyes were registered at specific pixels (Fig. 1). Next, the images were cropped to 130 x 150 pixels size and a mask was applied to remove most of the hair and background. The unmasked region was histogram equalized and normalized to mean zero and a unit standard deviation.

The system performance was evaluated by verification tests according to the FERET protocol [12]. Given a gallery image g and a probe image p, the algorithm verifies the claim that both were taken from the same subject. The verification probability P_V is the probability of the algorithm accepting the claim when it is true, and the false-alarm rate P_F is the probability of incorrectly accepting a false claim. The algorithm decision depends on the posterior probability score $si(k)$ given to each match, and on a threshold c. Thus, a claim is confirmed if $si(k) \leq c$ and rejected otherwise. A plot of all the combinations of P_V and P_F as a function of c is known as a receiver operating characteristic (ROC).

5 Results

Figure 2 shows the performance of the proposed verification system. The local FBT version performed at the same level of the best previous algorithm (PCA+LDA) on the expression dataset and achieved the best results on the age subset. The global version of the FBT algorithm was inferior at all conditions. Comparisons with the PFT representation indicate that this alternative features

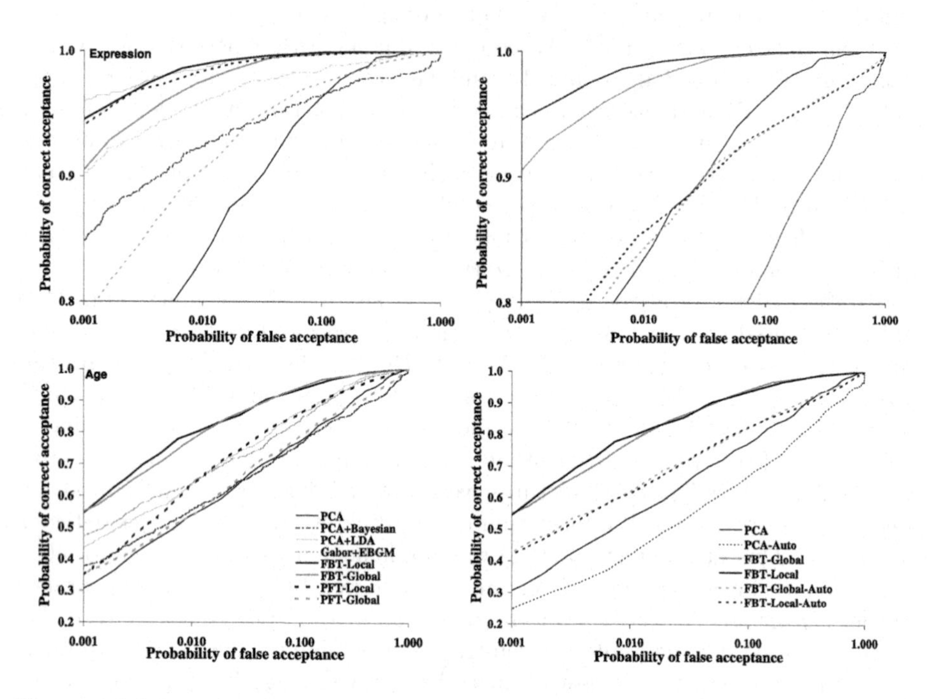

Fig. 2. ROC functions of the proposed and previous algorithms. Left panels: using semi-automatic FBT and PFT. Right panels: Using automatic FBT.

Table 1. Equal error rate (%) of the FBT, PFT and previous algorithms

	Semi-Auto		Auto	
Algorithm	Expression	Age	Expression	Age
FBT-Global	1.6	7	4.5	16
FBT-Local	1.1	8	7.1	16
PFT-Global	4.1	16		
PFT-Local	1.4	12		
PCA	5.9	17	14	23
PCA+Bayesian	4.9	18		
PCA+LDA	1.2	13		
Gabor-EBGM	2.5	13		

are less robust to age and illumination variations. Automation of the eye detection stage reduced the system performance by up to 20%. This reduction is expected, considering the variance property of the FBT to translation [20], and reflect sensitivity to registration errors typical to other algorithms, like the PCA.

We also computed the equal error rate (EER) of the proposed algorithms (Table 1). The EER occurs at a threshold level where the incorrect rejection and false alarm rates are equals (1-P_V = P_F). Lower values indicate better performance. The EER results reinforce the conclusions from the ROC functions.

6 Discussion

Most of the current biologically-inspired algorithms were validated only on very small databases, with the exception of the Gabor-EBGM algorithm that is based on Gabor wavelets transformation and can be viewed as analogous to human spatial filtering at the early stages. Here we presented a novel face verification system based on a local analysis approach and FBT descriptors. The system achieving top ranking on both the age and expression subset. These results are a clear demonstration of the system robustness in handling realistic situations of facial expression and age variations of faces.

The local approach is also superior to the global, a fact that have direct implication for the algorithm robustness for occlusions. In the local approach, the mouth region is ignored, thus its occlusion or variation (ex. due to a new beard) does not affect performance at all. From the computational point of view, the local analysis does not imply much more computation time: the FBT of each region consumes about half the time consumed by the global analysis. Preliminary results (not shown) of the global version with reduced resolution images indicate that computation time can be further with no performance loss, but we still have not tested the effect of image resolution on the local version.

The system have an automatic face detection version, but the trade-off is a certain performance loss. We currently work on the implementation of more precise face and eye detectors algorithms. For example, [21] learned the subspace that represents localization errors within eigenfaces. This method can be easily adopted for the FBT subspace, with the advantage of the option to exclude from the final classification face regions that gives high localization errors.

Currently, we are developing a series of psychophysical experiments with the aim of establishing the relation of the proposed system with human performance. The main questions are: (1) At what location and scale global spatial pooling occurs? (2) Are faces represented in a dissimilarity space? (3) How does filtering of specific polar frequency components affects the face recognition performance of humans and the proposed system?

In conclusion, the proposed system achieved state-of-the-art performance in handling problems of expression and age variations. We expect from future tests to show robustness to illumination variation and partial occlusion and our on-going work are focused on improving the performance of the automatic version.

References

1. DeValois, R.L., DeValois, K.K.: Spatial Vision. Oxford Sciences Pub. (1990)
2. Perret, D.I. Rolls, E., Caan, W.: Visual neurons responsive to faces in the monkey temporal cortex. Experimental Brain Research **47** (1982) 329–342
3. Gallant, J.L. Braun, J., VanEssen, D.: Selectivity for polar, hyperbolic, and cartesian gratings in macaque visual cortex. Science **259** (1993) 100–103
4. Wilson, H., Wilkinson, F.: Detection of global structure in glass patterns: implications for form vision. Vision Research **38** (1998) 2933–2947
5. Schwartz, E.: Spatial mapping in primate sensory projection: analytic structure and relevance to perception. Biological Cybernetics **25** (1977) 181–194
6. Tistarelli, M., Grosso, E.: Active vision-based face recognition issues, applications and techniques. In: NatoAsi Advanced Study on Face Recognition. Volume F-163. Springer-Berlin (1998) 262–286 Ed.: Wechsler, H. et al.
7. Bowman, F.: Introduction to Bessel functions. Dover Pub., New York (1958)
8. Fox, P., Cheng, J., Lu, J.: Theory and experiment of Fourier-Bessel field calculation and tuning of a pulsed wave annular array. Journal of the Acoustical Society of America **113** (2003) 2412–2423
9. Zana, Y., Cesar-Jr, R.M.: Face recognition based on polar frequency features. ACM Transactions on Applied Perception **2** (2005) To appear.
10. Duin, R., DeRidder, D., Tax, D.: Experiments with a featureless approach to pattern recognition. Pattern Recognition Letters **18** (1997) 1159–1166
11. Scurichina, M., Duin, R.: Stabilizing classifiers for very small sample sizes. In: Proceedings of the 13th International Conference on Pattern Recognition. Volume 2, Track B. (1996) 891–896
12. Phillips, P., Wechsler, H., Huang, J., Rauss, P.: The FERET database and evaluation procedure for face recognition algorithms. Image and Vision Computing Journal **16** (1998) 295–306
13. Turk, M., Pentland, A.: Eigenfaces for recognition. Journal of Cognitive Neuroscience **3** (1991) 71–86
14. Wiskott, L., Fellous, J., Kruger, N., VonDerMalsburg, C.: Face recognition by elastic bunch graph matching. IEEE Transactions on Pattern Analysis and Machine Intelligence **19** (1997) 775–779
15. Etemad, K., Chellappa, R.: Discriminant analysis for recognition of human face images. Journal of the Optical Society of America A-Optics Image Science and Vision **14** (1997) 1724–1733
16. Moghaddam, B., Jebara, T., Pentland, A.: Bayesian face recognition. Pattern Recognition **33** (2000) 1771–1782
17. Viola, P., Jones, M.: Rapid object detection using a boosted cascade of simple features. In: IEEE Conference on Computer Vision and Pattern Recognition (CVPR). (2001) 511–518
18. Cootes, T., Edwards, G., Taylor, C.: Active appearance models. IEEE Transactions on Pattern Analysis and Machine Intelligence **23** (2001) 681–685
19. Kothari, R., Mitchell, J.: Detection of eye locations in unconstrained visual images. In: IEEE International Conference on Image Processing. (1996) 519–522
20. Cabrera, J., Falc=n, A., Hernßndez, F., MTndez, J.: A systematic method for exploring contour segment descriptions. Cybernetics and Systems **23** (1992) 241–270
21. Martfnez, A.: Recognizing imprecisely localized, partially occluded, and expression variant faces from a single sample per class. IEEE Transactions on Pattern Analysis and Machine Intelligence **24** (2002) 748–762

Face Alignment and Adaptive Weight Assignment for Robust Face Recognition

Satyanadh Gundimada and Vijayan Asari

Department of Electrical and Computer Engineering,
Old Dominion University, Norfolk, VA 23529

Abstract. It is observed that only certain portions of the face images that are affected due to expressions, non uniform lighting and partial occlusions are responsible for the failure of face recognition. A methodology of identifying and reducing the influence of such regions in the recognition process is proposed in this paper. Dense correspondence is established between the probe image and a template face-model using optical flow technique. The face image is divided into modules and the summation of the magnitudes of the flow vectors in each module are used in determining the effectiveness of that module in the overall recognition. A low weightage is assigned to the modules whose summation of magnitudes of the flow vectors within that module is high and vice versa. An eye center location algorithm based on adaptive thresholding is implemented to align the test image with the face model prior to establishing the correspondence. Recognition accuracy has increased considerably for PCA based linear subspace approaches when implemented along with the proposed technique.

1 Introduction

Over the past 15 years, research has focused on making face recognition systems more accurate and fully automatic. Significant advances have been made in the design of classifiers for successful face recognition. Among appearance-based holistic approaches, eigenfaces [1] and Fisherfaces [2] have proved to be effective on large databases. PCA performs dimensionality reduction by projecting the original ndimensional data onto the lower dimensional linear subspace spanned by the leading eigenvectors of its covariance matrix. Its goal is to find a set of mutually orthogonal basis functions that capture the directions of maximum variance in the data and for which the coefficients are pair-wise de-correlated. Unlike PCA, LDA encodes discriminating information in a linearly separable space using bases that are not necessarily orthogonal. In addition to these methods there are other methods such as Independent Component Analysis. Kernel methods such as Kernel Principal Component Analysis (KPCA) and Kernel Fisher Discriminant Analysis (KFDA) [3] show better results in face recognition than linear subspace methods. Nonlinear projection based methods have been able to overcome the problem of expressions and lighting in face images to some extent. But there has not been a significant improvement in the recognition accuracy in situations where the face images undergo lot of variations including expressions, partial occlusions and lighting.

G. Bebis et al. (Eds.): ISVC 2005, LNCS 3804, pp. 191–198, 2005.

This paper implements a method of face recognition which is based on weighted modules in reduced dimensional space. The weights assigned to the image regions enhance the recognition accuracy by decreasing confidence in the modules which are affected due to facial variations. There are recent publications [4] [5] in this direction of expression, occlusion and lighting invariant face recognition. The technique presented in this paper is computationally efficient and has achieved a very high accuracy rates on certain freely available face databases. The paper is organized as follows. The second section describes the effect of facial variations on recognition accuracy and the role of modularization in reducing those effects. Third and fourth sections provide the implementation steps of the proposed technique along with the details of the face alignment technique. Section five explains the testing strategy and the obtained recognition rate on various databases.

2 Variations in Face Images

Variations caused in facial images due to expression, makeup and non uniform lighting tend to move the face vector away from the neutral face of the same person both in image space and reduced linear subspace. It has been observed that the dimensionality reduction techniques on individual modules of the face images improve the accuracy of face recognition compared to applying on the whole image. Figure 1 shows the classification accuracies of the individual modules of the images in the database divided into three separate sets. All the face

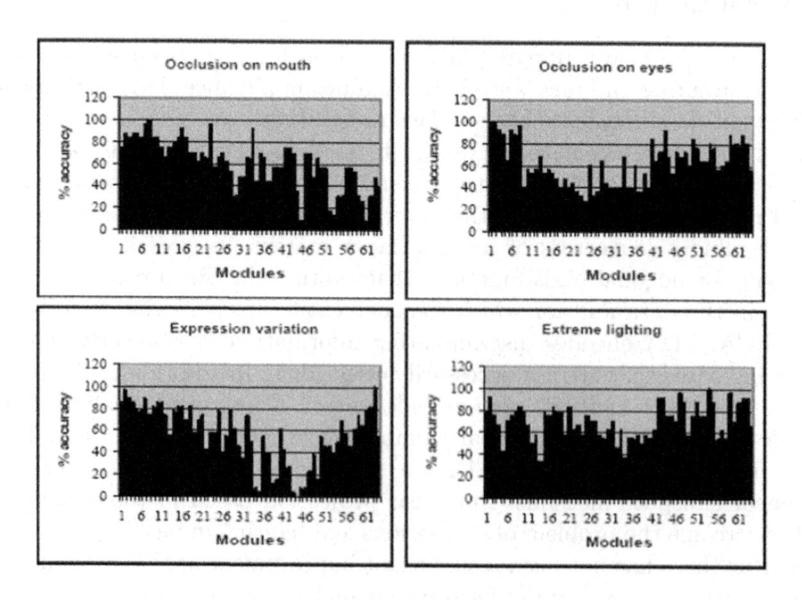

Fig. 1. Percentage of accuracies of each module in the images affected due to partial occlusion on mouth, partial occlusion on eyes, expression variation, and extreme lighting conditions

Fig. 2. Sample images affected due to partial occlusion on mouth, partial occlusion on eyes, change of expression, and non-uniform lighting

images in the first set have their eyes or mouth partially occluded. The second set consists of images with many expressions. The third set consists of face images whose mouth regions are partially occluded.Sample images from each set are shown in figure 2. Each module is projected into a space spanned by the 20 principal components and then classified using minimum distance measure. The result of classification indicates that the percentage of accuracy has worsened in the regions affected.

3 Weighted Modules

Each module of the test image is classified separately and the final decision of the overall classification of the test image is determined by employing a voting mechanism on the modules of the image. The classification is done in favor of the class or individual who obtains the maximum votes. Instead of a voting technique to classify the test image, a weighted module approach is implemented in this paper to reduce the influence of the affected modules. Initially images in the face database are divided into a predefined set of modules m. The directions of maximum variance are calculated for each module separately using principal component analysis and the weights are obtained after projecting the vectorised modules of each training image into their respective subspaces. The algorithm presented in this paper differs from the earlier works in using the image modules more effectively for the overall classification of the image. A less weight or confidence is given to those modules of the test image which are affected due to the variations caused because of expressions, makeup or decorations, occlusions, and lighting. Determination of the weights associated with each module is achieved by the application of an optical flow algorithm between the test image and a face template.

3.1 Optical Flow

Optical flow between the test image and a neutral face template is calculated to determine the regions with expressions, partial occlusions, and extreme lighting changes. The face model which is used as a reference image for a neutral face is the mean of all the face images in the training database. Lucas Kanades algorithm [6] is a classical technique and is implemented to find the optical flow between the test images and the face model in this paper. A brightness constancy constraint is assumed in the calculation of optical flow as given in equation 1.

$$I(x, y, t) = I(x + u\delta t, y + v\delta t, t + \delta t) \quad (1)$$

I(x,y,t) is the intensity at the image pixel (x,y) at time t. (u,v) is the horizontal and vertical veclocities, t is a very small time interval. Tailor series expansion of equation 1 results in the optical flow constraint as given in equation 2.

$$u\frac{\partial I}{\partial x} + v\frac{\partial I}{\partial y} + \frac{\partial I}{\partial t} = 0 \quad (2)$$

An additional smoothness constraint [6] is assumed to solve for the velocity vectors at each pixel of the image.

3.2 Assignment of Weights

Variations caused due to the reasons explained above can be identified in the test image by applying the optical flow algorithm with respect to the face template. The modules enclosing the regions with maximum variations are assigned lesser weight to minimize the influence of such modules on the overall accuracy of classification. Equations 3 and 4 explain the process of assignment of weights.

$$w_i = \frac{(G_{\max} - G_i)}{G_{\max}} \quad for\, G_i > T \quad (3)$$

$$w_i = 1 \quad for\, G_i \leq T \quad (4)$$

where G_i is the sum of the magnitudes of the optical flow vectors within each module. T is the magnitude threshold of the optical flow of the module, below which the module is given full confidence during classification. T is specific to each module and is set in such a way that variations that exist within the neutral face images i.e., without any expressions or decorations or lighting variations are not penalized.

$$G_k = \sum_{p=1}^{(N/m)} \sum_{q=1}^{(N/m)} \|F_{pq}\| \quad for\, k = 1, 2, 3, ...m \quad (5)$$

Where $\|F_{pq}\|$ is the magnitude of the optical flow between the test image and the average face template. The algorithm proposed by Lucas and Kannade for estimating optical flow is used for the estimation of the magnitude of the flow in this paper.

$$G_{\max} = Max(G_k)\forall k \quad (6)$$

The weights are set in such a way that the modules that enclose maximum variations are given zero weightage or no confidence. The modules whose flow magnitude does not exceed threshold T are given a weightage of 1 and the rest of the modules that lie between the limits are assigned weights according to equation 3.

3.3 Threshold Calculation

Threshold T represents the maximum variations that can be caused between the neutral face images of different individuals. The variations below this threshold are not considered as the ones that are caused because of expressions, occlusions and lighting. The mean image of the set of face images belonging to the same individual is selected to represent the neutral face of that individual. Then optical flow is calculated on the mean image of each individual and the face template. Sum of the magnitudes of flow vectors within each module is calculated. Maximum magnitude obtained for each module is taken as the threshold for that module. Equations 5 and 6 further explain the procedure of calculating threshold T.

$$G_{nr} = \sum_{i=1}^{(N/m)} \sum_{j=1}^{(N/m)} \|F_{ij}\| \;\; for\, r = 1, 2, 3, ..m \;\; and \;\; n = 1, 2, ..N \tag{7}$$

$$T_r = Max(G_{nr}) \tag{8}$$

G_{nr} is the summation of the magnitude of the optical flow vectors within each module for all the mean faces of the individuals with respect to the face template. T_r is the threshold for each of the module obtained by taking the maximum value of G_{nr}.

4 Face Alignment

It is necessary that the test image is properly aligned with the template face image before establishing the correspondence. In case of misalignment there is possibility of false motion being reported between the two faces. Figure 3 illustrates this reasoning.Optical flow vector magnitude at each pixel is calculated between the probe image and the face model as shown in the figure. The left-most image in the figure is properly aligned with the face model at the center where as the right-most image is not. The effect of misalignment can be clearly observed from the magnitude images which show a false motion between the faces. In order to overcome this problem a simple yet effective technique of alignment of faces using eye centers is proposed. Eye centers are located in the probe image and compared with those of the face model to align the faces.

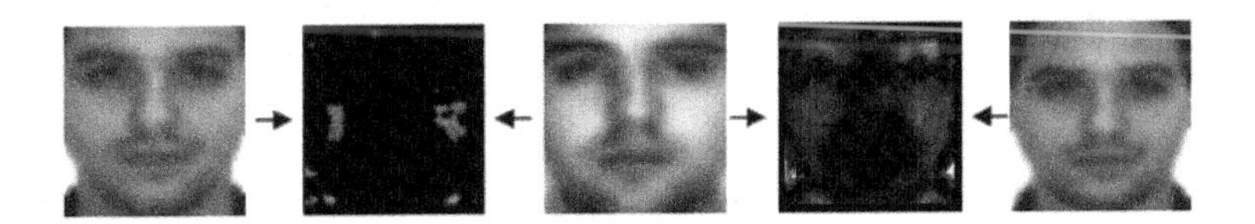

Fig. 3. Illustration of the effect of misalignment of test image with the face model in the center

4.1 Eye Center Location

The approximate area around the eyes is selected and is subjected to an adaptive thresholding technique explained in the next section. This step leaves an image that has maximum value for all pixels except at the eye centers. A weighted mean is obtained around each connected black region in the image giving the desired eye center locations. Figure 4 illustrates the process of selecting the region followed by thresholding and eye center location.

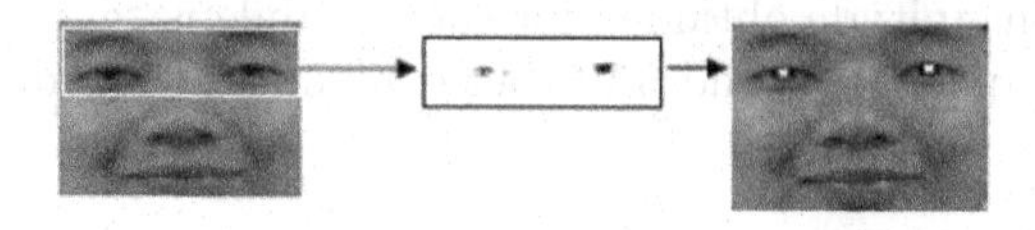

Fig. 4. Illustration of the process of thresholding and eye center location

4.2 Adaptive Thresholding

Adaptive thresholding approach presented here is robust against lighting variations and helps in locating the eye centers in images captured under non uniform lighting [7]. The technique implemented depends only on the spatial characteristics of the image. Given an image of size M × N pixels consists of L gray levels, the total gray levels are divided into two classes $P0 = \{0, 1, 2 \ldots t\}$ and $P1 = \{t+1, t+2 \ldots L-1\}$ at gray level t. The normalized between-class variance (σ_B^2/σ_T^2) is maximized to obtain the optimum threshold t^*. Where σ_B^2 is total variance and σ_T^2 the between-class variance. A cumulative limiting factor (CLF) is calculated for each progressive image as given in equation 9 and is compared with the seperability factor recursively [7].

$$CLF(\Delta) = \sigma_B^2(\Delta)/\sigma_T^2 \;\; for\, \Delta \geq 1 \tag{9}$$

$$SF = \sqrt{\frac{(\mu_T)^3}{\sigma_T^2}} \tag{10}$$

$$CLF(\Delta) = SF \tag{11}$$

where μ_T is the total mean. The process of recursive thresholding is stopped when the condition in equation 12 is satisfied. The separability factor (SF) thus helps in stopping the algorithm at a point where the pixels are present as dense clusters, which is a characteristic of the negative binomial distribution. This clustered nature of the pixels causes the object region to be prominent with the background completely thresholded.

5 Experimental Results

PCA which is a linear subspace approach is implemented to prove the efficiency of the proposed method in improving the recognition accuracy. The testing process is carried out on two face databases, AR and AT&T. In the case of AR database only 30 individuals with 13 images each are used for training. A leave-one-out strategy is implemented for testing. Probe image is aligned with the face model or the template. This step eliminates the possibility of false motion between the two images due to misalignment. A second step is to find out dense correspondence between the two face images using optical flow technique and the magnitudes of the flow vectors are calculated. The probe image is modularized and the summations of the magnitudes of the vectors within each module are calculated and the weight factor is assigned to each module. Each module of the probe image is projected into the corresponding linear subspace created from the training set and then a k nearest neighbor distance measure is used to classify that module. A final score for each class or individual in the training set is calculated by taking consideration of the weightage associated with each module. A winner takes all strategy is followed in determining the final classification result. The recognition accuracy comparison of PCA and the proposed WMPCA (weighted modular PCA) techniques are shown in Table 1. Results indicate a very high percentage increase in accuracy. It can be observed that the accuracy of the recognition increased on both databases by applying the proposed algorithm. The modules of the test image that vary a lot from the test image attributed to lighting variations, expressions and occlusions are given less weightage or less confidence in classification. Hence the good modules with high weightage or the ones that are not affected due to the reasons mentioned, determine the result

Table 1. Accuracy of PCA vs. WMPCA methods on AR and AT & T databases

Database	Percentage of Accuracy		
	PCA	WMPCA-16	WMPCA-64
AR	61.15	98.46	98.85
AT&T	96	98.5	99.25

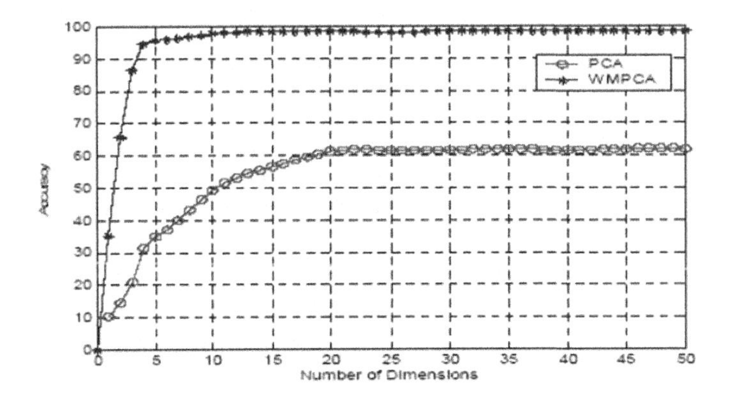

Fig. 5. Accuracy vs. number of dimensions of the subspace corresponding to AR database

of classification. This can be observed by the difference in accuracy levels of the same PCA algorithm on two different databases. The accuracy on AR database fell dramatically since the face images in this database are hugely affected due to the facial variations. Figure 5 shows the recognition accuracy of PCA and WMPCA algorithms on the AR database with respect to number of dimensions of the subspace. Each face image is divided into 16 modules for this case. It can be observed that a high level of accuracy is achieved for a low number of dimensions in the case of WMPCA.

6 Conclusion

An efficient methodology of identifying and reducing the influence of regions within the face images that cause a failure in the recognition process has been presented in this paper. A method of alignment of faces which removes the possibility of false variations has also been presented. The proposed technique could improve the face recognition accuracy in standard face databases.

References

1. Turk, M., Pentland, A.: Eigenfaces for recognition. Journal of Cognitive Neuroscience **3** (1991) 71–86
2. Zhao, W., Krishnaswamy, A., Chellappa, R., Swets, D., Weng, L.: Discriminant analysis of principal components for face recognition. Int. Conference on Automatic Face and Gesture Recognition **3** (1998) 336–341
3. Huang, J., Yuen, P., Chen, C., Sheng, W., Lai, J, H.: Kernel subspace lda with optimized kernel parameters on face recognition. IEEE International Conference on Automatic Face and Gesture Recognition (2004) 327–332
4. Martinez, A.: Recognition of partially occluded and/or imprecisely localized faces using a probabilistic approach. IEEE Computer Society Conference on Computer Vision and Pattern Recognition **1** (2000) 712–717
5. Zhang, Y., Martinez, A.: Recognition of expression variant faces using weighted subspaces. IEEE Computer Society Conference on Computer Vision and Pattern Recognition **1** (2000) 712–717
6. Lucas, B., Kanade, T.: An iterative image registration technique with an application to stereo vision. Proc. DARPA Image Understanding Workshop (1981) 121–130
7. Valaparla, D.P., Asari, V.K.: An adaptive technique for the extraction of object region and boundary from images with complex environment. environment, IEEE Computer Society Proceedings of 30th International Workshop on Applied Imagery and Pattern Recognition (2001) 194–199

Face Detection in Low-Resolution Images

Shinji Hayashi[1] and Osamu Hasegawa[1,2]

[1] Tokyo Institute of Technology, Yokohama, Japan
[2] PRESTO, Japan Science and Technology Agency (JST)
hayashi@isl.titech.ac.jp, hasegawa@isl.titech.ac.jp

Abstract. Face detection is a hot research topic in Computer Vision; the field has greatly progressed over the past decade. However face detection in low-resolution images has not been studied. In this paper, we use a conventional AdaBoost-based face detector to show that the face detection rate falls to 39% from 88% as face resolution decreases from 24 × 24 pixels to 6 × 6 pixels. We propose a new face detection method comprising four techniques for low-resolution images. As a result, our method improved the face detection rate from 39% to 71% for 6 × 6 pixel faces of MIT+CMU frontal face test set.

1 Introduction

In recent years, numerous methods for detecting faces in general scenes have been proposed[1]-[4]. Those methods work efficiently under various conditions such as illumination fluctuation and containing multiple face directions. On the other hand, considering the security use of discovering suspicious persons from surveillance images, it is better to detect a face immediately when a small face is captured in the distance. Nevertheless, conventional face detection technique usually detects face images larger than 20 × 20 pixel or 24 × 24 pixel. Face detection from low-resolution images has not been explicitly studied.

There are two studies related to this field. One is Torralba's psychological experiment[5]. That result indicates that a human can recognize a face in a low-resolution image better when using an upper-body image than using merely a face image. We use this knowledge to improve the face detection rate in section 3. The other is Kruppa and Schile's study[6]. They also used the knowledge of Torralba's experiment and applied "local context detector" for half resolution MIT+CMU ftontal face test set. However, the advantage of using "local context detector" is not clearly shown.

In this paper, we investigate the relation between resolution and the face detection rate systematically in section 2. We made four kinds of evaluation images from the MIT+CMU frontal face test set and trained four kinds of AdaBoost-based detectors. These four kinds indicate four levels of resolution. We evaluated face detection rates for these four kinds of detectors by plotting ROC curves as relations between false positives and the face detection rates. This evaluation shows that a detection rate decreases from 88% to 39% as the resolution of faces decreases from 24 × 24 pixel to 6 × 6 pixel. Section 3 presents our new method

G. Bebis et al. (Eds.): ISVC 2005, LNCS 3804, pp. 199–206, 2005.

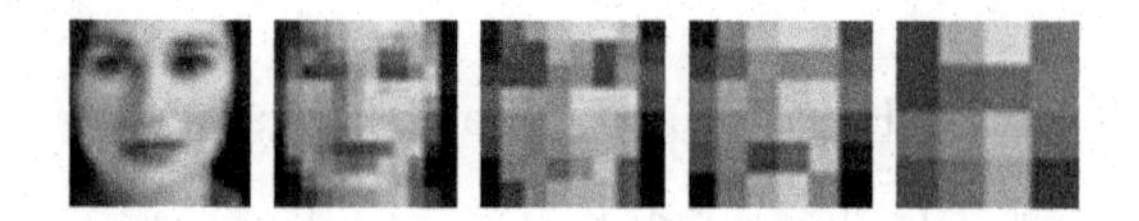

Fig. 1. face size is from left 24 × 24, 12 × 12, 8 × 8, 6 × 6, 4 × 4 pixel

for detecting faces from low-resolution images. This method comprises four techniques, "Using the upper-body", "Expansion of input images", "Frequency-band limitation of features", and "Combination of two detectors". Our results showed that a 39% face detection rate for 6 × 6 pixel faces increases to 71% by our proposed method. In section 4, we summarize our research.

In this paper, 'resolution' means the face size. We defined the face size as 2.4 times the interval between an individual's eyes.

2 Conventional Method

We use an AdaBoost-based face detector by Viola[7] for our research because it is used widely in face detection research[8]-[10]. We show the result of their application to low-resolution images.

2.1 Application to Low-Resolution Images

First, we determine the resolutions to investigate. Cropping faces in various sizes and observing, we judged that 6 × 6 pixel was near the boundary of resolution for an image to be recognizable as a face. Therefore, we designate 6 × 6 pixel as the minimum resolution to investigate in this study. Figure 1 shows cropped faces as 24 × 24, 12 × 12, 8 × 8, 6 × 6, and 4 × 4 pixels. We selected 24 × 24 pixel as the maximum resolution. 12 × 12, 8 × 8 pixel were added. These are the four kinds of resolution investigated here.

Next, we describe application of an AdaBoost-based face detector to low-resolution images. Resolution of training data is the minimum size of face detection because, in the face detection process, an input image pyramid is produced by scaling down. Consequently, it is necessary to lower the resolution of training data for detecting low-resolution faces. In this regard, not only the AdaBoost-based face detector but neural network-based face detectors and other devices are similar. We used MIT+CMU frontal face test set which is known as a standard test set for face detection[11]. This set comprises 130 images containing 507 frontal faces. A histogram of sizes of 507 faces is shown in Fig. 2. Because the minimum detectable face size is the size of the training data, most faces contained in the MIT+CMU set can be detected using a 24 × 24 pixel face detector. However, our research treats face detection from low-resolution images. This study is intended to detect faces smaller than 24 × 24 pixels. Therefore, the MIT+CMU set, in which the small face is not contained, cannot be used as it is. Evaluation images for face detection from low-resolution images were created as follows.

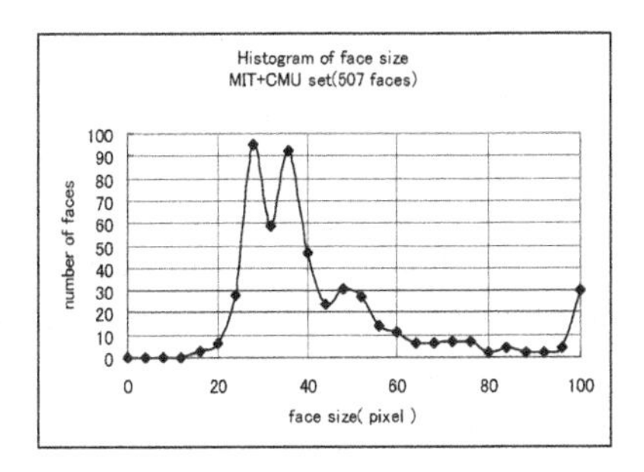

Fig. 2. Face size histogram of the MIT+CMU set

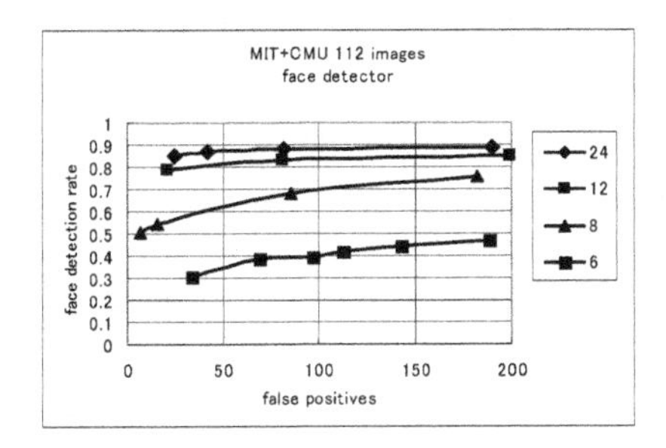

Fig. 3. Relation between resolutions and face detection rates

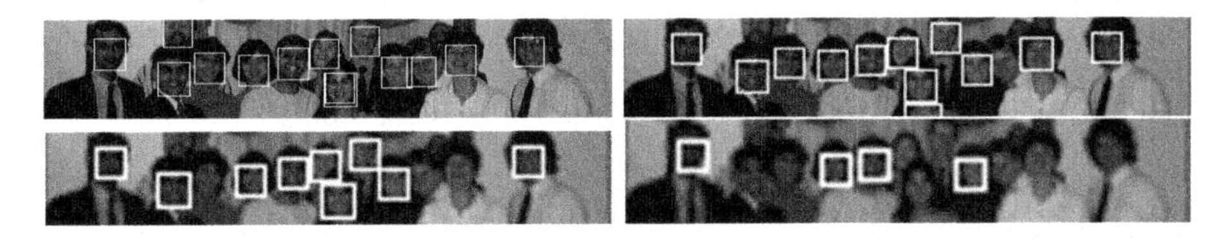

Fig. 4. Examples of detection results: average face size is 24×24(upper left), 12×12(upper right), 8×8(lower left), and 6×6(lower left) pixels. Thresholds were set to obtain almost the same number of false positives for 112 images.

– Eliminate 13 images that contain no faces and eliminate 5 images that contain line-drawn faces. Thereby, 130 images become 112 images.
– The whole image will be reduced with bicubic so that the "average face size" of the face might become a desired standard size (24 × 24, 12 × 12, 8 × 8, or 6 × 6 pixels). (Bicubic was chosen to perform the smoothest possible reduction)
– The above is repeated for 112 images and four kinds of sizes.

That process yielded four kinds of evaluation images. Respective averages of the face sizes contained in the four kinds of evaluation images are 24 × 24, 12 × 12, 8 × 8, or 6 × 6 pixels. Four kinds of detectors were made to evaluate the relation between a resolution and a face detection rate. These detectors were applied to four kinds of evaluation images. Four kinds of detectors were made using 5131 face images of 24 × 24, 12 × 12, 8 × 8, and 6 × 6 pixels and 5316 non-face images as training data. Evaluation results for the four detectors are shown in Fig. 3. This is the result obtained using conventional AdaBoost-based face detectors applied to low-resolution images. In Fig. 3, at the point of 100 false positives, the face detection rate declines from 88% to 39% as the face resolution is reduced from 24 × 24 pixel to 6 × 6 pixel. Therefore, it can be said that we can not obtain a sufficient face detection rate for 6 × 6 pixel faces merely using 6 × 6 pixel faces as training data. An example of detection results is shown in Fig. 4.

3 Proposed Method

When face size became 6 × 6 pixels, the detection rate fell extremely using conventional AdaBoost-based face detector. We chose 6 × 6 pixels as the minimum face size to detect; in this study, only 6 × 6 pixel evaluation images are used hereafter. In this section, we demonstrate that the face detection rate from low-resolution images is improved by our proposed method comprising four techniques.

3.1 Using Upper-Body Images

Getting a hint by Torralba's psychological experiment, we attempted to use upper-body images as training data. We choose 12 × 12 pixels as the size of upper-body images. This is double the resolution of face images. 4191 upper-body images of 12 × 12 pixels were prepared as training data; a detector was made using these images and 5316 non-face images. Figure 6 is a 12 × 12 upper-body image and a 6 × 6 face image. Each face size is the same.

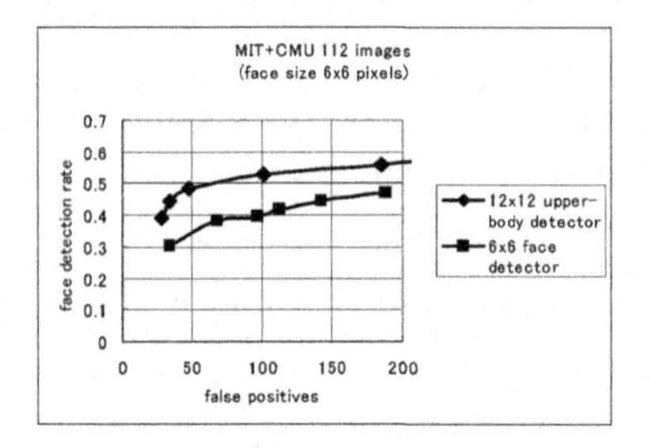

Fig. 5. Effect of using upper-body images

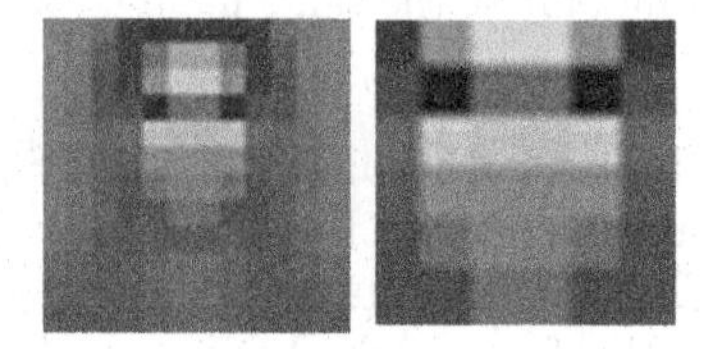

Fig. 6. Left:12 × 12 pixel upper-body image. Right:6 × 6 pixel face image.

Figure 5 portrays the result of 12 × 12 upper-body detector applied to 6 × 6 pixel evaluation images. For comparison, the result for a 6 × 6 face detector applied to 6 × 6 evaluation images is plotted. At the point of 100 false positives, the 6 × 6 face detector detects about 39% of faces, while the 12 × 12 upper-body detector detects 52% of faces. We noticed that there are faces that only the upper-body detector can detect and that only the face detector can detect. This indicates that these two detectors complement each other. Therefore, we use not only the upper-body detector, but also the face detector. Finally, we will try to combine these two detectors into one system.

3.2 Expansion of Input Images

In face detection, two or more "face coordinates candidates" usually occur around one face. This is because a detector judges the image as a face even

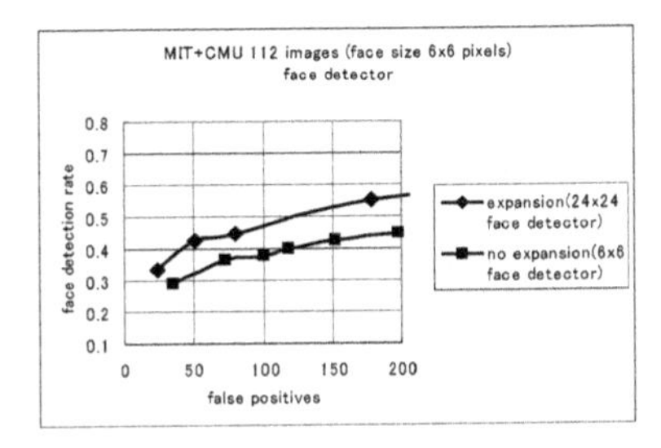

Fig. 7. Effect of expansion: face detector

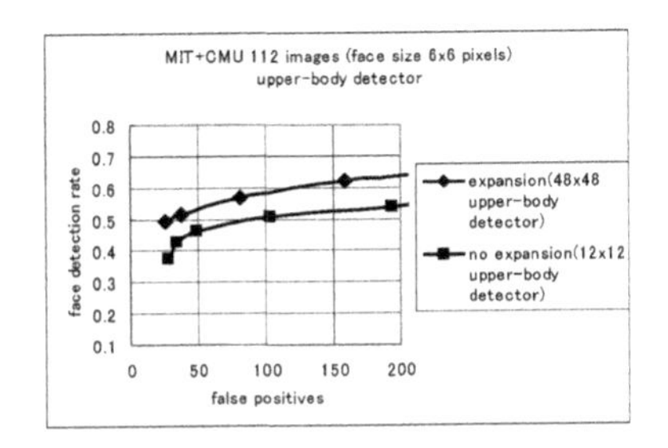

Fig. 8. Effect of expansion: upper-body detector

if the position and size vary somewhat. We counted number of face coordinate candidates by respectively applying a face detector to 100 24×24 pixel face images and 6×6 face images. For the 24×24 pixel face images, the average number of face-coordinate candidates is 20. For 6×6 pixel face images, the average number of face coordinates candidates is two. This difference is the difference of robustness for position and size changes.

Therefore, to detect 6×6 pixel faces, we propose to expand the whole input image by bicubic, and to detect faces using a 24×24 pixel face detector. Considering the size variation in 6×6 pixel faces, we choose six as a scaling factor. We expanded 6×6 pixel evaluation images by a factor of six, and applied the 24×24 face detector to these images. This result is depicted in Fig. 7. For comparison, the result of a 6×6 face detector applied to 6×6 pixel evaluation images is plotted. At the point of 100 false positives, the 39% face detection rate is improved to 48% using this expansion. To evaluate the effect of expansion for an upper-body detector, we made a 48×48 pixel upper-body detector using 4191 upper-body images of 48×48 pixels and 5316 non-face images. We applied it to 6×6 pixel expanded evaluation images. The result is shown in Fig. 8. For comparison, the result of the 12×12 pixel upper-body detector applied to 6×6 pixel evaluation images is plotted. At the point of 100 false positives, the 52% face detection rate is improved to 58% using expansion.

The face detection rate is improved through the use of expansion of input images for both the face detector and the upper-body detector.

3.3 Frequency-Band Limitation of Features

A classifier that constitutes a detector uses four simple features. We use the same features as Viola used. These features can take all positions and lengths possible in a 24×24 pixel image. When 6×6 pixel face images are expanded by a factor of four, fewer than 4 pixel cycle data in 24×24 pixel face images are meaningless. Therefore, we produced a new face detector and upper-body detector using conditions in eq. (1). H and W are shown in Fig. 9.

$$H \geq 4, W \geq 4 \tag{1}$$

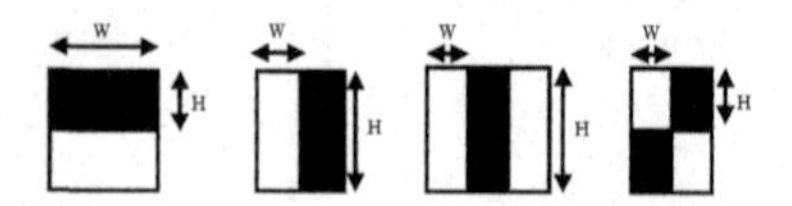

Fig. 9. W,H of features

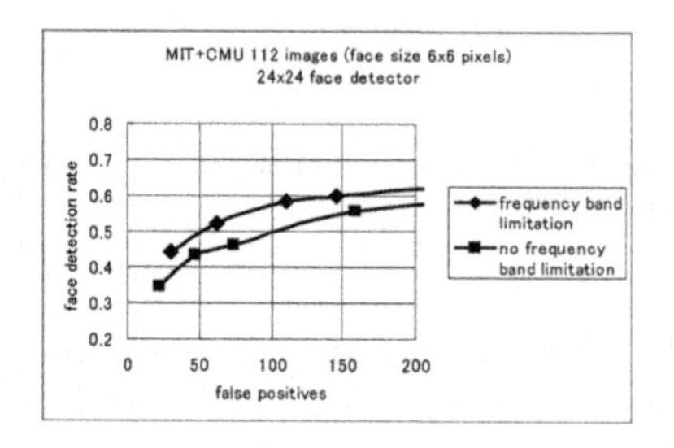

Fig. 10. Effect of frequency band limitation: face detector

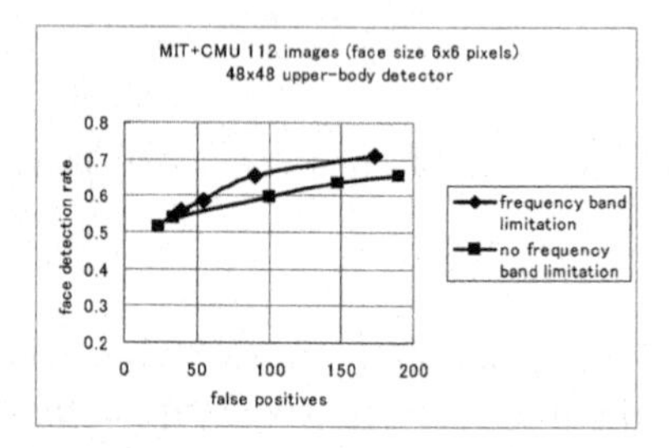

Fig. 11. Effect of frequency band limitation: upper-body detector

These two detectors were applied to 6 × 6 pixel evaluation images. The results are shown as "frequency-band limitation" in Fig. 10 and Fig. 11. In each evaluation, 6 × 6 pixel evaluation images are expanded by a factor of six; then a 24 × 24 face detector or 48 × 48 upper-body detector is used. For comparison, results before using frequency-band limitation are plotted as "no frequency band limitation" in Fig. 10 and Fig. 11. At the point of 100 false positives, the face detection rate of the face detector is improved from 48% to 58%. The face detection rate of an upper-body detector is improved from 58% to 67%.

3.4 Combination of Two Detectors

Because two detectors are used, two face-likenesses for the image are detected. In our research, we make a final judgment based on this information. This is achieved using a SVM. The face-likeness is defined as eq. (2). $h_i(x)$ is a weak learner and α_i is the weight of the weak learner. k is the number of "face coordinates candidates" and i is the number of weak learners.

$$p_k = \sum_{weak\ learners} \alpha_i h_i(x) \tag{2}$$

Two or more "face coordinate candidates" generated around one face are merged. Then one set of coordinates is finally made to correspond to one face in the detection process. When merging candidate locations,

$$P = \sum_k p_k \tag{3}$$

is calculated, which corresponds to "face coordinates" that were made by merging "face coordinate candidates". This value is inferred as a "face-likeness". Now,

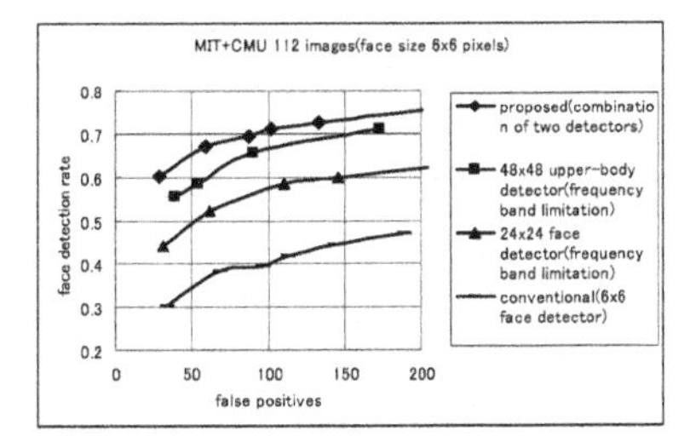

Fig. 12. Combination of two detectors in a SVM

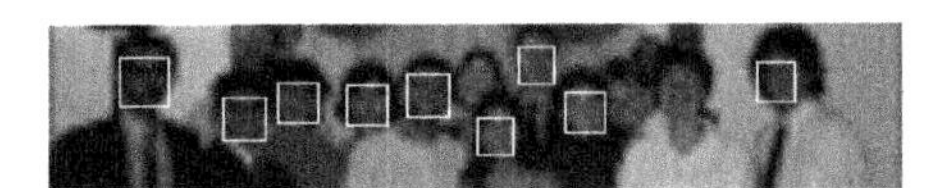

Fig. 13. Results of the proposed method as applied to 6 × 6 pixel evaluation images

two detectors are applied independently to an input image and the 2D vector Z is obtained for an image that is finally detected by further merging the result. Final judgement is made by a SVM whose input is this 2D vector Z.

We applied the proposed method to 6 × 6 pixel evaluation images. The result is presented in Fig. 12. The results before combined use are shown as "48 × 48 upper-body detector" and "24 × 24 face detector" in Fig. 12. At the point of 100 false positives, the face detection rates are improved to 71% from 58% (24 × 24 face detector) and 67% (48 × 48 upper-body detector). The result of the 6 × 6 face detector is plotted for comparison. The face detection rate is improved to 71% from 39% by our proposed method. Figure 13 is the result of our proposed

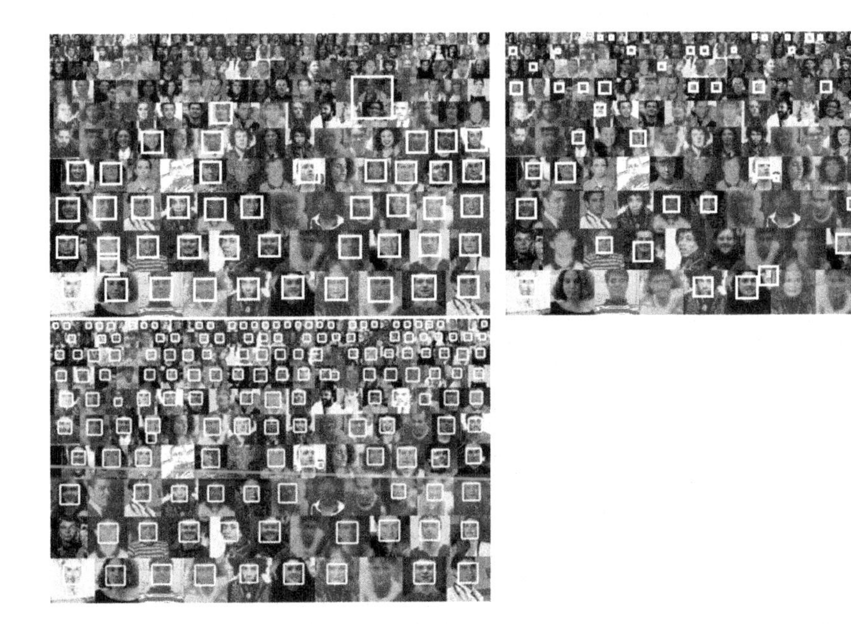

Fig. 14. Upper left: detected using a 24 × 24 face detector. Upper right: detected using a 6 × 6 face detector. Lower left: detected by the proposed method.

method applied to the lower left image in Fig. 4. In addition, although 6×6 pixel faces have been studied so far, the proposed method can also detect a higher-resolution face image. Figure 14 shows this. An image in Fig. 14 consists of 10 layers. The top layer's resolution is 6×6 pixels; the bottom layer's resolution is 24×24 pixels. The upper left is the detected result of 24×24 face detector. Low-resolution faces are not detected at all. Upper right represents the detection results of the 6×6 face detector. Faces of various sizes from 6×6 to 24×24 pixels are detected. However, the detection rate is very low. At lower left are the detection results of the proposed method. Faces of various sizes from 6×6 to 24×24 pixel are detected well. Thresholds of the three detectors are set to have the same number of false positives.

4 Conclusions

We proposed a new method comprising four techniques: "Using upper-body images", "Expansion of input images", "Frequency-band limitation", and "Combination of two detectors" to detect faces from low-resolution images. A conventional AdaBoost-based face detector can detect only 39% of faces in 6×6 pixel evaluation images, but our proposed method can detect 71% of faces in those same evaluation images.

References

1. M.H. Yang, D.J. Kriegman and N. Ahuja. "Detecting Faces in images:A Survey," IEEE Trans. on PAMI, vol.24, no.1, pp.34-58, January, 2002.
2. H. Schneiderman. "Feature-Centric Evaluation for Efficient Cascaded Object Detection," in Proc. of CVPR, vol.2, pp.29-36, June, 2004.
3. M. Osadchy and D. Karen. "Image Detection Under Varying Illumination and Pose," in Proc. of ICCV, vol.II, pp.668-673, July, 2001
4. B. Wu, H. Ai, C. Huang, and S. Lao. "Fast Rotation Invariant Multi-view Face Detection Based on Real Adaboost," in Proc. of FGR, pp.79-84, May, 2004.
5. A. Torralba and P. Shina. "Detecting Faces in Impoverished Images," AI Memo 2001-028, CBCL Memo 208, 2001
6. Hannes Kruppa, Bernt Schiele. Using Local Context To Improve Face Detection. in BMVC,2003
7. P. Viola and M. Jones. "Rapid Object Detection Using a Boosted Cascade of Simple Features," in Proc. of CVPR, vol.1, pp.511-518, December, 2001
8. R. Lienhart, A. Kuranov and V. Pisarevsky. "Empirical Analysis of Detection Cascades of Boosted Classifiers for Rapid Object Detection," in Proc. of DAGM'03, pp.297-304, September, 2003.
9. S.Z. Li, L. Zhu, Z.Q. Zhang, A. Blake, H.J. Zhang and H. Shum. "Statistical Learning of Multi-View Face Detection," in Proc. of ECCV, pp.67-81, May, 2002.
10. C. Liu and H.Y. Shum. "Kullback-Leibler Boosting," in Proc. of CVPR, vol.1, pp.587-594, June, 2003.
11. H.A. Rowley, S. Baluja, and T. Kanade. "Neural Network-Based Face Detection," IEEE Trans. on PAMI, vol.20, pp.23-38, January, 1998

Investigating the Impact of Face Categorization on Recognition Performance

Konstantinos Veropoulos[1], George Bebis[1], and Michael Webster[2]

[1] Computer Vision Laboratory
[2] Department of Psychology, University of Nevada, Reno NV 89557, USA
{kvero, bebis}@cse.unr.edu, mwebster@unr.edu

Abstract. Face recognition is a key biometric technology with a wide range of potential applications both in government and private sectors. Despite considerable progress in face recognition research over the past decade, today's face recognition systems are not accurate or robust enough to be fully deployed in high security environments. In this paper, we investigate the impact of face categorization on recognition performance. In general, face categorization can be used as a filtering step to limit the search space during identification (e.g., a person categorized as a middle-aged, Asian male, needs to be compared only to subjects having the same profile). Our experimental results demonstrate that face categorization based on important visual characteristics such as gender, ethnicity, and age offers significant improvements in recognition performance including higher recognition accuracy, lower time requirements, and graceful degradation. Additional performance improvements can be expected by implementing "category-specific" recognition subsystems that are optimized to discriminate more accurately between faces within the same face category rather than faces between other categories.

1 Introduction

Recently, there has been an increased interest in developing computer vision systems that can robustly and reliably recognize, track, monitor, and identify people and interpret their actions. Face recognition is a key biometric technology with a wide range of potential applications. Despite considerable progress in this research area, today's face recognition systems are not accurate or robust enough to be fully deployed in high security environments. Advances in this area are thus likely to make significant contributions in areas such as security, monitoring, surveillance and safety. Motivated by cognitive evidence, we believe that significant gains in recognition performance can be achieved by applying face categorization prior to recognition and optimizing recognition within each face category.

Specifically, there is cognitive evidence supporting the idea that humans utilize information from multiple visual cues for face recognition. It is well known, for example, that people are more accurate at recognizing faces of their own ethnicity than faces of another ethnicity [1]. Humans can also judge the gender of adults and children using feature sets derived from the appropriate face

G. Bebis et al. (Eds.): ISVC 2005, LNCS 3804, pp. 207–218, 2005.

age category, rather than applying features derived from another age category or a combination of age categories [2]. It has been also found that adaptation may routinely influence face perception and could have an important role in calibrating properties of face perception according to the subset of faces populating an individual's environment [3]. All this evidence suggests that people are better skilled than machines in recognizing faces because they have developed "specialized" perceptual processes through lifelong experiences while adaptation self-calibrates the human vision system to faces in their environment. These processes and the ability of the human visual system to adapt allow them to be more sensitive to certain types of visual information (e.g., age or gender), carrying more discriminative power for faces within the same category.

Despite the significant amount of evidence in this area, typical face recognition systems do not exploit, at least explicitly, information from multiple visual cues for recognition. In fact, in most cases faces are represented by extracting the same type features regardless to differences in gender, ethnicity, and age (e.g., middle-aged, Asian male vs young, Black female). Therefore, it is reasonable to expect that face recognition suffers from irrelevant and/or redundant information. In addition, many times face recognition systems yield inconsistent matches (e.g., matching a middle-aged, Asian male to a young, Black female). In principle, inconsistent matches can be avoided or reduced by simply restricting search only to faces having the same profile with the face in question.

Although some attention has been given to the problem of gender [4][5], ethnicity [6] and age classification [7], typical face recognition systems do not explicitly exploit information from such visual cues to limit the search space and reduce the number of inconsistent matches. An exemption is the recent work of Jain *et al.* [8] which shows that using ancillary information based on "soft biometrics" (e.g., gender and ethnicity) leads to improving the recognition performance of a fingerprint system. However, they have used this information along with the output of the fingerprint recognition system in order to verify the matching results, rather than exploiting this information to reduce the search space prior matching.

Our emphasis is this work is on investigating the impact of face categorization on recognition performance. In this context, we have designed and performed a large number of experiments using the FERET database to demonstrate the benefits of applying face categorization prior to recognition. Additional performance improvements can be expected by designing "specialized" (i.e., category-specific) recognition subsystems that are explicitly optimized to discriminate more accurately between faces in the same face category than faces in other categories. Coupling face categorization with category-specific recognition is essentially equivalent to incorporating an adaptation mechanism to the recognition process, allowing recognition to self-calibrate itself to different types of faces in the operating environment. Although we are not dealing here with the design and implementation of face categorization and category-specific recognition, we do discuss in Section 6 a number of important issues.

The rest of the paper is organized as follows: Section 2 presents a general methodology for coupling face categorization with recognition. Section 3 briefly describes the face recognition approach used in this study. The datasets and our evaluation methodology are presented in Section 4 while experimental results are presented in Section 5. Finally, in Section 6, we analyze the results of our experiments and elaborate on the design and implementation of face categorization and category-specific recognition algorithms.

2 Methodology

The key idea of employing face categorization is dividing faces into different categories prior to recognition using information from various visual cues. *First,* the face database (i.e., gallery set) is divided into different subsets by assigning faces into different face categories using gender, ethnicity and/or age information. It should be noted that, the purpose of age classification is to assign a given face to a particular age group (eg. between 20 to 40 years old) rather than estimating the age of the subject exactly. *Second,* a given face (i.e., query) is assigned to the appropriate face category using the same procedure. The query is then matched against faces belonging to its assigned category only, instead of being compared to all the faces in the database. A simple diagram illustrating the above procedure is shown in Fig. 1.

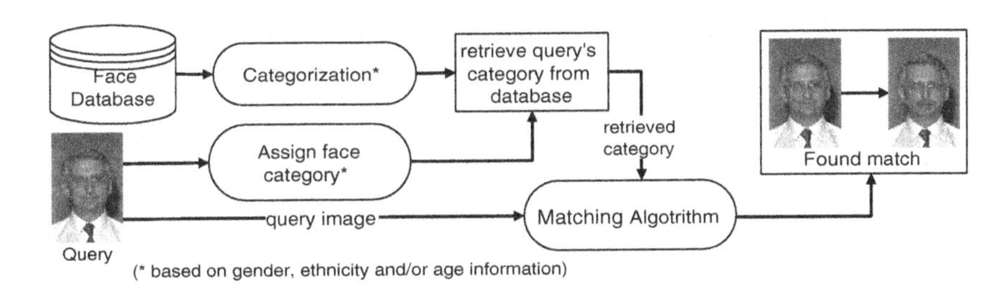

Fig. 1. Categorization and matching procedure for a query image

Applying categorization prior to recognition restricts the search space from the whole face database to the subset of images that belong to the same face category as the query image. This way, not only the number of comparisons is reduced to the size of the chosen face category, thus speeding up the matching process, but also the risk of mismatching a given face to a face from a completely different face category is reduced. In other words, it allows the system to degrade gracefully.

3 Recognition

To quantify the effects of face categorization on recognition, we performed recognition using the popular method of eigenfaces [9], although any other recognition methodology could have been used. The eigenface approach uses Principal Component Analysis (PCA) to represent faces in a low-dimensional subspace spanned by the "largest" eigenvectors of the covariance matrix of the data, that is, the eigenvectors corresponding to the largest eigenvalues or the directions of maximum variance. To create the eigenspace, 400 images were randomly chosen from the gallery set (see next section). In choosing the largest eigenvectors, we preserve 97% of the information in the data. For matching, we used a minimum-distance classifier based on Mahalanobis distance. Given a query face, we find the top N faces having the highest similarity score with the query face. To evaluate matching, we used the Cumulative Match Characteristic (CMC) curve [10] which shows the probability of identification against the returned 1-to-N candidate list size (i.e., it shows the probability that a given face appears in different sized candidate lists). The faster the CMC curve approaches the value one, which is an indication of that face being in the candidate list of a specified size, the better the matching algorithm is.

4 Datasets and Evaluation

To test our approach, we used the FERET database [10], released in October 2003, which contains a large number of images acquired during different photo sessions and has a good variety of gender, ethnicity and age groups. The lighting conditions, face orientation and time of capture vary. In this work, we concentrate on frontal face poses coded as *fa* (regular frontal image) or *fb* (alternative frontal image, taken *shortly* after the corresponding *fa* image)[1]. In our evaluations, the *fa* images were used as the gallery set while the *fb* images were used as the query set (i.e., face images in question). All faces were normalized in terms of orientation, position and size prior to experimentation. They were also masked to include only the face region (i.e., upper body and background were cropped out) yielding an image size of 48×60 pixels.

In order to evaluate the effect of different levels of face categorization, three sets of experiments were designed. First, we wanted to see what kind of improvements could be expected using one-level categorization where only one type of information was used to categorize faces (i.e., gender, ethnicity, or age). Next, we investigated a two-level categorization where two types of information were used at a time (i.e., gender and ethnicity, gender and age, or ethnicity and age). Finally, we investigated a three-level categorization where all three types of information (i.e., gender, ethnicity, and age) were used.

Before proceeding in describing our experiments and presenting our results, two important issues must be clarified. First, in practice, face categorization will be an automated process. In this study, however, face categorization was implemented manually since our main objective was to investigate the impact of categorization on recognition performance. Therefore, the results presented here can be thought as "best-case" performance since we have assumed error-free categorization. Second, recognition has not been optimized for each face category (i.e., we have applied the same recognition procedure for each face category). In

[1] It should be noted that, *shortly* could mean up to two years after the *fa* pose had been taken.

general, one can expect higher performance by optimizing recognition within each face category. There are important issues to be considered in both cases which we discuss in Section 6. In the following subsections, we provide a detailed description of our experiments.

One-Level Categorization: In one-level categorization, we only consider one category at a time, that is, gender, ethnicity or age separately. This type of categorization results in three different groups of experiments with the data organization shown in Table 1. Our notation for ethnicity categorization is as follows: Asian (As), Asian-Middle-Eastern (AME), Black-or-African-American (BAA), Hispanic (Hisp) and White (Wh).

Two-Level Categorization: In two-level categorization, we consider combinations of gender and ethnicity, gender and age, and ethnicity and age. This type

Table 1. Organization of data (total number of persons and, in parentheses, total number of images) for the gallery set (fa) and the query set (fb) assuming one-level partitioning

	Gender		Ethnicity				
	Male	**Female**	**As**	**AME**	**BAA**	**Hisp**	**Wh**
fa	501 (746)	365 (457)	130 (192)	40 (61)	72 (100)	51 (63)	558 (770)
fb	500 (740)	366 (456)	130 (190)	40 (60)	72 (99)	51 (63)	558 (767)

	Age					
	07–13	**17–23**	**27–33**	**37–43**	**46–53**	**57–63**
fa	17 (18)	402 (484)	201 (296)	144 (251)	79 (120)	21 (30)
fb	17 (18)	403 (480)	200 (296)	144 (247)	79 (120)	21 (31)

Table 2. Organization of data (total number of persons and, in parentheses, total number of images) for the gallery set (fa) and the query set (fb) after a two-level partitioning

	Gender+Ethnicity			
	fa		fb	
	Male	Female	Male	Female
As	83 (134)	47 (58)	82 (131)	48 (59)
AME	35 (53)		35 (53)	
BAA	33 (47)	39 (53)	33 (46)	39 (53)
Hisp	23 (28)	28 (35)	23 (28)	28 (35)
Wh	321 (478)	237 (292)	321 (476)	237 (291)

	Gender+Age			
	fa		fb	
	Male	Female	Male	Female
07–13	10 (11)		10 (11)	
17–23	183 (239)	219 (245)	183 (235)	220 (245)
27–33	131 (239)	70 (97)	130 (199)	70 (97)
37–43	102 (181)	42 (70)	102 (178)	42 (69)
47–53	55 (86)	24 (34)	55 (86)	24 (34)
57–63	19 (28)		19 (29)	

	Ethnicity+Age									
	fa					fb				
	As	AME	BAA	Hisp	Wh	As	AME	BAA	Hisp	Wh
07–13					10 (11)					10 (11)
17–23	72 (93)	19 (34)	31 (36)	31 (34)	241 (277)	73 (92)	19 (33)	31 (36)	31 (34)	241 (275)
27–33	41 (69)	10 (11)	15 (22)		123 (177)	40 (68)	10 (11)	15 (22)		123 (178)
37–43			17 (30)		104 (179)			17 (30)		104 (176)
47–53					58 (93)					58 (93)
57–63					29 (20)					20 (30)

of categorization results in three different groups of experiments with the data organization shown in Table 2. It should be noted that all categories including a small number of subjects (i.e., less than 10) have not been included in our evaluations (e.g., Hispanics between 27 and 33 years of age).

There-Level Categorization: In three-level categorization, we consider all three types of information (gender, ethnicity and age) together. This type of categorization results in several groups of experiments with the data organization shown in Table 3. Again, all groups containing less than 10 subjects have not been included in our evaluations.

Table 3. Organization of data (total number of persons and, in parentheses, total number of images) for the gallery set (fa) and the query set (fb) after a three-level partitioning

	Gender+Ethnicity+Age			
	fa		fb	
	Male	Female	Male	Female
As/17-13	33 (47)	39 (46)	33 (45)	40 (47)
As/27-33	35 (61)		34 (60)	
AME/17-13	14 (26)		14 (26)	
AME/27-33	10 (11)		10 (11)	
BAA/17-13	11 (13)	20 (23)	11 (13)	20 (23)
BAA/37-43	10 (16)		10 (16)	
Hisp/17-13	15 (17)	16 (17)	15 (17)	16 (17)
Wh/17-13	110 (136)	131 (141)	110 (134)	131 (141)
Wh/27-33	73 (109)	50 (68)	73 (110)	50 (68)
Wh/37-43	72 (128)	32 (51)	72 (126)	32 (50)
Wh/47-53	40 (68)	18 (25)	40 (68)	18 (25)
Wh/57-63	18 (27)		18 (28)	

5 Experimental Results

To quantify the effect of face categorization, we compared the CMC curves in two cases: (a) when search is restricted to a particular face category (best curve) and (b) when searching the whole gallery set (worst curve). As mentioned earlier,

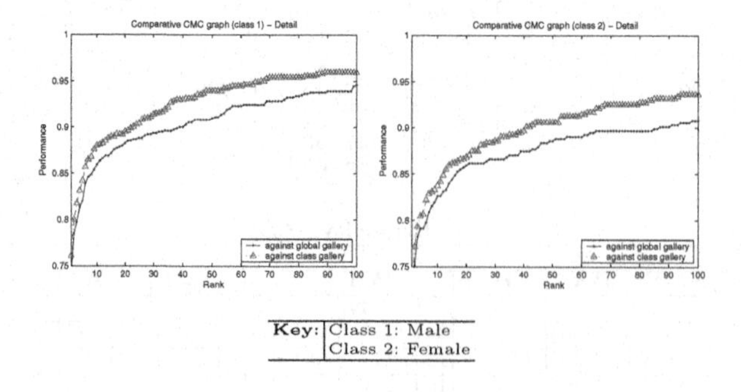

Fig. 2. CMC curves for Males and Females (one-level categorization)

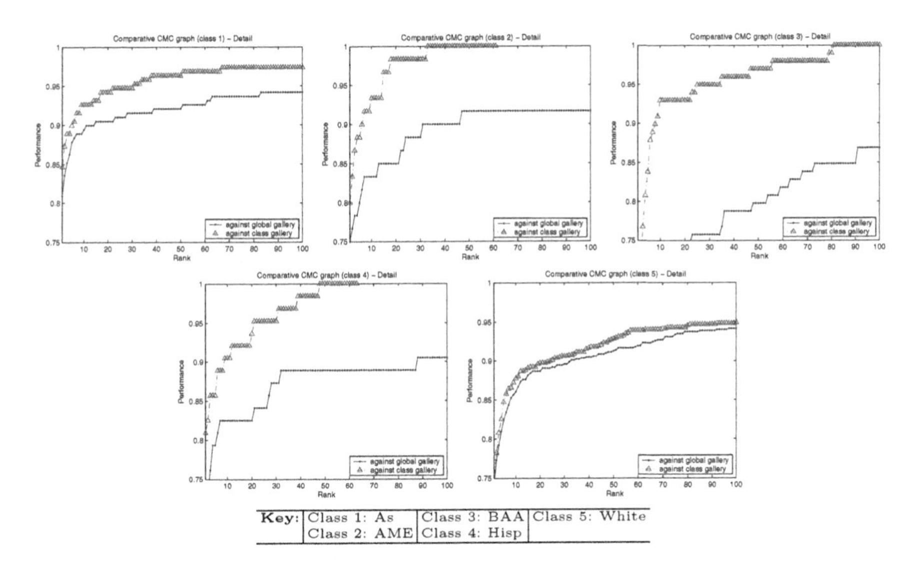

Fig. 3. CMC curves for different ethnicities (one-level categorization)

when the CMC curve reaches the value one, then the face in question (query) always appears in the candidate list. For example, the CMC curve for Asian-Middle-Eastern faces (class 2) shown in Fig. 3, indicates that the query face always appears in a candidate list of at least 27 persons assuming categorization, whereas to have the same effect without categorization, the candidate list needs to contain more than 100 persons.

Figs. 2–4 present the CMC plots obtained from experiments on one-level categorization. CMC plots obtained from experiments on two-level categorization are shown in Figs. 6–8. Finally, the CMC plots obtained from three-level categorization are given in Fig. 9. Fig. 5 shows several test cases where recognition failed when comparing each of the test faces against the whole gallery set (i.e., without face categorization). The purpose of the example is to demonstrate what kind of matching errors one should expect (e.g., mismatching a male/BAA (#854) to a female/Hispanic (#351)). Intuitively, one would expect recognition to degrade gracefully, that is, mismatching people within the same face category but not between different categories. Coupling face categorization with recognition has the potential to reduce the number of inconsistent matches.

6 Discussion and Conclusions

All CMC plots in Figs. 2–9 illustrate that applying face categorization prior to recognition leads to recognition improvements by reducing the search space and increasing accuracy. It is worth mentioning that, face categorization is independent of the recognition algorithm, therefore, it could be coupled with existing recognition systems without requiring any changes to the recognition engine or radical and costly changes in the current infrastructure.

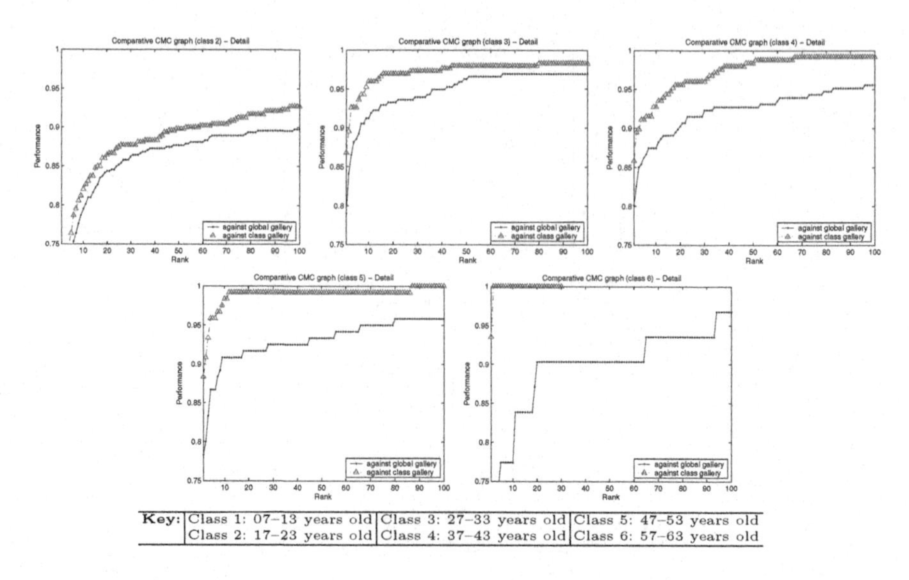

Key:	Class 1: 07–13 years old	Class 3: 27–33 years old	Class 5: 47–53 years old
	Class 2: 17–23 years old	Class 4: 37–43 years old	Class 6: 57–63 years old

Fig. 4. CMC curves for different age groups (one-level categorization)

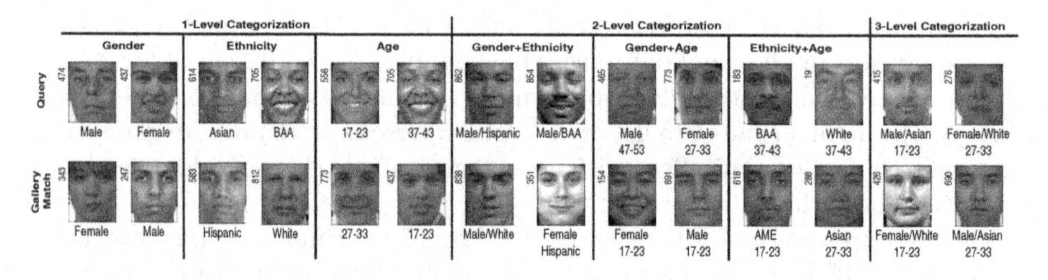

Fig. 5. Examples of mismatches without assuming face categorization. These cases were correctly matched assuming category-specific galleries.

There are a number issues related to implementing face categorization. One of them is what cues to select to define the face categories. Another one is whether to perform "hard" or "soft" categorization. "Hard" categorization implies assigning a face to a single face category while "soft" categorization implies assigning a face to several categories, each with a certain probability. In this study, we used some of the most obvious visual cues (e.g., gender, ethnicity, and age), and "hard" categorization. However, it might be possible to use additional visual cues (e.g., face shape) or even cues that do not necessarily have an obvious visual interpretation (e.g., generate the face categories using unsupervised learning [11]).

An other issue is the error introduced by the categorization step. As discussed earlier, the results presented in this study assume error-free face categorization (i.e., performed manually). In practice, however, face categorization is expected to introduce some errors by assigning faces to wrong categories, leading to incorrect matches. Employing "soft" categorization instead of "hard" categorization

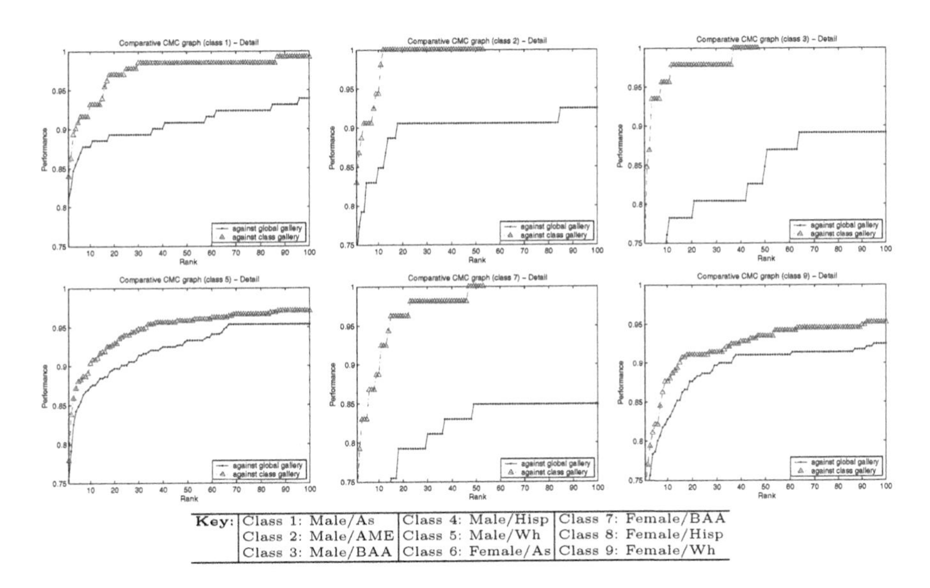

Fig. 6. CMC curves for two-level categorization using gender and ethnicity information

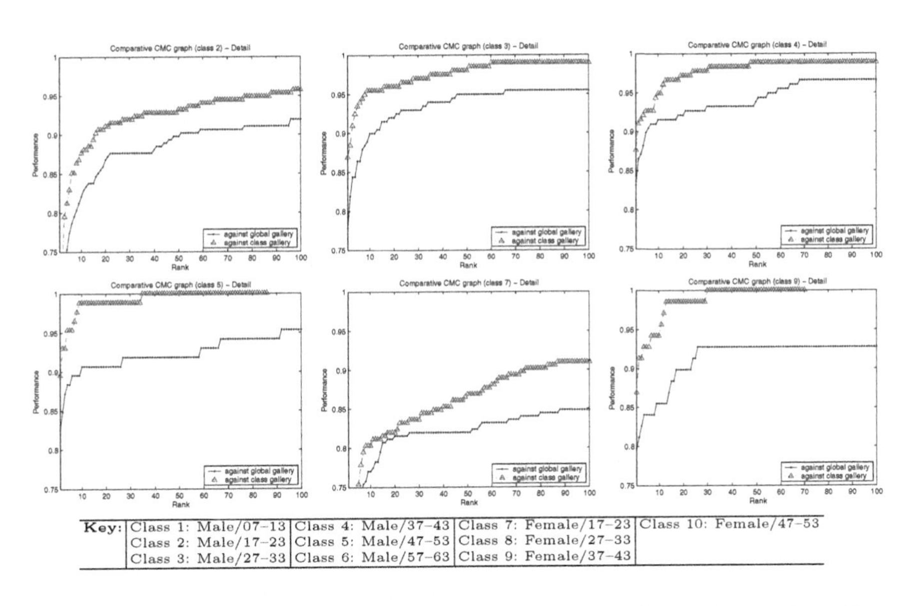

Fig. 7. CMC curves for two-level categorization using gender and age information

could help to reduce these errors. In general, however, it would be necessary to design highly accurate and robust face categorization algorithms in order to achieve high recognition accuracy. We believe that one way to deal with this issue is by capitalizing on recent advances in pattern recognition and machine learning.

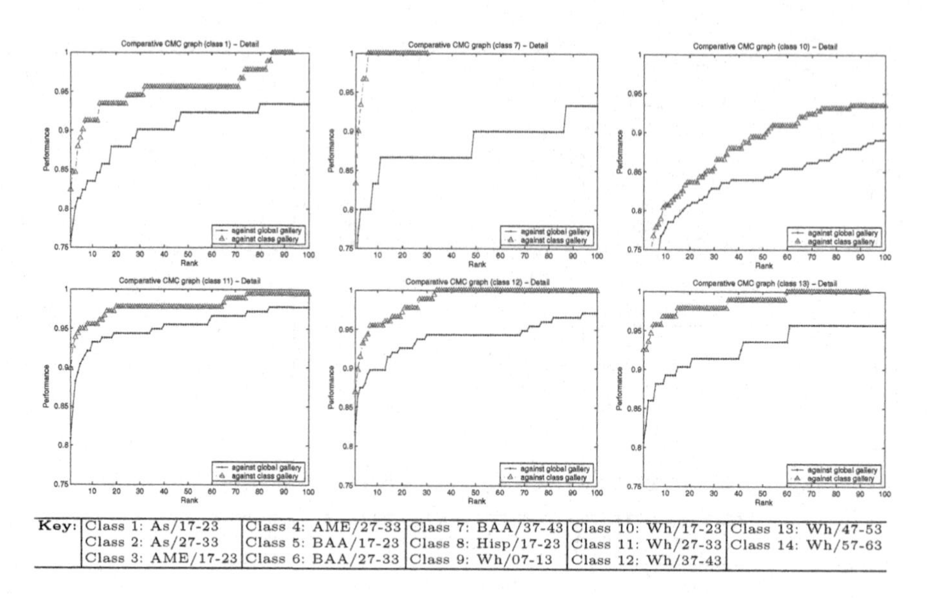

Key:					
	Class 1: As/17-23	Class 4: AME/27-33	Class 7: BAA/37-43	Class 10: Wh/17-23	Class 13: Wh/47-53
	Class 2: As/27-33	Class 5: BAA/17-23	Class 8: Hisp/17-23	Class 11: Wh/27-33	Class 14: Wh/57-63
	Class 3: AME/17-23	Class 6: BAA/27-33	Class 9: Wh/07-13	Class 12: Wh/37-43	

Fig. 8. CMC curves for two-level categorization using ethnicity and age information

First, we believe that it would be important to optimize the face representation scheme used for each category. Let us take, for example, the case of PCA that was used here to represent faces. For each face category, we chose a subset of eigenvectors by applying the same principle (i.e., choosing the "largest" eigenvectors). Although the "largest" eigenvectors preserve most of the information in the data, it is well known that they might not provide the best possible discrimination power. Therefore, it would be essential to optimize the face representation scheme for each category by selecting "category-specific" eigenvectors. This is essentially equivalent to performing feature selection. We have done preliminary work on eigenvector selection for gender classification [5], showing that it is possible to improve gender classification by selecting eigenvectors that encode mostly gender information. Alternatively, it might be more appropriate to consider other representation schemes or combinations of them such as Linear Discriminant Analysis (LDA), Independent Component Analysis (ICA), Canonical Correlation Analysis (CCA) [11] and their kernel counterparts [12].

Second, it would be important to employ more powerful classification algorithms such as Support Vector Machines (SVMs) and kernel methods [12]. Similar arguments can be made for the design of category-specific recognition subsystems. In addition to the above issues, there are also other issues such as how to deal with face categories containing a small number of subjects. As mentioned in Section 4, certain face categories in the FERET database contain less than 10 subjects. Training a classifier on a very small dataset becomes problematic and requires careful consideration. Our future work involves dealing with these issues.

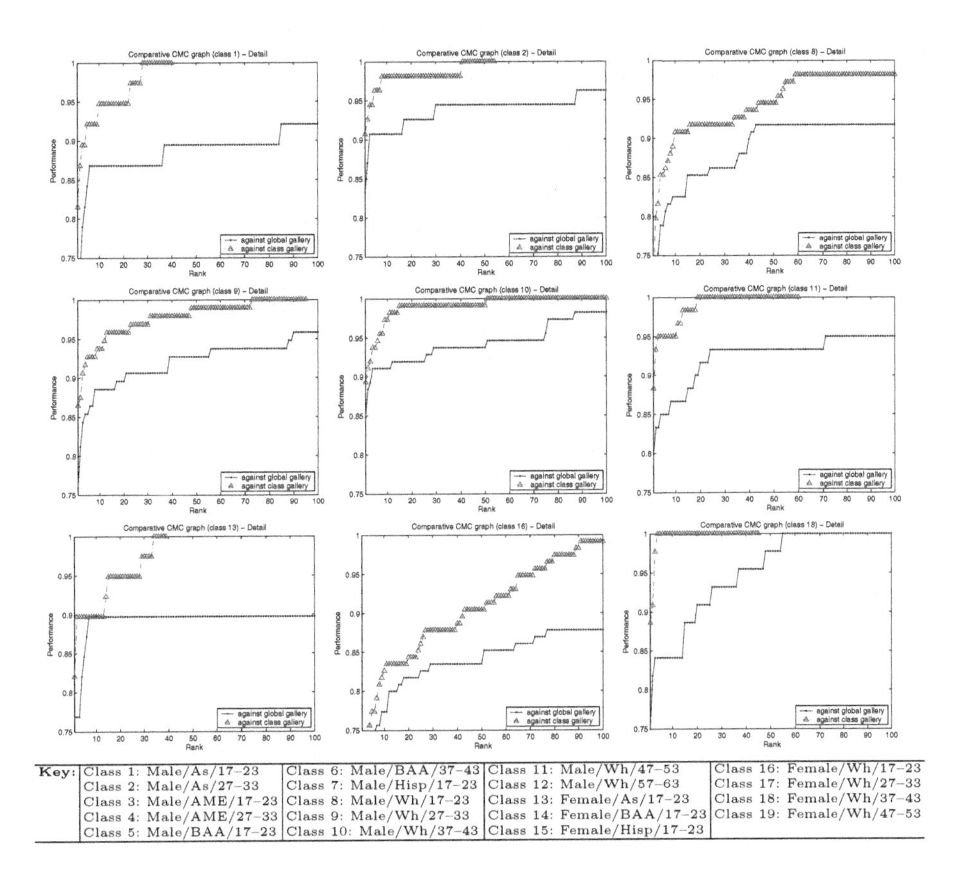

Key:				
	Class 1: Male/As/17–23	Class 6: Male/BAA/37–43	Class 11: Male/Wh/47–53	Class 16: Female/Wh/17–23
	Class 2: Male/As/27–33	Class 7: Male/Hisp/17–23	Class 12: Male/Wh/57–63	Class 17: Female/Wh/27–33
	Class 3: Male/AME/17–23	Class 8: Male/Wh/17–23	Class 13: Female/As/17–23	Class 18: Female/Wh/37–43
	Class 4: Male/AME/27–33	Class 9: Male/Wh/27–33	Class 14: Female/BAA/17–23	Class 19: Female/Wh/47–53
	Class 5: Male/BAA/17–23	Class 10: Male/Wh/37–43	Class 15: Female/Hisp/17–23	

Fig. 9. CMC curves for three-level categorization using gender, ethnicity and age information

References

1. O'Toole, A., Peterson, J., Deffenbacher, K.: An other-race effect for classifying faces by sex. In: Perception. Volume 25. (1996) 669–676
2. Cheng, Y., O'Toole, A., Abdi, H.: Classifying adults' and children's faces by sex: Computational investigations of subcategorical feature encoding. In: Cognitive Science. Volume 25. (2001) 819–838
3. Webster, M., Kaping, D., Mizokami, Y., Duhamel, P.: Adaptation to natural facial categories. In: Perception. Volume 428. (2004) 558–561
4. Moghaddam, B., Yang, M.: Learning gender with support faces. In: IEEE Transactions on Pattern Analysis and Machine Intelligence. Volume 24. (2002) 707–711
5. Sun, Z., Bebis, G., Yuan, X., Louis, S.J.: Genetic feature subset selection for gender classification: A comparison study. In: IEEE Workshop on Applications of Computer Vision, Orlando, FL (2002) 165–170
6. Gutta, S., Huang, J., Phillips, J., Wechsler, H.: Mixture of experts for classification of gender, ethnic origin, and pose of human faces. In: IEEE Transactions on Neural Networks. Volume 11. (2000) 948–960

7. Kwon, Y.H., Lobo, N.d.V.: Age classification from facial images. In: Computer Vision and Image Understanding. Volume 74. (1999) 1–21
8. Jain, A.K., Dass, S.C., Nandakumar, K.: Soft biometric traits for personal recognition systems. In: Lecture Notes in Computer Science. Volume 3072. (2004) 731–738
9. Turk, M., Pentland, R.: Eigenfaces for recognition. Cognitive Neuroscience **3** (1991) 71–86
10. Phillips, J., Moon, H., Risvi, S., Rauss, J.: The feret evaluation methodology for face recognition algorithms. In: IEEE Transactions on Pattern Analysis and Machine Intelligence. Volume 22. (2000) 1090–1104
11. R. Duda, P.H., Stork, D.: Pattern Classification. Jon-Wiley, 2nd edition (2001)
12. Taylor, J., Cristianini., N.: Kernel Methods for Pattern Analysis. Cambridge University Press (2004)

A Novel Approach on Silhouette Based Human Motion Analysis for Gait Recognition

Murat Ekinci and Eyup Gedikli

Computer Vision Lab. Dept. of Computer Engineering,
Karadeniz Technical University, Turkey
ekinci@ktu.edu.tr

Abstract. This paper[1] presents a novel view independent approach on silhouette based human motion analysis for gait recognition applications. Spatio-temporal 1-D signals based on the differences between the outer of binarized silhouette of a motion object and a bounding box placed around silhouette are chosen as the basic image features called the distance vectors. The distance vectors are extracted using four view directions to silhouette. Gait cycle estimation and motion analysis are then performed by using normalized correlation on the distance vectors. Initial experiments for human identification are finally presented. Experimental results on the different test image sequences demonstrate that the proposed algorithm has an encouraging performance with relatively robust, low computational cost, and recognition rate for gait-based human identification.

1 Introduction

The combination of human motion analysis and gait recognition based human identification, as biometrics, in surveillance systems has recently gained wider interest in the research studies [1][3][6]. There has also been considerable interest in the area of human motion classification [12], tracking and analysis [4] in recent years. Those are required as initial steps in gait recognition algorithms for human identification applications [1][3]. The main purpose and contributions of this paper are summarized as follows;

- We attempt to develop a simple but effective representation of silhouette for gait-based human identification using silhouette analysis. Similar observations have been made in [7][8], but the idea presented here implicitly more capture both structural (appearances) and transitional (dynamics) characteristics of gait.
- Instead of width/length time signal of bounding box of moving silhouette usually used in existing gait period analysis [10][11][3], here we analyze four distance vectors extracted directly from differences between silhouette and the bounding box, and further convert them into associated four 1D signals.

[1] This work is suported by KTU (Grant No: KTU-2002.112.009.1).

G. Bebis et al. (Eds.): ISVC 2005, LNCS 3804, pp. 219–226, 2005.

– The proposed method also presents the motion cues which can be used to determine human activities such as walking or running. Unlike other methods, this does not require on a geometrical shape models [9], not sensitivity to small noisy on silhouette data [4]. The proposed algorithm is not pixel-based implementation, and the idea can be applicable to real scenes in which objects are small and data is noisy.

The method presented is integrated into a low-cost PC based real-time view independent visual surveillance system for gait cycle estimation, human motion analysis their activities in monochromatic video, and then adapted into initial studies on gait recognition for human identification. The novel approach is basically to produce view directions based 1-D distance vectors represent the distances between silhouette and the bounding box. Thus, four 1-D signals are extracted for each view directions, they are top-, bottom-, left-, and right-views. Then correlation-based a similarity function is executed to estimate gait cycle of moving silhouette and to analysis human motions. The key idea in this work is that simple, view independent, fast extraction of the broad internal motion features of an object can be employed to analyze its motion and meanwhile for gait-based human identification. Finally, gait recognition results are also presented to show applicable the proposed method for human identification.

2 Spatio-temporal Human Motion Representation

Spatio-temporal human motion representation is based on the view directions to silhouette which is generated from a sequence of binary silhouette images *bs(t)= bs(x,y.t)*, indexed spatially by pixel location *(x,y)* and temporally by time *t*. There are four different image features: top-, bottom-, left- and right-view based distance vectors, as shown in figure 1. Form a new 2D image $F_T(x,t) = \sum_y bs(x,y,t)$, where each column (indexed by time *t*) is the top-view distance vector of silhouette image *bs(t)*, as shown in figure 1.a. Each value $F_T(x,t)$ is then a count of the number of the row pixels between the top side of the bounding box and the outer boundaries in that columns x of silhouette image *bs(t)*. The result is a 2D pattern, formed by taking the differences from the top view direction together to form a spatio-temporal pattern. A second pattern which represents the bottom-view direction $F_B(x,t) = \sum_y bs(x,y,t)$ can be constructed by counting the number of the row pixels between the bottom of the bounding box and its silhouette, as shown in figure 1.a. The third pattern $F_L(y,t) = \sum_x bs(x,y,t)$ is then constructed by taking the row differences (the number of the column pixels) from the left side of the bounding box to silhouette. The last pattern $F_R(y,t) = \sum_x bs(x,y,t)$ is also finally constructed by taking the row differences from the right side of the box to silhouette (figure 1.c).

From the temporal distance plots, it is clear that the view distance vector is roughly periodic and gives the extent of movement of the outer contours on the view direction of silhouette. The brighter a pixel in figure 1.b and 1.d, the larger value is the value of the view direction vector in that position. In this study, silhouette extraction is achieved by simple background subtraction using

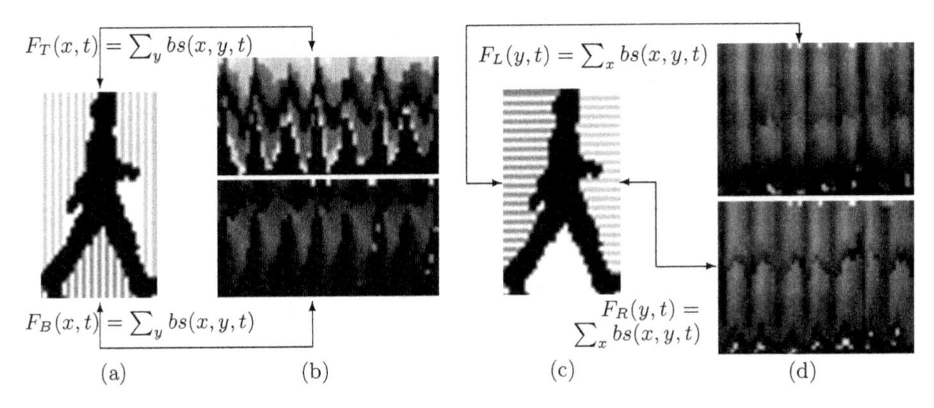

Fig. 1. Spatio-temporal motion representations. (a) Top-, bottom- (c) Left-, right-views to silhouette, (b) and (d) temporal plot of the distance vectors.

a dynamic background frame estimated and updated in time, more details could not given here because of page limitation of the paper, but it can be found in [2]. Then a 3x3 median filter operator is applied to the resulting images to suppress spurious pixel values. Once a silhouette generated, a bounding box is placed around silhouette. Silhouette across a motion sequence are automatically aligned by scaling and cropping based on the bounding box.

2.1 Features Derived from View Distance Vectors

The output of the detecting and tracking module gives a sequence of bounding boxes for every object [2]. Reference signals $R_v(x)$ and $R_v(y)$ for v view distances vectors at location column and row to silhouette are first obtained by assigning the distance signals produced from previous frame, respectively. In other words, the processes, $R_v(x,t) = F_v(x,t-1)$ and $R_v(y,t) = F_v(y,t-1)$, are executed. Then the same manner is sequentially repeated for the following frames to update the reference signals. In order to use in gait cycle estimation and motion discrimination, normalized correlation is performed to obtain maximum similarities between two view distance vectors produced from sequential two frames; for instance $F_T(x,t)$ in the current frame and $R_T(x,t)$ from the previous frame for top view. This is repeated for each view distance vectors.

3 Motion Analysis

We present a low-level approach to distinguish walking and running actions and to estimate the frequency and phase of each observed gait sequence, allowing us to perform dynamic time warping to align sequences before matching to achieve a gait based human identification. First, normalized correlation processes are executed as explained in previous section, and some of the experimental results are also shown in figure 2. For an input sequence (Fig. 2.a), once the person has been tracked for a certain number of frames, its spatio temporal gait parameters such as the normalized correlation based variations of the moving silhouette can be estimated.

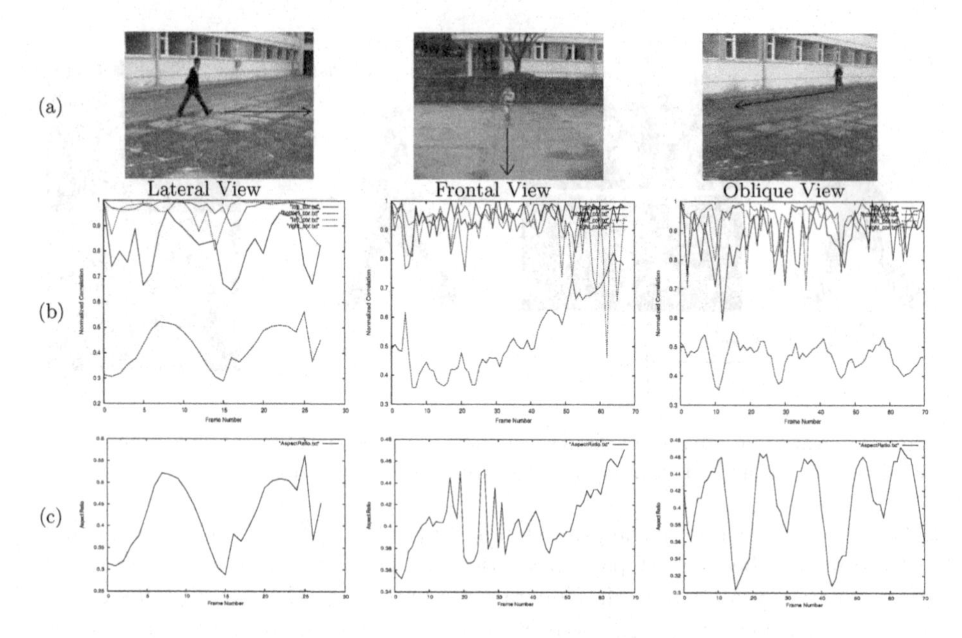

Fig. 2. (a) Example images used, (b) Normalized correlation results for walking and running, (c) Aspect ratio signals (i.e width/height.) of the bounding box

The normalized correlation results on four view distance vectors in the image sequence includes walking and running person's actions grabbed on different views are acquired as shown in figure 2.b. In that, the reference signals are automatically updated by copying the view distance vectors produced from previous frame in the sequence. To be able to produce optimum similarities on the distance vectors, the reference signals have naturally been normalized by selecting from previous frame in order to eliminate the influence of spatial scale and signal lengths.

The last line in figure 2 (i.e. Fig. 2.c) shows the aspect ratio signals (i.e. width/height in the bounding box) of the moving silhouettes. From the correlation plot, it is noted that view distance vectors change with time as the person transits through a period of view independent action, there is a high degree of correlation among the distance vectors across frames. In the experimental studies in the image sequence includes walking and running persons in lateral view, the normalized correlation results obtained from the all view distance vectors presented in this paper have exhibited the periodical signals. For oblique views, the top- and bottom-views distance vectors based normalized correlation processes have given more robust results than the left- and right-views distance vectors. The characteristics in their results on the test image sequences have given the similar signal characteristics with the aspect ratio signals for both lateral and oblique views, as shown in figure 2. For frontal view, the aspect ratio signals have not given a periodical signal on both actions (walking and running). But the view distance vectors-based correlation results have successfully exhibited the periodical signal characteristics.

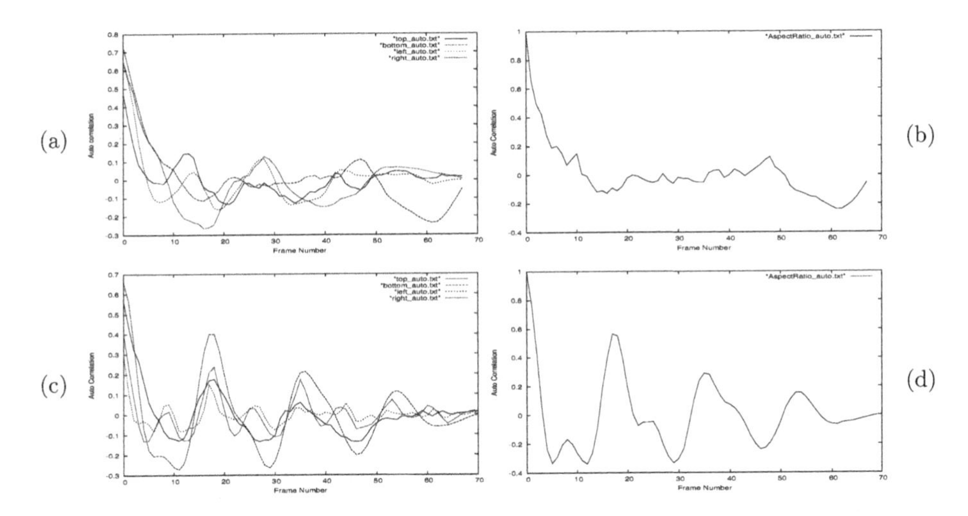

Fig. 3. Gait cyclic Estimation: Signals after removing the background then auto-correlation. (a) View distance based (b) Aspect ratio based auto-correlation results for walking person in frontal view, (c) View distance based (d) aspect ratio based auto-correlation results for running person in oblique view.

3.1 Gait Cycle Estimation

Human gait is a repetitive phenomenon, the appearance of a walking/running person in a video is itself periodic. Several vision methods have exploited this fact to compute the period of human gait from image features [10][11][3]. In [10][11], width time signal or height time signals of the bounding box of moving silhouette derived from an image sequence are used to analyze gait period. In [3], the aspect ratio of the bounding box of moving silhouette as a function of time is also used to determine the period of the gait. Different from them, here this paper presents four view distance vectors based variations on the moving silhouette as a function of time so as to enable them to cope effectively with both lateral view and frontal view.

Figure 2 displays a clear cyclical nature in the correlation results obtained on the view direction-based distance vectors. To quantify these signals, we may first remove their background component by subtracting their mean and dividing by their standard deviation, and then smooth them with a symmetric average filter. We finally compute their autocorrelation to find peaks, as shown in figure 3. For frontal view, although the periodical characteristics of moving silhouettes are correctly detected by left- and right-view distance vectors based gait cycle estimation (as plotted in figure 3.a), there has not been able to achieved any periodical characteristics on the results of the aspect ratio signals on the bounding box, as shown in figure 3.b. The proposed algorithm for gait cycle estimation has achieved more robust experimental results than the aspect ratio for frontal view. For oblique, as plotted in figure 3c-d, and lateral views, both the proposed method and the aspect ratio can easily detect the gait cycles.

3.2 Motion Discrimination

To determine if an object exhibits periodicity, an 1-D power spectrum, $P(f)$, of auto correlation is estimated. Periodic motion will show up as peaks in this spectrum at the motion's fundamental frequencies [5]. A peak at frequency f_i is significant if

$$P(f_i) = \mu_p + K * \sigma_p \tag{1}$$

where K is a threshold value (typically 0.7), μ_p is the mean of P, and σ_p is the standard deviation of P. In order to distinguish walking and running, the main motion frequency is estimated by determining the peak which has largest impulse from the significant peaks (eq. 1) in the power spectrum. One cycle of the movements is extracted using the indicated location of the largest impulse. Smaller impulses may also be present (harmonics) at integer multiplies of the fundamental.

Another point of interest to distinguish two actions from each other is that the variance of running frequencies is greater than that of walking frequencies. For each view distance vectors, the average variance of the amplitude in the power spectrum was determined on the experimental video sequences produced from different views (Lateral, frontal, oblique). Then the average variance values for each view distance vectors have also been used as threshold data. The threshold values for the variance of the motion, the running frequencies can be clearly distinguished from the that of walking. Those values only correctly classify 88% of the gaits (averaging of three different motion way). For the motion frequency determined by the largest impulse from the significant peaks, the average walking and running frequencies were found to be 3.571 (Hz)- 5.357 (Hz) for lateral, 3.521 (Hz)- 5.633 (Hz) for oblique, and 2.205 (Hz)- 2.941 (Hz) for frontal views, respectively. The average threshold values in frequency were used to discriminate the walking and running actions. At this work, typical threshold values were taken the mean of the averaging walking and running frequencies for each view. The values given were extracted from the video at a frame rate of 25 Hz. Then, four decision values based implementation correctly classify 94% for lateral view, 88% for oblique view, 76% for frontal view, of the gaits.

Finally, both threshold values on the variance of motion frequencies and largest impulses in the power spectrum were implemented to have more robust decision for motion analysis, then averaging correctly classify 94% of the human motion analysis even the silhouette data is produced from in noisy environments. At the experiments for motion discrimination, the database has 17 person (2 child, 15 adults), and their action includes walking and running in outdoor environment with three different way. Example frames are shown in figure 2.

3.3 Gait-Based Human Identification

We convert a two-dimensional silhouette shape into four one-dimensional distance vectors. The distance vector sequence is accordingly used to approximately represent a temporal pattern of gait. This process of original feature extraction is illustrated in Figure 1. To eliminate the influence of spatial scale and signal length of the distance vectors, we scale these distance vector signals with respect to magnitude and size through the sizes of the bounding boxes placed around silhouette. Next, eigenspace transformation based on Principal Component Analysis (PCA) is applied to time varying distance vectors derived from a sequence of silhouette images to reduce the dimensionality of the input feature space. A normalized Euclidean distance based pattern classification technique is final performed in the lower-dimensional eigenspace for recognition. The training process used is similar to the studies in [3].

4 Experimental Results and Conclusion

The database mainly contains video sequences on different days in outdoor and indoor environments. A digital camera (Sony DCR-TRV355E) fixed on a tripod is used to capture the video sequences. The algorithm presented here has been tried on a database includes 17 people walking and running for motion discrimination, and frame rate was 25 fps and the original resolution is 352x240. Test results given in section 3 encourage to implement this kind of parameters for human motion analysis for real time video surveillance applications, as long as human performs the same actions during the test sequence.

At the initial experiments on gait recognition, a gait database is established for our experiments. The database has 22 people, and subjects are walking laterally to the camera, the directions of walking is from left to right and from right to left. The database includes two sequences for each subject. One sequence includes 3 gait cycle for each direction, and the length of each gait cycle varies with the pace of the walker, but the average is about 26 frames. The subjects walk along a straight-line path at free cadence in lateral view with respect to the image plane, and 15 subjects were walking outside, an example frame is shown in figure 2.a-left, 7 subjects were walking inside, the inside platform is also shown in figure 2.a, but the subjects were walking in lateral view.

The initial results obtained using the proposed method are given in figure 4. Figure 4 shows the cumulative match scores for ranks up to 22, where figure

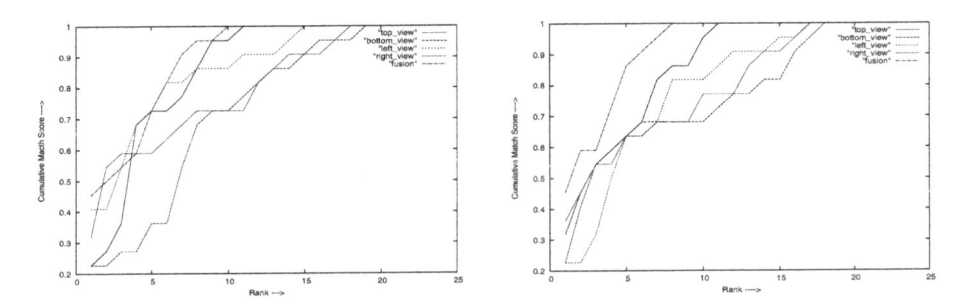

Fig. 4. Cumulative match score characteristics in the database, the subjects were walking (Left) from left to right, (Right) from right to left

uses the normalized Ecludiean distance similarity measures for each distance vectors and their fusion. Two cycles were used for training, and next one cycle was used for testing. Walking from left to right and the other direction are separately tested to obtain initial experimental results. The more details on the cumulative match score can be found in [13]. While only using alone each distance vectors without making a relationship between each others, we can see from experimental observations that recognition errors often happen when the two smallest values of the similarity function are very close for one view but not other view(s). Therefore, to have more robust classification, the classification processes of the distance vectors are finally re-implemented by fusing Euclidean distance measures. Then an increasing performance for the recognition has also been recorded at the initial experimental study, as shown in figure 4.

The novelty in the presented algorithm lies in its simplicity, the efficiency of the implementation, the usefulness in real-time applications, the effectiveness in view independent applications, the robustness to some factors such as motion object size and regular noise effects, and new approach includes multi-view and multi-purpose aspects to silhouette for silhouette based human identification.

References

1. M. S. Nixon, J. N. Carter, *Advances in Automatic Gait Recognition*, Proc. of IEEE Int. Conf. on Automatic Face and Gesture Recognition, 2004.
2. M. Ekinci, E. Gedikli, *Background Estimation Based People Detection and Tracking for Video Surveillance.* Springer LNCS 2869, ISCIS, 18*th* Int. Symp., Nov., 2003.
3. L. Wang, T. Tan, H. Ning, W. Hu, *Silhouette Analysis-Based Gait Recognition for Human Identification,* IEEE Trans. on PAMI, Vol.25, No. 12, December, 2003.
4. H. Fujiyoshi, A. J. Lipton, T. Kanade.: Real-Time Human Motion Analysis by Image Skeletonization. IEICE Trans. Inf.& SYST., Vol.E87-D, No.1, 2004.
5. R. Cutler, L. S. Davis, *Robust real-time periodic motion detection, analysis and applications* IEEE Trans. Pattern Analysis Machine Intelligence, Vol. 22, 2000.
6. S. Sarkar, *et. al*, *The HumanID Gait Challenge Problem: Data Sets, Performance, and Analysis.* IEEE Trans. on PAMI, Vol.27, No. 2, February 2005.
7. A. Kale, *et. al.*, *Identification of Humans Using Gait* IEEE Trans. on Image Processing, Vol.13, No.9, September 2004.
8. Yanxi Liu, R. T. Collins, T. Tsin, *Gait Sequence Analysis using Frieze Patterns,* Proc. of European Conf. on Computer Vision, 2002.
9. J. W. Davis, S. R. Taylor, *Analysis and Recognition of Walking Movements.* Proc., of int. Conference on Pattern Recognition, ICPR 2005.
10. C.BenAbdelkader,R. Cutler,L.Davis, *Stride and Cadence as a Biometric in Automatic Person Identification and Verification,* Proc. of Aut. Face Gest. Rec, 2002.
11. R. Collins, R. Gross, and J. Shi, *Silhouette-Based Human Identification from Body Shape and Gait,* Proc. Int. Conf. Automatic Face and Gesture Recognition, 2002.
12. O. Javed, S. Ali, M. Shah, *Online Detection and Classification of Moving Objects Using Progressively Improving Detectors,* IEEE, Proc. of Int. CVPR 2005
13. J. Phillips *et.al*, *The FERET Evaluation Methodology for Face recognition Algorithm,* IEEE Trans. Pattern Analysis and Machine Intel., vol.22, no.10, Oct. 2000.

A Hybrid HMM/DPA Adaptive Gesture Recognition Method

Stjepan Rajko[1,3] and Gang Qian[2,3,*]

[1] Dept. of Computer Science and Engineering
[2] Dept. of Electrical Engineering
[3] Arts, Media and Engineering Program,
Arizona State University, Tempe, AZ 85287, USA

Abstract. We present a hybrid classification method applicable to gesture recognition. The method combines elements of Hidden Markov Models (HMM) and various Dynamic Programming Alignment (DPA) methods, such as edit distance, sequence alignment, and dynamic time warping. As opposed to existing approaches which treat HMM and DPA as either competing or complementing methods, we provide a common framework which allows us to combine ideas from both HMM and DPA research. The combined approach takes on the robustness and effectiveness of HMMs and the simplicity of DPA approaches. We have implemented and successfully tested the proposed algorithm on various gesture data.

1 Introduction

Both Hidden Markov Model (HMM) and Dynamic Programming Alignment (DPA) approaches have been used extensively for gesture recognition[1]. Using HMMs, many good results have been achieved, for example with sign language [1, 2, 3]. While HMM-based methods usually prove accurate and robust, they require some effort in the proper training of the model (with notable exceptions such as [1]), and the implementation of the algorithms is not trivial. DPA approaches are much simpler, but only seem adequate for less challenging tasks, for example when the gesture vocabulary is small [4]. Although, there have been many attempts to improve DPA methods for gesture recognition, such as [5, 6].

DPA approaches have a long history, and an enormous body of research regarding various application areas and different optimization methods. For example, the Edit Distance problem [7], different kinds of DNA and protein sequence alignment [8, 9], and sound pattern recognition [10] can all be solved using DPAs. All of these areas offer common insights on various improvements, such as space-efficiency [11], or optimal implementations for parallel computers [12].

As HMMs are slowly pushing out DPAs in many application areas (including gesture recognition), improvements that have been developed in the context

* This material is based upon work supported by the National Science Foundation under CISE-RI No.0403428.

[1] Please note that many HMM algorithms can be implemented using Dynamic Programming, and that by DPA we refer only to non-HMM algorithms.

G. Bebis et al. (Eds.): ISVC 2005, LNCS 3804, pp. 227–234, 2005.

of DPAs have become less applicable. To facilitate the reuse of ideas from both bodies of work, we attempt to provide a common framework for the two methods. We do so by relying on the robustness of HMM theory, but deriving underlying algorithms that are very reminiscent of DPA approaches. Applying this to gesture recognition proved to result in a method both accurate and simple.

2 Problem Formulation

Since our method is general, we will formulate the problem in general terms, but give specific examples from our experiments. For the initial part of the discussion, we will assume that we are only trying to recognize a single gesture in the object being observed. Extending this to multiple gestures will be explained later.

Let $\mathbb{O}$ be a set of observations that we can witness by monitoring the object whose gestures we are trying to recognize. For example, in one of our experiments we monitor the direction of movement of a point in a 2D plane. We represent the direction by a point on the unit circle, so $\mathbb{O} = \{(x, y)|x^2 + y^2 = 1\} \bigcup \{(0, 0)\}$, where $(0, 0)$ indicates that the point is not moving.

We are initially given an example of the gesture to be recognized, expressed as a sequence of observations $M = M_1, M_2, \ldots, M_{n-1}$ with each $M_j \in \mathbb{O}$. We are also given a continuous stream or real-time observations of the object we are monitoring, denoted by $O_1, O_2, \ldots$ with each $O_i \in \mathbb{O}$. Both of the observation sequences are expected to be collected at a consistent frame rate, i.e. typical time series data. We will refer to times at which they are recorded as time steps.

The goal is to find continuous parts of the real-time observation sequence O that correspond to the gesture given by M. That is, we want to separate parts of O that are similar to the example gesture given by M (instances of the gesture) from parts that are not. We do so by modeling the gesture by a Hidden Markov Model (HMM) $\lambda = (S, a, \pi)$, defined by the set of states S, the state transition probability distribution a, and the initial state probability π.

Each state in $S = \{S_0, \ldots, S_n\}$ represents a phase in the execution of the gesture. The initial state is governed by $\pi = \{\pi_0, \ldots, \pi_n\}$, where π_j is the probability that the HMM will begin in state j. At each time step, the HMM changes its current state according to the state transition probability distribution $a = \{a_{k,j}\}$, with $a_{k,j}$ being the probability of transitioning from state k to state j.

$S_1 \ldots S_{n-1}$ correspond to the gesture example $M = M_1 \ldots M_{n-1}$. Upon entering one of these states, the HMM emits an observation $o \in \mathbb{O}$, according to a probability distribution function initialized from M. In our experiments, the p.d.f. for a state S_j, which we denote implicitly by $p(o|S_j)$, is initialized using a Gaussian-based model with mean M_j and variance determined from the average distance between successive observations in M.

States S_0 and S_n do not produce an observation (and for consistency we set $p(o|S_0) = p(o|S_n) = 1$ for all $o \in \mathbb{O}$), but are used to indicate the beginning and completion of the gesture. Hence, we enforce that the HMM begins in state 0 by setting $\pi_0 = 1$ and $\pi_j = 0$ for $j \neq 0$. We also assume that the gesture is executed by going through the states in a left to right fashion, which we model using a simplified form of the transition probabilities. In particular, we choose three constants, a_{stay}, a_{next}, and a_{skip}, which determine all state transition probabilities. a_{stay} gives the probability of staying in the same state from one time step to another, so a high value will allow gestures executed slower than the model to be recognized. a_{next} gives the probability of going to the next state, while the probability of going to the sth next state is given by $a_{skip}^{s-1} a_{next}$. Intuitively, a_{skip} is the probability of skipping a state, so a high value will allow gestures that that have parts of the model missing to be recognized.

In terms of a, we can write for all k and $j < n$

$$a_{k,j} = \begin{cases} 0, & \text{if } j < k \\ a_{stay}, & \text{if } j = k \\ a_{skip}^{j-k-1} a_{next}, & \text{if } j > k \end{cases}, \tag{1}$$

with the values for $a_{k,n}$ chosen so that $\sum_{j=1}^{n} a_{k,j} = 1$. In our experiments, we use $a_{stay} + a_{next} \sum_{j=k+1}^{\infty} a_{skip}^{j-k-1} = 1$, in which case $a_{k,n} = a_{next} \sum_{j=n}^{\infty} a_{skip}^{j-k-1}$.

3 The Algorithm

With $\lambda = (S, a, \pi)$ defined, the question of relating a part of the obervation sequence to the model of the gesture becomes the question of finding the most likely state sequence within λ to have produced it. In Section 3.1, we derive a modification of the Viterbi algorithm, which is commonly used to accomplish that task. In Section 3.2 we explain how we find the recognized gestures in the real-time observation sequence $O_1, O_2, \ldots$. Section 3.3 shows how the recognized gestures are used to improve the model of the gesture, and Section 3.4 explains how we deal with the recognition of multiple gestures.

3.1 A Modification of the Viterbi Algorithm

Given a particular sequence of v observations $O_{u+1}, O_{u+2}, \ldots, O_{u+v}$, we seek to find the most likely state sequence $(s_0 = S_0), s_1, \ldots, s_v, (s_{v+1} = S_n)$ of the HMM λ that would have produced it. The Viterbi algorithm does so using a dynamic programming variable, which captures the probability of partial state sequence generating a partial observation sequence, which we write as

$$\delta_{i,j}^{(u)} = \max p\left((s_0 = S_0), s_1, \ldots, (s_{v'} = S_j), O_{u+1}, \ldots, (O_{u+v'} = O_i) \,|\lambda\right) \tag{2}$$

$\delta^{(u)}$ can be thought of as an instance of λ that started its execution just prior to producing observation O_{u+1}, with $\delta_{i,j}^{(u)}$ representing the maximum probability of any partial state sequence starting with S_0 and ending with S_j producing the observation sequence $O_{u+1}, O_{u+2}, \ldots, O_{u+v'} = O_i$. It can be calculated as a table with initialization and recursive relationship

$$\delta_{u,j}^{(u)} = \begin{cases} 1, & \text{if } j = 0 \\ 0, & \text{otherwise} \end{cases} \tag{3}$$

$$\delta_{i,j}^{(u)} = \max_{k=1}^{n} \delta_{i-1,k}^{(u)} a_{k,j} p(O_i|S_j), \text{ for } i > u\,. \tag{4}$$

Using (1) and some simplification, we can separate (4) into

$$\delta_{i,j}^{(u)} = p(O_i|S_j) \max \begin{cases} a_{stay}\delta_{i-1,j}^{(u)} \\ a_{next} \max_{k=1}^{j-1} \delta_{i-1,k}^{(u)} a_{skip}^{j-k-1} \end{cases} . \tag{5}$$

However, we have no knowledge of when an intended instance of the gesture starts in the observation sequence $O = O_1, O_2, \ldots$, and calculating the $\delta^{(u)}$ table for all u is prohibitive. To that end we define $\delta_{i,j} = \max \delta_{i,j}^{(u)}$, which corresponds to choosing the optimal starting point (u value) at each point of the table, i.e. if $\delta_{i,j} = \delta_{i,j}^{(u)}$ then observations $O_{u+1} \ldots O_i$ are best explained by the HMM that started its execution just prior to O_{u+1} being observed. Conviniently, it is easy to show that $\delta_{i,j}$ can be calculated by compromising equations (3) and (4) with the superscript $^{(u)}$ dropped:

$$\delta_{0,j} = \begin{cases} 1, & \text{if } j = 0 \\ 0, & \text{otherwise} \end{cases} \tag{6}$$

$$\delta_{i,j} = \begin{cases} \max_{k=1}^{n} \delta_{i-1,k} a_{k,j} p(O_i|S_j), & \text{for } i > 0 \text{ and } j > 0 \\ 0, & \text{for } i > 0 \text{ and } j = 0 \end{cases} . \tag{7}$$

We now define $\gamma_{i,j} = \max_{k=1}^{j-1} \delta_{i,k} a_{skip}^{j-k-1}$, and note that

$$\gamma_{i,j} = \max \begin{cases} \gamma_{i,j-1} a_{skip} \\ \delta_{i,j} \end{cases} . \tag{8}$$

Hence, δ values for row i can now be calculated by first computing γ values for row $i-1$, and then using

$$\delta_{i,j} = p(O_i|S_j) \max \begin{cases} a_{stay}\delta_{i-1,j} \\ a_{next}\gamma_{i-1,j-1} \end{cases} . \tag{9}$$

Instead of calculating δ we set $\alpha_{i,j} = \log \delta_{i,j}$, and work with

$$\alpha_{i,j} = \max_{k=1}^{n} \{\alpha_{i-1,k} + \log a_{k,j} + \log p(O_i|S_j)\} . \tag{10}$$

This gives us

$$\alpha_{i,0} = 0 \tag{11}$$

$$\alpha_{i,j} = \log p(O_i|S_j) + \max \begin{cases} \log a_{stay} + \alpha_{i-1,j} \\ \log a_{next} + \beta_{i-1,j-1} \end{cases} , for j > 0 \tag{12}$$

$$\beta_{i,j} = \max \begin{cases} \beta_{i,j-1} + \log a_{skip} \\ \alpha_{i,j} \end{cases} , \tag{13}$$

which is more efficient and numerically stable, and has similarities with certain forms of DNA alignments and local alignments in particular[8].

Because $a_{k,n}$ is an exception to the rules given by (1), $\alpha_{i,n}$ needs to be calculated according to (4). Hence, we need three passes for each row of the table. One is to calculate α for all columns but the last, one to calculate β values, and for the last column of α. Since the work for each cell is constant, the time complexity to calculate a row of α and β is $\Theta(n)$.

3.2 Recognizing Gestures

The issues to address in relation to the gesture recognition are determining where a recognized gesture ended, where it started, and the most likely state sequence that generated the observations in between. To determine where a recognized gesture ends, we monitor the values in the last column of the α table. Whenever we encounter a local maximum at some row i, i.e. $\alpha_{i-1,n} \leq \alpha_{i,n} > \alpha_{i+1,n}$, we examine the value $\alpha_{i,n}$. If it is large enough, it means that a complete gesture (ending with S_n) has been executed with high enough probability.

To decide the treshold, consider the probability of the HMM generating a ficticious sequence of observations o such that $logp(o|S_j) \geq r$ for some constant r and all $j = 1, \ldots, n-1$, with n_{skip} states getting skipped and n_{stay} times that the HMM stays in the same state from time step to time step. Then,

$$\alpha_{i,n} \geq n_{skip} \log a_{skip} + (n - n_{skip})(r + \log a_{next}) + n_{stay}(r + \log a_{stay}) \quad (14)$$

After selecting appropriate values for r, a_{stay}, a_{next}, a_{skip}, different values for n_{stay}, and n_{skip} will give us the probabilities of different ficticious observation sequences, which can be used to determine a reasonable value for the treshold. In our experiments, we scale the probability distributions over $\mathbb{O}$ so that for an observation o that is one half of a standard deviation away from the mean of the Gaussian p.d.f. of a state S_j, $\log p(o|S_j)$ is expected to be 0 (it can vary slightly depending on the particular p.d.f.), so we set $r = 0$. We would also like to allow the gesture to be executed somewhat slower than the example M, and not allow a significant portion of the gesture to be omitted, so we set $a_{stay} = 0.75$ and $a_{next} = 0.25$, which gives $a_{skip} = \frac{1}{11}$. A borderline acceptable instance of the gesture would have $n_{skip} = \frac{1}{11}n$, and $n_{stay} = 0.75n$, yielding $\alpha_{i,n} \geq \frac{1}{11}n \log \frac{1}{11} + \frac{10}{11}n \log 0.75 + 0.25n \log 0.25$. Anything more probable than this will be accepted as a recognized instance of the gesture, and anything less probable will be rejected.

Once a local maximum in the righmost column of α exceeds the treshold, we employ a traceback technique to extract the correspondence between the observations and the HMM states. This is a simple modification of the traceback commonly used with the Viterbi algorithm. Basically, we maintain pointers along with the α and β table calculations which tell us the progression of the states. In our version of the algorithm, the pointers are maintained as follows:

$$\beta^*_{i,j} = \begin{cases} j, & \text{if } \beta_{i,j} = \alpha_{i,j} \\ \beta^*_{i,j-1}, & \text{otherwise.} \end{cases} \quad (15)$$

$$\alpha^*_{i,j} = \begin{cases} j, & \text{if } \alpha_{i,j} = a_{stay}\alpha_{i-1,j} \\ \beta^*_{i-1,j-1}, & \text{otherwise.} \end{cases} \quad . \quad (16)$$

If the end of the gesture was detected at $\alpha_{i,n}$, $\alpha^*_{i,n}$ tells us the previous state, $\alpha^*_{i-1,\alpha^*_{i,n}}$ the state before that, etc. When we reach S_0, that tells us where the gesture started. If the maximum length of a gesture instance is m, this requires us to keep m rows of the α table in memory, i.e. $\Theta(mn)$ space. However, the method of Hirschberg [11] (given in the context of the maximal common subsequence problem) can be adapted to reduce the space requirement to $\Theta(m + n)$.

3.3 Updating the Model

Once it has been detected that a gesture has been completed in the observation sequence, the traceback method tells us not only the most likely state sequence, but also what observation was generated by what state. This induces a mapping from the observations to the states of the model. In cases where the model was predicted to produce multiple observations from the same state, all of these observations are mapped to this state.

We can now update the model by incorporating the recently recognized gesture, which is similar to the approach taken by Lee and Xu[1]. We do so by updating each state which has an observation mapped to it. For each mapped observation we modify the p.d.f. related to the state to incorporate information given by the new observation. This can be done in many ways, for example by running a few iterations of the Expectation-Maximization algorithm with the new observation included. Here, we present a simpler approach as an example.

Suppose we represent the p.d.f. for each state by a mixture of Gaussians, with a given state S_j having g Gaussians, 1 through g, and each Gaussian i having mean μ_k, variance σ_k^2, weight γ_k, and $p(o|S_j) = \sum_{k=1}^{g} \gamma_k \mathcal{N}(o|\mu_k, \sigma_k)$.

To update S_j given a new observation o, we use a simple probabilistic technique that modifies the μ, σ, and γ parameters. We first choose a Gaussian from the mixture whose mean and variance we will update. The probability of choosing Gausian k is proportional to $\gamma_k \mathcal{N}(o|\mu_k, \sigma_k)$. If Gaussian i is chosen, we decide the new μ_i and σ_i by randomly drawing R points from the old Gaussian and adding o to the mix. Hence, R indicates how flexible the model is - a high R results in slow changes in the model, while a low R modifies the model more quickly. Furthermore, for well behaved observation sets the expected result of the above probabilistic method can be evaluated or approximated analytically.

Finally, we can update the weights so that

$$\gamma_k' = \begin{cases} \frac{R+1}{R+\gamma_k} \gamma_k, & \text{if } k = i \\ \frac{R}{R+\gamma_k} \gamma_k, & \text{otherwise} . \end{cases} \quad (17)$$

3.4 Recognizing Multiple Gestures

Up to this point in our discussion, we have assumed that we are only trying to find instances of a single gesture in the observation sequence. To recognize multiple gestures, we simply run multiple instances of the single gesture algorithm.

Each instance of the algorithm is initialized by an example of its gesture, and at each time step, a new row of each of the α tables is calculated using the newly recorded observation. The time complexity of the algorithm becomes $\Theta(\sum n_i)$, where n_i is the number of observations given in the example of gesture i.

Once a gesture is found, each instance of the algorithm reinitializes its α table, which corresponds to enforcing that no two recognized gestures overlap.

4 Experimental Results

We have implemented the proposed algorithms into the Motion Analysis and Visualization Engine (MAVE, *http://randomaxis.info/research/mave/*), which is released under the GNU GPL. Our initial tests dealt with the recognition of gestures of a point in a 2D plane, with the observations given to the algorithm being the point position (scenario A, $\mathbb{O} = \mathbb{R}^2$), velocity (scenario B, again $\mathbb{O} = \mathbb{R}^2$), or the direction of movement (scenarion C, $\mathbb{O} = \{(x,y)|x^2+y^2=1\} \bigcup \{(0,0)\}$).

The scenarios were each tested in a task involving recognition of 10 gestures representing digits 0-9, with the results summarized as follows. Velocity as the observation (scenario B) worked poorly, probably due to even slight changes in the speed of the gesture execution having dramatic effects on the observations. Position (scenario A) worked well, but only after incorporating a grid into the user interface, allowing the user to place the gestures in a similar position as the example gesture. Angle (scenario C) worked the best. In scenarios A and C, nearly all expressed gestures were recognized, and no misclassifications occured.

To illustrate the effects of model updating, we created some more detailed tests using scenario A and synthetic gestures of the form $y = a \sin t, x = t$ for $0 \leq t < 2\pi$ (see Figure 1). The gesture sequence to be recognized was generated by repeating the gesture $y = a \sin t$ with noise. Before every ten trials of the noisy gesture, non-gesture data of the form $y = 0, x = t$ was inserted. Also, we slowed down the model updating to see its effects over a longer period of time.

With $a = 0.3$, and very low noise (uniform distribution noise of ± 0.05 on both x and y) in the first test, the gesture data and the non-gesture data were very similar (Figure 1, left). The first 9 times the non-gesture was observed, it was misclassified as an instance of the gesture. However, after the 9th time (after observing 90 highly precise true gestures) it was no longer misclassified, showing the ability of the model updating to discriminate between very similar gestures.

In the second test, we used $a = 2.0$ (Figure 1, middle and right), and very high noise (± 0.75). In this case, the gesture was barely recognizable, but the recognition improved with time. The number of times it was recognized in each set of ten gesture trials was (in order) $1, 0, 1, 9, 10, 10, 10, 10, \ldots$. However, after recognizing these 51 instances of highly noisy data, the model became so flexible that it misclassified the non-gesture straight line as the gesture, showing that the model updating can adapt even to high noise, but at a cost in misclassification.

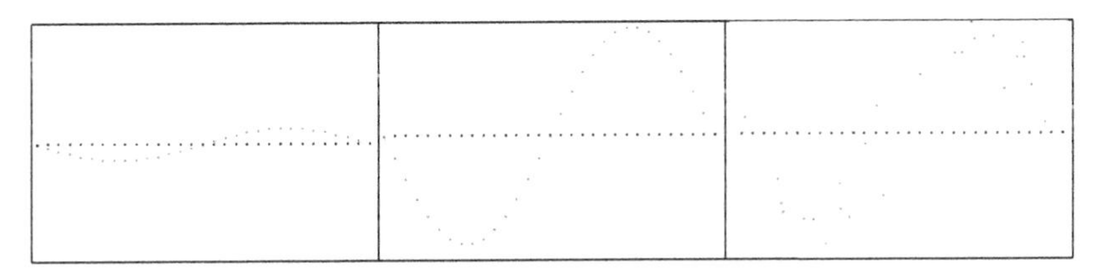

Fig. 1. gestures $y = 0.3 \sin t$ (left), $y = 2 \sin t$ (middle), and recognized portions of $y = 2 \sin t$ with large noise (right)

5 Conclusions and Future Work

We have presented a hybrid method applicable to gesture recognition, based on Hidden Markov Model theory but reminiscent of other Dynamic Programming Alignment methods. Our solution has both good accuracy (typical of HMM), and minimal training/initialization requirements (typical of DPA).

In addition to the 2D point results presented here, we have also succesfully applied the algorithm to 3D motion capture data, allowing us to recognize full body gestures. We are currently working on adapting our algorithm to sign language data[2], which will allow us to compare our approach to other methods.

References

1. Lee, C., Xu, Y.: Online, interactive learning of gestures for human/robot interfaces. In: 1996 IEEE International Conference on Robotics and Automation. Volume 4. (1996) 2982–2987
2. Vogler, C., Metaxas, D.: Handshapes and movements: Multiple-channel american sign language recognition. In: Lecture Notes in Computer Science. Volume 2915. (2004) 247–258
3. Hienz, H., Bauer, B., Kraiss, K.F.: Hmm-based continuous sign language recognition using stochastic grammars. In: GW '99: Proceedings of the International Gesture Workshop on Gesture-Based Communication in Human-Computer Interaction, London, UK, Springer-Verlag (1999) 185–196
4. Corradini, A.: Dynamic time warping for off-line recognition of a small gesture vocabulary. In: Proceedings of the IEEE ICCV Workshop on Recognition, Analysis, and Tracking of Faces and Gestures in Real-Time Systems (RATFG-RTS'01), Washington, DC, USA, IEEE Computer Society (2001) 82
5. Keogh, E., Pazzani, M.: Derivative dynamic time warping. In: First SIAM International Conference on Data Mining, Chicago, IL, USA (2001)
6. Wu, H., Kido, R., Shioyama, T.: Improvement of continuous dynamic programming for human gesture recognition. In: International Conference on Pattern Recognition. Volume 02. (2000) 945–948
7. Masek, W.J., Paterson, M.S.: A faster algorithm for computing string edit distances. Journal of Computer and System Sciences **20** (1980) 18–31
8. Setubal, J., Meidanis, J.: Introduction to computational molecular biology. PWS Publishing Company, Boston, MA (1997)
9. Smith, T.F., Waterman, M.S.: Identification of common molecular subsequences. Journal of Molecular Biology **147** (1981) 195–197
10. Kruskall, J.B., Liberman, M.: The symmetric time warping algorithm: From continuous to discrete. In: Time Warps, String Edits and Macromolecules: The Theory and Practice of String Comparison, Addison-Wesley (1983)
11. Hirschberg, D.S.: A linear space algorithm for computing maximal common subsequences. In: Communications of the ACM. Volume 18(6). (1975) 341–343
12. Rajko, S., Aluru, S.: Space and time optimal parallel sequence alignments. IEEE Transactions on Parallel and Distributed Systems **15** (2004) 1070–1081

Any opinions, findings and conclusions or recommendations expressed in this material are those of the authors and do not necessarily reflect the views of the National Science Foundation (NSF).

Hifocon: Object and Dimensional Coherence and Correlation in Multidimensional Visualization

Soon Tee Teoh[1] and Kwan-Liu Ma[2]

[1] Department of Computer Science, San Jose State University
[2] Department of Computer Science, University of California, Davis

Abstract. In any multidimensional visualization, some information has to be compromised when projecting multidimensional data to two- or three-dimensional space. We introduce the concepts of dimensional and object coherence and correlation to analyze and classify multidimensional visualization techniques. These concepts are used as principles for our design of Hifocon, a new multidimensional data visualization system.

1 Introduction

Multidimensional visualization is challenging because humans live in a three-dimensional world and have no intuition of higher dimensional space. Therefore, any attempt to visualize multidimensional data must find a projection from the high-dimensional space to a two- or three-dimensional visual space that is intelligible to humans. As a result, different multidimensional visualization ideas have been proposed.

To classify multidimensional visualization methods in terms of their emphases and tradeoffs, we introduce the principles of dimensional and object coherence and correlation. We discuss the strengths and limitations of existing multidimensional visualization techniques, and analyze and classify them using these principles.

We then introduce Hifocon (High-Dimensional Focus+Context), a multidimensional data visualization system designed to provide strong coherence and correlation. We show how Hifocon helps users to gain useful and interesting information. A particular strength of Hifocon is that it can be used to find hierarchical clusters, and clusters which are outliers in other dimensions.

2 Object and Dimension Coherence and Correlation

In high-dimensional visualization, not only are there too many objects to visualize at once, but there are also too many dimensions to visualize at once.

To discuss multidimensional visualization, we introduce a new concept: *object coherence* and *dimension coherence*. In a visual representation with object coherence, each object is represented as a single and coherent visual entity, such as a point. Lack of object coherence happens when an object is visually represented as separate visual entities such as several points. In such a visualization,

G. Bebis et al. (Eds.): ISVC 2005, LNCS 3804, pp. 235–242, 2005.

the user cannot see clearly the properties of the object all at once; therefore we say that the visualization of the object is "not coherent".

Dimension coherence is satisfied when the distribution of objects' attribute values in each dimension is clear. As we show in Section 3, many multidimensional visualization methods do not satisfy object and dimension coherence.

In general, object coherence is desirable when the user is interested in knowing the object's attribute values in many different dimensions and how they relate to one another. Dimension coherence is desirable when the user wants a clear picture of how objects are distributed in this dimension; for example, whether there are clusters present.

Correlation is another important aspect of understanding data. We define *object correlation* to be the property of a visualization that allows a user to tell whether two objects are similar in their attribute values, and to visually group similar objects. We say that a visualization has *dimension correlation* among a certain number of dimensions when the user is able to easily tell whether these dimensions are correlated according to the attribute values of the objects in the dataset.

Object and dimension correlation are very desirable and useful properties of a visualization, but because of the difficulty of visualizing high-dimensional data, they are often not achieved.

3 Related Work

Some existing techniques serve as examples to illustrate the concept of object and dimension coherence.

In parallel coordinates [6], each dimension is represented as a vertical line. Each object is mapped to one point on each line according to its attribute value in that dimension. A poly-line is then drawn to connect all the points. In parallel coordinates, there is good dimension coherence because for each dimension, the distribution of all the objects' attribute values for that dimension is clear. Furthermore, the correlation between adjacent dimensions is also visible. However, object coherence is not achieved in parallel coordinates because from the visualization, one cannot tell all the attribute values of any single oject. Similarly, object correlation is bad in parallel coordinates. In this respect, the primary focus of parallel coordinates is the dimensions, not the objects, and furthermore, when the user looks at a certain dimension, the focus is on that dimension and its adjacent dimensions because the relationship between those dimensions are obvious while all the other dimensions are still visible in context. Yang et al. [21] presented one way to enhance the perception of dimensional correlation in parallel coordinate is to order the dimensions such that similar dimensions are placed adjacent to each other.

Another popular multidimensional visualization method is the scatterplot matrix. In each position *(i,j)* in the matrix, a scatterplot is drawn with dimension i as the x-axis and dimension j as the y-axis. In this visualization, there is no object coherence because each object is shown as multiple points and the user cannot tell all the object's attribute values for any single object. There is dimension coherence because the user can tell the distribution of all the objects' attribute values for any dimension that the user is interested in. Furthermore, the correlation between any two dimensions i and j is clear from looking at the scatterplot in position (i,j). However, the user cannot simultaneously observe the correlation between more than two dimensions.

Dimension-reduction techniques are also commonly used in visualization. For example, Principal Component Analysis (PCA) [7] can be conducted on the data, and a scatterplot is shown with the first two principal components as the x- and y-axis. In such a visualization, there is no dimension coherence because each principal component is a combination of different original dimensions and therefore, from the visualization, one cannot tell an object's attribute value in any of the original dimensions. There is very good object coherence because each object is simple shown as a point, and the screen position of each object in relation to other objects can be easily observed. Similarly, there is also good object correlation because PCA tends to place objects similar in high-dimensional space close together in 2-D display. Another dimension-reduction method, MDS [19], is designed especially to preserve in 2-D the inter-object distances in higher dimensions. Projection Pursuit [5] methods provide more general projections of high-dimensional to low-dimensional space.

There are other existing multidimensional visualization techniques. Some are variants of the above-discussed methods, some combine different methods, and some, such as the Grand Tour methods [3], use animation and interaction techniques to enhance the visualization, linking multiple views. All these different methods can be analyzed based on their choices of what to show in focus and what to show in context, the smoothness of their transitions between focus and context, and their trade-offs between object and dimension coherence. For example, in animated visualizations, the correlation among the objects/dimensions shown between two adjacent frames is more obvious than between two frames separated by a long period of time.

Several multidimensional visualization systems have been built and are publicly available for download and use. The XGobi [17] package includes many built-in visualization tools such as scatterplots and parallel coordinates, and has the ability to link different scatterplots. Xmdv [20] is similar, and also includes dimensional stacking [12] and star glyphs [8]. VisDB [9] includes pixel-oriented techniques, and is used for visually exploring large databases These systems allow the user to conveniently choose different visualization display methods to explore the high-dimensional data.

4 Hifocon

Hifocon is the multidimensional visualization system we designed for improved coherence and correlation. In Hifocon, there are two display areas, called "primary" and "secondary". A scatterplot is shown in each. The user is allowed to choose which dimensions to use on the 4 axes. For example, the user may choose to use the first principal component for the x-axis and the second principal component as the y-axis in the primary display, and the original dimensions 5 and 8 as the x- and y-axes respectively in the secondary display.

Fisheye [4] magnification with star-glyph [8] are used to enhance coherence and correlation. A typical use of fisheye magnification is as follows. The user has chosen to display a scatterplot using MDS to layout the points. Then the user places a fisheye magnification lens on the display. This focuses the user's attention on the magnified objects, and these objects can be shown in more detail. Each magnified object is no longer shown as a single point, but as a star-shaped glyph. This star has n sticks radiating from the center, where n is the number of original dimensions the user has selected to focus on. The length of each stick is determined by the object's attributed value in the the stick's represented dimension; the larger the value, the longer the stick.

In this way, the user is allowed to select a subset of objects and a subset of dimensions to focus on simultaneously. Fisheye magnification with star-glyphs give good object coherence. However, there is not much dimension coherence because if MDS is used as the layout, the attribute values of the objects in any of the original dimensions cannot be discerned from the visualization. Furthermore, in star-glyphs, the focus dimensions are shown as disparate sticks on each object, so the distribution of the all the objects' values in any dimension cannot be clearly seen.

For better object coherence and dimension correlation, we designed another visualization metaphor: Arcs. In the two-scatterplot Hifocon display, each object is shown as two points, one in the primary and one in the secondary scatterplot. For better object coherence, a curved line is drawn between these two points. Now, an object is no longer two points, but one arc. Using arcs rather than straight lines to connect points give better perception of their endpoints. The arc representation has previously been used successfully in Thread Arcs [10].

Dimension correlation can also be enhanced in arcs. For example, if four different original dimensions were chosen as the four axes in the two scatterplot displays, dimension coherence is achieved for each of the four dimensions in focus. Dimension correlation is satisfied between the two dimensions shown in each scatterplot but not across the two scatterplots. Now, if arcs are drawn to connect objects in the two displays, then the dimension correlation between dimensions in the primary and secondary scatterplots becomes more obvious.

When there are too many objects in the display, the arcs can make it visually cluttered. When that happens, the user is allowed to move a focus lens (like the fisheye focus mentioned in the previous section). Only the objects covered by the lens would have arcs drawn in full color. Other objects are either displayed just as points, or have arcs drawn in less saturated color. These objects and arcs provide good context to the objects in focus.

Sometimes, a certain choice of axes provides a scatterplot visualization of the entire dataset that shows clearly the overall distribution of entire dataset. However, the visualization of parts of the data may not be clear. In such cases, Hifocon allows the user to *paint* a region of the display which the user is not satisfied with. A new pair of scatterplots will be shown and all objects falling on the painted region in the previous scatterplot will be re-displayed in this new scatterplot-pair. Different axes can be selected for this new display that would give a better visualization.

For example, a cluster in two dimensions *(a,b)* may become two clusters in two other dimensions *(c,d)*. In this case, the first two dimensions *(a,b)* can be chosen for the parent scatterplot, and a region is painted over the cluster, and a new scatterplot is plotted for the cluster, using dimensions *(c,d)*. In this way, hierarchical clustering can be observed.

PCA and MDS can also be performed only for this subset of data to more accurately show the statistical distribution and covariance of the subset.

Painting is performed simply by clicking on the mouse and dragging over the desired region of the display. The creation of regions and new scatterplots results in a heirarchy of scatterplots. Hifocon allows the simultaneous display of a scatterplot pair in focus together with its parent and children. Arcs can also be drawn to connect points representing the same object in the different scatterplots. This enhances object coherence and dimension correlation, so that the context shown by the parent scatterplot is more intuitive.

5 Examples

The Segment dataset from the Statlog [13] database is used to evaluate Hifocon. Each object in this dataset represents an image. Each image is of one of seven types: brickface, sky, foliage, cement, window, path or grass. These seven types are thus the classes an object can belong to. Each object is defined in 19-dimensional space. An example of a dimension is the average red value over the region. Another dimension is the contrast between vertically adjacent pixels, used to detect horizontal lines.

We use some examples from the visual exploration of the Segment dataset with Hifocon to illustrate how the visualization features of Hifocon can uncover important knowledge in high-dimensional data.

The left picture in Figure 1 shows a scatterplot pair with its parent scatterplot. In the secondary scatterplot, two clusters of red points are clearly distiguishable. However, in the primary scatterplot, there is only one cluster of red points. This shows that in the x-axis of the secondary scatterplot (which the user has chosen to be the original dimension *exred-mean*), there are two distinct clusters, however, in the other three axes (which the user has chosen to be original dimensions *region-centroid-row* , *wedge-mean* , and *exgreen-mean*), there is only one cluster.

Looking at the distribution of the red points on the secondary scatterplot along the y-axis, it is also clear that the left cluster has a higher value in the y-axis (which is *exgreen-mean*). This shows that even though the two clusters are not separately clustered in *exgreen-mean*, they are still separable. Now, the user is interested in finding out if there is any such correlation with the two dimensions used as axes in the primary scatterplot. This is done by drawing arcs and placing a focus point on one cluster and then the other, as shown in Figures 1. The results show that these two clusters are also separable in the two dimensions of the primary scatterplot, even though no clustering occurs in these two dimensions. This shows that there are two different types of class *brickface* surface type in this dataset, and these dimensions can be used to distinguish between the two types.

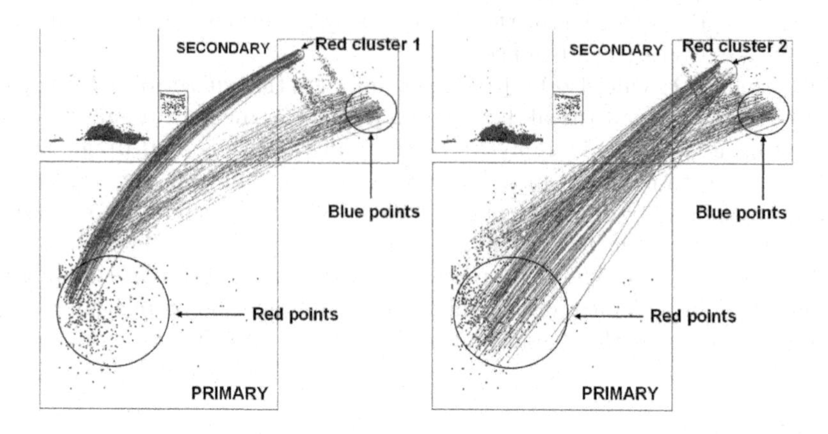

Fig. 1. Annotated screenshots. No clustering in the primary scatterplot, but the two clusters of the secondary scatterplot are separable in the primary scatterplot.

Another interesting discovery made in Hifocon visualization of the Segment dataset is that clusters in one dimension can be outliers in another dimension. This is shown when objects from one cluster in one plot has lines connected to objects which are outliers in another plot. This shows the interesting phenomenon that points in a cluster in one dimension can become outliers in other dimensions.

Figure 2 visualizes the objects belonging to the *sky* class. In the parent scatterplot (with *rawblue-mean* as the x-axis and *exred-mean* as the y-axis), there is a cluster with slightly larger value in *exred-mean* than *rawblue-mean*. By connecting the points in that cluster to the primary scatterplot (with *rawred-mean* as the x-axis and *intensity-mean* as the y-axis) with arcs, the user observes that the cluster also has slightly larger value in *rawred-mean* and smaller value in *intensity-mean*. Connecting lines to the child scatterplot shows that this cluster does not deviate in the two dimensions used for the child scatterplot. This shows that *sky* images contains a cluster that is slightly more red than other *sky* images.

6 Conclusions

We have defined the concepts of object coherence, object correlation, dimensional coherence, and dimensional correlation to help discuss and analyze multidimensional visualization. We find that object and dimension correlation are not satisfied in many existing multidimensional visualization methods. Using these concepts, we have provided an analysis of well-known existing multidimensional visualization methods.

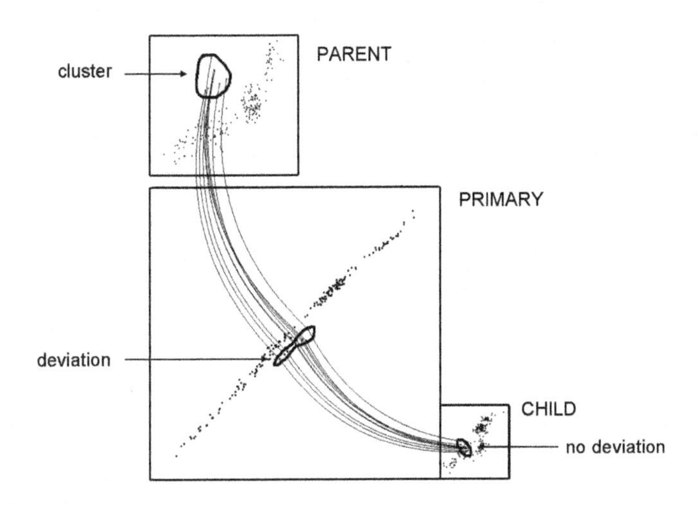

Fig. 2. Annotated screenshot. A cluster is observed in the parent scatterplot. This cluster is linked to the primary scatterplot and the child scatterplot. Deviation of the cluster is observed in the primary scatterplot but not in the child scatterplot. Such deviation is very hard to detect in parallel coordinates.

We then introduced Hifocon, a multidimensional visualization system we designed for better coherence and correlation. We incorporated dimension-reduction techniques like PCA and MDS to place objects on scatterplot displays, and used fish-eye magnification to show focus objects in detail with star-glyphs. We also use an arc to link two points representing the same object in two different scatterplots. This allows the relationship between four dimensions to be observed. Arcs are drawn for all points within a focus area specified by the user, while other points are shown as context. Coherence and correlation for both objects and dimensions are improved with arcs. With arcs, many interesting observations have been made. For example, we have shown an example of hierarchical clusters and an example of a cluster which becomes outliers in another dimension. Arcs are well-suited to discover such relationships because arcs link multiple dimensions together.

The ability to plot a new scatterplot for a subset of the data is also provided in Hifocon. This is important because axes can be custom-chosen to best reveal patterns, clusters and outliers in the subset. Arcs can be drawn back to the parent scatterplot for better object coherence and dimension correlation, so that the context shown by the parent scatterplot is more intuitive.

References

1. K. Alsabti, S. Ranka, and V. Singh. Clouds: A decision tree classifier for large datasets. In *Proc. 4th Intl. Conf. on Knowledge Discovery and Data Mining (KDD '98)*, pages 2–8, 1998.
2. M. Ankerst, M. Ester, and H.-P. Kriegel. Towards an effective cooperation of the user and the computer for classification. In *Proc. 6th Intl. Conf. on Knowledge Discovery and Data Mining (KDD '00)*, 2000.
3. D. Asimov. The grand tour: a tool for viewing multidimensional data. *SIAM Journal on Scientific and Statistical Computing*, 6(1):128–143, January 1985.
4. G. Furnas. Generalized fisheye views. In *Proc. ACM SIGCHI Conf. on Human Factors in Computing Systems (CHI'86)*, pages 16–23, 1986.
5. P.J. Huber. Projection pursuit. *The Annals of Statistics*, 13(2):435–475, 1985.
6. A. Inselberg. The plane with parallel coordinates. *Special Issue on Computational Geometry: The Visual Computer*, 1:69–91, 1985.
7. I.T. Jolliffe. *Principal Component Analysis.* Springer-Verlag, 1986.
8. E. Kandogan. Visualizing multi-dimensional clusters, trends, and outliers using star coordinates. In *Proc. ACM SIGKDD '01*, pages 107–116, 2001.
9. D.A. Keim and H.-P. Kriegel. Visdb: Database exploration using multidimensional visualization. *IEEE Computer Graphics and Applications*, 14(5):40–49, 1994.
10. B. Kerr. Thread arcs: An email thread visualization. In *Proc. IEEE Symposium on Information Visualization*, 2003.
11. J. Lamping, R. Rao, and P. Pirolli. A focus+context technique based on hyperbolic geometry for visualizing large hierarchies. In *Proc. ACM SIGCHI Conf. on Human Factors in Computing Systems (CHI'95)*, pages 401–408, 1995.
12. J. LeBlanc, M.O. Ward, and N. Wittels. Exploring n-dimensional databases. In *Proc. IEEE Visualization '90*, 1990.
13. D. Michie, D.J. Spiegelhalter, and C.C. Taylor. *Machine Learning, Neural and Statistical Classification.* Ellis Horwood, 1994.
14. R. Parekh, J. Yang, and V. Honavar. Constructive neural-network learning algorithms for pattern classification. *IEEE Trans. on Neural Networks*, 11(2), 2000.
15. R.M. Pickett and G.G. Grinstein. Iconographics displays for visualizing multidimensional data. In *Proc. IEEE Conference on Systems, Man, and Cybernetics*, pages 514–519, 1998.
16. J.C. Shafer, R. Agrawal, and M. Mehta. Sprint: A scalable parallel classifier for data mining. In *Proc. 22nd Intl. Conf. on Very Large Databases (VLDB '96)*, pages 544–555, 1996.
17. D.F. Swayne, D. Cook, and A. Buja. Xgobi: Interactive dynamic data visualization in the x window system. *Journal of Computational and Graphical Statistics*, 7(1):113–130, 1998.
18. S.T. Teoh and K.-L. Ma. Paintingclass: Interactive construction, visualization and exploration of decision trees. In *Proc. 9th Intl. Conf. on Knowledge Discovery and Data Mining (KDD '03)*, 2003.
19. W.S. Torgerson. Multidimensional scaling: I. theory and method. *Psychometrika*, 17:401–419, 1952.
20. M.O. Ward. Xmdvtool: Integrating multiple methods for visualizing multivariate data. In *Proc. IEEE Visualization '94*, pages 326–336, 1994.
21. J. Yang, W. Peng, M.O. Ward, and E.A. Rundensteiner. Interactive hierarchical dimension ordering, spacing and filtering for exploration of high dimensional datasets. In *Proc. IEEE Symposium on Information Visualization*, 2003.

Efficient Compression of Visibility Sets

Christian Bouville, Isabelle Marchal, and Loïc Bouget

France Télécom Recherche & Développement, Cesson-Sévigné, France
{christian.bouville, isabelle.marchal, loic.bouget}@francetelecom.com

Abstract. Interactive network-based walkthroughs in large urban environments raise difficult problems due to the size and density of these scenes. Thanks to the strong occlusion complexity of such environments, visibility streaming is a particularly efficient technique for minimizing the network load. In this paper, we present a solution which relies on client-side processing of visibility information so as to minimize the server workload. To solve the problem of transmitting the visibility data to the client, we suggest a bi-level compression scheme for the visibility sets that performs significantly better than previous methods. As a result, the visibility sets can be efficiently transmitted on-demand to the client and then used for adaptive streaming and rendering. Finally, we present our experimental results for a virtual city walkthrough.

1 Introduction

Efficient and fast automatic modeling tools allow generating huge 3D city models. However, using these large databases in network-based applications is a challenging problem. The usual download-and-play method of most existing Web3D applications is unworkable and the problem becomes even more difficult in the case of mobile networks and terminals given their limited memory resources. Furthermore, many applications require that viewing interactions begin once the network connection is on, even if the image is rendered with raw LODs.

An extensive literature addresses the problem of visualizing large and complex 3D databases [1]. Most of the proposed solutions use LOD and visibility culling to generate a simplified view-dependent model of the scene. In the case of urban walkthrough applications, visibility culling significantly reduces scene complexity since the foreground façades hide large parts of the scene. By implementing server-side visibility culling, network usage can be strongly decreased by sending only visible objects to the client [2]. However, some form of pre-fetching and caching is necessary to compensate for transmission lags [3]. Pre-fetching entails the visibility set be computed within a superset of all observer viewpoints possible within a given time period.

To avoid real-time server-side computation of the visibility set, these sets can be pre-computed for all view cells that form a partition of the viewpoint space [4]. Assuming that the potential visibility sets (PVS) have been pre-computed for all view cells of the viewpoint space, two methods of client-server cooperation are possible. In the first one, the client sends his viewpoint changes to the server

G. Bebis et al. (Eds.): ISVC 2005, LNCS 3804, pp. 243–252, 2005.

that locates the corresponding view cell and updates the client data according to the associated PVS. The drawback is that redundant data are sent to the client because the server does not know which data are already in the client cache. This problem can be solved if the client cache management procedure is known from the server or if the client informs the server about its cache content [5],[6]. But this is only possible with simple cache management procedures and nonetheless, it significantly impacts on the server workload. In the other method, we assume that the client has pre-fetched the PVS data for a sufficiently large area around the current viewpoint. The client can then determine by itself the objects that need to be requested from the server. This gives full freedom in the client cache management procedure and greatly simplifies the server task. Furthermore, the client renderer can take advantage of the local PVS data to perform visibility culling. However, this raises the problem of sending the PVS data to the client.

In the following, we will describe a solution based on an efficient hierarchical PVS data compression algorithm that allows sending visibility information at low transmission cost.

2 Related Work

In his early works on virtual environments walkthroughs, Funkhouser [3] suggests integrating visibility and detail control techniques for managing large amount of data during an interactive walkthrough. Since then, a significant research effort has been concentrated on visibility computation. Comprehensive surveys can be found in [4],[7]. Conservative methods in which for a given scene and viewpoint the occlusion culling algorithm determines a superset of the visible objects [8] are popular for urban environments. From-region algorithms partition the viewpoint space into cells, rather than attempting to build and store a complex aspect graph. The main advantage of these techniques is that their rather important computational cost can be transferred to a preprocessing step [9],[10]. Another interesting asset is that they make pre-fetching easier which is particularly useful for remote urban walkthrough systems as described in the introduction. In [11], Marvie describes a VRML/X3D implementation of this pre-fetching method through the introduction of new scene-graph nodes. However, the VRML syntax does not lend itself very well to the handling of very large scenes, in particular as regards compression. This is an important factor for urban walkthroughs since efficient objects pre-fetching requires fast transmission of visibility data to the client. In the literature, the problem of PVS data compression has mainly been considered under a storage point of view. The storage and the management of PVS data is indeed a difficult issue for large scenes involving millions of polygons. Most suggested compression techniques starts from a boolean *visibility array* in which the visibility of an object (column index) for a given view cell (row index) is encoded by a binary digit. In [12], van de Panne and Stewart suggest merging equal or similar rows/columns and using run-length binary compression. In [13], Gotsman et al. address the problem of visibility data compression in a 5D spatial hierarchy of the viewing space. They suggest reducing redundancies between hierarchy levels by creating visibility arrays at each nodes in which a zero is assigned when the object is not visible from the current node cell and all its descendants. Zach and Karner [14] use a similar technique for multiresolution mesh visualization. In [15], Nadler et al. make a theoretical analysis of visibility in urban scenes that leads them to an optimal view cell size as regards storage considerations. They also suggest using a hierarchical data structure to exploit cell-to-cell PVS coherency which results in saving up to 25% on total storage. Instead of using a PVS for each cell, Koltun [16] uses an intermediate representation called virtual occluder that aggregates occlusion for a region. These virtual occluders are pre-computed. As there are much less virtual occluders than individual occluders, this enables on-line PVS computation before the rendering stage. Moreira [17] breaks the PVS into several subsets according to geometric criteria so that the server can send the most relevant data first by using a visual importance metrics. Recently, Chhugani et al. [18] have suggested a new compression algorithm that they use for interactive display of huge models. It consists in computing the difference (the Δ sets) between the PVSs of adjacent view cells and compressing the Δs using a variable length encoding method that exploits the sparse distribution of the 1s.

3 Overview

Our goal is to allow interactive urban walkthrough applications in a mobile client/server configuration, that is with reduced network bandwidth and terminal resource. Furthermore, the server should be able to sustain thousands of connected clients. In this context, we have shown in the introduction that the best solution is a demand-driven client-server architecture in which the visibility data are pre-computed and exploited on the client-side (see Fig. 1). Therefore, the visibility sets serve three different purposes :

- reduce network and terminal resource usage by sending to the client a minimal subset of the scene and visibility data
- allow client-side visibility culling so as to minimize the client workload
- allow pre-fetching so as to cope with network latencies

The first two objectives lead us to minimize view cell size whereas the last one is better fulfilled with large view cells. Note however that too small view cells would bring about excessive protocol overhead and view cell management tasks. A hierarchical structure such as described in [13],[15] is a good solution for this. The low levels of the spatial hierarchy are appropriate for client-side visibility culling whereas the high levels are mostly beneficial to pre-fetching. Furthermore, this spatial hierarchy allows taking advantage of the strong cell-to-cell coherency when encoding PVS data.

Our system uses a two-level view cell hierarchy. The lower level is obtained through a Delaunay triangulation of the walkthrough area (i.e. all space left between building footprints) as suggested by Wonka [10]. To limit the number

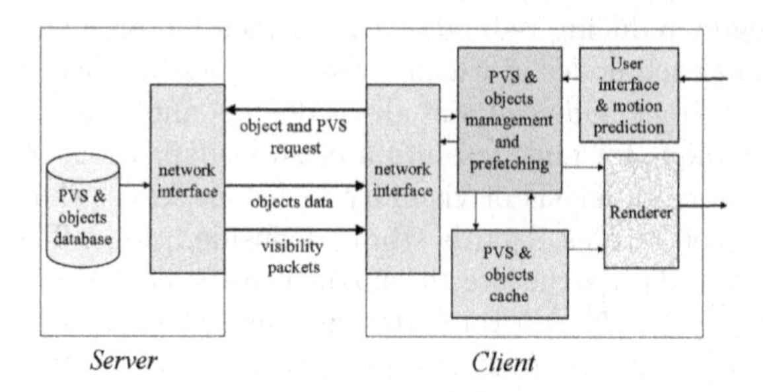

Fig. 1. Client-server architecture for remote interactive walkthroughs

of potentially visible objects in a cell, the largest cells are divided whenever the number of visible objects exceeds a fixed limit. The upper level consists in an axis-aligned subdivision of the whole urban area.

As our client-server architecture requires sending PVS data to the client, data compression is an important issue given that visibility data may be larger than scene data. Our method combines a hierarchical coding approach similar to Gotsman's [13] with a bi-level image compression technique for the visibility arrays so as to best take advantage of the cell-to-cell coherency. Pre-fetching is performed through a process which consists into requesting and storing the neighboring view cells within a viewpoint-centered lookahead area.

4 Visibility Data Compression

4.1 Original Visibility Data

The view cells have a triangular base and a constant height. The p view cells and n objects of the scene are indexed by single ID numbers. As explained in the previous section, the visibility data are structured in a two-level hierarchy. For this, the scene is subdivided in axis-aligned parallelepipedal regions such as provided by well-know tree structures (k-d tree, BSP,...) or simple uniform grid partitioning. We choose the later for the sake of simplicity.

A subdivision region takes in all view cells that intersect it. In most applications, the size of the subdivision regions is chosen so that each one contains an average of one hundred view cells. Experiments have shown that this size is sufficient to exploit cell-to-cell coherency for visibility array coding and it provides a good compromise between the data size of the subdivision regions and the pre-fetch range. Figure 3 shows a 2D example of spatial subdivision.

The PVS information is computed for each view cell of the scene and is stored in a boolean vector of n bits with each ith bit set to 1 to represent that the ith object is visible from the current view cell. A *visibility array* is built in which each row corresponds to one view cell and each column corresponds to one object.

4.2 PVS Compression

Dividing the global visibility array in as many visibility arrays as the number of subdivision regions is easily performed. It creates a set of much smaller visibility arrays though global redundancies are produced because some view cells belong to several subdivision regions. However the visibility arrays associated to the subdivision regions still have a prohibitive size because there is an entry for each object of the scene. Nevertheless there is a large number of zeros because many objects are not visible from any of the view cells included in the region. Such objects show up as all-zero columns in the visibility array. To remove this redundant zeros, we use a technique similar to Gotsmans's hierarchical compression scheme[13]. It consists in building a subdivision region visibility table (called *visibility table* from now on) as follows. A *visibility table* is a n-dimension boolean vector in which the ith entry is set to 1 when the object is potentially visible from at least one of the view cell of the subdivision region or else set to 0. The 0 entries of the *visibility table* show the columns of the visibility array which can be removed (see Fig. 2).

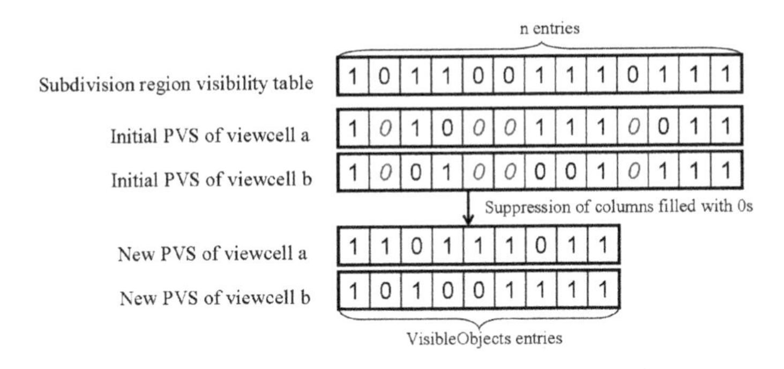

Fig. 2. Example showing columns removal in visibility arrays

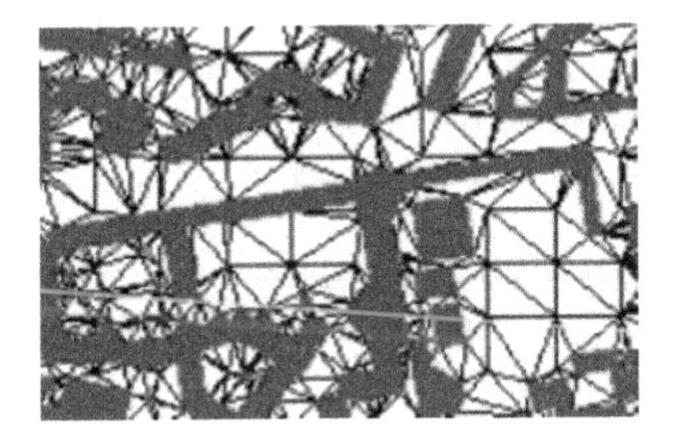

Fig. 3. An example of a 2D ground projection of the 3D scene with the buildings in dark and navigation space in white divided in triangular view cells

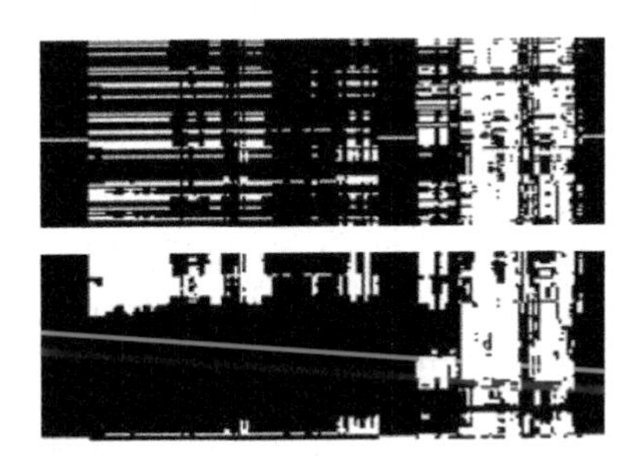

Fig. 4. A re-ordered visibility array (bottom image) compared to the original one (top image)

Visibility data are thus structured in two tables: the *visibility table* and the new compacted visibility array. Given the strong cell-to-cell coherency and the densely occluded nature of urban scene, this compression method significantly reduces the visibility data size. However, a lot of redundancies remain in visibility arrays. To further compress these arrays, we apply a bi-level image coding algorithm such as used in fax machines. Bi-level image coder such as JBIG are very effective at capturing the patterns and structure of any type of bi-level image. They provide much higher compression rate than run-length coder. However, visibility arrays appear to be very noisy images since there is little correlation between successive rows and columns. A reordering is necessary so that the bi-level coder can best exploit the cell-to-cell coherency. Correlation between rows can be improved if we permute them so that the Hamming distance between two consecutive rows (number of bit positions in which they differ) is minimal. If we take the sum of the Hamming distances between the $r-1$ consecutive row couples as an optimality criterion, an exhaustive search would lead to testing all $r!$ permutations (r is the row number i.e. the number of view cells included in the subdivision region). Given the average number of view cells per subdivision region, this appears to be too computationally expensive. The following simple algorithm provides a sub-optimal solution that proves to be sufficient in practice. A seed row is arbitrarily chosen and taken as the first row in the new visibility array. The closest to the first one according the Hamming metrics is searched among the remaining ones and moved to the second row, and so on until all the rows have been re-ordered. Figure 4 shows the effect of reordering on bi-level images and Fig. 5 summarizes the pseudo-code of the entire process.

This re-ordering algorithm requires $(r-1)!$ Hamming distance calculations. We also compare our reordering algorithm with the brute force method which consists in finding the row permutation which yields the smallest data size after applying bi-level image compression. In most cases (97%), the simple reordering algorithm leads to the same compressed array size as the brute force method.

As it can be expected, there is a strong correlation between row proximity in the re-ordered visibility array and view cells geometrical proximity in the viewing space (80% of adjacent rows correspond to adjoining cells) though no topological considerations have been taken into account when re-ordering. Concerning the columns of the array, it would cost a lot of CPU time to find the optimal re-ordering because of the huge number of objects. While building the scene database, we just try to number objects as coherently as possible using local proximity rules.

Once the rows have been re-ordered, we apply a lossless bi-level image coder or a binary compression algorithm. Four types of compression methods have been experimented:

- The run length compression algorithm used by de Panne and Stewart in [12]
- The JBIG1 compression standard
- The PNG compression format
- The generic GZIP compression method

```
Divide the scene in subdivision regions
For each region
   Assign view cells to regions
   Build the region visibility table
   Discard all-zero columns in the
   visibility arrays and build visibility tables
   Reorder the rows of the array:
      Build an empty new array called "newarray"
      Select a seed row
      Move it to top of newarray
      Current_row = First_row
      While un-ordered rows remain
          Search the closest row to Current_row
          Move it to Next_row in newarray
          Current_row = Next_row
   Apply bi-level image coding on newarray
```

Fig. 5. Pseudo-code for visibility data compression

4.3 PVS Decompression and Pre-fetching

When a visibility data packet (a visibility table plus a compressed visibility array) is received, the client builds an empty subdivision region visibility array with n (number of objects) columns and r rows. The *visibility table* is used to fill the columns which have only 0 values. The bi-level visibility image is decoded and used to fill the columns that are marked with a 1 in the visibility table.
Whenever the observer moves to a new subdivision region, new visibility data need to be requested from the server. To compensate for the network latencies, the server sends in advance to the client the visibility tables of the adjacent subdivision regions.

5 Results

We have implemented the client-server system described above so as to experiment the architecture and the algorithms. All the results given below were conducted on a PC platform with a 2.8GHz P4 CPU, 768MB of RAM.

The results with the virtual city of Rennes a view of which is shown in Fig. 6 are presented. PVSs have been computed with the method described by Wonka et al. in [10]. The scene is composed of buildings modeled either in 2.5D or 3D, façade textures and street furniture. The scene properties are described below in Table 1. The last item of this table is the size of the uncompressed global visibility table (one row for each cell and one column for each object). It is obviously too large to be transmitted in the context of an on-line application.

Table 2 gives the compression ratios for the scene described above. The size of the square subdivision regions is 50m which allows containing enough view cells

Table 1. Scene characteristic data with a 50 meters subdivision region

Scene properties	Rennes
surface of the city in km^2	19
average view cell surface in m^2	86
number of objects	22581
number of view cells	85210
avg. number of view cells in a subdivision region	43
avg. number of visible objects in a cell	428
avg. number of visible objects in a subdivision region	1475
global visibility table size without compression in MB	240.5

Table 2. Experimental results with the Rennes model. Compression ratios are given compared to the original visibility array

Compression methods	Average array size
Uncompressed binary	120541
M0: Uncompressed reduced	7891 (14.5x)
M1: Run-length encoding	5200 (23.2x)
M2: Gzip	2873 (42.0x)
M3: PNG	3263 (36.9x)
M4: JBIG1	2754 (43.8x)
M5: Gzip with reordering	2752 (43.8x)
M6: PNG with reordering	2474 (48.7x)
M7: JBIG with reordering	**1989 (60.6x)**

for the user to navigate during a few seconds without requesting new visibility data from the server.

The first item gives the average size of the visibility arrays with uncompressed binary coding (one column for each object of the scene). For M0, the size has been reduced by removing the all-0 columns. As mentioned above, this compression step requires sending a visibility table to allow the decoder to retrieve the removed columns. In all tested compression methods, this table is gzipped and sent in the same data packet as the view cells numbers and the compressed visibility array. The results given for M0 to M7 take into account the total size of the packets so as to allow a fair comparison between methods. The method M1 is the one suggested by van de Panne and Stewart. It consists in run-length encoding the TRUE entries of the visibility arrays. PNG compression (M3 and M6) has been implemented with libpng version 1.2.8. For JBIG compression (M4 and M7), we use the JBIG-KIT by Markus Kuhn. Better compression results are expected with a JBIG2 coder. The three methods M2, M3 and M4 lead to similar compression ratios. The results of M6 and M7 clearly show the advantage of re-ordering while M5 (gzip) is not very different from M2. The algorithm performs better with JBIG (M7) since the sophisticated prediction methods used by JBIG become effective only when image coherency is present. When applied to the whole scene, the overall gain is significant: the sum of all the compressed visibility arrays takes up only 6.7MB with M7 which is 36 times smaller than the original table (240.5MB).

6 Conclusion

We have presented a client-server system for urban walkthrough in very large and complex scenes. This system is based on visibility culling so as to minimize network and terminal resource usage. PVSs associated to view cells are precomputed and transmitted on-demand to the client. The client is then responsible for its own visibility culling and for the management of its local scene data, which minimizes data requests from the server. The cost of sending the visibility sets is negligible thanks to the two-step compression algorithms that we suggest. The last step uses a bi-level image coder which proves to be very effective. Furthermore, our compressed PVS data structure allows solving effectively the pre-fetching problem. Moreover, this client-side object selection method greatly facilitates a peer-to-peer implementation in which clients may act as servers for their peers. The above experimental results have been obtained on a PC platform. A mobile phone implementation based on OpenGL ES is underway. Due to the limited bandwidth of mobile network, further optimization is necessary in the streaming method.

References

1. Aliaga, D., Manocha, D.: Interactive Walkthrough of Large Geometric Datasets. http://www.cs.unc.edu/~geom/SIG00_COURSE (2000)
2. Cohen-Or, D., Fibich, G., Halperin, D., Zadicario, E.: Conservative Visibility and Strong Occlusion for Viewspace Partitioning of Densely Occluded Scenes. Computer Graphics Forum **17** (1998) 243–254
3. Funkhouser, T.A.: Database Management for Interactive Display of Large Architectural Models. In: Proc. Graphics Interface'96. (1996) 1–8
4. Cohen-Or, D., Chrysanthou, Y., Silva, C., Durand, F.: A Survey of Visibility for Walkthrough Applications. IEEE Transactions on Visualization and Computer Graphics (2003) 412–431
5. Gioia, P., Aubault, O., Bouville, C.: Real-Time Reconstruction of Wavelet Encoded Meshes for View-Dependent Transmission and Visualisation. IEEE Trans. on CSVT **14** (2004) 1009–1020
6. Schmalstieg, D., Gervautz, M.: Demand-Driven Geometry Transmission for Distributed Virtual Environments. Computer Graphics Forum **15** (1996) 421–432
7. Pantazopoulos, I., Tzafestas, S.: Occlusion Culling Algorithms : A Comprehensive Survey. Journal of Intelligent and Robot Systems (2002) 35:123–156
8. Cohen-Or, D., Zadicario, E.: Visibility Streaming for Network-based Walkthrough. In: Proc. Graphics Interface '98. (1998) 1–7
9. Leyvand, T., Sorkine, O., Cohen-Or, D.: Ray Space Factorization for From-Region Visibility. In: ACM Transactions on Graphics (Proceedings of SIGGRAPH'03). Volume 22. (2003) 595–604
10. Wonka, P., Wimmer, M., Schmalstieg, D.: Visibility Preprocessing with Occluder Fusion for Urban Walkthroughs. In: 11th Eurographics Workshop on Rendering. (2000) 71–82

11. Marvie, J.E., Bouatouch, K.: A Vrml97-X3D Extension for Massive Scenery Management in Virtual Worlds. In: Proceedings of the ninth international conference on 3D Web technology. (2004) 145–153
12. van de Panne, M., Stewart, A.: Effective Compression Techniques for Precomputed Visibility. In: 12th Eurographics Workshop on Rendering. (1999) 305–316
13. Gotsman, C., Sudarsky, O., Fayman, J.: Optimized Occlusion Culling Using Five-Dimensional Subdivision. Computer & Graphics (1999) 23(5):645–654
14. Zach, C., Karner, K.: Progressive Compression of Visibility Data for View-dependent Multiresolution Meshes. In: WSCG'2003. Volume 11. (2003)
15. Nadler, B., Fibich, G., Lev-Yehudi, S., Cohen-Or, D.: A qualitative and quantitative visibility analysis in urban scenes. Computer & Graphics (1999) 23:655–666
16. Koltun, V., Chrysanthou, Y., Cohen-Or, D.: Virtual Occluders : An efficient Intermediate PVS Representation. In: 11th Eurographics Workshop on Rendering. (2000) 59–70
17. Moreira, F., Comba, J., Freitas, C.: Smart Visible Sets for Networked Virtual Environments. In: SIBGRAPI. (2002) 373–380
18. Chhugani, J., Purnomo, B., Krishnan, S., Venkatasubramanian, S., Johnson, D., Kumar, S.: vLOD : High-Fidelity Walkthrough of Large Virtual Environments. IEEE Transactions on Visualization and Computer Graphics **11** (2005)

Fig. 6. A view over a part of the Rennes model

Rendering Optimizations Guided by Head-Pose Estimates and Their Uncertainty

Javier E. Martínez[1], Ali Erol[1], George Bebis[1], Richard Boyle[2], and Xander Twombly[2]

[1] Computer Vision Laboratory, University of Nevada, Reno, NV 89557
{javier, bebis, aerol}@cse.unr.edu
[2] BioVis Laboratory, NASA Ames Research Center, Moffett Field, CA 94035
{rboyle, xtwombly}@mail.arc.nasa.gov

Abstract. In virtual environments, head pose and/or eye-gaze estimation can be employed to improve the visual experience of the user by enabling adaptive level of detail during rendering. In this study, we present a real-time system for rendering complex scenes in an immersive virtual environment based on head pose estimation and perceptual level of detail. In our system, the position and orientation of the head are estimated using stereo vision approach and markers placed on a pair of glasses used to view images projected on a stereo display device. The main innovation of our work is the incorporation of uncertainty estimates to improve the visual experience perceived by the user. The estimated pose and its uncertainty are used to determine the desired level of detail for different parts of the scene based on criteria originating from physiological and psychological aspects of human vision. Subject tests have been performed to evaluate our approach.

1 Introduction

Virtual environments (VEs) are effective computing technologies that allow deployment of various advanced applications including immersive training systems, surgical simulations, and visualization of large data sets among others. Development of such computing environments raises challenging research problems. To allow high degree-of-freedom (DOF) natural interaction, new input modalities based on direct sensing of the hand, eye-gaze, head and even the whole human body motion are being incorporated. To create an immersion effect, advanced display technologies such as 3D stereo displays or CAVE environments are being engineered and high quality real-time rendering algorithms are being developed.

Among different input modalities, head pose and/or eye-gaze estimation provide an effective input mainly for navigation tasks in VEs. During navigation, head pose information (i.e., 6 DOF) can help to optimize the computational load of rendering and increase visual quality at regions where the user is focusing on by estimating where the user is looking at. Technically, it is possible to employ adaptive level of detail (LOD) in rendering to improve the visual experience perceived by the user without a major increase in the computational load.

In this study, we present a real-time system for rendering complex scenes in an immersive virtual environment based on head pose estimation and perceptual level of

G. Bebis et al. (Eds.): ISVC 2005, LNCS 3804, pp. 253 – 262, 2005.

detail (PLOD) [1]. In our system, the position and orientation of the head are estimated using stereo vision and markers placed on a pair of glasses that the user has to wear to view images projected on a stereo display device. The main innovation of our work is the incorporation of uncertainty estimates to improve the visual experience perceived by the user. The estimated pose and its uncertainty are used to determine the desired LOD for different parts of the scene based on criteria originating from physiological and psychological aspects of human vision. This work is part of a larger collaborative effort between our group and *BioVis* lab at NASA Ames to build a virtual simulator (i.e., Virtual Glove Box or VGX). VGX is intended to provide an advanced "fine-motor coordination" training and simulation system for astronauts to perform precise biological experiments in a Glovebox aboard the International Space Station [21][22].

In the next section, we present a brief review of previous work on PLOD. In Section 3, we describe of our system. The implementation details of head-pose estimation and PLOD calculation are presented in Sections 4 and 5 respectively. In Section 6, we report and discuss the results of our experiments. Finally, Section 7 contains our conclusions.

2 Previous Work

While the first work on PLOD dates back to '76 [1], most of the development has been done during the last decade. These advancements can be grouped into three areas, namely *criteria*, *mechanism* and *error measure*. The *criteria* are a set of functions that select areas from the objects that need to be drawn with a certain LOD. The *mechanism* is another set of functions that modify the geometry to achieve the desired LOD. They correspond to polygon simplification mechanisms that fall under four categories [5]: sampling, adaptive subdivision, vertex decimation and vertex merging. The *error measure* is an evaluation of the differences between the original object and the modified one, and it is used to control the mechanism. Measuring deviations from the original mesh to the modified mesh allows the quantification of the errors introduced when modifying the mesh. Common error measures in the literature include vertex-vertex, vertex-plane, vertex-surface, and surface-surface distances. Ideally, we would like these errors to be imperceptible to the user.

The most important part of a PLOD system is the set of criteria used to modulate the LOD. These criteria are related to or based on physiological and psychological aspects of human vision [2, 3]. We list below several important criteria [4]:

- **Contrast sensitivity:** The LOD is modulated depending on whether it is inside or outside of the Contrast Sensitivity Function (CSF) curve that shows the relationship between contrast and spatial frequency in human visual perception [4].
- **Velocity:** The LOD is modulated proportionally to the relative velocity of the eye across the visual field.
- **Eccentricity:** The LOD is modulated proportionally to the angular distance of the object to the viewpoint.
- **Depth of field:** The LOD is modulated proportionally to the distance to the Panum's fusional area [2]. This is used only in connection with stereo-vision.

There are several examples of systems that make use of eye-gaze for guiding perceptually motivated simplifications including Reddy [10], Luebke [3], Williams [18] and Murphy [17]. Both [3] and [17] make use of an eye tracker to estimate the eye-gaze vector. In [3], the user's head is placed in a chin rest to avoid having to calculate the position of the eyes. Only [17] tracks the head and the eyes simultaneously allowing the user to move in a more natural way.

3 System Design

Immersive VEs can be implemented in various operational environments, mainly deermined by the output devices. In this study, we targeted a stereo display system [21]. An ideal system would require tracking both the head and eye-gaze simultaneously to allow arbitrary motion of the user; however, eye-gaze tracking could be very costly and intrusive. In our application, users need to wear a pair of polarized glasses which makes eye-gaze tracking challenging since the user's eyes are not visible. To keep things simple, we decided to obtain a rough estimate of eye-gaze by tracking the head and estimating its orientation. Developing a more accurate eye-gaze tracking system (e.g., by mounting small cameras on the frame of the glasses) is a part of our future work.

Fig. 1. Hardware setup: (a) camera setup on the computer, (b) eye-glasses with IR reflective markers, (c) camera close-up with IR LEDs

To make head tracking fast and robust, we took advantage of the requirement that the users have to wear glasses by placing several markers on the frame of the glasses. This approach simplifies detecting the head without being intrusive. A challenging issue in designing the system was how to deal with illumination since any kind of external illumination could interfere with the stereo display device (e.g. projector-based) and disturb the user. To deal with this issue, we decided to use IR LEDs for illumination and IR reflective markers as shown in Figure 1. A high-pass filter was installed on the cameras to block visible light from entering the camera sensor. The filter used in our setup was the Kodak Wratten 97c filter which has a cut-off limit of 800nm.

The system contains three modules as shown in Figure 2: (a) a vision module, (b) a PLOD module and (c) a rendering module. The vision module detects the position, orientation and uncertainty of the user's head and passes it to the PLOD module, which takes into account the physiological and psychological aspects of the human vision to calculate the LOD at which to draw the elements. Finally, the rendering module draws everything on the screen at the calculated LOD.

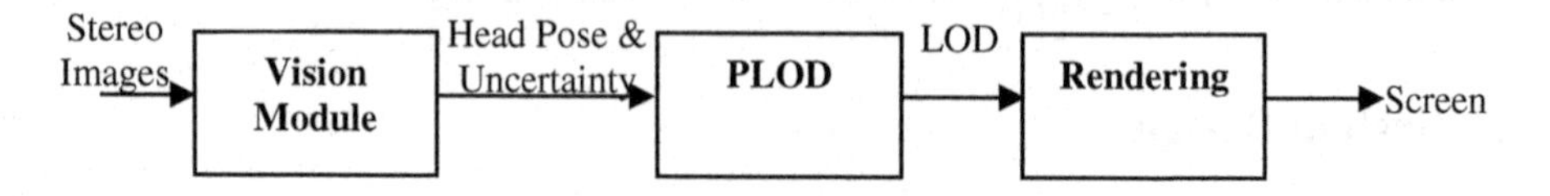

Fig. 2. Block diagram of the whole system

4 Head Pose Estimation

The vision module includes three processing steps: (a) marker extraction, (b) pose estimation, and (c) uncertainty estimation. First, the markers are extracted in each image. Then, the head pose is estimated by reconstructing the location of the markers in 3D through triangulation. Finally, uncertainty associated with the estimated pose is calculated.

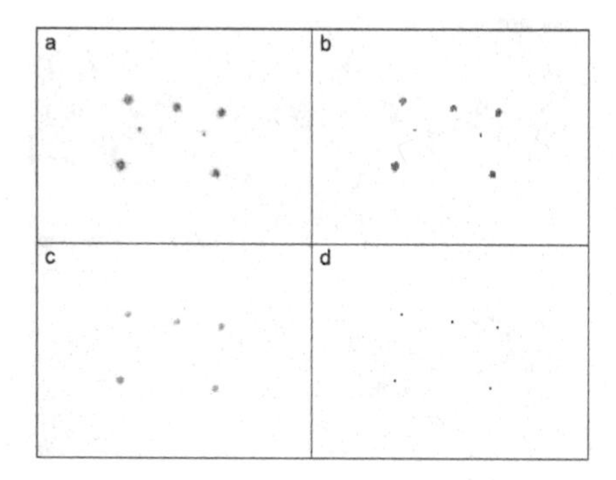

Fig. 3. Negative of the images from each stage of the process starting with: a) input image; b) thresholded with a value of 100; c) smoothed with a 9-pixel Gaussian filter; and d) final image showing the centers

4.1 Marker Extraction

The combination of IR illumination and IR reflective markers allows for fast and robust feature extraction. In the input images (see Figure 3(a)) the background is already suppressed due to the use of the filter that blocks visible light, allowing the detection and extraction of markers through a simple thresholding operation as shown in Figure 3(b). The thresholded image is then processed using a Gaussian filter to eliminate noise (see Figure 3(c)).

For each marker on the image, we estimate its center with sub-pixel accuracy (see Figure 3(d)). It should be noted that, it is still possible to get some extra blobs during segmentation due to light reflections on the eye-glasses; however, the special arrangement of markers (see Figure 4) can help us to eliminate them (e.g., by requiring that the upper 3 markers lie roughly on a line). This special marker configuration also allowed us to identify uniquely each marker on a single image (e.g. establish correspondences between the left and right images).

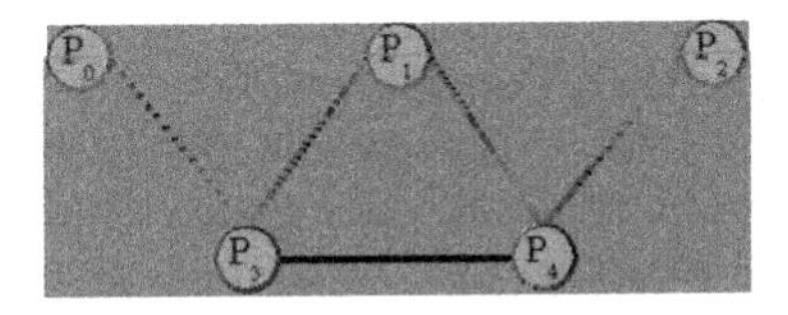

Fig. 4. Marker arrangement on the glasses

4.2 Pose Estimation

Once the markers have been extracted in each image, the center of each marker can be used to calculate its 3D location using triangulation. In our approach, the location of the head is estimated by the location of the middle marker P_1 while its orientation is estimated by averaging the normal vectors corresponding to the three triangles shown Figure 4. We have validated the accuracy of our head pose estimate algorithm using a magnetic tracker with an accuracy of 1.8mm in the position and 0.5° in the orientation.

4.3 Uncertainty Estimation

It is possible to associate an uncertainty measure to both the position and orientation estimates of the head; however, we have observed that the uncertainty in orientation has a much higher effect on the LOD mainly due to the amplification of the error in the calculation of the point of interest on the screen (see Section 5). Therefore, we are only considered estimating orientation uncertainty.

Uncertainty calculation in stereo vision is a well studied topic. In general, it is possible to propagate calibration and feature localization errors to the estimates of 3D position and local orientations [15]. However, estimating orientation uncertainty analytically in our system was rather difficult; therefore, we implemented a random sampling approach.

Specifically, in matching two markers, we assume that the correspondences between pixels belonging to each marker are unknown. Using the epipolar constraint and the distance of the pixels from the center of the marker, we generate a cloud of 3D points for each marker. Then, each cloud is randomly sampled and all possible combinations of the samples are used to generate orientation estimates by computing the covariance matrix of the samples.

5 Perceptual Level of Detail

We assumed that the scene is represented by a triangular mesh corresponding to the coarsest LOD. For each triangle in the mesh, we calculate the desired LOD and increase the resolution (i.e. generate smaller triangles) accordingly, using adaptive subdivision.

In the calculation of the desired LOD, we are interested in finding the highest spatial frequency that a person can see at a particular location under conditions determined by the triangle's contrast, eccentricity and angular velocity. The spatial frequency of a triangle is found by measuring the maximum angle between the vertices of the triangle projected on the screen plane with respect to the head position. The contrast level for a triangle is obtained by rendering the triangle at the coarsest level and examining the color content of the projection. To calculate the eccentricity, the triangle is represented by its geometric center. Uncertainty estimates mainly affect the eccentricity values.

When the user is looking at the screen, the direction of his (her) head intersects the plane formed by the screen at a point called the Point of Interest (POI). Uncertainty in head orientation affects the location of the POI, which in turn affects the eccentricity values of the triangles. We have incorporated orientation uncertainty in the eccentricity calculations by modifying the triangle's location with respect to the POI. Specifically, given a point P and the orientation uncertainty matrix Σ, an uncertainty corrected point P_u is calculated as follows:

$$P_u = e^{-\frac{1}{2}(P-POI)^T \Sigma^{-1} (P-POI)} (POI - P) + P \tag{1}$$

where point P is shifted towards POI proportionally to the probability that P itself is the POI.

The highest spatial frequency is determined by solving a system of equations given the contrast, angular velocity and the modified eccentricity values of triangles. Once the highest spatial frequency is known, it can be related to a certain LOD that is determined by the implementation. In our system, the depth of subdivision is taken to be the LOD measure.

6 Subject Tests

The objective of our tests was to quantify the improvement obtained by incorporating uncertainty correction on a perceptually oriented display system. The test application displays a terrain section or height map (see Figure 5), on which PLOD optimizations are applied. The user is shown three test cases (i.e. different views of the terrain), each containing three scenarios.

The first scenario presents the user with common optimizations found in the literature; namely velocity, contrast and eccentricity. The second scenario uses a constant uncertainty correction to modify the way eccentricity behaves. The constant uncertainty matrix is chosen to contain the maximum uncertainty values obtained using our algorithm on a large number of experiments. The third scenario uses uncertainty corrections like before; however, the covariance matrix is continuously updated through the sampling algorithm presented in Section 4.2.

In each case, the user was asked to judge the amount of changes perceived all over the screen while browsing the map by moving his/her head. The judgment of the user is constrained to be high, medium or low/no changes. This judgment is obviously very subjective but it helps establishing a baseline for comparing the results of different types of tests. We are only interested in the relative change rather than the absolute values of the responses.

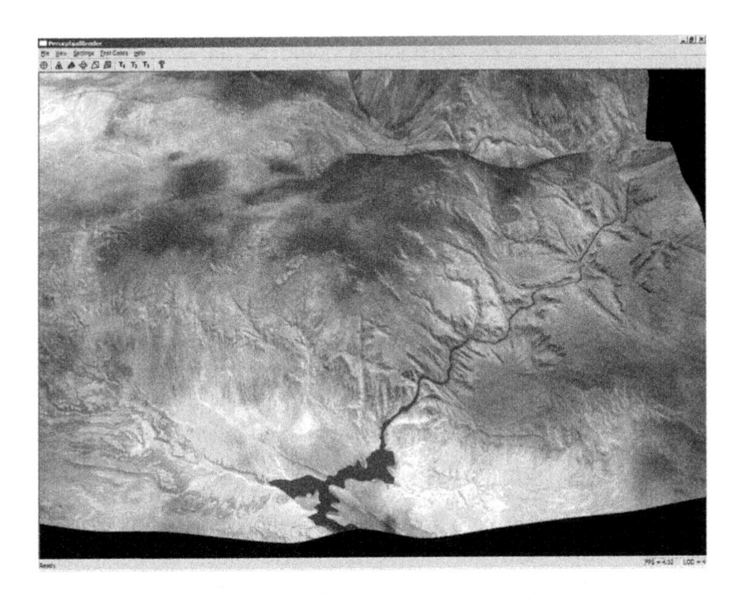

Fig. 5. Terrain view for test case 2

Our experiments were performed using 19 test subjects. Comparisons between different scenarios were performed, tabulating the increase and decrease rate of one test scenario versus the other. Our results are shown in Tables 1-4. In all tables, changes in user's satisfaction across the three scenarios are listed in the first column.

Table 1. Satisfaction comparison between test scenarios across all test cases

All cases	Increase	No Change	Decrease	Total
Fixed vs. None	63.16%	29.82%	7.02%	100.00%
Variable vs. None	26.32%	54.39%	19.30%	100.00%
Variable vs. Fixed	8.77%	33.33%	57.89%	100.00%

Table 2. Satisfaction comparison between test scenarios for test case 1

Case 1	Increase	No Change	Decrease	Total
Fixed vs. None	52.63%	47.37%	0.00%	100.00%
Variable vs. None	21.05%	52.63%	26.32%	100.00%
Variable vs. Fixed	10.53%	21.05%	68.48%	100.00%

Table 3. Satisfaction comparison between test scenarios for test case 2

Case 2	Increase	No Change	Decrease	Total
Fixed vs. None	63.16%	31.58%	5.26%	100.00%
Variable vs. None	21.05%	63.16%	15.79%	100.00%
Variable vs. Fixed	0.00%	42.11%	57.89%	100.00%

In all cases, a change in user's satisfaction could be an increase, no change or a decrease. Table 1 shows the average over all cases, while Tables 2, 3 and 4 show the results for test cases 1, 2 and 3 respectively.

Table 4. Satisfaction comparison between test scenarios for test case 3

Case 3	Increase	No Change	Decrease	Total
Fixed vs. None	73.68%	10.53%	15.79%	100.00%
Variable vs. None	36.84%	47.37%	15.79%	100.00%
Variable vs. Fixed	15.79%	36.84%	47.37%	100.00%

From Table 1, we can see that the use of fixed uncertainty greatly improves performance. In the case of fixed uncertainty, only 7% of the time people perceived worse performance compared to not having uncertainty optimizations enabled. The results for dynamic uncertainty are not as good as those for fixed uncertainty. About 55% of the time people did not notice any differences between using variable uncertainty and not using it. The direct comparison between dynamic and static uncertainty shows that dynamic uncertainty performance is clearly perceived as worse 57% of the time. Similar results can be observed for all test cases as shown in Tables 2-4.

Further analysis of our system's performance revealed that the main reason for the underperformance of the variable uncertainty approach was the jitter in the uncertainty covariance matrix. In particular, the calculation of the covariance matrix was not very stable and its values oscillated. These oscillations made the triangles that lie on the outer edges of the high resolution region to change levels back and forth from one level to the next. Since the human eye has an increased sensitivity to movements on the periphery compared to the center, this effect made the users more aware of changes in the periphery. The main reason for the oscillations was probably our sampling strategy. For the sake of high processing speed, we assumed a uniform distribution over the cloud of points which might not be a valid assumption. Several techniques that can be used to solve this problem including Monte Carlo, Shifted Hammersley, Latin Hypersquare, Equal Probability Sampling and others.

Another important observation was the increase in rendering speed when using the PLOD compared to rendering the same terrain at the highest LOD. The frame rate increased from 5 fps to 15 fps on a Pentium® 4 2.56MHz processor with 1 GB of RAM.

7 Conclusions

We have presented a real-time system that combines a vision module that estimates the user's head pose with a PLOD module that optimizes image rendering based on perceptual parameters. The system was implemented on a fairly modest PC using off the shelf components and it was able to improve the frame rate significantly compared to rendering the same terrain at full resolution. Subject tests were performed to assess the benefits of using uncertainty estimates in conjunction with other parameters. Our results indicated that uncertainty estimates help in making optimizations more seamless to the user. An approach for calculating orientation uncertainty was presented and employed as part of the vision module. However, the jitter in the uncertainty calculations prevented us from achieving the same level of performance compared to using fixed parameters. More details about this work can be found in [23]. Future work includes further investigation of these issues as well as estimating eye-gaze more accurately.

Acknowledgment

This work was supported by NASA under grant #NCC5-583.

References

1. J. H. Clark. "Hierarchical Geometric Models for Visible Surface Algorithms". Communications of the ACM, vol. 17(2), pages 547-554, 1976.
2. T. Oshima, H. Yamamoto, and H. Tamura. "Gaze-Directed Adaptive Rendering for Interacting with Virtual Space". Proceedings of 1996 IEEE Virtual Reality Annual International Symposium, pages 103-110, 1996.
3. David Luebke et al. "Perceptually Driven Simplification Using Gaze-Directed Rendering". University of Virginia Technical Report CS-2000-04.
4. David Luebke et al. Level of Detail for 3D Graphics. Morgan Kaufmann Publishers, 1st ed., 2003.
5. David Luebke. "A Developer's Survey of Polygonal Simplification Algorithms". IEEE Computer Graphics &Applications, May 2001.
6. Stephen Junkins and Allen Hux." Subdividing Reality". Intel Architecture Labs White Paper, 2000.
7. J. Warren and S. Schaefer. "A factored approach to subdivision surfaces". Computer Graphics and Applications, IEEE, pages 74-81, 2004.
8. David H. Eberly. 3D Game Engine Design. Morgan Kaufmann Publishers, 2001.
9. J. L. Mannos and D. J. Sakrison. "The Effects of a Visual Fidelity Criterion on the Encoding of Images". IEEE Transactions on Information Theory, vol. 20(4), pages 525-535, 1974.
10. M. Reddy. "Perceptually Modulated Level of Detail for Virtual Environments". PhD. Thesis. CST-134-97. University of Edinburgh, Edinburgh, Scotland, 1997.
11. Andrew T. Duchowski. "Acuity-Matching Resolution Degradation Through Wavelet Coefficient Scaling". IEEE Transactions in Image Processing, vol. 9(8), pages 1437-1440, August 2000.
12. Wilson S. Geisler and Jeffrey S. Perry, "Real-time Simulation of Arbitrary Visual Fields". ACM Symposium on Eye Tracking Research & Applications, 2002.
13. Jeffrey S. Perry and Wilson S. Geisler. "Gaze-contingent real-time simulation of arbitrary visual fields". Proceedings of SPIE: Human Vision and Electronic Imaging, San Jose, CA, 2002.
14. Qiang Ji and Robert M. Haralick. "Error Propagation for Computer Vision Performance Characterization". International Conference on Imaging Science, Systems, and Technology, Las Vegas, June, 1999.
15. Don Murray and James J. Little. "Patchlets: Representing Stereo Vision Data with Surface Elements". Workshop on the Applications of Computer Vision (WACV), 2005.

16. David A. Forsyth and Jean Ponce. Computer Vision A Modern Approach. Prentice Hall, 1st ed., 2003.
17. Hunter Murphy and Andrew T. Duchowski. "Gaze-Contingent Level Of Detail Rendering". EuroGraphics Conference, September 2001.
18. Nathaniel Williams et al. "Perceptually guided simplification of lit, textured meshes". Proceedings of the 2003 Symposium on Interactive 3D graphics, Monterrey, CA, 2003.
19. K. Arun et al. "Least-squares fitting of two 3-D point sets", IEEE Transactions on Pattern Analysis and Machine Intelligence, vol. 9(5), pages 698-700, 1987.
20. Robyn Owens. Lecture notes, http://homepages.inf.ed.ac.uk/rbf/CVonline/LOCAL_COPIES/OWENS/LECT11/node5.html
21. "VirtualgloveBox", http://biorvis.arc.nasa.gov/vislab/vgx.htm
22. "Effective Human-Computer Interaction in Virtual Environments", http://www.cse.unr.edu/CVL/current_proj.php
23. Javier Martinez, "Rendering Optimizations Guided by Head-Pose Estimates and Their Uncertainty", M.S. Thesis, Dept of Computer Science and Engineering, University of Nevada, Reno, August 2005.

Acceptance of Visual Search Interfaces for the Web - Design and Empirical Evaluation of a Book Search Interface

Olaf Thiele[1] and Gunnar Mau

[1] University of Mannheim, Germany
thiele@uni-mannheim.de

Abstract. Theoretically, visual search interfaces are supposed to outperform list interfaces for such task types as nonspecific queries because they make use of additional semantic information (like price, date or review for a book). But why are web sites like Amazon or eBay still using classical textual list interfaces? Many visual interfaces performed well on objective measures (retrieval time, precision or recall). But subjective factors (ease, joy, usefulness) determining their acceptance in practice are often neglected. Therefore, we created a graphical interface for searching books and evaluated it in a 51 participant study. The study builds on the technology acceptance model which measures users' subjective attitude towards using an interface. We found that the variable enjoyment is of higher relevance in both visual and textual search interfaces than previously stated. Finally, the novel interface yielded significantly better results for book searches than the textual one.

1 Introduction

Is "a picture worth a thousand words"? Blackwell tested this popular proverb and found that a picture is in fact only worth 84.1 words [1]. Like him, existing evaluation research focuses mainly on objective criteria (see [2] for a summary). But even if a visual interface replaces thousands of words, would one want to use or buy it? What subjective factors lead to the acceptance of visual search interfaces once their objective benefits have been shown? This question was evaluated in a user acceptance study. We designed and evaluated a simple graphical interface for searching books at Amazon. The well-tested technology acceptance model served as the theoretical foundation. We extended it to incorporate the factor joy of use because existing studies in adjoining research fields suggested that enjoyment plays a significant role in the acceptance of novel interfaces. We evaluated the extended model in a 51 participant experiment. An eye-tracking study was conducted as a back up for usability testing.

The paper is organized in the following way. The next section presents previous work in the field of acceptance research. Section three introduces the graphical book search interface built for the evaluation study. The fourth section describes the study in detail. The results of the study are reported in section five and are discussed in the subsequent section. The paper concludes with final thoughts in section seven.

G. Bebis et al. (Eds.): ISVC 2005, LNCS 3804, pp. 263–270, 2005.

2 Research on User Acceptance

In this section we present the theoretical model used in the study followed by a description of related studies.

2.1 Theoretical Model

The technology acceptance model (TAM) is the predominant model used for the evaluation of the acceptance of novel technologies. It was developed and initially tested by Fred Davis in 1989 [3]. The model has been extended in numerous evaluation studies over the last 15 years. Venkatesh et al. give a comprehensive summary [4]. The technology acceptance model suggests that the two factors 'perceived ease of use' and 'perceived usefulness' determine the 'intention to use' which in turn influences the actual usage of novel technology. The technology acceptance model is often extended to incorporate supplemental determinants. Several studies added 'perceived enjoyment' to the standardized technology acceptance model ([5], [6], [7]). 'Perceived enjoyment' measures the user's intrinsic motivation as compared to 'perceived usefulness' which taps into the user's extrinsic motivation. Koufaris, for example, emphasizes the importance of a joyful shopping experience, which typically leads to consecutive visits to the shop [6, p. 208]. Liaw and Huang explore the role of joy for using a classical web search engine. Their findings support the influential role of enjoyment for the acceptance of a new technology [7, p. 761].

2.2 Related Research on Acceptance

Even though many applications for information visualization have been developed, only some of them have been evaluated through a user study [8, p. 1594]. Thus, research on user acceptance in information visualization is still in an early stage. Chen and Yu present an overview of existing studies[2]. Only a fraction of the evaluations reviewed by them meets standardized criteria like those used in other scientific disciplines (e.g. psychology) [2, p. 864]. However, some researchers already apply subjective measurements to accompany objective results. Kobsa, for example, measured user satisfaction in a study comparing five tree visualization techniques to the built-in Windows Explorer [9]. While Kobsa's findings indicate that at least one of the visualization techniques is equivalent to the existent interface [9, p. 4], it remains unclear which interface users would choose. In addition to the factor ease of use as measured by Kobsa, our study measures both extrinsic and intrinsic motivation.

3 Book Search Interface

Following some background information in the next section, we describe both the textual baseline interface as well as the visual search interface.

3.1 Background Information

In a recent study, Hotchkiss et al. describe the search process as a series of query refinements [10, p. 5]. Users type only few words without using logical operators (e.g. and, or). If they cannot find the desired information on the first page, they usually refine their search by entering more specific terms found in the first result set [11, p. 20]. To ease this tedious process, White et al. propose to display more information about the contents of the result pages [12]. Their findings support our perception, that users like looking at a whole set of search results (20-30) to evaluate their search instead of seeing only few results as it is typical for today's search engines [12, p. 227]. Kim backs these findings in her cognitive study on information seeking characteristics on the web [13]. Her results also suggest that nonlinear navigation between search results (in contrast to checking results in order) is beneficial to the whole search process [13, p. 337]. Present search interfaces inhibit nonlinear navigation through the presentation of search results in a vertical list. Interconnections between search results as in our visual interface could facilitate finding the best results.

3.2 The Baseline Interface

Two interfaces were built for the study. The first is the baseline application which emulates the core functionality of the Amazon web page omitting side information. It presents search results in the same manner as the original Amazon web site. The interface is structured in the following way. The list that contains the search results is placed in the left half of the screen. In case one of the books is clicked on (either title or image), supplemental information on the book is given in the right half of the screen. The information presented corresponds to the data presented on the original Amazon web page. Besides selecting book information from the first result set, users can click on the appropriate option to view the next or previous twenty results. Users may also add items to the shopping basket. Its functionality is similar to that provided by the Amazon web site.

3.3 The Visual Book Search Interface

The book search visualization is a graphical interface built with web technology. It offers interaction features for exploring the underlying data. Figure 1 shows a sample screenshot with the cursor centered on a specific book after searching for linux related books. Similar to the textual interface, the right half of the screen shows the selected book. The information included is identical to that of the textual baseline interface. Generally, each book of the result set is represented by a book icon. Each graph is comprised of twenty individual book icons. They are organized in a scatter plot format. In the visualization shown in figure 1 the most recent books are placed on top while the oldest books are arranged towards the bottom of the image. The cheapest books are placed to the left side while the most expensive ones can be found on the right side. Arranging

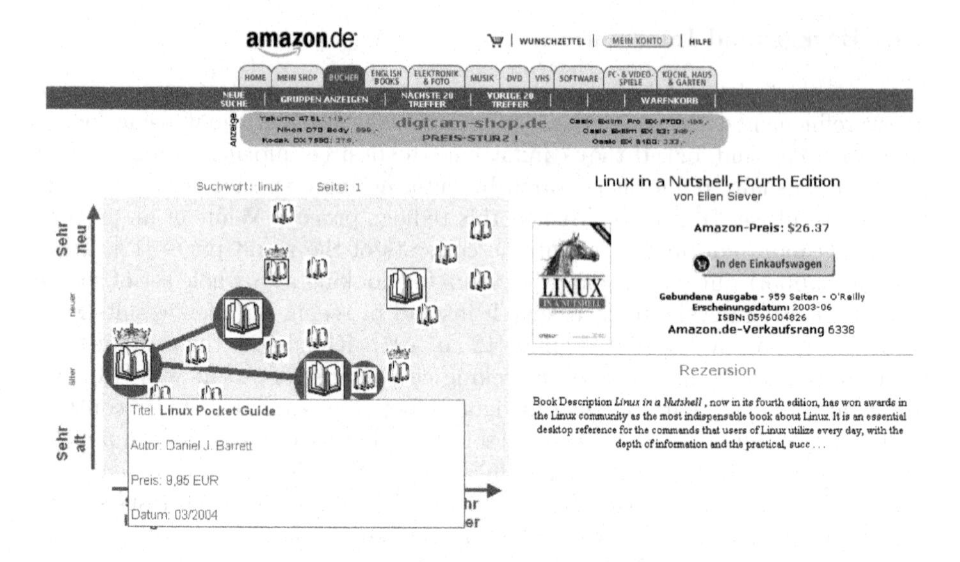

Fig. 1. Screenshot of the visual interface

data according to their relation has been widely used in other visual retrieval applications for the web. Kobayashi and Takeda offer a good overview of existing applications [14, p. 158]. The visual book interface represents a compromise between the magnitude of visualization techniques and the level of abstraction plausible for commercial web sites. Mukherjea emphasizes that abstraction is one of the key factors to be considered for acceptance of novel visual interfaces [15, p. 2]. Other semantic information shown in the graph: larger icon size represents customer reviews and axes may characterize price, date of publication, customer review, alphabetical order by author or average price per page. Furthermore, similar books are connected through lines once a book is selected. Huang gives a thorough explanation of the underlying principles [16]. In addition to these static features, the visualization offers an interactive element to facilitate browsing the search results. If the mouse cursor is placed over a book, detailed information about the book is displayed in a tool tip like manner. Weinreich and Lamersdorf introduced a similar feature to regular web browsing called Hyperscout [17].

4 Experimental Evaluation

Both interfaces were evaluated in an experiment. Subjective measures were derived from the technology acceptance model, objective results stem from the eye-tracking study.

4.1 Hypotheses

Following our line of thought presented in the preceding sections, we formulated two hypotheses: **H1** - The technology acceptance applies to the novel visual book search interface. **H2** - The new variable 'perceived enjoyment' functions as a mediator between 'perceived ease of use' and 'perceived usefulness'. The hypotheses were derived from the research presented in section two. Naturally, the technology acceptance model should prove as practical for visual information retrieval as it did for textual applications. Backed by other studies on intrinsic motivation, we believe that the influence of enjoyment is currently underrated.

4.2 Procedure

The experiment comprised 51 participants in an eye-tracking laboratory. The average participant was 25.4 years old. 31 female and 20 male test persons took part in the evaluation. 91% of the participants stated that their internet usage was high or very high. Moreover, 86% of them declared to query search engines frequently or very frequently. The design of the experiment includes one independent variable: 'interface'. This yielded two design categories: either first the textual and then the graphical interface or the other way around. The participants were randomly assigned to one of the two categories. First, the participants were briefly introduced to the experiment. Each test person was asked to solve two scenarios. Participants were shown a three minute introductory video with accompanying live demonstration. The video was meant to emulate experience with the search engine through presentation of standardized search queries. Test persons were then able to explore the respective interface alone for five minutes. Afterwards, the search task was explained to the test persons who then started to work on the task. Finally, participants were presented a questionnaire after each task and were asked to answer it.

5 Results

The presentation of the results is divided into the subjective results which evaluate the technology acceptance model and the results from the back up eye-tracking study.

5.1 Subjective Results

A questionnaire was used as the subjective measure for the study. It comprised items concerning perceived ease of use, perceived usefulness, enjoyment of use and intention to use. The items were derived from the acceptance studies presented in section two. The two hypotheses were tested for mediating effects using the analysis proposed by Baron and Kenny [18]. As for hypothesis H1, the results showed that all correlations were highly significant ($p < .001$). It can be stated that there exists a strong influence of both ease and usefulness on the intention to use. It is therefore reasonable to say that ease has an influence on both usefulness and intention to use. Furthermore usefulness is the key determinant of the intention to use. Hence, hypothesis H1 could be confirmed. While the hypothesis holds true for the graphical interface, results for the textual interface are different. The correlations indicate a much smaller influence on the intention to use. The succeeding regression analysis yielded no significant influence of the ease of use on the usefulness. It is plausible to state that the technology acceptance model does not explain the well-known textual interface. The results for the bivariate correlation of H2 are similar to those for hypothesis H1. Results for the graphical interface indicate once more high effect values and they are highly significant ($p < .001$). It can be stated that perceived enjoyment serves as a mediator between the factors ease of use and usefulness. Hypothesis H2 can be accepted for the graphical interface. Matching the preceding results for the textual interface, enjoyment does not serve as a mediator for the familiar textual interface. Both joy and ease of use have a strong influence on the usefulness of an application.

Finally, a regression analysis containing all major factors yielded overall results. To sum up, usefulness is the key determinant for the intention to use with respect to the graphical interface. In contrast, enjoyment has the strongest influence on usage of the textual interface. The most relevant results of this study, the differences of influence in both interfaces, are depicted in figure 2. A more detailed description of procedures and results can be found in [19].

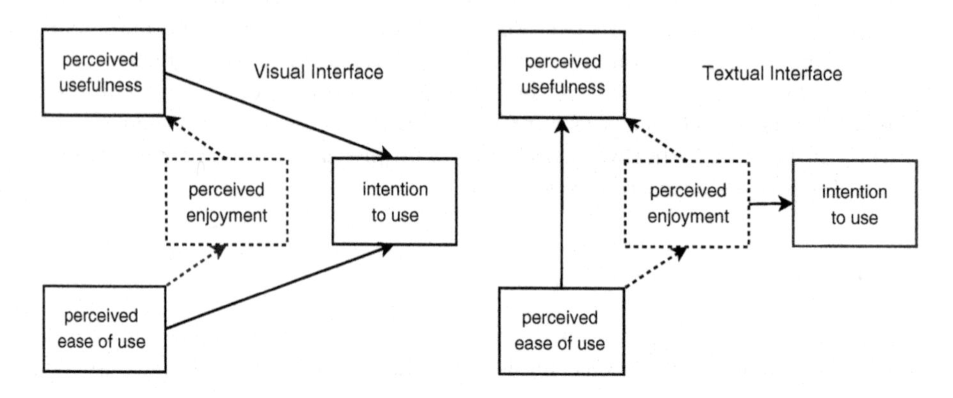

Fig. 2. Technology acceptance model for both interfaces (arrows = directed influences)

5.2 Objective Results

The objective results were derived from descriptive statistics in the eye-tracking back up study. In short, participants had to look at roughly 50 areas less to solve the task visually. Exemplary, navigational elements were looked at 8 times and 4.3 seconds using the visual interface and 9.3 times and 6.6 seconds using the textual interface. Less navigational elements need to be checked to complete the given task visually. Furthermore, the overall completion time was significantly smaller when the visual interface was used. The mean values are 3.21 minutes for the visual interface and 3.99 minutes for the textual interface (graphical sd 1.94, textual one 2.41). Both results are significant ($p < .05$). Using the visual interface, participants solved a task almost 50 seconds faster.

6 Discussion

This study has shown that the technology acceptance model can be applied to the novel user interface presented in this study. Since our findings are in line with many other studies that confirm the technology acceptance model, we argue that it would work for other visual information retrieval interfaces as well. In addition, we have shown that enjoyment is a very important factor for the acceptance of the visual and textual interface. The fact that the model cannot explain the textual interface is also congruent with the theory as it is meant to explain new technologies instead of existing ones. Interestingly, enjoyment is the sole variable that determines the intention to use existing textual interfaces. This might explain the popularity of Google because the search engine may look and feel more fun than others. This is supported by the fact that usefulness has had no direct effect on the intention to use. This does not imply that Google is useless, it states that other search engines (Yahoo, MSN) are equally good. It should also be mentioned that the sample consisted of 90% university students. It remains unclear whether a less educated sample would have produced similar results. In contrast, the typical internet user has an above-average education. The main focus of this study lay on the evaluation of acceptance of novel visual interfaces. However, we collected subjective data on how users rated the two interfaces as well. In short, participants thought that the textual interface is easier to use and in their perception leads to results in less time (objective results above show the opposite). The visual interface, on the other hand, is more enjoyable, more exciting and participants felt to be more in control. Eventually, participants liked the visual interface better than the textual one when asked for an overall assessment.

7 Conclusion

Joy is one of the most important factors for both novel and existing search interfaces. Novel interfaces are perceived as being more useful when they are enjoying. And existing interfaces are differentiated only through their perceived enjoyment. Therefore, we conclude that information visualization evaluations containing items on ease of use, usefulness and enjoyment will yield valid estimates on the acceptance of a novel visual search interface.

References

1. Blackwell, A.F.: Correction: A picture is worth 84.1 words. In: Proceedings of the First ESP Student Workshop. (1997) 15–22
2. Chen, C., Yu, Y.: Empirical studies of information visualization: a meta-analysis. Int. J. Hum.-Comput. Stud. **53** (2000) 851–866
3. Davis, F.: Perceived Usefulness, Perceived Ease of Use, and User Acceptance of Information Technology. MIS Quaterly, Vol. 13 (1989) 319 – 339
4. Venkatesh, V., Morris, M., Davis, G., Davis, F.: User acceptance of information technology: Toward a unified view. MIS Quarterly **27** (2003) 425 – 478

5. Davis, F.D., Bagozzi, R.P., Warshaw, P.R.: Extrinsic and intrinsic motivation to use computers in the workplace. Journal of Applied Social Psychology **22** (1992) 1111 - 1132
6. Koufaris, M.: Applying the technology acceptance model and flow theory to online consumer behavior. Info. Sys. Research **13** (2002) 205–223
7. Liaw, S.S., Huang, H.M.: An investigation of user attitudes toward search engines as an information retrieval tool. Computers in Human Behavior **19** (2003) 751–765
8. Belkin, N., Dumais, S., Scholtz, J., Wilkinson, R.: Evaluating interactive information retrieval systems: opportunities and challenges. In: CHI '04 extended abstracts on Human factors in computing systems, New York, ACM Press (2004) 1594–1595
9. Kobsa, A.: User experiments with tree visualization systems. In: INFOVIS '04: Proceedings of the IEEE Symposium on Information Visualization (INFOVIS'04), Washington, DC, USA, IEEE Computer Society (2004) 9–16
10. Enquiro: Search Engine Usage in North America. available online: http://www.enquiro.com/Downloads/ (2004)
11. Enquiro: Inside the Mind of the Searcher. available online: http://www. enquiro.com/Downloads/ (2004)
12. White, R.W., Jose, J.M., Ruthven, I.: A granular approach to web search result presentation. In Rauterberg, G.M., Menozzi, M., Wesson, J., eds.: Proceedings of the 9th IFIP TC13 Int. Conf. on HCI. Interact 2003., ISO Press (2003) 213–220
13. Kim, K.S.: Implications of user characteristics in information seeking on the world wide web. Int. J. Hum. Comput. Interaction **13** (2001) 323–340
14. Kobayashi, M., Takeda, K.: Information retrieval on the web. ACM Comput. Surv. **32** (2000) 144–173
15. Mukherjea, S.: Information visualization for hypermedia systems. ACM Comput. Surv. **31** (1999) 6
16. Huang, M.L.: Information visualization of attributed relational data. In: CRPITS '01: Australian symposium on Information visualisation, ACS (2001) 143–149
17. Weinreich, H., Lamersdorf, W.: Concepts for improved visualization of web link attributes. In: Proceedings of the 9th international World Wide Web conference on Computer networks, Amsterdam (2000) 403–416
18. Baron, R.M., Kenny, D.A.: The moderator-mediator variable distinction in social psychological research: Conceptual, strategic, and statistical considerations. Journal of Pe nality and Social Psychology **51** (1986) 1173–1182
19. Thiele, O., Mau, G.: Acceptance of visual search interfaces for the Web - Working paper. available online: http://www.olafthiele.de (2005)

Distributed and Collaborative Biomedical Data Exploration

Zhiyu He, Jason Kimball, and Falko Kuester

Calit2 Center of GRAVITY, University of California, Irvine
{zhe, jkimball, fkuester}@uci.edu

Abstract. Imaging techniques such as MRI, fMRI, CT and PET have provided physicians and researchers with a means to acquire high-quality biomedical images as the foundation for the diagnosis and treatment of diseases. Unfortunately, access to domain experts at the same physical location is not always possible and new tools and techniques are required to facilitate simultaneous and collaborative exploration of data between spatially separated experts. This paper presents a framework for collaborative visualization of biomedical data-sets, supporting heterogeneous computational platforms and network configurations. The system provides the user with data visualization, annotation and the middleware to exchange the resulting visuals between all participants, in real-time. A resulting 2D visual provides a user specifiable high-resolution image slice, while a resulting 3D visual provides insight into the entire data set. To address the costly rendering of large-scale volumetric data, the visualization engine can distribute tasks over multiple render nodes.

1 Introduction

The pervasive nature of imaging techniques such as MRI, fMRI, CT, OCT and PET has provided doctors in many different disciplines with a means to acquire high-resolution biomedical images. These data can serve as the foundation for the diagnosis and treatment of diseases. However, experts with a multitude of backgrounds, including radiologists, surgeons, and anatomists now contribute to the thorough analysis of the available data and collaborate on the diagnosis and development of a treatment plan. Unfortunately, access to these specialists at the same physical location is not always possible and new tools and techniques are required to facilitate simultaneous and collaborative exploration of volumetric data between spatially separated domain experts.

A distributed visualization environment for the collaborative analysis of biomedical data is presented, which allows researchers to virtually collaborate from any place with basic network support. All users have access to a HybridReality framework, which offers co-located 2D and 3D views of the volumetric data and enables collaborative information exchange via sketching and annotation. The HybridReality framework was designed with focus on the visualization of volume data-sets, supporting (i) heterogeneous computational platforms, ranging from high-end graphics workstations to low performance Tablet-

G. Bebis et al. (Eds.): ISVC 2005, LNCS 3804, pp. 271–278, 2005.

PCs and (ii) heterogeneous network configurations ranging from wireless networks to dedicated gigabit links. It was designed such that users can customize the middleware needed for the real-time exchange of the resulting visuals.

Both 2D and 3D visualization techniques contribute in different ways to obtain a better understanding of the data-set. Preim and Peitgen [1] stated that while 3D representations are more useful as overview, 2D visualizations enable more accurate interaction. In addition, 3D representations are useful to determine the position and orientations of the 2D slices while 2D slices are good to reduce occlusions [2]. A hybrid visualization approach was therefore selected for the targeted biomedical data, which combines 2D and 3D visuals. The 2D view currently provides a user specifiable high-resolution image slice, while the 3D view provides a volume rendered visual of the entire data set. Users can augment information onto the 2D and 3D rendered visuals using digital ink and share this information in real-time between multiple networked render nodes. Digital ink may simply consist of individual pixels, strokes, or interpreted geometric information.

2 Related Works

One possible approach towards starting a collaborative session between multiple users is to use remote desktop connections, enabling desktop contents to be shared with some support for user interaction. A broadly used example is VNC [3]. One limitation of VNC is that only one user can interact with an application at any given point time, constraining concurrent interactions with the provided

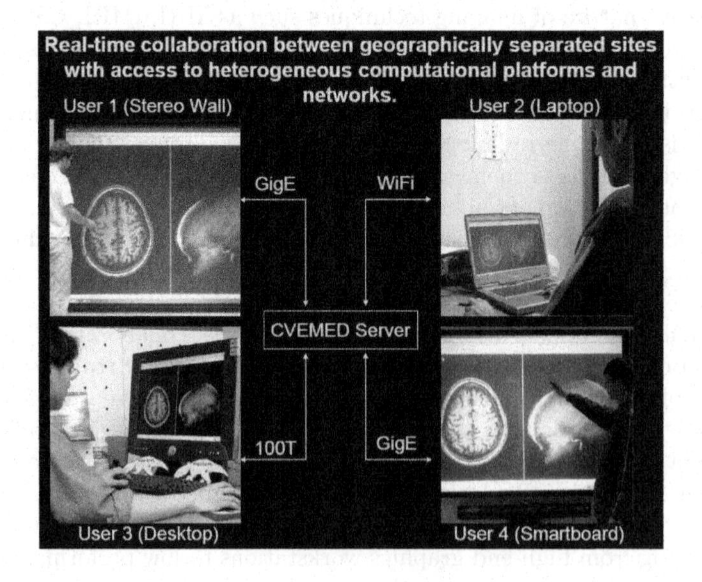

Fig. 1. The collaborative environment

data. This effectively undermines the ability for multiple users to simultaneously contribute to data analysis, modeling and interpretation.

Another example for collaborative visualization is given by Jern et al. [4], who introduced a lightweight application that is distributed as a plug-in and enables collaboration between multiple nodes. While the application is peer-to-peer, only one of the connected users is identified as an "active member", and can interact and change attribute and viewing parameters. The application uses DirectPlay to manage connection sessions and thereby is limited to Windows platforms.

Pang et al. [5], devised a shared-control visualization system based on the previous work of Spray. The improved CSpray system provides the user with particle primitives, used to highlight areas of interest in volumetric data. However, the user can not control the rendering parameters used for the creation of the final volumetric image, and interaction is restricted to data annotation.

Anupam et al. [6], introduced Shastra, a system supporting distributed graphics workstations for the rendering of large data set. Shastra enables the distribution of volume data in both object space and image space, providing near-linear speed-up for selected rendering tasks. Collaborative work is supported via a session manager that controls all of the participating nodes.

3 System Architecture

The system architecture focuses on separating the research and development paths for collaboration and visualization algorithms, middleware and tools. An important consideration was the design of a plug-in capable harness that can support user specific visualization algorithm and communication layers without affecting other framework components. The architecture is shown in Figure 2a, and consists of a set of discrete layers, including (1) an application layer, (2) a collaborative middleware layer and (3) a distributed rendering layer. The application layer serves as the foundation for the development of algorithms, tools and interfaces for distributed 2D/3D visuals and hides the middleware and rendering system from the user. The Collaborative Middleware Layer is built on TCP/IP for communications between instances of the client applications. Clients are connected through a communication server, responsible for synchronization and session management, including management of session logs that allow users to join and exit collaborative sessions at any point in time.

Based on the quality of the computational platforms and graphics pipes, rendering of large-scale volumetric data may be a very costly operation. To address this, render algorithms and middleware have to be able to adapt to quality of service requirements such as image quality and frame rates. Given a particular constraint, the system may select to render at one central location or to distribute the task over multiple render nodes, ie. a render farm. The Distributed Rendering System Layer is used to distribute the rendering tasks across attached rendering nodes and to composite the final visual. In order to support multiple users that simultaneously can interact with shared data, a client-server model is

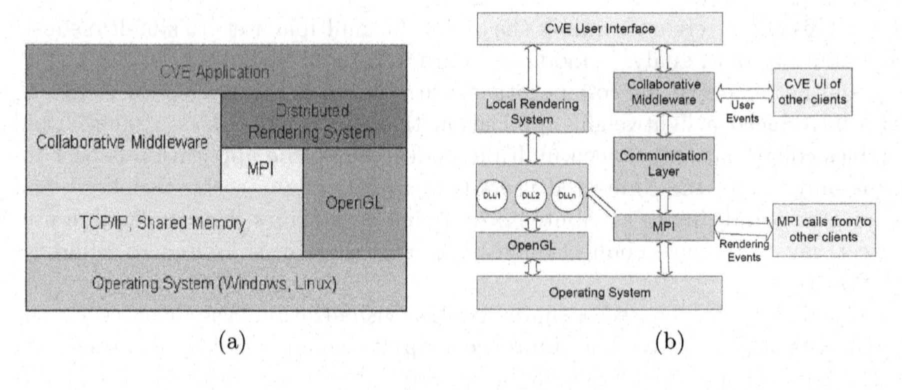

Fig. 2. (a) System architecture and (b) system framework

supported that uses a synchronization server, responsible for managing system wide data consistency and the processing and dissemination of user events as well as the shared visual contents. The server may select to distribute rendering tasks to client nodes and to function as a compositing node, to allow the real-time processing of larger datasets. As illustrated in Figure 2b2, data can be broken up and distributed among the rendering nodes. Each rendering node loads the provided rendering algorithm as a dynamically linked library (late binding), generates an image tile and returns it to the server where the resulting image tiles are gathered and combined into the final image.

This architecture facilitates the development of new visualization algorithm and communication software that can be easily integrated without affecting other layers. 2D/3D visuals, tools and interfaces that interact with the middleware and the rendering system layer are entirely built in the application layer. The independent nature of these layers provides a software test and development path to determine bottlenecks in the system. To provide portability and ease-of-use for all user interface related tasks we selected wxWindows, a portable windowing system which is readily supported on the most common operating systems.

3.1 Collaborative Middleware

Collaboration may have various definitions [7] and we define collaboration as a state in which multiple users are interacting upon one data-set. The collaboration (or collaborative) environment is designed such that all interactions can be synchronized in real-time, while guaranteeing data consistency. The system is designed with a centralized approach towards control, meaning that any one of the clients can be designated as the servant (server) of the session. This servant will receive events coming from all the clients within a session, handle events locally where appropriate, and then broadcast the results to the other connected clients. The advantage of this approach is inherent consistency of data. Event processing order is defined only by one central user, ensuring that modifications take place in the same order for all clients. More importantly, all transactions are tracked and logged, allowing proper state management as clients enter or leave a running session.

3.2 Data Transmission

The process of transmitting data is implemented in a server/client mode. Because of its distributed environment, the program adapts to a heterogeneous networking framework by compressing the image data that is transmitted among participating users. Besides image data, the sketching and annotation data is another source of data flow. Only a small region of the image will be affected during sketching. Therefore, the delay of sending the whole sketched image will be a huge overhead. There are two different strategies to solve this problem, either sending less information through the network or giving an immediate visual feedback to users currently sketching before receiving an answer from the servant of the current session. The second approach adds remarkable complexity to the application because it is difficult to ensure that events are shown in the same order that they are generated and it may be necessary to redraw the output at a connected user side because other users have done modifications before the changes introduced locally by another user. The first approach lacks of this complexity drawback because changes are sent to the servant of the collaborative session and only this node is responsible to decide the order that these changes are applied. A vector and color information is enough to define a stroke. Sending only this stroke information introduces less delay than sending the whole image and also make it easier to maintain the same stroke thickness even after the scaling of the image across different display devices.

4 Rendering System

The rendering system consists of a collection of distributed render nodes, residing on the desktop of participating users or being part of a designated render cluster. Based on the task at hand and desired interaction mode, users may select a stand-alone render mode, which utilizes only local graphics capabilities or a shared mode which uses the render cluster to generate and composite the final visual. Regardless of the mode selected, users can provide custom renderers via a run-time plug-in systems that allows algorithms used for image generation to be swapped on the fly. With the existing middleware layer it is possible to disseminate the results to all other users, as soon as the generated visual is available.

4.1 Collaborative Rendering

Network-centric applications are generally subject to network latency, jitter and data consistency constraints [8, 9]. Within the presented context, collaboration means real-time update of the data at all the connected sites, and therefore the need for minimized delays and data consistency, requiring a reliable control (see

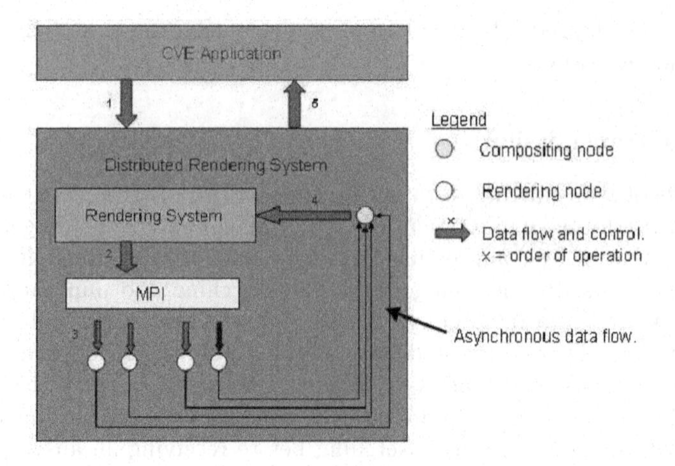

Fig. 3. Data flow in the system pipeline

section 3.1) and a rendering mechanism. The rendering system supports two modes of rendering, (1) local and (2) distributed. In both rendering modes, the rendering system is broken down into one or more compositing nodes and at least one rendering node.

For the local mode, visualization parameters are shared between all clients with each client node rendering its own final visual. This approach requires replication of the entire dataset on all clients and the renderer will only utilizes local system resources to store and process the volumetric data set. The performance of each node is therefore constrained by its own locally available resources, which may introduce quality-of-service variations, such as rendering speeds and accuracy, among the different nodes.

In the distributed mode, each client node renders a portion of the target dataset (volume). These individual image tiles are subsequently distributed between the participating nodes and composited into one final visual. Alternatively, a client node can connect to a pre-configured rendering farm that distributes the rendering task, composites a final visual and returns it to the client node via an MPI harness. One pass of the rendering system's pipeline(Figure 3) involves an inter-process signal from the compositor to the rendering nodes informing them to render their respective slabs. Each rendering node sends its result back to the compositor where they are uncompressed and composited for the final image.

4.2 Custom Renderers

The visualization of volume data is based on plug-ins (DLLs), which allows visualization algorithms to be changed at run-time to address different visualization objectives across different clients in the system. Two more commonly used render plug-ins for the target biomedical applications include back-to-front compositing and bump-mapping. The back-to-front module implements a hardware acceler-

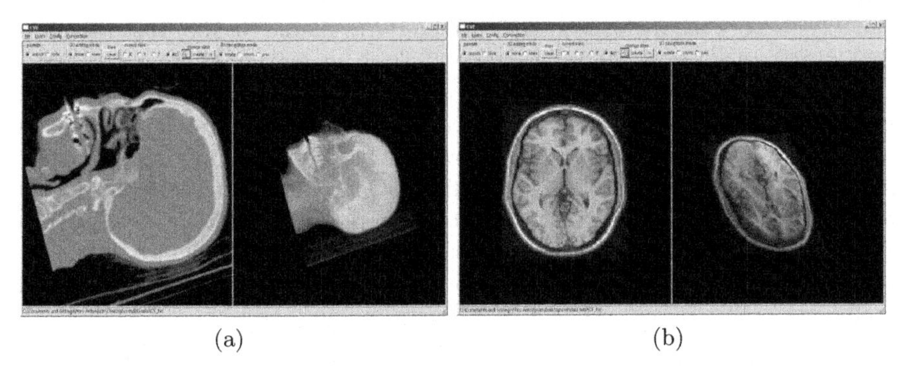

(a) (b)

Fig. 4. (a) The back-to-front rendering module and (b) the bumpmap module

ated volume rendering algorithm (Figure 4a). The volume data is converted into a 3D texture and a user defined number of slices is used to determine the number of textured quads to be drawn. Using the well known back-to-front volume rendering algorithm, the quads are drawn farthest first and the corresponding color and alpha values are adjusted by a user definable multi-dimensional transfer and opacity function. Finally, the framebuffer is read and used by the compositor to compose the final image. The bumpmap rendering module combines multiple imaging modalities by implementing a hardware accelerated bumpmap algorithm (Figure 4b). A 2D structural brain image(MRI) is used as the basemap and a 2D functional image(PET) is rendered as the heightmap. A color-mapped statistical image(z-map) is added as the third dimension and is overlayed on the basemap with adjustable transparency. All 3 images are pre-registered. This module visualizes multiple 2D imaging modalities in a 3D view and can be used in a stand-alone renderer with moderate hardware configurations.

5 Results

Tests were conducted on multiple computational platforms (Pentium4, Xeon) equipped with nVIDIA FX1000 and ATI Radeon 9700PRO graphics cards. The

Test Data Size	Time used to send	Time of receiving last package
22KBytes package, total 100 package = 2MB	8200ms	8514ms
103KBytes package, 1000 package, total size=100MB	103791ms	104086ms
103KBytes package, 1000 package, total size=100MB	35831ms	35914ms

(a)

	Image 1 (value 120/255)	Image 2 (value 185/255)
Voxels	6943	4282
512x512 window 1 rendering node	4.11 fps	4.19 fps
512x512 window 2 rendering nodes	7.65 fps	7.68 fps
256x256 window 1 rendering node	13.39 fps	13.42 fps
256x256 window 2 rendering node	25.44 fps	26.12 fps

(b)

Fig. 5. (a) Network performance and (b) distributed rendering results

available network bandwidth varied based on the available 10/100/1000 as well as 802.11b networks. Both image production as well as dedicated research network infrastructure was evaluated. Tests between the Brain Imaging Center (BIC) at UCI and the National Center for Microscopy and Imaging Research (NCMIR) at UCSD demonstrated the need for adaptive and progressive rendering algorithms that are capable to observe user specifiable QoS constraints. The results for the distributed test(Figure 5a) illustrate that real-time collaborative work is practical and distributed rendering greatly improves the performance. Figure 5b presents the results of the major image operations involved. The networking test result shows the tests of users collaboratively drawing strokes.

6 Conclusions

The paper introduces a distributed collaborative visualization framework, enhancing the distributed and collaborative visualization and analysis of biomedical data over commodity networks. The presented framework supports dynamic rendering plug-ins that may be used to implement, test and use various rendering techniques. Its flexible architecture enables it application to a wide range of hardware settings, from high-end graphics workstation with gigabit network to low-end laptops on wireless networks. The current work focuses on the overall architecture and integration of rendering and communication techniques.

References

1. Preim, B., Peitgen, H.O.: Smart 3d visualizations in clinical applications. In: Smart Graphics. (2003) 79–90
2. Tory, M.: Mental registration of 2d and 3d visualizations). In: Proceedings IEEE Visualization'03. (2003) 371–378
3. Richardson, T., Stafford-Fraser, Q., Wood, K.R., Hopper, A.: Virtual network computing. IEEE Internet Computing **2** (1998) 33–38
4. Jern, M., Palmberg, S., Ranlöf, M.: A robust and easy approach to collaborative visualization. In: International Conference on Information Visualisation IV 2002, IEEE Computer Society (2002) 281–289
5. Pang, A., Wittenbrink, C.M., Goodman, T.: Cspray: A collaborative scientific visualization application. In: Multimedia and Networking'95, SPIE (1995)
6. Anupam, V., Bajaj, C., Schikore, D., Schikore, M.: Distributed and collaborative visualization. Computer **27** (1994) 37–43
7. Wood, J., Wright, H., Brodlie, K.: Collaborative visualization. In: Proceedings of IEEE Visualization'97, IEEE Computer Society Press (1997) 253–260.
8. Kim, S.J., Kuester, F., Kim, K.: A global timestamp-based approach for enhanced data consistency and fairness in collaborative virtua. ACM/Springer Multimedia Systems Journal **10** (2005) 220–229
9. Strom, R., Banavar, G., Miller, K., Ward, M., Prakash, A.: Concurrency control and view notification algorithms for collaborative replicated objects. IEEE Transactions on Computing **47** (1998) 458–471
10. Banavar, G., Doddapaneni, S., Miller, K., Mukherjee, B.: Rapidly building synchronous collaborative applications by direct manipulation. In: ACM Conference on Computer supported Cooperative Work, ACM Press (1998) 139–148

Image Database Navigation: A Globe-Al Approach

Gerald Schaefer and Simon Ruszala

School of Computing and Informatics,
Nottingham Trent University, Nottingham, United Kingdom
gerald.schaefer@ntu.ac.uk

Abstract. Image database visualisation and navigation tools become increasingly important as image collections keep ever growing. Demanded are easily navigable and intuitive ways of displaying and browsing image databases allowing the user to view images from a collection that facilitates finding images of interest. In this paper we introduce a way of viewing a complete collection of images by projecting them onto a spherical globe for colour-based image database navigation. Taking median hue and brightness of images, features that are useful also for image retrieval purposes, and using these as a set of co-ordinates which then determine the location on the surface of the globe where the image is projected. Navigation is performed by rotation (e.g. choosing a different hue range) and zooming into areas of interest.

Keywords: image database navigation, image database visualisation, content-based image retrieval.

1 Introduction

Due to the large increase in use of digital capturing equipment for both personal and professional use, there is currently a large demand for ways of storing and exploring these image databases. With the size of collections ranging from the average home user owning around 1,000 images to companies with databases in excess of 1,000,000 images, efficient and effective ways of locating and searching for desired images are in high demand. Presently most tools display images in a 1-dimensional linear format where only a limited number of thumbnail images are visible on screen at any one time, thus requiring the user to search back and forth through pages of thumbnails to view all images. Obviously, this is a very time consuming, impractical and exhaustive way of searching images, especially in larger catalogues. Furthermore, the order in which the pictures are displayed does not reflect the actual image contents and hence cannot be used to speed up the search.

Some approaches which provide a more intuitive interface for image database navigation were recently introduced. Often the images are projected onto a 2-dimensional plane represented typically by the screen. Using multidimensional scaling, images can be arranged on screen in such a way that images that are

G. Bebis et al. (Eds.): ISVC 2005, LNCS 3804, pp. 279–286, 2005.

visually close to each other are also located close to each other on the display [4] hence providing an easy way for the user to zoom into an area of interest. Other methods incorporate the application of virtual reality ideas and equipment to provide the user with an interactive browsing experience [3].

In this paper we present a simple and fast approach to image database navigation. All images are projected onto a spherical globe; navigation through the image collection is performed by rotation of the sphere and zooming in and out. The use of a spherical object is not a coincidence, rather it stems directly from the type of features that are used for navigation. We utilise the median hue and median brightness (in HSV colour space) to calculate a pair of co-ordinates for each image in the database. As hue describes a circular quantity ($0° = 360°$) whereas brightness is not, a sphere seems a natural choice of geometrical body to encapsulate the combination of these two.

The rest of the paper is organised as follows: Section 2 describes some related work in the area of image database visualisation and navigation. Our proposed method is introduced in Section 3 whereas Section 4 describes how this system is used for database navigation. Section 5 concludes the paper.

2 Related Work

In here we briefly describe two previous methods for image database navigation: multi-dimensional scaling and MARS 3D. A more detailed review which also includes other approaches is given in [5].

2.1 Multidimensional Scaling

Rubner *et al.* were one of the first to suggest more intuitive interfaces for image database navigation [4]. They suggested the application of multidimensional scaling (MDS) [2] to calculate the locations of images and displaying them in a global 2-dimensional view on a single screen. Using this method all images in a database are (initially) shown simultaneously; their locations are dependent on their visual similarity (based on features such as colour, texture or shape descriptors) compared to all other images features in the database. If two images are very similar in content they will also be located close to each other on the screen and vice versa. The user can browse the database easily from a top-down hierarchical point of view in an intuitive way.

The main disadvantage of the MDS approach is its computational complexity. First a full distance matrix for the complete database, i.e. all pairwise distances between any two images in the collection, need to be calculated. MDS itself is then an iterative process which constantly rearranges the locations of each image minimising the (Euclidean) distances between images on screen and their actual (feature-based) database distances. Interactive visualisation of a large number of images is hence difficult if not impossible to achieve. Furthermore, adding images to the database requires re-computation of (part of) the distance matrix and rerunning MDS.

2.2 3D MARS and ImageGrouper

3D MARS [3] represents a virtual reality (VR) approach to image database navigation. Images are displayed on four walls in an immersive CAVE where browsing the database is done using a special wand to select images and make queries. While being an interesting novel idea it requires very specialist equipment not available for the average user wanting to explore their personal collections.

Although there exists also a desktop version called ImageGrouper which can be used with ordinary CRT displays, using this program is fairly difficult as there is no option for global browsing; only searching for an image first and then browsing from that location in the database is possible.

3 Visualisation on a Hue-Based Globe

Our aim is to provide a simple yet effective interface for image database visualisation and navigation. It should allow fast and intuitive browsing of large image collections and not rely on any specialised equipment not available to the average user.

We separate our approach into two tasks: selection of suitable features and visualisation of the image collection. Among typical features used for image retrieval those describing the colour content are certainly the most popular ones [8]. We follow this and describe each image by its median colour. However rather than employing the standard RGB colour space we use the HSV space [6]. Of this we take only the hue and value attributes as the saturation descriptor is deemed less important for describing image content. Value, which describes the brightness of a colour is defined in HSV as [6]

$$V = \frac{R+G+B}{3} \tag{1}$$

where R, G, and B are red, green and blue pixel values. V ranges between 0 and 1 where 0 corresponds to pure black and 1 to pure white. Hue "*is the attribute of a visual sensation according to which an area appears to be similar to one of the perceived colours, red, yellow, green and blue, or a combination of two of them*" [1] and is the attribute that is usually associated as 'colour'. Hue in HSV is defined as [6]

$$H = \cos^{-1} \frac{0.5[(R-G)+(R-B)]}{\sqrt{(R-G)(R-G)+(R-B)(G-B)}} \tag{2}$$

It is apparent that hue constitutes an angular attribute; H goes from red to yellow to green to blue back to red and is also often referred to as hue circle.

We now want to find a geometrical body that can be used to derive a coordinate system for placing thumbnails of the images contained in a database as well as to serve as the actual surface onto which those thumbnails are projected. Looking at the two attributes we have selected, H and V, we almost naturally end up with the body of a sphere, or a spherical globe. The hue circle describes

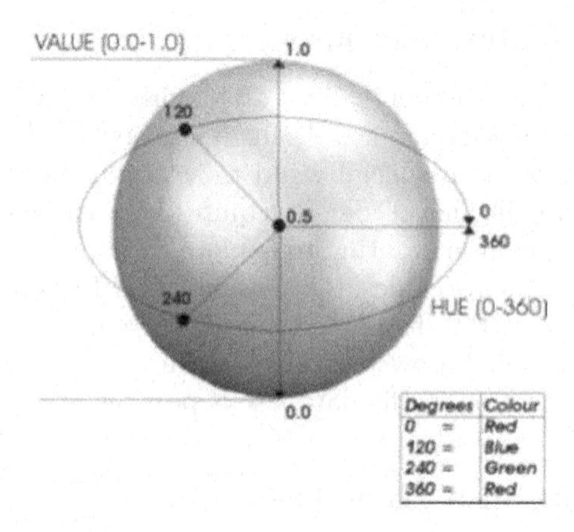

Fig. 1. Hue-Value co-ordinate system used

one dimension of the sphere. As all colours with high V values are similar i.e. close to white and the same holds true for those colours with low V which become similarly close to black, and as black and white by definition don't have a hue quality, the two points $V = 0$ and $V = 1$ describe the poles of the globe.

The use of a globe not only comes naturally with the choice of features, it also has other clear advantages. The concept of a globe will almost certainly be familiar to the average user as it is a direct analogy of the earth globe. It therefore provides a very intuitive interface to the user who will have experience on how to navigate and find something on its surface. Furthermore it allows us to employ a familiar co-ordinate system based on latitude and longitude. Longitude describes the circumference of the globe (i.e. the east-west co-ordinate) and lies in the interval $[0°, 360°]$. Latitude describes the north-south direction from pole to pole and ranges from $-90°$ at the south pole to $+90°$ at the north pole. Clearly each point on the surface of the globe can be uniquely described by a pair of longitude/latitude co-ordinates.

Our approach to visualising image databases is simple and straightforward. It also provides a very fast method for accessing the image collection. Images are transformed to an HSV representation and the median hue and value attributes are calculated. We make use of the median rather than the mean in order to provide some robustness with regards to the image background. Also, we actually calculate the median R, G, and B values and transform those to HSV which is computationally more efficient and results only in a slight deviation in terms of accuracy. From these the co-ordinates on the globe are then determined (see also Figure 1), where H directly translates to longitude and H is rescaled to match the latitude range ($V = 0.5$ corresponds to $0°$ latitude, i.e. a position on the equator). A thumbnail of the image is then projected onto the surface of sphere at the calculated co-ordinates[1]. Once the locations for all images have been

[1] Since those thumbnails are distorted more towards the poles we actually remap all images to be located between the great circles with $\pm 80°$ latitude.

Fig. 2. Initial globe view of the UCID dataset

calculated and their thumbnails projected the system shows an initial view of the globe and is ready for navigation as detailed in Section 4. Figure 2 shows the initial view of our image database globe based on the UCID [7] image database which contains some 1300 images.

Since the co-ordinates are extracted directly from the images our approach is very fast and hence much more efficient than methods such as MDS which rely on a comparably slow and computationally expensive iterative convergence procedure. Also does the addition of images to the database require only the computation of its median hue and brightness with no further calculations necessary as is the case for MDS and similar approaches. In addition are the features that we employ intrinsically suitable for query-based image retrieval [9]. Furthermore, the axes of the co-ordinate system are well defined and meaningful which is in contrast to those obtained by MDS or other similar techniques (such as principal components analysis) where axes are not associated with attributes. Finally, as the database globe is displayed on an ordinary CRT monitor no specialist equipment is necessary.

4 Image Database Navigation

As mentioned above the interface starts with an initial view such as the one shown in Figure 2 (which has a central point of 30° longitude, i.e. an average

Fig. 3. Globe view with central hue of 120° (left), 210° (middle), and 300° (right)

reddish/yellowish hue, and 0° latitude, i.e. medium brightness). From Figure 2 we can also see the controls the user has at his/her disposal for navigation purposes. As these are kept fairly simple and again due to the average user's familiarity of localising places on an earth globe, navigation is straightforward and intuitive.

The controls allow rotation of the globe around both the vertical and the horizontal axis and zooming in and out of a region of interest. The user can perform these operations using the keyboard where the cursor keys are translated to rotation of the sphere and the + and - keys are available for zooming. Similarly the mouse can be used for navigation: moving the mouse prompts a rotation whereas the left and right mouse buttons are responsible for zoom operations. Especially attractive is the application of a trackball: here the ball itself corresponds directly to the image globe, hence rotating the track ball rotates the sphere on screen whereas the two buttons are again used for zooming in and out.

From Section 3 it becomes clear that a rotation around the vertical axis will focus on a different average hue of the displayed images. In Figure 3 we show the view after rotating it clock-wise in 90° steps. While Figure 2 was centred around a red/yellow hue, the spheres in Figure 3 show the display centred around (from left to right) greenish, bluish, and magenta hues. In contrast, rotation around the horizontal axis will either shift the display to images that are darker (rotation towards south pole) or brighter pictures (rotation towards north pole).

While the global view of the sphere allows for easy selection of a general hue/brightness area, it is clear that in this view single images are hard to make out. Therefore a zoom function is provides which allows to user to restrict their attention to a smaller, more localised area of interest. In Figure 4 we show an example of a zoomed-in area where the user was interested in images with a beach/ocean view. It is clear that futher zoom operation(s) can be applied to localise single images of interest.

We note, that for none of the operations used for browsing the images, i.e. neither for rotation nor for changing the zoom factor, any additional calculations need to be performed (in contrast to e.g. MDS which will recalculate all co-ordinates for a zoomed-in area [4]) as the co-ordinates at which the pictures are placed do not change. We are therefore able to provide an image browsing environment that can operate in real time. Furthermore, while we provide a dedicated application for image database navigation we can also export our

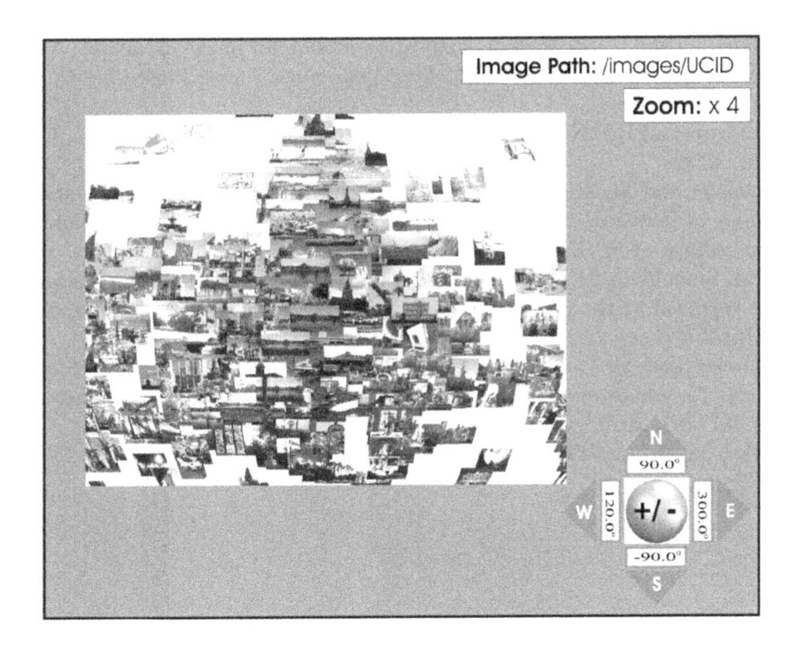

Fig. 4. Zoomed-in area displaying beach/ocean images

image globe to a VRML model [10] which can them be used and browsed with a suitable viewer.

5 Conclusions

We have introduced an efficient and effective approach to visualise and browse large image collections. Thumbnails of images are projected onto a spherical globe which acts as the medium users interact with. Navigation is simple, intuitive, and fast. While we have used colour features to determine the position of the thumbnails on the sphere's surface, the method is generic and other types of features can be equally employed.

References

1. CIE. *International Lighting Vocabulary.* CIE Publications 17.4, Commission International de L'Eclairage, 4th edition, 1989.
2. J.B. Kruskal and M. Wish. *Multidimensional scaling.* Sage Publications, 1978.
3. M Nakazato and T.S. Huang. 3D MARS: Immersive virtual reality for content-based image retrieval. In *IEEE Int. Conference on Multimedia and Expo*, 2001.
4. Y. Rubner, L. Guibas, and C. Tomasi. The earth mover's distance, multi-dimensional scaling, and color-based image retrieval. In *Image Understanding Workshop*, pages 661–668, 1997.

5. S.D. Ruszala and G. Schaefer. Visualisation models for image databases: A comparison of six approaches. In *Irish Machine Vision and Image Processing Conference*, pages 186–191, 2004.
6. J. Sangwine and R.E.N. Horne. *The Colour Image Processing Handbook*. Chapman & Hall, 1998.
7. G. Schaefer and M. Stich. UCID - An Uncompressed Colour Image Database. In *Storage and Retrieval Methods and Applications for Multimedia 2004*, volume 5307 of *Proceedings of SPIE*, pages 472–480, 2004.
8. A.W.M. Smeulders, M. Worring, S. Santini, A. Gupta, and R. Jain. Content-based image retrieval at the end of the early years. *IEEE Trans. Pattern Analysis and Machine Intelligence*, 22(12):1249–1380, 2000.
9. M. Stricker and M. Orengo. Similarity of color images. In *Conf. on Storage and Retrieval for Image and Video Databases III*, volume 2420 of *Proceedings of SPIE*, pages 381–392, 1995.
10. VRML Consortium. The Virtual Reality Modeling Language. *ISO/IEC IS 14772-1*, 1997.

Viewpoint Interpolation Using an Ellipsoid Head Model for Video Teleconferencing

Na-Ree Yoon and Byung-Uk Lee

Dept. of Information Electronic Engineering,
Ewha W. University, Seoul, Korea

Abstract. To establish eye contact in video teleconferencing, it is necessary to synthesize a front view image by viewpoint interpolation. After finding the viewing direction of a user, we can interpolate an image seen from the viewpoint, which will result in a front view image. There are two categories of previous research: image based method and model based method. The former is simple, however, it shows limited performance for complex objects. And the latter is robust to noise, whereas it is computationally expensive. We propose to model a face with an ellipsoid and show that the new method is simple and robust from various experiments.

1 Introduction

With recent development of the internet, video teleconference has become popular for business as well as personal use. When a participant of a teleconference looks at the eye of the other party, images taken by a camera give an impression that the user is looking at somewhere else. Front view images can be taken only when the user is gazing at the camera. However, it is physically impossible to locate a camera behind the face image of the remote party on the monitor. Since eye contact is an important factor in video teleconferencing, there have been many investigations to generate a face image with a front view and provide virtual eye contact by interpolating images taken from left and right side. Since we need to interpolate images in real time, the algorithm must be simple and robust.

There are two categories in the previous research: image based method [1][2] and model based method [3][4][5]. Image based methods interpolate images taken from various viewpoints in 2D image space. Therefore it is relatively simple and fast, which is suitable for real time applications. Model based methods generate 3D model of face obtained from captured images. It generates realistic images, however, generation of 3D model is computationally expensive.

We propose a simple and robust algorithm employing an ellipsoid as a head model. First we segment a face from captured images, and then build an ellipsoid from two images with known camera parameters. And then we project a point on the surface of the ellipsoid to the real images and a virtual image plane to establish correspondences among them. We obtain image intensity on the virtual camera plane by averaging the intensities of the corresponding points of real images. The algorithm is simple, however, the quality of the resulting images are satisfactory.

G. Bebis et al. (Eds.): ISVC 2005, LNCS 3804, pp. 287 – 293, 2005.

2 Previous Research

Viewpoint interpolation can be accomplished in image space. Disparities of two images are calculated after establishing correspondence between images, and a new image is synthesized by interpolating the disparities [1]. The focal point of the virtual camera is constrained to lie on the line segment joining the focal point of the two cameras. There are several methods finding the disparities developed for stereo matching [6]-[10]. Projective grid method [2] is similar to stereo but the search space is different. It searches for depth along a line connecting the focal point and image point of a virtual camera to find the best matching intensities after projecting the point onto two images. There can arise many false matches due to illumination or noise, therefore it may cause severe errors. Fig. 1 shows a result with many erroneous matches.

Fig. 1. An erroneous image from projective grid space method

Recently Yang and Zhang proposed a face modeling method [5] based on stereo analysis and a personalized face model. A 3D stereo head tracker with a personalized face model is used to compute initial correspondences across two views. More correspondences are then added through template and feature matching. Finally, all the correspondence information is fused together for view synthesis using view morphing techniques. The combined methods greatly enhance the accuracy and robustness of the synthesized views. This method can synthesize virtual video that maintains eye contact. The reported processing speed is 5 frames per second. Other model based methods are published using a generic rigid model [3] or a 2D face model [4].

3 Proposed Method: Ellipsoid Head Model

We propose to employ an ellipsoid to model a human head. Once we build a model in 3D space, it is straightforward to establish correspondence among a virtual image and real images. Therefore we can avoid stereo matching problem, which is computationally expensive and error prone. First we segment a face region from images [11][12] and approximate the boundary as an ellipse. Then we match the minor and major axis of the ellipses in 3D space using camera parameters and build an ellipsoid as shown in Fig. 2. It is clear that the points of ellipses do not correspond to the same point in 3D space; however, they are good approximations in building a 3D model. Yip and Jin employed an ellipse head model in a monocular setting [13] for face warping assuming fixed tilt angle. However, our method does not need to estimate tilt angle, since we are interpolating two images.

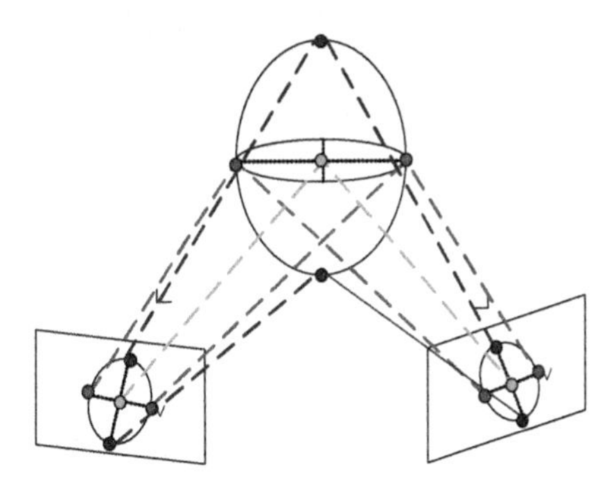

Fig. 2. Ellipsoid head modeling. An ellipsoid model for head is built by matching two face outline ellipses of images.

We can locate a virtual camera anywhere in space and synthesize an image seen from the position. We first connect a line from the focal point of the virtual camera to a pixel on the virtual image plane. If the line hits the ellipsoid head model, we project the point onto two image data planes and average their intensities. We can synthesize an image by repeating the process pixel by pixel.

Our method does not search for corresponding points between images; it is projection of a point on ellipsoid model onto image planes. Stereo matching depends on image intensity which is local information and subject to noise and camera characteristics. The proposed method uses global information of head position. This simple head model results in reliable face images, since the depth error of ellipsoid model from a real face is not significant compared to the distance from a camera to the face.

3.1 Intensity Calibration

Test images are taken with two cameras at the same time. Since the cameras are calibrated, the internal and external camera parameters are known [14]. Fig. 3 (a) and (b) show images taken from cameras. The two images show different intensities due to inconsistency of camera characteristics and viewing directions. We calculate the mean and standard deviation of intensities of face regions and match them by scaling and shifting the intensities as shown in the following equation.

$$I_{R'}(u,v) = \frac{\sigma_L}{\sigma_R}(I_R(u,v) - \mu_R) + \mu_L, u,v \in I_R ,$$

where I_R is the right image and $I_{R'}$ is the corrected image, μ_R and μ_L are the means, and σ_R and σ_L are the standard deviation of right and left images, respectively. Fig. 2 (c) shows a scaled image of Fig. 2 (b).

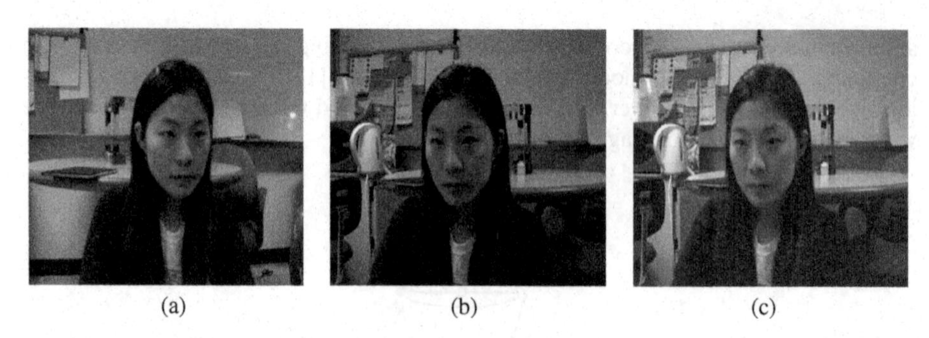

(a) (b) (c)

Fig. 3. (a) Left image (b) Right image (c) Brightness corrected version of image (b)

3.2 Head Modeling and Experiments

First we segment face and head in left and right images, and then calculate minimum mean square error (MMSE) ellipse from the face boundaries as shown in Fig. 4. We match the mean and standard deviation of face region intensities as a preprocessing step. We build an ellipsoid by matching the end points of minor and major axis of the ellipses. Since we have camera parameters, we can obtain an MMSE intersection point of two lines connecting the focal points and the ellipse boundary points. Now

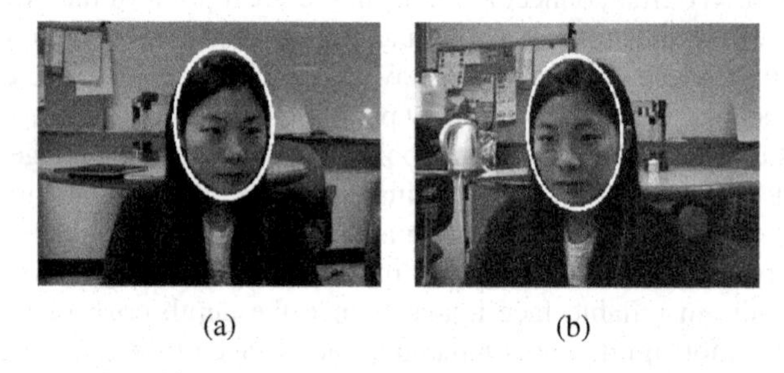

(a) (b)

Fig. 4. Ellipse model for head. (a) Left image (b) Right image.

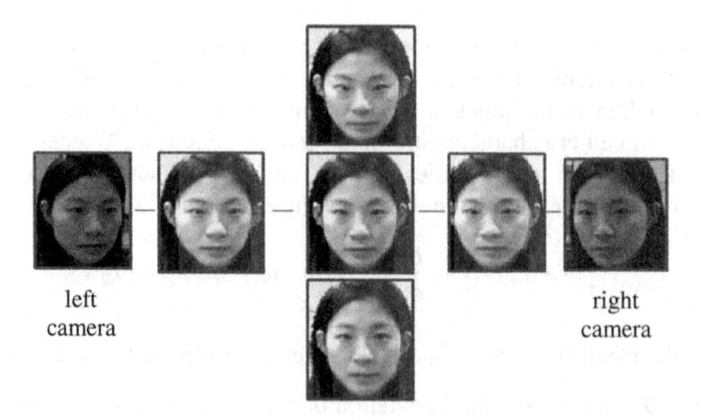

Fig. 5. Rendered images from given left and right images

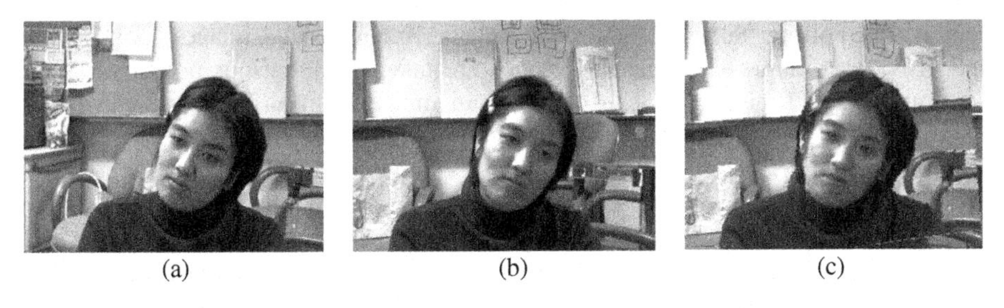

(a) (b) (c)

Fig. 6. Tilted pose of head (a) Left image (b) Right image (c) Interpolated image

(a) (b) (c)

Fig. 7. (a) Up image (b) Down image (c) Interpolated image

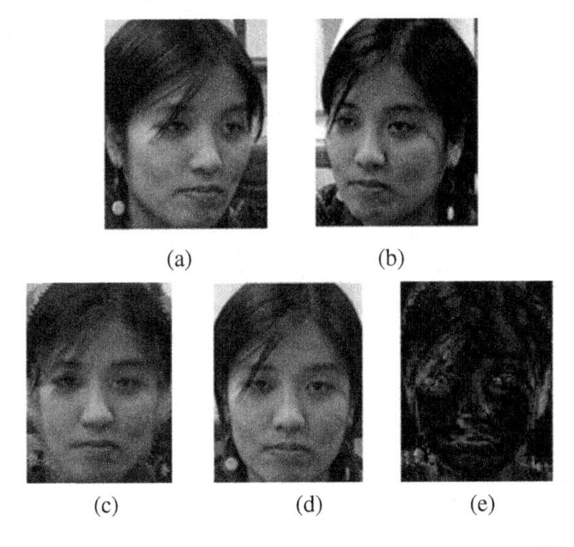

(a) (b)

(c) (d) (e)

Fig. 8. (a) Left image (b) Right image (c) Interpolated image using ellipsoid face model (d) Original image (e) Error image

we can choose a location of a virtual camera and synthesize an image. We can set the virtual camera at the eye gaze position [15][16] to obtain a front view image. We have obtained several synthetic images from various virtual positions. Fig. 5 shows left and right camera images, and five synthesized images seen from the center, top, bottom, near left, and near right. All synthesized images look natural and provide an impression that the images are taken from various positions. Since we employ a 3D model, we can generate an image from an arbitrary viewpoint. Therefore it is possible to generate a navigation video seen from a moving camera. The proposed method is robust to subject change or head tilting as shown in Fig. 6.

If we install two cameras with vertical separation, we can reduce the occlusion area between face images, compared to horizontal positioning of the cameras. Fig. 7 shows an experimental result interpolated from up and down images. We observe difference between a ground truth image and an interpolated image. Fig. 8 (a) and (b) are captured images. Fig. 8 (d) is a ground truth image taken from a camera, and (c) is a synthesized image at the same position by interpolating the left and right images. The synthesized image looks natural and the difference is not noticeable to a human viewer. Quantitative error analysis is beyond the scope of this work, since we need to separate error measures for position and brightness. Photometric intensity cannot be recovered by this method, since surface orientation and the reflectance properties are not taken into account.

4 Conclusions

We propose an algorithm to synthesize an image from any virtual position using two images, which enables us to maintain eye contact during video teleconferencing. We model a face from a captured image as an ellipse and then build an ellipsoid head model. We establish correspondence among images and virtual images by projecting the surface of the ellipsoid model onto the image planes and virtual image plane. We obtain a synthetic image after averaging the corresponding image intensities. The proposed method does not require complex calculation, therefore it is suitable for real time implementation. Since we have a 3D head model, the position of a virtual camera is not limited to the line segment joining the two focal points of taken images, as in the case of image based method. Our algorithm is not sensitive to specularity, camera aperture or image noise. The reason for the robustness is related to the fact that the depth error of ellipsoid is not significant compared to the distance of the camera and the face.

Our algorithm is limited to face region; it does not generate background images. Therefore we need to devise a computationally fast method to generate a background which looks natural. We also need to incorporate an eye gaze algorithm to establish accurate eye contact.

Acknowledgements

This research was supported by the MIC (Ministry of Information and Communications), Korea, under the ITRC (Information Technology Research Center) support program supervised by the IITA (Institute of Information Technology Assessment).

References

1. Ott, M., Lewis, J., Cox, I.: Teleconferencing Eye Contact Using a Virtual Camera, Proc. Conf. Human Factors in Computing Systems (1993) 109–110
2. Saito, H., Kimura, M., Yaguchi, S, Inamoto, N.: View Interpolation of Multiple Cameras Based on Projective Geometry, Proc. of Int'l Workshop on Pattern Recognition and Understanding for Visual Information Media (2002) 57–62
3. Gemmell, J., Zitnick, C.L., Kang, T., Toyoma, K., Seitz, S.: Gaze-Awareness for Videoconferencing, IEEE Multimedia, Vol. 7, No. 4 (2000) 26–35
4. Cham, T.J., Krishnamoorthy, S., Jones, M.: Analogous View Transfer for Gaze Correction in Video Sequences, Proc. Int'l Conf. Automation, Robotics, Control and Vision (2002)
5. Yang, R., Zhang, Z.: Eye Gaze Correction with Stereovision for Video-teleconferencing, IEEE Trans. on Pattern Analysis and Machine Intelligence, Vol. 26, No. 7 (2004) 956–960
6. Brown, M.Z., Burschka, D., Hager, G.D.: Advances in Computational Stereo, IEEE Trans. on Pattern Analysis and Machine Intelligence, Vol. 25, No. 8, (2003) 993–1008
7. Hartley, R., Zisserman, A.: Multiple View Geometry in Computer Vision, Cambridge University Press (2000)
8. Jain, R., Kasturi, R., Schunck, B.G.: Machine Vision, McGraw-Hill (1995)
9. Birchfield, S., and Tomasi, C.: Multiway Cut for Stereo and Motion with Slanted Surfaces, Proc. Int'l Conf. Computer Vision, Vol. 1, (1999) 489–495
10. Birchfield, S., and Tomasi, C.: Depth Discontinuities by Pixel-to-Pixel Stereo, Proc. of the Sixth IEEE International Conf. on Computer Vision, Mumbai, India (1998) 1073–1080
11. Huang, F.J., Chen, T.: Tracking of Multiple Faces for Human-computer Interfaces and Virtual Environments, IEEE Int'l Conf. on Multimedia and Expo., New York (2000)
12. Yang, M.H., Kriegman, D., Ahuja, N.: Detecting Faces in Images: A Survey, IEEE Trans. on Pattern Analysis and Machine Vision, Vol. 24, No. 1 (2004) 34–58
13. Yip, B., Jin, J.S.: Face Re-Orientation Using Ellipsoid Model in Video Conference, Proc. of the Seventh International Conference on Internet and Multimedia Systems and Applications, Hawaii (2003) 245-250
14. Tsai, R., A versatile Camera Calibration Technique for High Accuracy 3D Machine Vision Metrology Using off the shelf TV Cameras and Lenses, IEEE Journal of Robotics and automation, Vol. 3, No. 4 (1987) 323–344
15. Gee, A.H., Cipolla, R.: Determining the Gaze of Faces in Images, Image Vision Computing, Vol. 12, No. 10 (1994) 639–647
16. Hansen, D.W., Pece, A.: Eye Typing off the Shelf, IEEE Computer Society Conference on Computer Vision and Pattern Recognition, Washington D.C., U.S.A., Vol. 2 (2004) 159–164

Real-Time Video Annotations for Augmented Reality

Edward Rosten, Gerhard Reitmayr, and Tom Drummond

Department of Engineering, University of Cambridge, Cambridge CB1 2PZ, UK
{er258, gr281, twd20}@cam.ac.uk

Abstract. Augmented reality (AR) provides an intuitive user interface to present information in the context of the real world. A common application is to overlay screen-aligned annotations for real world objects to create in-situ information displays for users. While the referenced object's location is fixed in the view the annotating labels should be placed in such a way as to not interfere with other content of interest such as other labels or objects in the real world. We present a new approach to determine and track areas with less visual interest based on feature density and to automatically compute label layout from this information. The algorithm works in under 5ms per frame, which is fast enough that it can be used with existing AR systems. Moreover, it provides flexible constraints for controlling label placement behaviour to the application designer. The resulting overlays are demonstrated with a simple hand-held augmented reality system for information display in a lab environment.

1 Introduction

Augmented reality (AR) is an excellent user interface for mobile computing applications, because it supports an intuitive display of information. In an AR environment, the user's perception of the real world is enhanced by computer-generated entities such as 3D objects, 2D overlays and 3D spatialised audio [1]. Interaction with these entities occurs in real-time providing natural feedback to the user. A common application for augmented reality is information browsing. Annotations to real world objects are presented to the user directly within the view of the environment. Typical example are labels containing textual or pictorial information [2]. Such applications are especially interesting in the context of mobile augmented reality, where a user can roam a large area and subsequently request information on many objects.

Annotations can be general information displays such as heads-up displays that stay in fixed locations on the screen. Or they may be associated with objects in the view and appear close in the view. In the latter case they usually move with the objects or are connected to them by follower-lines which make the user aware of the relationship. However, placing annotations into the user's view is not trivial. To avoid distraction annotations should not move or jitter. They should also not overlap scene features or each other. Finally, readability of text annotations depends strongly on background colour and texture.

Automatically placing annotations is more difficult. Models of the environment may be limited to explicitly tracked objects and may not include a general description of the environment. Even where such a world model exists, it usually cannot capture fine details that determine the background clutter in images. Also, the application model may

G. Bebis et al. (Eds.): ISVC 2005, LNCS 3804, pp. 294–302, 2005.

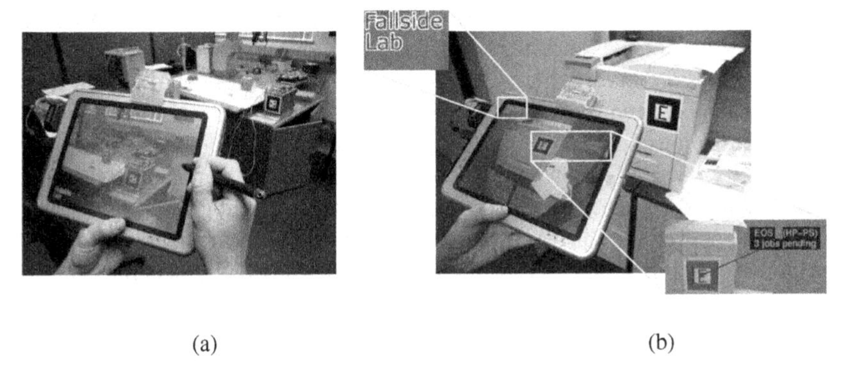

(a) (b)

Fig. 1. A hand-held augmented reality system for information browsing using labels attached to markers and "screen-stabilized" labels. The system determines the label locations in real-time in such a way that overlap with interesting parts of the image is minimised.

not even contain all possible objects of interests or have means to track them: for example, a person walking into view can be considered interesting to the user and should therefore not be occluded. However, mobile AR systems typically have no possibility of tracking all persons or mobile objects they encounter. To create useable information overlays in all such situations, image based methods are required.

To enable automated annotations for resource-constrained systems and unmodelled environments, we present a new, fast method which finds visually uninteresting areas in live video and hence determines candidate regions for label placement. The basic idea is to describe the fitness of a certain label location in terms of the number of occluded image features were the label to be placed in that location. The fitness distribution over the entire image is computed from features detected in each frame and tracked in a non-parametric filter framework over time (see section 3). Application designers can further modify the fitness distribution for each label to enforce constraints (see section 4) such as proximity to a location in the image or placement in one of several distinct locations such as image corners. The whole algorithm requires 5ms per frame (on a 1GHz Pentium-M) and is therefore suitable for real-time operation and integration into more complex systems (such as mobile augmented reality applications) as demonstrated in section 5.

2 Related Work

Traditional label placement research has focused on the problem of arranging large numbers labels on static display without overlap and unlimited computational time. Moreover, complete information about the display and any constraints on the labels is assumed as well. Many approaches exist and the Map-Labeling Bibliography [3] hosts an extensive selection. A good overview of typical approaches is given by Christensen et al. [4]. Azuma et al. [5] evaluate such label placement strategies for augmented reality displays both statistically and with a user study. Our work supplements this work by introducing a method to derive constraints for labels based on the visual content of the view. Therefore, we are not concerned with overlap between labels themselves, but rather with overlap of labels and interesting features of the environment. Once candidate locations of labels are known, global label placement strategies could be employed to reduce occlusion between labels.

Video annotations such as subtitles have been used for many years in the broadcasting industry. Typically such annotations are placed offline in a manual process and at fixed locations. In recent years, real time, world aligned annotations for sports casts have become possible such as the display of the first down line in American football [6] or live information for Nascar races [7]. These solutions rely on the accurate and expensive tracking of camera parameters and accurate models of the environment and pixel colours to achieve high precision. Moreover, manual fine-tuning by operators ensures robustness of the systems.

Information browsing is a common application for augmented reality systems. Feiner et. al [8] annotated persons and objects with application windows in an optical see-through setting. The NaviCam [2] demonstrated labels for objects tracked with optical fiducials. Simple rendering of annotations for multiple objects leads to clutter on the screen and overlap between labels themselves and other objects of interest. One approach is to reduce the number of labels by applying a filtering scheme [9] to select information based on properties of the tasks and the users as well as on proximity. Another promising approach is to directly manage the 2D display space and place labels only in regions that are not interesting. Bell et al. [10] describe a view management system that keeps track of free areas on the display. A 3D world model and tracking of real objects is required to accurately project the objects and environment back into the view and update the occupied areas as the user moves through the environment.

Other research investigates the properties of labels in augmented reality displays. Gabbard et al. [11] compare user performance in reading differently coloured text labels in optical see-through systems over various backgrounds. In contrast to that Leykin and Tuceryan [12] use a machine learning approach to automatically determine the readability of text over textured backgrounds. The information gained by classification can be incorporated in to our method by providing additional constraints.

Automatic placement without knowledge of the environment was attempted by Thanedar and Höllerer [13] to produce annotations for video sequences. Their approach selects candidate regions based on image properties such as absence of motion and uniformity of colour. The location is optimised over a series of frames, also taking future frames into account; it is therefore not suitable for real-time operation. In contrast to this approach, our method is causal and sufficiently optimised that it can be used as an additional component in a larger real-time system.

3 Tracking Candidate Locations

Our method finds uninteresting parts of the image in order to place labels without obscuring interesting parts of the image. To do this, a distribution of feature density is calculated in the current video frame. Areas with a high feature density are assumed to contain information interesting to the user. Labels are placed in the frame such that the integral of the density distribution over the label area is minimised. In principle any

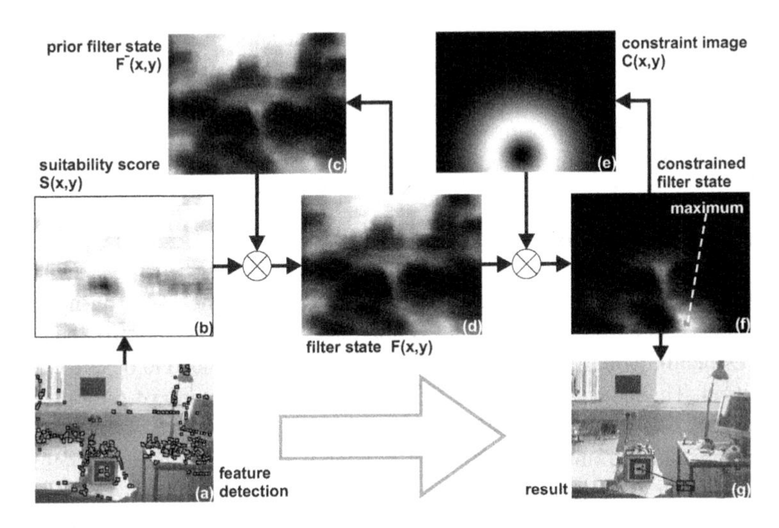

Fig. 2. Overview of the processing steps. (a) shows the detected features; the computed suitability score (b) updates the prior filter state (c) to arrive at the current filter state (d); a constraint image (e) is multiplied with it to compute the constrained filter state (f) and select the maximum location. (g) shows the resulting label placement. The maximum location is fed back to the constraint image as a location prior for the next frame.

feature detector could be used, for example the Harris [14] or SUSAN [15] detectors, or even edgel detectors. In our experience, corner detectors yield visually better results than edge detectors. Our method has a strong emphasis on low compute cost, so we use the very efficient FAST feature detector, presented in Appendix A.

For each label to be placed in the image a placement cost distribution $P(x, y)$ is calculated in the following manner. We define $P(x, y)$ to be the number of features occluded by the label if the label is placed at x, y. Our implementation uses an integral image [16] to quickly calculate this for each label. Locations with the lowest cost are the best locations for labels. However, the placement cost distribution is sensitive to noise. This can result local jitter of the optimal location or frequent large scale jumps if several locations are near optimal. Both effects are undesirable and can be avoided by filtering over time (see Fig.2 for an overview).

A non-parametric filter state $F_n(x, y)$ describes the suitability of a location for placing a given label within a frame n. The location of the maximum of $F_n(x, y)$, written as $(\overline{x}, \overline{y})$, describes the optimal location for the label. The first step is to update the last filter state for frame $n - 1$ with process noise by adding a constant c, yielding a prior $F_n^-(x, y)$. The prior is then updated with the suitability $S(x, y)$, defined as

$$S(x, y) = 1 - P(x, y)/\max_{x,y}(P(x, y)). \tag{1}$$

Then we multiply the suitability score with the prior state and normalise by a factor z. Therefore, the update step is

$$F_n(x, y) = F_n^-(x, y)S(x, y)/z. \tag{2}$$

The location $(\overline{x}, \overline{y})$ of the maximum of the filter state $F_n(x, y)$ at step n is then used as the optimal placement for a label, in the absence of any further information (see Section 4). The process noise parameter c controls the flexibility of the filter. Larger process noise results in a more responsive filter that quickly captures major changes in the distribution, but allows the label to jitter.

4 Placement Control

The filter state generated by the tracking process describes the overall fitness of locations for label placement. However, real applications require more control over the label location. Depending on the type of label different constraints need to be enforced on the label position. Thanedar and Höllerer [13] give a short taxonomy of possible labels in video overlays. Our method supports all of these label types.

To enforce a constraint on the location of a label, the application designer specifies a constraint image $C(x, y)$ that describes the suitability distribution of placing a label at a certain location. The constraint image is then multiplied with the filter state to yield a constrained filter state. The location of the maximum of the latter is the optimal placement for the associated label.

Such constraint images can either be static or changing over time depending on the type of label. For example, to place an annotation close to a tracked object an application multiplies a ring-like distribution around the object location with the filter state (see Fig.2). The resulting maximum and hence label will lie in an uninteresting part of the image near, but not too close, to the object being labelled. A directional constraint places the label in the approximate direction of the visible arrow on the marker (see Fig.3).

To place "screen-stabilised" (fixed) labels in one of a set of possible locations, a static constraint image is constructed that only contains support for the desired label locations. Again, the maximum of the resulting constrained suitability distribution is one of the chosen locations.

Even with these constraints, if large areas of the image are uninteresting, then there will be many equally suitable locations for the label, which can cause the label to jump around. To prevent this, a constraint is used which increases the value of the constrained filter at the previous location of the label. If this position is stabilised relative to the marker position, then this will bias the label towards moving smoothly around with the marker. If the absolute position of the label is used, the bias will be towards the label staying in the same place on the screen.

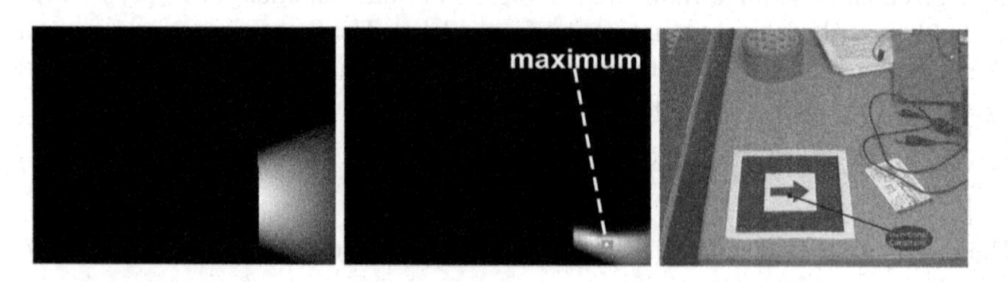

Fig. 3. Example of a directional contraint. The first column shows the constraint images, the second the constrained filter state, and the last the resulting location.

Avoiding overlap of multiple labels also becomes possible. A simple greedy algorithm can operate on a ranked list of labels: the first label is placed at the maximum location of its filter state (or a constrained filter state). The states for the remaining labels are then modified to discourage placement of subsequent labels in locations that could result in overlap with the first one. The modified state is then the input for placing the next label. The iterative modification of the filter states accumulates the information about all placed labels and constrains the placement of new ones to unused areas.

5 Results

To demonstrate the results of our automated label placement method, we created a small information browsing application for a hand-held AR system. A tablet PC with a 1GHz Pentium M processor and a Firewire camera mounted to its back becomes a lens-like tool to view annotations on real objects and locations in our lab (see Fig.1). To track objects and locations we employ the ARToolkit [17] library and a set of markers placed in the environment on interesting objects such as a printer. The system works at video frame rate of 30 fps recording the full 640×480 image but operating on quarter-sized images (320×240 pixels) for feature detection and filter representations. In this configuration, the system uses 17% of the available computing time.

When a marker becomes visible in the camera view, a corresponding label is placed next to it in an area free of any interesting features (see Fig.4 (a)). The distance to the marker is controlled by a circular constraint as described in section 4. The label is connected by a follower-line to the centre of the marker to disambiguate the association. As the tablet is moved about labels typically stay in the same location in the window to avoid unnecessary movement. However, if a label starts to occlude interesting image features it jumps to a different location with less overlap (see Fig.4 (b,c)). In general labels appear stable but can change their location instantly without any interpolation between locations, if required. The display also contains screen-stabilised information on the lab which is placed in one of the four screen corners.

Table 1 shows the average time spent calculating label placement for our demonstration system. All of the per-label costs are streaming operations on large quantities of pixel data, and so could be further optimised exploiting a streaming instruction set such as SSE2. Nevertheless, our portable C++ implementation exhibits good performance.

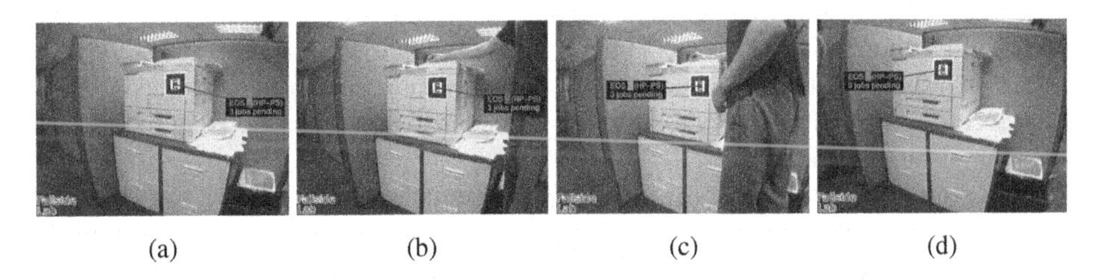

(a) (b) (c) (d)

Fig. 4. Example of the dynamic behaviour. (a) A label is placed in an uninteresting position. As a person moves into the view (b), the label jumps to another location (c). The weak position prior prevents the label from quickly jumping back to the previous position (d).

Table 1. Timings for various steps of the algorithm. A single precomputed constraint is used.

		Time (ms)
Per-frame cost	Feature detection	1.76
	Integral image	0.65
Per-label cost	Suitability measurement	1.03
	Filter measurements	0.63
	Insert constraint	0.51
Total cost	For one label	4.58
	For n labels	$2.41 + 2.17n$
Cost per frame over 10 frames		0.46

For real-time operation the label placement does not need to be computed for each frame, since large changes in label position happen infrequently. Therefore, another performance improvement consists in computing label placements only for every n^{th} frame and distribution computation over the intermediary frames to reduce the per-frame computation cost to $1/n^{th}$ of the total.

6 Conclusions

Our method implements a straightforward, yet flexible approach to determining annotation locations for overlays of live video images. Processing time per frame is minimal making it appropriate for inclusion into mobile and hand-held augmented reality systems that are constrained in terms of computing power. The bulk of the processor time is still left for other tasks such as tracking or interaction management. The non-parametric tracking of candidate locations can be tuned to select between slow or fast reaction to image changes or to prefer past locations over new ones. The complete modelling of state via a non-parametric representation captures the problem's multi-modal properties and allows for instant jumps to different locations. The inclusion of constraints gives application designers a flexible way to define label behaviour.

The underlying assumption that features appear predominantly in visually interesting areas is the key to the simplicity of the method. The assumption breaks down for feature rich areas of no importance to the user or task at hand. However, as long as there are some image regions with few features the label will be placed in a good position.

Direct comparisions to other methods described in section 2 are difficult, because none exhibit the same properties. Either they use models that include all interesting objects that should not be occluded, or they do not operate causally in that they optimise label locations using frames yet to be shown. The later can avoid surprising jumps, but is not applicable in real-time.

The presented approach is also applicable to general video feeds, but our work focuses on mobile augmented reality applications. Here the real-time constraints, limited availability of tracking solutions for model based annotation placement and ubiquitous use of video see-through displays match the features of the proposed method very closely. However, the method could also be adapted to optical see-through displays through the use of a calibrated camera that captures images that match the user's view.

An example video of a walk through our lab with annotations is available in the supplementary videos, and the FAST corner detection code is available from `http://savannah.nongnu.org/projects/libcvd`.

A FAST Feature Detection

We present here the FAST (Features from Accelerated Segment Test) feature detector. This is sufficiently fast that it allows on-line operation of the label placement system. A test is performed for a feature at a pixel p by examining a circle of 16 pixels (a Bresenham circle of radius 3) surrounding p. A feature is detected at p if the intensities of at least 12 contiguous pixels are all above or all below the intensity of p by some threshold t. This is illustrated in Fig.5. The test for this condition can be optimised by examining pixels 1 and 9, then 5 and 13, to reject candidate pixels more quickly, since a feature can only exist if three of these test points are all above or below the intensity of p by the threshold. With this optimisation the algorithm examines on average 3.8 pixels per location on a sample video sequence.

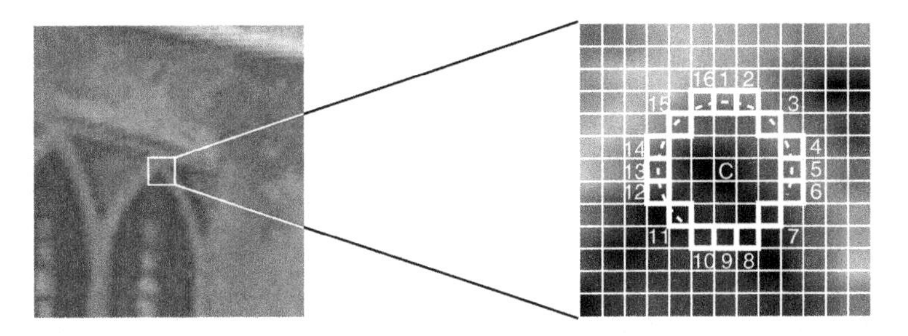

Fig. 5. FAST Feature detection in an image patch. The highlighted squares are the pixels used in the feature detection. The pixel at C is the centre of a detected corner: the dashed line passes through 12 contiguous pixels which are brighter than C by more than the threshold.

References

1. Azuma, R.T.: A survey of augmented reality. Presence - Teleoperators and Virtual Environments **6** (1997) 355–385
2. Rekimoto, J.: Navicam: A magnifying glass approach to augmented reality. PRESENCE - Teleoperators and Virtual Environments **6** (1997) 399–412
3. The Map-Labeling Bibliography. http://i11www.ira.uka.de/ awolff/map-labeling/bibliography/ (2005)
4. Christensen, J., Marks, J., Shieber, S.: An empirical study of algorithms for point-feature label placement. ACM Transactions on Graphics **14** (1995) 203–232
5. Azuma, R., Furmanski, C.: Evaluating label placement for augmented reality view management. In: Proc. ISMAR 2003, Tokyo, Japan, IEEE (2003) 66–75
6. Sportvision: 1st & Ten. http://www.sportvision.com/ (2005)
7. Sportvision: Race F/X. http://www.sportvision.com/ (2005)
8. Feiner, S., MacIntyre, B., Haupt, M., Solomon, E.: Windows on the world: 2D windows for 3D augmented reality. In: Proc. UIST'93, Atlanta, GA, USA (1993) 145–155

9. Julier, S., Lanzagorta, M., Baillot, Y., Rosenblum, L., Feiner, S., Höllerer, T.: Information filtering for mobile augmented reality. In: Proc. ISAR 2000, Munich, Germany, IEEE and ACM (2000) 3–11
10. Bell, B., Feiner, S., Höllerer, T.: View management for virtual and augmented reality. In: Proc. UIST'01, Orlando, Florida, USA, ACM (2001) 101–110
11. Gabbard, J.L., Swan II, J.E., Hix, D., Schulman, R.S., Lucas, J., Gupta, D.: An empirical user-based study of text drawing styles and outdoor background textures for augmented reality. In: Proc. IEEE VR 2005, Bonn, Germany, IEEE (2005) 11–18
12. Leykin, A., Tuceryan, M.: Automatic determination of text readability over textured backgrounds for augmented reality systems. In: Proc. ISMAR 2004, Arlington, VA, USA, IEEE (2004) 224–230
13. Thanedar, V., Höllerer, T.: Semi-automated placement of annotations on videos. Technical Report #2004-11, UC, Santa Barbara (2004)
14. Harris, C.J., Stephens, M.: A combined corner and edge detector. In: Proc. of the 4th Alvey Vision Conference. Number 4, Manchester, UK, Alvery Vision Conference (1988) 147–151
15. Smith, S., Brady, J.: SUSAN - a new approach to low level image processing. Int. Journal of Computer Vision **23** (1997) 45–78
16. Viola, P., Jones, M.: Robust real-time object detection. Int. Journal of Computer Vision (2002)
17. Kato, H., Billinghurst, M.: Marker tracking and HMD calibration for a video-based augmented reality conferenencing system. In: Proc. IWAR'99, San Francisco, CA, USA, IEEE CS (1999) 85–94

A Tree-Structured Model of Visual Appearance Applied to Gaze Tracking

Jeffrey B. Mulligan

NASA Ames Research Center

Abstract. In some computer vision applications, we may need to analyze large numbers of similar frames depicting various aspects of an event. In this situation, the appearance may change significantly within the sequence, hampering efforts to track particular features. Active shape models [1] offer one approach to this problem, by "learning" the relationship between appearance and world-state from a small set of hand-labeled training examples. In this paper we propose a method for partitioning the input image set which addresses two problems: first, it provides an automatic method for selecting a set of training images for hand-labeling; second, it results in a partitioning of the image space into regions suitable for local model adaptation. Repeated application of the partitioning procedure results in a tree-structured representation of the image space. The resulting structure can be used to define corresponding neighborhoods in the shape model parameter space; a new image may be processed efficiently by first inserting it into the tree, and then solving for model parameters within the corresponding restricted domain. The ideas are illustrated with examples from an outdoor gaze-tracking application.

1 Introduction

Many computer vision applications consist of analyses of large numbers of similar images; in this paper, we will be concerned with the problem of gaze estimation from images of the eye captured with a head-mounted camera. Assuming the camera platform does not move relative to the head, the images will vary within a restricted subspace. Variation within this subspace will be due both to the parameters of interest (the pose of the eye), and to parameters which are irrelevant for our purposes, such as variations in environmental illumination.

When images of the eye are collected in the laboratory, illumination can be carefully controlled, and the variations in pose are often restricted (e.g., we may only be interested in tracking the gaze within a display screen). In this case, simple methods which search for features known to be present are usually effective. When we attempt to measure gaze in natural behaviors outside of the laboratory, however, we may be confronted with a collection of images in which large gaze deviations cause expected features to disappear. Our inability to control the illumination outdoors during daylight also presents a new set of problems. Figure 1 presents a representative sample from the space of images in our study. Subjects recorded during the day, as in figure 1, generally maintain their eyelids in a relatively closed posture compared to subjects recorded at night,

G. Bebis et al. (Eds.): ISVC 2005, LNCS 3804, pp. 303–312, 2005.

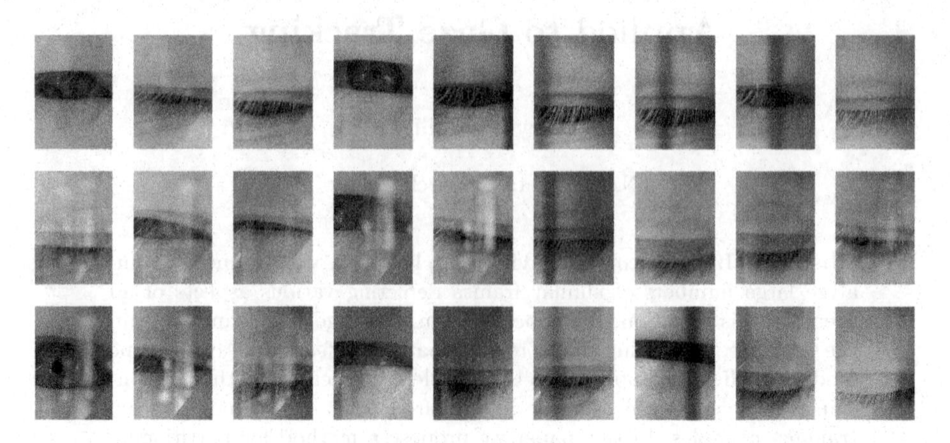

Fig. 1. A collection of images of a human subject's eye, collected during a behavioral experiment conducted outdoors, showing the variety of appearances encountered. In addition to changes in gaze direction, the images vary due to illumination; in this collection we see superimposed bright blobs (resulting from scattering or incomplete reflection at the imaging system's dichroic mirror), and dark vertical stripes, resulting from the shadow of the helicopter rotor blade passing in front of the sun.

or in a dark laboratory. In many of the images in figure 1, the eyelids appear closed. While some of these are certain to correspond to blinks, others correspond to downward fixations. In spite of the fact that in many of the images we cannot see any of the eyeball itself (and are so prevented from applying traditional eye-tracking methods), the position and shape of the lids are highly informative. When we have highly certain data regarding the position and orientation of the eyeball, the pose of the lids is irrelevant to determination of the line-of-sight, but for other frames the eyelid pose is our *only* observable. We seek a method to tell us which methods to apply to any given image.

Active Shape Models [1] have been proposed to recognize structures in medical images in the presence of variations in local image structure. In brief, these models work by learning an association between the local image appearance of model feature points, and the overall configuration of the features. Typically this association is learned from a collection of images in which the structures of interest have been hand-labeled. In selecting this training set, there are two important considerations: first, the training set must span the range of possible shapes (i.e., we must be sure to include the most extreme examples); second, the sampling density must be high enough to capture the variations of shape within the image space. Selection of the training set is therefore critical. One approach might be to simply add images until performance becomes acceptable (perhaps adding images chosen from the set of initial failures), but when the number of images is large, it may not be practical to have a human expert review the model fit for every frame, or even to view every image prior to selecting the training set. Therefore, we would like to have an automatic procedure to select a suitable training set.

Methods for sampling a space of images can be found in the field of *Vector Quantization* [2]. Vector Quantization (VQ) refers to a collection of techniques used in signal coding and compression. While many variants have been proposed for different applications, in every case the process begins with the generation of a *codebook*, which is a table of images chosen to coarsely represent the entire space. An arbitrary image is transmitted by simply sending the index of the most similar codebook entry; the receiver, which also possesses the codebook, uses the corresponding codebook entry to approximate the input image. The quality of the reconstruction depends on both the size and structure of the codebook, and many methods of codebook design have been proposed to meet the needs of different applications. While codebook design (which is a one-time computation, done ahead of time) is the most important determinant of reconstruction quality, another area which has received much attention is efficient mapping of arbitrary images into the codebook, which is critical for real-time encoding processes. It is desirable to avoid exhaustive search, in which the input image is compared to every codebook entry; a Tree-Structured Vector Quantizer (TSVQ) can reduce the number of comparisons from a codebook size of N to something on the order of log(N).

In the remainder of this paper, we present a variant of tree-structure vector quantization developed for a large set of eye images collected during helicopter flight tests. We then describe how the resulting codebook an be exploited to improve the performance of active shape models and other tracking procedures, by limiting the range of parameter values that must be searched for new images.

2 Codebook Generation

Given a set of images, we wish to find a subset which spans the entire set, in the sense that *any* image from the set will be "near" one of the *exemplars* from our special subset. The exemplars are analogous to the codebook entries in VQ, but unlike most VQ applications we are not particularly concerned with insuring that the exemplars are good matches to the nearby images; instead, it is simply sufficient for them to be near enough to point us in the right direction for subsequent processing.

Typical gaze records consist of a series of *fixations* in which the eye is steadily pointed at an object of interest, and *saccades*, which are rapid, ballistic movements from one position to another. In addition to these two types of eye movement, there are also smooth movements which are performed when the eye attempts to follow a moving target. Smooth movements of the eye in the head are also seen when the head moves while the eye is maintaining fixation on a stationary target. The interested reader can find a thorough introduction to the study of eye movements in [3] and [4].

Because gaze behavior typically consists of fixations lasting 250-500 milliseconds, when we process video sequentially it is highly likely that a given frame will be similar to the preceding frame. Therefore our algorithm proceeds as follows: we take the first frame as the first exemplar. Subsequent frames are processed

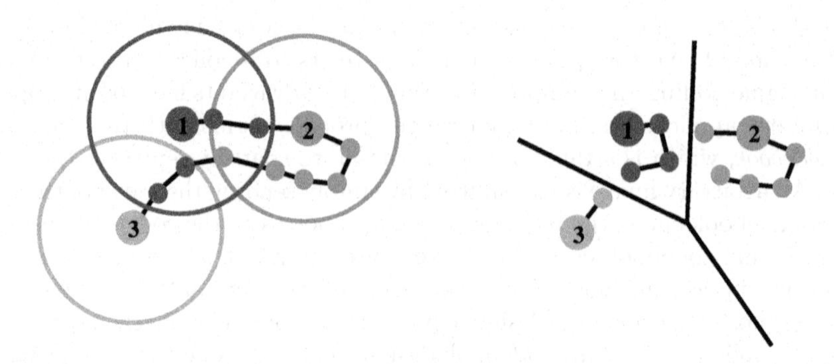

Fig. 2. Left panel: A two-dimensional cartoon of the codebook generation process. Each dot represents an image, with the connecting links indicating temporal order. The first image becomes the first exemplar (the large dot labeled 1), successive images are associated with it as long as their distance remains less than a threshold (δ) indicated by the circle. When a new image falls outside of this circle, a new exemplar is created, and successive images are associated with *it* until they leave its δ-neighborhood. Right panel: partition of the image space induced by the set of exemplars discovered by the codebook generation process. Each image is associated with the nearest exemplar; dark lines indicate boundaries between neighborhoods (Voronoi regions). Note that images which are linked in the sub-regions may not be temporally contiguous.

by first computing the similarity to the exemplar chosen to represent the immediately preceding frame. If the "distance" is below a threshold δ, then we accept the exemplar and move on to the next input frame. Otherwise, we search the set of remaining exemplars for one whose distance is less than δ, accepting the first one we find. If none of the current exemplars are within δ of the new image, then we add it to the set of exemplars. This procedure results in a set of exemplars with the following property: every image x in our collection is within δ of at least one of the exemplars, and every exemplar is separated by at least δ from from every other exemplar. Our goal is to choose δ as large as possible (to keep the size of the catalog small), but still small enough that the resulting classifier on the input images provides useful distinctions.

The left panel of figure 2 shows a two-dimensional cartoon of this process. The circles represent neighborhoods of radius δ centered at each exemplar, and the colors show how each image is associated with the exemplar representing the previous frame as long as the new distance is less than δ. We adopt this heuristic for two reasons: first, because the temporal sequence is continuous, and the behavior contains many stationary intervals, the previous exemplar is usually the best choice, and we can save time by simply accepting it. Second, during our sequential scan of the data there will be many occasions when the exemplar which will ultimately be found to be the nearest neighbor has not been scanned yet. Thus the purpose of the initial pass is simply to find a set of exemplars which completely covers the image space with δ neighborhoods. The association of each image with the nearest exemplar is accomplished by a second pass over the entire data set, performed after the catalog has been generated.

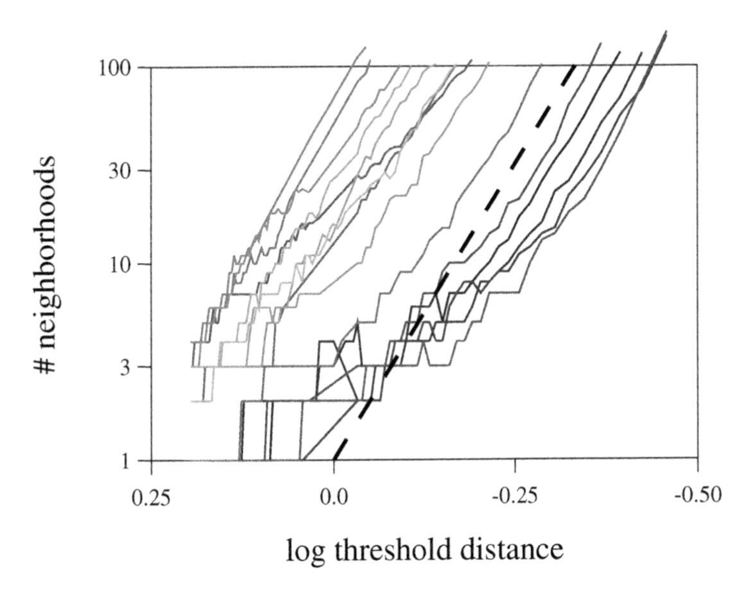

Fig. 3. Plot shows the number of neighborhoods formed for different values of the (angular) distance threshold. The heavy dashed line indicates a slope of 6 on the log-log axes; to the extent that this matches the slope of the curves generated from the empirical data, this suggests that the image manifold has an intrinsic dimensionality of 6. Each data curve represents a recording of approximately 100,000 frames. The five curves to the right of the dashed line represent images collected at night for which the only illumination was provided by the apparatus.

This process is effectively a nearest-neighbor classifier [5, 6], where the "classes" are defined implicitly by the exemplars. The results of the second pass are shown in the right-hand panel of figure 2.

The number of exemplars N found by this procedure depends on the choice of δ, and the dependence tells us something about the intrinsic dimensionality of the image manifold. The discovery of interesting structure from the topology of the manifold is the subject of a relatively new field of study known as *manifold learning*, exemplified by [7]. In figure 2, where we have represented the images as points in a two-dimensional space, the number of exemplars would be expected to grow in inverse proportion to the square of δ; in practice, the dimensionality is much greater. Figure 3 shows a plot of the number of exemplars generated as a function of δ for 15 individual video recordings from a head-mounted eye camera, each consisting of around 100,000 frames. The heavy dashed line indicates a slope of 6 on the log-log plot, which provides a reasonable fit to the asymptotic slope of the data graphs. The five records to the right of the dashed line correspond to the five night flights, for which the illumination is relatively constant. While there is a good deal of horizontal dispersion, each data set shows an asymptotic slope near 6, suggesting that the images vary in 6 dimensions. Four of these can be accounted for by physiological variables: two dimensions of gaze direction, and one each for pupil dilation and degree of eyelid closure.

The data shown in figure 3 are useful in two ways: first, they allow us to choose an initial value of δ which is small enough to generate more than one exemplar, but not so small that the number becomes unmanageable. Secondly, knowledge of the manifold's intrinsic dimension tells us how to decrease δ when we apply the procedure recursively to the neighborhoods generated by the first pass. If N is the intrinsic dimensionality of the image manifold, then to obtain k child nodes, we should divide δ by the Nth root of k.

3 Computational Efficiency

When δ is small relative to variation in the input set, many images are added to the catalog, and as the size of the catalog grows, the cost of testing a new image against the entire catalog grows apace. Can we reduce the number of tests which must be performed? Provided we retain the distances between the exemplar images, the answer is yes, by judicious application of the triangle inequality (see figure 4). Imagine we are processing a new image $\mathbf{x}$, which we have just compared to the exemplar $\mathbf{e}_i$ corresponding to the previous frame. We call the distance between these two images $d(\mathbf{x}, \mathbf{e}_i)$, which we assume to be greater than δ. There are two classes of exemplar which we can exclude from further testing: if $\mathbf{e}_i$ is far from $\mathbf{x}$, then we can reject any exemplars which are sufficiently near to $\mathbf{e}_i$; conversely, if $\mathbf{e}_i$ is near to $\mathbf{x}$, then we can reject any exemplars which are sufficiently far from $\mathbf{e}_i$. These notions are illustrated in figure 4. To reject a candidate exemplar (like $\mathbf{e}_k$ in figure 4) for being too far away from $\mathbf{e}_i$, we apply the triangle inequality to the lower triangle in figure 4, and find that we can reject $\mathbf{e}_j$ if $d(\mathbf{e}_i, \mathbf{e}_j) - d(\mathbf{e}_i, \mathbf{x}) > \delta$. Similarly, we can apply the triangle inequality to the upper triangle in figure 4, and see that we can reject $\mathbf{e}_j$ if $d(\mathbf{e}_i, \mathbf{x}) - d(\mathbf{e}_i, \mathbf{e}_j) > \delta$. The first test rejects all exemplars falling outside the

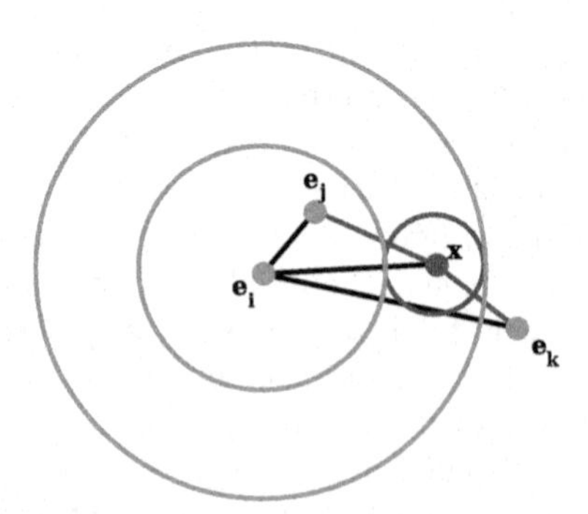

Fig. 4. Two-dimensional illustration of the use of the triangle inequality to cull unnecessary distance tests: the new input is $\mathbf{x}$, which has been tested against the exemplar chosen for the previous frame $\mathbf{e}_i$. We assume that the entire matrix of inter-exemplar distances is available. Exemplar $\mathbf{e}_j$ can rejected for being too close to $\mathbf{e}_i$, while $\mathbf{e}_k$ can be rejected for being too far. Exemplars falling in the annular region between the two large circles cannot be rejected and must be tested against $\mathbf{x}$.

largest circle in figure 4, while the second test rejects all exemplars falling inside the inner circle. Exemplars falling in the annular region bounded by the two concentric circles cannot be rejected, and must be compared directly to $\mathbf{x}$. The two cases can be combined into a single test: reject $\mathbf{e}_j$ if $|d(\mathbf{e}_i, \mathbf{x}) - d(\mathbf{e}_i, \mathbf{e}_j)| > \delta$.

Each time the distance between the new image $\mathbf{x}$ and an exemplar is computed, we can apply the test indicated above to all the remaining exemplars which have not yet been rejected. The computational savings resulting from this procedure cannot be predicted without knowledge of how the input images are distributed relative to one another. In our data set, the number of tests is reduced by more than half, compared to exhaustive search. Offset against this savings is the fact that we must maintain the symmetric matrix of distances between all the exemplars; when a new image is added to the catalog, we must tabulate the distances to all the other images in the catalog.

4 Distance Metrics

To this point, we have been deliberately vague about what we mean by the "distance" between two images; a common approach is to treat the images as points in an N-dimensional space (where N is the number of pixels, and the value of each pixel is the coordinate), and compute the standard Euclidean distance, as is done in [8]. This metrics, however, does not capture our intuitive idea of visual similarity under variable illumination. Scaling an image by a constant factor does not generally affect the visual appearance, but can result in a large distance. Normalized cross-correlation is often used to compare images when we wish to ignore scale changes of this sort:

$$r(\mathbf{x}, \mathbf{y}) = \frac{\mathbf{x}.\mathbf{y}}{|\mathbf{x}||\mathbf{y}|} . \tag{1}$$

The normalized correlation itself does not obey the triangle inequality; however, recalling that the dot product is related to the angle between two vectors by $\mathbf{x}.\mathbf{y} = |\mathbf{x}||\mathbf{y}|\cos(\theta)$, we use the correlation to compute an angular distance measure:

$$d(\mathbf{x}, \mathbf{y}) = \arccos(\ r(\mathbf{x}, \mathbf{y})\ ) . \tag{2}$$

We can visualize this for the case of three dimensional vectors: if each vector is projected to a point on the unit sphere, and the angle between the two vectors corresponds to the arc length of the great circle joining the two points. Because the triangle inequality holds on the sphere, the culling algorithm described above can be used with this distance measure.

5 Eye State Model

The primary parameters of interest in our application are the angles describing the rotational state of the eye within the orbit, which together with the position and orientation of the head determine the gaze vector in the world. The primary

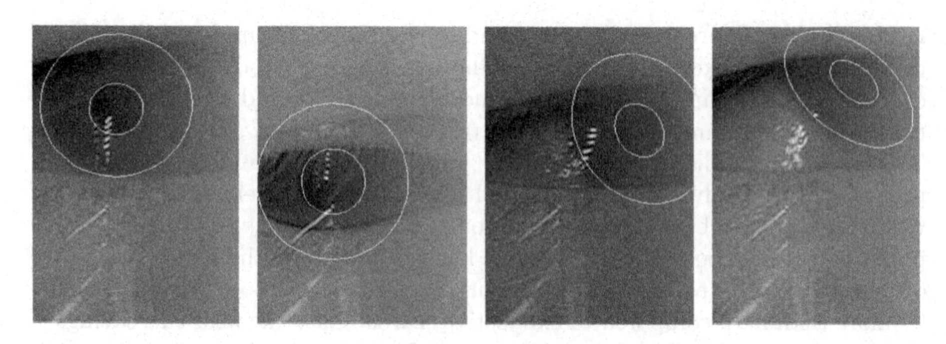

Fig. 5. Images of the eye with a rendering of a hand-tuned pupil-limbus model superimposed. The model has 5 global parameters (fixed for all images from a given run), and 3 parameters set on a frame-by-frame basis, consisting of two gaze angles and the pupil radius.

features we will use to determine these angles are the inner and outer margins of the iris, known as the *pupil* and the *limbus*, respectively. While the radius of the limbus is constant for a particular subject, the radius of the pupil varies in response to ambient light level, and is subject to continuous fluctuations due to the under-damped nature of the neural control system. Here we assume that pupil and limbus are concentric circles in the plane of the iris.

The problem is complicated by the fact that the pupil is not viewed directly, but lies behind the cornea, which is the eye's primary refracting surface. The effect of this is to increase the apparent size and reduce the apparent distance of the pupil relative to its physical location [9]. We approximate the appearance by a model with no refraction, with a tunable parameter for the depth separation between the planes containing the pupil and limbus. Other parameters which have a fixed value for all the images from a given subject are the limbus radius, and the distance of the plane of the limbus from the center of rotation. When the optical axis of the eye is directed toward the camera, the pupil and limbus appear as concentric circles in the image, and the location of their common center provides another pair of parameters, which are constant as long as there is no relative motion between the camera and the head. As gaze deviates from this direction, the images pupil and limbus are foreshortened and are well-fit by ellipses; lines drawn through the minor axes of these ellipses all intersect at the center point, which we use to find the center in our hand-labeling procedure. Figure 5 shows several images labeled with the pupil-limbus model. In addition to the iris parameters, we also label the eyelid margins in a separate labeling procedure.

The direction of gaze is the variable of primary interest for our application; while the tree-structure imposed on our set of images was based on overall image similarity (as captured by the correlation), it is our intuition that images which are similar will have similar gaze directions, and so the leaves of our tree can be associated with compact neighborhoods in gaze space. Note that the converse is not true: there can be images corresponding to the same direction of gaze which are very dissimilar, either because of lighting variations or a change in eyelid posture.

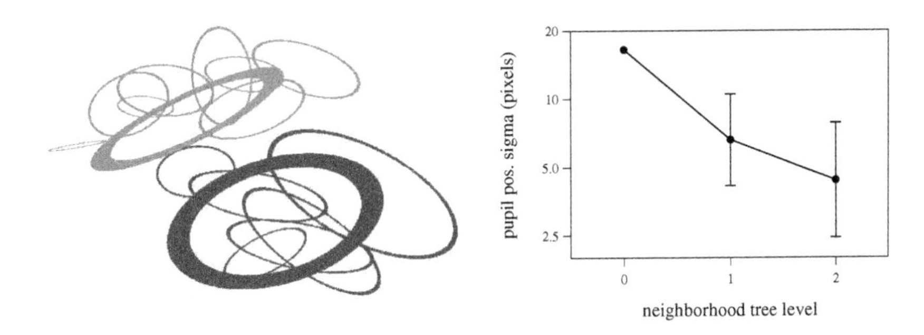

Fig. 6. Left panel: Ellipses depicting the variability in pupil position of child node exemplars for two first-level nodes (thick ellipses), and their corresponding second-level child nodes (thin ellipses). Right panel: Summary of variability in pupil position among subordinate nodes is shown for the first three levels in the hierarchy. The error bars show the standard deviation between the groups at the same level. (There are no error bars for the root node, because there is only one group.) The results validate our intuition that as image similarity increases, variation in gaze direction decreases.

To validate our intuition, we computed the variability in pupil position among the child exemplar images for the first three levels in the hierarchy for a single run (see figure 6). To generate this figure, 653 images were hand-labeled, consisting of the root node and the first three levels of the tree. For each image, we computed the position of the pupil center from the stored model parameters. For each node in the tree, we computed the mean pupil position over that node's children, and the corresponding standard deviations in x and y, and the covariance between the x and y deviations. In the left panel of figure 6, these derived measures are represented as ellipses, showing the scatter (in image space) of the pupil position in subordinate nodes. In the figure, 2 (of 14) first level nodes are represented, along with their all of their subordinate second-level nodes.

A crude univariate measure was formed by taking the Pythagorean sum of the x and y standard deviations, which is plotted for all the nodes on the right side of figure 6. At level 0, there is only a single node (the root of the tree); the average deviation among its children is plotted as the left-most point in figure 6. There are 14 level 1 nodes; for each of these we perform the same calculation over its children; we then compute the mean over the 14 nodes, plotting 1 standard deviation of this mean as an error bar in figure 6. Although the grouping was done on the basis of overall image appearance without regard to pupil position, we see from the data that the gaze directions do become more tightly clustered as we descend the tree.

6 Summary

We have described a method for decomposing a collection of images into subsets based on similarity of appearance; the resulting set of exemplars spans and uniformly samples the original collection, and is useful for application of techniques such as Active Shape Modeling which require hand-labeling of a training set. We have obtained useful results applying this process to a data set of eye images collected outdoors with uncontrolled illumination.

References

1. Cootes, T.F., Taylor, C.J.: Statistical models of appearance for medical image analysis and computer vision. In: Proc. SPIE Med. Imag. 2001. Volume 1. (2001) 236–248
2. A. Gersho and R. M. Gray: Vector Quantization and Signal Compression. Kluwer Academic Publishers (1992)
3. R. H. S. Carpenter: Movements of the Eyes. Pion (1977)
4. E. Kowler: Eye Movements and Their Role in Visual and Cognitive Processes. Elsevier (1990)
5. Cover, T.M., Hart, P.E.: Nearest neighbor pattern classification. IEEE Transactions on Information Theory **IT-13** (1967) 21–27
6. R. O. Duda and P. E. Hart and D. G. Stork: Pattern Classification. John Wiley and Sons (2001)
7. Tenenbaum, J.B., de Silva, V., Langford, J.C.: A global geometric framework for nonlinear dimensionality reduction. Science **290** (2000) 2319–2323
8. Christoudias, C.M., Darrell, T.: On modelling nonlinear shape-and-texture appearance manifolds. In Schmid, C., Soatto, S., Tomasi, C., eds.: Proc. IEEE Computer Society Conference on Computer Vision and Pattern Recognition (CVPR). (2005) 1067–1074
9. Ohno, T., Mukawa, N., Yoshikawa, A.: Freegaze: a gaze tracking system for everyday gaze interaction. In Duchowski, A.T., Vertegaal, R., Senders, J.W., eds.: Proc. Eye Tracking Research & Applications Symposium (ETRA), ACM (2002) 125–132

Emotional Expression in Virtual Agents Through Body Language

Vishal Nayak[1] and Matthew Turk[1,2]

[1] Media Arts and Technology Program, [2] Computer Science Department,
University of California, Santa Barbara, CA 93106
{v.nayak, mturk}@mat.ucsb.edu

Abstract. Virtual agents are used to interact with humans in a myriad of applications. However, the agents often lack the believability necessary to maximize their effectiveness. These agents, or characters, lack personality and emotions, and therefore the capacity to emotionally connect and interact with the human. This deficiency prevents the viewer from identifying with the characters on a personal level. This research explores the possibility of automating the expression of a character's mental state through its body language. Using a system that animates a character procedurally, we provide tools to modify the character's body movements in real-time, so that they reflect the character's mood, personality, interest, bodily pain, and emotions, all of which make up the current mental state of the character.

1 Introduction

Virtual agents must be able to interact and communicate effectively with a human. The major difficulty in this task is the fact that believability of the virtual character is essential for effective interaction. Believability is the ability of the agent to be viewed as a living, although fictional, character. We believe that only if the user views the agent as a living character will the user seriously mentally engage him/herself with the agent. Through this mental engagement, the virtual agents will be able to be maximally effective in their interaction with humans and will be able to connect with the human on a personal and emotional level. This connection is especially important for applications that attempt to significantly affect the user. These applications may include certain educational applications or games that aim to challenge the individual emotionally.

We believe that individuals will be able to better relate to virtual agents if these agents exhibit personality and emotions. Their believability would increase, since the expression of personality and emotions causes the agents to seem more like living characters. The objective of this research is to translate the high-level qualitative concepts of personality and emotion into low-level communicative physical gestures. In other words, we have enabled the character to perform body language based on his/her current mental state, which may include personality, emotions, mood, interest, or even bodily pain.

G. Bebis et al. (Eds.): ISVC 2005, LNCS 3804, pp. 313 – 320, 2005.

2 Background

Researchers have performed a considerable amount of research related to interactive virtual humans. One prominent area is that of Embodied Conversational Agents, which are agents that converse with humans. Justine Cassell, a pioneer of this area, has performed extensive research on the complex interaction between verbal cues (e.g., speech) and non-verbal cues (e.g., expressions, nods, gestures) [2]. Although our project does not deal with conversation, their research of communicative body language is very relevant to our work.

Laban Movement Analysis is a system for observing and notating all forms of movement. Researchers at the University of Pennsylvania have been using this system to mathematically gather essential gesture components from motion-capture and video data. These gesture components, which represent various characteristics, can then be applied to other motions [1]. Similar to our work, they are focusing on the implementation of movements that make up body language however our approaches are quite different.

The main goal of this research is to provide the capability to express a character's mental state through his/her body language in order to invoke an emotional response in the user. The character's expression will come in the form of facial expressions as well as body language. This system is meant to be a tool for the developer of any system with virtual agents. As the developer specifies the character's different personality or emotional characteristics, the character will modify its body structure, current movement, and/or create additional movements to reflect these characteristics.

The system presents the developer with control over seven main mental state characteristics that the character can express. These characteristics are confidence, anxiety, interest, thought, anger, defensiveness, and pain. The developer can control the quantities of the characteristics present in the character. These characteristics produce some body language, or automated change in the character's behavior, that is expressive of this mental state. We chose these seven characteristics because we felt that they were common characteristics that allowed for effective displays of body language. There is nothing inherently special about these seven characteristics, nor do they form a comprehensive set. Rather, these are the examples that we chose to demonstrate the power and effectiveness of using body language. The system can be extended to include any characteristic for which body language can be defined.

We use procedural animation to animate the character because of the real-time flexibility that the movements require. All body movements of the character are created algorithmically in real-time. For this project, we have used the PEAL character animation system and Playspace's emotion model (both described below).

2.1 Perlin Emotive Actor Library

Our system is built on the Perlin Emotive Actor Library (PEAL), which is a procedural, 3-dimensional, character animation system written in C++ using OpenGL [4]. We use a masculine character provided by the PEAL system, which supports the procedural animation of the body and facial features as well the character's walking action. We have built our system as a layer on top of the existing PEAL system.

Ken Perlin has won an Academy Award for his creation of Perlin Noise, which is noise created by a rhythmic stochastic noise function. Perlin Noise can be added to the joint angles of the body parts of the character in the PEAL system. This noise causes small irregular rhythmic movements, which give the impression of some natural fidgeting, the intensity of which can be adjusted.

2.2 Emotivation Model

Playspace, Inc., a game company in California, has performed extensive research on a model of emotion that can control facial expressions. This research includes analyzing, representing, and modeling facial expressions as well. They have developed a theory for understanding the expression of human emotion through facial expressions. They have broken down emotions into three primitive scales, called emotivations, each of which is a spectrum with two opposing notions at the ends. These three continuous dimensions are excite-depress, pain-pleasure, and aversion-desire. Each of these primitive scales directly maps onto a continuous range of facial movements between two extremes (see Figure 1). The facial expression of any emotion can be made up of some combination of values of these three spectrums.

Fig. 1. These facial expressions correspond to the extremes of the stated emotivations

The level on the depress-excite continuum directly relates to the amount of energy that is exhibited by the character. The aversion-desire continuum deals with the amount that the character is attracted to or repulsed by an object. The pain-pleasure continuum describes the amount of pain or pleasure that the character is experiencing. We have used this model for the facial expression component of this project.

2.3 Uses and Applications

As mentioned above, this system is meant to be a tool for the developer of applications with interactive agents. The various mental state characteristics and their parameters will be accessible to the programmer through an API.

Although any application with interactive agents will benefit from the addition of some personality or emotion-based body language, our system is particularly useful for agents in virtual worlds. Virtual reality and games would benefit hugely, since the agent interacts with the world and experiences different situations that may cause changes in his mental state.

3 Actions and Body Movements

In our system, when certain mental state conditions are met, the character may perform an action that is representative of this mental state. While an action is being performed, if the conditions change such that the action's conditions are no longer met, then the character terminates the action as soon as possible. All of the character's actions and movements at any given time make up his body language.

In our work, we have created body language by specifying the movements of various body parts as functions of the mental state characteristics over time. The PEAL system implements these movements in the geometry of the 3-dimensional character and handles the movements' repercussions to the rest of the body through the use of forward and inverse kinematics, which are crucial to procedural character animation.

All actions that make up body language are assigned a priority level depending on the importance of the action. Any actions created by the programmer should be assigned a priority level as well. In the case of a conflict between actions (e.g., two actions use the hands), this priority level will determine which action is performed.

The duration and delay time of actions are often determined probabilistically within a certain range. For an action that is representative of a certain mental state characteristic, often the average duration of the action is directly proportional to the level of the characteristic and the average delay of the action is inversely proportional to the level of the characteristic. The higher the characteristic level of the character, the sooner and for a greater amount of time he will perform the action. This timing helps to communicate the intensity of the characteristic to the user and the probabilistic nature helps to maintain unpredictability.

4 Mental State Characteristics

Emotions, personality traits, moods, and mental dispositions all contribute to a person's mental state. We have chosen to focus on seven main characteristics for this project: confidence, anxiety, interest, thought, anger, defensiveness, and pain. We have implemented a representative set of body language for each characteristic, which the programmer can set to any value on a continuous scale.

Fig. 2. The character in our system expressing (left to right) anger, defensiveness, and headache

If multiple characteristics affect the same body movements, then some of these movements (e.g., posture) can be averaged together by means of a weighted average, the weights of which are the levels of the characteristics causing the effects.

See Figure 2 for a few screenshots of different body language performed by the character in our system.

Confidence

The confidence scale is from total lack of confidence to complete confidence. The facial expression of the character is controlled by the depress and pleasure emotivations. As he becomes unconfident, the depress emotivation is added and the character gains a subdued expression. As he becomes increasingly confident, a slight amount of pleasure is added and the character forms a confident smile.

The posture of the character is directly proportional to the level of confidence. A complete lack of confidence will lead to a self-doubting hunched-over character. As confidence increases, the character's posture straightens with his chest out and chin up. The speed of the character's gait, which is affected by stride duration, stride size, and horizontal leg lift, is directly proportional to confidence.

As the character becomes increasingly confident, he occasionally places his hands behind his back with his chest protruding outward. If extremely confident, the character may clasp his hands behind his head in a relaxed resting position.

Anxiety

The anxiety scale goes from calmness to total anxiety. As the character's anxiety increases, he becomes slightly worried and gains a facial expression of excitement. The value of the depress-excite emotivation increases linearly with the anxiety level.

As anxiety increases, the level of Perlin noise increases linearly between a certain range. This increase creates the effect of the character becoming increasingly nervous and fidgety as his anxiety level goes up. The anxiety level of the character is also reflected in the stress carried in the character's shoulders. As anxiety increases, the character's shoulders gradually become increasingly tensed up, or shrugged.

If the anxiety level is greater than a certain value, the character may widen his lips and begin biting his nails.

Interest

If the agent is in a virtual environment or is a character in a game, then he may have a certain mental disposition towards various encountered objects (or characters). The interest scale is from dislike of the object to affinity for the object. The midpoint corresponds to being completely indifferent to the object. The emotivation of aversion-desire is directly proportional to the level of interest.

If the character has no feelings towards any object for an extended period of time and if the character has a certain amount of the depress emotivation (lacks energy), he gets bored and may yawn. However, if the character is interested in or is averse to an object, then it holds the character's attention and therefore his gaze. As these feelings of interest and aversion intensify to a certain amount, the character rotates towards and away from the object, respectively. As the feelings become even stronger, the character begins to walk towards or away from the object.

Thought

We must first define *thought* precisely. With the use of the five senses, an individual is taking in a constant stream of information through the process of perception. To think, however, is to go beyond this automatic perceptual reflex and to actually formulate a mental event. In order for a character to uphold the illusion of being a living non-robotic creature, it is necessary for the character to take part in, or pretend to take part in, natural actions such as thinking. In order to be effective, a character must allow the viewer to be able to see his thought process, which can be accomplished through the eye-accessing cues defined in neuro-linguistic programming (NLP) [3].

Neuro-linguistic programming (NLP) is essentially a model of communication and personality. It deals with the studying and modeling of human behavior. One relevant aspect of NLP is eye-accessing cues. According to NLP, when humans think, they commonly make short eye movements in observable directions. These movements can indicate to which of the five senses the thought relates and whether the thought is a memory or an imagination. Space does not permit us to go into greater detail here.

The thought scale is from lack of thought to deep thought. As the character becomes more deeply lost in thought, his natural fidgeting, or the Perlin noise in his joints, decreases. When maximally deep in thought, he is almost completely frozen.

Anger

The emotivations of excite, desire, and pain allow the character to facially express his anger. The feeling of anger can certainly cause one to become agitated or excited. An angered character has the desire to mentally involve and concern himself with a certain situation. Anger is a painful experience and, especially if present over a long period of time, can be unhealthy and harmful.

The natural fidgeting of the character, determined by the amount of Perlin Noise in the joints, is directly proportional to the level of anger. As the anger level rises, the character's body starts trembling and eventually seems to boil over with rage.

As the character's anger increases, he gradually begins to gaze towards the entity at which he is directing his anger and, at maximum anger, holds a steadfast gaze on this entity. If the anger level of the character rises above a certain point, the character performs the hostile gesture of clenching his fists tightly. If he is walking, he will swing his clenched fists as he walks.

Defensiveness

When protecting oneself from an outside force, whether the force is a serious threat or a mild social threat, it is common for individuals to put a barrier between themselves and the outside force. An individual may consciously or subconsciously defend him/herself by covering up or blocking part of his/her body.

The level of defensiveness is linearly related to the excite emotivation, which shows the amount of energy (physical and mental) that the character is expending in protecting himself. When experiencing defensiveness, the character will have a small amount of desire. He possesses the desire to protect himself from some entity.

When defensive, the character will periodically gaze away from the entity of which he is defensive. This action of gazing away prevents confrontation and prevents the character from giving any impression of aggressiveness. However, if the level of defensiveness is greater than a certain amount, then the character is facing an imminent threat and will not gaze away, since the avoidance of confrontation is no longer a possibility. He must physically protect himself by engaging in an action of self-defense. This action must be specific to the current threat, so we have implemented a generic action in which the character places both hands in fists in the air in front of him to protect himself. If the level of defensiveness is less than this self-defense threshold, then the character may cross his arms.

Physical Pain

The pain emotivation is directly proportional to the level of physical pain. Pain in a particular body part will affect the movements involving that body part. We have implemented some body language for pain in the character's head, stomach, hands/arms, and feet. Since the character will have a high compulsion to alleviate his pain, this body language is given a high priority, which will allow it to interrupt any other conflicting body language that has a lower priority.

Pain in the head, stomach, or feet is debilitating. Hence, the character's posture and, if he is walking, the walk speed are both inversely proportional to the level of pain. The character hunches over and slows down as pain increases. If the pain is greater than a certain value, he stops walking altogether. If the character is walking with hand pain, as pain increases, he will gradually stop swinging the arm in pain. For pain in any body part, as pain increases, the character becomes less concerned with any object at which he is looking and more concerned with the body part in pain. Therefore, he lowers his gaze from the current object to the ground in front of him and then, for pain in the hands or feet, moves his gaze to the body part in pain. This gaze change is given a priority level, so that the programmer may override this gazing action if he desires.

For pain in the head, stomach, and hands, if the pain rises above a certain point, the character holds the body part in pain. If he has a headache, he will first place one hand to his head and then, as pain increases, will place the second hand asymmetrically on his head as well. For a stomachache, he will hold his stomach with both hands asymmetrically. For hand pain, he will cradle the injured hand or arm with the healthy one.

5 Evaluation

We performed an informal evaluation of our system, in which we tested twenty-six subjects in a small experiment to gauge the effectiveness of the system. The subjects were given the program with an interface that consisted of seven anonymous sliders that controlled the quantities of the seven characteristics. They were also given a list of possible characteristics. Their task was to move the sliders, view the resulting body language, and match each slider to a characteristic on the given list. Their accuracy was measured by the percentage of sliders that they identified correctly.

The results, shown in Table 1, are encouraging. Accuracy ranges from 62% to 92%. A limitation of this evaluation is the fact that in an interaction with the user, and especially in virtual environments such as in games, the characters will have some context for their actions. We believe that the situational context of this body language is quite important to its identification.

Table 1. Accuracy percentages of the subjects' identification of the various characteristics

Mental	Confidence	Anxiety	Interest	Thought	Anger	Defensiveness	Pain
Accuracy	65 %	85%	62%	77%	92%	88%	88%

6 Conclusion

We have presented a system that allows a developer to endow a character with various personality characteristics, emotions, and mental attributes, such that the character automatically expresses this mental state through his body language. We strongly believe that these affective behaviors increase the believability of the character, which allows the user to better relate to and emotionally connect with the character.

With an emotional connection to the user, applications can affect the user in creative, innovative, and revolutionary ways. Educational games can challenge the player on a personal, emotional, or even ethical level. They can force users to make decisions that shape their personalities or allow them to grow as human beings. Educational applications can teach children values and life lessons. The ability of an interactive agent to personally affect the user undoubtedly allows the agent, and hence the application, to be significantly more effective.

References

1. Allbeck, J., Badler, N., Byun, M., Zhao, L., Representing and Parameterizing Agent Behaviors, Proceedings of Computer Animation, IEEE Computer Society, Center for Human Modeling and Simulation, University of Pennsylvania, 2002.
2. Cassell, J., Churchill, E., Prevost, S., Sullivan, J., Embodied Conversational Agents, MIT Press, Boston, Massachusetts, 2000.
3. Hall, L. Michael, Belnap, Barbara P.: The Sourcebook of Magic. A Comprehensive Guide to the Technology of NLP, Crown House Publishing Ltd., Williston, VT, 1999.
4. Perlin, Ken: Real Time Responsive Animation with Personality, IEEE Transactions on Visualization and Computer Graphics, Vol. 1 No. 1, Media Research Laboratory, Department of Computer Science, New York University, 1995.

Visual Tracking for Seamless 3D Interactions in Augmented Reality

C. Yuan*

Fraunhofer Institute for Applied Information Technology,
Collaborative Virtual and Augmented Environments,
Schloss Birlinghoven, 53754 Sankt Augustin, Germany
chunrong.yuan@fit.fraunhofer.de

Abstract. This paper presents a computer vision based approach for creating 3D tangible interfaces, which can facilitate real–time and flexible interactions with the augmented virtual world. This approach uses real–world objects and free–hand gestures as interaction handles. The identity of these objects/gestures as well as their 3D pose in the physical world can be tracked in real–time. Once the objects and gestures are perceived and localized, the corresponding virtual objects can be manipulated dynamically by human operators who are operating on those real objects. Since the tracking algorithm is robust against background clutter and adaptable to illumination changes, it performs well in real–world scenarios, where both objects and cameras move rapidly in unconstrained environments.

1 Introduction

Augmented Reality (AR) deals mainly with the visual enhancement of the physical world. The interactive aspect of AR requires tangible interfaces [1] that can invoke dynamic actions and changes in the augmented 3D space. On the one hand, the concept of tangible interfaces makes it possible to develop interactive AR applications. On the other hand, reliable systems that can retrieve the identity and location of real–world objects have to be developed. It is obvious that successful AR interactions depend among other things largely on the robust processing and tracking of real–world objects. According to [2], many AR systems will not be able to run without accurate registration of the real world.

Various means can be employed for the tracking of real–world objects including mechanical, electromagnetic, acoustic, inertial, optical and image based devices [3]. We favor the image based tracking method because it is non–invasive and can be applied in both static and dynamic situations. Unlike other approaches, image based visual tracking is a closed–loop approach that tackles simultaneously the registration and interaction problem. Images can provide a visual feedback on the registration performance so that an AR user can know how closely the real and virtual objects match each other. With this visual feedback, interactions with the virtual world can take place more naturally and efficiently.

* The author thanks the whole CVAE group as well as colleagues outside Fraunhofer for their kind support and discussions.

G. Bebis et al. (Eds.): ISVC 2005, LNCS 3804, pp. 321–328, 2005.

One popular approach to the visual tracking problem is using marker objects. In [4], 2D ARToolkit markers are used to render virtual objects onto them. A cube with different colors on each side of its surface has been used in [5], where the cube is localized in an image by the CSC color segmentation algorithm. In [6], the 3D pose of a dotted pattern is recovered using a pair of stereo cameras. Because these marker objects are designed only for tracking, they are not suitable for interaction purposes.

A few other works suggest using hand gestures as tangible interfaces. In [7], a pointing posture is detected based on human body segmentation by combining background subtraction method and region categorization. Another example is the augmented desk interface [8]. Here arms of a user are segmented from the infrared input image using a simple threshold operation. After that, fingertips are searched for within regions with fixed size using template matching algorithm. Gestures are then recognized based on multiple fingertip trajectories.

In this paper, we present a new approach which is capable of real–time tracking of the physical world as well as the creation of natural and easy to use interfaces. By relating real–world objects to their counterparts in the augmented virtual world one by one, a set of interaction units can be constructed so that the virtual world can be manipulated seamlessly by AR users operating on those real objects [9].

The proposed tracking approach contributes to the state–of–the–art in several aspects. First, both real–world objects as well as free–hand gestures are tracked simultaneously to satisfy different interaction purposes. Unlike the markers used in the references, the objects we have designed are much smaller, which makes it much easier to grasp. Second, our tracking system can support multiple users who can interact with the AR world either individually or cooperatively. Last but not least, the tracking cameras in our system are allowed to move freely in unconstrained environments, while most tracking systems can only handle static camera(s).

The remainder of this paper is organized as follows. Sect. 2. gives an overview of the tracking system. Sect. 3. presents the visual tracking algorithm. Interaction mechanisms based on the results of visual tracking are shown in Sect. 4. System performance is evaluated and discussed in Sect. 5., followed by a summary in Sect. 6.

2 System Overview

The tracking system is designed to be used in a multi–user AR environment, where several users need to interact collaboratively with the virtual world rendered on top of a round table (see Fig. 1(a)). For different purposes, different kinds of interaction mechanisms are needed. Hence we use various 2D/3D objects as well as hand gestures as input devices. The scene captured by the tracking system is very dynamic, as both foreground and background objects are changing constantly and unexpectedly.

The users can sit or stand, and can move around the table to examine the virtual world from different viewpoints. In order that the system keeps tracking the hand gestures while the users are moving freely, cameras are mounted on the head mounted displays (HMD). As a result, both the objects and the cameras are moving all the time. To enable dynamic interactions with the target objects in the virtual world, 3D pose parameters of the objects and gestures should be estimated precisely and in real time.

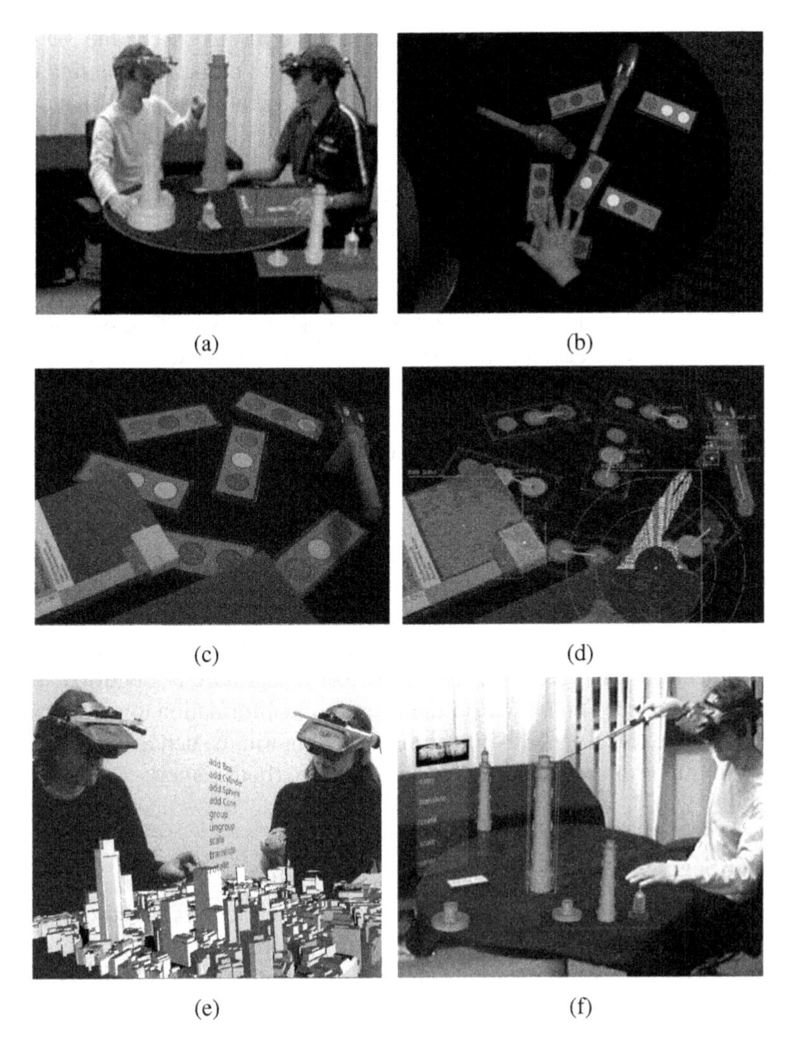

Fig. 1. (a). Multiple AR users interact with the augmented virtual world. (b). Objects and gestures used in the tracking system. (c). Offline color calibration. (d). Illustration of recognition and tracking results. (e). Manipulation of the virtual buildings. (f) Creation of new 3D models.

The central task of the vision based 3D interface is the identification and tracking of multiple colored objects appeared in the camera view. As shown in Fig. 1(b), the objects are made of six 2D place holder objects (PHOs), two 3D pointers, and a set of gestures. PHOs are 2D colored objects with 3DOF (degree of freedom) pose. They are called place holders because they are used mainly to be related to their virtual counterparts. The pose of the pointers is 6DOF. They are pointing devices that can be used to point at some virtual objects in 3D.

There are altogether six kinds of gestures used in the system, with the hand showing zero (a fist gesture) to five fingers. The gesture with one finger is a dynamic pointing gesture whose 6DOF pose can be tracked in the same way as that of the 3D pointers. The other five gestures are also tracked continuously. But unlike the pointing gestures, these gesture are tracked only in 3DOF, as they are generally used as visual command to trigger certain operations in the virtual world. Some HCI applications don't require the pose of a gesture to be known [8]. However, pose parameters of even a static gesture are indispensable for 3D interactions in location critical applications.

The tracking system uses a static camera (Elmo CC–491 camera unit with lipstick–size microhead QP–49H) hanging over the round table to recognize the PHOs. Each AR user wears a pair of head–mounted cameras (HMC), which is installed horizontally on the left and right side of the HMD. Each HMC is made of a pair of stereo cameras (JAI CV–M 2250 microhead camera) for 3D pose estimation. Pointers can be tracked by all the users' HMCs. Gestures made by an AR user are tracked only by the HMC on his own head. To increase tracking speed, the right image of a stereo pair will only be processed if pointers or gestures have been recognized in the left image.

3 Visual Object Tracking

Visual tracking for AR involves several steps such as object detection, object identification and object pose estimation. In the whole system, tracking is done using colors. First colored regions are detected. Then the shapes of the colored regions are analyzed to identify the objects and gestures. After an object or a gesture is identified, its 2D/3D pose will be estimated. Though we do use inter–frame information to guide tracking, it is not necessary to use a general–purpose tracking algorithm such as the condensation or mean–shift algorithm, as the scene is very dynamic (both cameras and objects move irregularly).

3.1 Color Segmentation

Color regions are segmented by identifying the different colors based on pixel–wise classification of the input images. For each of the colors used in the tracking system, a Gaussian model is built to approximate its distribution in the normalized red–green color space ($r' = \frac{r}{r+g+b}$, $g' = \frac{g}{r+g+b}$). Since color is very sensitive to the change of lighting conditions, adaptable color models are built in an offline color calibration process before the tracking system works online. The calibration is done interactively by putting objects in different locations. The adaptability of the color model can be visualized after calibration. To test the calibration result, the user just click on a color region and see whether it can be segmented properly, as is illustrated in Fig. 1(c), where the segmentation result of the right most circle on the top right PHO is shown.

After each of the used colors has been calibrated, the color models are completely built and can be made available for use in online tracking. Once new images are grabbed, the pixels that have similar statistics as those in the models are identified. Regions of different colors can now be established.

3.2 Object Recognition and Tracking

Recognition of the PHOs is done as follows. All the PHOs have a same background color. Once each region having this background color has been identified, the two colored regions within each can be localized and the geometric center of each circle can be computed . The lines connecting the two center points indicate the orientations of the PHOs (see Fig. 1(d)). Based on the identified colors, the identity of the PHOs can be determined. Using a calibrated camera, the 3DOF pose of the PHOs is easily calculated.

The recognition is quite robust. As can be seen from Fig. 1(d), all the six PHOs have been recognized despite occlusions. Neither does the existence of objects with similar colors in the image have any effect on the recognition results.

Recognition of the 3D pointers applies the same principle, i.e. by trying to locate the pointer's two colored regions. Shown in Fig. 1(d) on the right is the recognized pointer, whose 2D location and orientation have been marked with a line. The 3D pose estimation of pointers is not so straight forward as that of the PHOs, which will be explained in Sect. 3.3.

Gestures are identified through the analysis of skin–colored regions. The center of the palm is located by fitting a circle with maximal radius within the boundary of the segmented skin region. From here, fingers are sought after using circles with increasing radii. A region can be identified as a finger only if it can cross different circles with substantial pixels. Based on the number of found fingers, gestures can be differentiated. To suppress false alarms due to unintended hand movement of the user, only a gesture that has been recognized in three consecutive frames will be accepted as a gesture output. If the gesture is not a pointing gesture, then only the location of the hand (the center of the palm) will be computed. In case of a pointing gesture, calculation of its 3D pose is similar to that of the 3D pointers, i.e. by using the approach to be shown in Sect. 3.3.

For illustration purpose, the recognition result of a pointing gesture is shown in Fig. 1(d). The white point at the center of the hand shows the location of the palm. There are two big circles shown around the hand in Fig. 1(d). The interior one shows a circle which crosses the middle of the finger with an arc of maximal length. The exterior one crosses the finger with an arc whose distance to the fingertip is about one–sixth of the length the finger has. The center of this arc is regarded as the location of the fingertip. The line on the finger shows its orientation.

3.3 Multi–view 3D Pose Estimation

Since the HMC is not fixed in space, a multi–view based 3D pose estimation is approached. The calculation of the 3D pose of pointers and gestures is based on the triangulation of the points observed by both the HMC and the static overhead camera.

In principle there is no need to differentiate between a pointer and a pointing gesture, as in both cases, their 6DOF pose has to be computed. Due to this reason we will outline the algorithm by taking the pointer as an example.

In an offline process, the intrinsic camera parameters of the HMC and the transform matrix between the left and the right camera coordinate of the HMC is calibrated beforehand. Due to the constant movement of the HMC, it is necessary to estimate the extrinsic parameters of both the left and right cameras, i.e., to know the rotation and translation parameters of the HMC relative to the world coordinate. The idea is to use the PHOs to establish the transform matrices of the HMC.

Using the measurements of the static overhead camera, the 3D world coordinates of the colored circles on the PHOs can be computed. As long as two PHOs are in field–

of–view of the overhead camera, we can obtain at least four points whose 3D positions are known. If these PHOs are also in one of the HMC's field of view (e.g. the left or the right camera of the HMC), the 2D image coordinates of these four points in the HMC image are also computable. Let's suppose the left HMC camera sees the PHOs. Now its extrinsic camera parameters can be solved using a least square optimization algorithm. Based on the known transform between the two cameras of the HMC, the extrinsic parameters of the right camera can also be determined.

Since we have six PHOs, we can always have more than four points with known 3D–2D correspondences. This can guarantee a robust calculation of the projection matrices of the HMC even if some of the PHOs are moving or occluded. Once the location and orientation of the camera pair are known, a stereo–based reconstruction algorithm is applied to recover the 3D location of the pointer. If a pointer can be observed by more than one HMC, the pose computed by the two HMCs can differ. Hence we need to choose one with better quality. The criterion we use is to select the pose computed by a HMC that lies near to the pointer. By counting the total number of pixels the detected pointer has in both cases, the one with a larger size is chosen.

4 Vision Based 3D Interactions

With a working tracking system, users' intentions can be interpreted constantly and dynamically based on the captured status shift in the camera images. Using PHOs, pointers and gestures as tangible interface elements, AR users can interact with and manipulate objects in the virtual augmented world intuitively.

Shown in Fig. 1(e) are two AR users who need to cooperate with each other to accomplish the task of architectural design and city planing. In the users' HMDs, a virtual 3D model of a cityscape is visualized. With the objects in the physical world perceived and located, a number of dynamic interactions can be invoked seamlessly to support the design and construction process.

In the AR system, virtual objects can be selected and related to the PHOs by using either pointers or a pointing gesture. By pointing at a PHO first and a virtual building afterwards, a user can establish a one–to–one relationship between them. Correlation of a PHO and a virtual object can also be done by moving the PHO to the place where the virtual object is located.

An object is highlighted with a bounding box after selection so that users can know whether a virtual object is selected successfully (see Fig. 1(f)). For the same reason, the pointing directions can be visualized with highlighted virtual rays. A virtual object can be selected directly, when it is "touched" by the pointing gesture, as is shown in Fig. 1(a). Or the virtual object can be selected indirectly, so long the extension of the pointing ray intersects the virtual object, as is shown in Fig. 1(f).

If an AR user translates and rotates a PHO, the corresponding virtual building can be moved and rotated accordingly. Scaling of the buildings can be done if the user points at a corner of the highlighted bounding box and enlarges or shrinks it . Another way of scaling is to use gesture commands. Besides achieving scaling, gestures can also be used to activate such commands as "copy", "paste" or "delete". For example, after making a "copy" gesture command at the location where a virtual object resides, the user moves his hand to another place and makes a "paste" gesture command. A virtual object selected by the first gesture command will be duplicated. The duplicated building will now appear at the location where the second gesture has been made.

Similar to gestures, 3D virtual menus controlled by PHOs provide further means for the selection and creation of 3D buildings or 3D geometric parts. As shown in Fig. 1(e), the user on the left is using his pointer to select from the menu. With a menu item "translate", pointers or the pointing gesture can be used to move the selected virtual object to another place. By selecting and putting geometric parts together, new geometric models can be built on the fly. If one is not satisfied with the model just created, he can delete it using a simple "delete" gesture.

Take for example the top left object in Fig. 1(f). This virtual object is made of the three model objects shown on the bottom right. It is built by using the pointer to select and "glue" the three parts at the desired location. After the object is created, the user adds colors to its different parts by pointing at the part and utters a speech input at the same time. Although speech recognition is not the focus of this paper, we mention it just to show that tangible interfaces can be combined with other input methods such as 3D virtual menus or speech commands to assist interactions.

5 Performance Evaluation

System performance is evaluated based on experimental study and user tests. For the recognition of the objects and gestures, the approach of combining color and shape information leads to satisfactory recognition results: 99.2% for PHOs and pointers, 95.6% for gestures. Since PHOs and pointers are rigid objects, higher recognition rate has been achieved. The performance of gesture recognition is both encouraging and acceptable, since they are non–rigid and there exists a large variance of skin colors between different users. Furthermore, a user can make the same gesture in a number of different ways. For example, the gesture with three fingers shown can be made theoretically in ten different configurations by using any three fingers of a hand. Due to the user–friendly consideration, users are allowed to make the gesture in his own way.

Quantitative evaluation of the precision of the tracking is carried out by comparing the difference between the estimated pose and real pose. In average, the deviation is within 2 cm for translation parameters and 3° for rotation parameters. Based on the fact that different interaction tasks have been accomplished successfully and accurately, the quality of tracking and the effectiveness of the proposed interaction mechanisms have been positively evaluated by numerous AR users in different application scenarios.

Together with the other parts of our AR system, the tracking system runs in a distributed manner on several PCs. We can have one static camera tracking and three HMC tracking systems running simultaneously on three PCs, so that as much as three users wearing HMC can interact with the AR world. In average, the tracking speed ranges from 20 to 25 frames per second. The latency between tracking and visualization is negligible within the distributed AR environment. Extensive user tests show that the the tracking system achieves real–time performance for seamless 3D interactions in multi–user AR applications.

6 Conclusions

Interactions in AR require accurate, reliable and fast position tracking of the physical world. This paper presents a model–based visual tracking approach and its application in AR. The tracking system works in real time, is capable of robust tracking in multi–user AR environment. With a set of interaction units combining the real and the virtual, seamless interactions can be accomplished in 3D space intuitively. Using PHOs, pointers and free–hand gestures, users can interact with the AR system interchangeably. Having the visual object tracking system, the AR system always knows the user's intentions and can hence respond to the user's requests intelligently. By real–time rendering and visualization of the virtual objects together with added highlights, the AR users can see the interaction results immediately and this visual feedback can be used to guide their actions. In the future, we are aiming at developing more compact tracking system to enable pervasive interactions in mobile AR environments. We are planing to apply computer vision based tracking techniques in a number of real–world applications including AR enabled learning, pervasive gaming and human–robot interaction.

References

1. Patten, J., Ishii, H., Hines, J., Pangaro, G.: Sensetable: A wireless object tracing platform for tangible user interfaces. In: Conference on Human Factors in Computing Systems (CHI 2001), Seattle, USA (2001) 253–260
2. Azuma, R.: A survey of augmented reality. Teleoperators and Virtual Environments **6** (1997) 355–385
3. Hightower, J., Borriello, G.: Location systems for ubiquitous computing. IEEE Computer **34** (2001) 57–66
4. Poupyrev, I., Tan, D., Billinghurst, M., Kato, H., Regenbrecht, H., Tetsutani, N.: Developing a generic augmented-reality interface. IEEE Computer **35** (2002) 44–50
5. Schmidt, J., Scholz, I., Niemann, H.: Placing arbitrary objects in a real scene using a color cube for pose estimation. In: Pattern Recognition, 23rd DAGM Symposium, Munich, Germany (2001) 421–428
6. van Liere, R., Mulder, J.: Optical tracking using projective invariant marker pattern properties. In: IEEE Virtual Reality Conference 2003. (2003) 191–198
7. Kolesnik, M., Kuleßa, T.: Detecting, tracking and interpretation of a pointing gesture by an overhead view camera. In: Pattern Recognition, 23rd DAGM Symposium, Munich, Germany (2001) 429–436
8. Oka, K., Sato, S., Koike, H.: Real–time tracking of multiple fingertips and gesture recognition for augmented desk interface systems. IEEE Computer Graphics and Applications **22** (2002) 64–71
9. Yuan, C.: Simultaneous tracking of multiple objects for augmented reality applications. In: The Seventh Eurographics Symposium on Multimedia (EGMM 2004), Nanjing, P.R. China, Eurographics Association (2004) 41–47

ARISupport - Interaction Support for Augmented Reality Systems

Luiz Fernando Braga Lopes[1], Antonio Carlos Sementille [2,3], José Remo Ferreira Brega[2,3], Fátima L.S. Nunes Marques[2], and Ildeberto Aparecido Rodello[2]

[1] CESUMAR - Centro Universitário de Maringá
[2] UNIVEM - Centro Universitário Eurípides de Marília
[3] UNESP - Universidade Estadual Paulista Júlio de Mesquita Filho
lfbraga@cesumar.br
{semente, remo, fatima, rodello}@fundanet.br

Abstract. The communication between user and software is a basic stage in any Interaction System project. In interactive systems, this communication is established by the means of a graphical interface, whose objective is to supply a visual representation of the main entities and functions present in the Virtual Environment. New ways of interacting in computational systems have been minimizing the gap in the relationship between man and computer, and therefore enhancing its usability. The objective of this paper, therefore, is to present a proposal for a non-conventional user interface library called ARISupport, which supplies ARToolKit applications developers with an opportunity to create simple GUI interfaces, and provides some of the functionality used in Augmented Reality systems.

1 Introduction

Nowadays, the high degree of complexity imposed by tasks in different scientific areas is demanding more from man than their natural senses can provide. The interface with the user is constituted by the presentation of information, and it is this interface that asks for and receives data input, controls and commands. Finally it controls the dialog between the presentations and input. An interface defines both the strategies for carrying out the task as well as leads, guides, receptions, warns, assists and answers to the user during interactions [1]. Augmented Reality systems have the objective to make interactions in 3D environments possible, and to stimulate as many human senses as possible in order to connect the user in a way that is as close to reality as possible. However, to provide this connection, it is necessary that the user may be able to visualize, understand and carry out the necessary tasks in the Virtual Environment. In this article, we describe an interaction support for applications for Augmented Reality that provide components for the creation of geometrical forms, interaction tools and the development of the virtual environment. This support permits to developers to create sensitive interfaces by using markers from ARToolKit library [2], besides OpenGl and GLUT [3] functions.

G. Bebis et al. (Eds.): ISVC 2005, LNCS 3804, pp. 329–336, 2005.

2 Overview

In section 3 below, we describe the interactions in Augmented Reality, some interaction tasks and some interaction tools. In section 4 the ARToolKit library is presented, and as well as reporting on the use of this library in existing studies. In section 5 we find the support architecture as well as the functionalities provided. In section 6 the application tests using this support are illustrated. The limitations and future work are presented in section 7.

3 Interactions in Augmented Reality

The main requirement for the project of a computational graphical interface is the enhancing of the visualization task, i.e., the means that permits the user to access the system's contents. An interface may involve a highly interactive 3D control of computational processes, where the user enters the virtual space of applications, visualizes, manipulates and explores the application data in real time, using their senses, particularly the body's natural movements. To carry out this type of interaction, the user may use non-conventional devices such as visualization by HMD, gloves and others [4].

3.1 Interactions Tasks and Tools

According to Poupyrev [5], interaction tasks parameters are all the factors that influence the user's performance while he is carrying out an activity. They may classified according to their dependence on:

- **User:** experience, cognitive capability, perception and motor abilities, physical differences and others.
- **Input and output devices:** devices attributes such as freedom, resolution vision field and others.
- **Interaction techniques:** technique metaphors, their suggestions and implementation.
- **Application:** virtual environment configuration, size, form, use of objects, colors, lighting and others.
- **Context:** required precision, the tasks initial and final conditions, reaction to the tasks and others.

The interaction with virtual objects requires ways for the selection of objects, i.e., ways to indicate the interaction aim desired: Logical interfaces specify how the parameters for the environment and their objects may be altered, and physical interfaces, that consists of one or more visual, auditory or tactile equipment. The interaction controls may be [6]:

- **Direct User:** Hand tracking, gesture recognition.
- **Physical:** Joystick, trackball, mouse, gloves.
- **Virtual:** Virtual objects used to control movement.

Physical devices, however, do not always offer a natural mapping that facilitate the interaction task in the virtual world. By visually representing a physical device, anything that can be imagined may be implemented as a virtual control. This great flexibility is the main advantage of virtual controls. However, among the disadvantages is the loss of sensorial feedback.

4 Integration of Applications Using ARToolKit

ARToolKit is a set of libraries developed at the University of Washington that was designed for the quick development of Augmented Reality applications, providing computational vision techniques to calculate the position and orientation of markers printed in cards, by the use of a digital camera or HMD, so that these markers are correctly covered by 3D virtual objects. These markers supply a 4x4 projection matrix in reference to the spatial position in relation to capture device [5]. The reference elements for the calculations in the applications are values that came from the markers projection matrixes. In the next section we present works in which this library was used.

4.1 Related Work

Augmented Reality applications are developed to give the user the sensation of interaction with the real environment together with added information. To that aim, many tools have been developed.

In BUCHMANN et al. [8] it is presented an interaction technique in Augmented Real-ity environments denominated FingARTips, in which the ARToolKit library was used, where the markers are mounted on the finger tips to follow the user movements and establish an intention: manipulate virtual objects in an urban planning system.

Described by GEIGER [9], ARGUI offers the functionality of 2D interaction creating surfaces for Augmented Reality systems that need a virtual working area superimposed onto the real environment. Such project supplies a surface represented by a color pallet superimposed by a 2D panel sensitive to the touch of a cursor. After the interaction of the cursor with the panel, the meeting point is checked with a defined region. This region, for instance, may be defined as a button supplying an event.

5 The ARISupport Architecture

The use of libraries increases productivity and prevents unnecessary development efforts. They make available a set of elements already elaborated that may be promptly and easily used to build Augmented Reality systems. The support developed presents the following modules and characteristics:

Environment: Import figures as background images to obtain more realism in the environment, surface textures and functions such as sound and video.
Geometrical forms: Responsible for supplying complex graphical objects to be added to Augmented Reality applications, as well as to import 3D objects and images, and information that come from 2D texts.
Interaction: Mathematical functions capable of providing alterations of the objects position where there is freedom of movement.

The following diagram (Fig. 1) shows how Augmented Reality applications may interact with the services provided by the support developed. The functions are specific in the next item.

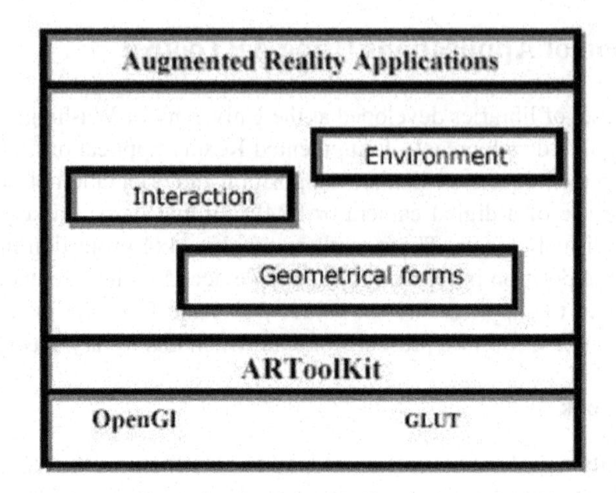

Fig. 1. ARISupport architecture diagram

5.1 Support Functions

The functions provided by this library are explained and illustrate as follow:

a) Environment Module
·**Load BMP and JPG Image as Texture Surface:** Adding textures to virtual objects of different shapes.
·**Colorful Lighting Function:** Lighting control of the virtual object (Supply more natural aspect to the virtual object projected onto the real environment) in different level of colors.
·**Play Sound:** To work as a return for the auditory information. To this function work correctly, a Thread must be implemented to prevent competition with the video.
·**Transparence Function:** Transparence effects to avoid that an object obstructs the access of the target object (Fig. 2).

Fig. 2. Transparent virtual object

·Play AVI Movies: Functions of importation and manipulation of videos in AVI format (Fig 3).

Fig. 3. Video added to the environment

b) Geometrical Forms Module
·Composed Geometrical forms: This function provides graphical objects that possess characteristics directed to Augmented Reality applications with parameters that quicken its build up as in for example: shapes, cylinder, spheres (mesh).
·2D Texts Drawing Routine: Projection of the elements in the user visual field by the use of a 2D text.
·Import 3DS Models: Import of 3D models developed in professional graphical environments [10].
·Import Numerical Keys: Offer 3D numerical objects for the building up of virtual keyboards. Bounding spheres options and the position established referring to the center of the marker (Fig. 4).

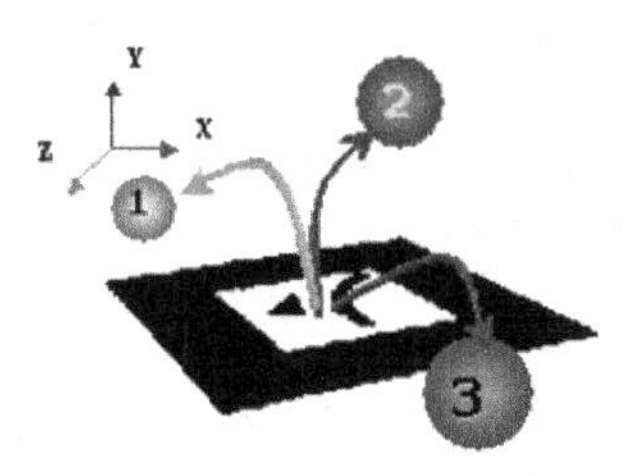

Fig. 4. Numerical keys as target point

·Projection of virtual objects in wireframes: To provide the surface elimination of 3D objects, developed in OpenGl or VRML (Fig 5).
c) Interaction Module
·Collision Distance between Markers: Mathematical calculation functions for distances between markers.
·Collision Function between Spheres: One of the classical collision detection means is to approximate each object, or part of it, to a sphere and check is this sphere intercepts the other. It is only necessary to observe if the distance between the centers of

the two spheres is smaller than the sum of both radius, which indicates that a collision has taken place.
·**Frame Rate Routines:** Provides the frame per second rate of an application.

Fig. 5. Wireframe of 3D object

6 Samples Applications

According to TISSIANI [11], the interface project with the user involvement finishes with the choice and the configuration of the presentation and the interaction objects behavior related to tools and objects that characterize a presentation unity. The description of the objects must include besides the image, their behavior in terms of their enabling (when it becomes enabled and when it becomes disabled), focus (when it possess the focus of the user actions), and user lead (guidance messages). Interfaces that were considered representative were then implemented.

6.1 Virtual Fingers Interactions

In the next prototype, two markers represent interaction objects and a marker represents a fixed object. After the interaction spheres collision with a fixed sphere, the objects changed color and the fixed object started to have a new behavior derived from the markers actions that simulate the fingers of the user: follow the same spatial changes of the colliding objects (Fig. 6).

A positive point observed after the execution of this prototype is the absence of specific manipulation hardware such as gloves or optical sensors. Improving this application, the user fingers is connected to markers, where the user is provided with the rep-

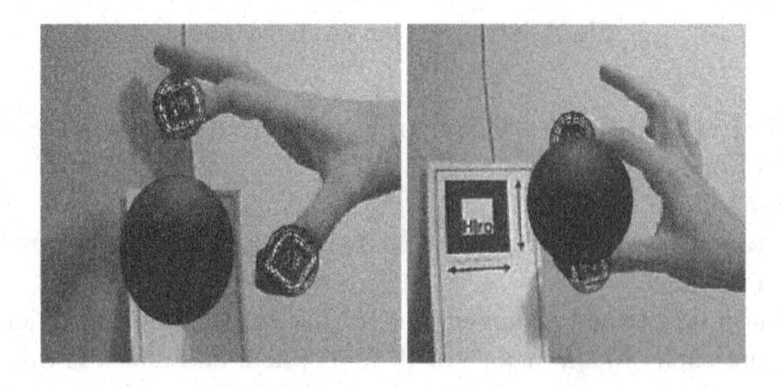

Fig. 6. Virtual fingers interaction

resentation of a virtual hand in the Virtual Environment, position and orientation are supplied to the system through the markers specified in the

6.2 Virtual Keyboards

Another prototype started from the creation of virtual menus. One of the concerns in the use of a prototype such as this is if the system target user is computer illiterate, since virtual objects drawn on a scene should provide familiarity to the users. It is of fundamental importance that there is a virtual return, i.e., the way that the result can be expressed after an interaction. It is important to provide an adequate selection return to the user, as for instance, a sound, a change of color or a confirmation message. The behavior must be defined by as a set of actions that are executed by an object when exposed to a certain stimuli, which may change its state or not. Transparent objects may also be used to avoid occlusion by another virtual object during a selection. The selection is carried out by the spatial proximity between the spheres drawn on the panel (Fig. 7), where the intersection point of the target object and the interaction object for the selection task must be obvious and accessible.

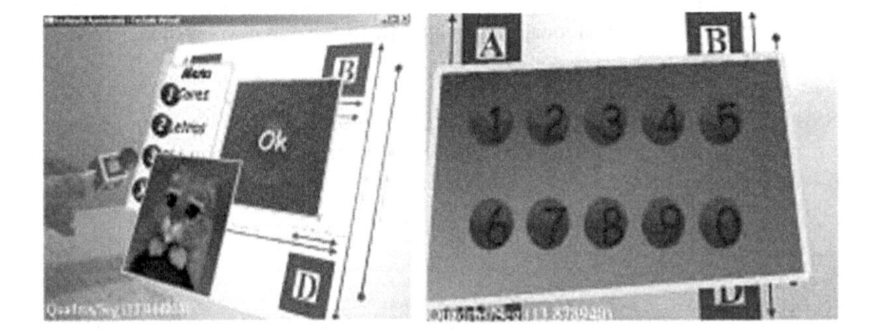

Fig. 7. A virtual keyboard application

7 Limitations and Future Work

One of the limitations found refers to the tracking results, which are affected by lighting conditions. The lighting must be constant and soft over all the area where the tracking will take place. To carry out the tracking in an environment with adequate lighting and use non-reflective materials (opaque) in the confection of markers. In future work we are going to (a) implementation of more precise collision detection algorithms, with the intention of empowering the system's achievements that do not demand too much computational effort as to compromise an application quality, i.e., the reduction of frames per second, and so losing the perception of realism, (b) the implementation of 2 or more cameras to avoid the occlusion of markers (work in progress) and (c) import other images and videos formats.

References

1. CYBIS, Walter de Abreu. Engenharia de usabilidade: uma abordagem ergonômica. Apostila. Disponível em: <http://www.labiutil.inf.ufsc.br/Apostila_nvVersao.pdf>. Acesso em: 29 dez. 2004.
2. www.hitl.washington.edu/research/shared_space/download
3. www.opengl.org
4. AZUMA, R., A Survey of Augmented Reality. Presence:Teleoperators and Virtual Environments, 1997. 6(4): pp. 355-385.
5. POUPYREV, Ivan. et al. A Framework and Testbed for Studying Manipulation Techniques for Immersive VR. ACM, 1997, p 21 - 28, Lausanne, Switzerland.
6. MINE, M., "Virtual environment interaction techniques". UNC Chapel Hill CS Dept.: Technical Report TR95-018. 1995.
7. KATO, H., BILLINGHURST, M., Marker Tracking and HMD Calibration for a Video-based Augmented Reality Conferencing System, Proc. of 2nd IWAR, pp.85-94 (1999). Proceedings of 2nd Int. Workshop on Augmented Reality. 1999. pp. 85-94.
8. BUCHMANN, Volkert. et al. FingARtips - Gesture Based Direct Manipulation in Augmented Reality. ACM, Proceedings of the 2nd International Conference on Computer Graphics and Interactive Techniques, Singapore, p. 212-221, Jun 2004.
9. GEIGER, Cristian. et al. 3D-Registered Interaction-Surfaces in Augmented Reality Space. In The Second IEEE International Augmented Reality Toolkit Workshop, Tokyo, Japan, Oct. 7, 2003.
10. www4.discreet.com/3dsmax
11. TISSIANI, Gabriela; GARCIAL, Fabiano Luiz Santos; CAMARGO, Fabio. Metodologia para criação de ambientes virtuais tridimensionais. Simpósio Nacional de Geometria Descritiva e Desenho Técnico, 15. Nov, 2001, São Paulo.

Background Updating for Visual Surveillance

Kyungnam Kim[1,2], David Harwood[2], and Larry S. Davis[2]

[1] IPIX Corporation 12120 Sunset Hills Rd, Suite 410, Reston, VA 20190, USA
[2] Computer Vision Lab, University of Maryland, College Park, MD 20742, USA
{knkim, harwood, lsd}@umiacs.umd.edu

Abstract. Scene changes such as moved objects, parked vehicles, or opened/closed doors need to be carefully handled so that interesting foreground targets can be detected along with the short-term background layers created by those changes. A simple layered modeling technique is embedded into a codebook-based background subtraction algorithm to update a background model. In addition, important issues related to background updating for visual surveillance are discussed. Experimental results on surveillance examples, such as unloaded packages and unattended objects, are presented by showing those objects as short-term background layers.

1 Introduction

Many background modeling and target detection literatures have focused on how well they model the underlying distributions of backgrounds or target foregrounds. They used the techniques such as a mixture of Gaussians [1], kernel density estimation [5, 7], high(region)-level analysis [6], color and gradient cues [3], depth measurements [2], Kalman filter [12], hidden markov model [9], markov random field [11], multiple views [10], combination with tracking [4], and so on. Many techniques tried to solve the challenging surveillance problems, for example, dynamic scenes [8, 12], crowded scene [14, 11], rain [13], underwater [17], illumination changes [18], beyond-visible-spectrum [19], non-stationary camera [15, 16], etc.

However, most background modeling techniques do not explicitly handle dynamic changes of backgrounds during detection, e.g., parked cars, left packages, displaced chairs. Even though they adapt to the changes in one way or another, they only forget the old backgrounds gradually and absorb the new background changes into the background model. Here, the meaning or importance of those background changes is ignored. Moreover, those changes are accommodated only within the capacity of the background model, i.e., the number of Gaussians in a mixture or the number of past samples in kernel density estimation. Hence, it is desirable, in the sense of intelligent visual surveillance, to have those background changes as short-term background layers, not just a binary output of forground/background.

G. Bebis et al. (Eds.): ISVC 2005, LNCS 3804, pp. 337–346, 2005.

Research on layers for motion segmentation, object tracking, or occlusion analysis can be found in [20, 21, 22, 23, 24, 25, 26]. [20] worked on motion and appearance in layers, [21] on subspace approach, [22] on Bayesian approach, [23] on depth ordering by tracking edges, [24] on transparency manifolds, [25] on depth layers from occlusions, [26] on a background layer model. [26] is most similar to ours in that the 'background' layers are handled. However, we are interested in static layers rather than motion layers which most previous methods have considered.

The motivation of layered modeling and detection is to still be able to detect foreground objects against new backgrounds which were obtained during the detection phase. If we do not have those short-term background layers, interesting foreground objects (e.g., people) will be detected mixed with other stationary objects (e.g., cars). The short-term backgrounds can be labelled with the time when they first appeared static so that they can be represented in temporal order.

In this paper, the background layers are embedded into the existing technique using a codebook model in [27]. Please note that it is a pixel-based approach which makes layers defined initially on a per-pixel basis.

A brief description about this codebook-based algorithm for background modeling is presented in Sec.2.1. The algorithm of layered modeling for background changes is given in Sec.2.2. Sec.3 discusses several important questions which need to be considered when constructing layered models. Experimental results showing surveillance examples are shown in Sec.4. Finally, conclusion is presented in the last section.

2 Algorithm

2.1 Codebook-Based Background Modeling

Let $\mathcal{X}$ be a training sequence for a single pixel consisting of N RGB-vectors: $\mathcal{X} = \{\mathbf{x}_1, \mathbf{x}_2, ..., \mathbf{x}_N\}$. Let $\mathcal{C} = \{\mathbf{c}_1, \mathbf{c}_2, ..., \mathbf{c}_L\}$ represent the codebook for the pixel consisting of L codewords. Each pixel has a different codebook size based on its sample variation. Each codeword $\mathbf{c}_i$, $i = 1 \dots L$, consists of an RGB vector $\mathbf{v}_i = (\bar{R}_i, \bar{G}_i, \bar{B}_i)$ and a 6-tuple $\mathbf{aux}_i = \langle \check{I}_i, \hat{I}_i, f_i, \lambda_i, p_i, q_i \rangle$. The tuple $\mathbf{aux}_i$ contains intensity (brightness) values and temporal variables described below.

- $\check{I}, \hat{I}$: the *min* and *max* brightness, respectively, that the codeword accepted;
- f: the *frequency* with which the codeword has occurred;
- λ: the *maximum negative run-length* (MNRL) defined as the longest interval during the training period that the codeword has NOT recurred;
- p, q: the *first* and *last* access times, respectively, that the codeword has occurred.

In the training period, each value, $\mathbf{x}_t$, sampled at time t is compared to the current codebook to determine which codeword $\mathbf{c}_m$ (if any) it matches (m is the matching codeword's index). We use the matched codeword as the sample's encoding approximation. To determine which codeword will be the best match, we employ the color distortion measure which uses rescaled RGB colors, not RGB values directly. To allow for brightness changes in detection, we store $\check{I}$ and $\hat{I}$ statistics, which are the min and max brightness of all pixels assigned to a codeword. We allow the brightness change to vary in a certain range determined by $\check{I}$ and $\hat{I}$. The matching condition is satisfied when the pure colors of $\mathbf{x}_t$ and $\mathbf{c}_m$ are close enough and the brightness of $\mathbf{x}_t$ lies between the acceptable brightness bounds of $\mathbf{c}_m$.

We refer to the codebook obtained from the previous step as the fat codebook. In the temporal filtering step, we refine the fat codebook by separating the codewords that might contain moving foreground objects from the true background codewords, thus allowing moving foreground objects during the initial training period. The true background, which includes both static pixels and moving background pixels, usually is quasi-periodic (values recur in a bounded period). This motivates the temporal criterion of MNRL (λ), which is defined as the maximum interval of time that the codeword has not recurred during the training period.

Let $\mathcal{M}$ denote the background model (a new filtered codebook):

$$\mathcal{M} = \{\mathbf{c}_m | \mathbf{c}_m \in \mathcal{C} \quad \wedge \quad \lambda_m \leq T_{\mathcal{M}}\}. \tag{1}$$

Usually, a threshold $T_{\mathcal{M}}$ is set equal to half the number of training frames, $\frac{N}{2}$.

A codeword having a large λ will be eliminated from the codebook by Eq.1. Even though one has a large frequency 'f', its large λ means that it is mostly a foreground event which was stationary only for that period f. On the other hand, one having a small f and a small λ could be a rare background event occurring quasi-periodically.

Subtracting the current image from the background model is straightforward. As done in the training phase, we simply compute the color distance of the sample from the nearest cluster mean with the brightness test. If no match is found, the pixel value is classified as foreground.

The detailed description and procedure are presented in [27] for reference.

2.2 Model Updating for Background Changes

As noted in Sec.1, the scene can change after initial training, for example, by parked cars, displaced books, etc. These changes should be used to update the background model. We achieve this by defining an additional model $\mathcal{H}$ called a *cache* and three parameters described below:

- $T_{\mathcal{H}}$: the threshold for MNRL of the codewords in $\mathcal{H}$;
- T_{add}: the minimum time period required for addition, during which the codeword must reappear;
- T_{delete}: a codeword is deleted if it has not been accessed for a period of this long.

The periodicity of an incoming pixel value is filtered by $T_{\mathcal{H}}$, as we did in the background modeling (Sec.2.1). The values re-appearing for a certain amount of time (T_{add}) are added to the background model as short-term background. Some parts of a scene may remain in the foreground unnecessarily long if adaptation is slow, but other parts will disappear too rapidly into the background if adaptation if fast. Neither approach is inherently better than the other. The choice of this adaptation speed is problem dependent.

We assume that the background obtained during the initial background modeling is long-term. This assumption is not necessarily true, e.g., a chair can be moved after the initial training, but, in general, most long-term backgrounds are obtainable during training. Background values not accessed for a long time (T_{delete}) are deleted from the background model. Optimally, the long-term codewords are augmented with permanent flags indicating they are not to be deleted*. The permanent flags can be applied otherwise depending on specific application needs.

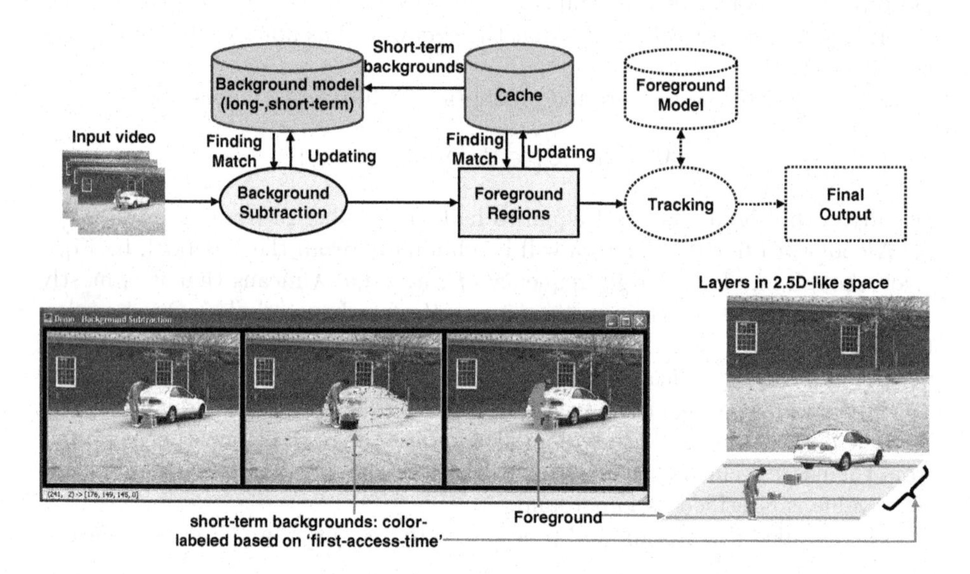

Fig. 1. The overview of our approach with short-term background layers: the foreground and the short-term backgrounds can be interpreted in a different temporal order. The diagram items in dotted line, such as Tracking, are added to complete a video surveillance system.

Thus, a pixel can be classified into four subclasses - (1) background found in the long-term background model, (2) background found in the short-term background model, (3) foreground found in the cache, and (4) foreground not found in any of them. The overview of the approach is illustrated in Fig.1. This adaptive modeling capability allows us to capture changes to the background scene. The detailed procedure is given below.

Algorithm for Background Update

I. After training, the background model $\mathcal{M}$ is obtained as in Eq.1. Create a new model $\mathcal{H}$ as a cache.

II. For an incoming pixel $\mathbf{x}$, find a matching codeword in $\mathcal{M}$. If found, update the codeword.

III. Otherwise, try to find a matching codeword in $\mathcal{H}$ and update it. For no match, create a new codeword $\mathbf{h}$ and add it to $\mathcal{H}$.

IV. Filter out the cache codewords which do not occur quasi-periodically (That is, their λ's are larger than the threshold $T_{\mathcal{H}}$).
$\mathcal{H} \leftarrow \mathcal{H} - \{\mathbf{h}_i | \mathbf{h}_i \in \mathcal{H},\ \ \lambda(\mathbf{h}_i) > T_{\mathcal{H}}\}$

V. Among the cache codewords which survive from the filtering in Step IV, move the ones, staying enough time in $\mathcal{H}$ to be determined as short-term backgrounds, to $\mathcal{M}$ (Their *first* access times are larger than T_{add}).
$\mathcal{M} \leftarrow \mathcal{M} \cup \{\mathbf{h}_i | \mathbf{h}_i \in \mathcal{H},\ \ p(\mathbf{h}_i) > T_{add}\}$

VI. Delete the codewords not accessed for a long time from $\mathcal{M}$ (Their *last* access times are larger than T_{delete}). But do not delete a codeword augmented with a permanent flag.
$\mathcal{M} \leftarrow \mathcal{M} - \{\mathbf{c}_i | \mathbf{c}_i \in \mathcal{M},\ \ q(\mathbf{c}_i) > T_{delete},\ \ permanent(\mathbf{c}_i) = \text{no}^*\}$

VII. Repeat the process from the Step II.

Many short-term background layers can be formed as changes to the background occur. The parameters $T_{\mathcal{H}}$, T_{add} and T_{delete} need to be controlled based on the specific application needs or the semantics of foreground objects.

The first-access-time of a codeword, p, can be used to label its background layer. Based on this temporal information, layers can be ordered in time-depth and temporal segmentation can also be performed.

3 Issues for Background Updating

There are several related background-updating issues that need to be considered for practical visual surveillance applications. In this section, those issues are discussed along with related references and possible solutions. As noted in [6], larger systems seeking a high-level understanding of image sequences use background subtraction as a component. A background maintenance module handles the default model for everything in a scene that is not modeled explicitly by other processing modules. Thus, the module performing background maintenance should not attempt to extract the semantics of foreground object on its own.

Spatial integration: Time-stamps of 'first-access-time' are assigned to background layers on each pixel as mentioned in the last paragraph in Sec.2.2. It is possible to segment the object by grouping pixels with similar time-stamps at close distance, without or with the help of 'spatial segmentation' (See [30] for segmentation techniques). However, note that a region of temporal segmentation may not correspond to a physical object, and vice versa.

Move in or out: There are two cases of background model updating - (1) A new object (blob) comes in to the scene or displaces, and then stops to be a short-term background, (2) An existing object modeled as background leaves the original place. The hole left behind would be labelled as short-term background.
The object is a connected component in a binary foreground map. Here, the object is assumed to be rigid. Over the boundary pixels, we can apply a color similarity test (or a symmetric neighbor filter [28]) to classify a move-in or move-out case as shown in Fig.2(a).

Human VS. stationary object: How to deal with a person who becomes almost stationary? There would be 'foreground aperture' or 'sleeping person' problems as addressed in [6]. Depending on the semantics of foreground objects, we may not want to let stationary people become background layers. A higher-level module needs to provide feedback to background maintenance about what pixels should not be adapted into the background. We could determine that the tracked object is a person or a group of people beforehand by keeping a foreground model. Sometimes, the human object boundary may not be perfectly motionless. Several heuristics to identify human objects by head detection, boundary analysis or vertical histograms were proposed in [14, 29]

Pre-labelled environments: Some fixtures like doors or gates need to be labelled before performing visual surveillance tasks since those are always in one of the pre-defined states - widely open, ajar, or closed. Many surveillance scenes involve doors or gates where interesting human activity events can occur. Moreover, in most cases, opening or closing a door causes illumination changes on the surrounding areas and, as a result, detection algorithms give false alarms.

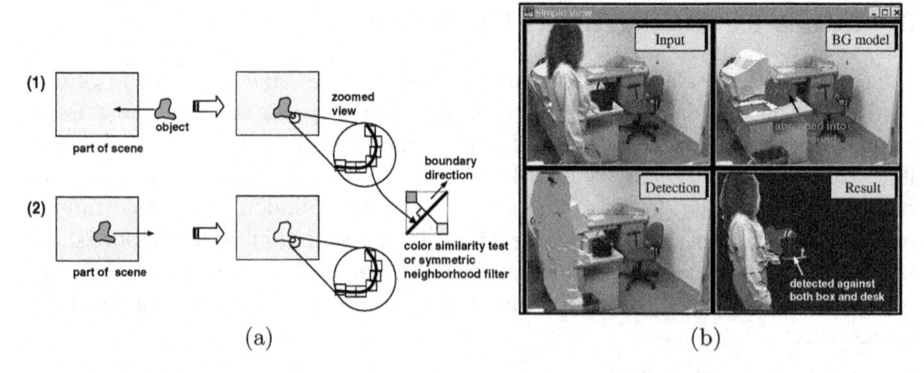

Fig. 2. (a): Two cases of changed backgrounds. The case (2) shows almost homogeneous neighborhoods over the boundary of the background hole, while different colors are observed on each side along the boundary of the newly moved object as in the case (1). (b): Layered modeling and detection - A woman placed a box on a desk and then the box has been absorbed into the background model as short-term. Then a purse is put in front of the box. The purse is detected against both the box and the desk.

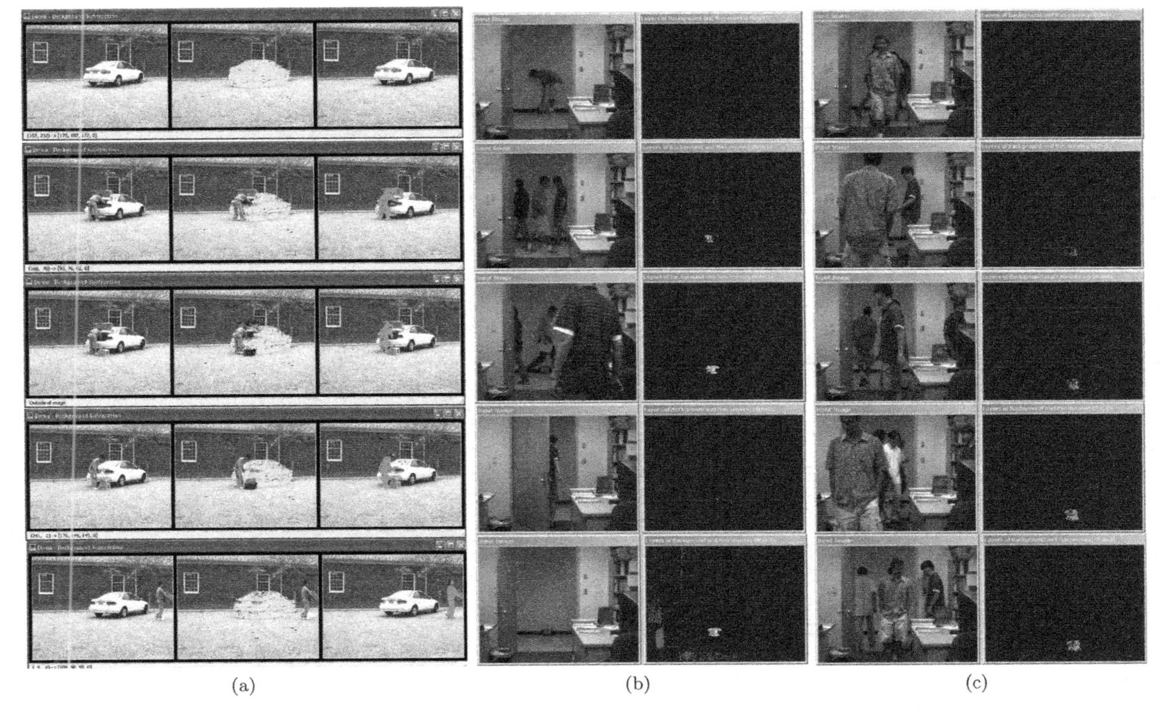

Fig. 3. (a): The leftmost column: original images, the middle column: color-labelled short-term backgrounds, the rightmost column: detected foreground. The video shows that a man parks his car on the lot and takes out two boxes. He walks away to deliver them. (b),(c): Detection of an object left unattended: The sample frames are shown in the order of time along with short-term background layers in the second column. (b): A bag is placed by somebody and left unattended. A short-term background layer is formed. It is still memorized as a layer after the door was closed and then opened. (c): While several people walk in and out the office, a bag has been left without any attention. Even with severe occlusion by walking people, the bag stands out as a layer.

One could manually store representative states of those areas as short-term backgrounds on the background model before performing actual detection. If that kind of pre-processing is not available or the environment is not controllable, the area needs to be specially labelled as a door or a gate, and then handled differently, i.e., detecting moving objects not by subtracting from a background model but by matching with foreground models only.

4 Experimental Results - Examples

Fig.2(b) shows detection of an object against both long-term backgrounds and a short-term background layer.

Fig.3(a) is a more interesting example which can be used for the further analysis of scene change detection. After parking a car, a man unloads two boxes one after another. The car and the two boxes are labelled with different coloring based on their 'first-access-times' as short-term backgrounds while the man is still detected as an active foreground. A car becomes a far-most background layer and then two boxes create two different layers against the car layer.

As shown in Fig.3(b),3(c), a package left unattended for a long time would be one of most demanding surveillance targets. Two such scenarios are presented here. To be precise on detection of unattended objects, a high-level analysis to identify 'unattendedness' is required along with this low-level detection.

5 Conclusion

The changes to a background scene, although implicitly modeled under limited modeling capacity, have not been handled explicitly by most background modeling techniques. Without short-term background updating, interesting foreground objects (e.g., people) will be detected mixed with other stationary objects (e.g., cars).

Layered modeling for these background changes is embedded into the codebook-based background subtraction algorithm. Several important issues were discussed from the point of view of visual surveillance. The experiments on surveillance examples show useful results such as background layers in different temporal depths as well as detection of an unattended object in crowded/occluded environments.

References

1. C. Stauffer and W.E.L. Grimson, "Adaptive background mixture models for real-time tracking", *IEEE Int. Conf. Computer Vision and Pattern Recognition*, Vol. 2, pp. 246-252, 1999.
2. M. Harville, "A framework for high-level feedback to adaptive, per-pixel, mixture-of-gaussian background models", *European Conf. Computer Vision*, Vol. 3, pp. 543-560, 2002.
3. O. Javed, K. Shafique, M. Shah, "A Hierarchical Approach to Robust Background Subtraction using Color and Gradient Information ", *IEEE Workshop on Motion and Video Computing (MOTION'02)*, 2002.

4. F. Porikli and O. Tuzel, "Human Body Tracking by Adaptive Background Models and Mean-Shift Analysis", *IEEE International Workshop on Performance Evaluation of Tracking and Surveillance (PETS-ICVS)*, 2003.
5. A. Elgammal, D. Harwood, and L.S. Davis, "Non-parametric model for background subtraction," *European Conf. Computer Vision*, Vol. 2, pp. 751-767, 2000.
6. K. Toyama, J. Krumm, B. Brumitt, and B. Meyers, "Wallflower: Principles and practice of background maintenance", *Int. Conf. Computer Vision*, pp. 255-261, 1999.
7. A. Mittal and N. Paragios, "Motion-based Background Subtraction Using Adaptive Kernel Density Estimation", *IEEE Conference in Computer Vision and Pattern Recognition*, 2004.
8. Antoine Monnet, Anurag Mittal, Nikos Paragios and Visvanathan Ramesh, "Background Modeling and Subtraction of Dynamic Scenes", *IEEE International Conference on Computer Vision (ICCV)*, Nice, France, Oct 2003.
9. B. Stenger, V. Ramesh, N. Paragios, F. Coetzee, and J.M. Buhmann, "Topology free hidden Markov models: application to background modeling", In *IEEE International Conference on Computer Vision*, Volume: 1, 2001, Page(s): 294 -301.
10. A. Mittal and L. S. Davis, "M2Tracker: A Multi-View Approach to Segmenting and Tracking People in a Cluttered Scene Using Region-Based Stereo", *Proc. of European Conf. on Computer Vision*, pp. 18-33, 2002.
11. N. Paragios and V. Ramesh, "A MRF-based Real-Time Approach for Subway Monitoring", *IEEE Conference in Computer Vision and Pattern Recognition*, 2001.
12. J. Zhong, S. Sclaroff, "Segmenting Foreground Objects from a Dynamic Textured Background via a Robust Kalman Filter", *IEEE International Conference on Computer Vision*, 2003.
13. K. Garg and S.K. Nayar, "Detection and Removal of Rain from Videos", *IEEE Computer Vision and Pattern Recognition (CVPR)*, Washington, July 2004.
14. Tao Zhao and Ram Nevatia, "Tracking Multiple Humans in Crowded Environment", *Proc IEEE Conf on Computer Vision and Pattern Recognition (CVPR)*, 2004.
15. Y. Ren, C. Chua, and Y. Ho, "Statistical background modeling for non-stationary camera", *Pattern Recognition Letters*, vol. 24, no. 1-3, pp. 183-196, January 2003.
16. Eric Hayman and Jan-Olof Eklundh, "Statistical Background Subtraction for a Mobile Observer", *IEEE International Conference on Computer Vision*, 2003.
17. Dirk Walther, Duane R.Edgington, and Christof Koch, "Detection and Tracking of Objects in Underwater Video", *IEEE International Conference on Computer Vision and Pattern Recognition*, 2004.
18. Yasuyuki Matsushita, Ko Nishino, Katsushi Ikeuchi, Masao Sakauchi, "Illumination Normalization with Time-Dependent Intrinsic Images for Video Surveillance", *IEEE Trans. Pattern Anal. Mach. Intell.*, 26(10): 1336-1347 (2004).
19. James W. Davis, Vinay Sharma, "Robust Background-Subtraction for Person Detection in Thermal Imagery", *Joint IEEE Workshop on Object Tracking and Classification Beyond the Visible Spectrum*, 2004.
20. Hulya Yalcin, Michael J. Black, Ronan Fablet, "The Dense Estimation of Motion and Appearance in Layers", *Proc IEEE Conf on Computer Vision and Pattern Recognition (CVPR)*, 2004.
21. Qifa Ke and Takeo Kanade, "A Robust Subspace Approach to Layer Extraction", *IEEE Workshop on Motion and Video Computing (Motion 2002)*, pages 37-43, 2002.

22. Philip H.S. Torr, Richard Szeliski, P. Anandan, "An Integrated Bayesian Approach to Layer Extraction from Image Sequences:, *IEEE Trans. Pattern Anal. Mach. Intell.* 23(3): 297-303, (2001).
23. Paul Smith, Tom Drummond, Roberto Cipolla, "Layered Motion Segmentation and Depth Ordering by Tracking Edges", *IEEE Trans. Pattern Anal. Mach. Intell.*, April 2004.
24. Brendan J. Frey, Nebojsa Jojic, Anitha Kannan, "Learning Appearance and Transparency Manifolds of Occluded Objects in Layers", *IEEE International Conference on Computer Vision and Pattern Recognition*, 2003.
25. Arno Schodl and Irfan A. Essa, "Depth layers from occlusions", *IEEE International Conference on Computer Vision and Pattern Recognition*, 2001.
26. Yue Zhou and Hai Tao, " Background Layer Model for Object Tracking through Occlusion", *IEEE International Conf. on Computer Vision, ICCV'03*, pp. 1079-1085, 2003.
27. K. Kim, T. H. Chalidabhongse, D. Harwood and L. Davis, "Background Modeling and Subtraction by Codebook Construction", IEEE International Conference on Image Processing (ICIP) 2004.
28. D. Harwood, M. Subbarao, H. Hakalahti, and L.S. Davis, "A New Class of Edge-Preserving Smoothing Filters", *Pattern Recognition Letters*, 6:155-162, 1987.
29. I. Haritaoglu, D. Harwood, L.S. Davis, "W^4: real-time surveillance of people and their activities" *IEEE Transactions on Pattern Analysis and Machine Intelligence*, Volume: 22, Issue: 8, Aug 2000, Page(s): 809 -830.
30. H.-D. Cheng, X.-H. Jiang, Y. Sun, J. Wang, "Color image segmentation: advances and prospects",, *Pattern Recognition*, 34 (12), 2001.

Pattern Discovery for Video Surveillance

Yunqian Ma[1], Pradeep Buddharaju[2], and Mike Bazakos[1]

[1] Honeywell International Inc., 3660 Technology Drive, Minneapolis, MN 55418
yunqian.ma@honeywell.com, mike.bazakos@honeywell.com
[2] Department of Computer Science, University of Houston, Houston, TX 77204
braju@cs.uh.edu

Abstract. There is a need in many surveillance applications to automatically detect certain events, such as activities and/or behaviors exhibited by people, vehicle, or other moving objects. Existing systems require that every event be custom coded, predefined, into the computer system. We present a novel system that can automatically capture and define (learn) new events by pattern discovery, and further presents the events to the operator for confirmation. The operator checks for validity of the newly detected events and adds them into the event library. We also propose a new feature selection procedure that can uniquely identify important events such as people falling. We present experimental results on real dataset, which shows the effectiveness of the proposed method.

1 Introduction

Many organizations, commercial and government have recognized the value of video in security management applications. In particular the digital video is far more useful in that it can be networked and interfaced with their computing infrastructure. Security people are not really interested in the 'video data', but rather in the 'information' contained in the video data. Every application has what is called 'application specific information needs', e.g. detect and track individuals or vehicles entering or leaving a building facility or security gate, or to monitor individuals within a store, office building, hospital.

Current Automated Video Surveillance (AVS) systems can process video sequences and perform almost all key low-level functions, such as motion detection, object tracking, and object classification. Recently, technical interest in video surveillance has moved from such low-level functions to more complex scene analysis to detect human and/or other object behaviors. i.e., patterns of activities or events [1, 2, 3, 4, 5]. Existing event detection/behavior analysis systems focus on the predefined events, for example, to combine the results of an AVS system with spatiotemporal reasoning about each object relative to the key background regions and the other objects in the scene. In [1], three levels of abstraction were presented: image features, mobile object properties and scenarios, whereas [3] defines an event recognition language that will let the user to define events of interest. In [6], recognition was performed by analyzing the static body parameters. For the predefined behaviors and patterns, we (already) developed a People Activity Detection System, which can detect people activities and behaviors and then alert operators, such as a person is 'walking', 'running', 'heading

G. Bebis et al. (Eds.): ISVC 2005, LNCS 3804, pp. 347–354, 2005.

in a direction', 'standing at a particular location', 'falling down', 'loitering', 'left an abandoned object', or that 'crowd is forming', just to name a few.

However, when the events are undefined, things are difficult. In this paper, we introduce a new way of modelling (defining) events to a computer system. We use low level function to extract information (feature) of activity. Further, the computer does pattern discovery to find new events, and through 'conversation' with human operator to model the events. We also propose a new feature selection procedure that can uniquely identify important events such as people falling.

This paper is organized as follows. Section 2 describes related video surveillance modules. Section 3 presents our proposed feature selection methods on the falling events and running events. Section 4 presents the pattern discovery. Section 5 presents experiment results. Conclusions are given in Section 6.

2 Video Surveillance Modules

The AVS system we rely to perform low level processing is Honeywell Advanced Video Processing Solutions (AVPS), The AVPS architecture is shown in Fig. 1. The following briefly describe the related ones.

Video Motion Detection: detects the moving objects by separating the input image into foreground and background regions. Color and edges are used to differentiate the foreground and background pixels. The method is a modification of the Gaussian Mixture Model, which represents the characteristics of a pixel with a set of Gaussian distributions.

Video Motion Tracking: tracks the moving object from frame to frame using a set of heuristic rules and a simplified particle filter operating on a set of shape and color features.

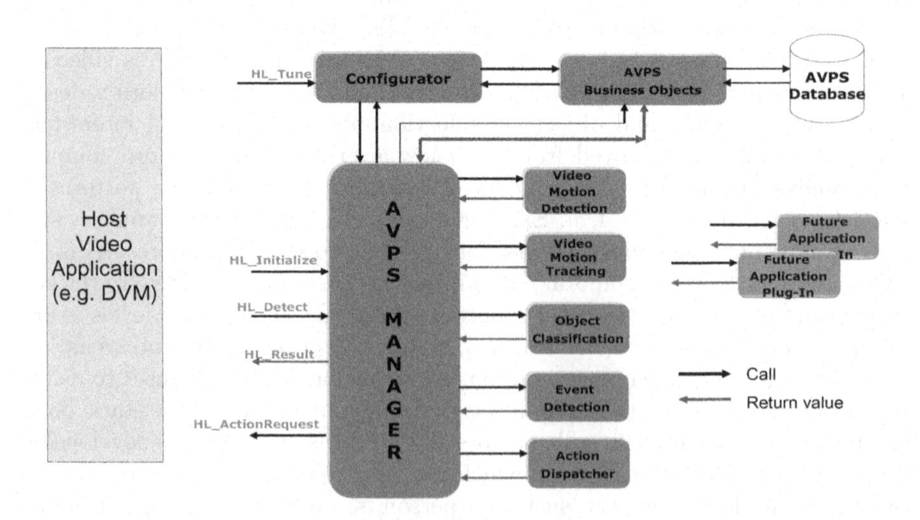

Fig. 1. Honeywell's Advanced Video Processing Solution (AVPS) architecture

Object Classification: Object classification classifies the object as 'human', 'vehicle' or 'others' using a statistical weighted average decision classifier. This classifier determines the object type based on a set of shape-, boundary-, and histogram-features, and their temporal consistency.

Another video surveillance model is a 3D site model. By using 3D site model, we can add physical features besides symbolic features (pixel-based features). Representing the features in physical measurements adds more discriminatory power to the behavioral analysis. Detail of our 3D site model can be found in [7]

3 Feature Extraction

After motion detection, motion tracking, and object classification, we extract information of moving objects. The appearance information of detected objects is recorded. This includes not only instantaneous information of the spatial features of objects [4, 6, 8] such as width, height, and aspect ratio, but also temporal information about changes in the objects' sizes as well as motion features, such as direction of movement and speed. All these information cues, which are important features for behavioral analysis, are organized to form a composite multi-dimensional feature vector. Each object being tracked is allocated a unique identifier; we maintain a history of the path taken by each object from frame to frame. In this section, we only present some key features extracted from the blob (mask) of the tracked object for specific people activities, such as running and falling. It is important that we select features that can distinguish these events well.

3.1 Feature for *Running* Event

We use the features from the star skeleton [8, 9], a computationally inexpensive feature to classify if the person is walking or running. [8, 9] extract the star

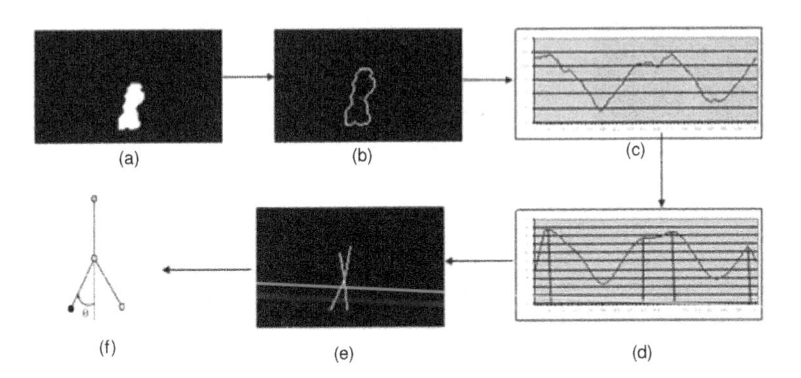

Fig. 2. Extraction of the star skeleton (a) Blob extracted by the AVPS system (b) Boundary of the blob with the centroid marked in red (c) Distance function from the boundary (d) Smoothed distance function with the local maxima extracted and (e) Star skeleton (f) LCP angle extracted from the star skeleton

skeleton from the blob and further analyze the motion of an individual target based on the angle made by left cyclic point (LCP) with the vertical (see angle θ in Figure 2(f)). As an improvement over this algorithm, we found that there is not necessary to use complex functions DFT, LPF, and Inverse DFT to smooth the distance function. Since the distance function doesn't exhibit great deal of signal noise, a simple Gaussian smoothing filter will reasonably smooth the signal as shown in Figures 2(c) and 2(d). This will improve the processing time which is critical for real-time event detection. The feature that can be clearly observed when a person is running is that there is an increase in the frequency of the cyclic motion, which means that the signal formed by the LCP angle (θ) will be at higher frequency.

3.2 Feature for *Falling* Event

Next, we propose a new feature to detect person falling event by extracting the waist skeleton from the blob. Further, we show that the feature extracted from this skeleton can identify the falling event very well. Following is the algorithm for extracting the waist skeleton:

i. Extract the boundary from the mask using a simple boundary following algorithm (see Figure 3(b)). Let the border points be represented by (x_i, y_i), $i = 1 \ldots N$ where N is the number of border points.
ii. Compute the centroid (x_c, y_c) of the mask.
iii. Compute the distance from the centroid to each border point. The distance vector is represented as a periodic one-dimensional signal $d(i)$ as shown in Figure 3(c). This signal should be smoothed using a simple smoothing filter, say Gaussian filter, as shown in Figure 3(d). Let the smoothed signal be $\hat{d}(i)$.

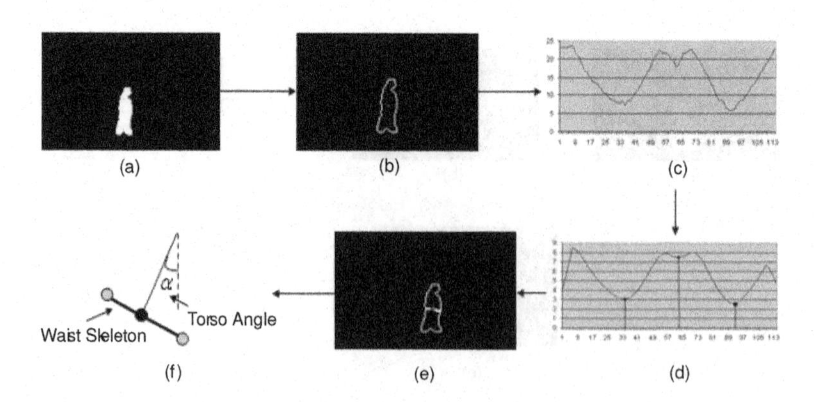

Fig. 3. Extraction of the waist skeleton and angle (a) Blob extracted by the AVPS system (b) Boundary of the blob with the centroid marked in red (c) Distance function from the boundary (d) Smoothed distance function with the local minima extracted (e) Waist skeleton and (f) Torso angle

iv. Find all local minima points by determining the zero-crossings of the second derivative ($\hat{d}''$) of the smoothed signal i.e., find the points (x_i, y_i) such that $\hat{d}'' > 0$. If there are more than two local minima, sort them all according to their distance to the centroid and pick the two points that are closest to the centroid. Connect the centroid to these two points and it represents the waist skeleton of the mask as shown in Figure 3(e).
v. Note from Figure 3(d) that even though three local minima are detected, we only find the two points that are close to the centroid and join them to it to form the waist skeleton. After the skeleton is extracted from the blob, we find the angle made by the line bisecting the skeleton with the vertical (torso angle, α) as shown in Figure 3(f). It is obvious that when a person is falling down, there will be an increase in the torso angle as shown in Figure 5.

4 Pattern Discovery

To handle non-predefined events, we introduce a new way of modelling (defining) events. As a result of feature vector formulation in section 3, event detection takes place in this multi-dimensional feature space. So, a particular event is described as a point cloud in the feature space with different events described by different point clouds. The system can learn to detect events by clustering points in the feature space into groups (or point clouds). In this section, we assume that one video clip contains one event (one consistent visual content). This can be done by automatic video temporal segmentation (partition a long/complex video in the temporal domain into short video clips [10]) or manually segmentation.

Table 1 outlines the steps for our proposed method. First, we have video clips to train the system. Each video clip will feed to the system by the 'open' clip function in Figure 4, the system will find a 'distance' between the new event clip and the existing ones, and alert the operator if it finds new candidate events(distance above some threshold). Then the operator will decide if a particular event is a valid event or an outlier or an existing event in the event library. For example, the operator can pick one of sequences, either play it or view the

Table 1. Proposed Method

Step 1: The user presents to the system a few sequences of digital video, containing examples of the new event which he wants to enter into his surveillance system.
Step 2: The system extracts a set of multi-dimensional features from these video sequences.
Step 3: The system does pattern discovery, give distance between the new video clip and existing ones, via a graphical user interface, how 'well' or how 'poorly' it can distinguish this new event from existing ones.
Step 4: The human operator will then give feedback to the system. The event library will be updated based on the interaction between the system and human operator's conversation.

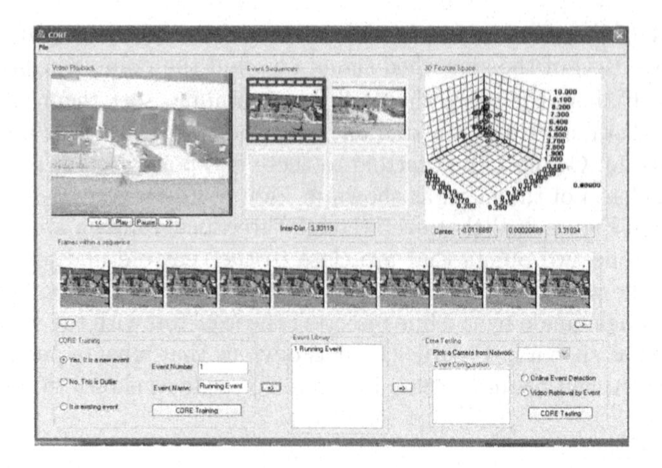

Fig. 4. The GUI of our proposed system

individual frames of those sequences. If the event candidate is a real new event, the operator will add it into the event library.

5 Experimental Results

We recorded several video clips representing the walking, running and falling events from a surveillance camera hooked to the dock side of the Honeywell lab building. We first show that the feature vectors described in Section 3 can be

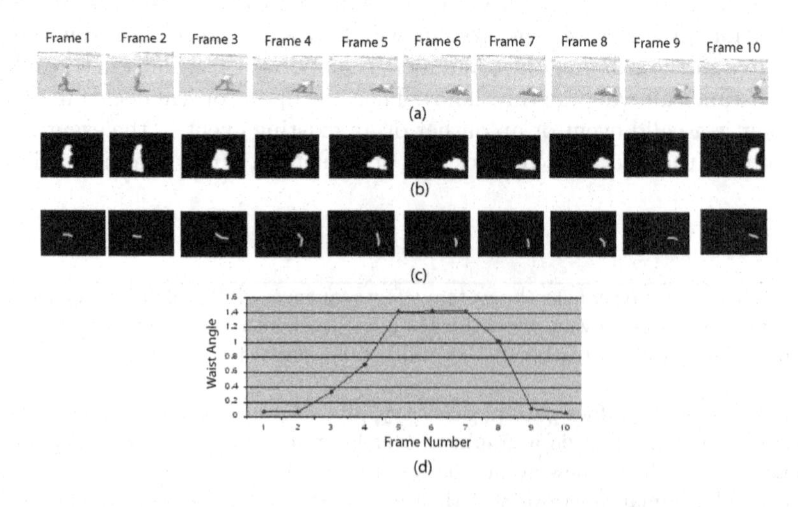

Fig. 5. (a) Individual frames from a video clip corresponding to falling event (b) Masks extracted from the AVPS system (c) Waist skeleton extracted using our algorithm and (d) Plot of torso angle

Table 2. Inter-distance between clusters formed by running and walking events

Seq.1	Seq.2	Inter-distance between Seq.1 and Seq.2
Running1	Walking1	3.21783
Running2	Walking1	2.94423
Running1	Running2	0.04278

Table 3. Inter-distance between clusters formed by Falling and walking events

Seq.1	Seq.2	Inter-distance between Seq.1 and Seq.2
Falling1	Walking1	3.076434
Falling1	Walking2	2.517798
Walking1	Walking2	0.5588628

used effectively to detect important events. Figure 5 shows that the system can detect the 'person falling' event effectively using our proposed waist angle. An increase in the torso angle represents that the falling event has occurred. Using additional information from other features increases the confidence of the event detection.

Next, we show pattern discovery results from the real data. We noticed that each event sequence forms a well defined and separate cluster in the feature space. The system can distinguish different events by using the inter-distance between the clusters. As shown in Table 2, the inter-distance between clusters formed by unusual event like running and usual event (walking) is large and hence our system can detect and report such unusual events effectively. Table 3 shows the inter-distance between falling (unusual) and walking (usual events).

6 Conclusion

In this paper, we introduce a new approach of modeling (defining) events for a video surveillance system. Our proposed methods automatically find what has happened of the associated camera, finds event candidates and turns to the human operator for opinion, to add/update the event library based on the human operator's feedback. In the feature selection for event detection, we also introduce a new feature for the falling down event. We used real world video data set to show the effectiveness of our proposed methods.

Our future work will focus on event prediction, when a pattern of behavior (by a person, or vehicle etc.), deviates 'significantly' from the expected normal patterns for the application at hand, we would like to detect it while it is still at its early stages of development and provide 'Early Warning' to the monitoring station. Providing early warning to security management about possible upcoming events will enable them to deploy effective response and protection.

References

1. Medioni, G., Cohen, I., Bremond, F., Hongeng, S., Nevatia, R.: Event detection and analysis from video streams. In: IEEE Transactions on pattern analysis and machine intelligence. Volume 23. (2001) 873 – 889
2. Hongeng, S., Nevatia, R.: Multi-agent event recognition. In: Proceedings of the 8th IEEE International Conference on Computer Vision (ICCV 2001). Volume 2., Vancouver, BC (2001) 84–91
3. Nevatia, R., Zhao, T., Hongeng, S.: Hierarchical language-based representation of events in video streams. In: IEEE Workshop on Event Mining, Madison, WI (2003)
4. Porikli, F., Haga, T.: Event detection by eigenvector decomposition using object and feature frame. In: Conference on Computer Vision and Pattern Recognition Workshop. (2004) 114 – 114
5. Bobick, A., Johnson, A.: Gait recognition using static activity-specific parameters. In: Proceedings of the 2001 IEEE Computer Society Conference on Computer Vision and Pattern Recognition. Volume 1., Kauai, Hawaii (2001) 423 – 430
6. Johnson, A.Y., Bobick, A.F.: A multi-view method for gait recognition using static body parameters. In: Proceedings of the Third International Conference on Audio- and Video-Based Biometric Person Authentication, Halmstad, Sweden (2001) 301 – 311
7. Ma, Y., Bazakos, M., Wang, Z., Wing, A.: 3d scene modeling for activity detection. In: 2nd International workshop on Conceptual Modeling for Geographic Information Systems (CoMoGIS 2005), Klagenfurt, Austria (2005) 304–313
8. Collins, R., Lipton, A., Kanade, T., Fujiyoshi, H., Duggins, D., Tsin, Y., Tolliver, D., Enomoto, N., Hasegawa, O.: A system for video surveillance and monitoring. Technical Report CMU-RI-TR-00-12, Robotics Institute, Carnegie Mellon University, Pittsburgh, PA (2000)
9. Hironobu, F., Alan, L.: Real-time human motion analysis by image skeletonization. In: Proc. of the Workshop on Application of Computer Vision. (1998)
10. Greenspan, H., Goldberger, J., Mayer, A.: Probabilistic space-time video modeling via piecewise gmm. In: IEEE Transactions on pattern analysis and machine intelligence. Volume 26. (2004) 384 – 396

Real-Time Crowd Density Estimation Using Images

A.N. Marana[1], M.A. Cavenaghi[1], R.S. Ulson[1], and F.L. Drumond

UNESP (Sao Paulo State University) - FC (School of Sciences),
DCo (Department of Computing) - LCAD (Laboratory of High Performance Computing),
Av. Eng. Luis Edmundo Carrijo Coube, sn, 17033-360, Bauru, SP, Brazil
[1]{nilceu, marcos, roberta}@fc.unesp.br

Abstract. This paper presents a technique for real-time crowd density estimation based on textures of crowd images. In this technique, the current image from a sequence of input images is classified into a crowd density class. Then, the classification is corrected by a low-pass filter based on the crowd density classification of the last *n* images of the input sequence. The technique obtained 73.89% of correct classification in a real-time application on a sequence of 9892 crowd images. Distributed processing was used in order to obtain real-time performance.

1 Introduction

For the problem of real-time crowd monitoring there is an established practice of using closed circuit television systems (CCTV), which are monitored by human observers. This practice has some drawbacks, like the possibility of human observers lose concentration during this monotonous task. Therefore, the importance of the development of robust and efficient automatic systems for real-time crowd monitoring is evident.

Efforts for crowd estimation in train stations, airports, stadiums, subways and other places, have been addressed in the research field of automatic surveillance systems. Davies et al. [1] and Regazzoni and Tesei [2, 3] have proposed systems for crowd monitoring and estimation based on existing installed CCTV. The image processing techniques adopted by theirs systems remove the image background and then measure the area occupied by the foreground pixels. The number of foreground pixels is used to estimate the crowd density. Lin et al. [4] proposed a technique based on the recognition of head-like contour, using Haar wavelet transform, followed by an estimation of the crowd size, carried out by a support vector machine. For crowd classification, Cho et al. [5] proposed a hybrid global learning algorithm, which combines the least-square method with different global optimization methods, like genetic algorithms, simulated annealing and random search. The techniques proposed by Marana et al. [6,7,8] estimate crowd densities using texture analysis with gray level dependence matrices, Minkowski fractal dimension and wavelets.

This paper presents a technique for real-time automatic crowd density estimation based on texture descriptors of a sequence of crowd images. The motivation for the use of texture descriptors to estimate crowd densities was inspired by the fact that

G. Bebis et al. (Eds.): ISVC 2005, LNCS 3804, pp. 355 – 362, 2005.

images of different crowd densities tend to present different texture patterns. Images of high-density crowd areas are often made up of fine (high frequency) patterns, while images of low-density crowd areas are mostly made up of coarse (low frequency) patterns. In order to improve the estimation accuracy and to provide real-time estimation, a distributed algorithm was developed. The technique obtained 73.89% of correct classification in a real-time application on a sequence of 9892 crowd images.

2 Material

The technique described in this paper for automatic crowd density estimation was assessed on a sequence of 9892 images extracted (one per second) from a videotape recorded in an airport area. From the total set of images, a subset of 990 images was homogeneously obtained (one image from each ten). Then, human observers manually estimated the crowd densities of these images. The manual estimations were used to assess the accuracy of the automatic technique.

After the manual estimation, the 990 images were classified into one of the following classes: very low (VL) density (0-20 people), low (L) density (21-40 people), moderate (M) density (41-60 people), high (H) density (61-80 people), and very high (VH) density (more than 80 people). Figure 1 shows samples of crowd density classes.

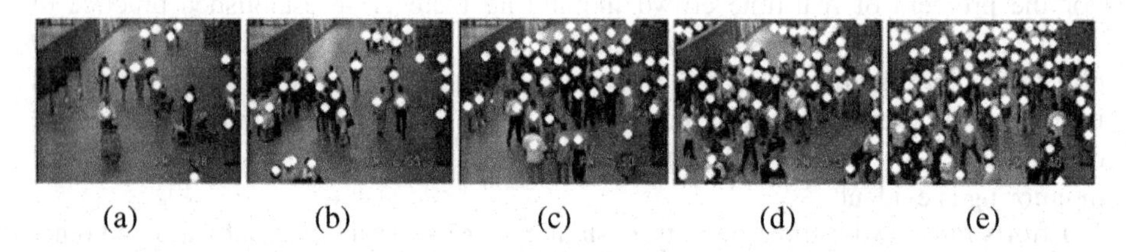

(a) (b) (c) (d) (e)

Fig. 1. Samples of crowd density classes. (a) Very low density (15 people); (b) Low density (29 people); (c) Moderate density (51 people); (d) High density (63 people); (e) Very high density (89 people).

Finally, the images of each class were grouped into train and test subsets. The train subset was used to train the neural network classifier and the test subset was used to assess the accuracy of the technique. Table 1 shows the distribution of the train and test subsets of images into the five classes of crowd densities.

Table 1. Distribution of the train and test subset of images into the five classes of crowd densities

	VL	L	M	H	VH
Train	14	179	169	101	33
Test	14	179	169	100	32
Total	28	358	338	201	65

3 Methods

Figure 2 presents a diagram of the technique proposed for crowd density estimation using texture descriptors. The first step of the technique consists in the classification of each pixel of the input image into one of the previously identified texture classes. The classification is carried out by a self-organizing map (SOM) neural network [9] using feature vectors composed of texture descriptors extracted from co-occurrence matrices [10], computed using a *wxw* window centered in the pixel being classified.

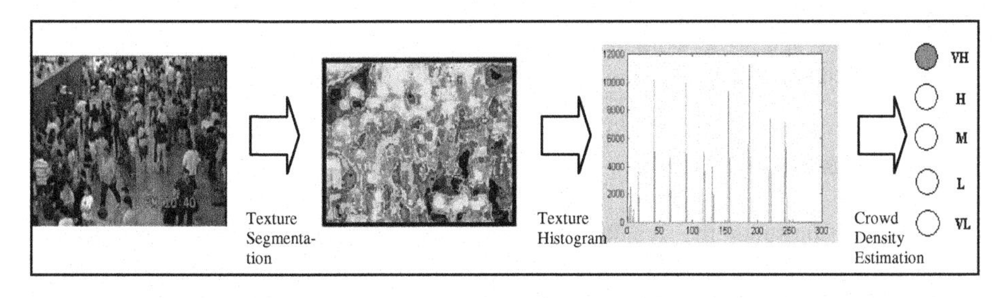

Fig. 2. Diagram of the technique for crowd density estimation using texture and neural network classifier

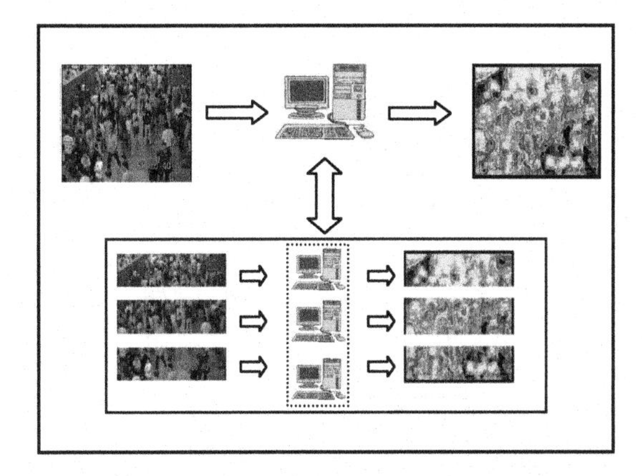

Fig. 3. Diagram of the proposed master-slave strategy for texture segmentation in PVM distributed environment, using *n* slave processors (in this example, *n=3*)

As the classification of all pixels of the image is a time-consuming process (more than 100 seconds per image), in order to obtain real-time estimation it was implemented a distributed algorithm for the Beowulf environment, using Parallel Virtual Machine (PVM) [11]. This algorithm has the following steps:

- The master processor divides the input image in n fragments (n is the number of slave nodes in the cluster);
- Each image fragment is sent to a slave processor;

- Each slave processor performs the texture classification of its image fragment pixels using a sequential algorithm;
- The slave processors send their classified fragments to the master;
- The master processor assembles all fragments into a final texture-segmented image.

Figure 3 shows a diagram of the master-slave strategy adopted in this work to obtain a texture-segmented image.

In the next step, the texture histogram, computed from the texture-segmented image, is used as feature vector by a second SOM neural network to classify the input crowd image into one of the crowd density classes.

The second neural network learns the relationship among the texture histogram profiles and the crowd density levels during the training stage, in a supervised way.

4 Experimental Results

This section presents the results obtained with the application of the proposed technique for real-time crowd density estimation on a sequence of 9892 crowd images.

During the experiments, it was used a cluster with eight Pentium IV processors, connected by a Fast-Ethernet switch.

Fig. 4. Texture patterns from where texture-training samples were extracted.

Pixel texture classification was carried out on a 15x15 window centered on the pixel, from where four co-occurrence matrices were calculated (distance d=1 and directions θ = 0°, 45°, 90° and 135°). From these four matrices, four texture features were extracted: energy, entropy, homogeneity and contrast [10], making up 16 features.

The SOM neural network used in the first step for texture classification was trained to classify crowd image pixels into 12 patterns of texture. Figure 4 shows the 12 texture patterns from where 100 training samples of each texture class were randomly extracted.

Figure 5(b) presents the result of the texture segmentation of the crowd image presented in Figure 5(a), obtained by the SOM neural classifier, using a 15x15 window and the texture patterns showed in Figure 4. Figure 5(c) presents the texture histogram obtained from the texture-segmented image.

It is possible to observe in Figure 5 that higher crowd density areas of the input image are associated with lighter gray level areas in the texture-segmented image, and that lower crowd density areas of the input image are associated with darker gray level areas in the texture-segmented image.

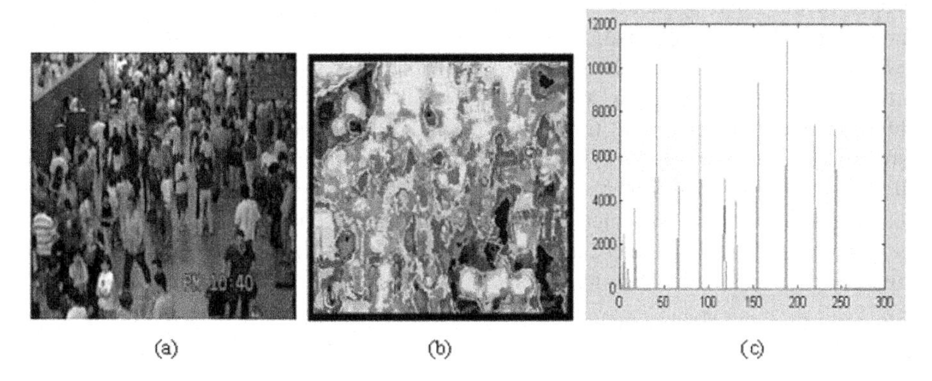

Fig. 5. Example of texture segmentation of a crowd image. (a) Input image; (b) Texture-segmented image; (c) Texture histogram obtained from the texture-segmented image.

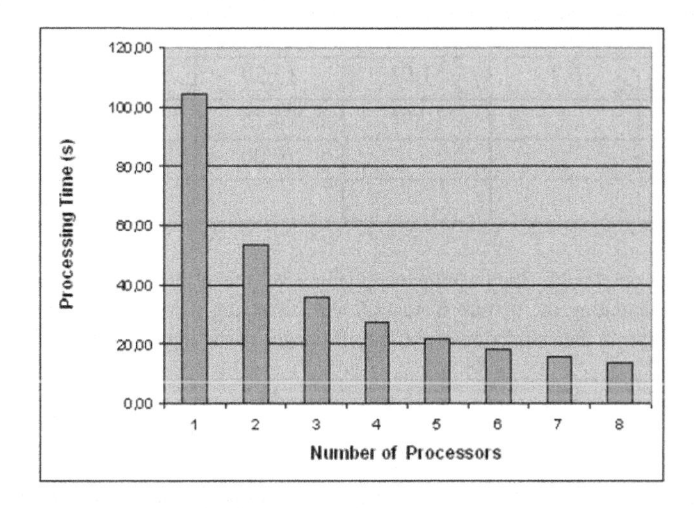

Fig. 6. Processing time (in seconds) necessary to classify all pixels of the input image (using a 15x15 window) and to estimate its crowd density, varying the number of processors of the cluster

Figure 6 shows the processing times for texture segmentation and crowd density classification of a single crowd image, using the 8-processors cluster. The efficiency obtained by the insertion of new processors in all cases was always almost maximum, since the decreasing of processing time was always near to 87%. The processing time for each crowd image was around 105 seconds when only one processor was used and around 14 seconds when all 8 processors were used.

Since the best processing time performance obtained (14 seconds) was not enough for real-time estimation, it was assessed the possibility of only part of pixels be classified.

In the first experiment carried out, the crowd images were divided into 4x4 sub-images and only one pixel from each sub-image (the top-left pixel) was classified. Table 2 shows the confusion matrix obtained in this experiment, where the last 7 images of the input sequence were used by a median low-pass filter to correct the current crowd density estimation. In this experiment, 73.89% of the 494 test crowd images were correctly classified. The best result (90.63% of correct classification) was obtained by the VH class, and the worst result (59% of correct classification) was obtained by the H class. Real-time requirement was reached, since the crowd density estimation for each image took 1.025 seconds. It is possible to observe in Table 2 that all miss-classified images were assigned to a neighbor class of the correct one. Some miss-classification was expected since the borders between the crowd density classes are very tenuous (for instance, an image with 20 people belongs to VL class, but it can be easily classified as belonging to L class).

Table 2. Results obtained when part of the input image pixels were classified and the crowd density classification were corrected applying the median low-pass filter in the last 7 estimations of the input sequence

	VL	**L**	**M**	**H**	**VH**
VL	64.29	35.71			
L	6.7	81.01	12.29		
M		10.65	72.78	16.57	
H			10.00	59.00	31.00
VH				9.38	90.63

Table 3. Results obtained by the technique applying a 3x3 mean filter on the texture-segmented image before calculating the texture histogram and correcting the estimation applying a low-pass (median) filter in the estimation of the last 10 images of the input sequence

	VL	**L**	**M**	**H**	**VH**
VL	71.43	28.57			
L	8.38	82.68	8.94		
M		13.02	77.51	9.47	
H			15.00	67.00	18.00
VH				18.75	81.25

In the second experiment, where all pixels of the input image were classified, it was obtained 77.33% of correct estimation. In this experiment, a 3x3 mean filter was applied to enhance (remove noise) the texture-segmented image and the last 10 estimations were used by a median low-lass filter to correct the crowd density classifications. But, in this case, the requirement for real-time estimation was not reached, since the estimations took 14 seconds. Table 3 shows the confusion matrix obtained in this experiment.

In the Table 3 it is also possible to observe that all miss-classified images were assigned to a neighbor class of the correct one (this is a very favorable result).

5 Conclusions

In this paper, the problem of crowd density estimation was addressed and a technique for real-time automatic crowd density estimation was proposed, based on texture features extracted from a sequence of images and processed in a distributed environment. The proposed approach takes into account the geometric distortions caused by the camera's position, since the farther areas (from the camera) under surveillance are mapped on finer textures and the closer areas are mapped on coarser textures. Crowd density estimations of a group of 494 test crowd images resulted in 77.33% of correct estimation. When real-time constraint was demanded, it was obtained 73.89% of correct estimation. These results can be considered quite good since the variance of crowd density estimations for each class were very small and their means were the expected values.

Acknowledgements

The authors thank FAPESP (process number: 01/09649-2) for the financial support.

References

1. Davies, A.C., Yin, J.H., and Velastin, S. A., "Crowd Monitoring Using Image Processing", *Electron. Commun. Eng. J.*, vol. 7, pp.37-47, 1995.
2. Regazzoni, C.S., and Tesei, A., "Distributed Data Fusion for Real-Time Crowding Estimation", *Signal Proc.*, vol. 53, pp. 47-63, 1996.
3. Tesei, A., and Regazzoni, C.S., "Local Density Evaluation and Tracking of Multiple Objects from Complex Image Sequences", *Proc. 20th Intern. Conf. IECON*, vol.2, Bologna, Italy, pp. 744-748, 1994.
4. Lin, S.F., Chen, J.Y., and Chao, H.X., "Estimation of Number of People in Crowd Scenes Using Perspective Transformation", *IEEE Trans. Sys., Man, Cyber. A*, vol.31, pp. 645-654, 2001.
5. Cho, S.Y., Chow, T.W.S., and Leung, C.T., "A Neural-Based Crowd Estimation by Hybrid Global Learning Algorithms", *IEEE Trans. Sys., Man, Cyber. B*, vol.29, pp. 535-541, 1999.
6. Marana, A.N., Velastin, S.A., Costa, L.F, and Lotufo, R.A., "Automatic Estimation of Crowd Density Using Texture", *Safety Science*, vol. 28, 165-175, 1998.

7. Marana, A.N., Costa, L.F., Lotufo, R.A., and Velastin, S.A., "Estimating Crowd Density with Minkowski Fractal Dimension", *IEEE Proceedings of the International Conference on Acoustics, Speech and Signal Processing,* vol. VI, 3521-3524, 1999.
8. Marana, A. N., Verona, V.V., "Wavelet Packet Analysis for Crowd Density Estimation", *Proc. IASTED Inter. Symposia on Applied Informatics,* Acta Press, pp. 535-540, Innsbruck, Austria, 2001.
9. Kohonen, T., "The Self-Organizing Map", *Proceedings of the IEEE,* vol.78, pp. 1464-1480, 1990.
10. Haralick, R. M., "Statistical and Structural Approaches to Texture", *Proceedings of the IEEE*, vol. 67(5), pp. 786-804, 1979.
11. 11.Geist, A.; Beguelin, A.; Dongarra, J.; Jiang, W.; Manchek, R.; Sunderan, V., "*PVM: Parallel Virtual Machine – A User's Guide and Tutorial for Networked Parallel Computing*", The MIT Press, 1994.

Automatic Robust Background Modeling Using Multivariate Non-parametric Kernel Density Estimation for Visual Surveillance

Alireza Tavakkoli, Mircea Nicolescu, and George Bebis

Computer Vision Laboratory, University of Nevada, Reno, NV 89557

Abstract. The final goal for many visual surveillance systems is automatic understanding of events in a site. Higher level processing on video data requires certain lower level vision tasks to be performed. One of these tasks is the segmentation of video data into regions that correspond to objects in the scene. Issues such as automation, noise robustness, adaptation, and accuracy of the model must be addressed. Current background modeling techniques use heuristics to build a representation of the background, while it would be desirable to obtain the background model automatically. In order to increase the accuracy of modeling it needs to adapt to different parts of the same scene and finally the model has to be robust to noise. The building block of the model representation used in this paper is multivariate non-parametric kernel density estimation which builds a statistical model for the background of the video scene based on the probability density function of its pixels. A post processing step is applied to the background model to achieve the spatial consistency of the foreground objects.

1 Introduction

An important ultimate goal of automated surveillance systems is to understand the activities in a site, usually monitored by fixed cameras and/or other sensors. This enables functionalities such as automatic detection of suspicious activities, site security, etc. The first step toward automatic recognition of events is to detect and track objects of interest in order to make higher level decisions on their interactions. One of the most widely used techniques for detection and tracking of objects in the video scene is background modeling.

The most commonly used feature in background modeling techniques is pixel intensity. In a video with a stationary background (i.e. video taken by a fixed camera) deviations of pixel intensity values over time can be modeled as noise by a Gaussian distribution function, $N(0, \sigma^2)$. A simplistic background modeling technique is to calculate the average of intensity at every pixel position, find the difference at each frame with this average and threshold the result. Using an adaptive filter this model follows gradual changes in the scene illumination, as shown in [1]. Kalman filtering is also used in [2], [3] and [4]. Also a linear prediction using Wiegner Filter is used in [5].

In some particular environments with changing parts of background, such as outdoor environments with waving trees, surface of water, etc., the background is

G. Bebis et al. (Eds.): ISVC 2005, LNCS 3804, pp. 363–370, 2005.

Table 1. Comparison of methods

Method	Color Independency	Automatic Threshold	Spatial Consistency
Parametric	Yes	No	No
Non-parametric	No	No	No
Proposed	Yes	Yes	Yes

not completely stationary. For these applications mixture of Gaussians has been proposed in [6], [7] and [8]. In order to find the parameters of the mixture of Gaussians, the EM algorithm is used while the adaptation of parameters can be achieved by using an incremental version of the EM algorithm. Another approach to model variations in the background model is to represent these changes as different states, corresponding to different environments; such as lights on/off, night/day, sunny/cloudy. For this purpose Hidden Markov Models (HMM) have been used in [9] and [10]. Edge features are also used as a tool to model the background in [11] and [12] based on comparing edges and fusion of intensity and edge information, respectively. Also block features are used in [13] and [14].

One of the most successful approaches in background subtraction is proposed in [15]. Here the background representation is drawn by estimating the probability density function of each pixel in the background model.

In this paper, the statistical background model is built by multi-variate non-parametric kernel density estimation. Then the model is used to automatically compute a threshold for the probability of each pixel in the incoming video frames. Finally a post processing stage makes the model robust to salt-and-pepper noise that may affect the video. Table 1 shows a comparison between the traditional parametric and non-parametric statistical representation techniques and our proposed method that addresses the above issues.

The rest of this paper is organized as follows. In Section 2 the proposed algorithm is presented and Section 3 describes our bi-variate approach to the density estimation. In Section 4 we discuss our proposed automatic selection of covariance matrix and suitable thresholds for each pixel in the scene. In Section 5 the noise reduction stage of the algorithm is presented by enforcing spatial consistency. Section 6 discusses our adaptation approach and in Section 7 experimental results of our algorithm are compared to traditional techniques. Section 8 summarizes our approach and discusses future extensions of this work.

2 Overview of the Proposed Algorithm

We propose an automatic and robust background modeling based on multivariate non-parametric kernel density estimation. The proposed method has three major parts. In the training stage, parameters of the model are trained and estimated for each pixel, based on their values in the background training frames. In the next stage, classification step, the probability that a pixel belongs to the background in every frame is estimated using our bi-variate density estimation. Then pixels are marked as background or foreground based on their probability

Trainin Stage:
1. For evey pixel in the scene:
1.1. Calculate its corresponding Kernel Bandwidth Matrix.
1.2. Estimate its suitable Threshold.

Classification Stage:
2. For every new frame:
2.1. For every pixel calculate its Estimated Probability (EP).
2.2. Assign median of EP for the 8-connected neighbor of every pixel as their new EP values.
2.3. If (EP>th) then label it as background pixel.
3. Remove very small foreground regions using connected component analysis.

Updating Stage:
4. Discard pixels in the oldest background frame corresponding to the background maks and add pixels of current frame.
5. If a large change in foreground regions is detected:
5.1. While all the background training frames are replaced:
5.1.1. Replace the background frame with current frame.
5.1.2. Proceed to next frame.
6. Perform training stage if adaptations (Gradual/Sudden) is performed.
7. Continue to next frame.

Fig. 1. Our Proposed Background Modeling Algorithm

values. The final stage of our proposed algorithm removes those pixels that do not belong to a true foreground region, but due to strong noise are selected as foreground.

In Fig. 1, the proposed algorithm is presented. The automation is achieved in the training stage, which uses the background model to train a single class classifier based on the training set for each pixel. Also by using step 2.2., we address the salt-and-pepper noise issue in the video.

3 Bi-variate Kernel Density Estimation

In [15], the probability density of a pixel being background is calculated by:

$$Pr(x_t) = \frac{1}{N}\sum_{i=1}^{N}\prod_{j=1}^{d}\frac{1}{\sqrt{2\pi\sigma_j^2}} \times exp\left[-\frac{1}{2}\left(\frac{x_{t_j}-x_{i_j}}{\sigma_j}\right)^2\right] \tag{1}$$

As mentioned in Section 2, the first step of the proposed algorithm is the bivariate non-parametric kernel density estimation. The reason for using multivariate kernels is that our observations on the scatter plot of color and normalized chrominance values, introduced in [15], show that these values are not independent. The proposed density estimation can be achieved by:

$$Pr(x_t) = \frac{1}{N}\sum_{i=1}^{N}\frac{1}{\sqrt{(2\pi)^2|\mathbf{\Sigma}|}} exp\left[-\frac{1}{2}\left(\mathbf{x}_t-\mathbf{x}_i\right)^T\mathbf{\Sigma}^{-1}\left(\mathbf{x}_t-\mathbf{x}_i\right)\right] \tag{2}$$

where $\mathbf{x} = [C_r, C_g]$, $C_r = \frac{R}{R+G+B}$ and $C_g = \frac{G}{R+G+B}$.

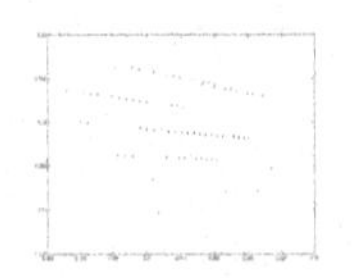
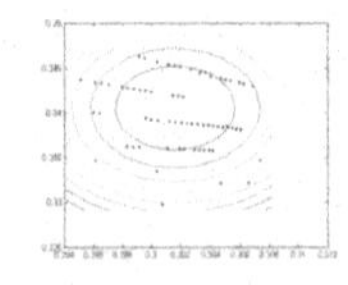
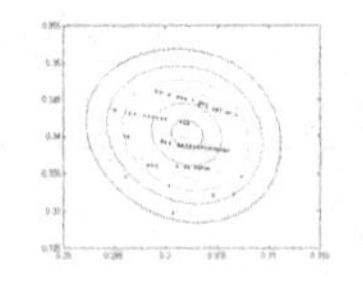
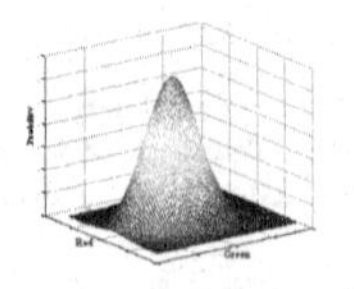

(a) Scatter Plot (b) Univariate (c) Bivariate (d) 3D illustration

Fig. 2. Red/Green chrominance scatter plot of an arbitrary pixel

In equation (2) $\mathbf{x}_t$ is the chrominance vector of each pixel in frame number t and $\mathbf{x}_i$ is the chrominance vector of the corresponding pixel in frame i of the background model. Also, $\mathbf{\Sigma}$ is the covariance matrix of the chrominance components. As it is shown in [16], kernel bandwidths are not important if the number of training samples reaches infinity. In this application, we have limited samples for each pixel, so we need to automatically select a suitable kernel bandwidth for each pixel. By using the the covariance matrix of the training data for each pixel, bandwidths are automatically estimated.

In Fig. 2, the scatter plot of red and green chrominance values of an arbitrary pixel shows that these values are not completely independent, and follow some patterns, as shown in Fig. 2(a). As expected the contours of simple traditional model are horizontal or vertical ellipses, while the proposed method gives more accurate boundaries with ellipses in the direction of the scatter of chrominance values.

Fig 2(c) shows the constant level contours of the estimated probability density function using the multi-variate probability density estimation from equation (2). In Fig. 2(d) a three dimensional illustration of the estimated probability density function is shown. The only parameters that we have to estimate in our framework are the probability threshold Th, to discriminate between foreground and background pixels, and the covariance matrix $\mathbf{\Sigma}$.

4 The Training Stage

As mentioned in Section 2, in order to make the background modeling technique automatic, we need to select two parameters for each pixel: the covariance matrix $\mathbf{\Sigma}$ in equation (2) and the threshold *Th*.

4.1 Automatic Selection of $\mathbf{\Sigma}$

Theoretically, the summation in Equation (2) will converge to the actual underlying bi-variate probability density function as the number of background frames reaches infinity. Since in practical applications, one can not use infinite number of background frames to estimate the probability, there is a need to find a suitable value of $\mathbf{\Sigma}$ parameters for every pixel in the background model.

In order to find the suitable choice of $\mathbf{\Sigma}$, for each pixel we first calculate the deviation of successive chrominance values for all pixels in the background model. Then the covariance matrix of this population is used as the $\mathbf{\Sigma}$ value. As a result the scene independent probability density of each chrominance value is estimated. In the case of a multi-modal scatter plot, observations that do not consider the successive deviations show global deviation not the local modes in the scatter plot.

4.2 Automatic Selection of Threshold

In traditional methods, both parametric and non parametric, the same global threshold for all pixels in the frame is selected, heuristically. The proposed method automatically estimates local thresholds for every pixel in the scene.

In our application we used the training frames as our prior knowledge about the background model. If we estimate the probability of each pixel in the background training data, these probabilities should be high. By estimating the probability for each pixel in all of the background training frames we have a fluctuating function shown in Fig. 3.

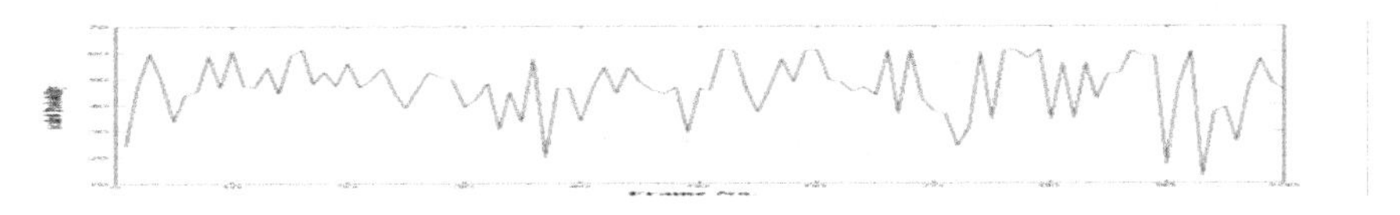

Fig. 3. Estimated probabilities of a pixel in the background training frame

We propose a probabilistic threshold training stage where we compute successive deviation of the estimated probabilities for each pixel in the training frames. The probability density function of this population is a zero mean Gaussian distribution. Then we calculate the 95 percentile of this distribution and use it as the threshold for that pixel.

5 Enforcing Spatial Consistency

Our observations show that if a pixel is selected as foreground due to strong noise, it is unlikely that the neighboring pixels, both in time and space, are also affected by this noise. To address this issue, instead of using the threshold directly on the estimated probability of pixels in the current frame, we calculate the median of probabilities of pixels in the 8-connected region surrounding current pixel. Then the threshold is applied on the median probability, instead of the actual one. Finally, a connected component analysis is used to remove the remaining regions with a very small area.

6 Adaptation to Gradual and Sudden Changes in Illumination

In the proposed method we use two different types of adaptation. To make the system adaptable to gradual changes in illumination, we replace pixels in the oldest background frame with those pixels belonging to the current background mask. To make the algorithm adaptable to sudden changes in the illumination, we track the area of the detected foreground objects. Once we detect a sudden change in their area, the detection part of the algorithm is suspended. Current frames replace the background training frames, and based on the latest reliable foreground mask, the foreground objects are detected.

Because the training stage of the algorithm is very time consuming the updating stage is is performed every few frames, depending on the rate of the changes and the processing power.

7 Experimental Results

In this section, experimental results of our proposed method are presented and compared to the existing methods.

Fig. 4 and Fig. 5 show frame number 380 of the "jump" and 28 of "rain" video sequences, respectively. The sequence in Fig. 4(a) poses significant challenges due to the moving tree branches, which makes the detection of true foreground (the two persons) very difficult. Rain in Fig. 5(a) makes this task very difficult. Results of [15] and the proposed method for these two video sequences are shown in Fig. 4 and Fig. 5 (b) and (c), respectively.

Fig. 6 shows the performance of the proposed method on some challenging scenes. In Fig. 6(a) moving branches of trees as well as waving flags and strips pose difficulties in detection of foreground. Fluctuation of illumination

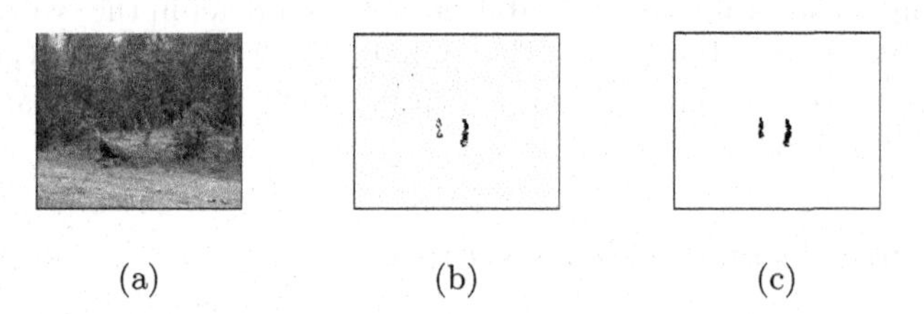

(a) (b) (c)

Fig. 4. Foreground masks selected from frame number 380 of the "jump" sequence: (a) Frame number 380. (b) Foreground masks detected using [15] and (c) using our proposed algorithm.

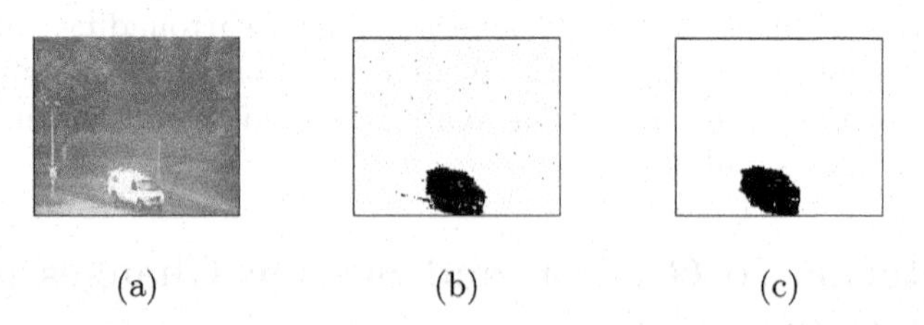

(a) (b) (c)

Fig. 5. Foreground masks selected from frame number 28 of the "rain" sequence: (a) Frame number 28. (b) Foreground masks detected using [15] and (c) using our proposed algorithm.

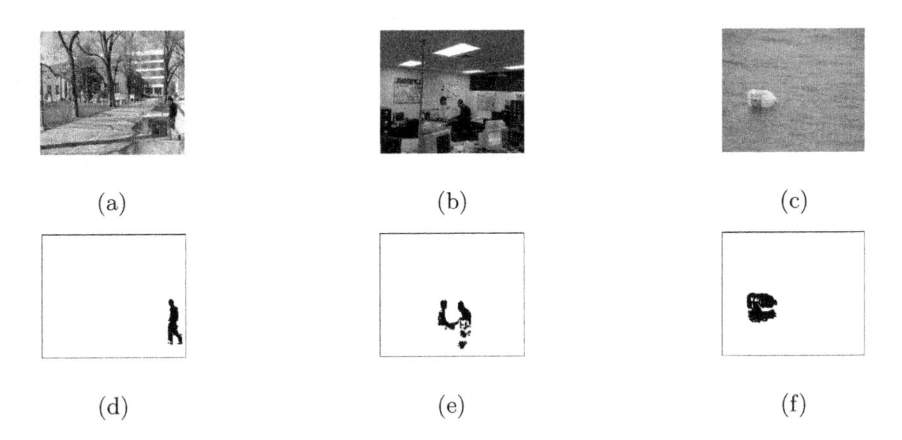

Fig. 6. Foreground masks selected from some difficult video scences using our proposed algorithm

in Fig. 6(b) due to flickering of monitor and light make this task difficult and waves and rain on the surface of water is challenging in Fig. 6(c). Results of the proposed algorithm for these scenes are presented in Fig. 6(d), (e) and (f), respectively.

The only time consuming part of the proposed algorithm is the training part, which is performed every few frames and does not interfere with the detection stage. Automatic selection of thresholds is another advantage of the proposed method.

8 Conclusions and Future Work

In this paper we propose a fully automatic and robust technique for background modeling and foreground detection based on multivariate non-parametric kernel density estimation. In the training stage, the thresholds for the estimated probability of every pixel in the scene is automatically trained. In order to achieve robustness and accurate foreground detection, we also propose a spatial consistency processing step.

Further extensions of this work include using other features of the image pixels, such as their HSV or L,a,b values. Also spatial and temporal consistency can be achieved by incorporating the position of pixels and their time index as additional features.

Acknowledgements

This work was supported in part by a grant from the University of Nevada Junior Research Grant Fund and by NASA under grant # NCC5-583. This support does not necessarily imply endorsement by the University of research conclusions.

References

1. Wern, C., Azarbayejani, A., Darrel, T., Petland, A.P.: Pfinder: real-time tracking of human body. IEEE Transactions on PAMI (1997)
2. Karman, K.P., von Brandt, A.: Moving object recognition using an adaptive background memory. Time-Varying Image Processing and Moving Object Recognition, Elsevier (1990)
3. Karman, K.P., von Brandt, A.: Moving object segmentation based on adaptive reference images. Signal Processing V: Theories and Applications, Elsevier Science Publishers B.V., (1990)
4. Koller, D., Weber, J., Haung, T., Malik, J., Ogasawara, G., Roa, B., Russel, S.: Toward robust automatic traffic scene analysis in real-time. In: ICPR. (1994) 126–131.
5. Toyama, K., Krumm, J., Brumitt, B., Meyers, B.: Wallflower: Principles and practice of background maintenance. In: ICCV. (1999) .
6. Grimson, W., Stauffer, C., Romano, R.: Using adaptive tracking to classify and monitor activities in a site. CVPR, (1998)
7. Grimson, W., Stauffer, C.: Adaptive background mixture models for real-time tracking. CVPR, (1998)
8. Friedman, N., Russel, S.: Image segmentation in video sequences: A probabilistic approach. Uncertainty in Artificial Intelligence, (1997)
9. J. Rittscher, J. Kato, S.J., Blake, A.: A probabilistic background model for tracking. In: 6th European Conf. on Computer Vision. Volume 2. (2000) 336–350.
10. B. Stenger, V. Ramesh, N.P.F.C., Bouthman, J.: Topology free hidden markov models: Application to background modeling. In: ICCV. (2001) 294–301.
11. Yang, Y., Levine, M.: The background primal sketch: An approach for tracking moving objects. Machine Vision and Applications, (1992)
12. S. Jabri, Z. Duric, H.W., Rosenfled, A.: Detection and location of people video images using adaptive fusion of color and edge information. In: ICPR. (2000) .
13. Y. Hus, H.H.N., Rekers, G.: New likelihood test methods for change detection in image sequences. Computer Vision and Image Processing, (1984)
14. Matsuyama, T., Ohya, T., Habe, H.: Background subtraction for non-stationary scenes. In: 4th Asian Conf. on Computer Vision. (2000) 662–667.
15. A. Elgammal, R. Duraiswami, D.H., Davis, L.S.: Background and foreground modeling using nonparametric kernel density estimation for visual surveillance. (In: IEEE) 1151–1163.
16. R. O. Duda, D.G.S., Hart, P.E.: Pattern classification. 2nd edn. Wiley John & Sons (2000)

Recognition of Complex Human Behaviors in Pool Environment Using Foreground Silhouette

How-Lung Eng[1], Kar-Ann Toh[2], Wei-Yun Yau[1], and Tuan-Kiang Chiew[1]

[1] Institute for Infocomm Research, 21 Heng Mui Keng Terrace, Singapore 119613
{hleng, wyyau, chiewtk}@i2r.a-star.edu.sg
[2] Biometrics Engineering Research Center,
School of Electrical and Electronic Engineering, Yonsei University, Korea
katoh@yonsei.ac.kr

Abstract. This paper presents a vision system which allows real-time recognition of temporal swimming activities and the detection of drowning incident. Operating with a set of techniques, the developed system focuses on two fundamental issues: i) way to analyze temporal behavior and ii) way to incorporate expert knowledge. To perform the recognition of different behaviors, data fusion and Hidden Markov Model (HMM) techniques are implemented. A polynomial classifier is introduced to deal with noisy foreground descriptors caused by poor resolution and sensory noise. It addresses the nonlinear interactions among different dimensions of foreground descriptors while preserving the linear estimation property. HMM is used to model the state transition process that yields a simple and efficient probabilistic inference engine. This work reports the results of extensive on-site experiments carried out. The results demonstrate reasonably good performance yielded, specifically, in terms of false alarm rates and detection of genuine water crises.

1 Introduction

The ability to automatically detect and recognize different human behaviors from videos is an important aspect of visual surveillance research. It enables high-level interpretation of events. Thus, occurrence of any undesirable incident could be detected efficiently. However, the problem remains a challenge due to the complexity of high variability in human movement and limitation to produce accurate foreground silhouette.

1.1 Related Work of Behavior Recognition

Among existing works, rule-based approach [1]-[2] is a popular choice, due to its simplicity for establishing a knowledge-based framework. A good example of rule-based approach could be referred to the work by [1]. It comprises a high-level module that operates on symbolic data and a set of heuristic rules. One advantage of the approach is that it provides the flexibility where the reasoning module could be progressively improved. Hence, this provides a simple yet convenient syntax for interfacing with expert knowledge. However, one limitation is that information is not being efficiently utilized, constrained by the simplicity of rules at each decision level.

G. Bebis et al. (Eds.): ISVC 2005, LNCS 3804, pp. 371–379, 2005.

In contrast to rule-based technique, probabilistic graph models such as Hidden Markov Models (HMMs) have also received enormous attention. For examples, in the work by Yamato et. al. [3], HMMs were applied to model the state transition process of feature vector sequences extracted from time sequential images. A similar work by Wilson and Bobick [4] used Parametric-HMMs to model gestures for representing different human's states. More recently, Oliver et. al. [5] applied Coupled-HMMs to model complex patterns of human activities, taking into account the causal connections among multiple temporal processes. One common limitation of the mentioned HMM-based methods is that these methods provide little semantic information. Semantic information is learnt indirectly through low-level features extracted from training sequences.

1.2 The Proposed Methodology

In this work, we emphasize the importance of modeling individual traits of behavior by referring to expert knowledge. Therefore, we resort to a hybrid of top-down and bottom-up framework, which comprises the incorporation of expert knowledge (high-level semantic meanings) and temporal behavioral analysis based on low-level features. With such objective, we propose a framework that comprises: a hierarchical representation of foreground descriptors, a data fusion module and a HMM modeling to describe the state transition process of analyzed behaviors.

In the hierarchical representation, a set of low-level descriptors are firstly defined and extracted from foreground silhouette. Intermediate-level descriptors that carry semantic meanings of different swimming behaviors are derived based upon these low-level descriptors. In the behavior recognition, the strength of data fusion is explored. A polynomial regression classifier algorithm is proposed to explore the non-linear input-output property among these descriptors. Lastly, the state transitions of various behaviors are modeled using Hidden Markov Model.

This paper is outlined as follows. Section 2 describes a background subtraction technique for obtaining foreground silhouette. Section 3 details the proposed water crises inference scheme. The hierarchical feature representation, data fusion mechanism and hidden markov modeling of state transition process are described in the respective subsections. Lastly, experimental results and concluding remarks are presented in Sections 4 and 5, respectively.

2 Foreground Silhouette Images

The first step involves a low-level module for generating foreground silhouette. Background subtraction proposed in our previous work [6] is applied. A brief summary of the main steps are provided below.

It involves the effort of constructing a set of homogeneous background regions with each of them can be statistically modeled using one single multivariate Gaussian distribution. This is achieved by firstly dividing a sequence of background frames into $n_1 \times n_2$ non-overlapping square blocks, and applying k-means algorithm on pixels collected to decompose each square block-(a, b) into homogeneous regions $\{\boldsymbol{R}_{a,b}^{1}, \ldots, \boldsymbol{R}_{a,b}^{c}\}$. We have shown in our previous work [6] that such modeling can facilitate an efficient spatial

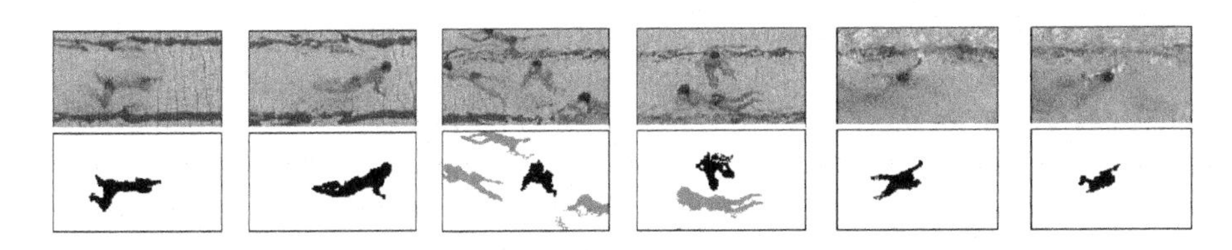

Fig. 1. Segmented foreground silhouettes of sample images with foreground targets demonstrating: normal swimming, treading and distress. Foreground targets are marked in black color.

searching scheme. This provides a better modeling of the dynamic property at aquatic environment.

A matching of a pixel $\boldsymbol{x}_{s,t}$ at position-(s,t) to a homogeneous region $\boldsymbol{R}^k_{a,b}$ is quantified by measuring a normalized distance. By thresholding on the difference image after subtracting a current frame from the background model, foreground pixels are detected as which correspond to large distance differences. Grouping of foreground pixels produces foreground silhouettes as presented in Figure 1.

3 Swimming and Water Crises Behaviors Modeling

The proposed framework of behavioral recognition comprises: a hierarchical representation of foreground descriptors, a data fusion step and a HMM modeling of the state transition process. The following subsections describe each of these modules respectively.

3.1 Swimmer Descriptors Extraction

Our approach of recognizing different behaviors in the context of swimming pool environment is to firstly understand the common visual indicators used by the professional lifeguarding community.

Drowning Research by Lifeguarding Community. In the drowning behavioral study [7]-[8], it is summarized that there are two types of water crises: distress and drowning. Both exhibit common visual indicators as follows:

1. There will be instinctive response with repetitive movements of extending the arm.
2. The body will be perpendicular (vertical up) in water with small movement in horizontal and diagonal directions.
3. The period of struggling on water surface is in the range of 20 to 60 seconds. Such rule of thumb is derived after referring to extensive real data obtained and validated over a 21 year period at Orchard Beach, Bronx, New York [8].

A Hierarchical Representation of Descriptors. To incorporate expert knowledge as highlighted above, a set of low-level descriptors is firstly formed from foreground silhouette map. They include: the centroid of segmented foreground, parameters of best-fit-ellipse, and cumulative area of pixels covered by a swimmer and its color information. These primitives contain important base information for higher level descriptors to build on.

Intermediate-level descriptors are defined to describe semantic meanings of motions based upon the computed low-level descriptors. They include: i) **Speed** (v_i): which is defined as the rate of translational displacement; ii) **Posture** (p_i): which is defined as a swimmer's dominant position. It is given by the principle axis's angle of a constructed best-fit ellipse enclosing the swimmer; iii) **Submersion index** (s_i): which is defined as the difference between a swimmer's current average saturation and the lowest value since it is being tracked. A sinking swimmer usually exhibits a higher colour saturation; iv) **Activity index** (Ac_i): which is defined as the ratio between the cumulative area of pixels covered by the swimmer and the average area of the best-fit ellipse; v) **Splash index** (Sp_i): which measures the number of splash pixels within a bounding box.

3.2 Data Fusion

Due to high variability in each class of behavior and inconsistency in foreground silhouette map, there exists high correlation among foreground descriptors extracted from different behavioral classes. Figures 2 (a)-(b) shows scatter plots when considering any two types of descriptors. Data of these plots is collected from videos containing swimmers demonstrating the actions: swimming, treading and simulated distress. To make accurate decision based on these descriptors, we describe in the following a method of data fusion to establish a nonlinear decision surface.

A Reduced Multivariate Polynomial. We consider a rth-order *generalized reduced multivariate polynomials* (GRM) [9] to describe the nonlinear input-output relationship as follows:

$$\text{(GRM):} \quad \hat{y}_{GRM} = \alpha_0 + \sum_{j=1}^{r} \alpha_{j+1}(x_1 + x_2 + \cdots + x_p)^j$$

$$+ \sum_{w=1}^{r} \sum_{j=w}^{r} (\boldsymbol{\alpha}_j^T \cdot \boldsymbol{x}^w)(x_1 + x_2 + \cdots + x_p)^{j-w} , \tag{1}$$

where $x_1 \ldots x_p$ denote the five defined descriptors ($p = 5$), $\boldsymbol{x}^w \triangleq [x_1^w, x_2^w, \cdots, x_p^w]$ and $r \geq 2$. During training with m training data sets, a regularized solution is considered in the computation:

$$\Theta = (\mathbf{X}^T\mathbf{X} + b\mathbf{I})^{(-1)}\mathbf{X}^T\mathbf{Y} , \tag{2}$$

where $\mathbf{I}$ is a $(p \times p)$ identity matrix, $\mathbf{Y} = [\boldsymbol{y}_1, \ldots, \boldsymbol{y}_m]^T$ and $\mathbf{X} = [\boldsymbol{x}_1, \ldots, \boldsymbol{x}_m]^T$. After training, the test output is computed based on: $\hat{\boldsymbol{y}}_{test} = \mathbf{X}\Theta$.

Figure 2 (c) shows the corresponding outputs of the developed GRM given by (1), after obtaining Θ using (2) from the training sequences.

3.3 State Transition Modeling

Temporal information is another important aspect of behavior analysis. We make use of the fact that there will not be possible of having rapid changes, alternating between two or more states within a short duration. Thus, we formulate the problem to identify the most likely state-transition process of a behavior within a local temporal window. To address the problem, we explore HMM [3]-[5],[10] to provide a probabilistic framework.

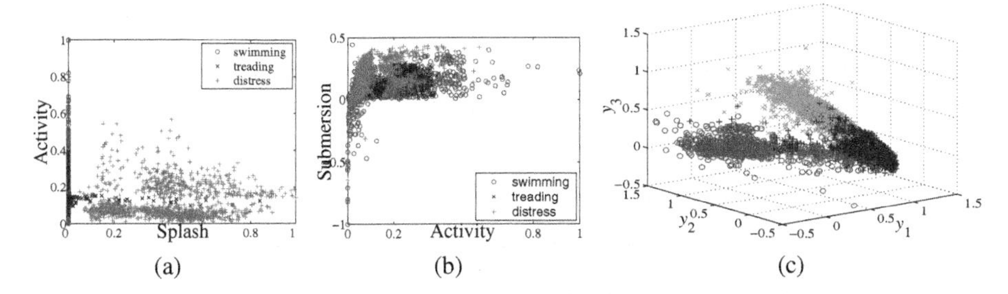

Fig. 2. (a)-(b) Scatter plots when considering two descriptors. Data is collected from videos of swimmers demonstrating: distress, treading and normal swimming. (c) Outputs of data fusion step, $\{\hat{\boldsymbol{y}}_i\}$. The true labeling for the three incidents are denoted as $[1\ 0\ 0]$, $[0\ 1\ 0]$ and $[0\ 0\ 1]$, respectively.

HMM Topology. The problem is formulated by considering a three discrete states of HMM, i.e., $S = \{S1, S2, S3\}$, which describe the swimming, treading and distress events, respectively. A state variable at time t is given by $s(t) \in S$. With the definition of HMM model $\lambda = (A, B, \pi)$, the problem is formulated to identify a state sequence $S = s(1), s(2), \ldots, s(T)$ so that the joint probability $P(O, S|\lambda)$ is maximized:

$$S = \underset{\{s(t)\}_{t=1}^{T}}{\text{argmax}}\, P(O, s(1), \ldots, s(T)|\lambda) . \tag{3}$$

Definition of (A, B, π). Referring to Figure 2 (c), the distribution of $\{\hat{\boldsymbol{y}}_i\}$ for each analyzed behavior could be reasonably modeled by one single multivariate distribution. Therefore, the observation probabilities $B = \{b_v\}$ is statistically defined to be:

$$b_v = \frac{1}{(2\pi)^{d/2}|\Sigma_v|^{1/2}} \times \exp\Big\{ -\frac{1}{2}(\hat{\boldsymbol{y}}_i - \boldsymbol{\mu}_v)^T \Sigma_v^{-1}(\hat{\boldsymbol{y}}_i - \boldsymbol{\mu}_v)\Big\} . \tag{4}$$

where Σ_v and $\boldsymbol{\mu}_v$ is the covariance and mean of $\{\hat{\boldsymbol{y}}_i\}$ for each behavior class.

Meanwhile, the state transition probabilities are empirically determined to be:

$$\begin{aligned} a_{1,1} &= 0.40 , & a_{1,2} &= 0.30 - \beta , & a_{1,3} &= 0.30 + \beta , \\ a_{2,1} &= 0.30 - \beta , & a_{2,2} &= 0.40 , & a_{2,3} &= 0.30 + \beta , \\ a_{3,1} &= 0.40 + 2\beta , & a_{3,2} &= 0.30 - \beta , & a_{3,3} &= 0.30 - \beta , \end{aligned} \tag{5}$$

where $\sum_v a_{u,v} = 1$ and β is a bias parameter imposed such that the state transition process is more sensitive in detecting any possibly distress behaviors. In our experiment, value of β is chosen in the range of $0.15 - 0.25$. The initial probabilities of different states are assigned to be $\pi_1 = \pi_2 = \pi_3 = 1/3$.

4 Experimental Results

4.1 Water Crises Detection

We created video sequences of *drowning*, *normal swimming* and *treading* events for the training process. From these sequences, an approximate number of 2000, 6000 and 6000

Table 1. Comparison on average error rates of the respective classifiers based on a 10-fold validation process

	$\%Error_{train}$	$\%Error_{test}$
GRM	≈ 8.20	≈ 10.13
GRM+HMM($T = 8$)	≈ 6.26	≈ 8.49
GRM+HMM($T = 16$)	≈ 5.00	≈ 7.25
OWM	≈ 11.80	≈ 13.55
OWM+HMM($T = 8$)	≈ 10.71	≈ 12.10
OWM+HMM($T = 16$)	≈ 9.11	≈ 10.98
FNN	≈ 9.24	≈ 10.63
FNN+HMM($T = 8$)	≈ 7.25	≈ 8.82
FNN+HMM($T = 16$)	≈ 6.60	≈ 8.51

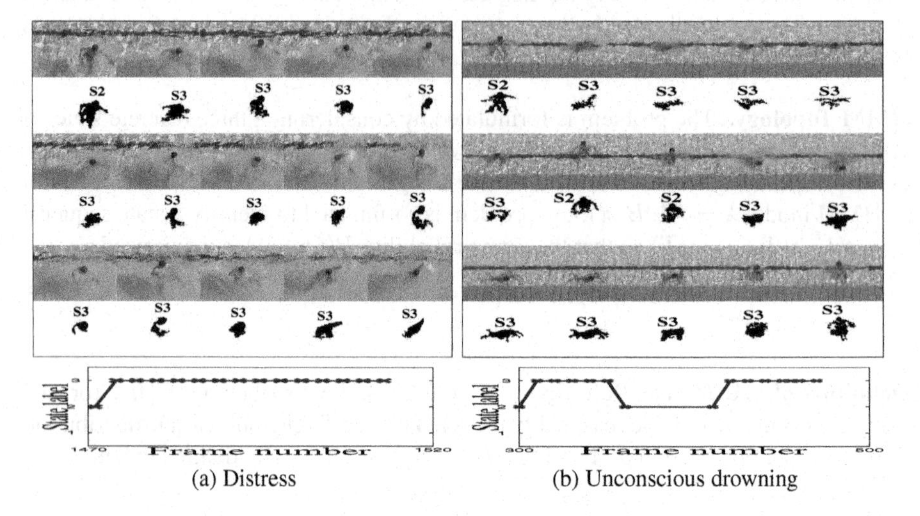

(a) Distress (b) Unconscious drowning

Fig. 3. Correct detections of simulated distress and unconscious drowning. There are large arm movement and small lateral body movement observed for victim of distress. For unconscious drowning, the victim sinks down beneath water surface without much arm movement. The corresponding state label $s(t)$ of these sample frames are displayed with the annotation: $S1 =$ swimming , $S2 =$ treading and $S3 =$ distress .

sets of swimmer descriptors were extracted for the respective class. Realistic simulated water distress was verified by lifeguard.

A 10-fold validation process has been performed. The testing involves selection of 90% of each class as $\mathcal{S}_{train}$ while the remaining as $\mathcal{S}_{test}$, and this process is repeated 10 times with different combinations of $\{\mathcal{S}_{train} , \mathcal{S}_{test}\}$. Referring to Table 1, the developed GRM has consistently attained satisfactory and better classification compared with a few commonly used classifiers e.g., *optimal weighting method* (OWM) [11] and *feedforward neural network* (FNN) (see e.g., [12]). It shows smaller error rates for both the training and test data sets. The reason that FNN has large classification error is due to its convergence to local error solution. The incorporation of HMM module together with data fusion has yielded further improvement. This is shown in the table with a reduction of about 2% to 3% of error rate for temporal windows $T = 8$ and $T = 16$, respectively.

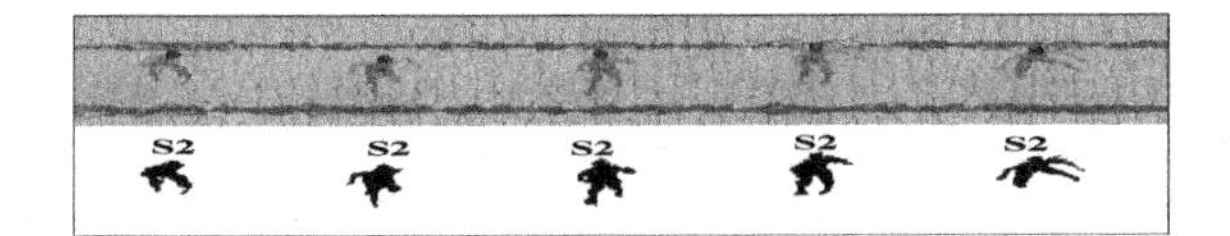

Fig. 4. Sample frames demonstrate correct detection of treading

In Figure 3, we show visual examples of correct detection of two water crisis situations: simulated distress and unconscious drowning. The system yields correct detection for almost all simulated genuine distress cases. We also observed that the developed system has demonstrated promising results of detecting "treading" event despite the significant overlapping between the swimmer's descriptors of treading and distress classes. Figure 4 shows one typical example of successful detection of treading behavior.

4.2 A Case Study of On-Site Trial

A case study of the on-site trial is performed by studying the performance of the developed system for a period of about 4 hours ($\approx$ 58000 frames) within which there is no drowning incident. Approximately 79000 sets of descriptors have been extracted within

Table 2. Numbers of alarm triggered at different intervals within a four-hours monitoring. The high alarm rate observed within the frame interval of 4000 – 19999 is due to the practicing of life saving technique by a group of children during a life-saving lesson.

	Numbers of alarms triggered	
Interval periods	HMM ($T = 8$)	HMM ($T = 16$)
000000 – 003999	0	0
004000 – 019999	16	10
020000 – 049999	7	0
050000 – 058000	5	4

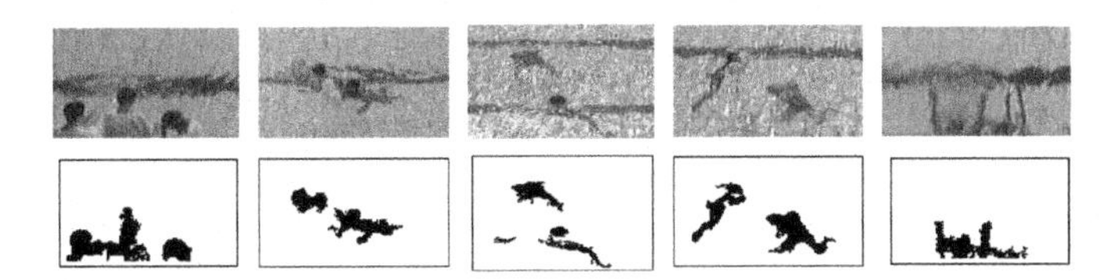

Fig. 5. Different scenarios that trigger alarms during an on-site trial. The 3rd and 4th columns are simulated distress cases demonstrated during an life-saving lesson.

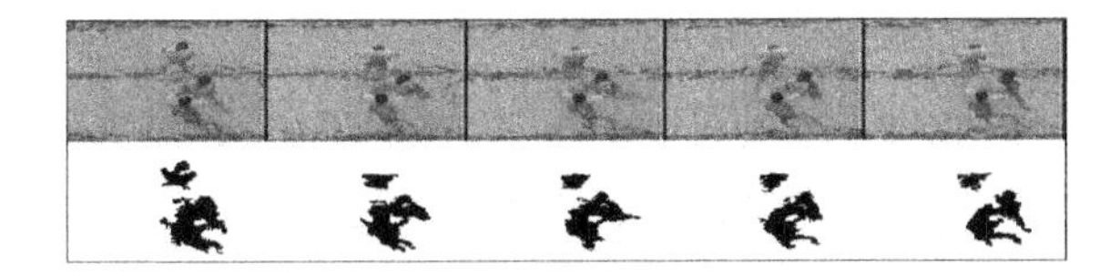

Fig. 6. Detection of a scenario which looks similar to a distress case during a life-saving lesson

these period at foreground detection rate of about 94% to 98%. The detection rate of foreground silhouette is based on the results reported in our previous work [6].

The number of false alarms triggered in four different intervals are illustrated in Table 2 for the HMM's temporal window settings of $T = 8$ and $T = 16$, respectively. For alarm triggering process, an accumulated score has been defined, which is increment by "2" when a distress state (i.e., $S3$) is detected; otherwise, decrement by "1" until reaching "0". A empirical threshold of value "80" is used in the testing. That means an alarm will be triggered after a continual detection of swimmer's status in distress state for 10 seconds at frame rate of 4 frame/second .

A higher alarm rate has been observed within the interval of 004000 – 019000 frames. It corresponds to a lifesaving lesson by a group of children with high swimming activities in contrast to normal situation. Figure 5 shows situations where alarms have been triggered. These have been mainly due to swimmers resting at pool border and practicing life-saving technique during swimming lesson. However, few scenarios which look similar to real water crises are detected as shown in Figure 6.

5 Conclusions and Future Work

We have presented in this paper a vision system that could detect early drowning symptom from the onset of a water crisis, and demonstrated its operation when applying on a public outdoor swimming pool. To approach the problem, we explored an approach of modeling individual traits of behavior rather than relying on precise geometry and temporal information.

A number of issues remain unexplored in this work, which will be considered in our future work. In this work, the system is tested on "quite realistic" simulated distress cases. A drowning incident may happen in a form which can be different from our simulations. This poses the challenge on how the system will react to the recognition of an event for which the system is not trained to. On the other hand, the complexity of the behavior recognition may grow exponentially when dealing with crowded situation.

References

1. R. Cucchiara, R., Piccardi, M., Mello, P.: Image analysis and rule-based reasoning for a traffic monitoring system. IEEE Trans. Intelligent Transportation Systems **1** (2000) 119–130
2. Su, M.C.: A fuzzy rule-based approach to spatio-temporal hand gesture recognition. IEEE Trans. Syst., Man and Cybernetics, Part C **30** (2000) 276–281
3. Yamato, J., Ohya, J., Ishii, K.: Recognizing human action in time-sequential images using hidden markov model. In Proc. IEEE Int. Conf. Computer Vision and Pattern Recognition (1992) 379–385
4. Wilson, A.D., Bobick, A.F.: Parametric hidden markov models for gesture recognition. IEEE Trans. Pattern Analysis and Machine Intell. (1999) 884–900
5. Oliver, N., Rosario, B., Pentland, A.: A bayesian computer vision system for modeling human interactions. IEEE Trans. Pattern Analysis and Machine Intell. **22** (2000) 844–851
6. Eng, H.-L., Wang, J.X., Kam, A.H., Yau, W.-Y.: Novel region-based modeling for human detection within highly dynamic aquatic environment. In Proc. IEEE Int. Conf. Computer Vision and Pattern Recognition **2** (2004) 390–397

7. Pia, F.: Observation on the drowning of nonswimmers. J. Physic. Edu. (1974) 164–167
8. Pia, F.: Reflections on lifeguarding surveilance programs. In Proc. Reflections on Lifeguarding Conf. (1974)
9. Toh, K.-A., Yau, W.-Y.: Fingerprint and Speaker Verification Decisions Fusion Using A Functional Link Network IEEE Trans. on Systems, Man, and Cybernetics Part C **35** (2005) 357–370
10. Rabiner, L.R.: A tutorial on hidden markov models and selected applications in speech recognition. Proc. IEEE **77** (1989) 257–288
11. Ueda, N.: Optimal linear combination of neural networks for improving classification performance. IEEE Trans. Pattern Anal. Machine Intell. **22** (2000) 207–215
12. Hornik, K., Stinchcombe, M., White, H.: Multi-layer feedforward networks are universal approximatorss. Neural Networks **2** (1989) 359–366

Adaptive Background Subtraction with Multiple Feedbacks for Video Surveillance

Liyuan Li, Ruijiang Luo, Weimin Huang, Karianto Leman, and Wei-Yun Yau

Institute for Infocomm Research,
21 Heng Mui Keng Terrace, Singapore, 119613
{lyli, rjluo, wmhuang, karianto, wyyau}@i2r.a-star.edu.sg

Abstract. Background subtraction is the first step for video surveillance. Existing methods almost all update their background models with a constant learning rate, which makes them not adaptive to some complex situations, e.g., crowded scenes or objects staying for a long time. In this paper, a novel framework which integrates both positive and negative feedbacks to control the learning rate is proposed. The negative feedback comes from background contextual analysis and the positive feedback comes from the foreground region analysis. Two descriptors of global contextual features are proposed and the visibility measures of background regions are derived based on contextual descriptors. Spatial-temporal features of the foreground regions are exploited. Fusing both positive and negative feedbacks, suitable strategy of background updating for specified surveillance task can be implemented. Three strategies for short-term, selective and long-term surveillance have been implemented and tested. Improved results compared with conventional background subtraction have been obtained.

1 Introduction

Background subtraction is the first fundamental step for video surveillance [1]. With a fixed camera, a background model is then generated and updated to keep the track of time-evolving background. The background model can be the mean value of gray levels or colors of the pixel [2], the color distribution parameters [7, 6], or the statistics of principal features for the background [5].

Existing methods of background subtraction almost all use a constant learning rate to update their background models. There is a dilemma to select a suitable learning rate. If a large learning rate is chosen, the system is prompt to adapt to various background changes. However, it would be easy to be disturbed by moving foreground objects. In addition, it would absorb the temporally stationary foreground objects into background very quickly. On the other hand, If a small learning rate is chosen, the system would perform smoothly and detect temporally motionless foreground objects for a longer time duration. But it would be less adaptive to the real background changes, especially once-off background changes.

In this paper, a new framework of integrating both positive and negative feedbacks to control the learning rate for different situations is proposed. The

G. Bebis et al. (Eds.): ISVC 2005, LNCS 3804, pp. 380–387, 2005.

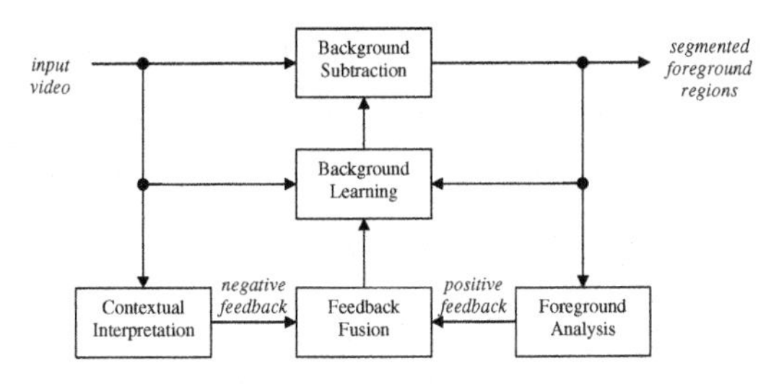

Fig. 1. The diagram of the proposed system

diagram is depicted in Figure 1. With the analysis of foreground regions obtained from background subtraction, the spatial and temporal features of them can provide positive feedback for background learning [3, 4]. However, positive feedback might not be able to correct some types of errors caused by background subtraction, e.g., a ghost due to a previously stationary person moving away. Negative feedback is introduced based on the contextual features of structural or homogeneous background regions, with which we can estimate whether the background parts are visible or not. Such global features are not related to the errors caused by background subtraction, and are stable and less affected by background changes. Fusing the positive and negative feedbacks, we can recognize the foreground regions as ghosts, noise, deposited objects, moving and stationary targets. For different surveillance tasks, different strategies of background updating can be applied. In this research, three strategies are implemented with both the positive and negative feedbacks.

The rest of the paper is organized as follows. Contextual descriptors for *region of interest* (ROI) in the background are defined and the visibility measures for different ROIs are derived in Section 2. Section 3 briefly describes a previous method for foreground region analysis. Section 4 has some experimental results, and conclusions and discussions are presented in Section 5.

2 Background Contextual Analysis

In natural scenes for video surveillance, the activities of foreground objects usually just happen in some areas (ROIs) of the scenes, e.g., persons walking on the ground surface, standing in front of a table. Therefore, whether those background parts are visible or not can be used to control the background updating. Global contextual features of the ROIs are used for such purpose.

2.1 Contextual Descriptors

Different ROIs of background may have different features. Some regions manifest significant structural features, while others may have homogeneous color distributions. In this paper, we employ *Orientation Histogram Representation* (OHR) to describe the structural features in a region and *Principal Color Representation* (PCR) to describe the distribution of dominant colors.

Let R^i_{bk} be a ROI of an empty scene, and more, $G(\mathbf{x})$ be the gradient image and $O(\mathbf{x})$ be the orientation image of the empty scene. Let us quantize the orientation values into 12 bins each corresponding to 30°, the orientation histogram for R^i_{bk} can be generated as

$$H_i(k) = \sum_{\mathbf{x}\in R^i_{bk}} B(G(\mathbf{x}))\delta_k(O(\mathbf{x})) \quad (1)$$

where $B()$ is a thresholding function and $\delta_k()$ is a delta function defined as

$$\delta_k(O(\mathbf{x})) = \begin{cases} 1, \text{ if } k \leq O(\mathbf{x})/30° < k+1 \\ 0, \text{ otherwise} \end{cases} \quad (2)$$

The OHR is less sensitive to illumination changes.

By scanning the region R^i_{bk} pixel by pixel, a table for the PCR of the region can be obtained as

$$T_i = \{p_i, \{E^k_i = (\mathbf{c}^k_i, p^k_i)\}^{N_i}_{k=1}\} \quad (3)$$

where p_i is the area of the region R^i_{bk}, $\mathbf{c}^k_i$ is the k-th most significant color of R^i_{bk} and p^k_i is its significance. The significance is computed by

$$p^k_i = \sum_{\mathbf{x}\in R^i_{bk}} \delta(\mathbf{I}_t(\mathbf{x}), \mathbf{c}^k_i) \quad (4)$$

$\delta(\mathbf{c}_1, \mathbf{c}_2)$ is a delta function. It equals to 1 when the color distance $d(\mathbf{c}_1, \mathbf{c}_2)$ is smaller than a small threshold ε, otherwise, it is 0. The color distance is

$$d(\mathbf{c}_1, \mathbf{c}_2) = 1 - \frac{2 < \mathbf{c}_1, \mathbf{c}_2 >}{\|\mathbf{c}_1\|^2 + \|\mathbf{c}_2\|^2} \quad (5)$$

where $< \cdot, \cdot >$ denotes the dot product [5]. The principal color components E^k_i are sorted in descendent order according to their significance measures p^k_i. The first N_i components which satisfies $\sum^{N_i}_{k=0} p^k_i \geq 0.95 p_i$ are used as the PCR of the region R^i_{bk}, which means the principal colors in the table cover more than 95% colors from the region R^i_{bk}. The *Principal Color Representation* (PCR) is efficient to describe large homogeneous regions, e.g., ground surfaces in the scene.

The descriptors of the global contextual features for ROIs are built off-line in advance. For some ROIs, both descriptors can be used, while for some other ROIs, just one of them is used.

2.2 Visibility Evaluation

We classify the ROIs into two types: strong structural regions (type-1) and large homogeneous regions (type-2). A type-1 region can be the image of a facility which may be occluded when it is occupied, e.g., a chair or a counter table. Both OHR and PCR descriptors are used for a type-1 region. A type-2 region is a large homogeneous background region, such as the ground or wall surface. Usually parts would be occluded when there are foreground objects in the region. Only PCR descriptor is used for a type-2 region.

Visibility for Type-1 ROI

A type-1 ROI usually has just two states: occluded or not. The visibility of it is evaluated on the whole region. Let R_{b1}^i be one of such ROIs, H_{b1}^i and $T_{b1}^i = \{p_{b,i}, \{E_{b,i}^k = (\mathbf{c}_{b,i}^k, p_{b,i}^k)\}_{k=1}^{N_{b,i}}\}$ are the contextual descriptors of it, and H_t^i and $T_t^i = \{p_{t,i}, \{E_{t,i}^n = (\mathbf{c}_{t,i}^n, p_{t,i}^n)\}_{n=1}^{N_{t,i}}\}$ are the OHR and PCR of the corresponding region in the current frame $I_t(\mathbf{x})$. If the region R_{b1}^i is not occluded at time t, both OHRs and PCRs are similar.

The visibility of R_{b1}^i according to OHRs can be defined as the similarity of the two orientation histograms (H_{b1}^i and H_t^i). This measure is defined as

$$v1_{b1}^{i,t} = \frac{2 < H_{b1}^i, H_t^i >}{\|H_{b1}^i\|^2 + \|H_t^i\|^2} \tag{6}$$

Obviously, if the background region R_{b1}^i is visible at time t, the orientation histograms H_{b1}^i and H_t^i are similar, so that the visibility value $v1_{b1}^{i,t}$ is close to 1, otherwise, it is close to 0.

The visibility of R_{b1}^i based on PCR can be defined as the likelihood of observing the background region at time t according to its original PCR T_{b1}^i. According to Bayesian law, the likelihood can be computed as

$$v2_{b1}^{i,t} = P(T_t^i|T_{b1}^i) = \sum_{k=1}^{N_{b,i}} P(T_t^i|E_{b,i}^k)P(E_{b,i}^k|T_{b1}^i) \tag{7}$$

The 2nd term in the right is the weight of the principal color $\mathbf{c}_{b,i}^k$ for the ROI R_{b1}^i. It is evaluated as $P(E_{b,i}^k|T_{b1}^i) = p_{b,i}^k/p_{b,i}$. The 1st term is the likelihood of observing the original appearance of R_{b1}^i in the current frame according to the corresponding principal color $\mathbf{c}_{b,i}^k$. It is evaluated from the PCRs of original and current appearances as

$$P(T_t^i|E_{b,i}^k) = \frac{1}{p_{b,i}^k} \min\left\{p_{b,i}^k, \sum_{n=1}^{N_{t,i}} \delta(\mathbf{c}_{b,i}^k, \mathbf{c}_{t,i}^n)p_{t,i}^n\right\} \tag{8}$$

Now, the visibility measure based on PCRs can be computed as

$$v2_{b1}^{i,t} = \frac{1}{p_{b,i}} \sum_{k=1}^{N_{b,i}} \min\left\{p_{b,i}^k, \sum_{n=1}^{N_{t,i}} \delta(\mathbf{c}_{b,i}^k, \mathbf{c}_{t,i}^n)p_{t,i}^n\right\} \tag{9}$$

Combining the two visibility measures based on OHR and PCR, the visibility of the ROI in the current frame is defined as

$$v_{b1}^{i,t} = w_1 v1_{b1}^{i,t} + w_2 v2_{b1}^{i,t} \tag{10}$$

where $w_1 \in [0,1]$ and $w_2 = 1 - w_1$ are weights for the OHR and PCR. w_1 is selected empirically. To be robust to various variations in the image sequence, a smooth filter is applied to the visibility measure as

$$\bar{v}_{b1}^{i,t} = (1-\beta)\bar{v}_{b1}^{i,t-1} + \beta v_{b1}^{i,t} \tag{11}$$

Here, $\beta = 0.2$ is chosen.

Visibility for Type-2 ROI

The type-2 ROIs are usually large homogeneous background regions with less or inconstant structural features, like ground or wall surfaces. Hence, just PCR descriptor is employed for them. To be robust to illumination changes, a few snapshots of the empty scene in different illumination conditions are captured for contextual modelling. Since a type-2 ROI is a large background region and usually parts of it are occluded when there are foreground objects in the scene, the visibility of it is evaluated pixel-by-pixel according to the local features.

Let $R_{b2}^{i,j}$ be the i-th type-2 ROI from the j-th snapshot and $T_{b2}^{i,j} = \{p_{i,j}, \{E_{i,j}^k = (\mathbf{c}_{i,j}^k, p_{i,j}^k)\}_{k=1}^{N_{i,j}}\}$ be the corresponding PCR descriptor. During the running, the visibility measures of the pixels in the ROI are evaluated with respect to each snapshot and the best ones are selected. Let $\mathbf{c}(\mathbf{x}) = I_t(\mathbf{x})$ is the color of the pixel $\mathbf{x}$ in the ROI from the current frame. The likelihood of observing $\mathbf{c}(\mathbf{x})$ according to the ROI's j-th snapshot can be estimated as

$$P(\mathbf{c}(\mathbf{x})|R_{b2}^{i,j}) = \frac{1}{p_{i,j}} \sum_{k=1}^{N_{i,j}} \delta(\mathbf{c}(\mathbf{x}), \mathbf{c}_{i,j}^k) p_{i,j}^k \tag{12}$$

Since a type-2 ROI is a large homogeneous region, the visibility of each pixel is defined on its local neighborhood, i.e.,

$$v_{b2}^{i,j,t}(\mathbf{x}) = \frac{1}{|W_{\mathbf{x}}|} \sum_{\mathbf{s} \in W_{\mathbf{x}}} P(\mathbf{c}(\mathbf{s})|R_{b2}^{i,j}) \tag{13}$$

where $W_{\mathbf{x}}$ is a small window centered at $\mathbf{x}$ and $|W_{\mathbf{x}}|$ is the size of it. Obviously, the visibility value $v_{b2}^{i,j,t}(\mathbf{x})$ is within $[0, 1]$ and the larger the value is, the greater the possibility of the pixel belonging to the background according to the j-th snapshot. Hence, the visibility of the whole region compared to the j-th snapshot is defined as $v_{b2}^{i,j,t} = \sum_{\mathbf{x} \in R_{b2}^{i,j}} v_{b2}^{i,j,t}(\mathbf{x})$. The best estimation over all the snapshots can be obtained as $j^* = \arg\max_j \{v_{b2}^{i,j,t}\}$ and the corresponding visibility measures for each pixel in the region at time t is determined as $v_{b2}^{i,t}(\mathbf{x}) = v_{b2}^{i,j^*,t}(\mathbf{x})$. Again, a smooth filter is applied like Equ. (11), that is

$$\bar{v}_{b2}^{i,t}(\mathbf{x}) = (1 - \beta)\bar{v}_{b2}^{i,t-1}(\mathbf{x}) + \beta v_{b2}^{i,t}(\mathbf{x}) \tag{14}$$

A Mask of Visible Background

From the visibility measures of type-1 and type-2 ROIs, a mask of visible background parts, or $V_t(\mathbf{x})$, can be obtained. For a type-1 region R_{b1}^i, if the visibility measure $\bar{v}_{b1}^{i,t}$ is larger than a threhold T_{b1}, all the pixels of the region are labelled as "0" denoting "visible", otherwise, all of them are marked as "1" indicating "occluded". For each pixel in type-2 region R_{b2}^i, if its visibility measure $\bar{v}_{b2}^{i,t}(\mathbf{x})$ is larger than a threshold T_{b2}, it is labelled as "0", otherwise, it is marked as "1". For the other parts of the image which do not belong to any ROIs, they are labelled as "0".

3 Foreground Region Analysis

Desired foregrounds are those of target objects, while the false positives are usually the non-interested objects or un-related changes according to the purpose of surveillance. Features from the foreground regions can provide information about whether the detected positive is desired. As in [4], both motion and shape features of the detected foreground regions are exploited to select desirable positives. For each stationary foreground region, a shape feature vector is generated according to the translation- and scale-invariant moments. Then a measure to describe the similarity to the target objects is computed. To control background updating, we are only interested in whether the foreground region is associated with a target object. If it does not look like any interested object, it might be a false positive.

4 Experiments

Fusing the information from background contextual interpretation and foreground region analysis, the detected changes at time t can be classified as four categories: moving object, stationary target, stationary non-interested objects, and ghosts. A ghost is a detected region with more than 90% parts belonging to the visible background. It may be caused by removing of an object that previously existed in the background or sudden change of lighting conditions.

With the recognition of the detected changes, various strategies can be implemented for different surveillance tasks. In this paper, three strategies for different surveillance purposes are implemented and tested. The images displayed in each row of the figure are arranged as the same format. From left to right, the images are: the frame, the background reference images maintained with controlled learned rate and constant learning rate, the segmented foreground image with controlled learning rate and constant learning rate, and the mask image of visibility for ROIs according to background contextual interpretation.

Short-Term Surveillance

The short-term surveillance is just interested in moving foreground objects, e.g., walking persons or running vehicles. Such system has a wide application for intruder detection in commercial buildings and forbidden zones. In this case, it is desirable to treat all stationary objects as parts of the background.

The test scene is taken from entrance of an official building. Only the type-2 contextual model for the ground surface in the hall was employed. The 1st row of Figure 2 shows a sample from the test, where the guarder in the left had stayed there for 1294 frames and the chair had placed there for 78 frames. From the images, it can be seen that three moving target objects were detected correctly while no false positive targets was detected with controlled learning rate. However, with constant learning rate, we still detected five target objects, among them two are not interested.

Selective Surveillance

In this case, the purpose of surveillance is to detect and track the target objects as long as possible but not be interested in other objects.

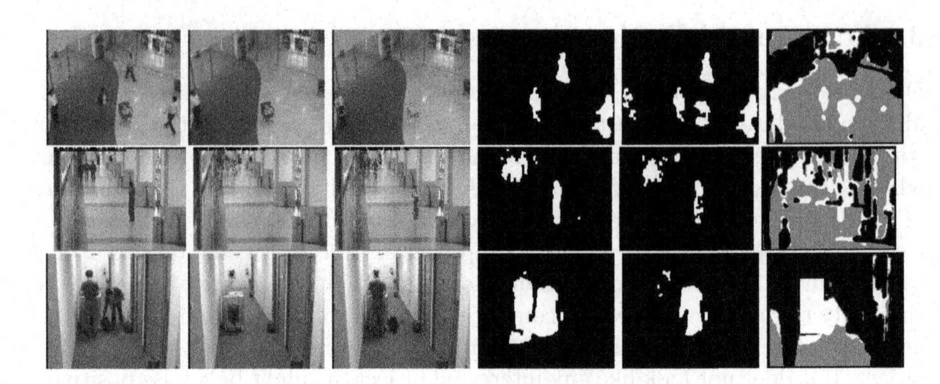

Fig. 2. Examples of tests for different surveillance tasks. From upper to lower are for short-term, selective, and long-term surveillance.

The test sequence comes from the open test database CAVIAR. It is the scene of a corridor in a shopping center. In this scenario, one person went into a shop and the other waited for him outside. The 2nd row of Figure 2 shows the results when the person had stood motionless for 374 frames. Part of his body had been learned as background with constant learning rate. With the controlled learning rate according to the contextual model of ground surface, the background updating was almost stopped when the person was standing there. Hence, the occluded part in the background reference image was clear and the person was detected with a good shape.

Long-Term Surveillance
In long-term surveillance, any foreground object that does not belong to the original background should be detected and tracked as long as it stays in the scene. So that the background updating should be stopped for any foreground objects.

The scene tested for long-term surveillance is a corridor of a public building in which there is a copy machine available for public to use. For this scene, one contextual models of type-1 ROIs were used for the copy machine, and a contextual model of type-2 ROI is employed for the carpet. In frame 729, a person was using the machine. He placed his bag beside him. In frame 1346 as shown in the 3rd row of Figure 2, another person took the bag away when its owner was concentrating on copying. It can be seen that the person and his bag had been absorbed into background with constant learning rate, whereas with the controlled learning rate according to the negative feedback based on the contextual interpretation, the person and his bag could still be detected completely.

5 Conclusions

In this paper, a novel framework of integrating both positive and negative feedbacks to control the background learning rate for adaptive background subtraction is proposed. Two descriptors of contextual features for background regions are proposed. Visibility measures for two types of ROIs of background are then derived. With the both background contextual interpretation and foreground region analysis, different strategies of adaptive background updating for different purposes of surveillance are implemented and tested. Experiments show that improved results of foreground segmentation can be obtained compared with background subtraction with constant learning rate.

References

1. I. Haritaoglu, D. Harwood, and L. Davis, W^4: Real-time surveillance of people and their activities. *IEEE Trans. Pattern Analysis and Machine Intelligence*, 22(8):809–830, August 2000.
2. D. Koller, J. Weber, T. Huang, J. Malik, G. Ogasawara, B. Rao, and S. Russel, Toward robust automatic traffic scene analysis in real-time. *Proc. Int'l Conf. Pattern Recognition*, pages 126–131, 1994.
3. M. Harville. A framework for high-level feedback to adaptive, per-pixel, mixture-of-gaussian background models. *Proc. European Conf. Computer Vision*, pages 543–560, 2002.
4. L. Li, I. Y. H. Gu, M. K. H. Leung, and Q. Tian. Adaptive background subtraction based on feedback from fuzzy classification. *Optical Engineering*, 43(10):2381–2394, 2004.
5. L. Li, W. Huang, I. Y. H. Gu, and Q. Tian. Statistical modeling of complex background for foreground object detection. *IEEE Trans. Image Processing*, 13(11):1459–1472, 2004.
6. C. Stauffer and W. Grimson. Learning patterns of activity using real-time tracking. *IEEE Trans. Pattern Analysis and Machine Intelligence*, 22(8):747–757, August 2000.
7. C. Wren, A. Azarbaygaui, T. Darrell, and A. Pentland. *Pfinder*: Real-time tracking of the human body. *IEEE Trans. Pattern Analysis and Machine Intelligence*, 19(7):780–785, 1997.

A Vectorial Self-dual Morphological Filter Based on Total Variation Minimization

Jérôme Darbon[1,2] and Sylvain Peyronnet[1]

[1] EPITA Research and Development Laboratory (LRDE),
14-16 rue Voltaire F-94276 Le Kremlin-Bicêtre, France
[2] Ecole Nationale Supérieure des Télécommunications (ENST),
46 rue Barrault, F-75013 Paris, France
{jerome.darbon, sylvain.peyronnet}@lrde.epita.fr

Abstract. We present a vectorial self dual morphological filter. Contrary to many methods, our approach does not require the use of an ordering on vectors. It relies on the minimization of the total variation with L^1 norm as data fidelity on each channel. We further constraint this minimization in order not to create new values. It is shown that this minimization yields a self-dual and contrast invariant filter. Although the above minimization is not a convex problem, we propose an algorithm which computes a global minimizer. This algorithm relies on minimum cost cut-based optimizations.

1 Introduction

One of the main issue for mathematical morphology is its extension to the vectorial case. The difficulty arises because a total order between elements is required using the classical approach of lattice theory [20]. However, such orders are required for technical reasons and not semantical purposes. Thus it is essential to propose a vectorial extension without such orders. Extensions of the lattice theory approach to the vectorial case have been tackled using vector ranking concepts [10, 21]. In this paper, we propose a new, self dual morphological filter for vectorial images, based on total variation minimization. Our approach does not require any order relation between vectors.

A lot of work has been devoted to the design of morphological operators for *color* images as a specific case of vectorial images. Main approaches consist in choosing a suitable color space representation and defining an ordering relationship [8, 13, 19]. In [5], Chambolle proposes a definition for contrast invariance of operators on colors. This definition is considered by Caselles *et al.* in [4] who present a morphological operator on color images.

Vector median filters are another approach for vector filtering, originally introduced by Astola *et al.* in [1]. The process consists of replacing the pixel value by the median of the pixels contained in a window around it. The median is defined as the value that minimizes the L^1-norm between all pixels in a window. This method has been used specially for noise filtering [14, 15, 16]. In [4], Caselles *et al.* connect vector median filters, morphological operators and partial

G. Bebis et al. (Eds.): ISVC 2005, LNCS 3804, pp. 388–395, 2005.

differential equations. They consider a lexicographic order to obtain these connections. Complementary results on these links for the scalar case can be found in [11].

In [6], the author deals with the scalar case and shows that minimization of the total variation (TV) under the L^1-norm as data fidelity yields a morphological filter. This model will be referred to as $L^1 + TV$. Assume that an observed image v is defined on Ω and takes values in $\mathbb{R}$. For sake of clarity, we assume here that Ω is a rectangle of $\mathbb{R}^2$ although all the results presented in the paper apply for any convex set in any dimension. The energy associated to the model $L^1 + TV$ is expressed as follows:

$$E(u) = \int_\Omega |u(x) - v(x)| dx + \beta \int_\Omega |\nabla u| \ , \qquad (1)$$

where the last term is the TV of u weighted by a non-negative coefficient β. Note that the gradient is taken in the distributional sense. An efficient algorithm is proposed in [7] to perform an exact minimization of (1), i.e, it provides a global minimizer. In [2], Blomgren *et al.* propose some extensions of the total variation definition to the vectorial case. They study them for image restoration purposes. However, no relation with mathematical morphology is introduced.

The contributions of this paper are the following. We propose a morphological filter based on the minimization of TV. Contrary to many previous approaches, our method does not require any order relationship between vectors. Our approach relies on extending the energy (1) to the vectorial case by simply applying the $L^1 + TV$ model on each channel. We further constrain the energy such that no new value is created. We show that this filter is a morphological one. Contrary to the minimization of (1), the problem is *not anymore convex*. We thus propose an algorithm which provides an exact minimizer for this new non-convex functional. This algorithm relies on minimum-cost cut ones. To our knowledge, these results are new.

The structure of the paper is as follows. Section 2 is dedicated to the presentation of the proposed approach for the design of our vectorial morphological filter. We present an algorithm to perform the minimization in Section 3, along with some results.

2 Vectorial Mathematical Morphology

In this section we briefly review the $L^1 + TV$ model. Then we show how to generalize the approach to the vectorial case. We define a continous change of contrast as follows [12]: any continuous non-decreasing function on $\mathbb{R}$ is called a continuous change of contrast. The following theorem is proved in [6] and in appendix A.

Theorem 1. *Let v be an observed image and g be a continuous change of contrast. Assume u to be a global minimizer of $E_v(\cdot)$. Then $g(u)$ is a global minimizer of $E_{g(v)}(\cdot)$. Besides, $-u$ minimizes $E_{-v}(\cdot)$.*

We now deal with the vectorial case. From now on, we consider vectorial images, $u = (u^1, ...u^N)$, defined on Ω which take values into $\mathbb{R}^N$. We define the L^1-norm $\|u\|_{L^1}$ for a vectorial image u as the sum of L^1-norms on each channel, i.e: $\|u\|_{L^1} = \sum_{i=1}^N \int_\Omega |u^i(x)|dx$. We extend the total variation $\overrightarrow{tv}(u)$ of a vectorial image u in the same way, i.e: $\overrightarrow{tv}(u) = \sum_{i=1}^N \int_\Omega |\nabla u^i|$. A straightforward extension of the scalar model $L^1 + TV$ to the vectorial case consists in applying *independently* $L^1 + TV$ on each channel, i.e:

$$E(u) = \|u - v\|_1 + \beta\, \overrightarrow{tv}(u) \ . \tag{2}$$

However, it is easily seen that if no constraint is added, minimization of this energy yields a minimizer which has new vectorial values. Consequently it breaks the morphological property. Thus we add a constraint to ensure that a global minimizer does not have new values. Let us denote by $\mathcal{C}$ the set of all vectorial values appearing in the observed image v. Our goal is to find a global minimizer of the following problem:

$$(\mathrm{P}) \begin{cases} \operatorname*{arginf}_u \|u - v\|_1 + \beta\, \overrightarrow{tv}(u) \\ \text{s. t. } \forall x \in \Omega \;\; u(x) \in \mathcal{C} \end{cases}$$

As one can see, our extension to the vectorial case reduces to the classical $L^1{+}TV$ model when images are scalar. We now give our definition for a vectorial change of contrast.

Definition 1. *Any continuous function $g : \mathbb{R}^N \mapsto \mathbb{R}^N$ is called a vectorial continous change of contrast if and only of its restriction to any canonic axis is a continuous change of contrast.*

Then it is easily seen that problem (P) defines a morphological filter according to our vectorial change of contrast definition (1).

Note that although minimization of the scalar model $L^1 + TV$ defined by equation (1) is a convex problem, *it is no longer the case for problem* (P). Indeed, the objective function is still convex, but the constraint is not. An algorithm for computing an exact solution of the non-convex problem (P) is given in the next section.

3 Minimization Algorithm and Results

In this section, we present an algorithm which computes a global optimizer for a discrete version of problem (P) along with some results. In the following we assume that images are defined on a discrete lattice S and take values in $\mathcal{C}$. We denote by u_s the value taken by the image u at the site $s \in S$. Two neighboring sites s and t are denoted $s \sim t$. The discrete version of energy (2) is thus as follows:

$$E(u) = \sum_{i=1}^N \sum_s |u_s^i - v_s^i| + \beta \sum_{(s\sim t)} |u_s^i - u_t^i| \ .$$

Now we present our algorithm for optimizing energy E.

```
Start with a labeling u such that ∀s u_s ∈ C
do
   success ← false
   forall α ∈ C
        u' = argmin_û E(û) where û is an α−expansion of u

        if E(u') < E(u)
             u ← u'
             success ← true
while success ≠ false
```

Fig. 1. Pseudo-code for our minimization algorithm

3.1 Minimimum Cost Cut Based Minimization

Our algorithm relies on the α-expansion moves algorithm proposed by Boykov *et al.* in [3]. An α-expansion move from a current labeling is defined as follows: given a value α, every pixel can either keep its current value or take α. We are interested in finding the optimal α-expansion move from a current labeling which minimizes the energy. Originally, this method is devoted to the approximation of non-convex Markovian energy [3].

In order to solve problem (P), we iterate optimal α-expansion moves. At each iteration we perform an optimal α-expansion move where α belongs to the set of observed values $\mathcal{C}$. The traversal on $\mathcal{C}$ stops when no α-expansion can furthermore decrease the energy. This algorithm is presented in Figure 1. We now prove, in the following proposition, that this algorithm provides a global minimizer for the non-convex problem (P).

Theorem 1. *Let u be an image such that*

$$E(u) > \inf_{u'} E(u') \ .$$

Then, there exists u^α which is within one $\alpha-$expansion move of u, such that

$$E(u) > E(u^\alpha) \ .$$

Proof: Before giving to the proof, we recall that for a one dimensional discrete convex function $f : \mathbb{Z} \mapsto \mathbb{R}$, the following inequality holds [17] :

$$\forall x \, \forall y \forall d \mid (y \geq x) \wedge (0 \leq d \leq (y-x)), \;\; f(x) + f(y) \geq f(x+d) + f(y-d) \ . \quad (3)$$

Let $\hat{u}$ be a global minimizer of E, i.e., $E(\hat{u}) = \inf_{u'} E(u')$ Given a value $\alpha \in \mathcal{C}$, we define an image δ as follows:

$$\forall s \;\; \delta_s = \begin{cases} \alpha - u_s & \text{if } \alpha \in [\![u_s, \hat{u}_s]\!] \text{ or } \alpha \in [\![\hat{u}_s, u_s]\!] \ , \\ 0 & \text{else.} \end{cases} \quad (4)$$

• We first prove the following inequality:

$$E(u) + E(\hat{u}) \geq E(u + \delta) + E(\hat{u} - \delta) \ . \tag{5}$$

We show it for the data fidelity and regularisation terms independently.
- Data fidelity terms: Since the absolute value is a convex function, we have the following inequality (obtained using equation (3)) for all data fidelity terms:

$$|u_s - v_s| + |\hat{u}_s - v_s| \geq |u_s + \delta_s - v_s| + |\hat{u}_s - \delta_s - v_s| \ .$$

This concludes the proof for the first case.
- *A priori* terms: Let $X_{st} = u_s - u_t$, $Y_{xt} = \hat{u}_s - \hat{u}_t$ and $D_{st} = \delta_s - \delta_t$. Assume that $X_{st} \leq Y_{st}$. Thus we have by definition of δ (equation (4)), $X_{st} \leq X_{st} + D_{st} \leq Y_{st}$. Applying inequality (3) we have the desired results. The case $X_{st} > Y_{st}$ is similar to this one.
• Let us denote by $\mathcal{M}$ the set of global minimizers of $E(\cdot)$. Let us define the norm $\|u\|_1$ on an image u as $\|u\|_1 = \sum_s |u_s|$. Let us define $u^\star$ as follows:

$$u^\star = \underset{u' \in \mathcal{M}}{\operatorname{argmin}} \|u' - u\|_1 \ . \tag{6}$$

From equation (5), we have $E(u) - E(u + \delta) \geq E(\hat{u} - \delta) - E(\hat{u}) \geq 0$, since $\hat{u}$ is a global minimizer. If the inequality is strict then the proof is finished. If this is not the case then we have $E(\hat{u} - \delta) = E(\hat{u})$. However, it is easy to show that $\|u + \delta - \hat{u}\|_1 < \|u - \hat{u}\|_1$. This is in contradiction with the definition of $\hat{u}$ (equation (4)). This concludes the proof. □

We use a minimum cost cut technique to find the optimal α−expansion move that must be done in order to decrease the energy [3]. This minimum cost cut is computed on a weighted graph corresponding to the energy associated with an α−expansion.

3.2 Results

We present some results on color images. Since, in this paper, we focus on demonstrating the effectiveness of our filter, we applied our model to the RGB space. We are aware that many other color spaces are available [18] and we are currently studying more suitable spaces. Figure 2 presents some results on the image *hand*. We note that the higher the coefficient β, the more the image is simplified. Details of the texture are removed while the geometry is kept. Moreover, the colors of the background of the hand do not merge. Finally, the color of the ring is well preserved. This result gives a very good initialization for a segmentation process. In [22], the authors perform the minimization of the $L^1 + TV$ model in order to decompose the image into two parts: the first one contains the geometry while the second one contains the textures. Figure 2 depicts the result of such a decomposition using our filter. We performed a change of contrast on gray levels to enhance the content of the textured image. Note how fine the decomposition is. Color version of these images are available at `http://perso.enst.fr/~darbon/papers/isvc05`.

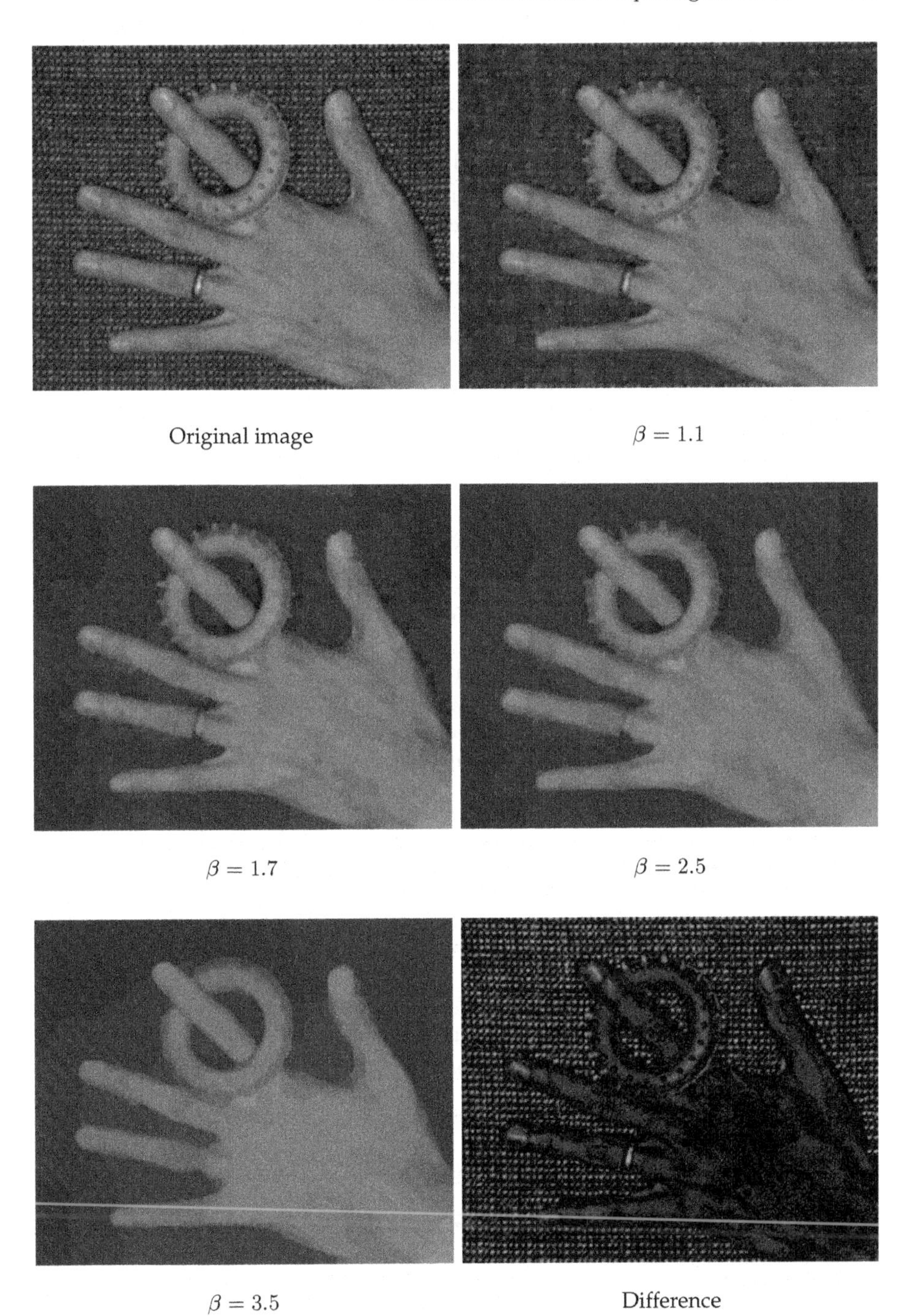

Fig. 2. Minimizers of problem (P) for different regularization coefficients for the image *hand*. The last image *difference* is the difference between the original image and the one for $\beta = 3.5$ (Note that we applied a change of contrast on the gray levels to enhance the colors).

4 Conclusion

In this paper we have proposed a new morphological filter for vectorial images. The main feature of this filter is that it does not involve any ordering between elements. We have also presented an algorithm to perform the filtering. Many opportunities for future work are considered. First, a faster algorithm is currently under investigation. The special case of color images must be handled by applying this filter on color spaces other than RGB [18], such as Lab. All these extensions will be presented in a forthcoming paper.

Acknowledgments. The authors would like to deeply thanks Didier Verna for his careful proofreadings and comments of this paper.

References

1. J. Astola, P. Haavisto, and Y. Neuvo. Vector median filters. *Proceedings of the IEEE*, 78(4):678–689, 1990.
2. P. Blomgren and T.F. Chan. Color tv: Total variation methods for restoration of vector-valued images. *IEEE Transactions on Image Processing*, 7(3):304–309, 1998.
3. Y. Boykov, O. Veksler, and R. Zabih. Fast approximate energy minimization via graph cuts. *IEEE Transactions on Pattern Analysis and Machine Intelligence*, 23(11):1222–1239, 2001.
4. V. Caselles, B. Coll, and J.-M. Morel. Geometry and color in natural images. *Journal Mathematical Imaging and Vision*, 16(2):89–105, 2002.
5. A. Chambolle. Partial differential equations and image processing. In *In the proceedings of the fourth IEEE International Conference on Image Processing (ICIP 94)*, pages 16–20, 1994.
6. J. Darbon. Total variation minimization with L^1 data fidelity as a contrast invariant filter. In *Proceedings of the 4th International Symposium on Image and Signal Processing and Analysis (ISPA 2005)*, Zagreb, Croatia, September 2005.
7. J. Darbon and M. Sigelle. A fast and exact algorithm for total variation minimization. In *Proceedings of the 2nd Iberian Conference on Pattern Recognition and Image Analysis (IbPRIA)*, volume 3522, pages 351–359, Estoril, Portugal, June 2005. Springer-Verlag.
8. M.C. d'Ornellas, R. Van Den Boomgaard, and J.-M. Geusebroek. Morphological algorithms for color images based on a generic-programming approach. In *In Brazilian Conf. on Image Processing and Computer Graphics (SIBGRAPI'98)*, pages 220–228, 1998.
9. L. Evans and R. Gariepy. *Measure Theory and Fine Properties of Functions.* CRC Press, 1992.
10. J. Goutsias, H.J.A.M. Heijman, and K. Sivakumar. Morphological operators for image sequences. *Computer Vision and Image Understanding*, 63(2):326–346, 1995.
11. F. Guichard and J.-M. Morel. *Image Iterative Smoothing and PDE s.* downloadable manuscript : please write email to fguichard@poseidon-tech.com, 2000.
12. F. Guichard and J.M. Morel. Mathematical morphology "almost everywhere". In *Proceedings of ISMM*, pages 293–303. Csiro Publishing, April 2002.
13. A.G. Hanbury and J. Serra. Morphological operators on the unit circle. *IEEE Transactions on Image Processing*, 10(12):1842–1850, December 2001.
14. R. Lukac. Adaptive vector median filter. *Pattern Recognition Letters*, 24(12):1889–1899, 2003.

15. R. Lukac, B. Smolka, K.N. Plataniotis, and A.N. Venetsanopoulos. Selection weighted vector directional filters. *Computer Vision and Image Understanding*, 94(1-3):140–167, 2004.
16. Z. Ma and H.R. Wu. Classification based adaptive vector filter for color image restoration. In *In the proceedings of the IEEE International Conference on Acoustics*, 2005.
17. K. Murota. *Discrete Convex Optimization.* SIAM Society for Industrial and Applied Mathematics, 2003.
18. K.N. Plataniotis and A.N. Venetsanopoulos. *Color Image Processing and Application.* Springer, 2000.
19. G. Sapiro. *Geometric Partial Differential Equations and Image Analysis.* Cambridge University Press, 2001.
20. J. Serra. *Image Analysis and Mathematical Morphology.* Academic Press, 1988.
21. J. Serra. *Mathematical Morphology in Image Processing*, chapter Anamorphoses and Function lattices, pages 483–523. Marcel-Dekker, 1992.
22. W. Yin, D. Goldfarb, and S. Osher. Total variation based image cartoon-texture decomposition. Technical report, UCLA, avril 2005.

A Proof of Theorem 1

We first introduce the notion of level sets of an image and give two lemma.

Definition 1. *The lower level sets of an image u, referred to as u^λ are defined as follows:*

$$u^\lambda(x) = \mathbb{1}_{u(x)\leq\lambda} \ .$$

Before we give the proof of Theorem 1, we give a lemma proved in [11], which stipulates that after a continuous change of contrast g, the level sets of an image $g(v)$ are some level sets of the image v.

Lemma 1. *Assume g to be a continuous change of contrast and u an image defined on Ω. The following holds: $\forall\lambda\,\exists\mu\ \ (g(u))^\lambda = u^\mu$.*

Lemma 2. *Let us denote χ_A the characteristic function of the set A. The energy $E_v(u)$ rewrites as follows for almost all λ: $E_v(u) = \int_{\mathbb{R}} E_v^\lambda(u^\lambda, v^\lambda)d\lambda$, where*

$$E_v^\lambda(u^\lambda, v^\lambda) = \int_\Omega \left(\beta\left|\nabla\chi_{u^\lambda}\right| + \left|u^\lambda(x) - v^\lambda(x)\right| dx\right) \ .$$

Proof: The fidelity term rewrites as follows: $|u(x) - v(x)| = \int_{\mathbb{R}} \left|u^\lambda(x) - v^\lambda(x)\right| d\lambda$. The co-area formula [9] states that for any function which belongs to the space of functions of bounded variation, we have: $\int_\Omega |\nabla u| = \int_{\mathbb{R}} \int_\Omega |\nabla\chi_{u^\lambda}|\, d\lambda$, for almost all λ. This concludes the proof of this lemma. □

Proof of theorem 1: First, we show that $L1+TV$ is invariant with respect to any change of contrast. It is sufficient to prove that for any level λ, a minimizer for $g(v)^\lambda$ is $g(u)^\lambda$. Using lemma 1, there exists μ such that $v^\mu = g(v)^\lambda$. A minimizer of $E_v^\mu(\cdot, v^\mu)$ is u^μ. Thus, u^μ is a minimizer of $E_v^\mu(\cdot, g(v)^\lambda)$. And we have $u^\mu = g(u)^\lambda$. Self dual invariance is easily obtained. It is enough to note that $\int_\Omega |\nabla u| = \int_\Omega |\nabla(-u)|$ and that $\int_\Omega |u(x) - v(x)|dx = \int_\Omega |(-u(x)) - (-v(x))|dx$. The conclusion is straightforward. □

Wavelet Transform Based Gaussian Point Spread Function Estimation

Qing-Chuan Tao[1], Xiao-Hai He[1], Hong-Bin Deng[2], Ying Liu[1], and Jia Zhao[1]

[1] College of Electronic Information, Sichuan University, Chengdu 610064, P.R. China
tqc104@163.com
[2] School of Information Engineering,
Beijing Institute of Technology, Beijing 100081, P.R. China

Abstract. Point spread function (PSF) estimation, an essential part for image restoration, has no accurate estimation algorithm at present. Based on the wavelet theory, a new Gaussian PSF accurate estimation algorithm is put forward in this paper. Firstly, the blurred images are smoothed, and their noise is reduced. Secondly, wavelet with varied scales is transformed, after which the local maxima of the modulus of the wavelet are computed respectively. Thirdly, on the basis of the relation deduced in this paper among the local maxima of the modulus of the wavelet at different scales, Lipschitz exponent and variance, the variance of a Gaussian PSF is computed. The experimental result shows that the proposed algorithm has an accuracy rate as high as 95%, and is of great application value.

1 Introduction

In the process of the image generation and transmission, images are degraded by some adverse factors, for example, the relative movement of the camera, defocusing, the torrent of the atmosphere as well as noise [1-2] etc. Such degradation can be commonly represented by a linear model of the form:

$$g(x,y) = f(x,y) * h(x,y) = \sum_{(m,n)} f(n,m)h(x-n, y-m) + n(x,y) \tag{1}$$

Where $g(x,y)$, $f(x,y)$, $h(x,y)$ and $n(x,y)$ denotes respectively the degraded image, the true image, the point-spread function (PSF), and additive noise. The process of the image restoration is estimating the true image from the observed image. The conventional algorithms, such as inverse filtering and Wiener filters, etc. require a priori knowledge of the PSF. However, in actual applications, the PSF of the degraded image is unknown. Therefore the true image has to be estimated from the degraded image due to the few (or no) priori knowledge of PSF and the original image [1]. This is called blind image restoration. At present, representative algorithms of the blind image restoration include maximum entropy algorithm, zero-sheet separation algorithm, simulated annealing algorithm, the expectation-maximization (EM) algorithm, the ARMA parametric algorithm, and the iterative blind deconvolution (IBD) algorithm, etc [1-2]. But the solution to the algorithm may not

G. Bebis et al. (Eds.): ISVC 2005, LNCS 3804, pp. 396–405, 2005.

be unique and the deconvolution is often ill-posed due to the lack of sufficient information and the existence of the additive noise. Therefore, the PSF estimation is of vital importance in image restoration. However, a precise estimation method has not yet been found. Because the PSF of a defocused system can be approximated in a Gauss function, an intensive study on the estimation of the Gauss PSF was undertaken. The typical Gaussian PSF is as follow:

$$PSF(x,y) = \frac{1}{\sqrt{2\pi\sigma_{bl}}} e^{-(x^2+y^2)/2\sigma_{bl}^2} \tag{2}$$

With σ_{bl} is the variance of the Gaussian function, which is called the smoothing factor.

The blurred image contains some information of the imaging system, such as the sharpness of the edge has close relationship with defocus of system and the depth of the 3-dimensional object[3-4], so Elder has provided an estimating algorithm of the Gaussian PSF based on the sharpness of the image edge [4-6] and achieved preferable experimental result. However, due to the lack of mathematic foundation, the accuracy of the algorithm is not high.

The sharpness of the edge can be measured by the Lipschitz exponent in the mathematic analysis. The exponent is bigger, the edge is smoother. In addition, according to wavelet theory, the Lipschitz exponent can be calculated by the maximum modulus of the wavelet transform. So based on the relationship of the Lipschitz exponent and the maximum of the wavelet transformation, we deduce, at the different scales, the mathematical relationship between the variance of the Gaussian function, Lipschitz exponent and modulus maximum of the wavelet transform. Applying the relationship, we can compute the variance of the Gaussian function in theory. But in practice, the precision is about the 95%.

2 Principles

2.1 Lipschitz Exponent

The wavelet transform has the characteristic of the multiresolution and can describe the local features the signal both in the time and frequency domain, so it can get the detail of the signal at the different scales [7,8]. From the view of the signal processing, the wavelet can recognize the singularity in the signal. In mathematics theory, the singularity of the signal as the sharp variation of the signal can be expressed precisely by the Lipschitz exponent. The definition is: assuming that around t_0 the function x(t) has the following characteristics:

$$|x(t_0+h) - p_n(t_0+h)| \le A|h|^{\alpha}, n < a < n+1, (n \in z) \tag{3}$$

Where h is a increment small enough, $p_n(t)$is the nth polynomial equation at $x(t_0)$, so we call the Lipschitz exponent of the $x(t_0)$ in the t_0 is α . Actually, $p_n(t)$ is the Taylor series' first n terms of the $x(t)$ in the t_0.

$$\begin{aligned} x(t) &= x(t_0) + a_1 h + a_2 h + a_2 h^2 + \ldots + a_n h^n + O(h^{n+1}) \\ &= p_n(t) + O(h^{n+1}) \end{aligned} \tag{4}$$

Apparently, α is not always equal to n+1; it must be greater than n, but it may be smaller than n+1. For example:

$$x(t) = x(t_0) + a_1 h + a_2 h + a_2 h^2 + ... + a_{2.5} h^{2.5} \quad (5)$$

In the t_0, there is: $2 < \alpha = 2.5 < 3$, so $n < a \leq n+1$. This demonstrates that, the Lipschitz exponent has the following features: if $x(t)$ is n times differentiable, but it is not continuity, that is n+1 times undifferentiable, so $n < a \leq n+1$; if the Lipschitz exponent of the $x(t)$ is α, the Lipschitz exponent of the $\int x(t)dt$ is $\alpha+1$, that is after each integral the Lipschitz exponent will add 1. For example, a signal that is differentiable once, has Lipschitz exponent 1, a step function has Lipschitz 0 and a dirac impulse Lipschitz -1.

Generally speaking, the function's Lipschitz exponent presents the greatness of that point's singularity, α is bigger, the point is smoother. In the next chapter we will discuss the relationship at one point between the Lipschitz exponent and modulus maximum of the wavelet transform.

2.2 Relationship Between Lipschitz Exponent and Modulus Maximum of the Wavelet Transform

Assuming the wavelet function $\varphi(t)$ is continuously differentiable and has a decay at infinity that is $O(\frac{1}{1+t^2})$. Mallat proved that when t is over [a,b], if the wavelet transform of the $f(t)$ satisfied [7]:

$$|W_s f(t)| \leq K s^{\alpha} \quad (6)$$

that is:

$$\log|Wsf(t)| \leq \log K + \alpha \log s \quad (7)$$

Where K is a constant, s is the scale of the wavelet transformation, so the Lipschitz exponent of $f(t)$ is α over [a,b]. In the equation (7), $\alpha \log s$ connects scale s and Lipschitz exponent, and it also implies the diversification of scale s. When $\alpha > 0$, the maximum of the wavelet transform will increase with the augment of scale s; when $\alpha < 0$, the maximum of the wavelet transform will decrease with the augment of scale s; when $\alpha = 0$, the maximum will not change with the alteration of scale.

2.3 Relationship Among Lipschitz Exponent and Modulus Maximum and Variance of the Gaussian Function

The edge of the image is the place where the signal is changed greatest, so the first differentiation of the smoothing function can be applied to be the wavelet function [7,8].

If $\theta(x, y)$ is the 2-dimensional smoothing function, the first differentiation in the x, y direction is used to be two wavelet function,

$$\varphi_s^{(1)}(x,y)=\frac{1}{s^2}\,\varphi^{(1)}\left(\frac{x}{s},\frac{y}{s}\right)=\frac{\partial\theta_s(x,y)}{\partial x} \tag{8}$$

where,

$$\theta_s\ (x,y)=\theta\left(\frac{x}{s},\frac{y}{s}\right) \tag{9}$$

So the arbitrary 2-dimensional function, in the scale s, its two fractions of the wavelet transform are:
In the x direction:

$$W_s^{(1)}f(x,y)=f(x,y)*\varphi_s^{(1)}(x,y)=s\frac{\partial}{\partial x}(f(x,y)*\theta_s(x,y)) \tag{10}$$

In the y direction:

$$W_s^{(2)}f(x,y)=f(x,y)*\varphi_s^{(2)}(x,y)=s\frac{\partial}{\partial y}(f(x,y)*\theta_s(x,y)) \tag{11}$$

in the equation, $*$ represents the convolution. From equation the (10) and (11), the image's fraction of the wavelet transform is the gradient in the x, y direction after the image being convolved by the smoothing function. The modulus of the wavelet transform is:

$$|W_s f(x,y)|=\sqrt{|W_s^{(1)}f(x,y|^2+|W_s^{(2)}f(x,y)|^2} \tag{12}$$

similar to the 1-dimensional signal, the relationship between the Lipschitz exponent of $f(x,y)$'s sharp variation point and the modulus of the wavelet transform is:

$$|W_s f(x,y)|\le Ks^{\alpha} \tag{13}$$

At the scale s, the x directional fraction of the wavelet transform of the blurred image $g(x,y)$ is:

$$W_s^{(1)}g(x,y)=s\frac{\partial}{\partial x}(g(x,y)*\theta_s(x,y)) \tag{14}$$

ignoring the noise and based on the property of the convolution the equation (14) can be rewritten:

$$W_s^{(1)}g(x,y)=s\frac{\partial}{\partial x}\{f(x,y)*[h(x,y)*\theta_s(x,y)]\} \tag{15}$$

$h(x,y)$ is the Gaussian function with the variance σ. Assuming $\theta_s\ (x,y)$ is also the Gaussian function with the variance $\sigma=s$, so based on the properties of the Gaussian function, there is:

$$h(x,y)*\theta_s(x,y)=\theta_{s0}\ (x,y),\ s_0=\sqrt{s^2+\sigma^2} \tag{16}$$

the equation (15) can be rewritten to:

$$W_s^{(1)} g(x,y) = s\frac{\partial}{\partial x}(f(x,y) * \theta_{s0}(x,y)) = \frac{s}{s_0} W_{s0}^{(1)} f(x,y) \tag{17}$$

the same as:

$$W_s^{(2)} g(x,y) = s\frac{\partial}{\partial y}(f(x,y) * \theta_{s0}(x,y)) == \frac{s}{s_0} W_{s0}^{(2)} f(x,y) \tag{18}$$

group the upper two equations, there is:

$$|W_s g(x,y)| = \frac{s}{s_0}\sqrt{|W_{s0}^{(1)} f(x,y|^2 + |W_{s0}^{(2)} f(x,y)|^2} = \frac{s}{s_0}|W_{s0} g(x,y)| \tag{19}$$

$$s_0 = \sqrt{s^2 + \sigma^2} \tag{20}$$

This equation shows that the wavelet transform at the scale s of a singular point which is smoothed by a Gaussian function with the variance σ equals to the wavelet transform at the scale $s_0 = \sqrt{s^2 + \sigma^2}$ of the unsmoothed original singular point.
The relationship between the magnitude and the measurement of wavelet transformation and the variance of the Gaussian PSF:

$$|W_s g(x,y)| \le K\frac{s}{s_0} s_0^{\alpha} \qquad s_0 = \sqrt{s^2 + \sigma^2} \tag{21}$$

Through no less than 3 different scales of the wavelet transform about the edges of the blurred image, we can get the modulus maxima of the wavelet transform correspondingly. Taking the equal in the equation (21) and grouping those equations, K, a, σ can be obtained.

3 The Details of the Estimation

3.1 The Choice of the Wavelet Function

Based on the wavelet function and former analysis, in this paper, the Gaussian function is used as the smoothing function and its differentiation is used as the wavelet function. The smoothing function and the wavelet function are as follows:

$$\theta(x,y) = \frac{1}{\sqrt{2\pi}} e^{-\frac{x^2+y^2}{2}} \tag{22}$$

$$\varphi^{(1)}(x,y) = \frac{\partial\theta(x,x)}{\partial x} = -\frac{1}{\sqrt{2\pi}} x e^{-\frac{x^2+y^2}{2}} \tag{23}$$

$$\varphi^{(2)}(x,y) = \frac{\partial\theta(x,x)}{\partial y} = -\frac{1}{\sqrt{2\pi}} y e^{-\frac{x^2+y^2}{2}} \tag{24}$$

the problem of the noise.

The relationship among the Lipschitz exponent, the modulus maximum of the wavelet transform and the variance of the Gaussian blurring function of the image edge is obtained by ignoring the noise. But the actually recorded image will be disturbed by the noise; in this case if the wavelet transform is directly used and the variance of the Gaussian function is calculated, the result will not be accurate. Therefore the noise has to be removed before computation. The usually used methods to remove the noise are: average filter, medial filter etc. But after smoothing, the variance will become bigger. In this paper, the Gaussian function is used as smoothing function to remove the noise,

$$\theta_\sigma(x,y)=\frac{1}{\sqrt{2\pi\sigma}}e^{-\frac{x^2+y^2}{2\sigma^2}} \tag{25}$$

Applying the former analytical results, we will get the following relationship:

$$\sigma_{bl}=\sqrt{\hat{\sigma}^2-\sigma^2_{no}} \tag{26}$$

σ_{bl} : The variance of the PSF.

$\hat{\sigma}$: The variance which is computed by the methods mentioned formerly after removing the noise.

σ_{no} : The variance which is used to remove the noise.

Firstly the Gaussian function is used to smooth the image and remove the noise, then the modulus maximum of the wavelet transform and the smoothing factors of the image after removing the noise, using equation (25) the smoothing factor of the PSF will be obtained by using the equation (26).

3.2 The Selection of the Edge Point (The Point of the Modulus Maximum)

The former computation is provided for the edge point of the image signal. So the first step is to find the edge of the image. From the equation (10) and (11), we know that the x and y fractions of the wavelet transform are the image's gradients, the modulus maximum of the wavelet transform is the image's edge point. Considering the very smoothing areas of the image will also produce the modulus maximum point with small value which will result in computational error easily. So, a threshold is used to remove those false edges in this paper. In practice, if the threshold is $35/\sigma_{bl}$, the result will be better.

3.3 The Solving Method

If scale s = 1,2,3, the corresponding modulus maxima of the wavelet transform are:

$$a_1=K(1+\sigma^2)^{\frac{a-1}{2}},a_2=2K(4+\sigma^2)^{\frac{\alpha-1}{2}},a_3=3K(9+\sigma^2)^{\frac{\alpha-1}{2}} \tag{27}$$

grouping these three equations, K, a, σ will be obtained. Let

$$y=\frac{4+\sigma^2}{1+\sigma^2},c=\ln\frac{a_3}{3a_1}\Big/\ln\frac{a_2}{2a_1},\ y\in[1,4]$$

eliminating a, K, we will get

$$y^c = \frac{8y-5}{3} \tag{28}$$

Because the range of c is between 1.6 and 2.6, it proves that y in the equation (28) will have a solution. In this paper, the gold section is used to get the result.

In actual computation, the edge points' smoothing factors are different, so the statistical histogram method is used. The interval of the histogram is 0.1, and the gravity center of the histogram is the smoothing factor of the image.

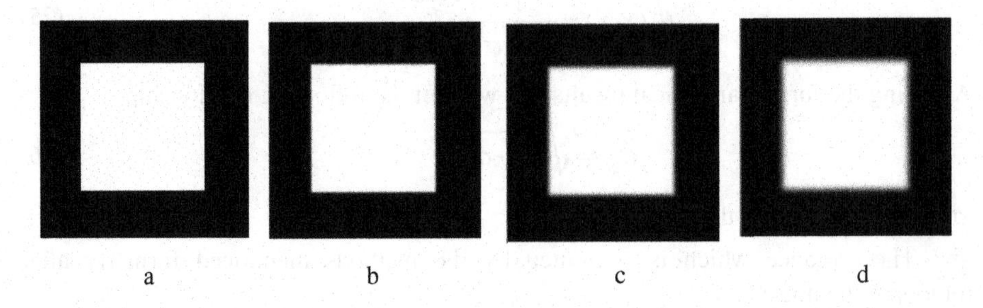

Fig. 1. a. original image; b. blurred image with $\sigma = 1$; c. blurred image with $\sigma = 2$; d. blurred image with $\sigma = 3$

4 Experiments

4.1 The Experiment 1

In order to validate the correctness of the algorithm, the rectangular is used to test it. The rectangle is the step signal, and its Lipschitz exponent is 0. The modulus maximum of the wavelet transform of the original and its blurred image are in the four apexes of the rectangle. Following the former estimating algorithm of the Gaussian PSF, we did the wavelet transform with the scale = 1, 2, 3 respectively, obtained the corresponding modulus maximum a_1, a_2, a_3, and then got the variance of the Gaussian PSF after solving the equation (28). The results of the experiment are as follows:

Table 1. The data of the experiment 1

σ / result	a_1	a_2	a_3	variance	error
σ=1	68.452530	89.34951	95.2530	1.0552	5.5%
σ=2	44.498755	71.10896	84.077352	2.1115	5.8%
Σ=3	31.895345	56.071590	71.63091	3.0277	0.9%

a. original image b. blured image $\sigma = 1.5$ c. blured image $\sigma = 2.5$ d. blured image $\sigma = 3.5$

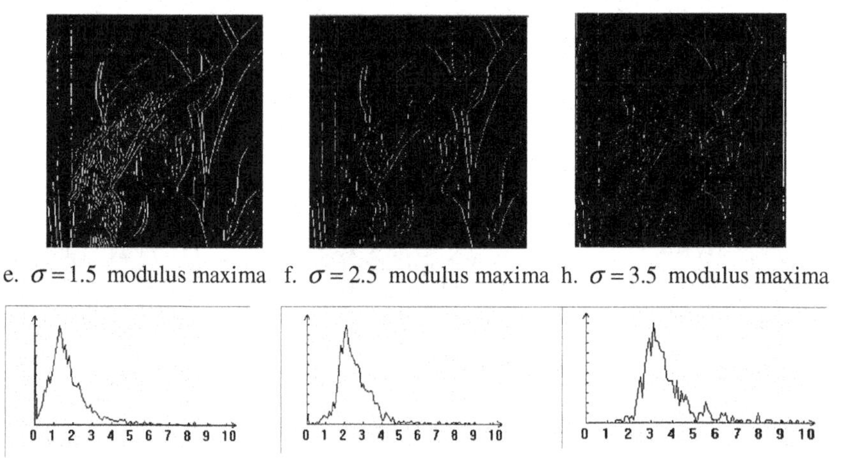

e. $\sigma = 1.5$ modulus maxima f. $\sigma = 2.5$ modulus maxima h. $\sigma = 3.5$ modulus maxima

i. $\sigma = 1.5$ Lipschitz histogram j. $\sigma = 2.5$ Lipschitz histogram k. $\sigma = 3.5$ Lipschitz histogram

Fig. 2. The result of the experiment 2

4.2 The Experiment 2 (Without Noise)

Fig. 2 shows that: the experiment used the Lena image as the original image, which was firstly blurred by the Gaussian function with the variance $\sigma = 1.5, 2.5, 3.5$. Then the experiment did the wavelet transform with the scale= 1, 2, 3, found the points with the modulus maximum (shown in fig. e, f, h), and then took the respective modulus maximum to the equation to solve the variance. The histogram distributions of the modulus maximum values are shown in the fig. i, j, k with the gravity center of the histogram as the estimate variance. The results are as follows:

Table 2. The data of the experiment 2

σ / result	The estimation mean value of the variance	error
σ= 1.5	1.56853	4.5%
σ=2.5	2.54928	1.9%
σ=3.5	3.59579	2.7%

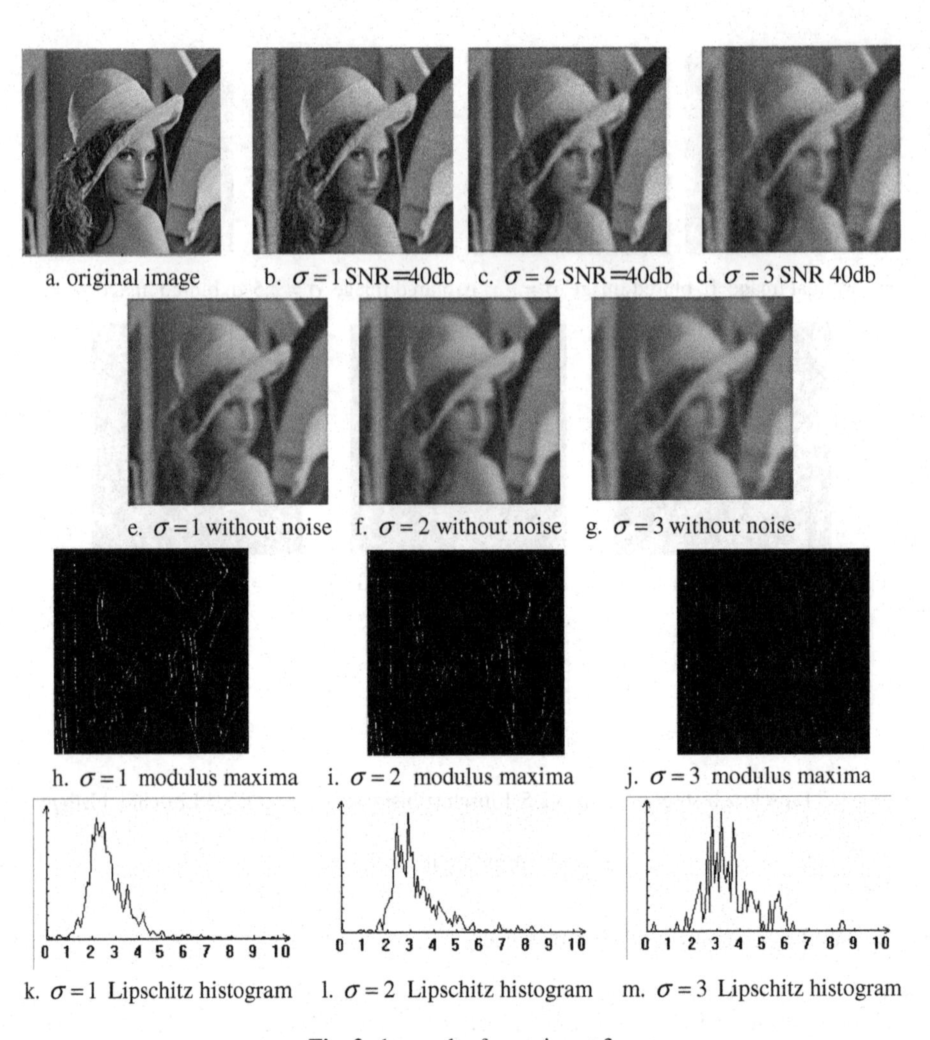

a. original image b. $\sigma=1$ SNR=40db c. $\sigma=2$ SNR=40db d. $\sigma=3$ SNR 40db

e. $\sigma=1$ without noise f. $\sigma=2$ without noise g. $\sigma=3$ without noise

h. $\sigma=1$ modulus maxima i. $\sigma=2$ modulus maxima j. $\sigma=3$ modulus maxima

k. $\sigma=1$ Lipschitz histogram l. $\sigma=2$ Lipschitz histogram m. $\sigma=3$ Lipschitz histogram

Fig. 3. the result of experiment 3

4.3 The Experiment 3 (With the Noise)

Fig.3 shows that: the experiment used the Lena image as the original image. It was blurred by the Gaussian function with the variance $\sigma=1.5,2.5,3.5$, then added the noise with the SNR= 40db. Because the existence of the noise will influence the computational result, it was smoothed before computing by the Gaussian function with the variance $\sigma=2$. Similar to experiment 2, we did the wavelet transform with the scale = 1, 2, 3, found the points with the modulus maximum (shown in fig. h, i, j), then took the respective maximum to the equation to solve the variance. The histogram distributions of the maximum values are shown in the fig. k, l, and m. The gravity center of the histogram was used as the estimate variance of the smoothed image. Based on the equation (28), the variance of the Gaussian function of the image before smoothing can be achieved. The results are as follows:

Table 3. The data of the experiment

σ / result	The estimate mean value of the variance after smoothing	The estimate mean value of the variance before smoothing	error
σ=1	2.2601	1.0526	5.3%
σ= 2	2.9184	2.1253	6.2%
σ= 3	3.6955	3.1075	3.2%

5 Conclusions

In this paper, according to the wavelet theory, the relationship among the modulus maximum, Lipschitz exponent and the variance of the Gaussian function of the wavelet with different scales is found. By way of this relationship, the variance of the Gaussian PSF can be computed accurately. The results show that the accuracy of this algorithm is around 95%. Although the algorithm mainly focuses on the circular symmetrical Gaussian PSF in this paper, it can also be used to estimate the non-circular symmetrical Gaussian PSF and used in the condition that the PSF is changed with the variance of the time or the space.

Acknowledgement

This paper is supported by Natural Science Foundation of China (60372079), and Hi-Tech Research and Development Program of China (863 Program 2004AA420090-2).

References

1. D.Kundur and D.hatzinakos.: Blind image deconvolution, IEEE Signal Processing mag.,vol.13,no.3, pp. 43-64,1996.
2. D.Kundur and D.hatzinakos.: A novel Blind scheme for image restoration using recursive filtering",IEEE Signal Processing Mag.,vol.26,no.2,pp.375-390,1998.
3. Yalin Xiong and Steve Shafer.: Depth from focusing and defocusing. in Proc. of IEEE Conf. on Computer Vision and Pattern Recognition, 1993.
4. Yoav Schechner and Nahum Kiryati.: Depth from defocus vs. stereo: How different really are they? in Proc. International Conf. on Pattern Recognition, 1998.
5. James Elder and Steven Zucker.: Local scale control for edge detection and blur estimation.IEEE Trans. Pattern Analysis and Machine Intelligence, vol. 20, no. 7, pp. 699–716, 1998.
6. V. Kayargadde and J.-B. Martens.: Estimation of edge parameters and image blur from local derivatives.Journal on Communications, pp. 33–34, 1994.
7. Stephane Mallat and Sifen Zhong.: Characterization of signals from multiscale edges.IEEE Trans. Pattern Analysis and Machine Intelligence, vol. 14, no. 7, pp. 710–732, 1992.
8. Stephane Mallat and Wen Liang Hwang.: Singularity detection and processing with wavelets. IEEE Trans. Information Theory, vol. 38, no. 8, pp. 617–643, 1992.

One-Point Hexagonal Inner Search for Fast Motion Estimation

Chorng-Yann Su and Cheng-Tao Chang

Institute of Applied Electronic Technology, National Taiwan Normal University,
162, Section 1, Heping East Road, Taipei, Taiwan
scy@cc.ntnu.edu.tw, think12381@yahoo.com.tw

Abstract. In this paper, we propose a novel inner search algorithm for fast motion estimation to speed up the coding of video compression. The proposed algorithm, called as one-point hexagonal inner search (OPHIS), is based on the characteristic of monotonically decreasing of distortion on a local area. The most probable inner point is checked when an inner search starts. Compared with the enhanced hexagon-based search algorithm (EHEXBS), the OPHIS not only decreases the number of search points but also gets a better video quality. Experimental results show that the speed improvement is about 12.06% on average and the percentage decrease of the mean squared error is near to 2.29% on average. Therefore, the proposed OPHIS is more suitable for the applications of fast motion estimation than the EHEXBS.

Index Terms: one-point hexagonal inner search, fast motion estimation, hexagonal search, enhanced hexagon-based search algorithm.

1 Introduction

In video coding standards, motion estimation plays a very important role. In order to reduce the execution time of motion estimation, many fast search algorithms have been proposed such as two-dimension search algorithm [1], three-step search algorithm (TSS) [2], new three-step search algorithm (NTSS) [3], block-based gradient descent search algorithm (BBGDS) [4], simple and efficient search (SES) [5], diamond search (DS) [6][7], hexagon-based search algorithm (HEXBS) [8], and enhanced hexagon-based search algorithm (EHEXBS) [9] *etc*..

The HEXBS algorithm [8] has shown that it performs well than the other algorithms such as the DS. The search pattern of the HEXBS is depicted in Fig. 1, which consists of seven checking points including a center point and six outer checking points. In the HEXBS, an inner search starts when the center point has the minimum distortion among the seven checking points. A shrunk pattern containing only the points 2, 4, 5, and 7 is used in the inner search. After the inner search, the best point for a macroblock is determined. On the other hand, if one of the six outer points has the minimum distortion, we should move the hexagonal pattern to the location in which the center point of the hexagonal pattern lies on the winning point. In each movement, only three new candidate points are checked. Figure 2 shows an

G. Bebis et al. (Eds.): ISVC 2005, LNCS 3804, pp. 406 – 412, 2005.

example of the consecutive steps of the HEXBS algorithm. This example contains two movements and a final inner search.

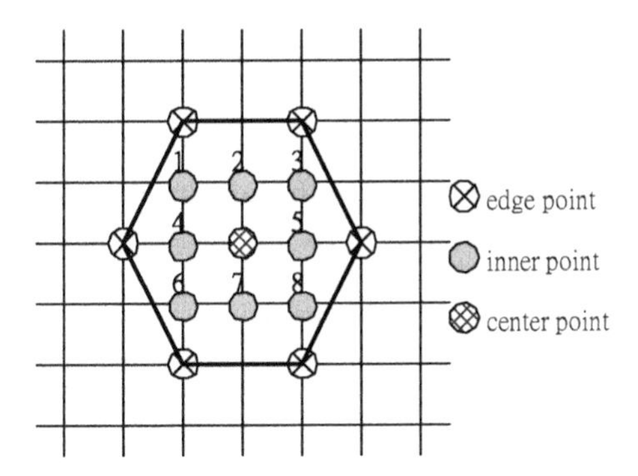

Fig. 1. The hexagon-shaped search pattern

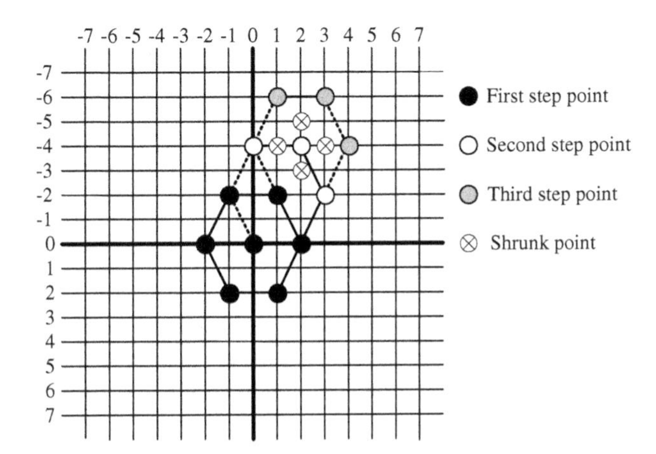

Fig. 2. An example of consecutive steps of the HEXBS to find the best point with coordinate (2, -4). There are three steps using the hexagonal pattern and one inner search using the shrunk pattern.

Although the HEXBS performs well, there is always room to improvement. By using the distortion information of the six outer checking points, the EHEXBS reduces the number of checking points of the inner search largely but only sacrifices a little mean-squared error value. The principle used in the EHEXBS is the monotonically decreasing of distortion in a local area. In this study, we use the same principle as the EHEXBS to investigate the possibility of further reducing the number of search points. We call this algorithm as one-point hexagonal inner search (OPHIS). We use eight representative video sequences for simulation.

The organization of this study is as follows. Section II briefly describes the EHEXBS for comparison. Section III describes our proposed algorithm. Section IV shows our experiment results with eight representative video sequences that vary in frame size and movement content. Finally, the concluding remarks are made in section V.

2 Brief Review of EHEXBS

The EHEXBS contains two main parts: a predictive HEXBS and a six-group fast inner search. They are described as follows.

2.1 Predictive HEXBS

It is well known that the motion vector of the current block is highly correlated with those of its neighboring blocks. Therefore, the motion information of neighboring blocks can be exploited to predict a well staring point. The algorithm adopts the typical predictive mode as shown in Fig. 3. The predictive motion vector of current block, denoted by P, is obtained by averaging the three motion vectors MV_i for i=1 to 3.

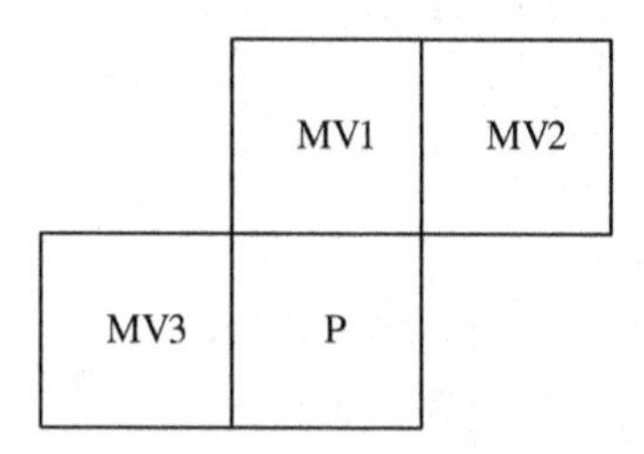

Fig. 3. A typical predictive mode. The predictive motion vector of current block, denoted by P, is obtained by averaging the three motion vectors MV_i for i=1 to 3.

2.2 Six-Group Fast Inner Search

In the HEXBS, four points surrounding the center point are checked in its inner search. In the EHEXBS, however, only two or three inner points are checked depending on which group having the minimum group distortion among the six

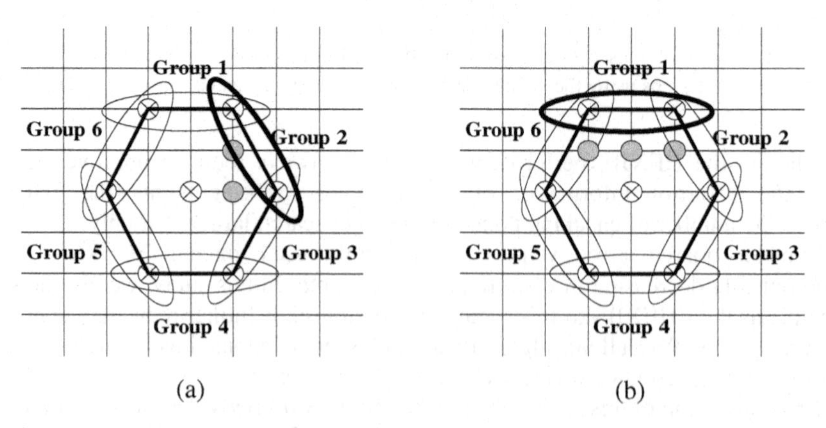

Fig. 4. (a) Two inner points nearest to Group 2 with the smallest group distortion are to be checked. (b) Three inner points nearest to Group 1 with the smallest group distortion are to be checked.

groups as shown in Fig. 4. If one of Group 2, Group 3, Group 5, or Group 6 has the minimum group distortion, two inner points nearest to the group are to be checked. Fig. 4(a) shows the two points if Group 2 wins. On the other hand, if Group 1 or Group 4 has the minimum group distortion, three inner points nearest the group are to be checked. Fig. 4(b) indicates the three points if Group 1 wins.

3 One-Point Hexagonal Inner Search

In the EHEXBS, six groups are formed for choosing the minimum group distortion. Assume that the distortions of the six edge points of the hexagon are denoted from d_1 to d_6. In the EHEXBS, the group distortions Gd_i, i=1, 2, ..6, can be defined as

$$Gd_i = \begin{cases} d_i + d_{i+1}, \text{for } 1 \le i \le 5, \\ d_i + d_1, \text{for } i = 6. \end{cases} \quad (1)$$

It needs to take six additions to calculate these group distortions and six memory units to store the calculated results before the comparison of group distortion. In our opinion, the six additions can be omitted if we define the group distortions as

$$Gd_i = d_i + d_c, \text{for } 1 \le i \le 6, \quad (2)$$

where d_c represents the distortion of center point of the hexagon. Note that the minimum group distortion chosen from (2) is always smaller than that chosen from (1) because the center point has the smallest distortion among those points of the hexagon when an inner search starts. Since each of the group distortions in (2) contains d_c, omitting d_c does not affect the comparison result. Thus, we can redefine the group distortions as

$$Gd_i = d_i, \text{for } 1 \le i \le 6. \quad (3)$$

Using this definition, we can save the six additions.

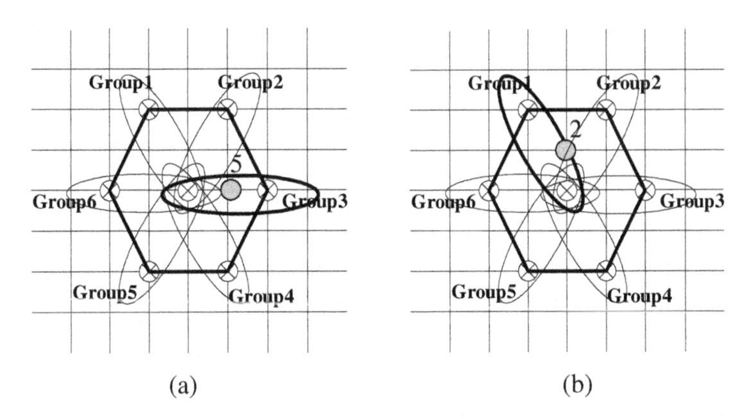

Fig. 5. The six groups used in the OPHIS and the examples of proposed strategies. (a) Group 3 has the minimum group distortion and the inner point labeled by 5 is to be checked. (b) Group 1 has the minimum group distortion and the distortion of Group 2 is smaller than that of Group 6. Therefore, the inner point labeled by 2 is to be checked.

Furthermore, to reduce the number of search points largely, we only check one inner point which is the most probable point with the smallest distortion. Our strategies are as following. If Group 3 or Group 6 has the minimum group distortion, the nearest inner point labeled by 5 or 4 is to be checked, respectively. Fig. 5(a) shows an example in which Group 3 has the minimum group distortion among the six groups. On the other hand, if one of Group 1, Group 2, Group 4, and Group 5 wins, the distortions of its neighboring groups are compared and the checked inner point is chosen near the winner. Fig. 5(b) depicts an example in which Group 1 has the smallest group distortion. Subsequently, comparing the distortions of Group 2 and Group 6 gets the winner Group 2 and thus the inner point labeled by 2 is to be checked. In this example, if Group 6 wins, the inner point labeled by 1 (see Fig. 1) is to be checked.

The proposed algorithm is summarized as following.

Step 1. Compare all Gd_is by using (3) and choose the smallest one called Gd_j

Step 2. Check the inner point 5 or 4 if j=3 or j=6, respectively. Otherwise, compare the neighboring two groups of Gd_j and then check the inner point near the winner.

4 Experimental Results

In order to evaluate the performance of the proposed OPHIS, we compare it with the TSS, 4SS, DS, and EHEXBS. In our experiments, the size of searching window is ±15

Table 1. Average number of search points per block for different algorithms

	Mother	Foreman	Container	Coastguard	Mobile	Bus	Football	Stefan
TSS	25.00	25.00	25.00	25.00	25.00	25.00	25.00	25.00
4SS	17.11	17.52	17.02	17.01	17.02	17.12	18.96	17.22
DS	13.30	14.00	13.03	13.03	13.12	13.33	16.31	13.44
EHEXBS	9.10	9.38	9.02	9.00	9.03	9.12	10.68	9.20
OPHIS	**8.10**	**8.38**	**8.02**	**8.00**	**8.02**	**8.12**	**9.69**	**8.19**

Table 2. Average MSE per frame for different search methods

	Mother	Foreman	Container	Coastguard	Mobile	Bus	Football	Stefan
TSS	13.07	56.72	12.29	53.08	327.06	215.18	118.48	212.64
4SS	12.29	53.10	12.55	49.40	271.54	204.87	121.74	204.60
DS	12.32	53.02	12.55	49.38	271.84	205.08	121.83	205.36
EHEXBS	13.24	60.36	12.65	52.55	282.58	215.02	134.66	217.45
OPHIS	**12.72**	**57.01**	**12.62**	**50.69**	**289.53**	**214.31**	**129.72**	**211.59**

Table 3. Speed improvement rate %SIR and MSE decrease percentage $\%D_{MSE}$ of the proposed OPHIS over the EHEXBS

	Mother	Foreman	Container	Coastguard	Mobile	Bus	Football	Stefan
%SIR	**12.33**	**11.98**	**12.47**	**12.49**	**12.45**	**12.32**	**10.21**	**12.25**
$\%D_{MSE}$	**4.09**	**5.88**	**0.27**	**3.68**	**-2.50**	**0.33**	**3.81**	**2.77**

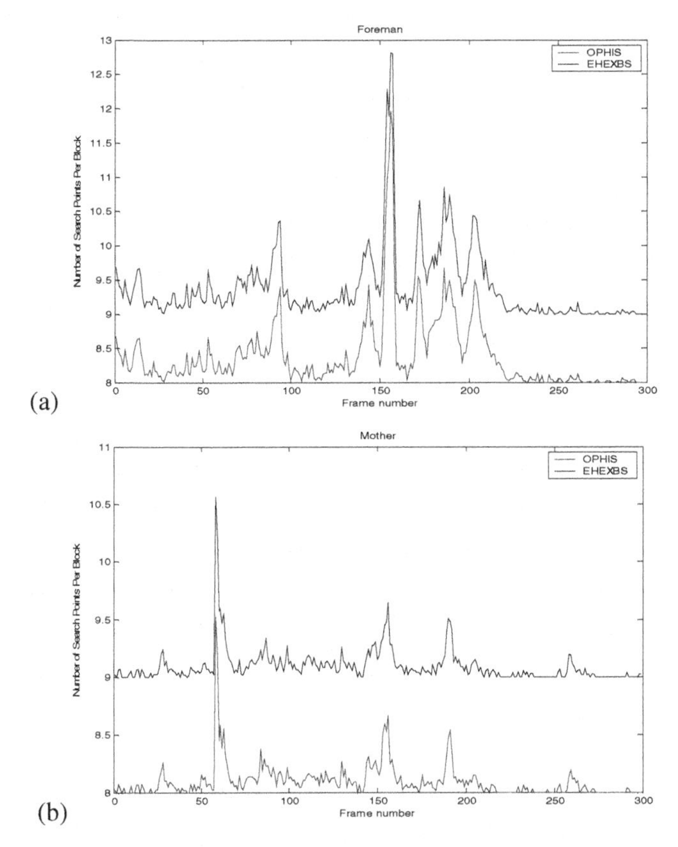

Fig. 6. Frame-by-frame comparison in the number of search points per block for different inner search methods and for different sequences. (a) "Foreman" sequence (b) "Mother" sequence.

and the block size is 16×16. The group of planes is one intra frame (I frame) followed by all the remainder inter frames (P frame). The measurements on I frame are not shown and only those on P frames are produced for comparison. We modify some of the source codes of Xvid [10] (version 1.0.3) to design these experiments.

Eight representative video sequences were used, which vary in frame size as well as motion content, named "Mother" (352×288, 299 P frames), "Foreman" (352×288, 299 P frames), "Coastguard" (176×144, 299 P frames), "Mobile" (352×240, 299 P frames), "Bus" (352×288, 149 P frames), "Football" (352×288, 89 P frames), "Stefan" (352×288, 89 P frames), and "Container" (176×144, 299 P frames). Table 1 tabulates the average number of searching points per block for different algorithms and the eight video sequences. Table 2 lists the average mean-squared-error (MSE) values per frame for different algorithms. Table 3 tabulates the speed improvement rate (%SIR) and the MSE decrease percentage (%D_{MSE}) in the average of the proposed OPHIS over the EHEXBS. These two measurements are defined as follows.

$$\%SIR = \frac{N_2 - N_1}{N_1} \times 100\% \tag{4}$$

$$\%D_{MSE} = \frac{MSE_2 - MSE_1}{MSE_1} \times 100\% \quad (5)$$

where N_1 and MSE_1 are the number of search points and the MSE of OPHIS, N_2 and MSE_2 are the number of search points and the MSE of EHEXBS. According to table 3, we find that the speed improvement of OPHIS is from 10.21% to 12.49% and the MSE decrease percentage is from -2.50% to 5.88% or near to 2.04% on average. Therefore, the proposed OPHIS can result in a more efficient inner search than the EHEXBS. Figure 6 shows a frame-by-frame comparison in the number of search points per block for different inner search methods and for different sequences.

5 Conclusion

In this paper, we proposed a novel one-point hexagonal inner search algorithm for fast motion estimation. The distortion information of the center point is well exploited. And only the most probable inner point is to be checked. Eight representative video sequences are used for experiments. Experimental results showed that the proposed method performs much better than EHEXBS in terms of the number of search points and the MSE values. Therefore, we can use the proposed method to perform more efficient searching and obtain a better visual quality.

References

[1] J. R. Jain and A. K. Jain, "Displacement measurement and its application in interframe image coding," *IEEE Trans. Commun.*, vol. COM-29, pp. 1799-1808, Dec. 1981.

[2] T. Koga, K. Iinuma, A. Hirano, Y. Iijima, T. Ishiguro, "Motion compensated interframe coding for video conferencing", proceedings, *National Telecommunications conference*, New Orleans, pp. G5.3.1-G5.3.5, Nov. 1981.

[3] R. Li, B. Zeng and M. L. Liou, "A new three-step search algorithm for block motion estimation," *IEEE Trans. Circuits Syst. Video technol.*, vol. 4, pp. 438-442, Aug. 1994.

[4] L. K. Liu and E. Feig, "A block-based gradient descent search algorithm for block motion estimation in video coding," *IEEE Trans. Circuits* and *Systems for Video Technology*, vol. 6, pp. 419-423, Aug. 1996.

[5] J. Lu and M. L. Liou, "A simple and efficient search algorithm for block-matching motion estimation," *IEEE Trans. Circuits* and *Systems for Video Technology*, vol. 7, pp. 429-433, Apr. 1997.

[6] J. Y. Tham, S. Ranganath, M. Ranganath and A. A. Kassim, "A novel unrestricted center-biased diamond search algorithm for block motion estimation," *IEEE Trans. Circuits* and *Systems for Video Technology*, vol. 8, pp.369-377, Aug. 1998.

[7] S. Zhu and K. K. Ma, "A new diamond search algorithm for fast block-matching motion estimation," *IEEE Trans. Image Processing*, vol. 9, pp. 287-290, Feb. 2000.

[8] C. Zhu, X. Lin and L. P. Chau, "Hexagon-based search algorithm for fast block motion estimation," *IEEE Trans. Circuits* and *Systems for Video Technology*, vol. 12, pp. 349–355, May 2002.

[9] C. Zhu, X. Lin, L. Chau and L.-M. Po, "Enhanced hexagonal search for fast block motion estimation," *IEEE Trans. Circuits* and *Systems for Video Technology*, vol. 14, pp. 1210-1214, Oct. 2004.

[10] http://www.xvid.org

Self-Describing Context-Based Pixel Ordering

Abdul Itani and Manohar Das

Oakland University, Rochester, Michigan
aitani@oakland.edu, das@oakland.edu

Abstract. In this paper we introduce a novel self-describing context-based pixel ordering for digital images. Our method is inherently reversible and uses the pixel value to guide the exploration of the two-dimensional image space, in contrast to universal scans where the traversal is based solely on the pixel position. The outcome is a one-dimensional representation of the image with enhanced autocorrelation. When used as a front-end to a memoryless entropy coder, empirical results show that our method, on average, improves the compression rate by 11.56% and 5.23% compared to raster-scan and Hilbert space-filling curve, respectively.

1 Space-Filling Curves

A space-filling curve is a bijection from the unit interval [0,1] into the unit square [0,1]×[0,1] that passes through every point of the unit square exactly once. The history of space-filling curves started in the nineteenth century when George Cantor, in 1878, proved that the number of points in a unit interval is the same as the number of points in a unit square. In 1890, Giuseppe Peano constructed the first such curve. More examples by David Hilbert and Waclaw Sierpinski, among other prominent mathematicians who have contributed to the field, soon followed.

2 The Hilbert Curve

Peano discovered the first space-filling curve, but it was Hilbert in 1891 who defined a general procedure to generate an entire class of space-filling curves. Hilbert observed that if the unit interval can be mapped onto the unit square then, after partitioning the unit interval into four congruent subintervals and the unit square into four congruent sub-squares, each subinterval can be mapped onto one of the sub-squares [1]. The number of subintervals, and similarly sub-squares, quadruples after every iteration of this procedure. The number of iteration is known as the order of the space filling curve. Hence, a Hilbert curve of order n partitions the unit interval into 2^{2n} subintervals and the unit square into 2^{2n} sub-squares. Figure 1 illustrates the order of the curve concept.

Hilbert demonstrated that the sub-squares can be arranged in such a way where if a square corresponds to an interval, then its sub-squares correspond to the subintervals of that interval. This property results in a clustering of points where adjacent points in the unit interval are adjacent in the unit square, but not vice versa. Thus, when the

G. Bebis et al. (Eds.): ISVC 2005, LNCS 3804, pp. 413 – 419, 2005.

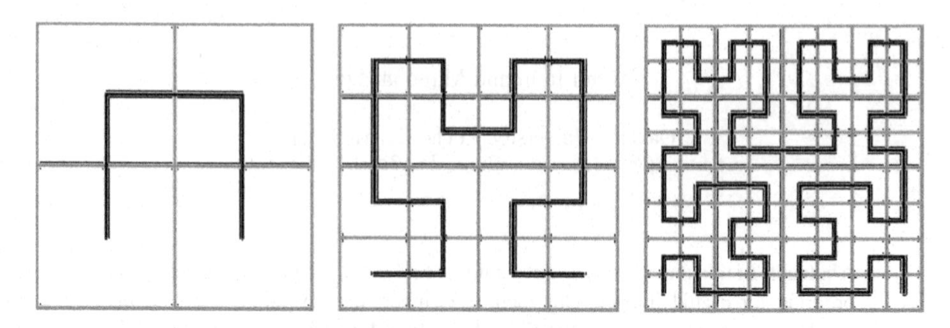

Fig. 1. First three orders of Hilbert-curve

$[0,1]\times[0,1] \rightarrow [0,1]$ mapping is applied to a digital image, the outcome is a one dimensional sequence of pixels with the two dimensional adjacency characteristics, even after the reduction of dimensionality from two to one, likely to be preserved. Figure 2 shows, side by side, the raster-scan and Hilbert-scan of the image "BIRD".

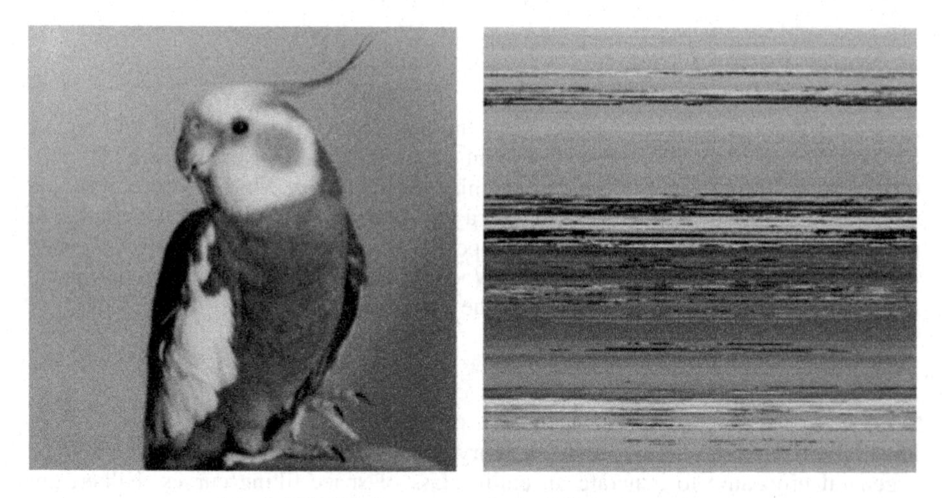

Fig. 2. "BIRD": Raster-scan (left), Hilbert-scan (right)

One fact that needs to be stressed is that space filling curves are spatial transformations that perform universal scans. The traversal is based solely on the pixel position, rather than a function of pixel value. In other words, the mappings are fixed and statically defined. Hence, given any two images of equal size, a space-filling curve will traverse both images, no matter how different their contents are, in the exact same order.

3 Context-Based Space-Filling Curves

Space-filling curves bring a lot of benefits to the image compression arena; however, one must admit that they are far from ideal. Their biggest drawback is the fact that they perform universal scans where the traversal is based solely on pixel position, rather than pixel value, thus underlining their inability to adapt to the images they traverse. There is no doubt that space-filling curves do posses the clustering property, but since they are not "aware" of the image being traversed, the traversal process has no knowledge regarding the edges contained within any image. Therefore, we have to assume that the traversal will cause an ample number of edge crossings.

An edge is a set of connected pixels that lie on the boundary between two regions. A region is defined as a connected set of pixels where the pixels are related to each other based on their gray-level value. Intuitively, connected pixels with very small transition in gray levels form a region. As such, the points in the image where the boundaries lie are places where the gray-level changes abruptly.

The main objective in designing a new traversal algorithm is to increase the autocorrelation between adjacent pixels by traversing the regions, one after the other, and only cross an edge when it is absolutely necessary. In other words, the ultimate objective is to minimize the number of edge crossings. The best approach to achieve this objective is to construct an undirected graph where the pixels in the image form the vertices, and the difference in gray-level between two pixels is used as the weight of the edge incident on the two pixels. In other words, the weight is considered as the cost we have to pay to move from one pixel to another. Therefore, based on this definition, our objective is to construct a path that connects all the vertices while keeping the cost at minimum. Such a path can be easily constructed by finding a spanning tree whose total edge-weight is a minimum. There are several algorithms that can be used to construct a minimum spanning tree; the easiest one to explain is most likely Prim's algorithm.

Prim's algorithm is a greedy, and at the same time optimal, method for constructing a minimum spanning tree for any weighted connected graph. The algorithm grows a spanning tree from a given vertex of a connected weighted graph G, iteratively adding the cheapest edge from a vertex already reached to a vertex not yet reached, finishing when all the vertices of G have been reached. Ties are broken arbitrarily.

We achieved the objective that was set, and thus the problem is solved, or so it seems. One caveat remains, however, which is the property that requires spatial transforms to be reversible. Unfortunately, the minimum spanning tree method is not inherently reversible. Therefore, we must package the minimum spanning tree along with "custom instructions" as overhead to assist in the reconstruction of the original image in two-dimensional space.

In the year 2000, Dafner et al. [2] published a paper describing a method to construct context-based space-filling curves that is based on graph theory. There too the authors stumbled across the same roadblock, mainly the overhead information. In their paper, the authors show that a context-based approach does indeed improve the autocorrelation of the new pixel ordering. However, in order to reconstruct the original image, a context-based pixel ordering needs to associate the specific ordering with the encoded image. The overhead hinders the effectiveness of the context-based ordering for lossless compression. While the re-ordered image compresses 5% to 10% better than the input image, when taking into account the overhead information, the resulting size is 4% to 7% larger when compared with the compressed original image [3].

3.1 A New Self-Describing Context-Based Pixel Ordering

In this section, we will introduce a novel approach for pixel ordering. We call our method self-describing context-based pixel ordering, SCPO for short. The method is context based, and therefore it uniquely adapts to any image at hand. The method is self describing, by that we mean it is inherently reversible; thus, no extra information is required to be transmitted to assist in finding the reverse transform. Lastly the method is a bijection from two-dimensional space to linear space, but it is not a space-filling curve because two consecutive pixels in the linear space are not necessary adjacent in the two dimensional space.

The intuitive idea behind SCPO is, given an image in raster-scan and a start pixel, to incrementally explore the image, region by region, starting with the region containing the start pixel. This is accomplished by maintaining a frontier of pixels that have been explored. As the traversal of the image proceeds, the frontier expands into the unexplored pixels. This process ends when all the pixels of the image have been explored.

At each iteration of the traversal process, we replace a pixel in the frontier by the pixel's 4 neighbors that have not yet been explored. The strategy as to which pixel of the frontier is selected defines the context-based pixel ordering. The strategy is simply to select the pixel that is closest in gray-level value to the previous pixel selected.

3.2 Initialization

The frontier is a vector, i.e. array, of two-dimensional space pixel positions. It initially contains the position of a start pixel. The start pixel has a fixed predetermined position in the original raster-scan, for example upper-left corner. SCPO also requires the labeling of each and every pixel in the two-dimensional space to track whether the pixel has been explored or not. Initially, all the pixels are unlabeled.

3.3 Mapping from Two-Dimensional Space to Linear Space

Start the process by labeling the start pixel and transmitting its gray-level value. Next, label the 4-neighbors of the start pixel, transmit their gray-level values, and then add them to the frontier. The 4-neigbors should be chosen, one by one, based on a fixed predetermined order, for example starting with the north neighbor and going through the remaining three in a clockwise fashion.

As long as the frontier is not empty, do the following: If this is the very first iteration of the loop, remove from the frontier the pixel closest in gray-level value to the start pixel. Otherwise, remove from the frontier the pixel closest in gray level value to the previous pixel removed. Ties should be broken using a fixed predetermined rule, for example last in first out. In either case, whether this is the very first iteration or not, perform the EXPLORE procedure as described in the next paragraph. After the EXPLORE procedure returns, do the next iteration.

EXPLORE: Check the labeling of the 4-neighbors, in the same order discussed earlier. If a neighbor is already labeled, do nothing. Otherwise, label it, transmit its gray-level value, and then add it to the frontier.

As a simple example of two-dimensional space to linear space mapping, consider the following 3×3 image sample

1	7	3
4	6	8
5	2	9

The steps to transform the image into linear space are as follows:

- Transmit the value1 and label it. Transmit the value 7 then the value 4, label them both, and then add both of them to the frontier.
- Since the value 4 is the closest number to 1, remove 4 from the frontier. Transmit the value 6 then the value 5, label them both, and then add both of them to the frontier.
- Since the value 5 is the closest number to 4, remove 5 from the frontier. Transmit the value 2, label it, and then add it to the frontier.
- Since the value 6 is the closest number to 5, remove 6 from the frontier. Transmit the value 8, label it, and then add it to the frontier.
- Since the value 7 is the closest number to 6, remove 7 from the frontier. Transmit the value 3, label it, and then add it to the frontier.
- Since the value 8 is the closest number to 7, remove 8 from the frontier. Transmit the value 9, label it, and then add it to the frontier.
- Even though the frontier is not empty yet, we can safely stop since all the pixels are labeled, and the rest of the iterations will have no impact on the outcome.

Therefore, the result in linear space is the sequence: 1 7 4 6 5 2 8 3 9.

Of course, this simple example does not reflect the effectiveness of SCPO. The image is too small and has no redundancy. However, it does demonstrate the fact the SCPO can handle a wide variety of dimensions. The image's width and height do not need to be a power of two; the width and the height do not even have to be equal. As a matter of fact, SCPO can handle any image that can be bounded by a closed two-dimensional geometrical shape, like a triangle for example.

3.4 Mapping from Linear Space to Two-Dimensional Space

The process starts by reading the start pixel gray-level value and labeling it. Next, read the gray-level value of the 4-neighbors, in the same order discussed previously, and label them.

As long as the frontier is not empty, do the following: If this is the very first iteration of the loop, remove from the frontier the pixel closest in gray-level value to the start pixel. Otherwise, remove from the frontier the pixel closest in gray-level value to the previous pixel removed, using the same tie-break rule discussed earlier. In either case, whether this is the first iteration or not, perform the BUILD procedure as described in the next paragraph. After the BUILD procedure returns, do the next iteration.

BUILD: Check the labeling of the 4-neighbors, in the same order discussed earlier. If a neighbor is already labeled, do nothing. Otherwise read its gray-level value, label it, and then add it to the frontier.

3.5 Visual Observations

A picture is worth a thousand words; this is definitely true in the case of the illustration in Figure 3. The two pictures show the original "BIRD" image and the scanning of the "BIRD" image using SCPO. In the SCPO-scan, the gray-level represents the order of traversal. The black pixels represent the pixels that were explored first, and the white pixels represent the pixels that were explored last. The gray-level increases as the exploration progresses from start to finish. The context-sensitivity of SCPO cannot be any clearer. SCPO successfully identified the distinct regions in "BIRD", and did a remarkable job in exploring the image's regions, one after the other.

Figure 4, shows, side by side, the Hilbert-scan and SCPO-scan of the image "BIRD". Notice how the clustering of pixels with, more or less, similar values is more evident in the SCPO scan than the Hilbert scan.

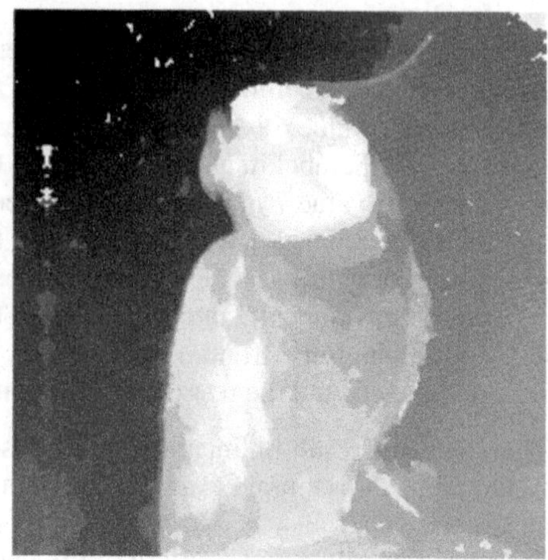

Fig. 3. "BIRD": Raster-scan (left), SCPO exploratory progression (right)

 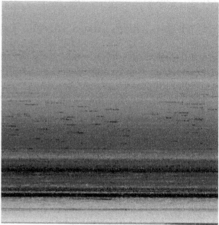

Fig. 4. "BIRD": Hilbert scan (left), SCPO-scan (right)

3.6 Experimental Results and Conclusion

In order to numerically evaluate the effectiveness of the SCPO algorithm in increasing the redundancy of the gray-level sequences in the linear space, we need to use a locally adaptive linear compression algorithm. A couple of options are Lempel Ziv Welch (LZW) [4] or the combination of move-to-front (MTF) coder [5] along with a memoryless entropy coder. We decided that the latter serves our purposes best.

MTF is a very simple domain transform that exploits locality of reference, i.e. cases where gray-levels are used frequently over short intervals and then fall into long periods of disuse. The scheme uses a self-organizing list of gray-levels so that frequently accessed gray-levels are located near the front of the list. A gray-level is encoded by transmitting its position in the list. As such, MTF produces a highly skewed distribution with the index corresponding to the front of the list consistently prominent.

Table 1 compares the compression rates for several 256×256, 8-bit standard test images. The results reflect an improvement of 6.33% and 11.56%, contributed to the Hilbert-scan and SCPO-scan, respectively, over the traditional raster scan. The numerical values clearly show a significant advantage in using a contest based pixel ordering over traditional space-filling curves.

Table 1. Comparison between Raster-scan, Hilbert-scan, and SCPO-scan

	MTF + Memoryless Entropy (in bits per pixel)		
	Raster-scan	Hilbert-scan	SCPO-scan
bird	4.94	4.25	4.05
bridge	7.34	7.01	6.91
camera	5.96	5.44	5.48
goldhill	6.87	6.51	6.34
lena	7.16	6.26	5.92
montage	5.02	4.50	4.07
slope	3.98	3.76	2.01
Average	5.90	5.39	4.97

References

1. Fabrizio Angiulli, and Clara Pizzuti, "Approximate k-Closest-Pairs with Space Filling Curves",4th International Conference on Data Warehousing and Knowledge Discovery, pp. 124-134, Aix-en-Provence, France, September 2002.
2. Revital Dafner, Daniel Cohen-Or, and Yossi Matias, "Context-based Space Filling Curves", Eurographics, vol 19, no. 3, 2000.
3. Ziv Bar-Joseph, and Daniel Cohen-Or, "Hierarchical Context-based Pixel Ordering", Eurographics, vol 22, no. 3, 2003.
4. Terry A. Welch, "A Technique for High-Performance Data Compression", Computer, June 1984.
5. J.L. Bentley, D.D. Sleator, R.E. Tarjan, and V.K.Wei, "A Locally Adaptive Data Compression Algorithm", Communications of the ACM, vol. 29, no. 4, pp. 320 330, April 1986.

Lossless Compression of CCD Sensor Data

Gerald Schaefer and Joanna Obstoj

School of Computing and Informatics,
Nottingham Trent University, Nottingham, United Kingdom
gerald.schaefer@ntu.ac.uk

Abstract. An evaluation of lossless image compression methods applied to CCD sensor data is provided. Ten different image compression algorithms were tested on an image set of more than 200 images organised according to the Bayer pattern configuration. The results show that Glicbawls is the best performing algorithm providing the highest compression ratio followed by CALIC, JPEG-LS, and JPEG2000.

Keywords: CCD sensor, Bayer pattern, image compression, lossless compression.

1 Introduction

The growing popularity of digital cameras demands every attempt of improvements in terms of quality, quantity and speed of the features they offer. One of the very basic features of a digital camera is that it enables users to store the captured image data. The most popular format available that is provided is JPEG which is a lossy compression format and hence discards some of the original information. More advanced cameras also allow to store images in raw format which maintains the original data but also requires much more space.

In this paper we investigate the application of lossless image compression algorithms for such raw images. These images differ from ordinary digital pictures in the way colour information is stored. As most CCD sensors capture essentially only intensity but no colour information they are coupled with filters whose elements capture either red, green, or blue light. Usually the filter elements are organised in such a way that in each 2×2 square of CCD diodes, 2 green, 1 red, and 1 blue element are placed as in the Bayer pattern configuration [2]. Our aim is to evaluate how well lossless image compression algorithms perform on Bayer pattern data. For this we generated a test image data set of 200+ images organised into 8 groups of image types. The colour channels of the CCD data are split and compressed using 10 lossless image compressors. The results show that interestingly Glicbawls [8], a rarely used compression algorithm, provides the highest compression ratios followed by CALIC [13], JPEG-LS [5] and JPEG2000 [6].

The rest of the paper is organised as follows. Section 2 explains how CCD data is structured and stored. In Section 3 we describe our image data set acquired for the evaluation. Section 4 briefly describes the lossless image compression algorithms we have used while Section 5 presents how they perform on the test images. Section 6 concludes the paper.

G. Bebis et al. (Eds.): ISVC 2005, LNCS 3804, pp. 420–426, 2005.

2 CCD Sensor Data

Generally a CCD can be described as a 2-dimensional array of many tiny, light-sensitive diodes (photosites) which convert photons into electrons. The value of the generated electrical charge is proportional to the intensity of incident light and is, using an analog-to-digital converter, transformed to a digital value.

Photosites capture intensity only and hence no information on colour. In order to capture colour images, sensors in digital cameras use a Colour Filter Array (CFA) which covers the detector array and is placed between the lens and the sensors. A CFA has one colour filter element for each sensor which means that the recovery of full-colour images from a CFA-based detector requires a method of calculating values of the other colours at each pixel which is usually achieved through interpolation. One of the most popular CFA configurations is the Bayer pattern [2] which uses the three additive primary colours, red, green and blue (RGB) for the filter elements. Figure 2 shows on the left how an image is stored according in Bayer pattern format. In every 2×2 pixel square there are 2 green, 1 red, and 1 blue element; the reason for putting more emphasis on green is the human visual system's higher sensitivity to that colour.

3 Test Image Data Set

As there is no standard CCD sensor data set available we have decided to capture our own image database for the evaluation process. In total there are 211 images, all in Bayer pattern form and originally captured with a Minolta Dimage V digital camera. All images are of size 2048×1536 and have been converted to 8 bits per channel (from 12) so that all algorithms can handle the data. The content of the images was chosen so as to resemble those an average user might take.

In order to see whether there is any correlation between the type of image content and the compression performance we have divided the dataset into eight image groups as follows:

Fig. 1. Sample image of each category: nature, carving, car, people, shopping, graphic, water, city (from left to right, top to bottom)

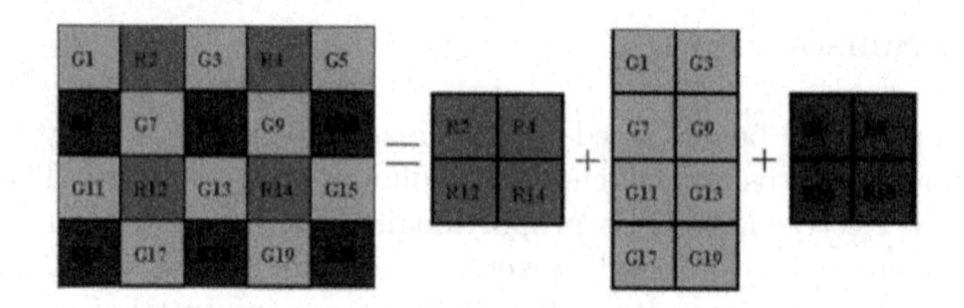

Fig. 2. Illustration how Bayer pattern data is split into 3 colour channels

- nature: landscape images of flowers, trees, grass etc.
- carvings: images of sculptures and boss reliefs.
- cars: images of various cars in different colours.
- people: images of persons and images resembling passport photos.
- shopping: images of window displays and adverts on bus stops.
- graphics: images containing text, patterns, and cartoon posters.
- water: images of river (with swans) and fountains.
- city: images of buildings and streets.

An image of each category is shown in Figure 1. Following [1] each of the raw images was split into three images, one for each colour channel as indicated in Figure 2. The resulting files were stored in PGM format.

4 Image Compression Algorithms

In total we evaluated 10 different lossless image compression algorithms. Brief details on them are given in the following:

- **PNG:** The Portable Network Graphic (PNG) is the file format for lossless compression and storage of images that is recommended as a web standard by the WWW Consortium [14]. Its compression scheme uses preprocessing to remove data redundancy, deflating which is based on the LZ77 method [15] and Huffman coding. We used the `pnmtopng` implementation (version 2.37.6, part of the NetPBM 10.25 toolkit, `http://netpbm.sourceforge.net/`) compiled with libraries `libpng` (version 1.2.8, `http://libpng.sourceforge.net/`) and `zlib` (version 1.2.2, `http://www.gzip.org/zlib/`).
- **BTPC:** Binary Tree Predictive Coding (BTPC) is a lossless or lossy image compression algorithm based on multi-resolution decomposition [10]. It creates a binary pyramid of the image by recursively dividing it into two subimages: high and low resolution images. The pixels in the high-resolution image are predicted based on patterns in the neighboring pixels. The remaining error is then encoded with an adaptive Huffman coder. We used the implementation provided by the author (version 5.0, `http://www.intuac.com/userport/john/btpc5/`).
- **APT:** Adaptive Prediction Trees (APT) is a compression algorithm which supersedes BTPC and uses hex-trees rather than binary trees [9]. The method

uses a spatial predictor, an inter-component predictor, a quantizer and adaptive runlength and Huffman coding. Again, we used the implementation provided by the author (version 1.0, `http://www.intuac.com/userport/john/apt/`).

- **FELICS:** Fast Efficient Lossless Image Compression System (FELICS) is based on context modeling and Rice coding [4]. The context of a pixel consists of the two nearest neighbours which are utilised in a raster scan order to estimate the probability distribution of the pixel intensity. Afterwards, the most suitable error model is chosen and intensities encoded with the Rice code of the model. We used the implementation of the Managing Gigabytes (MG) System (`http://www.cs.mu.oz.au/mg/`).
- **SPIHT:** Set Partitioning In Hierarchical Trees (SPIHT) is an algorithm which transforms the image to a multi-resolution representation using, in the case of lossless compression, the S transform followed by arithmetic coding [11]. We used the QccPackSPIHT package (`http://www.cipr.rpi.edu/research/SPIHT/`).
- **Glicbawls:** Grey Level Image Compression By Adaptive Weighted Least Squares (Glicbawls) [8] processes images in scanline order. A probability distribution for each pixel is calculated by using a least squares predictor based on all of the previously encoded pixels and by using prediction errors. The contribution of each pixel is weighted according to its Manhattan-distance from the current pixel. Finally the data is encoded using arithmetic coding. We used the implementation provided by the author (`http://byron.csse.monash.edu.au/glicbawls/`).
- **Lossless JPEG:** Lossless JPEG is the former JPEG committee standard for lossless image compression [7]. The standard describes predictive image compression algorithm with Huffman or arithmetic entropy coder. We used the Cornell University implementation (version 1.0, `ftp://ftp.cs.cornell.edu/pub/multimed/ljpg.tar.Z`) which applies Huffman coding.
- **JPEG-LS:** JPEG-LS is the current standard of the JPEG committee for lossless and near-lossless compression of still images [5]. The standard describes low-complexity predictive image compression algorithm with entropy coding using modified Golomb-Rice family. The algorithm is based on the LOCO-I algorithm [12]. We used the University of British Columbia implementation (version 2.2, `ftp://ftp.netbsd.org/pub/NetBSD/packages/distfiles/jpeg_ls_v2.2.tar.gz`).
- **JPEG2000:** JPEG2000 is a recent JPEG committee standard describing an algorithm based on wavelet transform image decomposition and arithmetic coding [6]. Apart from lossy and lossless compressing and decompressing of whole images it delivers many interesting features (progressive transmission, region of interest coding, etc.) [3]. We used the JasPer implementation by Adams (version 1.700.0, `http://www.ece.uvic.ca/~mdadams/jasper/`).
- **CALIC:** Context-based Adaptive Lossless Image Coding (CALIC) is a relatively complex predictive image compression algorithm using arithmetic entropy coder [13]. We used the implementation by Wu and Memon (`ftp://ftp.csd.uwo.ca/pub/from_wu/`).

5 Experimental Results

As mentioned in Section 3 each picture comprises three images, one for each channel. These images were compressed separately using all the compressions algorithms listed in Section 4. As performance indicator we use the compression ratio which is defined as O/C where O is the filesize of the original image (i.e. the sum of the sizes of the three channel images) and C is that of the compressed version. The results for all algorithms are given in Table 1 and are provided in terms of the average compression ratios for all groups and the average ratio for all images (since there are different numbers of images in the categories the average over all images will differ slightly from the average over all groups).

The columns in Table 1 are sorted in ascending order of compression ratio to ease interpretation. From there we can see that the best performing algorithm is Glicbawls followed by CALIC, JPEG-LS, and JPEG2000. The rest of the algorithms perform significantly worse with Lossless JPEG providing the lowest compression ratios. APT provides only marginally higher compression ratios than its predecessor BTPC. That Glicbawls is outperforming all other methods might seem a bit surprising as it is an algorithm not often used or cited. Its average compression ratio of 2.68 is significantly better than that of the next best algorithm which is CALIC with an average ratio of 2.54. However, Glicbawls is also computationally much more expensive compared to the other algorithms as it performs a least squares search. This complexity might therefore prevent its practical application embedded in digital cameras.

Looking again at Table 1 we see that the relative performance of the algorithms is independent of the image categories. The ranking of the compressors is the same for all image groups (with a slight exception for the *city* images).

We have also analysed the compression ratios obtained for the different colour channels. The results, averaged over the whole data set, are listed in Table 2. We see that while the compression ratios for red and blue are fairly similar, those for the green channel are significantly lower. A possible explanation might be the way the pixels of the green channel were merged (as was shown in Figure 2) which results in pixel neighbours which originally had different distances to each other which in turn might cause lower prediction performance by the compressors.

Table 1. Average compression ratios for all image groups and compression algorithms

category	LJPG	PNG	BTPC	APT	FELICS	SPIHT	JPG2000	JPG-LS	CALIC	Glicbawls
nature	1.79	1.95	1.99	2.00	2.02	2.08	2.09	2.20	2.24	2.30
carvings	1.95	2.15	2.18	2.19	2.21	2.31	2.32	2.39	2.45	2.58
cars	1.97	2.14	2.22	2.23	2.28	2.35	2.39	2.47	2.53	2.70
people	2.08	2.24	2.31	2.32	2.33	2.43	2.47	2.47	2.54	2.71
shopping	2.04	2.18	2.27	2.28	2.34	2.40	2.43	2.53	2.58	2.74
graphics	2.10	2.28	2.37	2.38	2.39	2.47	2.50	2.56	2.62	2.77
water	2.13	2.32	2.44	2.45	2.48	2.58	2.66	2.70	2.75	2.98
city	2.20	2.45	2.54	2.55	2.54	2.62	2.72	2.81	2.86	3.04
all	**2.02**	**2.20**	**2.27**	**2.28**	**2.30**	**2.37**	**2.41**	**2.48**	**2.54**	**2.68**

Table 2. Average compression ratios for different colour channels

channel	LJPG	PNG	BTPC	APT	FELICS	SPIHT	JPG2000	JPG-LS	CALIC	Glicbawls
red	2.07	2.24	2.36	2.37	2.37	2.45	2.47	2.60	2.61	2.75
green	1.89	2.08	2.10	2.10	2.12	2.22	2.27	2.33	2.40	2.51
blue	2.11	2.28	2.40	2.42	2.42	2.43	2.50	2.63	2.67	2.79

Fig. 3. Red, green, blue channel of a sample image

6 Conclusions

We have analysed the performance of lossless image compression algorithms for the application of compressing raw CCD sensor data based on the Bayer pattern configuration. A test image set of more than 200 images was acquired and used to evaluate 10 lossless compression methods. The results show that Glicbawls provides the highest compression ratio (though at a higher computational expense), followed by CALIC, JPEG-LS, and JPEG2000. The relative performance of algorithms was found to be independent of image characteristics while a lower compression ratio was noted for the green compared to red and blue channels.

In this study, each image was split into its three channels, and each component compressed independently. As Figure 3 shows for a sample image there is a high correlation between the three colour channels. We are currently working on exploiting this correlation for CCD sensor data which will provide an improvement in compression performance.

References

1. S. Battiato, A. Bruna, A. Buemi, and F. Naccari. Coding techniques for CFA data images. In *12th Int. Conference on Image Analysis and Processing*, pages 418–423, 2003.
2. B.E. Bayer. Color imaging array. *U.S. Patent 3,971,065*, 1976.

3. C. Christopoulos, A. Skodras, and T. Ebrahimi. The JPEG2000 still image coding system: and overview. *IEEE Trans. Consumer Electronics*, 46(4):1103–1127, 2000.
4. P.G. Howard and J.S. Vitter. Fast and efficient lossless image compression. In *3rd Data Compression Conference*, pages 351–360, 1993.
5. ISO. Lossless and near-lossless compression of continuous-tone images (JPEG-LS). *ISO Working Document ISO/IEC JTC1/SC29/WG1 N522*, 1997.
6. ISO. JPEG2000 image coding system. *ISO/IEC FCD 15444-1 JPEG2000 Part I Final Committee Draft Version 1.0*, 2000.
7. G. Langdon, A. Gulati, and E. Seiler. On the JPEG model for lossless image compression. In *2nd Data Compression Conference*, pages 172–180, 1992.
8. B. Meyer and P.E. Tischer. Glicbawls - grey level image compression by adaptive weighted least squares. In *11th Data Compression Conference*, page 503, 2001.
9. J. Robinson. Apt website. `http://www.intuac.com/userport/john/apt/`.
10. J.A. Robinson. Efficient general-purpose image compression with binary tree predictive coding. *IP*, 6(4):601–608, April 1997.
11. A. Said and W.A. Pearlman. An image multiresolution representation for lossless and lossy compression. *IEEE Trans. Image Processing*, 5(9):1303–1310, September 1996.
12. M.J. Weinberger, G. Seroussi, and G. Sapiro. The LOCO-I lossless image compression algorithm: Principles and standardization into JPEG-LS. *IEEE Trans. Image Processing*, 9(8):1309–1324, 1996.
13. X.L. Wu. Lossless compression of continuous-tone images via context selection, quantization, and modeling. *IEEE Trans. Image Processing*, 6(5):656–664, May 1997.
14. WWW Consortium. PNG (Portable Network Graphics) specification. *Version 1.0*, 1996.
15. J. Ziv and A. Lempel. A universal algorithm for sequential data compression. *IEEE Trans. Information Theory*, 32(3):337–343, 1977.

Geometric Approach to Segmentation and Protein Localization in Cell Cultured Assays

S. Raman, B. Parvin, C. Maxwell, and M.H. Barcellos-Hoff*

Lawrence Berkeley National Laboratory, Berkeley, Ca 94720

Abstract. Cell-based fluorescence imaging assays are heterogeneous requiring collection of a large number of images for detailed quantitative analysis. Complexities arise as a result of variation in spatial nonuniformity, shape, overlapping compartments, and scale. A new technique and methodology has been developed and tested for delineating subcellular morphology and partitioning overlapping compartments at multiple scales. This system is packaged as an integrated software platform for quantifying images that are obtained through fluorescence microscopy. Proposed methods are model-based, leveraging geometric shape properties of subcellular compartments and corresponding protein localization. From the morphological perspective, convexity constraint is imposed to delineate, partition, and group nuclear compartments. From the protein localization perspective, radial symmetry is imposed to localize punctate protein events at sub-micron resolution. The technique has been tested against 196 images that were generated to study centrosome abnormalities. Computed representations are evaluated against the ground truth annotation for comparative analysis.

1 Introduction

The response of tissues and biological material in general to exogenous stimuli is often heterogeneous and requires a large set of samples for each experimental variable, e.g., tissue type, type of stimuli, dosage, and concentration. These responses are often multidimensional and multispectral and can be imaged using different type of microscopy. Quantitative analysis of these responses is a necessary step toward visualization of large scale co-localization studies and construction of predictive models. Research in this area has spanned from learning techniques using texture-based features for characterizing patterns of protein expression [3] to geometric techniques using nonlinear diffusion [1, 12], curve evolution, and shape regularization for segmentation of subcellular compartments [4, 12, 5]. Often segmentation provides context for quantifying protein expression. However when protein expression is not diffuse within a compartment, additional processing is needed within the specific context. This paper

* Research funded by the Low Dose Radiation Research Program, Biological and Environmental Research (BER), U.S. Department of Energy, under contract number DE-AC02-05CH11231 with the University of California. LBNL publication number is LBNL-58749. Points of contact: SRaman@lbl.gov and parvin@media.lbl.gov.

G. Bebis et al. (Eds.): ISVC 2005, LNCS 3804, pp. 427–436, 2005.

outlines a complete methodology and its evaluation for quantitative assessment of co-localization studies in cell culture assays. Although the technique has been tested against studying centrosomal abnormalities (CA), it is extensible to other phenotypic studies. As CA occur in less than 2% of normal tissue and in about 80% of breast cancers [9]. CA may serve as valuable prognostic and therapeutic targets. Various cellular stresses such as viral infection, exposure to ionizing radiation and altered microenvironmental stimuli, can augment the frequency and type of CA [8]. Within resting animal cells, the centrosome represents a major microtubule organizing center and is composed of a pair of centrioles and pericentriolar material. Prior to division, the centrosome will replicate during the DNA synthesis phase of the cell cycle. During mitosis replicated centrosomes will separate and nucleate a bipolar spindle that equally contacts and segregates the replicated genetic information into two daughter cells. One facet of CA refers to additional centrosomes (more than two), which leads to abnormal cell division. As CA are rare events in cell culture assays, large numbers of samples within and between treatment groups must be analyzed for objective results. Complexities arise as a result of nonuniform staining, overlapping nuclei, touching centrioles, and scales of these subcellular compartments. In the proposed system, these complexities are addressed through model-based techniques that are driven by the inherent geometries. These geometric constraints take advantage of the convexity features of the nuclear compartment and the radial symmetry of the centrosome. Nuclear extraction is initiated from differential spatial operators as opposed to intensity thresholding, which is a common practice in most ad-hoc solutions. These differential operators lead to edge fragments that are linked for high-level geometric analysis, partitioning, and grouping. Nuclear regions provide context for quantitative protein localization. When localization is not diffused, additional analysis is required to characterize punctate signals. These punctate signals may vary in shape, scale, and intensity. Furthermore, they often overlap and create additional complexity. These complexities are addressed through a special class of iterative voting, which is kernel-based, and its topography favors radial symmetries. It is robust with respect to variation in size and intensity, and delineates overlapped compartments.

Organization of this paper is as follows. Section 2 reviews previous research. Section 3 summarizes geometric segmentation of the nuclear regions which provide the context for protein localization. Section 4 outlines the spatial voting technique for protein localization. Section 5 provides (1)the experimental results for 196 images, and (2)the comparison of the system performance against manual analysis.

2 Previous Work

The difficulties in localization of subcellular compartments are often due to variations in scale, noise, and topology. Other complexities originate from missing data and perceptual boundaries that lead to diffusion and dispersion of the spatial grouping in the object space. Techniques for extraction of nuclear compartments are either through global thresholding or adaptive (localized) thresholding followed by watershed method for separating adjacent regions. Techniques in radial symmetries, as evident by centrosome configuration, can be classified into three different categories: (1) point operations leading to dense output, (2) clustering based on parameterized shape models or voting schemes, and (3) iterative techniques. Point operations are usually a series of cascade filters that are tuned for radial symmetries. These techniques use image gradient magnitudes and orientations to infer the center of mass for regions of interest [6, 7, 10]. Parametric techniques tend to be more robust as long as the geometric model captures pertinent shape features at a specific scale, e.g., Hough transform. Iterative methods, such as watershed [11], regularized centroid transform [12], and geometric voting Yang04, produce superior results because they compensate for larger variation of shape feaures.

The method implemented here falls into the category of iterative techniques which are adaptive to geometric perturbation and typically produce more stable results. This method shares several attributes with tensor-based voting [2], but it differs in that it is scalar and iterative.

3 Segmentation

In a typical 2D cell culture assay that is stained for nuclear compartment, some nuclei are isolated and others are clustered together to form clumps. Thus, the strategy is to detect isolated ones first, and then impose additional processing for the clumped regions. The image signature suggests that thresholding may be sufficient as an initial step; however, shading, nonuniform staining, and other artifacts demands a localized strategy. This localized strategy is an edge-based technique with a geometric convexity optimization approach for improved reliability. Edges are collected to form contours and then tested for convexity. If convexity fails then the clumped region is partitioned into multiple convex regions according to a geometric policy. Several intermediate steps are shown in Figure 1, and steps are as follows.

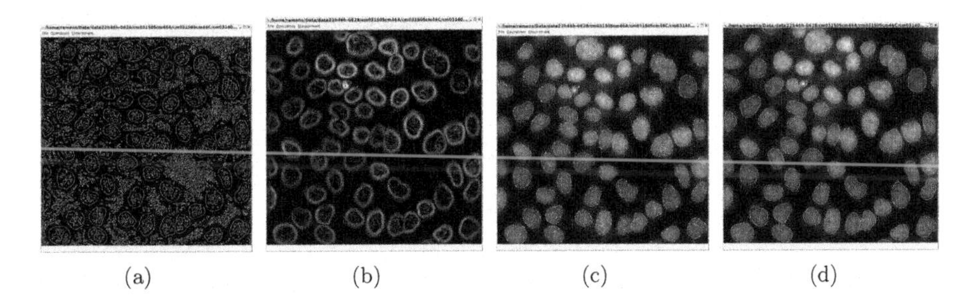

(a) (b) (c) (d)

Fig. 1. Steps in segmentation: (a) Zero-crossing of Laplacian; (b) gradient image; (c) points of maximum curvature along contours; and (d) partitioning of clumped nuclei

3.1 Boundary Extraction and Convexity

Let $I(x, y)$ be the original image with 2D image coordinates. An initial boundary is extracted by linking zero-crossing edges that are filtered by the gradient magnitude at the same scale. Zero-crossing (computed from Laplacian, $\nabla^2 I$) assures that boundaries are closed, and the gradient threshold assures that spurious contours are eliminated. Two gradient thresholds (low and high) are used to initiate linking from strong edges and fill the gaps with weak edge points. Next, each computed contour is approximated with a polygon and total angular change is computed to test for convexity. If the region is not convex then additional processing is initiated.

3.2 Grouping and Partitioning

Partitioning of clumped nuclei into distinct convex objects is through iterative decomposition and constraint satisfaction. Intuitively, these partitions should be terminated by folds in the boundary corresponding to positive curvature maxima. The main purpose of the constraint-based grouping is to limit the number of hypotheses and reduce computational cost. The net result of this process is a set of corresponding candidates for each positive curvature maxima point for potential decomposition. The following geometric constraints are enforced.

Positive Curvature Constraint. The curvature at any point along the contour is given by $k = \frac{\delta' x \delta'' y - \delta' y \delta'' x}{(\delta' x^2 + \delta' y^2)^{3/2}}$. The contour derivatives are computed by convolving derivatives of a Gaussian with the contour information. The intent is to partition a clump of nuclei from the points of maximum curvature along the contour.

Antiparallel Constraint. The antiparallel constraint asserts that each pair of positive curvature maxima along the contour must be antiparallel, which is estimated by computing the tangent directions at each candidate point. This constraint reduces the number of hypotheses for a potential partition thus reducing the computational cost.

Non-intersecting Constraint. The Non-intersecting constraint asserts that a partition cannot intersect existing boundaries corresponding to the entire blob or other hypothesized partitions.

Convexity Constraint. The nuclear regions that occur in the cell culture are always convex, the convexity constraint enforces that the partition obtained has to be convex to avoid incorrect segmentation.

Grouping and Partitioning. Each clump is partitioned by linking pairs of positive curvature maxima that satisfy the above conditions. Each configuration has its own cost function, and the optimum configuration satisfies all the above mentioned constraints and will minimize $C = \Sigma_{i=1}^{n} \frac{\phi_i - \Pi}{\Pi}$, where n is the number of partition in a clump, determined by the system as follows. Essentially, the problem if reduced to grouping of curvature maximas in such a way that certain geometric constraints are satisfied.

Decomposition Algorithm

1. *Localize positive curvature maxima along the contour*
2. *Set initial number of compartments n:= 2*
3. *Construct a set of all valid configurations of n compartments by connecting valid pairs of positive curvature maxima satisfying the antiparallel, non-intersecting and convexity constraints*
4. *Evaluate cost of each configuration (per Equation 2)*
5. *Increment the compartment count n:=n+1 and repeat steps 3 and 4 until there is at least one configuration that has all convex compartments*
6. *Select the configuration with the least cost function*

---

4 Protein Localization

The problem of localizing punctate protein expression was first evaluated using Hough transform, cross correlation against training samples, and analysis of local intensity distribution. These Clustering based on Hough method proved to be scale sensitive, while correlation and intensity-based methods suffers from false positives and lack of geometric models. A geometric model is essential in the presence of scale varying and overlapping protein signals. A spatial class of spatial iterative voting is introduced to facilitate these requirements. Voting along gradient direction provides a hypothesis profile for saliency, e.g., punctate protein events. A specific kernel design (1) encodes the knowledge for saliency, (2) applied at each edge location along the gradient direction, and (3) refined and reoriented at each iteration step. The shape and evolution of these kernels, inferring center of mass, is shown in Figure 2. A brief review of the technique [13] is as follows: Let $I(x, y)$ be the original image, where the domain points (x, y) are 2D image coordinates. Let $\alpha(x, y)$ be the voting direction at each image point, where $\alpha(x, y) := (\cos(\theta(x, y)), \sin(\theta(x, y)))$ for some angle

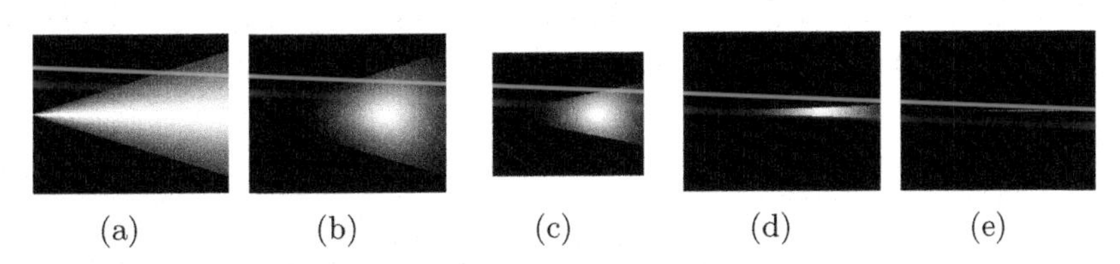

(a) (b) (c) (d) (e)

Fig. 2. Kernel topography: (a-e)The Evolving kernel, used for the detection of radial symmetries (shown at a fixed orientation) has a trapezoidal active area with Gaussian distribution along both axes

$\theta(x,y)$ that varies with the image location. Let $\{r_{\min}, r_{\max}\}$ be the radial range and Δ be the angular range. Let $V(x,y;r_{\min},r_{\max},\Delta)$ be the vote image, dependent on the radial and angular ranges and having the same dimensions as the original image. Let $A(x,y;r_{\min},r_{\max},\Delta)$ be the local voting area, defined at each image point (x,y) and dependent on the radial and angular ranges, defined by

$$A(x,y;r_{\min},r_{\max},\Delta) := \{(x \pm r\cos\phi, y \pm r\sin\phi) \mid r_{\min} \le r \le r_{\max} \text{ and } \theta(x,y) - \Delta \le \phi \le \theta(x,y) + \Delta\} \quad (1)$$

Finally, let $K(x,y;\sigma,\alpha,A)$ be a 2D Gaussian kernel with variance σ, masked by the local voting area $A(x,y;r_{\min},r_{\max},\Delta)$ and oriented in the voting direction $\alpha(x,y)$. Figure 2 shows a subset of voting kernels that vary in topography, scale, and orientation.

The iterative voting algorithm is outlined below for radial symmetry.

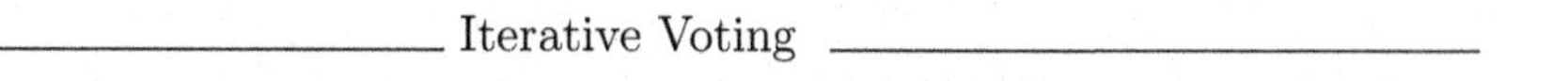

Iterative Voting

1. *Initialize the parameters:* Initialize $r_{\min}, r_{\max}, \Delta_{\max}$, and a sequence $\Delta_{\max} = \Delta_N < \Delta_{N-1} < \cdots < \Delta_0 = 0$. Set $n := N$, where N is the number of iterations, and let $\Delta_n = \Delta_{\max}$. Also fix a low gradient threshold, Γ_g and a kernel variance, σ, depending on the expected scale of salient features.
2. *Initialize the saliency feature image:* Define the feature image $F(x,y)$ to be the local external force at each pixel of the original image. The external force is often set to the gradient magnitude or maximum curvature depending upon the the type of saliency grouping and the presence of local feature boundaries.
3. *Initialize the voting direction and magnitude:* Compute the image gradient, $\nabla I(x,y)$, and its magnitude, $||\nabla I(x,y)||$. Define a pixel subset $S := \{(x,y) | \, ||\nabla I(x,y)|| > \Gamma_g\}$. For each grid point $(x,y) \in S$, define the voting direction to be

$$\alpha(x,y) := -\frac{\nabla I(x,y)}{||\nabla I(x,y)||}$$

4. *Compute the votes:* Reset the vote image $V(x,y;r_{\min},r_{\max},\Delta_n) = 0$ for all points (x,y). For each pixel $(x,y) \in S$, update the vote image as follows:

$$V(x,y;r_{\min},r_{\max},\Delta_n) := V(x,y;r_{\min},r_{\max},\Delta_n) + \sum_{(u,v)\in A(x,y;r_{\min},r_{\max},\Delta_n)} F(x - \tfrac{w}{2} + u, y - \tfrac{h}{2} + v) K(u,v;\sigma,\alpha,A),$$

where $w = \max(u)$ and $h = \max(v)$ are the maximum dimensions of the voting area.

5. *Update the voting direction:* For each grid point $(x, y) \in S$, revise the voting direction. Let

$$(u^*, v^*) = \arg \max_{(u,v) \in A(x,y;r_{\min},r_{\max},\Delta_n)} V(u, v; r_{\min}, r_{\max}, \Delta_n)$$

Let $d_x = u^* - x, d_y = v^* - y$, and

$$\alpha(x, y) = \frac{(d_x, d_y)}{\sqrt{d_x^2 + d_y^2}}$$

6. *Refine the angular range:* Let $n := n - 1$, and repeat steps 4-6 until $n = 0$.
7. *Determine the points of saliency:* Define the centers of mass or completed boundaries by thresholding the vote image:

$$C = \{(x, y) \mid V(x, y; r_{\min}, r_{\max}, \Delta_0) > \Gamma_v\}$$

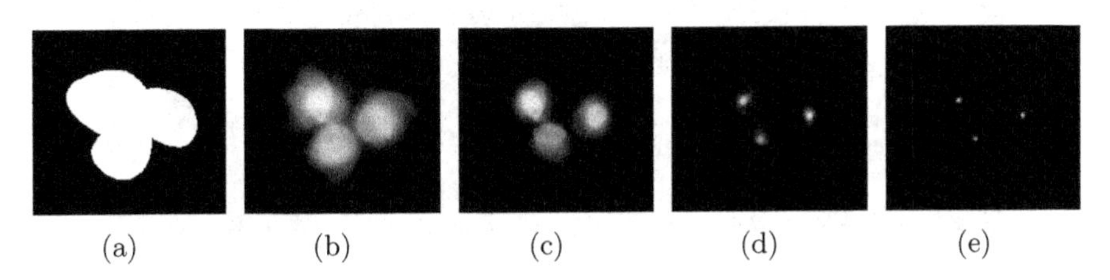

Fig. 3. Detection of radial symmetries for a synthetic image simulating three overlapping centrosomes (a protein event): (a) original image; (b)-(e) voting landscape at each iteration

An example of the application of radial kernels to overlapping objects is shown in Figure 3 together with the intermediate results. The voting landscape corresponds to the spatial clustering that is initially diffuse and subsequently refined and focused into distinct islands.

5 Experimental Results and Conclusion

A total of 196 images were processed to quantify number of abnormal centrosomes for each nucleus in the image. This result was then compared against manual count for validation, as shown in Figure 4. The system's error is at 1% and 10% for nuclear segmentation and quantitation of centrosome abnormality, respectively. Figure 5 shows the performance of the system on overlapping nuclear regions. It should be noted that in some cases there is no intensity decay when adjacent nuclei overlap; watershed-based techniques can fail to produce proper decomposition of nuclear compartments under these conditions. In

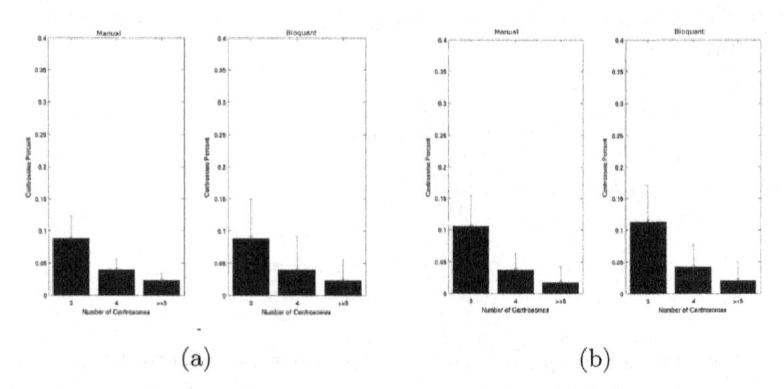

Fig. 4. Comparative results of abnormal centrosomes between manual and automated counting for two separate treatments. Each chart shows manual (on the left) and automated quantitation (on the right).

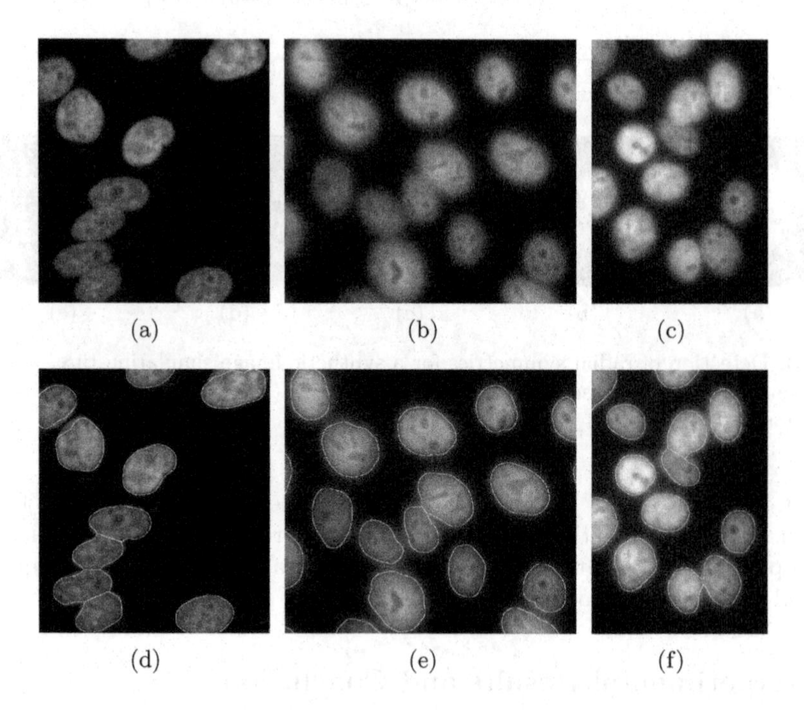

Fig. 5. Decomposition of overlapping nuclei: (a)-(c) original images; (d)-(f) decomposition results

contrast, proposed geometric approach is invariant to intensity distribution as a basis for decomposition. An example of localization of centrosomes through voting is shown in Figure 6, where a rare event due to CA is captured in region 20 and region 45. Each punctate signal is assigned to the closest nuclear boundary.

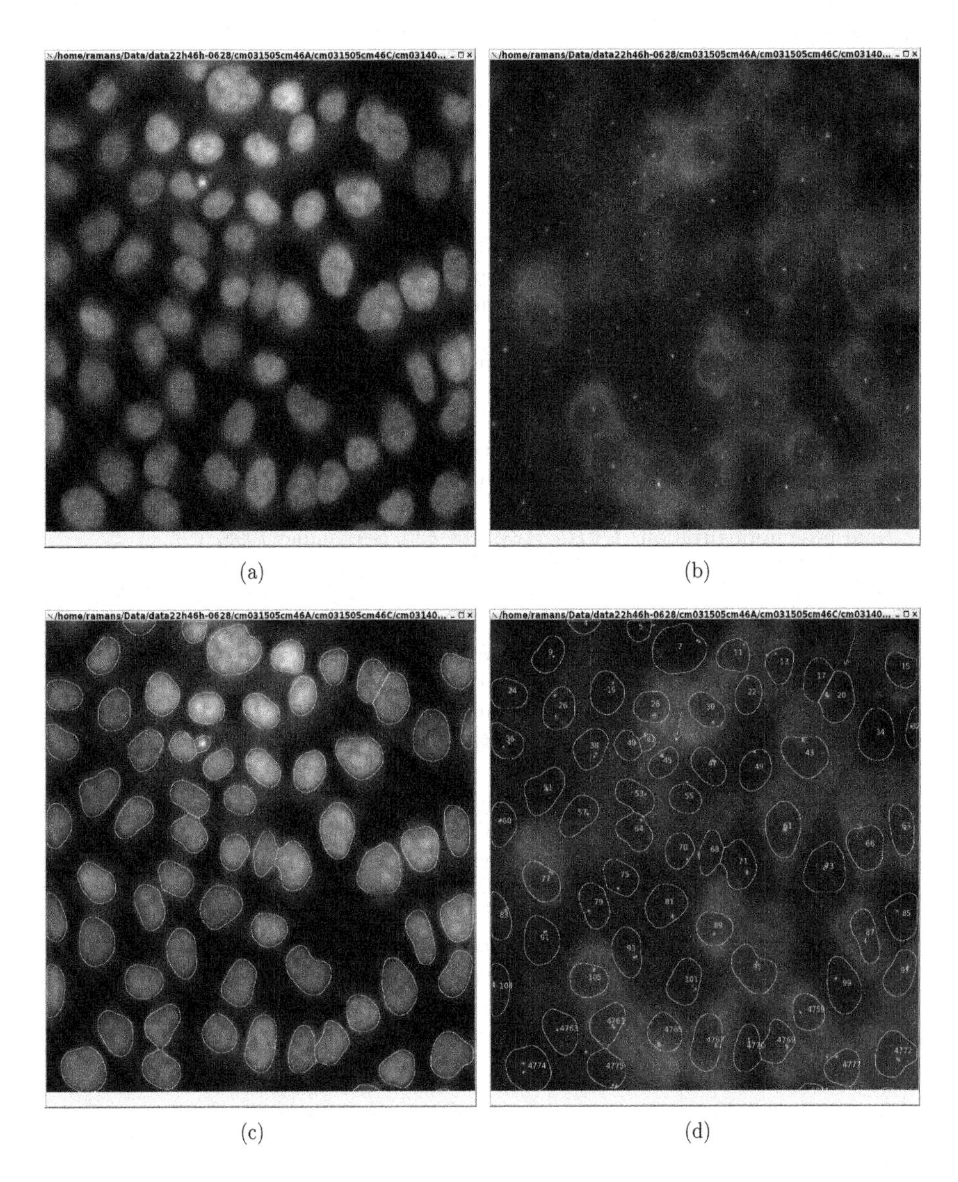

Fig. 6. Nuclear segmentation and centrosome localization indicates decomposition of overlapping nuclear compartments and detection of nearby punctate events corresponding to centrosome organelle: (a) original nuclear image; (b) corresponding centrosomes image; (c) segmented nuclear compartments; and (d) localized centrosomes. A rare event in nuclei 20 and 45 indicates four and three centrosomes, respectively. Nuclear and centrosome regions are represented by cyan contours and cyan dots, respectively. Ambiguities due to adjacent and overlapping regions (both nuclear and centrosomes) are resolved. Furthermore, pertinent events are measured in context. For example, centrosome abnormality of region 20 is referenced against correct nuclear size of morphology.

References

1. R. Malladi and J. Sethian. A unified approach to noise removal, image enhancement, and shape recovery. *IEEE Transactions on Image Processing*, 5(11):1554–1568, 1995.
2. G. Medioni, M.S. Lee, and C.K. Tang. *A Computational Framework for Segmentation and Grouping.* Elsevier, 2000.
3. R. Murphy. Automated interpretation of subcellular locatoin patterns. In *IEEE Int. Symp. on Biomedical Imaging*, pages 53–56, April 2004.
4. C. et. al. Ortiz De Solorzano. Segmentation of nuclei and cells using membrane protein. *Journal of Microscopy*, 201:404–415, March 2001.
5. B. Parvin, Q. Yang, G. Fontenay, and M. Barcellos-Hoff. Biosig: An imaging bioinformatics system for phenotypic analysis. *IEEE Transactions on Systems, Man and Cybernetics*, 33(B5):814–824, October 2003.
6. D. Reisfeld, H. Wolfson, and Y. Yeshurun. Context-free attentional operators: The generalized symmetry transform. *IJCV*, 14(2):119–130, March 1995.
7. D. Reisfeld and Y. Yeshurun. Preprocessing of face images: Detection of features and pose normalization. *CVIU*, 71(3):413–430, September 1998.
8. J. L. Salisbury. The contribution of epigenetic changes to abnormal centrosomes and genomic instability in breast cancer. *Journal of Mammary Gland Biology and Neoplasia*, 6(2):203–12, April 2001.
9. J. L. Salisbury, A. B. D'Assoro, and W. L. Lingle. Centrosome amplification and the origin of chromosomal instability in breast cancer. *Journal of Mammary Gland Biology and Neoplasia*, 9(3):275–83, July 2004.
10. G. Sela and M.D. Levine. Real-time attention for robotic vision. *Real-Time Imaging*, 3(3):173–194, June 1997.
11. L. Vincent and P. Soille. Watersheds in digital spaces: An efficient algorithm based on immersion simulations. *PAMI*, 13(6):583–598, June 1991.
12. Q. Yang and B. Parvin. Harmonic cut and regularized centroid transform for localization of subceullar structures. *IEEE Transactions on Biomedical Engineeing*, 50(4):469–475, April 2003.
13. Q. Yang and B. Parvin. Perceptual organization of radial symmetries. In *Proceedings of the Conference on Computer Vision and Pattern Recognition*, pages 320–325, 2004.

Multi-level Thresholding Using Entropy-Based Weighted FCM Algorithm in Color Image

Jun-Taek Oh, Hyun-Wook Kwak, Young-Ho Sohn, and Wook-Hyun Kim

School of EECS, Yeungnam University, 214-1 Dae-dong,
Gyeongsan, Gyeongbuk 712-749, South Korea
{ohjuntaek, psthink, ysohn, whkim}@yumail.ac.kr

Abstract. This paper proposes a multi-level thresholding method based on a weighted FCM(Fuzzy C-Means) algorithm in color image. FCM algorithm can determine a more optimal thresholding value than existing methods and be extended to multi-level thresholding, yet it is sensitive to noise, as it does not include spatial information. To solve this problem, a weight based on the entropy obtained from neighboring pixels is applied to FCM algorithm, and the optimal cluster number is determined using the within-class distance in the code image based on the clustered pixels for each color component. Experiments confirmed that the proposed method was more tolerant to noise and superior to existing methods.

1 Introduction

Image segmentation plays an important role in understanding and analyzing image. In particular, region segmentation and object detection in image are both essential procedures for practical applications. Methods for image segmentation[1] include texture analysis-based methods, histogram thresholding-based methods, clustering-based methods, and region-based split and merging methods, among which threshold-based image segmentation is widely used in many applications, such as document processing and object detection, as it is simple and efficient as regards dividing image into the foreground and background.

Histogram thresholding-based methods use various criteria, such as Otsu's method[7], the entropy method[8], minimum error thresholding, and etc. However, none of these histogram thresholding-based methods include spatial information, which can lead to serious errors in the case of image segmentation. Plus, the selection of a threshold is very difficult, as the histograms of most real-images have an ambiguous and indistinguishable distribution. To solve the problem, fuzzy clustering[2, 3] algorithms, such as FCM(fuzzy c-means), fuzzy ISODATA, and PCM(possibilistic c-mean), have become a powerful tool that has been successfully applied to image thresholding to segment image into meaningful regions. However, certain problems like noise still remain, as no spatial information is included.

In general, threshold-based segmentation of color image segments image using a threshold extracted from gray image after converting color image into gray image. As such, this method is simple and can reduce the computational time, yet some of the color information can be lost when color image is converted into gray image. In this case, objects with the same gray information yet completely different color information

G. Bebis et al. (Eds.): ISVC 2005, LNCS 3804, pp. 437 – 444, 2005.

can be erroneously classified as identical objects. Therefore, the threshold needs to be determined based on the color space of image. Y. Du[5, 6] used a histogram thresholding-based method, such as Otsu's method and entropy-based method, for each color component in color image, and then multi-level image thresholding is performed according to optimal clusters determined by the within–class and between-class distance of the clusters, which are classified for each color component. Yet, this method is difficult to extend to multi-level thresholding for each color component and the reclassification of cluster-units to detect optimal clusters leads to incorrect image segmentation.

This paper uses entropy as a weight to supply the spatial information between the current pixel and its neighbors, while applying FCM algorithm for each color component in color image. The final segmentation is then based on the within-class distance for all the clusters in the code image. The proposed algorithm can be extended to multi-level thresholding using FCM algorithm and is robust against noise. Furthermore, correct image segmentation can be accomplished by pixel-based reclassification based on the within-class distance, and the optimal number of clusters defined using the average of the within-class distance.

2 Weighted FCM Algorithm

2.1 FCM Algorithm

FCM(fuzzy c-means) algorithm[2, 3] is widely used in image segmentation as an unsupervised segmentation algorithm. The objective function $J_m(U,V)$ in FCM algorithm is given by :

$$J_m(U,V)=\sum_{i=1}^{c}\sum_{j=1}^{n}(u_{ij})^m \left\| v_i - x_j \right\|^2 \tag{1}$$

where x_j is the gray-level value of j'th pixel and v_i is the mean value of i'th cluster. A solution of the objective function $J_m(U,V)$ can be obtained via an iterative process, where the degrees of membership and the mean value of cluster are updated via:

$$u_{ij}=\frac{1}{\sum_{k=1}^{c}\left(\left\| v_i - x_j \right\| / \left\| v_k - x_j \right\|\right)^{2/m-1}} \qquad v_i=\sum_{j=1}^{n}(u_{ij})^m x_j \Big/ \sum_{j=1}^{n}(u_{ij})^m \tag{2}$$

where u_{ij} is the degree of membership between the j'th pixel and i'th cluster, v_i is the mean value of i'th cluster, c is the number of clusters, and m is an arbitrarily chosen FCM weighting exponent that must be greater than one.

The objective function is minimized when high membership values are assigned to those pixels whose intensities are close to the center of their particular cluster, and low membership values are assigned when the point is far from the center. Plus, when the algorithm has converged, the maximum membership procedure is used to defuzzy the partition matrix. FCM algorithm can classify most of noise-free real-images, which have an uncertain and complex data distribution. However, as FCM algorithm does not incorporate spatial information, it may fail to segment image corrupted by noise and other imaging artifacts.

2.2 Entropy-Based Weighted FCM(EWFCM) Algorithm

The neighborhood information is incorporated into FCM algorithm to remove any noise. In image, since the center pixel has a relationship with its neighbors, the probability that the center pixel and its neighbors will be classified in the same cluster is high. As such, Y. Yang[4] proposed a spatially weighted FCM algorithm using k-NN(nearest neighbor) algorithm, which is based on a distance between a mean gray-value of a cluster and a gray-value of a current pixel. However, Y. Yang's method may be lead to an incorrect classification if the histogram distributions of clusters are different. And it needs to define a parameter in advance. Therefore, this paper proposes an improved entropy-based weighted FCM(EWFCM) algorithm, where a weight based on entropy that takes into account the spatial relationship between the current pixel and its neighbors is applied to FCM algorithm.

The improved degrees of membership u_{ij}^* and v_i^* are given by:

$$u_{ij}^* = \frac{w_{ij}}{\sum_{k=1}^{c}\left(\| v_i - x_j \| / \| v_k - x_j \|\right)^{2/m-1}} \qquad v_i^* = \sum_{j=1}^{n} (u_{ij}^*)^m x_j \Big/ \sum_{j=1}^{n} (u_{ij}^*)^m \tag{3}$$

For i'th cluster, j'th pixel possessed a high ratio of belonging to i'th cluster when many neighbors of j'th pixel belong to i'th cluster. Then w_{ij} possesses a high weight as regards belonging to i'th cluster, and w_{ij} is calculated as:

$$w_{ij} = 1 - \frac{e_i}{e_i + e_k} = 1 - \frac{p_i \log(p_i)}{p_i \log(p_i) + p_k \log(p_k)} \tag{4}$$

$$p_i = \frac{1 + \#\text{ of } x_{en} \text{ in the set } N_j^i}{1 + \#\text{ of } x_{en} \text{ in the set } N_j} \qquad p_k = \frac{1 + \#\text{ of } x_{en} \text{ in the set } N_j^k}{1 + \#\text{ of } x_{en} \text{ in the set } N_j} \tag{5}$$

where x_n is the neighboring pixel of j'th pixel that is the center pixel, N_j is the set of the neighbors nearest to the center pixel, N_j^i is the subset of N_j composed of the pixels belonging to i'th class, N_j^k is the subset of N_j except N_j^i, p_i is the ratio that the neighbors of the j'th pixel belong to the same cluster, and p_k is the ratio that the neighbors of the j'th pixel do not belong to the same cluster. w_{ij} is then obtained by the entropy of Shannon based on those ratios. w_{ij} is set to 1 when all the neighbors of the pixel x_j belong to the same cluster and the weight value of the remaining clusters is set to 0. The weights of all the clusters are the same when the ratios are same. EWFCM algorithm is consecutively performed based on the centers and membership values obtained from FCM algorithm as it may be faced with local minima. EWFCM algorithm can correctly classify pixels by only using a classification index between a current pixel and the neighbors and is performed faster than Y. Yang's method.

3 Color Image Multi-level Thresholding Using EWFCM Algorithm

Color image consists of 3-dimensional color information(red, green, blue). To obtain this color information, this paper first applies EWFCM algorithm to each color component, then creates the code image based on the clustered data. Finally, the multi-level thresholding for a given color image is achieved by a reclassification procedure based on the within-class distance of all the clusters in the code image.

The number of clusters in the code image is determined according to the cluster number from EWFCM algorithm for each color component. If the number of clusters for each color component is set to 2, the code image consists of all 8 clusters, and each cluster is assigned a cluster number from 0 to 7. Yet, the number of clusters needs to be reduced in the reclassification step. But, before performing the reclassification of the clusters in the code image, noise is removed from the original image based on the cluster information. As such, the code image does not include noise, yet the original image does. However, since the pixel-based reclassification step uses the color information from the original image, the color information related to noise must be modified. Therefore, the difference between the color value of a pixel in a cluster and the average color value of all the clusters is compared, and then the cluster with the smallest difference is selected. If the selected cluster is equal to the cluster that includes the pixel in the code image, then the pixel maintains the original color value. Otherwise, the color value of the pixel is replaced with the average color value of the cluster that includes the pixel. In the pixel-based reclassification procedure, the cluster with the highest within-class distance is first selected, and then the difference between the color value of the pixels that are included in the cluster and the average color value of the remaining clusters is compared. The pixels are then reclassified in the cluster with the smallest difference. The optimal number of clusters in the code image is defined based on the average within-class distance for all the clusters. The cluster number with the minimum average within-class distance is selected after repeating the reclassification procedure until the number of clusters is 2. Fig. 1 shows the clustered images for each color component in the experimental image and the finally-clustered images in the code image.

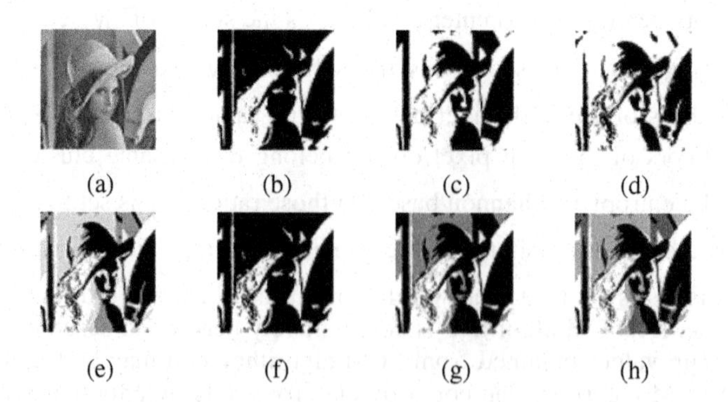

Fig. 1. Clustered images using EWFCM algorithm and pixel-based reclassification based on within-class distance. (a): Original image. (b)~(d): Clustered images for each color component(red, green, blue). (e): Code image. (f)~(h): Finally-clustered images, where the number of clusters is 2, 3, 4, respectively.

4 Experiment

All the algorithms in this paper were coded using SDK Version 1.4.1 in Window XP. The experimental images were color images, including Lena, House, Baboon, and Peppers. And a function developed by M. Borsotti[13] was used for the performance evaluation.

$$Q(I) = \frac{\sqrt{R}}{10000(N \times M)} \times \sum_{i=1}^{R} \left(\frac{e_i^2}{1+\log(A_i)} + \left(\frac{R(A_i)}{A_i} \right)^2 \right) \tag{6}$$

where I is the segmented image, N and M are the width and height of the image, respectively, R is the number of regions in the segmented image, A_i and e_i are the area and average color error for the i 'th region, respectively. $R(A_i)$ represents the number of regions with an area equal to A_i. The smaller the value of $Q(I)$, the better the segmentation result.

Fig. 2 shows the resulting images that are classified into a given cluster number(2, 3, 4) for gray-level images. Figs.2(a1) and (b1) are the original images; figs.2(a4) and (b4) are the noisy images with 10% Gaussian noise. Figs.2(a2), (b2), (a5) and (b5) are the resulting images that are classified by Y. Yang's method, and Figs.2(a3), (b3), (a6) and (b6) by EWFCM algorithm. As be seen in Fig.2, EWFCM algorithm shows a better segmentation result than Y. Yang's method, especially for MRI noisy image. Plus, based on pixel-united classification, when the number of clusters is 2, the average processing time per iteration of EWFCM algorithm approximately shows 55% of that of Y. Yang's method, and in the case that the number of clusters increases, the difference between the average processing times of Y. Yang's method and EWFCM algorithm is increased. Fig.3 shows the optimally clustered images based on the code images for the experimental images. Figs.3(a) and (b) show the experimental images that are widely used in image processing. Figs.3(c) and (d) show the resulting images that were clustered by Y. Du's method. First, after classifying each color component into 2 clusters with thresholds given by Otsu's method, it obtained the code image. The optimally clustered image is then given by the cluster-based reclassification procedure based on the within-class distance and between-class distance. Figs.3(e) and (f) show the resulting images that were clustered by the proposed method. The numbers under the figures show the optimal number of clusters for each image. In spite of the fewer clusters, the proposed algorithm segmented more exactly than the existing methods. Plus, in the case of the noisy images, using the average brightness of a cluster instead of the noise brightness in the reclassification step prevented the reproduction of noise. Fig.4 shows the results using the performance evaluation function(Q). The proposed method exhibited the better performance than Y. Du's method for all the experimental images. Fig.5 shows the performance evaluation results between the traditional FCM algorithm and EWFCM algorithm proposed in this paper. In this experiment, the number of clusters was set at 2, 3, and 4 for each color component in the experimental images. And the processing procedure for the reclassification step was the same. Clearly, EWFCM algorithm was superior to FCM algorithm for the noisy images, indicating that applying EWFCM algorithm to each color component was more effective than FCM algorithm. However, in the procedure for creating the code image, EWFCM algorithm showed approximately 2.5 times longer processing time than that of FCM algorithm. And the number of clusters for each color component is a very important factor in segmenting image. Therefore, multi-level thresholding for each color component needs to be performed before the reclassification step. In Figs.5(a) and (b), the proposed method obtained the best result for all the experimental images when pixels of each color component were classified into 3 clusters.

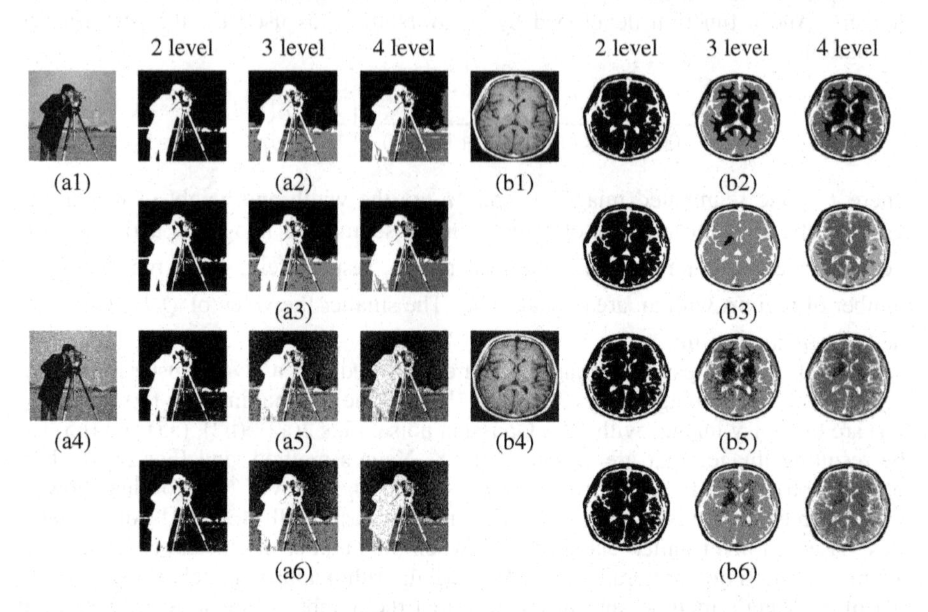

Fig. 2. Clustered images by the proposed method and Y. Yang's method(1). (a1), (b1) : Experimental images. (a4), (b4) : Noisy images with 10% gaussian noise. (a2), (a5), (b2), (b5) : Clustered images by Y. Yang's method. (a3), (a6), (b3), (b6) : Clustered images by the proposed method(EWFCM).

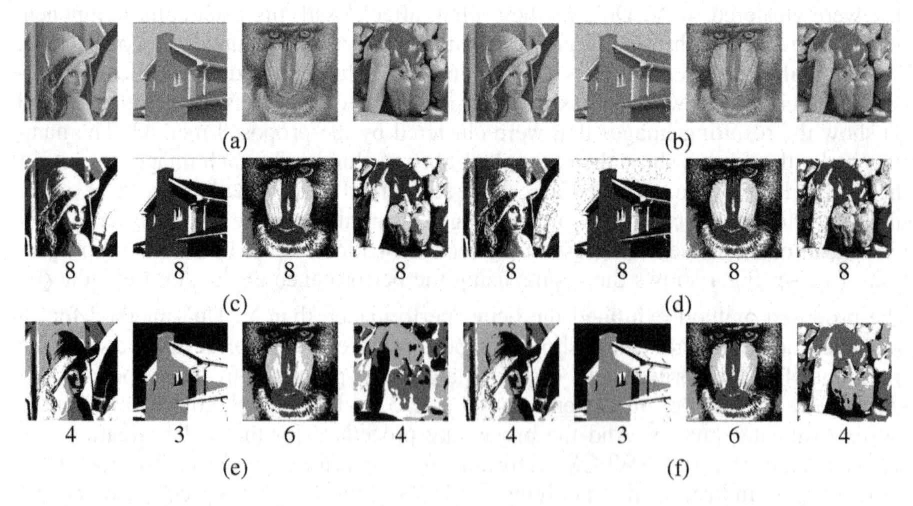

Fig. 3. Optimally clustered images (a): Experimental images without noise. (b): Experimental images with added salt & pepper noise, such that SNR = 5. (c), (d): Clustered images by Y. Du's method. (e), (f): Clustered images by the proposed method.

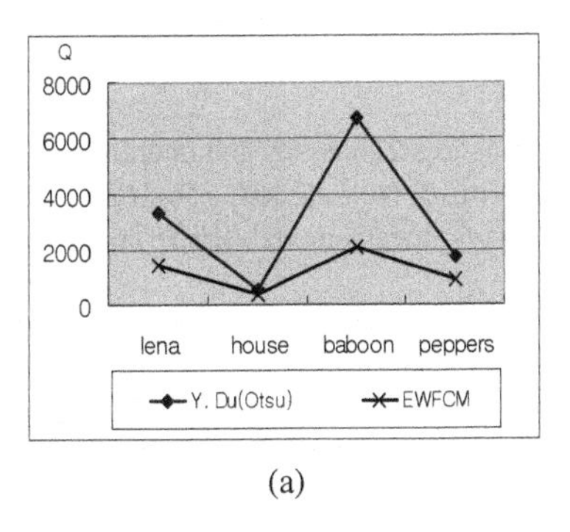

(a)

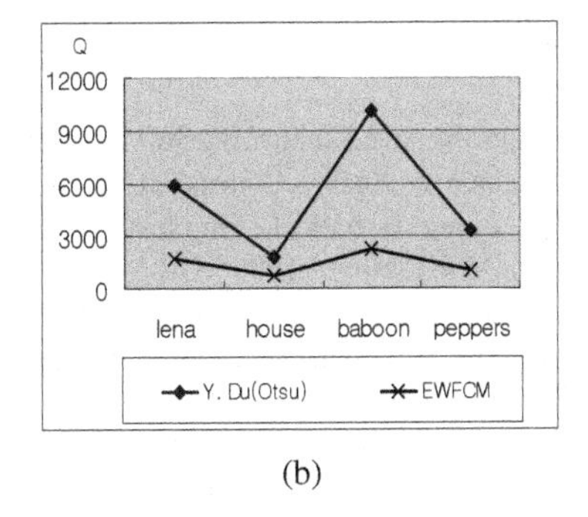

(b)

Fig. 4. Comparison of performance evaluation by Y. Du's method and the proposed method (a): for Fig.3(a). (b): for Figs.3(b).

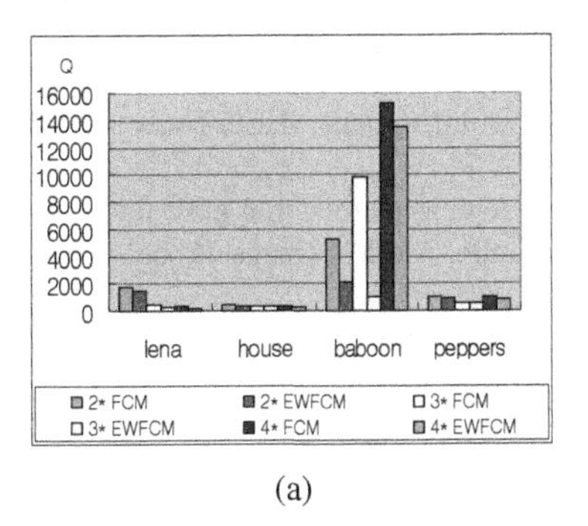

(a)

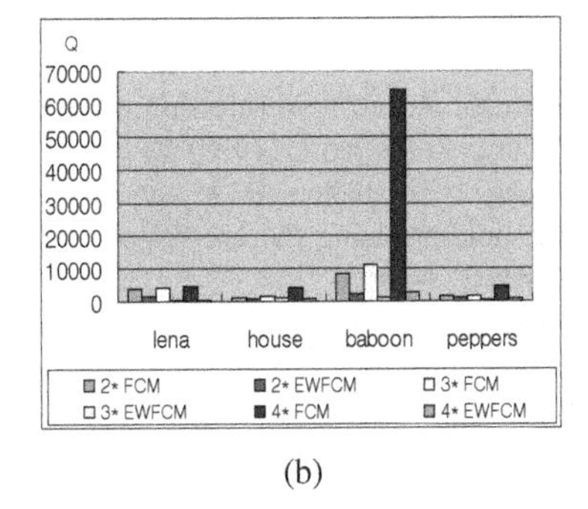

(b)

Fig. 5. Multi-level thresholding performance evaluation of FCM algorithm and EWFCM algorithm (a): for Figs.3(a). (b): for Figs.3(b).

5 Conclusion

This paper proposed a multi-level thresholding method for color image using the entropy-based weighted FCM algorithm and pixel-based reclassification. The entropy-based weighted FCM(EWFCM) algorithm can effectively remove noise by using entropy as the spatial information and be extended to multi-level thresholding founded on the advantage of FCM algorithm. Plus, based on the within-class distance of the clusters in the code image, multi-level thresholding of a color image can be performed by pixel-based reclassification that can precisely segment edges. The optimal number of clusters can also be determined according to the average distance of the within-class distance for all the clusters. As be seen in experiments, the proposed method shows more superior segmentation results than the existing methods. But, the processing time of EWFCM algorithm is excessive as before. Therefore, with reducing the processing time, region-based reclassification than pixel-based are areas under further study.

References

1. Sezgin, M. and Sankur, B.: Survey over image thresholding techniques and quantitative performance evaluation. Journal of Electronic Imaging, Vol.13, No.1, (2004) 146-165
2. Pal, N., and Bezdek, J.: On cluster validity for the fuzzy c-means model. IEEE Trans. Fuzzy Syst., Vol.3, No.3, (1995) 370-379
3. Krishnapuram, R., Frigui, H., and Nasraoui, O.: Fuzzy and possibilistic shell clustering algorithms and their application to boundary detection and surface approximation. IEEE Trans. Fuzzy Syst., Vol.3, No.1, (1995) 44-60
4. Yang, Y., Zheng, C., and Lin, P.: Image thresholding based on spatially weighted fuzzy c-means clustering. Proc. of IEEE Conf. on Computer and Information Technology, (2004) 184-189
5. Du, Y., Chang, C., and Thouin, P. D.: Unsupervised approach to color video thresholding. Opt. Eng. Vol.32, No.2, (2004) 282-289
6. Du, Y., Change, C. I., and Thouin, P. D.: An unsupervised approach to color video thresholding. Proc. of IEEE Conf. on Acoustics, Speech and Signal Processing, Vol.3, (2003) 373-376
7. Otsu, N.: A threshold selection method from gray level histograms. IEEE Trans. Syst. Man Cybern. Vol.9, No.1, (1979) 62-66
8. Kapur, J. N., Sahoo, P. K., and Wong, A. K. C.: A new method for gray level picture thresholding using the entropy of the histogram. Graph. Models Image Process., Vol.29, (1985) 273-285
9. Borsotti, M., Campadelli, P., and Schettini, R.: Quantitative evaluation of color image segmentation results. Patt. Recogn. Lett. Vol.19, No.8, (1998) 741-747

Adaptive Robust Structure Tensors for Orientation Estimation and Image Segmentation

Sumit K. Nath and Kannappan Palaniappan

MCVL, Department of Computer Science, University of Missouri-Columbia,
Columbia MO 65211, USA
{naths, palaniappank}@missouri.edu

Abstract. Recently, Van Den Boomgaard and Van De Weijer have presented an algorithm for texture analysis using robust tensor-based estimation of orientation. Structure tensors are a useful tool for reliably estimating oriented structures within a neighborhood and in the presence of noise. In this paper, we extend their work by using the Geman-McClure robust error function and, developing a novel iterative scheme that adaptively and simultaneously, changes the size, orientation and weighting of the neighborhood used to estimate the local structure tensor. The iterative neighborhood adaptation is initialized using the total least-squares solution for the gradient using a relatively large isotropic neighborhood. Combining our novel region adaptation algorithm, with a robust tensor formulation leads to better localization of low-level edge and junction image structures in the presence of noise. Preliminary results, using synthetic and biological images are presented.

1 Introduction

Structure tensors have been widely used for local structure estimation [1, 2, 3], optic-flow estimation [4, 5] and non-rigid motion estimation [6]. Robust statistical estimators have been shown to provide better results when compared with traditional least-squares based approaches [7]. In our work on motion analysis using biological image sequences [6, 8],we have reported the advantages of using structure tensors for segmentation. This is due to the fact that smoothing is minimized in the direction of the orientation vector, resulting in features that are less blurred at object discontinuities.

Combining robust estimators with structure tensor-based orientation estimation is a recent development that holds promising potential to improve localization accuracy in the presence of noise. Boomgaard and Weijer [2] apply robust tensor-based estimation for texture analysis and boundary detection while demonstrating the limitations of a total least-squares based approach. Robust estimators are computationally more expensive than their least-squares counterparts. An iterative approach is required to solve a robust structure-tensor matrix, as it becomes non-linearly dependent on the orientation of the patch [2]. However, robust structure tensors significantly improve orientation estimates. Instead of using a fixed local neighborhood, an adaptive area for integration has been shown to be beneficial for optic-flow estimation [5].

G. Bebis et al. (Eds.): ISVC 2005, LNCS 3804, pp. 445–453, 2005.

A spatially varying Gaussian kernel that adjusts to local image structure, size and shape is presented in this paper. We also show how this kernel can be efficiently embedded in the fixed-point iteration scheme proposed by Boomgaard and Weijer [2]. In addition, we also investigate the use of the Geman-McClure robust error function which is experimentally shown to yield improvements in localization of low-level image structures.

The paper is organized as follows. In Section 2, we discuss mathematical concepts associated with 2D structure tensor estimation. Section 3 describes our proposed adaptive spatially varying Gaussian kernel algorithm. Section 4 presents some results and discussion when using our algorithm on synthetic and biological images. A conclusion is provided in Section 5.

2 2D Structure Tensor Based Orientation Estimation

Let $\mathbf{v}(\mathbf{x})$ be the true gradient of an image patch $\mathbf{\Omega}(\mathbf{y})$, centered at $\mathbf{x}$. The norm of the error vector between the estimated gradient $\mathbf{g}(\mathbf{y})$ at location $\mathbf{y}$ and $\mathbf{v}(\mathbf{x})$ is given by $\mathbf{e}(\mathbf{x},\mathbf{y})$ as

$$||\mathbf{e}(\mathbf{x},\mathbf{y})|| = ||\mathbf{g}(\mathbf{y}) - (\mathbf{g}^{\mathbf{T}}(\mathbf{y})\,\mathbf{v}(\mathbf{x}))\mathbf{v}(\mathbf{x})|| \tag{1}$$

This can also be seen in Fig. 1. For clarity, we omit the positional arguments in some instances. In order to estimate $\mathbf{v}$, we will minimize an error functional $\rho(||\mathbf{e}(\mathbf{x},\mathbf{y})||^2)$ integrated over the image patch $\mathbf{\Omega}$, subject to the condition that $||\mathbf{v}|| = 1$ and $||\mathbf{g}|| = 1$ (as these are direction vectors).

The *least-squares* error functional is $\rho(||\mathbf{e}(\mathbf{x},\mathbf{y})||) = ||\mathbf{e}(\mathbf{x},\mathbf{y})||^2$ and the error over the image patch e_{LS} can be written as,

$$e_{LS}(\mathbf{x}) = \int_{\mathbf{\Omega}} \rho(||\mathbf{e}(\mathbf{x},\mathbf{y})||^2)\, W(\mathbf{x},\mathbf{y})\, d\mathbf{y} \tag{2}$$

On simplifying this expression, we obtain

$$e_{LS} = \int_{\mathbf{\Omega}} (\mathbf{g}^{\mathbf{T}}\mathbf{g})\, W(\mathbf{x},\mathbf{y})\, d\mathbf{y} - \int_{\mathbf{\Omega}} (\mathbf{v}^{\mathbf{T}}(\mathbf{g}\mathbf{g}^{\mathbf{T}})\mathbf{v})\, W(\mathbf{x},\mathbf{y})\, d\mathbf{y} \tag{3}$$

Here, $W(\mathbf{x},\mathbf{y})$ is a spatially invariant weighting function (e.g., Gaussian) that emphasizes the gradient at the central pixel within a small neighborhood, when evaluating the structure tensor.

Minimizing e_{LS} with respect to $\mathbf{v}$, subject to the condition that $||\mathbf{v}|| = 1$, is equivalent to maximizing the second term of Eq. 3. Using Lagrange multipliers, we can write this criterion as

$$\mathcal{E}_{LS}(\mathbf{x},\mathbf{y}) = \mathbf{v}^{\mathbf{T}}\,\Big(\int_{\mathbf{\Omega}} (\mathbf{g}\mathbf{g}^{\mathbf{T}})\, W(\mathbf{x},\mathbf{y})\, d\mathbf{y}\Big)\,\mathbf{v} + \lambda(1 - \mathbf{v}^{\mathbf{T}}\mathbf{v}) \tag{4}$$

Differentiating $\mathcal{E}_{LS}(\mathbf{x},\mathbf{y})$ to find the extremum leads to the standard eigenvalue problem for solving for the best estimate of $\mathbf{v}$, given by $\hat{\mathbf{v}}$.

$$\mathbf{J}(\mathbf{x},W)\,\hat{\mathbf{v}} = \lambda\,\hat{\mathbf{v}}, \tag{5}$$

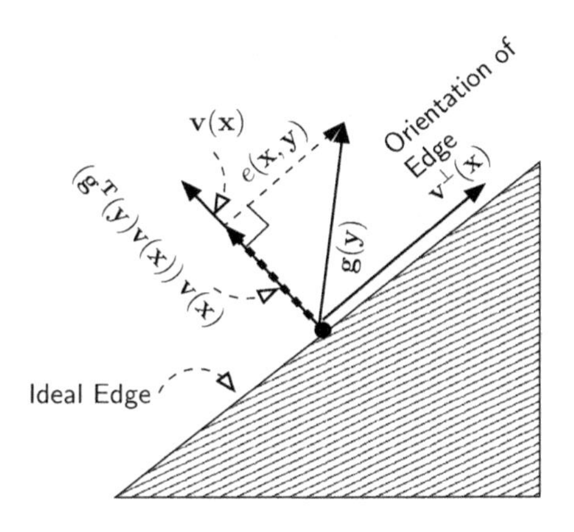

Fig. 1. Gradient and edge orientations of a pixel located in an ideal edge

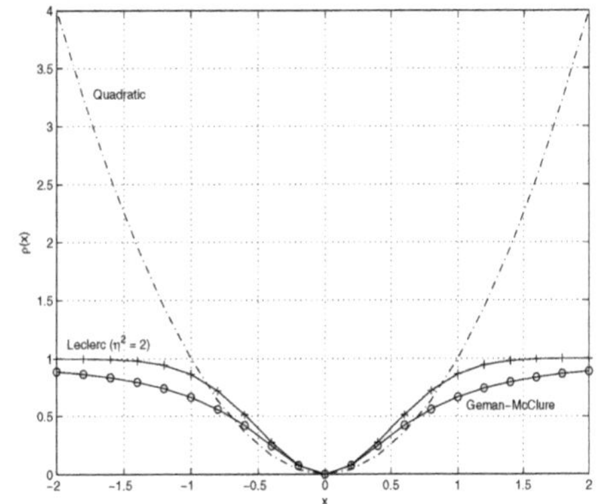

Fig. 2. Plot of Error Measures. $m^2 = 0.5$ for robust error measures.

For clarity, we replace $\hat{\mathbf{v}}$ with $\mathbf{v}$ in the remaining part of the paper.

In Eq. 5,

$$\mathbf{J}(\mathbf{x}, W) = \int_{\mathbf{\Omega}} (\mathbf{g}\mathbf{g}^{\mathbf{T}})\, W(\mathbf{x}, \mathbf{y})\, d\mathbf{y}$$

is the least-squares structure tensor at position $\mathbf{x}$ using the weighting kernel W. The maximum eigenvector solution of Eq. 5 gives the least-squares estimate for the gradient at pixel $\mathbf{x}$ using the surrounding gradient information. Although $\mathbf{v}^{\perp}(\mathbf{x})$ could be determined using the minimum eigenvector, it should be noted that for an ideal edge, the smaller eigenvalue will be zero. Hence it is numerically more reliable to estimate the maximum eigenvector.

Unlike the least-squares (or quadratic) error measure, robust error measures are noise tolerant by imposing smaller penalties on outliers [7]. In this paper, we use the *Geman-McClure* robust error function [7], instead of the *Gaussian* robust error function used in [2]. The Geman-McClure robust error function is defined as,

$$\rho(||\mathbf{e}(\mathbf{x}, \mathbf{y})||, m) = \frac{||\mathbf{e}(\mathbf{x}, \mathbf{y})||^2}{m^2 + ||\mathbf{e}(\mathbf{x}, \mathbf{y})||^2} = 1 - \frac{m^2}{m^2 + ||\mathbf{e}(\mathbf{x}, \mathbf{y})||^2} \tag{6}$$

where, m is a parameter that determines the amount of penalty imposed on large errors. The *Gaussian* robust error function is a special case of the *Leclerc* robust error function [7, p. 87, Fig. 29],

$$\rho(||\mathbf{e}(\mathbf{x}, \mathbf{y})||^2, m, \eta) = 1 - e^{-\frac{||\mathbf{e}(\mathbf{x}, \mathbf{y})||^2}{(\eta\, m)^2}}$$

with $\eta^2 = 2$. Fig. 2 shows that both robust error measures 'clamp' the influence of large outliers to a maximum of one, whereas the quadratic measure is unbounded. The Geman-McClure function clamps the error norm more gradually, when compared with the Leclerc function. Moreover, we experimentally obtained improved results when using the Geman-McClure function than with the Leclerc function.

Using Eq. 6, the error function to be minimized can be written as

$$e_{GM} = \int_{\Omega} W(\mathbf{x}, \mathbf{y})\, d\mathbf{y} - \int_{\Omega} \frac{m^2}{(\mathbf{g^T g} - \mathbf{v^T}(\mathbf{gg^T})\mathbf{v} + m^2)} W(\mathbf{x}, \mathbf{y})\, d\mathbf{y} \tag{7}$$

Minimization of e_{GM}, subject to the constraint that $||\mathbf{v}|| = 1$, is equivalent to maximizing the second term of Eq. 7 within the region $\mathbf{\Omega}$. Using Lagrange multipliers, this can be written as follows,

$$\mathcal{E}_{GM}(\mathbf{x}, \mathbf{y}) = \int_{\Omega} \frac{m^2}{(\mathbf{g^T g} - \mathbf{v^T}(\mathbf{gg^T})\mathbf{v} + m^2)} W(\mathbf{x}, \mathbf{y})\, d\mathbf{y} + \lambda(1 - \mathbf{v^T v}) \tag{8}$$

Differentiating $\mathcal{E}_{GM}(\mathbf{x}, \mathbf{y})$, with respect to $\mathbf{v}$, and setting it to zero gives

$$\mathbf{J}(\mathbf{x}, \mathbf{v}, W)\, \mathbf{v} = \lambda\, \mathbf{v} \ \text{ where,} \tag{9}$$

$$\mathbf{J}(\mathbf{x}, \mathbf{v}, W) = \int_{\Omega} \frac{m^2}{(\mathbf{g^T g} - \mathbf{v^T}(\mathbf{gg^T})\mathbf{v} + m^2)^2} (\mathbf{gg^T})\, W(\mathbf{x}, \mathbf{y})\, d\mathbf{y} \tag{10}$$

is the Geman-McClure robust structure tensor.

The following iterative equation,

$$\mathbf{J}(\mathbf{x}, \mathbf{v_i}, W)\, \mathbf{v_{i+1}} = \lambda\, \mathbf{v_{i+1}} \tag{11}$$

is a fixed-point functional iteration scheme for numerically solving $(\lambda, \mathbf{v})$ in Eq. 9 that usually converges to a local minimum [2]. Several convergence criterion can be used. Some of them include $||\mathbf{v_{i+1}} - \mathbf{v_i}|| < \epsilon$, $\mathrm{Tr}(\mathbf{J}(\mathbf{x}, \mathbf{v_i}, W) < k_{trace}$ (a trace threshold), and the size of W (for which we refer the reader to the next section). The total least-squares solution is used to initialize the iterative process in Eq. 11.

3 Spatially Varying Gaussian Kernel Adaptation

The structure tensor estimates in the neighborhood $\mathbf{\Omega}$ can be weighted to increase the influence of gradients close to the central pixel and less influence from the surrounding region. A soft Gaussian convolution function was used in [2]. In this work, we propose a spatially varying kernel, $W(\mathbf{x}, \mathbf{y})$, that is a Gaussian function with *adaptive size and orientation* within $\mathbf{\Omega}$. The neighborhood $\mathbf{\Omega}$ is initialized as a circular region and subsequently adapted to be an oriented elliptical region. Spatially varying adaptation of the kernel (local neighborhood shape and coefficients) is beneficial for improving the estimation of oriented image structures. When computing the structure tensor at a pixel located on an edge, it would be beneficial to accumulate local gradient information along a thin and parallel region to the edge. At the same time, influence of local gradients parallel to the gradient at the pixel should be minimized. Such a strategy would lead to an improved estimate of the gradient. A neighborhood where two

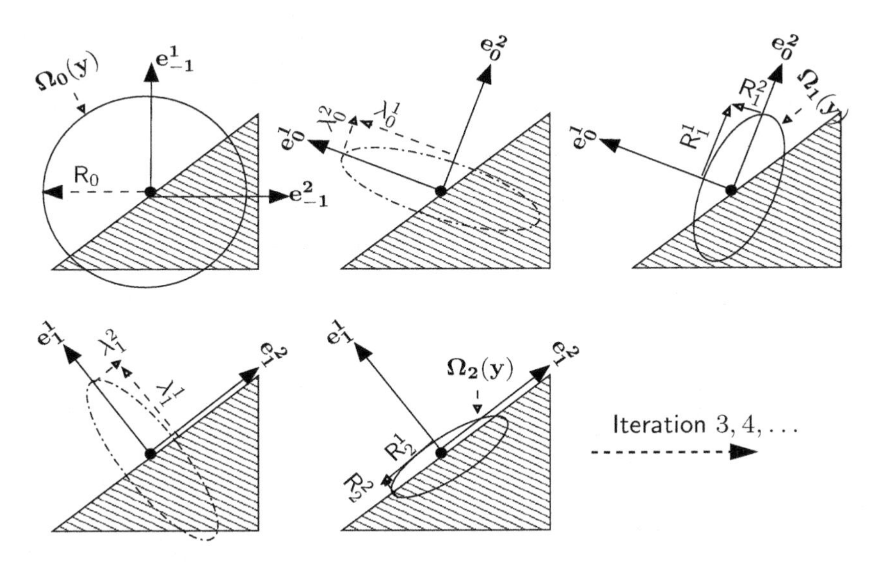

Fig. 3. The first three steps of the adaptive tensor algorithm at an ideal edge. $\mathbf{\Omega_i}(\mathbf{y})$ is the local neighborhood, $[\lambda_i^1,\, \lambda_i^2]$ the eigenvalues and $[\mathbf{e}_i^1,\, \mathbf{e}_i^2]$ the eigenvectors at the ith iteration step. R_0 is the radius of the initial (circular) local neighborhood while $[\mathrm{R}_{i+1}^1,\, \mathrm{R}_{i+1}^2]$ are the semi-major and semi-minor axes of the new local neighborhood at the $(i+1)^{th}$ iteration step. Adaptation updates for region size and orientation are shown in Eqs. 13 and 14. $\mathbf{\Omega_i}(\mathbf{y})$ is initially circular and subsequently becomes an oriented elliptical region.

or more edges meet is referred to as corners. For localizing such regions, it would be beneficial to select a region that is very small. The proposed adaptive structure tensor algorithm describes the approach by which appropriate small regions can be derived.

Fig. 3 shows the adaptive algorithm at an ideal edge. In this figure, the dashed-line elliptical region is oriented along the gradient while the solid-line elliptical region (that is scaled and rotated by 90°) is oriented along the edge. The spatially varying kernel $W_i(\mathbf{x}, \mathbf{y})$ that is used with Eq. 10 is defined as

$$W_i(\mathbf{x}, \mathbf{y}) = K\, e^{-\left(\frac{1}{2}\,(\mathbf{y}-\mathbf{x})^T\, \mathbf{U}_{\mathbf{i-1}}^{\mathbf{T}}\, \Lambda_i^{-2}\, \mathbf{U}_{\mathbf{i-1}}\,(\mathbf{y}-\mathbf{x})\right)}$$

$$\Lambda_i = \begin{bmatrix} \sqrt{2}\mathrm{R}_i^1 & 0 \\ 0 & \sqrt{2}\mathrm{R}_i^2 \end{bmatrix} \tag{12}$$

where K is a scaling factor associated with the Gaussian function. We initialize the kernel $W_0(\mathbf{x}, \mathbf{y})$ as an isotropic Gaussian with $\mathrm{R}_0^1 = \mathrm{R}_0^2 = \mathrm{R}_0$. A fairly large number is chosen (typically $\mathrm{R}_0 = 8$), in order to reduce the influence of noise when evaluating the structure tensor. The columns of $\mathbf{U_i}$ are the eigenvectors $(\mathbf{e_i^1}, \mathbf{e_i^2})$, with the columns of $\mathbf{U_{-1}}$ initialized as the co-ordinate axes. Let λ_i^1 and λ_i^2 (with $\lambda_i^1 > \lambda_i^2$) be the eigenvalues of the structure tensor $\mathbf{J}(\mathbf{x}, \mathbf{v_{i-1}}, W_i)$ at the ith iteration. Scaled versions of these eigenvalues are used to update the semi-major and semi-minor axes for the $(i+1)^{th}$ iteration as

$$\mathrm{R}_{i+1}^1 = \frac{\lambda_i^1}{\lambda_i^1 + \lambda_i^2}\,\mathrm{R}_i^1 \quad \text{and, } \mathrm{R}_{i+1}^2 = \frac{\lambda_i^2}{\lambda_i^1 + \lambda_i^2}\,\mathrm{R}_i^2 \tag{13}$$

The eigenvectors obtained from the current iteration, along with $(\mathrm{R}_{i+1}^1, \mathrm{R}_{i+1}^2)$ are used to update the kernel as follows

$$W_{i+1}(\mathbf{x}, \mathbf{y}) = K\, e^{-\left(\frac{1}{2}\,(\mathbf{y}-\mathbf{x})^T\, \mathbf{U_i^T}\, \Lambda_{i+1}^{-2}\, \mathbf{U_i}\,(\mathbf{y}-\mathbf{x})\right)}$$
$$\Lambda_{i+1} = \begin{bmatrix} \sqrt{2}\mathrm{R}_{i+1}^1 & 0 \\ 0 & \sqrt{2}\mathrm{R}_{i+1}^2 \end{bmatrix} \tag{14}$$

This kernel is used to compute a new structure tensor $\mathbf{J}(\mathbf{x}, \mathbf{v_i}, W_{i+1})$ as per Eq. 10. To account for the spatially varying Gaussian kernel, Eq. 11 is modified to the following form

$$\mathbf{J}(\mathbf{x}, \mathbf{v_i}, W_{i+1})\, \mathbf{v_{i+1}} = \lambda\, \mathbf{v_{i+1}} \tag{15}$$

We experimentally determined that two or three iterations were sufficient to achieve the convergence criteria presented in the previous section.

4 Results and Discussion

We demonstrate the performance of our algorithm using synthetic and biological images. Edges and junctions at which two or more edges meet (i.e., corners) are typical low-level image structures. Fig. 4(a) depicts a synthetic image having different types of edges (i.e., horizontal, vertical and slanted) and corners. Fig. 4(b) shows the least-squares estimate for the structure tensor, using a circular region for $W(\mathbf{x}, \mathbf{y})$. Smeared edges and corners, that result from this process, are shown in the intensity maps of confidence measures (Figs. 4(b), 4(e)).

The proposed (spatially varying) adaptive robust tensor method produces better localization of edges and corners, as shown in Figs. 4(c) and 4(f). Along ideal edges, one of the eigenvalues is nearly equal to zero. Consequently, there would be no adaptation in the size of the kernel (Eq. 12). Thus, the improved localization of edges in Fig. 4(c) is due to the robust component of our algorithm. With noisy edges, however, both eigenvalues will be non-zero. Hence, both kernel adaptation and robust estimation contribute to the improved localization of noisy edges as shown in Fig. 4(f). At junctions, both eigenvalues are greater than zero and can be nearly equal to each other for 90° corners [9, Ch. 10]. Hence, there is a nearly isotropic decrease in the kernel (Eq. 12) which leads to improved localization of corners as seen in both Figs. 4(c) and 4(f).

We also show the effect of using different robust error measures with real biological images. Fig. 5(a) shows a *Lilium longiflorum* pollen tube, imaged using high resolution Nomarski optics (diameter of pollen tube is 20 microns). These images are used to study the movement of the tip and small interior vesicles that actively contribute to the growth dynamics of pollen tubes [10]. Fig. 5(e) shows a section of the *Arabidopsis thaliana* root from the meristem region, with root hairs and internal cellular structures (diameter of the root is approximately

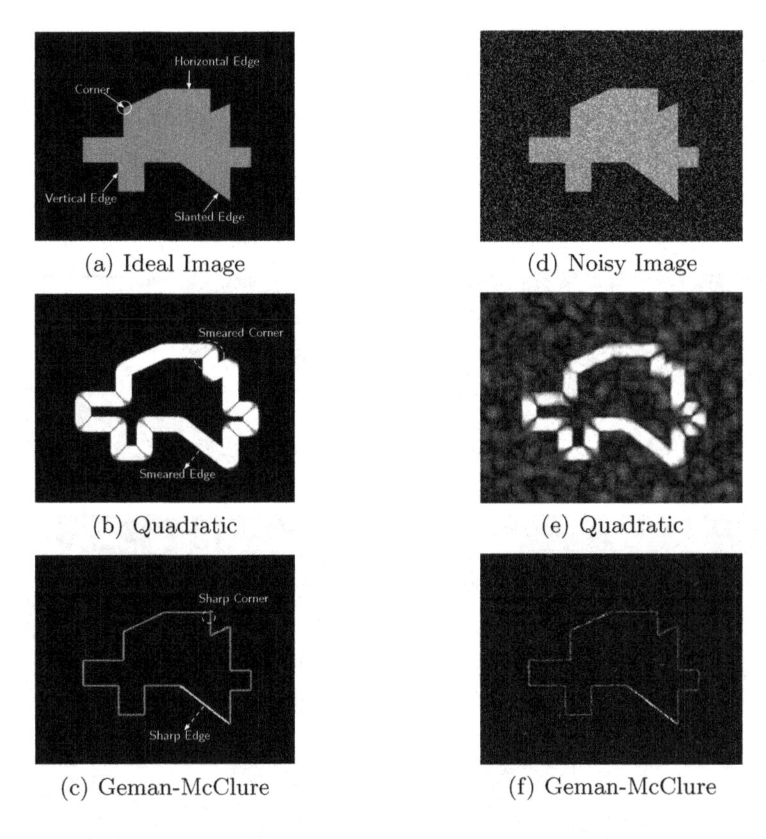

(a) Ideal Image (d) Noisy Image

(b) Quadratic (e) Quadratic

(c) Geman-McClure (f) Geman-McClure

Fig. 4. An ideal image and the same image corrupted with 60% additive Gaussian noise $\mathcal{N}(0,1)$. Corresponding, scaled, intensity plots of the confidence measure $\lambda_i^1 - \lambda_i^2$ (i.e., converged eigenvalues) using least-squares (quadratic) and Geman-McClure error measures are also shown. $\mathrm{R}_0 = 8$ (use to defined both $W(\mathbf{x}, \mathbf{y}$ and $\mathbf{\Omega}(\mathbf{y}))$, $k_{trace} = 0.005$ for both error measures, and the number of iterations is 8. Original image dimensions are 262×221.

100 microns). Temporal stacks of such root images were used to automatically compute the most spatiotemporally accurate growth profile along the medial axis of the root, for several plant species [8]. As seen from Fig. 5(d) and 5(h), the Geman-McClure function does a better job at detecting more salient image features, such as vesicles in the pollen tubes and internal cellular structures in the root, that are important in characterizing the physiology of biological motions.

In a previous paper, we have presented growth characterization results using a least-squares based robust tensor algorithm for computing velocity profiles of root growth in *Arabidopisis thaliana* [8]. The accurate localization and segmentation feature of the proposed adaptive robust structure tensor algorithm can be suitably extended for computing such velocity profiles, or growth in other biological organisms.

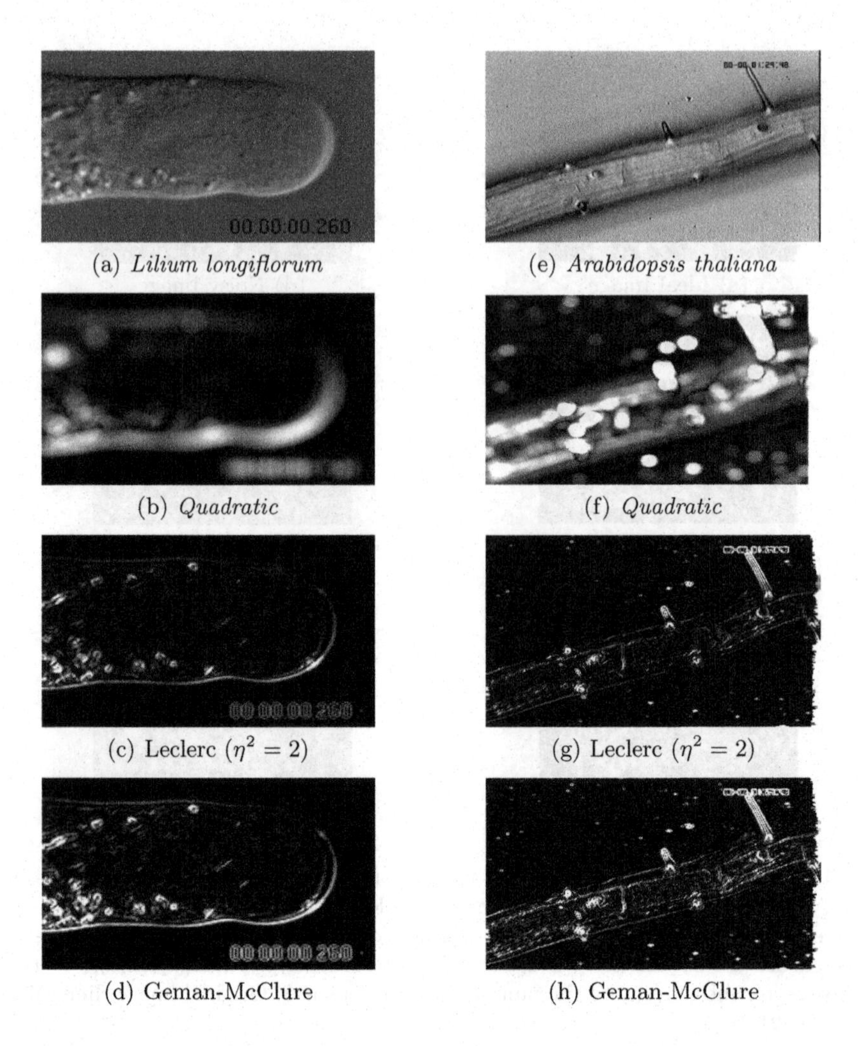

(a) *Lilium longiflorum* (e) *Arabidopsis thaliana*

(b) *Quadratic* (f) *Quadratic*

(c) Leclerc ($\eta^2 = 2$) (g) Leclerc ($\eta^2 = 2$)

(d) Geman-McClure (h) Geman-McClure

Fig. 5. *Lilium longiflorum* pollen tube and meristem region of an *Arabidopsis thaliana* root image, with corresponding scaled intensity plots of confidence measure $\lambda_i^1 - \lambda_i^2$ (i.e., converged eigenvalues). $\mathrm{R_O} = 8$ (used to define both $W(\mathbf{x}, \mathbf{y}$ and $\mathbf{\Omega}(\mathbf{y}))$, $m^2 = 0.5$ and $k_{trace} = 0.005$ with a maximum of 8 iterations. Original image dimensions are 197×133 for the pollen tube and 640×480 for the root images, respectively.

5 Conclusion and Scope for Future Work

An adaptive, robust, structure tensor algorithm has been presented in this paper that extends the robust orientation estimation algorithm by Boomgaard and Weijer [2]. The adaptation procedure for local orientation estimation uses a new, spatially varying, adaptive Gaussian kernel that is initialized using the total least-squares structure tensor solution. We adapt the size, orientation and weights of the Gaussian kernel simultaneously at each iteration step. This leads to improved detection of edge and junction features, even in the presence of noise. In a future work, we intend to explore the relationship between the proposed adaptive robust-tensor algorithm and *anisotropic diffusion* [11, 12].

Acknowledgements

This research was supported in part by the U.S National Institutes of Health, NIBIB award R33 EB00573. The biological images were provided by Dr. Tobias Baskin at the University of Massachusetts, Amherst.

References

1. G.H.Granlund, H.Knutsson: *Signal Processing for Computer Vision.* Kluwer Academic Publishers, Dordrecht, Netherlands (1995)
2. R.van den Boomgaard, J.van de Weijer: Robust estimation of orientation for texture analysis. In: 2nd *Intl. Work. Text. Anal. Synt.*, Copenhagen, Dennmark (2002) 135–138
3. U.Köthe: Integrated edge and junction detection with the boundary tensor. In: *Proc. IEEE Int. Conf. Computer Vision.* Volume 1., Nice, France (2003) 424–431
4. B.Jähne, H.Haußecker, H.Scharr, H.Spies, D.Schmundt, U.Schurr: Study of dynamical processes with tensor-based spatiotemporal image processing techniques. In: *LNCS-1407: Proc.* 5th *ECCV*. Volume 2., Freiburg, Germany, Springer-Verlag (1998) 322–336
5. H.H.Nagel, A.Gehrke: Spatiotemporally adaptive estimation and segmentation of OF-Fields. In: *LNCS-1407: Proc.* 5th *ECCV*. Volume 2., Freiburg, Germany, Springer-Verlag (1998) 86–102
6. K.Palaniappan, H.S.Jiang, T.I.Baskin: Non-rigid motion estimation using the robust tensor method. In: *CVPR - IEEE Workshop on Articulated and Nonrigid Motion.* Volume 1., Washington, DC (2004) 25–33
7. M.J.Black, A.Rangarajan: On the unification of line processes, outlier rejection, and robust statistics. *Intern. J. Comput. Vis.* **19** (1996) 57–91
8. C.Weele, H.Jiang, K.K.Palaniappan, V.B.Ivanov, K.Palaniappan, T.I.Baskin: A new algorithm for computational image analysis of deformable motion at high spatial and temporal resolution applied to root growth: Roughly uniform elongation in the meristem and also, after an abrupt acceleration, in the elongation zone. *Plant. Phys.* **132** (2003) 1138–1148
9. B.Jähne, H.Haußecker, P.Geißler: *Handbook of Computer Vision and Applications-Vol. 2 (Signal Processing and Pattern Recognition).* Academic Press, San Diego, CA (1999)
10. T.L.H-Clarke, N.M.Weddle, S.Kim, A.Robi, C.Parris, J.G.Kunkel, P.K.Hepler: Effect of extracellular calcium, pH and borate on growth oscillations in *Lilium formosanum* pollen tubes. *J. Exp. Bot.* **54** (2003) 65–72
11. J.Weickert: *Anisotropic Diffusion in Image Processing.* Teubner-Verlag, Stuttgart, Germany (1998)
12. T.Brox, R.van den Boomgaard, F.Lauze, J.van de Weijer, J.Weickert, P.Mrázek, P.Kornprobst: Adaptive structure tensors and their applications. In J.Weickert and H.Hagen, ed.: *Visualization and Image Processing of Tensor Fields.* Springer-Verlag, Berlin, Germany (2005)

Structural and Textural Skeletons for Noisy Shapes

Wooi-Boon Goh and Kai-Yun Chan

School of Computer Engineering, Nanyang Technological University,
Nanyang Avenue, Singapore 639798
{aswbgoh, askychan}@ntu.edu.sg

Abstract. The extraction of consistent skeletons in the presence of boundary noise is still a problem for most skeletonization algorithms. Many suppress skeletons associated with boundary perturbation, either by preventing their formation or removing them subsequently using additional operations. A more appropriate approach is to view a shape as comprising of structural and textural skeletons. The former describes the general structure of the shape and the latter its boundary characteristics. These two types of skeletons should be encouraged to remaining disconnected to facilitate gross shape matching without the need for branch pruning. Such skeletons can be formed by means of a multi-resolution gradient vector field (MGVF), which can be generated efficiently using a pyramidal framework. The robust scale-invariant extraction of the skeletons from the MGVF is described. Experimental results show that the MGVF structural skeletons are less affected by boundary noise compared to skeletons extract by other popular iterative and non-iterative techniques.

1 Introduction

Skeletons are widely adopted as a basis for shape description [4],[10]. Kimia [5] recently highlighted several psychophysical evidences that suggest some role for medial axis in the human visual system. However, it is still a challenge to extract robust skeletons in the presence of boundary noise. A shape's skeleton can be defined as the locus of centers of maximal discs contained within the shape [2] and it is well-known that small boundary perturbations can significantly alter the structure of such skeletons. This problem has been traditionally addressed using some form of pre-smoothing technique or branch pruning strategy. In the case of the former, pre-smoothing the shape contour using curvature flow smoothing techniques [4] could be carried out before skeleton extraction. Alternatively, topology preserving pruning methods can be employed [11]. Multiscale pruning strategies such as the iteratively pruned trees of Voronoi edges have also been proposed [7]. Pizer *et al.* [8] described the medialness function (cores) of a shape over a width-proportional scale. By selecting cores from appropriate scales, shapes can be made relatively insensitive to boundary noise. In summary, most approaches seek to suppress spurious skeletons either by preventing their formation or removing them subsequently. However, it has been acknowledged that selecting an appropriate scale or pruning threshold that can properly define what constitutes an insignificant skeleton is non trivial [9]. Moreover, such 'spurious' skeletons may be useful in describing

G. Bebis et al. (Eds.): ISVC 2005, LNCS 3804, pp. 454 – 461, 2005.

boundary characteristics. A more appropriate approach is to view a shape as comprising of two types of skeletons, namely structural and textural skeletons (see Fig. 1b). In our work, the *structural skeleton* is formally defined as the fully connected skeletal segment that has as its member, the skeletal point with the largest Euclidean distance from any boundary point. It describes the general structure and topology of the shape. This skeleton is relatively stable to boundary noise. *Textural skeletons* on the other hand, describe the shape's boundary characteristics and they emanate from the boundary towards the interior. Pizer *et. al* in [9] used the term *topological skeleton* to refer to the part of the skeleton which cannot be further contracted without altering its corresponding topology. Skeletal branches emanating from the topological skeleton towards the boundary (see Fig. 1a) represent define finer details and can be deleted without affecting the topology. These skeletons are usually fully connected and in cases where they are not, homotopy preserving algorithms are employed to maintain connectivity [13]. Pruning must therefore be employed to remove spurious branches before the 'noise-free' skeleton can be extracted for subsequent robust shape analysis.

We argue that structural and textural skeletons should be encouraged to remain disconnected. In this way, both the gross shape structure and boundary perturbations are simultaneously represented and accessible without need for costly branch pruning. This seems to run contrary to the homotopic nature of most skeletonization algorithms. A fully connected skeleton can be represented with a single graph but such a graph resulting from a noisy shape can be dense. This makes subsequent graph matching complicated and costly. The edit distance algorithm of Sebastian *et. al* [10] prunes away leaf edges in the shock graph and associate an appropriate splice cost for such an operation. Nonetheless, pruning numerous spurious edges arising from boundary noise can increase the time taken to compute the optimal match between shapes. However, if the relatively 'noise-free' structural skeletons are disconnected from the textural skeletons (see Fig. 1c), they can be easily compared to determine their gross shape match before textural skeletons are employed for refined matching.

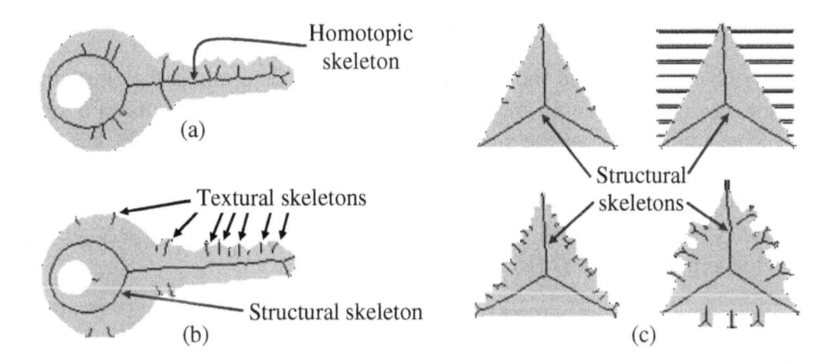

Fig. 1. (a) Sensitivity of a homotopic skeleton to boundary perturbation. (a) The structural skeleton is connected in order to maintain topology of the shape and disconnected textural skeletons capture prominent boundary artifacts such as the serrated teeth of the key. (c) Structural and textural skeletons of four triangular shapes with varying boundary characteristics.

2 The MGVF Skeleton

2.1 The Gradient Vector Field and Disparity Map

Several researchers have proposed the use of vector fields to analyze symmetry in shapes [1], [13]. In our work, a gradient vector field is used as a basis for generating a scalar 2D surface from which the skeleton can then be extracted by detecting the local maxima on this surface. A computational efficient pyramidal framework is proposed for generating a gradient vector field that exhibits characteristics that facilitates the extraction of a disconnected 'noise-free' structural skeleton. Integration of gradient information over different spatial resolutions allows the gradient vectors in the interior to be constituted with noise free low spatial frequencies whilst vectors near the boundary are constituted with high spatial frequencies that will retain the boundary characteristics. Pyramid operations such as *REDUCE* and *EXPAND* can be reviewed in [3]. It is assumed that the input image is a binary silhouette image $I(x, y)$. Firstly, a Gaussian pyramid $G(l,x,y)$ of $N+1$ levels is created by iteratively applying the *REDUCE* operation N times on each consecutive output image, starting with $I(x, y)$. From the scalar Gaussian pyramid, we then derived the vectorial Gradient pyramid $\boldsymbol{H}(l,x,y)$, which consist of two pyramids $H^x(l,x,y)$ and $H^y(l,x,y)$ given by

$$H_l^x(\boldsymbol{x}) = \nabla g_{\sigma_H}^x(\boldsymbol{x}) * G_l(\boldsymbol{x}) \text{ and } H_l^y(\boldsymbol{x}) = \nabla g_{\sigma_H}^y(\boldsymbol{x}) * G_l(\boldsymbol{x}) \qquad \text{for } 0 \le l \le N \tag{1}$$

where $\boldsymbol{x} = (x, y)$ and the convolution kernels are first-order Gaussian derivatives in the x and y directions, respectively and are given by

$$\nabla g_{\sigma_H}^x(\boldsymbol{x}) = -\frac{x}{\sigma_H^2}\exp(-\frac{x^2+y^2}{2\sigma_H^2}) \text{ and } \nabla g_{\sigma_H}^y(\boldsymbol{x}) = -\frac{y}{\sigma_H^2}\exp(-\frac{x^2+y^2}{2\sigma_H^2}) \tag{2}$$

Each level $\boldsymbol{V}_l$ of the Gradient Vector Field pyramid, for $0 \le l < N$, is constructed by iteratively applying *EXPAND* to a proportioned sum of the corresponding level $\boldsymbol{H}_l$ of the Gradient pyramid and *EXPAND* $[\boldsymbol{V}_{l+1}]$, starting with $l=N$-1. More formally,

$$\boldsymbol{V}_l = \alpha \boldsymbol{H}_l + (1-\alpha)\, EXPAND\, [\boldsymbol{V}_{l+1}] \qquad \text{for } 0 \le l < N \tag{3}$$

where $\boldsymbol{V}_l = \boldsymbol{H}_l$ for $l = N$ and the parameter $\alpha \in [0, 1]$ determines the smoothness of the gradient vector field within the object. A small value of α results in a smoother vector field in the interior of the shape. Given the gradient vector field $\boldsymbol{V}_l(\boldsymbol{x})$ in (3), the shape axes can be located by detecting locations in the vector field where the local gradient vectors exhibit high vector directional disparity. Using the directional disparity operator Δ, the normalized Vector Field Disparity pyramid $D(l,x,y)$ is derived from $\boldsymbol{V}_l(\boldsymbol{x})$ where each level $D_l(\boldsymbol{x})$ is defined as

$$D_l(\boldsymbol{x}) = \Delta(\boldsymbol{V}_l(\boldsymbol{x}),\sigma_D) = \frac{g_{\sigma_D}(\boldsymbol{x}) * \|\boldsymbol{V}_l(\boldsymbol{x})\| - \|g_{\sigma_D}(\boldsymbol{x}) * \boldsymbol{V}_l(\boldsymbol{x})\|}{g_{\sigma_D}(\boldsymbol{x}) * \|\boldsymbol{V}_l(\boldsymbol{x})\|} \qquad \text{for } 0 \le l \le N \tag{4}$$

The local disparity measure is computed within a weighted locality defined by the Gaussian kernel $g_{\sigma D}$ given by $\exp[-(x^2+y^2)/2\sigma_D^2]/\sqrt{2\pi}\sigma_D$. The normalized vector field disparity measure $D_l(\boldsymbol{x}) \in [0, 1]$ gives a value close to 1 in localities of high directional disparity such as at the center of a circle. In order to detect consistent shape axes over different scales of a shape, a full resolution vector field disparity map $M(x,y)$ is obtained by iteratively applying *EXPAND* to the sum of D_l and *EXPAND* $[D_{l+1}]$, starting with at $l=N$-1 to $l=0$. The final summed output is divided by $N+1$ to normalize the disparity map such that $M(x,y) \in [0,1]$.

2.2 Skeleton Extraction and Structural Skeleton Connectivity

Given the disparity map $M(x,y)$, the shape axes can be extracted by detecting local maximas on this disparity surface using a simple local ridge detection algorithm, which flags out a pixel as a ridge pixel when a specified number of its neighbouring pixels have disparity values less than its own. In our implementation, a 5×5 square neighbourhood was used and at least 14 pixels must have disparity values less than the centre pixel to classify it as a ridge point. However, shape axes near bifurcation points cannot be properly extracted because the ridges in the interior of the shape has been significantly blurred due to the multiple *EXPAND* operations used to derive $M(x,y)$. A more robust method of extracting the shape axes can be achieved by first computing $\boldsymbol{M}_V(x,y)$, the first-order Gaussian derivative of $M(x,y)$ in the x and y directions. The resulting disparity gradient map $\boldsymbol{M}_V$ is a vector consisting of the x and y derivatives given by M_V^x and M_V^y respectively. The directional disparity operator Δ in (4) is then applied to $\boldsymbol{M}_V$ to obtained an enhanced vector field disparity map $M_E(x,y)$ defined by $\Delta(\boldsymbol{M}_V, \sigma_E)$, where σ_E determines the size of the effective neighbourhood in which the vector disparity is computed. Since vectors around ridge points are always outward flowing, a landscape map $M_L(x,y)$ that highlights 'ridgeness' and 'valleyness' in the disparity map can be constructed using

$$M_L(x,y) = \sum_{i=x,y} \nabla g_{\sigma_R}^i(x,y) * M_V^i(x,y) \tag{5}$$

where the Gaussian derivative kernels $\nabla g^i{}_{\sigma R}$ are defined in (2). $M_L(x,y)$ gives large positive values at ridge points and negative values at valley points. A ridge-enhanced disparity map $M_R(x,y)$ can now be created using

$$M_R(x,y) = M_E(x,y)\, M_L(x,y) \tag{6}$$

The local maximas on the ridge-enhanced disparity map $M_R(x,y)$ are detected using the same ridge detection algorithm described earlier. Standard disparity-weighted morphological thinning is then applied to thin the extracted ridges to unit-width skeletons. The intentional use of a non homotopy-preserving local ridge detection algorithm is to encourage disconnectivity between structural and textural skeletons. However, in order to connect broken structural skeletal segments, a modified version of the *directional-uphill climbing* (DUC) algorithm proposed by Shih and Pu [12] was adopted. It employs directional information of the current skeletal end points within a small 3×3 neighborhood and it adds skeletal pixels to current end point by climbing up the slope with the steepest gradient. The DUC starts at an unconnected end point $\boldsymbol{p}$ that has the lowest disparity value $M_R(\boldsymbol{p})$. This ensures connectivity is achieved by climbing uphill towards larger disparity values. The DUC algorithm appends a skeletal point to the current end point $\boldsymbol{p}$ by determining which of the directional-neighbor has the steepest disparity gradient from $\boldsymbol{p}$. Once this neighboring point $\boldsymbol{p}_{next}$ has been identified, the DUC algorithm is then iteratively applied to $\boldsymbol{p}_{next}$ until the current neighborhood N_P contains a structural skeletal pixel. A single parameter criterion is introduced to decide if a given end point should be connected to the structural skeleton or should remain as an unconnected textural element. Given that an object is defined by a set of boundary points $B=\{\boldsymbol{b}_i\}_{i=1}^{N}$ and there is a set of skeletal end points $P=\{\boldsymbol{p}_j\}_{j=1}^{M}$ detected within its interior. To determine if DUC should be applied to end point $\boldsymbol{p}_j$, a circle c_j with radius r_j is first obtained, where r_j is given by

$$r_j = \lambda R_j, \qquad \text{where} \quad R_j = \min_{1 \le i \le N} \left\{ \left\| \boldsymbol{b}_i - \boldsymbol{p}_j \right\| \right\} \tag{7}$$

and $\| \;\|$ gives the Euclidean distance between two points. The circle c_j is termed the *λ-maximal disk* of $\boldsymbol{p}_j$ since λ relates its radius r_j to R_j, the radius of the maximal disk centred about $\boldsymbol{p}_j$. The parameter $\lambda \in (0, 1]$ is called the *connectivity factor* and is used to control the size of the λ-maximal disk. DUC is only applied to end point $\boldsymbol{p}_j$ if there exist at least one structural skeletal pixel within the λ-maximal disk region. The connectivity factor λ governs the disk's diameter and has a direct influence over the sensitivity of the process that recruits disjointed skeletal segments to form part of the structural skeleton. Typical values of $\lambda = 0.7$ were used in most of the experiments presented in section 3. Other default parameters adopted by the MGVF algorithm are $\sigma_H = 1.0$, $\sigma_D = 1.5$, $\sigma_E = 1.0$, $\sigma_R = 1.0$ and $\alpha = 0.8$, unless otherwise stated. Discussion of the effects of parameters such as α and λ is beyond the scope of this paper.

3 Experimental Results

3.1 Scale and Rotation Invariance

Fig. 2a shows the MGVF structural skeleton can be extracted consistently over scales spanning two octaves. The textural skeletons is more numerous and prominent with increasing scale but such artifacts are not problematic since they are mostly disconnected from the structural skeletons. This cannot be said of the skeletons produced by the two-pass parallel thinning algorithm of Zhang & Suen [14] in Fig. 2b and the skeleton extracted from the Euclidean distance transform (EDT) surface in Fig. 2c, which employs the squared Euclidean distance metric and the same local skeleton extraction/connectivity algorithm presented in section 2. As the scale increase, more runners were observed. In these cases, scale invariant shape analysis would require some additional post-processing such as insignificant branch pruning.

The rotation invariance of the MGVF algorithm is clearly observed in Fig. 3a since only isotropic Gaussian-based operators are employed in generating the MGVF and disparity maps. Good isotropic behavior is difficult to achieve in iterative algorithms [6]. The results from the Zhang & Suen iterative parallel algorithm in Fig. 3b produced different skeletons for shapes rotated by 30° and 45°. Skeletons extracted from distance transform are only rotationally invariant if the distance metric employed is truly Euclidean. Unfortunately, the more computationally efficient city block and chessboard distances are not rotation invariant. Since the EDT algorithm used the squared Euclidean distance metric, complete rotation invariance is observed in Fig. 3c. The least consistent result seen in Fig. 3d is from the binary morphological *bwmorph*( ) function from Matlab® version 5.3.

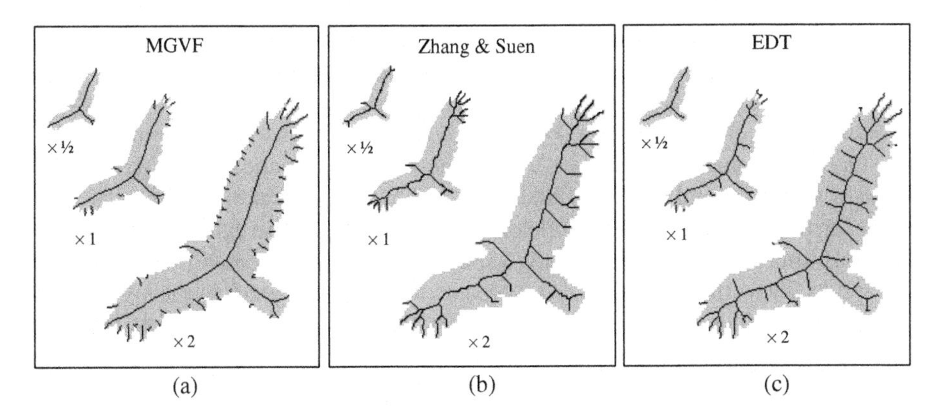

Fig. 2. Skeletons extracted at various scales indicated using (a) the proposed MGVF, (b) Zhang and Suen and (c) EDT ($\lambda = 0.7$) algorithms

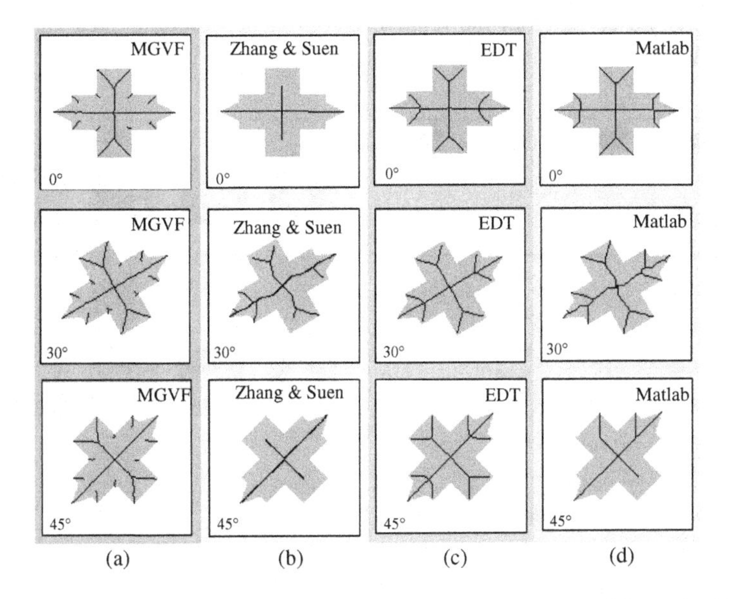

Fig. 3. Results of the rotation invariance experiment. Skeletons extracted from the (a) MGVF, (b) Zhang and Suen, (c) Euclidean distance transform and (d) Matlab®'s *bwmorph*('skel') algorithms. Rotation angles are indicated at bottom-left corner of each image.

3.2 Analysis of Boundary Texture and Boundary Noise Sensitivity

Fig. 4a shows the extracted MGVF structural and textural skeletons of four different boundary-textured hare shapes. Both these classes of skeleton remain unconnected allowing simultaneous skeletal analysis of the gross shape form and boundary textural characteristics. Another experiment was conducted to evaluate the accuracy of the MGVF skeleton in the presence of Gaussian boundary noise. A known reference skeleton with N skeletal points is first extracted from an undistorted square shape. The boundary of the square is then perturbed in the x and y directions by varying degree of zero-mean Gaussian noise with varying standard deviation σ_n. For each test image generated, the Euclidean distance between the each skeletal pixel in the reference skeleton and the closest skeletal pixel of newly extracted skeleton is computed, resulting in a distance array x_i, where $1 \le i \le N$. The standard deviation of the skeletal discrepancy as derived in [1] is computed. Fig. 4b shows the variations in the mean value of SD for the MGVF and EDT skeletons, for $0 \le \sigma_n \le 4$. The experiment was conducted 10 times and for each run, the value of σ_n was incremented by steps of 0.2. The results show that the skeletal discrepancy of skeletons extracted using the proposed MGVF algorithm is consistently lower than those extracted using the EDT algorithm, especially at higher levels of the Gaussian boundary noise. The boundary noise robustness of the skeletons extracted using the MGVF algorithm is due to the fact that the gradient vector field within the interior of the shape is derived mainly from the low spatial frequency components of the shape's boundary. The skeletal information embedded with the gradient vector field disparity is therefore less susceptible to high frequency distortions present in the noisy and jagged boundaries. This can be clearly observed from the relatively consistent structural skeletons extracted using the MGVF algorithm in Fig. 4c, even at noise levels of $\sigma_n = 4.0$.

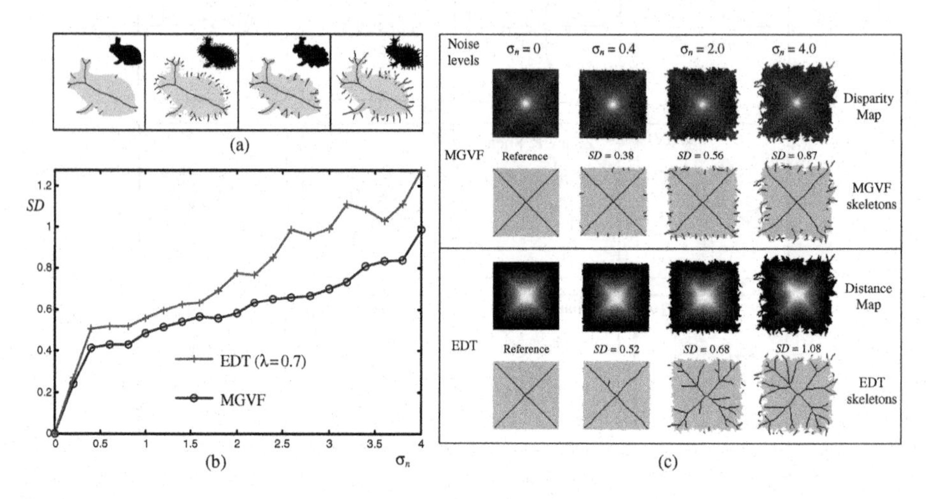

Fig. 4. (a) MGVF skeletons extracted from the boundary texture experiment with $\alpha = 0.6$. (b) Plots of standard deviation (SD) in the skeletal discrepancies of the MGVF and EDT skeletons. (c) Skeletons extracted from the disparity and distance maps at selected boundary noise levels of $\sigma_n = 0$, 0.4, 2.0 and 4.0. The SD of each extracted skeleton from their respective reference skeleton are also indicated. The skeletons at $\sigma_n = 0$ are the reference skeletons.

4 Conclusions

This paper suggests that the homotopy-preserving approach of many skeletonization algorithms may not produce medial structures suitable for robust and efficient shape representation under noisy conditions. Instead, medial representation should consist of structural and textural skeletons. It was shown that such skeletons can be recovered from the loci of local directional disparity maximas in the proposed MGVF. Advantages of the proposed dual skeletal representation were highlighted in experiments, which showed that the MGVF-based structural skeletons can be extracted consistently in the presence of boundary noise and are invariant to large scale changes and arbitrary rotation. Subsequent skeletal analysis of shapes can also be simplified by the fact that these structural skeletons, which describe the general shape of the object, remain disconnected from the numerous textural skeletons present at the boundary.

References

1. G.J. Abdel-Hamid, Y.H. Yang. Multiresolution skeletonisation: an electrostatic field-based approach. Proc. of Int. Conf. on Image Processing 1994 (1) pp. 949-953.
2. H. Blum. A transformation for extracting new descriptors of shape," in W. Wathen-Dunn, ed., Models for the Perception of Speech and Visual Form, pp. 363-380, Cambridge, MA: MIT Press, 1967.
3. P.J. Burt. The pyramid as a structure for efficient computation. in A. Rosenfeld, ed., Multiresolution Image Processing & Analysis, pp. 6-35, Berlin, Springer-Verlag, 1984.
4. B.B. Kimia, A. Tannenbaum, S.W. Zucker. Shape, shocks and deformation, i: the components of 2-d shape and the reaction-diffusion space. International Journal of Computer Vision1 5 (1995) 189-224.
5. B.B. Kimia. On the role of medial geometry in human vision, to appear in the *Journal of Physiology*, currently available online at author's web site at www.lems.brown.edu/vision/publications/Kimia's_Publication/Journal/journals.htm.
6. L. Lam, S.W. Lee and C.Y. Suen, "Thinning Methodologies – A Comprehensive Survey," IEEE Trans. on Pattern Analysis and Machine Intelligence 14 (9) (1992) 869-885.
7. R.L. Ogniewicz, O. Kübler. Hierarchic voronoi skeletons. Pattern Recognition 28 (3) (1995) 342-359.
8. S.M. Pizer, D. Eberly, D.S. Fritsch, B.S. Morse. Zoom-invariant vision of figural shape: the mathematics of cores. Computer Vision and Image Understanding 69 (1) (1998) 55-71.
9. S.M. Pizer, K. Siddiqi, G. Székely, J. N. Damon, S.W. Zucker. Multiscale medial loci and their properties. International Journal of Computer Vision 5 (2-3) (2003) 155-179.
10. T.B. Sebastian, P.N. Klein, B.B. Kimia. Recognition of shapes by editing shock graphs. IEEE Trans. on Pattern Analysis and Machine Intelligence 26 (5) (2004) 550-571.
11. D. Shaked, A.M. Bruckstein. Pruning medial axes. Computer Vision and Image Understanding 69 (2) (1998) 156-169.
12. F.Y. Shih, C.C. Pu. A skeletonization algorithm by maxim tracking on euclidean distance transform. Pattern Recognition 28 (3) (1995) 331-341.
13. K.S. Siddiqi, S. Bouix, A. Tannenbaum, S. W. Zucker. Hamilton-Jacobi skeletons. International Journal of Computer Vision 48 (3) (2002) 215-231.
14. T.Y. Zhang, C.Y. Suen. A fast parallel algorithm for thinning digital patterns. Communications of the ACM 27 (3) (1984). 236-239.

Accurate and Efficient Computation of High Order Zernike Moments

Gholamreza Amayeh, Ali Erol, George Bebis, and Mircea Nicolescu

Computer Vision Laboratory, University of Nevada, Reno, NV 89557
{amayeh, aerol, bebis, mircea}@cse.unr.edu

Abstract. Zernike Moments are useful tools in pattern recognition and image analysis due to their orthogonality and rotation invariance property. However, direct computation of these moments is very expensive, limiting their use especially at high orders. There have been some efforts to reduce the computational cost by employing quantized polar coordinate systems, which also reduce the accuracy of the moments. In this paper, we propose an efficient algorithm to accurately calculate Zernike moments at high orders. To preserve accuracy, we do not use any form of coordinate transformation and employ arbitrary precision arithmetic. The computational complexity is reduced by detecting the common terms in Zernike moments with different order and repetition. Experimental results show that our method is more accurate than other methods and it has comparable computational complexity especially in case of using large images and high order moments.

1 Introduction

Moment functions of image intensity values are used to capture global features of the image in pattern recognition and image analysis [1]. Among many moment based descriptors, Zernike moments have minimal redundancy (due to the orthogonality of basis functions [2]), rotation invariance and robustness to noise; therefore they are used in a wide range of applications on image analysis, reconstruction and recognition [3]. However, there are also some technical difficulties in the calculation of Zernike moments due to the very high computational complexity and lack of numerical precision. It is usually not possible to calculate them accurately in reasonable time when the desired moment order is high and/or the images to be processed are large.

Little attention has been paid to the efficient and accurate calculation of Zernike moments [4, 5, 6]. Mukundan et al. [4] proposed a recursive algorithm for computing the Zernike and Legendre moments in polar coordinates. Belkasim et al [5] introduced another recursive algorithm using radial and angular expansions of Zernike orthonormal polynomials. Finally in a more recent study, Gu et al. [6] employed the square to circular transformation of Mukundan et al. [4] and more efficient recursive relations to develop an even faster algorithm but its accuracy is still limited to that of [4] because of approximate coordinate transformation.

In this paper, we propose an algorithm to reduce the computation cost of Zernike moments without sacrificing accuracy. To preserve accuracy we do not

G. Bebis et al. (Eds.): ISVC 2005, LNCS 3804, pp. 462–469, 2005.

use any form of coordinate transformations and employ an arbitrary precision arithmetic library [7]. The computational complexity is reduced by computing the common terms in Zernike moments with different order and repetition only once.

In the next section, we briefly summarize the definition of Zernike moments. Then in section 3, we present our method. In section 4, the accuracy and computational complexity of our method are compared against other algorithms. Section 5 concludes the study.

2 Zernike Moments

Zernike moments are based on a set of complex polynomials that form a complete orthogonal set over the interior of the unit circle [8]. Zernike moments are defined to be the projection of the image function on these orthogonal basis functions. The basis functions $V_{n,m}(x, y)$ are given by

$$V_{n,m}(x, y) = V_{n,m}(\rho, \theta) = R_{n,m}(\rho)e^{jm\theta} \tag{1}$$

where n is a non-negative integer, m is non-zero integer subject to the constraints $n - |m|$ is even and $|m| < n$, ρ is the length of the vector from origin to (x, y), θ is the angle between vector ρ and the x-axis in a counter clockwise direction and $R_{n,m}(\rho)$ is the Zernike radial polynomial. The Zernike radial polynomials,$R_{n,m}(\rho)$, are defined as:

$$R_{n,m}(\rho) = \sum_{k=|m|,n-k=even}^{n} \frac{(-1)^{\frac{n-k}{2}} \frac{n+k}{2}!}{\frac{n-k}{2}!\frac{k+m}{2}!\frac{k-m}{2}!}\rho^k = \sum_{k=|m|,n-k=even}^{n} \beta_{n,m,k}\rho^k \tag{2}$$

Note that $R_{n,m}(\rho) = R_{n,-m}(\rho)$. The basis functions in equation 1 are orthogonal thus satisfy

$$\frac{n+1}{\pi}\iint_{x^2+y^2\leq 1} V_{n,m}(x, y)V^*_{p,q}(x, y) = \delta_{n,p}\delta_{m,q} \tag{3}$$

where

$$\delta_{a,b} = \begin{cases} 1 & a = b \\ 0 & otherwise \end{cases} \tag{4}$$

The Zernike moment of order n with repetition m for a *digital* image function $f(x, y)$ is given by [9]

$$Z_{n,m} = \frac{n+1}{\pi}\sum\sum_{x^2+y^2\leq 1} f(x, y)V^*_{n,m}(x, y) \tag{5}$$

where $V^*_{n,m}(x, y)$ is the complex conjugate of $V_{n,m}(x, y)$. To compute the Zernike moments of a given image, the image center of mass is taken to be the origin. The function $f(x, y)$ can then be reconstructed by the following truncated expansion [9]:

$$\tilde{f}(x,y) = \sum_{n=0}^{N} \frac{C_{n,0}}{2} R_{n,0}(\rho) + \sum_{n=1}^{N} \sum_{m>0} (C_{n,m} cosm\theta + S_{n,m} sinm\theta) R_{n,m}(\rho) \quad (6)$$

where N is the maximum order of Zernike moments we want to use, $C_{n,m}$ and $S_{n,m}$ denote the real and imaginary parts of $Z_{n,m}$ respectively.

3 Proposed Algorithm

A way to improve the speed of Zernike moment calculation is to use a quantized polar coordinate system. In [4] and [6], a square to a circle transformation is utilized for this purpose. In [5], for a $M \times M$ image the angles are quantized to $4M$ and radii are quantized to M levels. A side effect of quantization is that some error is introduced especially in high order Zernike moments. In our method we avoid using any quantization, therefore, it's as accurate as the classical method. We obtain speed-up by detecting common terms in Zernike moments.

By substituting equations 2 and 1 in 5 and re-organizing the terms the Zernike moments can be calculated in the following form:

$$\begin{aligned} Z_{n,m} &= \frac{n+1}{\pi} \sum \sum_{x^2+y^2 \leq 1} \left(\sum_{k=|m|}^{n} \beta_{n,m,k} \rho^k \right) e^{-jm\theta} f(x,y) \\ &= \frac{n+1}{\pi} \sum_{k=|m|}^{n} \beta_{n,m,k} \left(\sum \sum_{x^2+y^2 \leq 1} e^{-jm\theta} \rho^k f(x,y) \right) \\ &= \frac{n+1}{\pi} \sum_{k=|m|}^{n} \beta_{n,m,k} \chi_{m,k} \end{aligned} \quad (7)$$

The $\chi_{m,k}$'s defined in the equation 7 become a common term in the computation of Zernike moments with the same repetition as shown in Figure 1 for the case of repetition m=0. In general, to compute Zernike moments up to order N, we need to compute $\chi_{m,k}$ for each repetition as demonstrated in Table 1. The table shows all the $\chi_{m,k}$ to be computed for each repetition up to order 10.

$$\begin{aligned}
Z_{0,0} &= \beta_{0,0,0}\,\boxed{\chi_{0,0}} \\
Z_{2,0} &= \beta_{2,0,0}\,\boxed{\chi_{0,0}} + \beta_{2,0,2}\,\boxed{\chi_{0,2}} \\
Z_{4,0} &= \beta_{4,0,0}\,\boxed{\chi_{0,0}} + \beta_{4,0,2}\,\boxed{\chi_{0,2}} + \beta_{4,0,4}\,\boxed{\chi_{0,4}} \\
Z_{6,0} &= \beta_{6,0,0}\,\boxed{\chi_{0,0}} + \beta_{6,0,2}\,\boxed{\chi_{0,2}} + \beta_{6,0,4}\,\boxed{\chi_{0,4}} + \beta_{6,0,6}\,\boxed{\chi_{0,6}} \\
Z_{8,0} &= \beta_{8,0,0}\,\boxed{\chi_{0,0}} + \beta_{8,0,2}\,\boxed{\chi_{0,2}} + \beta_{8,0,4}\,\boxed{\chi_{0,4}} + \beta_{8,0,6}\,\boxed{\chi_{0,6}} + \beta_{8,0,8}\,\boxed{\chi_{0,8}} \\
Z_{10,0} &= \beta_{10,0,0}\,\boxed{\chi_{0,0}} + \beta_{10,0,2}\,\boxed{\chi_{0,2}} + \beta_{10,0,4}\,\boxed{\chi_{0,4}} + \beta_{10,0,6}\,\boxed{\chi_{0,6}} + \beta_{10,0,8}\,\boxed{\chi_{0,8}} + \beta_{10,0,10}\,\boxed{\chi_{0,10}}
\end{aligned}$$

Fig. 1. The common terms to compute Zernike moments up to 10 orders with zero repetition

Table 1. $\chi_{m,k}$'s needed to compute Zernike moments up to 10 order and m repetition

repetition m	$\chi_{m,k}$
0	$\chi_{0,0}, \chi_{0,2}, \chi_{0,4}, \chi_{0,6}, \chi_{0,8}, \chi_{0,10}$
1	$\chi_{1,1}, \chi_{1,3}, \chi_{1,5}, \chi_{1,7}, \chi_{1,9}$
2	$\chi_{2,2}, \chi_{2,4}, \chi_{2,6}, \chi_{2,8}, \chi_{2,10}$
3	$\chi_{3,3}, \chi_{3,5}, \chi_{3,7}, \chi_{3,9}$
4	$\chi_{4,4}, \chi_{4,6}, \chi_{4,8}, \chi_{4,10}$
5	$\chi_{5,5}, \chi_{5,7}, \chi_{5,9}$
6	$\chi_{6,6}, \chi_{6,8}, \chi_{6,10}$
7	$\chi_{7,7}, \chi_{7,9}$
8	$\chi_{8,8}, \chi_{8,10}$
9	$\chi_{9,9}$
10	$\chi_{10,10}$

Table 2. The difference between magnitude of Zernike moments computed by classical method using double precision and *Big Number class* variables

Order , repetition	0	2	4	6	8	10	...	40	42	44	46	48	50
42	7.28e-4	6.60e-4	1.91e-4	2.72e-4	1.72e-4	6.54e-6	...	1.17e-17	3.82e-17				
44	3.50e-3	5.57e-3	1.11e-3	1.18e-3	1.05e-4	1.49e-4	...	1.52e-15	1.30e-17	1.04e-17			
46	3.97e-1	6.48e-3	5.25e-3	2.04e-3	2.57e-3	1.07e-3	...	2.12e-14	1.48e-15	9.06e-17	2.60e-18		
48	1.86e0	6.91e-2	4.39e-2	2.83e-2	1.66e-2	3.50e-3	...	5.23e-14	5.92e-14	3.11e-16	1.20e-16	3.47e-18	
50	1.38e1	1.81e0	1.06e-1	9.39e-2	6.92e-2	7.12e-2	...	7.52e-12	2.67e-13	1.60e-14	8.60e-16	4.65e-17	2.17e-18

The second row of the table corresponds to the $\chi_{m,k}$ shown in Figure 1. Once all the entries in the table 1 are computed, Zernike moments with any order and repetition can be calculated as a linear combination of $\chi_{m,k}$ as shown in equation 7. Also note that the coefficients $\beta_{n,m,k}$ does not depend on the image or the coordinates; therefore, they are stored on a small lookup table to save further computation.

Another important issue in high order Zernike moment computation is numerical precision. Depending on the image size and the maximum order, double precision arithmetic does not provide enough precision. This fact is demonstrated in table 2, which shows the magnitude of the difference between Zernike moments computed using double precision and arbitrary precision arithmetic for a 300×300 image up to order 50. It can be seen that the error becomes more and more significant with increasing order and decreasing repetition. Figure 3 shows the effect of this error on the orthogonality of basis functions. It can be clearly seen that in Figure 2(a) ,which is obtained using the double precision, equation 3 is violated to a great extent while in Figure 2(b), which is obtained using arbitrary precision, the orthogonality is preserved.

To calculate the computational complexity of our algorithm, let the size of the image be $M \times M$ pixels, and the maximum order of Zernike moments be N. At the beginning we need M^2N multiplications to compute $\rho^k f(x,y)$ for $k = 0, 1, ..., N$ for once. Note that for $k = 0$ we don't need any multiplication. In

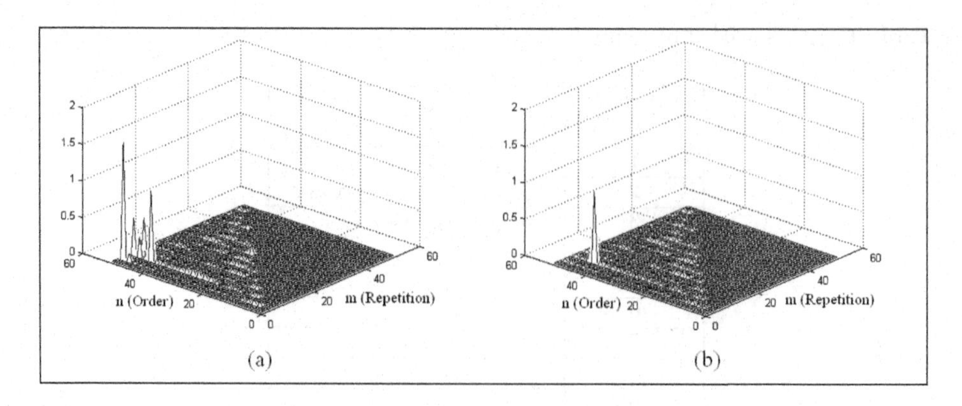

Fig. 2. Dot product of basis function with $n = 43, m = 7$ and other basis functions up to order 50 using (a) double precision and (b) arbitrary precision arithmetic

the next step, we must compute $\chi_{m,k} = \sum_x \sum_y e^{-jm\theta} \rho^k f(x,y)$. The number of $\chi_{m,k}$ to compute Zernike moments up to $N(even)$ order is $\frac{N}{2}(\frac{N}{2}+1)$. As there is no need for any multiplication for $m = 0$ and $\chi_{m,k}$ is a complex number, this step requires $M^2N(\frac{N}{2}+1)$ multiplications and $2(M^2-1)(\frac{N}{2}+1)^2$ additions. For large N and M the number of multiplications and additions to compute $Z_{n,m}$ according equation 7 is negligible.

4 Experimental Results

We compare the accuracy of the existing algorithms [4, 6, 5] and our algorithm based on the fidelity of reconstruction. The test image that we used in our experiments is shown in Figure 3. This is a 64×64 image and Zernike moments up to order 40 are utilized for reconstruction. Figures 4(a), 4(b) and 4(c) show the results of Mukundan's [4], Gu's [6] and our method respectively. It can be seen that the former two algorithms give poor reconstructions mainly because of the square to circle transformation. The effect of the transformation is clearly visible in the reconstructed images.

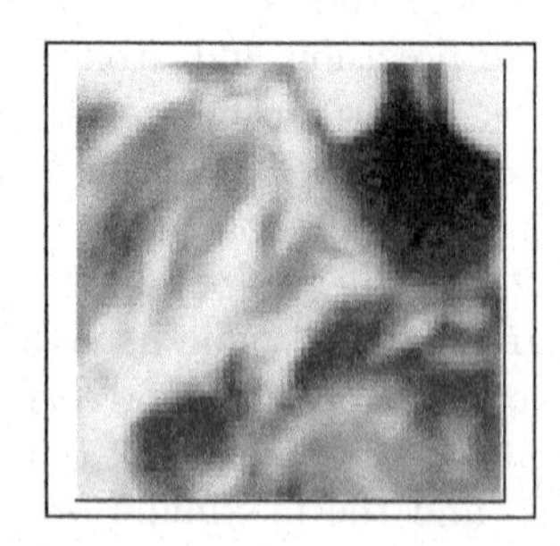

Fig. 3. Original gray level image

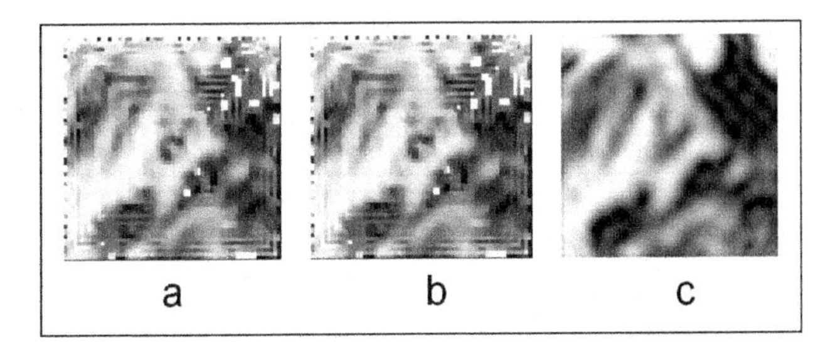

Fig. 4. The reconstructed images using the moment of order up to 40 by (a) Mukundan's method, (b) Gu's method and (c) our method

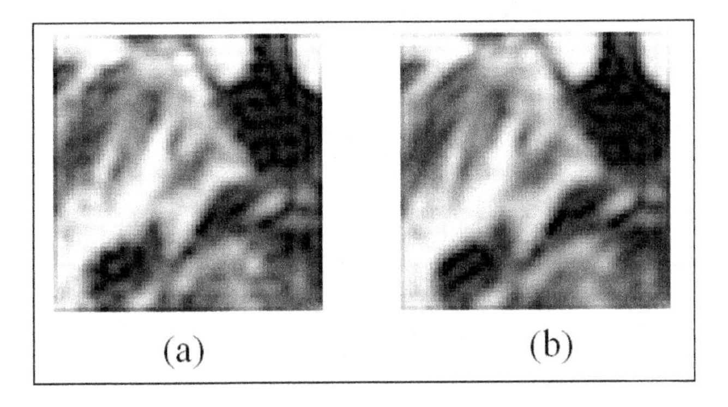

Fig. 5. The reconstructed images using the moment of order up to 60 by (a) Belkasim's method and (b) our method

The reconstruction result of Belkasim's [5] method using Zernike moments up to order 60 is shown in Figure 5(a). We used arbitrary precision arithmetic in the implementation of Belkasim's method as well. Our method's output is shown in Figure 5(b). It is possible to see that the Belkasim's method introduces some distortions at the edges. Our method's output is smoother in general. To make the difference more clear we computed reconstruction errors at different orders for the two algorithms. The error is computed using:

$$\varepsilon_r = \frac{\sum_x \sum_y |\tilde{f}(x,y) - f(x,y)|^2}{\sum_x \sum_y f(x,y)^2} \tag{8}$$

where $f(x,y)$ is the original image function and $\tilde{f}(x,y)$ is the reconstructed image. Table 3 shows the results of error computation. We would expect the error to decrease with the increasing order and our method (See column 1) behaves as expected; however, the behaviour of Belkasim's method is quite different, which shows that the quantization of polar coordinates has its effect mainly at higher order moments.

Table 3. Reconstruction error of Figure 3 by our method and Belkasim's method

Order	Our method	Belkasim's method
35	0.0647	0.0648
40	0.0621	0.0628
45	0.0596	0.063
50	0.0370	0.0557
55	0.0203	0.0645
60	0.0133	0.0665

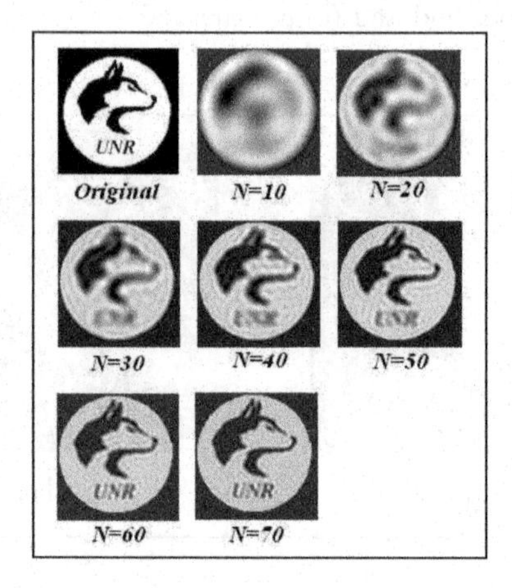

Fig. 6. Original image and reconstructions using different orders of Zernike moments

High order Zernike moments are used when there is a need to capture the details of the image. Figure 6 demonstrates this behavior using a 300×300 binary logo shown at the top left corner of the figure. Other images show reconstruction results using different orders. The reconstructed images up to order 20 only contains a rough silhouette of the wolf. In reconstructions up to order 50, it is possible to see the head of wolf. At order 50, the head of the wolf is clearly visible but letters in the logo are still blurred. At order 70 it becomes possible to see the letters clearly.

Table 4. The comparison of the computational complexity of different methods

	Number of Addition	Number of Multiplication
Mukundan's method	$\frac{N^2M^2}{2} + \frac{1}{8}NM^3$	$2N^2 + N^2M^2 + \frac{1}{4}MN^3$
Belkasim's method	$N(M+2)(M-1)$	$\frac{N^2M^2}{2} + 2MN$
Gu's method	$\frac{3}{8}N^2M + 2NM^2 + \frac{1}{12}N^3M + \frac{1}{4}N^2M^2$	$\frac{N^2M}{2} + 2M^2N$
Our method	$2(\frac{N}{2}+1)^2(M^2-1)$	$\frac{N^2M^2}{2} + 2M^2N$

Table 4 shows the number of multiplication and addition needed in our method and the others for $M \times M$ image using moments up to order N. It is clear that our method is not the fastest method; however, it is not extremely slow either. In our method, the number of multiplications stands close to Belkasim's method for large images ($M \gg 1$) and high order moments ($N \gg 1$).

5 Conclusion

We designed and implemented an accurate and efficient algorithm for high order Zernike moment calculation. We were able to compute very high order Zernike moments with reasonable computational complexity while preserving accuracy. According to the definition of Zernike moments for a digital image (See Equation 5) our computation is exact. The computational efficiency is provided by detection of common terms in Zernike moments. In our experimental results we also pointed out that polar coordinate quantization and double precision arithmetic are important sources of error in high order Zernike moment calculation.

Acknowledgments

This work was supported by NASA under grant # NCC5-583.

References

1. Prokop, R.J., Reeves, A.P.: A survey of moment based techniques for unoccluded object representation. Graph. Models Image ProcessCVGIP **Vol. 54,No. 5** (1992) 438 460.
2. Teague, M.R.: Image analysis via the general theory of moments. J. Opt. Soc. Am. **Vol. 70,Issue. 8** (1980) 920 930.
3. Teh, C.H., Chin, R.T.: On image analysis by the method of moments. IEEE Trans. Pattern Anal. Mach. Intell. **Vol. 10** (1988) 485 513.
4. Mukundan, R., Ramakrishnan, K.: Fast computation of legendre and zernike moments. Pattern Recognition **Vol. 28,No. 9** (1995) 1433 1442.
5. Belkasim, S.O., Ahmadi, M., Shridhar, M.: Efficient algorithm for fast computation of zernike moments. IEEE 39th Midwest symposium on Circuits and Systems **Vol. 3** (18-21 Aug. 1996) 1401 – 1404.
6. Gu, J., Shua, H.Z., Toumoulinb, C., Luoa, L.M.: A novel algorithm for fast computation of zernike moments. Pattern Recognition **Vol. 35** (2002) 2905 2911.
7. GMP: (GNU multiple precision arithmetic library) *http://www.swox.com/gmp.*
8. Zernike, F.: Physica. (1934)
9. Khotanzad, A., Hong, Y.H.: Invariant image recognition by zernike moments. IEEE Trans. on Pattern Anal. and Machine Intell. **Vol. 12** (1990) 489 – 498.

3D Model Generation from Image Sequences Using Global Geometric Constraint

Masayuki Mukunoki, Kazutaka Yasuda, and Naoki Asada

Department of Intelligent Systems,
Hiroshima City University, Hiroshima 731-3194, Japan
{mukunoki, kazutaka, asada}@cv.its.hiroshima-cu.ac.jp
http://www.cv.its.hiroshima-cu.ac.jp/

Abstract. This paper describes a method for generating a three-dimensional model from an uncalibrated image sequence taken around an object. Our method is based on feature tracking and minimization of re-projection errors. To cope with mis-matchings in the result of feature tracking, we introduce two types of global geometric constraints. The one is "affine constraint" which imposes the positional relationship between pixels on the images. The other is "depth constraint" which imposes the three-dimensional structure of the object. First, we use the affine constraint to reconstruct the object roughly and then we refine the feature tracking and shape reconstruction using the depth constraint. Experimental results show that our method can automatically generate accurate three-dimensional models from real image sequences.

1 Introduction

Generating 3D models of real objects is the central concern in computer vision, and many works have been done to recover 3D information from image sequences. When intrinsic and extrinsic camera parameters are known, 3D shape information of the object can be recovered using the geometric relationships between cameras[1],[2]. When the extrinsic camera parameters are unknown, they must be also recovered from the feature points extracted from images[3],[4],[5]. We focus on the latter cases. Most of the methods so far assume that the result of calibration is correct. However, the matching of feature points usually include several errors because of the feature extraction errors, tracking errors, quantization errors of pixel sampling, and so on. As the result, the extrinsic camera parameters and the object shape are poorly reconstructed.

In this paper, we describe a method for generating a three-dimensional model from an image sequence taken around an object, where the extrinsic camera parameters (camera motion) are unknown, while the intrinsic ones are given. Our method is based on feature tracking and minimization of re-projection errors. The method using the minimization of re-projection errors is quite robust for small amount of errors in the feature tracking. However, if the tracking results contain large errors, we cannot reconstruct the object shape. We additionally introduce two types of global geometric constraints. At first, we introduce the "affine constraint" which approximate the transformation between two images by affine transform and restrict the search area for feature tracking within the neighbor of transformed position of the point. Secondly, we reconstruct the

G. Bebis et al. (Eds.): ISVC 2005, LNCS 3804, pp. 470–477, 2005.

object shape and camera motion from the feature tracking result by minimizing the re-projection errors. Then we eliminate the feature points that have large re-projection errors since such feature points can be wrong matching and decrease the accuracy of the reconstruction. Thirdly, we apply the "depth constraint" which imposes the three-dimensional structure of the reconstructed object. We repeat the second and third stages and refine the feature tracking and shape reconstruction. Finally, we generate a three-dimensional model with texture mapping.

2 3D Model Generation

2.1 Initial Feature Tracking Using Affine Constraint

First, feature points are extracted from each image by Harris operator[6]. We denote the two images of interest as I and I'(Fig. 1). Each feature point P extracted from I is compared with the feature points Q from I' using the Sum of Square Differences (SSD).

$$SSD(P,Q) = \sum_{(u,v)\in\Omega,(u',v')\in\Omega'} |I(u,v) - I'(u',v')|^2,$$

where Ω and Ω' are neighboring region of P and Q respectively, and $I(u,v)$ and $I'(u',v')$ are pixel values at the (u,v) and (u',v') of image I and I' respectively.

These points are corresponded in the order of SSD. Here, we introduce the affine constraint. The 3×3 affine transform matrix A is calculated using the global matching of the images.

$$\arg\min_{A} \sum_{(u,v)} |I(u,v) - I'(u',v')|^2,$$
$$\text{where} \quad [u' \ v' \ 1]^\top = A\,[u \ v \ 1]^\top .$$

We calculate above equation by two steps. In the first step, only the translation parameters are changed all over the image and the optimum parameters are obtained. Then the all 6 parameters of the affine transform is optimized using the gradient descent algorithm where the initial parameters are set as the obtained translation parameters.

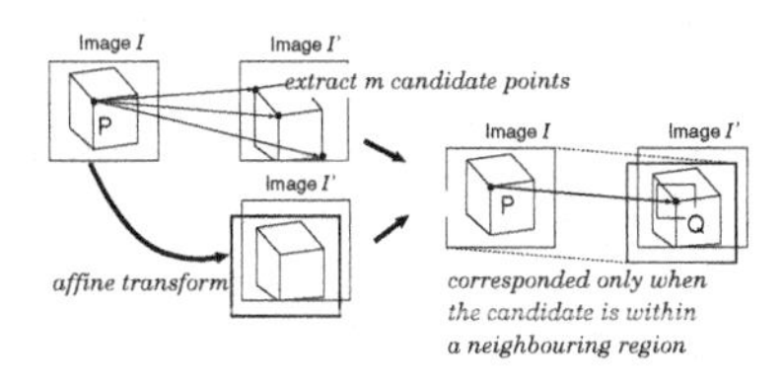

Fig. 1. Feature tracking using affine constraint

A feature point Q are corresponded to P only when Q has within the m-th smallest SSD and Q is transformed by affine matrix A within the d-pixels away from P. In the experiments, we use m=5 and d=15.

2.2 Shape Reconstruction

When the result of feature tracking is given, we reconstruct the object shape and camera motion by minimizing the re-projection errors[7][8].

Suppose objects are represented by a set of feature points whose 3D coordinates $\boldsymbol{s}_p$ $(p = 1 \cdots P)$ are defined in the world coordinates, and those feature points are projected onto the fth image $(f = 1 \cdots F)$ (Fig. 2). 2D coordinates of the projected pth point on the fth image are denoted by $\boldsymbol{u}_{fp}$. Note that when the pth point is not observed from the fth camera, the corresponding $\boldsymbol{u}_{fp}$ is undefined in the fth image.

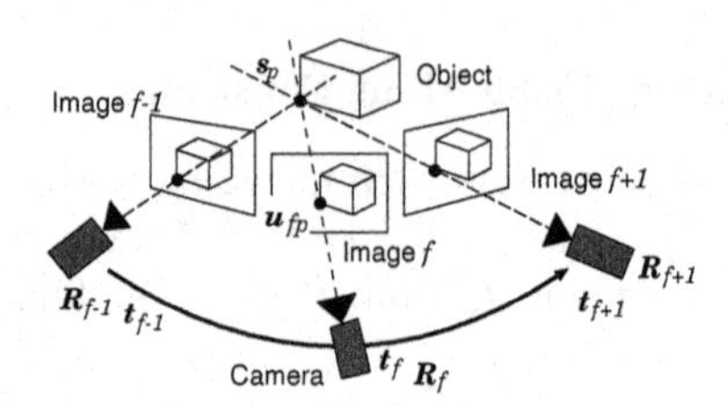

Fig. 2. Shape reconstruction

The pose and position (motion) of the fth camera are represented by the rotation matrix R_f and translation vector $\boldsymbol{t}_f$. The perspective projection operator $\mathcal{P}$ is defined by $\mathcal{P}(x, y, z)^T = \frac{l}{z}(x, y)^T$, where l is the focal length of the camera. Using these notations, reconstruction of object shape and camera motion is formulated by minimizing the re-projection error $E(\boldsymbol{x})$, as follows.

$$E(\boldsymbol{x}) = \sum_{(f,p)} |\mathcal{P}[R_f \boldsymbol{s}_p + \boldsymbol{t}_f] - \boldsymbol{u}_{fp}|^2 \tag{1}$$

where $\boldsymbol{x}$ denotes a composite vector consisting of $\boldsymbol{s}_p$, $\boldsymbol{q}_f$, $\boldsymbol{t}_f$, where $\boldsymbol{q}_f$ is a quaternion representation of the rotation matrix. Since Eq.(1) includes non-linear representation such as perspective projection, the problem is solved by using non-linear optimization method, e.g. Levenberg-Marquardt algorithm, preconditioned conjugate gradient one[9].

In order to solve the non-linear optimization problem stably, we need appropriate initial values that lead to the global minimum of re-projection error function $E(\boldsymbol{x})$. In our study, we assume that the image sequence is taken from a camera that moves around the object. This camera motion is modeled as a uniform motion along circular path with gazing at the center where the object is located. Based on this idea, we define the generalized initial values for circular motion, as follows.

$$R_f = R(\omega f),\ \boldsymbol{t}_f = (0, 0, r)^T,\ \boldsymbol{s}_p = (0, 0, 0) \tag{2}$$

where the fth camera is located on a circle of radius r with gazing at the center. ω indicates the motion direction and step of every one frame. Since the object shape is unknown at the beginning, the initial shape is given by $\boldsymbol{s}_p = (0, 0, 0)$ which means all feature points meet at the center of the circle; that is, object is reduced to a point. While this setting of initial values is very simple, it works successfully for many image sequences taken by the circular motion[10].

The principle of shape reconstruction by minimizing the re-projection errors is very simple but it gives the optimum result in terms of maximum likelihood estimation for the pixel errors. The method is same as the so called "bundle adjustment[8]", and widely used for refining and/or integrating the initial and/or partial reconstruction result obtained by other method. We directly apply this method for both of initial reconstruction and refinement steps since it can reconstruct reasonable shape and camera motion even when a small amount of errors exists in the feature tracking result.

On the other hand, the result of feature tracking contains several mis-matchings, which leads to large amount of errors. In general, robust estimation method, such as LMedS estimation or M-estimation[11], is used to cope with this. However, when we use these methods, the convergence of the nonlinear optimization becomes worse and it takes more computational cost. We use the affine constraint for initial feature tracking, which suppresses the outliers. Thus, we directly apply the nonlinear optimization. After the optimization is converged, we calculate the re-projection error for each feature point and delete the point if its re-projection error is large. After that, we again apply the nonlinear optimization to the rest feature points and obtain the object shape and camera motion.

2.3 Refinement of Reconstruction Using Depth Constraint

Once the object shape and camera motion are reconstructed, we refine them using the depth constraint.

In order to calculate the depth from the camera to the object at each pixel, we make a surface model from the reconstructed feature points. Suppose the feature points are expressed by the 3D coordinates that are centered at the object center and the z-axis is along the object height direction. The feature points are projected to the cylindrical coordinates in order to apply the 2D Delaunay method. When a feature points is expressed (x, y, z) in 3D coordinates, its projection to the cylindrical coordinates is (R, θ), where

$$R = z \qquad \theta = \tan^{-1} \frac{y}{x}.$$

In cylindrical coordinates, θ and $\theta + 2\pi$ denotes the same position. Considering this, feature points projected near the $\theta = -\pi$ and $\theta = \pi$ are also projected to the $\theta + 2\pi$ and $\theta - 2\pi$ respectively. Then we apply 2D Delaunay method. Finally, we delete the duplicated surfaces and generate the surface model.

Once the surface model is generated, the depth for each pixel can be calculated. The search area of feature tracking is limited within the following area:

$$\begin{bmatrix} u' \\ v' \end{bmatrix} = \mathcal{P} \left[R' \hat{\lambda} \begin{pmatrix} u \\ v \\ l \end{pmatrix} + \boldsymbol{t}' \right] + \begin{bmatrix} 0 \\ \alpha \end{bmatrix}$$
$$where \quad \hat{\lambda} \in [\lambda - \delta, \lambda + \delta] \tag{3}$$

R' and $\boldsymbol{t}'$ denotes the camera motion of image I' relative to image I and l is the focus length. λ is the depth of the feature point in the image I and δ is the search area along the depth. Theoretically, the matching feature points lies on the epipolar line. However, the estimated camera motion contains some errors. To cope with this, we also search the feature points along the vertical direction to the image. α denotes this search area. (Note that this should be vertical to the epipolar line, but for simplicity we employ this setting. Epipolar lines are usually horizontal to the image in our camera motion.)

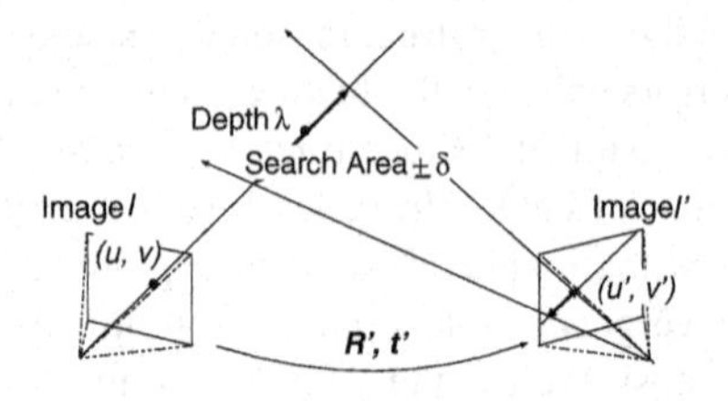

Fig. 3. Feature tracking using depth constraint

Feature points are extracted from image I and the matching is searched from image I' of the area restricted by the depth constraint using the SSD. This is done to all the successive pair of images and the new feature tracking result is obtained. The shape reconstruction and the feature tracking are repeated until the number of extracted feature points is converged.

2.4 Texture Mapping

In order to generate 3D model, texture is mapped onto the surface model. For each patch of surface, the texture is extracted from the image where all the vertexes of the patch can be observed and the area of the projected patch is the maximum.

3 Experiments

In order to evaluate the applicability and characteristics of our method, we apply our method to a real image sequence. The object is a model house with $10 \times 8 \times 12cm$ large. We take 25 images around the object, each of which has 720×480 pixels.

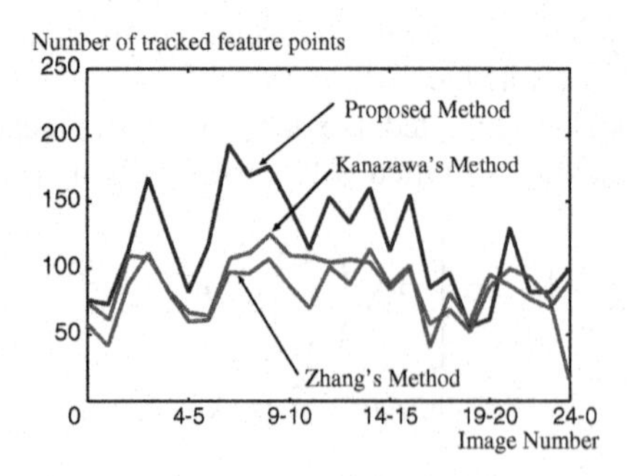

Fig. 4. Number of tracking points by Zhang's method, Kanazawa's one and the proposed one(affine constraint)

Fig. 4 shows the number of tracked feature points for each image. For comparison, we applied Zhang's method[12] and Kanazawa's method[13] to the same image sequence. The mean number of tracked feature points was 113 points by our method (with affine constraint) and 78 points by Zhang's method and 87 points by Kanazawa's method. Fig. 5 is another example for demonstrating the characteristics of our method. Zhang's method can track smaller number of feature points and the points are not

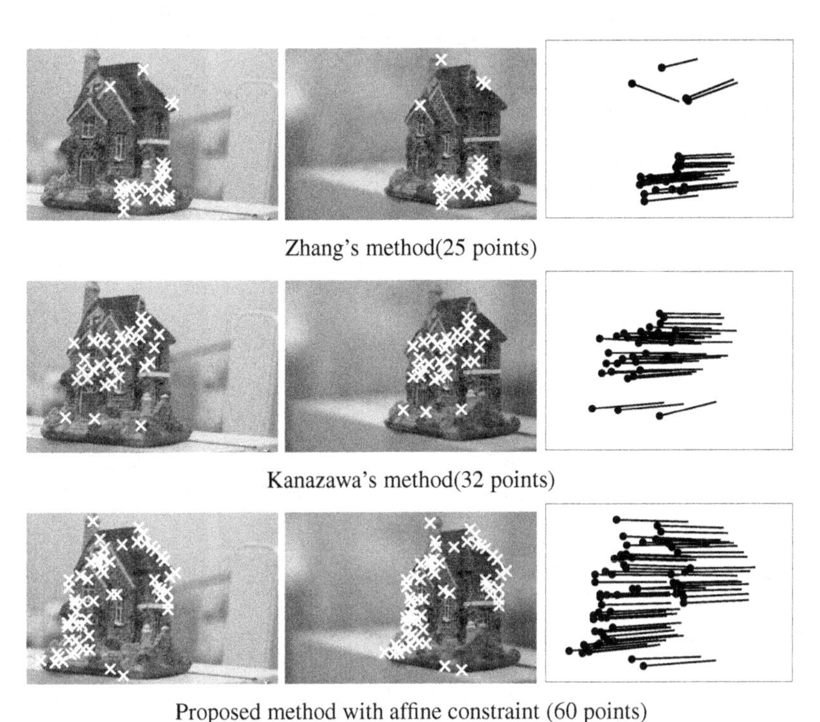

Fig. 5. Feature points and optical flow

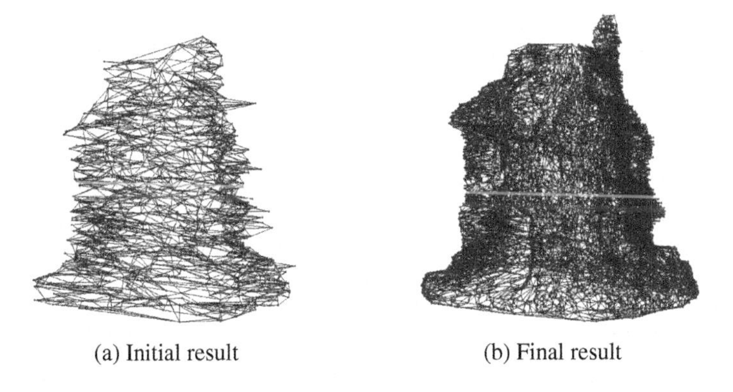

Fig. 6. Reconstruction result

Fig. 7. Generated 3D model

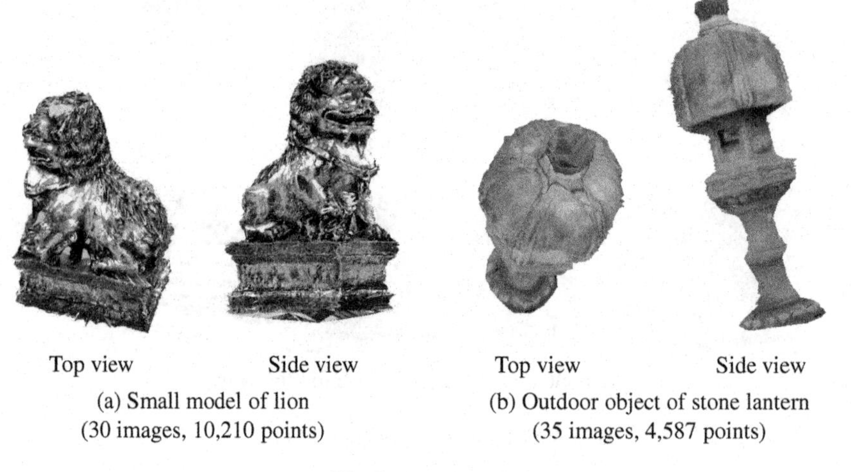

Fig. 8. Other results

uniformly distributed on the object. The optical flow obtained by our method shows that the result of our method does not contain obvious outliers. Although Kanazawa's method does not contain obvious outliers as well, it apts to track smaller number of feature points.

Fig. 6(a) shows the initial reconstruction result using affine constraint. The result consists of 1,294 unique feature points. The initial result holds the substantial object shape and camera motion although it contains some errors and the generated model is rough.

Fig. 6(b) shows the final reconstruction result using depth constraint. The result consists of 15,751 unique feature points. Fig. 7 shows the generated 3D model with texture mapping. Fig. 8 shows the other results of generated 3D models. We can automatically generate these 3D models from the given image sequences.

4 Conclusion

We have proposed a stepwise refinement approach for 3D shape reconstruction. We employed the minimization of re-projection errors for shape reconstruction method and introduced two types of global constraints. We could stably obtain initial reconstruction using affine constraint and refine it using depth constraint. Our procedure has applied to several kinds of real image sequences and we can obtain fine 3D models. We think our method is applicable to relatively wide variety of real image sequences.

At present, we assume that the camera motion is circular around the object. The texture on the top of the object cannot be obtained under this camera motion. It is remained as future works to use the images from every direction for reconstruction and 3D model generation.

References

1. L. Matthies, T. Kanade and R. Szeliski: "Kalman filter-based algorithms for estimating depth from image sequences," *International Journal of Computer Vision*, vol. 3, pp. 209–239, 1989.
2. G. L. Gimel'farb and R. M. Haralick: "Terrain reconstruction from multiple views," *Proc. 7th Int. Conf. on Computer Analysis of Images and Patterns (CAIP'97)*, LNCS 1296, Springer, pp. 694–701, 1997.
3. P. Beardsley, P. Torr and A. Zisserman: "3D Model Acquisition from Extended Image Sequences," *Proc. ECCV'96,* Cambridge, UK., vol. 2, pp. 683–695, 1996.
4. R. Koch, M. Pollefeys and L. V. Gool: "Multi Viewpoint Stereo from Uncalibrated Video Sequences," *Proc. ECCV'98*, LNCS, Springer, pp. 55–71, 1998.
5. R. Hartley and A. Zisserman, : "Multiple View Geometry in Computer Vision,"*Cambridge University Press*, Cambridge, U.K, 2000.
6. C. Harris and M. Stephens: "A Combined Corner and Edge Detector," *Proc. Alvey Vision Conf.*, pp. 147–151, 1988.
7. R. Szeliski and S. B. Kang: "Recovering 3D Shape and Motion from Image Streams using Non-Linear Least Squares," CVPR, pp.752–753, (1993).
8. B. Triggs, P.F. McLauchlan, R.I.Hartley, A. W. Fitzgibbon: "Bundle Adjustment – A Modern Synthesis," Vision Algorithms: Theory and Practice, LNCS 1883, Springer, pp.298-375 2000.
9. A. Amano, T. Migita and N. Asada: "Stable Recovery of Shape and Motion from Partially Tracked Feature Points with Fast Nonlinear Optimization," *Proc on Vision Interface*, pp. 244–251, 2002.
10. N. Asada, M. Mukunoki, T. Migita, M. Aoyama: "Large Object Shape Recovery from Uncalibrated Camera Motion by Non-Linear Optimization," *Proc. Int. Conf. on Signal and Image Processing*, pp.151-156, 2004.
11. Z. Zhang: "Determining The Epipolar Geometry And Its Uncertainty: A Review," *IJCV*, **27**, pp. 161–195, 1998.
12. Z. Zhang, R. Deriche, O. Faugeras and Q.-T. Luong : "A robust technique for matching two uncalibrated images through the recovery of the unknown epipolar geometry," *Proc. 3rd Artif. Intell.*, **78**, pp. 87–119, 1995
13. Y. Kanazawa and K. Kanatani: "Robust Image Matching Preserving Global Consistency", Proc. 6th ACCV, pp.1128–1133, 2004.

Efficient Shot Boundary Detection for Action Movies Using Blockwise Motion-Based Features

Min-Ho Park[1], Rae-Hong Park[2], and Sang Wook Lee[3]

[1] Dept. of Electronic Engineering, Sogang University, Sinsu Dong, Mapo-Gu, Seoul, Korea
minhohihi@sogang.ac.kr

[2] Dept. of Electronic Engineering and Interdisciplinary Program of Integrated Biotechnology, Sogang University, Sinsu Dong, Mapo-Gu, Seoul, Korea
rhpark@sogang.ac.kr

[3] Dept. of Media Technology, Sogang University, Sinsu Dong, Mapo-Gu, Seoul, Korea
slee@sogang.ac.kr

Abstract. Conventional shot boundary detection (SBD) algorithms have limitations in handling video data that contain fast illumination changes or rapid motions of objects and background. This paper presents a SBD algorithm that is efficient for action movies/videos. A measure of discontinuity in camera and object/background motion is proposed for SBD based on the combination of two motion features: the modified displaced frame difference (DFD) and the blockwise motion similarity. A variant of the block matching algorithm (BMA) is developed for the former and we find that it is a robust SBD feature for fast motion video. The latter measures the similarity of motion directions of small local region such as macroblock (MB). Experimental results with seven test action movies show the effectiveness of the proposed algorithm. The proposed features can be easily applied to compressed video.

1 Introduction

The huge amount of digital multimedia content available today in digital libraries and on the Internet requires adequate tools for efficiently accessing such data. Shot boundary detection (SBD) is a critical step for efficient video search and browsing, and a large number of SBD algorithms have been developed. Most SBD methods are reasonably effective for the specific types of video data they are developed for, however it is inconceivable that a single algorithm based on a low-level image feature can identify all types of scene transitions in general video sequences as human viewers can do. We note that most of the previous algorithms have their limitations in handling videos that contain rapid illumination changes or fast moving objects and background. In this paper, we focus on the problem of SBD in video sequences with fast moving objects/background such as action movies.

A commonly used method for SBD computes the absolute difference of pixel intensity between frames k and k+1 [1], [2]. This method is easy and fast but gives an incorrect result when the sequence contains abrupt changes in illumination, camera motion, or object motions. An improved method [3] uses motion estimation to avoid

G. Bebis et al. (Eds.): ISVC 2005, LNCS 3804, pp. 478–485, 2005.

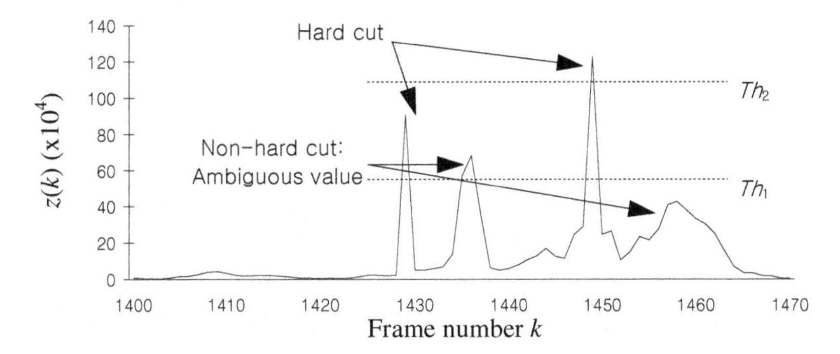

Fig. 1. Conventional discontinuity value $z(k)$ as a function of the frame index, showing the difficulty of optimal threshold selection

performance degradation by motions. This approach considers both camera and object motions, however, still shows low detection performance in action movies. Other motion-based methods [4], [5], [6] consider dominant or global camera motions and detect shot boundaries by finding abrupt changes in dominant motions.

Although the methods mentioned above consider global or local motions such as camera motion or object motion, the detection performance is sensitive to fast motion as in action movies [7]. The image frames in a video sequence are easily blurred by fast motion, and the conventional features computed from the blurred images are often ineffective for determining whether the frame is a shot boundary or not. Fig. 1 shows some discontinuity measure plotted as a function of frame index and illustrates the optimal threshold selection for SBD. A discontinuity measure is usually computed using image features such as color, edge, shape, motion or their combination. With a low (high) threshold value Th_1 (Th_2), false detection or miss detection occurs due to the ambiguous discontinuity value. Recent work [8] uses adaptive thresholding to overcome this problem but with limited effectiveness. Instead of varying thresholds adaptively, our approach is to develop special motion features suitable for SBD in the presence of fast moving objects/background. This paper addresses the problem of false/miss detection of shot boundaries in fast-motion action scenes and presents a new algorithm that can overcome the problem. The algorithm reduces the possibility of miss/false detection using the proposed motion-based features: the modified displaced frame difference (DFD) and the blockwise motion similarity.

The rest of the paper is organized as follows. In Section 2, two new features, modified DFD and blockwise motion similarity, are presented. In Section 3, experimental results are shown and in Section 4 conclusions are given.

2 Proposed Motion-Based Features

In this section, two new features are presented that are sensitive to shot boundaries: the modified DFD and the blockwise motion similarity. The discontinuity measure for SBD is proposed based on the combination of the two features.

2.1 Modified DFD

As mentioned above, the DFD has been widely used as a measure of discontinuity, because motion-based difference defined between two successive frames is a more efficient feature than other intensity-based feature. The blockwise DFD $d_i(u_i,v_i,k)$ computed by the block matching algorithm (BMA) [9] is defined by

$$d_i(u_i,v_i,k) = \min_{-M \le u,v \le M} \frac{1}{M^2} \sum_{x=0}^{M-1} \sum_{y=0}^{M-1} (I_i(x+u, y+v, k+1) - I_i(x,y,k))^2 \tag{1}$$

where $I_i(x,y,k)$ signifies the intensity at (x,y) of $M \times M$ macroblock (MB) i at frame k, and u and v denote horizontal and vertical displacements, respectively. The framewise DFD $d(k)$ at frame k is computed by averaging the blockwise DFD:

$$d(k) = \frac{1}{N_b} \sum_{i=1}^{N_b} d_i(u_i,v_i,k) \tag{2}$$

where u_i and v_i signify the horizontal and vertical components of the motion vector (MV) for MB i, respectively, and $N_b=XY/M^2$ denotes the number of MBs at frame k with $X \times Y$ signifying the image size. The DFD value at a shot boundary is high whereas low at a non-shot boundary. It is useful when video sequences have slow motions and constant illumination. But the DFD value obtained from fast motion sequences such as action movies is too ambiguous for accurate SBD because blur produced by fast motion gives motion estimation errors. Most sequences in movies are somewhat blurred because the exposure time of movie cameras is long enough to produce blurring, in which motion blur cannot be ignored.

We assume that the DFD in a motion-blurred image is larger than that in a non-blurred image [10], and that the larger the motion magnitude, the higher the DFD. To get a DFD value for accurate SBD, we propose a modified DFD by employing the motion magnitude term and the distribution of the DFD value that is computed in a sliding window with length N+1 (N: even). First, we simply divide the conventional blockwise DFD $d_i(u_i,v_i,k)$ by the motion magnitude. The normalized DFD $d^*(k)$ at frame k is defined as

$$d^*(k) = \frac{1}{N_b} \sum_{i=1}^{N_b} d_i^*(k) \tag{3}$$

where

$$d_i^*(k) = \begin{cases} d_i(u_i,v_i,k), & \text{if } u_i(k) = v_i(k) = 0 \\ d_i(u_i,v_i,k) / \sqrt{u_i(k)^2 + v_i(k)^2}, & \text{otherwise} \end{cases} \tag{4}$$

is the modified DFD for MB i. In the video sequences we tested, we observed that the normalized DFDs $d^*(k)$s due to fast motion are reduced to some degree while those due to shot boundaries are not significantly affected. Therefore, the normalization in equation (4) reduces ambiguous values that yield false classification in fast motion video and diminishes the possibility of false detection at shot boundaries. We can

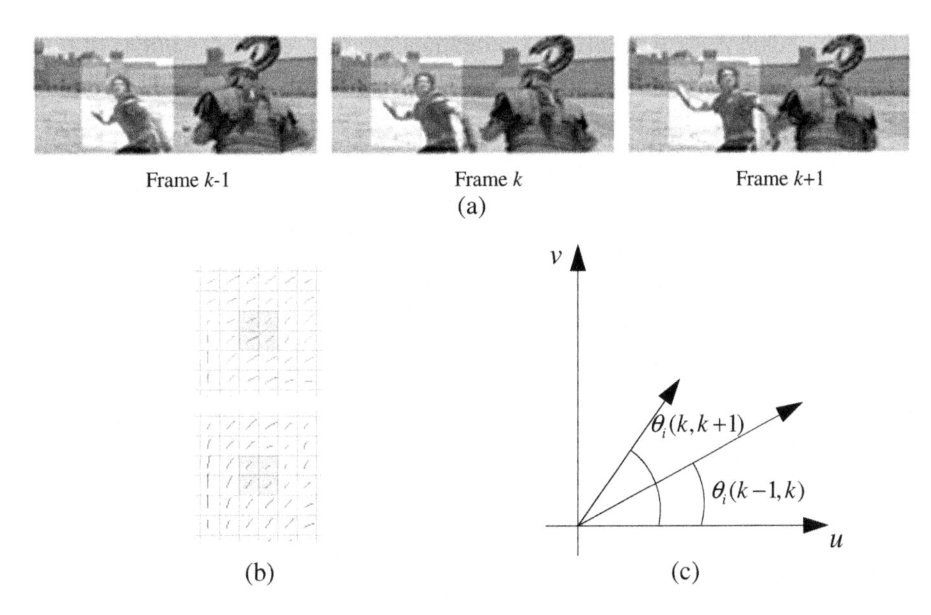

Fig. 2. Blockwise motion similarity: (a) Three successive frames k-1, k, and k+1. (b) MVs obtained by the BMA in the highlighted region of Fig. 2(a): top to bottom are shown representation of MVs with frames k-1 and k, and MVs with frames k and k+1. (c) Blockwise motion similarity in MB i obtained by MVs of frames k-1, k and k+1.

reduce miss detection by choosing shot boundary candidates that satisfy the following condition:

$$d^{**}(k)=\begin{cases} d(k), & \text{if } d(k)=\max\limits_{-N/2\le j\le N/2} d(k+j) \text{ and } \dfrac{1}{3}\sum\limits_{j=-1}^{1} d(k+j)\ge \dfrac{C_1}{N+1}\sum\limits_{j=-N/2}^{N/2} d(k+j) \\ d^{*}(k), & \text{otherwise} \end{cases} \tag{5}$$

where C_1 is a constant. In most of the video sequences we examined, we found that, at a shot boundary k, the DFD $d(k)$ is usually maximum among the consecutive N frames and the average value of $d(k)$s in the three frames around the shot boundary k is substantially larger than those of N frames. When this is the case, $d(k)$ is not normalized just to enhance the chance of being detected as a shot boundary. The constant C_1 is determined empirically.

2.2 Blockwise Motion Similarity

We can determine the shot boundary as the time at which motion directions of objects and background change abruptly. The motion flow of objects and background in the same shot is usually smooth whereas different shots contain different objects and background. In this subsection, we focus on the motion directions of the matched MBs in three successive frames and propose a blockwise motion similarity.

Conventional methods do not consider object motions as an important feature, instead regard dominant or global motion by a camera as an important feature. The proposed method deals with all block-based motions that represent motions of each object. Fig. 2 illustrates the computation method of the blockwise motion similarity. Fig. 2(a) shows three consecutive frames *k*-1, *k*, and *k*+1 in a movie clip, and Fig. 2(b) shows the two MVs computed for frames *k*-1 and *k* and for frames *k* and *k*+1 in the highlighted region of Fig. 2(a). Fig 2(c) shows the direction angles $\theta_i(k-1,k)$ and $\theta_i(k,k+1)$ of those two MVs in the coordinates (u, v).

The measure of the motion direction similarity at MB *i* is defined as

$$MS_i(k) = \begin{cases} 1, & \text{if } \left|\theta_i(k,k+1) - \theta_i(k-1,k)\right| \le Th_\theta \\ 0, & \text{otherwise} \end{cases} \tag{6}$$

where Th_θ is the angle threshold. The motion similarity $MS(k)$ at frame *k* is defined as the average of $MS_i(k)$:

$$MS(k) = \frac{1}{N_b} \sum_{i=1}^{N_b} MS_i(k) \tag{7}$$

This measure of motion similarity $MS(k)$ is higher when more block pairs around frame *k* have similar motion directions.

2.3 Computation of the Discontinuity Measure and SBD Rules

By examining many video sequences, we have found that both the modified DFD and the motion direction similarity measure are highly effective for detecting shot boundaries. We present a measure of discontinuity based on the combination of the two features:

$$Z(k) = \frac{d^{**}(k)}{\frac{1}{N+1} \sum_{j=-N/2}^{N/2} d^{**}(k+j)} \times \exp\left(\frac{-C_2 MS(k)}{\frac{1}{N+1} \sum_{j=-N/2}^{N/2} MS(k+j)} \right) \tag{8}$$

where C_2 is a constant that determines the rate of decrease of $Z(k)$ by the motion similarity at shot boundaries. Equation (8) shows that the discontinuity measure $Z(k)$ is large when two features change abruptly whereas it is small when they have little change. This different characteristic of the discontinuity measure can be utilized for separation of shot boundaries from non-shot boundaries and reduces the ambiguity in SBD. We employ a sliding window to consider the temporal variation of the discontinuity measure. We can determine shot boundaries using following detection rules:

$$Z(k) > Z(k+j), \ -N/2 \le j \le N/2, j \ne 0 \quad \text{and} \tag{9}$$

$$Z(k) \ge \frac{C_3}{N+1} \sum_{j=-N/2}^{N/2} Z(k+j) \tag{10}$$

If the discontinuity measure at frame *k* satisfies detection rules, it is assumed that an abrupt shot change occurs at frame *k*. The first detection rule in equation (9) finds shot boundary candidates whereas the second one in equation (10) prevents non-hard cuts from being selected.

3 Experimental Results and Discussions

Our method is applied to seven test action movies, which are sampled at 24 frames per second (fps). A full search BMA is used to estimate blockwise motion. For each sequence, a human observer identifies the shot boundaries as the ground truth.

For performance evaluation of the proposed SBD algorithm in terms of the detection accuracy, two quantitative measures are used: the precision $P=N_C/(N_C+N_F)$ and the recall $R=N_C/(N_C+N_M)$, where N_C, N_F , and N_M are the numbers of correct, false and miss shot detections, respectively. The problem of SBD using low-level image features is inherently heuristic and it is not easy to mathematically justify the choice of optimal parameters. With the video sequences we tested, the set of parameters (C_1, C_2, C_3) that minimizes the detection error is experimentally found to be (3.1, 1.5, 6). The size N of a temporal sliding window is defined as the maximum size that does not exceed the average shot length [9], in which the optimal size of N is experimentally set to 12.

Fig. 3 shows the proposed motion-based features as a function of the frame index. As can be observed from Fig. 3, the modified DFD gives better performance, in terms of separability between shot boundaries and non-shot boundaries, than the conventional DFD. It is true that the ambiguity in SBD is significantly reduced by the modified DFD, however the modified DFD at some non-shot boundaries is not small enough to be ignored. It can be reduced further by combining the modified DFD with the blockwise motion similarity that is assumed to be constant within a shot.

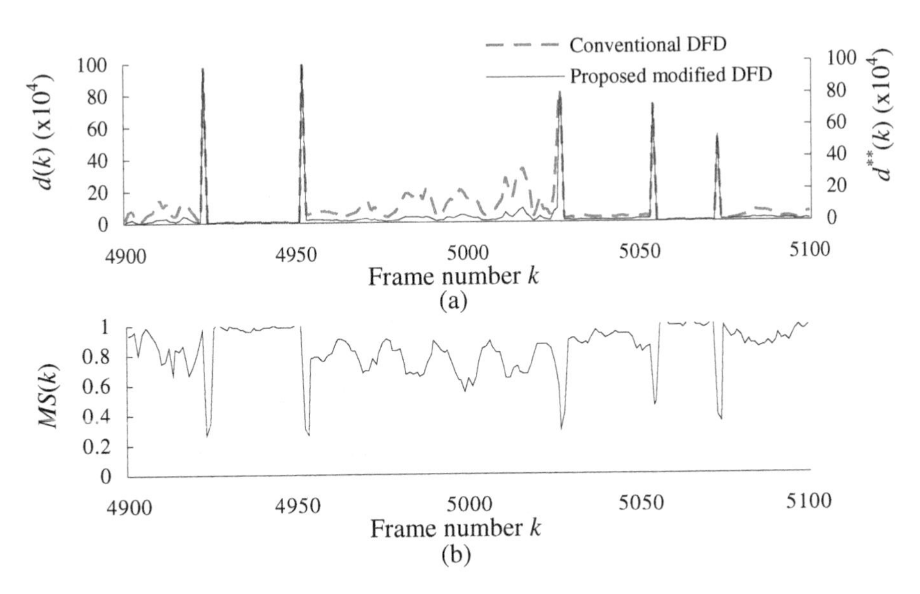

Fig. 3. Proposed motion-based features: (a) Conventional DFD and the proposed modified DFD. (b) Blockwise motion similarity $MS(k)$ as a function of the frame index.

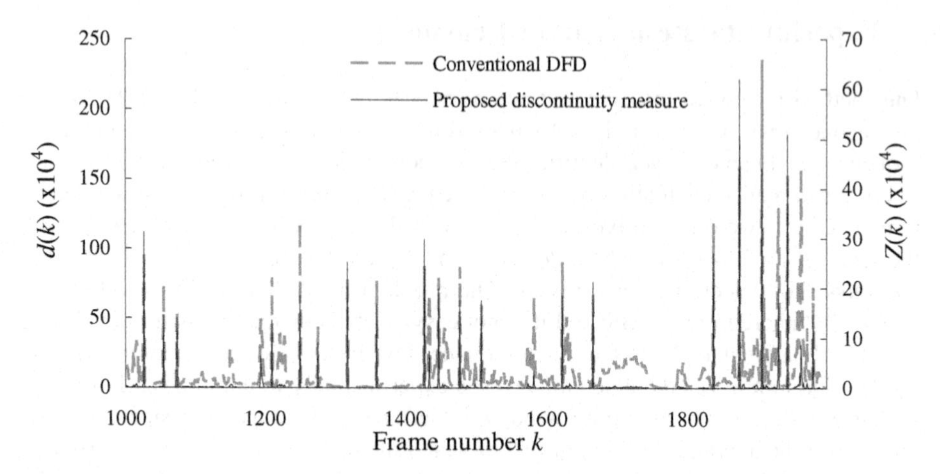

Fig. 4. Performance comparison between the conventional DFD and the proposed discontinuity measure

Table 1. Performance evaluation of the proposed SBD algorithm

Test sequence	N_C	N_M	N_F	Precision (%)	Recall (%)	Ground Truth	# of frames
1	109	4	2	98.2	96.5	113	9220
2	56	2	2	96.6	96.6	58	12000
3	122	6	6	95.3	95.3	128	6470
4	180	8	8	95.7	95.7	188	12470
5	56	3	17	76.7	94.9	59	8370
6	206	5	14	93.6	97.6	211	9590
7	136	4	3	97.8	97.1	140	14010

Fig. 4 shows performance comparison between the conventional DFD and the proposed discontinuity measure. As shown in Fig. 4, with the proposed motion-based features, the discontinuity measure easily determines the optimal threshold value in action movies, in which the difference between the minimum value for hard cuts and the maximum value for non-hard cuts is increased so that the probability of miss classification is reduced.

As mentioned above, most significant problem is how to determine shot boundaries using the effective discontinuity measures, and then how to increase the detection performance. With two detection rules that consider the discontinuity measures of temporally adjacent frames, we can efficiently handle unexpected non-hard cuts due to fast motions and abrupt illumination changes. Table 1 summarizes the performance evaluation of the proposed SBD algorithm. Note that the proposed algorithm gives high detection performances for all test sequences considered, because of the motion-based discontinuity measure that is suitable for detecting shot boundaries in action movies.

4 Conclusions

We propose two motion-based features for SBD of fast motion sequences: the modified DFD using the BMA and the blockwise motion similarity. The former is robust to fast motions by explicitly considering the motion magnitude, reducing the possibility of classification in SBD due to motion blur. The latter is defined by comparing motion directions of the MBs in consecutive frames. To compute the accurate motion similarity, we make use of blockwise motions of both objects and background that are important to our perception of movie content. SBD results by the proposed discontinuity measure show the effectiveness of the proposed algorithm for action movies, in which ambiguity in classification is greatly reduced.

Further research will focus on the development of the SBD algorithm for different types of shot boundaries, and on the investigation of a shot grouping method to summarize the movie content. Also application of the proposed algorithm to compressed video such as moving picture experts group (MPEG) is to be studied further, in which motion features can be easily obtained.

Acknowledgement

This work was supported by Brain Korea 21 Project.

References

1. Rasheed, Z., Shah M.: Scene Boundary Detection in Hollywood Movies and TV Shows. Proc. Comput. Vis. Pattern Recognit., Vol. 2. Madison WI USA (2003) 343–348
2. Kikukawa, T., Kawafuchi, S.: Development of an Automatic Summary Editing System for the Audio Visual Resources. Trans. Inst. Electron., Inform., Commun. Eng., Vol. J75-A. 2 (1992) 204–212
3. Zhang, H.J., Kankanhalli, A., Smoliar, S.W.: Automatic Partitioning of Full Motion Video. Proc. ACM Multimedia Systems, Vol. 1. Secaucus NJ USA (1993) 10–28
4. Ngo, C.W., Pong, T.C., Zhang, H.J.: Motion Analysis and Segmentation through Spatio-Temporal Slices Processing. IEEE Trans. Image Processing, 12 3 (2003) 341–355
5. Lan, D.J., Ma, Y.F., Zhang, H.J.: A Novel Motion-based Representation for Video Mining. Proc. Int. Conf. on Multimedia and Expo, Vol. 3. Baltimore MD USA (2003) 469–472
6. Ma, Y.F., Zhang, H.J.: Motion Texture: A New Motion based Video Representation. Proc. Int. Conf. on Pattern Recogn., Vol. 2. Quebec QU Canada (2002) 548–551
7. Lienhart, R.: Comparison of Automatic Shot Boundary Detection Algorithms. Proc. SPIE Storage and Retrieval for Image and Video Databases VII, Vol. 3656. San Jose CA USA (1998) 290–301
8. Yeo, B.-L., Liu, B.: Rapid Scene Analysis on Compressed Video. IEEE Trans. Circuits Syst. Video Technol., 5 (1995) 533–544
9. Moschetti, F., Kunt, M., Debes, E.: A Statistical Adaptive Block-Matching Motion Estimation. IEEE Trans. Circuits Syst. Video Technol., 13 5 (2003) 417–431
10. Damon, L., Tull, Katsaggelos, A.K.: Regularized Blur-Assisted Displacement Field Estimation. Proc. Int. Conf. on Image Processing, Vol. 3. Lausanne Switzerland (1996) 85–88

Text Localization and Extraction from Complex Color Images

S. Sabari Raju, P.B. Pati*, and A.G. Ramakrishnan

Department of Electrical Engineering,
Indian Institute of Science, Bangalore, INDIA – 560 012
pati@ee.iisc.ernet.in

Abstract. Availability of mobile and hand-held imaging devices, such as, cell phones, PDA's, still and video cameras have resulted in new applications, where the text present in the acquired images is extracted and interpreted for various purposes. In this paper, we present a new algorithm for automatic detection of text in color images. Proposed system involves Gabor function based multi-channel filtering on the intensity component of the image along with Graph-Theoretical clustering applied on the color space of the same image, there-by utilizing the advantages of texture analysis as well as those of connected component for text detection. Our approach performs well on images with complex background.

1 Introduction

Embedded text in images and videos provides useful information for automated annotation and indexing. Such text eventually helps in mining the relevant images from the database [1]. An efficient scheme for detection, localization and extraction of textual information from images is needed for such a task. Images may have text of various styles and sizes in simple or complex background. Document analysis softwares, generally, assume high scanning resolution, high quality document images with fairly simple layout structure. These assumptions do not hold for camera captured scenic or document images. Performance of any Optical Character Recognizer (OCR) greatly depends on such a text localization task.

Numerous approaches on text localization have been reported in the literature. Majorly, color and texture are the information being employed for this task. Messelodi *et. al.* [2] have extracted connected components to characterize text objects, based on their size information, in book cover color images. They utilize the heuristics which depend both on the geometrical features of a single component as well as its geometrical and spatial relationship with other components. Zhong *et. al.* [3] segment the image into connected components with uniform color. They use several heuristics on size, alignment and proximity to select the components as likely text characters. In the gray-scale version of the obtained image, the regions with higher local variance are termed as text regions. The algorithm is reported to work fine for (a) CD and book cover images,

* Corresponding author.

G. Bebis et al. (Eds.): ISVC 2005, LNCS 3804, pp. 486–493, 2005.

and (b)traffic scene videos. Jain and Yu [4] extract a set of images by analyzing the color space of the input image. They employ connected component (CC) analysis on each of the derived images to locate possible text regions. Finally, they merge the information so obtained to locate text regions in the original image. Strouthpoulos *et. al.* [5] have proposed a technique to determine the optimal number of unique colors present in the input image. In the first step, an unsupervised neural network clusters the color regions. In the subsequent step, a tree-search procedure, using *split-and-merge* conditions decides whether color classes must be split or merged. They use a page layout analysis technique, on each of the obtained optimal color images. Finally, they add the information obtained from each of the optimal color images to extract the text region. Smith [6] uses vertical edge information for localizing caption text in images. Jung [7] has used a neural network based filtering technique to classify the pixels of input image as belonging to text or non-text regions.

2 System Description

The proposed text extraction scheme (refer Fig. 1) is demonstrated with texture based method and color clustering. It can be assumed that text regions in an image contain a lot of abrupt changes in the gray values, in various directions, making it rich in edge information [8]. So an ideal feature to discriminate between text and non-text areas should invariably involve directional frequency. Gabor function based filters are well known to accomplish this task of directional frequency selectivity. So, in the proposed algorithm, Gabor filter based multi-channel filtering is adapted followed by Block Energy Analysis (BEA), which

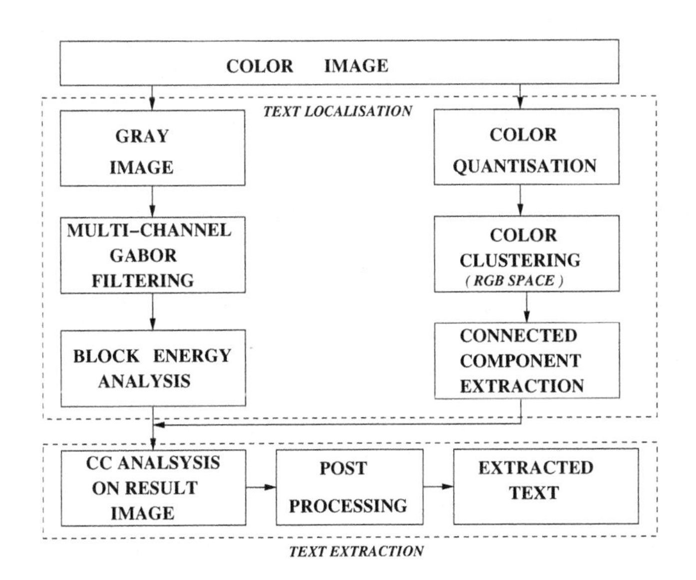

Fig. 1. Overview of the proposed approach

is employed on the energy image, *i.e.*, output of the Gabor filter. Parallelly, the color image is quantized and color components in the image are analyzed using Graph-Theoretical cluster technique. The results of the Gabor based multi-channel filter and color component analysis are merged, and CC analysis is done based on geometrical and statistical information of the individual components. Components which are present inside the bounding box of another component are removed at the post-processing stage.

2.1 Gabor Filter Bank

In a given image, consisting of text and non-text regions, the text regions are quite rich in high frequency components. The technique involving multi-channel filtering with Gabor function based filters, for page layout analysis, is developed due to convergence of biological [9, 10] and machine learning approaches. Such a method is meant to detect text regardless of the type of script, size of font or the layout the text is embedded in, and is more robust than other kinds of feature detection models. Besides, it has a low sensitivity to various kinds of noise.

A bank of Gabor filters are chosen for extraction of the above mentioned features. A Gabor function is a Gaussian modulated by a complex sinusoid.

$$h(x, y) = g(x', y') \, exp[j2\pi \, Ux] \quad (1)$$

where x' and y' are the rotated components of the x and y co-ordinates, in the rectangular co-ordinate system, rotated by angle θ. U is the radial frequency in cycles/image width.

$$g(x, y) = \frac{1}{(2\pi\sigma_x\sigma_y)} exp\left(-\frac{1}{2}\left[\left(\frac{x}{\sigma_x}\right)^2 + \left(\frac{y}{\sigma_y}\right)^2\right]\right) \quad (2)$$

σ_x and σ_y explain the spatial spread and the bandwidth of the filter function $h(x, y)$. If B_r is the radial frequency bandwidth in octaves and B_θ is the angular bandwidth in degrees, then,

$$\sigma_x = \frac{\sqrt{2}}{2\pi U}\frac{2^{B_r}+1}{2^{B_r}-1}, \qquad \sigma_y = \frac{\sqrt{2}}{2\pi U \tan\left(\frac{B_\theta}{2}\right)} \quad (3)$$

The power of discrimination of the different filters are dependent on the values of B_r and B_θ.

Any combination of B_r, B_θ and U involves two filters, corresponding to the sine and the cosine functions respectively, in the exponential term in Eqn. 1. Gabor filters of $B_r = 1$ octave and $B_\theta = 45^o$ at four different orientations ($\theta = 0^o$, 45°, 90°, 135°) have been used for the reported work. Three different radial frequency, U, values ($U = 0.2, 0.3 \; and \; 0.5$) have been chosen as they have been observed to be working well for all kinds of images used in our work.

2.2 Block Energy Analysis (BEA)

A *space-frequency* filter bank, using Gabor filters, has been designed and implemented for separating the text and non-text areas in a gray level document image. The filter response of a complex filter (refer Eqn. 1) at any pixel (i, j) is:

$$E(u_l,\ \theta_k) \ = \ \sqrt{e(u_l,\theta_k)^2 + o(u_l,\theta_k)^2} \qquad (4)$$

where $e(u_l,\theta_k)$ and $o(u_l,\theta_k)$ are the outputs of the cosine(even) and sine(odd) filters, with radial frequency u_l and angle θ_k, at that pixel location, respectively. The total local energy is the sum total of the outputs of all the complex filters at that given pixel.

$$E_T \ = \ \sum_{l=1}^{3}\sum_{k=1}^{4} E(u_l,\ \theta_k) \qquad (5)$$

We low pass filter the magnitude response image of the Gabor filter bank (the E_T image) with a Gaussian filter. A 11×11 Gaussian mask ($\sigma_x = \sigma_y = 3$) is employed for this purpose. It is seen that this removes artifacts and irregularities present and, thereby, helps in text detection. We evaluate block energy at each pixel by considering blocks of 15×15 size. An average of the block energies is evaluated across all the blocks in the image. Twice this average energy (decided heuristically) is the threshold for block wise text and non-text separation, *i.e.*, if the block energy is found to be above the threshold value, thus calculated, the block is considered as text area.

2.3 Color Component Generation and Analysis

The methodology for the color component generation is as follows:

1 Quantize the color space into prototype colors. The prototypes are found by masking the two least significant bit.
2 Compute the 3-D histogram (RGB color space with 256 pixel level) of the color image.
3 Construct lists of pixels representing each histogram bin.
4 For every unique color in the histogram, link to the bin which has maximum vote in the neighborhood of 20, forming non-overlapping unimodal clusters in tree structure. (The self-referencing bins are the local maximum and representative of the cluster, C_i, $i = 1,\ 2,\ \cdots,\ N$.)
5 Generate connected components from each cluster to construct binary images
6 Connected Component Analysis:
    FOR each cluster
        N_i is the no. of ON pixels in i_{th} cluster.
        $N_m \ = \ Max\ \{N_i\};\ i = 1,\ 2,\ \cdots,\ N.$
        If ON pixel in the cluster, N_i, is greater than 5% of N_m.
            FOR each connected component in the cluster:
            Select text components based on geometrical and statistical information of the components.
            END FOR each
        END IF each
    END FOR each
7 At the end of the CC analysis, final image is constructed by merging all components obtained from different color planes.

3 Experimental Results and Discussion

Our image database consists of 150 color images. These images are (i) scanned with 300 dpi and stored at 24-bit color representation, (ii) captured with **Minolta Dimage 2330 Zoom** still camera, (iii) captured with the camera present in the **Sony Ericsson T610** mobile phone, (iv) frames extracted from videos and (v) downloaded from WWW sources. The proposed algorithm performs consistently well on a majority of these images.

The algorithm is evaluated by counting the number of detected characters. The following *rates* are formulated as a quantitative measure for the effectiveness of the algorithm.

$$Precision\ Rate = \frac{No.\ of\ correctly\ detected\ text\ characters}{No.\ of\ detected\ characters} X\ 100 \quad (6)$$

$$Recall\ Rate = \frac{No.\ of\ correctly\ detected\ text\ characters}{No.\ of\ characters\ present\ in\ original\ Image} X\ 100 \quad (7)$$

The accuracy of detection is evaluated on 70 images from the database. 91.7% of precision rate is attained in an average while the average recall rate achieved is 89.2%.

Fig. 2 illustrates the comparison between general color clustering technique with CCA and the proposed algorithm. A camera-captured image is shown in

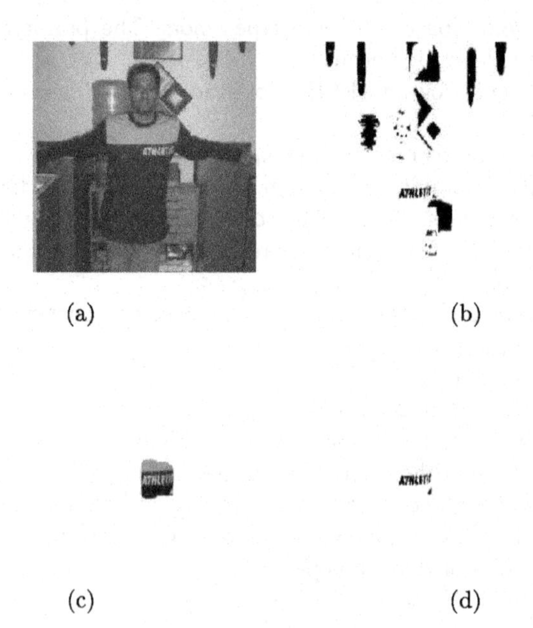

Fig. 2. Text localization Results (a) Original Camera Image (b) Result only with Color Clustering and standard connected component analysis (c) Output of the Gabor filter (d) Result of proposed scheme

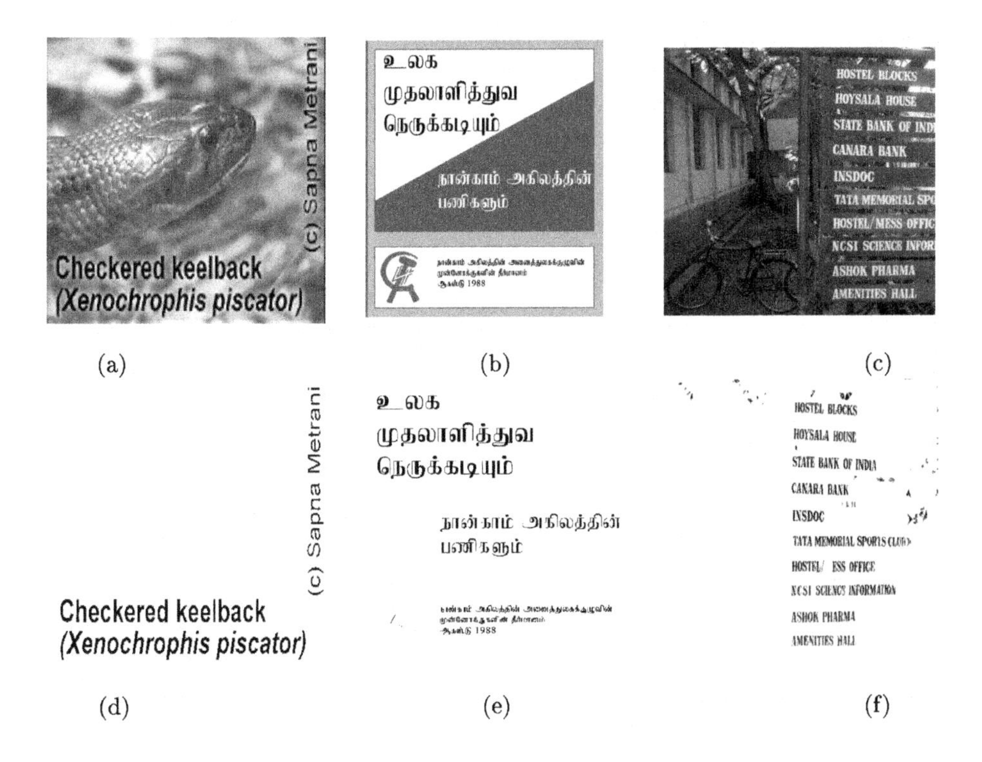

Fig. 3. Experimental Results (a) WWW image (b) scanned book cover image (c) Camera Image (d)-(f) Extracted text regions

Fig. 2(a) which has very less text in the image. Fig. 2(b) shows the text region using color clustering and CC analysis and Fig. 2(c) shows the output using the Gabor filters. Fig. 2(d) shows the output of the proposed system where regions of text are well detected in-spite of the dominance of natural background.

A natural image with synthetic text is shown in Fig. 3(a). This image has 40098 unique colors. The interesting point of this example is the gradual change of the background colors. The application of the proposed text extraction technique, gives results shown in Fig. 3(d). Test image 3(b) has background of two principal color tones. In addition, this document has white as text and back-

Table 1. Processing Time for Video Frame (240×320) and Camera Image (520×640) in seconds

Operation	**Video Frame (secs)**	**Camera Image (secs)**
Gabor Filtering	3.0	7.0
Computing 3-D histogram	0.03	0.035
Constructing and Linking Tree	0.37	0.45
CC analysis in one cluster	0.07	0.08

ground regions. Complexity in the connected component analysis here is the background of the black text region (bounding box of the character) has white color, which also satisfies the characteristics of character. The text areas are correctly obtained and are shown in figure 3(e). Fig. 3(c) shows a color image with complex background. The number of unique colors in this image is 88399. It can be observed that the majority of the text areas are correctly obtained and this is shown in Fig. 3(f).

Table 1 presents the time taken by each module of the algorithm for a typical camera captured image (520 × 640) and for a frame extracted from a video sequence of size 240 × 320. It may be noted that the Gabor filtering part of the algorithm is computationally expensive.

4 Conclusion

In this paper, an approach to automatically localize and extract text, on camera captured (still and mobile) as well as on scanned document images, is proposed and implemented. The results obtained thus far are encouraging.

The algorithm is able to detect and localize text in document images as well as in scenic images with complex background. It has the ability to deal with high resolution scanned images and camera captured images with equal efficiency. Not only is the proposed algorithm script invariant, it also is invariant to skew present in the document images. The disadvantage of our algorithm is the computational cost. The running of the algorithm on the mobile images shown in figure 2 takes about 3.5s and camera captured images shown in Fig. 3(f) takes 7.82s on a PC with Pentium-IV processor at 2.2 GHz with 512 MB of RAM. When text extraction performance is the criteria, our scheme performs consistently well.

Integrating an OCR which can perform well on low-resolution images with the proposed text extraction method is proposed as a scope for future investigations. The proposed approach could also be applied to handwritten documents.

References

1. Antani, S., Kasturi, R., Jain, R.: A survey on the use of pattern recognition methods for abstraction, indexing and retrieval of images and video. Pattern Recognition **35** (2002) 945–965
2. Messelodi, S., Modena, C.M.: Automatic identification and skew estimation of text lines in real scene images. Pattern Recognition **32** (1999) 791–810
3. Zhong, Y., Karu, K., Jain, A.K.: Locating text in complex color images. Pattern Recognition **28** (1995) 1523–1535
4. Jain, A.K., Yu, B.: Automatic text location in images and video frames. Pattern Recognition **31** (1998) 2055–2076
5. C.Strouthpoulos, N.Papamarkos, Atsalakis, A.E.: Text extraction in complex color document. Pattern Recognition **35** (2002) 1743–1758
6. Smith, M.A., Kanade, T.: Video skimming for quick browsing based on audio and image characterization. Technical report, Technical Report CMU-CS-95-186, Carnegie Mellon University (1995)

7. Jung, K.: Neural network-based text location in color images. Pattern Recognition Letters **22** (2001) 1503–1515
8. S, S.R., Pati, P.B., Ramakrishnan, A.G.: Gabor filter based block energy analysis for text extraction from digital document images. In: Intl. Workshop on Document Image Analysis for Libraries. (2004)
9. Porat, M., Zeevi, Y.Y.: The generalized gabor scheme of image representation in biological and machine vision. IEEE Trans. on PAMI **10** (1988) 452–467
10. Morrone, M.C., Burr, D.C.: Feature detection in human vision: a phase dependent energy model. Proceedings of the Royal Society of London(B) **235** (1988) 221–245

Using Linguistic Models for Image Retrieval

Brian Zambrano, Rahul Singh, and Bibek Bhattarai

Department of Computer Science,
San Francisco State University, San Francisco, CA 94132
bzambran@sfsu.edu, rsingh@cs.sfsu.edu, bdb@sfsu.edu

Abstract. This research addresses the problem of image retrieval by exploring the semantic relationships that exist between image annotations. This is done by using linguistic relationships encoded in WordNet, a comprehensive lexical repository. Additionally, we propose the use of a reflective user-interface where users can interactively query-explore semantically related images by varying a simple parameter that does not require knowledge about the underlying information structure. This facilitates query-retrieval in context of the emergent nature of semantics that complex media, such as images have. Experiments show the efficacy and promise of this approach which can play a significant role in applications varying from multimedia information management to web-based image search.

1 Introduction

Since the past decade, image retrieval has been a key area of research within the broader domain of information retrieval. Applications of image retrieval transcend multiple domains including web-based image search, object recognition, motion recognition, personal information management, satellite imagery and bio-medical imaging. The classical approaches to this problem have their origins primarily in signal and image processing and computer vision. A detailed review of the area may be obtained from [1, 14] and references therein. Ultimately, the classical formulations are based on image matching and involve selecting an appropriate image representation such as shape [12], texture [7] or color [15] along with a suitable similarity function. The query is then formulated as a set of constraints on the selected descriptors (such as the percentage of pixels in an image having a specific color(s)), or geometric constrains on image features, or an entire example image. Finally, executing the retrieval requires searching the images in the repository to find those images that satisfy the constraints or maximize the similarity value. In spite of their intuitive theoretical appeal and a large number of academic and commercial efforts [7, 6, 4, 11], the classical approach has had limited success. This can be envisaged by the lack of broadly available image retrieval systems today notwithstanding the ubiquity of image-based information in the digital world. Salient factors leading to this apparent paradox include:

- *The Signal-to-Symbol Barrier:* Queries to an image database are based on the need to satisfy a semantically meaningful information goal. Traditional retrieval formulations however, act only at the signal level. This leads to unsatisfactory performance. For instance, searching for a red colored car on a large image database using the color red typically would yield few meaningful results.

G. Bebis et al. (Eds.): ISVC 2005, LNCS 3804, pp. 494–501, 2005.

- *Data modeling for large-scale retrieval:* There is a critical paucity of formal and well validated data models for complex media-based information such as images. Most models have typically focused on the development of powerful features to describe the corresponding media and the use of similarity functions to answer queries based on these features [9]. Essentially, these are efforts to store signal-level attributes and do not facilitate bridging the signal-to-symbol barrier. A further element of complexity is introduced by the fact that semantic attributes that can be associated with images are often poorly structured. This implies that the type, number, and very presence of these attributes may cardinally vary from image to image. This is possible even in cases where the images belong to a distinct domain.
- *The emergent nature of image semantics:* The semantics associated with complex media (like video or images) is *emergent*, i.e. media is endowed with meaning by placing it in context of other similar media and through user interactions [10]. This implies that facilitating user interactions and exploratory behavior are essential components of a successful image retrieval approach.

The goal of our research has been to rethink image retrieval in context of the aforementioned issues. We propose using knowledge about the semantic content of an image to facilitate image retrieval. To do so, we utilize WordNet [16], an electronic lexical system to discern the linguistic relationships between descriptions of image content. A semi-structured data model is used to capture any available semantic or media-level information related to specific images. The model is implemented using an XML database to support large scale storage and query-retrieval. Finally, we employ a *reflective* user interface to support user-media interactions. The interface allows immediate visual feedback and response as users vary retrieval parameters. This allows retaining user context and reduces the cognitive load on the user as they engage in query-exploration.

The reader may note that our formulation presupposes the presence of semantic image descriptions or annotations. While a major departure from classical image recognition formulations, the advent of technology increasingly makes such as assumption less limiting than what may appear at the first glance. Indeed, large annotated image databases such as [5] are available today. Further, the WWW contains significant number of mixed text-image pages which forms the basis of keyword indexed image search on the web provided by facilities such as Media RSS (Yahoo), video search and image search (Google), and MSN Video (Microsoft). Finally, advances in the development of integrated annotation systems such as [13, 8] are expected to further ameliorate the process of media (and image) annotation, allowing for broader use of approaches such as the one proposed in this paper.

A series of recent works have attempted to utilize either feature-annotation correlations [3, 18] or linguistic relations within annotations [2, 17] to facilitate image retrieval. While we share the idea of using WordNet-supported relationships with the aforementioned works, the key distinctions of our research lie in conjoining this capability with support for emergent semantics in user-image interactions as well as application of a semi-structured data model to support large scale query-retrieval.

2 A Brief Introduction to WordNet and Its Utilization

The design of WordNet has been motivated by psycholinguistic theories of human lexical memory [16]. For a given word or phrase, WordNet provides lexical relationships that include among others, *synsets* (sets of synonyms), *hypernyms*, *hyponyms* (is-a relationships), and *holonyms* (part-of-a relationship). This data is available for up to four parts of speech (noun, verb, adjective and adverb). The word "bat", for instance, can either represent a noun or a verb. For each part of speech, every sense of the word will have the associated lexical information as described above. In our system, we currently focus exclusively on nouns and use the first sense of the word. Further, we use hypernyms which is the "is-a" relationship. As an example, a subset of the hypernym WordNet results for "flamingo" is shown in Figure 1. Hypernyms are returned in a hierarchy with the top level description being the most specific for the search term. Each subsequent description becomes more general. It should be noted that the proposed approach is equally extensible to other relationships that exist in WordNet.

flamingo -- (large pink to scarlet web-footed wading bird with down-bent bill; inhabits brackish lakes)
=> wading bird, wader-(any of many long-legged birds that wade in water in search of food)
=> aquatic bird-(wading and swimming and diving birds of either fresh or salt water)
=> bird-(warm-blooded egg-laying vertebrates characterized by feathers and forelimbs modified as wings)

Fig. 1. A subset of the hypernym WordNet results for "flamingo". As can be seen, a flamingo is a "wading bird, wader", which is an "aquatic bird", which is a "bird", etc. This hierarchy extends from more specific semantic concepts to less specific concept.

3 System Description

There are three major components to the system: (1) Algorithmic mechanism for computing term similarity, (2) A Semi-structured data storage and query-execution infrastructure, and (3) A front-end reflective GUI for displaying thumbnails, controlling searches, and exploration. Each of these components is described in detail below.

- **The Retrieval Strategy:** In order to calculate the similarity between two terms, we use a weighted score based on the top to bottom comparison of descriptions within the hypernym hierarchy of these terms. After the WordNet results are obtained for a query and annotation term, we step through the query term's hypernym descriptions. If any one of these descriptions is found within the hypernyms of the annotation, the match score is incremented by an amount that is in the range [1, n], where n is the total number of hypernyms of the term, with matches at the top scoring higher (n corresponding to the top of the hierarchy and 1 to the bottom). This score is then normalized by dividing it by the maximal possible match score.

  Formally, let Q denotes the query term and A the annotation term. Further, for any term T let T_k denote the k_{th} term in the hypernym hierarchy of T. Let also the predicate *depth(T)* denote the depth of the hypernym hierarchy of the term T. Finally, let $depth(T_k)$ indicate the position of the k_{th} term in the hypernym hierarchy of T. The similarity between Q and A, denoted as $S(Q,A)$ can be described by formula (1), where the set-theoretic intersection of two terms T_i and V denotes their match/mismatch and takes values in {0,1}.

$$S(Q,A) = \frac{\sum_{i=0}^{depth(Q)}((depth(Q) - depth(Q_i) \times (Q_i \cap A))}{(depth(Q) \times (depth(Q)+1))/2} \tag{1}$$

Figure 2 shows results for the query/annotation pair of flamingo/penguin and penguin/flamingo. It is important to note that the direction of our search plays a key role and produces different results. Note that if the query string exactly matches a label, the corresponding image is treated as the closest match. This is done to avoid ties since, for certain label/query combinations, a relative score could be found to be 100 even though the search term did not match exactly. Using the results in Fig. 1, we see that this may happen if we searched for "wader" and we have images labeled as "wader" and "wading bird". In Fig. 1, we can see that the hypernym hierarchies for both terms would be the same producing similarities of 100. So, if we search for "wader" and we have an image labeled "wader", the proposed approach ensures that it is returned ahead of any images labeled "wading bird".

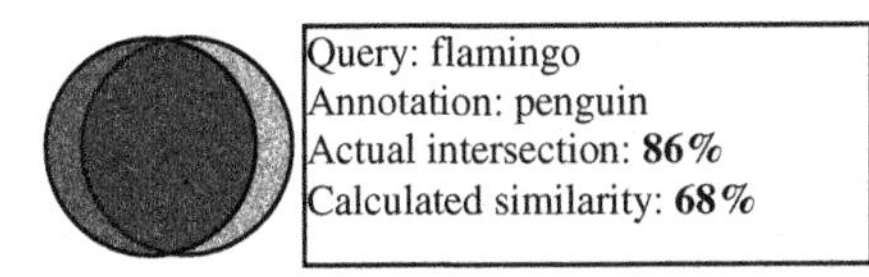

Query: flamingo
Annotation: penguin
Actual intersection: **86%**
Calculated similarity: **68%**

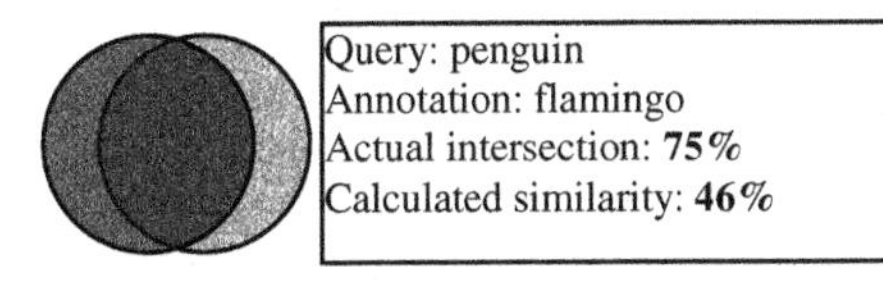

Query: penguin
Annotation: flamingo
Actual intersection: **75%**
Calculated similarity: **46%**

Fig. 2. Intersections of two query(left)/annotation(right) pairs. Although the actual intersections only vary by 11%, the calculated similarities vary by 24%. The difference in weighted scores suggests that a flamingo is more similar to a penguin than a penguin is to a flamingo.

- **Semi-Structured Data Storage:** Berkeley XML is a native XML database which we use for persistent data storage of search scores, image locations and image labels. This provides us with the scalability and efficiency needed for a large-scale image retrieval system. Due to the relatively high expense of a term similarity calculation (two WordNet lookups and the similarity algorithm), we store the score for a given query-label combination in our database. Subsequent searches first lookup into the database to ensure that this operation is only performed once per query-label combination. Queries into Berkeley XML are in the XQuery format which closely follows XPath syntax. Schemas for the internal representation of system data is shown in Fig. 3.
- **Graphical User Interface:** The reflective user interface provides three primary functions: creating and viewing thumbnails, labeling of images and search-exploration capabilities. Once a user has browsed to a folder containing images and created thumbnails, a single keyword can be applied to one or more selected images. A slider bar resides below the label controls and is used for specifying the relevance of search results. Below the slider bar is a text field where the user types the query term and clicks the Search button. During a search, the slider specifies a similarity value which results should be at or above. For example, when the slider bar is at 50, all results will be at least 50% similar to the search term as determined by the algorithm described above. Thumbnail images are displayed from most to least similar. In addition to partially controlling the initial search result set, the

slider bar also provides reflective feedback after the search has been performed. Moving the slider to the right (increasing the similarity) causes images with a similarity value less than the slider bar value to disappear from the displayed results. Likewise, lowering this value will cause potentially new images to appear.

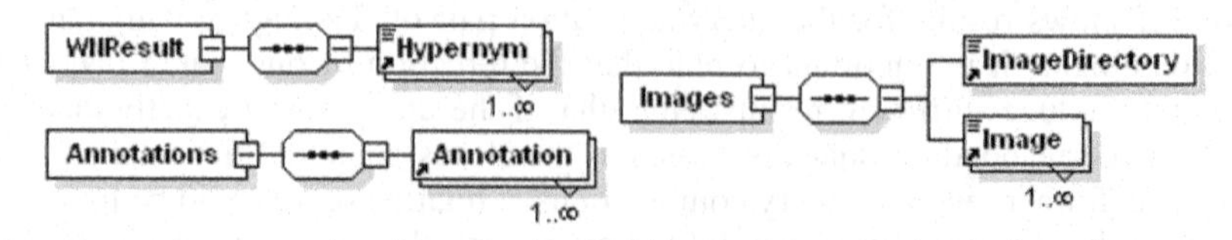

Fig. 3. Schemas for the XML database

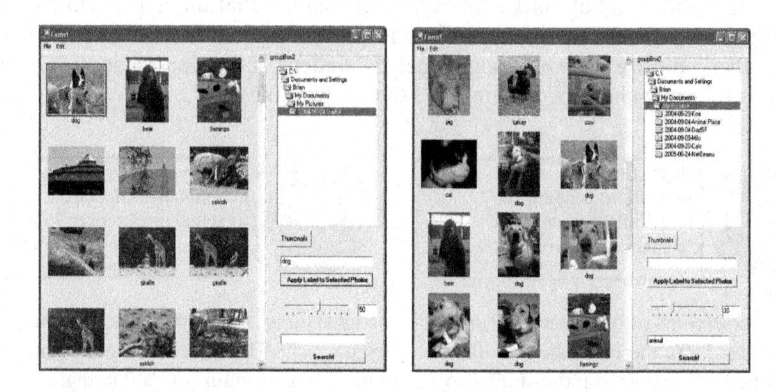

Fig. 4. The user interface. The left view shows browsing and labeling support for images. The right view shows results for the query involving the label "animal" at 30% similarity.

4 Experimental Results

Experiments were performed on a collection of 2113 images of which 388 had annotations from a group of 110 unique annotations. Various queries were performed at 10 %, 30 %, 50 %, 70 %, and 90 % similarities. For each query, the time to go through all labeled photos and calculate similarities, if needed, was recorded. Because the similarity value for each query-label pair is made only once before being stored in the database and cached in memory, we report the maximum retrieval time of 31.1s during initialization and the average of 0.28s.

After results were displayed, we manually count the total number of images returned and determine whether they are accurate to find precision and recall. It should be noted that hard boundaries may not exist when determining whether an image is correct for a given query. As an example, the word "chinchilla" as a noun has three senses. The first sense is related to its pelt: "the expensive silvery gray fur of the chinchilla". Sense three is related to a rodent as one might expect: "small rodent with soft pearly gray fur". Because we use the first sense exclusively, a query for "rodent" will not return chinchillas; however chinchillas will show up when searching for "fur" or "pelt". This is semantically correct, but may be counterintuitive and blurs the boundaries on correctness.

Table 1. Precision and recall for different queries at various term similarity thresholds

	Similarity Threshold				
	90	70	50	30	10
			Query: cat		
Precision	100	100	40	26.7	9.9
Recall	75	100	100	100	100
			Query: bird		
Precision	100	30	30	25.7	11.1
Recall	77.8	100	100	100	100
			Query: animal		
Precision	100	100	46.9	46.9	26
Recall	85.4	85.4	92.7	92.7	92.7
			Query: friend		
Precision	none	70.8	21	21	8.5
Recall	none	81	81	81	81
			Query: party		
Precision	100	100	100	100	81.8
Recall	27	27	27	27	48.6

Table 1 shows experimental results for four randomly selected queries at varying similarity thresholds. This dataset provides a fairly consistent picture of the system's efficacy across a broad range of queries. The standard measures of precision and recall are used to access performances. For all the query terms, the recall is quite high across the range of similarity values. This can be attributed to our use of hypernyms as the basis of our retrieval algorithm. Many annotations were for various animals including dogs, cats, elephants and penguins. When searching for "animal", we cast a large net and include nearly every image of an animal. Recall for "animal" would have been 100% at all levels had the first sense of "chinchilla" not been related to fur. More constrained or specific terms such as "bird" and "cat" produce more consistent recall across all levels.

Precision is more variable across all search terms. At very low similarities, we see many photos which bare little resemblance to the query term. As we deal exclusively with nouns, almost everything will be somewhat related. This accounts for the low precision at very low similarities. As the threshold value increases, loosely related images fall off. For all queries except "party", the 100% precision included photos which labels unequal to the query. Results for "bird" included "penguin" and "flamingo". Likewise, "cat" included "lion". Some of the images retrieved from the query "animal" are shown in Figure 2.

An interesting example that illustrates the potentially complex and distal semantic relationships such an approach can unearth is the search for the concept *friend*. As shown in table 1, this example has a large range for precision and relatively low recall. A *friend* is defined as a type of person which causes concepts like *Uncle* and *ostrich* to appear, both of which are people (the first sense of ostrich is related to a person who refuses to face reality).

A significant observation that can be made from these examples is that many of the retrieved results have significant semantic relationship to the query, even though at the image descriptor level, the corresponding images may share low similarities. This is a key asset of such an approach.

Figure 5 graphically shows how precision increases dramatically and the recall tends to decrease as the term similarity value is raised. As we constrain our results by increasing the threshold, very few unrelated images appear (high precision). At the same time, several related photos are not returned (lower recall). Lower values of similarity produce the opposite effect returning a large set of images include nearly all expected images as well as many which are extraneous.

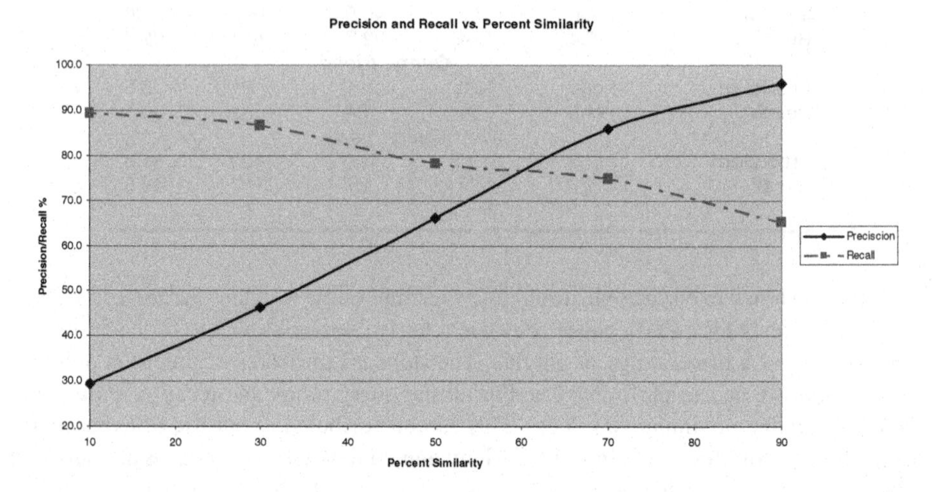

Fig. 5. A plot of precision and recall vs. query/annotation similarity averaged across 20 randomly generated queries

5 Conclusions

The proposed research addresses three cardinal challenges encountered in query-retrieval of complex media such as images. These include bridging the signal-to-symbol gap, supporting emergent semantics of complex media, and formal storage models that can support the lack of structure in real-world information related to such media. Departing fundamentally from classical research in image matching, we use linguistic relationships amongst descriptions of image content as the key mechanism for information retrieval. We propose an algorithm that allows determining similarity between images using the categorical, hierarchy-based relationship model of WordNet. Further, a reflective user interface allows direct query-exploration of the images. Within it, users can explore images that are semantically proximal or distal to the query. This allows support for the emergent nature of image semantics. Finally, we use a semi-structured data model, implemented through an XML database to support queries over large datasets. Experiments verify the promise of this approach which can play a key role either independently or in conjunction with classical image processing techniques towards solving the complex challenge of image retrieval.

References

[1] S. Antani, R. Kasturi, and R. Jain, "A survey on the use of pattern recognition methods for abstraction, indexing and retrieval of images and video", Pattern Recognition 35(4): 945-965, 2002

[2] Y-A. Aslandogan, C. Their, C. Yu, J. Zou, and N. Rishe, "Using Semantic Contents and WordNet in Image Retrieval", Proc. SIGIR 1997

[3] K. Barnard and D. Forsyth, "Learning the Semantics of Words and Pictures", ICCV, Vol. 2, pp. 408 – 415, 2001

[4] M. Flickner, et al. "Query by Image and Video Content: The QBIC System", IEEE Computer, 28(9): 23-32,1995.

[5] http://www.gettyimages.com

[6] Gupta, S. Santini, and R. Jain: In Search of Information in Visual Media. Commun. ACM 40(12): 34-42, 1997

[7] Pentland, R. Picard, and S. Sclaroff, "Photobook: Content-Based Manipulation of Image Databases", Int. J. of Computer Vision, Vol. 18, No. 3, 1996

[8] J. Pinzon and R. Singh, "Designing An Experiential Annotation System For Personal Multimedia Information Management", IASTED Int. Conf. on Human-Computer Interaction, 2005 (To Appear)

[9] S. Santini and A. Gupta, "Principles of Schema Design for Multimedia Databases", IEEE Trans. On Multimedia, Vol. 4, No. 2, 2002

[10] S. Santini, A. Gupta, and R. Jain, "Emergent Semantics Through Interaction in Image Databases", IEEE Trans. On Knowledge and Data Engineering, Vol. 13, No. 3, 2001

[11] http://www.scimagix.com

[12] R. Singh and N. P. Papanikolopoulos, "Planar Shape Recognition by Shape Morphing", *Pattern Recognition*, Vol. 33, No. 10, pp. 1683-1699, 2000

[13] R. Singh, Z. Li, P. Kim, D. Pack, and R. Jain, "Event-Based Modeling and Processing of Digital Media", *Proc. First ACM SIGMOD Workshop on Computer Vision Meets Databases (CVDB)*, pp. 19-26, 2004

[14] Smeulders, M. Worring, S. Santini, A. Gupta, and R. Jain: Content-Based Image Retrieval at the End of the Early Years. IEEE Trans. Pattern Anal. Mach. Intell. 22(12): 1349-1380 (2000)

[15] T-F. Syeda-Mahmood, "Data and Model Driven Selection Using Color Regions", Int. J. of Computer Vision, Vol. 21, 1997

[16] http://wordnet.princeton.edu

[17] Yang, M. Dong, and F. Fotouhi, "Learning the Semantics in Image Retrieval – A Natural Language Processing Approach", Proc. CVPR Workshops, 2004

[18] R. Zhao and W. Grosky, "Narrowing the Semantic Gap – Improved Text-based Web Document Retrieval Using Visual Features", IEEE Trans. on Multimedia, Vol4, No. 2, pp. 189 – 200, 2002

Content-Based Image Retrieval Via Vector Quantization

Ajay H. Daptardar and James A. Storer

Computer Science Department,
Brandeis University, Waltham, MA 02454, USA
ajay@brandeis.edu, storer@cs.brandeis.edu

Abstract. Image retrieval and image compression are each areas that have received considerable attention in the past. However there have been fewer advances that address both these problems simultaneously. In this work, we present a novel approach for content-based image retrieval (CBIR) using vector quantization (VQ). Using VQ allows us to retain the image database in compressed form without any need to store additional features for image retrieval. The VQ codebooks serve as generative image models and are used to represent images while computing their similarity. The hope is that encoding an image with a codebook of a *similar* image will yield a better representation than when a codebook of a *dissimilar* image is used. Experiments performed on a color image database over a range of codebook sizes support this hypothesis and retrieval based on this method compares well with previous work.

1 Introduction

A core problem for image databases and digital libraries is that of *Content-Based Image Retrieval* (CBIR), where images specified by a query must be retrieved from a large image database. With the ever increasing amounts of machine generated imagery (digital cameras, scientific and medical instruments, remote sensors, etc.), the need has never been greater for efficient and effective systems to manage visual data and understand the content within these media. The need to "google" imagery will become increasingly important in the future. We follow the *query-by-example* model [1], where the user supplies an image and the system returns the best matching images in the database.

In much of the past work on CBIR, images are first represented by feature vectors which capture certain contents of the image. Perhaps the most important discriminating feature for image classification and retrieval is color [2, 3]. Color distribution in an image can be accurately modeled by a histogram of the intensities. A typical color image, however, is capable of representing 2^{24} different colors and building a histogram of this size is infeasible. The color space is thus first quantized into a fixed number of colors (bins) and images are compared by comparing their color histograms using some vector norm of the difference between the histogram vectors. Examples of schemes for image retrieval based on color historgrams are [4, 5, 6] and an analysis of color histograms can be found in

G. Bebis et al. (Eds.): ISVC 2005, LNCS 3804, pp. 502–509, 2005.

[7]. Since global color based retrieval considers only single pixels, it does cannot account for spatial correlation between pixels. To take into account the spatial properties of images based on the histogram approach, color coherence vectors (CCVs) [8] along with geometric histograms [9] have been proposed. CCVs measure the spatial coherence of the pixel for a given color, i.e. a large coherent regions of a color corresponds to a high coherence value, where as the geometric histograms consider the distribution of certain fixed geometric configurations over the entire image. In this work, spatial information is incorporated implicitly when we perform quantization on image blocks instead of single pixels.

VQ based image classification and retrieval has been proposed in the past. Idris and Panchanathan [10] use VQ to index compressed images and video data. Images are initially compressed using a universal VQ codebook, then for each code vector in the codebook, a histogram of image pixels is generated (the number of pixels is taken to be the number of colors in the image). Thus a linear combination of the code vector histograms weighted by the frequency of occurrence of a code vector approximates the per pixel (color) histogram of the entire image. Their results compare favorably to methods based on color histograms. They also propose another method that compares images based on which of the code vectors is used in an image. Even in this case, the reduced complexity similarity evaluation performs as well as color histograms [11]. Lu and Teng [12] also employ a universal codebook to represent each image and use the histogram intersection (HI) between code vector usage histograms to compute similarity. The VQ based methods described so far make use of a universal codebook where if images with different statistical properties (classes) were to be later added to the database, then the codebook may need to be updated to maintain retrieval accuracy. One way to solve this is to design separate codebooks for each image. Schaefer [13, 14] uses this approach and constructs a separate codebook for each image. The images are then compared indirectly by computing a modified Hausdorff distance (MHD) between the image codebooks. In this work as well, we make use of the VQ codebooks, but instead comparing codebooks, we evaluate the similarity between a query image and a database image by evaluating the encoding distortion when the query image is compressed with the database image codebook. This idea is similar to that of maximum likelihood classification where data is classified as belonging to one of several class models (codebooks) depending upon which model results in the maximum probability (minimum distortion). Jeong and Gray [15] use a similar method called minimum distortion image retrieval (MDIR). Gaussian mixtures are used as image models and retrieval takes place by encoding the query image with the Gaussian mixture codebooks. The best match is the image corresponding to the codebook for which the query image had minimum distortion. Although the Gaussian mixture codebooks are robust, they are unsuitable for image compression since the number of mixture components is usually quite small, eight in this case.

Section 2 briefly describes vector quantization, Section 3 explains our method for image similarity along with the MHD based method. Section 4 presents experiments. Section 5 concludes.

2 Vector Quantization

Vector Quantization (see the book by Gersho and Gray [16]) is a lossy encoding method used to quantize and compress source signal vectors. Traditional VQ works by training on a set of training vectors to construct a codebook and then using this codebook to encode source vectors. For image VQ, the image is blocked into N, k-dimensional source vectors, $\{x_i\}_{i=1}^{N}$, then using a clustering algorithm such as the LBG [17], a codebook $\mathcal{C}$ with M code vectors is built. For example, if $k = 16$, the image can be partitioned into 4×4 sub-images. Encoding takes place by assigning, to each source vector x, a code vector $y_i \in \mathcal{C}$ following the nearest-neighbor mapping:

$$Q(x) = y_i \text{ only if } d(x, y_i) \leq d(x, y_j) \text{ for all } j \neq i \ , \tag{1}$$

where $d(x, y)$ is the cost or distortion function usually taken to be, as it is in this work, the squared Euclidean distance between two vectors:

$$d(x, y) \equiv \|x - y\|^2 = \sum_{i=1}^{k} (x_i - y_i)^2 \ . \tag{2}$$

3 VQ Based Image Similarity

In this section we describe our approach to image similarity using VQ. It can be seen that because we quantize image blocks rather than single pixels, VQ captures some amount of interpixel (intrablock) spatial correlation along with some textural attributes. The VQ codebooks along with the usage frequencies of code vectors form a generative model for the image and code vectors represent the principle regions or modes in the images. Thus we expect that encoding an image with a codebook of a similar image will yield a better representation than when a codebook of a dissimilar image is used. Schaefer [13] uses a separate codebook for each image as its feature. Image similarity is assessed by directly comparing the codebooks of the respective images. The distance measure is modified version of the Hausdroff Distance between two point sets. Basically, the distance measure computes how far, on average, a code vector from a codebook is from another codebook. For our experiments, we compare our approach with that of Schaefer's MHD approach since to our knowledge is the only one that uses separate codebooks for each image and advocates compressed domain image retrieval. In the following section we define our similarity measure and also explain the MHD measure.

3.1 Encoding Distortion Distance

To determine the similarity between a query image A, and a database image B, our system computes a simple retrieval distance which is defined to be the mean squared error when A is encoded with B's codebook. To make the distance symmetric, we consider the maximum of the mean squared error in the both directions. Specifically, given two images A and B with M-level, codebooks C_A and C_B respectively with k-dimensional code vectors, the encoding distortion distance (EDD) is determined by

$$d_{\mathrm{EDD}}(A, B) = \max\{d_{\mathrm{ED}}(A, C_B), d_{\mathrm{ED}}(B, C_A)\} , \tag{3}$$

where

$$d_{\mathrm{ED}}(X, C) = \frac{1}{Nk} \sum_{i=1}^{N} \min_j \|x_i - y_j\|^2 \tag{4}$$

is the average per component squared Euclidean distance between source vectors $X = \{x_i\}_{i=1}^N$ and code vectors $C = \{y_j\}_{j=1}^M$.

3.2 Modified Hausdorff Distance

We compare the EDD approach with a similar method based on the modified Hausdorff distance between image codebooks. For images A and B with M-level, k-dimensional codebooks C_A and C_B respectively, the MHD is determined by

$$d_{\mathrm{MHD}}(A, B) = \max\{d_{\mathrm{mhd}}(C_A, C_B), d_{\mathrm{mhd}}(C_B, C_A)\} , \tag{5}$$

where

$$d_{\mathrm{mhd}}(C_A, C_B) = \frac{1}{M} \sum_{i=1}^{M} \min_j \|y_i^{(A)} - y_j^{(B)}\|^2 . \tag{6}$$

This measure computes how far two codebooks are by computing the maximum of the average distance of a codebook from the other.

4 Experiments

To test our method, we use the database due to Wang, Li and Wiederhold [18] available on the web[1]. It is a subset of the COREL collection containing generic mostly photographic images. The database consists of a 1000 JPEG images which are either 256×384 or 384×256 with 100 images per class. The classes are semantically classified as: *Africans, Beach, Architecture, Buses, Dinosaurs (graphic), Elephants, Flowers, Horses, Snow Mountains and Foods.* Sample images from each class are shown in figure 1. Retrieval effectiveness is evaluated using two standard quantities: *precision* and *recall*. The precision is defined as the fraction of the images retrieved that are relevant (belong to the same class as the query) and recall is the fraction of the relevant images that are retrieved. For a given query, let a be the number of relevant images that are retrieved, b, the number of irrelevant items and c, the number of relevant items that were not retrieved. Then, precision is given by

$$p = \frac{a}{a + b} \tag{7}$$

[1] `http://wang.ist.psu.edu/docs/related/`

Fig. 1. Sample database images from each class. *Africans, Beach, Architecture, Buses, Dinosaurs* (left) and *Elephants, Flowers, Horses, Snow Mountains, Foods* (right).

and the recall is given by

$$r = \frac{a}{a+c} . \tag{8}$$

Generally the precision and recall are shown on a single graph so that they may show the change in precision as the recall increases. Since the precision typically drops as the recall increases, a retrieval system is said to be more effective if it has higher precision at the same recall values.

4.1 Image Features

We consider simple pixel image features for our experiments. However, the images are first transformed from the RGB color space to the perceptually uniform *CIE* $L^*u^*v^*$ color space where the Euclidean distance between colors closely approximates their perceptual distance [19]. For computational convenience, the system retains the central 256×256 region of each image. With our current system, when an image is added to the database, its VQ codebook is computed with a standard splitting algorithm (e.g., see the book of Gersho and Gray [16]). Codebook training and generation is done on 4×4 arrays of 3-byte pixels, and feature vectors (codebook entries) are 48-dimensional ($4 \times 4 \times 3$) real vectors.

4.2 Results

Figure 2(a)-(f) shows the database average precision vs. recall curves for various codebook sizes. The curves are the average for all 1000 database images when each of them is queried in turn. The plots show that the EDD method outperforms the MHD method over all codebook sizes. A possible reason for higher precision at a given recall could be because the average distortion per vector is

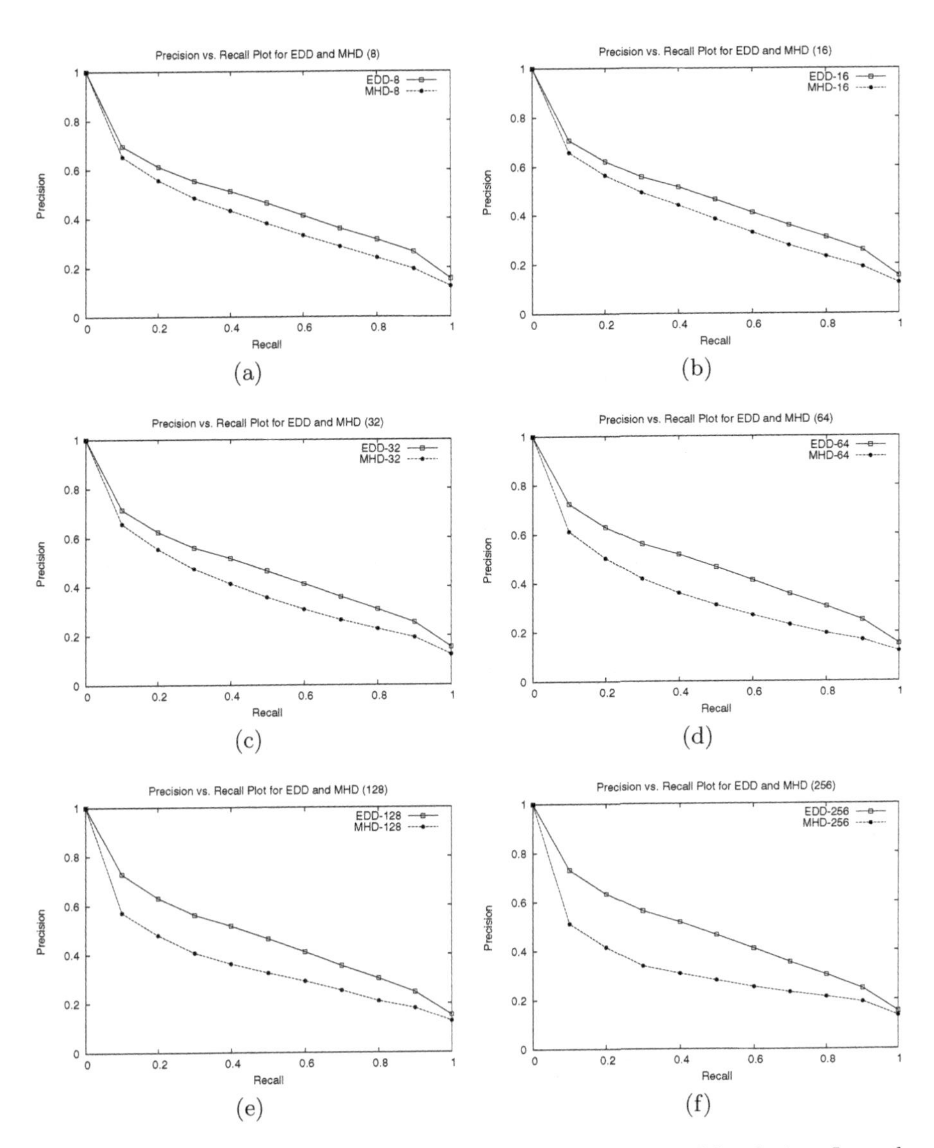

Fig. 2. Database average precision vs. recall curves for various codebook sizes. It can be seen that the EDD method performs better over the entire range. Also as the codebook size increases, the gap between EDD and MHD widens.

smaller when considering the entire image (all image vectors) than when only the image codebooks are considered. As a consequence the MHD assigns a lower similarity value (higher distortion) for intraclass images and this degrades the retrieval precision. We can also see in figure 3 that the codebook size has almost no effect on the EDD retrieval performance, this is not unexpected since a bigger codebook most likely contains the smaller codebooks. Thus a larger codebook will better represent intraclass images but it can also represent extraclass

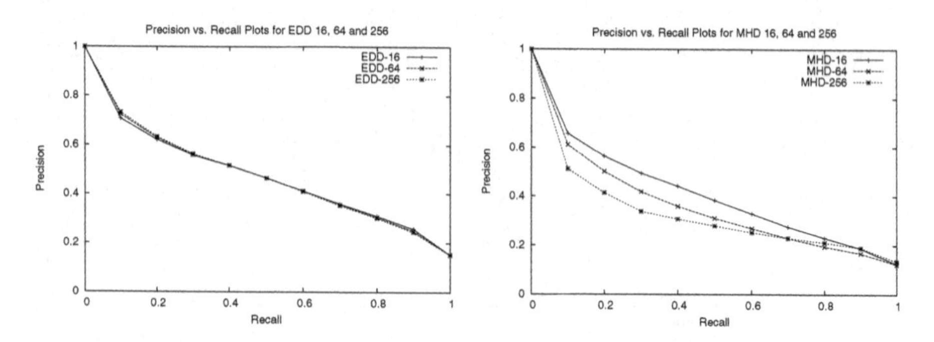

Fig. 3. Precision vs. recall curves for EDD (left) and MHD (right) for various codebook sizes

images better. Thus we see only a slight improvement in the retrieval precision. The same however cannot be said about the MHD method which performs best when codebooks are small. Again the reason could be due to high intraclass distortion.

5 Conclusion and Future Work

A simple image retrieval method based on VQ compression has been introduced. By considering VQ codebooks as image descriptors, a query can be assigned to class whose codebook best encodes the query. The similarity measure has been shown to be robust with respect to codebook sizes and compares favorably with current VQ based systems. In future work we wish to compare our work with that of Jeong and Gray [16]. We do not report the comparison in this work since their approach requires fixed sizes for the model components (codebooks) and remains to be implemented. However we did compare our results for codebook size eight and although the image feature are not the same (they use a more robust HSV color space), our work improves retrieval precision for some classes (like *Beach* and *Horses*) but on average compares well with their work. Also we wish to further investigate retrieval systems which operate either partially or completely in the compressed domain.

References

1. Eakins, J.P., Graham, M.E.: Content-Based Image Retrieval. Technical report, JISC Technology Applications Programme (1999)
2. Furht, B., Smoliar, S.W., Zhang, H.: Video and Image Processing in Multimedia Systems. Kluwer Academic Publishers (1995)
3. Gevers, T.: Color in Image Search Engines. In: Principles of Visual Information Retrieval. Springer-Verlag (2001)
4. Swain, M.J., Ballard, D.H.: Color Indexing. International Journal of Computer Vision **7** (1991) 11–32

5. Flickner, M., Sawhney, H., Niblack, W., Ashley, J., Huang, Q., Dom, B., Gorkani, M., Hafner, J., Lee, D., Petkovic, D., Steele, D., Yanker, P.: Query by Image and Video Content: The QBIC System. IEEE Computer **28** (1995) 23–32
6. Smith, J.R., Chang, S.F.: VisualSEEk: A Fully Automated Content-Based Image Query System. In: Proceedings of the fourth ACM International Conference on Multimedia. (1996) 87–98
7. Stricker, M., Swain, M.: The Capacity of Color Histogram Indexing. In: IEEE Conference on Computer Vision and Pattern Recognition. (1994) 704–708
8. Pass, G., Zabih, R., Miller, J.: Comparing Images Using Color Coherence Vectors. In: ACM Multimedia. (1996) 65–73
9. Rao, A., Srihari, R.K., Zhang, Z.: Geometric Histogram: A Distribution of Geometric Configurations of Color Subsets. In: Proceedings of SPIE on Internet Imaging. Volume 3964. (2000) 91–101
10. Idris, F., Panchanathan, S.: Image and Video Indexing using Vector Quantization. Machine Vision and Applications **10** (1997) 43–50
11. Idris, F., Panchanathan, S.: Storage and Retrieval of Compressed Images. IEEE Transactions on Consumer Electronics **43** (1995) 937–941
12. Lu, G., Teng, S.: A Novel Image Retrieval Technique based on Vector Quantization. In: Proceedings of International Conference on Computational Intelligence for Modeling, Control and Automation. (1999) 36–41
13. Schaefer, G.: Compressed Domain Image Retrieval by Comparing Vector Quantization Codebooks. In: Proceedings of the SPIE Visual Communications and Image Processing. Volume 4671. (2002) 959–966
14. Schaefer, G., Naumienko, W.: Midstream Content Access by VQ Codebook Matching. In: Imaging Science, Systems and Technology. Volume 1. (2003) 170–176
15. Jeong, S., Gray, R.M.: Minimum Distortion Color Image Retrieval Based on Lloyd-Clustered Gauss Mixtures. In: Proceedings of the IEEE Data Compression Conference. (2005) 279–288
16. Gersho, A., Gray, R.M.: Vector Quantization and Signal Compression. Kluwer Academic Publishers (1992)
17. Linde, Y., Buzo, A., Gray, R.M.: An Algorithm for Vector Quantizer Design. In: IEEE Transactions on Communications. Volume 28. (1980) 84–95
18. Wang, J.Z., Li, J., Wiederhold, G.: SIMPLIcity: Semantics-sensitive Integrated Matching for Picture LIbraries. IEEE Transactions on Pattern Analysis and Machine Intelligence **23** (2001) 947–963
19. Wyszecki, G., Stiles, W.: Color Science: Concepts and Methods, Quantitative Data and Formulae. 2 edn. Wiley-Interscience (2000)

Multi-aspect Target Tracking in Image Sequences Using Particle Filters

Li Tang, Vijay Bhaskar Venkataraman, and Guoliang Fan

School of Electrical and Computer Engineering,
Oklahoma State University, Stillwater, OK 74078

Abstract. This paper addresses the issue of multi-aspect target tracking where target's aspect is modeled by a continuous-valued affine model. The affine parameters are assumed to follow first-order Markov models and augmented with target's kinematic parameters in the state vector. Three particle filtering algorithms, Sequential Importance Re-sampling (SIR), the Auxiliary Particle Filter (APF1), and a modified APF (APF2) are implemented and compared along with a new initialization technique. Specifically, APF2 involves two likelihood functions and a re-weighting scheme to balance the diversity and the focus of particles. Simulation results on simulated infrared image sequences show the proposed APF2 algorithm significantly outperforms SIR and APF1 algorithms for multi-aspect target tracking in terms of robustness, accuracy and complexity.

1 Introduction

Target tracking is usually formulated as an estimation problem of a dynamic state-space system, where the state stores the kinematic characteristics of the target and two models are involved, i.e., the system model and the observation model. Given a probabilistic state-space formulation, the tracking problem is well suited for the Bayesian approach which attempts to construct the posterior probability density function (PDF) of the state based on all state/observation information available. In order to process sequentially received data efficiently, a recursive Bayesian filtering approach is needed which is composed of two steps: predict and update. The former one uses the system model to predict the stage PDF forward based on the past state, and latter one modifies the predicted PDF based on the lately received observation. If the posterior PDF at every time step is Gaussian, and both system and observation models are linear functions, the Kalman filter can offer the optimal solution to the tracking problem. If the system/observation models are not linear, the extended Kalman filter (EKF) linearizes the non-linear functions by using the first term in the Taylor series expansion. Still the EKF always approximates the posterior PDF to be Gaussian [1]. The sequential importance sampling (SIS) algorithm, or so called particle filtering, is a recently proposed technique to deal with nonlinear/non-Gaussian Bayesian tracking problems [2]. It implements a recursive Bayesian filter by Monte Carlo (MC) simulations. The key idea is to represent the required posterior density function by a set of weighted particles and to estimate the state based on these particles and their weights.

G. Bebis et al. (Eds.): ISVC 2005, LNCS 3804, pp. 510–518, 2005.

In this paper, we want to consider a specific non-linear tracking problem where the variation of target's aspect is modeled by an affine model. Specifically, we incorporate a continuous-valued affine model into the state/observation models to accommodate variant rotation and scaling factors of a given target. We assume that the dynamics of aspect parameters follow a first-order Markov process. Previous work assumes that multi-aspect target signatures are stored in a library and a discrete-valued aspect index is included in the state vector [3]. We propose a new algorithm to deal with the problem of multi-aspect target tracking, where the aspect parameters are continuous and can be estimated during the tracking process. Three specific SIS algorithms, Sequential Importance Resampling (SIR), the Auxiliary Particle Filter (APF1), a modified APF (APF2) are implemented. APF2 involves two likelihood functions and a re-weighting scheme to improve the particle distribution, and a new initialization technique is developed to improve the performance of multi-aspect target tracking.

2 System, Observation and Multi-aspect Models

2.1 System and Observation Models

Let Δ denotes the time interval between two consecutive frame. The state vector at instant $t = k\Delta$ ($k \in \mathbb{N}$) of a target typically consists of position (x_k,y_k), and velocity ($\dot{x_k}$,$\dot{y_k}$), of its centroid in a 2D Cartesian coordinate system: $\mathbf{x}_k = [x_k\ \dot{x_k}\ y_k\ \dot{y_k}]$. The random sequences of the position and the velocity are assumed to be statistically independent and evolve over time according to the white noise acceleration model [3]. The state update equation can be written as

$$\mathbf{x}_k = \mathbf{F}\mathbf{x}_{k-1} + \mathbf{w}_{k-1} \ , \tag{1}$$

where the transitional matrix $\mathbf{F} = [1\ \Delta;\ 0\ 1]$, and the process noise $\mathbf{w}_k$ is assumed to be white and zero-mean Gaussian. The observation matrix $\mathbf{z}_k$ collects the observations $\{(i,j)|1 \le i \le L, 1 \le j \le M\}$ at instant $t = k\Delta$:

$$\mathbf{z}_k = \mathbf{H}(\mathbf{x}_k) + \mathbf{v}_k \ . \tag{2}$$

This observation model is generated by adding a noise field $\mathbf{v}_k$ with a template of a specific intensity distribution. $\mathbf{H}$ is a function of the state of the target, i.e., $\mathbf{x}_k$. Process noise $\mathbf{w}_k$ in the state model is statistically independent of the clutter field $\mathbf{v}_k$ in the observation model [4]. The clutter frames $\{\mathbf{v}_k|k \in \mathbb{N}\}$ are assumed to be an independent, identically distributed (i.i.d.) Gaussian random sequences with zero mean and non-singular covariance matrices. It is described by the first order GMRF field given by [5]:

$$\mathbf{v}_k(i,j) = \beta_v^c[v_k(i-1,j)+v_k(i+1,j)]+\beta_h^c[v_k(i,j-1)+v_k(i,j+1)]+\varepsilon_k(i,j) \ , \tag{3}$$

where the unknown parameters β_v^c and β_h^c are, respectively, the vertical and horizontal predictor coefficients, and ε_k is the prediction error such that [6]

$$E[v_k(i,j)\varepsilon_k(l,r)] = \sigma_{c,k}^2\delta_{i-l,j-r} \ .$$

We can estimate the GMRF parameters, i.e., $\hat{\beta}_h$, $\hat{\beta}_v$ and $\hat{\sigma}_c^2$, for each frame $\mathbf{z}_k$ via suboptimal approximate maximum likelihood (AML) estimator in [7].

2.2 Multi-aspect Model

Traditional tracking methods assume that a target has one or several fixed aspects. However in practice, a target may appear in the image sequence with arbitrary aspects of many possibilities. The idea of discrete-valued aspect characterization in [6] inspires us to generalize multi-aspect tracking by introducing the continuous-valued multi-aspect model. Specifically, we incorporate an affine model to account for target's various aspects in each time step as follows:

$$\mathbf{T} = \begin{bmatrix} 1 & \alpha & -\alpha y \\ 0 & 1 & 0 \\ 0 & 0 & 1 \end{bmatrix} \begin{bmatrix} s_x & 0 & (1-s_x)x \\ 0 & s_y & (1-s_y)y \\ 0 & 0 & 1 \end{bmatrix} \begin{bmatrix} \cos\theta & \sin\theta & (1-\cos\theta)x-(\sin\theta)y \\ -\sin\theta & \cos\theta & (1-\cos\theta)y+(\sin\theta)x \\ 0 & 0 & 1 \end{bmatrix} \tag{4}$$

where α, s_x, s_y and θ are the shearing, scaling along x-axis, y-axis and rotation parameter, respectively. All of them are continuous-valued random variables which follow the first order Markov chain with equal transition probability (i.e., 1/3) of increasing, decreasing by a quantization step (Δ_α, Δ_{s_x}, Δ_{s_y}, Δ_θ) or staying at the same value in each time instant. Process noise (γ_α, γ_{s_x}, γ_{s_y}, γ_θ) is added to each random variable to reduce the quantization effect of parameter estimation. Therefore, we can define a new augmented state vector as:

$$\mathbf{x}_k = [x_k \ \dot{x_k} \ y_k \ \dot{y_k} \ s_x \ s_y \ \alpha \ \theta]^T. \tag{5}$$

Due to the nature of (4), the present observation model shows strong nonlinearity which cannot be tackled well by the Kalman filters. For simplicity, we set the shearing factor $\alpha = 0$ and $s_x = s_y$ to avoid unrealistic distortion.

2.3 Likelihood Functions of Observation

Let Z_k and $h(\mathbf{x}_k)$ be the 1D representations of the observed frame $\mathbf{z}_k$ and the clutter free target frame $H(\mathbf{x}_k)$ in (2) obtained by reading a frame row by row and stacking the rows as a long vector. Similarly, let V_k denote the 1D vector representation of the clutter frame defined in (3). For a given observation and given target state, the likelihood function is given by

$$p(Z_k|\mathbf{x}_k) \propto \exp\frac{2\lambda(Z_k)-\rho(\mathbf{x}_k)}{2\sigma_{c,k}^2}, \tag{6}$$

where $\rho(\mathbf{x}_k)$ is the *energy term* depending on the current target template (with certain rotation and scaling factors)

$$\rho(\mathbf{x}_k) = h^T(\mathbf{x}_k)(\sigma_{c,k}^2 \Sigma_v^{-1})h(\mathbf{x}_k), \tag{7}$$

and $\lambda(Z_k)$ is the *data term* depending on observation Z_k and target state $\mathbf{x}_k$,

$$\lambda(Z_k) = Z_k^T(\sigma_{c,k}^2 \Sigma_v^{-1})h(\mathbf{x}_k). \tag{8}$$

The calculation of $\lambda(Z_k)$ and $\rho(x_k)$ is discussed in detail in [4]. It is worth mentioning that the computation of $\rho(\mathbf{x}_k)$ and $\lambda(Z_k)$ involves linear interpolation of the original target template under the affine model according to (4). In the following, we will briefly review the SIS theory, and then three specific SIS algorithms will be discussed to implement multi-aspect tracking [1].

3 Multi-aspect Baysian Tracking Using Particle Filters

From the Bayesian perspective, the tracking problem is to recursively calculate some degree of belief in the state $\mathbf{x}_k$ at time k, taking different values, given the observation $\mathbf{z}_{1:k}$ up to time k. Thus, it is required to construct $p(\mathbf{x}_k|\mathbf{z}_{1:k})$ which may be obtained in two stages. With the Markov assumption, the prediction stage uses the system model to obtain the prior PDF of the state at time k as

$$p(\mathbf{x}_k|\mathbf{z}_{1:k-1}) = \int p(\mathbf{x}_k|\mathbf{x}_{k-1})p(\mathbf{x}_{k-1}|\mathbf{z}_{1:k-1})d\mathbf{x}_{k-1}, \tag{9}$$

where $p(\mathbf{x}_k|\mathbf{x}_{k-1})$ is given in the system model (1). Then the update stage modifies the prior via Bayes' rule based on the new observation $\mathbf{z}_k$:

$$p(\mathbf{x}_k|\mathbf{z}_{1:k}) \propto p(\mathbf{z}_k|\mathbf{x}_k)p(\mathbf{x}_k|\mathbf{z}_{1:k-1}), \tag{10}$$

where $p(\mathbf{z}_k|\mathbf{x}_k)$ is the likelihood function defined by the observation model in (2). The recursive relationship between (9) and (10) form the basis of the optimal solution. However, in general, the analytical solution is not tractable, and particle filters or SIS approximate the optimal Bayesian solution. The detailed algorithm implementation of particle filtering can be found in [1]. We will discuss a few new issues related to the problem of multi-aspect target tracking.

3.1 Initialization

The initialization, i.e., the initial particle distribution, plays an important role in most SIS algorithms, especially when the dimension of the state vector (i.e., $\mathbf{x}_k$) is increased. In [3], it was assumed that the target is initially located within a given region. In this work, we want to consider a more general case with no prior knowledge of the initial particle distribution, and we hope that the initial target state includes both kinematic variables and affine parameters. Therefore, we generate a number of target templates with different rotation and scaling parameters, i.e., θ and s, which are uniformly drawn from $[\theta_{min}, \theta_{max}]$ and $[s_{min}, s_{max}]$ respectively. Given a rotated and scaled template $\mathbf{G}(s, \theta)$, we can compute a similarity map $\mathbf{M}(s, \theta)$ to show the possibility that it is present in different positions. To do so, we need to remove the structured clutter by convolving $\mathbf{z}_1$ with the template of the GMRF model $\mathbf{H} = [0 \ -\beta_v \ 0; \ -\beta_h \ 1 \ -\beta_h; \ 0 \ -\beta_v \ 0]$. Then the resulting image is convolved with the given target template $\mathbf{G}(s, \theta)$:

$$\mathbf{M}(s, \theta) = [\mathbf{z}_1 * \mathbf{H}] * \mathbf{G}(s, \theta). \tag{11}$$

Given rotation and scaling parameters, θ and s, which is associated with a similarity map, i.e., $\mathbf{M}(s, \theta)$, we assign an appropriate weight to each position which is in proportion to the convolution output. A reasonable number of initial particles are selected according to their weights from all similarity maps, for which the initial affine parameters are determined in accordance with the rotation and scaling factors of the associated similarity map. We expect the proposed initialization technique will improve the performance of multi-aspect target tracking by providing a set of good particles with complete state parameters.

3.2 SIR and APF

In the SIR, *resampling* is used in each time step in order to reduce the degeneracy problem, and the prior $p(\mathbf{x}_k|\mathbf{x}_{k-1}^i)$ is used as the importance density for drawing samples. Since the optimal importance density relies on both $\mathbf{x}_{k-1}$ and $\mathbf{z}_k$ which is not considered in the SIR [1], the sampling process is usually less effective. The APF filter is another SIS algorithm with a more effective sampling process [8]. The idea is to draw samples twice so that the present observation is considered in the sampling process. First, we draw samples from the prior and compute the weights $\widehat{w}_n^j$. Then we draw an auxiliary sample indices k^j from set $1, 2, ..., N_p$ with $p(k^j = i) = \widehat{w}_n^i$ for all $j = 1, 2, ..., N_p$. This step helps us to identify those particles at time $k-1$ which will propagate with larger weights at time k. This information is stored in the auxiliary index table k^j based on which we will re-draw samples by propagating those "promising" particles more times. The pseudo-codes of SIR and APF filters are shown in Table 1.

However, there is a potential problem with the two-step particle drawing in the APF where the particle diversity may suffer due to two properties of the likelihood function defined in (6). The likelihood function has a bias towards smaller scaling factors due to fact that the ρ term depends heavily on the tar-

Table 1. Pseudo-code of the SIR and APF algorithms

Implementation of SIR Filter	Implementation of APF Filter
1. Initialization for $j = 1, \cdots, N_p$ Draw $x_{0,1}^j \sim p(x_{0,1}), x_{0,2}^j \sim p(x_{0,2})$ $r_0^j \sim p(r_0),\ s_{0,x}^j \sim p(s_{0,x}), s_{0,y}^j \sim p(s_{0,y})$ and set $w_0^j = 1/N_p, n = 1$ end 2. for j=1, $\cdots, N_p$ Draw $\widetilde{x}_{n,1}^j \sim p(x_{n,1}\|x_{n-1,1}^j)$ $\widetilde{x}_{n,2}^j \sim p(x_{n,2}\|x_{n-1,2}^j), \widetilde{r}_n^j \sim p(r_n\|r_{n-1}^j)$, $\widetilde{s}_{n,x}^j \sim p(s_{n,x}\|s_{n-1,x}^j)$, $\widetilde{s}_{n,y}^j \sim p(s_{n,y}\|s_{n-1,y}^j)$ and compute $w_n^j \propto p(y_n\|\widetilde{x}_{n,1}^j, \widetilde{x}_{n,2}^j, \widetilde{r}_n^j, \widetilde{s}_{n,x}^j, \widetilde{s}_{n,y}^j)$ end 3. Normalize such that $\sum_{j=1}^{N_p} w_n^j = 1$ 4. Resample to generate a new set of samples $[x_{n,1}^j, x_{n,2}^j, r_n^j, s_{n,x}^j, s_{n,y}^j]$ such that $p([x_{n,1}^j, x_{n,2}^j, r_n^j, s_{n,x}^j, s_{n,y}^j] =$ $[\widetilde{x}_{n,1}^k, \widetilde{x}_{n,1}^k, \widetilde{r}_n^k, \widetilde{s}_{n,x}^k, \widetilde{s}_{n,y}^k]) = w_n^k$ 5. Set $w_n^j = 1/N_p$ for $1 \leq j \leq N_p$ and estimate the mean values 6. Set $n = n + 1$ and return to step 2	1. Initialization: same as SIR 2. for j=1, $\cdots, N_p$ Draw $\widetilde{\mu}_{n,1}^j \sim p(x_{n,1}\|x_{n-1,1}^j)$ $\widetilde{\mu}_{n,2}^j \sim p(x_{n,2}\|x_{n-1,2}^j), \widetilde{\mu}_{n,r}^j \sim p(r_n\|r_{n-1}^j)$ $\widetilde{\mu}_{n,sx}^j \sim p(s_{n,x}\|s_{n-1,x}^j)$, $\widetilde{\mu}_{n,sy}^j \sim p(s_{n,y}\|s_{n-1,y}^j)$ and compute $\widehat{w}_n^j \propto p(y_n\|\widetilde{\mu}_{n,1}^j, \widetilde{\mu}_{n,2}^j, \widetilde{\mu}_{n,r}^j, \widetilde{\mu}_{n,sx}^j, \widetilde{\mu}_{n,sy}^j)$ end 3. Normalize such that $\sum_{j=1}^{N_p} \widehat{w}_n^j = 1$ 4. for $j = 1, \cdots, N_p$ Draw $k^j \sim \{1, 2, ..., N_p\}$ such that $p(k^j = i) = \widehat{w}_n^i$ for $i = 1, 2, ..., N_p$ Draw $x_{n,1}^j \sim p(x_{n,1}\|x_{n-1,1}^{k^j})$, $x_{n,2}^j \sim p(x_{n,2}\|x_{n-1,2}^{k^j}), r_n^j \sim p(r_n\|r_{n-1}^{k^j})$, $s_{n,x}^j \sim p(s_{n,x}\|s_{n-1,x}^{k^j})$, $s_{n,y}^j \sim p(s_{n,y}\|s_{n-1,y}^{k^j})$ and compute $w_n^j \propto \frac{p(y_n\|x_{n,1}^j, x_{n,2}^j, r_n^j, s_{n,x}^j, s_{n,y}^j)}{p(y_n\|\widetilde{\mu}_{n,1}^{k^j}, \widetilde{\mu}_{n,2}^{k^j}, \widetilde{\mu}_{n,r}^{k^j}, \widetilde{\mu}_{n,sx}^{k^j}, \widetilde{\mu}_{n,sy}^{k^j})}$ end 5. Normalize such that $\sum_{j=1}^{N_p} w_n^j = 1$ 6. Estimate the mean values 7. Set $n = n + 1$ and return to step 2

get size. Also, the particle weights tend to have a large dynamic range which encourages particles drawn from a small set of particles in the second-step.

3.3 APF1 and APF2

To mitigate the above mentioned problems we propose two techniques to modify the existing APF algorithm. Specifically, we use an alternative likelihood function in the first step that is less sensitive to the target aspect (rotation and scaling), and we also adopt a re-weighting scheme to increase the diversity of particles drawn in the second-step. The modified APF algorithm is called APF2 in contrast to the original one, i.e., APF1. The new likelihood function, as defined in (12), is independent of the ρ term, implying that the likelihood will be less sensitive to the affine parameters. Also $\sigma^2_{c,k}$ is omitted as it is almost a constant over different frames.

$$\tilde{p}(Z_k|\mathbf{x}_k) \propto \exp\left(\lambda(Z_k)\right). \tag{12}$$

To balance the need of diversity (having multiple distinct samples) with the need of focus (multiple copies of samples with large weights), a re-weighting scheme applies a monotone function to the existing weights to meet a specific need [9]. In this work, we prefer to have a diverse set of particles at the first-step, so all weights W computed from (12) are re-weighted by function $\ln(W)$ thereby reducing the non-linear stretching effect imposed by the exponential function in (12). The original likelihood function defined in (6) is used in the second-time particle drawing when the high selectivity is desired for accurate state estimation.

4 Simulation Results

Similar to [6], we have generated simulated infrared image sequences by adding independent GMRF noise fields with a real infrared image of 240×240 pixels. Then the target template (15×35 pixels) is added to the simulated sequence whose centroid moves according to the white noise acceleration model with mean velocity of (-2,-0.5) and whose aspect (rotation and scaling) also varies according to the first-order Markov model. The simulated peak target-to-clutter ratio (PTCR) is 11.9dB. Additionally, the first-order Markov models of time-varying rotation and scaling are parameterized as follows. The rotation angles vary within $[-30°, 30°]$, and $\Delta_\theta = 2°$ with an additional uniform process noise depending on the step size. The scaling factors are changing within $[0.5, 1.5]$, and $\Delta_s = 0.05$ with an additional uniform process noise depending on the step size.

4.1 Comparison Between SIR, APF1 and APF2

We first evaluate and compare the tracking performance of SIR and APF. We also study the contribution of the match filtering based initialization. There are four criteria to be used for algorithm evaluation, i.e., the number of convergent

Table 2. Comparison of SIR, APF1 and APF2

Algorithms	Initia-lization	Particle number	# convergent runs	Steps to converge	Mean of error			Stdev of error		
					(x, y)	θ	s	(x, y)	θ	s
SIR	Yes	10k	9	4.7	0.78	0.74	0.012	0.44	0.72	0.016
	No	50k	2	2.5	1.23	0.97	0.049	1.52	1.28	0.063
APF1	Yes	10k	15	4.1	0.95	0.69	0.015	0.59	0.86	0.033
	No	50k	4	6.8	1.19	0.94	0.026	0.75	1.25	0.048
APF2	Yes	3k	20	2.5	0.76	0.87	0.011	0.69	0.64	0.021

runs out of 20 Monto Carlo runs, the mean of *convergence time* (the tracking error of position is below 2 pixels and never get larger than that thereafter), the mean and the standard deviation of estimation errors for all state variables. The results are shown in Table 2.

Remarks: It is shown that the proposed initialization improves both SIR and APF in terms of multi-aspect target tracking performance, with much less particles, higher percentages of convergent runs, and faster convergence speeds, compared with the case without initialization (i.e., uniform initialization). Specifically, APF2 outperforms SIR and APF1 algorithms almost in all aspects, showing the usefulness of two different likelihood functions and the re-weighting scheme

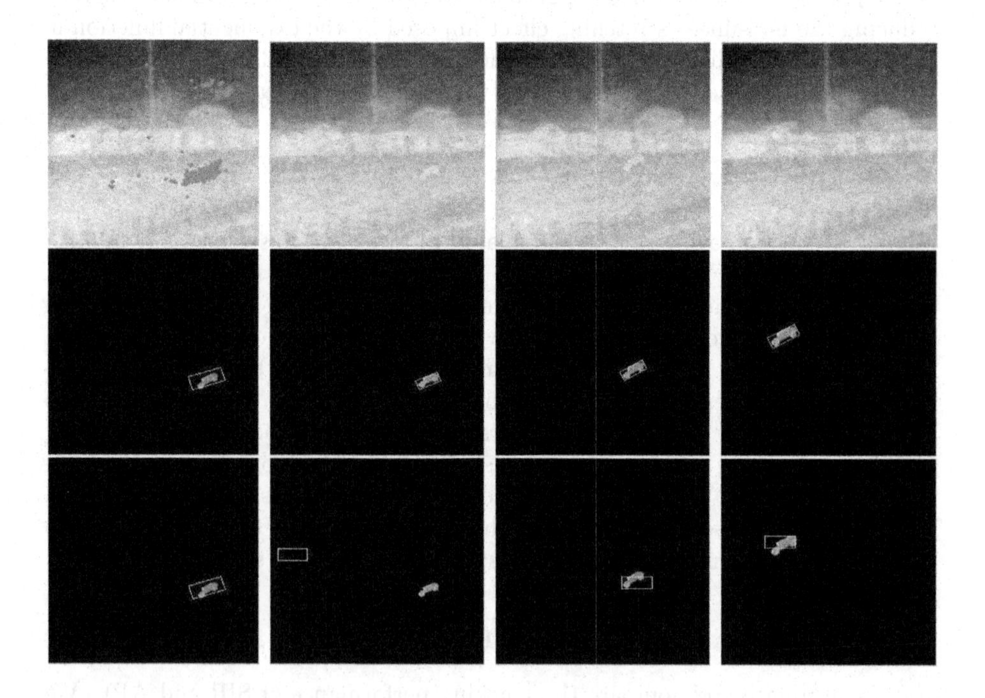

Fig. 1. Multi-aspect target tracking results of a 50-frame simulated image sequence. The dark dots represent the initial particle distribution in the first frame.

to balance the diversity and the focus of the particle distribution. Also, the match-filtering based initialization improves the efficiency and robustness of the tracking performance significantly with 100% convergent runs for APF2.

4.2 Tracking With/Without Affine Modeling

To demonstrate the effectiveness of incorporating the affine model into the system/observation models, we also evaluate the proposed APF2 algorithm by comparing it with the one without aspect modeling. As before, in addition to the motion model, the target has time-varying rotation and scaling parameters in the simulated image sequence. The simulation results are depicted in Fig. 1.

Remarks: It is shown that the proposed APF2 algorithm can accurately track the target with time-varying aspects. On the other hand, the particle filter without aspect modeling fails to track the target. With the help of match-filtering based initialization, APF2 can work very well with only about 3000 particles, and it also converges quickly, usually within the first 3 steps.

5 Conclusions

We have discussed a specific multi-aspect target tracking problem, where a continuous-valued affine model is incorporated in the state vector for multi-aspect modeling. Specifically, we have implemented three SIS algorithms, i.e., SIR, APF1 and APF2, as well as a new initialization scheme. APF2 is a modified APF1 which is able to balance the diversity and the focus of particles by involving two likelihood functions and a re-weighting scheme. Simulation results on simulated image sequences show that APF2 outperforms other two methods with the improved tracking performance and reduced computational complexity.

Acknowledgements

This work is supported by the Army Research Lab under Grant W911NF-04-1-0221.

References

1. Arulampalam, M.S., Maskell, S., Gordon, N., Clapp, T.: A tutorial on particle filters for online nonlinear/non-gaussian bayesian tracking. IEEE Trans. Signal Processing **50** (2002) 174–188
2. Gordon, N.J., Salmond, D.J., Smith, A.F.M.: Novel approach to nonlinear/non-gaussian bayesian state estimation. In: Inst. Elect. F. Volume 140. (1993) 107–113
3. Bruno, M.G.S.: Bayesian methods for multiaspect target tracking in image sequences. IEEE Trans. Signal Processing **52** (2004) 1848–1861
4. Bruno, M.G.S., Moura, J.M.F.: Multiframe detection/tracking in clutter: optimal performance. IEEE Trans. Aerosp. Electron. Syst. **37** (2001) 925–946

5. Moura, J.M.F., Balram, N.: Noncausal gauss markov random fields:parameter structure and estimation. IEEE Trans. Inform. Theory **39** (1992) 1333–1355
6. Bruno, M.G.S.: Sequential importance sampling filtering for target tracking in image sequences. IEEE Signal Processing Letters **10** (2003) 246–249
7. Moura, J.M.F., Balram, N.: Recursive structure of noncousal gauss markov random fields. IEEE Trans. Inform. Theory **38** (1992) 334–354
8. Pitt, M., N.Shephard: Filtering via simulation: auxiliary particle filters. J. Amer. Statistic. Assoc. **94** (1999) 590–599
9. Doucet, A., Freitas, J.F.G., Gordon, N.J.: Sequential Monte Carlo Methods in Practice. 1st edn. Springer-Verlag, Eds. New York (2001)

Segmentation and Recognition of Traffic Signs Using Shape Information

Jun-Taek Oh, Hyun-Wook Kwak, Young-Ho Sohn, and Wook-Hyun Kim

School of EECS, Yeungnam University, 214-1 Dae-dong,
Gyeongsan, Gyeongbuk 712-749, South Korea
{ohjuntaek, psthink, ysohn, whkim}@yumail.ac.kr

Abstract. This paper proposes a method for traffic sign recognition and segmentation using shape information of traffic sign. First, a connected component algorithm is used to segment candidate traffic sign regions from a binary image obtained based on the RGB color ratio of each pixel in image. Then actual traffic sign regions are segmented based on their X- and Y-axes symmetry. The recognition step utilizes shape information, including a moment, edge correlogram, and the number of times a concentric circular pattern from the region center intersects with the frequency information extracted by the wavelet transform. Finally, recognition is performed by measuring the similarity with templates in a database. Experimental results confirm the validity of the proposed method as regards geometric transformations and environmental factors.

1 Introduction

Recognition and segmentation of traffic sign have already been widely studied and the existing methods can be essentially classified as either color-based or shape-based. Color-based methods perform region segmentation based on the typical colors of traffic signs(i.e. red, blue, and yellow) to provide candidate regions. For example, H. Akatsuka[1] used a look-up table in Nrgb color space to specifically segment speed limit signs(red, white, and blue), and the same scheme was used by R. Ghica[2] in RGB(red, green, and blue) color space. N. Kehtarnavaz[3] focused on detecting stop signs with a specific range of HSI color space based on a statistical study of stop signs. In addition, G. Nicchiotti[4] performed a shape analysis of regions obtained using region growing in HSI color space. Based on the fact that traffic signs are usually painted with distinctive colors, color-based methods would be expected to be efficient. However, reliable segmentation of traffic signs using only color information has certain limitations, as color information is sensitive to changes in the weather or lighting conditions. Shape-based methods are already used in many fields, including object recognition, robot vision, solid (3D) object recognition and so on. However, the methods are more difficult, as complex real-images invariably include a loss of shape and changing view-points. In addition, road images can also contain numerous objects with similar shapes to traffic sign, so segmentation of traffic signs in road images requires complex processing steps. Y. Aoyagi[6] used genetic information and circular pattern matching based on edges extracted by a Laplacian filter, J. H. An[7]

G. Bebis et al. (Eds.): ISVC 2005, LNCS 3804, pp. 519 – 526, 2005.

applied a circular pattern to segmented candidate regions obtained using dominant color information in RGB color space.

This paper proposes a new method for segmenting and recognizing traffic signs in real-image. The segmentation step uses color ratio and the symmetric properties in X- and Y-axes directions of traffic sign. The color ratio, which is robust to changes in the light and weather, is used to create a binary image including candidate traffic sign regions. Then, the symmetric properties in X- and Y-axes directions, which are robust to scaling, are used to finally segment traffic sign regions. The recognition step consists of extracting the shape information and measuring the similarity. In this study, a moment, edge correlogram, and concentric circular pattern are used as the shape information, since they are robust to rotation and scaling. The segmented regions are then recognized by measuring their similarity to templates in a predefined database, where the similarity is measured based on the Euclidean distance.

2 Segmentation of Traffic Sign Regions

2.1 Binary Image Creation Using Color Ratio

Most images use RGB color space that consists of three components, i.e. red, green, and blue. Although RGB color space is simple, it is very sensitive to lighting changes. Therefore, a method that only uses the pixel brightness will be limited as regards segmenting traffic signs. HSI color space, which consists of hue, saturation, and intensity, is invariant to lighting changes, yet the transformation formula from RGB color space to HSI color space is nonlinear and computationally expensive. Moreover H may be undefined in accordance to S or I. Thus, a color ratio that uses the relation between color components obtains the characteristics of HSI color space as well as reducing the computation time. Plus, it can directly detect ROI(region of interest). A binary image using a color ratio can be obtained by:

$$g(x,y) = k_1 \begin{cases} T1_{low} \le f_g(x,y)/f_r(x,y) \le T1_{high} \\ T2_{low} \le f_b(x,y)/f_r(x,y) \le T2_{high}, \\ T3_{low} \le f_b(x,y)/f_g(x,y) \le T3_{high} \end{cases} \quad g(x,y) = k_2 \quad otherwise \tag{1}$$

where $f_r(x,y)$, $f_r(x,y)$, and $f_r(x,y)$ are the brightness values for each color component, red, green, and blue, respectively, and $T1_{low}$, $T1_{high}$, $T2_{low}$, $T2_{high}$, $T3_{low}$, and $T3_{high}$ are the thresholds that indicate the minimum and maximum value for a traffic sign within the brightness value range for each color component and k_1 and k_2 are the constants that represent the brightness for black and white, respectively, in the resulting image.

2.2 Region Segmentation Using the Symmetric Properties in X- and Y-axes Directions

In this study, traffic sign regions are segmented based on the region size, the number of crossing-points between edges and 8 directional scanning lines, and the symmetric properties in X- and Y-axes directions. After removing the candidate regions, which are not traffic signs, by the region size and the number of crossing-points, traffic sign regions are finally segmented according to the symmetric properties for remaining regions. The symmetric property can robustly discriminate a traffic sign region, except for the rotated regions. Based on the fact that the horizontal and vertical shape at the center of traffic sign is symmetric, the symmetric property is a way to compare the distance of the edge that is furthest in X-axis and Y-axis direction. Fig. 1(a) shows that any sign has the symmetric property in X-axis direction. Thus, the furthest edge points (i.e. LP and RP) in X-axis direction from the center of the region are identified, then the distance between the center and LP and the center and RP is divided into N sections. After calculating the distance of the furthest edge in the upper direction from the basis axis for region A and region B, the distances with the same index are compared using the Euclidean distance. Meanwhile, for region C and region D, the width of the candidate region is divided into N sections. Then, after calculating the distance (i.e. aldi and ardi) of the furthest edge in the lower direction from the basis axis, the distances are compared. If the measured value using the Euclidean distance is small, this means that the region has the symmetric property in X-axis direction. Therefore, in this study, if the value was less than 0.3, the region was considered a traffic sign region. Fig. 1(b) presents the symmetric property in Y-axis direction. The furthest edge points (i.e. TP and BP) in Y-axis direction from the center of the region are identified, and then the distance between TP and LP is divided into N sections. After calculating the distance (i.e. bldi and brdi) of the furthest edge in the right and left directions of Y-axis, the distances with the same index are compared. The following processes are then the same as mentioned above.

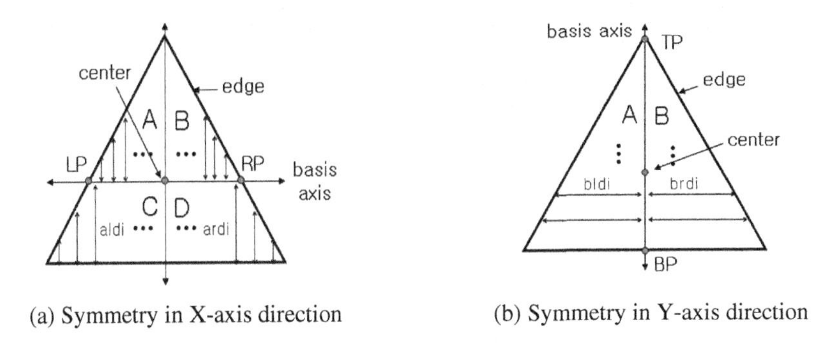

(a) Symmetry in X-axis direction (b) Symmetry in Y-axis direction

Fig. 1. Extraction of shape information using the symmetric properties in X- and Y-axes directions

3 Recognition of Traffic Sign Regions

Before performing the recognition step, first, the segmented regions as a traffic sign region are classified in accordance with color information, as a traffic sign consists of specific color, such as red and blue. Then, after enhancing a color of the regions using a histogram stretch, their size is normalized using a linear interpolation method. Finally, we extract shape information in binary images based on frequency information extracted by wavelet transform.

Wavelet transform decomposes the original signal into different frequency components and can be widely used as a tool to extract these components. Plus, it can perform multi-scale decomposition, similar to the human visual function. 2-dimensional wavelet transform is treated by iteratively performing 1-dimensional wavelet transform in horizontal and vertical direction. Fig.2 shows the image binarized by an adaptive threshold after decomposing a traffic sing region using daubechies-4 as the mother wavelet. In this study, we use binary images of all sub-bands by 2 levels to extract the following shape information.

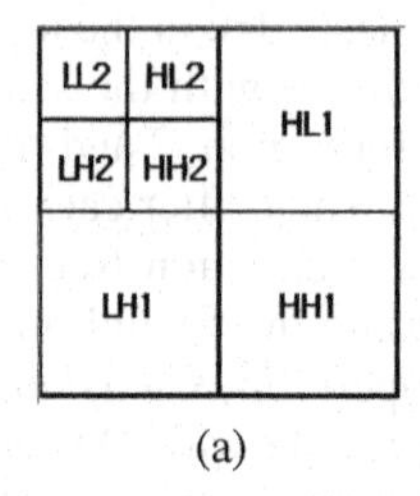

(a)

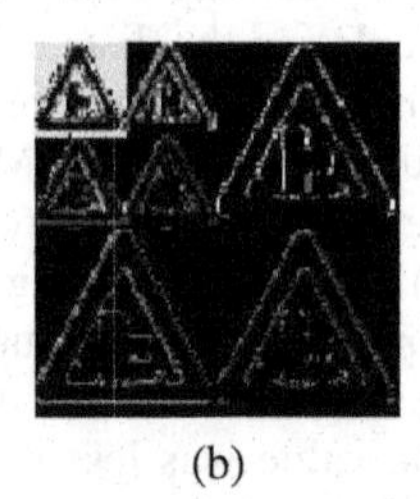

(b)

Fig. 2. Wavelet sub-band decomposition(2 level). (a) : As sub-bands decomposed by 2 level, 'L' and 'H' indicate a low and high frequency, respectively. (b) : Image binarized by an adaptive threshold after performing wavelet transform using daubechies-4 as the mother wavelet.

3.1 Moment, Edge Correlogram, and Circular Pattern as Shape Information

Moment. Moment is a superior shape descriptor in the field of pattern recognition and is widely used as feature information. The central moment for the digital function is given as Eq.(2) and the normalized moment η_{pq} is defined as Eq.(3).

$$u_{pq} = \sum_x \sum_y (x-x')^p (y-y')^q f(x,y) \qquad x' = m_{10}/m_{00}, \quad y' = m_{01}/m_{00} \tag{2}$$

$$\eta_{pq} = \frac{\mu_{pq}}{\mu_{00}^{\gamma}} \quad \gamma = \frac{p+q}{2} + 1 \quad (p+q) = 2,3,4... \tag{3}$$

An invariant moment set ϕ_i is easily derived from the normalized central moment and is invariant to various transforms, such as translation, rotation, and scaling.

Edge Correlogram. Correlogram was proposed by J. Hung[8, 9] to solve the problem that existing histogram-based methods retrieve images that have a similar color distribution despite a perceptively different image. Thus is due to the absence of spatial information. As such, correlogram includes spatial information between colors as well as color information. Thus, correlogram is widely used in the field of image retrieval. In this study, we perform correlogram based on edge in binary images to reduce the demanded computational time and memory size.

$$r_C^k(I) = P_{p_a \in I_C} \left[p_b \in I_C \,\middle|\, \| p_a - p_b \| = k \right] \tag{4}$$

$$\begin{gathered} \| p_a - p_b \| = \max(abs(x_a - x_b),\ abs(y_a - y_b)) \\ p_a = (x_a, y_a) \in I, \quad p_b = (x_b, y_b) \in I \end{gathered} \tag{5}$$

Where $r_C^k(I)$ is the probability that an edge(p_a) in image encounters another edge(p_b) at k distance away from itself, and the distance was set as $k = \{1,3,5,7\}$. Plus, I_C is the set of all edges existing in binary image.

Concentric Circular Pattern. We use the number of crossing-points between edges in binary image and imaginary circles with N different radii. This information is invariant to rotation and scaling, and shows the complexity of the edges according to the radius. Fig. 3 shows how a concentric circular pattern is applied to a '+' traffic sign.

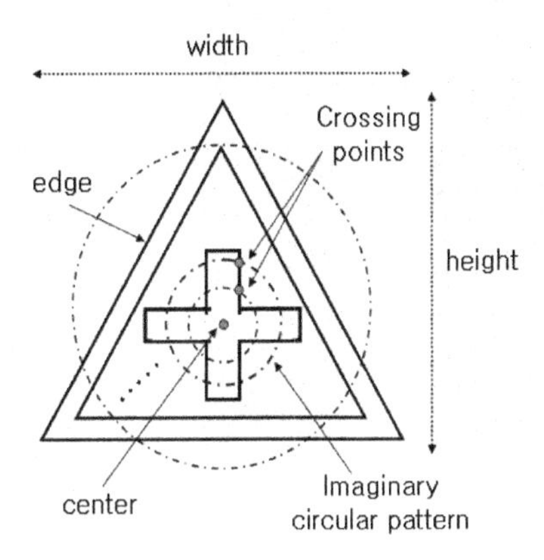

Fig. 3. Extraction of shape information using concentric circular patterns

Similarity. The similarity is measured between the features of the segmented traffic sign regions and a predefined database. The similarity measure function uses the Euclidean distance as follows:

$$ED_S = \sum_{j=0}^{m}(weight_j \times \sqrt{\sum_{i=0}^{n}(f_{i_{input}}^{j} - f_{i_{DB}}^{j})^2}) \tag{6}$$

where ED_S is the total similarity, $weight_j$ is the weight of the similarity between the j'th features, where the value of a weight is given in accordance with the degree of importance, $f_{i_{input}}^{j}$ and $f_{i_{DB}}^{j}$ are the features of the segmented region and predefined database, respectively, and m is the number of shape information and n is the number of features used for each shape information. If the value of ED_S is lower, this shows that the similarity is higher.

4 Experiment

The proposed system was implemented using JAVA SDK version 1.4.1 on Windows XP, and warning, regulatory, and indicatory signs obtained using Sony DSC-F505V in various environments were used as the experimental images. To obtain a red-binary image, the color ratio of red to green and blue as set at 0.6 as a threshold, and to obtain a blue-binary image, the color ratio of green and blue to red was set at 1.5 and the color ratio of blue to green was set at 1.5. If the proposed system did not segment any candidate regions, the thresholds were reset at 0.8 and 1.3 to create a red-based and blue-based binary image, respectively. In addition, the candidate regions were normalized at 128×128. The weights for the shape information, i.e. the moment, edge correlogram, and concentric circular pattern, were set at 0.35, 0.25, and 0.3, respectively. These thresholds and weights are determined by experiments with various images.

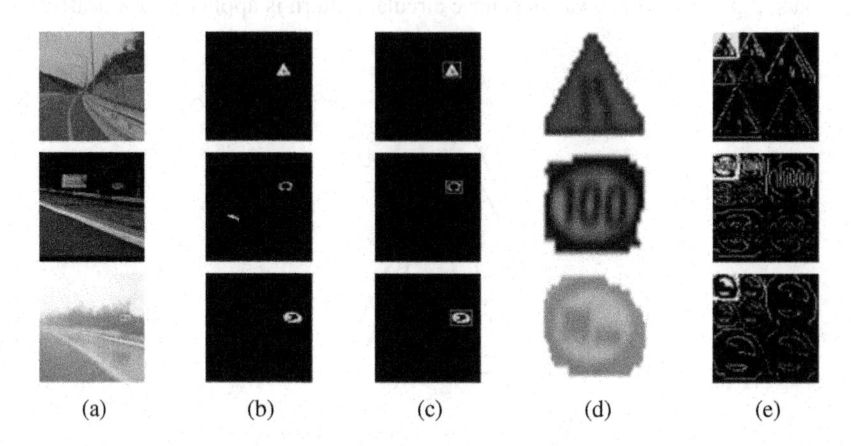

Fig. 4. Segmentation and wavelet transform of traffic sign regions. (a) : Experimental images. (b) : Candidate regions segmented by color ratio. (c) : Finally segmented traffic sign regions using the symmetric properties in X- and Y-axes directions. (d) : Normalized images of the segmented regions. (e) : Wavelet sub-band decomposition images of the segmented regions.

Fig. 4 shows the experimental images obtained in various environments. In Fig.4(b), the candidate traffic sign regions existing in certain environments, such as at night and in rainy and foggy weather, were effectively segmented by using color ratio. And as be seen in Fig4.(c), the traffic sign regions are finally segmented by using the symmetric properties in X- and Y-axes directions though the shape of them is a little lossy. Fig. 4(d) and (e) are the 128×128 normalized images by a liner interpolation method and the sub-band decomposition images for them, respectively. Tables 1 and 2 show the computational time and accuracy rate, respectively, for the segmentation and recognition of the traffic signs, including warning, regulatory, and indicatory signs. In the aspect of the computational time, the average computational time for segmenting a

Table 1. Processing time for region segmentation and recognition

	# of images	Computational time(msec)	
		Segmentation	Recognition
Warning	35	3777	1265.5
Regulation	30	4142	1030.4
Indication	35	3701	1235.21
Average	33.33	3873.33	1177.03

Table 2. Accuracy rate for region segmentation and recognition

	# of regions	Succession			Rate of segmentation (%)	Rate of recognition(%)	
		Segmentation	Recognition				
			# within 1 rank	# within 5 rank		# within 1 rank	# within 5 rank
Warning	45	44	33	41	97.77	75.00	93.18
Regulation	35	34	26	32	97.14	76.47	94.11
Indication	40	38	30	35	95.00	78.94	92.10
Average	40	38.66	29.66	36	96.66	76.72	93.10

Table 3. Similarity values for warning and regulatory signs. Row : Signs stored in database. Column : Signs segmented in the experimental images.

	Do not pass	Yield	Speed limit	No right turn
Do not pass	**0.083312**	0.180022	0.134764	0.110324
Yield	0.180305	**0.076962**	0.195615	0.204133
Speed limit	0.132568	0.188941	**0.117383**	0.148838
No right turn	0.127546	0.229555	0.139384	**0.101518**

Table 4. Similarity values for indicatory signs. Row : Signs stored in database. Column : Signs segmented in the experimental images.

	Crosswalk	Parking	Right turn	Roundabout
Crosswalk	**0.086898**	0.242694	0.233313	0.333459
Parking	0.257214	**0.127595**	0.141886	0.267155
Right turn	0.313318	0.254940	**0.195169**	0.199155
Roundabout	0.357787	0.296628	0.254066	**0.174285**

traffic sign was 3873.33msec and most of the time was spent on the labeling step involving the connected component algorithm. Plus, average computational time for recognizing the segmented region was 1177.03msec. In the aspect of the accuracy, an average of 38.66 sign regions were correctly segmented from 45 warning sign regions, 35 regulatory sign regions, and 40 indicatory sign regions. As such, the average accuracy rate for segmentation was 96.66%. Plus, an average of 29.66 sign regions was recognized, representing an average accuracy rate of 76.72%. However, in the latter case, only the region with the highest rank of similarity was considered. Moreover, the database used only included shape information on 102 standard traffic signs, yet real traffic signs can slightly vary from standard traffic signs. For example, the number notifying a speed limit will differ according to the road situation. In addition, if the size of the segmented region was very small, a lower accuracy rate was achieved even though a linear interpolation method was used to normalize the region. Therefore, when the five regions with the highest rank of similarity were considered, an average of 36 sign regions were recognized, representing an average accuracy rate of 93.1%. Tables 3 and 4 show the measured similarities between the features of the segmented region and the predefined database for traffic signs where the principal colors were red and blue, respectively. First row and column show the standard traffic sign images stored in database and the segmented traffic sign images. In Table 3 and 4, the same type of traffic signs had the highest similarity. Therefore, it indicates that the shape information used in this study is valid for recognition of traffic sign.

5 Conclusion

This paper proposed an improved method using shape information to segment and to recognize traffic sign regions in real-image. Color ratio is used to segment traffic sign regions, which avoids a transformation into another color space and is robust to weather and lighting conditions. In addition, the symmetric properties in X- and Y-axes directions are robust to scaling as well as a slight loss of shape, yet sensitive to rotation. Based on binary images created by wavelet transform, traffic sign regions are then accurately recognized using shape information, such as moment, edge correlogram, and concentric circular pattern information, which is robust to rotation and scaling. Future works will investigate an effective normalization algorithm for the scaling and recognition of a figure and number.

References

1. Akatsuka, H., and Imai, S.: Road signposts recognition system. In Proc. of SAE vehicle highway infrastructure: safety compatibility, (1987) 189-196
2. Ghica, R., Lu, S., and Yuan, X.: Recognition of traffic signs using a multilayer neural network. In Proc. of Canadian Conf. on Electrical and Computer Engineering (1994)
3. Kehtarnavaz, N., Griswold, N. C., and Kang, D. S.: Stop-sign recognition based on color shape processing. Machine Vision and Applications, Vol.6, (1993) 206-208
4. Nicchiotti, G., Ottaviani, E., Castello, P., and Piccioli, G.: Automatic road sign detection and classification from color image sequences. In Proc. 7th Int. Conf. on Image Analysis and Processing, (1994) 623-626
5. Estable, S., Schick, J., Stein, F., Janssen, R., Ott, R., Ritter, W., and Zheng, Y. J.: A real-time traffic sign recognition system. In Proc. of Intelligent Vehicles, (1994) 213-218
6. Aoyagi, Y., and Asakura, T.: A study on traffic sign recognition in scene image using genetic algorithm and neural networks. In Proc. of IEEE Conf. on Industrial Electronics, Control and Instrumentation, (1996) 1838-1843
7. An, J. H., and Choi, T. Y.: Dominant Color Transform and Circular Pattern Vector for Traffic Sign Detection and Recognition. IEICE Trans. on Fundamentals of Electronics Communications and Computer Science, Vol.E81, No.6, (1998) 1128-1135
8. Huang, J.: Color-Spatial Image Indexing and Applications. Thesis of Ph. of Doc. in the Faculty of the Graduate School of Cornell Univ., (1998)
9. Huang, J., Kumar, S. R., Mitra, M., Zhu, W. j., and Zabih, R.: Spatial Color Indexing and Applications. Int. J. of Computer Vision, Vol.35, No.3, (1999) 245-268

Detection and Tracking Multiple Pedestrians from a Moving Camera

Jong Seok Lim and Wook Hyun Kim

Department of Computer Engineering, Yeungnam University, Korea
{robertlim, whkim}@yumail.ac.kr

Abstract. This paper presents a method to detect and track multiple pedestrians from a moving camera. First, a BMA(Block Matching Algorithm) is used to obtain a motion vector from two consecutive input frames. A frame difference image is then generated by the motion compensation with the motion vector. Second, pedestrians are detected by the step that the frame difference image is transformed into binary image, a noise is deleted and a projection histogram is processed. And a color histogram is applied on the obtained pedestrian region to separate from adjacent pedestrians. Finally, color segmentation and color mean value is used to track the detected pedestrians. The experimental results on our test sequences demonstrated the high efficiency of our method.

1 Introduction

In this paper we present a method to detect and track multiple pedestrians in video sequences obtained from a moving camera. The class of applications we are interested in is the unmanned automobile system [1] with a car-mounted monocular color camera. In this system, pedestrian detection and tracking is an essential part. That is, a collision can be preventing from each other as previously perceiving a dangerous traffic situation. Therefore this can be used in various applications of a real world such as security or surveillance system and crosswalk signal control system [2].

The pedestrian detection is a previous step to track pedestrians. If pedestrians are detected correctly, the pedestrian tracking also can be achieved smoothly. Some of conventional pedestrian detection algorithms mainly detected one person and used a fixed camera. Generally, it is very ease to detect one pedestrian from a fixed camera. Because all moving objects can be detect by the frame difference from two consecutive input frames.

However, it is very difficult to detect and track multiple pedestrians from a moving camera because pedestrians are occluded or existed close at hand each other. Our goal is to obtain a robust algorithm able to cope with this situation.

There are many algorithms for moving object detection and tracking such as correlation based method, optical flow based method, shape based method, motion based method, frame difference based method, model based method, and contour based method. The correlation based method [3] is operated in case of a moving camera but it is difficult to detect nonrigid objects. The optical flow

G. Bebis et al. (Eds.): ISVC 2005, LNCS 3804, pp. 527–534, 2005.

based method [4] has drawbacks that obtains poor result in case that an interval between frames is wide, a illumination is change, a consistent shape can not keep it because of noise. The shape based method [5] should be consider conditions of a wide scope such as a shape of an object, a movement of flux, illumination, and a color. Both motion based method [6] and frame difference based method [7] do not detect pedestrians in case of having a subtle movement of background. The model based method [8] should be present an exact geometrical model and tracking model is limited to a minority. The contour based method [9] is difficult to track in case that a target object is occluded partially.

The traditional methods detected mostly one pedestrian from the fixed camera. In this paper, it is proposed an efficient novel algorithm that can detect and track multiple pedestrians from a moving camera. Our method has advantages that algorithm is simple and processing time is fast. The rest of this paper is organized as follows. In the next section, the proposed algorithm is described in detail. Section 3 shows the experimental results. Finally, Section 4 concludes this paper.

2 The Proposed Approach

The proposed algorithm is divided into six major steps as shown in Fig. 1. The first step is to calculate the motion vector by BMA from two consecutive input frames. This motion vector is our primary information for pedestrian detection from a moving camera. The second step is to calculate the frame difference using the motion vector from two consecutive input frames. In the third step, pre processing is carried out for the smooth work.

The frame difference image is transformed into binary image and noises also eliminated by the proposed noise deletion method. Then, pedestrians are detected by the projection histogram which is generated by counting pixels in the pre processed image with vertical and horizontal direction respectively. However, if pedestrians are adjacent to each other, it is very difficult to detect them and can know only the region of pedestrians.

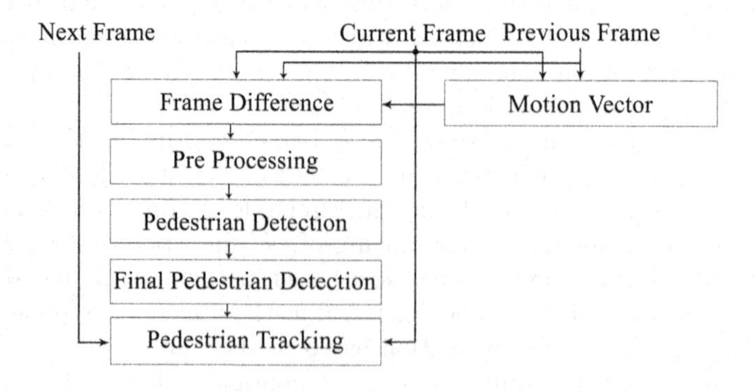

Fig. 1. Block diagram of proposed algorithm

The region of pedestrians which is not detected in the fourth step is separated by the color histogram in the fifth step. And the detected pedestrians are surrounded by bounding box. The sixth step is to track multiple pedestrians by comparing the color mean value in the region of pedestrians detected in the fifth step with that in a certain region of the next frame which is segmented by a color value.

The details of each step will be discussed in the following subsections.

2.1 Motion Vector

In case of a moving camera, the background in the image is change. In this status, it is very difficult to detect only moving objects using the frame difference between two consecutive input frames since a background region also is detected together with it. Therefore, we detect moving objects by the motion compensation using the motion vector which is calculated by the BMA.

The motion vector is founded by the direction dx, dy that minimized the total sum D of the difference between the region of the current frame and that of the previous frame while scanning in the four direction. Their relation is shown as follows:

$$D = \Sigma\Sigma|f_n(x_i, y_j) - f_{n-1}(x_i + dx, y_j + dy)| \quad (1)$$

where F_n is the current frame and F_{n-1} is the previous frame. x_i denotes the pixel location in the horizontal direction and y_j denotes the pixel location in the vertical direction. And the size of the region is set with 16×16 each and the maximum value of the moving in the region is set to the eight pixels in the all direction.

Once the motion vector is calculated, we find the representative motion vector to process the motion compensation. The representative motion vector is set to the motion vector that it emerged the most frequently among the entire motion vector. If the representative motion vector calculated in the image is $x = 4$ and $y = 3$, it means that the previous frame is moved as the four pixels to the x direction and the three pixel to the y direction.

2.2 Frame Difference

The frame difference between two consecutive input frames is widely used to detect moving objects because the computation complexity is very low. However, this method does not detect moving objects in case that the background change by the moving camera. Therefore, we use the representative motion vector founded the previous subsection to detect moving objects.

In this paper, we compute the frame difference by the motion compensation using the representative motion vector and the equation is shown as follows:

$$d(i, j) = |f_n(i + x, j + y) - f_{n-1}(i, j)| \quad (2)$$

where x and y is a component of the representative motion vector.

2.3 Pre Processing

After the frame difference step, moving objects is detected. However, due to the irregular camera movement, there exist some noise regions in the frame difference image. Therefore, a pre processing step to eliminate these noise regions is necessary.

First, the binary image is generated by thresholding the frame difference obtained in previous subsection. Then, noise regions are removed. A traditional way to remove the noise regions is using the morphological operations. However, these operations can remove not only noise regions, but also the object boundary.

We propose an effective noise removing method. This method is to remove all of the pixels existing in the window if the sum total of the pixels existing in the window which has an $n\times n$ size is smaller than a threshold value. The window size is set to a width 25 and a height 30. The threshold value is set to 72 pixels which is a size of the circumference inscribed in the window. That is, it deserves a face size of the pedestrian who want to detect.

2.4 Pedestrian Detection

The pedestrian detection step generates the bounding box around the pedestrian using the projection histogram. The projection histogram makes by the counting pixels which is the bigger than 0 through scanning to the horizontal and the vertical direction respectively. In [7] this method detects the position of pedestrians.

After generating the projection histogram, pedestrians are detected using human's shape information. The human being is very different from an automobile or an animal. In the case of dog and cat, the height is small and the width is big as compared with the human. In the case of automobile, the width is very big. Therefore it can distinguish human being from them using this information. However, this method can not detect pedestrians in case that multiple pedestrians are adjacent or some occluded each other.

Fig. 2 shows the projection histogram and the image which pedestrians are detected. As shown in Fig. 2, the pedestrian of the left was detected but pedestrians of the right were not detected individually because pedestrians are adjacent each other.

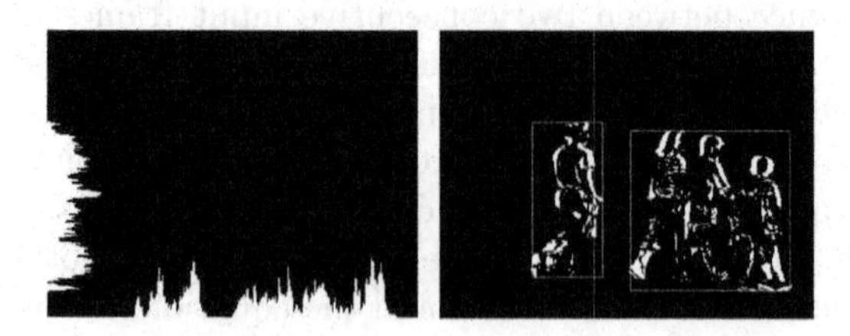

Fig. 2. Projection histogram and pedestrian detection result. The left is a projection histogram image and the right is a pedestrian detection result image.

2.5 Final Pedestrian Detection

If it fails to detect pedestrians with the projection histogram method, a color histogram approach is used. In the previous step, we founded the area existing pedestrians by the projection histogram. To separate pedestrians who exist in the area, we use a color histogram method based on RGB.

Generally, pedestrians who are adjacent each other can detect as separating the head part of them. In this paper, we assume that the size of the pedestrian's head is about 30 pixels. Because the size of the pedestrian's head that we want to detect correspond to it.

The method generating a color histogram for the area of pedestrians in the current frame is as follows:

- It draws a histogram with the RGB component of each pixel which exists on the first line of the pedestrian's region.
- It repeats the previous step from the second line to the thirty lines.

Fig. 3 shows the color histogram of the RGB component for the head part of pedestrians. As shown in the Fig. 3, it is possible to separate pedestrians with the only R component.

Fig. 3. RGB component color histogram. The left is a R component and the center is a G component. The right is a B component.

2.6 Pedestrian Tracking

After detecting pedestrians, the pedestrian tracking is processed using the color mean value. First, to track pedestrians effectively, the next frame is segmented as follows:

- On the round of the bounding box, it set the area of the 5 pixels.
- In the next frame, all of the region exclude the previous area is filled with the white color.

The pedestrian tracking method compares the color mean value of the current frame with that of the next frame which is segmented and finds the most well matching part. At this moment, the search area is limited to five pixels around the bounding box in the current frame. That is, it subtracts the color mean value in the bounding box of the current frame from that of the next frame in the search area and finds the region which the minimum value has and generates a new bounding box at the position.

3 Experimental Results

Simulations have been carried out on the video sequences captured in our city. And test platform is a personal computer with a 1.4 GHz Pentium 4 processor. The format of the test sequence is 320×240 at 15 fps. The quality evaluations for the both the pedestrian detection and tracking are applied on our algorithm.

3.1 Pedestrian Detection Evaluation

Both the error rate and the failure rate of the pedestrian detection are adopted to present the effectiveness of our algorithm. The error rate is defined as the following equation:

$$Error\ Rate = \frac{Error\ Pedestrian\ Count}{Pedestrian\ Count\ per\ Frame} \tag{3}$$

where the error pedestrian count(EPC) is the number of none pedestrians who is detected in error.

The failure rate is defined as the following equation:

$$Failure\ Rate = \frac{Failure\ Pedestrian\ Count}{Pedestrian\ Count\ per\ Frame} \tag{4}$$

where the failure pedestrian count(FPC) is the number of pedestrians who is not detected.

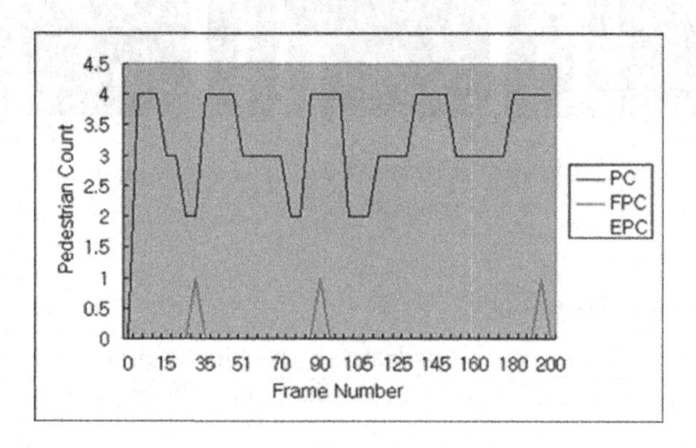

Fig. 4. Error rate and failure rate

Fig. 4 shows both the error rate and the failure rate of the video sequence. The error rate is 0% and the failure rate is 3% most of the time. This behavior corresponds to a much occlusion of pedestrians.

Fig. 5 shows the detection results for several benchmark sequences. The sequences are regular, slow, fast, and running pedestrian in JPG format. The detection results at frame #30, #60, and #90 of each sequence are shown in the figure. The regular and slow pedestrian sequences do not have occlusion so their detection results tend to be better than that of other sequences.

Fig. 5. Segmentation results for three benchmark sequences

3.2 Pedestrian Tracking Evaluation

The error of the pedestrian tracking is also adopted to present the effectiveness of our algorithm. The tracking error e is defined as the following equation:

$$e = \sqrt{(x - x')^2 + (y - y')^2} \tag{5}$$

where x and y denotes the location of the left upper corner point which is tracked by the full search method. $x^{'}$ and $y^{'}$ denotes the location which is tracked by our method.

Fig. 6 shows the tracking results for the regular, slow, fast, and running pedestrian sequences. As shown in Fig. 6, a high tracking error is due to a big camera movement.

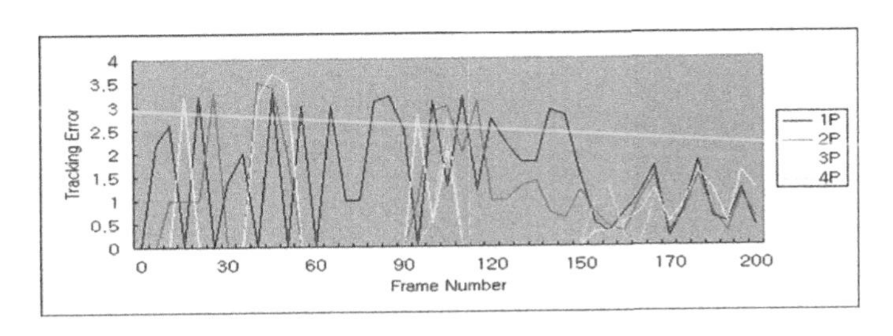

Fig. 6. Tracking result for all sequences

4 Conclusions

In this paper, we proposed an efficient method to detect and track multiple pedestrians in video sequences obtained from a moving camera. A BMA is used to compensate camera movement from the video sequence. And the moving object is detected by the frame difference and the pre processing is performed. Then, pedestrians are detected by the projection histogram. If pedestrians are adjacent or occluded each other, it is separated by the color histogram. Finally, after performing color segmentation, pedestrians are tracked using color mean value. The experimental results demonstrate the high efficiency of our approach as it have shown error rate of 0% and failure ratio of 3% and excellent tracking.

References

1. Franke U., Gavrila D., Goerzig S.:Autonomous Driving Approaches Downtown to Appear. IEEE Expert (1997)
2. Wohler C., Aulaf J.K.,Portner T., Franke U.: A Time Delay Neural Network Algorithm for Real-time Pedestrian Detection. Proc. of the IEEE Intelligent Vehicles Symposium'98, Stuttgart Germany (1998) 247-251
3. Inoue H., Tachikawa T., Inaba M.: Robot Vision System with a Correlation Chip for Real-time Tracking, Optical Flow and Depth Map Generation. Proc. of the IEEE International Conf. on Robotics and Automation. (1992) 1621-1626
4. Yamamoto S., Mae Y., Shirai Y.: Real-time Multiple Object Tracking based on Optical Flows. Proc. of the Robotics and Automation, Vol. 3 (1995) 2328-2333
5. Broggi A., Bertozzi M., Fascioli A.: Shape-based Pedestrian Detection. Proc. of the IEEE Intelligent Vehicles Symposium 2000 (2000) 215-220
6. Mori H., Charkari N.M., Matsushita T.: On-Line Vehicle and Pedestrian Detection based on Sign Pattern. IEEE Trans. On Industrial Electronics, Vol. 41 (1994) 384-391
7. Lim J.S., Kim W.H.: Multiple Pedestrians Tracking Using Difference Image and Projection Histogram. Proc. of the International Conf. on Imaging Science, Systems and Technology, Vol. 1 (2002) 329-334
8. Rohr K.: Towards Model-based Recognition of Human Movements in Image Sequences. CVGIP:Image Understanding, Vol. 59 (1994) 94-115
9. Paragios N., Deriche R.: Geodesic Active Contours and Level Sets for the Detection and Tracking of Moving Objects. IEEE Trans. on PAMI, Vol. 22(2000) 266-280

Event Detection in Underground Stations Using Multiple Heterogeneous Surveillance Cameras

Andrea Cavallaro

Multimedia and Vision Lab,
Queen Mary, University of London, Mile End Road, E1 4NS, London, UK
andrea.cavallaro@elec.qmul.ac.uk

Abstract. An automatic event detection system is presented that addresses the problem of safety in underground and train stations. The proposed system is based on video analysis from multiple heterogeneous cameras, including sensors in the visible and in the infrared spectrum. Video analysis on surveillance footage from underground stations is a challenging task because of poor image quality, low contrast between pedestrians and the platform, reflections and occlusions. To overcome these problems, statistical analysis, information fusion and domain knowledge are exploited. First, we perform robust object detection in each sensor using statistical colour change detection and a continuously updated background model. Then, we integrate the results using domain knowledge and a common ground plane for all cameras. Finally, a binary decision tree is defined to detect events of interests. The effectiveness of the method is demonstrated on the dataset of the Challenge for Real-time Events Detection Solutions (CREDS).

1 Introduction

The increasing processing power of low-cost microprocessors, the decreasing cost of storage devices and the shift from analogue to digital video CCTV cameras are enabling the automation of tasks that otherwise would require the intervention of a human operator. Digitalization and automation may result in more efficient and cost effective monitoring of pedestrians in underground and train stations. As an example, Figure 1 reports the number of accidents on London Underground between 1993 and 2003. The objective is to reduce the number of accidents and causalities in non patrolled stations and to increase the safety in transportation networks with autonomous trains.

The growing interest in automated analysis for monitoring underground and train station has been recently highlighted by the Challenge for Real-time Events Detection Solutions (CREDS) [1]. In the context of this challenge, a public dataset is provided, which was generated by the RATP, the Paris transport company, in the P.te des Lilas underground station. The dataset contains data for four different video cameras configurations (Fig. 2). For each configuration, three synchronised cameras (in the visible or infrared spectrum) cover the platforms and the tracks.

Several scenarios have been recorded with different camera configurations (Fig. 3). Each scenario consists of three video sequences corresponding to three video cameras in different positions.

G. Bebis et al. (Eds.): ISVC 2005, LNCS 3804, pp. 535 – 542, 2005.

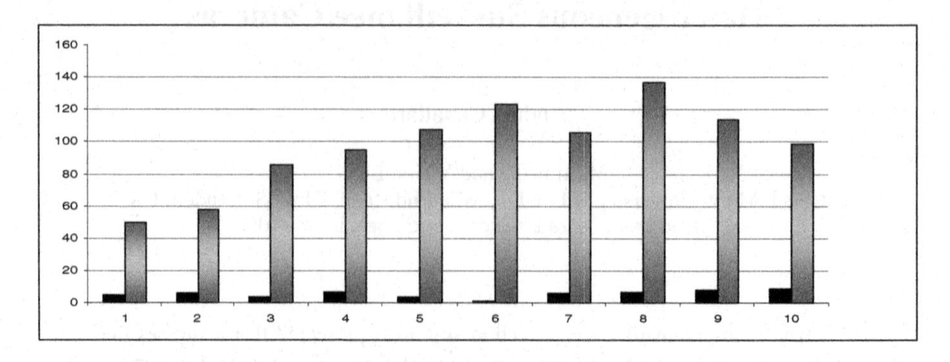

Fig. 1. Number of people killed (black bar) and injured (grey bars) each year on London Underground between 1993/1994 (1) and 2002/2003 (10). Source: Transport for London[1].

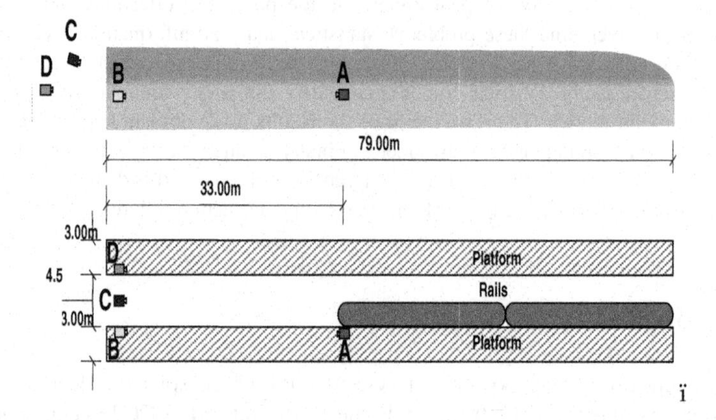

Fig. 2. Layout of the underground station and camera positions that have been used for the generation of the CREDS dataset [1]

The dataset presents a number of realistic and challenging image analysis problems. These problems include low contrast between the pedestrians and the platform, reflections on the surface of the platform and changes in illumination generated by the presence/absence of the train in the station. Additional complexity is introduced by the automatic gain control of the cameras, which is particularly strong for the infrared camera when people pass close to the sensor. Moreover, distortions are introduced in the data by the lenses of the cameras and the long field of view.

Given the camera configuration, traditional scene analysis methods based on carving objects' visual hulls or on stereo vision cannot be applied.

In this paper, we describe how we solved the above mentioned problems using image analysis techniques and the generation of a binary decision tree for event classification. In Section 2 the four major modules for image analysis are described. Section 3 reports on the experimental results and Section 4 concludes the paper.

---

[1] http://www.tfl.gov.uk/tfl/reports_library_stats.shtml

Fig. 3. Examples of camera configurations and events. *(top)* Configuration 1: video and infrared camera in A and video camera in C. *(centre)* Configuration 2: three video cameras in A, B, and C. *(bottom)* (a) a warning event; (b) an alarm event; (c) a critical alarm event (courtesy of RATP from CREDS dataset).

2 Proposed Approach

To classify the events of interest in the underground station, we use domain knowledge, video object detection and information fusion. The proposed system is organized in four major steps, namely object detection, object classification, object localization, and event classification. The *object detection* module filters each sensor input and generates a set of connected blobs. The filtering depends on the type of sensor. Statistical colour change detection [2] with continuous background update [3] is used for the video sensors. Background subtraction and edge detection [4] are used for the infrared sensors (Fig. 4).

To account for the perspective view and the different size of objects, the parameters of the statistical change detection are adapted to the distance from the camera. For the infrared camera, morphological operations and contour filling are used to generate the final blobs. The blobs are then classified into one of the following classes: *pedestrian*, *train* or *object* (e.g., paper, thrown object).

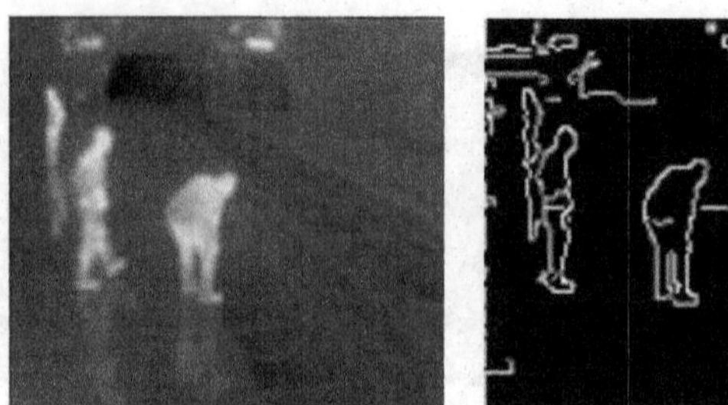
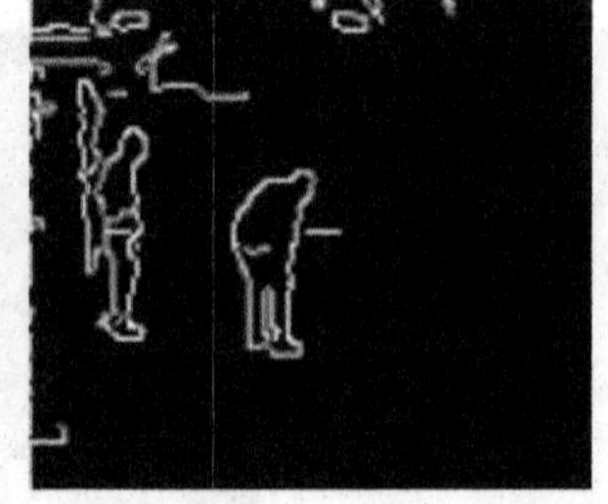

Fig. 4. Example of change detection based on edges for the infrared camera

The *object classification* module determines the class of the blobs based on rules that use the attributes of each blob. These attributes are size, location and direction of motion. For example, pedestrians and pieces of paper are classified based on their apparent size, whereas the train is classified based on its location (on the track), direction of motion (along the platform), and size (apparent width larger than half the track size).

Object localization is a particularly difficult task because of the perspective view of the cameras and because of possible accumulated errors from the object detection and classification modules. As the layout of the station is known (Fig. 2) and the cameras are fixed, an object position is defined using Regions of Interest (ROIs) in the scene. Five ROIs are defined, namely two platforms, R_1 and R_5, two proximity regions, R_2 and R_4, and the tracks, R_3. Moreover, three blob features are used for object localization: (i) the lower middle pixel of its bounding box; (ii) its contour; (iii) the size of the area, if any, overlapping R_2 or R_4. The first feature helps in predicting the position of the feet of a pedestrian [5], whereas the second and third features enable the localization of blobs that are overlapping more than one region. When the contour points of one blob overlap two regions, voting is used to decide which region the blob belongs to. This information is exploited in the *event classification* module.

There are three types of events of interest: warnings, alarms and critical alarms. The events of interest and their description are summarized in Table 1. Examples of events are given in Fig. 3, bottom. Events of interest are defined by the following object attributes: (i) type, (ii) position, and (iii) direction. Direction is used only for objects in R_3. Note that event classification requires the tracking of the object generating the event in order to correctly define the duration of each event.

Proximity warnings (ID1) are generated by pedestrians that are too close to the edge of the platform or that are kneeling along the edge of the platform. This event is detected when even a minor blob area is either in R_2 or in R_4 or if any contour point is on the white line and no contour point is on R_3. Warnings such as objects thrown on the tracks (ID2) are more difficult to detect as they require the use of the direction of motion as additional information. Moreover, the detection of ID2 events is more difficult because of the small size of the objects and the short life-span of the event. In fact, spatio-temporal regularization filtering that is used in the object detection module can classify objects generating ID2 events as noise and therefore remove them. A trade-off between small object detection and noise filtering is required with different parameters for each camera view.

Table 1. Events of interest in underground station

Event description	Event type	Event ID
Proximity warning	Warning	1
Objects dropped on tracks	Warning	2
Objects thrown across tracks	Alarm	3
Person trapped in doors of moving train	Alarm	4
Person walking on the tracks	Critical alarm	5
Person falling/jumping on the tracks	Critical alarm	6
Person crossing the tracks	Critical alarm	7

Alarms include an object thrown across the tracks (ID3) and a person trapped between the doors of a moving train (ID4). ID3 events are detected based on the object size and the direction of motion. For ID4 events the system should first detect the presence of moving train and then verify the presence of a person with the train and that also overlaps with the platform (R1 or R5). The detection of ID3 and ID4 events presents similar challenges to warning events. An ID3 event is similar to an ID2 event both in terms of detection strategy and problems associated with the classification.

Critical alarms (ID5-ID7) have a unique feature: they are generated only by pedestrians on the tracks. The direction of motion differentiates between people walking along the tracks (ID5) and people crossing the tracks (ID7). In addition to the above, object tracking is necessary to maintain the identity of the event over time. Object tracking is based on a combination of nearest neighbor filter and colour histogram intersection between subsequent observations of an object. Finally, as for the ID2 event, the detection of a person falling on the tracks (ID6) is more difficult because the duration of the event is very short and requires and ad-hoc analysis. To this end, the transition from region R2 or R4 to region R3 is checked as well as the direction of the object's motion.

Based on the above description of the events of interest, we perform event classification using a binary decision tree (Fig. 5). The proposed tree has branching factor B=2 and number of levels L=4. The leaf nodes represent the result of event classification and the root is a query whether an object is in R_3. The ID follows the definitions

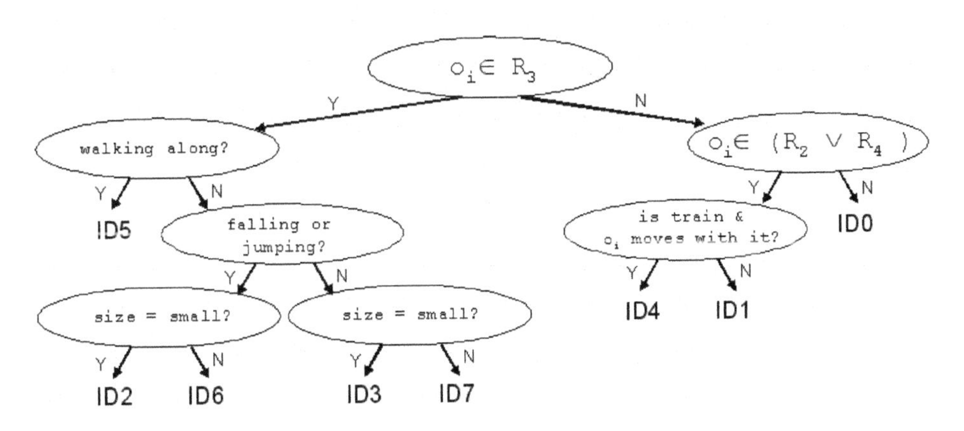

Fig. 5. Binary decision tree for event classification

in Table 1 and in addition there is ID0, which means no event. The tree is applied for each frame in which an object, o_i, is detected; and it is repeated for each object i, i=1, 2,…, N_f, with N_f number of objects in frame f.

3 Results

This section presents sample results of the proposed event detection and classification solution using the CREDS data set, and discusses its performance and limitations. The test sequences are in QCIF format at 25 Hz.

To visualize the events, red lines delimitate the ROIs and objects are color-coded in red (objects generating alarms), yellow (objects generating warnings), and green (normal behavior on the platform). The train is color-coded in blue.

In Fig. 6 shows different type of events that are detected under different camera views. It is possible to notice, clockwise from the top left image, a normal situation with a train approaching, a proximity warning with the event close to the camera, a proximity warning with the event far from the camera, and three alarms.

Fig. 6. Sample results from the CREDS data set

In general, we observed that the major limitations of the system are related to the object detection module, at the beginning of the processing chain. Fig. 7 shows two errors of the current implementation of the system, namely the missed detection of thrown paper (see zoom on the top right portion of Fig. 7 (a)) and the misclassification of a pedestrian as part of the train. The first problem can be solved by defining a strategy for decreasing the local variance of the statistical change detector. The second problem can be overcome by including models of the object in the scene.

(a) (b)

Fig. 7. Limitations of the current implementation of the system. (a) Small object thrown on the tracks; (b) illumination variations generated by the train on the platform.

The fusion of the information derived from multiple cameras is based on the projection of the blob position onto a common ground plane. Fig. 8 shows the accumulated object path over time generated by a pedestrian walking along the tracks (crosses of different colour represent information from different views). Voting is used to decide among contrasting outputs from the three cameras, with larger weight given to the sensor in the most favorable position.

An important observation about the use of the ground plane for the CREDS events: although the ground plane view of the scene can be used as support to event classification, it cannot be used as only element of decision, as it does not provide relevant information for the detection of some of the events of interest. For example, the height from ground is necessary for object classification and the detection of objects activity like bending, kneeling, and throwing objects requires the image plane view. For this reason, the fusion of information takes place not only between cameras to generate the ground plane view, but also between the camera plane and the ground plane for object and event classification.

Fig. 8. Image plane view and ground plane view of the scene

4 Conclusions

We presented an automatic event detection system that addresses the problem of safety in underground stations. The system uses image analysis, object description and a binary decision tree. Domain knowledge is exploited to define areas of interest in the scene and information from different views is combined in a common ground plane.

Current work includes the use of models to facilitate the discrimination of objects and of homographic transformations to make the solution more general and to reduce set-up time. Finally, we are planning an extensive evaluation and comparison with the solutions recently proposed at the CREDS challenge [1].

References

1. Ziliani, F., Velastin, S., Porikli, F., Marcenaro, L., Kelliher, T., Cavallaro, A., Bruneaut, P.: Performance evaluation of event detection solutions: the CREDS experience. Proc. of IEEE International Conference on Advanced Video and Signal based Surveillance (2005)
2. Cavallaro, A., Ebrahimi, T.: Interaction between high-level and low-level image analysis for semantic video object extraction. Journal on Applied Signal Processing, Special Issue on: Object-based and semantic image and video analysis, vol. 2004, n. 6, (2004) 786-797
3. Stauffer, C., Grimson, W.: Adaptive background mixture models for real-time tracking. Proc. of IEEE International Conference on Pattern Recognition (1999) 246–252
4. Cavallaro, A., Ebrahimi, T.: Change detection based on colour edges. Proc. of IEEE International Symposium on Circuits and Systems (2001)
5. Khan, S., Shah, M.: Consistent labelling of tracked objects in multiple cameras with overlapping fields of view. IEEE Trans. Pattern Analysis and Machine Intelligence, vol. 25, n. 10 (2003) 1355-1360

Large-Scale Geospatial Indexing for Image-Based Retrieval and Analysis

Kenneth W. Tobin[1,*], Budhendra L. Bhaduri[2], Eddie A. Bright[2], Anil Cheriyadat[2], Thomas P. Karnowski[1], Paul J. Palathingal[3], Thomas E. Potok[3], and Jeffery R. Price[1]

[1] Image Science and Machine Vision Group, Oak Ridge National Laboratory, Oak Ridge, Tennessee 37831-6010
{Tobinkwjr, Karnowskitp, Pricejr}@ornl.gov
http://www.ornl.gov/sci/ismv

[2] Geographic Information Science and Technology Group, Oak Ridge National Laboratory, Oak Ridge, Tennessee 37831-6017
{Bhaduribl, Brightea, Cheriyadatma}@ornl.gov
http://www.ornl.gov/sci/gist/gisthome.html

[3] Applied Software Engineering Research Group, Oak Ridge National Laboratory, Oak Ridge, Tennessee 37831-6085
{Palathingalp, Potokte}@ornl.gov
http://www.epm.ornl.gov/~v8q/

Abstract. We describe a method for indexing and retrieving high-resolution image regions in large geospatial data libraries. An automated feature extraction method is used that generates a unique and specific structural description of each segment of a tessellated input image file. These tessellated regions are then merged into similar groups and indexed to provide flexible and varied retrieval in a query-by-example environment.

1 Introduction

Large geospatial data libraries of remote sensing imagery are being collected today in higher resolution formats both spatially and spectrally and at an unprecedented rate. These libraries are being produced for many applications including hazard monitoring, drought management, commercial land use planning, estuary management, agricultural productivity, forestry, tropical cyclone detection, homeland security, and other intelligence and military applications [1, 2]. While these systems do provide end-users with useful geographic information data products, it is typically required that a user know precise information in a world-oriented dataset regarding a region of study if they are to achieve effective results.

Techniques that facilitate search and retrieval based on image content, for example in a query-by-example environment, can provide an analyst or researcher with a rapid method for searching very large geospatial libraries with minimal query specification. Content-based image retrieval (CBIR) refers to techniques used to index and retrieve

---

* Prepared by Oak Ridge National Laboratory, managed by UT-Battelle, LLC, for the U.S. Department of Energy under Contract No. DE-AC05-00OR22725.

G. Bebis et al. (Eds.): ISVC 2005, LNCS 3804, pp. 543 – 552, 2005.

images from databases based on their pictorial content [3, 4]. Pictorial content is typically defined by a set of statistical or semantic features extracted from an image to describe the spectral content, texture, and/or shape of the entire image or of specific image regions. Region-based image retrieval is referred to as RBIR [5].

In a geospatial library environment these searches produce results such as the fraction of queried cover type existing in a defined region, e.g., describing the coverage of city, urban/suburban, or forest content. Many CBIR methods for geospatial data attempt to produce a description of image primitives at the pixel level (e.g., based on local structures, textures, or spectral content) [5, 6]. Yet as the resolution of these data sources increases, the ability to automatically identify cover types by classifying pixels becomes problematic due to the highly-resolved mixture of man-made and natural structures that are present in complex spatial arrangements.

Fig. 1 demonstrates this point through several examples of the high-resolution imagery that will be used throughout this discussion. These image regions represent a wide variety of cover types ranging from mixed deciduous and conifer forest lands to suburban and industrial settings. At these resolutions and with the complex proximities of the various man-made and natural structures, it is difficult to apply pixel classification methods to segment image content.

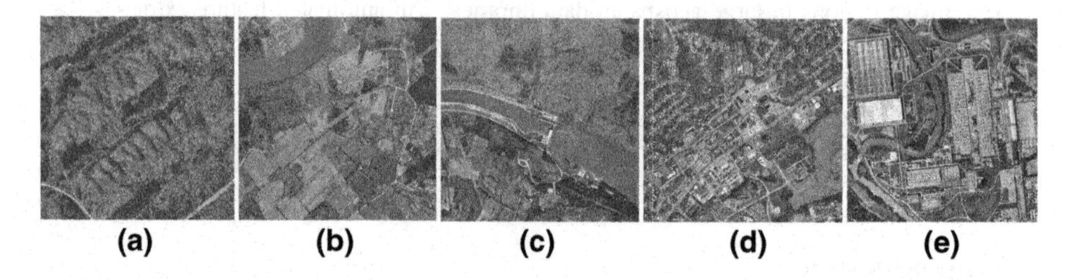

Fig. 1. Examples of a wide variety of spatial data regions that may exist in a large geospatial image database including, (a) forest, (b) agriculture, (c) water structure (locks, dams, etc.), (d) urban/suburban area, and (e) industrial sites. Resolution of these scenes are 0.5m per pixel.

At the Oak Ridge National Laboratory (ORNL) we are developing methods to automatically describe these region types so that a large image library can be efficiently assembled and indexed to perform content-based retrievals that will accommodate searches for specific spatial structure. This system encompasses three main development areas: a software agent architecture to support distributed computing and to gather image content and metadata from the web, a geospatial data modeling component to register the imagery in a consistent world-coordinate system, and a RBIR component to index imagery for search and retrieval. In this paper we will focus primarily on the RBIR aspects of search and retrieval. In Section 2 we give a brief overview of the architecture of the archive generation system that has been developed. In Section 3 we review the critical components of our image region description and indexing approach. Finally, in Section 4 we present and discuss results obtained using the data set represented in Fig. 1, a total indexed land area of approximately 153 km^2 (59 mi^2) at 0.5m per pixel resolution.

2 Overview of Geospatial Library System Architecture

At ORNL we have developed a system and architecture by combining novel approaches from three distinct research areas: software agents, georeferenced data modeling, and content-based image retrieval. The resulting technology represents a comprehensive image data management and analysis system. This system allows us to meet the challenges of organizing and analyzing large volumes of image data, and of automating the image consumption process to populate the database. The overall system approach breaks down into three components: (1) an innovative software-agent-driven process that can autonomously search through distributed image data sources to retrieve new and updated information, (2) a geo-conformance process to model the data for temporal currency and structural consistency to maintain a dynamic data archive, and (3) an image analysis process to describe and index spatial regions representing various natural and man-made cover types.

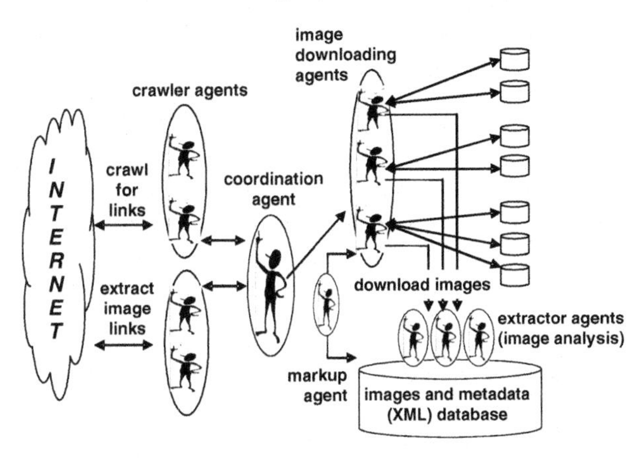

Fig. 2. Schematic representation of the agent architecture

Fig. 2 represents the agent-based architecture of our design. There are five types of agents that are represented in this system. The Coordination Agent controls the workflow between the different agents. The Crawler Agent performs a depth-first search for image links on potential websites (in our case, only URL's ending with .edu, .gov and .net). The Download Agent downloads images for all the image links generated by the Crawler Agent. The Download Agent coordinates with the image repository to ensure that the image does not already exist in the repository or that the image is newer or has a higher resolution than the existing one.

The fourth type of agent is the Markup Agent. This type of agent creates XML files that have images marked up with their properties and metadata. For each image in the repository, this agent extracts image properties like height, width, bit planes, etc. In addition, this agent extracts geospatial information like the images bounding box coordinates from the accompanying metadata/world file. After collecting this information, it creates an XML file for each image in the image repository using all of the above-deduced properties. The XML files are then stored in a separate XML Repository.

Finally the fifth agent type, Extractor Agents, perform preprocessing of the images. Typically each Extractor Agent runs on a separate processor so that images can be processed in parallel. An image is first segmented into block segments of size 128×128 pixels. Once the image segments are created, a feature vector file describing each segment is created by making use of the image properties in the XML file and the feature extraction methods described below.

To deploy this agent architecture, we used the Oak Ridge Mobile Agent Community (ORMAC) framework [7]. This framework has been under development over the course of several agent-based research projects. ORMAC is a generic agent framework providing transparent agent communication and mobility across any Internet connected host.

3 Image Analysis

Once the imagery has been downloaded by the software agents, our goal is to generate a succinct description of an image-dependent number of contiguous areas. Fig. 3

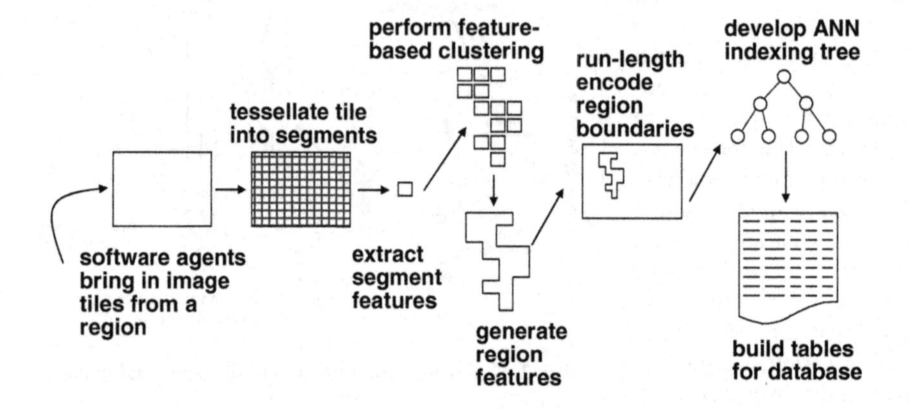

Fig. 3. Process flow shows tessellation of the input tile, feature extraction, segment clustering, indexing, and database building for query-based search and retrieval

provides an overview of the process. For this application we are restricting our analysis to a single spatial resolution. In general, for our architecture, multiple resolution data is handled independently and searches can be drilled into by performing a query at one resolution to locate candidate regions, followed by a step-up or step-down in resolution based on longitude and latitude coordinates. Our approach begins with an image tile, for example of the size represented in Fig. 1. These image tiles are 3100x3100 pixels representing a size of 1,750m on a side.

Fig. 4. Example image segments representing four cover types

The tiles are tessellated into 128×128 pixel segments corresponding to 64m×64m area. The segment size was determined heuristically by ensuring that various cover structure would be adequately represented in each segment. Fig. 4 shows examples in clockwise order from the upper left of four cover types: agricultural, forested, suburban, and industrial. A number of structure-oriented features are extracted from each segment. These features are reduced using a PCA/LDA method [8] to provide a short-length vector for segment clustering by a region growing procedure to organize similar segments into contiguous groups. Each contiguous group represents a sub-region in the original image tile and a summary feature description is generated for indexing. Also, the region boundary is run length encoded for efficient storage in the database. Finally, an indexing tree is developed using the region features by application of an approximate nearest neighbor (ANN) method as described in Ref. [9]. The indexing tree provides $O[log_2(n)]$ retrieval efficiency from the database through a query-by-example RBIR.

3.1 Feature Analysis

For this research, we have experimented with features that measure the texture and structure of the image segments. These features are not intended to be exhaustive in their characterization of these attributes, but rather to demonstrate the feasibility of the approach. The spectral attributes of an image segment are also valuable and have been used by many researchers to classify cover types in geospatial data [5, 6, 10]. But over large geospatial extents, spectral information can unintentionally limit a query-based search to a confined region. This is demonstrated by the Landsat Thematic Mapper (TM) data shown in Fig. 5 (30m per pixel resolution). Although we are not using Landsat TM data for this study, the four regions show agricultural areas over a large geographical distance and include Maine, Virginia, Tennessee, and Florida. Although the same three spectral bands were used to visualize crop regions, the spectral content varies tremendously. To avoid this unintentional bias in our indexing and retrieval process, we have adapted two feature sets that rely primarily on edge information to describe texture and structure.

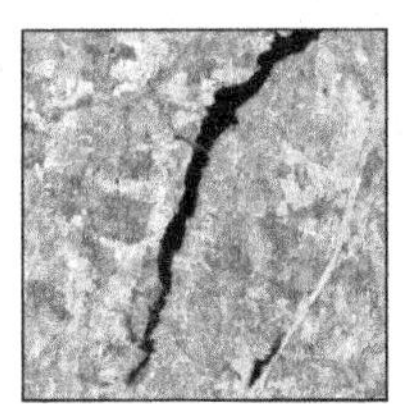
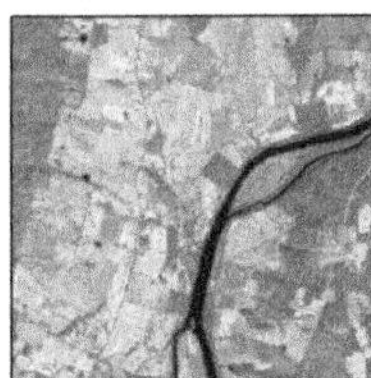
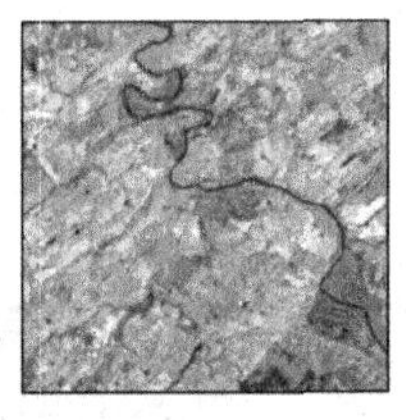

Fig. 5. Examples from the Landsat Thematic Mapper showing variation in spectral response across large geospatial extents. Three of six spectral bands have been selected for display that emphasize variations in crop cover. From left to right, Maine, Virginia, Tennessee, Florida.

We characterize image segment texture using local binary patterns (LBP) [11] and local edge patterns (LEP) [12]. In the rotation-invariant LBP texture operator, each 3×3 pixel neighborhood in the intensity image is thresholded by the intensity value of the center pixel. As there are 8 neighboring pixels, each of which can be represented as a 1 or 0 (if above or below the center pixel value, respectively), it is evident that there are 256 (2^8) possible patterns that can result from this thresholding. Since, however, we desire rotational invariance, we note only those patterns that are unique under rotation. For example, the three patterns in Fig. 6 are all (approximately) equivalent under rotation about the center pixel. Applying this equivalence-under-rotation idea, it can be shown that there are only 36 unique patterns. This implies that every pixel in the image can be assigned a number from 1-36 depending upon its LBP. The 36-bin normalized distribution (i.e., histogram) of the LBP values in a given 128×128 image segment hence provides 36 features for that region.

The LEP is computed almost identically to the LBP, except that we examine 3×3 pixel neighborhoods in the image edge map rather than the image intensity values. When considering the edge map, we must also consider the state of the center pixel, which is a 1 if the center pixel is an edge, or a 0 if not. This doubles the number of potential patterns from 36 to 72 so that every pixel in the image can be assigned a number from 1-72 depending upon its LEP. The 72-bin normalized distribution of the LEP values hence provides 72 features.

1	0	0
0		0
1	0	0

0	1	0
1		0
0	0	0

1	0	1
0		0
0	0	0

Fig. 6. Three local binary patterns (LBP) that are equivalent under rotation about the center pixel

To characterize structure in a segment, we analyze the distribution of edge orientations. The motivation to this approach is that man-made structures generally have regular edge features oriented in only a few directions (usually two for buildings) while natural image regions have randomly oriented edges. Different mixtures of man-made and natural structures will result in a variety of descriptions.

We compute local image orientation at each edge pixel using steerable filters [13]. We then find the 64-bin histogram of the edge orientation over angles from -90 to +90 degrees. The edge orientation distribution for a man-made structure is shown in the top of Fig. 7 (a) and that for the natural image is shown in the bottom of Fig. 7 (a). Note in the top of Fig. 7 (c) that there are two peaks in the edge orientation distribution near -80 degrees and +10 degrees that correspond to the orientations of the building. The distribution for the natural scene in the bottom of Fig. 7 (c) however, is approximately uniform. Since we require that the stored features be invariant to rotations of the source image, we next take the discrete or fast Fourier transform of the 64-point edge ori-

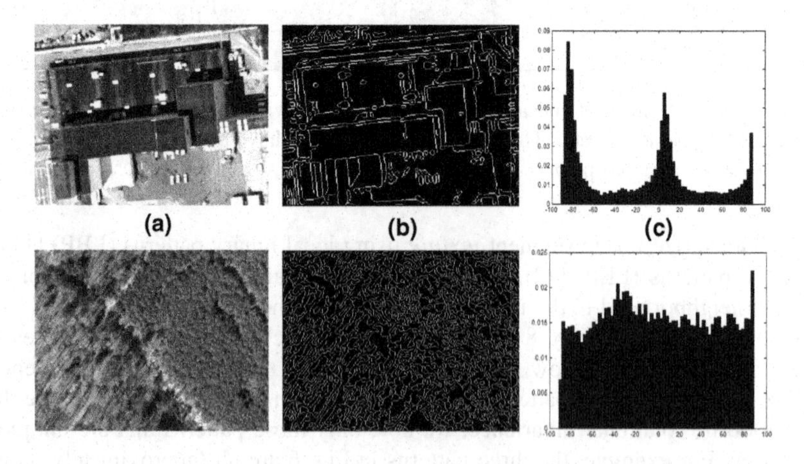

Fig. 7. Image segment in (a), edge map in (b), and edge orientation of (b) in (c). The top row represents a man-made structure and the bottom row a natural scene.

entation histogram and keep the magnitude of the first 32 points as the final features. The magnitude of the DFT or FFT is invariant to circular shifts of the data.

The total number of texture and structure features used at this point is therefore 140 (i.e., 36+72+32). Subsequent to the feature extraction step we apply a PCA and LDA process that results in a reduction from 140 to 8 features per image segment. These features are the basis of geospatial clustering and indexing for search and retrieval.

3.2 Geospatial Clustering

Once the features of the image segments have been extracted, it is possible to use this feature vector as an index for retrievals. Since there are generally a large number of contiguous 128×128 segments that define a content-based region (e.g., forested, suburban, etc.), we seek to group neighboring segments with similar features together to form a sub-region within an image tile or tiles. We perform a geospatial clustering procedure using a region growing technique to connect large contiguous and homogeneous segments of similar structure and texture characteristics.

Region growing is initialized by randomly selecting a seed segment at location (x,y), where (x,y) designates a coordinate of the corner or centroid of a segment. A segment with feature vector $\boldsymbol{v}(x,y)$ is merged with a neighboring segment with feature vector $\boldsymbol{v}'$, or with a segment group with mean vector $<\boldsymbol{v}'>$ if,

- the coordinate of the neighboring segment or of the closest segment group is an element of the set $\{(x\pm 1, y\pm 1)\}$,
- $|\boldsymbol{v}-\boldsymbol{v}'| < T_1$ or $|\boldsymbol{v}-<\boldsymbol{v}'>| < T_1$, where T_1 is a user-specified threshold,
- the resulting variance, σ^2, of the new segment group is less than T_2, where T_2 is a user-specified threshold used to limit the variance.

The merging process is continued until all the segments in the image tile have been tested. Fig. 8 shows typical results of this merging process.

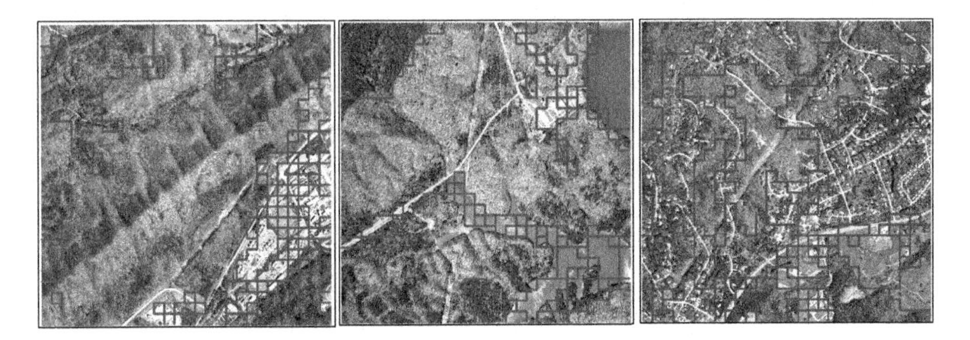

Fig. 8. Region growing results across three tiles from the image library. Each bordered region represents one homogeneous, connected group of segments as determined by their texture and structure features.

Once the contiguous segment regions have been determined, each segment group (image sub-region) has 16 descriptive features associated with it, i.e., each sub-region is described by vector $\boldsymbol{w} = (<f_1>, <f_2>, \ldots, <f_N>\ldots, \sigma_1^2, \sigma_2^2, \ldots, \sigma_N^2)^t$, for N=8, where

$\langle f_n \rangle$ is the average of the n-th feature across the ensemble of segments in that group, and σ_n^2 is the corresponding variance of that feature. It is this sub-region description that is used for indexing and retrieval in the RBIR library.

4 Results

The results presented here are for a geospatial library composed of 50 image tiles (3500x3500 pixels, 1750m×1750m, 0.5m per pixel) representing approximately 153 km^2 of land in and around the U.S. Department of Energy's Oak Ridge Reservation [14]. For this demonstration, the image regions (i.e., over all tiles) were tessellated into 39,200 segments of size 128×128 pixels. Features were then extracted for each of the segments, which were subsequently clustered as described in Sections 3.1 and 3.2 above. The number of sub-regions developed through geospatial clustering was 4,810, resulting in a reduction of 88% in the number of unique, spatially distinct objects indexed for retrieval.

For demonstration purposes, we have indexed the original 39,200 segments in one descriptive dataset, and the 4,810 sub-regions in another dataset. Fig. 9 shows an example retrieval of several cover types at the image segment level. In the figure, each of the images in the left-hand column represents a query. The remaining five images in each row represent the top five matching results of the query for an industrial complex in (a), suburban area in (b), an agricultural area in (c), and a specific search for striped parking lots and roadways in (d). Note the flexibility of the system to locate imagery of an extreme variety of cover types and detail using only eight features (from the original 140).

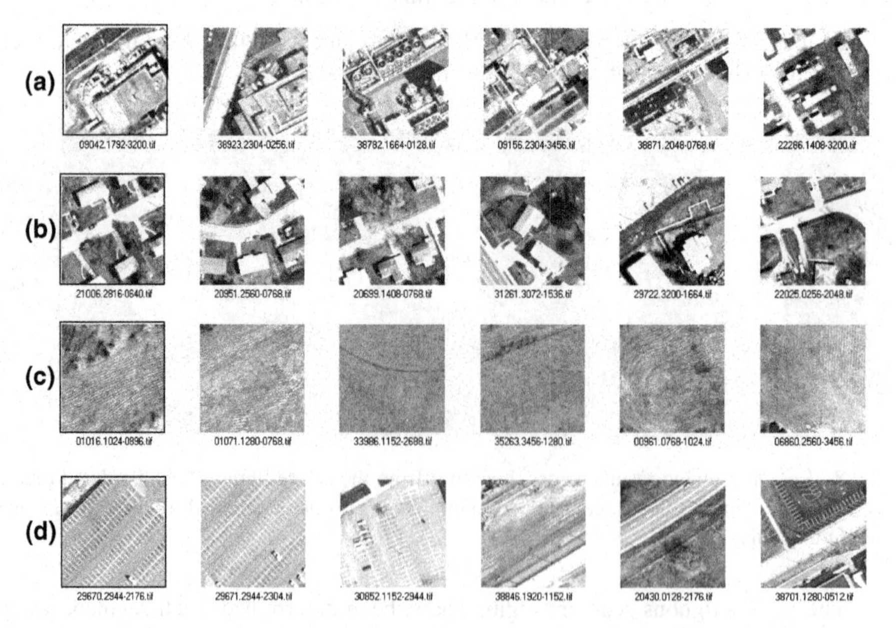

Fig. 9. Examples of the retrieval of image segments. The query images are in the left column. (a) an industrial complex, (b) a suburban setting, (c) agriculture, and (d) striped pavement.

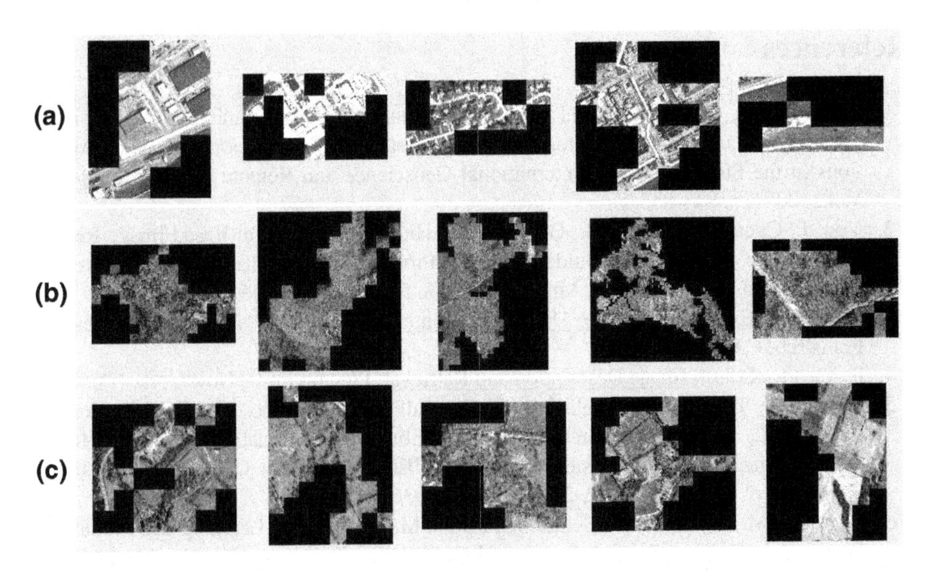

Fig. 10. Examples of the retrieval of geospatial clusters. (a) An industrial complex, (b) a large expanse of deciduous forest, (c) an agricultural region.

Although this type of segment-level query can be useful to an analyst, it can also provide too much redundant information regarding large spatial extents of visually similar imagery. For example, forested or agricultural regions may occupy a large percentage of the data library in a rural region such as this. An ability to collect together these large geospatial regions, or alternatively, to search for small man-made structures of a particular type distributed throughout large contiguous rural areas (i.e., a needle in a haystack) would also be useful. Therefore, in Fig. 10, we show examples of three queries performed on the geospatially clustered regions of the image library. Once again, the query region is represented by the left most column of images. In (a) we see an industrial complex, in (b) a large deciduous forest region, and in (c) an example of large, contiguous agriculture areas.

5 Conclusion

In this paper we have presented a novel method for automated feature extraction, spatial clustering, and indexing of a large geospatial image library. Although retrieval experiments were described for a relatively small geospatial data set, the system architecture and processing methodology have been developed to facilitate very large data libraries that can be maintained and updated in a dynamic manner through distributed computing with a software agent architecture. The feature analysis and indexing approach used in this research provides an efficient and flexible method for describing a broad range of cover types while allowing a user to locate very specific structural detail in a query-by-example environment. Future work in this area includes the incorporation of other geographical information metadata into the query process along with the addition of spectrally-based features for augmenting the specificity of local searches within a geospatial region of interest.

References

1. Tapley, B.D., Crawford, M.M., Howard, T., Hutchison, K.D., Smith, S., "A Vision for Creating Advanced Products From EOS Core System Data to Support Geospatial Applications in the State of Texas," International Geoscience and Remote Sensing Symposium, Vol.2, 2001, p. 843-845.
2. You, J., Cheung, K.H., Liu, J., Guo, L., "On Hierarchical Content-Based Image Retrieval by Dynamic Indexing and Guided Search," Proceedings of SPIE, Storage and Retrieval Methods and Applications for Multimedia, Vol. 5307, 2004, p. 559-570.
3. S. Santini, Exploratory Image Databases, Content-based Retrieval, Academic Press, San Fransisco, CA, 2001.
4. E. Vicario, Editor, Image Description and Retrieval, Plenum Press, New York, NY, 1998.
5. Datcu, M., Daschiel, H., Pelizzari, A.,Quartulli, M., Galoppo, A., Colapicchioni, A., Pastori, M., Seidel, K., Marchetti, P.G., D'Elia, S., "Information Mining in Remote Sensing Image archives: System Concepts," IEEE Trans. On Geoscience and Remote Sensing, Vol. 41, No. 12, Dec. 2003, p. 2923-2936.
6. Schroder, M., Rehrauer, H., Seidel, K., Datcu, M., "Interactive Learning and Probabilistic Retrieval in Remote Sensing Image archives," IEEE Trans. on Geoscience and Remote Sensing, Vol. 28, No. 5, Sept. 2000, p. 2288-2298.
7. Potok, T., Elmore, M., Reed, J. and Sheldon, F.T., "VIPAR: Advanced Information Agents Discovering Knowledge in an Open and Changing Environment," Proc. 7th World Multiconference on Systemics, Cybernetics and Informatics, Orlando FL, pp. 28-33, July 27-30, 2003.
8. Bingham, P.R., Price, J.R., Tobin, K.W., Karnowski, T.P., "Semiconductor Sidewall Shape Estimation," SPIE Journal of Electronic Imaging, Vol. 13, No. 3, July 2004.
9. Tobin, K. W., Karnowski, T.P., Arrowood, L.F., Ferrell, R.K., Goddard, J.S., Lakhani, F., "Content-based Image Retrieval for Semiconductor Process Characterization", EURASIP Journal on Applied Signal Processing, Special Issue on Applied Visual Inspection, Vol. 2002, No. 7, 2002.
10. Harvey, N.R., Theiler, J., Brumby, S.P., Perkins, S., Szymanski, J.J., Bloch, J.J., Porter, R.B., Galassi, M., Young, C., "Comparison of GENIE and Conventional Supervised Classifiers for Multispectral Image Feature Extraction," IEEE Transactions on Geoscience and Remote Sensing, VOl. 40, No. 2, Feb. 2002, p. 393-404.
11. Pietikainen, M., Ojala, T. and Xu, Z. Rotation-invariant texture classification using feature distributions. Pattern Recognition, vol. 33, no.1, pp. 43-52, 2000.
12. Yao, C.-H. and Chen, S.-Y. Retrieval of translated, rotated and scaled color textures. Pattern Recognition, vol. 36, pp. 913-929, no. 4, 2003.
13. Freeman, W. and Adelson, E. The design and use of steerable filters. IEEE Transactions on Pattern Analysis and Machine Intelligence, vol. 13, no. 9, pp. 891-906, 1991.
14. Tuttle, M., Pace, P., "ORNL Basemapping and Imagery Project: Data Collection, Processing, and Dissemination," Geographic Information System (GIS) Environmental management conference, Reno, NV, CONF-9603148-1, 1996.

An Interactive Visualization Method for Integrating Digital Elevation Models and Geographic Information Systems Vector Layers

J. Stuart[1], J. Jaquish[1], S. Bassett[2], F. Harris[1], and W. Sherman[2]

[1] Department of Computer Science and Engineering,
University of Nevada, Reno, Reno, NV, 89557
[2] Desert Research Institute, Reno, NV, 89510

Abstract. Currently there are software packages that allow a user to analyze GIS data. The problem is that the software is limited in the interaction provided. This paper presents a method for merging digital elevation models (DEM) and GIS vector layers, and also provided is an interactive visualization tool for analyzing the output.

Keywords: DEM, GIS layers, Visualization.

1 Introduction

Training is an essential part in military effectiveness [1, 2]. Generally, the more realistic training is to the soldier, the better prepared that soldier will be when an actual scenario arises [3, 4]. Creating a realistic training environment requires significant preparation in planning, coordination, time, money, etc. Resources such as equipment, fuel, vehicle parts, and maintenance time are used extensively, making it difficult to provide consistent, thorough training for every one.

The advent of computer technology has significantly impacted the way the military trains its personnel. Specifically, the field of computer graphics and visualization has become crucial for the creation of realistic training environments. With modern technology, the military can train its personnel in computer simulated situations, thus alleviating much of the need for travel and equipment transportation. Also, personnel can work their way through a simulation several times, honing their skills while using minimal resources.

Visualization techniques help to establish realism, but real-world geographic data is also necessary to achieve a fully immersive and realistic simulation. The geographic data represents a true-to-life landscape in the simulated environment. The data can be visualized via computer graphics and virtual reality techniques. The end goal is to give personnel the feeling they are at the real-world location, even though they are actually in a simulated environment.

In order to obtain accurate information about a location, specialists in geographic and geological disciplines must first visit and thoroughly analyze the location. This is viewed as a necessary expenditure of time and resources. However, situations occur where the resources and access necessary to collect ample data is simply not available. This lack of data can endanger missions, especially

G. Bebis et al. (Eds.): ISVC 2005, LNCS 3804, pp. 553–561, 2005.

when specific training, such as helicopter flight, requires accurate knowledge and representation of an area.

There is some data that can be gathered and then later analyzed off-site. One such piece of data is a Digital Elevation Model (DEM) [5]. The name has pragmatic significance in that it consists of spatially explicit digital values of height data. Other important data are Geographic Information Systems (GIS) vector layers [6]. GIS vector layers are maps (i.e. represent a location) that store two-dimensional shapes (polygons) with attributes. Attributes can be assigned from a variety of sources including satellite imagery, site visits, etc. DEMs are also referred to as GIS raster layers, but from this point forward, any mention of a GIS layer refers to a GIS vector layer.

DEMs and GIS layers have been combined before, but this paper proposes a method for merging the two so as to be efficiently displayed in a three-dimensional virtual environment. Such an environment would give specialists better interaction with the data being visualized. It is also believed that an environment such as this would reduce the amount of time and other resources necessary to perform a thorough analysis of geographic sites.

The remainder of this paper is structured as follows. Section 2 presents background information on geographic applications, computer graphics, and immersive virtual environments. Section 3 presents our method for combining DEMs and GIS layers and displaying them in a manner conducive to fluid interactivity. We present the results of our methods in Section 4 and state our conclusions in Section 5. Section 6 presents several possibilities for future work on this topic.

2 Background

The fields of geography and computer graphics must be combined for this project to become a practical application. Geography is the study of earth and its features. Computer graphics refers to methods of creating visual imagery with computing techniques. It is incredibly difficult to interpret hundreds of tables of geographic data if it is not visualized (i.e. with computer graphics). Thus the combination of geographic data and computer visualization techniques is unavoidable.

There are several applications in use by geographic specialists that help them consolidate and visualize geographic data. One such program is called ArcGIS™ [7]. ArcGIS is designed for the desktop environment on a typical two-dimensional monitor. It works primarily with GIS layer data files (mentioned in Section 1). It is useful for portraying and altering region data and associated attributes. ArcGIS is not meant to display three-dimensional data, that task is left to another application (typically packaged with ArcGIS) called Arc Scene™. However, users do not feel immersed into the environment because the data is visualized on a two-dimensional screen.

The feeling of immersion and realism is important because it allows a specialist to notice and analyze more features of a landscape, and to analyze those features with higher accuracy. To achieve complete immersion, we use a computer graphics technique called Virtual Reality (VR).

Effective VR is created in a virtual/immersive environment by means of several projection screens and accompanying projectors. In this environment, users are required to wear a headset or a pair of specialized glasses. Via the combination of the glasses, projection screens, and the projectors, users are given a realistic sense of depth unattainable on modern desktop systems. Several companies such as FakeSpace™ and Silicon Graphics Inc.™ sell full VR projection systems.

Beyond immersion in a VR environment, one must also have the means to interact with and manipulate the data being visualized. For this project, the immersive environment must allow the user to pick regions of a map and see all associated attributes. Attributes assigned to regions in GIS layers depend on the context of the research. The user must also have the ability to add, remove, and update attributes as they see fit, all while inside the VR environment.

This interaction must be done in real-time, as one of the main points of the purpose is to cut-down on a crucial resource, experts' time. For many reasons, allowing real-time interaction can be quite difficult. Geographical experts need to interact with large areas of the world at once, and the size of the area to be visualized is directly proportional to the amount of data stored and processed. The second reason is we are striving for realism and the amount of realism is also directly proportional to the amount of data stored. This all amounts to longer and longer computation time. Optimization methods are a must to visualize this data as fast and realistically as possible. We can now begin discussing our methods for quickly visualizing this data to allow for fluid interaction.

3 Proposed Methods

The primary elements of visualization dealt with by this paper are three dimensional digital elevation maps (DEMs), stored using the BIL File Format [8], and two dimensional Geographical Information Systems (GIS) layers, stored using the ESRI™ Shapefile Format [9]. It is common for both DEMs and GIS layers to be complex in terms of size and structure, thus requiring special methods for visualization.

3.1 Digital Elevation Map Manipulation

Three-dimensional rendering APIs such as OpenGL [10] and Direct3D [11] expect display primitives to be represented as collections of triangles. DEMs are easily represented using triangles, so rendering a DEM can be trivial. Figure 2 shows a DEM and all of the triangles used to approximate it. However, the size of modern DEMs are approaching the point that real-time rendering with modern graphics hardware is not possible. Also, this paper uses DEMs to assign an extra dimension to a GIS layer, not just for visualization.

In order to efficiently deal with DEMs, this paper applies a lossy compression technique to DEMs called Triangle Decimation [12, 13] and Mesh Simplification [14, 15, 16]. Triangle Decimation works by examining coincident triangles, and removing unnecessary triangles. Figure 1 shows a set of triangles that can be reduced

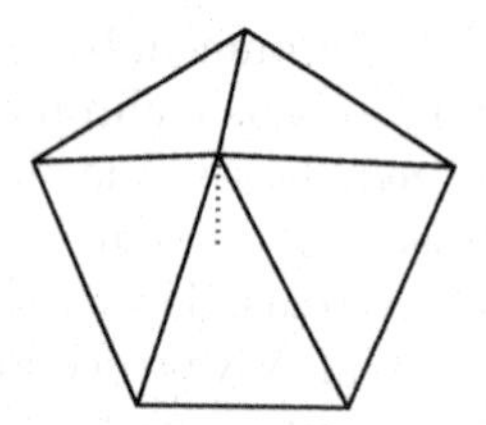
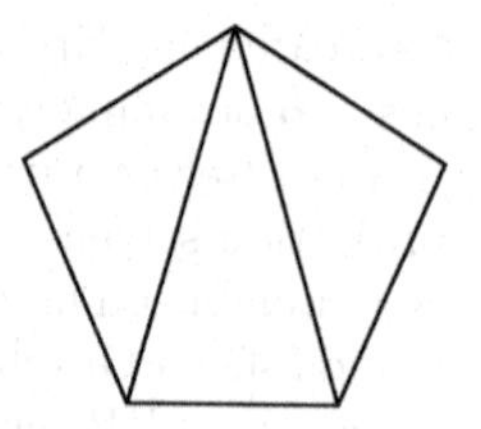

Fig. 1. Candidate triangles and the result of their decimation. The small amount of height lost in the left area is barely noticeable in the right area.

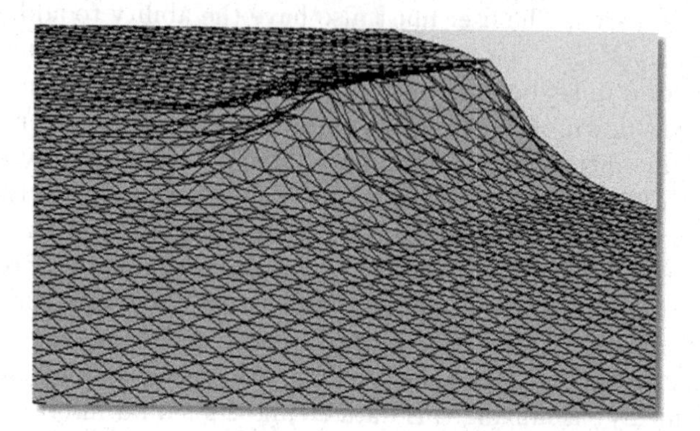

Fig. 2. Approximated Digital Elevation Map

and the possible effects of triangle decimation. Triangle decimation is called lossy because once it is performed, it is not always possible to regain the full representation of the DEM. However, the effects of the decimation aim to have little-to-no visual side effects. Figure 2 shows a DEM that is a prime candidate for triangle decimation since it has many coincident triangles that are nearly coplanar.

3.2 GIS Layer Manipulation

As mentioned previously, rendering APIs expect primitives to be broken into triangles. The GIS layers found in Shapefiles are represented using two-dimensional polygons. These polygons are clean, meaning they contain no self-intersecting lines. Examples for both clean and non-clean polygons are shown in Figure 3.

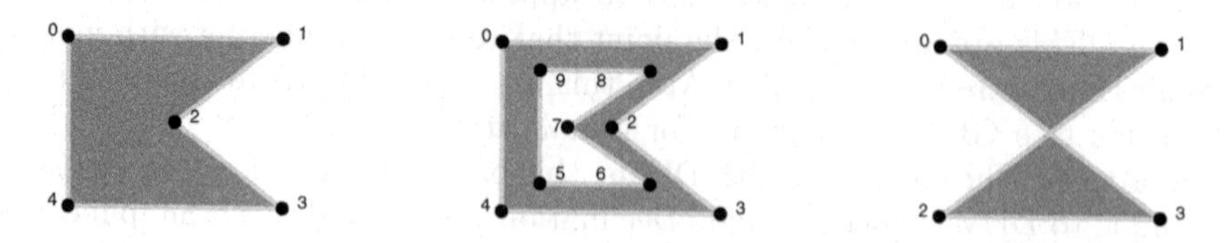

Fig. 3. Two clean (left, middle) polygons and a non-clean (right) polygon

Since there is no restriction on the structure of the polygons beyond that of "cleanness," one cannot assume anything of the convexity of the polygons in GIS layers. This paper uses several techniques to triangulate the polygons in the GIS layer; ear-clipping [17], monotone decomposition [18], and trapezoidilization [17]. The output of all these techniques is a set of two-dimensional, non-intersecting triangles.

3.3 Combining DEMs and GIS Layers

In order to combine the DEM and the GIS layer, a six step approach is proposed:

1. Read and store the raw DEM and GIS layer
2. Convert the GIS layer into sets of two-dimensional triangles
3. Convert the DEM into triangles
4. Perform triangle decimation on the DEM
5. Add a third dimension to the GIS layer
6. Add the DEM points to the GIS layer

Step 1 of the approach is trivial. Steps 2, 3, and 4 can be done using the algorithms discussed in 3.1 and 3.2. Step 5 can be accomplished using the $O(t_d * v_g)$ algorithm presented Figure 4, where t_d is the number of triangles in the DEM and v_g is the number of vertices in the GIS layer. Step 6 can be computed using the $O(v_d * t_g)$ algorithm shown in Figure 5, where v_d is the number of vertices in the DEM and t_g is the number of triangles in the GIS layer.

```
T0 ← Triangles in DEM
V0 ← Vertices in GIS layer
for all t0 ϵ T0
  for all v0 ϵ V0
    if v0 has only two dimensions
      if v0 is contained by t0
        v1 ← v0 projected onto t0
        V0 ← V0 − {v0}
        V0 ← V0 ∪ {v1}
```

Fig. 4. Algorithm for assigning height values to a GIS layer

```
V0 ← Vertices in DEM
T0 ← Triangles in GIS layer
for all v0 ϵ V0
  for all t0 ϵ T0
    if v0 is contained by t0
      T1 ← SPLIT (t0, v0)
      V0 ← V0 − {v0}
      T0 ← T0 − {t0}
      T0 ← T0 ∪ T1
```

Fig. 5. Algorithm for incorporating DEM points with a GIS layer

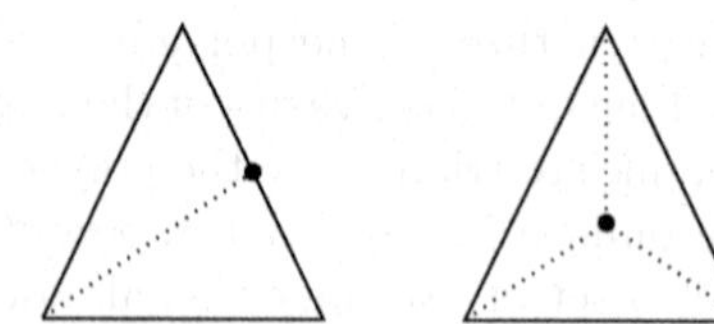

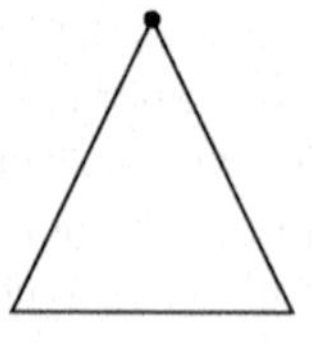

Fig. 6. Cases for **SPLIT**: Splitting a triangle into (from left to right), 2 triangles, 3 triangles, and 1 triangle

The algorithm relies on the ability to split a triangle into one, two, or three triangles new triangles. The algorithm, which we call **SPLIT**, takes as parameters a triangle and a point. **SPLIT** works by examining the location of the point; if the point lies on a vertex of the triangle, **SPLIT** returns the original triangle. If the point lies on the perimeter of the triangles, but not on a vertex of the triangle, **SPLIT** returns two new triangles with the point being a vertex on both triangles. Finally, if the point resides in the interior of the triangle, **SPLIT** creates three new triangles using the vertices of the triangle and the new point. Examples for the three cases of **SPLIT** can be seen in Figure 6. In the figure, the dark dot represents the second parameter to **SPLIT**.

4 Results

The overall algorithm we presented takes two pieces of data for its input. The first is a DEM, with an example given in Figure 2. The second is a GIS layer, presented in Figure 7. The algorithm combines its input and produces a set of three-dimensional triangles. The algorithm was implemented as a preprocessing stage for our visualization tool.

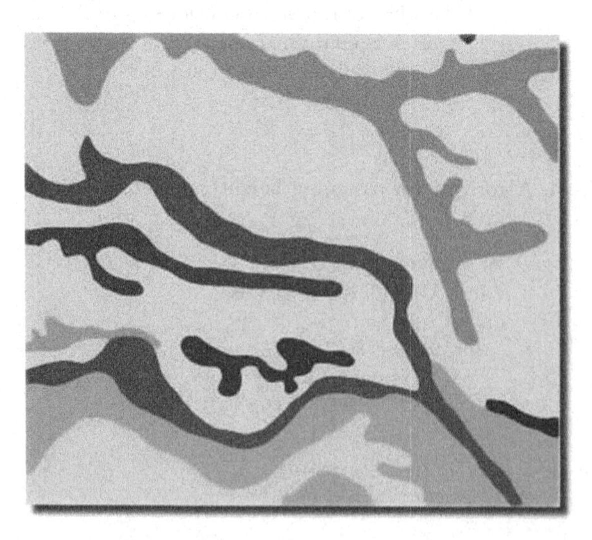

Fig. 7. Two-dimensional GIS Layer

Fig. 8. Three-dimensional visualization of combined DEM and GIS layer. Outlining the triangles helps accentuate the height.

With our data in hand, we constructed an interactive visualization tool. This tool provides better interaction with GIS data than current packages because of the ability to accentuate specific features of the data, and because unlike other packages you can interact with and manipulate the data. Using our tool, one can accentuate the data by stretching, in various directions, the data set. This, combined with the ability to become immersed in the data in three dimensions and the capability to "fly through" the data and view the data from multiple angles, provides the user a greater ability to discover features that would have otherwise been missed. A screenshot of the visualization is shown in Figure 8.

5 Conclusions

The visualization methods presented in this paper will serve as the basis for larger and more complex visualizations. The methods presented have proven to be robust, capable of handling a wide array of data. The improved interaction and immersion in the VR environment provides a more efficient and beneficial experience for GIS experts than some of the common packages available today.

The method devised by this paper is by no means the end to a line of work. In fact, the work presented by this paper will serve as the foundation for a series of visualization tools. Because the VR environment is geared towards better interaction, experts can work more efficiently. The added sense of depth provides the user with more detail than is typical with two-dimensional displays, allowing a user more accurately and efficiently analyze GIS data.

Data set sizes used ranged from tens of polygons, less than a thousand triangles, and a 100×100 DEM, all the way to hundreds of polygons, tens of thousands of triangles, and a DEM that was bigger than 1300×1100. While the running time and response time of our methods are affected by the size of the input, they still cope excellently with large input sets and allow for real-time interaction.

Packages like ArcGIS and Arc Scene provide users a rich set of features for handling GIS data. However, these packages aim to provide as many services as relevant (and rightfully so), instead of focusing on one or two very specific areas. Since our method runs as a standalone application, we have the ability to fine-tune the visualization and the level of interaction.

6 Future Work

The possibilities for future work are numerous. As stated before, the methods we proposed will serve as the foundation for more advanced visualizations. Another immediate possibility is the refinement of our code.

One larger goal we have in mind is to visualize dust kick-up in real-time. A significant analysis of terrain is key to modeling dust, and we believe that the methods implemented for this paper will serve as an excellent aid to this project.

The source code written for this paper is robust, capable of handling a wide variety of data sets. However, this robustness comes at a sacrifice to speed. An immediate avenue of future work is to optimize the source code, and to integrate faster algorithms into our visualization methods.

References

1. Smith, R.: Essential Techinques for Military Modeling and Simulation. Volume 1 of Simulation Conference Proceedings. (1998) 805–812
2. Walton, G.H., Patton, R.M., Parsons, D.J.: Usage Testing of Military Simulation Systems. Winter Simulation Conference (2001) 771–779
3. Service, D.M.F.P.: Former POW learns value of military training. TRADOC News Service (2003)
4. Leu, M.C., Hilgers, M.G., Agarwal, S., Hall, R.H., Lambert, T., Albright, R., Nebel, K.: Training in Virtual Environments for First Responders. ASEE Midwest Section Meeting (2003)
5. geo Community: USGS SDTS format Digital Elevation Model data (DEM). http://www.dofactory.com/Patterns/Patterns.aspx (Accessed June 13. 2005)
6. Meuser, M.R.: What is GIS and How Does it Work? http://www.dofactory.com/Patterns/Patterns.aspx (Accessed June 13. 2005)
7. ESRI: ArcGIS. http://www.esri.com/software/arcgis/ (Accessed June 13. 2005)
8. Softwright: TopoScript .BIL File Format. http://www.softwright.com/faq/support/toposcript_bil_file_format.html (Accessed April 2. 2005)
9. ESRI: ESRI Shapefile Technical Description. http://www.esri.com/library/whitepapers/pdfs/shapefile.pdf (Accessed March 17. 2005)
10. Board, O.A.R.: OpenGL - The Industry Standard for High Performance Graphics. http://www.opengl.org/ (Accessed June 13. 2005)
11. Corporation, M.: Microsoft DirectX: Home Page. http://www.microsoft.com/windows/directx/default.aspx (Accessed June 13. 2005)

12. Schroeder, W.J., Zarge, J.A., Lorensen, W.E.: Decimation of Triangle Meshes. ACM SIGGRAPH (1992) 65–70
13. Schroeder, W.J.: A Topology Modifying Progressive Decimation Algorithm. IEEE Visualization (1997) 205–212
14. Kobbelt, L., Campagna, S., Seidel, H.: A General Framework for Mesh Decimation. Graphics Interface Conference (1998)
15. Schaufler, G., Sturzlinger, W.: Generating Multiple Levels of Detail from Polygonal Geometry Models. Virtual Environments ́95 (1995) 33–41
16. Algorri, M.E., Frances-Schmitt: Mesh Simplification. Volume 15 of Computer Graphics Forum. (1996) 77
17. O'Rourke, J.: Computational Geometry in C. 2 edn. Cambridge University Press (1998)
18. de Berg, M., van Kreveld, M., Overmars, M., Shcwarzkopf, O.: Computational Geometry - Algorithms and Applications. 2 edn. Springer (1998)

Splines Interpolation in High Resolution Satellite Imagery

José A. Malpica

Departamento de Matemáticas, Universidad de Alcalá, 28871 Madrid, Spain
josea.malpica@uah.es

Abstract. In this paper some insights into the behavior of interpolation functions for resampling high resolution satellite images are presented. Using spatial and frequency domain characteristics, splines interpolation performance is compared to nearest-neighbor, linear and cubic interpolation. It is shown that splines interpolation injects spatial information into the final resample image better than the other three methods. Splines interpolation is also shown to be faster than cubic interpolation when the former is implemented with the LU decomposition algorithm for its tridiagonal system of linear equations. Therefore, if the main purpose for high resolution satellite resampling is to obtain an optimal smooth final image, intuitive and experimental justifications are provided for preferring splines interpolation to nearest-neighbor, linear and cubic interpolation.

1 Introduction

IKONOS, successfully launched on September 24, 1999, was the first civilian earth observation satellite with high-resolution sensors. It has 1-m panchromatic (Pan) and 4-m multiband (XS) images: blue (0.45–0.52 μm), green (0.52–0.60 μm), red (0.63–0.0.69 μm), and near infrared (0.76–0.90 μm). Since that date more high-resolution (HR) satellites have been launched with sensor resolutions in panchromatic ranging from 0.61 m (QuickBird) to 5 m (SPOT-5). Like IKONOS, most of these satellites simultaneously provide high-resolution panchromatic and low-resolution multispectral images.

An effective fusion of the panchromatic and multispectral images to produce a high quality pan-sharpened colour image is important for many remote sensing applications worldwide. Specifically, this type of fused image is used for photo interpretation or simple visual analysis in such applications as urban planning and ecological, agricultural or general decision-making. Fusion is also important in order to obtain cartographic feature extraction. Image fusion involves two processes: registration and resampling. Image registration is the process of finding a mapping from each XS multispectral onto the Pan such that each pixel representing the same position in the two images corresponds to the same point in the ground of the imaged scene; image resampling is the processes of obtaining for the low-resolution XS the same resolution as the Pan image. Apart from resampling for pan-sharpening, interpolation is also essential in a variety of satellite image processing applications, such as magnification, image geo-referenciation and orthophoto production.

G. Bebis et al. (Eds.): ISVC 2005, LNCS 3804, pp. 562 – 570, 2005.

Four interpolation methods have been tested on a portion of a scene from IKONOS, a relatively flat area of terrain on the Alcala University campus that is 2 km wide by 2 km long. The image was taken at 11:04 AM on June 6, 2000. A Pan and four XS bands of 1 and 4 meters resolution respectively were taken, with 11 bits per pixel for all bands. The Pan and XS grey values represent reflectivity responses of terrain features at different wavelengths. The Pan band is used as a reference to see how well each interpolation method performs on the XS bands.

The focus in this paper will be the resampling stage, since special care was taken for an accurate registration. Resampling could be considered a magnification operation on the XS bands in order to obtain the same resolution the Pan band has, i.e., going from 4m to 1m resolution. In remote sensing and photogrammetry, resampling is done mostly through nearest-neighbour, linear and cubic methods and it is rare to see splines interpolation in the science literature of the remote sensing community. There is a misunderstanding among those working in these communities that splines interpolation is computationally more expensive than cubic interpolation, and when a smooth product is needed the last method is always applied.

The experimental work that is going to be reported in this paper is to resample (through magnification) several bands of XS with 4m resolution pixels in order to obtain the same 1m resolution as the Pan has. Four interpolation methods will be compared to find out which one obtains the closest image to the Pan band. However, the objective of this paper is not only to determine an overall best method, but to present a comprehensive list of properties of the four methods and to enable the user of high satellite image similar to Ikonos to select which is optimal for his application.

2 Interpolation as Convolution

In image resampling the interpolation process must reconstruct a two-dimensional continuous signal g(x,y) from its discrete samples $f(x_i, y_j)$ i=1...m, j=1...n, where m represents the lines and n the columns of the image. Interpolation can be interpreted as the convolution of the discrete image samples with the continuous two-dimensional impulse response h(x,y) of a two-dimensional reconstruction filter

$$g(x,y) = \sum_k \sum_l c_{k,l}\, h\left(\frac{x - x_k}{\Delta_x}, \frac{y - y_l}{\Delta_y}\right), \tag{1}$$

where c_{kl} are parameters which depend upon the sampled data $f(x_i,y_j)$, and Δ_x and Δ_y represent the sampling increments in the abscises and ordinates, respectively. The range of summation of indices k and l depend on the neighbourhood chosen for interpolation. The impulse response h is the interpolation kernel. The kernels for the four types of interpolation methods studied in this paper are symmetric and separable; therefore computational complexity can be reduced considering that the following equation is fulfilled,

$$h(x,y) = h(x) \cdot h(y). \tag{2}$$

This allows us to study image resampling in one dimension since extension to two dimensions will be obvious.

For equally spaced data many one-dimensional interpolation functions (among them the four studied in this paper) should be expressed by the following equation:

$$g(x) = \sum_k c_k h\left(\frac{x - x_k}{\Delta_x}\right). \tag{3}$$

The c_k is selected so that the interpolation condition $g(x_k)=f(x_k)$ for each x_k is satisfied.

The ideal one-dimensional interpolator is given by the sinc function [1]:

$$\sin c(x) = \frac{\sin(\pi x)}{\pi x}. \tag{4}$$

Some fundamental properties of any interpolator can be derived from this ideal interpolation function. Although the sinc function provides an exact reconstruction of g(x,y), it is unlimited. For band-limited data the response of the sinc function ideal interpolation kernel is a unit step function which has the value of one for frequencies between $-\pi/\Delta$ and $+\pi/\Delta$, and zero elsewhere. If the sampling increment is sufficiently small, this kernel would pass every frequency of a band-limited function without change.

Behaviour of the various interpolation methods can be examined by comparing the Fourier transforms of their interpolation kernels. Deviations from the ideal spectrum given by the Fourier transform of the sinc function in the interval $(-\pi/\Delta, +\pi/\Delta)$ cause a loss of frequency information and the image would appear blurred. Deviations from the ideal spectrum outside the interval conduce to aliasing. In what follows we are going to give a brief survey of the general behavior for each interpolator, see [1-4] and the two recent papers by Unser and T. Blu [5] and [6] for a more detail study.

2.1 Nearest-Neighbour Interpolation

The value g(x) is taken as the closest known $g(x_k)$ value. The nearest-neighbour algorithm is exact only when the sampled function is a constant

$$h_1(x) = \begin{cases} 1, & 0 \le |x| < 0.5 \\ 0, & elsewhere. \end{cases} \tag{5}$$

The main advantage of this interpolation method is its simplicity, which results in the most efficient of all implementations. However strong aliasing and blurring effects are associated with this method.

2.2 Linear Interpolation

This method will reproduce at most a first-degree polynomial. The value for g(x) is calculated by weighting both direct neighbours with the opposite distance to the point of interpolation x. Therefore, the linear approximation of the sinc function follows the triangular function given by the equation

$$h_2(x) = \begin{cases} 1-|x|, & 0 \le |x| < 1 \\ 0, & elsewhere. \end{cases} \tag{6}$$

The main disadvantages of linear interpolation are the attenuation of high frequency (it acts like a low-pass filter) and aliasing into the low frequencies.

2.3 Cubic Interpolation

Key [7] obtained the following cubic interpolation kernel

$$h_3(x) = \begin{cases} \frac{3}{2}|x|^3 - \frac{5}{2}|x|^2 + 1, & 0 < |x| \le 1 \\ -\frac{1}{2}|x|^3 + \frac{5}{2}|x|^2 - 4|x| + 2, & 1 < |x| < 2 \\ 0, & elsewere. \end{cases} \tag{7}$$

Key also studies the convergence rate of this method and compares it with the previous nearest-neighbour and linear methods. He found that the nearest-neighbour algorithm has a $O(\Delta)$ convergence rate while the linear has $O(\Delta^2)$ and the cubic has $O(\Delta^3)$. This means that the cubic interpolation function will generally be a more accurate approximation to the sampled function than the linear or nearest-neighbour interpolations.

2.4 Splines Interpolation

Splines interpolation can be derived by several self-convolutions of a so called basis function. Actually the kernel of the linear interpolation can be obtained from the convolution of the nearest-neighbour with itself.

$$h_2 = h_1(x) * h_1(x). \tag{8}$$

Therefore, the kernel h_1 can be used for the construction of splines of order n. For n=3 the quadratic splines is obtained and the cubic splines for n=4. When $n \rightarrow \infty$ this process converges to a Gaussian function, see Lehman et al. [1],

$$h_n = h_1(x) * h_1(x) * \ldots * h_1(x). \tag{9}$$

There are several methods and kernels for splines interpolation. In this paper we always refer to splines.

2.5 Implementation

When (x,y) is the point in the rectangular subdivision $[x_i, x_{i+1}]x[y_j, y_{j+1}]$ the cubic and spline interpolation is given by equation (1) in the following form:

$$g(x,y) = \sum_{k=-1}^{2} \sum_{l=-1}^{2} c_{i+k,j+l}\, h\left(\frac{x - x_{i+k}}{\Delta_x}, \frac{y - y_{j+l}}{\Delta_y} \right), \tag{10}$$

$$c_{ij} = f(x_i, y_j). \tag{11}$$

Boundary conditions are stronger for spline than for cubic, but this is not traduced into a longer computational execution time as usually thought.

We will follow Press et al. [8] for the implementation. Splines and cubic have a similar algorithm since both are high smoothing interpolators. To interpolate one functional value in a 4x4 neighbourhood, one performs 4 one-dimensional splines across the rows of the grid in the x direction. This is followed by one additional one-dimensional spline down the newly created column. Instead of pre-computing and storing all the derivative information (as in cubic interpolation), spline users typically pre-compute and store only one auxiliary table of second derivatives in one direction only. Then one need only do spline evaluations (not constructions) for the m row splines; one must still do a construction and evaluation for the final column spline. Spline construction is a process of computational complexity O(n), while a spline evaluation is only of order O(log n) (to find the place in the table using quick-sort search method).

Splines are especially practical because not only the set of equations that generated them but also the boundary conditions, are not only linear, but also tridiagonal; that is, it has nonzero elements only on the diagonal plus or minus one column. For tridiagonal sets, the procedures of LU decomposition, forward- and back- substitution each take only O(n) operations, and the whole solution can be solved very concisely. Therefore the equation can be solved in O(n) operations.

3 Comparison of Interpolation Methods

The image registration process is crucial for the accuracy of the produced pan-sharpened image. Therefore special care was taken to put the pixels of the XS and Pan effectively into correspondence through ground control points. Next the XS bands are interpolated to obtain the 1 meter pixel resolution. In order to know how the interpolation has worked, several indices are going to be defined, some for spectral and some for spatial quality.

In order to evaluate interpolation kernels a common used approach is to compare the spectral and spatial characteristics of interpolation kernels with those of the sinc function. The problem with such approaches is that they are based on the fundamental assumption that in all cases, the sinc function is the optimal interpolation kernel, as stated in previous section, but in our case the optimal kernel would be the one giving the Pan image as the convolution result.

CCs (Correlation Coefficients) are the most popular index for evaluating spectral properties among the remote sensing community; they measure the correlation between each RGB colour band and the original colour reference in the XS images.

Let us now define a spatial quality index. Let Pan(x_i, y_j) be the panchromatic original image, normalized to the interval [0,1], and f(x_i, y_j) the intensity of the resample colour image, f(x_i, y_j) =(R+G+B)/3. The coefficient δ is defined as the difference between both images:

$$\delta = \frac{\sum_{i=1}^{m}\sum_{j=1}^{n}\left|f(x_i, y_j) - Pan(x_i, y_j)\right|}{m \cdot n}. \tag{12}$$

Table 1. Indices for resampling with nearest-neighbour, bilinear, cubic and splines

	Nearest	Linear	Cubic	Splines
CCR	1	0,9426	0,9400	0,9394
CCG	1	0,9400	0,9367	0,9367
CCB	1	0,9428	0,9395	0,9396
δ_{x1000}	72,5079	69,8884	67,1531	60,7070

The Pan image should be identical to the theoretical continuous signal g(x,y). The smaller the factor δ is, the more spatial information from the Pan original is injected into the resample images. Since the coefficient δ measures only information from isolated pixels without considering the neighbouring pixels, it could be considered as a first-order statistic for spatial conservation. It would be useful also to take into account second-order statistic coefficients, which would allow comparing to what degree of spatial structure is preserved. It is obvious that only a very small fraction of the spatial information is addressed by this coefficient, since it would have required filters with different windows sides, as well as third- and higher-order statistics through texture.

It can be observed in Table 1 that first order spatial quality rises from left to right while spectral correlation decreases in the same direction. The correlation in cubic and splines are very similar; however, a tiny decrement is observed in the correlation coefficient CCR from cubic to splines, while opposing increments are found in the δ factor. Contrary to CC indices the contribution of δ to the conservation of spatial information is not conclusive due to a high standard deviation of around 45. Further

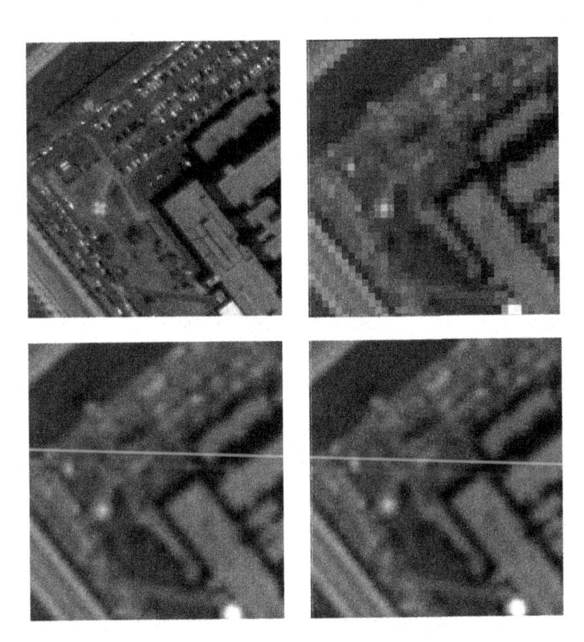

Fig. 1. Detail of Ikonos image scene from Alcala University Campus. From upper left, in clockwise direction, Pan image, nearest-neighbor, splines, linear interpolation.

research is necessary in order to find coefficients which properly represent spatial information.

It can be seen clearly in Figure 1 that nearest-neighbour resampling produced the worst quality of all four resampling methods, as stated in previous sections. The Pan image is shown here for comparison purposes only. Linear and spline resampling are very similar, but very small differences can be observed. The cubic resampling has not been shown in Figure 1 as it seems it is totally similar to spline resampling to the naked eye. The images have 11 bits of digital level resolution, but it has to be normalized to 8 bits in order to be shown as an image, and the eye cannot perceive the fine differences in 256 digital levels.

In order to investigate the spatial distribution of δ factor "error" images were built by subtracting the interpolated images from the panchromatic image (Figure 2) and taking absolute values. Minimum intensity (black) corresponds to the maximum absolute error in the interpolation image. Error magnitudes between maximum linear interpolation error and none are represented by corresponding shades of gray. Therefore, decreasing intensity denotes an increase magnitude of error in Figure 2.

It can be observed how nearest-neighbor error image in Figure 2 is highly cluttered, with the typical saw structure for this method. Nearest-neighbor interpolation will be useful when spectral properties must be conserved, such as when some type of classification has to be performed after interpolation. Besides being the fastest of the four methods as will be seen bellow.

From Figure 2 can be also note that splines give to the straight lines and other high frequency features a smoother representation than linear interpolation; and splines

Fig. 2. Error images obtain as subtraction of each interpolation image for the Ikonos in Figure 1 and the Pancromatic. The darker the pixel is the greater the difference. From upper left, in clockwise direction, nearest-neighbor, linear, splines and cubic interpolation.

also give a more homogeneous representation than cubic interpolation. Note that the roofs of buildings are uniformly lighter in splines and cubic than in linear interpolation. As expected, spline and cubic are better approximations to the sampled function than linear.

It can be observed that in general linear has a bigger contrast than splines which means that the differences to the pan image are smaller in the latter.

An overall picture shows that the splines interpolation intensity is closer in spatial characteristics to the Pan image than nearest-neighbour, linear or cubic for this IKONOS sub-scene. However, since not interpolation method is universal the selection could depend of the application at hand

In Table 2 execution times are given in seconds for a Pentium processor 1.5 GHz with 512 MB RAM. This was to convert an image of 500x500 pixels into an image of 2000x2000. Interpolation employed in this manner is equivalent to digital image magnification.

Table 2. Execution time for nearest-neighbour, bilinear, cubic and splines

	Nearest	Linear	Cubic	Splines
CT	15.31	42.99	55.18	46.90

4 Conclusions

From the analysis of the four kernels corresponding to the four interpolation methods, splines interpolation is shown to have a less blurred appearance and less aliasing. However, analysis in section 3 shows that the splines and cubic images suffer from a lost of spectral information.

Even if the final purpose of the resampling process is only visualization, and there is no difference to the naked eye between cubic and splines, splines interpolation is faster and could be more convenient. An added reason for using splines instead of the other three methods is that when further calculations (of spatial characteristics) are going to be performed in the final resample image (such as cartographic feature extraction), splines interpolation is the more accurate in conserving spatial information.

Acknowledgements

The author wishes to thank the Spanish MCYT for financial support; project number BTE2003-08657, the company Aurensa SA for providing the Ikonos image and the anonymous referees for their comments, which help to improve the presentation of this paper.

References

1. Lehmann T. M., Gönner C., Spitzer K.: Survey: Interpolation Methods in Medical Image Processing, IEEE Transaction on Medical Imaging, **18**, no. 11, (1999) 1049-1075.
2. Thévenaz P., Blu T., Unser M.: Interpolation Revisited, IEEE Transactions on Medical Imaging, **19**, no. 7, (2000) 739-758.

3. Unser M., Aldroubi A., Eden M.: Fast B-spline transforms for continuous image representation and interpolation, IEEE Transactions on Pattern Analysis and Machine Intelligence, **13**, no. 3, (1991) 277-285.
4. Bartels R., Beatty J. and Barsky B.: An Introduction to Splines for Use in Computer Graphics and Geometric Modeling. Elsevier, (1987), 476 pages.
5. Unser M., Blu, T.: Cardinal exponential splines: part I - theory and filtering algorithms, IEEE Transactions on Signal Processing, **53**, no. 4, (2005) 1425–1438.
6. Unser M.: Cardinal exponential splines: part II - think analog, act digital, IEEE Transactions on Signal Processing, **53**, no. 4, (2005) 1439-1449.
7. Key R. G.: Cubic Convolution Interpolation for Digital Image Processing, IEEE Transaction on Acoustics, Speech, and Signal Processing, **29**, no. 6, (1981) 1153-1160.
8. Press W. H., Teukolsky S. A., Vetterling W. T., Flannery B. P.: Numerical Recipes in C++. The Art of Scientific Computing. 2nd edn. Cambridge University Press, (2002) 126-132.

Tool for Storm Analysis Using Multiple Data Sets

Robert M. Rabin[1,2] and Tom Whittaker[2]

[1] NOAA/National Severe Storms Laboratory, Norman OK 73069, USA
[2] Cooperative Institute for Meteorological Satellite Studies (CIMSS), University of Wisconsin-Madison, Madison, WI 53706, USA

Abstract. This note describes a web-based tool for storm analysis using multiple data sets developed for use in research of thunderstorms and forecasting applications. The tool was developed for users to monitor atmospheric changes along the path of storm systems. It demonstrates the use of the Thematic Real time Environmental Data Distributed Services (THREDDS) and other data sets.

1 Introduction

The functionality of integrating and overlaying data from multiple sources has been useful in atmospheric and multidisciplinary research. Several tools have been developed over years to meet this need. These include the Man Computer Interactive Data Access System (McIDAS) [1], VIS5D [2], VisAD [3], and more recently the Interactive Data Viewer (IDV).

The basic functionality of such systems includes the ability to animate imagery, usually as time sequences, overlay gridded or point data, provide statistical comparisons between images and other data, and to rotate the viewing angle in the case of three dimensional (3-D) gridded data. In the case of atmospheric data, the ability to visualize the distribution of data in space (3-D) and time is useful. The wind is an example of an important atmospheric parameter to be viewed in 3-dimensions and time. In this case, the air flow can be visualized from plots of streamlines at an individual time, or as trajectories over a span of time.

In some cases, the ability to focus on an organized atmospheric system, such an individual thunderstorm is desirable. Since storms are rarely stationary, they must be identified and tracked in space and time in order to evaluate their evolution. Often the process of identification and tracking is done manually. Given a storm position and movement vector, wind or other data can be displayed in a storm relative frame of reference. Viewing imagery in a storm relative frame of reference provides insight into the interaction of the storm with its near environment, such storm relative inflow. In other applications, tools have been developed to automatically track storms and to plot attributes of the moving storm versus time (in the form of time-series plots). Examples of such applications include the Warning Decision Support System (WDSS) [4] which evaluates properties of storm rotation, hail signatures, etc. from Doppler radar data. The

G. Bebis et al. (Eds.): ISVC 2005, LNCS 3804, pp. 571–578, 2005.

output has wide applications, from severe storm research to warning guidance for the National Weather Service forecasters.

This paper reports on a prototype tool which provides automated tracking of cloud systems from radar and satellite and interactive functionality to obtain time-series on-line. The application reported here is unique because of its on-line interactive capability. The time-series include attributes of: 1) the cloud systems, and 2) atmospheric conditions in a user selectable region relative to the moving cloud system. The tool uses on-line databases of satellite, radar, and model analysis data to provide both near-real time and archived information on storm attributes, and on the atmospheric environment surrounding them to users of the Internet. The tool has the capability to provide relatively quick access to a wealth of information relevant to the atmospheric research community on thunderstorm behavior. To date, this capability has yet to become widely available by other means.

2 Data Access

Data are obtained in near-real time through the Internet from a variety of sources. Currently, forecast model data are available using the Thematic Real time Environmental Data Distributed Services (THREDDS) being developed by University Corporation for Atmospheric Research's Unidata [5] and the NOAA Operational Model Archive and Distribution System (NOMADS) by the National Climatic Data Center (NCDC), National Centers for Environmental Prediction (NCEP) and the Geophysical Fluid Dynamics Laboratory (GFDL) [6]. Data retrieval is efficient in that only desired subsets of large data files are transfered from the remote servers for local archival and processing. Conceivably, all environmental data sets may become available from THREDDS in the future. Meteorological fields which are derived from the NOAA Rapid Update Cycle (RUC) model and observed surface data are obtained directly from the NOAA Storm Prediction Center (SPC). Satellite and radar data are obtained from McIDAS Abstract Data Distribution Environment (ADDE) servers which also allow efficient transfer of compressed subsets of data. Satellite data are from the geostationary operational environmental satellite imager (GOES-12) . Radar data are based on a national composite from individual WSR-88D radars across the U.S. produced at Unidata.

3 Analysis of Cloud Clusters

The analysis of cloud systems is based on the automated identification and tracking of features in satellite or radar images which are deemed to be associated with deep convective thunderstorms. Often such storms form into clusters known as Mesoscale Convective Systems (MCS) during the summer months in the central U.S. These storms bring a variety of significant weather including heavy rain, high wind and hail. The initiation, movement, and decay of MCSs are relatively difficult to forecast. Although the individual storm elements may be short-lived, the clusters often last for several hours.

In the case of satellite imagery, storms are identified by unusually cold cloud top temperatures in the window infrared (IR) band (wavelength near 11 microns). A simple scheme for identification and tracking of these features has been employed following that of [7]. Other more sophisticated techniques could be substituted in the future. The technique is based on choosing a cloud top temperature threshold which contains most of the anvil cloud above the MCS. The selection of colder thresholds will identify and track sub-scale features, such as overshooting tops, possibly associated with individual storm updrafts. Tracking is obtained from movement of centroid positions of each identified cluster between successive IR images. The association of clusters in successive images is based on observed spatial overlap. This limits the analysis to features of a minimum horizontal scale which depends on the interval between images and propagation speed of the features. To allow for interactive user selection of cloud top temperature thresholds, the identification and tracking is automatically computed for temperature increments of 1^oC covering a range of possible conditions (-75 to -30 ^oC). Centroid location, cloud top size, and statistics such as mean and minimum temperature within each cloud cluster are stored in a file for display and relation to other variables, as described later.

An analysis similar to that of cloud top temperature is performed using patterns of radar reflectivity. In this case, thresholds of radar reflectivity correspond to echoes of different intensity.

Uncertainties in satellite and radar data are relatively small factors in the positioning and coverage of the cloud systems with horizontal scales of 100 km or more. However, local weather conditions at the ground (severity of wind and rainfall) can not be inferred from these data alone.

4 Display

The display interface is based on a Java applet which allows client machines to interact with the server database of imagery and output analysis described in Section 3. Upon opening the tracker web page from any Java-enabled web browser: http://tracker.nssl.noaa.gov, the user can select movies of IR satellite images (3-hour duration) from the entire archive of data (since June 2003). The display can be magnified (zoomed) for closer examination of desired storms. Tracks of each cloud cluster during a 3-hour period are displayed corresponding to the default cloud top temperature threshold of -43 ^oC . The images can be enhanced to display only the cloud areas defined by the temperature threshold. This depicts the cloud features being tracked for this particular threshold. Smaller features within major clusters, such as overshooting tops, can then be examined by choosing progressively colder thresholds.

Images of radar reflectivity can be overlaid on the satellite IR movies. In this case, the selectable thresholds are levels of reflectivity in dBZ. The same functionality described above for the satellite imagery can be applied to the radar data. In this case, choosing progressively larger reflectivity values will identify the location and tracks of smaller scale features in the radar data.

After selecting an individual cloud or reflectivity cluster with the cursor, time series of variables associated with the cluster can be displayed. This includes variables associated with the satellite or radar data discussed in Section 3, such as cloud top size and mean temperature or reflectivity within each cloud cluster. The time series computed from additional data sets can also be selected for computation and display. Computation utilizes the VisAD library to facilitate sampling parameters from the model grids in space and time. These data sets include observations from other sensors such as fields of atmospheric parameters. Of particular interest are factors which influence storm behavior, such thermodynamic stability and wind shear. By default, these variables are evaluated at the centroid position of the cluster for each time period. Uncertainties in atmospheric variables depend on the availability of surface and upper air observations and the amount of variability caused by storm dynamics. The user can interactively define any other location displaced from the default position. This is particularly useful in examining the environment of the inflow region to a storm which has not yet been modified by rain cooled air.

5 Examples

An example of a long-lived MCS in its mature and dissipating stage is shown in Figs. 1-2. The selected centroid track appears in grey. Figures 3-4 show time series corresponding to the mature and dissipating stages. Gridded atmospheric variables were obtained at hourly intervals from the NOAA Storm Prediction Center (SPC). Three variables are selected for display. The cloud top temperature (CTT) warms and the deep layer shear (6 km shear) weakens (0715-1030

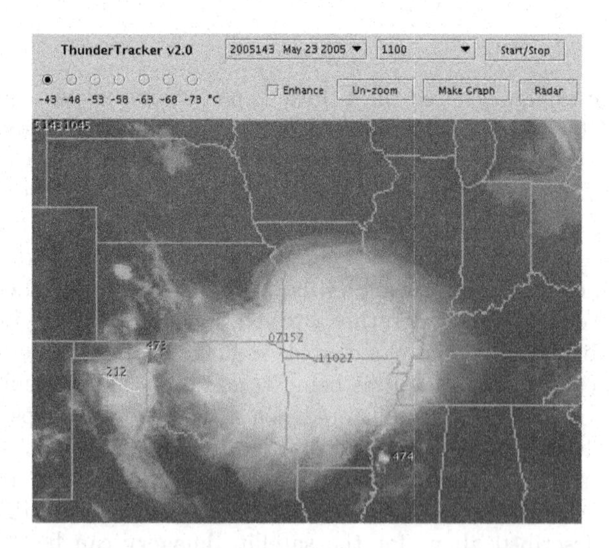

Fig. 1. Mesoscale Convective Complex, mature stage. Selected track (grey) 0715-1102 UTC, 23 May 2005.

Fig. 2. Mesoscale Convective Complex, decaying stage. Selected tracks (grey) 1045-1432 UTC, 23 May 2005.

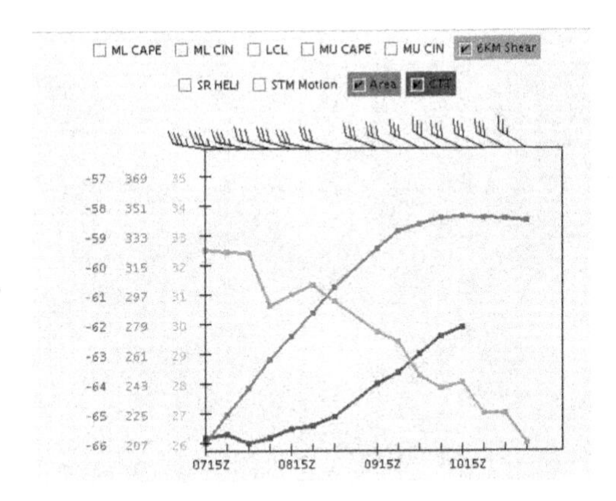

Fig. 3. Time series plots from Mesoscale Convective Complex (mature stage). Parameters plotted: 1) Size of cloud cluster (Area, 10^4 km^2), 2) Cloud top temperature (CTT, ^{o}C), 3) Deep layer shear (6 km Shear, knots).

UTC) as the initial growth of the cloud cluster ceases (Fig. 3). The warming and decreasing shear signal future weakening of the storm system. During the dissipating stage (Fig. 4, 1045-1400 UTC), the cloud size rapidly decreases as the atmospheric conditions stabilize (Most Unstable Convective Available Potential Energy, MU CAPE decreases). The average cloud top temperature remains relatively steady during this period.

Another example of MCS tracks is given in Fig. 5. The storm cluster highlighted with the grey track produced a series of tornadoes in central Illinois between 1930-2030 UTC. The trends of atmospheric parameters are given in

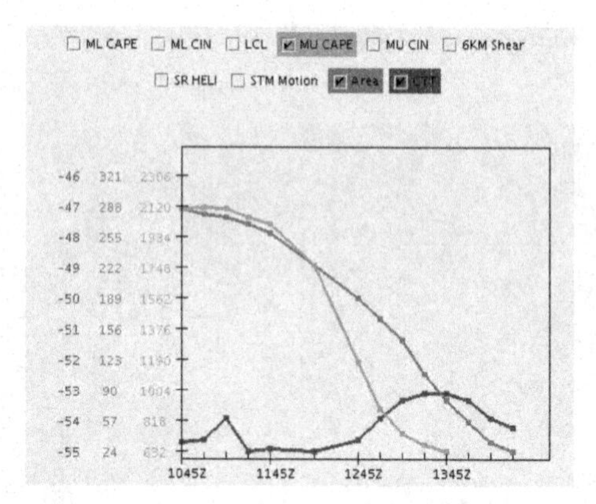

Fig. 4. Time series plots from Mesoscale Convective Complex (decaying stage). Same parameters as in Fig.3 except, 3) Most Unstable Convective Available Potential Energy (MU CAPE, J kg^{-1}).

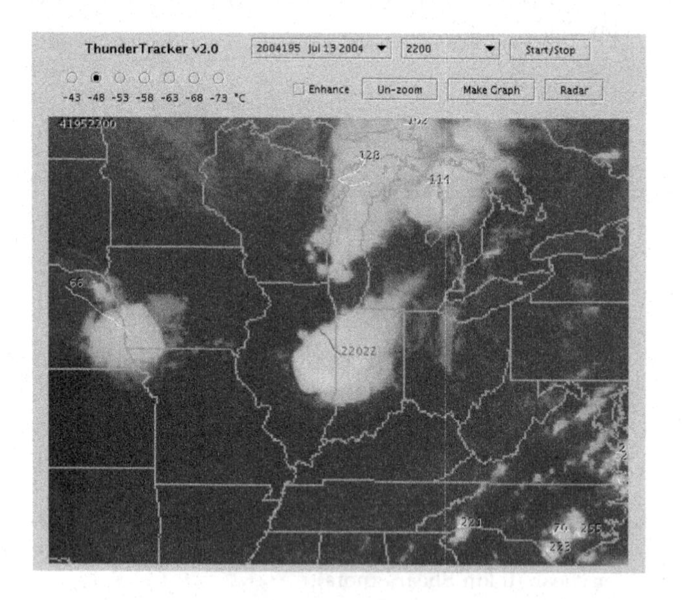

Fig. 5. Storm track, MCS associated with central Illinois tornadoes, 13 July 2004

Fig. 6. Gridded atmospheric variables were obtained from the NOMADS in this case. Plotted are convective inhibition, CAPE, and helicity. The inhibition is a measure of required energy to initiate storms. Helicity is a measure of wind shear conducive to development of rotating updrafts (with potential for tornado-genesis), [8]. There appears to be strong correlations between the time of the tornadoes and a maximum in helicity and a minimum in convective inhibition.

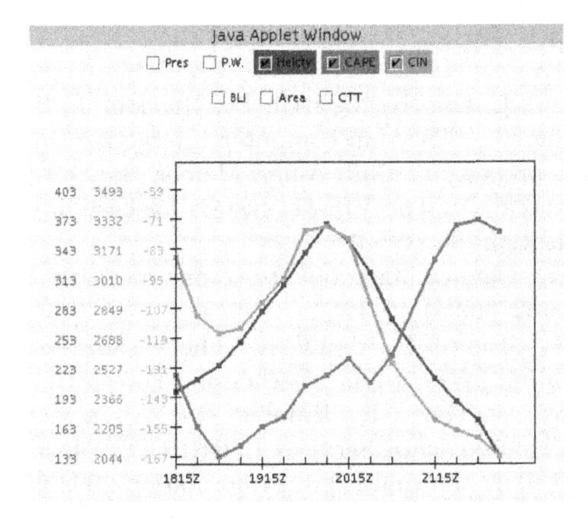

Fig. 6. Time trends of atmospheric variables associated with MCS in Fig. 5. Variables plotted are: helicity (Helcty), Convective Available Potential Energy (CAPE, J kg^{-1}), and Convective Inhibition (CIN, J kg^{-1}).

6 Conclusions

This note describes a web-based tool for storm analysis using multiple data sets developed for use in research of thunderstorms and forecasting applications. The functionality includes: 1) access to a wide range of archived data, and 2) cross-referencing of trends in radar, satellite, and other atmospheric data in the moving frame of reference of storm clusters. The software allows users to animate satellite and radar images and to view trends of cloud top temperature, radar reflectivity, environmental conditions, etc. In addition to being a research tool, forecasters can monitor changes which might alter the strength and longevity of a storm as it moves along, such as atmospheric stability, wind shear, and moisture. In principle, additional data can be included for analysis. For example, lightning frequency, high resolution visible imagery from GOES, and factors such as convergence from surface and Doppler radar data could be used to monitor and forecast the initiation of storms from developing cumulus clouds.

Acknowledgments

This work was funded by the National Oceanic and Atmospheric Administration (NOAA) High Performance Computing and Communications (HPCC) program. Thanks to Dr. Brian Mapes for contributing his tracking code, Daphne Zaras of NOAA/NSSL for adapting the code for real time processing, and Dr. Phillip Bothwell of the NOAA/SPC for making the gridded atmospheric data available in real-time.

References

1. Lazzara, M., Benson, J., Fox, R., Laitsch, D., Rueden, J., Santek, D., Wade, D., Whittaker, T., Young, J.: The Man computer Interactive Data Access System: 25 Years of interactive processing. Bull. Amer. Meteor. Soc. **80** (1999) 271–284
2. Hibbard, W.and Santek, D.: The VIS-5D system for easy interactive visualization. Proc. IEEE Visualization '90 (1990)
3. Hibbard, W.: VisAD: Connecting people to communications and people to people. Computer Graphics **32** (1998) 10–12
4. Lakshmanan, V.S.T., Stumpf, G., Hondl, K.: The warning decision support system - integrated information (WDSS-II). Weather and Forecasting:in review (2005)
5. Domenico, B., Caron, J., Davis, E., Kambic, R., Nativi, S.: Thematic Real-time Environmental Distributed Data Services (THREDDS): Incorporating interactive analysis tools into NSDL. Journal Digital Information 2002-05-29 (2002)
6. Rutledge, G., Alpert, J., Ebuisaki, W.: NOMADS a climate and weather model archive at the National Oceanic and Atmospheric Administration. Bulletin of the American Meteorological Society:accepted (2005)
7. Mapes, B.E.and Houze Jr., R.: Cloud clusters and superclusters over the oceanic warm pool. Mon. Wea. Rev **121** (1993) 1398–1416
8. Kerr, B.W., Darkow, G.L.: Storm-relative winds and helicity in the tornadic thunderstorm environment. Weather and Forecasting **11** (1996) 489–505

3D Modeling and Adaptation for Virtual Heritage System

Minh Tuan Le[1,3], Hae-Kwang Kim[1], and Yong-Moo Kwon[2]

[1] Dept. of Computer Software, Sejong University, Seoul 143-747, Korea
tuanlm@sju.ac.kr, hkkim@sejong.ac.kr
[2] Imaging Media Research Center, KIST, Seoul 136-791, Korea
ymk@kist.re.kr
[3] Center for Development of Information Technology,
Posts and Telecommunications Institute of Technology, Hanoi, Vietnam

Abstract. Recently, virtual heritage has emerged as a promising technology for conservation, preservation, and interpretation of our culture and natural history. We implemented a virtual heritage system with real data acquisition and a MPEG-21 based graphics adaptation architecture for transmitting adapted 3D contents to multiple target devices. Our system consists of 3D modeling tools, 3D content authoring tools, 3D database system and 3D graphics adaptation system. In this paper, we provide a overview of our system, including our approach in 3D modeling, a web-based interactive presentation over network and proposed a graphics adaptation system within MPEG-21 framework for transmitting adapted 3D contents to multiple target devices with different user preferences.

1 Introduction

Virtual heritage has become increasingly important in the conservation, preservation, and interpretation of our cultural and natural history. Rapid advances in digital technologies in recent years offer virtual heritage new direction [1]. Especially, new media technologies, from 3D media technology to virtual reality, are very promising ones expected to satisfy heritage representation such as the naturalness, the sensation of depth and realism [2],[3].

In this paper, our main point is how to create and present 3D contents over network on wide range of target devices with different user preferences. In previous system [4], we use digital camera with MR-MBS technique [5] and laser based scanning technique for the 3D modeling of culture heritages. A problem of the approach is its only focus on visible object. In presentation of 3D virtual heritage, PCs and high speed network are used for rendering and transmitting. The problem is how to present the 3D contents through network with different devices capabilities and user preferences. To solve the problems, we first show a overview of our virtual heritage system. Then, we introduce approaches for 3D modeling of various kind of culture heritages and show some results. Finally, a graphics adaptation system within MPEG-21 framework is designed allowing access to the same 3D contents with different devices and user preferences.

G. Bebis et al. (Eds.): ISVC 2005, LNCS 3804, pp. 579–586, 2005.

The paper is structured as followings: Our virtual heritage system will be presented in section 2. Section 3 describes 3D modeling techniques. Interactive presentation of 3D culture heritage service is showed in section 4. The conclusion and some future development are summarized in section 5.

2 Virtual Heritage System Architecture

Our main goal are the 3D modeling of culture heritages and presentation of 3D virtual heritage through a network. User can use PC or PDA to access to the same 3D content on heterogeneous devices with user chose geometry quality. We design a virtual heritage system which focuses on the following four issues:

(1) Automatic generation of 3D models.
(2) Management of 3D models using DBMS.
(3) Creation of new 3D contents through authoring tools.
(4) 3D graphics adaptation and service system.

Figure 1 shows a schematic representation of our 3D virtual heritage system.

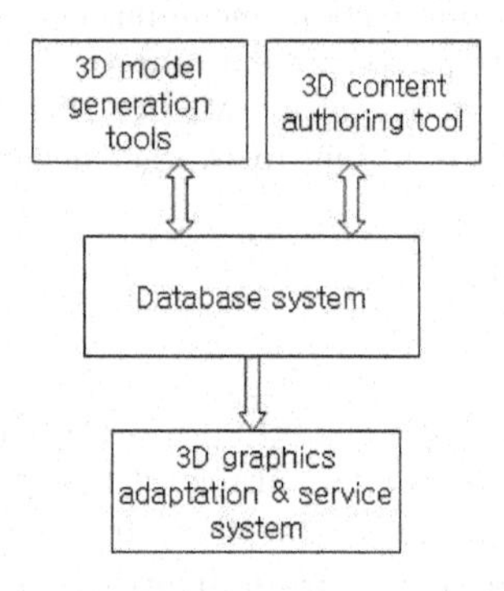

Fig. 1. 3D virtual heritage system

3 Generation of 3D Models

3.1 Image Based Generation

3D Model Generation Using Digital Camera. We use computer vision technique for the 3D modeling of visible culture heritage. By using single digital camera, a multiview images is captured while controlling the image capture position. Range information is extracted by analyzing the disparity of the object. The disparity map is extracted by using MR-MBS technique [5] because the proposed MR-MBS method matches faster than the MBS method. After extracting the disparity map, the object is segmented using the disparity histogram in assumption that the background is far from the object. The image-based 3D modeling scheme using digital camera is based on our approach in [4].

3D Model Generation Using X-ray Camera. We also develop X-Ray techniques for the 3D modeling of invisible objet. We are towards two research issues. One is the 3D modeling of ancient sword without opening the boxes where the swords are stored using shape from silhouette method and exploit parallel geometry of X-ray camera [6]. Our approach is very cheap, fast and need no X-ray camera parameters to reconstruct convex shape of culture heritage. Fig. 2 and Fig. 3 shows an modeling procedure of an ancient sword and 3D reconstructed model. For the 3D modeling of invisible culture heritage with concavity, we use the back projection technique as shown in Fig. 4. Basically, the well-known inverse radon transform is used for the reconstruction of each section data. Then, the marching cube algorithm is used for the 3D modeling.

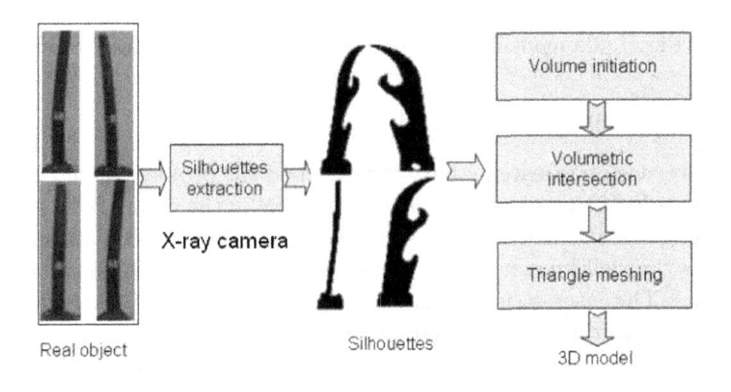

Fig. 2. 3D modeling procedure using shape from silhouette

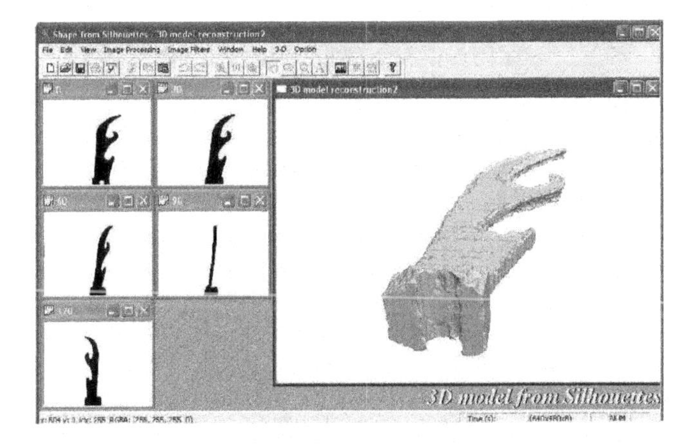

Fig. 3. The X-ray image and 3D model of a ancient sword

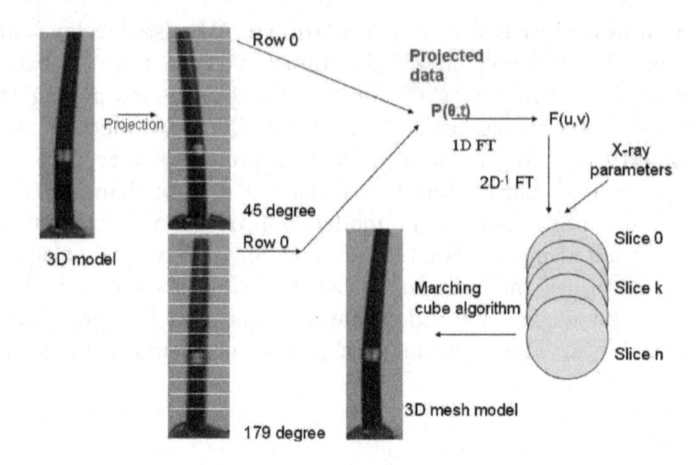

Fig. 4. 3D modeling procedure using Computed Tomography

3.2 Laser Scanning Based Generation

The computer vision researches have long studied the problem of determining the shape of an object from a set of photographs. One of the common forms of active range sensing for 3D modeling is optical triangulation [7]. One example of this technique is the well-known laser scanning technique. The fundamental principle is as follows: The laser stripe is casted onto the surface of the object, which is then captured by the conventional CCD camera. Then the range information can be captured by analyzing the captured pattern of the laser stripe. Thus each captured image gives us a range profile and sweeping the light over the surface of the object, we can capture its shape. Here, we apply the laser scanning scheme for 3D modeling of Korea cultural heritage. We use the Vivid 700 laser scanner

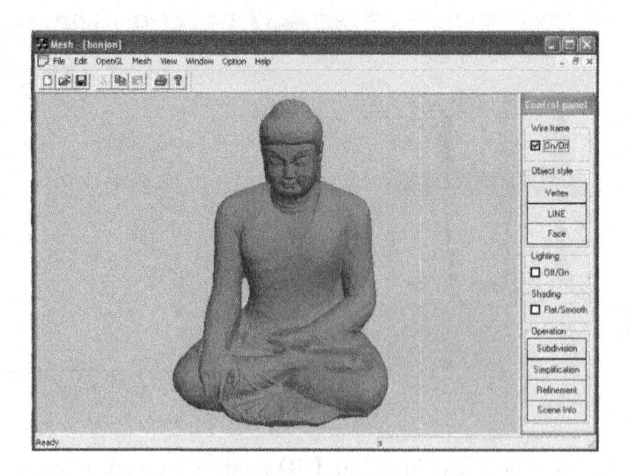

Fig. 5. 3D model of Buddha statue

made by Minolta Co. For 3D modeling from point clouds of laser scanning, we use RapidForm [8] that has functions of polygon generation using triangulation, and registration and merge of polygon models. Fig. 5 shows the 3D model of a Korean Buddha statue.

4 Interactive Presentation

4.1 Web Service of 3D Models

Web-based virtual museum is developed for servicing 3D models through the internet. On the homepage of a heritage service (http://culture.kist.re.kr), a search engine for 3D models using keyword is provided. In more detail, the search can be performed through technology, category and media type. A 3D model tour scheme based on image-map is also provided. The system also provides a scheme for creating a schedule of a tour course. Visitor can see 3D models sequently as scheduled by clicking the tour button.

4.2 Service of 3D Models Within the MPEG-21 Framework

Problems in the Web based service of the virtual culture heritage content is how to access the 3D models through network with different terminals capabilities such as PDA, mobile phone, PCs and user preferences such as quality of geometry, texture, animation, file format information. The vision for MPEG-21 is to define multimedia framework to enable transparent and augmented use of multimedia resources across a wide range of networks and devices used by different communities [9]. Digital Item (DI) is a structured digital object and is combined by resource and descriptor. One of main MPEG-21 parts is Digital Item Adaptation (DIA). The goal of DIA is to achieve interoperable transparent

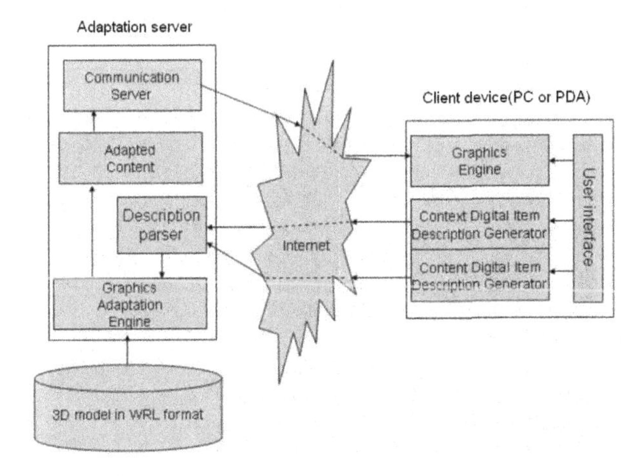

Fig. 6. Architecture of MPEG-21 DIA based graphics adaptation system

access to (distributed) advanced multimedia content by shielding users from network and terminal installation, configuration, management, and implementation issues [10]. A system based on MPEG-21 DIA for servicing 3D models through network is developed to solve the problems and and its adopted in the adaptation model document of the MPEG-21 DIA [9]. Fig. 6 shows the architecture of our MPEG-21 DIA based graphics adaptation system.

Currently, our MPEG-21 DIA based graphics adaptation system includes a adaptation server and clients(PC and PDA) where our 3D models are adapted through network according to user preference such as quality of geometry [9]. At the client side, main modules are a Context Digital Item Description Generator (CDI), Content Digital Item Description Generator (XDI) and Graphics Engine. User chooses user preferences, a CDI that produces CDI.xml, a XDI that produces XDI.xml, and Graphics Engine that display adapted content. The resource is stored in CDI.xml. Two descriptors stored in XDI.xml are GeometryEmphasis and TextureEmphasis. The user at the client using user interface sends a request for a 3D graphics contents to the adaptation server. The XML files are transmitted to the Adaptation server. At the adaptation server, description parser is an

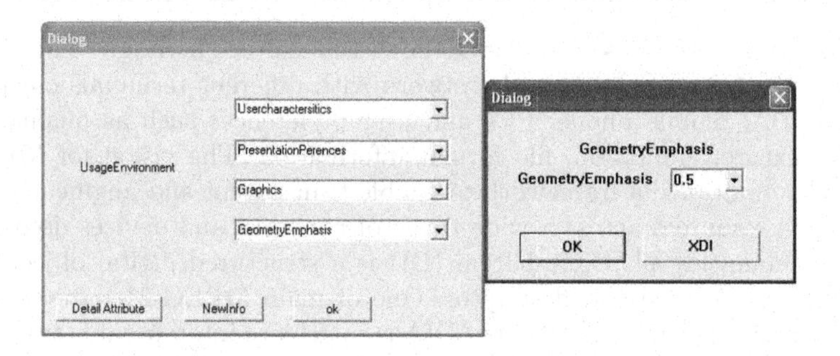

Fig. 7. The client user preferences window

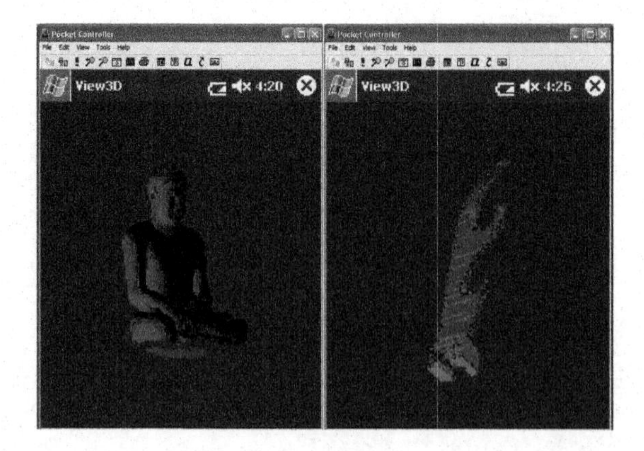

Fig. 8. 3D models of virtual heritage display on PDA with 0.5 geometry quality

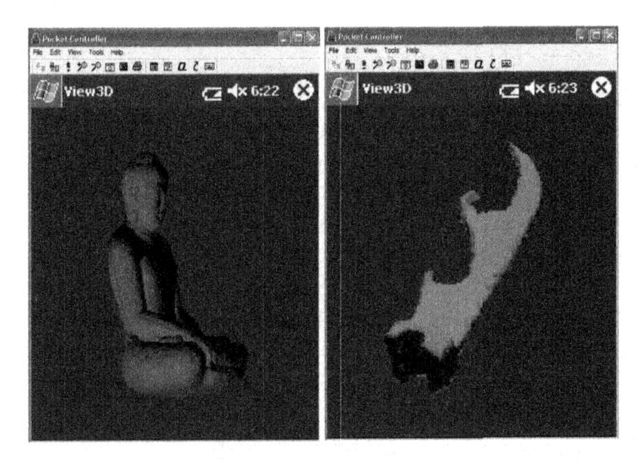

Fig. 9. 3D models of virtual heritage display on PDA with full geometry quality

xml parser that parses the XML files. The resource and two descriptors are sent to graphics adaptation engine to adapt the 3D graphics contents. The 3D content is parsed into geometry and material parts and sends to the geometry adaptation and material adaptation engine. Each specialized adaptation engine adapts the received parts of graphics to adapted parts. The adapted content includes the adapted parts of graphics. For geometry part, the geometry adaptation engine is built on a 3D triangle mesh simplification algorithm [11] . For material part, we are implementing a size reduction method to change the texture quality. The adapted graphics content is transfer to the communication server. Finally, the communication server sends formatted graphics contents to graphic engine of the client to display on the screen.

Fig. 7 shows the client's user preferences windows setting the value of geometry quality that would be stored in XDI.xml and sent to the graphics adaptation server. The 3D resource located in the CDI.xml file is also delivered to the adaptation server. Then, graphics adaptation server parses the XDI.xml and CDI.xml files and adapts the 3D VRML model to simplified model according to the descriptions in XDI.xml. The simplified model is transfer to the client device to display. Fig. 8 and Fig. 9 shows our 3D model of virtual heritage display on PDA according to different user preferences.

5 Conclusions

In this paper, we introduce our virtual heritage system of which main goal is the service 3D models and contents of natural heritages over network with a wide range of target devices. We first show 3D modeling approaches for various type of heritages. Then, we introduce our 3D graphics adaptation system for interactive cultural heritage presentation on different target devices and user preferences. In future work, we are investigating on various algorithms for geometry, material and animation adaptation.

References

1. S. T. Refsland, T. Ojika, A.A., Stone, R.: Virtual heritage: breathing new life into our ancient past. In: IEEE Multimedia. Volume 7. (2000)
2. SIGGRAPH, A.: Applications of computer vision to computer graphics. In: Computer Graphics. Volume 33. (1999)
3. Kannade, T., Tander, P.: Virtualized reality: Constructing virtual worlds from real scenes. In: IEEE MultiMedia 4. (1997) 34–37
4. Y. M. Kwon, I. J. Kim, S.C.A.H.D.K., Kim, H.: Virtual heritage system: Modeling, database and presentation. In: VSMM 01, Proceedings of the Seventh International Conference on Virtual Systems and Multimedia (VSMM01) Proceedings of the Seventh International Conference on Virtual Systems and Multimedia (VSMM01), UC Berkeley, USA (2001)
5. Kwon, Y.M.: Multiresolution approach to depth extraction for arbitrary view synthesis. In: Proceedings of 3D Image Conference '98, Tokyo, Japan (1998) 135–140
6. Le, M.T., Kim, H.K.: Automatic 3d model generation from 2d x-ray images. In: ICIEC 2004 Conference, Hanoi, Vietnam (2004)
7. Curless, B.: From range scans to 3d models. In: Computer Graphics. Volume 33. (1999) 38–41
8. RapidForm: (www.rapidform.com)
9. group, M.M.: Mpeg-21 digital item adaptation am v.5.0. In: mpeg document no. n5613, Pattaya, Thailand (2003)
10. Hellwagner, H., Timmerer, C.: Towards universal multimedia access using the mpeg-7 and mpeg- 21 standards. In: The 9th IASTED International Conference on Internet and Multimedia systems and applications, Grindelwald, Switzerland (2005)
11. Garland, M., Heckbert, P.: Simplification using quadric error metrics. In: Computer Graphics. Volume 31., ACM Press, New York (1997) 209–216

Direct Point Rendering on GPU

Hiroaki Kawata[1] and Takashi Kanai[2]

[1] Keio University, Faculty of Environmental Information,
5322 Endo, Fujisawa, Kanagwa 252-8520, Japan
[2] RIKEN, Integrated Volume-CAD System Research Program,
2-1 Hirosawa, Wako-shi, Saitama 351-0198, Japan

Abstract. In this paper, we propose a method for directly rendering point sets which only have positional information by using recent graphics processors (GPUs). Almost all the algorithms in our method are processed on GPU. Our point-based rendering algorithms apply an image buffer which has lower-resolution image than a frame buffer. Normal vectors are computed and various types of noises are reduced on such an image buffer. Our approach then produces high-quality images even for noisy point clouds especially acquired by 3D scanning devices. Our approach also uses splats in the actual rendering process. However, the number of points to be rendered in our method is in general less than the number of input points due to the use of selected points on an image buffer, which allows our approach to be processed faster than the previous approaches of GPU-based point rendering.

1 Introduction

In recent years, point-based surface representation is becoming more and more important and drawing increasing attention thanks to recent advances of 3D scanning technology. Though a large number of points can be acquired by using 3D scanning devices, it is difficult to handle large meshes constructed from these point primitives. Therefore, approaches to point-based modeling or rendering, which directly handle point primitives instead of constructing meshes or high-order surfaces, have been a focus of constant attention.

Among these point-based approaches, point-based rendering is suitable for visualizing a large number of point primitives. In the process of rendering a mesh with millions of triangles, an overhead to rasterizing a triangle is too high because the area of a triangle projected to a screen buffer is often smaller than that of a pixel. This fact marks a watershed to alter a point-based rendering instead of a surface rendering based on triangles. Moreover, the process of point-based rendering can be accelerated using recent graphics processors (GPUs).

In this paper, we propose a direct rendering approach of point primitives using GPU. "*Direct*" in our case means that points are rendered using *only* their position information. Our approach is effective especially for rendering a large number of points acquired from 3D scanning devices. This is because that those acquired points mainly consist of only 3D positions and colors. On the other

G. Bebis et al. (Eds.): ISVC 2005, LNCS 3804, pp. 587–594, 2005.

hand, a normal vector is also needed to compute shading effects when rendering. These normal vectors are usually calculated from 3D positions of points (e.g. [1, 2]) as a pre-process. If we define a normal vector for each point, large space equivalent to the same size as 3D positions will be required to store such normal vectors. This would cause a large bottleneck when rendering points on PCs with a little DRAM memory.

The idea of our approach is based on the method proposed by Kawata and Kanai [3]. However, our algorithm is mostly executed on GPU, and is essentially different from the algorithm in [3] when implemented on GPU. The main features of our approach are described as follows:

Ad-hoc normal vector calculation. Normal vectors needed for shading effects are calculated in the rendering process on GPU. This saves the calculation time of such vectors in the pre-processing stage.

Noise reduction. Noise reduction of points is applied on GPU. In general, points acquired from 3D scanning devices involve several types of noises. Our approach is effective for rendering such noisy points.

Fast rendering algorithm. Splats are used in the final rendering stage. Texture filtering needed for this stage is applied for only selected points on an image buffer. The number of such selected points are in general less than input points. Our algorithm then renders points quickly compared to the previous approaches of GPU-based point rendering.

2 Related Work

Details of the approaches of point-based computer graphics are described in [4, 5]. Here we mainly describe related researches of point-based rendering. Point based rendering was first introduced by Levoy and Whitted [6]. One important process is to fill holes between neighboring points. There are two types of approaches for such hole-filling; screen-based approach and object-based approach. Our approach is basically of the former approach.

On the other hand, most of GPU-based point-rendering approaches focus on the implementation of the filtering phase when overlapping splats. Ren et al. [7] proposed an object-space anisotropic EWA filtering on GPU. In [7], a rectangle is used as a rendering primitive which has the problem of rendering speed, because four vertices in each splat have to be transferred to GPU. Guennebaud et al. [8] and Botsch et al. [9] independently addressed this issue by using point sprites. Zwicker et al. [10] proposed a high-quality object-space EWA texture filtering on GPU. Botsch et al. [11] realized a per-pixel lighting (Phong shading) by using a normal vector field for each splat. Other approaches include a method to transfer points effectively to GPU by using linear point lists [12], and an implementation of point-selection algorithm [13].

In our approach, splats are used to render points as done by most of the approaches described above. In addition, both the normal vector computation and noise reduction processes are also implemented on GPU.

3 Rendering Algorithm Using GPU

Figure 1 illustrates an overview of our direct point rendering algorithm on GPU. The input for our algorithm is a set of points $\mathcal{P}$: $p_i \in \mathcal{P}$ ($i = 1 \ldots n$, n is the number of points). Although only a 3D position $\mathbf{p}_i$ is required for each point, in some cases it is also possible to attach color information $\mathbf{c}_i$.

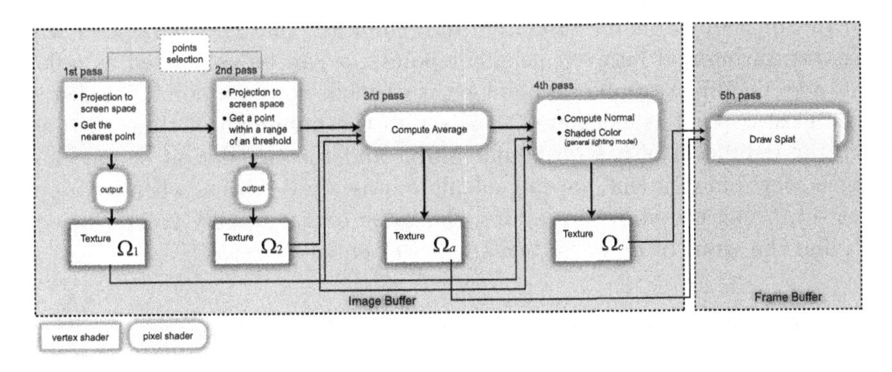

Fig. 1. Overview of our direct point rendering algorithm on GPU

Our approach adopts a totally five-pass algorithm. In the process of filling holes, we use an *image buffer* as proposed in [3] which has a lower resolution than a frame buffer. In our approach, an image buffer is used from the first to the fourth passes. In the fifth pass, we magnify a buffer to the resolution of an actual frame buffer and apply splat rendering in this pass. We allocate several floating-point textures Ω in VRAM memory on GPU. They have the same resolution as an image buffer and are used as inputs/outputs for each pass of our whole algorithm.

3.1 Setting the Resolution of an Image Buffer

In the first and second passes, we project each point to an image buffer[1] (details are described in Section 3.2).

In these processes, an appropriate resolution of an image buffer has to be determined for filling holes. This resolution is dynamically determined by the resolution of a point set and by camera parameters (a view position, field of view, the size of view frustum, etc.).

Let the width and height of a frame buffer and an image buffer be w_s, h_s, w_i, h_i, respectively. w_i, h_i are then calculated by the following equations derived from the perspective projection:

$$w_i = w_s / \rho, \quad h_i = h_s / \rho, \tag{1}$$

[1] For the image buffer, we use a floating-point buffer on GPU. In case of DirectX, IEEE-format `D3DFMT_A32B32G32R32F` is available. In case of OpenGL, pbuffer can be used.

$$\rho = \frac{\sigma}{\tan(f/2)} \cdot \frac{1}{\lambda} \cdot w_s, \tag{2}$$

$$\lambda = \frac{z_f \cdot z_n}{z_f - z_n} \cdot |\mathbf{v} - \tilde{\mathbf{p}}| + 1. \tag{3}$$

where f denotes a view angle (*fov*), $\mathbf{v}$ denotes a view position, z_f, z_n denote the distance from a view position to the far plane and the near plane respectively, and $\tilde{\mathbf{p}}$ denotes a barycentric point of a point set.

σ in Equation (2) is *the resolution of a point set*, that is, a parameter which estimates an interval between neighbor points. σ can be calculated as follows: First, a $k-$neighbor graph of a point set is defined. For each point, the distance to the closest point is calculated. σ is set as the minimum of these distances. Since the definition of a $k-$neighbor graph and the calculation of the closest point is view-independent, we can calculate σ as a pre-process when we input a point set. Using the above equations, the value of ρ is usually greater or equal to 1, and the value of w_i, h_i is then smaller or equal to w_s, h_s.

3.2 Points Selection for Noise Reduction and Averaging

In the first and second passes described in Figure 1, the selection of a point set to an image buffer is processed by using vertex shader. These processes are done to reduce noises of a point set. Note that only a point can be stored for each pixel on current GPUs. We then add rendering passes to store multiple points. In our case, a two-pass rendering algorithm is applied.

For each pass, we apply perspective projection for each point and store a projected point to an image buffer. This process is done by both vertex shader and pixel shader on GPU. In the vertex shader, the perspective projection to a camera coordinate for each point is applied. In the pixel shader, a projected point is simply written to an image buffer. After the process of the pixel shader, the contents of an image buffer are copied to a floating-point texture Ω. In this case, a projected point is stored in a corresponding pixel of a texture as a floating point value.

Figure 2 shows the procedure for selective storage of points to an image buffer. When multiple points are projected to the same pixel, only the closest

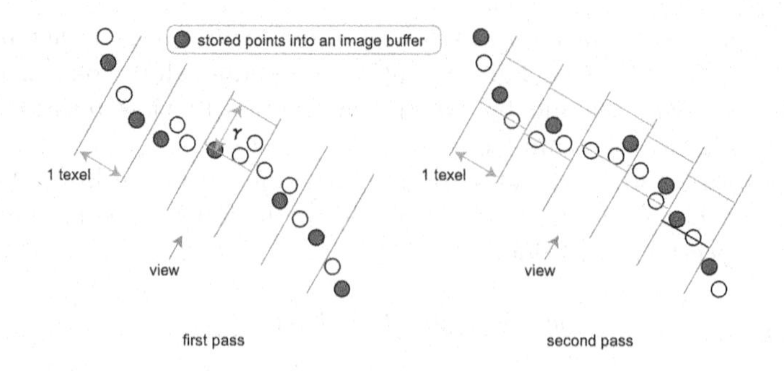

Fig. 2. Overview of selective storage process

point to a view position is selected and stored to a pixel of a texture Ω_1 in the first pass (Figure 2 left).

In the second pass, we also apply perspective projection for each point and store the projected one to an image buffer. In this case, we select a point whose depth from a point selected in the first pass is in the range of γ, and which is the farthest point within this range (Figure 2 right). There are two purposes for this selective storage: One is to omit isolated points (called *outliners*), and the other is to reduce bumpy noises by averaging.

To implement this selective storage on GPU, we first look up a point on Ω_1 and investigate whether the depth of a projected point is within the range of γ or not in the vertex shader of the second pass. If a point is out of range, we omit this point. By setting γ, we can omit later processes for outliners or for points of back faces. γ is a view-independent parameter, then a constant value can be set in the pre-processing stage. According to our experiments, we found that 0.5-1.0% over a diagonal length of a bounding box surrounding at an object is suitable for our results.

Next, the farthest point within the range of a threshold γ is selected by setting "write if the depth of a pixel is larger than that which has already been written"[2]in the depth test on GPU. A selected point by this test is stored in a pixel of a texture Ω_2.

Even if a point has both its position and a color, both results can be written to separate buffers in each pass by using MRT (*Multiple Renger Target*). Moreover, we also use *Vertex Texturing* to look up a point stored in a texture Ω_1 in the vertex shader of the second pass. These two functionalities are supported from Shader Model 3.0, and can be used by only *n*VIDIA GeForce 6 series GPU.

In the third pass, we look up two corresponding points on floating-point textures Ω_1 and Ω_2 in the pixel shader to compute their average value. An average value is then stored to a texture Ω_a. This value is used only as a position for drawing splats in the final pass described in Section 3.4.

3.3 Computation of Normal Vectors

In this sub-section, we describe our novel approach to compute normal vectors on GPU. The computation of normal vectors is processed in the pixel shader of the fourth pass in Figure 1.

In the process of computing normal vectors, information on neighboring points for each point is needed. To rapidly acquire neighboring points, we utilize textures Ω_1 and Ω_2 created in the selective storage process described before. Figure 3 shows the principle of computing normal vectors. In the left figure of Figure 3, a normal vector at a point p is computed by using its neighboring point p_i (18 points at a maximum).

We approximate here the proximity of a point p defined on the camera coordinate system to a plane,

$$f(x, y) = z = Ax + By + C, \quad (4)$$

[2] In case of DirectX, we can use `D3DCMP_GREATER` flag for this process.

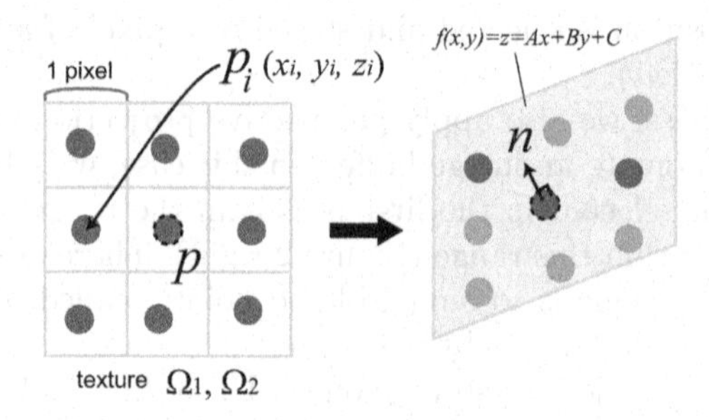

Fig. 3. Plane-fitting process and computation of normal vector

by using least-square fitting (Figure 3 right). We first look up neighboring points $p_i = \{x_i, y_i, z_i\}$ $(i = 1 \ldots N \leq 18)$ from Ω_1, Ω_2. For point p, we compute coefficients A, B, C by solving the following equation:

$$\sum_{i=1}^{N} \{z_i - (Ax_i + By_i + C)\}^2 \rightarrow min. \tag{5}$$

A, B, C are the solution of a 3×3 linear equation. Here we try to solve this equation by using both Cramer's formula and Gauss's elimination method. Although the latter is the numerical solution, we can expand the code and write it to the pixel shader directly. Compared to these two solutions, we found that the computation time and thus the number of instruction sets in the pixel shader is almost equal (Gauss's elimination: 336, Cramer's formula 340). By using such computed coefficients, a normal vector can be defined as $(A, B, -1)$. We then apply shading to compute a color by using a normal vector and a point from Ω_a and store a color to a texture Ω_c.

We approximate a plane in Equation (4) to the proximity of a point p. However, in this equation, we cannot define a plane parallel to a viewing direction. In our case, situations which a normal vector is completely perpendicular to the viewing direction rarely occur. We then think that it is a trivial problem for practical use. We also think that more general equations such as $Ax+By+Cz+D = 0$ can be used to fit to a plane. In this case, complicated numerical approaches such as Newton's method are required to compute coefficients, which tend to increase the number of instruction sets and thus the computation time.

3.4 Rendering with Splats

We now draw splats in the fifth pass with two floating-point textures Ω_a and Ω_c where positions and colors are contained respectively in Figure 1. Along with Botsch et al.'s approach [9], each splat is rendered with alpha-blending by using a *Point Sprite* with an attached *Gaussian kernel texture*. A Gaussian kernel texture is a 2D texture sample (point sprite) in which a Gaussian function is embedded. Each vertex of this texture has its own 2D texture coordinate (u_i, v_i) whose origin is

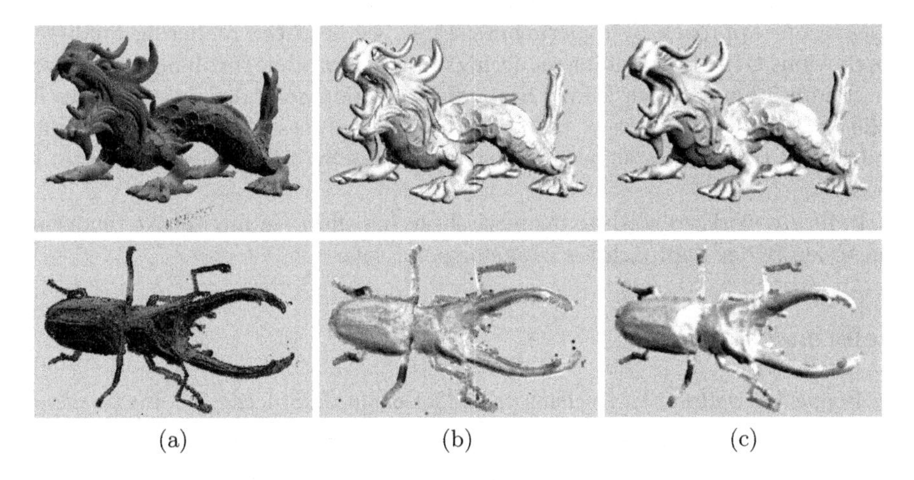

Fig. 4. Rendering results for actual range images. Top: Stanford Asian Dragon. Bottom: Beetle. (a) Range image. (b) Rendering results by approach in [9]. (c) Rendering results by our approach.

the center point. The rendering process is done in both vertex shader and pixel shader. The final color in a frame buffer is a weighted sum of splat colors. The resolution of textures Ω_a, Ω_c is smaller than that of a frame buffer. We therefore need to magnify them to the same size as a frame buffer in this pass.

4 Results

Figure 4 shows visual comparisons between our approach and an approach in [9] for actual range images. The upper part of Figure 4 denotes the results for a point set of Stanford Asian Dragon (3,609,600 points). This point set is acquired from a 3D scanning device, however it looks “good”, namely, it has less bumpy noises. For such point sets, we found that the approach in [9] produces higher-quality images than our approach, because normal vectors can be computed correctly. In contrast, some blurring effects appear as a result of our approach. This is thought to be a certain loss of points in the selective storage process.

The bottom of Figure 4 shows results for a point set of Beetle (559,327 points). This point set has high bumpy noises and considerable outliners, and it is difficult to compute normal vectors correctly in this case. In the result of [9], the blob patterns appear, while our approach can produce better quality image even for such point sets, proving that our approach fully demonstrates it's ability for noisy point sets.

5 Conclusion and Future Work

In this paper, we have proposed a direct rendering approach for GPU to points which only have positional information. We have demonstrated three advantages of our approach by experiments: First, we keep the rendering quality as the previous GPU-based point rendering approaches, while involving normal vector computation for each frame. Secondly, our approach fully demonstrates it's ability for noisy point sets by the noise reduction process. Finally, the computation time is twice faster than previous approaches by using the selective storage process.

In future work, we wish to decrease flickering effects in interactive rendering, and to apply our approach for irregular point sets.

References

1. Hoppe, H., DeRose, T., Duchampy, T., McDonald, J., Stuetzle, W.: Surface reconstruction from unorganized points. Computer Graphics (Proc. SIGGRAPH 92) **26** (1992) 71–78
2. Jones, T., Durand, F., Zwicker, M.: Normal improvement for point rendering. IEEE Computer Graphics & Applications **24** (2004) 53–56
3. Kawata, H., Kanai, T.: Image-based point rendering for multiple-range images. In: Proc. 2nd International Conference on Information Technology & Applications (ICITA 2004), Macquarie Scientific Publishing, Sydney (2004) 478–483
4. Krivanek, J.: Representing and rendering surfaces with points. Technical Report DC-PSR-2003-03, Department of Computer Science and Engineering, Czech Technical University in Prague (2003)
5. Kobbelt, L.P., Botsch, M.: A survey of point-based techniques in computer graphics. J. Computers & Graphics **28** (2004) 801–814
6. Levoy, M., Whitted, T.: The use of points as a display primitive. Technical Report 85-022, Computer Science Department, University of North Carolina at Chapel Hill (1985)
7. Ren, L., Pfister, H., Zwicker, M.: Object space EWA surface splatting: A hardware accelerated approach to high quality point rendering. Computer Graphics Forum (Proc. Eurographics 2002) **21** (2002) 461–470
8. Guennebaud, G., Paulin, M.: Efficient screen space approach for hardware accelerated surfel rendering. In: Proc. 8th International Fall Workshop on Vision, Modeling and Visualization (VMV 2003), IOS Press, Amsterdam (2003) 1–10
9. Botsch, M., Kobbelt, L.P.: High-quality point-based rendering on modern GPUs. In: Proc. Pacific Graphics 2003, IEEE CS Press, Los Alamitos CA (2003) 335–343
10. Zwicker, M., Rasanen, J., Botsch, M., Dachsbacher, C., Pauly, M.: Perspective accurate splatting. In: Proc. Graphics Interface 2004, Morgan Kaufmann Publishers, San Francisco, CA (2004) 247–254
11. Botsch, M., Spernat, M., Kobbelt, L.P.: Phong splatting. In: Proc. Symposium on Point-Based Graphics 2004, Eurographics Association (2004) 25–32
12. Dachsbacher, C., Vogelgsang, C., Stamminger, M.: Sequential point trees. ACM Transactions on Graphics (Proc. SIGGRAPH 2003) **22** (2003) 657–662
13. Guennebaud, G., Barthe, L., Paulin, M.: Deferred splatting. Computer Graphics Forum (Proc. Eurographics 2004) **23** (2004) 653–660

An Artistic Portrait Caricature Model

V. Boyer

Group of Research in Images Synthesis,
Intelligence Artificial Laboratory, University Paris 8
boyer@ai.univ-paris8.fr
http://www.ai.univ-paris8.fr/~boyer

Abstract. We present a new model for artistic portrait caricature modeling and rendering. It is composed of a caricature model and a rendering system. The computer portrait caricature is based on an exaggeration of the face features depending on measures realized on the head. A canon provides "golden proportions" to idealize adult male or female head. According to automatic measures realized on a 3D head mesh, the model produces a new deformed mesh. Using the deformed mesh, the renderer produces images in real-time with an hand-like line drawing style.

Keywords: Mesh deformation, Non-Photorealistic rendering, hand-like line drawing.

1 Introduction

Artistic portrait and moreover caricature are new topics of Non-Photorealistic Rendering[1]. Perkins[2] defines a caricature as a symbol that exaggerates measurements relative to any measure which varies from one person to another. Brennan[3] has produced a caricature generator. Based on a 2D image, it produces a caricature. But with this system only one viewpoint is possible. Our aim is to produce 3D images of caricature portrait in real-time. Our model is composed of a caricature model and a rendering system. The caricature model focuses on the facial features. The renderer produces an image with a hand-like line-drawing style. In a portrait, the silhouette can be realized with this method[4] and for a caricature portrait, it enhances the distortions produced by the artist. In the following, we present our caricature model, the renderer and images produced.

2 Caricature Model

The input of our caricature model is a 3D triangle mesh. Our caricature model is designed to produce a distorted triangle mesh which is then the input to the rendering system. This model is inspired by artistic books dealing with portraits[5],[6]. In the following, we present a brief discussion on the facial anthropometry consideration compared to the attempts of artist. Then our canon and our model are presented.

G. Bebis et al. (Eds.): ISVC 2005, LNCS 3804, pp. 595–600, 2005.

2.1 Craniofacial Anthropometry and Artistic Aesthetic Ideals

Craniofacial anthropometry involves measurement of the skull and face. Generally, some particular points of the head are used, measures are realized and compared to anthropometric landmarks[7]. This can be used in medicine to prevent and treat assymmetries for example. Artists use generally a grid system named **canon** and **rules** which provide "golden proportions" to idealize adult male or female head. But they were not intented to represent typical cranonical morphology (some of these do not exist in normal head face). As this paper deals with caricature portrait, we focus on artistic aesthetic ideals. We propose a caricature model based on a canon.

2.2 The Canon

A canon can be viewed as a set of rules which determinate the proportion of the face. It produces a gird system. In our canon, the head is delimited by a bounding box. Vertically, we compute the distance, named d_h, which is equal to 2/7 of the head height. Idealy, starting from the bottom of the bounding box:

- the lower lips is at a distance equal to $\frac{1}{2} \times d_h$,
- the lower part of the nose is at a distance equal to d_h,
- the top of the eyes, the bottom of the eyebrows and the top of the ears are at a distance equal to $2 \times d_h$
- the top of the forehead is at a distance equal to $3 \times d_h$.

Horizontally, we compute the distance, named d_v, which is equal to 2/5 of the head width. Idealy, starting from the right of the bounding box:

- the left limit of the left eye is at a distance equal to $\frac{1}{2} \times d_v$,
- the right limit of the left eye is at a distance equal to d_v,
- the center of the nose is at a distance equal to $\frac{5}{4} \times d_v$,
- the left limit of the right eye is at a distance equal to $\frac{3}{2} \times d_v$,
- the right limit of the right eye is at a distance equal to $2 \times d_v$.

The left part of the figure 1 presents this canon with these "golden proportions". The thick lines are used to represent the integer values of d_h and d_v.

2.3 The Caricature Model

Caricature modeling is performed in five steps.

1. A model is loaded[1] and an half-edge data structure is created to maintain the edge adjacency information[8].

[1] Additional Informations concerning front-facing, back-facing and material properties are maintained.

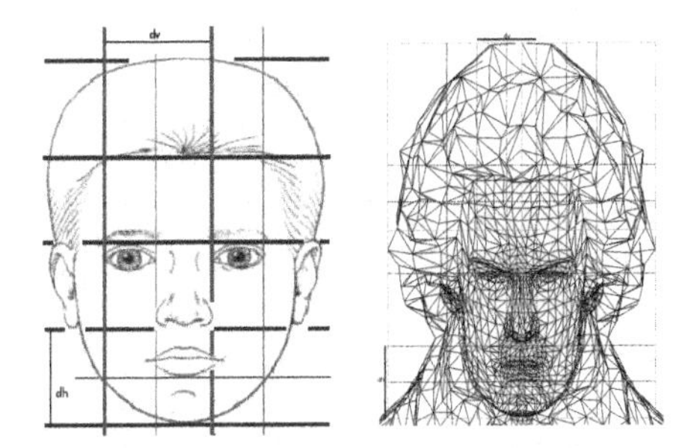

Fig. 1. left: Canon model, right: Canon of the Beethoven's head

2. Creation of a bounding box around the head of the model. The user specifies the lower limit of the head with an horizontal line[2]. The following steps use this box as a limit.
3. Creation of the **canon**. The user specifies an horizontal line, named $\mathcal{H}$ (top of the eyes), and a vertical line, named $\mathcal{V}$ (left of one eye), and our system computes the canon of the face based on our canon model defined above. The right part of the figure 1 presents the results of this step on the Beethoven's head.
4. Detection and extraction of significant parts of the head. This step is realized automatically using the canon and if available material properties of the model. Note that the material properties simplifies the detection of significant part limits. For all of these significant parts, at least one chain of edges is created with the half-edge data structure. The significant parts are:
   - **eyes** are localized with the canon. At the previous step, the user have specified the upper left corner of the left eye. Based on curvature and material properties if available[3], a closed chain is created for each eye representing the limit of the eye.
   - **eyebrows:** the curvature and material properties are used. A closed chain is created for each eyebrows.
   - **nose:** two chains are created. The first one is a set of segments describing the curvature of the nose bone. The set of segment is composed by vertices with a high Z-value placed horizontally between the eyes and vertically starting between the eyes and finishing with a high Z-value. Note that the expected value for the curvature of the nose bone is a set of segments which have the same vector. The second one is composed by vertices describing the triangle mesh of the nose. In this case curvature is used.
   - **shape of the head:** the shape of head's chain starts from the chin, includes the ears and the top of the forehead excluding the hairs. Chin

[2] To help the user, an orthographic projection is used and only the front-facing polygons are drawn as outlined polygons.

[3] Note that for some models, eyes are composed by edges incident to only one polygon and so the detection is very easy.

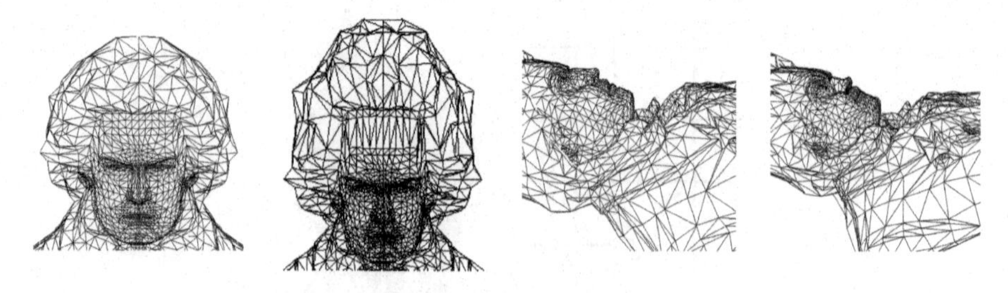

Fig. 2. Original and distorted Beethoven's head and nose

is at the bottom of the canon and a vertical symmetry is used to find other parts. Materials properties can also be used to find the limit with the hair.

At the end of this step, the user can verify and modify the detection realized if needed. Eyes, nose and shape of the head are often well detected. Some problems remains for eyebrows chains.

5. Measure computation and generation of a new triangle mesh: using the chains generated above and the canon, we compute measures on the head. These are the nose curvature and size, the eyes size and tilt, the fronthead size, the height of the hair and the eyebrows. We deform the triangle mesh according to the measures and the expected values of the canon. The deformation is weighted by a user-specified value. The order of the deformations is the hair, the forehead, the width of the head, the eyes and the nose[4]. This assures that there is not discontinuity on the new 3D mesh. The number of vertices and edges is constant. The figure 2 presents the results of this step on the Beethoven's head (left to right: global view (original, distorted), focus on nose (original, distorted)[5].

3 Rendering

The rendering process produces images in real-time in NPR style using hand-like line-drawing. Our method is based on the Sousa et al. method[9]. The main steps of the algorithm are:

1. extraction of additional feature lines. We search the *silhouette edges* (**SE**), the *border edges* (**BE**) and the *creases* (**CE**). The creases are edges which separate two front-facing triangles whose normal vectors make an angle θ. The limits of θ are given by the user and can be changed dynamically.

[4] There are two deformations for the nose: one for the curvature and the other for sub-mesh of the nose.

[5] Note that for Beethoven's nose, two vertices do not follow the curvature (starting from the top of the nose, the second one is above the expected curvature and the next to the last is below the curvature and one can see the exaggeration of the nose curvature produced.

2. creation of graphs. Three graphs, one for each kind of edge, are created. They maintain an adjacency list represented by an array of vertices (see[9] for details).
3. generation of list of chains: a chain corresponds to a path in the graph (**SE**, **BE**, **CE**) starting from a source (vertex with indegree equal 0) and finishing at a skin (vertex with outdegree equal 0). Contrary to Sousa, the sources are sorted by lowest *indegree* and highest *outdegree* and we build all chains for a graph composed at least by two vertices (possible chains with less than two vertices are not considered). Note that when a vertex is selected, its indegree and outdegree are updated. This permits to obtain the same chains at any time. This process is iterated until no valid chain remains in the graph.
4. creation of B-splines: at this step we have obtained chains from graphs and we add chains extracted for significant parts of the head (eyes, eyebrows, nose...). Vertices of chains are considered as control points of a B-Spline then rendered. The thickness of the B-Splines depends on two parameters:
   – the kind of edges: B-Spline of silhouette and border have globally a thickness greater than creases and the chains created during the caricature process have the same thickness.
   – the measure of curvature: for each control point of the B-Spline, we compute the thickness of the curve depending on the curvature (a high curvature increases the thickness).

The triangle mesh is drawn with the background color and the curves are drawn with the foreground color. Using the Z-buffer, the visibility computation is realized. Remark that for the other views (i.e. when triangles are displayed with lines) the back face culling is used to display only the lines of the visible triangles. The images have been produced on a Pentium IV 2,4Ghz with an X800 graphic card. The figure 3, presents different views of the Beethoven's head rendered with our system. The frame rate is 30 frames/second for images in 800x600. Other examples are given in figure 4. It is impossible to compare images produced with our system with other methods because there is no other 3D portrait caricature model.

Fig. 3. Different view of the Beethoven's head with different values for creases rendered with our system

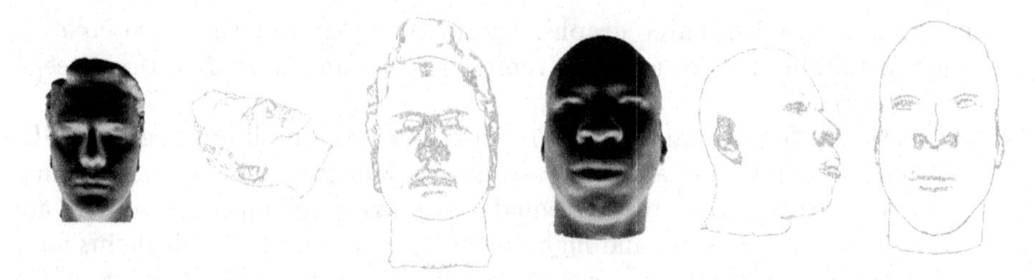

Fig. 4. Two other examples: Original mesh, images produced by our rendering system with different deformation ratios and creases values

4 Conclusion

We have presented a model to design artistic portrait caricature rendering. It is the first working directly on 3D models, other ones distort only 2D images. It produces distortions of a 3D triangle mesh and a real-time rendering in an artistic style. The distortions depend on the measures between the model and a canon. The rendering is a 3D NPR method that automatically enhance the distortions with pure line drawings.

References

1. Gooch, A., Gooch, B.: Non-Photorealistic Rendering. AK Peters, Ltd. (2001)
2. Perkins, D.: A definition of caricature and recognition. Studies in the Anthropology of Visual Communication **2** (1975) 1–24
3. Brennan, S.: The caricature generator. Leonardo **18** (1985) 170–178
4. Wong, E.: Artistic rendering of portrait photographs. Master's thesis, Cornell University (1999)
5. Dunster, J.: Drawing Portraits: Fundamentals. Green Verdugo Press (2003)
6. Zhao, W., Chellappa, R., Phillips, P., Rosenfeld, A.: Face recognition: A literature survey. ACM Computing Surveys **35** (2003) 399–458
7. Kolar, J., Salter, E.: Craniofacial Anthropometry: Practical Measurement of the Head and Face for Clinical, Surgical,and Research Use. Springfield (1997)
8. Mantyla, M.: An Introduction to Solid Modeling. Computer Science Press (1988)
9. Sousa, M., Prusinkiewicz, P.: A few good lines: Suggestive drawing of 3d models. In: Computer Graphics Forum. Volume 22(3). (2003) 381–390

Capturing and View-Dependent Rendering of Billboard Models

Oliver Lee, Anusheel Bhushan, Pablo Diaz-Gutierrez, and M. Gopi

Computer Graphics Lab, University of California, Irvine

Abstract. In this paper, we propose a method for obtaining a textured billboards representation of a static scene, given a sequence of calibrated video images. Each billboard is a textured and partially transparent plane into which the input images are mapped using perspective projection. Binning using Hough transform is used to find the position of the billboards, and optic flow measures are used to determine their textures. Since these billboards are correct only from specific view-points, view-dependent rendering is used to choose and display appropriate billboards to reproduce the input.

1 Introduction

A fundamental problem in Computer Vision is the retrieval of a geometric model from a set of images. Even when the input images are accurately calibrated, it is easy to find two different objects that yield identical images after being projected. However, some applications do not require exact reconstruction, but only a compelling reproduction, and a simple model representation. Billboards are a good approach, as they provide an unstructured, light weight representation of an object that can be combined with other rendering systems. The automatic billboard generation from calibrated video sequences is our goal in the present paper.

The problem we try to solve can be shortly stated as finding a minimal number of textured planes that reproduce the input images when seen from the appropriate position. *We define an* **equivalent geometry** *to a textured geometry G for a set of viewpoints V as a textured geometry E that looks identical to G when viewed from V.* The set of geometries equivalent to (G, V) forms an equivalence class. Our target is to find an equivalent geometry for the static scene in the input. Finding the accurate geometry might be neither feasible nor desirable, as explained. Since our input is a calibrated video sequence of *unknown scene geometry*, our computation of billboards is purely image-based and shall not assume anything about the shape of the objects in the scene. In essence, all planes in the object geometry are perfect choices for billboards, but not all billboards belong to the object geometry.

Since the goal of stereo-based techniques is to extract exact geometry, such a reconstruction is overly restrictive for our purposes of obtaining an approximate reproduction of the input. On the other hand, our approach tolerates certain

G. Bebis et al. (Eds.): ISVC 2005, LNCS 3804, pp. 601–606, 2005.

geometric distortion between the original scene and the obtained representation, so long as the result is visually equivalent to the input.

Specifically, the following are the main contributions of this paper.

- Given a calibrated video sequence of an unknown geometry, we calculate an equivalent geometry using optical flow properties.
- We reduce the complexity of the set of billboards using Hough transform and also based on the constraint of maintaining the geometric equivalence.
- We show the use of these billboards in the reconstruction of video images from viewpoints not completely aligned with any input viewpoint.

2 Related Work

The trade-off between representing a scene with geometry and images is a classical conflict in image based rendering (IBR) in computer graphics. Image-based methods take a collection of images as input, construct a representation of the color or radiance of the scene, and use it to synthesize new images from arbitrary viewpoints. The methods tend to differ in the number of input images they use, the representation of the data, the degree to which they incorporate geometric information about the scene into the image representation, and the compression techniques they employ. Almost all image based rendering techniques avoid explicitly extracting geometric information from the images. Nevertheless, they use such an information, if provided, to improve the efficiency of storage and rendering.

Levoy and Hanrahan [1] acquire many hundreds of images, which are resampled to lie on a regular grid in a two-plane parameterization. They apply vector quantization to obtain compressed representations of light fields. Gortler et al. [2] present a similar two-plane parameterization that they call a lumigraph. They use approximate surface geometry derived from photograph silhouettes to perform a depth correction that substantially reduces ghosting and blurring artifacts. Schirmacher et al. [3] use light field and per pixel quantized dense depth for rendering.

Heigl et al. [4] uses unstructured camera images to perform image-based rendering from such an unstructured data. A similar algorithm is presented by [5] where an IBR method known as unstructured light fields is designed to satisfy a set of goals that includes making use of information about surface geometry, if available. This method also generalizes many IBR algorithms, including lightfield rendering and view-dependent texture mapping. In all these methods, input images are directly used for rendering, without any resampling or reformatting to any other representation.

Another class of algorithms require geometric proxies to approximate the scene geometry and are closely related to this paper. View-dependent texture mapping [6, 7, 8] uses geometric information to re-project each input image from the desired camera viewpoint. The re-projected input images are then blended together using weights based on primarily the view direction, and possibly other factors such as sampling rate. In these works, the geometric information about the scene is provided by the user and the input set of images are retained and used during rendering from novel viewpoints. Similarly, Decoret et al. [9] automatically refactor the triangulated model into a representation purely based on billboards. Our system extracts the required equivalent geometry, and the input video sequence, once reindexed into this geometry, is not used any longer. These are the primary differences between our work and view-dependent texture mapping techniques. A formal analysis of the trade off between the number of images from different camera positions and the fidelity of geometry in order to produce satisfactory IBR from novel viewpoints is presented in [10].

For compression of light field data, Magnor and Girod [11, 12]develop an MPEG-like scheme to compress two-plane lightfields that achieves better compression ratios than those obtained by Levoy and Hanrahan. Further in [13], they use the accurate scene geometry to develop two methods for multi-view coding: one is the texture-based coding where the scene geometry is used to convert images to view-dependent texture maps and the other is the model-aided predictive coding where the geometry is used for disparity compensation and occlusion detection between images. In either case, the geometry of the scene has to be provided as input. Further, the representation is used for multi-view coding and rendering of scenes and not directly applicable for video compression.

The final category of IBR algorithms require accurate geometry of the scene. Surface light field Nishino et al. [14, 15] uses the user specified surface of the object to index and compress the view dependent radiance information. The accurate geometry of the object is used for two purposes. The colors indexed on the surface of the object would exhibit high degree of coherence, and the rendering of the object can use the traditional geometry rendering pipeline.

In this paper, we use ideas similar to those used in image based modelling to compress video of static scenes; but with additional complexity of extracting the *equivalent geometry* automatically from the video sequence.

3 Optic Flow as a Measure of Geometric Proximity

Our goal is to find the *equivalent geometry* of a model as a set of billboards. Instead of operating at a per-pixel level, we obtain geometric proxies for contiguous pixels regions. A region on a plane that is proximate to geometry has the property that texture projected from multiple input viewpoints will match in the region. So, we apply projective texturing to map the input images onto the billboard and then use texture similarity as a measure of geometric proximity.

We can use different measures of texture matching: Color distance at each pixel is noisy and unreliable, while using intensity correlation can return good results, but is expensive. We use optical flow between the projected images as a measure of texture matching. Regions with low optic flow project similar textures from the input viewpoints and thus are candidates for being part of the *equivalent geometry*. We use an optic flow algorithm for texture matching. Given the optic flow value, we perform an adaptive thresholding to get regions of low flow, based on the location of the cameras and the billboard.

4 Algorithm Description

Our algorithm takes a set of calibrated images of a video sequence and produces an *equivalent geometry* for the represented scene. That is, a set of textured planes, or billboards, that look like the input when seen from the input viewpoints. The process comprises two fundamental steps, repeated until the input data has been exhausted. These steps are the spatial sampling of the input scene and the search for fitting planes. In the first one, the geometry of the objects in the input scene is sampled using measures of optic flow. In the second step, we find a set of planes that fit the approximate sampled geometry obtained in the first step.

4.1 Spatial Sampling of the Input Scene

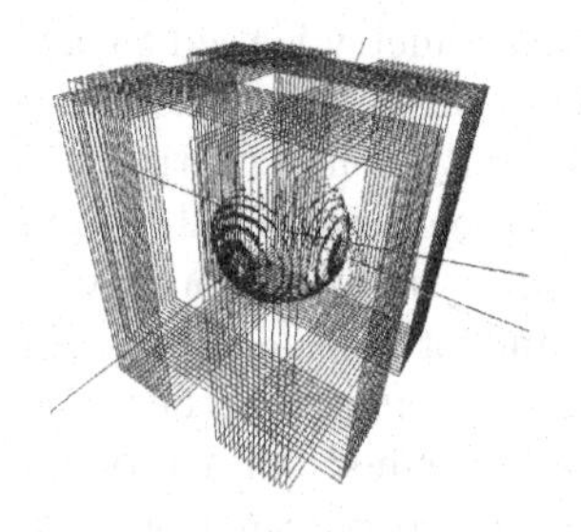

Fig. 1. Grid of planes for dense spatial sampling of the input geometry

The first step in the process of finding an equivalent geometry sampling the input scene to calculate an estimate of the geometry contained in the input. Such sampling can be as well split in two stages. First we must roughly identify the area where the input geometry is to be located. In the second one, we actually sample that geometry. The first sampling stage can be accomplished in a number of ways. Under constrained conditions, such as controlled video capture or when using synthetic models like in this paper, the approximate location of the object might be already known, and this step can be skipped.

The second stage in the sampling procedure is a dense sampling of the volume resulting in the first stage. In order to extract a set of points near the input geometry, we place a regular grid of parallel planes along the three dimensions, spanning all the sampling volume found in the previous stage. For each of those planes, we project pairs of images from the input viewpoints and use an optic flow measure, as explained in Section 3, to determine which points on the plane lie nearby the input geometry. Points on the plane with an optic flow value under a threshold are treated as being near the input geometry. After this operation has been performed on all sampling planes, we triangulate the obtained 3D points (see Figure 1) to produce an approximation to the surface in the input scene. This set of triangles will be the input to the next part of the algorithm, described in the following subsection.

4.2 Finding Fitting Billboards

This step in the algorithm takes a set of triangles near the surface, and returns the equivalent geometry for the input scene. We say a plane fits a triangle if all its three vertices lie within a user defined distance from the plane. The equivalent geometry is made of planes fitting the triangles that approximate the geometry. To find a set of planes that fit a large number of triangles, we use a variant of the stochastic method RANSAC: Iteratively, we choose three points from different

Fig. 2. **Left:** Input images for the Blob and Armadillo scenes. **Right:** Resulting billboard sets for the same scenes.

triangles in the surface approximation. These three planes define a plane P that fits n triangles from the surface. n is a measure of the *goodness* of P fitting the data. RANSAC methods guarantee that a good solution will be reached with high probability after a certain number of samplings are done. After we have a set of good fitting planes, we do a local optimization of the position and orientation of the candidate planes to maximize surface coverage.

Finally, we texture the obtained planes with the projection of one input image. In order to reduce texel distortion, the input image with the most normal orientation with respect to the plane is chosen.

The two described steps of the algorithm are repeated several times, with a number of new billboards added to the result in each iteration. Every time a billboard is added to the result, part of the input is *covered*. Covering of an image is defined as follows. Given an input image I, a pixel $I(x, y)$ with color c in I is said to be covered when visualizing the billboards onto I produces an image with color c at position (x, y). Covered pixel regions are removed from the input images, and when all the input pixels have been covered, the algorithm terminates and the set of billboards is returned.

5 Results and Conclusion

Although the algorithm described in Section 4 finishes after a bounded number of iterations, convergence is slow. To speed up the process, we associate a quadtree that keeps track of the covered regions in each input image. This way, the termination condition is checked more effifiently. Furthermore, increasing the granularity of billboard texturing from one pixel at a time to block sizes reduces the run time at the cost of a small decrease in the quality of results, like those in Figure 2.

We have introduced a novel method to construct a billboard-based representation of an unknown-geometry object from a sequence of calibrated images. We demonstrate it with a number of pairs of images from the input and the results. Planned future work includes an accurate sampling volume estimation, a more structured billboard identification and the necessary modifications to handle more general models, such as a room or an open space.

References

1. Levoy, M., Hanrahan, P.: Light field rendering. In: Proceedings SIGGRAPH 96, ACM SIGGRAPH (1996) 31–42
2. Gortler, S.J., Grzeszczuk, R., Szeliski, R., Cohen, M.F.: The lumigraph. In: Proceedings SIGGRAPH 96, ACM SIGGRAPH (1996) 43–54
3. Schirmacher, H., Heidrich, W., Seidel, H.P.: High-quality interactive lumigraph rendering through warping. In: Graphics Interface. (2000)
4. Heigl, B., R.Koch, Pollefeys, M., Denzler, J., Gool, L.: Plenoptic modeling and rendering from image sequences taken by hand-held camera. In: Proceedings of DAGM. (1999) 94–101
5. Buehler, C., Bosse, M., McMillan, L., Gortler, S., Cohen, M.: Unstructured lumigraph rendering. In: Proceedings SIGGRAPH 2001, ACM SIGGRAPH (2001) 425–432
6. Debevec, P., Taylor, C., Malik, J.: Modelling and rendering architecture from photographs: A hybrid geometry and image based approach. In: Proceedings SIGGRAPH 96, ACM SIGGRAPH (1996) 11–20
7. Debevec, P., Yu, Y., Borshukov, G.: Efficient view-dependent image-based rendering with projective texture-mapping. In: Eurographics Rendering Workshop, Eurographics (June, 1998) 105–116
8. Pulli, K., Cohen, M.F., Duchamp, T., Hoppe, H., Shapiro, L., Stuetzle, W.: View-based rendering: Visualizing real objects from scanned range and color data. In: Proceedings Eurographics Rendering Workshop 97, Eurographics (1997) 23–34
9. Décoret, X., Durand, F., Sillion, F.X., Dorsey, J.: Billboard clouds for extreme model simplification. ACM Trans. Graph. **22** (2003) 689–696
10. Chai, J.X., Tong, X., Chan, S.C., Shum, H.Y.: Plenoptic sampling. In: Proceedings SIGGRAPH 2000, ACM SIGGRAPH (2000) 307–318
11. Magnor, M., Girod, B.: Adaptive block-based light field coding. In: Proc. 3rd International Workshop on Synthetic and Natural Hybrid Coding and Three-Dimensional Imaging. (September,1999) 140–143
12. Magnor, M., Girod, B.: Hierarchical coding of light fields with disparity maps. In: Proc. IEEE International Conference on Image Processing. (October, 1999) 334–338
13. Magnor, M., Ramanathan, P., Girod, B.: Multi-view coding for image-based rendering using 3-d scene geometry. IEEE Transactions on circuits and systems for video technology **13** (November, 2003) 1092–1106
14. Nishino, K., Sato, Y., Ikeuchi, K.: Appearance compression and synthesis based on 3d model for mixed reality. In: Proceedings of IEEE ICCV, IEEE (September, 1999) 38–45
15. Nishino, K., Sato, Y., Ikeuchi, K.: Eigen-texture method: Appearance compression based on 3d model. In: Proceedings of Computer Vision and Pattern Recognition. (June, 1999) 1:618–624

Error-Bounded Solid Voxelization for Polygonal Model Based on Heuristic Seed Filling

Jianguang Weng[1], Yueting Zhuang[1], and Hui Zhang[2]

[1] College of Computer Science and Technology, Zhejiang University, Hangzhou, China
wengjg@zju.edu.cn
[2] Department of Computer Science, Indiana University, Bloomington, USA
huizhang@cs.indiana.edu

Abstract. Although surface voxelization is now becoming a matured field, solid voxelization still lags quite behind due to the lack of robust and efficient means of processing complex polygonal models. Our paper presents a fast and easy to implement error-bounded solid voxelization algorithm in three subtasks: (i) PVM (Primary Volume Model), in which most of the non-object voxels are eliminated. (ii) BVM (Boundary Volume Model), which provides reliable discrete object boundary. (iii) RVM (Revised Volume Model), which is the result of Heuristic Seed Filling as the critical portion of our algorithm. In the third subtask, the non-object voxels from PVM and the object voxels from BVM form the boundaries and seeds are computed from PVM and BVM as well. Unlike traditional seed filling, our approach achieves significantly improved performance and produces error-bounded experimental results. Furthermore, our method is more robust compared to 3D scan-filling.

1 Introduction

Volume model has many natural advantages over surface model by being viewpoint independent, insensitive to scene/object complexity, and suited to the representation of sampled dataset, inner information as well as block operations [1]. With the enhancements of hardware, volume graphics technology has been applied widely in diverse fields. However, surface graphics is so far the primary branch of computer graphics. Thus in order to benefit from volume graphics, we need to convert surface model into volume model in variant applications. This conversion, termed as voxelization, can be basically classified as surface voxelization and solid voxelization. Another common classification results in binary and non-binary voxelization. The core focus of our paper is to develop a solid binary voxelization for complex polygonal models which 3D scan-filling is not able to process correctly.

From 1980s, firstly being introduced by Kaufman [2]-[5], a few voxelization algorithms have been proposed. Surface voxelization is used as a fundamental aspect for solid voxelization[6]-[10]. Furthermore, the topological theory of surface voxelization in discrete 3D space is a particularly key problem. There are three kinds of separability for a discrete boundary (i.e. 6, 18, and 26-separability) [3], generally, an n-separating boundary doesn't have any n-connected tunnels from inside to the outside.

G. Bebis et al. (Eds.): ISVC 2005, LNCS 3804, pp. 607 – 612, 2005.

Solid voxelization is usually based on surface voxelization, but so far it still lacks robust and efficient means. Seed filling and 3D scan-filling, as the two main approaches of solid voxelization, have limitations. As a robust way to eliminate all non-object voxel with *n*-separating discrete boundary, the performance of seed filling algorithm decays dramatically when the number of filled voxels increases [11]. 3D scan-filling is efficient yet sensitive to the behavior property of ray intersection points [9] [10]. By taking advantages of graphics hardware, Karabassi et al. voxelized a surface model based on six depth buffer images only, which were read from depth buffer memory by rendering the model in six views of a bounding-box [12]. Although Karabassi's method is the fastest for binary solid voxelization, it might produce some errors in resultant volume models. Passalis tried to alleviate errors by adding more depth buffer images [13], but his method still suffered from lack of error control.

Therefore in this paper, we are motivated to develop a novel solid binary voxelization approach for complex polygonal model based on heuristic seed filling. Our paper improves performance of seed filling algorithm for solid voxelization, which reduces the number of filled voxels by narrowing the filling space. To ensure the correctness, reliable 6-separating surface voxelization is proposed. Compared to Karabassi's method, ours not only eliminate most errors but provide mean of error control.

In particular, our approach is the best candidate for polygonal models where enclosed and non-enclosed surface boundaries coexist. The rest of this paper is organized as follows: PVM and BVM computations are presented in section 2. Details of Heuristic seed filling are given in section 3. And experimental results and conclusions in section 4 and 5 respectively.

2 PVM and BVM

Karabassi's method judges whether a voxel is an object voxel by 6 depth-buffer images, i.e. **X1**, **X2**, **Y1**, **Y2**, **Z1**, **Z2**, obtained from rendering the polygonal model six times. The camera is placed on each of the six faces surrounding the computed bounding box of the object and the depth-buffers are retrieved using parallel projection [11]. For each pair of opposite directions (e.g., +**X**, -**X**), the values of the two associated depth-buffers provide a regular sampling of the object's surface from the front and back views. On one hand Karabassi's method is fast and able to eliminate most non-object voxels, while on the other hand its resultant model might leave some errors without error control. We adapt Karabassi's method to improve the robustness by relaxing ε voxels' size for the value of each pixel in depth-buffer images. It results in PVM (Primary Volume Model) with uncontrollable errors.

Separating boundary is essential to filling algorithm. In order to obtain a 6-separating discrete solid boundary, we adopt POLYGON algorithm [5] for polygon face voxelization. The method of 3rd dimensional coordinate computation in POLYGON is applied to edge voxelization. 2D Amanatides and Woo's line traversal algorithm is used to discretize edges on the other two dimension plane [6].

Without losing of any generality, assume $ax+by+cz+d=0$ is the polygon plane equation satisfying $c \geq a, c \geq b$. Further assume that the polygon projects on **XY** plane, with $\boldsymbol{p}(x, y)$ as the projection of a voxel central point, $\boldsymbol{p}(x+1, y)$ and $\boldsymbol{p}(x, y+1)$ are projections of two neighbor voxel central points. Define $\Delta z_X = -a/c$, $\Delta z_Y = -b/c$.

Now we label **Z** coordinate at $\boldsymbol{p}(x, y)$ as z, then **Z** coordinate at $\boldsymbol{p}(x+1, y)$ and $\boldsymbol{p}(x, y+1)$ can be deduced as $z_{x+1} = z + \Delta z_{\mathbf{X}}$ and $z_{y+1} = z + \Delta z_{\mathbf{Y}}$ respectively. Such **Z** coordinate computation method in principle guarantees 6-connection of resultant voxels. POLYGON only takes care of the voxels whose central point projections are enclosed by the polygon. We adopt the same method to consolidate computation of **Z** coordinate for all voxels whose projections intersect with edges. As long as the result of 2D edge discretization is 4-connected, we can guarantee the result of polygon voxelization is 6-separating. Since Bresenham algorithm results in 8-connected and LINE algorithm results in 26-connected [2], we exploit Amanatides 2D line traversal algorithm which is one of the most efficient methods for 4-connected discretization [6]. The resultant model of surface voxelization, named as BVM (Boundary Volume Model), includes a part of object voxels that compose a 6-separating boundary.

3 Heuristic Seed Filling

With 6-separatability property, BVM guarantees that 6-connected seed filling algorithm will not affect object voxels as long as seed filling begins from any outside non-object seed. Conventional seed filling is slow because it usually begins from a corner voxel and fills a tremendous number of outside voxels. Starting from this point, we thoroughly present a heuristic seed filling algorithm here, which improves the performance remarkably.

So far most non-object voxels have been affirmed by PVM, and can be neglected in this step. Meanwhile, no non-object voxels from PVM would be suitable as seed candidates anymore. However, these non-object voxels along with the boundary object voxels from BVM can serve as outer and inner boundary in our seed filling algorithm respectively. The solution to our remaining key problem, i.e. how to seek heuristic seeds, can now be reach by seeking fake boundary object voxel in PVM. The resultant model from heuristic seed filling, named as resultant volume model (RVM), eliminates most errors in PVM, with bounded error left only.

Before we enter the critical portion of the algorithm, some neighbor operations for expressing voxel topological properties are in order.

$$\boldsymbol{N}_{26}(\boldsymbol{V}_{ijk},\xi) = \{\boldsymbol{V}_{lmn} \mid |i-l| \le \xi, |j-m| \le \xi, |k-n| \le \xi\} \tag{1}$$

$$\boldsymbol{N}_6^{\mathbf{X}}(\boldsymbol{V}_{ijk},\xi) = \{\boldsymbol{V}_{lmn} \mid |i-l| \le \xi, m = j, n = k\} \tag{2}$$

$$\boldsymbol{N}_6^{\mathbf{Y}}(\boldsymbol{V}_{ijk},\xi) = \{\boldsymbol{V}_{lmn} \mid |j-m| \le \xi, i = l, n = k\} \tag{3}$$

$$\boldsymbol{N}_6^{\mathbf{Z}}(\boldsymbol{V}_{ijk},\xi) = \{\boldsymbol{V}_{lmn} \mid |k-n| \le \xi, i = l, m = j\} \tag{4}$$

$$\boldsymbol{N}_6(\boldsymbol{V}_{ijk},\xi) = \boldsymbol{N}_6^{\mathbf{X}}(\boldsymbol{V}_{ijk},\xi) \cup \boldsymbol{N}_6^{\mathbf{Y}}(\boldsymbol{V}_{ijk},\xi) \cup \boldsymbol{N}_6^{\mathbf{Z}}(\boldsymbol{V}_{ijk},\xi) \tag{5}$$

Let $\boldsymbol{SOV}_{\mathrm{PVM}}$, $\boldsymbol{SNOV}_{\mathrm{PVM}}$ and $\boldsymbol{SBOV}_{\mathrm{PVM}}$ denote the set of object voxels, non-object voxels and boundary object voxels in PVM respectively.

$$\boldsymbol{SOV}_{\mathrm{PVM}} = \{\boldsymbol{V}_{ijk} \mid \boldsymbol{V}_{ijk} = 1 \quad \text{in} \quad \mathrm{PVM}\} \tag{6}$$

$$SNOV_{\mathrm{PVM}} = \{V_{ijk} \mid V_{ijk} = 0 \quad \text{in} \quad \mathrm{PVM}\} \tag{7}$$

$$SBOV_{\mathrm{PVM}} = \{V_{ijk} \mid V_{ijk} \in SOV_{\mathrm{PVM}}, \exists V_{lmn}(V_{lmn} \in N_6(V_{ijk},1) \wedge V_{lmn} = 0)\} \tag{8}$$

Similar naming is applied to BVM too. These sets are affirmed from previous computation. We obtain the set of checking voxels as follows:

$$SCHV = \{V \mid V \in SOV_{\mathrm{PVM}} - SBOV_{\mathrm{BVM}}\} \tag{9}$$

Then a set of candidate heuristic seed could be collected.

$$SCDV = \{V \mid V \in SCHV, \exists N(N \in N_6(V,1) \wedge N \in SNOV_{\mathrm{PVM}})\} \tag{10}$$

At the last step, fake boundary object voxel set, i.e. heuristic seed set, can be defined as follows:

$$SFBOV(\xi) = \{V_{ijk} \mid V_{ijk} \in SCDV, N_{26}(V_{ijk},\xi) \cap SBOV_{\mathrm{BVM}} = \varnothing\} \tag{11}$$

where ξ is an integer parameter satisfying $0 \le \xi \le \varepsilon$. ε is the relaxing factor PVM computation. $SFBOV(0)$ is the set defined with ideal accuracy and increased ξ would improve stability.

We remark that some unlocated fake boundary object voxels are produced, however, it doesn't necessarily result in errors because all fake object voxels in a 6-connected block would be eliminated as long as there is only one fake boundary object voxel being detected in the block. Furtherly, we have relaxed PVM computation by relaxing factor ε so that we can detect fake boundary object voxel more reliably by setting $\xi < \varepsilon$. At last, even if some fake boundary object voxels haven't been detected, errors are bounded by a narrow band. Fake object voxels in PVM will be eliminated by heuristic seed filling algorithm which takes $SFBOV(\xi)$ as seeds. Let $SFOV$ denote the set of fake object voxels.

4 Examples

We choose three typical polygonal models as examples to analyze the algorithm performance. As shown in Fig. 1, Fig. 2 and Fig. 3. Boundary object voxels, fake object voxels and inner object voxels are labeled using different gray scales, from

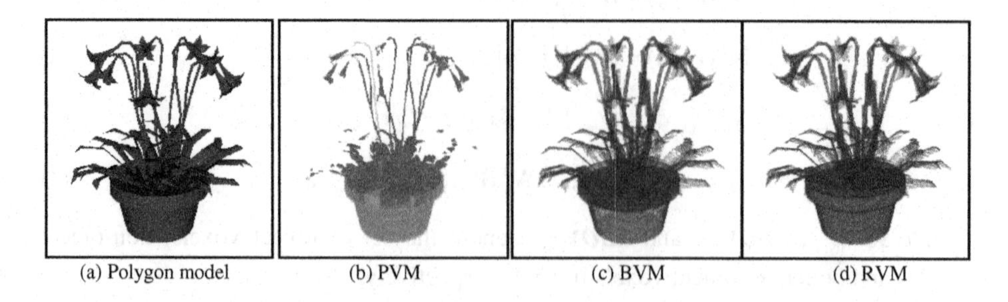

(a) Polygon model (b) PVM (c) BVM (d) RVM

Fig. 1. (a) Polygonal model of potted plant is complex in that closed and non-closed surface boundaries coexist in the model. 3D-Scan filling doesn't treat such models correctly.

dark to bring, accordingly. We choose the opacity value as 0.8 for boundary object voxels and inner object voxels, 1 for fake object voxels. The experiments were performed on a 3000MHZ Pentium IV with 512M RAM and ATI RADEON 9600 display adapter. $\xi = 1$ for *SFBOV* computation. The fake object voxels are eliminated while object voxels are very well kept intact. As suggested in Table 1, the time complexity has been reduced remarkably by applying heuristic seed filling. The examples proves the correctness of our method, including 6-separatability of BVM, the ability of seeking suitable seeds for heuristics seed filling, as well as performance improvement.

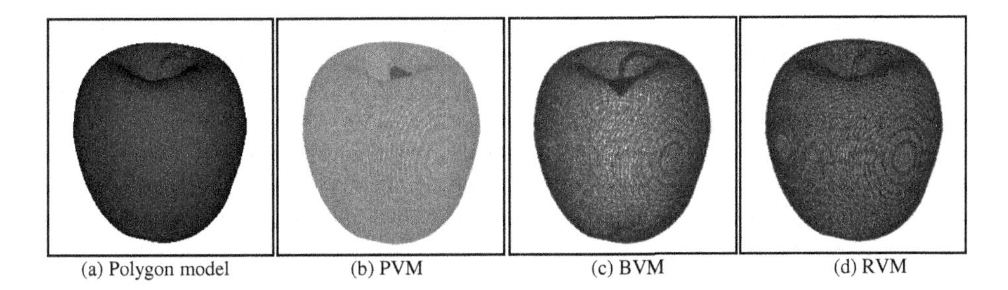

(a) Polygon model (b) PVM (c) BVM (d) RVM

Fig. 2. Voxelization of polygonal apple model

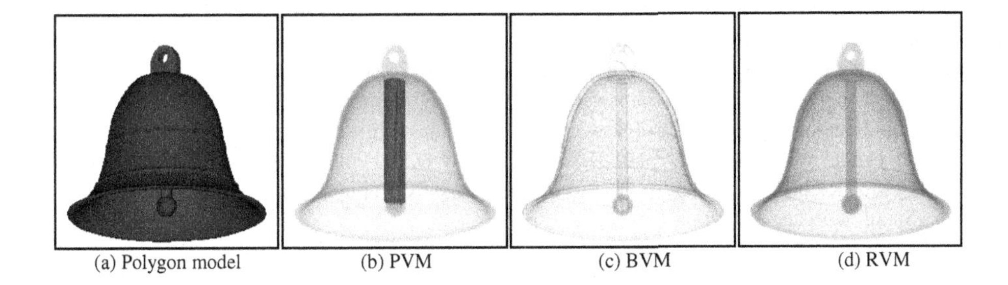

(a) Polygon model (b) PVM (c) BVM (d) RVM

Fig. 3. Voxelization of polygonal bell model

Table 1. Comparison of timing. $\delta = 0$ for PVM computation. $\xi = 1$ for SFBOV computation.

Model	Conventional	Heuristic	Time Ratio
Plant	1814628	23402	77.74
Apple	860517	1421	605.57
Bell	1733082	1681	1030.98

5 Conclusion

The method proposed in this paper improves performance of polygonal model solid voxelization remarkably, by saving time and space cost. The experiment's result has proven the method's correctness and efficiency. In addition to polygonal model, the method could be flexibly extended to other representations as well. In this paper, we didn't consider inner cavities hidden in surface, which is a difficult problem for random polygonal model when it might be solved by ray shooting method for some models owning parity property of crossing point number.

References

1. Kaufman, D. Cohen and R. Yagel. Volume Graphics. IEEE Computer, vol. 26, no. 7, 1993, pp. 51-64.
2. Kaufman and E. Shimony. 3D Scan-conversion Algorithms for Voxel-based Graphics. Proc. of ACM Workshop on Interactive 3D Graphics, 1986, 45–76, 1986.
3. D. Cohen and A. Kaufman. Fundamental of Surface Voxelization. Graphical Models and Image Processing vol. 57, no. 6, 1995, pp.453-461.
4. D. Cohen D. and A. Kaufman. 3D Line Voxelization and Connectivity Control. IEEE Computer Graphics and Applications. vol. 17, no. 6, 1997, pp.80-87.
5. Kaufman. Efficient Algorithms for Scan-converting 3D Polygons, Computers and Graphics. vol. 12, no. 2, 1988, pp.213-219.
6. J. Amanatides and A. Woo. A Fast Voxel Traversal Algorithm for Ray Tracing. Eurographics, 1987, pp. 3-9.
7. E. Andres, P. Nehlig, and J. Françon. Tunnel-free Supercover 3D Polygons and Polyhedra. Computer Graphics Forum vol. 16, no. 3, 1997, pp.3-13.
8. J. Huang, R. Yagel, V. Filippov and Y. Kurzion. An Accurate Method for Voxelizing Polygon Meshes. Proc. of the 1998 IEEE Symposium on Volume Visualization, Research Triangle Park, North Carolina, USA, 1998, pp. 119-126.
9. S.F. Fang and H.S. Chen. Hardware Accelerated Voxelization. Computers and Graphics, vol. 24, no. 3, 2000, pp.433-442.
10. Z. Dong, W. Chen, H.J. Bao, H.X. Zhang and Q.S. Peng. Real-time Voxelization for Complex Polygonal Models. Pacific Conference on Computer Graphics and Applications, Seoul, Korean, 2004, pp.43-50.
11. J. Huang, Y. Li, R. Crawfis, S. C. Lu and S.Y. Liou. A Complete Distance Field Representation. Proc.of the Conference on Visualization, San Diego, California, USA, 2001, pp.247-254.
12. E.A. Karabassi, G. Papaioannou and T. Theoharis. A Fast Depth-buffer-based Voxelization Algorithm. Journal of Graphics Tools, vol. 14, no. 4, 1999, pp.5-10.
13. G. Passalis, I.A. Kakadiaris and T. Theoharis. Efficient Hardware Voxelization. Proc. of the Computer Graphics International, 2004, pp.374-377.

Riemannian Mean Curvature Flow

Raúl San José Estépar, Steve Haker, and Carl-Fredrik Westin

Laboratory of Mathematics in Imaging, Brigham and Women's Hosptial,
Harvard Medical School, Boston, MA, USA
{rjosest, haker, westin}@bwh.harvard.edu

Abstract. In this paper we explicitly derive a level set formulation for mean curvature flow in a Riemannian metric space. This extends the traditional geodesic active contour framework which is based on conformal flows. Curve evolution for image segmentation can be posed as a Riemannian evolution process where the induced metric is related to the local structure tensor. Examples on both synthetic and real data are shown.

1 Introduction

Motion of a front by its mean curvature has been extensively studied. It is well-known that a planar curve moving with normal speed equal to its curvature will shrink to a point while its shape becomes smoother and circular [1, 2]. The smooth shrinkage to a point is what makes this type of motion attractive since in many problems solutions are required to be smooth.

Mean curvature evolution schemes for segmentation, implemented with level set methods, have become an important approach in computer vision [3, 4]. Evans and Spruck [5] and Chen, Giga, and Goto [6] independently framed mean curvature flow of any hypersurface as a level set problem and proved existence, uniqueness, and stability of viscosity solutions. Extension of Evans et al. and Chen et al. to manifolds was presented by Ilmanen in [7]. Sarti et al [8] have presented a Riemannian mean curvature flow of graphs, however the authors limit their final analysis to an extension of the conformal case. In this paper, we provide expressions that take into account a general metric.

Motion by curvature is characterized by the curve evolution equation, in its level set formulation,

$$\frac{\partial \Psi}{\partial t} = \operatorname{div}\left(\frac{\nabla \Psi}{\|\nabla \Psi\|}\right)\|\nabla \Psi\| = \kappa \|\nabla \Psi\|, \tag{1}$$

where Ψ is the level set function and κ is the mean curvature. In this paper we present a natural generalization of eq. (1) to a Riemannian metric space. Section 2 introduces some basic concepts and the notation of differential operators in a Riemannian space. In Section 3 we provide a formulation of the level set equation in a general Riemannian metric space. Section 4 presents the Riemannian Mean Curvature Flow (**RMCF**) given by eq. (11). Here also the particular case of RMCF when the metric is conformal is presented. Finally, Section 5 shows some experimental results on synthetic metric fields and real data.

G. Bebis et al. (Eds.): ISVC 2005, LNCS 3804, pp. 613–620, 2005.

2 Background

2.1 Riemannian Geometry

A metric tensor, also called a *Riemannian metric*, is a symmetric and positive definite second-order tensor, $\mathbf{G} = [g_{ij}]$. The arc length, ds_G, between two infinitely close points $\mathbf{x}$ and $\mathbf{x} + d\mathbf{x}$ in a Riemannian metric space is given by $ds_G^2 = d\mathbf{x}^T \mathbf{G}\, d\mathbf{x}$

Let $\mathbf{a}(\mathbf{x})$ and $\mathbf{b}(\mathbf{x})$ be two vectors defined at a point $\mathbf{x} \in \mathbb{R}^n$. In Riemannian geometry, the inner product is generalized by using the metric tensor. For each $\mathbf{x} \in \mathbb{R}^n$, there is a positive definite symmetric metric tensor $\mathbf{G}(\mathbf{x})$, that can be represented as a $n \times n$ matrix. The metric tensor is used to define a new inner product $\langle \mathbf{a}(\mathbf{x}), \mathbf{b}(\mathbf{x}) \rangle_G$, the G-inner product, by

$$\langle \mathbf{a}(\mathbf{x}), \mathbf{b}(\mathbf{x}) \rangle_G = \mathbf{a}(\mathbf{x})^T \mathbf{G}(\mathbf{x}) \mathbf{b}(\mathbf{x}). \tag{2}$$

The space $\mathbb{R}^n$ together with the G-inner product is a *Riemannian metric space.*

2.2 Definitions

Many of the concepts from multivariate vector calculus generalize in a straightforward way to Riemannian metric spaces [9]. Let $u : \mathbb{R}^n \to \mathbb{R}$ be a smooth function and $\mathbf{v} : \mathbb{R}^n \to \mathbb{R}^n$ a vector field. The generalization of the Euclidean gradient and divergence to a Riemannian space with metric $\mathbf{G}$ is given by the G-gradient and G-divergence with formulae

$$\nabla_G u = \mathbf{G}^{-1} \nabla u, \qquad \mathrm{div}_G\,(\mathbf{v}) = |\mathbf{G}|^{-\frac{1}{2}} \mathrm{div}\left(|\mathbf{G}|^{\frac{1}{2}} \mathbf{v} \right), \tag{3}$$

where $|\mathbf{G}|$ is the determinant of the tensor $\mathbf{G}$. The Laplacian of u, $\mathrm{div}\,(\nabla u)$ can be generalized in the *Laplace-Beltrami operator*

$$\mathrm{div}_G\,(\nabla_G u) = |\mathbf{G}|^{-\frac{1}{2}}\, \mathrm{div}\left(|\mathbf{G}|^{\frac{1}{2}} \mathbf{G}^{-1} u \right). \tag{4}$$

3 Riemannian Level Sets

In this section we present the level set equation on a Riemannian manifold. We are going to study the evolution of a front given by the n-dimensional hypersurface $\mathcal{C}(\mathbf{s}, t) : [0,1]^{n-1} \times [0, \infty) \to \mathcal{M}$ where $\mathcal{M}$ is a Riemannian manifold with metric $\mathbf{G}(\mathbf{x})$, and $\mathbf{x}$ is a point in $\mathbb{R}^n$. This front propagates in $\mathcal{M}$ with a speed F. Let us embed the propagating front $\mathcal{C}(t)$ as the zero level set of a function $\Psi(\mathbf{x}, t) : \mathcal{M} \times \mathbb{R} \to \mathbb{R}$. Since $\mathcal{C}(t)$ is the zero level set of Ψ, $\Psi(\mathcal{C}, t) = 0$.

Theorem 1. (Riemannian level set equation)
The evolution of a function $\Psi(\mathbf{x}, t)$ in a Riemannian manifold $\mathcal{M}$ defined by the metric $\mathbf{G}$ with a embedded front propagating in the normal direction of the manifold $\mathcal{M}$ under the speed function F is given by

$$\frac{\partial}{\partial t} \Psi(\mathbf{x}, t) = F \| \nabla_G \Psi(\mathbf{x}) \|_G. \tag{5}$$

In order to prove the Riemannian level set equation we proceed as follows, in analogy to [10]. The evolution of a front $\mathcal{C}(t)$ in its normal direction is given by

$$\frac{\partial \mathcal{C}(t)}{\partial t} = F\hat{\mathbf{N}}_G \tag{6}$$

for all t, where $\hat{\mathbf{N}}_G$ is the unit normal to the front in the Riemannian manifold with metric $\mathbf{G}$. Taking the total derivative of $\Psi(\mathcal{C}(t), t) = 0$ with respect to t and applying the chain rule we get

$$\langle \nabla \Psi(\mathcal{C}(t), t), \frac{\partial \mathcal{C}(t)}{\partial t} \rangle + \frac{\partial \Psi(\mathcal{C}(t), t)}{\partial t} = 0. \tag{7}$$

Writing Ψ_t for $\frac{\partial \Psi}{\partial t}$ and using eq. (6) we get

$$\Psi_t = \langle -\nabla \Psi(\mathcal{C}(t), t), F\hat{\mathbf{N}}_G \rangle. \tag{8}$$

The unit normal, $\hat{\mathbf{N}}_G$, to the front can be written in terms of the level set function as

$$\hat{\mathbf{N}}_G = -\frac{\nabla_G \Psi}{||\nabla_G \Psi||_G}. \tag{9}$$

Then, eq. (8) can be expanded as

$$\begin{aligned} \Psi_t &= -F \langle \nabla \Psi, -\frac{\nabla_G \Psi}{||\nabla_G \Psi||_G} \rangle = \frac{F}{||\nabla_G \Psi||_G} \left(\mathbf{G} \nabla_G \Psi\right)^T \nabla_G \Psi \\ &= \frac{F}{||\nabla_G \Psi||_G} ||\nabla_G \Psi||_G^2 = F ||\nabla_G \Psi||_G. \end{aligned} \tag{10}$$

□

4 The Riemannian Mean Curvature Flow

Here we generalize the Euclidean mean curvature flow to mean curvature flow in a Riemannian manifold. Essentially, we warp the Euclidean space into a new space, the Riemannian manifold, and we solve the evolution for that space. The benefit of this approach is that we are free to choose the metric tensor, and thus the nature of the space in which the flow will take place. In image processing, this is crucial since the metric for the space may be derived from the image, resulting in a flow adapted to the image characteristics.

Mean curvature flow appears naturally within the problem of *curve shortening* and the solution has been already introduced in eq. (1). This montion has also been extended to the case where the curves evolve in a space having a special kind of Riemannian metric, a conformal metric. See [4] and sub-section 4.3 of this paper.

In this paper, we extend the method to the case of a general Riemannian metric G. Indeed, the minimization of the curve length functional

$$L_G = \int_0^1 ||C_p||_G \, dp = \int_0^1 ds_G$$

in a Riemannian space with metric $\mathbf{G}$ leads to the mean curvature flow $C_t = \kappa_G N_G$, and the corresponding partial differential equation

$$\Psi_t = \kappa_G \|\nabla_G \Psi\|_G = \text{div}_G \left(\frac{\nabla_G \Psi}{\|\nabla_G \Psi\|_G} \right) \|\nabla_G \Psi\|_G . \tag{11}$$

4.1 Explicit Formulation

Here an explicit formulation of eq. (11) in terms of the Euclidean gradient is presented. The explicit formulation makes possible an interpretation of the forces that act in a RMCF. The Riemannian mean curvature flow can be rewritten in the following form

$$\Psi_t = \underbrace{\text{Tr}\{\mathbf{P}_G \mathbf{G}^{-1} \mathbf{H}\}}_{\text{smoothing term}} + \underbrace{\text{Tr}\left\{ \left(\mathbf{I} - \mathbf{G}^{-1} \frac{\nabla \Psi \nabla \Psi^T}{2\|\nabla_G \Psi\|_G^2} \right) \mathbf{A} \right\}}_{\text{Advection term type 1}} + \underbrace{\frac{|\mathbf{G}|^{-1}}{2} \langle \mathbf{G}^{-1} \nabla \Psi, \nabla |\mathbf{G}| \rangle}_{\text{Advection term type 2}} . \tag{12}$$

where $\mathbf{H}$ is the Hessian of the level set, $\mathbf{I}$ is the identity matrix, $\mathbf{A}$ is a matrix with elements $a_{ik} = \frac{\partial g^{ij}}{\partial x_k} \frac{\partial \Psi}{\partial x_j}$, and $\mathbf{P}_G$ is the G-projection operator defined as $\mathbf{P}_G = \mathbf{I} - \mathbf{G}^{-1} \frac{\nabla \Psi \nabla \Psi^T}{\|\nabla_G \Psi\|_G^2}$. The projection operator defines the projection onto the tangent plane to the manifold $\mathcal{M}$ with metric $\mathbf{G}$. The interested reader can find details on the derivation of eq. (12) in [11], as well as a numerical implementation.

4.2 Interpretation

Equation (12) reveals that the motion under mean curvature in a Riemannian manifold with metric $\mathbf{G}$ is the result of three action forces:

- **Smoothing term** (F_s): This term is the result of projecting the Hessian of the level set function into the tangent plane to the manifold. The projected Hessian is weighted by the metric inverse. Therefore, smoothing along sheets tangent to the manifold will be allowed while smoothing in other directions will be restrained.
- **Advection term type 1** (F_{a1}): This advection term is due to a change in the rotationally dependent part of the metric as well as the rotationally invariant part. In other words this term attracts the evolving contour to areas where the metric changes in orientation as well as where the metric changes in magnitude.
- **Advection term type 2** (F_{a2}): This advection term is only due to a change in the rotationally invariant part of the metric. Basically, this term attracts the evolving front to areas where the metric changes in magnitude. $\nabla|\mathbf{G}|$ is a doublet that forces the G-gradient of the propagating front to get attracted toward the extrema of $\nabla|\mathbf{G}|$.

4.3 Conformal Case

In this section we analyze the particular case where our metric $\mathbf{G}$ is conformal. A conformal metric space is characterized by a metric of the form

$$\mathbf{G}(\mathbf{x}) = \phi(\mathbf{x})\mathbf{I} \tag{13}$$

where $\phi(\mathbf{x}) : \mathbb{R}^n \to \mathbb{R}$. Here ϕ defines the cost for a front to travel in an isotropic medium. For this metric, the following relations hold: $|\mathbf{G}| = \phi^n$, $\|\nabla_G \Psi\|_G = \phi^{-\frac{1}{2}}\|\nabla\Psi\|$ and $\nabla|\mathbf{G}| = n\phi^{n-1}\nabla\phi$. Using these relations, eq. (12) can be made specific to the conformal metric case by the expression

$$\Psi_t = \frac{1}{\phi}\text{div}\left(\frac{\nabla\Psi}{\|\nabla\Psi\|}\right)\|\nabla\Psi\| + \frac{n-1}{2\phi^2}\langle\nabla\Psi, \nabla\phi\rangle. \tag{14}$$

For the 2D case, i.e. planar curve evolution $n = 2$.

The evolution of curves by mean curvature in conformal metric spaces has been studied by other authors [3, 4]. Both of these works conclude that the evolution equation in 2D is

$$\Psi_t = \phi^{\frac{1}{2}}\text{div}\left(\frac{\nabla\Psi}{\|\nabla\Psi\|}\right)\|\nabla\Psi\| + \frac{1}{2\phi^{\frac{1}{2}}}\langle\nabla\Psi, \nabla\phi\rangle. \tag{15}$$

The discrepancy between our result and their result is given by a factor $\phi^{\frac{3}{2}}$. Appendix A elaborates on the source of this discrepancy.

5 Experiments

5.1 The Pullback Map

We have tested the connection between the Euclidean mean curvature flow and its Riemannian counterpart in the warped space by means of pullback maps. Let B be a n-dimensional Euclidean space, so $\mathbf{G}_B = \mathbf{I}$, and let $\mathbf{w} : A \to B$ be a smooth injective mapping from $A = \mathbb{R}^n$ into B. The mapping $\mathbf{w}$ defines a warping of the Euclidean space B into A. Let $\mathbf{G}_A = \mathbf{J}_w^T\mathbf{J}_w$ where $\mathbf{J}_w$ is the Jacobian matrix of $\mathbf{w}$ given by

$$[\mathbf{J}_w]_{ij} = \frac{\partial w_i}{\partial x_j}, \tag{16}$$

and $\mathbf{w} = (w_1, w_2, \ldots, w_n)$. Then $\mathbf{G}_A$ is the *pullback* of $\mathbf{G}_B$ to A via $\mathbf{w}$. This results in two Riemannian spaces $(A, \mathbf{G}_A)$ and $(B, \mathbf{G}_B)$ that are isometric. This means that if we have a curve $\mathcal{C}$ in $(B, \mathbf{G}_B)$ of some length, then $\mathcal{C} \circ \mathbf{w}$ in $(A, \mathbf{G}_A)$ is a curve of the same length. Let Ψ be a level set function on B undergoing mean curvature flow given by the partial differential equation (1). We define a new level set function $\Psi^* = \Psi \circ \mathbf{w}$ that is the pullback of Ψ via $\mathbf{w}$. Since the two spaces $(A, \mathbf{G}_A)$ and $(B, \mathbf{G}_B)$ are isometric, the mean curvature with respect to G_B of

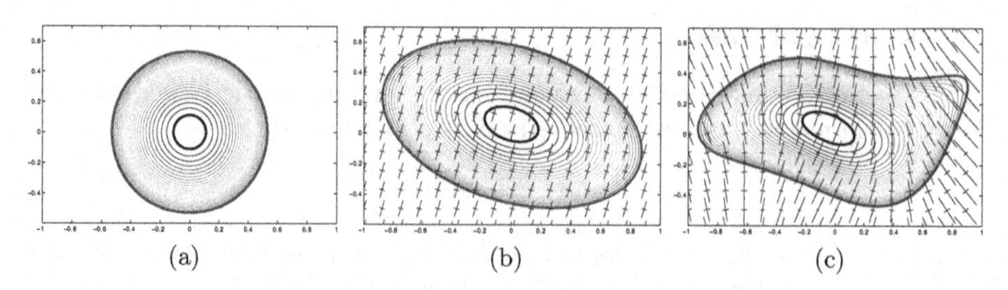

Fig. 1. Level Set Evolution in a Riemannian metric space. (a) Level Set Evolution of a circular contour in a Euclidean space. (b) Evolution with a metric given through the Jacobian eq. (17). (c) Evolution in a metric space with a non-trivial metric.

the level set Ψ at a point $\mathbf{w}(\mathbf{x})$ is the same that the mean curvature with respect to $\mathbf{G}_A$, i.e. in the warped space, of the level set Ψ^* at $\mathbf{x}$. Therefore, through the pullback map we can test the correctness of our formulation.

To that end, we have considered the following situation. We have embedded an initial circular contour as the zero level set of a function $\mathbf{\Psi} : [-1,1]\times[-1,1] \to \mathbb{R}$. This level set function has undergone mean curvature flow in the Euclidean space as given by eq. (1). Contours corresponding to the zero level set during the evolution process are shown in Figure 1a. We have tested two different mappings $\mathbf{w}$, namely, an affine map and a less trivial map.

Affine Map. The affine map used to pull back is given by $\mathbf{w}(x,y) = (x+y, 2y-x)$. The metric of the space described by this map is

$$\mathbf{G}_{aff} = \begin{bmatrix} 2 & -1 \\ -1 & 5 \end{bmatrix}. \tag{17}$$

An initial level set, $\Psi^*(\mathbf{x},0)$, in the space A has been obtained by applying the map to the initial circular contour $\Psi^*(\mathbf{x},0) = \Psi(\mathbf{w}(\mathbf{x}),0)$. The initial zero level set is shown in Figure 1b in thick line. This new level set function Ψ^* has been evolved under eq. (12) using the metric $\mathbf{G}_{aff}$. The resulting evolving zero level sets are shown in Figure 1b. In this figure the metric is represented by means of local coordinate systems in the orientation given by the main eigenvector of the metric $\mathbf{G}_{aff}$, with axes shown with length proportional to the corresponding eigenvalue. As we can see the evolution shrinks the contour to an ellipse.

Non-trivial Map. The map used to pull back in this case is given by $\mathbf{w}(x,y) = (x + \frac{y^2}{3} + \frac{\cos(\pi y)}{3.5}, -\frac{(x+0.5)^2}{4} + 2y + \frac{\sin(\pi x)}{3.5})$. In this case the metric tensor is a function of x and y. As in the previous case, the initial level set is defined as $\Psi^*(\mathbf{x},0) = \Psi(\mathbf{w}(\mathbf{x}),0)$. This initial contour in A is shown in Figure 1c as the outermost thick contour. The Riemannian mean curvature flow equation has been solved in the domain. The zero level sets for the evolution process are shown in Figure 1c. The corresponding metric tensor that defines the space where the evolution takes place is also displayed. It is possible to go from one of the zero level sets at $t = t_0$ in Figure 1c to the corresponding one in Figure 1a via $\mathbf{w}$, i.e. $\Psi^*(\mathbf{x}, t_k) = \Psi(\mathbf{w}(\mathbf{x}), t_k)$.

5.2 Image Example

The RMCF can be used in a framework for performing image segmentation. In this case, the metric of the Riemannian space is defined by the image that we want to segment given by the local structure tensor. A balloon force term is added to allow the initial level set to expand. The Riemannian curvature flow acts on the expanding level set as a attracting force to the location where the metric changes. At the same time it tries to keep the level set smooth. Figure 2a shows an example of the RMCF segmentation result of an MRI image. In blue we show the initial contour. A detailed view of the image metric used to define the Riemannian space is shown in Figure 2b.

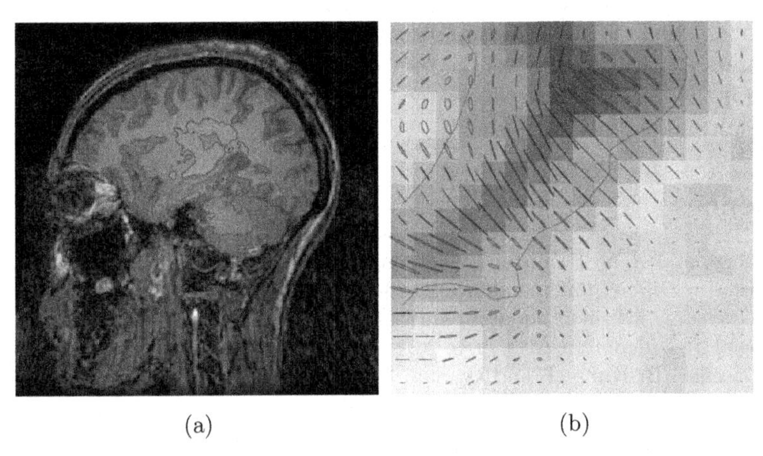

(a) (b)

Fig. 2. Image segmentation by RMCF. (a) Segmentation result, in blue the initial contour and in red the final result. (b) Metric induced by the image.

6 Conclusions

We have proposed a RMCF equation using level set theory. The mean curvature flow takes place in a space endowed with a Riemannian metric. This case can be seen as a generalization of what it has been called geodesic active contours. We provide an explicit formulation for the flow, showing it comprises three forces. We have analyzed the particular case where the metric used in the RMCF is conformal. Experimental results have built an insight into the proposed evolution.

A Conformal Case Discrepancy

Eq. (14) and eq. (15) differ by a factor $\phi^{\frac{3}{2}}$. The discrepancy can be accounted for by revisiting the derivation of the evolution equation. In appendix B of [3], the authors show the derivation of their evolution equation. They minimize a length functional L by computing the first order variation. At a given point they derive

$$L_t = \int_0^L \left\langle \langle \nabla \phi^{\frac{1}{2}}, \mathcal{N} \rangle \mathcal{N} - \phi^{\frac{1}{2}} \kappa \mathcal{N}, \mathcal{C}_t \right\rangle ds. \tag{18}$$

From this equation the steepest-descent method, connecting a initial curve $\mathcal{C}$, with a local minimum of $L(\mathcal{C})$, is used to yield the evolution equation given by eq. (15). It is our understanding that eq. (18), although being the right integral, should be expressed in terms of the intrinsic inner product and length, i.e. $\langle , \rangle_\phi$ and ds_ϕ respectively, i.e.

$$L_t = \int_0^L \left\langle \left(\langle \nabla \phi^{\frac{1}{2}}, \mathcal{N} \rangle \mathcal{N} - \phi^{\frac{1}{2}} \kappa \mathcal{N} \right) \phi^{-\frac{3}{2}}, \mathcal{C}_t \right\rangle_\phi ds_\phi. \tag{19}$$

In this case, the way to achieve the minimum of the function L is by solving the evolution given by eq. (14) with $n = 2$.

Although the flow in eq. (15) implies that the functional L is decreasing, it is not the mean curvature flow in the image space with the conformal metric, and in general the use of the two flows eq. (15) and eq. (14) will not produce the same result.

References

1. M. Gage and R. S. Hamilton. The heat equation shrinking convex plane curves. *Journal of Differential Geometry*, 23:69–96, 1986.
2. M. Grayson. The heat equation shrinks embedded plane curves to round points. *Journal of Differential Geometry*, 26:285–314, 1987.
3. V. Caselles, R. Kimmel, and G. Sapiro. Geodesic active contours. *International Journal of Computer Vision*, 22(1):61–79, 1997.
4. S. Kichenassamy, A. Kumar, P. Olver, A. Tannenbaum, and A. Yezzi. Conformal curvature flows: from phase transitions to active vision. *Archives on Rational Mechanics and Analysis*, 134:275–301, 1996.
5. L. C. Evans and J. Spruck. Motion of level sets by mean curvature. *Journal of Differential Geometry*, 33:635–681, 1991.
6. Y. Giga Y.G. Chen and S. Goto. Uniqueness and existence of viscosity solutions of generalized mean curvature flow equations. *Journal of Differential Geometry*, 33:749–786, 1991.
7. T. Ilmanen. Generalized flow of sets by mean curvature on a manifold. *Indiana J. Math.*, 41(3):671–705, 1992.
8. A. Sarti and G. Citti. Subjective surfaces and riemannian mean curvature flow of graphs. *Acta Math. Univ. Comenianae*, LXX:85–103, 2001.
9. M. DoCarmo. *Riemannian Geometry.* Birkhäuser, 1992.
10. S. J. Osher and J. A. Sethian. Fronts propagation with curvature dependent speed: Algorithms based on hamilton-jacobi formulations. *Journal of Computational Physics*, 79:12–49, 1988.
11. Raúl San José Estépar. *Local Structure Tensor for Multidimensional Signal Processing. Applications to Medical Image Analysis.* PhD thesis, University of Valladolid, Spain, 2005.

3D Shape from Unorganized 3D Point Clouds

George Kamberov[1], Gerda Kamberova[2], and Amit Jain[1]

[1] Department of Computer Science,
Stevens Institute of Technology, Hoboken, NJ 07030
[2] Department of Computer Science,
Hofstra University, Hempstead, NY 11549

Abstract. We present a framework to automatically infer topology and geometry from an unorganized 3D point cloud obtained from a 3D scene. If the cloud is not oriented, we use existing methods to orient it prior to recovering the topology. We develop a quality measure for scoring a chosen topology/orientation. The topology is used to segment the cloud into manifold components and later in the computation of shape descriptors.

1 Introduction

In this paper we are concerned mainly with inferring the topology and shape of the components of complex 3D scenes. We are after a methodology that works: for scenes involving multiple surfaces; with data which are possibly sparse and/or noisy; with partial views of some objects. The geometric features at each surface point that we search for are the mean and Gauss curvature and the principal curvatures directions. To meet our goals, we use a novel approach to define and extract topology on the cloud so that surface points have neighborhoods that are as tight as possible in surface distance, not simply in Euclidean distance; we use redundant stable calculations to infer the geometric features. We develop a new scoring function for evaluating the fit of the assigned orientation and topology to the point cloud.

2 Related Work

There is a substantial body of work on the recovery of geometry from point clouds. One approach is to reconstruct a parametrization or a polygonal mesh [1, 2, 3, 4, 5, 6, 8, 9, 10, 13, 15, 16, 19, 21, 25, 35] and then use differential geometric formulae or a tailor-made approach to compute differential properties. The existing surface reconstruction methods are not well suited to deal automatically with sparse, noisy samples from multiple surfaces and surfaces with boundary. Such methods will benefit if combined with a reliable approach for extracting differential properties from the cloud prior to the reconstruction. Some key recent techniques for computing differential properties include [7, 11, 18, 26, 29, 31, 34] and the eleven methods in [33]. They will work better if the neighborhoods used in the computation are tight in surface distance. [36] extends tensor voting to

G. Bebis et al. (Eds.): ISVC 2005, LNCS 3804, pp. 621–629, 2005.

estimate the curvature tensor but not at the original cloud points but at perturbed "re-adjusted" point locations. This position adjustment is not justified in many applications.

A key component in reconstruction and in computation of differential properties is to establish good estimates of the surface orientation and topology (in the correct mathematical sense of a "neighborhood structure").

3 The Framework

3.1 Oriented Cloud

An *oriented point cloud* $M = \{(p, \mathbf{N}) \in \boldsymbol{R}^3 \times S^2\}$ is a set $\{p\}$ of 3D *base points* with a normal vector attached to each base point. Sometimes one can pull orientation directly from the experiment [12, 20, 38]. If a point cloud is not oriented we compute orientation using one of the many existing methods [8, 14, 19, 21, 27, 28, 30].

Our methodology addresses fundamental questions arising in geometric processing of unorganized point clouds: how to segment the cloud into components equipped with topology which accounts for surface distance, and how to compute differential properties of surface components. The framework includes methods to: quantify the likelihood that two points are neighbors in terms of an implicit measure of *surface distance*; build topology based on neighborhoods which are tight in terms of *surface distance*; and measure (score) how well a given choice of orientation and topology fit the cloud in terms of surface distance.

3.2 Topology of an Oriented Cloud

Let $\mathbf{f}$ be a local parametrization of an oriented surface in $\boldsymbol{R}^3$ and let $\mathbf{N}$ be the Gauss map (the normal field), and let $< \cdot | \cdot >$ denote the Euclidean dot product in $\boldsymbol{R}^3$. The fundamental identity $-\left\langle \frac{d\mathbf{N}}{ds} \middle| \frac{d\mathbf{f}}{ds} \right\rangle = \left\langle \mathbf{N} \middle| \frac{d^2\mathbf{f}}{ds^2} \right\rangle$, can be used to quantify the proximity between two points P and Q in an oriented point cloud. Here s is an arc-length parameter of a curve on the surface.

Proximity Likelihood. To incorporate multi-scale analysis we use a scale/ resolution parameter $\rho > 0$. It can be selected according to the needs of the application at hand, or be set to be the diameter of the 3D point cloud of base points. To define the neighbors of an oriented cloud point $P = (p, \mathbf{N}_p)$ we use a weight function Δ_P, which weights all oriented cloud points $Q = (q, \mathbf{N}_q)$ whose base points q are inside a 3D volume $B_\rho(p)$ centered at the base point p. The volume could be a ball of radius at most ρ or a cubic voxel with side at most 2ρ. $\Delta_P(Q)$ quantifies the *proximity likelihood that* Q *is nearby* P on the sampled surface. It accounts for Euclidean distance, surface distance, and the deviation of the normals:

$$\Delta_P(Q) = \left(1 - \frac{|p-q|}{M_1(P)}\right) t(P,Q), \quad \text{where } M_1(P) = \max_{(q',N'),q' \in B_\rho(p)} (|p-q'|), \tag{1}$$

and $t(P, Q)$ depends on the cosine between the normals, $\langle \mathbf{N}_p | \mathbf{N}_q \rangle$, and on an implicit measure of surface distance derived from the identity, $-\left\langle \frac{d\mathbf{N}}{ds} \middle| \frac{d\mathbf{f}}{ds} \right\rangle = \left\langle \mathbf{N} \middle| \frac{d^2\mathbf{f}}{ds^2} \right\rangle$. We choose, [23],

$$t(P, Q) = \left(\frac{1}{2} + \frac{1}{2} \langle \mathbf{N}_p | \mathbf{N}_q \rangle\right) \left(1 - \frac{\delta_P(Q)}{M_2(P)}\right), \quad M_2(P) = \max_{(q', N'), q' \in B_\rho(p)} (\delta_P(Q'))$$
$$\delta_P(Q) = |\langle \mathbf{N}_q + \mathbf{N}_p | \overrightarrow{pq} \rangle|.$$

Note that $\delta_p(Q) = O(s^3)$, where $p = \mathbf{f}(0)$ and $q = \mathbf{f}(s)$ and that $t(p, Q)$ is a product of two terms: the first depends on the cosine of the angle between the normals at P and Q, and the second, expresses the implicit measure of surface distance. In the case of exact samples of oriented planar or spherical patches, $\Delta_P(Q)$ encodes exactly the surface distance between the base points.

In addition to the construction of neighborhoods the proximity likelihood also provides a tool to score the pair of orientaion/topology.

Δ Neighborhoods on an Oriented Point Cloud. Following [23] we use the proximity likelihood to build a topology on an oriented cloud which accounts for *surface distance.* Given an oriented cloud M and a scale $\rho > 0$, a collection $\mathcal{U}(P) \subset M$ is called neighborhood of $P = (p, \mathbf{N})$ of likelihood $\lambda \geq 0$, if for every neighborhood point $Q = (q, \mathbf{N}_q) \neq P$ we have: (i) the likelihood $\Delta_P(Q) \geq \lambda$; (ii) the base point q is inside the volume $B_\rho(p)$ and the vector $q - p$ is not collinear to the normal $\mathbf{N}$ at the base point p.

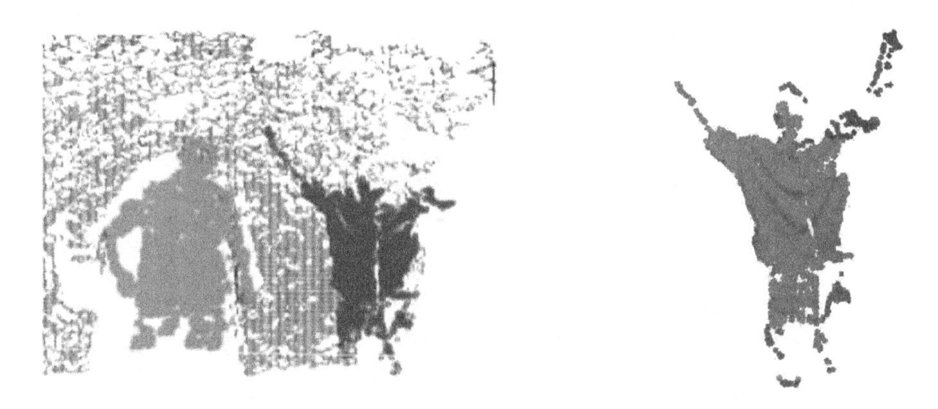

Fig. 1. On the left we show segmentation of an unorganized oriented cloud generated using stereo [12]. The components are recovered automatically using the extracted Δ *neighborhoods topology.* The three largest components are displayed, they account for 97% of the total 17500 points. On the right we show a point based rendering of one of the objects in the scene (consisting of three components) which uses the computed differential shape descriptors.

The points in oriented clouds fall into two classes: *interior surface points* and *boundary* points. The boundary points include *boundary surface points, isolated points,* and *curve points.* The isolated points do not have neighborhoods with positive likelihood. The surface and curve points do have neighborhoods with positive likelihood. P is a surface point if one can use the neighborhood to estimate the orientation along at least two orthogonal directions emanating from the base point. P is an interior surface point if one can use a positive likelihood neighborhood $\mathcal{U}(P)$ to compute the orientation in a full circle of directions centered p and perpendicular to $\mathbf{N}$. A point is a curve point if it is not a surface or an isolated point. The surface points are samples of 2D manifolds and we can compute differential properties at each such point see Section 3.3.

Finding a Δ neighborhood of a point P is a pretty straightforward local procedure. There is no extra cost to treat scenes with multiple objects and surfaces with boundary.

Segmentation. The neighborhoods $\mathcal{U}(P)$ of the points P in the oriented cloud define a graph. The vertices of the graph are the points in the oriented cloud, and two vertices P and Q are connected by an edge if either P is a neighbor of Q ($P \in \mathcal{U}(Q)$), or if Q is a neighbor of P ($Q \in \mathcal{U}(P)$). The connected components of this graph are (discrete samples of) the manifold components of the scene. See Figure 1. This scene segmentation algorithm has time complexity $\Theta(n+k)$, where n is the number of points in the oriented cloud and k is the number of pairs of neighbors (edges in the graph).

Orientation/Topology Scoring. For non-oriented clouds one can choose one of the many existing techniques to assign orientation, see Section 2. Topology

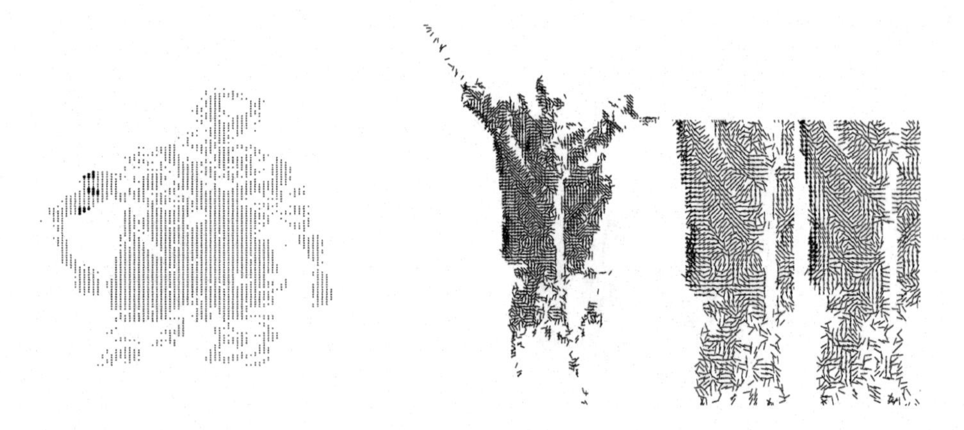

Fig. 2. On the left, we show one of the connected components and in bold the computed Δ neighborhoods of one interior surface point and two surface boundary points. This 2D connected component is automatically segmented from the cloud in Figure 1. In the center, we show one family of principal directions for another connected component, and on the right we "zoom" and show detail of the two families of principal directions recovered on this component.

is build using Δ neighborhoods. There are alternative topologies, for example using neighborhoods provided by the orientation algorithm. To decide which orientation/topology choice is appropriate we use $\Delta_P(Q)$ from (1) to assign a loss L for an orientation/topology choice. Our main concern is to find neighborhoods which are tight in surface distance in order to minimize the error in computing differential properties. Thus the loss is associated with the radius of a neighborhood in *surface distance.* This radius controls the step size of the difference quotients approximating differential properties at the center of the neighborhood. More precisely, given an oriented cloud and its corresponding topology and a scale parameter ρ, we define the expected loss L for the chosen orientation/topology as a weighted average, over all cloud points, of the deviation of the mean likelihood for each neighborhood from the ideal likelihood, 1. The weight for each neighborhood is its normalized likelihood. In math terms,

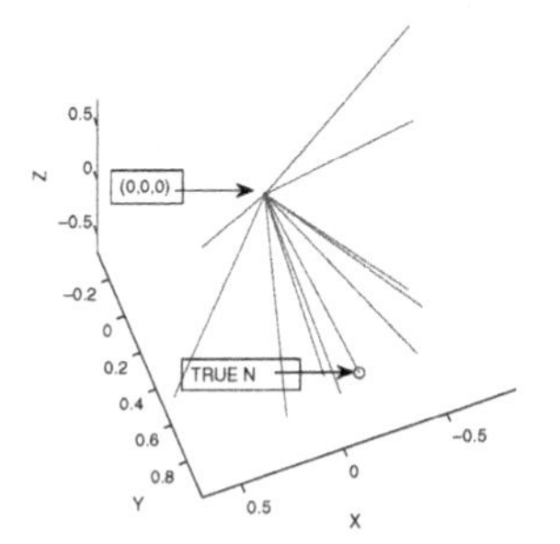

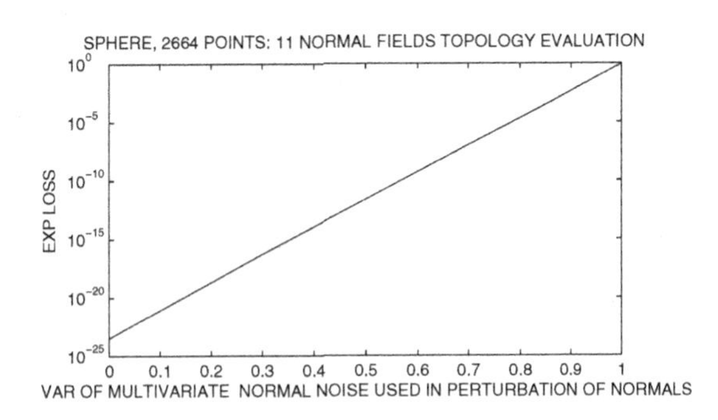

Fig. 3. Example evaluating 11 different orientation/topology selections for a point cloud sampled randomly from a unit sphere. One of the normal fields consists of the true normals, the other 10 are generated using increasing level of noise. On the left, we show for a fixed point of the sampled sphere the 11 unit normals used: the true unit normal is marked with a circle; the perturbed unit normals, for $k = 1 \ldots 10$, are generated as follows, $N_k = X_k/|X_k|$ where X_k is a 3D random vector with a multivariate normal distribution with mean the true unit normal at the point and a variance-covariance matrix $var_k * I$, where $var_k = 0.1k$ and I is the 3 by 3 identity matrix. Note that the generated noisy normals allow for increasingly large deviations from the true normal. For the particular point illustrated here, the angles between the true normal and the perturbed normals vary from 10.6 to 106.9 degrees. On the right, we show the scoring of the 11 normal fields (same point cloud, 11 different normal fields) and the corresponding Δ *neighborhood topologies* which are computed using our likelihood measure of closeness which incorporates surface distance, deviation of normals, and Euclidean distance: On the horizontal axis, are the variances, var_k that were used in generating the perturbed normal fields, the mark 0 on the horizontal axis corresponds to the exact normal field. On the vertical axis, are the expected loss scores, L, for the various orientation/topologies. A lower expected loss L indicates a better normal filed/topology fit for the original unorganized point cloud. Note that since the expected loss in this case happened to be exponential we used a semilog plot to display it, the marks on the vertical axis are the correct expected losses, but the graph is linear exhibiting the log of the exponential function.

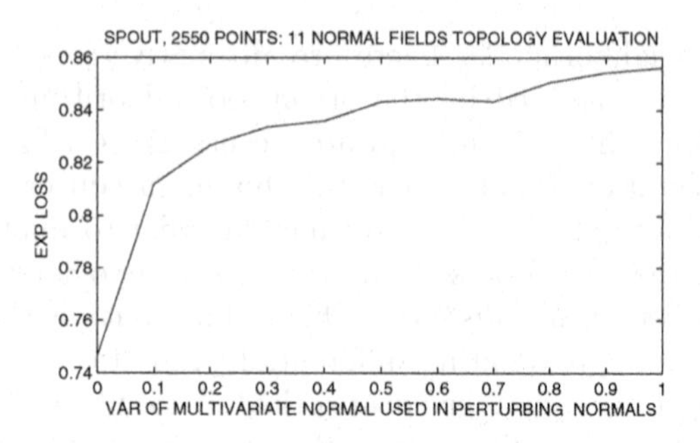

Fig. 4. Example evaluating the 11 different orientations and computed topologies for a point cloud sampled from the Utah teapot spout. The generation of the perturbed normals, and the labelling conventions of the figure are as those in Figure 3(right) with the exception that the graph is the expected loss itself, not its log.

$L = \sum_P (1 - \bar{\Delta}_P) \frac{\bar{\Delta}_P}{\sum_P \bar{\Delta}_P}$, where P is a point that runs over the whole cloud, and $\bar{\Delta}_P$ denotes the mean, over all neighbors Q of P, of all likelihoods $\Delta_P(Q)$. We have been testing this loss function for different synthetic surfaces providing ground truth and for different noise levels, see Figures 3 and 4.

3.3 Geometric Descriptors of Oriented Point Clouds

We follow the approach in [22] to compute differential properties from an oriented point cloud equipped with topology. Recall the classical identities relating the mean and Gauss curvatures, H and K, to the directional derivatives of the parametrization $\mathbf{f}$ and the Gauss map $\mathbf{N}$

$$-Hd\mathbf{f}(\mathbf{u}) = \frac{1}{2}\left(d\mathbf{N}(\mathbf{u}) - \mathbf{N} \times d\mathbf{N}(\mathbf{v})\right) \tag{2}$$

$$\omega(\mathbf{u}) = \frac{1}{2}\left(d\mathbf{N}(\mathbf{u}) + \mathbf{N} \times d\mathbf{N}(\mathbf{v})\right) \tag{3}$$

$$K = H^2 - (a^2 + b^2) \tag{4}$$

where $(\mathbf{u}, \mathbf{v})$ is any positively oriented basis of the tangent plane, and $a =< \omega(\mathbf{u}) | d\mathbf{f}(\mathbf{u}) >$, and $b =< \omega(\mathbf{u}) | d\mathbf{f}(\mathbf{v}) >$. Furthermore, the principal curvature directions are expressed in closed form in terms of a and b, [22]. These identities allow us to define and compute the "surface type" differential features at a "surface point" $P = (p, N)$. In our framework P is a surface point if we can use a neighborhood of P, $\mathcal{U}(P)$, to compute the Gauss map in at least two orthogonal directions in the tangent plane passing through p and perpendicular to the normal $\mathbf{N}$. Cloud components that contain surface points are samples of 2D surfaces. To compute the differential features (mean and Gauss curvature and principle curvature directions) at a surface point P we use the distribution of the normals in $\mathcal{U}(P)$. With every neighbor $Q_i \neq P$ we associate a positively oriented frame $\phi_i = (\mathbf{u}_i, \mathbf{v}_i)$ where $\mathbf{u}_i$ is the unit vector in direction of the orthogonal projection of the vector $\overrightarrow{pq_i} = q_i - p$ on the tangent plane and $\mathbf{v}_i = N \times \mathbf{u}_i$. The neighbor Q_i gives us an estimate of the directional derivative $d\mathbf{N}(\mathbf{u}_i)$. For each such neighbor Q_i, for which we can estimate the directional derivative $d\mathbf{N}(\mathbf{v}_i)$ from the distribution of the normals in $\mathcal{U}(P)$, we obtain an estimate H_{ϕ_i} of the mean curvature using (2). The mean curvature, H, at the point is estimated statistically by averaging the measurements $\{H_{\phi_i}\}$ after throwing out the minimal and maximal. The principal curvature axes and the Gauss curvature are estimated in a similar fashion, from (4), and by noticing that the principal curvature vectors can be expressed in closed form in terms of the entries $< \omega(\mathbf{u}_i)|\mathbf{u}_i >$, $< \omega(\mathbf{u}_i)|\mathbf{v}_i >$, and $< \omega(\mathbf{v}_i)|\mathbf{v}_i >$.

Thus we use multiple estimates of the mean and Gauss curvatures and the principal curvature directions at each surface point P. The redundancy is crucial when dealing with discrete, possibly sparse, and noisy data. Results are shown in Figures 1, 2. By design, the technique only involves first order numeric differentiation and avoids matrix diagonalization. The technique does not need parametrization – all that is needed is a method to define orientation and topology (if not given). Comparisons with results evaluating methods for quantitative shape extraction [17, 29, 33] demonstrate that independently of the surface type tested or the shape parameters sought (mean or Gauss curvature) our approach always gives empirical results better or comparable to the best published in [17, 29, 33]. (See [24].)

4 Summary

We present a framework for computing topology and geometry for unorganized point cloud sampled from a complex 3D scene with multiple objects and possibly occlusions. If the cloud is not oriented we use one of the existing methods to orient it. The advantage we have is that we also developed a scoring function that quantifies the fit of a given orientation and topology to a point cloud. The crucial ingredient in computing the topology is a proximity likelihood function that accounts simultaneously for Euclidean distance, deviation of the normals, and implicitly for surface distance. Once the topology is computed, the cloud is partitioned into 2D manifold components, isolated points and curve components. Next, shape descriptors are estimated for the points that belong to the 2D manifold components. These computations are local, work directly on the cloud, exploit redundancy, avoid unstable computations like diagonalization of general symmetric matrices and taking of square roots. They do not use surface/mesh reconstructions. Our approach to extracting topology is unique in incorporating the unknown surface distance. Empirical studies show that our geometry extraction method is admissible in decision-theoretic sense and outperforms the dominant approaches developed up to 2003.

References

1. M. Alexa, J. Behr, D. Cohen-Or, S. Fleishman, D. Levin, C. T. Silva, "Computing and Rendering Point Set Surfaces", *Trans. Vis. Comp. Graph.*, Volume 9(1): 3-15, 2003.
2. Nina Amenta and Yong Joo Kill, "Defining Point-Set Surfaces", ACM Transactions on Graphics, volume 23(3), 264-270, Special Issue: Proceedings of SIGGRAPH 2004.

3. J. Boissonnat, Cazals, F., "Smooth surface reconstruction via natural neighbour interpolation of distance functions", *Proc. 18th Annual Symp. Comp. Geom.*, pp. 223-232, 2000.
4. E. Boyer, Petitjean, S., "Regular and Non-Regular Point Sets: Properties and Reconstruction", Comp. Geometry, vol. 19, 101-131, 2001.
5. M. Capps and Teichmann, M., "Surface reconstruction with anisotropic density-scaled alpha shapes," IEEE Visualization '98 Proceedings, 67-72, October 1998.
6. F. Cazals, Giesen, J., Pauly, M., Zomorodian, A., "Conformal Alpha Shapes", Eurographics Symposium on Point-Based Graphics (2005), M. Pauly, M. Zwicker, (Editors)
7. F. Cazals, Pouget, M., "Estimating Differential Quantities Using Polynomial Fitting of Osculating Jets", Proceedings Eurographics/ACM SIGGRAPH Symposium on Geometry Processing, pp. 177-187, 2003.
8. S.-W. Cheng, Dey T. K., Ramos E., Ray, T., "Sampling and meshing a surface with guaranteed topology and geometry" Proc. 20th Ann. Symp. on Comp. Geometry, ACM, pp. 280-289, 2004.
9. T. K. Dey, Sun, J., "An Adaptive MLS Surface for Reconstruction with Guarantees" , Tech. Rep. OSU-CISRC-4-05-TR26, Apr. 2005.
10. S.-W. Cheng, Dey T. K., Ramos E., "Manifold Reconstruction from Point Samples", Proc. ACM-SIAM Sympos. Discrete Algorithms, 2005, 1018–1027.
11. D. Cohen-Steiner and Morvan, Jean-Marie, "Restricted Delaunay triangulations and normal cycle," Proc. 19 ACM Symp. Comp. Geometry, pp 312-321, 2003.
12. K. Daniilidis and Zabulis, X., "Multi-camera reconstruction based on surface normal estimation", 2nd Intl. Symp. 3D Data processing, Visualization and Transmission, Thessaloniki, Greece, 2004, IEEE Proc. Series, in cooperation with Eurographics and ACM SIGGRAPH
13. T. K. Dey, Goswami, S., "Provable surface reconstruction from noisy samples", Proc. 20th Annual Symposium on Computational Geometry, ACM, pp. 330-339, New York, 2004.
14. T. K. Dey, Li, G., Sun, J., "Normal Estimation for Point Clouds: A Comparison for a Voronoi Based Method", Eurographics Symposium on Point-Based Graphics (2005), M. Pauly, M. Zwicker, (Editors).
15. T. K. Dey, Sun, J., "Extremal Surface Based Projections Converge and Reconstruct with Isotopy", Tech. Rep. OSU-CISRC-05-TR25, Apr. 2005.
16. H. Edelsbrunner, Mucke, E.P., "Three-dimensional alpha shapes," ACM Trans. Graph., Volume 13(10, 43-72, 1994.
17. Flynn, P.J., and Jain, A.K. On Reliable Curvature Estimation, *Proc. IEEE Conf. Comp. Vis. Patt. Rec.*, pp 110-116, 1989.
18. J. Goldfeather and Interrante, V., "A Novel Cubic-Order Algorithm for Approximating Principal Direction Vectors", ACM Transactions on Graphics, 23(1), pp. 45-63, 2004.
19. M. Gopi, Krishnan, S., Silva, C. T., "Surface reconstruction based on lower dimensional localized Delaunay triangulation", EUROGRAPHICS 2000, Computer Graphics Forum, Volume 19(3), 2000.
20. J.-Y. Guillemaut, Drbohlav, O., Sara, R., Illingworth, J., "Helmholtz Stereopsis on rough and strongly textured surfaces ", 2nd Intl. Symp. 3D Data Processing, Visualization and Transmission, Thessaloniki, Greece, Sept 2004, IEEE Proc. Sers., in cooperation with Eurographics and ACM SIGGRAPH 2004
21. H. Hoppe, DeRose, T., Duchamp, T., McDonald, J., Stuetzle, W. "Surface reconstruction from unorganized points", *Comp. Graph. (SIGGRAPH '92 Proceedings)*, 26, 71–78, (1992)

22. G. Kamberov, Kamberova, G., "Recovering Surfaces from the Restoring Force", *Proc. ECCV 2002*. Lecture Notes in Comp. Science, Volume 2351, pp 598-612, Springer-Verlag Berlin Heidelberg 2002.
23. G. Kamberov, Kamberova, G., "Topology and Geometry of Unorganized Point Clouds", 2nd Intl. Symp. 3D Data processing, Visualization and Transmission, Thessaloniki, Greece, Sept 2004, IEEE Proc. Series, in cooperation with Eurographics/ACM SIGGRAPH
24. G. Kamberov, Kamberova, G., Conformal Method for Quantitative Shape Extraction: Performance Evaluation, ICPR 2004, Cambridge, UK, August, 2004, IEEE Proceedings Series, 2004
25. D. Levin, "Mesh-Independent Surface Interpolation", To appear in *Geometric Modeling for Scientific Visualization*, Brunnett, Hamann, Mueller, and Linsen eds. Springer-Verlag, 2003.
26. D. Meek, Walton, D., "On surface normal and Gaussian curvature approximations given data sampled from a smooth surface." Computer-Aided Geometric Design, 12:521-543, 2000.
27. G. Medioni, Tang, C, "Curvature-Augmented Tensor Voting for Shape Inference from Noisy 3D Data", *IEEE PAMI*, vol. 24, no. 6, June 2002
28. N. Mitra, Nguyen, A., Guibas, L., "Estimating Surface Normals in Noisy Point Cloud Data", *Proc. 19th ACM Symp. Comput. Geometry (SoCG)*, pp. 322-328, 2003.
29. M. Meyer, Desbrun, M., Schröder, P., Barr, A., "Discrete Differential-Geometry Operators for Triangulated 2-Manifolds", Preprint. See *http://www.cs.caltech.edu/ mmeyer/*
30. R. Šára and Bajcsy, R., "Fish-Scales: Representing Fuzzy Manifolds", *Proc. Int. Conf. on Computer Vision*, Bombay, India, Narosa Publishing House, 1998.
31. S. Rusinkiewicz, "Estimating Curvatures and Their Derivatives on Triangle Meshes", 2nd Intl. Symp. 3D Data processing, Visualization and Transmission, Thessaloniki, Greece, 2004, IEEE Proc. Ser., in cooperation with Eurographics and ACM SIGGRAPH, 2004.
32. E. M. Stokley, Wu, S. Y., "Surface Paremeterization and Curvature Measurement of Arbitrsary 3D Objects: Five Practical Methods", *IEEE Trans. PAMI*, vol 14, 1992.
33. T. Surazhsky, Magid, E., Soldea, O., Elber, G., and Rivlin, E., "A comparison of Gaussian and mean curvatures estimation methods on triangular meshes", 2003 IEEE Interntl. Conf. on Robotics & Automation (ICRA2003)
34. G. Taubin, "Estimating the Tensor of Curvature of a Surface from a Polyhedral Approximation", In *Proc. 5th Intl. Conf. on Computer Vision (ICCV95)*, 902–907, (1995)
35. T. Tasdizen, Whitaker, R., Burchard P., Osher, S., "Geometric surface processing via normal maps", ACM Transactions on Graphics, v.22 n.4, p.1012-1033, Oct. 2003
36. W.S. Tong, Tang, C.K., "Robust Estiation of Adaptive Tensors of Curvature by Tensor Voting", *IEEE Trans. PAMI*, vol 27(3), 434-449, 2005.
37. E. Trucco, Fisher, R. "Experiments in Curvature-Based Segmentation of Range Data", *IEEE Trans. PAMI*, vol 17, 1995.
38. T. Zickler, Belhumeur, P. N., and Kriegman, D. J., "Helmholtz Stereopsis: Exploiting Reciprocity for Surface Reconstruction." Int. Jour. Comp. Vis. (IJCV), **49**(2/3), 215-227.

3D Hand Pose Reconstruction with ISOSOM

Haiying Guan and Matthew Turk

Department of Computer Science, University of California, Santa Barbara, CA 93106
{haiying, mturk}@cs.ucsb.edu

Abstract. We present an appearance-based 3D hand posture estimation method that determines a ranked set of possible hand posture candidates from an unmarked hand image, based on an analysis by synthesis method and an image retrieval algorithm. We formulate the posture estimation problem as a nonlinear, many-to-many mapping problem in a high dimension space. A general algorithm called ISOSOM is proposed for nonlinear dimension reduction, applied to 3D hand pose reconstruction to establish the mapping relationships between the hand poses and the image features. In order to interpolate the intermediate posture values given the sparse sampling of ground-truth training data, the geometric map structure of the samples' manifold is generated. The experimental results show that the ISOSOM algorithm performs better than traditional image retrieval algorithms for hand pose estimation.

1 Introduction

Despite the rapid advances in computing communication and display technologies, the development of Human Computer Interaction (HCI) still lags behind. Gesture is a good candidate for the next generation input devices. It has the potential ability to relieve the interaction bottleneck between users and the computer. Vision-based gesture interpretation is a promising research area for this problem due to its passive and non-intrusive sensing properties.

Many approaches of 3D hand pose estimation to support gesture recognition may be classified into two categories: model-based approaches with 3D data [1] and appearance-based approaches with 2D data [2] [3]. Athitsos *et al.* [4] formulated the problem of hand pose estimation to a problem of image database indexing. Shimada *et al.* [5] generated 125 possible candidate poses with 128 view points with a 3D model of 23 degrees of freedom (DOF). The real input hand image was matched to pre-computed models with a transition network, and possible pose candidates were found for their hand tracking system.

In this research, we take an image retrieval approach based on analysis by synthesis method. It utilizes a 3D realistic hand model and renders it from different viewpoints to generate synthetic hand images. A set of possible candidates is found by comparing the real hand image with the synthesis images. The ground truth labels of the retrieved matches are used as hand pose candidates. Because hand pose estimation is such a complex and high-dimensional problem, the pose estimate representing the best match may not be correct. Thus, the retrieval

G. Bebis et al. (Eds.): ISVC 2005, LNCS 3804, pp. 630–635, 2005.

is considered successful if at least one of the candidates in top N matches is sufficiently close to the ground-truth (similar to [4]). If N is small enough, with additional distinguishable contextual information, it may be adequate for automatic initialization and re-initialization problems in hand tracking systems or sign language recognition systems, where the correct estimation could be found and the incorrect ones could be eliminated in the later tracking.

The hand is modeled as a 3D articulated object with 21 DOF of the joint angles (hand configuration) [1] and 6 DOF of global rotation and translations [1]. A hand pose is defined by a hand configuration augmented by the 3 DOF global rotation parameters. The main problem of analysis by synthesis is the complexity in such a high dimension space. The size of the synthesis database grows exponentially with respect to the parameter's accuracy. Even though the articulation of the hand is highly constrained, the complexity is still intractable for both database processing and image retrieval. Wu *et al.* [6] and Zhou *et al.* [7], for example, reduced the dimensionality to 6 or 7 based on data collected with the data glove.

In this paper, we formulate hand pose reconstruction as a nonlinear mapping problem between the angle vectors (hand configurations) and the images. Generally, such mapping is a many-to-many mapping in high dimension space. Due to occlusions, different hand poses could be rendered to the same images. On the other hand, the same pose is rendered from the different view points and generates many images. To simplify the problem, we eliminate the second case by augmenting the hand configuration vector with the 3 global rotation parameters. The mapping from the images to the augmented hand configurations becomes a one-to-many mapping problem between the image space and the augmented hand configuration space (the hand pose space). The dimensionality of image space can be reduced by feature extraction. Finally, we establish the one-to-many mapping between the feature space and the hand pose space with the proposed ISOSOM algorithm. The experimental results shows that our algorithm is better than traditional image retrieval algorithms.

The paper is organized as follows. The ISOSOM algorithm is proposed in Section 2. The experimental results are shown in Section 3. Finally, the conclusions are given in Section 4.

2 ISOSOM

Instead of representing each synthesis image by an isolated item in the database, the idea of this research is to cluster the similar vectors generated by similar poses together and use the ground-truth samples to generate an organized structure in low dimension space. With such structure, we can interpolate the intermediate vector. This will greatly reduce the complexity. Based on Kohonen's [8] Self-Organizing Map (SOM) and Tenenbaum's ISOMAP algorithm [9], we propose an ISOmetric Self-Organizing Mapping algorithm (ISOSOM). Instead of

[1] The translation parameters could be estimated by hand segmentation algorithms or neglected if translation and scale invariant features are adopted.

organizing the samples in the 2D grids by Euclidian distance, it utilizes the topological graph and geometric distance of the samples' manifold to define the metric relationships between samples and enable the SOM to follow better the topology of the underlying data set. The ISOSOM algorithm compresses information and automatically clusters the training samples in a low dimension space efficiently.

2.1 ISOSOM Initialization, Training, and Retrieval

Although the ISOSOM algorithm is robust with respect to the initialization, the appropriate initialization allows the algorithm to converge faster to the solution. Before the training, initial vectors associated with neurons on the ISOSOM map are linearly interpolated by the sample nodes of the manifold's topological graph.

We generate the topological graph of the manifold using the approach described in the first two steps of the ISOMAP algorithm. We define the graph G over all data points by connecting node i and j if i is one of the k nearest neighbors of j. We set the edge lengths equal to the Euclidean distance of i and j. On the graph, the distance of any two nodes is defined by the cost of shortest path between them. This distance is approximately the geometric distance on the manifold. Such distance preserves the high-dimension relationship of the samples in low dimension space.

The neurons of the ISOSOM map are connected with their neighbors on the low dimension manifold. In each training step, we randomly choose a sample vector from the training samples and find its Best-Matching Unit (BMU) in the ISOSOM map. Instead of using Euclidean distance, we measure the similarities of the input sample vector with each neuron vector in the ISOSOM map by the geometric distance between the two nodes on the manifold of the training samples. In order to measure this similarity, the nearest nodes of input vector and the neuron vector on the topological graph are retrieved by the Euclidean measurements. The shortest path between the two retrieved nodes on the manifold graph is approximated as the distance of the input vector and the neuron vector of the ISOSOM map. The BMU is the neuron on the ISOSOM map with the smallest geometric distance to the input training vector.

After obtaining the BMU, its associated vectors and its topological neighbors on the ISOSOM map are updated and moved closer to the input vector in the input space as in the classical SOM algorithm.

Given a vector with full components or partial components, similar neurons are found and sorted by the similarity measurement described above. The mask is used for the vector with partial components and the similarity measurements are also modified to handle such cases.

2.2 ISOSOM for Hand Pose Reconstruction

Due to the projection and the feature extraction, feature samples of the different poses are highly overlapping in the feature space. In order to separate the mixed-up features, we form large vectors consisting of both feature vectors and their

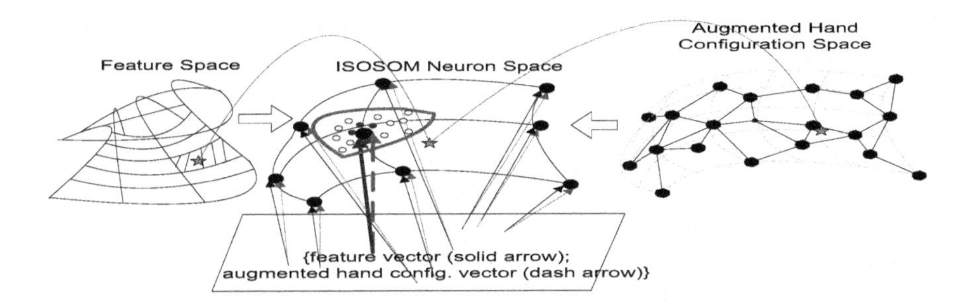

Fig. 1. The ISOSOM for Hand Pose Reconstruction

corresponding hand pose vectors. These vectors are used as training samples in our algorithm. In other words, after training, each neuron of the ISOSOM is associated with two vectors: the feature vector and the hand pose vector. Figure 1 gives an intuitive depiction of the ISOSOM map.

In the retrieval step, for a given input hand image, we calculate its feature vector. Using a mask to handle the missing hand pose components, we compare the similarity of this feature vector with all feature vectors associated with the ISOSOM neurons. The possible candidates of the hand pose are retrieved by the top n best matches. Because the mapping from the feature space to the hand pose space is a one-to-many mapping, one feature vector could have several possible hand pose candidates. This is desirable because it reflects the intrinsic nature of the mapping. The confidence of each candidate is also measured by the error measurement of ISOSOM.

3 Experimental Results

We generate a training database containing 25 commonly used poses. Three camera parameters (roll: $0° - 360°$, pitch: $-90° - 90°$, and yaw: $0° - 360°$, interval: $36°$) control the global rotation of the camera viewpoints. For each pose, 726 images are rendered in different view points and there are totally 18150 synthesis images in the database. For each hand configuration, 48 joint angle parameters are saved as the joint angle vector, which are 3 rotation parameters for hand, 9 parameters (3 rotation parameters for 3 joints respectively) for each finger and thumb. In addition to the 3 global rotation parameters of the camera, the hand pose vector is composed of these 51 parameters.

In the experiments, we adopt traditional Hu moments features [10] to represent given images. It should be pointed out that ISOSOM is a general algorithm for nonlinear mapping and dimension reduction, it does not specify the features. The following experimental shows that even with less descriptive Hu features, our algorithm still can achieve good estimation results.

We generate another synthesis database containing the same 25 poses but more dense samples for the testings. Because Hu features are invariant to in-plane rotation, translation, and scale, we focus on pitch and yaw rotation of

Table 1. The comparisons of the reconstruction performance by the traditional retrieval algorithm, the SOM and the ISOSOM algorithms. (The number of images measured: 21525.)

	The percentages of hits of the similar hand pose (except roll rotation)								
	Threshold 10			Threshold 20			Threshold 40		
Number	IR	SOM	ISOSOM	IR	SOM	ISOSOM	IR	SOM	ISOSOM
Top 40	23.21%	16.13%	36.73%	36.25%	34.27%	59.97%	47.93%	55.64%	78.01%
Top 80	27.13%	23.20%	48.71%	44.48%	44.52%	72.11%	58.36%	67.03%	86.85%
Top 120	29.28%	28.63%	55.77%	49.14%	50.97%	78.82%	63.69%	73.04%	91.64%
Top 160	31.41%	32.39%	61.14%	53.17%	55.37%	83.32%	68.39%	76.28%	94.33%
Top 200	33.35%	35.28%	65.26%	56.98%	58.62%	86.13%	72.78%	78.64%	95.56%

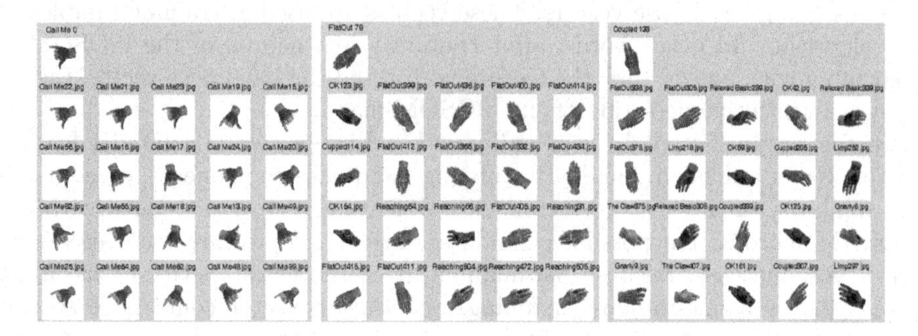

Fig. 2. The ISOSOM retrieval results (The name of each image indicates the hand configuration. The number for query image is the index number in the query dataset. The number for retrieved image is the index number in the ISOSOM neuron graph.)

the camera. Instead of using 36° as a interval, we use 9° as a interval for the pitch and yaw rotations. In this dense sampling database, 21525 hand images are generated as testing data set. It turns out that 92.33% of the testing images in the dense sampling database cannot find the exact match in the sparse sampling database (the training data set). Because the training samples are from the sparse sampling training set and the testing samples are from the dense sampling set, the difficulty for retrieving the correct hits increases.

We compare the performance of the traditional image retrieval algorithm (IR), SOM, and ISOSOM in Table 1. For a given testing image in the dense set, we count a hit if there are one or more hand poses in the retrieved poses which satisfy two criteria: first, they have a similar hand configuration as the query image; that is, the hand configuration's parameter components changes within a small range without changing the physical meaning of the posture. Second, the global rotation parameters are close to the query image within evaluation threshold 10°, 20° and 40° respectively. Table 1 shows that the performance of ISOSOM is the best among the three algorithms. Compared to the traditional image retrieval algorithm for the top 40 matches, the hit rates of ISOSOM increase around 13% − 31%. This also indicates that the ISOSOM algorithm not only has the clustering ability, but also has interpolation ability. The ISOSOM retrieval results are shown in figure 2. The first image is the query image. The rest 20 images are the retrieval results from the ISOSOM neurons.

4 Discussion and Conclusion

We have investigated a nonlinear mapping approach for 3D hand pose estimation from a single image. Traditional image retrieval algorithms just compare the image features in feature space and retrieve the top matches. Our approach utilizes both the feature vectors and their corresponding augmented hand configuration vectors to avoids the feature overlapping problem in nature. To deal with the complexity, we reduced the redundancy by clustering the similar feature vectors generated by similar poses together and represented them by neurons in our low dimension ISOSOM map. The ISOSOM algorithm could be considered as a variant of the SOM algorithm which aims at enabling SOM to follow the better topology of the underlying data set. The experimental results confirm that the ISOSOM algorithm greatly increase the hit rates in the pose retrievals.

References

1. Lee, J., Kunii, T.L.: Model-Based analysis of hand posture. IEEE Computer Graphics and Applications **15** (1995) 77–86.
2. Rosales, R., Athitsos, V., Sclaroff, S.: 3d hand pose reconstruction using specialized mappings. In: International Conference on Computer Vision (ICCV). (2001) 378–385.
3. Nolker, C., Ritter, H.: Visual recognition of continuous hand postures. IEEE Transactions on Neural Networks **13** (2002) 983–994.
4. Athitsos, V., Sclaroff, S.: An appearance-based framework for 3d hand shape classification and camera viewpoint estimation. In: Proceedings of the Fifth IEEE International Conference on Automatic Face and Gesture Recognition, Washington, DC, USA, IEEE Computer Society (2002) 45–50.
5. Shimada, N., Kimura, K., Shirai, Y.: Real-time 3d hand posture estimation based on 2d appearance retrieval using monocular camera. In: IEEE ICCV Workshop on Recognition, Analysis, and Tracking of Faces and Gestures in Real-Time Systems. (2001) 23–30.
6. Wu, Y., Lin, J.Y., Huang, T.S.: Capturing natural hand articulation. In: ICCV. (2001)
7. Zhou, H., Huang, T.S.: Tracking articulated hand motion with eigen dynamics analysis. In: Ninth IEEE International Conference on Computer Vision. (2003) 1102–1109.
8. Kohonen, T.: Self-Organizing Maps. Springer Series in Information Sciences (2001)
9. Tenenbaum, J.B., Silva, V.D., Langford, J.C.: A global geometric framework for nonlinear dimensionality reduction. Science (2000) 2319 –2323.
10. Hu, M.K.: Visual pattern recognition by moment invariants. IRE Trans. on Information Theory (1962) 179 –187.

A Motion Capture System for Sign Language Synthesis: Overview and Related Issues*

László Havasi[1] and Helga M. Szabó[2]

[1] PannonVision, Csap utca 4., H-6727 Szeged, Hungary
havasi@pannonvision.hu
[2] National Association of the Deaf, Benczúr utca 21, H-1068 Budapest, Hungary
szabo.helga@sinosz.hu

Abstract. HANDY[1] is a project for the synthesis of articulatory sign-language as used by the deaf. This paper describes a sub-project named HANDYCap, which is used as a prior stage to the actual sign-language synthesis. HANDYCap is a low-cost hand-motion capture and data-processing system which we use to enable semi-automatic construction of the sign database. Additionally, the paper gives a broad survey of the technical and linguistic issues relating to the signing task. The optical tracking system used for motion-capture is described, together with related issues. In performing the database-construction task it is necessary to pay attention to the linguistic background, as well as to the problems of loading and storing the data efficiently and correctly.

1 Introduction

The paper introduces the process and way of data from native signer to the sign data. This paper describes a part of a sign-language synthesis project which is necessary as a prior stage to the actual sign-synthesis. We outline the handling of sign-data from its origination (the symbols articulated by the native signer) to its intermediate destination, the sign database which is to be built up. The process is designed so as to enable a semi-automatic construction of the sign database. The digitization of a sign entails the capture of the hand-motions of the native signer. In our project, the motion information is then converted into a format appropriate for use by the subsequent sign-synthesis module. There are several previous publications on sign and gesture synthesis, motion planning and data representation; most of them however focus exclusively on either linguistic or on technical issues. In contrast, this overview attempts to concern itself both with all the technical tasks involved in sign capture, and also with the linguistic aspects necessary for generation of the sign database introduced in [1].

HANDYCap is based on the use of (relatively) low-cost optical motion capture hardware to capture the hand movement. Our other goal was to achieve real-time computation without the necessity for special high-performance computer hardware. In order to achieve correct results from motion capture (detecting movement paths

* This work is supported under contract no. TST-00014/2003 from the Hungarian Ministry of Education.

G. Bebis et al. (Eds.): ISVC 2005, LNCS 3804, pp. 636 – 641, 2005.

and relevant body parts) it is necessary to take account of the linguistic characteristics of sign language; and for the synthesis operation also, it is vital to generate grammatically correct utterances in sign language.

2 Why Is Sign Language Synthesis Important?

Sign synthesis is a way to achieve the conversion of a sign-language message sequence from a stored, textual form into the "fluid" medium used in conversation. In more and more countries, deaf persons have now gained recognition as a special language-minority group. This is quite justified since, for a number of reasons, their access to information using normal language is restricted. However, beyond this, many deaf people have difficulty in reading the written form of a spoken language. Sign synthesis may be grouped into two types: articulatory, where the output is synthesized by rules that are intended to correspond to the process by which humans articulate speech; and concatenative, where prerecorded signs (motions) are broken down into small segments that are recombined to create new signs.

Sign synthesis is today still an active research topic. There are reports on several re-search projects, and some commercial applications have been released. In Japan, two concatenative synthesis systems have been developed for a larger speech-to-text sys-tem by Hitachi and the Communications Research Laboratory. The companies Vcom3D and SignTel have released synthesis applications that generate a North-American variety of Signed English, with Vcom3D using motion capture data and SignTel using videos. A British company has developed a prototype captioning system named "Simon the Signer" [4]. The extended system known as ViSiCAST, which likewise generates signed English, uses concatenations of DataGlove data [5]. Sign-Synth is a prototype system which uses ASCII-Stokoe encoding for the underlying data representation and produces H-Anim compliant Web3D output.

3 Motion Capture

Some sign synthesis applications use synthetic signing [4], while others make use of recorded signs (captured motion) directly [6]. A possible method of capturing a sign is that the hand and other motions of the signer are tracked using several different input devices: an optical system (with markers on the face) for tracking facial expression, a magnetic body-suit for posture sensing, and data gloves for sensing hand and finger shapes [5].

In [2], the reader can find a good survey of the solution methods and the devices employed. The two main types are based on optical and on magnetic devices; at the present time neither type has a clear advantage over the other [3]. A short description of the technical parameters of both systems and the importance of these systems in sign language research can be found in [3]. The HANDYCap system uses three cameras, which operate at a high frame-rate of 120 Hz (120 frames/second). Two cameras are focused on the whole body, while the third one is focused only on the face and provides data for further processing (for sensing facial expressions).

The basis of the optical systems is the camera calibration, also called homography computation. It means that the intrinsic parameters (focal length, aspect ratio, principal point) and extrinsic parameters (rotation and translation) of the cameras are known and can be correlated to a world coordinate-frame. This computation can be accomplished using a calibration rig, which consists of a printed pattern (of a type designed to be easy to automatically detect) placed onto two orthogonal planes. The equation system is linear and can be solved using SVD (Singular Value Decomposition) or by other methods (e.g. Gold Standard) [7]. After calibration, the 3D coordinate computation is possible from coherent points on two cameras by using the triangulation method. The average and the maximal 3D errors of our system were found to be 2.3mm and 12mm, respectively. For body part localization the optical motion-tracking system records the positions and movements of markers placed on the subject's (signer's) body. The first task is the retargeting, which is the mathematical "fitting" of skeleton model parameters to the native signer's physical characteristics. Current solution is to waiting the signer in a predefined rest position while the system computes and fits model parameters from 3D coordinates.

The critical point of the optical system is the spatio-temporal tracking of the detected markers. The markers are easy to detect because their emitted light lies in a part of the infrared spectrum to which these digital cameras are very sensitive. The motion of a marker is called its trajectory; the computation to predict the position of the marker in the next frame is performed using the sliding-window technique from frame to frame. In the final step, the tracked 3D points will be fitted to the skeleton model to determine the model parameters (joint rotations) required during the movement; this task is solved by a non-linear optimization. Most of the above-mentioned tasks are challenging in themselves, and have given rise to a considerable amount of literature.

Because HANDYCap uses only two cameras for data-capture for the subsequent 3D computations, this restricts the number of body-markers which can be distinguished. We in fact placed markers on the signer's wrists, elbows, shoulders and on the lower part of the neck. This arrangement allows us to determine the movement of the hands and estimate the position on the head.

4 Sign Visualization

There are several methods for visualization (display of signing output): simple skeleton, VRML, anatomy-based modeling, and others. Briefly, our visualization engine uses a spline-based interpolated (B-spline) surface (Figure 1c) from the skeleton model (Figure 1a) and the predefined base point set around the bones (Figure 1b); these points can be generated easily with a simple rotation around the starting positions of the bones, and with a translation. Because the HANDY project focuses on sign language synthesis, our 3D model contains only the upper part of the body. This approach assists us to achieve real-time animation.

Thanks for the spline interpolation technique; the surface can in fact be dynamically modified during the animation. In our experiments using different orders for the splines a more realistic effect can be achieved around the joints. The hand is built up from 6 parts (surface segments), and every part is defined with 3D B-spline control lines (1D splines) and not with B-spline surfaces (2D splines).

The final visualization requires the support of the DirectX Direct3D software technology.

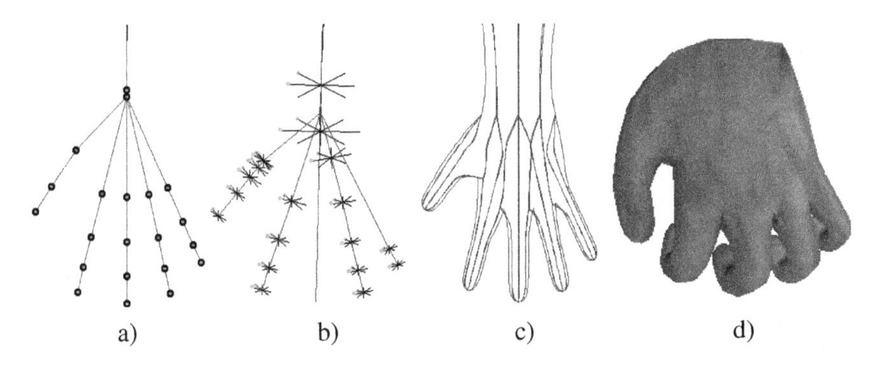

Fig. 1. Hand model for sign visualization: a) General skeleton model. b) Reference points around the bones (short illustration). c) B-spline control lines. d) Hand with texture.

5 Linguistic Issues Storing Data

As mentioned above, for efficient motion capture and sign synthesis an essential precondition is to carefully examine the inherent structure of signs. There are several distinct types of signs; a primary dichotomy is that signs can be one-handed or two-handed. It has also been suggested by many investigators that phonological units of sign languages are organized into syllables. Where two signs follow one another, either the handshapes or the movements can be assimilated – they are phonological processes in sign languages. Sign languages differ from spoken languages in having two distinct, anatomically similar articulators – namely, the two hands. However, while many signs do involve both hands, the hands do not have equal roles. We must reflect this fact when storing data in the HANDY database. In case of symmetrical two-handed signs both hands move independently during articulation of a sign, then both hands must be specified for the same handshape and the same movement (simultaneously or in alternation), and specialization for orientation must be symmetrical or identical. That's why the parameters for the active hand can be copied into the control for the weak hand, of course giving due consideration to the mirror image of the articulator itself, and the mirrored path of movement. In case of asymmetrical signs the two hands do not share the same specification for handshape, then the specification for the passive hand must belong to a restricted set.

Many significant similarities between oral and sign languages have been found to exist. Within the models of the inherent structure of signs, static (location) elements correspond to consonants, and dynamic (movement) elements correspond to vowels, much the same as an LML syllable may be compared to CVC.

The movement performed between the two points can be referred to as macro movement. This movement, which can be further divided into lexical movement and transitional movement, is characterized by the displacement of the hand between two distinct points in space. The purpose of the transitional movement is to bring the articulator(s) back to the starting position of the lexical (primary) movement which has just been completed; or, within signs, between adjacent lexical units; or to move the hands from a resting position to the point where the sign starts. Therefore this transitional type of movement is not stored in the database, in contrast with the lexical type movements. The single unidirectional movement, the repeated unidirectional movement and the cyclic movement constitute different categories of these.

There is also a type of movement in signs that can be referred to as micro movement (movement in fingers; handshape change; movement in fingers) Handshape changes can be involved only in finger configurations: from closed to open shapes, or vice versa. In detecting parameters of movement and handshape, HANDYCap must pay attention to all these phenomena. In a later phase, in order to generate fluent signed utterances we must pay attention to the management of some inflexions and other phonological processes. The shape of passive hand assimilates to the form of the active hand if two or more signs form a compound. Signs can be morphologically extremely complex too. Derivation causes changes at the sublexical level to result in systematic changes in meaning as well (derived forms of pronouns; change of aspects or action arts; changes to express plural, or differences in size). That is why it is necessary to survey the main cases of these processes. These parameters in HANDY must be modified manually, and so we can generate many variations from the basic signs.

6 Conversion of Motion into Database Format

Because rough motion in the captured data presents the possibility of some traps or errors, we have chosen a middle-way solution, namely that signs are constructed only semi-automatically from the captured motion. If we note some errors in the animation, we can then manually modify the appropriate parameter(s). This method also renders possible some retrospective investigations, e.g. on variable speed and movement.

For sign-generation, HANDY builds up signs from lexical and sublexical components stored in the database [1]. During sign editing, the operator first defines the start and end positions of a sign in the captured data. From this information the hand location can be determined. The handshape and hand orientation in the sign are adjusted manually. The advantage of the motion capture system appears during the motion planning. The highest-priority aim is the ability of the "clients" (deaf people) to understand the signing output.

The module which is principally responsible for realism in the generated signing is called the motion planner. The characteristics of lifelike animation have been studied e.g. in [8]. Generally the motion data is confined by keyframe-like constraints defined in the database [1]. In our case these keyframes are built up from sublexical elements and the points of motion trajectory; they form a lexical component in the database. In our implementation the motion planner uses spline (Bezier, or B-Spline) interpolation to approximate the captured trajectories. This results in a very smooth trajectory even when the captured motion data shows irregularities and variations (such fluctuations are inherent to natural live motion). The motion capture system was used to extract the properties of these small motions. We generated some "typical" additional fine motions from the differences between the captured motion and the spline interpolation. For improved naturalness, the motion planner module adds-on one of these components to the synthesized motion.

7 Conclusions

The aims of our research project are 3D sign synthesis, computer aided sign design and uniform sign-data representation, employing cost efficient methods.

The paper has surveyed the sign capture procedure from the input stage, the body-movements of the native signer, to the construction of the sign database. Most of the technical tasks involved have been summarized, together with the linguistic aspects. HANDYCap is based on a comparatively cheap optical motion capture system. It employs basically a two-camera (stereoscopic) system, which does set limits on the system's capabilities; our main goal however was not the complete motion capture which would be required for the purpose of concatenative sign synthesis. The technology which is now available allows researchers to simulate the real-time articulation of sign language with great fidelity.

References

1. Havasi, L., Szabó, H.: HANDY: Sign Language Synthesis from Sublexical Elements Based on an XML Data Representation. TSD, LNAI, Springer-Verlag, (2004) pp. 73-80
2. Moeslund, T. B.: Interacting With a Virtual World Through Motion Capture. In: Virtual interaction: interaction in virtual inhabited 3D worlds. Springer-Verlag, pp. 221-234.
3. Tyrone, M. E.: Overview of Capture Techniques for Studying Sign Language Phonetics. International Gesture Workshop, LNAI, Springer-Verlag, (2001), pp. 101-104
4. Kennaway, R.: Synthetic Animation of Deaf Signing Gestures. International Gesture Workshop, LNAI, Springer-Verlag, (2001), pp. 146-157
5. Verlinden, M., Tijsseling, C., Frowein, H.: A Signing Avatar on the WWW. International Gesture Workshop, LNAI, Springer-Verlag, (2001), pp. 169-172
6. Bangham, J.A.,Cox, S.J., Lincoln, M., Marshall, I., Tutt, M., Wells, M.: Signing for the Deaf Using Virtual Humans. IEE Seminar on Speech and language processing for disabled people, London (2000)
7. Hartley, R., Zisserman, A.: Multiple View Geometry in Computer Vision, Cambridge, Cam-bridge University Press (2003)
8. Kopp, S., Waschsmuth, I.: A Knowledge-based Approach for Lifelike Gesture Animation. European Conference on Artificial Intelligence (2000), pp. 663-667

Dynamic Visualization of Spatially Referenced Information

Wu Quan and Mao Lin Huang

Faculty of Information Technology, University of Technology, Sydney, Australia
{kevinqw, maolin}@it.uts.edu.au

Abstract. This paper proposes a dynamic visualization approach that combines the graph metaphor and the spatial metaphor for visualizing and navigating spatially referenced data. It provides users with a "marching" scheme for viewing a series of graphs G_1, G_2, ... G_n that are related to a spatial map. Moreover, It provides three types of navigation mechanisms. This dynamic visualization can facilitate the processes of spatially referenced data mining.

1 Introduction

The recent estimates show that over 80 percent of information today contains geospatial referencing, such as geographic coordinates, addresses, and postal codes [1]. Therefore, many researches [2, 3] have been done in discovering spatially related knowledge from the huge datasets, such as predicting the spread of a disease, finding crime hot spots, and detecting instability in traffic.

Many geographic information systems provide functions for generating spatial maps that can be used for viewing, referencing, exploration and manipulation of data that contains spatial attributes. We call these maps "spatial frame of references" that can significantly amplify the cognition process in identifying geographic locations. Graph visualization uses a graph metaphor to map the extracted patterns into one or more graphs. A good graph layout allows users to understand data much easier. Many recent applications like [4] and [5] have combined graph visualization with thematic maps for exploring spatially referenced data.

However, most of the existing visual spatial data mining methods separate the spatial metaphor from graph metaphor into two visual objects (such as windows, widgets). This, thereby, limits the correlation between two visual metaphors, which will probably cause two problems: 1) Lack of the overall context of visualization; 2) Impossibility of cross navigation.

M. Kreuseler and H. Schumann have proposed a new approach called *Marching Sphere* [6] in 2002, which integrated the spatial metaphor and the graph metaphor into a single visualization. While Marching Sphere is a good solution to combining two visual metaphors to visualize complex information, it has the following weaknesses: 1) the implementation of 3D graphics is computationally expensive in ordinary PCs; 2) it is practically difficult to navigate across 2D and 3D visual metaphors.

G. Bebis et al. (Eds.): ISVC 2005, LNCS 3804, pp. 642 – 646, 2005.

In this paper, we proposed a dynamic visualization called *Marching Graph* that replaces 3D spheres used in [6] with 2D graphs. We use spring layout algorithms to layout the data structure and allow users to "march" through the geospatial map interactively.

2 Terminology

Spatial Frame *SF:* is an interactive thematic map which consists of a set of spatial regions. We have $SF = \{R_1, R_2, \dots, R_n\}$. There is a independent graph G_i can be derived from a corresponding spatial region R_i, and it can be expressed by $R_i \rightarrow G_i$.

Spatial Region *R:* is a sub-area of the spatial frame. We define each spatial region as $R_i = (name_i, x_i, y_i, w_i, h_i, polygon_i, SF_{Ri})$, in which the $name_i$ is the identifier of the region, x_i *and* y_i are coordinators of the top-left point of the rectangle that just bounds the polygonal boundary of R_i, w_i and h_i is the width and height of the rectangle respectively, $polygon_i$ contains a series of the boundary points of the region, SF_{Ri} is a lower level nested spatial frame which contains the sub-regions information of R_i.

Circular Region *C(G_i):* is a display space which contains the drawing of a graph G_i.

Historic Trail *HT:* consists of a sequence of small circles displayed above the spatial frame that represent the recent history of explored graphs.

3 Technical Details

Marching Graph is implemented in Java. It displays a thematic map (the spatial frame) and a series of circular areas above the map (see Figure 1(a)). At a time only one circular area is fully opened with the green background color and the display of a graph

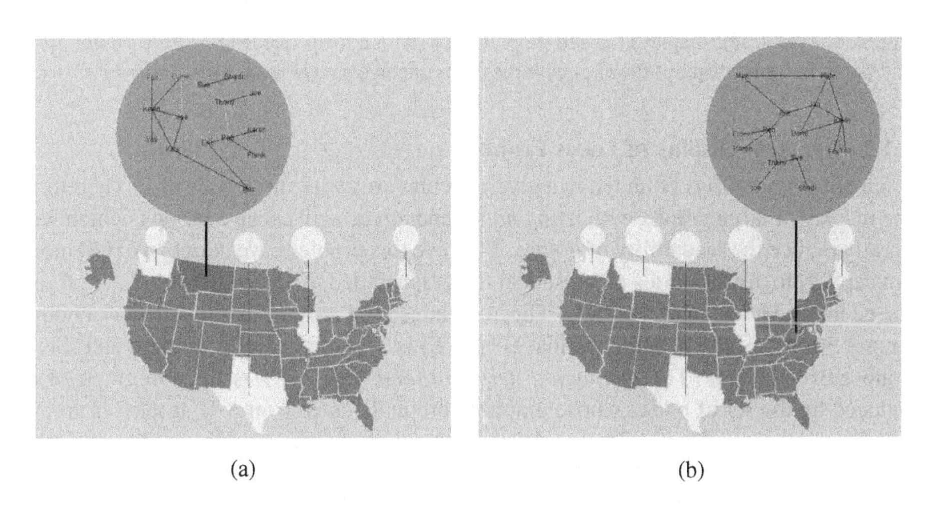

(a) (b)

Fig. 1. (a) A display of Marching Graph with the focus on "Montana" state. (b) A display of Marching Graph with state "West Virginia" focused.

layout $D(G_i)$, while other small yellow circular areas are displayed as a historic path of the navigation without the display of graph layouts.

3.1 Graph Visualization

We use graphs G_1, G_2, ... G_n to visually present the relational data that are associated with particular geographic regions on the thematic map. To generate such a visual metaphor we need to extract the implicit/explicit relational structures from the spatially referenced data. The modeling of such structures is essential for the analysis and process of data.

To visually represent the relational structures on the screen, we use a physical model called *force-directed layout* algorithm to draw the abstract graphs G_1, G_2,...G_n on a 2D geometric space according to the aesthetics rules that ensure the quality of layouts. Figure 2 shows examples of force-directed layout graphs produced by our visualization.

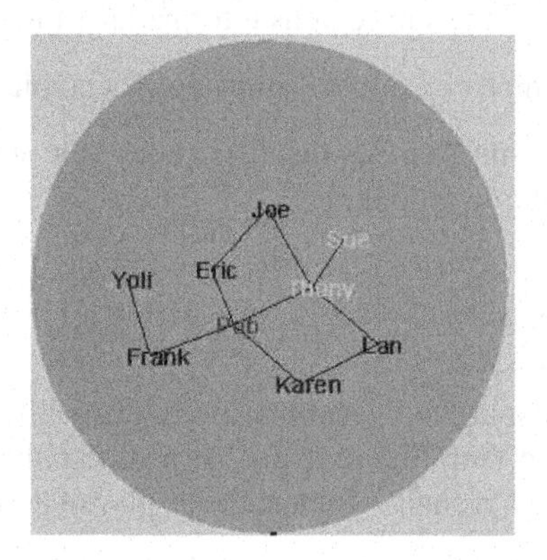

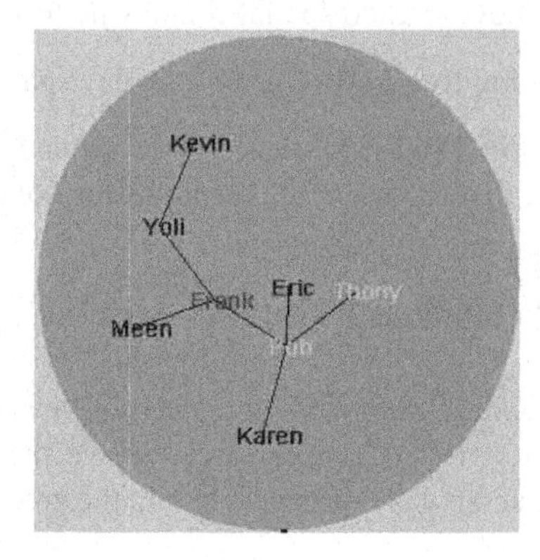

Fig. 2. The left frame displays the sub-graph G_i of G with a focus queue Q_i ={*Pob, Thony, Sue*}, and the right frame displays the G_{i+1} with the focus queue Q_{i+1} ={*Frank, Pob, Thony*}

3.1.1 Dynamic Display of Focus Frames

Each drawing $D(G_i)$ is bounded in a given circular area with the certain size. Therefore, the display of large graphs with many *nodes* and *edges* may cause overlaps, which will greatly reduce the readability of graphs. To solve this problem, we adopt an exploratory concept [7] to draw a series of subsets of the graph called *focus frames* F_1, F_2, ..., F_n on the geometric plane incrementally. This method is used only when the number of nodes excess 30 in the graph. Suppose that $G=(V, E)$ is a graph, $v \in V$ is a node, and d is a nonnegative integer. The *distance-d neighborhood* $N_d(v)$ of v is the sub-graph of G induced by the set of nodes whose graph-theoretic distance from v is at most d. In our implementation we have chosen d=2, and we write $N_2(v)$ as $N(v)$ and call it the *neighborhood* of v ($v \in N_2(v)$). Given a queue $Q=(v_1,v_2,...v_s)$ of nodes, and the current focus node $v \in N_2(v)$, the sub-graph of G induced by the union of $N_2(v)$ and Q is called a focus frame. The nodes $v_1,v_2,...v_s$ are the focus nodes of the focus frame.

3.1.2 Graphic Design and Positioning

To display the drawings $D(G_1)$, $D(G_2)$, …, $D(G_n)$ on the screen, we need to assign a set of graphical attributes, such as *shape, color, size, thickness, brightness, z-coordinator* etc, to the drawings for improving their visibility. To place the drawing of graph G_i in the visualization, two parameters are needed: 1) the position of its related geographic region of the map and 2) the amount of display space currently used. The graph position is given by a reference point of the map coordinate system. A graph is positioned by translating its local center point (i.e. the center of a polygon) into its reference point on the map. We draw a line to link the graph to its corresponding geographic region.

3.2 Navigation Within (and Cross) Visual Metaphors

The success of visual data retrieval and analysis depends very much on the ability of supporting a variety of exploration tasks provided by the visualization. In our visualization, the abstract relational data is represented by graph metaphors that are located above a spatial region of the spatial metaphor. Consequently, during the navigation the user usually maintains two focuses. One is on a particular region of the thematic map. Another is on a data item of the corresponding graph. These dual focuses are independent. In our visualization, there are three types of navigation: 1) Intra-Graph Navigation, 2) Inter-Graph Navigation, 3) Marching on the Map (cross metaphors navigation).

3.2.1 Marching on the Map

Our system provides users with a kind of marching effect when users navigate on the map. Particularly, we use the small symbolic circles to show the history of visited graphs. Also the sizes of symbolic graphs are different. The smaller the circle is, the earlier the visiting time is. During the "marching", we always maintain a *Historic Trail (HT)* showing the history of recent visits. This HT consists of a sequence of small circles in the display representing the recent history of explored graphs. Each recently visited graph is presented by a small yellow symbolic circle without the display of detailed layout of graph (see Figure 1(b)).

3.2.2 Intra-graph Navigation

Since the circular display area $C(G_i)$ assigned to a graph G_i is limited, it is unable to display a large number of nodes (say more than 30 nodes) comprehensively. Therefore, we adopt "filtering" technique to provide dynamic display of graphs. In a given circular area $C(G_i)$ of display, the user's view is focused on a small subset of the entire graph G_i. at any time. Figure 2 shows an example of the change of focus frames from F_i to F_{i+1} progressively.

3.2.3 Inter-graph Navigation

We also allow users to navigate across two graph layouts $D(G_i)$ and $D(G_{i+1})$ based on the inter-relationships among graphs. The user can move the focus over a small symbolic circle (see Figure 1(a)) to highlight it with different color ("blue" in our system). If the user clicks on this small circle, it will be enlarged with the display of detailed graph layout and the corresponding region on the map will be focused simultaneously.

4 Conclusion

This research was initially motivated by a health data mining application that attempts to predict the spread of diseases over Germany [6]. In the paper, we proposed a new visualization framework, called *Marching Graph* that uses a force-directed layout algorithm to draw the relational structure in a 2D geometric space. We allow users to "march" through the whole geospatial map, region by region, to find out particular data items of interest through the display and navigation of a series of relational structures presented by graphs $G_1, G_2, \ldots, G_n$. Moreover, we provide three types of navigation mechanisms that allow users to freely navigate through the complex information space across two visual metaphors.

References

1. MacEachren, A. M. & Kraak, M.: Research Challenges in Geovisualization. In Cartography and Geographic Information Science, Vol. 28, No.1, (2001) 3-12
2. Overbye, T. J. & Weber, J. D.: New Methods for the Visualization of Electric Power System Information. In IEEE Symposium on Information Visualization (InfoVis'00). (2000)
3. Shekhar, S., Chawla, S., Ravada, S., Fetterer, A., Liu, X. & Lu, C. T.: Spatial databases-accomplishments and research needs. Transactions on Knowledge and Data Engineering 11, (1999) 45-55
4. Keim, D. A., Noth, S. C., Panse, C. & Schneidewind, J.: Visualizing geographic information: VisualPoints vs Carto-Draw. Information visualization, 2 (2003) 58-67
5. Andrienko, G. L. & Andrienko, N. V.: Interactive maps for visual data exploration. International Journal for Geographical Information Science, 13(4) (1999) 355-374
6. Kreuseler, M. & Schumann, H.: A Flexible Approach for Visual Data Mining. In IEEE Transactions on Visualization and Computer Graphics, Vol. 8, No.1, January-March (2002)
7. Huang, M. L., Eades, P. & Lai, W.: On-Line Visualization and Navigation of the Global Web Structure. International Journal of Software Engineering and Knowledge Engineering, Vol. 13, No.1, (2003)

WYSIWYG-Tool Tips: Enhancing Tool Tips with Translucent Preview Bitmaps

Heiko Drewes and Albrecht Schmidt

Embedded Interaction Research Group,
Media Informatics, University of Munich, Germany
{albrecht, heiko}@hcilab.org, www.hcilab.org

Abstract. This paper suggests to enhance the concept of tool tips by presenting translucent preview bitmaps. The basic idea is to give the user a preview of what would happen when a certain operation is invoked. We have implemented two prototypes to evaluate the concept. One provides WYSIWYG (What You See Is What You Get) tool tips for documents and applications on the desktop. The second one is an application that provides previews of dialogs while browsing through the menu. Initial experience shows that this can provide a benefit for the user as she or he sees what is going to happen rather than only providing feedback on what has happened. This is in particular of interest to actions that can not be undone.

1 Introduction

A central rule when designing interactive systems is to give the user control over the system [1]. To feel comfortable and in control when interacting with a computer, it is necessary to have an expectation about what will happen as a result of the intended action. The user interface combined with the user's knowledge must allow to predict what a command or action will result in. In graphical user interfaces descriptive names of menu items give the user a hint what will happen when she or he is invoking this menu item. For further assistance of the users, it is common to provide more information about a menu item by displaying a tool tip. Such a tool tip (or balloon help) is a small window, which displays a textual or iconic description of what to expect when choosing the item under the current mouse cursor position.

It is hard to provide useful textual tool tips. On one hand they should be short so that the user can instantly recognize the message. On the other hand if the text in a tool tip is too long it becomes cumbersome to read all the text. Tool tips normally display the menu item text and do not carry more information. It is common to display additional help texts in the status bar of an application, but very often just the name of the menu item is repeated or the menu item text is made into a sentence., e.g. 'Save' and 'Saves the document'.

The following example shows shortcomings of current textual tool tips. The tool tip that commonly appears when the mouse cursor is over the tool bar button for saving a document in Microsoft Word says "Save Document". The resulting action on pressing the button is however different depending on whether the document was

G. Bebis et al. (Eds.): ISVC 2005, LNCS 3804, pp. 647 – 652, 2005.

already saved or whether it is the first time that the document is saved. In the first case no dialog will appear and the document will be saved in the background. In the second case a dialog will appear where the user can choose a name for the document. Similarly the resulting action on pressing the print button in the toolbar can not be determined from the label or tool tip in current applications. E.g. in Microsoft Word it commonly prints the whole document to the default printer whereas in the Adobe Acrobat Reader a dialog appears. This motivated the development of prototypes, where additionally to the tool tip a semi transparent bitmap preview of the result of the action is displayed.

For the convenience of the users, most software applications provide several ways to invoke the same dialog – from the menu, from a toolbar, from a property context menu or even from outside the application by the control panel. Multiple ways to the same dialog support the intuitive use. The other side of the coin is, that if a user is searching for a specific setting, she or he may end up again and again in the same dialog, which was searched for the specific setting already. Here too providing a preview of what is going to be displayed when selecting an option can make searching quicker.

2 Preview and Feedback

Feedback is an important topic for human computer interaction. Providing a confirmation that the intended action had taken place is reassuring for the user [1]. With the spread of computers the question in the users head shifted from 'Does the computer do this?' to 'How to get the computer to do this?'. So the answer to the question how to assist the user controlling a computer shifts from feedback to preview. A preview message like 'This will delete all your data' is more helpful to the user, than the feedback message 'All your data have been deleted'.

In cases where interaction with the computer has a permanent effect and where undo is not possible, feedback is too late for guiding the user. Typical tasks in desktop applications that have a permanent effect are printing or sending email. These actions can not be undone as they either change the physical world or have effects in areas where the user has no control anymore. When looking beyond desktop systems into physical computing or embedded computing this becomes even more critical, e.g. shutting down a pump in a power plant or accelerating a vehicle will in general have effects that are not easily reversible.

For communicating what is going to happen we considered different options for presentation, such as texts, icons, and graphics. From informal user interviews we learned that people are reluctant to read long tool tips and that icons require learning of their meaning. To make a preview work it has to be instantaneously recognizable by the user. Therefore the best options are images of what will happen. However presenting solid and large images on top of the application will hide information. This is an annoying effect with the existing small textual tool tips. Also solid images as a preview for dialogs can not be distinguished from the real dialog. The main two parameters of interest for WYSIWYG tool tips are the size and the transparency of the presented preview picture. To explore this further we have implemented prototypes.

3 Application Tool Tips

The basic concept of providing previews of dialogs that will appear is implemented in the application tool tip prototype. When moving the mouse over the toolbar a preview of the dialog, that would appear when this button is pressed, will be shown additionally to the textual tool tip (see figure 1). This is implemented similarly for menu items as menu tips. When a menu item is highlighted a preview of the dialog, which will appear when this action is chosen, is presented, see figure 2.

The application demonstrated is an empty Win32 application, generated by the framework of the integrated development environment, extended with the dialog preview. Based on this application example any application can be developed including WYSIWYG tool tips, but it could also be implemented into the operating system without the need to code it within any application. Whenever the mouse cursor stays a while over a button on the toolbar or an item of the menu, a translucent preview of the corresponding dialog appears at exactly the position it will appear when clicking the item. In our prototype we can change the value for transparency. An extensive discussion on the use of transparency can be found in [2]. Alternatively to the use of transparent visualization multiblending, as introduced in [3], could be used.

The save button of this application shows the typical behavior of applications. It behaves different depending on whether the document has been saved already or not. The first time a document is saved, the application pops up a save dialog to enter a filename. Pressing the save button again does not show a dialog but simply saves the document under the given name. This is reflected in the bitmap tooltip.

Presenting a preview of the dialog that will appear has two advantages. One is speed. The user can already see in the dialog preview if this provides the options she or he needs. In general this saves two clicks (one for opening the dialog and one for canceling the dialog) and the mouse movement in between. The second advantage is to avoid unwanted actions, e.g. when there is no preview for the save action it is clear that the user will not have the chance to give the document a new name.

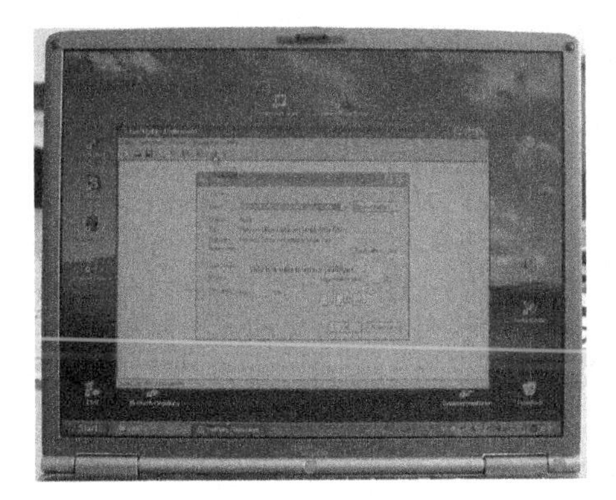

Fig. 1. When the mouse cursor is over a button in the toolbar, additionally to a textual tool tips a preview of the dialog to expect is visualized

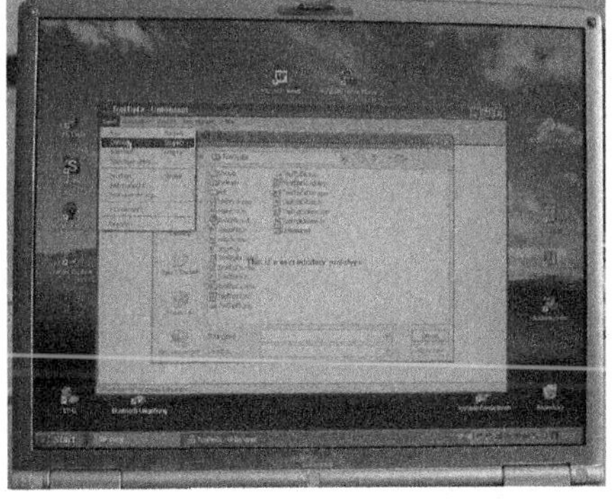

Fig. 2. While navigating in a menu a preview of the expected dialog is presented. This allows the user to avoid choosing menu items which lead to unwanted dialogs.

4 Desktop Tool Tips

In the desktop tool tips we generalize the concept to the preview of applications and documents. The basic idea demonstrated in this prototype is to provide a preview of what happens when an icon on the desktop is double clicked (or clicked depending on the setup of the system).

This prototype implements translucent previews of applications for the icons on the desktop. Whenever the mouse cursor stays a while over an icon on the desktop, a translucent preview of the application appears on the desktop. On an application icon the preview shows the opened application, on a document icon the preview shows the opened application with the document loaded.

In the current version of the prototype the previews are static images and taken from a preconfigured bitmap. For a product implementation we would expect that the application will store a bitmap of the window when closing together with the position where the window was presented. This can be done by the operation system using the representation in the display memory.

When moving the mouse pointer over a desktop icon of an application a preview of the application as it will open appears translucent on the screen. It is visualized on the desktop how and where the application would start. In figure 3 this is shown for a document. A translucent picture of the application, as last opened, is presented. In this case it shows that the document was open in full screen and would open in full screen if double clicked. We extended the prototypes for our experiment to allow to select the level of transparency and the size of the window.

5 Implementation of the Prototypes

Both prototypes are written for the Windows XP platform using C++ and Visual Studio. They make use of functionality of the operating system to overlay transparent windows. The prototypes are available for download in the internet on the project web page, see [4].

Both prototypes catch notifications from the operating system. The application tool tips prototype does this by overriding the GetMessageString-function of the framework, which is asking for a help text for the status bar. The desktop tool tips prototype runs in the background. It installs a system wide hook, which catches the notifications from the operating system for displaying and hiding a tool tip (TTN_SHOW, TTN_POP).

In contrast to the application tool tips prototype, where all message handling takes place within the same address space, the desktop tool tips prototype has to handle messages and share data across processes. As a technical consequence, the hook function must reside in a dynamic link library, as dynamic link libraries map their address space into each of its client processes, see [5].

6 Interviews with Users

We have used the prototypes to discuss the idea and design considerations for WYSIWYG tool tips. Over the last month we conducted informal interviews with users from different backgrounds.

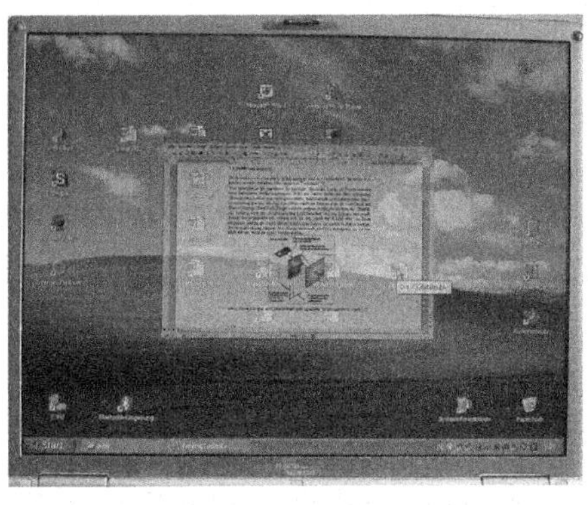

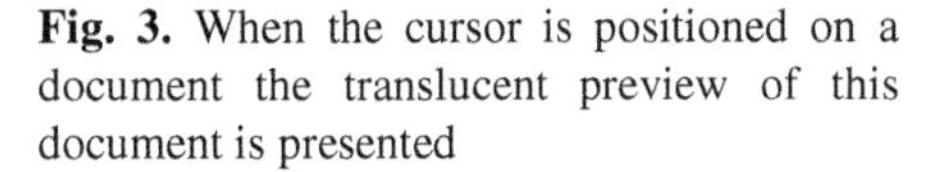

Fig. 3. When the cursor is positioned on a document the translucent preview of this document is presented

Fig. 4. In the interviews users could experiment with the settings of transparency and size of the preview

When presenting the application tool tips prototype, nearly all persons stated something like: "This is nice, but I know how an open or save dialog looks like. The idea will make more sense for dialogs which I do not know." This statements suggest that it is important to use a real and complex application for a larger user study. In general there was agreement that the presentation of the dialog to expect is providing additional control over the system as one knows what the system will do. Most users were happy with the visualization of the dialogs in real size and did not feel that it obstructs their view on the document, as they are navigating in a menu or a toolbar anyway.

Talking with the users about the desktop tool tips gave similar results. People normally know how an application looks like if they put it on their desktop, but they appreciated the preview of their documents. Some of the users asked for the preview of the documents laying on the desktop toolbar. Others asked for such previews in the explorer for documents like Word, PDF and HTML files. The existing thumbnail previews are helpful, but it is impossible to read a line of text in this reduced bitmap.

With regard to size most users preferred larger previews of documents and applications (50% to 100% of the original size) as this allowed them to really see the document details. In terms of transparency the preferred levels depended on the used background and on the size of the preview. It appears that users would like to have full size previews with a high level of transparency and that smaller previews are preferred with less transparency, see figure 3 for an example of a full screen 60% transparent document preview and figure 4 for a half size 30% transparency preview of the same document.

One of the interview partners gave a hint to a psychological effect. Clicking or double-clicking something invokes an action. If it is not clear what kind of action will take place, a shy user avoids to click anything; maybe this click will destroy something or change some settings and the system won't work anymore. Moving the mouse doesn't invoke any action and the preview of a dialog or an application does not have the obligation to read the displayed text and to decide, whether to press 'OK' or 'Cancel'.

7 Conclusions

In this paper we introduced the concept of translucent WYSIWYG tool tips to provide preview information on action that may happen if the user invokes a command. In two prototypical implementations we demonstrated how this can be realized within applications and on the desktop.

Providing a preview helps the user to anticipate what will happen if a button is pressed. From the participatory design sessions it can be concluded that such functionality is helpful when working with a new, unknown (e.g. guest account), or complex system.

The native Win32 implementation that was developed shows that current computer hardware has enough performance to provide such functionality.

Acknowledgments

This work has partly been conducted in the context of the research project Embedded Interaction ('Eingebettete Interaktion') which is funded by the DFG ('Deutsche Forschungsgemeinschaft').

References

1. B. Shneiderman, Designing the User Interface, Addison Wesley, 1998, Third Edition.
2. B. L. Harrison, G. Kurtenbach, K. J. Vicente: An experimental evaluation of transparent user interface tools and information content. Proc. of the 8th ACM symposium on User interface and software technology. Nov 95, Pittsburgh, p.81-90.
3. P. Baudisch, C. Gutwin: Multiblending: displaying overlapping window simultaneously without the drawbacks of alpha blending. Proc. of CHI 2004, April 2004, pp. 367-374.
4. WYSIWYG tool tip project and software download page: http://www.hcilab.org/projects/tooltips/tooltips.htm
5. Microsoft Developer Network: http://msdn.microsoft.com/library/default.asp?url=/library/en-us/winui/winui/windowsuserinterface/windowing/hooks/abouthooks.asp

Motion Visualization of Ultrasound Imaging

Dong C. Liu[1], Longlong Hou[1], and Paul S. Liu[2]

[1] College of Computer Science, Sichuan University, China
[2] Department of Electrical Engineering and Computer Science, University of California, Berkeley, USA

Abstract. This paper presents a method for motion visualization of medical ultrasound imaging based on line integral convolution (LIC) algorithms. The motion vector is derived by a hierarchical-type of block matching algorithm with sub-pixel accuracy. Then, the original pixel-based LIC algorithm has been extended to block-based processing and the proposed method can handle both the steady and unsteady motion where the size of the convolution filter is a function of the motion strength. Test results are reported to verify the effectiveness of the proposed approach both in synthetic and in-vivo ultrasound images. We also present a display technique to show the grey-scale LIC image for the motion direction and color coded motion amplitude to enhance the motion strength.

1 Introduction

Ultrasound has become a standard clinical tool in the diagnosis and treatment of illness and injury. Applications in the measurement of tissue motion include the identification of ischemia by analyzing heart, and arterial walls motion [1]. Furthermore, motion analysis of passive tissues, due to the heart or due to external forces such as compression, may show the response as a function of its elasticity, which is directly related to the healthiness of the tissue [2].

Virtually all methods proposed up to now for measuring tissue/flow motion rely on two approaches [3]: estimating the displacement/velocity field on B-mode images; and computing the flow velocity using Doppler techniques [3]. The derived velocity field from the current methods, however, has not been processed in such a way that the clinician can simultaneously visualize both the magnitude and direction for extracting the information of motion dynamics. In this paper, we apply the line integral convolution (LIC) algorithm [4] for motion visualization in medical ultrasound imaging.

2 Motion Detection from Image Registration

The use of 2-D correlation to estimate motion from ultrasound B-mode images was proposed by Akiyama *et al.* [5] for soft tissue motion and by Trahey *el al.* [6] for blood flow detection. The simplest method of the correlation estimation is the Sum-Absolute-Difference (SAD),

$$\text{SAD}\ (i_c, j_c; i, j) = \sum_{m=1}^{g_y} \sum_{n=1}^{g_x} | H^{(l)}(i_c, j_c; m, n) - H^{(l+1)}(i, j; m, n) | \qquad (1)$$

G. Bebis et al. (Eds.): ISVC 2005, LNCS 3804, pp. 653–658, 2005.

In Eqn (1), the registration error has been calculated between the windowed target region of $g_x \times g_y$ on frame l centered at (i_c,j_c) and a search region on frame l+1 centered at (i,j). The location (i_0,j_0) which has a minimum in SAD(i,j) for all (i,j) within a searching area of $S_x \times S_y$ determines the motion vector of (i_c,j_c) on the frame l.

In this report, we present a hierarchical type of search where the size of search area is a function of the initial SAD. Mathematically, this will be

$$(i^{(k)}, j^{(k)}) = \min_{(i,j)\in\Omega_k} \mathrm{SAD}(i_c, j_c; i, j) \tag{2}$$

and the minimum SAD corresponds to the pixel $(i^{(K-1)},j^{(K-1)})$ where

$$\begin{aligned} \Omega_k &= [i^{(k-1)} - c(K-k), i^{(k-1)} + c(K-k); K-k] \times \\ &[j^{(k-1)} - c(K-k), j^{(k-1)} + c(K-k); K-k] k = 1,2,\ldots K-1 \end{aligned} \tag{3}$$

defines the searching area used in the k-th iteration with $(i^{(0)},j^{(0)})=(i_c,j_c)$.

To achieve the sub-pixel accuracy of the minimum SAD (MSAD) approach, we present a quadratic interpolation to estimate the local minimum around the MSAD derived from Eqn (2). From three SAD values of h_1, h_2 and h_3 along the X direction where h_2 is the MSAD value with the x-component of x_2. The floating-number pixel with the local minimum can be obtained by

$$x^* = x_2 + \frac{(h_1 - h_3)\Delta_x}{2(h_1 - 2h_2 + h_3)} \tag{4}$$

where Δ_x is the x-interval of the last searching area. Similarly, the y component of the local minimum can be derived from three SAD values along the Y direction.

3 Algorithm Development of Motion Visualization

The LIC algorithm is a technique used in computer graphics and scientific visualization for imaging vector fields with image intensity and directional information, see [4] and some extensions in [7]. The basic idea of the LIC is displaying a texture that has been locally filtered according to the vector field. The LIC algorithm takes as input a vector field and a texture (e.g., a white noise bitmap) and outputs an image. The texture could represent the local vector field, i.e., the local texture captures the curvature features of the vector field.

3.1 Line Integral Convolution in Vector Field

The streamline vector of a velocity lattice is defined by the line segment which passes through the current lattice with a direction parallel to the velocity vector. In Fig. 1, the vector $(B^{(k)}, B^{(k+1)})$ is the streamline vector at the lattice k. Mathematically, the pixel $B^{(k+1)}$ can be written as, also see [4],

$$B^{(k+1)} = B^{(k)} + V^{(k)}\Delta S_k \tag{5}$$

where ΔS_k is the distance between $B^{(k)}$ to the boundary of the current lattice along $V^{(k)}$, or,

$$\Delta S_k = \min(S_x^{(k)}, S_y^{(k)}) \tag{6}$$

where

$$S_d^{(k)} = \max(0, \frac{C_d^{(k)} - B_d^{(k)}}{V_d^{(k)}}), \quad V_d^{(k)} \neq 0 \tag{7}$$

In Eqn (7) the subscript d represents the d-component (e.g., the x or y component from Eqn (6)) of a vector. If $V_x^{(k)} = V_y^{(k)} = 0$ then set $\Delta S_k = 0$ for a static velocity lattice and the search stops.

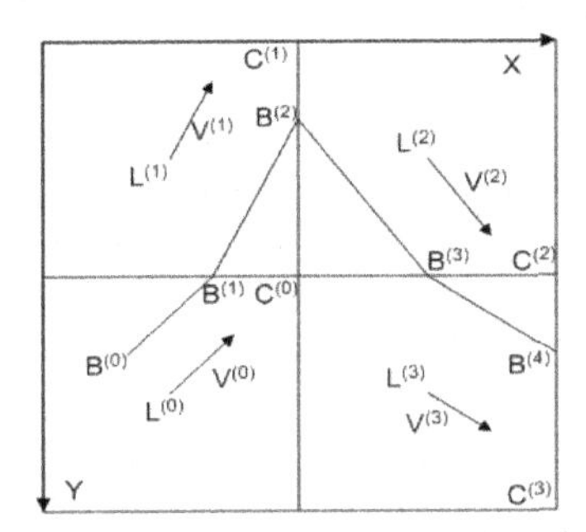

Fig. 1. A vector field which determines the local forward streamline

It is clear that, from Eqn (6), one needs two searches to determine the next streamline boundary, one in x and the other in y direction. The corner pixel $C^{(k)}$ used in Eqn (7) will be estimated along the velocity vector of the current lattice, also see Fig. 1.

The new velocity lattice $L^{(k+1)}$ could be determined by updating its center pixel:

$$L_x^{(k+1)} = \begin{cases} L_x^{(k)} + w_x \operatorname{sgn}(V_x^{(k)}) & \text{if } w_y \mid V_x^{(k)} \mid \geq w_x \mid V_y^{(k)} \mid \\ L_x^{(k)} & \text{otherwise} \end{cases} \tag{8}$$

and

$$L_y^{(k+1)} = \begin{cases} L_y^{(k)} + w_y \operatorname{sgn}(V_y^{(k)}) & \text{if } w_y \mid V_x^{(k)} \mid \leq w_x \mid V_y^{(k)} \mid \\ L_y^{(k)} & \text{otherwise} \end{cases} \tag{9}$$

where the function sgn(V) is equal to 1 or −1, according to the sign of ψ.

Therefore, for each pixel $F(x, y)$ in the output image, it will be determined by the 1D convolution of a filter kernel and the texture pixels along the local streamline indicated by the vector field from the following formula:

$$F(x, y) = \sum_{k=0}^{L} [h_k \sum_{i=0}^{N_1} I(i; B^{(k)}, B^{(k+1)})] + \sum_{k=0}^{L} [h_k^{'} \sum_{i=0}^{N_2} I(i; B_{-1}^{(k)}, B_{-1}^{(k+1)})] \tag{10}$$

where h_k is a line integral of a convolution kernel $h(\omega)$,

$$h_k = \int_{S_k}^{S_{k+1}} h(\omega)d\omega \tag{11}$$

where $S_{k+1} = S_k + \Delta S_k$, $S_0 = 0$ and ΔS_k is defined in Eqn (6). The value $I(i;B^{(k)},B^{(k+1)})$ of Eqn (10) is the i-th texture pixel between the line segment $B^{(k)}$ and $B^{(k+1)}$, where there are $N_1 + 1$ pixels.

The size of the velocity lattice (w_x,w_y) in Eqns (8) and (9) is a function of the motion vector, i.e., using a larger lattice in convolution for a stronger motion. To have a smooth change of the size of the velocity lattice, we apply a sigmoid function $A(v)$ to be the area of the velocity lattice,

$$A(v) = \frac{A_{\max}}{1+e^{-a(v-v_0)}} \qquad a = \begin{cases} a_1 & \text{if } v \geq v_0 \\ a_2 & \text{if } v < v_0 \end{cases} \tag{12}$$

where $a_1 = \alpha a_2$, $\alpha \geq 1$ defines a constant to change the shape so that the stronger motion always has a longer convolution kernel. The two unknown v_0 and a_2 in Eqn (12) can be computed from the following conditions: $A(0)=A_{\min}$ and $A(v_{\max})=A_{\max}$-0.5 where $A_{\max}$ is the maximal area of the velocity lattice. The window size w is then the square root of A.

3.2 Display of Motion Dynamics

In this Section we will apply the color transparency to the grey-scale LIC image and color coded motion amplitude to enhance the motion strength on display. Mathematically, the color transparency image could be seen as an interpolation between I_1, the grey scale LIC image and the color coded I_2, the motion amplitude image:

$$I_{(r,g,b)} = (1-\beta)I_1 + \beta\, C[I_2]_{(r,g,b)} \tag{13}$$

Where $C[.]_{(r,g,b)}$ denotes a color map and β is the transmission coefficient ranged from 0 to 1.

As discussed in [1] the radial and the tangential components of a motion vector can represent the contraction (expansion) and the rotational motion along a predefined direction vector. In our application, we can define an examined box centered at (x_c,y_c) and oriented along a vector starting from (x_0,y_0), see Fig. 2a. The radial and the tangential velocity components V_r and V_t will be

$$V_r = (\vec{V} \bullet \vec{R})/|\vec{R}| \quad \text{and} \quad V_t = \text{sgn}(\vec{V} \times \vec{R})\sqrt{|\vec{V}|^2 - (V_r)^2} \tag{14}$$

where $\vec{R}$ is the position vector of $(x_c$-x_0, y_c-$y_0)$ and sgn($\vec{A}$) is equal to one if the z-component of $\vec{A}$ is positive; otherwise it's negative one.

4 Computer Simulations and Results

Because the accuracy of the motion detection is the key to a high quality LIC image, we have investigated the detected error of MSAD-based methods by looking at the angular error between the theoretical and the estimated motion vectors,

$$\Phi = \arccos\left(\frac{\vec{V}_{ref} \bullet \vec{V}_{est}}{|\vec{V}_{ref}||\vec{V}_{est}|}\right) \tag{15}$$

To obtain moving tissues governed by known motion vectors, we make a sequence of synthetic images as follows: start from a phantom speckle image and then generate more images by shifting and interpolating with respect to its previous image with predefined motion patterns.

Simulation results show that angular error has a range from 4 to 20 degrees corresponding to the local motion of 5.5 to 1 pixel shifting when we apply a 24x24 hierarchical MSAD search. The LIC imaging of a simulated rotational field derived from theoretical motion vectors is visually the same as that from MSAD search.

Finally, we tested our motion visualization algorithms to a sequence of cardiac images acquired from a Siemens Elegra system. In Fig. 2, the user is asked to draw a region of interest with significant motion and the LIC algorithm only works for that region.

Fig. 2a shows the detected motion vectors superimposed on the original image. Fig. 2b shows the LIC image which was derived by the particle flow going through seven successive image frames. In Fig. 2b the motion intensity has been color coded and blended with the grey scale LIC texture where brown is used as background (i.e., zero to low velocity) and green for motion intensity changes.

At the bottom of Fig. 2 we show the radial and tangential velocity components within a used defined ROI and display them as a function of time. In the left radial velocity panel, the motion profile looks like a sinusoidal which means the local tissue in this ROI moves back and forth in a radial manner. The tangential velocity curve in the right panel is low and flat because, in this case, the tissue is moving almost in a radial manner inside the ROI.

Consequently, we have proposed motion visualization algorithms based on the LIC technique for ultrasound imaging. The LIC image with reliable motion fields can display motion patterns with more information in direction, amplitude, singularity. It also displays the interface of different velocity fields, which may not be obtained from the conventional B-mode and color-flow ultrasound imaging.

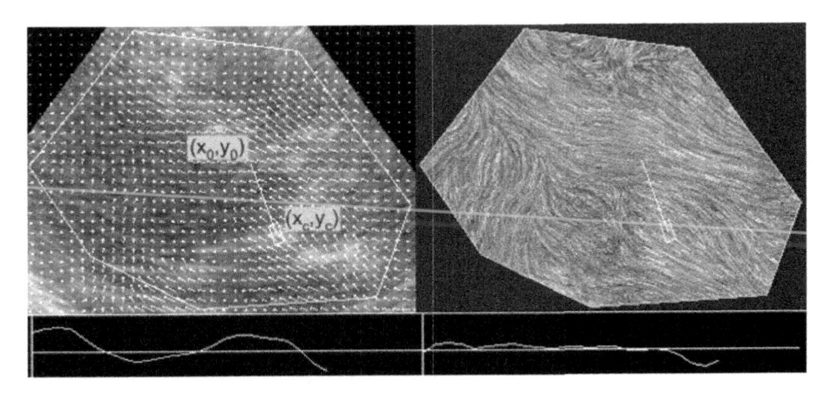

Fig. 2. a. Derived velocity field plus a display of radial velocity component as a function of time; **b.** The color transparency LIC image plus a display of tangential velocity component

References

1. Mailloux G.E., Bleau A., Bertrand M., Petitclerc R.: Computer Analysis of Heart Motion from Two-dimensional Echocardiograms, IEEE Trans. Biomed. Eng. 34, (1987) 356–364
2. O'Donnell M., Skovoroda A.R., Shapo B.M., Emelianov S.Y.: Internal Displacement and Strain Imaging Using Ultrasonic Speckle Tracking, IEEE Trans. Ultrason., Ferrolec. Freq. Contr., 41, (1994) 314–325
3. Hein I.A., O'Brien W.O.: Current Time-Domain Methods for Assessing Tissue Motion by Analysis from Reflected Ultrasound Echoes – A Review, IEEE Trans. Ultrason., Ferrolec. Freq. Contr., 40, (1993) 84–102
4. Cabral B., Leedom C.: Imaging Vector Fields Using Line Integral Convolution, Computer Graphics Proc., (1993) 263-270
5. Akiyama I., Hayama A., Nakajima M.: Movement Analysis of Soft Tissues by Speckle Patterns, JSUM Proc. (1986) 615–616
6. Trahey G.E., Allison J.W., Von Ramm O.T.: Angle Independent Ultrasonic Detection of Blood Flow, IEEE Trans. Biomed. Eng. 34, (1987) 965–967
7. Forssell L.K., Cohen S.D.: Using Line Integral Convolution for Flow Visualization: Curvilinear Grids, Variable-Speed Animation, and Unsteady Flows, IEEE Trans. Visualization and Comp. Graphics, 1, (1995) 133-141

Two Novel Complete Sets of Similarity Invariants

Hongchuan Yu and Mohammed Bennamoun

School of Computer Science and Software Engineering,
University of Western Australia, Perth WA6009, Australia
{yu, bennamou}@csse.uwa.edu.au

Abstract. In this paper, we propose two complete sets of similarity invariant descriptors under the Fourier-Mellin Transform and the Analytical Fourier-Mellin Transform (AFMT) frameworks respectively. Furthermore, their numerical properties are presented and be revealed through image reconstruction. Experimental results indicate that our proposed invariant descriptors can fully reconstruct the original image eliminating any existing similarity transformation (such as rotation, translation and scale) from the original image.

1 Introduction

A central issue in pattern recognition is the recognition of objects independently of their position, orientation and scale. For this purpose, the extraction of invariant descriptions with respect to similarity transformations remains a crucial challenge. It is important that the invariants fulfill certain criteria such as low computational complexity, numerical stability and completeness [1-3]. The first two criteria are easy to be understood while the third criterion is generally ignored. Indeed the completeness is one of important criteria for the invariant evaluation. The complete invariant means that two objects have the same form if and only if their invariant descriptions are the same. Whereas the invariant property is only relative to a certain transformation. It may only contain partial information of an object and not the whole information. Thus, invariant description based on partial information of an object is usually prone to an incorrect recognition. It is clear that the complete set of invariants can effectively be used for an accurate object discrimination. Nevertheless, many invariant descriptors are incomplete [4], such as geometric moments, complex moments, Legendre moments and Zernike moments. In this paper, we will pursue the research line of Brandt and Lin in [2,6] and Ghorbel in [3] to develop two novel complete sets of hybrid invariants with respect to similarity transformations, and further give some numerical problems of our proposed hybrid invariants. For evaluation, the proposed complete invariants are used to reconstruct image. This because when describing an image by a set of invariants it is very useful to investigate which invariants give rise to which characteristics of the image or vice versa. Indeed, there exist some successful examples of image reconstruction by the invariant descriptors [4,5].

The paper is organized as follows: two complete sets of similarity invariants are first presented in Section 2. Then, some numerical properties (or problems) of the

G. Bebis et al. (Eds.): ISVC 2005, LNCS 3804, pp. 659 – 665, 2005.

proposed hybrid complete invariants are presented in Section 3. Image reconstruction and experimental analysis are presented in Section 4. Finally, our conclusions and the future works are given in Section 5.

2 Proposed Complete Invariants

2.1 Translation

The Taylor Invariant Descriptor [2]:
With this invariant descriptor, the basic idea is to eliminate the linear part of the phase spectrum by subtracting the linear phase from the phase spectrum. Let $F(u,v)$ be the Fourier transform of an image $I(x,y)$, and $\phi(u,v)$ be its phase spectrum. The following complex function is called the Taylor invariant,

$$F_T(u,v) = \exp(-j(au+bv))\, F(u,v), \tag{1a}$$

where, a and b are respectively the derivatives with respect to u and v of $\phi(u,v)$ at the origin (0,0), i.e. $a = \phi_u(0,0)$, $b = \phi_v(0,0)$. Due to the property of reciprocal scaling, it can be modified as follows:

$$F_T(u,v) = (u^2+v^2)\, F(u,v) \exp(-j(au+bv)). \tag{1b}$$

The Hessian Invariant Descriptor [2]:
With this invariant descriptor, the basic idea is to differentiate the phase spectrum twice so as to eliminate the linear phase. It can be written in a vector form as follows,

$$F_H(u,v) = (|F(u,v)|, \phi_{uu}(u,v), \phi_{uv}(u,v), \phi_{vv}(u,v))^T. \tag{2a}$$

Due to the rotational symmetry and the reciprocal scaling, it is modified as follows,

$$H(u,v) = \Omega(u,v)\, F_H(u,v), \tag{2b}$$

where, the definition of $\Omega(u,v)$ refers to [2]. $H(u,v)$ is referred to as the **Symmetric Hessian Invariant**.

2.2 Rotation and Scaling

In [6], the Fourier-Mellin transform was adopted to construct the rotation and scaling invariants. First the image $I(x,y)$ is mapped to its corresponding Log-polar image $I(\rho,\theta)$ with its Fourier transform $F(u,v)$. The complete rotation and scaling invariant is then obtained through the application of the Taylor invariant of Eq.(1a) to $I(\rho,\theta)$,

$$M_T(u,v) = \exp(-j(au+bv))\, F(u,v). \tag{3}$$

$M_T(u,v)$ is called the **Mellin-Taylor invariant**. Similarly, one can also apply the Hessian invariant of Eq.(2a) to $I(\rho,\theta)$ to get the Mellin-Hessian invariant $M_H(u,v)$.

In [3], the Analytical Fourier-Mellin Transform (AFMT) was adopted to construct a complete invariant to rotation and scaling. Different from the Fourier-Mellin transform, the AFMT adopts the **polar coordinate** instead of the **Log-polar coordinate**. Its definition and inverse transform refer to [3]. Under the AFMT, the rotation and scaling transform in a polar coordinate, i.e. $I_1(r,\varphi) = I_0(\lambda r,\varphi+\beta)$, are transformed through the AFMT as follows,

$$AF_1(u,v) = \lambda^{-c+ju} \exp(jv\beta)\, AF_0(u,v). \tag{4}$$

It can be noted that the magnitude spectrum is no longer invariant to scaling because of the λ^{-c} term. Several of the AFMT numerical algorithms were presented in [7].

The basic idea of the AFMT complete invariant in [3] is to eliminate the scaling term λ^{-c+ju} and the linear phase $\exp(jv\beta)$ in Eq(4). On this basis, the **AFMT complete invariant** with respect to rotation and scaling is defined as follows,

$$AI(u,v) = AF(0,0)^{\frac{-c+ju}{c}} \exp\left(-jv\arg\left(AF(0,1)\right)\right) AF(u,v). \tag{5}$$

2.3 Proposed Hybrid Complete Invariants

When considering the translation, rotation and scaling together, we can apply the translation property of Fourier transform into the complex domain to combine the translational invariant with the rotation and scaling invariant to construct a hybrid complete invariant as follows,

$$S(\cdot) = M_T(F_T(\cdot)), \tag{6}$$

where, $M_T(\cdot)$ is as defined in Eq.(3) and applied to a complex spectrum, and $F_T(\cdot)$ is as defined in Eq.(1) and applied to a real image. Similarly, we can also construct another hybrid invariant based on the Mellin-Hessian invariant, i.e. $M_H(F_T(\cdot))$. Accordingly, because $M_T(\cdot)$ (or $M_H(\cdot)$) is applied directly to a complex spectra but not separately to a magnitude spectrum and a phase spectrum, the resulting hybrid invariant of Eq.(6) is complete.

Similarly, we can also exploit Eq.(4) in the complex domain to construct a hybrid descriptor under the AFMT. But then, due to the reciprocal scaling property of the Fourier transform, i.e. $F(I(\lambda x,\lambda y)) = \lambda^{-2}F(\lambda^{-1}u,\lambda^{-1}v)$, when the property of Eq.(4) is applied in the polar domain of the Fourier spectra, it would be modified as follows,

$$AF_1(k,w) = \lambda^{c-2-jk} \exp(jw\beta)\, AF_0(k,w). \tag{7}$$

The AFMT invariant of Eq.(5) is also modified as follows,

$$AI(k,w) = \left|AF(0,0)\right|^{\frac{-c+2+jk}{c-2}} \exp\left(-jw\arg\left(AF(0,1)\right)\right) AF(k,w). \tag{8}$$

By the same manner as Eq.(6), we can construct a hybrid complete invariant under the AFMT scheme as follows,

$$S(\cdot) = AI(F_T(\cdot)). \tag{9}$$

3 Numerical Problems of Our Proposed Hybrid Invariants

3.1 Scaling Invariant Problem

Consider the complete invariant $S(k,w)$ of Eq.(6). Under the Fourier-Mellin transform scheme, the similarity transform is eliminated through the elimination of the linear phase in $S(k,w)$. Indeed, the elimination of the linear phase only results in a cyclic shift but not eliminates the scale factor in the original domain. We refer to it as the

scaling invariant problem of the Fourier-Mellin transform. This can be justified as follows.

The key idea is that converting $I(x,y)$ to Log-polar coordinates $I(\rho,\theta)$ will change the domain of I in the scale dimension as $(-\infty, \max\{\ln(x^2+y^2)^{0.5}\}]$, which is infinite, while the length of the discrete sampling on $I(\rho,\theta)$ is finite. Therefore, eliminating the linear phase $\exp(ju\ln\lambda)$ will result in a circular shift of I in the spatial finite domain. Since the reconstructed I is not infinite. This is summarized as follows.

Proposition 1. Eliminating the linear phase cannot overcome the scaling factor under the Fourier-Mellin Transform scheme.

Because of the scaling invariant problem, the Fourier-Mellin transform results in a circular shift in the scaling dimension, while the Analytical Fourier-Mellin transform can alleviate this problem. Expanding the reciprocal scaling formula of AFMT can yield to, $AFMT(I(\lambda r,\varphi)) = \lambda^{-c} \exp(ju\ln\lambda)\, AF(u,v)$. It can be noted that when the linear phase $\exp(ju\ln\lambda)$ results in a circular shift in the scaling dimension, λ^{-c} can make the magnitude of AFMT reciprocally scaled and the coordinate u needs not to be reciprocally scaled. This is different from the reciprocal scaling property of Fourier transform. When λ^{-c} is eliminated in Eq.(9), the contraction or dilation can be eliminated but not converted to a circular shift after taking the inverse AFMT. This can effectively alleviate the circular shift of scaling, which results from the linear phase $\exp(ju\ln\lambda)$.

3.2 Phase Diffusion Problem

In the complete invariant of Eq.(6), eliminating the linear phase usually brings about the phase diffusion in the phase spectrum. The chief reason is that the complete invariant of Eq.(6) requires the estimated coefficients of the linear phase to be integer.

Our starting point is the following two well-known propositions, (1) Discrete sampling results in a periodic spectrum; (2) The periodic signal results in a discrete spectrum. When the phase $\phi(u,v)$ is linearly modified as, $\phi_c(u,v) = \phi(u,v) - au - bv$, the resulting phase $\phi_c(u,v)$ is required to be periodic modulo 2π, i.e. $\phi_c(u,v) \bmod (2\pi) = 0$. In general, a finite spatial signal (such as an image) is always regarded as a periodic signal. This results in a discrete spectrum. Due to the discrete spectrum, the magnitude is zero in between integer grids, and the phase in between integer grids is undefined. Thus, the above equation can be rewritten as follows,

$$(\phi(2\pi u/M, 2\pi v/N) - 2\pi(au/M + bv/N)) \bmod (2\pi) = 0,$$

where $u = 0$ or M, and $v = 0$ or N. For this reason, in the Taylor or Hessian invariants, the centroid of the phase spectrum should correspond to an integral cyclic translation in the spatial image plane. This is summarized as follows.

Proposition 2. The coefficients of the linear phase should be integers, and correspond to an integral circular translation in the original coordinate plane.

Because the Mellin-Taylor invariant is applied directly to a complex frequency domain in Eq.(6), the linear phase estimate becomes very sensitive to the centroid of the phase spectrum. The inaccurate estimate fails to make the resulting phase periodic modulo 2π. Thus, this results in a diffused spectrum. From the above analysis, one can see that the main error of Eq.(6) is from the linear phase estimate and the scaling factor.

With the complete invariant of Eq.(9), the phase diffusion problem can be avoided. Considering Eq.(8), one can note that only the linear phase coefficient of rotation is estimated, which is $AF(0,1)$. Because the spectrum $AF(k,w)$ is a discrete spectrum, thus, $(2\pi AF(0,1)) \bmod (2\pi) = 0$. It is clear that no phase diffusion takes place. The main error of Eq.(9) is from the scaling problem, though it is alleviated.

4 Image Reconstruction and Analysis

Image reconstruction consists in the adoption of the inverse procedure that was used to compute the hybrid complete invariant. For comparison, the numerical procedures of the hybrid invariant computation and reconstruction are briefly described in Fig.1.

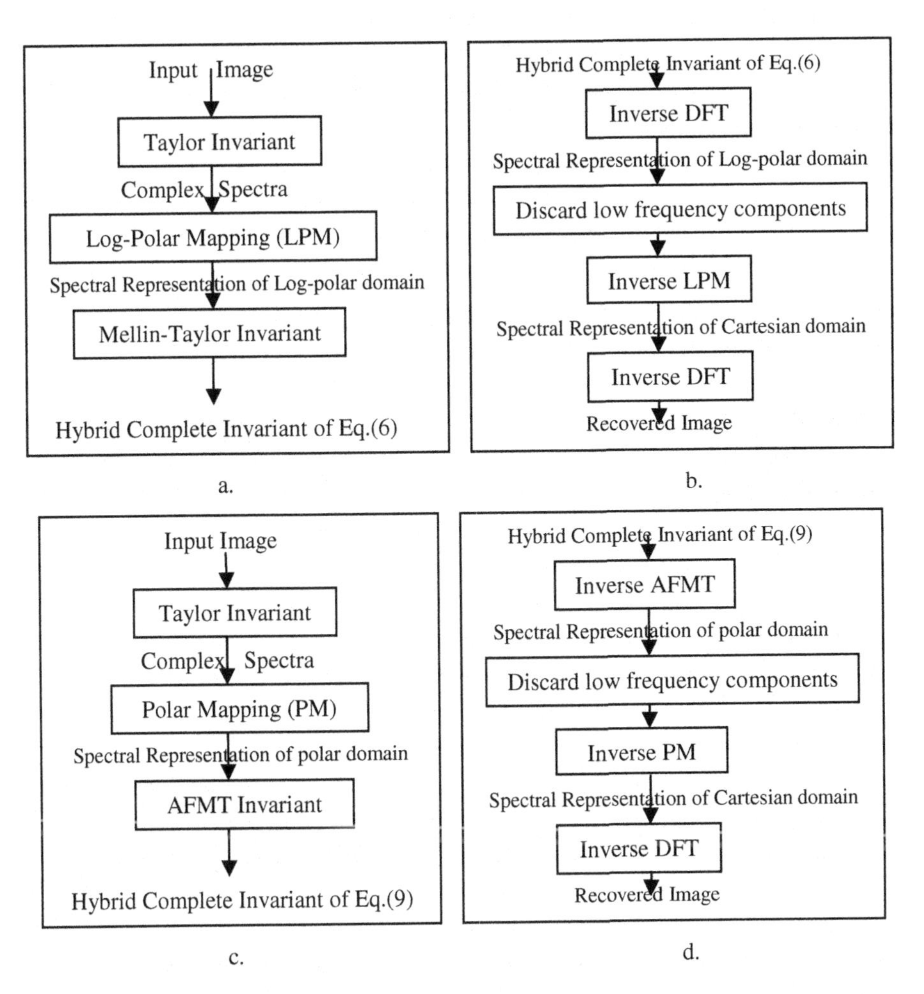

Fig. 1. The computational procedures of the complete invariants of Eq.(6) and Eq.(9) are shown in (a) and (c), while image reconstruction procedures based on Eq.(6) and Eq.(9) are shown in (b) and (d) respectively

The **Zero-Padding Approach** for discarding these low frequency components: **1)** Extend the size of $F_T(\rho,\theta)$ (or $F_T(r,\varphi)$) and pad $F_T(\rho,\theta)$ (or $F_T(r,\varphi)$) with zero in the frequency Log-polar (polar) domain along the scale dimension; **2)** Take the DFT (or AFMT) of the padded $F_T(\rho,\theta)$ (or $F_T(r,\varphi)$). This will lead to a more finely sampled version of the continuous Fourier transform (or continuous AFMT); **3)** Compute the hybrid invariant $S(k,w)$ of Eq.(6) (or Eq.(9)); **4)** Take the inverse DFT (or inverse AFMT) of $S(k,w)$; **5)** Select the original size of the scale dimension in $F_T(\rho,\theta)$ (or $F_T(r,\varphi)$), i.e. $[0,\rho_{max}]$ or $[0,r_{max}]$.

The zero-padding has the effect of adding a large gap between the low frequency and the high frequency domains in $F_T(\rho,\theta)$ (or $F_T(r,\varphi)$). By selecting the original size in the scale dimension, we can discard those low frequency components.

On the other hand, since the DC component in the frequency Cartesian domain $F_T(u,v)$ corresponds to $\rho = 0$ (or $r = 0$) in the frequency Log-polar (or polar) domain $F_T(\rho,\theta)$ (or $F_T(r,\varphi)$), and the magnitude spectrum of $F_T(u,v)$ follows an approximately negative exponential distribution around the DC component. Thus, discarding some DC components resulted in the reconstructed image darker than the original, and a change of some essential structure (similar to an affine transform). One can observe that the aspect ratios of Fig.(2e,2f) and Fig.(3e,3f) are slightly different from the original images in Fig.1. Furthermore, one can also note that the aspect ratios and gray levels are also slightly different between Fig.(2e) and Fig.(2f) (or Fig.(3e) and Fig.(3f)). This is due to the fact that the quantities of the discarded low frequency components are different in Fig.(2c) and Fig.(2d) (or Fig.(3c) and Fig.(3d)). However, discarding the circular low frequency components is carried out in image reconstruction. Hence, the hybrid complete invariant $S(k,w)$ should be unaltered.

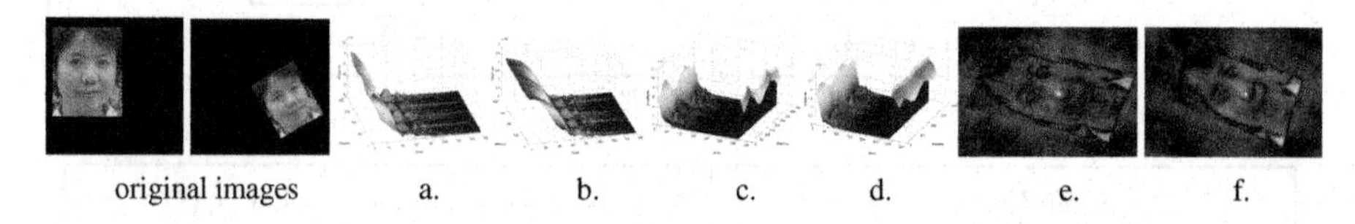

Fig. 2. Image reconstruction using the hybrid invariant descriptor of Eq.(6). The magnitude spectra illustrate the scaling invariant problem of the Fourier transform while the quality of the reconstructed images is used to evaluate this hybrid invariant. a) and b) are the magnitude spectra before the application of the Mellin-Taylor descriptor; c) and d) are the magnitude spectra after the Mellin-Taylor descriptor is applied; e) and f) are the reconstruction results.

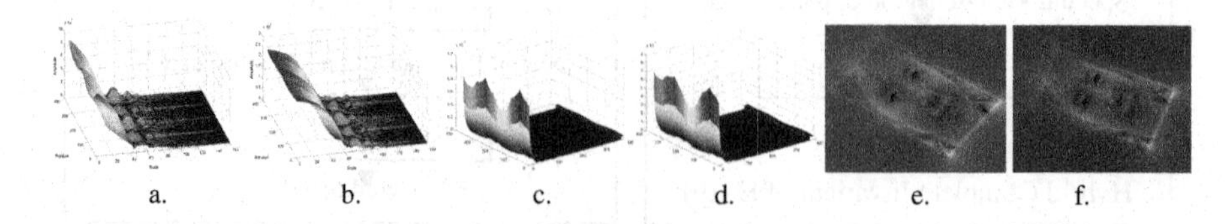

Fig. 3. Image reconstruction using the hybrid invariant descriptor of Eq.(9). The magnitude spectra illustrate the scaling invariant problem of the Fourier transform while the quality of the reconstructed images is used to evaluate this hybrid invariant. a) and b) are the magnitude spectra before the application of AFMT invariant; c) and d) are the magnitude spectra after the application of AFMT invariant; e) and f) are the reconstruction results.

Comparing Fig.(2e,2f) with Fig.(3e,3f), one can note that the reconstructed results based on the complete invariant of Eq.(9) do not appear distinct artifacts. This means that the complete invariant of Eq.(9) can avoid the phase diffusion problem as described in section 3.2.

5 Conclusions

In this paper, we presented two complete sets of hybrid similarity invariants under the Fourier-Mellin transform and the analytical Fourier-Mellin transform frameworks respectively. Furthermore, some numerical problems of our proposed complete invariants were presented. Through image reconstruction, we could intuitionally and effectively reveal these numerical problems for further evaluation.

However, the AFMT-base hybrid complete invariant maintains some good numerical properties. In future work, we will apply it to 3D object registration and recognition.

Acknowledgement. The authors would like to thank Dr Brandt and Prof. Lin for their fruitful discussions.

References

[1] Stephen L. Adler, General Theory of Image Normalization, Computing Research Repository, Report-No. IASSNS-HEP-95/89, http://arxiv.org/abs/cs.CV/9810017
[2] R.D. Brandt, F. Lin, Representation that uniquely characterize image modulo translation, rotation and scaling, Pattern Recognition Letters, Vol.17, pp.1001-1015, 1996
[3] Faouzi Ghorbel, A complete invariant description for gray-level images by the harmonic analysis approach, Pattern Recognition Letters, Vol.15, pp.1043-1051, 1994
[4] R. Mukundan and K.R. Ramakrishnan, Moment Functions in Image Analysis: Theory and Applications, World Scientific Publishing Co. Pte Ltd, Singapore, 1998
[5] S.X. Liao, M. Pawlak, On image analysis by moments, IEEE Trans. Pattern Anal. Mach. Intell., Vol.18, pp.254–266, 1996
[6] F. Lin, R.D. Brandt, Towards absolute invariants of images under translation, rotation and scaling, Pattern Recognition Letters, Vol.14, pp.369-379, 1993
[7] S. Derrode and F. Ghorbel, Robust and efficient Fourier-Mellin transform approximations for gray-level image reconstruction and complete invariant description, Computer Vision and Image Understanding, Vol.83, pp.57-78, 2001

Detection of Text Region and Segmentation from Natural Scene Images

Jonghyun Park[1] and Soonyoung Park[2]

[1] Institute for Robotics and Intelligent Systems,
University of Southern California, Los Angeles, California 90089-0273
jhpark@iris.usc.edu
[2] Dept. of Electronic Engineering, Mokpo National University, South Korea
sypark@mokpo.ac.kr

Abstract. In this paper, we present an approach to the segmentation and detection of text region from natural scenes. Clustering-based natural scene segmentation is first considered based on the histogram of hue and intensity components separately. Secondly, text region extraction method is proposed by using wavelet-based features for representing the input patterns and neural network architecture for the classifier. The effectiveness and reliability of the proposed method is demonstrated through various natural scene images. The experimental results have proven that the proposed method is effective.

1 Introduction

We easily accumulate natural scene image by personal digital assistant, mobile phone, and robot, equipped with a digital camera according as diverse media has been widespread. And it is natural that the demand of detection and recognition of text region has been increased. Texts are ubiquitous in traffic signs, indicators, video sequences, documents, etc. Therefore, segmentation, detection, and recognition of text region from a color natural scene are useful in many field and very important technologies. Detecting text region generally consists of two processing procedures; the first is separating text region from natural scene, and then verifying text region is followed as a post-processing. The quality of separating text region affects on the whole performance directly.

Some approaches have been proposed on the detection and recognition of texts from document images or from simple natural scenes. Researches [1-5] have been developed as a prototype of sign translation system, where [1-3] were for handheld device and [4,5] were for PC. Works related to segmentation have been presented in [6,7]. The previous works can be classified in terms of color space based on and segmentation method. RGB space was used in [1,4,5] and work in [2] was based on RGB and HSI spaces. Diverse segmentation methods were used, such as edge detection [2][4], Gaussian mixture model [2], color quantization [4], binarization method [3], histogram-based color clustering [5].

In this paper, we analyze the performance of several color components in terms of segmentation of text regions. And then we perform the detection of text region using wavelet-based features and neural network.

G. Bebis et al. (Eds.): ISVC 2005, LNCS 3804, pp. 666–671, 2005.

2 Clustering-Based Natural Scene Segmentation

The k-means clustering algorithm is applied to each component of hue and intensity separately to perform segmentation of text region. K-means algorithm has the complexity $O(nkdL)$ where n is number of pixels, d is the number of dimensions, k is the number of clusters, and L is the number of loops. Since we use each of color components separately, d is 1. So the time complexity is $O(nkL)$.In addition, the time complexity could be reduced drastically since the processing was carried out on the histogram space. Algorithm I shows the modification of the clustering algorithm originally proposed by Zang et al. [8].

Algorithm I. Histogram-based k-means clustering algorithm

---

1. Compute histogram H or I with m bits for the n pixels;
2. Initialize k clusters, u_i°, $1 \leq i \leq k$;
3. L = 0;
4. REPEAT {
5. L = L+1;
6. Assign each sample to the closest cluster center;
7. Compute new cluster centers, u_i^L;
8. } until($u_i^{L-1} = u_i^L$, $1 \leq i \leq k$);

In the line 7, new cluster center value is computed by

$$u_i^L = \frac{1}{N} \sum_{b \in B[i]} H[b] * b \tag{1}$$

where $B[i]$ represents the set of bits assigned to $i-th$ cluster by the line 6 and b is bin value of histogram assigned to $i-th$ cluster. Now the time complexity is $O(mkL)$. m may be regarded to be 256(if hue component, m is 360) since the intensity component is quantized into 1 byte.

Because the hue is a value of angle, the cyclic property of the hue must be considered. Hue space is a 2π cyclic space. A new definition of the distance of cyclic hue space that was proposed by C. Zhang and P. Wang is used in this paper [8]. The center point of a cluster is computed by the definition of center point proposed by them. The k-means clustering algorithm requires the number of clusters to be known beforehand. The number of clusters is not only most important factor for the quality of clustering algorithm, but also increasing the complexity of the problem segmenting text region in the next post-processing step. The number that is less than the proper number of clusters makes text region blurred, and a character is divided into multiple characters for the case where the number of clusters is more than the proper one. Many approaches to solve the problem have been proposed over the years [9]. Our text segmentation can be described as algorithm II.

Algorithm II. Text segmentation using k-means clustering

---

1. **for**($k = 2; k < max\_number\_of\_clusters; k^{++}$) {
2. **Apply the algorithm I by letting number of clusters to be k;**
3. **Compute the validity measure in [9],** v_k;
4. }
5. $k' =$ **arg max** v_k;
6. **Using** $k' - th$ **clustering result, for each of** n **pixels in the image, assign region label,** i,
7. **if the pixel belongs to** $i - th$ **cluster;**

---

3 Text Region Extraction

There are many problems in obtaining efficient and robust text region detection from natural scenes. We will consider the classification of the potential text regions and the detection of the text from its backgrounds. We develop a simple method for the text region detection from segmentation image. Each candidate text region is normalized using nearest neighbor interpolation when scaling is simple region resampling. The input feature vectors for the neural network are directly extracted from 64×64 normalized text region.

3.1 Feature Extraction from Candidate Regions

The feature extraction is one of the most important tasks in pattern classification and recognition. In this Section, we develop a wavelet-based feature extraction method for text and non-text regions. The wavelet features are extracted from the high-frequency and low-frequency by using the same method proposed by Park et al. [10].

Agorithm. Wavelet-based feature extraction method
Input : arbitrary-sized segmented sub-image with grayscale tone.
Output : wavelet features.
Procedure :
1. size-normalize the input image into 64×64 image
2. perform wavelet transformation using Daubechies kernels by 2-levels.
3. partition using mesh schemes in [10].
4. compute the first and second moments from the blocks by (1)
5. take the moments as the features.

$$\mu = \frac{1}{n^2}\sum_{i=0}^{n-1}\sum_{j=0}^{n-1} b(i,j), \sigma = \sqrt{\frac{1}{n^2}\sum_{i=0}^{n-1}\sum_{j=0}^{n-1}[\mu - b(i,j)]^2} \quad (2)$$

here, $b(i,j)$ represents a block sub-image.

3.2 Multi-layer Perceptrons Classifier

The modular neural network architecture is used as the classifier, usually consisting of multiple layers of one input layer, hidden layers and one output layer. Let us assume that we have K classes, each represented as w_i. The modular neural network classifier consists of K subnetworks, each responsible for one of K classes [11].

The database is divided into a training set and a test set. Training and testing sets are performed using a neural network classifier. The neural network classifier is trained using standard programming technique. In the text region detection step, we are using wavelet feature vectors of 3.1.

4 Experimental Results

To test the effectiveness of proposed method, we have performed experiments on all color natural scene images supported from ICDAR. The conversion of the RGB color image to HSI model is carried out and the hue and intensity components are only used as values of the feature vectors. The ICDAR database includes diverse images, such as simple, complex, distorted images, and the sizes and distribution of color of natural scene images are various.

4.1 Natural Scene Segmentation

Clustering-based segmentation algorithm has been applied to the histogram of hue and intensity components of natural scene images in Figure 1. Figure 1 (a), (d) and (g) show the original image with highlights being included. Figure 1 (b), (e) and (h) show the segmented results using intensity component and Figure 1 (c), (f) and (i) are the results of segmentation using hue component. We can observe that segmentation based on intensity causes the division and blurring of characters due to the variation of intensity components in the highlighted image. However, the segmentation on the hue space is robust to the highlighted natural scene images although there are many separated regions on characters. The experimental results can be summarized; 1-dimensional clustering method based on either H or I components is sufficient for application of mobile device. And the processing time is important for the efficiency of running on mobile devices. The running time of our method is millisecond level in 640×480 size.

4.2 Text Region Detection

The text region detection algorithms have been designed and trained on an ICDAR database. The feature extraction, training and testing procedures described in Section 3 have been applied on this database. More precisely, 2000 pattern containing both true text region and non-text region have been selected from the output of the natural scene segmentation step applied this database.

Some experimental results using neural network are shown in figure 2. Here, text regions are overlapped with regular bars or line. Although the lighting is uneven, most of the text regions in the natural scenes can be located. In figure, some lowercase text region are false alarm and missing, because they are of similar patterns between text region and non-text region. Of course, this problem could be avoided using precision segmentation and feature extraction algorithms.

Fig. 1. Segmentation result of natural scene image using I and H components

Fig. 2. Examples of text region detection from natural scene : (a),(b) detected result in I, (c),(d) detected result in H

5 Conclusion

In this paper, we present a general scheme for the segmentation and detection of embedded text region using intensity and hue value in natural scene images. The method is split into two parts : the segmentation of natural scene and detection of text region. The performance of color components hue and intensity are analyzed and compared in terms of segmentation of text region in color natural scene images. We conclude that intensity component is dominant among the other components, but the hue component is better than intensity component for the color natural scene image whose text region is highlighted. From the experimental results, the following conclusion is drawn : the proposed method can locate most of text region in natural scene images, although mistakes sometime occur, missing text region and causing false alarms. Also, segmentation using only hue component works well when the intensity might fail. The performance of text segmentation can be improved by combining both results. Future work will be concentrated on varied feature extraction and improvement the robustness of algorithm.

References

1. Datong Chen, Herve Bourlard and Jean-Philippe Thiran, "Text identification in complex background using SVM," Proc. of the Int. Conf. on Computer Vision and Pattern Recognition, vol. 2, pp. 621-626, 2001.
2. J. Ohya, A. Shio and S. Aksmatsu, "Recognizing characters in scene images," IEEE Trans. Pattern Analysis and Machine Intelligence, vol. 16, pp. 214-220, 1994.
3. Y. Zhong, K. Karu and A.K. Jain, "Locating text in complex color images," Pattern Recognition, vol. 28, pp. 1523-1536, 1995.
4. K. Sobottka, H. Bunke and H. Kronenberg, "Identification of text on colored book and journal covers," International Conference on Document Analysis and Recognition, pp. 57-63, 1999.
5. V. Wu, R. Manmatha and E. M. Riseman, "Textfinder: An automatic system to detect and recognize text in images," IEEE Trans. on Pattern Analysis and Machine Intelligence, vol. 20, pp. 1224-1229, 1999.
6. Chuang Li, Xiaoqing Ding and Youshou Wu, "Automatic text location in natural scene images," International Conference on Document Analysis and Recognition, pp. 1069-1073, 2001.
7. Kongqiao Wang and Jari A. Kangas, "Character location in scene images from digital camera," Pattern Recognition, vol. 36, pp. 2287-2299, 2003.
8. C. Zhang and P. Wang, "A new method of color image segmentation based on intensity and hue clustering," International Conference on Pattern Recognition, vol. 3, pp. 3617-3621, 2000.
9. Siddheswar Ray and Rose H. Turi, "Determination of number of clusters in K-means clustering and application in colour image segmentation," International Conference on Advances in Pattern Recognition and Digital Techniques, pp. 27-29, 1999.
10. Jong-Hyun Park and Il-Seok Oh, "Wavelet-based feature extraction from character images," Lecture Notes in Computer Science, vol. 2690, pp. 1092-1096, 2003.
11. Il-Seok Oh and Ching Y.Suen, "Distance features for neural network-based recognition of handwritten characters," International Journal on Document Analysis and Recognition, vol. 1, pp. 73-88, 1998.

ARM Based Microcontroller for Image Capturing in FPGA Design

Chi-Jeng Chang[1], Wu-Ting Wu[1], Hui-Ching Su[2], Zen-Yi Huang[1], and Hsin-Yen Li[1]

[1] Department of Industrial Education, National Taiwan Normal University, Taipei, Taiwan
[2] Chunghwa Telecom Co., Ltd. Taipei, Taiwan
t07022@cc.ntnu.edu.tw

Abstract. This paper presents how a ARM7 was designed by repeated adding group-instructions and the system was verified in a self-developed FPGA board. This ARM7 was then connected with a CMOS image capturing and processing unit (IPU) implemented in other FPGA board. ARM7 now become a microcontroller for this IPU. IPU integrates image capturing, convolution and sorting in FPGA to perform 3-stage pipelined operations to seed up system operations. Convolution and sorting help further filter out the Fixed Patten Noise (FPN) and dark current noise in CMOS image sensor and result in better image qualities. The FPGA board with ARM7 and IPU could be used for teaching CPU design, controller design and a system-on –chip (SoC) design since all circuits are in a single FPGA chip.

1 Introduction

This paper presents how a ARM7 CPU[1,2,3,4] was designed by adding group-instructions and was tested in a FPGA board. Then this ARM7 was connected with a CMOS image capturing and processing device implemented in other FPGA board. ARM7 now becomes a microcontroller for this image capturing and processing unit which sometimes is called image accelerator for its high speed operations. ARM7 may contains more than 5 instruction groups, namely, data-processing, branch, data-transfer, status/exception and coprocessor. The first 3 groups of instruction design and system verification are described in section 2 through 4. FPGA image accelerator combining the image capturing algorithm was usually done in 8051 series CPU. Section 5 describes the SoC architecture and verification results of the ARM7 as an interface controller for the image accelerator. Some concluding remarks are described in section 6.

Peoples are usually familiar with using CPUs, such as 8051.80×86, ARM, MIPS. But very few of them think about designing them. Section 2 and 3 describe a way by repeated adding more and more group-instructions to obtain a ARM7 CPU.

Since CPU circuit can be added up, it can also be shrunk down in FPGA design by taking out unused instructions. So it is possible to construct a tailor-made ARM CPU in FPGA for a specific application.

G. Bebis et al. (Eds.): ISVC 2005, LNCS 3804, pp. 672 – 677, 2005.

2 ARM7 System Configuration

ARM7 system shown in Fig. 1 includes a register bank (REG) containing 16 32-bit registers, a main memory (MEM), a data processing unit (DTU), and control unit (CON) for organizing and sequencing the system operations. Fig. 1 also shows the datapath between these 4 units for the execution of 28 DPU instructions (16 for alu, 6 for shifting, 6 for multiply), not including the 4 condition bits of NZCV (Negative, Zero, Carry, Overflow). If the condition bits are included (as many other computers do) the maxima number of instructions may reach 112 (28×4). More detailed DPU is not shown for simplicity. It is a ordinary combinational circuit composed of an arithmetic-logic unit a shifter and a multiplier.

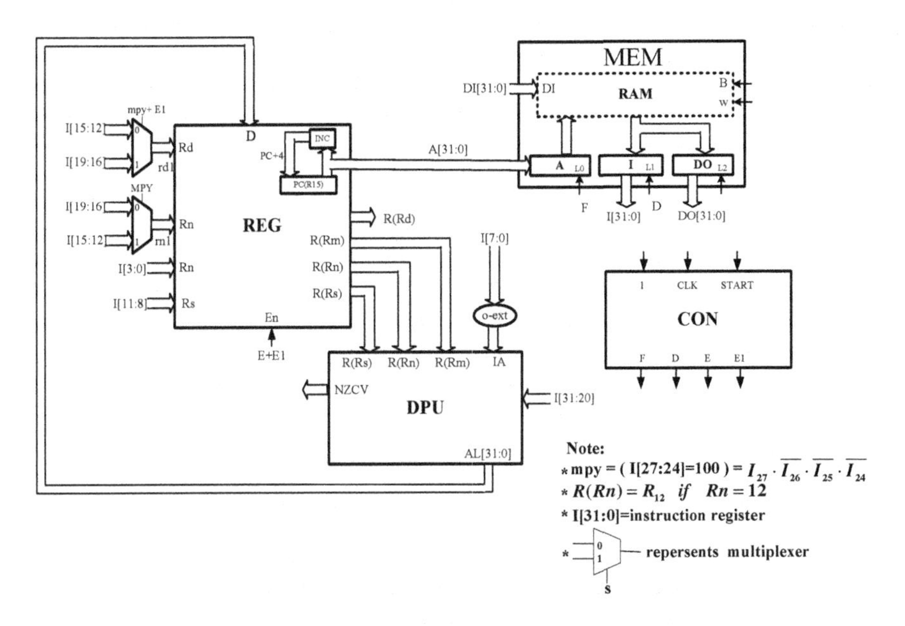

Fig. 1. ARM7 System Configuration for 28 DPU instructions

3 Added Branch and Data Transfer Instructions and Control Unit

3.1 Branch and Data Transfer Circuit

Fig. 2 shows the block diagram, datapath and control for the adding of branch and data transfer instruction groups. Comparing Fig. 2 with Fig. 1, an increasing complexity can be found in datapath structure, multiplexing inputs to IA of DPU, and the control unit CON. The 4-bit bus rd2, m2 in Fig. 2 are the outputs form 2 multipliers that connect to rd and rn for addressing REG. The inputs of the 2 multiplexer are not shown for simplicity.

Branch instructions used for changing the program execution sequence, are usually accomplished by changing the values of program counter (R15). Data transfer instructions are concerned with the single or multiple data transfer between registers and memory as shown in Figure 2. The a gray-dotted bus DO [31:0] in Fig. 2 from memory to D terminal of REG and the other dotted bus R(Rd) form REG block to the DI[31:0] terminal of MEM were added for the data transfer purpose.

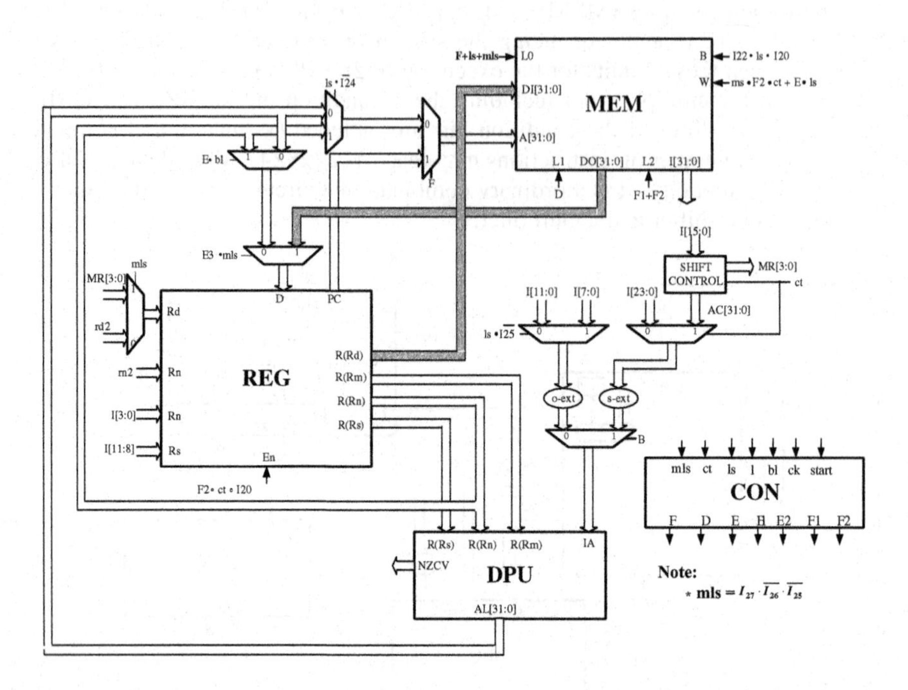

Fig. 2. Block diagram of Arm7 contains branch, data-transfer and DPU instructions

3.2 Control Unit

When more instructions were added, the control unit became larger and more complicated. The control unit (CON) at lower right corner in Fig. 2 has more inputs and outputs than those in Fig. 1. CON actually is a finite state machine realization form the state diagram shown in Fig. 3. Most of the instructions in ARM use only 3 states during instruction execution, namely F(fetch), D(decode), E (execute). Long (l) mul-

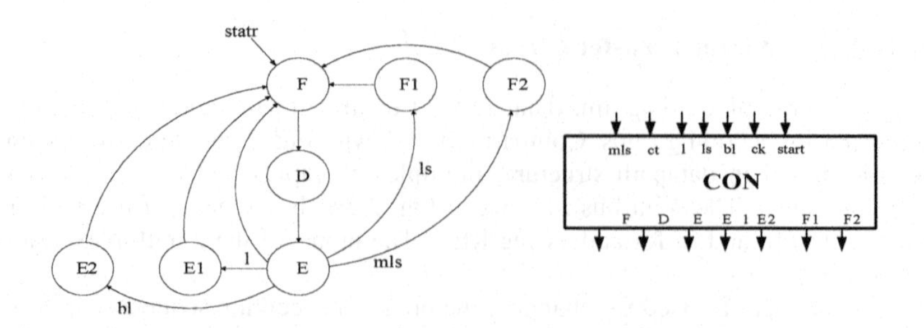

Fig. 3. Control state diagram and Enlarged Control unit block diagram from Figure 2

tiplication (64 bit product) and Branch Link (bl) instruction, both needed extra E1 or E2 state, respectively. The data transfer included Load/Store (ls), multiple Load/ Store (mls) need extra states F1 and F2. So the inputs of the CON block are the decoded instruction signals l, bl, ls, mls, as mentioned above, and ct represented the multiple register transfer counts, the outputs are the states F, F1, F2, D, E, E1, E2 as shown in the enlarged block in Fig. 3 for easy reading.

4 Platform Board Demonstration

Fig. 4 showed the self-develop FPGA board with an 0.8 million gate count XILINX FPGA chip (xcv800) at the center. Each of the 36 instructions in ARM7 was verified in the board. Several programs such as sorting, arithmetic calculations, counters were keyed in for verification. Fig. 5 shows the board was running a 24-hour clock program which was keyed in through the key pad at lower right corner and the total 24-hour clock circuit was loaded through parallel port into FPGA chip. The 7-segment showing 030903 was the snap shot at the 3 o'clock 9 minutes and 3 seconds while 24-hour clock program was running.

Fig. 4. Self-made platform board

Fig. 5. Self-made platform board snap shot at 03:09:03 during program running

Section 2 through 4 are briefly described the design approach of adding group-instructions and the verification of our ARM7 CPU. This approach works fine so far and can be continued adding more and more instruction groups. But in the following sections, the focus is in the application of the ARM7 CPU interfacing with an image capturing and processing unit (IPU) [5], implemented in a 300k gate-count FPGA chip (xc2s300e).

5 ARM7 as Microcontroller or SoC Based Design

Image Processing Unit (IPU) includes image capturing, 2-D convolution and 2-D sorting. Image capturing is a self-developed FPGA version based on 8051 software program. 2-D convolution and 2-D sorting are based on the FPGA version of image processing algorithms from Crookes[6,7] and Maheshwari[8], respectively.

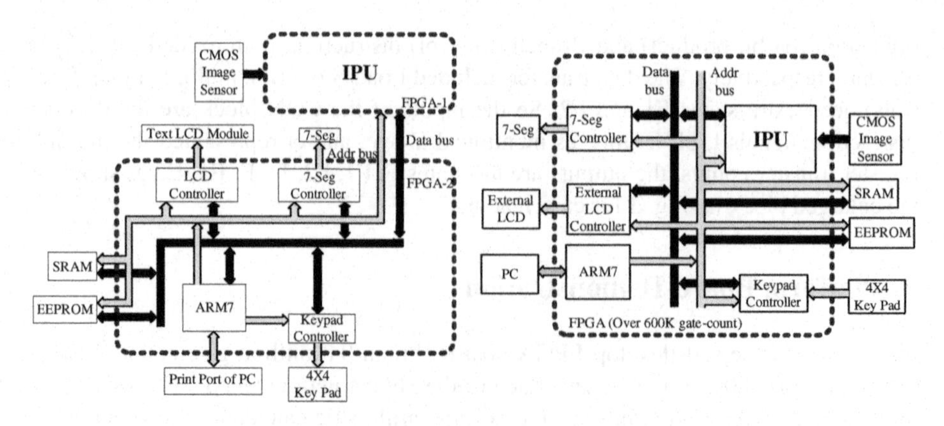

Fig. 6. a. ARM7 and IPU in separate FPGA board. **b.** ARM7 and IPU merge in a single FPGA chip

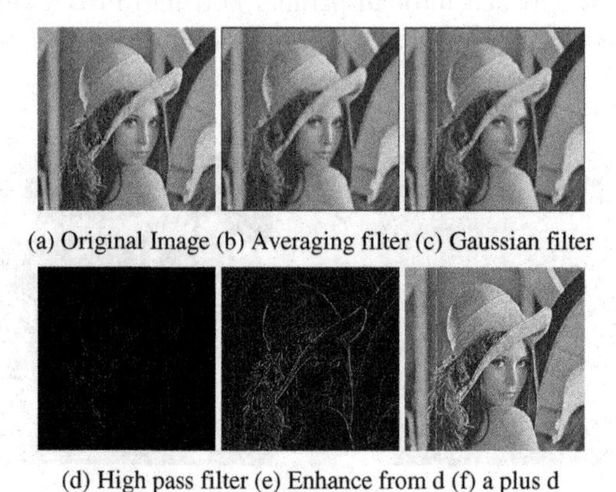

Fig. 7. Photo of Lena through this experiment

Capturing, convolution and sorting were usually done in series. They are now integrated in a single FPGA chip. IPU can be connected to the self-developed ARM7 microcontroller as shown in Fig. 6a. Fig. 7 shows the experiment result by using photo of Lena as an original image. In Fig. 6a ARM7 used up to 600k gate-count out of an total 800k gate-count FPGA-2 chip, IPU used up to 70k gate-count out of a 300k gate-count FPGA-1 chip. IPU can be merged to the 800k chip as shown in Fig. 6b since both are using FPGA design. This architecture becomes a kind of SoC design in FPAG version.

6 Concluding Remarks

Since FPGA is reconfigurable the microcontroller CPU can be tailored to fit a special purpose. For example, supposed a 800k FPGA chip was fully occupied by the circuits of ARM7 and had no room for putting in another 70 k gate-count image accelerator.

Since all calculations during image processing are done in the image accelerator circuits. Then it is possible to take out the unused 32x32 multiplier (occupied about 150k gate-count) and make room available for 70k gate-count image accelerator to be included in.

ARM7 embedded with many device controllers in a FPGA chip shown inside the dash-lined area in Fig. 6b demonstrates a kind of SoC architecture design. It might gradually become a platform for CPU design capable of adding controllers for controlling special accelerators or for interfacing the devices, such as image processing, mechantronics, nano-optics.

References

1. Steve Furber, "ARM System-on-Chip Architecture (2nd Edition)," Maidstone, Kent, USA : Addison-Wesley, 2000.
2. Seal, D. ARM Architectural Reference Manual, 2nd edition, Addison Wesley, 2000.
3. Chang, C.J., Tsai, C.A., Using XILINX for Computer Architecture Laboratory. Engineering Education for the 21st century, Conference Proceedings, pp. 31-34, Sheffield, England, 17-20 April, 2000.
4. Djordjevic, J., MilenKovic, A., An Integrated Environment for Teaching Computer Architecture, IEEE-MICRO, May-June, pp.66-74, 2000.
5. Zen-Yi Huang, "FPGA Platform for Capturing and Filtering CMOS Image Sensor," Master thesis, National Taiwan Normal University, 2004.
6. Crookes D., Benkrid K., Bouridane A., Alotaibi K., and Benkrid A., "Design and implementation of a high level programming environment for FPGA-based image processing," Vision, Image and Signal Processing, IEE Proceedings , vol. 147, Issue: 4 ,pp. 377-384, Aug. 2000.
7. Benkrid K., Crookes D., and Benkrid A., "Towards a general framework for FPGA based image processing using hardware skeleton," *Parallel Computing* vol. 28, Issue: 7-8, pp. 1141-1154,Aug, 2002.
8. Maheshwari R., Rao S.S.S.P., and Poonacha P.G., "FPGA implementation of median filter," *Tenth International Conference on VLSI Design*, pp. 523-524, June. 1997.

Contraction Mapping Calibration

Nicolas Guilbert[1] and Anders Heyden[2]

[1] Lund Institute of Technology
nicolas@maths.lth.se
[2] Division of Mathematics, Malmö University, Sweden

Abstract. In this paper a new calibration scheme for recovering Euclidian camera parameters from their affine of projective primitives is presented. It is based on a contraction mapping implying that the obtained solution is unique, i.e. no local minimas threaten to yield a non-optimal solution. The approach unifies Euclidian calibration from affine and projective configurations and fewer cameras ($m \geq 2$) need to be available than in traditional schemes. The algorithm is validated on synthetic and real data.

1 Introduction

The structure from motion problem has been studied extensively during the last two decades. In particular the problem of autocalibration, i.e. how to automatically calculate the intrinsic parameters of the observing camera, can be solved if the aspect ratio and the skew are known which is shown in [2].

The problem has received a lot of attention in the projective case, but also in the affine case [3], making extensive use of projective geometry. The central idea of this paper is to use a well known result from functional analysis, the Contraction Mapping Theorem, which states that if a function is a contraction, then it has an associated unique fixed point. This unique fixed point can be evaluated with arbitrary precision through iteration of the contraction mapping, *independently* of the starting point.

It would thus be interesting to know of a function $\mathcal{P} \mapsto \mathcal{P}$, $\mathcal{P}$ denoting all possible projective or affine camera configurations, whose fixed point were to be the optimal Euclidian calibration of the cameras, since this would by iteration yield the optimal calibration.

The challenge addressed here is that of finding such a function, which has led to an algorithm with an experimental success rate of 100% for affine calibration and less for projective calibration, depending on the constraints imposed. Success is here defined as reaching the optimal (ground truth) least squares estimate of the calibration parameters. The guarantee of success is only shown experimentally, however strong arguments are presented suggesting that the guarantee could be proved theoretically too.

In Section 2 we describe the fundamental notions necessary to understand the calibration problem the way we address it. In Section 3 the upgrading from an affine to a Euclidian camera configuration by means of a contraction mapping is treated and in Section 4 the results are sought extended to projective → Euclidian calibration. Experimental validation on both synthetic and real data is eventually done in Section 5 and Section 6 concludes the paper.

G. Bebis et al. (Eds.): ISVC 2005, LNCS 3804, pp. 678–683, 2005.

2 Notation and Background

2.1 Generalities

The perspective camera matrix, which models a classical pinhole camera, may be decomposed as

$$\mathbf{P} = \underbrace{\begin{bmatrix} f & sf & fx_c \\ 0 & af & fy_c \\ 0 & 0 & 1 \end{bmatrix}}_{\mathbf{K}} \underbrace{\begin{bmatrix} \mathbf{r}_1^\top & t_1 \\ \mathbf{r}_2^\top & t_2 \\ \mathbf{r}_3^\top & t_3 \end{bmatrix}}_{[\mathbf{R}^\top \quad \mathbf{t}]} \tag{1}$$

where f denotes the focal length, a the aspect ratio, s is the skew and (x_c, y_c) the principal point. The $\mathbf{r}_i$ are the 3 columns of the rotation matrix $\mathbf{R}$ indicating the orientation of the camera, i.e. $\mathbf{r}_1$ and $\mathbf{r}_2$ are the horizontal and vertical axis of the image plane respectively and $\mathbf{r}_3$ the focal axis. $c = -\mathbf{R}(t_1, t_2, t_3)^\top$ is the camera centre. In most practical cameras, x_c and y_c are highly correlated to the camera rotation, highly ambiguous and only of interest if the rotation needs to be determined very precisely. They are thus often, and will be in the sequel be, assumed to be zero.

The affine camera matrix has the form

$$\mathbf{P}' = \begin{bmatrix} \bar{\mathbf{P}} & \mathbf{t} \\ \mathbf{0}_{1\times 3} & 1 \end{bmatrix}, \tag{2}$$

where the uncalibrated state is expressed by the prime ($'$). It may when calibrated be decomposed as

$$\mathbf{P} = \begin{bmatrix} \gamma_x & s & 0 \\ 0 & \gamma_y & 0 \\ 0 & 0 & 1 \end{bmatrix} \begin{bmatrix} \mathbf{r}_1^\top & t_1 \\ \mathbf{r}_2^\top & t_2 \\ \mathbf{0}_{1\times 3} & 1 \end{bmatrix} \tag{3}$$

where γ_x and γ_y are analogous to f and af in (1).

3 Affine to Euclidian Calibration

3.1 Euclidian Calibration

Classical autocalibration for affine cameras is described in the method in [3], i.e. by assuming skew $s = 0$ and aspect ratio $a = 1$ and determining an upgrading 3D homography $\mathbf{H}$ that maps (2) to (3), i.e. $\mathbf{P} = \mathbf{P}'\mathbf{H}$.

We here propose an alternative iterative scheme which in practice guarantees convergence to a least squares estimate of the three parameters up to an overall scaling (i.e. 100% success rate).

The basic idea of the algorithm is to iteratively find a homography $\mathbf{H}_c$ that will transform the uncalibrated affine cameras so as to get them as close to the calibrated form (3) as possible. The idea is very simple, although the formal presentation within the framework of the contraction mapping theorem tends to make it somewhat opaque: the information needed for the calibration of an affine camera is contained in 1) the upper triangular form of the intrinsic calibration matrix K, and 2) in the orthonormality of the two vectors $\mathbf{r}_1$ and $\mathbf{r}_2$ defining the rotation of the camera. In order to recover the form (6) we start out by aligning our existing estimate of the form (6) with a plausible candidate, the plausible candidate being the current $\mathbf{r}_1$ and $\mathbf{r}_2$ of each camera. These current $\mathbf{r}_1$ and $\mathbf{r}_2$ are obtained via QR-factorisation of each of the current matrices and subsequently stacked in a large matrix. In this alignment, the aligned estimate will hopefully inherit some of the structure of the target. Furthermore, repeating the alignment brings the camera matrices as close as possible to the desired form, as we shall see. The algorithm proceeds as follows:

1. Stack the 2×3 camera matrices in a $2m \times 3$ matrix $\mathcal{P}$; Perform a QR factorisation of each of the camera matrices;
2. Stack the resulting rotation matrices in a $2m \times 3$ matrix $\mathcal{R}$.
3. Align $\mathcal{P}$ to $\mathcal{R}$, i.e. minimise/reduce the Frobenius norm $\|\mathcal{P}\mathbf{H} - \mathcal{R}\|_F$ over an arbitrary homography $\mathbf{H}$
4. Go to 1. unless the algorithm has converged.

Even though the algorithm is iterative, it converges very fast, and in fact 1 iteration would seem to suffice to obtain useful parameters. Each iteration takes a few milliseconds ($m \leq 15$, standard PC) and scales linearly with the number of calibrated cameras.

The Contraction Mapping Theorem. Before addressing the central problem, we define a *contraction* and introduce a common tool from functional analysis, the so-called Contraction Mapping Theorem here reproduced from [1]:

Definition 1. Contraction: *A mapping $\mathbf{T} : \mathcal{X} \mapsto \mathcal{X}$ where $\mathcal{X}$ is a subset of a normed space N is called a* contraction mapping, *or simply a* contraction, *if there is a positive number $a < 1$ such that*

$$\|\mathbf{T}\mathbf{k}_1 - \mathbf{T}\mathbf{k}_2\| \leq a\|\mathbf{k}_1 - \mathbf{k}_2\|, \quad \forall \mathbf{k}_1\mathbf{k}_2 \in \mathcal{X} \quad . \tag{4}$$

The definition is central to

Theorem 1. Contraction Mapping Theorem: *If $\mathbf{T} : \mathcal{X} \mapsto \mathcal{X}$ is a contraction mapping a closed subset $\mathcal{X}$ of a Banach space, then there is exactly one $\mathbf{x} \in \mathcal{X}$ such that $\mathbf{T}\mathbf{x} = \mathbf{x}$. For any $\mathbf{x}_0 \in \mathcal{X}$, the sequence $(\mathbf{x}_n)$ defined by $\mathbf{x}_{n+1} = \mathbf{T}\mathbf{x}_n$ converges to $\mathbf{x}$.*

The challenge is thus to determine a contraction $\mathbf{T}$ with a suitable fixed point, i.e. a fixed point solution which minimises the sum of squared errors between the $3m$ estimated intrinsic parameters and the wanted parameters from (3).

We introduce $\mathcal{P}$ as the $2m \times 3$ stack of all the 2×3 matrices $\bar{\mathbf{P}}$ from (2), i.e.

$$\mathcal{P} = \begin{bmatrix} \bar{\mathbf{P}}_1 \\ \vdots \\ \bar{\mathbf{P}}_m \end{bmatrix} = \begin{bmatrix} \mathbf{K}_1\mathbf{R}_1 \\ \vdots \\ \mathbf{K}_m\mathbf{R}_m \end{bmatrix},$$

where the rightmost expression is a *RQ-factorisation* of each of the $\bar{\mathbf{P}}$'s, i.e. $\mathbf{K}_i$ is 2×2 upper triangular containing 3 entries form $\mathbf{k}$ and $\mathbf{R}_i$ has two orthonormal rows.

Furthermore, we define the block-diagonal $2m \times 2m$ matrix $\mathcal{K}$ and the $2m \times 3$ matrix $\mathcal{R}$ such that

$$\mathcal{K} = \begin{bmatrix} \mathbf{K}_1 & & \\ & \ddots & \\ & & \mathbf{K}_m \end{bmatrix}, \quad \mathcal{R} = \begin{bmatrix} \mathbf{R}_1 \\ \vdots \\ \mathbf{R}_m \end{bmatrix},$$

i.e.

$$\mathcal{P} = \mathcal{K}\mathcal{R}.$$

Let $\mathbf{H}$ denote the homography that minimises the distance between $\mathcal{P}$ and $\mathcal{R}$ i.e.

$$\min_{\mathbf{H}} \|\mathcal{P}\mathbf{H} - \mathcal{R}\|_F, \tag{5}$$

where $\|\mathbf{A}\|_F$ denotes the Frobenius-norm, i.e. the square root of the sum of the squares of all the elements of the matrix $\mathbf{A}$. Note that $\mathbf{H}$ may be considered as the affine transformation that optimally aligns the point clouds described by the rows of the two $2m \times 3$ matrices $\mathcal{P}$ and $\mathcal{R}$ and let

$$\hat{\mathcal{P}} = \mathcal{P}\mathbf{H} = \hat{\mathcal{K}}\hat{\mathcal{R}} \tag{6}$$

denote the optimally aligned point cloud. By extracting the new estimate of the intrinsic parameters from $\hat{\mathcal{K}}$, denoted $\hat{\mathbf{k}}$, the output of $\mathbf{T}$ is obtained.

We now conjecture that aligning two point clouds $\mathcal{K}_1\mathcal{R}_1 \in \mathcal{V}$ and $\mathcal{K}_2\mathcal{R}_2 \in \mathcal{V}$ to the point clouds $\mathcal{R}_1$ and $\mathcal{R}_2$ which have the local structure (orthogonal point pairs) brings each of the local structures closer to each other from an overall least squares point of view, i.e.

$$\|\mathbf{T}\mathbf{k}_1 - \mathbf{T}\mathbf{k}_2\|_2 \leq \alpha\|\mathbf{k}_1 - \mathbf{k}_2\|_2, \tag{7}$$

with $\alpha < 1$. As formulated in (7), the conjecture seems to be somewhat false and overly general, which we are only able to show experimentally. Two instances $\mathcal{K}_1\mathcal{R}_1$ and $\mathcal{K}_1\mathcal{R}_1$ and their corresponding $\mathbf{k}_1$ and $\mathbf{k}_2$ are created by applying two random transformations $\mathbf{H}_1$ and $\mathbf{H}_2$ according to (5). They are subsequently transformed by $\mathbf{T}$ and it is verified whether they fulfill (7). It turns out that (7) is satisfied in only 97% of the tries. This would indicate that $\mathbf{T}$ might not truly be a contraction. It could however also be due to the implementation of the minimisation in (5) which is not guaranteed to yield a global minimum. It is noteworthy that for the second iteration, i.e. if $\mathbf{T}$ is applied twice, the (7) is satisfied *every* time. Also, the algorithm converges to the unique fixed point every time, thus guaranteeing an optimal Euclidian calibration of the affine cameras.

Validity of the Fixed Point. Equation (7) implies that $\mathbf{T}$ is a contraction. It follows from the Contraction Mapping Theorem that the equation $\mathbf{k} = \mathbf{T}\mathbf{k}$ has a unique solution $\mathbf{k}_0$. It now remains to be proven that the fixed point $\mathbf{k}_0$ is a least squares estimate of the affine intrinsic parameters (up to an undefined scale factor).

Since $\mathbf{k}_0$ is a fixed point $\mathbf{k}_0 = \mathbf{T}\mathbf{k}_0$ and accordingly $\mathbf{H} = \mathbf{I}_{3\times3}$ (according to (6)) and the point clouds $\mathcal{K}_0\mathcal{R}_0$ and $\mathcal{R}_0$ are thus optimally aligned, i.e.

$$\|\mathcal{K}_0\mathcal{R}_0 - \mathcal{R}_0\|_F = \min_{\mathcal{K}\mathcal{R}\in\mathcal{V}} \|\mathcal{K}\mathcal{R} - \mathcal{R}\|_F . \tag{8}$$

Also, considering each pair of points separately and decomposing each $\mathbf{R}_i$ into

$$\mathbf{R}_i = \begin{bmatrix} u_1 \; u_2 \; u_3 \\ v_1 \; v_2 \; v_3 \end{bmatrix}$$

and each $\mathbf{K}_i - \mathbf{I}$ into

$$\mathbf{K}_i - \mathbf{I} = \begin{bmatrix} k_1 \; k_3 \\ 0 \; k_2 \end{bmatrix} - \begin{bmatrix} 1 \; 0 \\ 0 \; 1 \end{bmatrix} = \begin{bmatrix} \epsilon_1 \; \epsilon_3 \\ 0 \; \epsilon_2 \end{bmatrix},$$

we see that

$$\begin{aligned} \|\mathbf{K}_i\mathbf{R}_i - \mathbf{R}_i\|_F^2 &= \|(\mathbf{K}_i - \mathbf{I})\mathbf{R}_i\|_F^2 \\ &= \epsilon_1^2(u_1^2 + u_2^2 + u_3^2) + \\ &+ \epsilon_2^2(v_1^2 + v_2^2 + v_3^2) + \\ &+ \epsilon_3^2(v_1^2 + v_2^2 + v_3^2) \\ &= \epsilon_1^2 + \epsilon_2^2 + \epsilon_3^2, \end{aligned} \tag{9}$$

which is valid for every of the m point pairs. Thus the minimisation in (8) which is the one that is performed, is equivalent to the minimisng (9) for all the $i = 1..m$ cameras, which affirms the estimate as a least squares estimate.

Finally, if the estimated $\mathbf{H}$ at each iteration is denoted $\mathbf{H}_j$, $j = 1..,m_i$, j denoting the iteration number and m_i the number of iterations, the upgrading (calibrating) transformation $\mathbf{H}_c$ is obtained as

$$\mathbf{H}_c = \prod_{j=1}^{m_i} \mathbf{H}_j$$

and is applied to each camera $\mathbf{P}'_i$ according to

$$\mathbf{P}_{Ai} = \mathbf{P}'_i\mathbf{H}_c \,. \tag{10}$$

4 Projective $\longrightarrow$ Euclidian Calibration

The projective $\rightarrow$ Euclidian case is conceptually very similar to the affine $\rightarrow$ Euclidian case. The difference is that the stacked camera matrices $\mathcal{P}$ now consist of m 3×4 matrices, and that the regularised parameters of $\mathbf{K}_i$ are the 5 parameters from (1). The conjecture is not as well satisfied as in the affine case.

5 Experiments

5.1 Comparison to the Traditional Approach, Affine Case

In the traditional approach to affine autocalibration described by Quan in [3] the problem is formulated as that of solving a set of homogeneous quadratic equations in a least squares sense which is done using Levenberg-Marquardt minimisation. Such an approach is generally prone to stranding in local minimas.

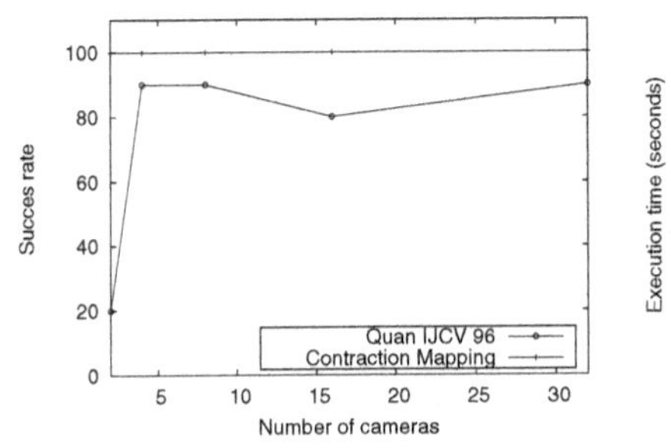

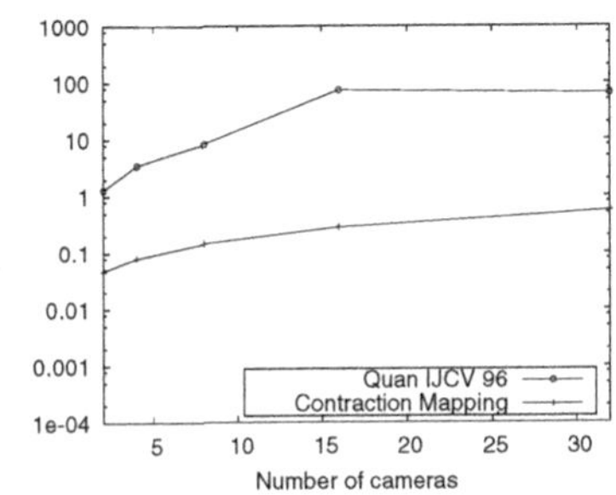

Fig. 1. Comparison to traditional affine calibration, see [3] Top: Success rate. The existing state-of-the art algorithm works quite well, i.e. the underlying Levenberg-Marquardt minimisation reaches the global minimum $\approx$ 90% of the time. The proposed algorithm however shows a 100% success rate. Bottom: Execution times. Even though the proposed algorithm is iterative, every iteration is very fast, only few iterations are needed and the execution time scales linearly with the number of cameras. Note: Quan's algorithm was implemented using numerically (as opposed to analytically) calculated derivatives.

In the following experiments, a varying number (2,4,8,16 and 32) of random cameras were generated and transformed by a random 3×3 homography $\mathbf{H}_r$.

The success rates of Quan's and the proposed algorithm were compared together with their execution times. Quan's algorithm reached the global minimum approximately 90% of the time, compared to a 100% for the contraction mapping scheme.

The results, success rates and execution times, are shown in Figure 1.

6 Summary and Conclusions

A new autocalibration framework was presented uniting affine and projective calibration. For affine calibration, the implemented algorithm achieves a 100% success rate at reaching the optimal least squares estimate, independently of the number of available cameras. This is better than the state-of-the-art algorithm [3], which at best has a 90% success rate. This was shown experimentally, and with a strong argument for it being valid theoretically too.

References

1. D. H. Griffel. *Applied Functional Analysis*. Dover Publications, 1985.
2. A. Heyden and K. Åström. Euclidean reconstruction from image sequences with varying and unknown focal length and principal point. In *Proc. Conf. Computer Vision and Pattern Recognition*, pages 438–443, 1997.
3. L. Quan. Self-calibration of an affine camera from multiple views. *Int. Journal of Computer Vision*, 19(1):93–105, 1996.

Discrimination of Natural Contours by Means of Time-Scale-Frequency Decompositions

Leandro A. Loss and Clésio L. Tozzi

Department of Computer Science and Engineering,
School of Electrical and Computer Engineering,
State University of Campinas

Abstract. This paper evaluates the discriminative potential of time-scale-frequency decompositions for contour-based recognition of natural shapes. Specifically, it provides the analysis and comparison of descriptors derived from the Fourier Transform, the Short-Time Fourier Transform, the Wavelet Transform and the Multi-Resolution Fourier Transform. Linear Discriminant Analysis and Backward Sequential Selection are employed for dimensionality reduction and selection of the most significant features, respectively. A Bayesian Classifier is used for class discrimination. To improve discrimination, a hierarchical classification is adopted. The approaches are analyzed and compared considering experiments developed over digitalized leaves.

1 Introduction

Natural shapes are often irregular and thus characterized by great intra-class variability. Therefore, recognition systems of natural shapes must consider, in addition to suitable descriptors for the class differentiation, classification approaches capable of dealing with the large variance of measured features.

Approaches based on scale and/or frequency decompositions are frequently considered for shape description because the domain change resulting from them usually reveals features which contribute to a most efficient classification system. Examples of scale decomposition approaches are the Curvature Scale Space [1] and the Wavelet Transform [2]. Frequency decomposition approaches are, in general, based on the Fourier Transform [3] or on variations of it, such as the Short-Time Fourier Transform [4] and the Generic Fourier Transform [5]. Due to its characteristics, Multi-Resolution Fourier Transform [6] can be included in both approaches.

To evaluate the potential of the time-scale-frequency transforms, four different approaches are tested and compared in this paper: the Fourier Transform (FT), the Short-Time Fourier Transform (STFT), the Wavelet Transform (WT), and the Multi-resolution Fourier Transform (MFT). Methods for dimensionality reduction, feature selection, theoretical decision and error estimation are employed for the improvement and evaluation of the discriminative potential of the approaches. The cost, accuracy and discriminative potential of the approaches are analyzed and compared based on the results of experiments developed over a database of 300 digitalized leaves of 15 different plant species.

G. Bebis et al. (Eds.): ISVC 2005, LNCS 3804, pp. 684–689, 2005.

2 Time-Scale-Frequency Decompositions

2.1 The Fourier Transform

Through the FT [3], temporal measurements are decomposed and represented by their spectral information. By definition, given a periodic function $x(t)$, its FT $X(\omega)$ is obtained by:

$$X(\omega) = \int_{-\infty}^{\infty} x(t)e^{-j\omega t}dt \tag{1}$$

where ω is the analyzed frequency. Since $e^{-j\omega t} = \cos(\omega t) - j\sin(\omega t)$, the simplest interpretation of the equation (1) is that the signal $x(t)$ is decomposed through sinusoids and co-sinusoids of different frequencies.

Advantages of using FT in shape description emerge from the speed and ease by which its coefficients can be normalized to possible signal variances, such as rotation, reflection, scale and position changes [5].

2.2 The Short-Time Fourier Transform

The STFT [4] makes possible the differentiation of signals whose FT spectral representations are identical (resulting from integration between ($-\infty,\infty$) of equation (1)). In this approach, a function $x(t)$ is multiplied by some fixed-width window function which is, typically, non-zero only in a region of interest. Therefore, by centering the window in different positions over the signal, it is possible to decompose it in the spectral domain, keeping the relationship between the analyzed frequencies and their occurrence locations. The STFT of $x(t)$ is computed by:

$$X(t_g, \omega) = \int_{-\infty}^{\infty} x(t)g(t - t_g)e^{-j\omega t}dt \tag{2}$$

where $g(t - t_g)$ is a window function and t_g is its center. A Gaussian is usually used as window, leading to the least uncertainty for the transformation [7].

Invariance normalizations from FT are mostly preserved here. However, signature shifts cause proportional shifts in the STFT time axis. This can be overcome by either time shifting the whole result to start at a pre-defined position (e.g. max or min) or using some measurement taken along the time axis.

2.3 Wavelet Transform

The WT [2] is based on the signal decomposition through a family of functions called *wavelets.* A *wavelet* family is built from a function limited in time, usually called the *mother wavelet* (ψ), and dilations and translations of this function. The decomposition of a signal $x(t)$ by WT is obtained through the equation (3):

$$X(a, b) = \frac{1}{\sqrt{a}} \int_{-\infty}^{\infty} x(t)\psi(\frac{t - b}{a})dt \tag{3}$$

where a and b are the respective scale and translation parameters.

A time x scale space results from wavelet decomposition, and from it, feature vectors can be composed by its coefficients or by any other measurement taken along the axes. Regarding invariance acquisition, scale changes and translations can be treated directly during the contour parameterization, dividing the whole signature by its maximum value and using coordinates relative to the shape centroid. Rotations, reflections and changes on sampling initial point result in signature shifts and, consequently, time shifts on wavelet coefficient. Invariances can be acquired through the use of measurements taken along the time axis.

2.4 The Multi-resolution Fourier Transform

Extending the STFT concepts, the MFT [6] performs signal decomposition using the same equation (2) but with variable window width σ. Thus, time, scale and frequency are correlated to form a space capable of representing arbitrary signals in a non-ambiguous fashion. However, the main difficulty associated with this transform is its high computational cost.

One alternative, called Instantaneous Multi-Resolution Fourier Transform (IMFT) [8], is an approach to reduce the MFT dimensionality through time fixation. Time is fixed by centering the window over a relevant position t_g of the signal $x(t)$, and freeing the window width σ and the analysis frequency ω. It is important to notice that this procedure retains the local analysis capability of the descriptor.

Since IMFT is the multiple application of FT over larger parts of the signal, invariances can be acquired, at each change of σ, the same way as with FT, except the selection of t_g, which must be done by manually indication or higher level knowledge. Its coefficients can be used as descriptors, as can any other measurements which exploit the variation of coefficients due to the successive increase of the window.

3 Evaluation Methodology

3.1 Preprocessing and Feature Extraction

Leaf samples (Figure (1a)) were digitalized with a scanner, configured to generate 8-bit monochromatic images with 70 ppi. The sample contours were extracted using 8-neighborhood sequential capture of thresholded boundaries. The apex reference position was indicated manually for each sample, but this information was used only by IMFT descriptors. The contours were thus represented by their centroid distance signature normalized in amplitude $(0 - 1)$, resampled to 512 points and decomposed by the transforms under consideration.

Features were extracted from the resulting decompositions, helping to identify descriptors which could make viable the complete discrimination of the tested species. Thus, as descriptors, feature sets composed by the transform coefficients or measurements, as energy, moment and entropy, were analyzed, observing always their invariance acquisition procedures. For the WT, the features were also extracted using decompositions through Morlet and Mexican Hat wavelet families.

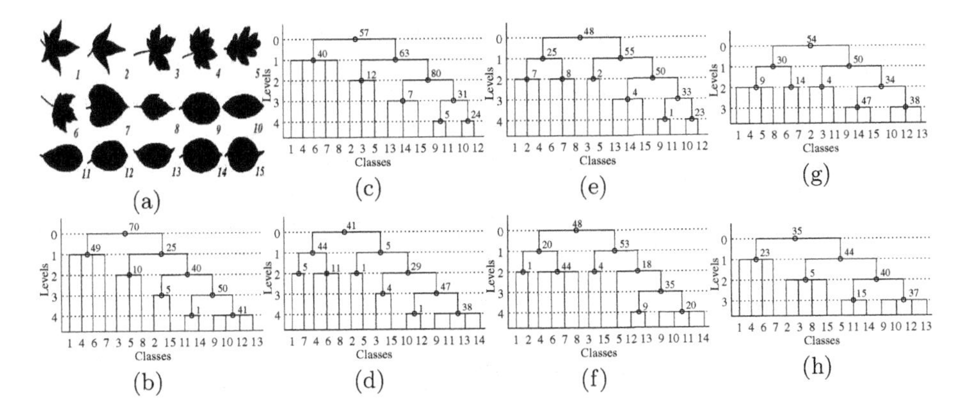

Fig. 1. Hierarchical classification trees for dataset illustrated in (a): (b) FT Coefficients, (c) STFT Coefficients, (d) Energies of STFT, (e) Energies of WT (Morlet), (f) Energies of WT (Mexican Hat), (g) IMFT Coefficients and (h) Energies of IMFT

3.2 Dimensionality Reduction and Feature Selection

For all approaches, dimensionality reduction was performed by Linear Discriminate Analysis (LDA). LDA transforms the original feature space maximizing the distances between classes and minimizing the distances within classes. The transformation which best achieves this is determined by the eigen-decomposition of $C_W^{-1}C_B$, where C_B and C_W are the between- and within-class covariance matrices, respectively.

Taking advantage of the its calculation conditions, dimensionality reduction was achieved by determination of the most relevant features, made through sequential elimination of those features which presented the smallest relationships var^B/var^W. For classification purposes, only the first two components of the LDA space are considered, which will likely be formed by the best features.

3.3 Theoretical Decision and Error Estimation

A Bayesian Classifier, applied over the LDA space formed by the first two components, was used to evaluate the discriminative capability of the tested descriptors. The Bayesian discriminant function between a class ω_i and an unknown sample x_k can be calculated by $S_i(x_k) = p(x_k|\omega_i)P(\omega_i)$, where $p(x_k|\omega_i)$ is the probability that x_k belongs to the class ω_i, and $P(\omega_i)$ is the occurrence probability of the class ω_i. The sample x_k is assumed to belong to the class ω_i which yields the largest numerical value for $S_i(x_k)$.

In general, the identification of a large number of classes increases overlappings and decision ambiguities, thus reducing the system classification capability. To minimize overlappings and improve classification capability, the sample classification was made in steps, in a hierarchical tree fashion, whose branches were formed through the successive subdivision of the population into smaller groups every time a decision ambiguity did occur. However, until this moment, the subdivision of the population has been performed through visual inspection, as gaps between classes are noted. Feature selection was made in each classification step and the minimum number of features was assigned to the respective tree node (Figure (1)).

The method Leave-One-Out was employed for estimating the classification accuracy. This method was chosen because it generates the most realistic estimations for relative small populations and, in addition, allows the exact reproduction of the results, due to its independence on random choices.

4 Experiments and Result Analysis

As database, 300 images of leaves equally distributed over 15 plant species were used (Figure (1a)). For comparison purposes, results of the two best feature sets of each approach will be shown, except for FT, which only one feature set, composed initially by the first 120 lowest order coefficients, was used. For the STFT, descriptors initially formed by (1) 340 normalized coefficients and (2) 64 coefficient energies were analyzed. For the IMFT, descriptors initially formed by (1) 200 normalized coefficients and (2) 60 coefficient energies were used. Since the WT coefficients are influenced by horizontal shifts of the signatures caused by the shape rotation, reflection and changes on contour sampling, feature sets were formed by coefficient energies calculated from the signal decomposition through the bases *Morlet* and *Mexican Hat.*

Figures (1b-h) illustrate the hierarchical classification trees for the mentioned descriptors. For each illustrated result, a transform was applied over the centroid distance signature of the signals, and, after feature extractions from the resulting space and respective invariance normalizations, descriptors were formed and then classified by a Bayesian Classifier in a hierarchical fashion, as overlapping of classes did occur. For Bayesian equation, Gaussian distributions were assigned to the classes, and all classes were assumed to have equal occurrence probability.

Cost factors reflect the efficiency of each approach and can be compared with an eye to the establishment of a methodology for natural shape recognition. Aspects which influence the classification cost of the approaches are: (1) the number

Table 1. Summary of results (see text for details)

Approaches		Levels (Nodes)	Feats.[1]	Cost [sec][2]			Accuracy	
				Descrip.	Classif.	Total	No Tree	Tree
FT	Coeffs.	4(8)	102	0.002	0.940	0.942	24%	100%
STFT	Coeffs.	4(8)	92	0.045	0.820	0.865	27%	100%
	Energ.	4(10)	63	0.150	0.670	0.820	29%	100%
WT	Morlet	4(10)	60	0.800	0.580	1.380	31%	100%
	Mex.Hat	4(10)	58	0.780	0.570	1.350	32%	100%
IMFT	Coeffs.	3(8)	62	0.030	0.442	0.472	34%	100%
	Energ.	3(6)	60	0.150	0.440	0.590	37%	100%

[1] Union of feature sets of each node.
[2] Estimated by a Matlab algorithm on 333MHz/512MB-RAM SUN station.

of nodes in the tree, since it is directly related to the number of applications of the classification algorithm; and (2) the number of minimum features needed to differentiate the classes, which influences the cost for feature extraction and dimensionality reduction. In the tests performed, the number of minimum features was obtained through the union of the feature subsets from each tree node. Table (1) summarizes the results of the tested descriptors.

5 Conclusions

The four tested approaches resulted in good accuracy in the identification of the species being examined after the hierarchical approach was adopted. However, the descriptors extracted from IMFT showed slightly better discriminative capability. This conclusion is based both on the smaller number of tree subdivisions needed for the complete identification of the classes and on the smaller number of features required for each tree node. Although the number of levels contributes to an increase in computational cost, it was possible to observe that the processing cost associated with the sample feature extraction was a major influence in the computational performance of the approaches, and the main factor responsible for the greater time demand by WT descriptors. As expected, the FT approach showed the best performance during the feature extraction step, but due to its greater number of features and classification levels, more time was consumed in the classification step than in the same step in the approaches derived from it (STFT and IMFT).

The disadvantage of the IMFT, compared to the other approaches, is its dependence on the user interaction or higher level knowledge necessary to determine the most suitable position for the analysis window. This procedure could, eventually, limit the use of this approach for automatic systems. Nevertheless, the identification of this position could be made through search methods over the sample contours, an issue not raised in this work.

References

1. Mokhtarian, F.: Silhouette-based isolated object recognition through curvature scale space. IEEE Transactions on PAMI **17** (1996) 539–544
2. Mallat, S.: A Wavelet Tour of Signal Processing. 2 edn. Volume 1. Academic Press (1999)
3. Kammler, D.W.: A First Course in Fourier Analysis. Prentice Hall (2000)
4. Allen, J., Rabiner, L.: A unified approach to short-time fourier analysis and synthesis. Proceedings of the IEEE **65** (1977) 1558–1564
5. Zhang, D.: Image Retrieval Based on Shape. PhD thesis, Faculty of Information Technology, Monash University (2002)
6. Calway, A.D.: The Multiresolution Fourier Transform: A General Purpose Tool for Image Analysis. PhD thesis, Warlick University (1989)
7. Gabor, D.: Theory of communication. IEE Journal **93** (1946) 429–457
8. Loss, L.A.: Discrimination of natural contours through the analysis of time-scale-frequency decompositions (portuguese). Master's thesis, State University of Campinas (2004)

Color and Edge Refinement Method for Content Based Image Retrieval

Taesu Park, Minhyuk Chang, and Jongan Park

Department of Information & Communications Engineering, Chosun University,
375 Seosuk-dong, Dong-gu, Gwangju, 501-759, Korea
japark@chosun.ac.kr

Abstract. Standard histograms, because of their efficiency and insensitivity to small changes, are widely used for content based image retrieval. But the main disadvantage of histograms is that many images of different appearances can have similar histograms because histograms provide coarse characterization of an image. Color histograms too are widely used and suffer from the same problem. In this paper, the technique defined is based on Histogram Refinement [1] and we call it Color and Egde Refinement. Color and Egde Refinement method splits the pixels in a given bucket into several classes just like histogram refinement method. The classes are all related to colors & edges and are based on color & edge coherence vectors.

1 Introduction

There are queries that require the comparing of the images on their overall appearance. In such cases, color histograms can be employed because they are very efficient regarding computations. Plus they offer insensitivity to small changes regarding camera position. But the main problem with color histograms is their coarse characterization of an image. That may itself result in same histograms for images with different appearances. Color histograms are employed in systems as QBIC[2], Chabot[3] etc.

In this paper, a modified scheme based on histogram refinement [1] method is presented. The histogram refinement method provides that the pixels within a given bucket be split into classes based upon some local property and these split histograms are then compared on bucket by bucket basis just like normal histogram matching but the pixels within a bucket with same local property are compared. So the results are better than the normal histogram matching. So not only the color and edge features of the image are used but also spatial information is incorporated to refine the histogram. The results are obtained by testing the algorithm on a database of images provided in MPEG-7 data.

2 Related Work

Hsu [4] exploits the degree of overlap between regions of the same color. They used a database of 260 images. Smith & Chang's method also partitions the image. However, they allow each region to contain multiple different colors instead of one predominant color like in Hsu method described above [5]. They used database of 3100 images.

G. Bebis et al. (Eds.): ISVC 2005, LNCS 3804, pp. 690 – 695, 2005.

Rickman and Stonham [6] provide a method based on small equilateral triangles with fixed sides. Stricker and Dimai [7] finds the first three moments of the color distributions in an image. Huang et al. [8] method is called Color Correlogram and it captures the spatial correlation between colors.

Pass and Zabih [1] method is Histogram Refinement. They partition histogram bins by the spatial coherence of pixels. They further refine it by using additional feature. The additional feature used is the center of the image. The center of the image is defined as the 75% centermost pixels. Jong-An, Bilal et al. [9] provided shape description based on histogram based chain codes.

3 Method

3.1 Color Refinement

Color Refinement is based on histogram refinement [1] method. The histogram refinement method provides that the pixels within a given bucket be split into classes based upon some local property and these split histograms are then compared on bucket by bucket basis and the pixels within a bucket are compared.

Pre-processing

Three different methods can be used for preprocessing:

a) Convert to HSV Space. Quantize so as to obtain 8:2:2 (HSV) from 256:256:256 (RGB). Then obtain the histogram.
b) Convert to HSV Space. Quantize so as to obtain 8:2:2 (HSV) from 256:256:256 (RGB). Consider only the hue value. Then obtain the histogram.
c) Convert to grayscale intensity image. Uniformly quantize into eight quantized values. Then obtain the histogram.

Methods (b) and (c) are considered for preprocessing so as to reduce the feature vector size which is associated with the image.

Color Refinement Method

Color histogram buckets are partitioned based on spatial coherence just like computed by Pass and Zabih [1]. A pixel is coherent if it is a part of some sizable similar colored region, otherwise it is incoherent. So the pixels are classified as coherent or incoherent within each color bucket. If a pixel is part of a large group of pixels of the same color which form at least one percent of the image then that pixel is a coherent pixel and that group is called the coherent group or cluster. Otherwise it is incoherent pixel and the group is incoherent group or cluster.

Then two more properties are calculated for each bin. First the numbers of clusters are found for each case, i.e., coherent and incoherent case in each of the bin. Secondly, the average of each cluster is computed. So for each bin, there are six values: one each for percentage of coherent pixels and incoherent pixels, number of coherent clusters and incoherent clusters, average of coherent cluster and incoherent cluster.

These values are calculated by computing the connected components. A connected component C is a maximal set of pixels such that for any two pixels $p,p' \in C$, there is a path in C between p and p′. Eight connected neighbors method is used for computing connected component. A pixel is classified as coherent if it is part of a connected component whose size is equal to or greater than τ ($\tau = 1\%$ of the image size). Otherwise it is classified as incoherent. And the connected component is classified as coherent connected component if it equals or exceeds τ. Otherwise it is classified as incoherent connected component. Finally the average for coherent and incoherent connected component is calculated.

For each discretized color j, let the number of coherent pixels as α_j, the number of coherent connected components as $C_{\alpha j}$ and the average of coherent connected component as $\mu_{\alpha j}$. Similarly, let the number of incoherent pixels as β_j, the number of incoherent connected components as $C_{\beta j}$ and the average of incoherent connected component as $\mu_{\beta j}$. For each discretized color j, the total number of pixels are $\alpha_j+\beta_j$ and the color histogram summarizes the image as $<\alpha_1+\beta_1,\ldots,\alpha_n+\beta_n>$.

Post-processing
We use the L_1 distance to compare two images I and I′. Using the L_1 distance, the jth bucket's contribution to the distance between I and I′ is:

$$\Delta_1 = |(\alpha_j-\alpha'_j)| + |(\beta_j-\beta'_j)| \quad (1)$$

$$\Delta_2 = |(C_{\alpha j}-C'_{\alpha j})| + |(C_{\beta j}-C'_{\beta j})| \quad (2)$$

$$\Delta_3 = |(\mu_{\alpha j}-\mu'_{\alpha j})| + |(\mu_{\beta j}-\mu'_{\beta j})| \quad (3)$$

So we get a very finer distinction with this method. In original scheme [1], only equation (1) is used and for comparison, the following equation is used:

$$\Delta_1 = |(\alpha_j+\beta_j)| - |(\alpha'_j+\beta'_j)| \quad (4)$$

Also equations (1) to (3) provide for incorporating the scalability. And remove problems identified by Huang et al. [8] which cannot be removed by only using CCV (Color Coherent Vector) defined in [1].

3.2 Edge Refinement

Edge Refinement is also based on histogram refinement [1] method.

Pre-processing
Two different methods can be used for preprocessing:

a) Apply the Sobel operator to find the horizontal and vertical edges.
b) Apply the Compass operator to find the edges in eight directions.

Method (a) is considered for preprocessing so as to reduce the feature vector size.

Edge Refinement Method
First the buckets are formed based on edge direction in the pre-processing stage. Then for each bucket, total number of pixels is computed. We used the Sobel operator to compute the edges. We computed horizontal and vertical edges only. Hence two buckets were formed in our case. Here, another improvement is made by classifying each pixel in the bucket as coherent or incoherent.

Then four more values are calculated in each bucket. First the numbers of clusters are found in each bucket by 8-neighborhood rule and secondly, the average of the cluster is computed in each bucket. Then based on the number of pixels and the clusters, number of straight edges and slanted edges are computed. So for each bin, there are five values: one each for total number of pixels, number of clusters, average of cluster, number of straight edges and number of slanted edges.

These values are calculated by computing the connected components. The connected component is classified as straight edge cluster if it occupies rows (in case of horizontal edges) or columns (in case of vertical edges) equal to or less than τ ($\tau = 3$ rows/columns in our case). Otherwise it is classified as slanted edge cluster. Also, one more condition is added that the straight or slanted edge cluster must have at least 3 pixels. For each edge direction j, let the number of pixels as α_j, the number of connected components as C_j, the average of connected component as μ_j, the number straight edge cluster as γ_j, and the number of slanted edge cluster as Γ_j. Again we used the L_1 distance to compare two images I and I′.

4 Results and Discussion

We implemented the color refinement and used it for image retrieval from a database of images provided in CD 6 and CD 8 of the MPEG-7 test material. We conducted the tests for methods (b) and (c) listed in the pre-processing stage in section 3.1. This was done to reduce the feature vector size. We obtained six values for each of the bucket in the histogram. The six values include percentage of coherent pixels (α_j), percentage of incoherent pixels (β_j), number of coherent clusters ($C_{\alpha j}$), number of incoherent clusters ($C_{\beta j}$), average of coherent cluster ($\mu_{\alpha j}$) and average of incoherent cluster ($\mu_{\beta j}$) for each jth bucket. We used total of eight buckets. So the total length of the feature vector associated with an image is 48 integer values.

We compared the results with L_1 distance. First, we used equation (1) for identifying the similarity between images. Then we used equation (2) to further refine the results and finally we used equation (3) to get the final result. Descriptor values for some of the still images from CD 6 are provided in Appendix 1.

Edge refinement was used to further refine results of color refinement method. We conducted the tests for method (a) listed in the section 3.2. We obtained five values for each of the bucket in the histogram. We used total of two buckets. The total length of feature vector associated with image is 10 integer values. We compared the results with L1 distance. Descriptor values for some of the still images for edge refinement are shown in appendix 2. As can be seen from the tables in appendix 2, the values for total number of pixels (αj) vary greatly and there analysis form the first step in matching an image with the other. That search is further refined by number of clusters (Cj).

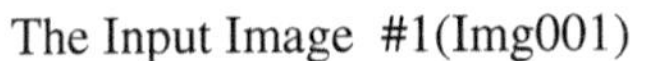

The Input Image #1(Img001) The result for Image #1 (Img002)

For image number one shown above (Img001 in the tables), we got only one result. On inspection of all the images of the database, we found that this was the closest result. With further experiments, we found that this was also the case for many more images. For example in appendix 1, Img005 was found to be the result for Img004, Img006 was found to be the result for Img008, Img009 was found to be the result for Img007 and so on. However, we also got multiple results for our input image, for example, we found Img4, Img5 and Img 6 as the results for Img 3.

5 Conclusions

Usage of method (a) in section 3.1 and 3.2, described in pre-processing, give better results. However, the length of the feature vector is increased from 48 integer values to 192 integer values. So, that method was not implemented.

Color refinement method takes care of the color as well as the spatial relation feature. And hence, it provides better results than the equivalent methods.

Application of edge refinement method to the results of color refinement method provides significant improvement and provides more accurate and precise results.

Acknowledgements

This study was supported by research fund from the Chosun University, Gwangju, Korea (2005).

References

1. Greg Pass and Ramin Zabih. Histogram Refinement for content–based image retrieval. In IEEE Workshop on Applications of Computer Vision, pages 96-102, December 1996.
2. M. Flickner et al. Query by image and video content: The QBIC system. IEEE computer, 28(9):23-32, September 1995
3. Virginia Ogle and Michael Stonebraker. Chabot: Retrieval from a relational database of images. IEEE computer, 28(9):40-48, September 1995.
4. Wynne Hsu, T. S. Chua and H. K. Pung. An integrated color-spatial approach to content based image retrieval. In ACM Multimedia Conference, pages 305-313, 1995.
5. Michael Swain and Dana Ballard. Color indexing. International Journal of Computer Vision, 7(1):11-32, 1991.
6. Rick Rickman and John Stonham. Content based image retrieval using color tuple histograms. SPIE proceedings, 2670:2-7, February 1996.
7. Markus Stricker and Alexander Dima. Color indexing with weak spatial constraints. SPIE proceedings, 2670:29-40, February 1996.
8. Jing Huang, S. Ravi Kumar, Mandar Mitra, Wei-Jing Zhu, and Ramin Zabih. Image indexing using color correlograms. In IEEE Conference on Computer Vision and Pattern Recognition, pages 762-768, 1997.
9. Jong-An Park, Min-Hyuk Chang, Tae Sun Choi and Muhammad Bilal Ahmad, "Histogram based chain codes for shape description," IEICE Trans. On Communications, vol.E86-B, no.12, pp. 3662-3665, December 2003.

Appendix 1. Descriptor Values (Color Refinement Method) for Images from CD 6

Image #	α_j	β_j	$C_{\alpha j}$	$C_{\beta j}$	$\mu_{\alpha j}$	$\mu_{\beta j}$
Img0017	0	0	0	0	0	0
Img0018	0	0	0	0	0	0
Img0019	0	0	0	0	0	0
Img0041	0	0	0	0	0	0
Img0042	0	0	0	0	0	0
Img0043	0	0	0	0	0	0
Img0085	0	0	0	0	0	0

Bin 1 (Above), Bin 2 (Below)

Image #	α_j	β_j	$C_{\alpha j}$	$C_{\beta j}$	$\mu_{\alpha j}$	$\mu_{\beta j}$
Img0017	98	2	1	11	8178	16
Img0018	100	0	1	5	14503	1
Img0019	99	1	1	5	14897	25
Img0041	98	2	2	1	7596	233
Img0042	100	0	1	23	11772	1
Img0043	98	2	2	20	8136	17
Img0085	98	2	1	8	2283	5

Bin 3

Image #	α_j	β_j	$C_{\alpha j}$	$C_{\beta j}$	$\mu_{\alpha j}$	$\mu_{\beta j}$
Img0017	0	100	0	19	0	8
Img0018	0	100	0	18	0	7
Img0019	0	100	0	8	0	11
Img0041	0	100	0	2	0	7
Img0042	0	100	0	4	0	6
Img0043	0	100	0	7	0	9
Img0085	0	100	0	14	0	16

Appendix 2. Descriptor Values for Edge Refinement Method

Bin 1: Horizontal Edges

Image #	α_j	C_j	μ_j	γ_j	Γ_j
Img001	1334	372	4	127	29
Img002	1317	359	4	136	28
Img003	1147	232	5	88	20
Img004	1028	205	5	73	26
Img005	1110	208	5	70	34
Img006	996	219	5	84	25
Img007	856	174	5	49	34
Img008	1062	239	4	102	30
Img009	775	159	5	48	40
Img010	890	199	4	68	30

Bin 2: Vertical Edges

Image #	α_j	C_j	μ_j	γ_j	Γ_j
Img001	1159	404	3	111	36
Img002	1204	446	3	123	38
Img003	978	364	3	82	34
Img004	925	241	4	49	29
Img005	957	315	3	73	30
Img006	937	187	5	61	31
Img007	825	133	6	52	22
Img008	944	187	5	64	28
Img009	824	158	5	57	35
Img010	1043	216	5	83	32

Selecting a Discriminant Subset of Co-occurrence Matrix Features for Texture-Based Image Retrieval

Najlae Idrissi[1,2], José Martinez[1], and Driss Aboutajdine[2]

[1] Atlas-GRIM, INRIA & LINA (FRE CNRS 2729) Polytechnic School of the University of Nantes BP 50609, 44306 Nantes cedex 03, France
[2] GSCM Science Faculty of Rabat, University Mohamed V Rabat, Morocco
aboutaj@fsr.ac.ma, {prnom.nom}@lina.univ-nantes.fr

Abstract. In the general case, searching for images in a content-based image retrieval (CBIR) system amounts essentially, and unfortunately, to a sequential scan of the whole database. In order to accelerate this process, we want to generate summaries of the image database. In this paper, we focus on the selection of the texture features that will be used as a signature in our forthcoming system. We analysed the descriptors extracted from grey-level co-occurrence matrices's (COM) under the constraints imposed by database systems.

1 Introduction and Motivation

For one or two decades, with content-based image retrieval (CBIR) systems, images can directly be retrieved by their visual content such as colour [1], texture [2], shape, and others [3]. The use of texture proved its effectiveness and usefulness in pattern recognition and computer vision. Texture is generally hard to be described using key words because our vocabulary for textures is limited. This is a strong motivation to use them in a CBIR. Also, texture is recognised as an essential feature in order to classify, recognise, and, as of this work, query images. However, no general definition of texture exists despite its importance in digital images [4] [5].

Several techniques have been proposed and compared to analyse and describe the texture. Strand and Taxt [6] compared filtering features [7] and co-occurrence statistics and found that co-occurrence matrices were the best. Buf et al. [8] report that several texture features offer roughly the same performance when evaluating co-occurrence features [9], fractal dimension, transform and filter bank features, number of grey-level extrema per area, and curvilinear integration features. Compared to run-length difference, grey-level difference density, and power spectrum, co-occurrence-based features were found better as reported by Conners and Harlow [10].

Consequently, the first aim of this study is to evaluate the performance of texture features extracted from grey-level co-occurrence matrices (COM) for retrieving similar textures. An additional and salient requirement is that such features must be used within an *actual* image database system, i.e., a

G. Bebis et al. (Eds.): ISVC 2005, LNCS 3804, pp. 696–703, 2005.

general-purpose database management system (DBMS) rather than an *ad hoc* CBIR. Due to hard limitations of multi-dimensional indexing [11] [12], still harder for standard DBMSs, the feature vector's size has to be quite low, in the order of only four up to, say, twelve for high-dimensional indexing techniques, e.g., X-trees [13] or SR-trees [14] (not yet available as standard tools). Therefore, firstly, they have to be as *discriminative* as possible, they can distinguish between different classes of textures, and secondly as *uncorrelated* as possible, the features must be independent to avoid the redundancy's problem which may influence the analyses. Let us note that the second property should be verified outside the DBMS world too. Finally, we also want the used properties to be interpretable and understandable by the human point of view since we will also have to translate them into linguistic variables during a following stage of our work.

The rest of the paper is organised as follows. The co-occurrence matrices method is presented in section 2 for texture analysis and the various descriptors that can be taken into consideration. In section 3, the Experiments are conducted and presented in order to select a subset of descriptors that satisfy our requirements. Finally, in the conclusion in section 5 we indicate how the results of this paper will be used in the next step of our work.

2 Texture Description

2.1 Co-occurrence Matrices

A co-occurrence matrix (COM) is the joint probability of occurrences of grey-levels i and j between pairs of pixels. Each value x at coordinate (i, j) in the matrix reflects the frequency of the grey-levels i and j separated by a given distance d (offset) along a given direction θ. The pair (d, θ) is the key of a COM. Formally, the definition of COM matrix for an $N \times M$ image f is the normalised square matrix $K \times K$ given as follows, where K is the maximum grey-level and $i, j \in \{1 \dots K\}$:

$$P_{d,\theta}(i,j) = \frac{\left| \left\{ (n,m) : \begin{array}{c} f(n,m) = i, \\ f(n + d\cos\theta, \\ m + d\sin\theta) = j \end{array} \right\} \right|}{N \times M} \quad (1)$$

As an example, figure 1 shows a bark texture and some of its related COMs.

2.2 COM-Based Selected Descriptors

From COM, one derives numerical parameters that are more convenient and useful to analyse and describe textures. In the early 70's, Haralick et al. [9] proposed fourteen parameters. This approach explored the grey-level spatial dependence of texture.

For our work, we considered that, among the proposed fourteen, eight are *a priori* pertinent. The rationale for the choice of these features is multiple: (i) a

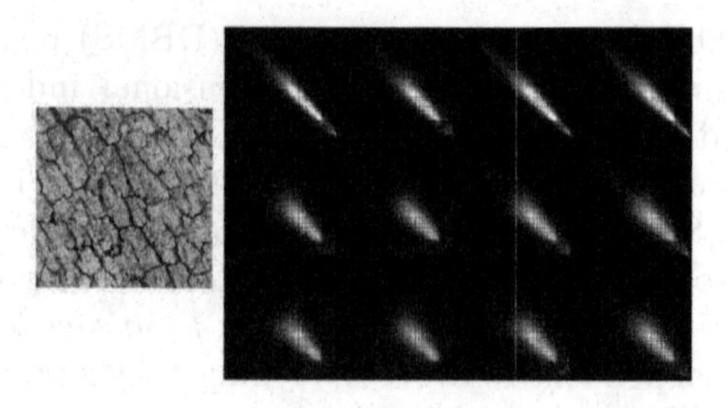

Fig. 1. A Bark texture and some of its grey-level co-occurrence matrices calculated respectively for $d = 1, 3, 5$ (in row) and $\theta = 0, 45, 90, 135$ (in column)

Table 1. The eight retained Haralick' descriptors

Feature	Formula
energy (eng)	$\sum_{i=0}^{n}\sum_{j=0}^{n} p_{d,\theta}(i,j)^2$
uniformity (unif)	$\sum_{i=0}^{n} p_{d,\theta}(i,i)^2$
local homogeneity (homloc)	$\sum_{i=0}^{n}\sum_{j=0}^{n} \frac{1}{1+(i-j)^2} p_{d,\theta}(i,j)$
entropy (ent)	$-\sum_{i=0}^{n}\sum_{j=0}^{n} p_{d,\theta}(i,j) \log p_{d,\theta}(i,j)$
variance (var)	$\sum_{i=0}^{n}\sum_{j=0}^{n} (i-\mu)^2 p_{d,\theta}(i,j)$
contrast (cont)	$\sum_{i=0}^{n}\sum_{j=0}^{n} (i-j)^2 p_{d,\theta}(i,j)$
correlation (corr)	$\sum_{i=0}^{n}\sum_{j=0}^{n} \frac{(i-\mu_i)(j-\mu_j) p_{d,\theta}(i,j)}{\sigma_i \sigma_j}$
directionality (dir)	$\sum_{i=0}^{n} p_{d,\theta}(i,i)$

careful reading of the literature indicates that the other six parameters are seldom used, (ii) they are computationally less expensive, an important constraint to be taken into account when dealing with large image databases, (iii) we found ourselves uneasy to attribute a "natural" semantics (such as "coarse", "smooth", "contrasted", "directional", etc.) to the eliminated parameters, and (iv) we are searching for a minimal though discriminant set of descriptors, and eight is already large for us. The eight retained descriptors are presented in the Table 1.

3 Experiments

Experiments have been conducted on two consecutive stages. The first one consists in determining, among the previous eight features, the smallest subset of discriminant and uncorrelated ones. Next, we verify their discriminative power by computing precision/recall graphs for each of them individually, then for their combination using an Euclidean distance as a similarity measure.

3.1 Experimental Databases

These experiments have been conducted on images of:

- the Brodatz's album [15] as a training database (148 grey-level images being divided into 15 different classes),

- on images of the Meastex's collection [16] [17] (69 grey-level images divided into 5 different classes: Asphalt, 4; Concrete, 12; Grass, 18; Rock, 25; Misc, 10),
- and another excerpt, much more diverse, of the Brodatz's album as test databases (111 images labelled from D1 to D112 consisting of 31 classes).

3.2 Feature Extraction

A main problem with COM is the choice of the key. For the distance, we used $d = 1, 3, 5$ without observing differences (the presented results correspond to $d = 1$). For the direction, we used $\theta = 0, 45, 90, 135$. To obtain invariance by translation and rotation, we summed the four feature values $f_{\theta,d}$, for a given distance d of feature f (See Table 1):

$$f_d = \sum_{\theta \in \{0,45,90,135\}} f_{\theta,d} \tag{2}$$

4 Results

Firstly, we selected a sub-subset of the Haralick's features thanks to experiments on the first Brodatz's album sample. Then, we verified, on the two other image collections, that this selection is valid.

4.1 Selection of a Minimal Feature Vector

We studied the correlations between the eight descriptors calculated from COM in order to avoid redundancy as well as to reduce the size of the feature vector. Table 2 provides the correlation coefficients r (given for $d = 1$) on the first excerpt of the Brodatz's collection. By grouping the features depending on very strong (r is near to ± 1) or less strong (r is near to 0) correlations between them, we can further reduce the feature vector from eight dimensions to only five. Let us note that direction is a strong texture indicator that ought to be analysed differently in order to extract the actual orientation (otherwise it is strongly correlated to uniformity, a fact that can also be derived from equations in Table 1). Then, we analysed the effectiveness of the features thanks to the well-know precision/recall graph of information retrieval:

$$precision = \frac{retrieved \cap relevant}{relevant} \tag{3}$$

$$recall = \frac{retrieved \cap relevant}{retrieved} \tag{4}$$

Figure 2(a) gives the different graphs of the different features taken individually, to illustrate the discriminative power for each one. Secondly, thanks to this graph and the correlations of Table 2, we conducted the same test with

Table 2. Correlation coefficients between the eight descriptors on the excerpt of the Brodatz's collection (for $d = 1$)

	eng	unif	hom	ent	var	cont	corr	dir
eng	1	**0.99**	0.43	-0.20	-0.40	-0.19	-0.03	0.70
unif		1	0.39	-0.16	-0.42	-0.20	-0.02	0.67
hom			1	**-0.81**	-0.32	-0.38	-0.15	**0.88**
ent				1	0.43	0.37	0.25	-0.60
var					1	**0.91**	0.02	-0.08
cont						1	0.02	-0.05
corr							1	-0.13
dir								1

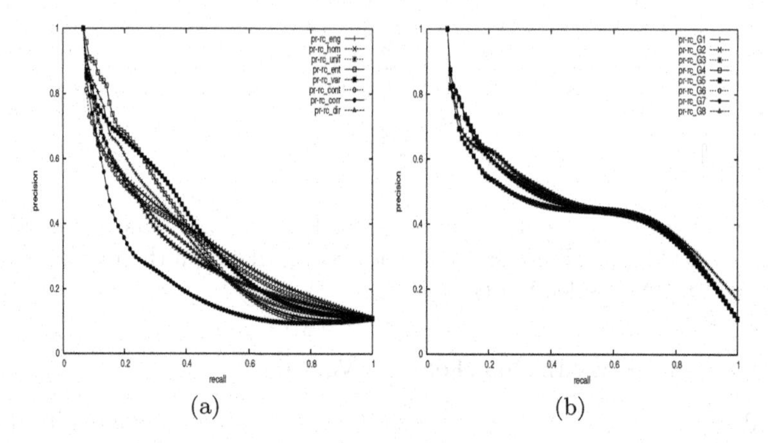

Fig. 2. Plot of different curves of precision/recall (a) for all descriptors individually, and (b) for possible combinations of these descriptors, for the "training" subset of the Brodatz's album

the eight possible combinations of uncorrelated features (i.e., $\{eng, unif\} \times \{ent, homloc\} \times \{var, cont\} \times \{corr\} \times \{dir\}$). Figure 2(b) shows the corresponding precision/recall graph, where the Euclidean distance is used as the similarity measure. The "best" feature vector consists of *energy*, *variance*, *entropy*, *correlation*, and *directionality*. Note the significative improvement in precision and recall of using several features.

4.2 Validation

Next, we validated this result on the two other sample databases. Interestingly enough, the results turned out to be disappointing for the Meastex database (See Figure 3(a)), whereas they were much better for the second excerpt of the Brodatz's album (See Figure 3(b)). Nevertheless, the selected combination remains the good one. Moreover, the differences between some variants do not

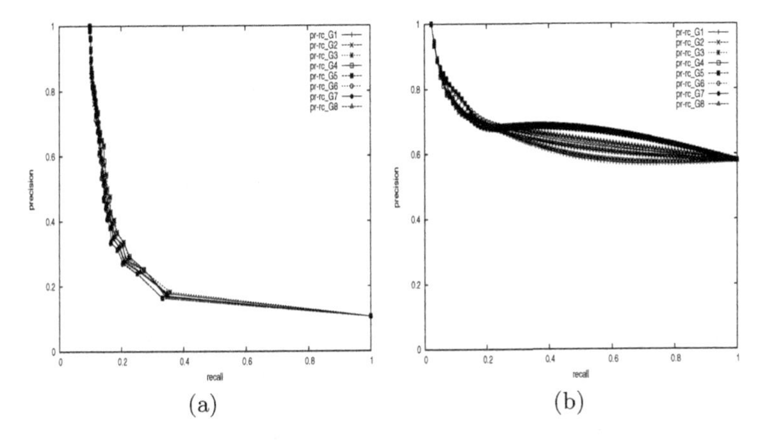

Fig. 3. Plot of different curves of precision/recall for the possible combinations of descriptors for (a) the Meastex database, and (b) the second excerpt of the Brodatz's album

seem statistically significant, which allows the designer to choose among two subsets. However, in order to understand such large a difference in the graphs, we went trough the correlation test for these two additional image collections. The respective correlations of the Meastex and the second excerpt of the Brodatz's album are given in Table 3(a) and (b). The additional correlations found in Table 3(a) with respect to Table 2 are easily explainable: the classes of the Meastex database demonstrate strong visual similarities between them (especially between Asphalt, Concrete, and Rock). However, the curve being so bad, a further reduction of the size of the feature vector is not an option. Conversely, the second Brodatz's sample demonstrates that additional features could have been used, since the correlation between variance (var) and contrast (cont) has disappeared. However, the curve being very good, a less rigorous reduction of the feature vector is certainly inappropriate; moreover, it could introduce a bias [18].

Table 3. Correlation coefficients between the eight descriptors (for $d = 1$) on (a) the Meastex collection, and (b) the second sample of the Brodatz's collection

	eng	unif	hom	ent	var	cont	corr	dir
eng	1	**0.96**	**0.96**	**-0.86**	-0.42	-0.50	-0.09	**0.98**
unif		1	**0.89**	-0.71	-0.29	-0.36	-0.13	**0.98**
hom			1	**-0.90**	-0.44	-0.61	-0.14	**0.98**
ent				1	0.71	0.80	0.09	**-0.84**
var					1	**0.86**	-0.09	-0.38
cont						1	-0.03	-0.52
corr							1	-0.15
dir								1

(a)

	eng	unif	hom	ent	var	cont	corr	dir
eng	1	**0.98**	0.80	-0.84	0.27	-0.11	-0.31	0.86
unif		1	0.78	-0.79	0.31	-0.35	0.31	**0.98**
hom			1	**-0.91**	0.34	-0.09	0.28	0.84
ent				1	-0.18	0.34	-0.32	**-0.93**
var					1	0.30	-0.35	0.41
cont						1	-0.15	-0.30
corr							1	0.24
dir								1

(b)

5 Conclusion

In this work, we analysed the benefit of using descriptors derived from grey-level co-occurrence matrices of images for these have been widely used and accepted as good texture descriptors. The aim was to decide which (1) *small subset* of (2) *discriminant* and (3) *uncorrelated* features to retain for future work.

The selection process was based on *a priori* selection, where general considerations have been taken into account, followed by an experiment conducted on well-known test collections of textured images in order to extract the descriptors that fit our needs. This selection work has led to the following set of texture descriptors: *energy*, *entropy*,*variance*, *correlation*, and *direction*.

These descriptors could be used directly into an image database. However, standard DBMSs are not at ease with computing complex functions (i.e., distances) because they cannot be efficiently indexed. More generally, *clustering* is unavoidable when dealing with large collections of images. Also, in order to offer different ways to query and browse an image database, we also want textures to be described, to some extents, thanks to key words.

Therefore, the next step in our work is to study the actual range of values for the various descriptors, their variations, their impact on the human perception, and finally their translation into *fuzzy linguistic variables.* These linguistic terms could be used are mere key words. In fact, an efficient and incremental algorithm has already been developed in our research team and used to cluster images based on colour features [19]. We shall extend it with these texture features.

References

1. Swain, M.J., Ballard, D.H.: Color indexing. International Journal of Computer Vision **7** (1991) 11–32
2. Ma, W.Y., Manjunath, B.S.: NETRA: A toolbox for navigating large image databases. In: Proceedings of the IEEE International Conference on Image Processing (ICIP'97). (1997)
3. Rui, Y., Huang, T.: Image retrieval: Current techniques, promising directions and open issues. Journal of Visual Communication and Image representation (1999)
4. Lin, H.C., Wang, L., Yang, S.: Extracting periodicity of a regular texture based on autocorrelation function. Pattern Recognition Letters **18** (1997) 433–443
5. Tamura, H., Mori, S., Yamawaki, T.: Texture features corresponding to visual perception. IEEE Transaction on Systems, Man and Cybernetics **8** (1978) 460–473
6. Stand, J., Taxt, T.: Local frequency features for texture classification. Pattern Recognition **27** (1994) 1397–1406
7. Randen, T., Husø y, J.: Filtering for texture classification: A comparative study. IEEE Transaction on Pattern Analysis and Machine Intelligence **21** (1999) 291–310
8. Buf, J., Kardan, H., Spann, M.: Texture feature performance for image segmentation. Pattern Recognition **23** (1990) 291–309
9. Haralick, R., Shanmugan, K., Dinstein, I.: Textural features for image classification. IEEE Trans. On Systems, Man, and Cybernetics **SMC-3** (1973) 610–621
10. Conners, R., Harlow, C.: A theorical comparison of texture algorithms. IEEE Transactions on Pattern Analysis and Machine Intelligence **2** (1980) 204–222

11. Beckmann, N., Kriegel, H.P., Schneider, R., Seeger, B.: The r*-tree: An efficient and robust access method for points and rectangles. Proceedings of ACM SIGMOD International Conference on Management of Data (1990) 322–331
12. Guttman, A.: R-trees: A dynamic index structure for spatial searching. proceedings of ACM SIGMOD International Conference on Management of Data (1984) 47–54
13. Berchtold, S., Keim, D.A., Kriegel, H.P.: The X-tree: An index structure for high-dimensional data. In: 22nd International Conference on Very Large Data Bases (VLDB), Mumbai (Bombay), India (1996) 28–39
14. Katayama, N., Satoh, S.: The SR-tree: an index structure for high-dimensional nearest neighbor queries. In: ACM International Conference on Management of Data (SIGMOD), Tucson, Arizona (1997) 369–380
15. (Brodatz's Texture Album) http://www.ux.his.no/ tranden/brodatz.html.
16. (Meastex database) http://ccsip.elec.uq.edu.au/ guy/meastex/meastex.html.
17. Smith, G., Burns, I.: Measuring texture classification algorithms. Pattern Recognition Letters **18** (1997) 1495–1501
18. Smeulders, A., Worring, M., Santini, S., Jain, R.: Content-based image retrieval at the end of the early years. IEEE Transactions on Pattern Analysis and Machine Intelligence **22** (2000) 1349–1380
19. Loisant, E., Saint-Paul, R., Martinez, J., Raschia, G., Mouaddib, N.: Browsing clusters of similar images. In: Acte des 19e Journes Bases de Donnes Avances(BDA'2003), Lyon, France (2003) 109–128

An Automatic Relevance Feedback in Image Retrieval Using Belief Functions

Saïd Kharbouche, Patrick Vannorenberghe, Christèle Lecomte, and Pierre Miché

Perception Systèmes Information, Laboratoire PSI FRE 2645 CNRS, Université de Rouen
UFR des sciences, Place Emile Blondel, 76821 Mont Saint Aignan Cedex, France
said.kharbouche@univ-rouen.fr
patrick.vannorenberghe@univ-rouen.fr
christele.lecomte@univ-rouen.fr, pierre.miche@insa-rouen.fr

Abstract. This paper proposes an automatic relevance feedback approach for content-based image retrieval using information fusion and without any user input. This method is proposed as an alternative of the simple ranking of result images. The idea consists to pass from a simple user selected query image to multi-images query in order to get more information about the query image type. Given a query image, the system first computes its feature vector to rank the images according to a well-chosen similarity measure. For each retrieved image, the degree of belief about the relevance is then assigned as a function of this measure. This degree of belief is then updated using an iterative process. At each iteration, we evaluate, for each retrieved image, the degree of relevance using the combination of belief functions associated to previously retrieved images. Then, each retrieved image is not found by the query image only but it is found by the query image and previously retrieved images too. Some experimental results will be proposed in this paper in order to demonstrate that the methodology improves the efficiency and accuracy of retrieval systems.

1 Introduction

The goal of any CBIR system (Content Based Image Retrieval) is to find the most similar images to a user selected query image. But CBIR is generally based on low-level visual features like colour, texture and shape. These low-level visual features can't always express the user's high-level concepts due to the richness of human semantics. That is because a lot of attention is given to systems based on the relevance feedback in order to explore user favorites for improving and enhancing retrieval performance. Various techniques have been proposed [1][2][3][4] for relevance feedback. They consist to update system parameters after each user reaction to a set of result images proposed by the system. These reactions are obtained by manual annotation of the user for each result image. When the user decides what best images are and what worst images are, the system uses these user inputs to recompute new ranked images, looking for more user satisfaction. There are other methods [5] based on automatic feedback but only to gather the recognized personal faces in order to use it later on identifying images of person in large collections. The

G. Bebis et al. (Eds.): ISVC 2005, LNCS 3804, pp. 704–709, 2005.

rest of this paper is organized as followed: we review the belief functions theory in section 2, our method of automatic relevance feedback using belief functions is presented in section 3. Section 4 summarizes experimental results. Finally, we give a conclusion in section 5.

2 Dempster-Shafer Theory

Dempster-shafer theory (or belief functions theory) has been already used in image retrieval systems to combine a lot of information sources (text analyzers, image content based analyzers) and it has been successfully compared with linear combination [6]. In this section, several concepts of the DS theory of evidence [7] are recalled, which allows introducing notations used in this paper. Let us denotes $\Omega=\{\omega_1, \omega_2, \ldots, \omega_M\}$ a finite set of mutually exclusive and exhaustive hypotheses, generally called the frame of discernment. Given an information source S and an unlabeled pattern X, which we look to recognize its unique label between the M subsets of the frame Ω. A basic belief assignment (bba) m[S,X] on Ω is defined as a function from 2^Ω to [0,1] verifying:

$$m[S,X](\emptyset)=0 \text{ and } \sum_{A\subseteq\Omega} m[S,X](A)=1. \tag{1}$$

Each subset A, such as m[S,X](A) > 0, is called a focal element of m[S,X]. An α-discounted bba $m^\alpha[S,X]$ can be obtained from the original bba m[S,X] as follows:

$$\begin{aligned} m^\alpha[S,X](A) &= \alpha.m[S,X](A) \qquad \forall\, A\subset\Omega, \qquad A\neq\Omega \\ m^\alpha[S,X](\Omega) &= 1-\alpha+\alpha.m[S,X](\Omega) \ \text{ with } 0\leq\alpha\leq 1. \end{aligned} \tag{2}$$

The discounting operation is useful when the source of information S, from which m[S,X] has been derived, is not fully reliable. In this case, coefficient α represents a form of metaknowledge about the source reliability, which could not be encoded in m[S,X]. Let S_1 and S_2 two sources of information and $m[S_1,.]$ and $m[S_2,.]$ their pieces of evidence. For an unlabeled pattern X, theses two bba can be aggregated with the Dempster's rule of combination (orthogonal sum $\oplus$), yielding to a unique belief function m[.,X] defined as:

$$m\,[.,.X](A)=\frac{\sum_{B\cap C=A}(m\,[S_1,X](B).m\,[S_2,X](C))}{\sum_{B\cap C=\phi}(m[S_1,X](B).m[S_2,X](C))}. \tag{3}$$

Based on rationality arguments developed in the TBM (Transferable Belief Model), Smets [8] proposes to transform m[S,X] into a pignistic probability function BetPm[S,X] used for decision making and defined for all $\omega_l\in\Omega$ as:

$$BetPm[S,X](\omega_l)=\sum_{A\subseteq\Omega\,/\,\omega_l\in A}\frac{m[S,X](A)}{|A|} \tag{4}$$

where |A| denotes the cardinality of A; and $l = \{1, 2\ldots M\}$. In this transformation, the mass of belief m[S,X](A) is distributed equally among the elements of A.

3 Automatic Feedback in Image Retrieval

Often the image which has the shortest distance to the query image is a relevant image; we will exploit this propriety in order to accumulate more information about the category of the query image. Our idea is simple: given an input image I_q (query image) and an information source S_q derived from this query image I_q with a reliability α_q, the image retrieval system returns an image I_1 (the higher ranked image). We can say that the information source S_q decides that the image I_1 is the most similar image to the query image I_q. Now we will consider another information source S_1 derived from the first retrieved image I_1 with a reliability α_1 and $\alpha_1 \leq \alpha_q$. The second most similar image will be retrieved by both sources S_q and S_1. After obtaining the second most similar image I_2, an information source S_2 will be derived from this image with a reliability coefficient α_2 where $\alpha_2 \leq \alpha_1 \leq \alpha_q$. The sources S_q, S_1 and S_2 will decide together which the third similar image is. The system follows this way until getting the desired number of retrieved images. Generally, to find the nth similar image, we consider n images (the query image and (n-1) previously retrieved images) as information sources (S_q, S_1, $S_2, \ldots S_{n-1}$) with different reliabilities ($\alpha_{n-1} \leq \ldots . \alpha_2 \leq \alpha_1 \leq \alpha_q$). Each one of these sources takes part on the decision of the next retrieved image I_n, combining all information issued from these information sources. Let B a set of *N* images in the database, and $R \subset B$ a set of the result images. At the beginning, the set R is empty: $R=\emptyset$. The set B/R represents the complementary of R into B (called the candidate images). The coefficient α_i denotes the reliability associated to information source S_i issued from the ith retrieved image I_i while α_q denotes the reliability coefficient related to information source S_q issued from the query image I_q. Theses values are chosen into the interval [0,1] (1 if the source is fully reliable and 0 if it is completely unreliable).

Let Ω= {relevant, not-relevant} the frame of discernment. So, we have three possible focal elements, two assumptions ("image is relevant" and "image is not relevant") and a composite assumption Ω also called uncertainty. Each information source $S_{i,}$ presented by an image $I_i \in R \cup \{I_q\}$ (i can be q) examines each image I_j in the set (B/R): is it a relevant image, not-relevant image or is there no opinion for this image I_j. For this reason, we propose a basic belief assignment $m[S_i,I_j]$, which distributes the belief quantity between three elements: relevant, no-relevant and uncertainty (Ω) and satisfyes:

$$m[S_i,I_j](\text{relevant}) + m[S_i,I_j](\text{not-relevant}) + m[S_i,I_j](\Omega)=1 \quad (5)$$

where $I_i \in R \cup \{I_q\}$ and $I_j \in (B/R)$. The quantity of belief given to the assumption "relevant" by S_i to I_j must be proportional to the distance between the two images I_i and I_j.. This distance, noted by $d(I_i,I_j)$, can be computed by the measure of the distance between their feature vectors d: $(\text{Features space})^2 \rightarrow [0,1]$ with $d(I_i,I_j)=d(V_i,V_j)$ where V_i and V_j are the feature vectors extracted respectively from the image I_i and the image I_j. The more the two images are similar, the smaller their distance is ($I_i=I_j \Rightarrow d(I_i,I_j)=0$). The basic belief assignment $m[S_i,I_j](.)$ which is discounted by a coefficient α_i according to the reliability of source S_i can be computed as follows:

$$\begin{aligned} m^{\alpha_i}[S_i,I_j](\text{relevant}) &= \alpha_i.(1-d(I_i,I_j)) \\ m^{\alpha_i}[S_i,I_j](\text{not relevant}) &= \alpha_i.d(I_i,I_j) \\ m^{\alpha_i}[S_i,I_j](\Omega) &= 1-\alpha_i. \end{aligned} \quad (6)$$

For each image I_j from B/R, we combine all basic belief assignments using the Dempster's combination rule (formula (3)). The aggregated bba is:

$$m[., I_j]= m^{\alpha_q}[S_q,I_j] \oplus m^{\alpha_1}[S_1,I_j] \oplus m^{\alpha_2}[S_2,I_j] \oplus..\oplus m^{\alpha_r}[S_r,I_j] \quad (7)$$

where r denotes the cardinality of R. After the discounting and combination phases, the system computes the pignistic probability using formula (4). Finally, the system decides what the most similar image (relevant image) is, by selecting, from B/R, the image which has the biggest value of pignistic probability for the subset "relevant" of the frame Ω. $I_a \in B/R$ is the most similar image if:

$$BetPm[., I_a](relevant) > BetPm[., I_b](relevant) \;\forall\; I_b \neq I_a \in B/R. \quad (8)$$

This retrieved image will be included into the set R of retrieved images. The retrieval operation can be stopped by putting a threshold on the cardinality of R or/and putting another threshold on pignistic probability.

4 Experiments

The feature vector used in this evaluation is based on colour histograms of nine sub-images [10] in order to represent the local information in different zones of the image. We reduce number of colours in space HSV (Hue, Saturation, Value) by a uniform and static quantization in 162 bins [9]: 18 bins for hue axis, 3 bins for saturation and 3 bins for value. With this method, the sub-image is now presented by a feature vector within a space of dimension 162. Thus, the image is presented by a matrix 9×162 (number of sub-images × number of quantified colours):

$$V_a = \begin{pmatrix} v^1_{a,1},\ldots\ldots,v^9_{a,1} \\ \vdots \\ v^1_{a,162},\ldots\ldots,v^9_{a,162} \end{pmatrix} \quad (9)$$

where $v^k_{a,c}$ is the proportion of colour c in the kth sub-image of the image I_a. The similarity function between the two images I_a et I_b is given by the following equation:

$$d(I_a,I_b) = \frac{1}{9}\sum_{k=0}^{9} \frac{\sum_{c=1}^{162} \min(v^k_{a,c}, v^k_{b,c})}{\min(\sum_{c=1}^{162} v^k_{a,c}, \sum_{c=1}^{162} v^k_{b,c})}. \quad (10)$$

Our database contains 1115 colour images obtained from the database COLOMBIA: (http://www.cs.washington.edu/research/imagedatabase/groundtruth/). These images are distributed in 20 categories (football, Barcelona, flowers, mountains,...). Reliabilities of information sources are computed in the following manner. Let $\alpha \in [0.1]$, $\alpha_i=(\alpha)^i$ for each source S_i issued from i[th] retrieved image. All the time, the S_q issued from the query image is fully reliable then $\alpha_q=1$. In our tests, we have fixed α at 0.9. Then $\alpha_1= 0.9$, $\alpha_2=0.81$, $\alpha_3= 0.729$,... The figure 1-a shows the 9 result images for a query images (the 1st image) using a simple ranking. The 5th, 6th, 7th, and the last result image are not relevant. In the figure 1-b, where we have used our approach, all the 9 result images are relevant. The figure 2 illustrates the average precision-recall for the 48 images of football category. We can see that our proposed approach is better than a simple ranking for this category.

5 Conclusions

In this paper, an automatic relevance feedback approach for content-based image retrieval using information fusion and without any user input has been proposed. Given a query image, the system first computes its feature vector to rank the images according to a well-chosen similarity measure. For each retrieved image, the degree of belief about the relevance is then assigned as a function of this measure. This degree of belief is then updated using an iterative process. We can note that using belief functions in relevance feedback, in attempt to gather more information about query image category, gives more precision than systems based on a simple ranking. Moreover, the system becomes more robust, and it can be integrated easily with any image retrieval system. This technique has some critical points as the measurement of reliability. Another critical point is the accumulation of errors. We will try to solve these problems in future works by analysing the conflict information.

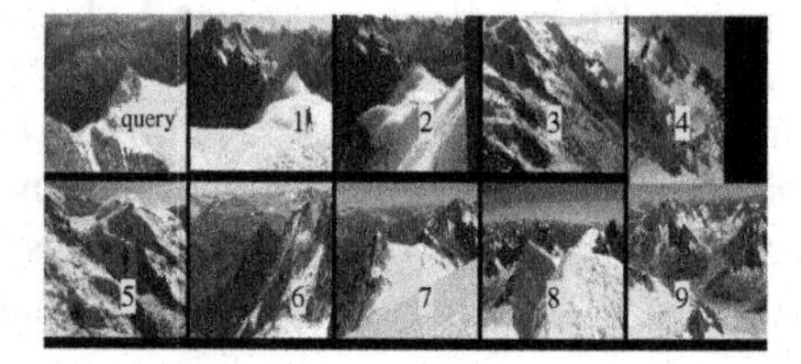

Fig. 1. Query image and its result images by simple ranking (a) and our approach (b)

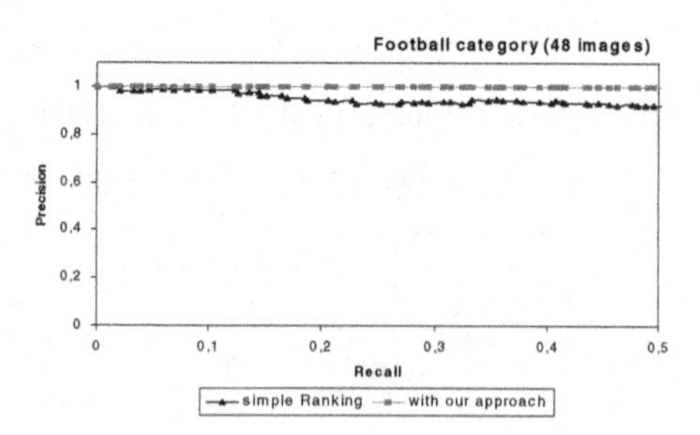

Fig. 2. Average precision vs. retrieval effectiveness of 48 images of football category using the simple ranking and using our approach

References

[1] Young Rui and al , Relevance Feedback: A Power Tool for Interactive Content-Based Image Retrieval Storage and Retrieval for Image and Video Databases (SPIE 1998).

[2] Qasim Iqbal and J.K.Aggawal, Feature Integration, Multi-image Queries and Relevance Feedbackin Image Retrieval, Visual 2003, Miami, Florida, Sep 2003, pp 467-474.

[3] Arnold W.M and al. Content-Based Image Retrieval at the end of the early years. IEEE Transactions on Pattern Analysis and Machine Intelligence, Vol 22, N° 12. December 2000.

[4] Hum-Woo Yoo and al, Visual information retrieval via content-based approach, Pattern Recognition 35 (2002) 749-769.

[5] Y.Alp Aslandogan, Clement T. Yu, Automatic Feedback for Content Based Image Retrieval on The Web, ICME 2002.

[6] Y.Alp Aslandogan, Clement T. Yu, Diogenes: A web Search Agent for Content Based Indexing of Personal Images, SIGIR 2000.

[7] G.Shafer, A Mathematical Theory of Evidence, Princeton University Press, 1976.

[8] P.Smets and R.Kennes, The Transferable Blief Model, Artificial Intelligence, vol. 66, no. 2,pp. 191-234, 1994.

[9] J.R Smith and S.F.Chang Li, Decoding image semantics using composite region templates, IEEE Workshop, CBAIVAL 1998.

[10] R.Schettini and al, A survey of methods for colour image indexing and retrieval in image databases, (R. Luo, L. MacDonald eds.), J. Wiley, 2001. (Invited paper).

A Fast Full Search Algorithm for Variable Block-Based Motion Estimation of H.264

Chan Lim[1], Hyun-Soo Kang[2], Tae-Yong Kim[3], and Kook-Yeol Yoo[4]

[1] Graduate School of AIM, Chung-Ang University, Seoul, Korea
mj23cb@wm.cau.ac.kr
[2] School of Electrical & Computer Eng., ChungBuk University, Chungju, Korea
hskang@chungbuk.ac.kr
[3] Graduate School of AIM, Chung-Ang University, Seoul, Korea
kimty@cau.ac.kr
[4] Dept. of Info. and Comm. Eng., YeungNam University, Gyeongsanbuk-do, Korea
kyoo@yu.ac.kr

Abstract. In this paper, we propose a novel fast motion estimation algorithm based on successive elimination algorithm (SEA) which can dramatically reduce complexity of the variable block size motion estimation in H.264 encoder. The proposed method applies the conventional SEA in the hierarchical manner to the seven block modes. That is, the proposed algorithm can remove the unnecessary computation of SAD by means of the process that the previous minimum SAD is compared to a current bound value which is obtained by accumulating current sum norms and reused SAD of 4x4 blocks for the bigger block sizes than 4x4. As a result, we have tighter bound in the inequality between SAD and sum norm than the bound in the ordinary SEA. If the basic size of the block is smaller than 4x4, the bound will become tighter but it also causes to increase computational complexity, especially addition operations for sum norm. Compared with fast full search algorithm of JM of H.264, our algorithm saves 60 to 70% of computation on average for several image sequences.

1 Introduction

The motion estimation and the compensation play an important role in the digital video compression system. Block matching algorithm (BMA) is widely used for the motion estimation, which searches a block in the previous frames correlated most highly with the current block [1][2]. In H.264, the blocks for the motion estimation vary in size, i.e. from 16x16 to 4x4. Variable block-based motion estimation algorithm (VBMEA) supplies the huge gain in compression efficiency. Full-search algorithm (FSA), the most simple algorithm used in VBMEA, checks all allowed reference blocks within search range to get the optimal vector but suffers from crucial computational cost as considering all blocks in the search range [3][4]. Successive elimination algorithm (SEA), which improves the searching process by removing unnecessary computation, was proposed as a solution to reduce computational cost [5]. In this paper, we propose a fast search algorithm using SEA which may be useful to decide the optimal mode among seven variable blocks (4x4, 4x8, 8x4, 8x8, 8x16,

G. Bebis et al. (Eds.): ISVC 2005, LNCS 3804, pp. 710 – 717, 2005.

16x8, and 16x16). The proposed method, in which sum norm or SAD of 4x4 blocks for each mode is stored produces the necessary condition with tighter bound than the traditional SEA depending on the availability of SAD. As the hierarchical process from 4x4 to 16x16 needs the additional operations like addition, we should take into account the computational overhead consumed in the hierarchical process to decide whether SAD computation is needed or not for the candidate blocks. Nevertheless, the proposed algorithm is of great advantage to computation reduction by keeping away from unnecessary SAD computation with hierarchical SEA.

The organization of this paper is as follows. In Section 2, we give the general introduction and the problem for variable block-based motion estimation and full search algorithm of JM 7.3. Section 3 describes SEA and variable block-based motion estimation using SEA. Section 4 presents our experimental results by which our scheme is evaluated. Conclusions are presented in Section 5.

2 Variable Block-Based Motion Estimation with FSA

The purpose of BMA is to search the optimal reference block in the previous image for a block in a current image. To do this, Sum of absolute difference (SAD) is widely used as a criterion for finding the most correlated block. The variable block-based motion estimation (VBME) of H.264 supports block matching of the variable sizes. Moreover, due to adopting multiple reference frames in H.264, it is feasible that the blocks over 8x8 refer to different reference frames [2][7][8]. The hierarchically-structured motion estimation may be efficient since the blocks are organized in the hierarchical manner. That is, the region with low activity like background is more probable to be decided to a mode of large block while the region with high activity is more likely to be done to small block size modes. However, the use of various block modes causes complexity problem. To make matters worse, applying FSA to VBME makes the computational cost heavier.

Fast full search algorithm (FFSA) was used in JM 7.3 of H.264. As presented in the flowchart of Fig. 1, SADs of other six modes are computed by accumulating pre-computed 4 x 4 SADs. Although the SADs of 4x4 blocks are reused for larger blocks

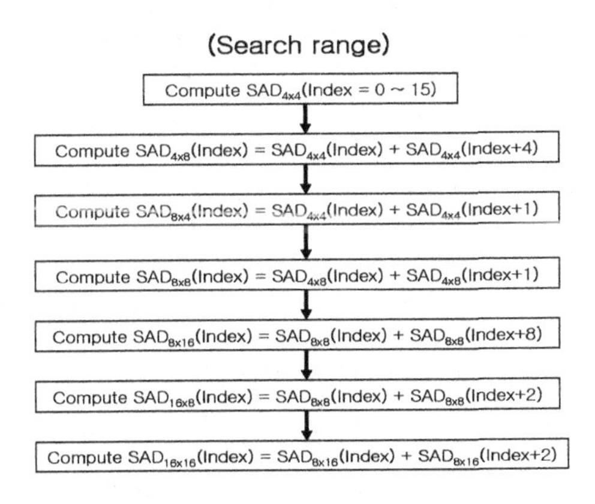

Fig. 1. Flowchart of the fast full search algorithm in H.264

than 4 x 4 blocks, the hierarchical structure for the seven modes needs more intensive computation than a 16x16 MB mode. That is, variable block approach requires more cost than fixed size approach in computation for block matching in spite of high compression efficiency.

3 Proposed Variable Block-Based Motion Estimation Algorithm

SEA among many fast algorithms is quite an efficient method to reduce computational complexity by removing unnecessary blocks for SAD computation with a necessary condition for a reference block to be the optimal block. The necessary condition is well-known as Minkowski's inequality which identifies the relationship between SAD and sum norm.

On the assumption that the size of a block is NxN and the search range is (2N+1)x(2N+1), the inequality in [5] for the optimal motion vector to have to satisfy the necessary condition is as follows

$$R^i - SAD^i_{\min}(m,n) \le M^i(x,y) \le R^i + SAD^i_{\min}(m,n), \quad (1)$$

where i is each mode, R and $M(x,y)$ are sum norms of a block in the current frame and in the previous frame, and $SAD_{\min}(m,n)$ denotes the minimal SAD among SADs of the candidate blocks before the current search point. (x,y) and (m,n) are the motion vectors of each position. The optimal block matching is performed only for the blocks whose sum norms meet the condition of Eq. (1). It is sure that the number of the blocks that satisfies the condition of Eq. (1) is less than the number of all blocks within the search range. Therefore it is feasible that the algorithm reduces computational complexity of search process without excluding the optimal position. The performance of the algorithm is depending on an initial motion vector and computation of sum norm for each block.

3.1 Variable Block-Based Motion Estimation with SEA

In this paper, we propose a method to remove unnecessary computation by combining the pre-computed SADs with sum norms of 4x4 blocks. The method excludes the blocks for which SAD computation is not needed by the inequality which compares the minimal SAD with SAD or sum norm of a block. In case that the inequality in [9] is applied to 4x4 blocks, an 8x8 sub-block satisfies Eq. (2).

$$\left|\sum_{k=1}^{4}(R_k - M_k(x,y)\right| \le \sum_{k=1}^{4}\left|R_k - M_k(x,y)\right|, \quad (2)$$

where k is the index of each 4x4 block. Eq. (2) means that the sum of the sum norms of four 4x4 sub-blocks to which an 8x8 block is partitioned is larger than the sum norm of the 8x8 block. That is to say, the sum of sum norms of the split blocks makes bound of SEA tighter than the sum norm of the original block before splitting. Undoubtedly, being split smaller, the bound is getting tighter by the sum of the partial sum norms because the sum of sum norms of a pixel by a pixel is SAD of the block in case of being split by pixels. Therefore, if pre-computed SADs are partially reused, we can get almost SAD for the tight bound of SEA without SAD computation for the mode (larger blocks than 4x4) and it is feasible that unnecessary SAD computation is reduced by the inequality of SEA. Fig. 2 shows the relationship of SADs according to the ways of block partitioning and the selections of SAD or sum norm. Furthermore, suppose that the reuse of SADs of the second and the third 4x4 blocks, denoted by $SAD_2(x,y)$ and $SAD_3(x,y)$, are available by the mean to make the bound of the 8x8 block tighter. Then, we have the following relationship.

$$\begin{aligned}\sum_{k=1}^{4}|R_k - M_k(x,y)| &\le |R_1 - M_1(x,y)| + SAD_2(x,y) + SAD_3(x,y)\\ &+ |R_4 - M_4(x,y)| \le \sum_{k=1}^{4} SAD_k(x,y) = SAD(x,y),\end{aligned} \tag{3}$$

The above inequalities can be generalized to the other type sub-blocks (16x8, 8x16, 8x4, and 4x8) of 16x16 MB. Eq. (3) denotes that the combination of the sum norms or the SADs of 4x4 blocks, the second term, is closer to the SAD(x,y) than the sum of only sum norms of 4x4 blocks. Thus, if the SADs of smaller blocks were pre-computed, we use the SADs instead of the sum norms, which gives tighter bound.

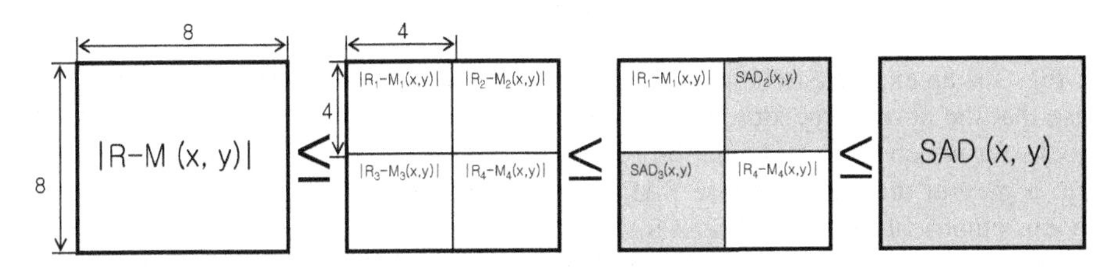

Fig. 2. The comparison of the bound of 8x8 block by the accumulation of SAD and sum norm for 4x4 blocks

The proposed algorithm reduces whole SAD computation for the motion estimation by making the inequality's bound of larger blocks tighter by reusing pre-computed SAD of 4x4 blocks. The following procedure presents the method to remove the reference blocks which SAD computation is unnecessary with slight modification and generalization to various blocks of SEA in the initial block-size of 4x4.

Step1. When search range equals 0, compute R_{4x4} and $SAD(0, 0)_{min4x4}$ for each index of 4x4 block.

Step2. When search range is larger than 0, compute $M(x, y)_{4x4}$ for each index of 4x4 blocks.

Step3. Compare $|R - M(x, y)|_{4x4}$ with $SAD(m, n)_{min4x4}$.

- 3.1. If $|R - M(x, y)|_{4x4} > SAD(m, n)_{min4x4}$, go to Step 7.
- 3.2. If $|R - M(x, y)|_{4x4} \le SAD(m, n)_{min4x4}$, go to Step 4.

Step4. Compute $SAD(x, y)_{4x4}$ and replace $|R - M(x, y)|_{4x4}$ with it.

Step5. Compare $SAD(x, y)_{4x4}$ with $SAD(m, n)_{min4x4}$.

- 5.1. If $SAD(x, y)_{4x4} \ge SAD(m, n)_{min4x4}$, go to Step 7.
- 5.2. If $SAD(x, y)_{4x4} < SAD(m, n)_{min4x4}$, go to Step 6.

Step6. Replace SAD (m, n) $_{min4x4}$ with SAD (x, y) $_{4x4}$ as the minimum SAD of current (x, y) position for 4x4 blocks.

Step7. Maintain the minimum SAD of previous position for 4x4 blocks as it of current position.

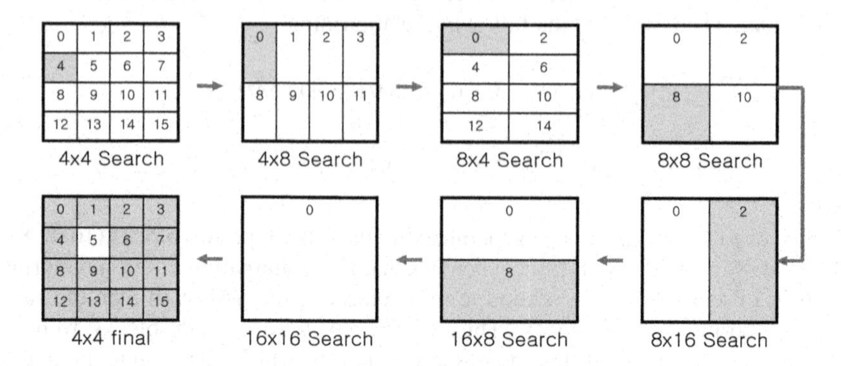

Fig. 3. The search process for each mode to need SAD computation in the proposed algorithm

Fig. 3 is an example to help understanding for the algorithm. As shown in Fig. 3, in case that the above procedure is repeated according to each mode, the number of the blocks for which SAD computation is needed will be obtained. The shaded regions in Fig. 3 present the blocks whose SADs were computed in the process of each mode. By our empirical results, we need SAD computation only for tiny ratio of 4x4 blocks per 16x16 MB. We should not miss that the proposed method finds the optimal vector like FSA. As a result, the proposed method has advantage of complexity reduction without performance degradation.

4 Experimental Results

For the performance evaluation, we compare the proposed method with FFSA in JM. We assume ADD (addition), SUB (subtraction), and COMP (comparison) as one cycle operation and ABS (absolute value) as two cycle operations considering 2's complement operations. The experiment was performed for five QCIF (176x144) standard image sequences (Foreman, Coast guard, Mother & daughter, Stefan and Table tennis). The input image sequences of 100 frames were used and only one previous frame was referenced as a reference frame. The number of search points for motion estimation was (2N+1)*(2N+1) = 1089, when N=16. Table 1 shows the ratio of the number of 4x4 blocks with SAD computation to the total number of 16x16 MBs, without and with pre-computed SAD_{4x4}, according to each mode and test images.

As presented in Table 1, the difference of the computational costs between NOT and REUSED for pre-computed SAD_{4x4} is remarkable except 4x4 mode. NOT is the application for sum of only sum norms of split blocks like the second block in the inequality of Fig. 2 and REUSED is the application for accumulation of not only sum norms but also pre-computed SADs of split blocks like the third block of Fig. 2. That supports that the proposed algorithm reduces unnecessary SAD computation by the tight bound of the larger modes than 4x4 with reusing pre-computed SAD_{4x4} in Minkowsi's inequality as shown in Fig. 2.

Table 1. Without and with reusing pre-computed SAD_{4x4}, the comparison for the average ratio of the number of each mode with SAD computation to the total number of each block-size per 16x16 MB

mode	Foreman		Coastguard		Mother & daughter		Stefan		Table tennis	
SAD_{4x4}	Not	Reused	Not	Reused	Not	Reused	Not	Reused	Not	Reused
4x4	7.828	7.828	17.205	17.205	6.525	6.525	13.427	13.427	19.183	19.183
4x8	3.662	0.457	10.734	0.364	4.219	0.626	7.701	0.587	14.327	0.665
8x4	3.936	0.421	13.666	0.369	4.197	0.481	9.333	0.614	14.077	0.606
8x8	2.195	0.296	8.625	0.239	3.455	0.451	5.379	0.435	10.906	0.446
8x16	1.271	0.284	5.461	0.234	2.487	0.332	3.291	0.38	8.646	0.459
16x8	1.361	0.281	6.595	0.228	2.234	0.276	3.894	0.384	8.331	0.407
16x16	0.918	0.24	4.22	0.222	1.492	0.22	2.614	0.331	6.878	0.439
4x4total	10.694	8.364	24.372	17.483	10.087	7.496	19.273	14.067	29.23	20.109

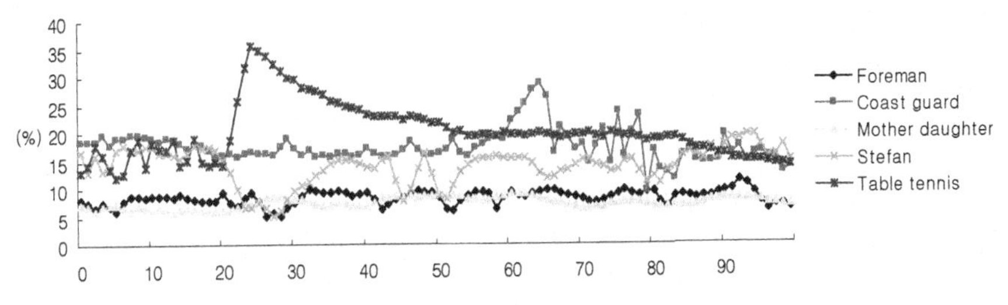

Fig. 4. The average rate of the number of 4x4 blocks for which SAD was computed the total number of 4x4 block-sizes per 16x16MB in each frame

Fig. 4 shows the percentage of the 4x4 blocks for which SAD was computed according to each frame and image. As shown in Table 1, in contrast with Foreman and Mother & daughter, Table tennis and Coast guard have the higher percentage of 4x4 blocks to undergo SAD computation. In Table tennis, it is noticeable that 4x4 blocks with SAD computation are suddenly increased around the 25th frame where zoom-out happens. And in Coast guard, global motion by camera movement and two objects overlapping takes place around the 65th frame. On the other hand, Foreman and Mother & daughter have the small motion of the objects which is the reason why the percentage is consistent. Stefan has the large motion of an object without zooming. Therefore, in case that the image has sudden changes in motion and size of objects or there is global motion in the sequences, the number of blocks which need the SAD

Table 2. The comparison of the computational cost of SAD and that of sum norm per 4x4 block: the computational cost for each step was represented in this table

<table>
<tr><td colspan="2"></td><td>SAD4x4</td><td colspan="4">|R-M|4x4</td></tr>
<tr><td colspan="2">Search range</td><td>0 ~ 1088</td><td>0</td><td>1 ~ 1088</td><td>1</td><td>2 ~ 1088</td></tr>
<tr><td rowspan="3">ADD (+)</td><td>SAD</td><td>15</td><td></td><td></td><td></td><td></td></tr>
<tr><td>R</td><td></td><td>15</td><td></td><td></td><td></td></tr>
<tr><td>M</td><td></td><td></td><td></td><td>15</td><td>4</td></tr>
<tr><td colspan="2">SUB (-)</td><td>16</td><td></td><td>1</td><td></td><td>4</td></tr>
<tr><td colspan="2">ABS (| •|)</td><td>16</td><td></td><td>1</td><td></td><td>4</td></tr>
</table>

Table 3. The comparison of the computational cost of fast full search algorithm of JM 7.3 and that of the proposed algorithm for all test image sequences ① |R-M| ② COMP (|R-M| vs. SAD_{min}) ③ SAD_{4x4} ④ SAD+|R-M| ⑤ COMP (SAD+|R-M| vs. SAD_{min})

Image	Common All		Individual (Proposed + SEA) Foreman		Coast guard		MOT&DAU		Stefan		Table tennis		FFSA (JM 7.3)
Operation	①	②	③	④+⑤	③	④+⑤	③	④+⑤	③	④+⑤	③	④+⑤	
SAD4x4		1008	91854		191709		82215		154287		220563		1097712
|R-M|4x4	155872												
4x4(+)		17408		1353		2957		1170		2305		3347	
4x8(+)	8712	8704		80		64		110		102		116	8712
8x4(+)	8712	8704		74		64		84		108		106	8712
8x8(+)	4356	4352		26		20		40		38		38	4356
8x16(+)	2178	2176		12		10		14		16		20	2178
16x8(+)	2178	2176		12		10		12		16		18	2178
16x16(+)	1089	1088		6		4		4		8		10	1089
Sum	228713		93417		194818		83649		156878		224218		1124973
Common+ Individual			322130		423531		312362		385591		452931		
(Proposed x 100) / FFSA (%)			**28.6**		**37.6**		**27.8**		**34.3**		**40.3**		**100**

computation increases. However, the proposed algorithm is still available, since the sudden changes are not frequently happened in the overall image sequences.

Table 2 shows the computational complexity of SAD and sum norm for a 4x4 block. For the computation of M in Table 2, we refer to [5] where it is shown that the sum norms of reference blocks can be computed with just a little computation since the previously obtained sum norm of a neighbor block is used to compute a current block's sum norm. Adopting [5], complexity of M is 8 cycles on average. Provided that there are two 4x4 blocks which are horizontally overlapped by 3 pixels, the block on the right requires four addition operations and four subtraction operations. That is, the sum norm of the block on the right can be calculated by adding the 4 new supplementary pixels to the sum norm of the block on the left and subtracting the 4 left most pixels of the right block.

Table 3 shows the computational complexity of FFSA in JM7.3 and the complexity of the five operation processes in the proposed algorithm for all test image sequences, respectively. The computational complexity of the proposed algorithm comes from the operation frequency for five main processes as presented in Table 3. We can get the outstanding result from the table. The ratio for FFSA denotes the complexity of our method when we consider FFSA as 1. As presented in Table 3, the proposed algorithm has gain of 60~70% in complexity with the same optimal motion vector as FFSA has.

5 Conclusion

In this paper, we proposed a fast search method based on SEA for the variable block size motion estimation in H.264. It was realized that SAD computation for 4x4 blocks was reduced by accumulating not only sum norm but also pre-computed SAD. It originates from the fact that the bound of the inequality gets tighten by the sum of sum norm of sub-blocks split from a whole block and the reuse of pre-computed SADs. Thus, the proposed algorithm can make the bound of the inequality tighter without additional SAD computation because the SADs available from previous processing are considered in company with sum norms into the inequality of SEA.

In experimental results, we showed that our method had the consistent gain of 60~70% without degradation of performance with the various test images whose motion characteristics are quite different from one another.

Acknowledgement. This work supported by the IT Research Center (ITRC), Ministry of Information and Communication, Korea.

References

1. M. Brunig, W. Niehsen, "Fast full-search block matching", IEEE Trans. on Circuits and Systems for video Technology, Vol.11, No.2, pp. 241-247, Feb. 2001.
2. S. Y. Huang, J. R. Chen, J. S. Wang, K. R. Hsieh, and H. Y. Hsieh, "Classified variable block size motion estimation algorithm for image", IEEE International Conference on Image Processing, Vol.3, pp. 736-740, Nov 1994.
3. A. Ahmad, N. Khan, S. Masud, and M. A. Maud, "Selection of variable block sizes in H.264", IEEE International Conference on Acoustics, Speech, and Signal Processing (ICASSP '04), Vol.3, pp. 173 -176, May 2004.
4. T. G. Ahn, Y. H. Moon, J. H. Kim, "Fast Full-Search Motion Estimation Based on Multilevel Successive Elimination Algorithm", IEEE Trans. on Circuits and Systems for Video Technology, Vol.14, No.11, pp. 1265-1269, Nov. 2004.
5. W. Li, E. Salari, "Successive elimination algorithm for motion estimation", IEEE Trans. on Image Processing, Vol.4, No.1, pp. 105-107, Jan. 1995.
6. T. M. Oh, Y. R. Kim, W. G. Hong, and S. J. Ko, "A fast full search motion estimation algorithm using the sum of partial norms", International Conference on Consumer Electronics, pp. 236-237, June 2000.
7. Z. Zhou, M. T. Sun, and Y. F. Hsu, "Fast variable block-size motion estimation algorithm based on merge and slit procedures for H.264 / MPEG-4 AVC", International Symposium on Circuits and Systems, Vol.3, pp. 725-728, May 2004.
8. W. Choi, J. Lee, S. Yang, and B. Jeon, "Fast motion estimation and mode decision with variable motion block sizes", Proc. of SPIE, Visual Communications and Image Processing (VCIP), July 2003.
9. Y. Noguchi, J. Furukawa, H. Kiya, "A fast full search block matching algorithm for MPEG-4 video", International Conference on Image Processing, Vol.1, pp. 61-65, 1999.

Adaptive Switching Linear Predictor for Lossless Image Compression

Abdul Itani and Manohar Das

Oakland University, Rochester, Michigan
aitani@oakland.edu
das@oakland.edu

Abstract. Linear prediction has been extensively researched and a significant number of techniques have been proposed to enhance its effectiveness, among them switching linear predictors. In this paper, we propose a general framework for designing a family of adaptive switching linear predictors. In addition, we will utilize the proposed framework to construct a concrete implementation based on set partitions and relational operators.

1 Introduction

Since the introduction of CALIC [1], and JPEG-LS [2], the data compression scene is witnessing a revived interest in lossless data compression after being dominated by the lossy sibling. One theme that is playing a role in most recent compression algorithms is predictive coding.

Predictive coding has uses in image, speech, and audio compression. It has been extensively researched and a significant number of techniques have been proposed to enhance its effectiveness. One such technique, commonly known as switching linear predictors, uses a combination of linear predictors where, at each pixel, it selects which linear predictor to use next based on some predefined rules.

In this paper, we propose a general framework for designing a family of adaptive switching linear predictors. In addition, we will utilize the proposed framework to introduce a new adaptive switching linear predictor. Finally, the performance of our new predictor will be compared to the one used by the JPEG-LS coder.

2 Monochrome Digital Images

The term monochrome (or gray-level) digital image is defined as a function, denoted by $f(r,c)$, where r and c are spatial coordinates, and the value or gray-level of f at any pair of coordinates (r,c) is a nonnegative integer representing the brightness in the image at that point. The origin is assumed to be at the upper left corner of the image; values on the horizontal, or c, axis increase from left to right, and values on the vertical, or r, axis increase from top to bottom.

G. Bebis et al. (Eds.): ISVC 2005, LNCS 3804, pp. 718 – 722, 2005.

3 Predictive Coding

Predictive coding consists of two major steps: pixel prediction, and entropy coding. Pixel prediction is accomplished by traversing an image using some predetermined order, such as raster-scan, where the value of each pixel is predicted based on a number of past pixels. The prediction, $\hat{f}(r,c)$, is then rounded to the nearest integer and used to form the difference between the actual and predicted value of that pixel.

$$e(r,c) = f(r,c) - \hat{f}(r,c) \tag{1}$$

Finally, when the image traversal ends, the prediction errors are encoded using some entropy coder. The order of a predictor is a quantitative measure and it is equal to the number of past pixels, a.k.a. causal neighboring pixels, used in the prediction.

3.1 Linear Predictors

Linear predictors use a linear combination, such as weighted sum, of the causal neighboring pixels. As an example, consider the following first-order linear predictor

$$\hat{f}(r,c) = \alpha f(r,c-1) \tag{2}$$

Despite its simplicity, a first-order linear predictor is an effective method for removing much of the horizontal dependencies between pixels. A second-order linear predictor similar to the following

$$\hat{f}(r,c) = \alpha f(r,c-1) + \beta f(r-1,c) \tag{3}$$

takes advantage of both horizontal and vertical dependencies to deliver even more impressive compression results, provided 2-dimensional correlation exists between pixels.

3.2 Nonlinear Predictors

Simply stated, any predictor that is not linear belongs to the nonlinear category. In this section, we will focus our attention on a particular nonlinear predictor, the one known as MED [3]. This nonlinear predictor is part of the JPEG-LS coder, which is a relatively new standard in lossless and near–lossless compression of continuous tone images.

MED performs a test on three causal neighboring pixels to detect vertical or horizontal edges. If an edge is not detected, then the guessed value is an interpolation based on the three neighboring pixels. This expresses the expected smoothness of the image in the absence of edges. Specifically, for $\alpha = f(r,c-1)$, $\beta = f(r-1,c)$, $\chi = f(r-1,c-1)$, the LOCO-I predictor guesses

$$\hat{f}(r,c) = \begin{cases} \min(\alpha,\beta) & \text{if } \chi \geq \max(\alpha,\beta) \\ \max(\alpha,\beta) & \text{if } \chi \leq \min(\alpha,\beta) \\ \alpha+\beta-\chi & \text{otherwise} \end{cases} \tag{4}$$

The predictor can be interpreted as picking β in most cases where a vertical edge exists left of the current location, α in most cases of a horizontal edge above the current location, or a plane predictor if no edge has been detected.

4 A New Family of Adaptive Switching Linear Predictors

We will now introduce a new family of adaptive switching linear predictors using a formal framework for the definition of such predictors. Our new predictor is a family because for any given positive parameter *n*, a unique context-based adaptive switching linear predictor is constructed. The number of context-classes is directly related to the value of *n*, but the two are not equal. In general, *n* is much smaller than the number of context classes, and each and every context class has exactly one linear sub-predictor of order *n*.

Starting with the n past neighbors, the encoder classifies the current context to adaptively select which sub-predictor to use in the prediction step. Furthermore, the sub-predictor coefficients are, themselves, adaptive since they are dynamically adjusted to enhance the prediction of the sub-predictor belonging to the respective context class.

One way to interpret the classification method is to treat it as a relation *R* on a set of pixels *I* that gives rise to a partition *P* in which the members of *P* are the context classes of *R*. The union of all context classes, therefore, is the set of pixels *I* that make the digital image. In addition, the intersection of any two context classes is empty.

Each class context keeps track of the n sub-predictor coefficients. Initially, the coefficients start with the value zero. In order to predict the value of a pixel $f(r,c)$, we first classify the current context, based on the yet to be defined relation R, then use the corresponding sub-predictor to find the prediction $\hat{f}(r,c)$. The prediction, $\hat{f}(r,c)$, is then rounded to the nearest integer and used to form the final prediction value.

What follows next is a simple reward system, where the coefficient corresponding to the neighbor closest in value to $f(r,c)$ is adjusted to increase its value. As a result, the next time this same context class is encountered, the adjusted coefficient will have a bigger influence on the prediction outcome.

What we described thus far is a general-purpose framework for the description of adaptive switching linear predictors. In order to construct a concrete implementation, we need to define the one thing that remains so far undefined, mainly the relation *R*.

The relation *R* is a set of Boolean predicates, i.e. propositions that can be either True or False. The number of Boolean predicates is equal to the number of context classes. Each and every predicate allows or denies membership to a corresponding context class.

One of the several definitions of *R* that we experimented with uses the relational operator <, the relational operator =, along with the values of the *n* past neighbors as operands, to define the predicates. The predicates describe all possible comparative relationships that the operands might have with respect to each other. For the sake of brevity, we will refer to this particular implementation as ASLP, Adaptive Switching Linear Predictor.

For the case when $n = 1$, we have exactly one predicate whose value is always True. Therefore, when n is 1, ASLP behaves exactly like a regular first-order linear predictor with coefficient $\alpha = 1$.

For the case when $n = 2$, we have exactly three predicates. They are

$$a < b \qquad b < a \qquad a = b$$

As a final example, the case when $n = 3$, we have exactly thirteen predicates

$$\begin{array}{llll} a < b < c & c < a < b & c < (a = b) & a = b = c \\ a < c < b & c < b < a & (a = b) < c & \\ b < a < c & a < (b = c) & (a = c) < b & \\ b < c < a & b < (a = c) & (b = c) < a & \end{array}$$

The predicates, for any value of n, can be found using a simple algorithm that permutes the operators along with the operands, then removes the duplicates. Two predicates, p and q are duplicates if and only if $p \leftrightarrow q$ is a tautology. Theoretically, we can always limit the number of predicates from above using the formula $2^{n-1}n!$. The higher the value of n, the bigger the discrepancy is between the upper bound and the actual number of predicates needed. For example, for $n = 1$, the upper bound and the actual value are the same. On the other hand, for $n = 3$, the upper bound is 24, while the actual value is 13.

4.1 Experimental Results

Table 1 shows the entropy (in bits per pixel, assuming memoryless Markov processes) before and after applying various predictors to several 512×512, 8-bit standard test images.

Table 1. Comparison between the MED and ASLP for various values of n

	Original	MED	ASLP		
			$n = 3$	$n = 4$	$n = 5$
f-16	6.71	4.25	4.40	4.34	4.35
goldhill	7.48	4.92	5.06	5.02	5.02
Lena	7.45	4.60	4.66	4.50	4.52
mandrill	7.36	6.30	6.27	6.25	6.25
peppers	7.57	4.87	4.79	4.66	4.68
Zelda	7.27	4.24	4.25	4.15	4.16
Average	7.30	4.86	4.90	4.82	4.83

The results reflect a slight advantage in favor of ASLP when using four or five causal neighboring pixels, with the best results obtained at $n = 4$ The causal neighboring pixels used to obtain the results reported, for all $n \leq 5$, are given in Figure 1.

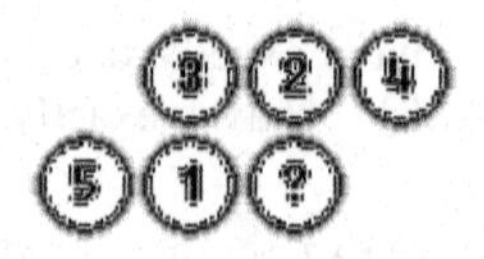

Fig. 1. ASLP causal neighboring pixels for values of n ≤ 5

The empirical results presented do echo the results of a more comprehensive study which involved standard test images in addition to medical images and satellite images. We applied the ASLP algorithm using values of n ranging from 1 to 6, inclusive. The ASLP with parameter $n = 4$ did better, on average, than the rest of the parameter values we tested.

We must stress that the empirical results presented reflect only the performance of the MED and ASLP prediction algorithms. These two algorithms are not meant to be used as full-fledged compression systems. Prediction is just one step in the compression process, and the final outcome of any compression algorithm typically yields better results than the ones achieved by the prediction step alone.

5 Conclusion and Future Work

The advantages that ASLP has over the MED predictor are not statistically significant. However, the major contributions of this paper are the formal definition of the adaptive switching linear predictors framework, and the particular implementation of the relation *R* presented earlier.

The current reward-based system does not perform exceptionally well because it only allows positive weights. By making room for negative weights, we believe our predictor will gain a significant boost in performance. In addition, the initial conditions we used for the weights, a vector of zeros, is not a particularly good idea. We suspect that a static set of non-zero vectors tailored to the contexts defined by the relation *R* might further enhance the performance of our predictor.

References

1. X.Wu and N. Memon, "Context-based, adaptive lossless image coding," IEEE Trans. Commun., vol. 45, pp. 437–444, April 1997.
2. M.J. Weinberger, G. Seroussi, and G. Sapiro, "LOCO-I: A Low Complexity, Context-Based, Lossless Image Compression Algorithm", Proceedings of the IEEE Data Compression Conference, March-April 1996.
3. S. A. Martucci, "Reversible compression of HDTV images using median adaptive prediction and arithmetic coding", Proc. IEEE International Symposium on Circuits and Systems, pp. 1310-1313, IEEE Press, 1990.

Toward Real Time Fractal Image Compression Using Graphics Hardware

Ugo Erra

ISISLab - Dipartimento di Informatica ed Appl. "R.M. Capocelli",
Università degli Studi di Salerno, 84081 Baronissi, Italy
ugoerr@dia.unisa.it

Abstract. In this paper, we present a parallel fractal image compression using the programmable graphics hardware. The main problem of fractal compression is the very high computing time needed to encode images. Our implementation exploits SIMD architecture and inherent parallelism of recently graphic boards to speed-up baseline approach of fractal encoding. The results we present are achieved on cheap and widely available graphics boards.

1 Introduction

Fractal compression is a lossy compression method introduced by Barnsley and Sloan [1] for compactly encoding images. The main idea of fractal compression is to exploit local self-similarity in images. This permits a self-referential description of image data to be yielded.

The general approach is firstly to subdivide the image using a fixed partition in simple case or adaptive partition in an advanced approach, and then to find the best matching image portion for each part. This searching phase is known to be the most time consuming part and numerous strategies have been presented to speed-up encoding. On the other hand, fractal image compression offers interesting features like fast decoding, independent-resolution and good image quality at low bit-rates which is useful for off-line applications.

Today's GPUs (graphics processing units) have high-bandwidth memories and more floating-point units. One of the most recently presented GPUs, the NVIDIA 7800, has peak performance of 165 Gflops and memory bandwidth of 38.4 GB/sec. Recently, all this computational power has become cheap and widely available. As side effects, several researches has began to exploit GPUs for general purpose applications such as scientific computation, database operations, matrix multiplications and many more as shows in [2].

This paper presents a novel approach to perform fractal compression on programmable graphics hardware; to our knowledge, this is the first application that uses the GPU for image compression. Using programmable capabilities of the GPUs, we exploit the large amount of inherent parallelism and memory bandwidth to perform fast pairing search between portions of the image. As a result, we show that GPUs are effective co-processors for fractal compression.

G. Bebis et al. (Eds.): ISVC 2005, LNCS 3804, pp. 723–728, 2005.

2 Fractal Compression

The basic idea of fractal compression is to find similarities between larger and smaller portions of an image. This is accomplished partitioning the original image into blocks of fixed size, called *range* and creating a shape codebook from the original image of double size of the range, called *domain*. Range blocks partition the image so that every pixel is included while the domain blocks can be overlapped and/or to not contain every pixel. We give below the baseline approch, the mathematical theory about these principles can be found on [3].

Given a range block R we must find a domain D from codebook such that $R \approx sD + o\mathbf{1}$ where s and o are called *scaling* and *offset* respectively. These values define the optimal transformation by which we can encode an image portion using another part. The encoder must scan all the codebook to find optimal D, s, and o. The domain block must be shrunk by pixel averaging to match the size of range block.

Given the two blocks R and D with n pixel intensities, $r_1, \ldots, r_n$ and $d_1, \ldots, d_n$, the quantity to minimize is $\sum_{i=1}^{n} (s \cdot d_i + o - r_i)^2$ where coefficients s and o are given by

$$s = \frac{n\left(\sum_{i=1}^{n} d_i r_i\right) - \left(\sum_{i=1}^{n} d_i\right)\left(\sum_{i=1}^{n} r_i\right)}{n\sum_{i=1}^{n} d_i^2 - \left(\sum_{i=1}^{n} d_i\right)^2} \qquad o = \frac{1}{n}\left(\sum_{i=1}^{n} r_i - s\sum_{i=1}^{n} d_i\right) \tag{1}$$

The values s, o, and the position of domain block D are the encoded values for range R. The steps of the baseline encoder with fixed block are the following:

1. *Range blocks* R_i. Given a fixed size (4×4, 8×8, and so on) create a set of range blocks overlapping the entire image.
2. *Shape codebook* D_i. The shape codebook is created in two steps:
   (a) Using a step size of l pixel horizontally and vertically create a set of domain blocks which are double the range size.
   (b) Shrink the domain blocks by averaging four pixel to match range size.
3. *The search.* For each range block R an optimal approximation $R \approx sD + o\mathbf{1}$ is computed in the following steps:
   (a) For each domain block D_i compute $R \approx sD_i + o\mathbf{1}$ using formulas (1).
   (b) Among all codebook D_i output the code for current range $[k, s, o]$ such that the error $R \approx sD_k + o\mathbf{1}$ is minimum.

Related works. Fractal compression allows fast decompression but has long encoding times. The most time consuming part is the domain blocks searching from each range. In [4] Beaumont adopts a search strategy using an outward spiral starting from the coordinate of range and halts when a necessary condition has been reached. This strategy reduces encoding time but image quality could suffer due to the overlook of some possible optimal pairing. Categorized search proposed by Boss, Fisher and Jacobs [5, 6] and features vector methods proposed by Saupe [7] are efficient classification techniques. They reduce the encoding complexity using a classification of the domain codebook block in such way that for each range the search is essentially more efficient.

The use of general purpose high performance architecture has been used to accelerate the encoding phase without a decrease of image quality. Related work has been done concerning the encoding phase on SIMD architecture. In [8] massively parallel processing approach has been used on an APE100/Quadrics SIMD machine. For testing, they used 512 floating point processors, offering a peak power of 25.6 GFLOPS. They are able to compress a gray level image of 512×512 using a scalar quantization techniques in about 2 seconds.

3 Programmable Graphics Hardware

Today, GPUs are fundamentally programmable stream processors [9]. In this computational model stream are collections of data requiring similar computation. Every object in the stream is processed by the some function called kernel. GPUs has a screen-space stream engine called fragment processor. The fragment processor supports a fully orthogonal instruction set optimized for 4-component vector processing. Furthermore, as stream architecture, the fragment processor exploits spatial parallelism; it runs the same fragment program for each pixel.

This processor presents limits and advantages. For each incoming pixel the fragment program is invoked at a specific location and returns the final value in the same location as output. That is not possible to write in a different location or to do scattering. Instead the kernel can do gathering using textures as lookup table to read precomputed values.

The textures can be used as lookup tables during computation though access to them is restricted to write-only or read-only. Floating-point texture vectors can be of two, three of four components. Each fragment can fetch a component vector as input from one or more textures and returns a vector components. This feature and the fact that fragment processor has enormous throughput make fragment engine well suited to fractal compression.

4 Mapping Fractal Compression on the GPU

In order to exploit the specialized nature of the GPU and its restricted programming model we must map the fractal compression as a streaming computation. The goal is to perform pairings test between range and domain exploiting parallel architecture of the GPU and high bandwidth access to pixels. The entire process uses a gray level image as input data and returns the textures T_{POS} with the position of optimal domain blocks and T_{SO} with scaling/offset coefficients as outputs.

The underlying idea is to use a producer/consumer scheme. The producer gathers from the domain pool a block which is broadcasted to all consumers that are the ranges. Each range stores the current domain as soon as it appears as the best pairing block. The entire process continues until all domain blocks have been consumed. In this scenario, a pixel appears as a single floating-point processor responsible for only one range. Then, the GPU mimics a computational grid rendering a sized-range rectangular upon which performs parallel pairing test among all the ranges for a given domain.

4.1 Data Structures Organization

Fractal compression is implemented as fragments programs. These programs are executed via multi-pass rendering of a screen-sized rectangle where each pixel is an encoding range. Notice that during encoding the same range will be paired among all other domains and from another point of view the same domain will be paired among all ranges. Then, for each range block and for each domain block we precompute all the related quantities that remain constant during the entire encoding. These constant values are the summations of the scaling and offset formulas in 1 and will be stored in the lookup textures T_R and T_D using one 32-bit component for T_R and two 16-bit component for T_D.

In order to exploit SIMD parallelism and efficient bandwidth, during the encoding, the source image is stored compactly into texture. An RGBA texture which uses 32-bit per component is capable to store up to 256 bit per pixel. Usually, for a gray level image, 8-bit per pixel are necessary. Thanks to the specialized instruction `pack` we are able to store up to 16 pixels into a single RGBA pixel's texture. Using this representation of the image it is possible to read 16 pixels simultaneously in a single texture access followed by a `unpack` instruction.

4.2 Fractal Compression Kernels

The entire flow diagram for the streaming fractal compression is illustrated in Figure 1. The following sections detail the implementation of each kernel and the read/write textures access. In the following, the kernels always take as input the compact version of source image.

Ranges summation. This kernel precomputes the range summation using the technique described in the previous section. It takes the original image as input and returns a texture T_R as output. This buffer is a previously declared one 32-bit color component texture. The size of this buffer is 1/4 of the input image if we choose a range block size of 4×4, or 1/8 for a range block of 8×8, and so on.

Domains summation. The kernel precomputes the domains summations. It takes the original image as input and returns the texture T_D as output. This buffer is a previously declared two 16-bit color components texture.

Stream range generator. This is the only party performed in the CPU and it is not a computational stage. It serves as a start-up routine to generate a stream of fragment programs. It draws a texture of size T_R to force the "Pairing Test" fragment program execution for each range. Furthermore, it passes to the next stage the position of the current domain and the entire group of pixels belongs to the current domain as parameters. This permits to store an entire domain into registers of fragment processor avoiding continuous texture fetches.

Pairing test. This kernel performs all possible tests for optimal pairing. At each rendering pass this kernel has T_R as input textures, coordinate of current

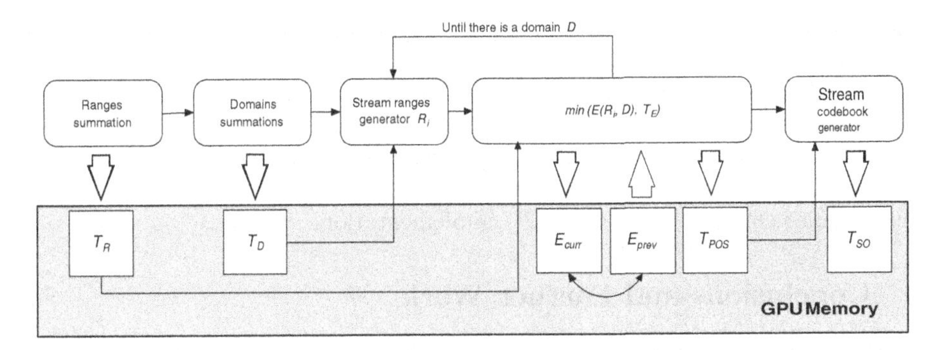

Fig. 1. A streaming fractal compressor

domain and pixels' domain from the previous stage. It returns a sized range texture T_{POS} with the coordinates of current optimal blocks as output. More precisely, due to hardware limits which not allow read/write access on the same texture, pairing tests are not performed for a given range R among all domains D_i. We must invert pairing tests as follows: given a domain D performs pairing tests among all ranges R_i updating minimal errors for each range. This schema use a double buffer to read previous errors in texture T_{prev} and to store current errors in texture T_{curr}. Thus, given a domain block D at each rendering pass each fragment program computes and stores the following value: $T_{curr} = min\left(E\left(R_i, D\right), T_{prev}\right)$. Before the next rendering pass the errors textures T_{curr} and T_{prev} are swapped and another domain block is passed as input.

Stream codebook generator. The last stage computes and writes into texture T_{SO} final scaling s and offset o. The kernel has textures T_{POS} as input and returns a texture T_{SO} with optimal coefficients. This operation is performed here in order to avoid useless write operations and therefore optimizes the amount of memory bandwidth required for texture accesses.

5 Experimental Results

In order to compare the amount of pairing tests that GPU is capable to perform, we implemented heavy brute force algorithm on GPU as well as on CPU. We have experimented on a Pentium IV based machine with 3.2GHz processor speed and 1GB of RAM. The used graphics card was a GeForce FX 6800, with 128MB of video memory, core speed of 300MHz and memory speed of 800MHz. We used OpenGL Cg shading language to implement our GPU-based compressor.

The test image has a resolution of 256×256 pixels. Choosing a range size of 4×4 pixels we obtain 64×64 ranges. The domain blocks must be twice the size of range blocks and using a step of one pixel to scan the image, the domain pool contains $(128 - 4 + 1)^2 = 15,625$ elements. In total, using a heavy brute force strategy $4,096 \times 15,625 = 64,000,000$ possible pairings require testing.

The CPU version takes about 280 seconds to perform all pairing test whereas the GPU version takes about 1 second. Then, the amount of paring test that the GPU is capable to perform is about 64 millions per second whereas the CPU performs about 220 thousands paring test per second. These results arise considering fractal compression a random-memory-access intensive problem. The memory bandwidth together arithmetic intensity advantages GPU over CPU. Moreover, our work shows its advantages when compared to expensive parallel architecture as for instance in [8] which uses 512 floating-point processors with performance comparable to our GPU implementation.

6 Conclusions and Further Work

Fractal image compression is well suited for parallel system due to its high computation complexity and regular algorithmic structure. Today, we think that graphics board offers substantial computational power to take full advantages of the baseline approach. We are going to investigate two scenarios. The former is to further exploit the graphics hardware to obtain more efficient compression schema and taking into account also color image. The latter is to use GPU as an efficient co-processor. The general purpose architecture of the CPU permits to excel on arranging data. The GPU could be used as an efficient pairing engine while the CPU arranges pairings tests.

Today, the consumers for less than $500 can buy an off-the-shelf graphics card with performances comparable to SIMD parallel machines that cost hundreds of thousands of dollars several years ago. Furthermore, as the GPU consumes less power than a high-end CPU, it is evident how using the graphics card can extend the life-time of an existing computer system. In conclusion, we think that GPUs offer the great opportunity to take full advantages of the fractal compression on consumer desktop personal computers.

References

1. Barnsley, M.F., Sloan, A.: Chaotic compression. Computer Graphics World (1987)
2. GPGPU. (Website) `http://www.gpgpu.com`.
3. Yuval, F.: Fractal Image Compression - Theory and Application. Springer-Verlag, New York (1994)
4. Beaumont, J.M.: Image data compression using fractal techniques. British Telecom Technol. Journal **9** (1991) 93–109
5. Jacobs, E.W., Fisher, Y., Boss, R.D.: Image compression: A study of the iterated transform method. Signal Processing **29** (1992) 251–263
6. Yuval, F.: Fractal image compression. Fractals: Complex Geometry, Patterns, and Scaling in Nature and Society **2** (1994) 347–361
7. Saupe, D.: Accelerating fractal image compression by multi-dimensional nearest neighbor search. In Storer, J.A., Cohn, M., eds.: Proceedings DCC'95 Data Compression Conference, IEEE Computer Society Press (1995)
8. Palazzari, P., Coli, M., Lulli, G.: Massively parallel processing approach to fractal image compression with near-optimal coefficient quantization. J. Syst. Archit. **45** (1999) 765–779
9. Venkatasubramanian, S.: The graphics card as a stream computer. In: SIGMOD-DIMACS Workshop on Management and Processing of Data Streams. (2003)

Motion Based Segmentation Using MPEG Streams and Watershed Method

Renan Coudray and Bernard Besserer

Laboratoire Informatique Image Interaction, University of La Rochelle,
Av. Michel Crepeau, 17042 La Rochelle Cedex 1, France
renan.coudray@univ-lr.fr, bernard.besserer@univ-lr.fr

Abstract. Many computer vision applications require the calculation of motion present in image sequences, such as video indexing, summarization, motion segmentation and others. In previous work, we have presented a new technique which performs Global Motion Estimation on MPEG compressed video. This article presents a method to extend the process to allow fast motion-based segmentation of a video. The method enables the segmentation of the background and objects which have their own local motion in real time. The motion information belonging to each area is also given. Moreover, some indicators warn if the estimation is not reliable.

1 Introduction

As the amount of archived videos continuously grows, the demand for video annotation and metadata generation increases in order to catalog, sort or categorize the huge amount of sequences often stored in digital form[1]. Several approaches for video indexing based on single image (snapshots) have been investigated [2], but the analysis of the dynamic behavior of the sequences could improve sequence characterization [3].

Since the MPEG1 or MPEG2 standards are widely used for digital video storage and for digital video broadcasting (DVB [4]), the input data of the presented approach is a MPEG stream [5]. Global Motion Estimation (GME) performed in MPEG4 or MPEG7 is not exploited because its use is still marginal. Instead, Global Motion Estimation is based upon existing motion vectors carried along in the MPEG stream for block-based motion compensation.

In [6], the model for the estimation was a simplified affine motion model. We presented here an extension of the method, fitting the complete affine model.

The GME algorithm calculates global translation by forming an accumulation space of the motion vectors where the different translation movements are separated. By this accumulation space, a motion based segmentation is carried out with a watershed algorithm. An alternative method is also proposed, more adapted to our sparse data. Finally visual results will be presented and discussed.

2 Global Motion Estimation

Since MPEG is a data compression standard, the motion compensation vectors stored in MPEG streams are not necessarily accurate with regard to real motion

G. Bebis et al. (Eds.): ISVC 2005, LNCS 3804, pp. 729–736, 2005.

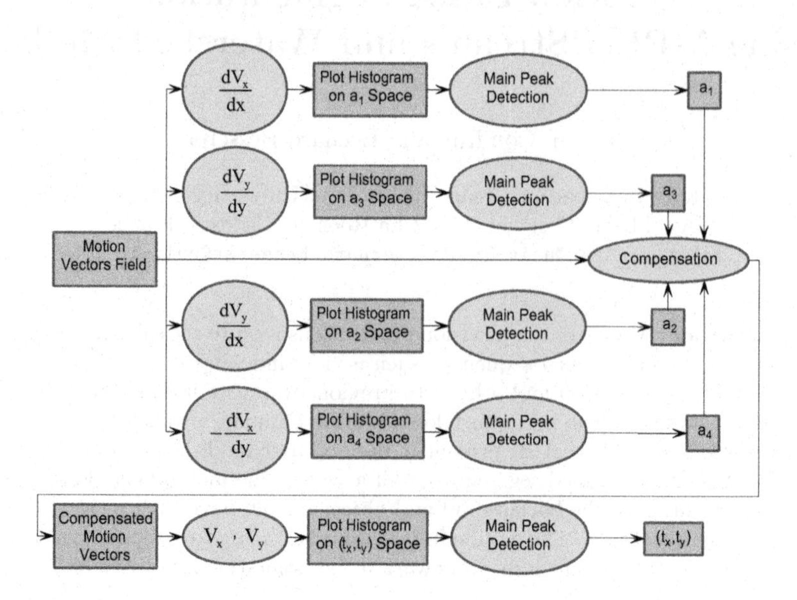

Fig. 1. Scheme of the Global Motion Estimation using affine model

in the scene. The motion estimation is for reducing temporal redundancy and not for estimating the real displacements. In a previous work [6], we have presented a method to set up one motion field per Group Of Picture (GOP, often 12-15 successive frames) and to reject wrong vectors ([7], areas with poor visual surface characteristics like flat shades often lead to meaningless motion vectors) by the use of the Discrete Cosine Transform (DCT) coefficients computed for each bloc in the compressed stream.

For the GME (Global Motion Estimation), the motion vectors are plotted in appropriate accumulation spaces, and the estimation is fast. In [6], the used motion model was the simplified affine model (4 parameters). Here, the motion is represented with the affine model (6 parameters, Eq. 1, Fig. 1). The same method is still used, each sample (motion vector) contributes to a globally consistent solution. The most redundant values point to the parameters of the global motion.

In a first stage (upper part of Fig. 1), the motion vector spatial derivatives are computed to estimate a first set of deformation parameters (zoom, rotation). As a second stage, all motion vectors are compensated to estimate the remaining translational motion (lower line of Fig. 1).

$$V = \begin{pmatrix} a_1 & a_2 \\ a_3 & a_4 \end{pmatrix} \begin{pmatrix} x \\ y \end{pmatrix} + \begin{pmatrix} t_x \\ t_y \end{pmatrix} \tag{1}$$

$$V = V - \begin{pmatrix} a_1 & a_2 \\ a_3 & a_4 \end{pmatrix} \begin{pmatrix} x \\ y \end{pmatrix} \tag{2}$$

As the MPEG motion vectors can be inaccurate, each contribution from a motion vector to an accumulation space is weighted by a Gaussian distribution. This accumulation method congregates close contributions in a same peak within the accumulation space. The simple search of the most redundant value gives the global parameter. To refine the estimation, for each one-dimensional accumulation space (a_1, a_2, a_3, a_4), a second order polynomial regression is carried out around the maximum. The top position of the regression curve gives the parameter value (i.e. where the curve derivative is zero). All the motion vectors are compensated (Eq. 2) before being added up in the two-dimensional accumulation space (t_x, t_y). In this space, the mode represents the translation parameters of the global motion, and each remaining peak represents an object movement.

The extension of the Global Motion Estimation by fitting the complete affine model is the natural continuity of previous works. The main contribution of this paper is the complete investigation of the accumulation space to compute a motion based segmentation.

3 Motion Based Segmentation

Efficient motion-based segmentations usually rely on a dense motion vectors field (so-called optical flows). Being based on the work published in [8], our concept is similar : estimation of the affine movement for each picture area and classification of the obtained parameters. However, using a sparse motion field, the deformation parameters (a_1, a_2, a_3, a_4) are problematic to estimate on small areas. Given a video shot, the foremost deformations are caused by camera motion.

So, our compromise is to estimate the global deformation and to classify each vector only on the translation values.

Fig. 2 is a representation of our translation accumulation space after to have compensate the global deformation. With a standard watershed method, all the relevant peaks can be easily extracted. The first step is to threshold the accumulated data in order to eliminate noise. All location (or cells) in this accumulation space holding less than 5 occurrences are discarded. Then, the accumulation space is inverted (making valleys from peaks, Eq. 3). Finally, the standard wa-

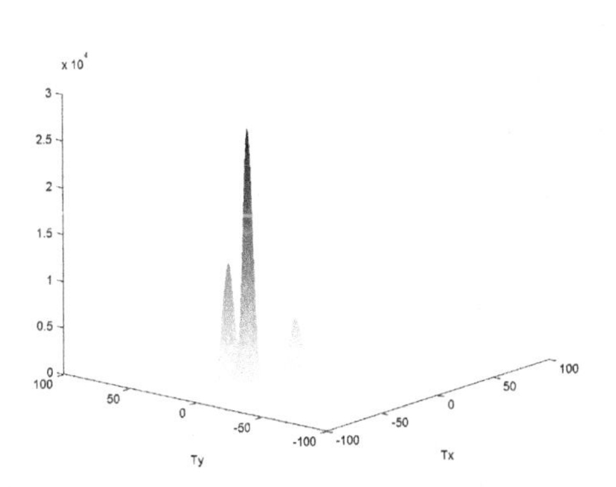

Fig. 2. (t_x, t_y) accumulation space visualization

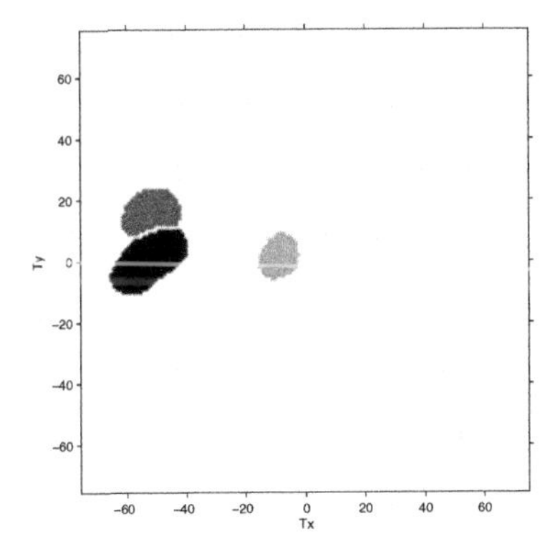

Fig. 3. Watershed result

tershed algorithm [9] is applied. Fig. 3 presents the result of the watershed, and three movements are easily distinguished.

$$v = M - v \qquad \textit{Where } v \textit{ is one value and } M \textit{ the maximum value of the accumulation space} \tag{3}$$

For clarity, only the center of our accumulation space is shown in the figures. In fact, the accumulation space is rather large to enable the segmentation of large motion (-1024 to 1024, with half-pixel precision). This accumulation space is also very sparse, so a recursive method has been developed which gives equivalent results to the watershed. The optimization is not presented in details, but this approach allows to treat only nonnull positions. Basically, the position of each accumulation is registered, and this registration map is used in the next step, making computation cost fairly independent of the size of the accumulation space.

Firstly, the maximum position (mode) within the accumulation space is detected. For each position related to the maximum one, the directional Gradient in the direction of the mode is computed. While the Gradient is positive, points are assumed to belong to the same peak and the algorithm is repeated in a neighborhood. At this step, all points which belong to the highest peak are aggregated, and this aggregate is labelled. *Prog. 1* presents the code (in C language) which computes the gradient for each position and labels the accumulation space for all the data of the same peak.

Prog. 1: *(mx,my) is the maximum position, (x,y) the actual position and n the identification number of the peak. _histoT is a global array which contains the accumulation space data and _mask is the array which contains the label of each position.*

```
void DilatPeakRec(int x,int y,int mx,int my, __int64 n){
    // is this point already agregated
    if(!(_mask[x+y*_histoWidth]&n)){
        // compute the direction of the maximum position
        int tx,ty;int dx=mx-x;int dy=my-y;
        int adx=abs(dx);int ady=abs(dy);
        if((adx==0)||(adx<ady/2.0)) tx=0;
        else tx=dx/adx;
        if((ady==0)||(ady<adx/2.0)) ty=0;
        else ty=dy/ady;
        // verification of the gradient direction
        if(_histoT[x+y*_histoWidth]<_histoT[x+tx+(y+ty)*_histoWidth]){
            // the position belongs to the peak
            _mask[x+y*_histoWidth]+=n;
            // recursion on the neighborhood
            DilatPeakRec...
}   }   }
```

The process is iterated until all non-zero positions belong to a peak : the maximum in the remaining positions is located and a new aggregation around it is started, and so on. If a position belongs to several aggregates, it becomes a member of the peak which has the nearest maximum position. In this case,

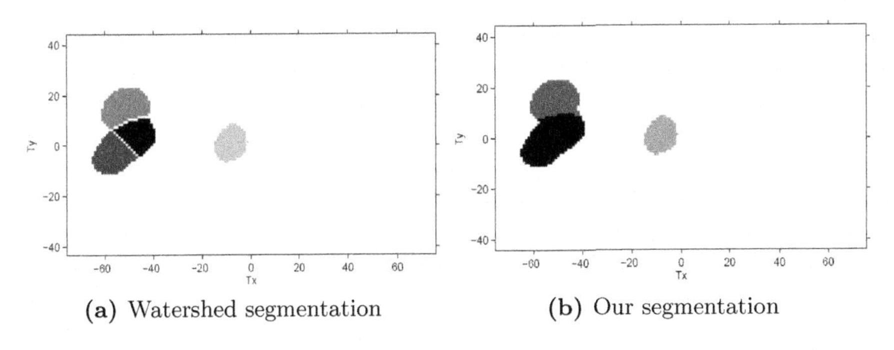

(a) Watershed segmentation (b) Our segmentation

Fig. 4. Peak over segmentation with watershed algorithm

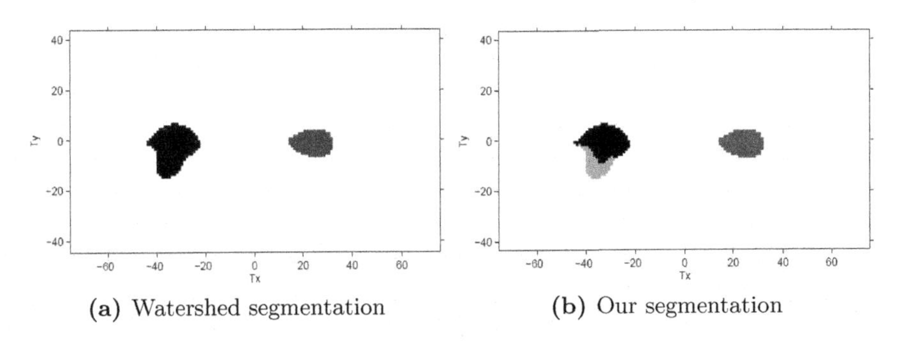

(a) Watershed segmentation (b) Our segmentation

Fig. 5. Contiguous peaks confusion with watershed algorithm

borders are perhaps less well delimited than with the watershed algorithm, but without much consequence on the picture segmentation result.

For contiguous peaks, our segmentation results differ to those issued by the watershed algorithm. But the watershed technique gives also different results according to the Structural Element chosen : if the Structural Element is too small (4 connections) then wrong local maxima can be detected (Fig. 4). In other cases, contiguous peaks are not distinguished with a 4- or 8-connex Structural Element (Fig. 5). Our method gives more stable results for this situation.

Some time, the segmentation is bad. This occurs on very difficult scenes, for example scenes with high motion amplitude or scenes with an important and moving foreground object. For a good segmentation, each peak and its aggregation must have a small standard deviation (ideally the same one used for the Gaussian distribution at the accumulation stage). The ratio between main peak's energy (sum of contributions located within the aggregation) and overall energy (occurrences for the whole accumulation space) should be high. A bad segmentation is often due to a bad estimation of the early deformation parameters (zoom, rotation). In the actual implementation, no re-estimation of the motion parameters is proposed when the situation is difficult (i.e, if the main peak have a too large standard deviation), but some kind of temporal filtering could be designed (the segmentation results should be consistent from GOP to GOP in the sequence).

Instead of showing the segmentation in the accumulation space, the next section illustrates the matching segmentation for the sequence's frames.

4 Results

Tests are carried out on the "Mobile and Calendar" sequence[1]. A train is moving to the left while the calendar moves vertically and the camera zooms and pans to the left.

When the accumulation space is segmented, all the macroblocks whose motion vectors belong to the same peak's aggregate are marked with the same label and displayed with the same color. For visualization clarity, Fig. 6 shows the results of the first three segmented peaks. Underlying frames are the intra-coded picture of each GOP and 4 pixels per macroblocks are drawn (the DC components of each DCT block).

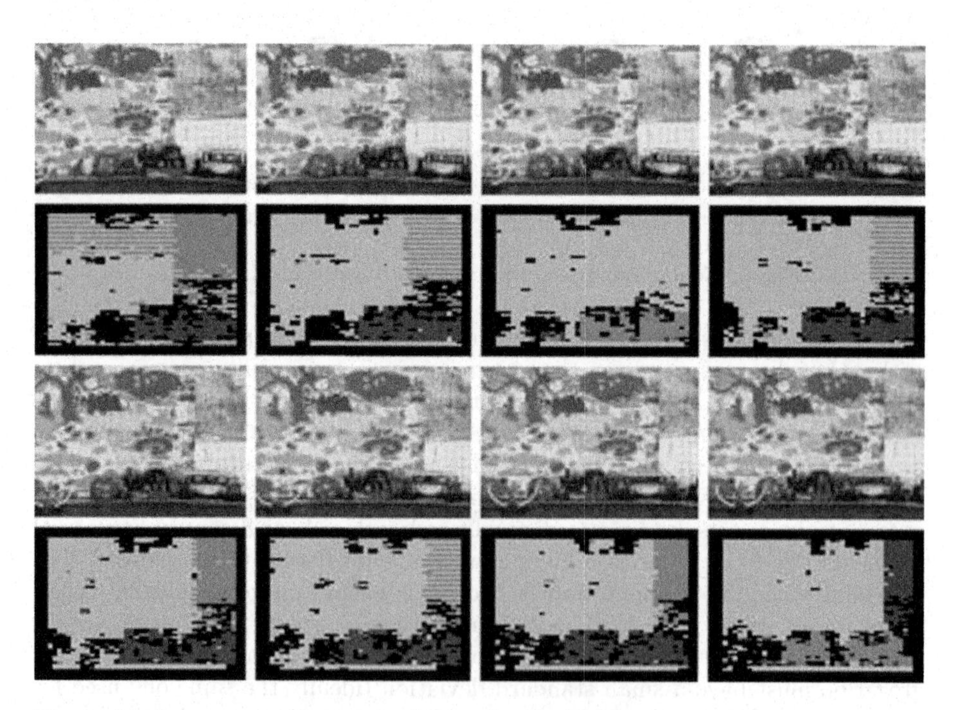

Fig. 6. Motion segmentation of "mobile and calendar" sequence. Frames are sequentially arranged from left to right and from top to bottom.

For illustrating this paper, we focused on frames taken when the calendar stops before moving upwards. This is a difficult step for the motion-based segmentation because background and calendar motion are very similar. Black color represents unsegmented areas, and segmented areas are drawn with gray levels,

[1] http://www.mpeg2.de/video/streams/tek.htm

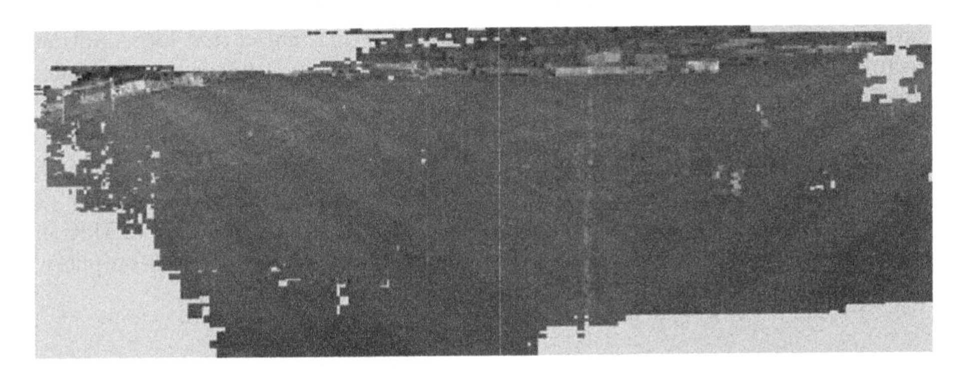

Fig. 7. Mosaicing on Sport Event. *For each GOP, only I-frame DC coefficients which belong to the background are drawn and each frame is adjusted to others with the global motion parameters.*

coupled to the peak energy. The background shows the most intensive value and the calendar the second one, except when its motion becomes null (on frame 3) and when it has almost disappeared (frame 8). Interlacing artifacts can be seen because, according to the MPEG2 standard, odd and even lines can be compensated separately. Fig. 5(b) corresponds to the segmentation of the first frame, the tangle of the 2 peaks explains the bad calendar affectation (for the odd lines only).

Although the exposed approach allows to estimate and compensate the global motion according to the affine model (zoom, rotation and translation), segmentation of moving objects are only based on translations. Even with a complete analysis of the accumulation space, the ball, which rotates pushed by the train, would not be segmented.

The "Mobile and Calendar" example shows that MPEG motion can be used for motion segmentation with a fair precision. Complex movements appear in this sequence (zoom, objects with similar displacements), fortunately, their motion amplitude is rather small. In the case of large motion, the precision of the MPEG motion vectors decrease. Our algorithms have been tested on some sport events. When the movements are too large, the estimation of the background motion gives good results, but the segmentation is more inaccurate. Fig. 7 shows the result of a background mosaicing uses our Global Motion Estimation and motion based segmentation methods. We notice a flaw for wide and fast panning : the background is then oversegmented in two or three distinct regions. Players are too small to be represented by peaks in the accumulation space, but they are not assimilated to the background when they are in movement. At last, the mosaicing is good, since all the GOPs of the sequence contribute to and complete this display, hiding possible bad segmentations.

The difficulty of the presented method is to choose a suitable Gaussian filter variance. As the Gaussian distribution congregates motion vectors which must represent the same movement, the segmentation result depends to this setting : with a large variance, similar motion can not be segmented while with a small variance, objects can be over segmented. Moreover, it is noted that large motion vectors have less precision that small ones. The use of a non-linear accumulation space is being investigated to resolve that matter.

The complete approach is implemented using C language. The test video sequence parameters are : 12 frames per GOP, 30 fps and frame size is 704×480. The motion segmentation is carried out at GOP frequency, for each I-Frame (2 times per second). The partial decoding of the MPEG stream, the Global Motion Estimation and the segmentation takes about 200 ms on a 2.4 GHz computer, so 200ms are still available for real-time, application related, tasks.

5 Conclusion

This contribution demonstrate that it is possible to obtain, with computationally efficient techniques, the camera motion and foreground objects position and movement from compressed video sequences. Based on MPEG compressed data (that means possibly inaccurate, block-based motion estimation), the results are beyond our expectations. Current work focuses on performing automatic sport events summarization using these results. The main advantage of this algorithm is its performance and it is intended that this method could be used in collaboration with traditional methods (which are using uncompressed data) to improve the visualization of the results.

References

1. Tekalp, A.M.: Digital video processing. Prentice Hall Ed. (1995)
2. Kobla, V., Doermann, D., Lin, K.: Indexing and retrieval of mpeg compressed video. Journal of Electronic Imaging **7** (1998)
3. Porter, S., Mirmehdi, M., Thomas, B.: Video indexing using motion estimation. The British Machine Vision Conference (2003)
4. Benoit, H.: Digital Television MPEG-1, MPEG-2 and Principles of the DVB System, second edition. Focal Press (2002)
5. : ISO/IEC 13818-1 and ISO/IEC 13818-2. (2000)
6. Coudray, R., Besserer, B.: Global motion estimation for MPEG-encoded streams. Proc. of IEEE Int. Conf. on Image Processing (2004)
7. Coudray, R., Besserer, B.: Agregation, selection et utilisation de l'information de mouvement issue d'un flux MPEG. GRETSI (2005)
8. Wang, J., Adelson, E.: Spatio-temporal segmentation of video data. SPIE Proc. Image and Video Processing II **2182** (1994) 120–131
9. Vincent, L., Soille, P.: Watersheds in digital spaces: An efficient algorithm based on immersion simulations. IEEE Transactions of Pattern Analysis and Machine Intelligence **13** (1991)

Efficient Depth Edge Detection Using Structured Light

Jiyoung Park[1], Cheolhwon Kim[1], Juneho Yi[1], and Matthew Turk[2]

[1] School of Information and Communication Engineering, Sungkyunkwan University, Korea
Biometric Engineering Research Center
{jiyp, ani4one, jhyi}@ece.skku.ac.kr
[2] Computer Science Department, University of California,
Santa Barbara, CA 93106
mturk@cs.ucsb.edu

Abstract. This research features a novel approach that efficiently detects depth edges in real world scenes. Depth edges play a very important role in many computer vision problems because they represent object contours. We strategically project structured light and exploit distortion of the light pattern in the structured light image along depth discontinuities to reliably detect depth edges. Distortion along depth discontinuities may not occur or be large enough to detect depending on the distance from the camera or projector. For practical application of the proposed approach, we have presented methods that guarantee the occurrence of the distortion along depth discontinuities for a continuous range of object location. Experimental results show that the proposed method accurately detects depth edges of human hand and body shapes as well as general objects.

1 Introduction

Object contour is valuable information in image analysis problems such as object recognition and tracking. Object contours can be represented by depth discontinuities (a.k.a. depth edges). However, the use of traditional Canny edges cannot distinguish between texture edges and depth edges. We describe a structured light based framework for reliably capturing depth edges in real world scenes without dense 3D reconstruction.

Depth edges directly represent shape features that are valuable information in computer vision [1, 2]. Unfortunately, few research results have been reported that provide only depth discontinuities without computing 3D information at every pixel in the input image of a scene. On the other hand, most effort has been devoted to stereo vision problems in order to obtain depth information. In fact, stereo methods for 3D reconstruction fail in textureless regions and along occluding edges with low intensity variation [3]. Recently, the use of structured light was reported to compute 3D coordinates at every pixel in the input image [4, 5]. However, the fact that this approach needs a number of structured light images makes it hard to be applicable in realtime. One notable technique was reported recently for non-photorealistic rendering [6]. They capture a sequence of images in which different light sources illuminate the scene from various positions. Then they use shadows in each image to assemble a depth edge map. This technique was applied to finger spelling recognition [7]. Although very attractive, it only works where shadows can be reliably created. In

G. Bebis et al. (Eds.): ISVC 2005, LNCS 3804, pp. 737 – 744, 2005.

contrast, our method is shadow free. In addition, by a slight modification of the imaging system so that it can capture white and structured images at the same time, it can be easily applied to dynamic scenes where the camera moves.

The remaining of this paper is organized as follows. In section 2, we describe the procedure to detect depth edges in a patterned image. Section 3 presents our methods that guarantee the occurrence of the distortion along depth discontinuities for a continuous range of object location. We report our experimental results in section 4. Finally, conclusions and future work are discussed in section 5.

2 Detecting Depth Edges

We detect depth edges by projecting structured light onto a scene and exploiting distortion of light pattern in the structured light image along depth discontinuities. Fig. 1 illustrates the basic method to compute depth edges. First, as can be seen in Fig. 1 (a), we project a white light and structured light consecutively onto a scene where depth edges are to be detected. Second, we extract horizontal patterns simply by differencing the white light and structured light images. We call this difference image the 'patterned image' (see Fig. 1 (b)). Third, we exploit distortion of light pattern in the structured light image along depth edges. We use 2D Gabor filtering that is known to be useful in segregating textural regions. The amplitude response of the Gabor filter is very low where distortion of light pattern occurs. We then accurately locate depth edges using edge information from the white light image. Fig. 1 (c) illustrates this process and a final depth edge map is shown in Fig. 1 (d).

However, distortion along depth discontinuities may not occur or be sufficient to detect depending on the distance from the camera or projector. Fig. 2 shows an example situation. Along the depth edges between objects A and B and between objects C and D, the distortion of pattern almost disappears. This makes it infeasible to detect these depth edges using a Gabor filter. For practical application of the proposed approach, it is essential to have a solution that guarantees the occurrence of the distortion along depth discontinuities irrespective of object location.

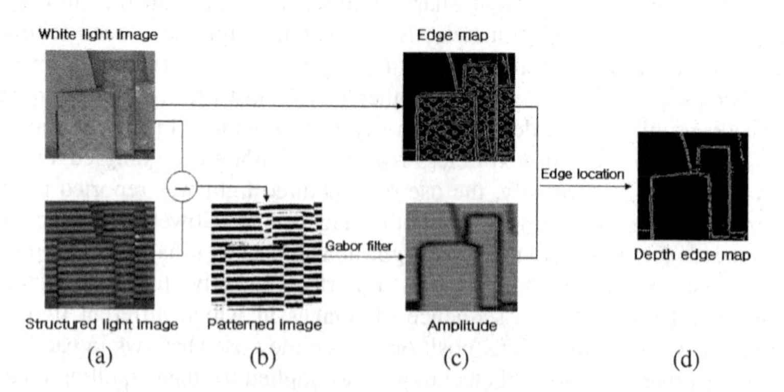

Fig. 1. The basic idea to compute a depth edge map: (a) capture of a white light and structured light image, (b) patterned image, (c) detection of depth edges by applying a Gabor filter to the patterned image with edge information from the white light image, (d) final depth edge map

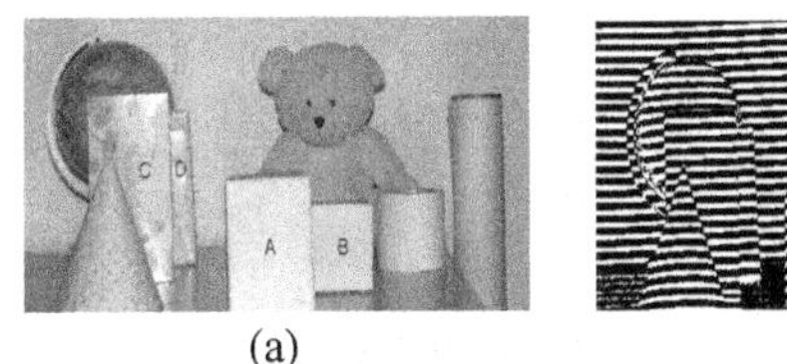

(a)

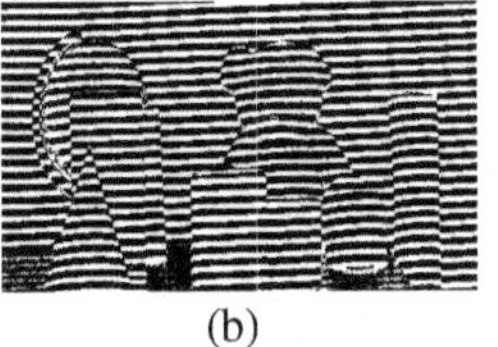

(b)

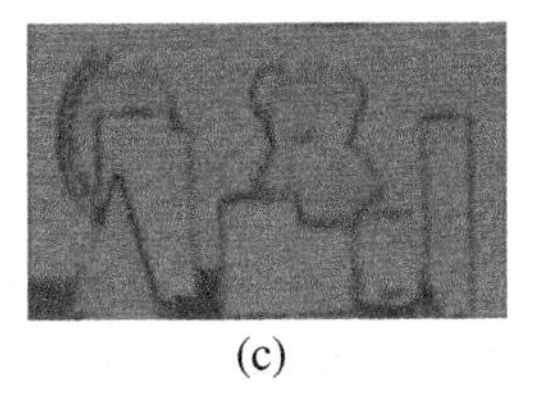

(c)

Fig. 2. Problem of disappearance of distortion along depth edges depending on the distance of an object from the camera and projector: (a) white light image (b) patterned image (c) amplitude response of Gabor filter applied to the patterned image

3 Detectable Range of Depth Edges

We have described that we can easily detect depth edges by exploiting the distortion along depth discontinuities in the patterned image. However, as previously mentioned, the distortion may not occur or be sufficient to detect depending the distance of depth edges from the camera or projector. In this section, we present methods to guarantee the occurrence of the distortion for a continuous range of object location.

3.1 Reliably Detectable Distortion

In order to compute the exact range where depth edges are detectable, we have modeled the imaging geometry of the camera, projector and object as illustrated in Fig. 3. The solid line represents a light ray from the projector. When structured light is projected onto object points A and B, they are imaged at different locations in the image plane due to different depth values. That is, distortion of horizontal pattern occurs along the depth discontinuity. The amount of distortion is denoted by Δ . Note that the width of horizontal stripes projected onto object locations A and B are the same in the image plane although they have different depth values. This is because the perspective effect of the camera and projector cancel each other out. From this model, we can derive the following equation using similar triangles:

$$\Delta = fd\left(\frac{1}{a}-\frac{1}{b}\right) = \left(\frac{fdr}{a(a+r)}\right) \tag{1}$$

In order for a depth edge to be detectable by applying a Gabor filter, the disparity of the same horizontal stripe, Δ , in the image plane should be above a certain amount. We have confirmed through experiments that an offset of at least 2/3 of the width of the horizontal stripe (w) is necessary for reliable detection of the distortion. Thus, the range of Δ for reliable detection of pattern distortion can be written:

$$2wk + \frac{2w}{3} \le \Delta \le 2wk + \frac{4w}{3}, \quad k = 0,1,\cdots. \tag{2}$$

From equation (2), we can know that there are ranges where we cannot detect depth edges due to the lack of distortion depending the distance of a depth edge from the camera or projector. Therefore, for practical application of the proposed approach, we need to guarantee that we are operating within these detectable regions.

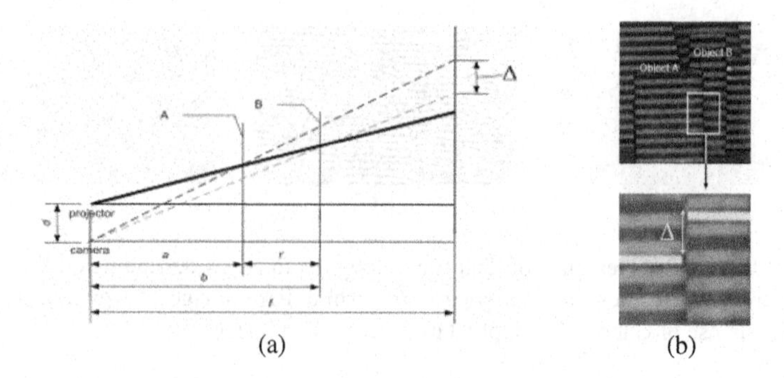

(a) (b)

Fig. 3. Imaging geometry and the amount of distortion: (a) spatial relation of camera, projector and two object points viewed from the side (b) the magnitude of pattern distortion, Δ, in a real image

3.2 Extending the Detectable Range of Depth Edges

We propose two methods to extend the range so that detection of distortion is guaranteed. The first method is based on a single camera and projector setup that uses several structured light images with different width of horizontal stripes. We use additional structured light whose spatial period is halved such as, $w_2=2w_1$, $w_3=2w_2$, $w_4=2w_3$, $\cdots$. When n such structured light images are used, the range of detectable distortion, Δ , is as follows.

$$2/3 w_1 < \Delta < \left(2^n - 2/3\right) w_1 \cdot \tag{3}$$

The second method exploits an additional camera or projector. As illustrated in Fig. 4, this method is equivalent to adding a new curve, $d=d_2$ (the dotted line), that is different from d_1. Recall that d denotes the distance between the camera and the projector. The new detectable range is created by partially overlapping the ranges by the two curves. A and B represent respectively detectable and undetectable ranges in Δ . They correspond to X and Y regions in a. When $a_1>a_2$ and $a_4>a_3$, the undetectable range B in X is overlapped with the detectable range A in Y. Similarly, the undetectable range B in Y is overlapped with the detectable range A in X. Therefore, if we consider both X and Y, we can extend the range where the detection of the distortion is guaranteed. To satisfy the condition $a_1>a_2$ and $a_4>a_3$, equation (4) must hold where the range of Δ is $\gamma wk + \alpha w < \Delta < \gamma wk + \beta w,\ k = 0,1,\cdots$.

$$\frac{\alpha+\gamma+\gamma k}{\beta+\gamma k} d_1 < d_2 < \frac{\beta+\gamma k}{\alpha+\gamma k} d_1 \tag{4}$$

3.3 Computation of the Detectable Range of Depth Edges

The detectable range of depth edges $[a_{\min}, a_{\max}]$ is computed in the following two steps:

- Step 1: Determination of the width of a stripe, w, in the structured light

First, we set $a_{\max}$ to the distance from the camera to the farthest background. Given $r_{\min}$, w can be computed by equation (5) which is derived from equation (1).

$$w = \frac{3 f d_1 r_{\min}}{2 a_{\max}(a_{\max} + r_{\min})} \tag{5}$$

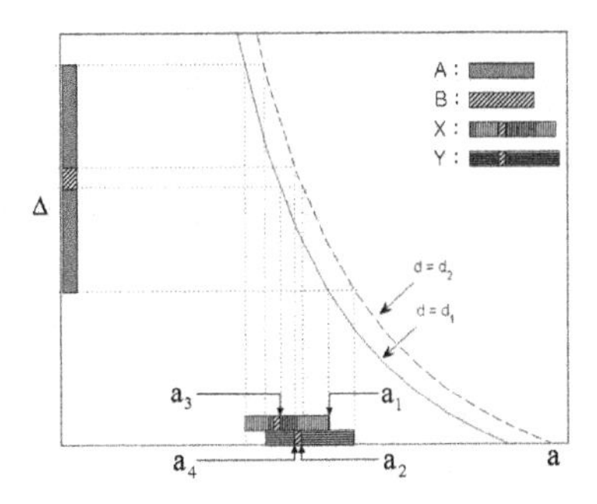

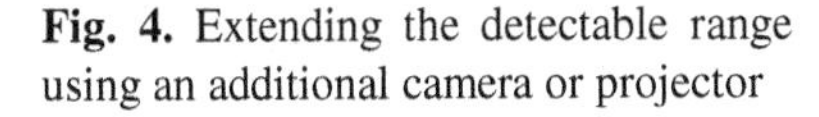
Fig. 4. Extending the detectable range using an additional camera or projector

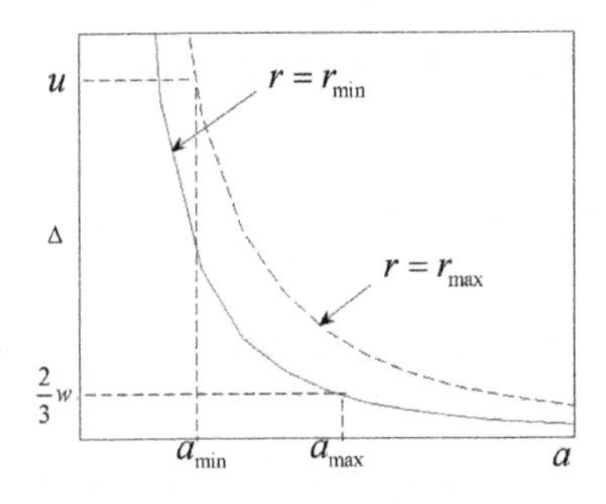

Fig. 5. Computation of the detectable range of depth edges

Thus, given a_{max} and r_{min}, we can compute the ideal width of stripes of the structured light. Using this structured light, we can detect depth edges of all object points that are located in the range, $a = [0, a_{max}]$, and apart from each other no less than r_{min}.

- Step 2: The minimum of the detectable range, a_{min}

Given w from step 1, we can compute a_{min} that corresponds to the upper limit of Δ, u, as shown in Fig. 5. We have described two methods in section 3.2 for extending the detectable range of depth edges. The expression for u is different depending on which method is used. After determining u and r_{max}, a_{min} can be computed by equation (1). r_{max} denotes the maximum distance between object points in the range $[a_{min}, a_{max}]$ that guarantees the occurrence of the distortion along depth discontinuities. Clearly, the distance between any two object points is bounded by (a_{max}.- a_{min}). Therefore, when a_{min} and r_{max} satisfy equation (6), we are guaranteed to detect depth edges of all object points located in the range $[a_{min}, a_{max}]$, and apart from each other no less than r_{min} and no more than r_{max}

$$a_{max} - a_{min} = r_{max} \tag{6}$$

In this case, u, a_{min} and r_{max} have the following relationship.

$$u = \frac{fd_1 r_{max}}{a_{min}\left(a_{min} + r_{max}\right)} \tag{7}$$

Then r_{max} becomes:

$$r_{max} = \frac{a_{max}^2 u}{fd_1 + a_{max} u} \tag{8}$$

Substituting equation (8) into equation (6), we obtain the following equation.

$$a_{min} = \frac{fd_1 a_{max}}{fd_1 + u a_{max}} \tag{9}$$

This way, we can employ structured light of optimal spatial resolution that is most appropriate for given application. Furthermore, we can use this method in an active way to collect information about the scene.

4 Experimental Results

For capturing structured light images, we have used a HP xb31 DLP projector and Canon IXY 500 digital camera. In this section, we present experimental results for two different experimental setups.

A. 1 camera and 1 projector

In order to extend detectable range of depth edges, this setup uses the first method (as explained in section 3.2) that just employs additional structured light whose spatial frequency is halved. Fig. 6 shows the result of depth edge detection using three structured light images with different width of horizontal stripes. Setting f=3m, a_{max}=3m, d=17.3cm and r_{min}=10 cm, w_1 and a_{min} are determined as 0.84cm and 2.33m, respectively. Each Gabor amplitude map (Fig. 6 (c)~(e)) shows that we cannot detect all the depth edges in the scene using a single structured light image. However, combining the results from the three cases, we can obtain the final Gabor amplitude map as in Fig. 6 (f). The result Fig. 6 (g) shows that this method is capable of detecting depth edges of all the objects located in the detectable range. We have also compared the result with the output of the traditional Canny edge detector Fig. 6 (h).

B. 1 camera and 2 projectors

We can apply both extension methods when using a single camera and two projectors. The detectable range can be extended more than setup A when the same number of the structured light images is used. Fig. 7 shows the experimental result when two

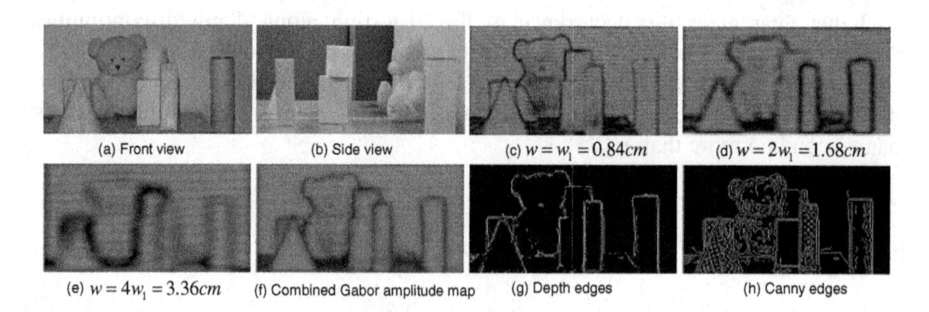

(a) Front view (b) Side view (c) $w = w_1 = 0.84cm$ (d) $w = 2w_1 = 1.68cm$

(e) $w = 4w_1 = 3.36cm$ (f) Combined Gabor amplitude map (g) Depth edges (h) Canny edges

Fig. 6. Detecting depth edges using a single camera and projector

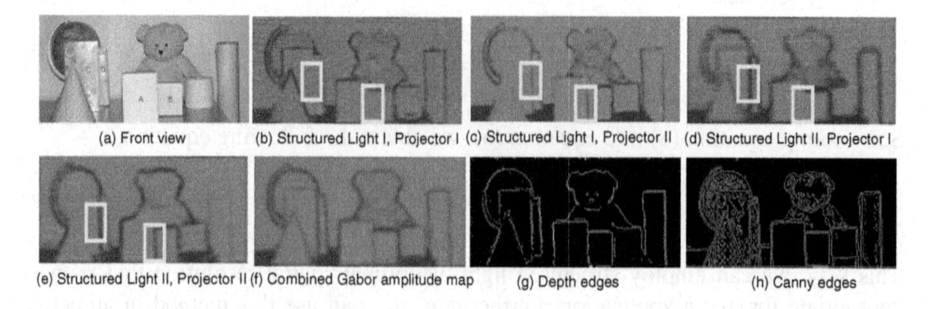

(a) Front view (b) Structured Light I, Projector I (c) Structured Light I, Projector II (d) Structured Light II, Projector I

(e) Structured Light II, Projector II (f) Combined Gabor amplitude map (g) Depth edges (h) Canny edges

Fig. 7. Detecting depth edges using a single camera and two projectors

structured lights are used for each projector. When f =3m, a_{max} =3m, d_1= 17.3cm, d_2=20.7cm, r_{min} =10cm are used, w_1 and a_{min} are determined as 0.84cm and 1.94m, respectively. Fig. 7 (b)~(e) show how the four structured light images play complementary roles to produce a final depth edge map.

Fig. 8 shows the result of detecting of hand and human body contours. Our method accurately detects depth edges by eliminating inner texture edges by using only a single camera and one structured light image. The result shows that our method is effectively applicable to gesture recognition.

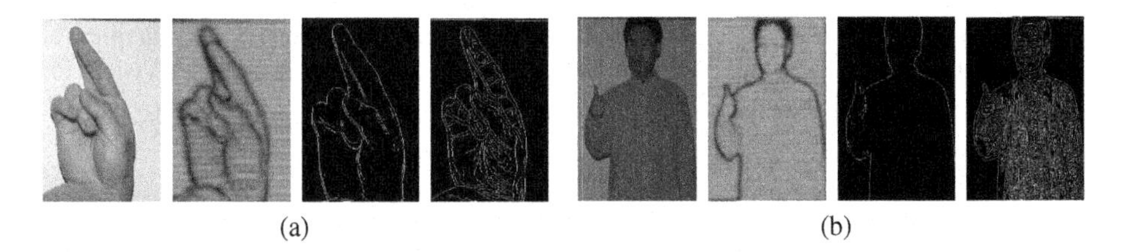

(a) (b)

Fig. 8. (a) Detection of depth edges in the case of hand gestures for fingerspelling, (b) Detecting human body contours for gesture recognition, from left to right: white light image, Gabor amplitude map, depth edges and canny edges

5 Conclusions

We have proposed a new approach using structured light that efficiently computes depth edges. Through a modeled imaging geometry and mathematical analysis, we have also presented two setups that guarantee the occurrence of the distortion along depth discontinuities for a continuous range of object location. These methods enable the proposed approach to be practically applicable to real world scenes. We have demonstrated very promising experimental results.

We have also observed that infrared projectors show the same distortion characteristics in patterned images. This makes us directly apply the same analysis from the LCD projectors to infrared projectors. By bypassing dense 3D reconstruction that is computationally expensive, our methods can be easily extended to dynamic scenes as well. We believe that this research will contribute to great improvement of many computer vision solutions that rely on shape features.

Acknowledgement

This work was supported in part by the Korea Science and Engineering Foundation (KOSEF) through the Biometrics Engineering Research Center (BERC) at Yonsei University.

References

1. T. A.Cass, "Robust Affine Structure Matching for 3D Object Recognition," *IEEE Transactions on Pattern Analysis and Machine Intelligence*, pp. 1264-1265, 1998.
2. I. Weiss and M. Ray, "Model-based recognition of 3D object from single vision," *IEEE Transactions on Pattern Analysis and Machine Intelligence*, pp. 116-128, 2001.

3. T. Frohlinghaus and J. M. Buhmann "Regularizing phase-based stereo," Proceedings of 13th International Conference on Pattern Recognition, pp. 451-455, 1996.
4. S. H. Lee, J. M. Choi, D. S Kim, B. C. Jung, J. K. Na, and H. M. Kim, "An Active 3D Robot Camera for Home Environment," Proceedings of 4th IEEE Sensors Conference, 2004.
5. D. Scharstein and R. Szeliski, "High-Accuracy Stereo Depth Maps Using Structured Light," IEEE Computer Society Conference on Computer Vision and Pattern Recognition, Vol. 1, pp. 195-202, 2003.
6. R. Raskar, K. H. Tan, R. Feris, J. Yu, and M. Turk, "Non-photorealistic Camera: Depth Edge Detection and Stylized Rendering Using Multi-Flash Imaging," Proceedings of ACM SIGGRAPH Conference , Vol. 23, pp. 679-688, 2004.
7. R. Feris, M. Turk, R. Raskar, K. Tan, and G. Ohashi, "Exploiting Depth Discontinuities for Vision-based Fingerspelling Recognition," IEEE Workshop on Real-Time Vision for Human-Computer Interaction, 2004.

Image Smoothing and Segmentation by Graph Regularization

Sébastien Bougleux[1] and Abderrahim Elmoataz[2]

[1] GREYC CNRS UMR 6072, ENSICAEN,
6 BD du Maréchal Juin, 14050 Caen Cedex, France
sebastien.bougleux@greyc.ensicaen.fr
[2] LUSAC, Site Universitaire, BP 78,
50130 Cherbourg-Octeville, France
abder.elmoataz@greyc.ensicaen.fr

Abstract. We propose a discrete regularization framework on weighted graphs of arbitrary topology, which leads to a family of nonlinear filters, such as the bilateral filter or the TV digital filter. This framework, which minimizes a loss function plus a regularization term, is parameterized by a weight function defined as a similarity measure. It is applicable to several problems in image processing, data analysis and classification. We apply this framework to the image smoothing and segmentation problems.

1 Introduction

Image smoothing, denoising and segmentation are fundamental problems of computer vision. The goal of image smoothing and denoising is to remove spurious details and/or noise for a given possibly corrupted image, while maintaining essential features such as edges. The goal of segmentation is to divide a given image into parts that belong to distinct objects in the image. There exists several methods to solve these problems. The variational ones, based on regularization, are particularly well suited to impose constraints on the solution, such as regularity. These methods, solved with partial differential equations (PDE), constitute a significant framework in image processing and data analysis. In the case of an image regularization, a classical methodology first supposes the image to be defined on a continuous domain. Then it considers a continuous variational function which typically involves a regularization term (internal energy), and a constraint term (external energy). The problem is formalized by a minimization problem which can be solved by finding the steady-state solution of a heat equation corresponding to the Euler-Lagrange equation. Finally, the resulting PDE are numerically discretized [1], [2].

However, many data can be represented by graphs of arbitrary or complex topology. With these representations, the continuous regularization cannot work. The idea is to consider a discrete regularization on graphs, which can be reduced to solve linear systems or nonlinear systems by iterative methods. This was proposed for images represented by grid graphs [3]. For example, the total

G. Bebis et al. (Eds.): ISVC 2005, LNCS 3804, pp. 745–752, 2005.

variation (TV) digital filter [4], which is a discretization of the continuous one, is used for denoising and enhancing images, or more generally data living on graphs. In the context of data classification, a discrete regularization method is applied on weighted graphs, using discrete differential operators [5], [6], [7]. We propose a regularization framework on weighted graphs of arbitrary topology, which corresponds to a family of nonlinear filters. This family includes the bilateral filter [8] and the TV digital filter. It is parameterized by a weight function defined as a similarity measure. Each filter can be implemented by a simple and fast algorithm. We apply our framework on the image smoothing, denoising and segmentation problems.

This article is organized as follows: In Section 2, we present differential geometry on weighted graphs, which is similar to the one introduced in [6]. In Section 3, we present discrete regularizations on graphs. In Section 4, we present algorithms for image filtering and segmentation by the construction of a graph corresponding to an initial adapted partition and by a diffusion on this graph. The partition of the graph is realized by an energy partition [9].

2 Differential Geometry on Weighted Graphs

A *graph* $G = (V, E)$ consists of a finite set V of vertices and a finite set $E \subseteq V \times V$ of edges. We assume G to be undirected, connected, with no self-loops and no multiple edges. Let (u, v) be the edge that connects the vertices u and v, G is *weighted* if it is associated with a weight function $w : E \to \mathbb{R}_+$ satisfying $w(u, v) = w(v, u)$, for all the edges in E. The *degree* function $d_w : V \to \mathbb{R}_+$ of a vertex v, is a measure on the neighborhood of v: $d_w(v) = \sum_{u \sim v} w(u, v)$, where $u \sim v$ denotes all the vertices u connected to v by an edge of E.

Let $H(V)$ be the Hilbert space of real-valued functions $f : V \to \mathbb{R}$. Similarly define $H(E)$, the *graph gradient* operator $\nabla : H(V) \to H(E)$ of f on an edge (u, v) is:

$$(\nabla f)(u, v) = \sqrt{\frac{w(u, v)}{d_w(u)}}(f(u) - f(v)). \tag{1}$$

The amplitude of the gradient, or the *local variation* of f at the vertex v, is defined to be:

$$\| \nabla_v f \|_{H(V)} = \sqrt{\sum_{u \sim v} (\nabla f)^2(u, v)}. \tag{2}$$

It can be viewed as a measure of the regularity of a function around a vertex. Meanwhile the *global variation* of f (or the 2-Dirichlet form), defined by:

$$R_p(f) = \frac{1}{p} \sum_{v \in V} \| \nabla_v f \|^p_{H(V)}, \tag{3}$$

measures of the regularity of f over the graph.

The *graph Laplace* operator $\Delta : H(V) \rightarrow H(V)$, of f at a vertex v, is defined to be:

$$(\Delta f)(v) = \left.\frac{\partial R_2(f)}{\partial f}\right|_v = d_w(v)f(v) - \sum_{u \sim v} w(u,v)f(u). \quad (4)$$

3 Regularization of Weighted Graphs

Given a graph $G = (V, E)$ and a function $g \in H(V)$, the regularization of G consists in the search of a function $f \in H(V)$, which is not only smooth enough on G, but also close to g. It is an optimization problem formalized by the minimization of a weighted sum of two energy terms:

$$f^* = \arg \min_{f \in H(V)} \left\{ R_p(f) + \frac{\mu}{2} \|f - g\|^2_{H(V)} \right\}, \quad (5)$$

where $R_p(f)$ represents the regularization term defined by (3), and the second term represents the closeness to the function g. The positive constant μ corresponds to the Lagrange relaxation parameter. Since the energy terms in (5) are strictly convex functions, then the optimization problem has a unique solution f^* which satisfies the equation:

$$\frac{\partial R_p(f^*)}{\partial f^*} + \mu(f^* - g) = 0. \quad (6)$$

Depending on the choice of $p \in \mathbb{N}_*$, the equation (6) leads to different kinds of regularizations. In the particular case of $p = 2$, the equation (6) can be considered as the discrete analogue of the Euler-Lagrange equation on a graph. Using the Laplace operator of the equation (4), we rewrite the equation (6) for each vertex of V:

$$(\mu + d_w(v))f^*(v) - \sum_{u \sim v} w(u,v)f^*(u) = \mu g(v), \forall v \in V. \quad (7)$$

This is a system of linear equations in f^* which is strictly positive definite. Its solution is unique and depends on g and μ. Among the existing methods to solve the system (7), the local iterative ones converge to the solution with efficiency, even if the graph has a large size or a complex topology. The Gauss-Jacobi method is the simplest of them. Let n be the iteration step, $f^{(n)}$ be the function f^* at the step n, and $f^{(0)} = g$. At each vertex v of V, the computation of $f^{(n+1)}(v)$ only depends on $f^{(0)}$ and on the values of $f^{(n)}$ in the neighborhood of v. The following equation expresses an iteration of the algorithm:

$$f^{(n+1)}(v) = \frac{1}{\mu + d_w(v)} \sum_{u \sim v} w(u,v)f^{(n)}(u) + \frac{\mu}{\mu + d_w(v)} f^{(0)}(v). \quad (8)$$

The above method is a forced low-pass digital filter. We call it, the *anisotropic weighted Laplace filter* and note it $AWL(n, G, g, \mu)$.

The cases where $p \neq 2$ are not the purpose of this article since they do not use the Laplace operator. As in the case of $p = 2$, they have been used in numerous applications with other definitions of the gradient operator (1), see [6], [7] for example.

4 Application to Image Filtering and Segmentation

4.1 Graph Representation and Energy Partition

Let $g : \mathbb{Z}^2 \to \mathbb{R}$ be a grey level image of pixels. We modelize g by a weighted graph $G = (V, E)$ such that each vertex of V corresponds to a pixel of g, and the weight function

$$w(v_i, v_j) = exp(-\lambda|g(v_i) - g(v_j)|), \lambda \in \mathbb{R}_+ \tag{9}$$

estimates the similarity between two pixels. Since the proposed framework enables to deal with arbitrary graphs, we experiment two graph representations: (i) regular grid graphs generated by 4-adjacency, and (ii) graphs of arbitrary topology generated by a pre-segmentation of g. In the case (ii), we first modelize g by a regular grid graph generated by 4-adjacency. Then, we compute an energy partition of G which is analogue to the energy partition of the image domain [9]. In the following, we present the mathematical framework associated to the energy partition of graphs.

A *path* $c(u, v)$ is a sequence of vertices $(v_1, \ldots, v_m)$ such that $u = v_1$, $v = v_m$, and $(v_i, v_{i+1}) \in E$ for all $1 \leq i < m$. Let $C_G(u, v)$ be the set of paths connecting u and v. We define the pseudo-metric $\delta : V \times V \to \mathbb{R}_+$ to be:

$$\delta(u, v) = \min_{c \in C_G(u,v)} \left(\sum_{i=1}^{m-1} w(v_i, v_{i+1}) \right) . \tag{10}$$

Given a finite set of source vertices $S = \{s_1, \ldots, s_k\} \subset V$, the *energy* induced by δ is given by the minimal individual energy: $\delta_S(v) = \inf_{s_i \in S} \delta(s_i, v), \forall v \in V$. Based on the pseudo-metric δ, the *influence zone* of a source vertex s_i is defined to be the set of vertices that are closer to s_i than to any other source vertex: $Z_\delta(s_i, S) = \{v \in S | \delta(s_i, v) \leq \delta(s_j, v), \forall s_j \in S\}$. The *energy partition* of G, with respect to the set of sources S and the pseudo-metric δ, corresponds to the set of influence zones: $E_\delta(S, \Gamma) = \{Z_\delta(s_i, S), \forall s_i \in S\}$.

With these definitions, the image pre-segmentation consists in finding a set of source vertices and a pseudo-metric. We use the set of extrema of the intensity of g as a set of source vertices. To obtain exactly an energy partition which considers the total variation of g along a path, we use the following weight function in (10): $w(u, v) = |g(u) - g(v)|$. Then, the energy partition of the graph represents an approximation of the image, by assigning a model to each influence zone of the partition. The model is determined by the distribution of the graph values on the influence zone. Among the different models, the simplest are the constant ones, as mean or median value of the influence zone. The resultant graph $G' = (V', E')$, is a connectivity graph where $V' = S$ and E' is the set of edges connecting two vertices $s_i, s_j \in S$ if $Z_\delta(s_i, S) \cap Z_\delta(s_j, S) \neq \emptyset$.

4.2 Image Smoothing and Denoising

Given an image g as defined in Section 4.1, an integer n, and two reals λ (for the weight function (9)) and μ, the image g is transformed into an image

$f^* = AWF(n, g, G, \mu)$. The method described in Section 3 gives the iterative algorithm of the AWL filter. The action of the filter is illustrated in Fig.1 on a grid graph for denoising, and on an arbitrary graph in Fig.2 for smoothing. The arbitrary graph is a connectivity graph obtained by an energy partition of g.

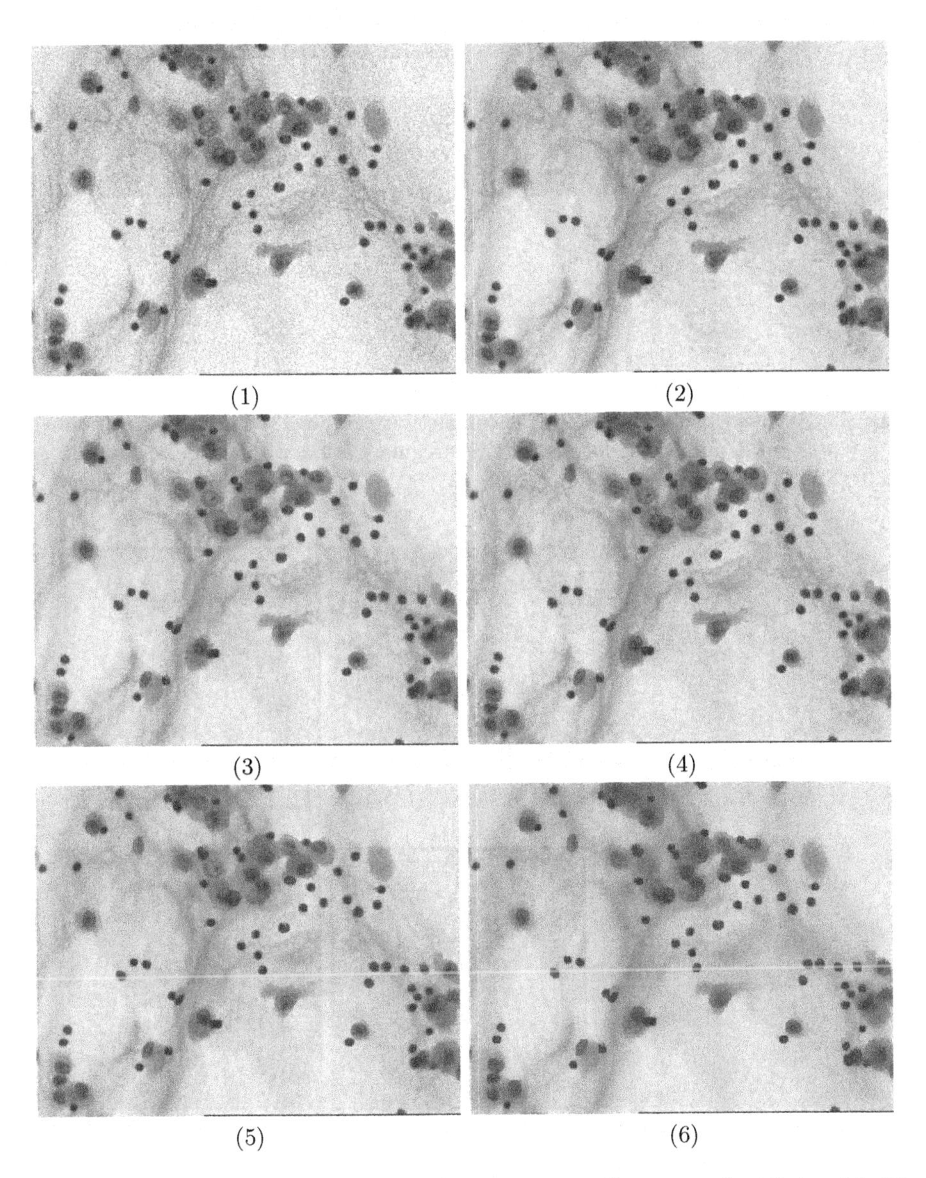

Fig. 1. (1) The original image. The regularizations are all computed with $\lambda = 10$: (2) 5 iterations and $\mu = 0.8$, (3) 5 iterations and $\mu = 0.2$, (4) 100 iterations and $\mu = 0.8$, (5) 100 iterations and $\mu = 0.5$, (6) 100 iterations and $\mu = 0.2$

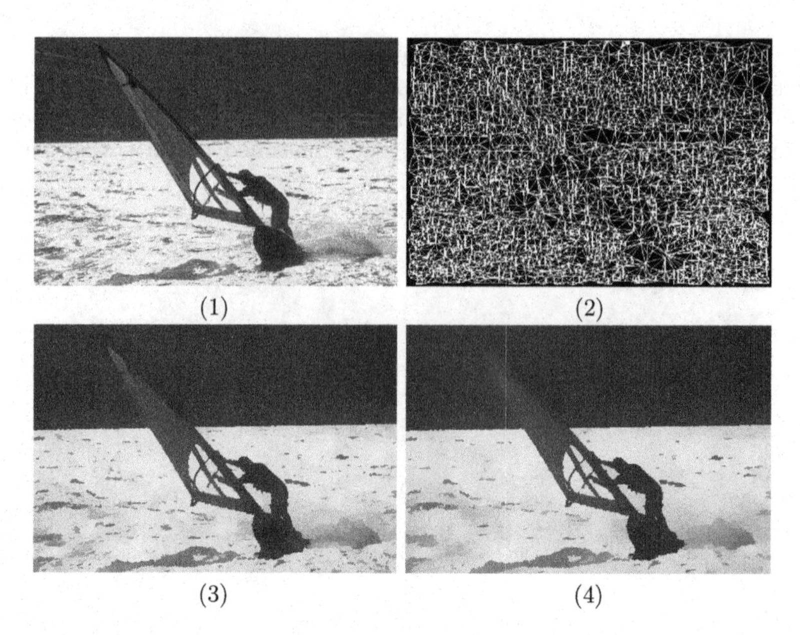

Fig. 2. (1) The original image. (2) The connectivity graph. (3) The regularization with $\mu = 0.5$, $\lambda = 0.5$ and 20 iterations. (4) The regularization with $\mu = 0.5$, $\lambda = 1/5$ and 20 iterations.

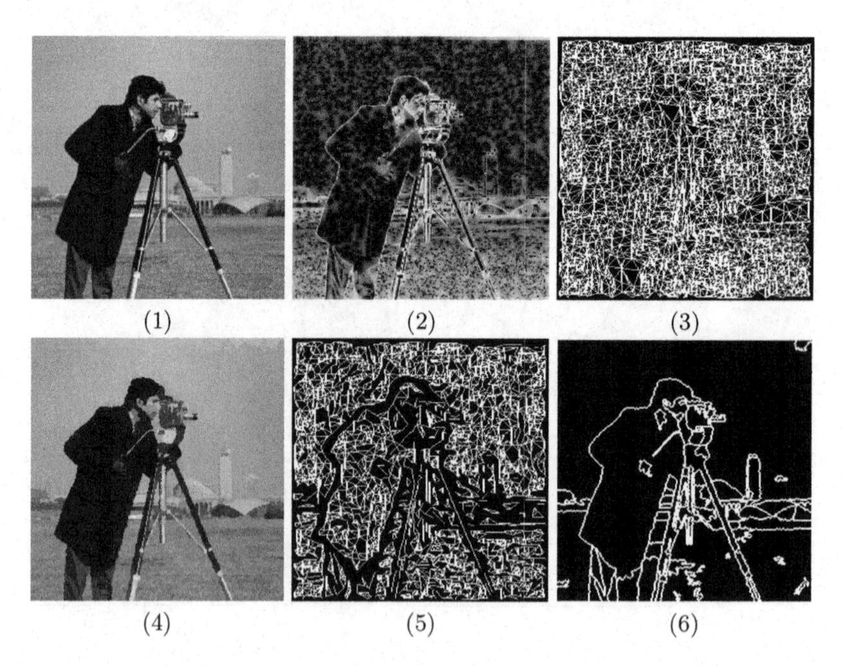

Fig. 3. (1) The original image. (2) The energy image. (3) The initial connectivity graph. (4) The pre-segmented image. (5) The connectivity graph that has been cut after the regularization process with $\lambda = 1/5$, four iterations and $t = 5$. (6) The segmented image.

4.3 Image Segmentation

Given an image g as defined in Section 4.1, an integer n, and three reals λ (for the weight function (9), μ and t, the segmentation algorithm is organized in four main steps:

(i) Pre-segmentation of g from its associated grid graph G, which gives a graph G' and a pre-segmented image g' (see Section 4.1).
(ii) Regularization of G' by the iterative algorithm: $f^* = AWL(n, G', g', 0)$.
(iii) We cut the edges of G' which have a weight less than a fixed threshold t (the weight is computed from f^*).
(iv) We merge the influence zones of g' that remain connected by an edge.

The segmentation algorithm is illustrated in Fig.3, where g' is a model of g based on the mean value (step (i)).

4.4 Related Digital Filters

The bilateral is a nonlinear filter on digital images. It has recently been proposed as an alternative to anisotropic diffusion [10]. Unlike the anisotropic diffusion, the bilateral filtering does not involve the solution of partial differential equations and can be implemented in a single iteration [11]. While the bilateral filtering has been originally proposed as an heuristic algorithm, it can be derived as a solution of the regularization of grid graphs. The AWL filter is equivalent to the bilateral filter if in the iteration (8) we have $\mu = 0$ and $w(u,v) = \exp\left(-(u-v)^2/2\sigma_D^2\right)\exp\left(-(g(u)-g(v))^2/2\sigma_R^2\right)$, where g is an image, σ_D is the geometric spread in the domain, and σ_R is the photometric spread in the image range.

The total variation digital filter is another nonlinear filter on digital images, and more generally on arbitrary graphs, which is use for denoising data [4]. It is the discrete version of the total variation formalized by the minimization of (5) with $p = 1$ and $w = 1$ for all edges. Moreover, it can be implemented by the AWL filter by taking the weight function: $w(u,v) = \frac{1}{\|\nabla_v g\|} + \frac{1}{\|\nabla_u g\|}$.

5 Conclusion

We have proposed a family of nonlinear filters, based on weighted graph regularization. This family, which is parameterized by a weight function, includes standard filters as the bilateral filter and the TV digital filter. Moreover, we have shown two applications of the regularization framework in the domain of image processing. As a continuation of this work, we will define a hierarchical segmentation and other weight functions that could realize other fusion processes than the one based on the difference of image intensity. Also, we will apply the regularization to the segmentation of non-organized set of points and to the supervised classification of color images.

Acknowledgments

We would like to thank the blind reviewers for their valuable and detailed comments.

References

1. Morel, J.M., Solimini, S.: Variational methods in image segmentation. Birkhauser Boston Inc., Cambridge, MA, USA (1995)
2. Tsai, Y.H.R., Osher, S.: Total variation and level set methods in image science. Acta Numerica **14** (2005) 509–573
3. Osher, S., Shen, J.: Digitized PDE method for data restoration. In Anastassiou, E.G.A., ed.: Analytical-Computational methods in Applied Mathematics. Chapman & Hall/CRC (2000) 751–771
4. Chan, T., Osher, S., Shen, J.: The digital TV filter and nonlinear denoising. IEEE Trans. Image Processing **10** (2001) 231–241
5. Zhou, D., Schölkopf, B.: A regularization framework for learning from graph data. In: ICML Workshop on Statistical Relational Learning and Its Connections to Other Fields. (2004) 132–137
6. Zhou, D., Schölkopf, B.: Regularization on discrete spaces. In: Proceedings of the 27th DAGM Symposium, Berlin, Germany, Springer (2005) 361–368
7. Belkin, M., Matveeva, I., Niyogi, P.: Regularization and semi-supervised learning on large graphs. In: COLT. (2004) 624–638
8. Mumford, D., Shah, J.: Optimal approximation of piecewise smooth functions and associated variational problems. Comm. Pure Appl. Math. **42** (1989) 577–685
9. Arbeláez, P.A., Cohen, L.D.: Energy partitions and image segmentation. Journal of Mathematical Imaging and Vision **20** (2004) 43–57
10. Barash, D.: A fundamental relationship between bilateral filtering, adaptive smoothing, and the nonlinear diffusion equation. IEEE Trans. Pattern Analysis and Machine Intelligence **24** (2002) 844–847
11. Tomasi, C., Manduchi, R.: Bilateral filtering for gray and color images. In: ICCV '98: Proceedings of the Sixth International Conference on Computer Vision, Washington, DC, USA, IEEE Computer Society (1998) 839–846

Author Index

Lecture Notes in Computer Science

For information about Vols. 1–3707

please contact your bookseller or Springer

Vol. 3835: G. Sutcliffe, A. Voronkov (Eds.), Logic for Programming, Artificial Intelligence, and Reasoning. XIV, 744 pages. 2005. (Subseries LNAI).

Vol. 3814: M. Maybury, O. Stock, W. Wahlster (Eds.), Intelligent Technologies for Interactive Entertainment. XV, 342 pages. 2005. (Subseries LNAI).

Vol. 3809: S. Zhang, R. Jarvis (Eds.), AI 2005: Advances in Artificial Intelligence. XXVII, 1344 pages. 2005. (Subseries LNAI).

Vol. 3807: M. Dean, Y. Guo, W. Jun, R. Kaschek, S. Krishnaswamy, Z. Pan, Q.Z. Sheng (Eds.), Web Information Systems Engineering – WISE 2005 Workshops. XV, 275 pages. 2005.

Vol. 3806: A.H. H. Ngu, M. Kitsuregawa, E.J. Neuhold, J.-Y. Chung, Q.Z. Sheng (Eds.), Web Information Systems Engineering – WISE 2005. XXI, 771 pages. 2005.

Vol. 3805: G. Subsol (Ed.), Virtual Storytelling. XII, 289 pages. 2005.

Vol. 3804: G. Bebis, R. Boyle, D. Koracin, B. Parvin (Eds.), Advances in Visual Computing. XX, 755 pages. 2005.

Vol. 3803: S. Jajodia, C. Mazumdar (Eds.), Information Systems Security. XI, 342 pages. 2005.

Vol. 3799: M. A. Rodríguez, I.F. Cruz, S. Levashkin, M.J. Egenhofer (Eds.), GeoSpatial Semantics. X, 259 pages. 2005.

Vol. 3798: A. Dearle, S. Eisenbach (Eds.), Component Deployment. X, 197 pages. 2005.

Vol. 3796: N.P. Smart (Ed.), Cryptography and Coding. XI, 461 pages. 2005.

Vol. 3795: H. Zhuge, G.C. Fox (Eds.), Grid and Cooperative Computing - GCC 2005. XXI, 1203 pages. 2005.

Vol. 3793: T. Conte, N. Navarro, W.-m.W. Hwu, M. Valero, T. Ungerer (Eds.), High Performance Embedded Architectures and Compilers. XIII, 317 pages. 2005.

Vol. 3792: I. Richardson, P. Abrahamsson, R. Messnarz (Eds.), Software Process Improvement. VIII, 215 pages. 2005.

Vol. 3791: A. Adi, S. Stoutenburg, S. Tabet (Eds.), Rules and Rule Markup Languages for the Semantic Web. X, 225 pages. 2005.

Vol. 3790: G. Alonso (Ed.), Middleware 2005. XIII, 443 pages. 2005.

Vol. 3789: A. Gelbukh, Á. de Albornoz, H. Terashima-Marín (Eds.), MICAI 2005: Advances in Artificial Intelligence. XXVI, 1198 pages. 2005. (Subseries LNAI).

Vol. 3785: K.-K. Lau, R. Banach (Eds.), Formal Methods and Software Engineering. XIV, 496 pages. 2005.

Vol. 3784: J. Tao, T. Tan, R.W. Picard (Eds.), Affective Computing and Intelligent Interaction. XIX, 1008 pages. 2005.

Vol. 3781: S.Z. Li, Z. Sun, T. Tan, S. Pankanti, G. Chollet, D. Zhang (Eds.), Advances in Biometric Person Authentication. XI, 250 pages. 2005.

Vol. 3780: K. Yi (Ed.), Programming Languages and Systems. XI, 435 pages. 2005.

Vol. 3779: H. Jin, D. Reed, W. Jiang (Eds.), Network and Parallel Computing. XV, 513 pages. 2005.

Vol. 3777: O.B. Lupanov, O.M. Kasim-Zade, A.V. Chaskin, K. Steinhöfel (Eds.), Stochastic Algorithms: Foundations and Applications. VIII, 239 pages. 2005.

Vol. 3775: J. Schönwälder, J. Serrat (Eds.), Ambient Networks. XIII, 281 pages. 2005.

Vol. 3773: A. Sanfeliu, M.L. Cortés (Eds.), Progress in Pattern Recognition, Image Analysis and Applications. XX, 1094 pages. 2005.

Vol. 3772: M. Consens, G. Navarro (Eds.), String Processing and Information Retrieval. XIV, 406 pages. 2005.

Vol. 3771: J.M.T. Romijn, G.P. Smith, J. van de Pol (Eds.), Integrated Formal Methods. XI, 407 pages. 2005.

Vol. 3770: J. Akoka, S.W. Liddle, I.-Y. Song, M. Bertolotto, I. Comyn-Wattiau, W.-J. van den Heuvel, M. Kolp, J. Trujillo, C. Kop, H.C. Mayr (Eds.), Perspectives in Conceptual Modeling. XXII, 476 pages. 2005.

Vol. 3768: Y.-S. Ho, H.J. Kim (Eds.), Advances in Multimedia Information Processing - PCM 2005, Part II. XXVIII, 1088 pages. 2005.

Vol. 3767: Y.-S. Ho, H.J. Kim (Eds.), Advances in Multimedia Information Processing - PCM 2005, Part I. XXVIII, 1022 pages. 2005.

Vol. 3766: N. Sebe, M.S. Lew, T.S. Huang (Eds.), Computer Vision in Human-Computer Interaction. X, 231 pages. 2005.

Vol. 3765: Y. Liu, T. Jiang, C. Zhang (Eds.), Computer Vision for Biomedical Image Applications. X, 563 pages. 2005.

Vol. 3764: S. Tixeuil, T. Herman (Eds.), Self-Stabilizing Systems. VIII, 229 pages. 2005.

Vol. 3762: R. Meersman, Z. Tari, P. Herrero (Eds.), On the Move to Meaningful Internet Systems 2005: OTM 2005 Workshops. XXXI, 1228 pages. 2005.

Vol. 3761: R. Meersman, Z. Tari (Eds.), On the Move to Meaningful Internet Systems 2005: CoopIS, DOA, and ODBASE, Part II. XXVII, 653 pages. 2005.

Vol. 3760: R. Meersman, Z. Tari (Eds.), On the Move to Meaningful Internet Systems 2005: CoopIS, DOA, and ODBASE, Part I. XXVII, 921 pages. 2005.

Vol. 3759: G. Chen, Y. Pan, M. Guo, J. Lu (Eds.), Parallel and Distributed Processing and Applications - ISPA 2005 Workshops. XIII, 669 pages. 2005.

Vol. 3758: Y. Pan, D.-x. Chen, M. Guo, J. Cao, J.J. Dongarra (Eds.), Parallel and Distributed Processing and Applications. XXIII, 1162 pages. 2005.

Vol. 3757: A. Rangarajan, B. Vemuri, A.L. Yuille (Eds.), Energy Minimization Methods in Computer Vision and Pattern Recognition. XII, 666 pages. 2005.

Vol. 3756: J. Cao, W. Nejdl, M. Xu (Eds.), Advanced Parallel Processing Technologies. XIV, 526 pages. 2005.

Vol. 3754: J. Dalmau Royo, G. Hasegawa (Eds.), Management of Multimedia Networks and Services. XII, 384 pages. 2005.

Vol. 3753: O.F. Olsen, L.M.J. Florack, A. Kuijper (Eds.), Deep Structure, Singularities, and Computer Vision. X, 259 pages. 2005.

Vol. 3752: N. Paragios, O. Faugeras, T. Chan, C. Schnörr (Eds.), Variational, Geometric, and Level Set Methods in Computer Vision. XI, 369 pages. 2005.

Vol. 3751: T. Magedanz, E.R. M. Madeira, P. Dini (Eds.), Operations and Management in IP-Based Networks. X, 213 pages. 2005.

Vol. 3750: J.S. Duncan, G. Gerig (Eds.), Medical Image Computing and Computer-Assisted Intervention – MICCAI 2005, Part II. XL, 1018 pages. 2005.

Vol. 3749: J.S. Duncan, G. Gerig (Eds.), Medical Image Computing and Computer-Assisted Intervention – MICCAI 2005, Part I. XXXIX, 942 pages. 2005.

Vol. 3748: A. Hartman, D. Kreische (Eds.), Model Driven Architecture – Foundations and Applications. IX, 349 pages. 2005.

Vol. 3747: C.A. Maziero, J.G. Silva, A.M.S. Andrade, F.M.d. Assis Silva (Eds.), Dependable Computing. XV, 267 pages. 2005.

Vol. 3746: P. Bozanis, E.N. Houstis (Eds.), Advances in Informatics. XIX, 879 pages. 2005.

Vol. 3745: J.L. Oliveira, V. Maojo, F. Martín-Sánchez, A.S. Pereira (Eds.), Biological and Medical Data Analysis. XII, 422 pages. 2005. (Subseries LNBI).

Vol. 3744: T. Magedanz, A. Karmouch, S. Pierre, I. Venieris (Eds.), Mobility Aware Technologies and Applications. XIV, 418 pages. 2005.

Vol. 3740: T. Srikanthan, J. Xue, C.-H. Chang (Eds.), Advances in Computer Systems Architecture. XVII, 833 pages. 2005.

Vol. 3739: W. Fan, Z.-h. Wu, J. Yang (Eds.), Advances in Web-Age Information Management. XXIV, 930 pages. 2005.

Vol. 3738: V.R. Syrotiuk, E. Chávez (Eds.), Ad-Hoc, Mobile, and Wireless Networks. XI, 360 pages. 2005.

Vol. 3735: A. Hoffmann, H. Motoda, T. Scheffer (Eds.), Discovery Science. XVI, 400 pages. 2005. (Subseries LNAI).

Vol. 3734: S. Jain, H.U. Simon, E. Tomita (Eds.), Algorithmic Learning Theory. XII, 490 pages. 2005. (Subseries LNAI).

Vol. 3733: P. Yolum, T. Güngör, F. Gürgen, C. Özturan (Eds.), Computer and Information Sciences - ISCIS 2005. XXI, 973 pages. 2005.

Vol. 3731: F. Wang (Ed.), Formal Techniques for Networked and Distributed Systems - FORTE 2005. XII, 558 pages. 2005.

Vol. 3729: Y. Gil, E. Motta, V. R. Benjamins, M.A. Musen (Eds.), The Semantic Web – ISWC 2005. XXIII, 1073 pages. 2005.

Vol. 3728: V. Paliouras, J. Vounckx, D. Verkest (Eds.), Integrated Circuit and System Design. XV, 753 pages. 2005.

Vol. 3726: L.T. Yang, O.F. Rana, B. Di Martino, J.J. Dongarra (Eds.), High Performance Computing and Communications. XXVI, 1116 pages. 2005.

Vol. 3725: D. Borrione, W. Paul (Eds.), Correct Hardware Design and Verification Methods. XII, 412 pages. 2005.

Vol. 3724: P. Fraigniaud (Ed.), Distributed Computing. XIV, 520 pages. 2005.

Vol. 3723: W. Zhao, S. Gong, X. Tang (Eds.), Analysis and Modelling of Faces and Gestures. XI, 4234 pages. 2005.

Vol. 3722: D. Van Hung, M. Wirsing (Eds.), Theoretical Aspects of Computing – ICTAC 2005. XIV, 614 pages. 2005.

Vol. 3721: A.M. Jorge, L. Torgo, P.B. Brazdil, R. Camacho, J. Gama (Eds.), Knowledge Discovery in Databases: PKDD 2005. XXIII, 719 pages. 2005. (Subseries LNAI).

Vol. 3720: J. Gama, R. Camacho, P.B. Brazdil, A.M. Jorge, L. Torgo (Eds.), Machine Learning: ECML 2005. XXIII, 769 pages. 2005. (Subseries LNAI).

Vol. 3719: M. Hobbs, A.M. Goscinski, W. Zhou (Eds.), Distributed and Parallel Computing. XI, 448 pages. 2005.

Vol. 3718: V.G. Ganzha, E.W. Mayr, E.V. Vorozhtsov (Eds.), Computer Algebra in Scientific Computing. XII, 502 pages. 2005.

Vol. 3717: B. Gramlich (Ed.), Frontiers of Combining Systems. X, 321 pages. 2005. (Subseries LNAI).

Vol. 3716: L. Delcambre, C. Kop, H.C. Mayr, J. Mylopoulos, Ó. Pastor (Eds.), Conceptual Modeling – ER 2005. XVI, 498 pages. 2005.

Vol. 3715: E. Dawson, S. Vaudenay (Eds.), Progress in Cryptology – Mycrypt 2005. XI, 329 pages. 2005.

Vol. 3714: H. Obbink, K. Pohl (Eds.), Software Product Lines. XIII, 235 pages. 2005.

Vol. 3713: L.C. Briand, C. Williams (Eds.), Model Driven Engineering Languages and Systems. XV, 722 pages. 2005.

Vol. 3712: R. Reussner, J. Mayer, J.A. Stafford, S. Overhage, S. Becker, P.J. Schroeder (Eds.), Quality of Software Architectures and Software Quality. XIII, 289 pages. 2005.

Vol. 3711: F. Kishino, Y. Kitamura, H. Kato, N. Nagata (Eds.), Entertainment Computing - ICEC 2005. XXIV, 540 pages. 2005.

Vol. 3710: M. Barni, I. Cox, T. Kalker, H.J. Kim (Eds.), Digital Watermarking. XII, 485 pages. 2005.

Vol. 3709: P. van Beek (Ed.), Principles and Practice of Constraint Programming - CP 2005. XX, 887 pages. 2005.

Vol. 3708: J. Blanc-Talon, W. Philips, D.C. Popescu, P. Scheunders (Eds.), Advanced Concepts for Intelligent Vision Systems. XXII, 725 pages. 2005.